Twentieth-Century Literary Criticism

Guide to Gale Literary Criticism Series

When you need to review criticism of literary works, these are the Gale series to use:

If the author's death date is: **You should turn to:**

After Dec. 31, 1959
(or author is still living)

CONTEMPORARY LITERARY CRITICISM

for example: Jorge Luis Borges, Anthony Burgess,
Ernest Hemingway, Iris Murdoch

1900 through 1959

TWENTIETH-CENTURY LITERARY CRITICISM

for example: Willa Cather, F. Scott Fitzgerald,
Henry James, Mark Twain, Virginia Woolf

1800 through 1899

NINETEENTH-CENTURY LITERATURE CRITICISM

for example: Fyodor Dostoevsky, Nathaniel Hawthorne,
George Sand, William Wordsworth

1400 through 1799

***LITERATURE CRITICISM FROM 1400 TO 1800
(excluding Shakespeare)***

for example: Anne Bradstreet, Alexander Pope,
François Rabelais, Phillis Wheatley

SHAKESPEAREAN CRITICISM

Shakespeare's plays and poetry

Antiquity through 1399

CLASSICAL AND MEDIEVAL LITERATURE CRITICISM

for example: Dante, Homer, Plato, Sophocles, Vergil

Gale also publishes related criticism series:

CHILDREN'S LITERATURE REVIEW

This series covers authors of all eras who have written for the preschool through high school audience.

SHORT STORY CRITICISM

This series covers the major short fiction writers of all nationalities and periods of literary history.

POETRY CRITICISM

This series covers poets of all nationalities, movements, and periods of literary history.

DRAMA CRITICISM

This series covers playwrights of all nationalities and periods of literary history.

BLACK LITERATURE CRITICISM

This three-volume set presents criticism of works by major black writers of the past two hundred years.

WORLD LITERATURE CRITICISM, 1500 TO THE PRESENT

This six-volume set provides excerpts from criticism on 225 authors from the Renaissance to the present.

ISSN 0276-8178

Volume 19

Twentieth-Century Literary Criticism

**Excerpts from Criticism of the
Works of Novelists, Poets, Playwrights,
Short Story Writers, and Other Creative Writers
Who Lived between 1900 and 1960,
from the First Published Critical
Appraisals to Current Evaluations**

**Dennis Poupard
Editor**

**Marie Lazzari
Thomas Ligotti
Associate Editors**

 Gale Research Inc. • *DETROIT* • *WASHINGTON, D.C.* • *LONDON*

STAFF

Dennis Poupard, *Editor*

Marie Lazzari, Thomas Ligotti, *Associate Editors*

Serita Lanette Lockard, Lee Schreiner, *Senior Assistant Editors*

Sandra Giraud, Paula Kepos, Sandra Liddell, Joann Prosyniuk, *Assistant Editors*

Sharon R. Gunton, Phyllis Carmel Mendelson, James E. Person, Jr., *Contributing Editors*
Melissa Reiff Hug, *Contributing Assistant Editor*

Lizbeth A. Purdy, *Production Supervisor*
Denise Michlewicz Broderick, *Production Coordinator*
Eric Berger, *Assistant Production Coordinator*
Robin Du Blanc, Sheila J. Nasea, *Editorial Assistants*

Victoria B. Cariappa, *Research Coordinator*
Jeannine Schiffman Davidson, *Assistant Research Coordinator*
Daniel Kurt Gilbert, Maureen R. Richards, Keith E. Schooley,
Filomena Sgambati, Vincenza G. Tranchida, Valerie J. Webster, Mary D. Wise, *Research Assistants*

Linda M. Pugliese, *Manuscript Coordinator*
Donna Craft, *Assistant Manuscript Coordinator*
Maureen A. Puhl, Rosetta Irene Simms, *Manuscript Assistants*

Jeanne A. Gough, *Permissions Supervisor*
Janice M. Mach, *Permissions Coordinator, Text*
Patricia A. Seefelt, *Permissions Coordinator, Illustrations*
Susan D. Battista, *Assistant Permissions Coordinator*
Margaret A. Chamberlain, Sandra C. Davis, Kathy Grell,
Mary M. Matuz, *Senior Permissions Assistants*
Colleen M. Crane, Josephine M. Keene, Mabel C. Schoening, *Permissions Assistants*
Margaret Carson, H. Diane Cooper, Dorothy J. Fowler, Anita Williams, *Permissions Clerks*

Library of Congress Catalog Card Number 76-46132
ISBN 0-8103-2401-6
ISSN 0276-8178

Computerized photocomposition by
Typographics, Incorporated
Kansas City, Missouri

Printed in the United States of America

Published simultaneously in the United Kingdom
by Gale Research International Limited
(An affiliated company of Gale Research Inc.)

10 9 8 7 6 5 4 3 2

Contents

Preface

It is impossible to overvalue the importance of literature in the intellectual, emotional, and spiritual evolution of humanity. Literature is that which both lifts us out of everyday life and helps us to better understand it. Through the fictive lives of such characters as Anna Karenina, Jay Gatsby, or Leopold Bloom, our perceptions of the human condition are enlarged, and we are enriched.

Literary criticism can also give us insight into the human condition, as well as into the specific moral and intellectual atmosphere of an era, for the criteria by which a work of art is judged reflects contemporary philosophical and social attitudes. Literary criticism takes many forms: the traditional essay, the book or play review, even the parodic poem. Criticism can also be of several types: normative, descriptive, interpretive, textual, appreciative, generic. Collectively, the range of critical response helps us to understand a work of art, an author, an era.

Scope of the Series

Twentieth-Century Literary Criticism (TCLC) is designed to serve as an introduction for the student of twentieth-century literature to the authors of the period 1900 to 1960 and to the most significant commentators on these authors. The great poets, novelists, short story writers, playwrights, and philosophers of this period are by far the most popular writers for study in high school and college literature courses. Since a vast amount of relevant critical material confronts the student, *TCLC* presents significant passages from the most important published criticism to aid students in the location and selection of commentaries on authors who died between 1900 and 1960.

The need for *TCLC* was suggested by the usefulness of the Gale series *Contemporary Literary Criticism (CLC)*, which excerpts criticism on current writing. Because of the difference in time span under consideration *(CLC* considers authors who were still living after 1959), there is no duplication of material between *CLC* and *TCLC*. For further information about *CLC* and Gale's other criticism series, users should consult the Guide to Gale Literary Criticism Series preceding the title page in this volume.

Each volume of *TCLC* is carefully compiled to include authors who represent a variety of genres and nationalities and who are currently regarded as the most important writers of this era. In addition to major authors, *TCLC* also presents criticism on lesser-known writers whose significant contributions to literary history are important to the study of twentieth-century literature.

Each author entry in *TCLC* is intended to provide an overview of major criticism on an author. Therefore, the editors include approximately twenty authors in each 600-page volume (compared with approximately fifty authors in a *CLC* volume of similar size) so that more attention may be given to an author. Each author entry represents a historical survey of the critical response to that author's work: some early criticism is presented to indicate initial reactions, later criticism is selected to represent any rise or decline in the author's reputation, and current retrospective analyses provide students with a modern view. The length of an author entry is intended to reflect the amount of critical attention the author has received from critics writing in English, and from foreign criticism in translation. Critical articles and books that have not been translated into English are excluded. Every attempt has been made to identify and include excerpts from the seminal essays on each author's work. Additionally, as space permits, especially insightful essays of a more limited scope are included.

An author may appear more than once in the series because of the great quantity of critical material available, or because of a resurgence of criticism generated by events such as an author's centennial or anniversary celebration, the republication of an author's works, or the publication of a newly translated work or volume of letters. Generally, a few author entries in each volume of *TCLC* feature criticism on single works by major authors who have appeared previously in the series. Only those individual works that have been the subjects of vast amounts of criticism and are widely studied in literature classes are selected for this in-depth treatment. Rainer Maria Rilke's *The Notebooks of Malte Laurids Brigge* and Mark Twain's *Adventures of Huckleberry Finn* are examples of such entries in *TCLC,* Volume 19.

Organization of the Book

An author entry consists of the following elements: author heading, biographical and critical introduction, principal works, excerpts of criticism (each followed by a bibliographical citation), and an additional bibliography for further reading.

- The *author heading* consists of the author's full name, followed by birth and death dates. The unbracketed portion of the name denotes the form under which the author most commonly wrote. If an author wrote consistently under a pseudonym, the pseudonym will be listed in the author heading and the real name given in parentheses on the first line of the biographical and critical introduction. Also located at the beginning of the introduction to the author entry are any name variations under which an author wrote, including transliterated forms for authors whose languages use nonroman alphabets. Uncertainty as to a birth or death date is indicated by a question mark.

- The *biographical and critical introduction* contains background information designed to introduce the reader to an author and to the critical debate surrounding his or her work. Parenthetical material following many of the introductions provides references to biographical and critical reference series published by Gale, including *Children's Literature Review, Contemporary Authors, Dictionary of Literary Biography, Something about the Author,* and past volumes of *TCLC.*

- Most *TCLC* entries include *portraits* of the author. Many entries also contain illustrations of materials pertinent to an author's career, including holographs of manuscript pages, title pages, dust jackets, letters, or representations of important people, places, and events in an author's life.

- The *list of principal works* is chronological by date of first book publication and identifies the genre of each work. In the case of foreign authors where there are both foreign language publications and English translations, the title and date of the first English-language edition are given in brackets. Unless otherwise indicated, dramas are dated by first performance, not first publication.

- *Criticism* is arranged chronologically in each author entry to provide a useful perspective on changes in critical evaluation over the years. All titles by the author featured in the critical entry are printed in boldface type to enable the user to ascertain without difficulty the works being discussed. Also for purposes of easier identification, the critic's name and the publication date of the essay are given at the beginning of each piece of criticism. Unsigned criticism is preceded by the title of the journal in which it appeared. When an anonymous essay is later attributed to a critic, the critic's name appears in brackets at the beginning of the excerpt and in the bibliographical citation.

- Critical essays are prefaced by *explanatory notes* as an additional aid to students using *TCLC.* The explanatory notes provide several types of useful information, including: the reputation of a critic; the importance of a work of criticism; the specific type of criticism (biographical, psychoanalytic, structuralist, etc.); a synopsis of the criticism; and the growth of critical controversy or changes in critical trends regarding an author's work. In many cases, these notes cross-reference the work of critics who agree or disagree with each other. Dates in parentheses within the explanatory notes refer to a book publication date when they follow a book title and to an essay date when they follow a critic's name.

- A complete *bibliographical citation* designed to facilitate location of the original essay or book by the interested reader follows each piece of criticism. An asterisk (*) at the end of a citation indicates that the essay is on more than one author.

- The *additional bibliography* appearing at the end of each author entry suggests further reading on the author. In some cases it includes essays for which the editors could not obtain reprint rights. An asterisk (*) at the end of a citation indicates that the essay is on more than one author.

An appendix lists the sources from which material in each volume has been reprinted. It does not, however, list every book or periodical consulted in the preparation of the volume.

Cumulative Indexes

Each volume of *TCLC* includes a cumulative index to authors listing all the authors who have appeared in *Contemporary Literary Criticism, Twentieth-Century Literary Criticism, Nineteenth-Century Literature Criticism,* and *Literature Criticism from 1400 to 1800,* along with cross-references to the Gale series *Children's Literature Review, Authors in the News, Contemporary Authors, Contemporary Authors Autobiography Series, Dictionary of Literary Biography, Something about the Author,* and *Yesterday's Authors of Books for Children.* Users will welcome this cumulated author index as a useful tool for locating an author within the various series. The index, which lists birth and death dates when available, will be particularly valuable for those authors who are identified with a certain period but whose death date causes them to be placed in another, or for those authors whose careers span two periods. For example, F. Scott Fitzgerald is found in *TCLC,* yet a writer often associated with him, Ernest Hemingway, is found in *CLC.*

Each volume of *TCLC* also includes a cumulative nationality index. Author names are arranged alphabetically under their respective nationalities and followed by the volume numbers in which they appear.

A cumulative index to critics is another useful feature in *TCLC.* Under each critic's name are listed the authors on whom the critic has written and the volume and page where the criticism may be found.

Acknowledgments

No work of this scope can be accomplished without the cooperation of many people. The editors especially wish to thank the copyright holders of the excerpted criticism included in this volume, the permissions managers of many book and magazine publishing companies for assisting us in securing reprint rights, and Anthony Bogucki for assistance with copyright research. We are also grateful to the staffs of the Detroit Public Library, the Library of Congress, University of Detroit Library, University of Michigan Library, and Wayne State University Library for making their resources available to us.

Suggestions Are Welcome

In response to various suggestions, several features have been added to *TCLC* since the series began, including: explanatory notes to excerpted criticism that provide important information regarding critics and their work; a cumulative author index listing authors in all Gale literary criticism series; entries devoted to criticism on a single work by a major author; and more extensive illustrations.

Readers who wish to suggest authors to appear in future volumes, or who have other suggestions, are cordially invited to write the editors.

Authors to Be Featured in *TCLC*, Volumes 20 and 21

Arnold Bennett (English novelist)—Bennett is credited with introducing techniques of European Naturalism to the English novel. Set in the manufacturing district of the author's native Staffordshire, Bennett's novels tell of the thwarted ambitions of those who endure a dull, provincial existence.

Hermann Broch (Austrian novelist, poet, and essayist)—Broch was a philosophical novelist whose works are considered profound reflections upon the social and moral disintegration of modern Europe. His major works, which include his masterpiece *The Sleepwalkers,* have been compared to James Joyce's *Ulysses* and *Finnegans Wake* for their contribution to the Modernist exploration of language.

Sãdeq Hedãyat (Iranian novelist)—Considered the most important prose writer in modern Persian literature, Hedãyat has been compared to Edgar Allan Poe and Franz Kafka for his gruesome outlook on the human condition and for the often fantastic quality of his works.

James Hilton (English novelist)—Hilton was the author of *Goodbye Mr. Chips* and *Lost Horizon,* two of the most popular and well-loved works of twentieth-century English fiction.

Julia Ward Howe (American poet and biographer)—A famous suffragette and social reformer, Howe was also a popular poet who is best known as the composer of "The Battle Hymn of the Republic."

T. E. Hulme (English poet)—A major influence on the work of T. S. Eliot, Ezra Pound, and other important twentieth-century poets, Hulme was the chief theorist of Imagism and Modernism in English poetry.

Ilya Ilf and Evgeny Petrov (Russian novelists and short story writers)—Among the most prominent humorists of post-Revolutionary Russia, Ilf and Petrov collaborated on numerous works satirizing the weaknesses of Soviet society. Their humorous but pointed stories and novels earned them a reputation as "the Soviet Mark Twain."

Sheila Kaye-Smith (English novelist)—Kaye-Smith is best known for her novels of the Sussex countryside. Often compared to Thomas Hardy's Wessex novels, the works of Kaye-Smith also portray strong-willed male and female characters who demonstrate the natural vitality of an agrarian way of life.

Velimir Khlebnikov (Russian poet)—Khlebnikov was a leading member of the Russian Futurists, a literary movement whose adherents sought to revitalize poetry by rejecting traditional aesthetic principles. The author of experimental poetry and multi-genre works he called "super-tales," Khlebnikov is considered among the twentieth century's most brilliant linguistic innovators and poetic craftsmen.

Thomas Mann (German novelist)—In novels characterized by irony and a deep, often humorous, sympathy for humanity, Mann singlehandedly raised the German novel to an international stature it had not enjoyed since the time of the Romantics. In his most important novel, *The Magic Mountain,* Mann explored such themes as the nature of time, the seduction of the individual by disease and death, and the conflict between the intellect and the spirit. *TCLC* will devote an entry to critical discussion of this work, which is considered the twentieth century's foremost representative of the German bildungsroman.

Ferenc Molnár (Hungarian dramatist)—The author of comedies praised for their wit, charm, and technical excellence, Molnár was the first Hungarian dramatist to achieve international acclaim. His most successful play, *Liliom,* gained fame through its adaptation by Richard Rodgers and Oscar Hammerstein as the musical *Carousel.*

Horacio Quiroga (Uruguayan short story writer)—Represented in English translation by the recently published *Decapitated Chicken, and Other Stories,* Quiroga's tales of death and madness in the jungles of South America reflect the influence of Edgar Allan Poe as well as the sensational tragedies of Quiroga's own life.

Raymond Roussel (French novelist and dramatist)—Roussel was a wealthy eccentric who staged expensive but entirely unsuccessful productions of his own plays and published elaborate but ignored editions of his novels. He was claimed as a forerunner by the Surrealists for the extravagant and often shocking imagination demonstrated in his works and is today recognized as one of the oddest and most ingenious authors in modern literature.

John Ruskin (English critic)—Most renowned for his critical writings on art and architecture, particularly *Stones of Venice* and the five-volume series *Modern Painters,* Ruskin was also an important social critic. His advocacy of various reforms and his association with the Pre-Raphaelite circle of artists, writers, and thinkers place him at the intellectual and cultural center of Victorian England.

Bernard Shaw (Irish dramatist, critic, novelist, and essayist)—Considered the greatest dramatist of the English language since Shakespeare, Shaw revolutionized English theater by disposing of the romantic conventions of the "well-made" play and instituting a theater of ideas firmly grounded in realism. In *Man and Superman,* which he called "a dramatic parable of Creative Evolution," Shaw described his theory of a life-force that guides the evolution of humanity. *TCLC* will devote an entire entry to critical discussion of this work.

Olaf Stapleton (English novelist)—An important influence on the works of C. S. Lewis, Arthur C. Clarke, and Stanislaw Lem, Stapleton was the author of what he described as "fantastic fiction of a semi-philosophical kind." Today, critics regard his novels as among the most significant and accomplished examples of science fiction and speculative writing.

Lincoln Steffens (American journalist and autobiographer)—Steffens was one of a group of writers in the early twentieth century who were described as "muckrakers" by President Theodore Roosevelt. Steffens's call for radical reforms in American government and society forms the substance of his best works, including *The Shame of the Cities* and *The Struggle for Self Government,* and serves as the background to his highly readable *Autobiography.*

George Sterling (American poet)—A poet whose work was traditional in form yet modern in the nihilist sensibility it expressed, Sterling was one of the major figures in the bohemian society of writers and artists who congregated around Carmel, California, in the early decades of the twentieth century.

Beatrice and Sydney James Webb (English social writers)—Prominent members of the progressive Fabian society, the Webbs wrote sociological works significant to the advent of socialist reform in England and influenced the work of several major authors, including H. G. Wells and George Bernard Shaw.

Owen Wister (American novelist)—Considered the founder of modern fiction about the Old West, Wister is best known as the author of *The Virginian,* a novel that established the basic character types, settings, and plots of the Western genre.

Virginia Woolf (English novelist)—Woolf is one of the most important English novelists of the twentieth century. *Mrs. Dalloway* is perhaps the most frequently studied of her novels and a landmark work in the history of modern fiction for its use of the literary device known as stream of consciousness. *TCLC* will devote an entire entry to this important work.

Emile Zola (French novelist, dramatist, and critic)—Zola was the founder and principal theorist of Naturalism, perhaps the most influential literary moveme..t in modern literature. His twenty-volume series *Les Rougon-Macquart* is one of the monuments of Naturalist fiction and served as a model for late nineteenth-century novelists seeking a more candid and accurate representation of human life.

Additional Authors to Appear
in Future Volumes

Abbey, Henry 1842-1911
Abercrombie, Lascelles 1881-1938
Adamic, Louis 1898-1951
Ade, George 1866-1944
Agustini, Delmira 1886-1914
Akers, Elizabeth Chase 1832-1911
Akiko, Yosano 1878-1942
Aldanov, Mark 1886-1957
Aldrich, Thomas Bailey 1836-1907
Aliyu, Dan Sidi 1902-1920
Allen, Hervey 1889-1949
Archer, William 1856-1924
Arlen, Michael 1895-1956
Austin, Alfred 1835-1913
Austin, Mary 1868-1934
Bahr, Hermann 1863-1934
Bailey, Philip James 1816-1902
Barbour, Ralph Henry 1870-1944
Barreto, Lima 1881-1922
Benét, William Rose 1886-1950
Benjamin, Walter 1892-1940
Bennett, James Gordon, Jr. 1841-1918
Benson, E(dward) F(rederic) 1867-1940
Berdyaev, Nikolai Aleksandrovich
   1874-1948
Beresford, J(ohn) D(avys) 1873-1947
Bergson, Henri 1859-1941
Binyon, Laurence 1869-1943
Bishop, John Peale 1892-1944
Blackmore, R(ichard) D(oddridge)
   1825-1900
Blake, Lillie Devereux 1835-1913
Blum, Leon 1872-1950
Bodenheim, Maxwell 1892-1954
Bowen, Marjorie 1886-1952
Byrne, Donn 1889-1928
Caine, Hall 1853-1931
Campana, Dino 1885-1932
Cannan, Gilbert 1884-1955
Chand, Prem 1880-1936
Churchill, Winston 1871-1947
Coppée, Francois 1842-1908
Corelli, Marie 1855-1924
Croce, Benedetto 1866-1952
Crofts, Freeman Wills 1879-1957
Cruze, James (Jens Cruz Bosen) 1884-
   1942
Curros, Enriquez Manuel 1851-1908
Dall, Caroline Wells (Healy) 1822-1912
Daudet, Leon 1867-1942
Davidson, John 1857-1909
Day, Clarence 1874-1935
Delafield, E.M. (Edme Elizabeth Monica
   de la Pasture) 1890-1943
Deneson, Jacob 1836-1919
DeVoto, Bernard 1897-1955

Douglas, (George) Norman 1868-1952
Douglas, Lloyd C(assel) 1877-1951
Dovzhenko, Alexander 1894-1956
Drinkwater, John 1882-1937
Drummond, W.H. 1854-1907
Durkheim, Emile 1858-1917
Duun, Olav 1876-1939
Eaton, Walter Prichard 1878-1957
Eggleston, Edward 1837-1902
Erskine, John 1879-1951
Fadeyev, Alexander 1901-1956
Ferland, Albert 1872-1943
Feydeau, Georges 1862-1921
Field, Rachel 1894-1924
Flecker, James Elroy 1884-1915
Fletcher, John Gould 1886-1950
Fogazzaro, Antonio 1842-1911
Francos, Karl Emil 1848-1904
Frank, Bruno 1886-1945
Frazer, (Sir) George 1854-1941
Freeman, R. Austin 1862-1943
Freud, Sigmund 1853-1939
Fröding, Gustaf 1860-1911
Fuller, Henry Blake 1857-1929
Futabatei, Shimei 1864-1909
Gladkov, Fydor Vasilyevich 1883-1958
Glaspell, Susan 1876-1948
Glyn, Elinor 1864-1943
Golding, Louis 1895-1958
Gosse, Edmund 1849-1928
Gould, Gerald 1885-1936
Guest, Edgar 1881-1959
Gumilyov, Nikolay 1886-1921
Gyulai, Pal 1826-1909
Hale, Edward Everett 1822-1909
Hall, James 1887-1951
Harris, Frank 1856-1931
Hawthorne, Julian 1846-1934
Hernandez, Miguel 1910-1942
Hewlett, Maurice 1861-1923
Heyward, DuBose 1885-1940
Hope, Anthony 1863-1933
Hudson, W(illiam) H(enry) 1841-1922
Huidobro, Vincente 1893-1948
Hviezdoslav (Pavol Orszagh) 1849-1921
Ilyas, Abu Shabaka 1903-1947
Imbs, Bravig 1904-1946
Ivanov, Vyacheslav Ivanovich 1866-
   1949
Jacobs, W(illiam) W(ymark) 1863-1943
James, Will 1892-1942
Jammes, Francis 1868-1938
Jerome, Jerome K(lapka) 1859-1927
Johnson, Fenton 1888-1958
Johnston, Mary 1870-1936
Jorgensen, Johannes 1866-1956

King, Grace 1851-1932
Kirby, William 1817-1906
Kline, Otis Albert 1891-1946
Kohut, Adolph 1848-1916
Korolenko, Vladimir 1853-1921
Kuzmin, Mikhail Alexseyevich 1875-
   1936
Lamm, Martin 1880-1950
Lawson, Henry 1867-1922
Ledwidge, Francis 1887-1917
Leipoldt, C. Louis 1880-1947
Lemonnier, Camille 1844-1913
Lima, Jorge De 1895-1953
Locke, Alain 1886-1954
Long, Frank Belknap 1903-1959
Louys, Pierre 1870-1925
Lucas, E(dward) V(errall) 1868-1938
Lyall, Edna 1857-1903
Maghar, Josef Suatopluk 1864-1945
Manning, Frederic 1887-1935
Maragall, Joan 1860-1911
Marais, Eugene 1871-1936
Martin du Gard, Roger 1881-1958
Masaryk, Tomas 1850-1939
McClellan, George Marion 1860-1934
McCoy, Horace 1897-1955
Meyrink, Gustave 1868-1932
Mirbeau, Octave 1850-1917
Mistral, Frederic 1830-1914
Monro, Harold 1879-1932
Moore, Thomas Sturge 1870-1944
Morley, Christopher 1890-1957
Morley, S. Griswold 1883-1948
Mqhayi, S.E.K. 1875-1945
Murray, (George) Gilbert 1866-1957
Nansen, Peter 1861-1918
Nobre, Antonio 1867-1900
Nordhoff, Charles 1887-1947
Norris, Frank 1870-1902
Obstfelder, Sigborn 1866-1900
O'Dowd, Bernard 1866-1959
Ophuls, Max 1902-1957
Orczy, Baroness 1865-1947
Owen, Seaman 1861-1936
Page, Thomas Nelson 1853-1922
Papini, Giovanni 1881-1956
Parrington, Vernon L. 1871-1929
Peck, George W. 1840-1916
Péret, Benjamin 1899-1959
Phillips, Ulrich B. 1877-1934
Pickthall, Marjorie 1883-1922
Pinero, Arthur Wing 1855-1934
Pontoppidan, Henrik 1857-1943
Prem Chand, Mushi 1880-1936
Prévost, Marcel 1862-1941
Quiller-Couch, Arthur 1863-1944

Randall, James G. 1881-1953
Rappoport, Solomon 1863-1944
Read, Opie 1852-1939
Reisen (Reizen), Abraham 1875-1953
Remington, Frederic 1861-1909
Riley, James Whitcomb 1849-1916
Rinehart, Mary Roberts 1876-1958
Ring, Max 1817-1901
Rohmer, Sax 1883-1959
Rolland, Romain 1866-1944
Rozanov, Vasily Vasilyevich 1856-1919
Saar, Ferdinand von 1833-1906
Sabatini, Rafael 1875-1950
Saintsbury, George 1845-1933
Sakutaro, Hagiwara 1886-1942
Sanborn, Franklin Benjamin 1831-1917
Santayana, George 1863-1952
Sardou, Victorien 1831-1908
Schickele, René 1885-1940
Schwob, Marcel 1867-1905
Seabrook, William 1886-1945

Seton, Ernest Thompson 1860-1946
Shestov, Lev 1866-1938
Shiels, George 1886-1949
Skram, Bertha Amalie 1847-1905
Smith, Pauline 1883-1959
Sodergran, Edith Irene 1892-1923
Solovyov, Vladimir 1853-1900
Sorel, Georges 1847-1922
Spector, Mordechai 1859-1922
Spengler, Oswald 1880-1936
Squire, J(ohn) C(ollings) 1884-1958
Stavenhagen, Fritz 1876-1906
Stockton, Frank R. 1834-1902
Subrahmanya Bharati, C. 1882-1921
Sully-Prudhomme, Rene 1839-1907
Thoma, Ludwig 1867-1927
Trotsky, Leon 1870-1940
Tuchmann, Jules 1830-1901
Turner, W(alter) J(ames) R(edfern) 1889-1946
Vachell, Horace Annesley 1861-1955

Van Dine, S.S. (William H. Wright) 1888-1939
Van Dyke, Henry 1852-1933
Vazov, Ivan Minchov 1850-1921
Veblen, Thorstein 1857-1929
Villaespesa, Francisco 1877-1936
Wallace, Edgar 1874-1932
Wallace, Lewis 1827-1905
Walsh, Ernest 1895-1926
Webb, Mary 1881-1927
Webster, Jean 1876-1916
Whitlock, Brand 1869-1927
Wilson, Harry Leon 1867-1939
Wolf, Emma 1865-1932
Wood, Clement 1888-1950
Wren, P(ercival) C(hristopher) 1885-1941
Yonge, Charlotte Mary 1823-1901
Zecca, Ferdinand 1864-1947
Zeromski, Stefan 1864-1925

Readers are cordially invited to suggest additional authors to the editors.

James (Rufus) Agee

1909-1955

American novelist, journalist, critic, essayist, screenwriter, and poet.

Known primarily as a journalist during his lifetime, Agee has since been recognized as a versatile writer of outstanding talent through the posthumous publication of critically respected works in a variety of genres. His most highly regarded writings include the autobiographical novel *A Death in the Family,* which was awarded the 1958 Pulitzer Prize in fiction, and *Let Us Now Praise Famous Men,* considered one of the most important works to document the social trauma of the Great Depression.

Agee was born in Knoxville, Tennessee. His father was the poorly schooled son of a rural Southern family and his mother the daughter of an educated Northern family, a dichotomy which preoccupied Agee throughout his life and decisively affected his literary career. When Agee was six years old his father was killed in an automobile accident, and the boy was raised by his mother. The loss of his father prompted in Agee's later life what commentators have called a crisis of identity, which was at least partially due to Agee's conviction that he had betrayed his father's Southern heritage by becoming a successful member of Northern society. From 1919 to 1924 Agee attended St. Andrew's, an Episcopal boarding school in the Cumberland Mountains, where he first met Father James Flye and initiated a friendship that provided him with encouragement and guidance throughout his life. He continued his education at Phillips Exeter Academy in Maine and began earnest preparation for a career as an author, contributing numerous poems, short stories, dramas, and essays to the *Phillips Exeter Monthly.* He continued to write prolifically at Harvard, where a successful academic career culminated in graduation with honors, despite periodic bouts of severe depression and his reluctance to become part of the social establishment represented by the prestigious university. Upon graduation in 1932, Agee was offered a position as a staff writer on *Fortune* magazine, which he accepted despite misgivings about his potential for success in writing for a magazine devoted to capitalism, given his own poetic temperament and leftist political leanings. The association proved difficult; Agee later wrote that his attitude toward *Fortune* varied from ''a sort of hard, masochistic liking without enthusiasm or trust, to direct nausea at the sight of this symbol $ and this % and this *biggest* and this blank billion.'' Nevertheless, the work provided him with a steady income and enough free time to continue his other literary projects, and he remained with *Fortune* for the next seven years.

In 1934 Agee's first volume of poetry, *Permit Me Voyage,* was published to generally favorable reviews. Critics admired the technical excellence of the poems, written primarily in the tradition of Elizabethan and Jacobean English verse, and predicted for Agee a distinguished career in poetry. However, Agee soon abandoned poetry for prose, a medium which, according to Robert Fitzgerald, was better suited to his literary ambitions. In 1936 Agee was assigned by *Fortune* to the project that eventually became the central work of his career, *Let Us Now Praise Famous Men. Fortune* conceived the project as a series of articles, illustrated with photographs by Walker Ev-

Photograph by Florence Homolka

ans, which was to document the lives of tenant farmers in the Deep South, examining farm economics and evaluating the efficacy of relief efforts. The work resulting from Agee's eight weeks among Alabama sharecroppers, however, was a lengthy, subjective, and deeply personal account of three tenant families and Agee's stay among them. *Fortune* rejected the work, and Agee devoted the next three years to expanding and reworking his manuscript, which was eventually published in book form, with photographs by Evans, in 1941. Although many critics of the 1940s objected to the work's departure from conventional documentary methods, finding particularly offensive Agee's personal participation in the narrative and his frank treatment of sexuality, critical reaction to *Let Us Now Praise Famous Men* was generally favorable. The book was nevertheless ignored by the reading public, with the first edition selling only five hundred copies. Upon its reissue two decades later, however, *Let Us Now Praise Famous Men* was acclaimed by critics and readers alike as a brilliant and original work, judged by Granville Hicks to be ''one of the extraordinary, one of the great books of our time.''

In 1939 Agee moved from *Fortune* to *Time,* hoping that a position as a literature and film critic for *Time* would be better suited to his talents and temperament. In his film reviews for *Time,* and particularly in those written for the *Nation* beginning in 1942, Agee produced what critics consider America's first serious body of film criticism. Praised for their intelligence, insight, and wit, Agee's critiques prompted W. H. Auden to proclaim the weekly *Nation* column "Agee on Films" "the most remarkable regular event in American journalism today." Agee remained with *Time* and the *Nation* until 1948, when he resigned both positions in order to concentrate on a variety of literary projects. He devoted the rest of his life to writing fiction and Hollywood film scripts, most notably a treatment of C. S. Forester's novel *The African Queen* in collaboration with John Huston. In 1951 he suffered his first heart attack, after which he was advised by doctors to limit his drinking, smoking, and habitual overwork. According to friends, Agee was unwilling to adopt a sedate lifestyle after years of overindulgence, and his health rapidly deteriorated. He died of a heart attack in 1955.

Let Us Now Praise Famous Men, Agee's least orthodox and most famous work, is also considered by critics to be the pivotal work of his literary career. In returning to the rural South after years at Eastern schools and as a member of New York's literary community, Agee was presented with an opportunity to rediscover the Southern heritage that he felt he had betrayed, as well as to confront the memories of his childhood in Knoxville and at St. Andrews. Empathetic toward the farmers of the South and sensitive to their situation, he objected to the assignment as delineated at *Fortune,* and to social documentary in general, in the following terms: "It seems to me curious, not to say obscene and thoroughly terrifying . . . to pry intimately into the lives of an undefended and appallingly damaged group of human beings, an ignorant and helpless rural family, for the purpose of parading the nakedness, disadvantage, and humiliation of these lives before another group of human beings." He also disapproved of the often patronizing attitude of journalists toward their subjects in essays designed to elicit pity rather than respect and understanding from the reader. Agee therefore took particular care to present his subjects as individuals, not as class victims or representatives of a social group. He departed most radically from conventional documentary methods in his personal participation in the narrative. Critics observe that the work is as much a record of Agee's reaction to his subjects and their plight as it is a documentary; Richard H. King has commented that in *Let Us Now Praise Famous Men* "a (perhaps *the*) central concern was an investigation of his own motives and intentions." Basing his aesthetic approach to the project on his conviction that life is superior to art, Agee relied heavily on bare description in an attempt to transcend the artifice of literature, meticulously cataloging the contents of the tenants' houses down to the texture of the dust in a corner of a drawer. Lamenting the inadequacy of words to express what he had observed, he regretted that the book could not include "fragments of cloth, bits of cotton, lumps of earth, records of speech, pieces of wood and iron, phials of odors, plates of food and of excrement." Critics often comment on the shapelessness of the text, which is a disorderly assembly of topics and digressions that appear to have been arranged, as William Stott has observed, "on the spur of the moment, in pencil, on a scrap of paper, with casual arrows shifting tens of thousands of words about." While some critics see this formlessness as evidence of an unfocused approach to the subject, others consider it a conscious expression by Agee of the impossibility of communicating reality, or, in the words of Lionel Trilling, "an inevitable failure, for failure alone can express the inexpressibleness of his matter."

Agee's fiction is primarily autobiographical. In *The Morning Watch,* a novella concerning the emotional and spiritual ma-turation of a twelve-year-old boy at a religious school in Tennessee, the setting and many of the characters are modeled closely after Agee's experiences at St. Andrew's. The novella has been praised for its subtle rendering of the protagonist's development from immature idealism to a mature awareness of life's complexity. At the same time, commentators have frequently criticized the work for sacrificing substance to technique, particularly in its overly rhetorical style and excessive reliance on symbolism. Richard Chase refers to the language in *The Morning Watch* as "a kind of free-lance, predatory agent" and comments that "one feels that the author has turned loose a kind of ravenous metaphorical beast who has swallowed up the hero." More highly regarded by critics is Agee's only novel, *A Death in the Family.* Like *The Morning Watch,* Agee's novel is based on an autobiographical episode, in this case the death of the author's father. Agee wrote that he intended the book to be "chiefly a remembrance of my childhood, and a memorial to my father." Left unfinished at his death, the novel was pieced together by editors who inserted several passages from outside the time frame of the story between major divisions in the narrative. Critical comment has centered on this editorial decision. While some critics maintain that the interpolations detract from the narrative by creating internal contradictions and by further complicating Agee's attempt to present the event from a variety of viewpoints, others contend that the inserted passages surpass the main narrative in the quality of their prose and contribute to the cohesiveness of the novel by focusing the narrative more exclusively on the principal character, Rufus.

Agee published relatively few works during his lifetime, and was at the time of his death widely considered a gifted writer who did not fulfill his promise due to an unwillingness to concentrate his abilities on any particular genre. The publication of *A Death in the Family,* however, and its subsequent receipt of the Pulitzer Prize in 1958, regenerated interest in Agee and his works; the resulting reissue of *Let Us Now Praise Famous Men* and publication of six volumes of previously unpublished poetry, prose, screenplays, and letters have established Agee's reputation as one of the most talented and accomplished writers of his generation.

(See also *TCLC,* Vol. 1; *Contemporary Authors,* Vol. 108; *Dictionary of Literary Biography,* Vol. 2: *American Novelists since World War II;* and *Dictionary of Literary Biography,* Vol. 26: *American Screenwriters.*)

PRINCIPAL WORKS

Permit Me Voyage (poetry) 1934
Let Us Now Praise Famous Men [with photographs by
      Walker Evans] (essay) 1941
The Morning Watch (novella) 1951
A Death in the Family (novel) 1957
Agee on Film: Reviews and Comments (criticism) 1958
Agee on Film, Vol. II: Five Film Scripts (screenplays)
      1960
Letters of James Agee to Father Flye (letters) 1962
Four Early Stories by James Agee (short stories) 1964
The Collected Poems of James Agee (poetry) 1968
The Collected Short Prose of James Agee (prose) 1968
Selected Journalism (prose) 1985

ARCHIBALD MacLEISH (essay date 1934)

[*A Pulitzer prize-winning American poet and dramatist, MacLeish has also served as a lawyer, university professor, Librarian of Congress, and Assistant Secretary of State. His philosophy of art rejects isolationism in favor of activism; he argues: "To declare, as the American aesthetic seems to do, that the effort to act upon the external world in the making of a work of art is a betrayal of the work of art is a misconception of the nature of art. The nature of art is action, and there is no part of human experience, public or private, on which it cannot act or should not." MacLeish was a staff member at* Fortune *during the time Agee worked there as a writer. In the following excerpt from his introduction to* Permit Me Voyage, *MacLeish favorably appraises Agee's poetic talent. For an interpretation of the collection contradicting MacLeish's view, see the excerpt by Horace Gregory dated 1935.*]

I find Agee's first book [*Permit Me Voyage*] of more interest than any first book of poems I have seen for a long time. It will not excite the new-generationers, left wing or right. Agee does not assume what is usefully known as a Position. He obviously has a deep love of the land. Equally obviously he has a considerable contempt for the dying civilization in which he has spent twenty-four years. By both he comes honestly. He spent his boyhood, with his fair share of the disadvantages so generously bestowed by the not-quite-existing order, in and about the Cumberland Mountains, and some of his vacation time during his Harvard years he spent as a harvest stiff in the Kansas and Nebraska wheat fields. But neither emotion overrides his work and neither is capitalized to carry off the book. The whole emphasis is upon the work. And the work shows it. What appears is a technical apprenticeship successfully passed, a mature and in some cases a masterly control of rhythms, a vocabulary at once personal to the poet and appropriate to the intention and, above everything else, the one poetic gift which no amount of application can purchase and which no amount of ingenuity can fake—a delicate and perceptive ear. The book in other words is the book of a young poet laboring at an art rather than the book of a young poet laboring a distinction. And because the labor is severe and ardent and successful, because the poet is clearly recognizable in the labor, the book achieves an integral and inward importance altogether independent of the opinions and purposes of its author. What is always presented in the first work of any true artist is not an accomplishment but an instrument. The instrument which has been exercised in the making of these poems is one which is capable of enduring work. (pp. 6-7)

> *Archibald MacLeish, in a foreword to* Permit Me Voyage *by James Agee, Yale University Press, 1934, pp. 5-7.*

ROBERT FROST (letter date 1934)

[*Frost was one of America's most popular twentieth-century poets. In the following excerpt from a letter to Louis Untermeyer concerning the poems in* Permit Me Voyage, *he critiques "Ann Garner" (referred to in the letter as "that long one") and an untitled poem ("the very first little lyric") that runs as follows: "Child, should any pleasant boy/ Find you lovely, many could,/ Wind not up between your joy/ The sly delays of maidenhood:/ Spread all your beauty in his sight/ And do him kindness every way,/ Since soon, too soon, the wolfer night/ Climbs in between, and ends fair play."*]

And now Agee—Oh gee! Ain't that long one a terrible travesty of Birches, Home Burial, and The Fear combined! And the psychology of having a woman so bothered over a still-born child! Take the very first little lyric in the book. What is such

a thing if it isn't pretty flawless? There are five flaws to eight lines. You can't have anything between a joy—one joy. "Many could" is painful outside parenthesis. The euphuism of "everyway" is unpleasant. Why not say every which way? What does "wind not up" mean? I've heard this being kind to a boy called winding up a little ball of yarn. Wolfer night doesn't interrupt love. Night brings lovers together. He means wolfer *day*. Of course he means Death, if you'll only help him with a little understanding. "Climbs!" Why climbs? No luck at all in my first two dips. What am I going to say to the kid? "Hereafter in a better book than this I shall desire more love and knowledge of you."

> *Robert Frost, in a letter to Louis Untermeyer on November 2, 1934, in his* Robert Frost on Writing, *edited by Elaine Barry, Rutgers University Press, 1973, p. 109.*

HORACE GREGORY (essay date 1935)

[*Gregory is a highly regarded American poet, critic, and translator. In the following excerpt he favorably reviews* Permit Me Voyage *and concurs with Archibald MacLeish's positive evaluation of Agee's talent, but disagrees with MacLeish's interpretation of Agee's message (see the excerpt by MacLeish dated 1934).*]

After reading Archibald MacLeish's ill-advised, if not downright neurotic, foreword [see excerpt dated 1934] to James Agee's first book [*Permit Me Voyage*], the temptation is to continue critical argument indefinitely and to forget the younger poet. I shall not yield entirely to that attractive prospect, for I believe that Mr. MacLeish's general enthusiasm for James Agee's work is visibly justified. Mr. Agee has a quick eye for words and has discovered the means of using them in a closely packed line of verse. He is "literary" in the fortunate sense, and there is evidence that he has exercised no little discrimination in selecting his models. Throughout his book there is also evidence of a sensitive mind and with it the presence of a swift imagination. He is, I think, a genuine poet, and a number of his poems reveal those qualities by which he may become a very good one.

In his foreword (in which the bearded face of Karl Marx is the King Charles' Head) Mr. MacLeish says: "Agee does not assume what is usefully known as a Position." At this point I am positive that Mr. MacLeish is wrong, and wilfully wrong, for his statement is an attempt to dismiss or override one of the most interesting items in James Agee's book. I am thinking of an eight-page dedication, which is a cross between a prose poem and an exercise in pulpit oratory. The fact that Agee's rostrum is a pulpit and not a soap-box does not change the nature of his purpose, which is an effort to make clear (and recite in public) a number of his many preferences.

Fifty-nine names (including God) are listed here; the list is so long that notable omissions become significant: Where nearly everyone from God to Toscanini and Charlie Chaplin is mentioned I was unable to find the names of Herbert Hoover, Earl Browder, Franklin D. Roosevelt, Mae West, or Satan. I concluded that he had not forgotten them, for such a list presupposes an excellent memory; and though the dedication reminded me of a college fraternity membership list (including the Columbia Hall of Fame) I am sure that Mr. Agee's choices were deliberate. It is, in short, a statement of Position, and here are social and esthetic and religious prejudices set down in no uncertain terms. First of all, I would say that James Agee is a bit stage-struck at the idea of becoming *famous*, and he is eager to take a seat upon the side of established reputations; and thus we have such diversely assorted dead as Christ and Shelley, Homer and Van Gogh, and among the living, Rivera, Roy Harris, and Picasso. I think it is obvious that he dislikes the Communists and Wall Street as heartily as does his master A. MacLeish; that he is for God against the anti-Christ.

At this point we enter directly into the nature of James Agee's poetry. I can think of no single poem in the book that is good in its entirety, but even the worst selection for this volume (a narrative, ''Ann Garner'') contains excellent lines. Throughout the book there is a desperate, almost hysterical necessity for the poet to sustain his Position, his faith in God; the poems are often shattered by this necessity; the inward conflict becomes too great and the poet's equipment at this moment is inadequate. Therefore, the shorter poems are the most effective, and we find such stanzas as:

> A summer noon, the middle sun
> Stunned me full of waking sleep
> And spread me slack as stone upon
> The grass in water foundered deep:

and two fine lines such as

> His hottest love and most delight
> The rooster knows for speed of fear.

A conscious and valuable esthetic produced these lines, and, more than that, I think James Agee possessed what is loosely called ''poetic vision.'' He can penetrate a given moment of experience and reproduce it in vivid imagery; yet should his emotional need become too great (and this is often the case) the ''vision'' is destroyed by an effort to be merely ''poetic'' and the elaborated image falls short of its intention. (pp. 48-51)

> *Horace Gregory, ''The Beginning of Wisdom,'' in*
> Poetry, *Vol. XLVI, No. I, April, 1935, pp. 48-51.*

SELDEN RODMAN (essay date 1941)

[*Rodman is an American art and literature critic, poet, biographer, and travel writer. As president of the Haitian Art Center of New York and codirector of the Centre d'Art in Haiti, Rodman has been instrumental in encouraging Haitian artists and promoting Haitian art in the United States. The following excerpt is taken from one of the earliest favorable reviews of* Let Us Now Praise Famous Men.]

[''**Let Us Now Praise Famous Men**''] is not a book for those who consider Kenneth Robert a realist, nor yet for those whose lukewarm passion for poetry and England is satisfied by ''The White Cliffs.'' In fact it is easy (and not unpleasant) to picture the rage that is going to draw blood to the faces of certain self-righteous reviewers of books when they shall innocently start their daily commutation through its pages. Not that these connoisseurs of stylized fiction and high-minded, politically impeccable war-reportage will travel much farther that the introductory pages (unless frightened into Hansenesque neutrality by the sheer bulk of the thing), but that the author has set his traps for them so cunningly, and with such calculated cruelty, that opening almost at random should serve to produce the desired result.

Take the opening pages. If the reader does not like the kind of naked realism which is the truth as Walker Evan's camera-eye sees it, he is through before he even reaches the text. If he passes the photographs he is immediately warned: ''Serious readers are advised to proceed to the book proper after finishing the first section of the Preface.'' The next warning, which he will take according to his share of arrogance or humility, is a statement of the book's purpose: the documented, ''unimagined'' record of three tenant families in Alabama, but ''more essentially, an independent inquiry into certain normal predicaments of human divinity.'' Next (and this is no doubt intended for those in the trade with pretensions): ''If complications arise, that is because we are trying to deal with it not as journalists, sociologists, politicians, entertainers, humanitarians, priests, or artists, but seriously . . . This is a book *only* by necessity.'' From that point on for seventeen pages, our nimble arbiter of what is still called ''taste'' will be unmercifully slugged, drugged, browbeaten, and outraged, at the end of which (but by no means for the last time) if he can still take it (which he can't, and why should he?) he will begin to become a small but integral part of the home, house, food, clothes, sleep, work, filth, excrement, blood, and spirit of Three Tenant Families.

Even if the reader should be humble about the meaning of life, and not be sure that he always understands what such indefinable, unclassifiable, and by-nature-once-occurring things as ''art'' and ''poetry'' are—even then (and this reviewer does not pretend that he began with nearly enough humility for either ''art'' or life) he will from time to time fall into one or another of the springs and masked batteries, throw down the volume in a rage, and curse the author for a confused adolescent, an Ezra Pound in Wolfe's clothing, a shocking snob, or a belligerent mystic posing with a purple pencil on the Left Bank of *Fortune*.

Part of the greatness and unique quality of ''**Let Us Now Praise Famous Men**,'' then, is its structural failure, its over-all failure as the ''work of art'' it does not aim or presume to be and which from moment to moment it is. Were it written *straight*, proceeding logically without these savage asides from the arrival of its ''spies'' (Agee and Evans) through their initiation and undoing and departure, it would be dishonest. The unparalleled intensity of much of the writing, the extraordinary nightmarish and yet sacred sense of the *whole*—the feeling that this is the tragedy of most of the two billion inhabitants of the planet extended backward and forward in space and time—the communication of Christian (most anti-churchly) brotherly love, the extreme reverence for man and nature—none of these would be remotely possible coming from a ''sophisticated,'' ''sensitive,'' ''confused,'' ''upper class,'' ''American,'' ''writer'' in the year 1941 without an accompaniment of the most profound guilt. And it is because this guilt is shamelessly exposed in its most raw and unattractive shape, that ''**Let Us Now Praise Famous Men**'' will be spat upon—and years hence (unless the country is given over to the fascists or the faith-healers of ''far away'' democracy) read. . . .

It is typical of Agee (and perhaps of the perceptive writers of our generation as a whole) that he should begin such a monumental history of three tenant families by explaining to his readers that the proper way to listen to Schubert's C Major Symphony is not to go to a concert hall but to lie down on the floor and subject one's head to the blasting sound-box of the phonograph. A writer of the 20's might have confined himself to a personal description of the music. A writer of the 30's would have pleaded the tenants' cause with moral indignation and material ''solutions.'' Our generation not only sees the connection, but, for reasons which I have already suggested, insists on it stridently. For one thing, acceptance of great art and complacence before human poverty and degradation is so incompatible and soul-damaging an attitude that its prevalence may be considered a contributing cause of the current crisis in Western society. Agee, because he leans so far in the opposite direction, will be called a romanticist of poverty by the orthodox Marxist, and a nihilist by the Progressive Education Association. But to those who believe, as this reviewer does, that the road to the ultimate cynicism is alternately paved with Resignation and Pride, it is the combined fury and humility of **"Let Us Now Praise Famous Men"** that endows it with its special truth.

> Selden Rodman, *"The Poetry of Poverty," in* The Saturday Review of Literature, *Vol. XXIV, No. 18, August 23, 1941, p. 6.*

W. H. AUDEN (essay date 1944)

[*Often considered the poetic successor of W. B. Yeats and T. S. Eliot, Auden is also highly regarded for his literary criticism. As a member of a generation of British writers strongly influenced by the ideas of Karl Marx and Sigmund Freud, Auden considered social and psychological commentary important functions of literary criticism. As a committed follower of Christianity, he considered it necessary to view art in the context of moral and theological absolutes. Thus, he regarded art as a "secondary world" which should serve a definite purpose within the "primary world" of human history. This purpose is the creation of aesthetic beauty and moral order, qualities that exist only in imperfect form in the*

Agee as a student at Harvard. Reproduced by permission of Alma Neuman.

primary world but are intrinsic to the secondary world of art. Consequently, it is both morally and aesthetically wrong for an artist to employ evil and suffering as subject matter. Auden concluded that "to write a play, that is to construct a secondary world, about Auschwitz, for example, is wicked: author and audience may try to pretend that they are morally horrified, but in fact they are passing an evening together, in the aesthetic enjoyment of horrors." While he has been criticized for significant inconsistencies in his thought throughout his career, Auden is generally regarded as a fair and perceptive critic. In the following excerpt from a letter to the editor of the Nation, *he praises the weekly column "Agee on Films."*]

Dear Sirs: In the good old days before pseudo-science and feminism ruined her, it was considered rude to congratulate one's hostess on her meals, since praise would imply that they could have been bad, and by the same rule of courtesy it should be unnecessary to write grateful letters to editors.

Astonishing excellence, however, is the exception, and James Agee's film column seems to this reader, and to many others he has spoken with, just that.

I do not care for movies very much and I rarely see them; further, I am suspicious of criticism as the literary genre which, more than any other, recruits epigones, pedants without insight, intellectuals without love. I am all the more surprised, therefore, to find myself not only reading Mr. Agee before I read anyone else in *The Nation* but also consciously looking forward all week to reading him again.

In my opinion, his column is the most remarkable regular event in American journalism today. What he says is of such profound interest, expressed with such extraordinary wit and felicity, and so transcends its ostensible—to me, rather unimportant—subject, that his articles belong in that very select class—the music critiques of Berlioz and Shaw are the only other members I know—of newspaper work which has permanent literary value.

One foresees the sad day, indeed, when Agee on Films will be the subject of a Ph.D. thesis.

> W. H. Auden, *"Agee on Films," in* The Nation, *Vol. 159, No. 21, November 18, 1944, p. 628.*

JOHN S. PHILLIPSON (essay date 1961)

[*In the following excerpt, Phillipson examines the themes and techniques of* The Morning Watch.]

In the one hundred and twenty pages of James Agee's **The Morning Watch**, symbols and motifs act, interact, and interrelate complexly. In their ordered complexity they contrast with the disorder and confusion within the mind of the book's protagonist, a twelve-year-old named Richard (we do not learn his last name) who, in a little over two hours' time, discovers some important truths about himself and the consequences of being a human being. (p. 359)

Running through this study in character-maturation are the dual concepts of God and death and, deriving from these, a third motif of suffering. All three of these are intimately associated with the day on which the story takes place—the most solemn and tragic not only in Christian history, but, from the orthodox Christian point of view, in the history of the world. In the midst of his reveries and fantasies concerning the Passion, Richard recalls the death of his own father, a surrogate-deity, and the two words *God* and *Death* are joined if not actually identified. There is a recollection of his father in his coffin six years before and the accompanying memory of the conviction that had come then of death as a fact, irrevocable and eternal. A brief prayer for that lost father, and the memory vanishes before the new recollection of a different and more important Death. As the memories depart, the boy is left with only the two words mysteriously interrelated in the fact of suffering. At the end of the novellette the three motifs are restated and interrelated in another memory from his childhood, as he recalls his mother's words: "'Daddy was terribly hurt so God has taken him up to Heaven to be with Him and he won't come back to us ever any more.'" But in their restatement at the end, they are enriched and given new significance.

To understand this significance, one must return to an earlier page, to the time when Richard, freshly wakened, prays that he may know Christ's suffering that day. For Richard, in a way, becomes a kind of *alter Christus*. Almost his first thought, on awakening, concerns the parallel between that day and the actual day of the Passion, a parallel that is frequently restated. (pp. 360-61)

[The] Lenten period is ending. It has been a period whose events have produced memorable feelings—"something like the feeling of his birthday, and of Christmas, and of Easter, and it was still more like the feeling he now seldom and faintly recalled, during the morning just after he learned of his father's death, and during the day he was buried." Here again is the father-death motif.

We have suggested here one outstanding characteristic of Richard's religiosity: his insistence upon an appropriate accompanying emotion. As he luxuriates in fanciful imaginings concerning the Passion and anticipates the triumphant joy of Easter, he recognizes (as later in the chapel) that he has been indulging in puerile self-satisfaction and ingenious explorations of consciousness and memory. This has not been pure worship, pure sorrow. Too much of himself and his subjective states have been intermingled.

Using mainly a modified omniscient technique, Agee takes us constantly within the mind of his protagonist; almost all that we see is from the boy's point of view. Rarely do we enter the minds of one of the others, but, like Richard, we hear their talk. A surprising fact, in view of Richard's sincere piety, is his overt ignoring of the profanities and obscenities of the others. Their effect has been to produce in him a kind of nausea—the kind of feeling he has "when, without being too mad or too desperate to care, he knew it was impossible not to fight." He has met something against which his protest is as useless as the protest of Christ would have been against the blasphemies of the Roman soldiers. His companions are the soldiers on this commemorative night. He fights to restore to his mind "the thorn-crowned image of his Lord" that he has envisioned when kneeling in prayer beside his cot; but the picture that comes resembles "a pious painting he knew." And here enters the motif of reality-artificiality that ramifies throughout the tale.

For Richard tries desperately to find reality, to escape from subjective states of mind, which he recognizes for what they are. In rare moments he succeeds; more often he falls into vainglorious musings. So it is that he can think on his follies of a year before and, "for the first time in his life," lose "himself in reflective remembrance." A year ago he had aspired to sainthood (an unpermissible aspiration from his new point of view); now his fancies carry him to actual imitation of the crucifixion. The imagined flash of the newspaper photographer's bulb awakens him from his revery to the humili-

ating discovery that even as he mocked his earlier puerilities he was liable to perpetrate them anew. The contrast here moderates to one between reality and fantasy. Yet Richard becomes increasingly aware of how difficult true holiness is—holiness inspired not by vainglorious love but pure, unadulterated by self-consideration. A year before, he would not have found such awareness possible. That he perceives it is evidence of religious growth.

Another significant detail, the donning and shedding of shoes, relates to the reality-artificiality motif and the death-life opposition. When the three boys leave the dormitory for the chapel, they carry their shoes. On entering the chapel, they put on their shoes, but on quitting it an hour later, they once more walk barefoot, and it is in this state that they undergo the experience at the Sand Cut.

From the point that this detail is introduced, the quality of vitality is stressed in connection with bare feet and contact with the living earth. Indeed, this is the season when the earth's ability to revive is seen and felt at its most intense. Emerging from the dormitory and touching the bare earth with his unshod feet, Richard feels as though "he had put his hand on living flesh," and the vitality of the awakening earth penetrates the gravel-strewn ground so that "its aliveness soared through him like a sob." When, an hour later, they leave the chapel, "a wave of energy [sweeps] upward through their bare feet." This is in sharp contrast to the scene and mood of death within the chapel, heated by the flames of many candles, insufficiently ventilated, so that Richard is forced to go out to avoid fainting. Within, the wildflowers gathered from the neighboring mountains in profusion are dying fast; without, all nature is being restored, with the coming of day and the renewal of the spring. Thus we find a new motif: that of death and rebirth. It has been shown in several ways—in the passage from sleep to waking, from dormitory to out-of-doors, from chapel to out-of-doors, and in the pervasive fact of Christ's impending death and resurrection.

When Richard leaves the chapel at six o-clock, he is not satisfied; he has felt a grief stemming from an awareness of Christ's passion, and he has experienced an actual physical suffering from kneeling against an uneven board and from breathing the heated, exhausted air. Now, although his soul is "filled to overflowing with a reverent and marveling peace and thankfulness," what he sees within is "a dry chalice, an empty Grail." He is troubled by "something . . . which he had done or had left undone, some failure of the soul or default of the heart which he could not now remember or was it perhaps foresee," and he recognizes a certain, though subtle, failure.

When he steps outside, Richard is transformed by the vitality he encounters. The three wonder what punishment will be theirs for having outstayed their assigned watch and, concurrently, what to do now, for with the vitality of the earth surging through them, a return to sleep has become impossible. Richard offers the first possibility: tennis; Hobe's suggestion of swimming is briefly debated and then Richard settles the matter by two words—"Come on"—and a setting-out. The others follow.

While this discussion is ensuing, three cock-crows have been heard. In the context of this night, the parallel is inescapable. As Peter has sinned in denying his Lord, so the boys are sinning through a simple failure of obedience. Within the chapel, Richard was willing in fantasy to undergo crucifixion; now, back in the "real" or everyday world, he fails in the performance of a simple obligation, without even the excuse of continued worship which might otherwise have exculpated him. Ironically he worries about the sin of pride (because the boys follow him and his command) at the moment that he sins by disobedience. For the moment, both as leader and as sinner, he has assumed the role of Peter.

The religious imagery returns as we see the rooster, "in the silence before daylight a priest, vesting himself for Mass." A stone hits the heavy netting about chicken house and the rooster's proud carriage and demeanor alter as his underlying cowardice manifests itself. And Richard, observing this, identifies himself with the rooster, knowing fear. For he fears the other boys and their knowledge of his fear. Confusedly his fear becomes mingled with his supposed pride and he meditates upon how and to whom he will confess this "sin."

On their way to the Sand Cut, two significant events occur: as they slow their steps by a hogpen, the foul-mouthed Hobe (appropriately) speaks to the hogs in their language and is answered. The sensualist Jimmy slides his hand inside his overalls against his naked body. Of Richard's thoughts and actions at this point we are told nothing, for Richard's discovery lies ahead, at a clearing in the now magic-haunted woods, when he discovers a locust shell, "the whole back split." Here again is the double motif of suffering and death, expressed in what will become Agee's perhaps most important symbol. Associated with it in Richard's mind are age and angels, the terrestrial and supernatural—two contrasts which run parallel throughout the work—in a vast hierarchy extending "to the central height." Like a human being, whom, in embryonic form, it resembles, the locust represents suffering; and in its tenacity of grip by which (it is suggested) the broken back was produced, we have suggested the universal wedding of existence and suffering. For Richard, the shell becomes an object of veneration, symbolizing, as it does, tenacity in the face of suffering and even, perhaps, by its fierce grip, acceptance of the suffering. "With veneration, talon by talon, he re established the shell in its grip against the rigid bark."

The events at the Sand Cut are also revealing and significant. Now, at the onset of puberty, the three boys take an interest, in this remote, alien place, in the others' physical development. Richard, modest, is uneasy before the others' bravado. Then comes the plunge into the water, colder than imagined, with its pain and shock, and Richard offers up the physical trial that he knows will be his as he plunges beneath "the smashing cold." Desiring to prolong the suffering, he grips a rock near the bottom of the pond to hold himself down; then, fearful that he has stayed down too long, he pushes upward frantically, half by instinct, and reaches the air in time. Here again is the death motif, linked with the motif of life or rebirth. In the Christian symbolism which permeates the story, the plunge into the pool is a symbolic baptism, which, by its very nature, implies a rebirth, going back as it does to Christ's statement in John III:5, "Unless a man be born again of water and the Spirit, he cannot enter into the kingdom of God." Standing in the water, near the shore; gazing at the rising sun, Richard epitomizes the newly baptized. His feet, in the dark water, touch the realm of cold and death from which he has just escaped; his body without is in the realm of the sun and the reviving day. In these first few moments of return to life he seeks once more "to make himself aware of the suffering to which at this moment Jesus was submitting Himself."

Of all this, Richard, understandably, says nothing to the others, except that he "was just swimming under water." And then appears a snake. Richard is both the first to see it and also its

killer. His attitude is ambiguous and ambivalent: admiration and fear are mingled. When the others set out to kill it, Richard for a moment seeks to stop them; then, as they bungle the task with a large rock, Richard, snatching up a small one, moves in close to the snake's head and effects the kill. From this come several significances.

The snake may, of course, be interpreted as a phallic symbol and, as this, an object of mingled attraction and repulsion. The boys' eagerness to kill it suggests the vehemence of their feelings. The whole context of the story, however, suggests a Christian interpretation. Traditionally the serpent has been the symbol of Satan and sin; previously Judas has been presented in metaphor as a snake. Of the three boys, Richard is the best suited for this symbolic slaying of sin; and here he becomes not just St. George in miniature but, again, an *alter Christus* in his triumph both over death (in escaping from the pond) and over the personification of sin. The snake, incidentally, serves through its newly acquired skin to restate the theme of rebirth.

Richard has been traditionally gentle to animals, and it is this gentleness which moves him to spare the snake; yet there is "something new in him which he could not understand, about which he was profoundly uneasy." This "something new" involves the matter of suffering; for the snake, Richard knows, as do the others, will not die at once: it will live to sundown. And thus a prolongation of suffering: a whole day of dying lies before it. This knowledge haunts the boy until at last he achieves a resolution of it and its implications which ends the story. Suffering and death have just been close to Richard; now, gazing at the slime on his hand, he throws the rock into the water and submerges the hand. In consciously deciding not to wash the hand, he is asserting his will against Hobe's. Having escaped death, he is approaching life newly, and the essence of that new attitude is self-knowledge combined with self-assurance.

It should be noted that when Richard throws into the pond the rock with which he has just killed the snake, it hits the water "just about where I dove in." Here we have a clearly implied restatement of a relationship between the pool-dive and the killing of the snake, with Richard as the central figure in both actions.

After the killing, the snake passes into the hands of Hobe; the three dress and, "without consultation, or imitation," put on their shoes. There is an awareness in each that the "adventures" of the night are over, and there remains now only a return to the "normal" world of convention marked by the putting on of shoes. By the killing, Richard has achieved a new stature in the eyes of his fellows, and even his refusal of the dead snake cannot diminish that stature entirely. He has become "one of them in a way he had never been before." For the moment, at least, his music lessons, his studiousness, and his lack of athletic skill are outweighed by this one act of desperate violence.

On the way back, Richard begins again to meditate upon the crucifixion and the events of that first Good Friday. The spit of the Roman soldiers is drying on Christ's face as the water and slime are drying upon his own hand; when Richard trips upon a root, his immediate thought is "Jesus falls the first time," and he asks forgiveness at once for the implied blasphemous identification.

With the donning of shoes there has come a transformation of the scene: the magic has departed: "The woods were full of ordinary sunlight now; the colors were no longer strange and the deep perspectives were no longer mysterious, but pleasant and casual." It is under these conditions of the ordinary that Richard detaches the locust shell from the tree and puts it gently into his breast pocket. He is hungry, yet he is determined to pass the day without food or water. "He thought again of the thorns, and the spittle, and the patience and courage, and of his maculate hand." And here we approach a climax, as the snake, and the boy Richard, and Christ merge in the oneness of suffering. For Christ suffered the fate of all mankind—suffering and, at the last, death, though in an extraordinary way. The hours of Christ's passion are lengthened and the day-long dying of the snake is prolonged so that suffering and dying become matters of a lifetime—Richard's and all men's. In "His: his; so hard and so long" we have the final identification of Christ with Richard, seen now in the common humanity that God assumed in becoming man, and in man's common fate.

Back in the chapel, in the artificial world of heat and death, the stifling world where breathing became difficult, Richard had fancied himself a knight-errant and, later, as Christ crucified. Later, as a minor St. George, he does indeed do a knightly deed; and identification with Christ is adumbrated throughout. Now, back in the world of the everyday, he achieves a new knowledge, a new awareness: for the first time the meaning of sin and of the Redemption come to him with a clarity and force from which the histrionic and melodramatic are wholly absent; and so it is that perfect contrition comes to him—that which he sought in vain before. In his walking on, though with difficulty, seemingly carrying a burden almost too great to be borne, the *Christus* motif receives a final restatement. The boy's last action is to throw the snake to the hogs, who devour it greedily. Richard feels a brief "horror and pity" at the renewed thought that, mangled and dismembered as it is, the snake will live till sundown; then there is a renewed recollection of his father's suffering and death and a coming of peace in the acceptance of the fact that life, suffering, and death are inextricably intermingled. His right hand (undoubtedly that with which he killed the snake) hangs at his side subtly enlarged, so it seems; and, clasped to his heart, is the locust shell. Richard's acceptance of life and its burdens—a lifetime of them—is complete. (pp. 361-66)

> John S. Phillipson, "Character, Theme, and Symbol in 'The Morning Watch'," in Western Humanities Review, Vol. XV, No. 4, Autumn, 1961, pp. 359-67.

DWIGHT MACDONALD (essay date 1967)

[*An American essayist and critic, Macdonald was a noted proponent of various radical causes from the mid-1930s until his death in 1982. Founder of the journal* Politics (*1944-49*), *which welcomed "all varieties of radical thought," he pursued Trotskyism, anarchism, pacifism, and anti-communism before eventually settling on "conservative anarchism"—a humanistic libertarian ethic of which Thoreauesque civil disobedience is a part—as his personal ethic. In the following excerpt from an essay originally published in 1967, Macdonald discusses Agee's film criticism and praises his natural writing ability.*]

Agee brought to film criticism some qualities not as common in the trade as they might be. The most distinctive one I have already mentioned: he fell in love with movies at an early age and the affair didn't cool off—on the contrary! Although he never actually brought her to bed (i.e., made a movie), love makes one observant of subtleties and nuances. Agee's reviews are suffused with intimate understanding. Most of the films he dealt with are not much—with his usual bad luck in timing,

he dealt with cinema between 1943 and 1948, a period that was pretty much a blank (except for the Italian neo-realists) compared to the silent twenties or to the renascence of the sound film that began with Bergman in the mid-fifties. However, Agee's film criticism is still good, and important, reading. Who cares, after all, about the musical performances Corno di Bassetto, alias Bernard Shaw, covered so diligently and copiously in London from 1888 to 1894; and who can resist reading his critiques today? Nor does one read Max Beerbohm's reviews of the Edwardian theatre to find what he thought of the latest work of Pinero or Henry Arthur Jones or John Galsworthy but rather to find why, and how, he thought what he thought. So with *Agee on Film*, v. I.

Not that his infatuation with the movies didn't have its drawbacks. A lover sees many aspects, mostly interesting ones, of his beloved that more objective observers miss, but he also sees many aspects, mostly interesting ones, that aren't there. Jim could always fill out the botched, meagre, banal outlines of what was actually projected on the screen with his own vision of what, to his sympathetic, imaginative eye, the director had clearly intended to be there—and what would, had he been the director, undoubtedly have been there. I remember more than once seeing some Hollywood mess on his recommendation, finding it a bore, complaining to him and being told either that it was so boring that is was exciting (an argument which impressed me then as much as it does now) or else being shaken by his interpretation of certain parts— he always looked at the parts, I always at the whole—which was so ingenious, concrete and convincing as to make me wonder how I could have missed such beauties. Convincing, that is, until I saw the film again, as with two of his favorites, Chaplain's *Monsieur Verdoux* and Wyler's *The Best Years of Our Lifes*.

His critiques, in short, are usually more interesting than their subjects. A fatal defect in a reviewer, whose job is the modest one of a tipster oriented toward the consumer: which book or play or movie will entertain not the reviewer but the customer? A venial sin, however, in a critic, whose scope is broader and whose conclusions, therefore, are not as important as the way he arrives at them—i.e., what one learns on the trip. Although I disagree, excepting a few splendid low-comedy scenes in the old Sennett tradition, with Agee's three-part *Nation* eulogy of *Verdoux*, the social, political and even some of the aesthetic arguments he develops in the course of arriving at his erroneous conclusion seem to me of the greatest interest. For, besides his lover's dedication, Agee brought to bear other qualities that are also rare in the field: intellectual power; a knowledge of books and music and other arts that I hate to call "a broad cultural background" but can think of no more concise term; a moral independence (sorry again, I mean I can't imagine him taking seriously the late "*auteur* theory" or the "in" inanities of the Mekas-Warhol high-fashion underground—he has some bleak remarks about the late Maya Deren, one of their *ur* culture-heroines). And he knew how to write, a knack not common in cinematic literature.

Agee was in fact the most copiously talented writer of my generation, ready, like the players in *Hamlet*, to take on anything: tragical, comical, historical, pastoral and, to bring Polonius's categories up to date, critical, polemical, analytical, factual, poetical and journalistical. An all-around, all-in professional word-slinger, the kind editors dream about. Also the kind that gives them nightmares, for this surface versatility and adaptability was cross-ripped by deeper tides—very private standards, commitments, reluctances, refusals so deep in his psyche as to appear to be quirks or, as we say now, hang-ups—which frustrated them. He was never able to get down on paper anywhere near as much of his prodigal gifts as some of his less prodigious but more practical contemporaries were. No sneer, intended at thrifty exploitation of one's talent—it's always been one of my strong points—nor do I mean to endorse the "mute, inglorious Miltons" line of romantic argument. If they're mute, they're not Miltons. A writer is judged by what he writes, not by what we (or he) think or hope he might have written if only . . . (As an idea cannot claim more meaning than can be deduced, without unreasonable strain, from its verbal expression: "thoughts too deep for words" are also too deep for thought.) But there are exceptions to every practical rule, or ought to be, because experience is varied—as against certain philosophical systems whose logic works smoothly because it is abstracted from the friction of imperfect reality—and I think the works Agee never got around to writing, or rather to finishing, may be such an exception. I can think of no other writer of my generation who could when he was in the vein, rise to a more powerful, original style, formally; or a style more flexibly adapted to express the particular subject. Agee was a "natural" writer, as Honus Wagner and Shoeless Joe Jackson were "natural" ballplayers. He also had something not common in American writers—a peculiar ability, again when he was going good, to combine emotion and thought, a mailerbellow cameleopard. In his best writing the conventional antithesis between "feeling" and "intellect" disappears, merging into something beyond talent or craft, something which only the old-fashioned word "genius" adequately describes. (pp. 6-8)

> Dwight Macdonald, "Agee and the Movies," in his Dwight Macdonald on Movies, *Prentice-Hall, Inc., 1969, pp. 3-14.*

ROBERT FITZGERALD (essay date 1968)

[*Fitzgerald was an American journalist, poet, and translator who has earned particular praise for his translations of* Antigone *(1937; with Dudley Fitts) and* Oedipus at Colonus *(1957). A Harvard classmate, coworker, and close friend of Agee, Fitzgerald was the editor of* The Collected Poems of James Agee *and* The Collected Short Prose of James Agee. *In the following excerpt from his introduction to* The Collected Poems, *Fitzgerald discusses the themes and techniques of Agee's poetry and the place of poetry in his literary development.*]

The earliest work in *Permit Me Voyage* is **"Ann Garner,"** written at Phillips Exeter Academy in 1928 and revised in 1929 for publication in *The Hound and Horn,* at that time edited in Cambridge by Lincoln Kirstein, a junior at Harvard College where Agee was a freshman. The latest work in the book, half a dozen of the lyrics and a few of the sonnets (by the author's direct testimony) as well as the **"Dedication,"** the **"Chorale"** and the title lyric (by all reasonable conjecture) were written in 1934, the year of publication. In these six years, then, Agee had grown from a precocious schoolboy to a strong and subtle maker of verse. He had gained an easy command of the classical tradition in English verse, of the learned Elizabethan and Jacobean poets whose learning, at least in Latin, he shared and whose resources of rhetoric and metric he made, for a short time, his own.

Of few poets in our century can this be said with more precision. The songs, the sonnets and the **"Chorale"** are in a direct line of descent from English achievements of the period between 1550 and 1640, and yet it would be foolish to consider

Agee as a young man. Photograph courtesy of Phillips Exeter Academy

them merely imitative; they are poems in their own right, new increments to the tradition. In his Foreword to the book, Archibald MacLeish justly noted "a mature and in some cases a masterly control of rhythms" and "a delicate and perceptive ear" [see excerpt dated 1934]. Consider, among the lyrics, the four beautiful modulations of rhythm in the fourth, fifth, seventh and last, and the extraordinary camera-change from rain to snow, life to death, in the last. As to the sonnets, Agee's best, notably his fifth, sixth and twentieth, can stand comparison with any but the greatest in our language.

But the cultivated gift, the literary preparation, is not the most notable thing about *Permit Me Voyage*. More notable, and in the long run more important, is something that might be called preparation of spirit. This was religious. No one can fail to perceive that, but it is not so easy to define it. After boyhood, the *anima naturaliter Christiana* in Agee had taken on endless complications, complications that arose in part from the use of his mind, a good one, curious and angry and highly trained, and from his artistic conscience, one of the most spacious and inflammable of the age. The **"Dedication"** is pertinent here. No one could possibly confuse the honor roll in this litany with a kind of *Vanity Fair* name-dropping. The reader feels, and is right in feeling (though he can barely imagine it), that every single one of those named was a living presence to the author, a possession and a vision to the author, who could not therefore accept any account of the world that excluded, say, Bach's, Chaplin's, Frederick Burrhus Skinner's . . . and so on.

That is why the achievement of his book of poems, a sufficient and indeed a remarkable achievement of its kind, represented for Agee principally what he felt to be over and done with in his work. For the range he already embraced, the scale of things he had it in him to do, the forms of verse as he understood them were inappropriate and the possibilities of verse inadequate. I speak of the essential truth as realized and more than intimated in his first book by himself, true though it may also be that the circumstances of his life affected the matter. Briefly after 1934, as the reader can see from some of the poems in Part II of this book, he groped his way ahead a little in one direction, then another, but in a few years more he had in effect abandoned verse. His hand at verse had begun to lose its cunning. In Part IV you can see how kinds of crudity and callowness came back into his verse rhythms, as though rhyming were now—not always but most often—only doodling in the margins of his prose.

It is conceivable that the scope of Agee's prose work could have been attained, through concentration, by an equally great artist in verse. I do not quite see how. It seems to me that his two principal gifts demanded the realization in prose that he at length and with suffering and difficulty triumphantly gave them. One of these gifts was a capacity for major musical form, the sustained and various shaping of movement in time. Here again the **"Dedication"** is significant, a herald and a harbinger. So is **"Theme with Variations"** in Part II. E. M. Forster said that music is the deepest of the arts and deep beneath all the arts, and to this Agee would surely have assented. The luxuries and spaced elaborations of music, the leisures and agitations and returns, the rake and dance and fluidity of it—these entered into his writing as it developed from *Let Us Now Praise Famous Men* through the film scripts, through *The Morning Watch*, to its consummation, *A Death in the Family*.

His other great gift may be called a sense of being—first of all, a raging awareness of the sensory field in depth and in detail. How could the forms of metrical statement explored by Sidney or Spenser or Donne content this twentieth-century soul, so moved and fascinated by the visual world about him, as he was by photography and film? A living prosody for him would govern the timing of camera shots, the speed and gain and hue of images, the cutting of sequences. After the classic fieldwork of his Alabama book with Walker Evans, his school and training ground was cinema, the art of the moving picture, and I suspect that in exerting himself with this medium as critic and writer he tested most of those visions of the world, mentioned in his **"Dedication,"** that had gone to make up his own. Sidetrackings, failures, times of soddenness and waste were inevitable, and traces of all are to be found in the present book. Yet the preparation of spirit to which *Permit Me Voyage* testified stayed with him during those twenty years, brought him back on course in time and held him there steadily enough. Gradually in his art he rose above his influences and his *personae* and into himself. Out of complication (this nettle) he plucked simplicity (this flower), along with other ancient virtues, coming out in his prose work at the end into a most limpid purity and piety toward the good living of good people in the fathomless world of God.

All that hard-earned beauty still lay ahead when most of these poems were written, though in the best of them you could see what lay ahead. (pp. x-xii)

Robert Fitzgerald, in an introduction to The Collected Poems of James Agee *by James Agee, edited by Robert Fitzgerald, Houghton Mifflin Company, 1968, pp. ix-xii.*

WILFRID SHEED   (essay date 1969)

[*The son of Frank Sheed and Maisie Ward, founders of the Catholic publishing house of Sheed & Ward, Sheed is an English-born American critic and fiction writer whose works in both fields are marked by his erudition and wit. In the following excerpt from an article originally published in 1969, Sheed negatively reviews* The Collected Short Prose of James Agee *and discusses the effect of Agee's journalistic experience on his prose style as well as the reflection of Agee's personality in his work.*]

James Agee was so much the American idea of a writer—wild, lunging, unfulfilled; boozy, self-destructive, sufficiently Southern; a refined model from the Thomas Wolfe prototype—that we still keep sniffing around his literary remains for the one work that would clinch it, the missing sonnet.

It will not be found in [*The Collected Short Prose of James Agee*], which is mainly a waste basket job, and published to look like one. But there are some clues and confirmations. The early stories are just early stories, no better or worse than most people's early stories. Promising. But not terribly promising. The romantic death of feeling is much on hand. "Waning moons and the wind in the trees, etc. [my etc.] . . . I could no longer get excited over these things; I could no longer even think of them without a slight sickened feeling of shame, without ending by laughing at them and myself." Amory Blaine could not have put the problem more poignantly.

There is also a burst of near-Benchley humor, suitable to a Harvard man. "[Sex] is my hobby. Sex and Stamps. But Sex is lots more fun. Where would we be without it? Probably off shooting pool somewhere." Otherwise, the stories tell us mostly what we already know about Agee; that his powers of observation were extraordinary, but with a tendency to float free from his purpose, and that his prose was vivid but sometimes pretentious (e.g., pointless inversions: "I told of Maine a lie or two") and sometimes strangely harsh on the ear.

The two satires that follow are so bad that even a college magazine would hesitate to publish them (and the second has the added burden of being dated to the point of inscrutability). In his introduction, Robert Fitzgerald says "you do not hear much of his parodies" but fails to draw the correct conclusion from this. Agee's versatility has been much commended, but he was versatile chiefly in the sense of attempting a lot of things (remember Beachcomber's famous chess master, who played seventy-six games simultaneously and lost them all?). Agee's best work in one form is surprisingly like his best work in another. Two of the four short descriptive bits that follow the disastrous satires could easily be inserted into one of his movie scripts. Both are crowd scenes so painstakingly described that your eyes almost begin to hurt from reading them. One would not be surprised to see camera instructions inserted. And as Pauline Kael has said, his power of visual evocation was also his outstanding gift as a movie critic. So his versatility was different ways of doing the same thing.

What comes next is the book's principal excuse, probably the most revealing thing that has ever been written about Agee by anyone. It is his Guggenheim application for 1937, surely the strangest application ever compiled by a sane man. It lists no fewer than forty-seven projects, several of them multiple, covering practically the whole of human experience from sex to politics. The good judges must have thought he was mad. This kind of scatterbrained fertility is usually associated with the cracked men in the patent office. And a look at the projects themselves indicates that Agee belongs as much to the line of wild-eyed American boy inventors and tinkerers as to any line of writers.

Two themes recur in a number of places. One has to do with experiments in mixed media—plays merged with film, music with photography, books with records; and along with these, audience participation á la (or perhaps not) the Living Theater, an assault on Art "in any of its contemporary meanings," and a return to "directness" and "organic necessity" in the arts. These proto-McLuhanisms are probably not too startling as prophecies, being, even then, the obvious next jumps for fashion to take. But they are interesting in view of Agee's own work and what he was trying to do with it.

The second theme is a kind of split-screen approach to psychology. He has a notion to make a triptych of people's portrait photographs: one with the left side duplicated on the right, one with the right duplicated on the left, and one in natural full face. This would give us the sitter's conscious, unconscious and workaday characters: and by extension, his whole biography. He also suggests a triptych of different sort for people's relationships to be seen as through "mirrors set in a triangle"— "[the] interflections, as the mirrors shift [being] analogous to the structures of contrapuntal music." Fitzgerald mentions that Agee's obsession with different points of view could drive you crazy in conversation, too.

One gets the feeling as one lowers this brainstorm of an application that what Agee really wanted was to produce a complete history of human sensibility using all the art forms at once while simultaneously transcending them. Writing happened to be the thing he did, but you often sense his impatience with the written word, as if it can't do enough for him. Even in an application for money, he bolts his syntax to keep up with the rush of his thought. It seems automatic to call him a natural writer because that sprawling proliferation looks natural, yet here he says that "I am at least as interested in moving pictures as in writing." And it seems a good bet that had he gone on living, he would have done less and less writing, outside of movie scenarios.

The Guggenheim people turned down his application, no doubt backing away gingerly, and the projects mostly came to nothing. Agee was a man of quick enthusiasms. And when I asked his old colleague Manny Farber to describe him, he used that single word "projects." It wasn't that magazine work had shortened his wind: he could pursue one of his projects into an enormous book. But there is something manic about this, as if it must be kept a white-hot project until completed. And the overwriting, the sentences all twisted and writhing for effect, the Mailer-like eagerness to define and redefine his task in *Let Us Now Praise Famous Men,* seems to be the result.

His magazine work may have helped him to keep his observation so fastidiously exact: although to judge from a few lines quoted by Fitzgerald, he seems to have had this conscience about getting things right, down to the color on the bird's left wing, from boyhood on. I can think of no recent writer except John Updike with so puritanical a sense of obligation to the small truths; to the point of occasional tedium. Still, his fact-packed essay on Brooklyn, rejected by *Fortune* and printed here, possibly profits from having been written for *Fortune*

and not for the ages: precisely because he was obliged to put in all the topological and architectural minutiae that constitute the essay's real poetry and to ration the "boozy pseudo-poetry" (to use E. Wilson's phrase about Chesterton). Agee is always at his best down among the facts; and I have often wondered whether the original version of *Let Us Now Praise Famous Men* (also unfavored by *Fortune*) was not better than the windy masterpiece he finally published.

Not that there was a lack of wind over at the *Time-Life* of the thirties. *Time* in particular was notorious for its bursts of portentous fine writing, and these played straight to Agee's weakness. Fitzgerald quotes with approval an editorial, or whatever they called those company croonings, that Agee wrote for *Time* after the first atom bombs had been dropped. Here is a whiff of it:

> . . . in the dark depths of men's minds and hearts, huge forms moved and silently arrayed themselves. Titans, arranging out of the chaos in an age in which victory was already only the shout of a child in the street . . . the promise of good and of evil bordered alike on the infinite . . . Man's fate has forever been shaped between the hands of reason and spirit, now in collaboration, again in conflict. Now reason and spirit meet on final ground. If either or anything is to survive, they must find a way to create an indissoluble partnership.

Leaving aside the merits of this as free verse (I had an English English teacher who said once, sighting me along the length of his nose, "This sort of thing is much easier to write than many people suppose"), it will be noted that its content can be paraphrased down to a Chinese fortune cookie. And this cranking up of the rhetorical machinery in the service of an unexceptionable platitude was something that a man of Agee's temperament should not have been asked to do.

The years of vassalage at Time Inc. lent a spurious slickness of style and emotion to a naturally rugged talent. Fitzgerald describes Agee's piano-playing as "battered conclamant notes, quite a few near misses, very little sweet shading or pianissimo," and the same could be said of his best prose. One talks lightly of sellouts, but a writer of Agee's vitality can survive a lot of cheap work—so long as it does not exaggerate some weakness already there. The balance sheet is hard to keep with Agee. Time Inc. did send him to Alabama and Brooklyn and it did put him into movies, where his contribution was enormous (unfortunately, all his movie reviews have been previously collected, so there is no excuse to talk about them now). On the other hand, Fitzgerald says that after the war he "found Jim in a corduroy jacket, a subtle novelty, and in a mood far more independent of Left or 'Liberal' attitudes. He had become a trace more worldly." This was a period when *Time* was puffed up like a pouter pigeon, and Agee's alleged mood matched that of his masters to a nicety.

Fitzgerald briefly raises the question of why Agee entered that organization so quickly and stayed so long. He writes: "Was it weakness that kept James Agee at *Fortune*, or was it strategy and will, for the sake of the great use he would make of it? . . . When you reflect on it in this way, weakness and strategy, instinct and destiny seem all one thing." Foraging the text for our own clues, we find in one of the early stories "that mood of sustained callousness and irony which I thought one desert afternoon had perpetuated in me, still serves me well. Although it has achieved a few complexities of perception which may perhaps enrich it, it remains my habitual state of mind, it dilutes experience to a fairly palatable beverage of dubious concoction.'' More romantic death of feeling, perhaps. But it sounds like good equipment for working on the old Time Inc.

And one finds on the Guggenheim application a project on the pathology of laziness. ''A story,'' he explains, ''of cumulative horror.'' One doesn't write such stories from the outside. Laziness in a busy writer suggests that some call is going unheeded, that writing is being used as an evasion, like non-stop talking. His pious boyhood might have set him off in one direction, writing in some sense for the Glory of God; but then as that faded he seemed reluctant to take on another motive in case it might war too bitterly with his first one: a common problem with partially lapsed Christians. He fended off aesthetic and political allegiances, from left and right, looking for truth in his triple mirrors. It is typical of Agee that he never quite gave up religion but never reembraced it either. As with Time Inc., he just hung on and raged.

The refusal to become anything in particular—Christian or atheist, aesthete or philistine, husband or bachelor, North or South, hobo or Time-Lifer—explains the fascination with multiple points of view and with the noncommittal art of the camera: itself to be used multiply, so that one statement can contradict another. This produced admirable effects in the way of kinetic prose, verbal photographs. But, for creative purposes, it had the effect of a slightly arrested development. Whether one plays what Seymour Krim has called the Great American Postponement game out of cowardice or out of a greed to choose everything, it leaves one similarly unformed and psychically incomplete. Agee remained, even in his face, the quintessential promising young writer to the day of his death at forty-five. And the masterwork of his maturity (*A Death in the Family*) is not the first American masterwork to be told in the first person of a child. (pp. 52-8)

> Wilfrid Sheed, ''Collected Short Prose of James Agee,'' in his The Morning After: Selected Essays and Reviews, *Farrar, Straus and Giroux, 1971, pp. 52-8.*

SAMUEL HYNES (essay date 1969)

[*An American critic and educator, Hynes has written and edited numerous studies of English literature and literary figures. In the following excerpt, he discusses the themes and techniques of* Let Us Now Praise Famous Men.]

In the library of a small college where I once taught, James Agee's *Let Us Now Praise Famous Men* is shelved with books on the history of Alabama. This is rather like classifying *Moby Dick* as a book about whales, but one can understand the librarian's dilemma, for Agee's book is fundamentally unclassifiable. It is neither fiction nor poetry, though it is full of sensitive poetic writing; it is factual and descriptive, but it is not documentary; it has no imaginary characters or situations, but it is a work of the imagination. (p. 328)

The book has a place in time; it is a product of the 1930's, but it is not topical: or at least what is most valuable in it is not. Agee chose to write about three white tenant families living in rural Alabama, but he wrote about them, not as typical examples of a social and economic problem, but as human beings, as a ''portion of unimagined existence.'' His book is above all a book about *knowing,* about how one human being

may realize the extistence of another, and of the obstacles to such knowledge. The obstacles are moral and psychological, and, in the expression, aesthetic, and Agee wrote about them all. It is this effort at knowing human actuality that gives the book its peculiar form—the form of a series of new approaches to an insoluble central problem—and its tone of painstaking tenderness and love.

Let me try to describe some of these approaches. There are, first of all, Walker Evans' photographs—thirty-one of them in the first edition, placed together at the beginning of the book. Agee put them there because he wanted them to be seen, not as illustrations to his text, but as ''Book One,'' a unit equivalent in importance to the five hundred pages of prose which are ''Book Two.'' ''One reason I so deeply care for the camera,'' he wrote, ''is just this. So far as it goes . . . and handled cleanly and literally in its own terms, as an ice-cold, some ways limited, some ways more capable, eye, it is, like the phonograph record and like scientific instruments and unlike any other leverage of art, incapable of recording anything but absolute, dry truth.'' Evans' photographs are not ice-cold, but they are very clean, honest-looking pictures of the people and places that Agee writes about; they show without artfulness the grain in the unpainted boards of the houses, the seams in the weathered faces, and the naked poverty of the life. They demonstrate the first principle of the book—that knowing depends on seeing, really seeing things and people as they exist.

Agee's prose text embodies three approaches, each in its way a correlative of the photographs. First, the descriptive approach: Agee's attempt to realize in words the thoroughness of the camera's record. Second, the personal approach: the equivalent of the human sensitivity that chose these poses, these faces, these scenes, and made them seem significant and true. Third, the aesthetic: the artist's meditations on the problems of reality, truth, and art that the occasion poses. The book sets these approaches, each with its characteristic style, in a pattern of repetitions, so that one comments on another, and each alone is seen to be inadequate to the whole truth of the subject. There is nothing that could be described as movement or development in this structure; the effect is rather of hovering, failing, and trying again to express the whole of this human actuality in words.

The descriptive matter is gathered into one section titled simply ''Some Findings and Comments,'' and divided into ''Money,'' ''Shelter,'' ''Clothing,'' ''Education,'' and ''Work.'' Each part is an effort to describe, objectively and without judgment, the subject as it touched the lives of the three tenant families. Agee did this by including everything he observed, and by treating each object, however trivial, with the same scrupulous care. The description of a tenant house, for example, includes this careful catalog of the objects at the bottom of a dresser drawer:

> The two parts of a broken button.
> A small black hook, lying in its eye.
> Another small black hook.
> In the corners of the pale inward wood, fine gray dust and a sharp-grained unidentifiable brown dust.
> In a split in the bottom of the drawer, a small bright needle, pointed north. . . .

The central section of the book, some two hundred pages, is devoted to this kind of detailed writing, and it is one of the poignancies of the experience that the entire contents of the tenants' lives, every scrap of paper, every broken toy or abandoned garment, *could* be recorded—that these lives were so bare that they *could* be contained within the limits of a few pages in a book.

Yet paradoxically, though this book is full of particulars the particulars in themselves are not important. What *is* important is the attitude implied in the details. (pp. 330-32)

[Agee's] rendering of the odors that identify the house identifies also the quality of the life lived there—the meager materials of the building itself, the poor and monotonous food, the smell of labor and of sleep. And it describes that life without repugnance or indignation, which are removed, superior emotions, but with careful and reverent precision. Agee's respect for the actual was great, but it did not lead him to literary realism or to mere documentation; "description," he wrote, "is a word to suspect." His subject, as he said, was "certain normal predicaments of human divinity"; so that I suppose he might properly be described as a Christian realist. He strove to realize in his writing the divinity in each individual, by treating each person as he was; no one in this book is mythologized, not even the author, and no one becomes a representative case; Agee leaves his people alone, as separate and unique souls. (pp. 332-33)

His conviction, manifested here and everywhere in his work, that it is demeaning to a man to treat him as a representative case, makes his writing more than either mere documentary or mere propaganda.

Agee shared with many people of his time a deep concern for the miseries of the poor, but he knew that such concern had no political or historical limits, and he reminded his readers of this truth by placing at the head of his text two very different but related epigraphs. One is from the *Communist Manifesto:* "Workers of the world, unite and fight. You have nothing to lose but your chains, and a world to win." The other is from *King Lear:*

> Poor naked wretches, whereso'er you are,
> That bide the pelting of this pitiless storm,
> How shall your houseless heads and unfed sides,
> Your loop'd and window'd raggedness, defend you
> From seasons such as these? O! I have ta'en
> Too little care of this! Take physick, pomp;
> Expose thyself to feel what wretches feel,
> That thou may'st shake the superflux to them,
> And show the heavens more just.

Agee said of these two quotations that they were the first and second themes of a sonata: politics and poetry, action and compassion, woven together into a complex musical form. But one's final impression is of a book nearer in tone to Lear than to Marx. Compassion means "feeling with," and Agee's book is a work of fellow-feeling, a sensitive man's careful efforts to enter into the beings of other men.

This fellow-feeling made the second of Agee's approaches, the personal method, a necessary complement to the descriptive matter. Agee had what many religious men have: the need to testify. This is probably almost the opposite of the will to reform; it places the testifier in a relation of sympathetic equality to the subject, whereas reform implies a degree of elevation, a point of view. Agee's testimony is an agonized account of his love for, and separateness from, the people he met, his awareness of each person, but also of the distance between them, which even love cannot bridge. . . . [There are] tender accounts of meetings with the members of the white tenant families, of their shy good manners, and of his inarticulate affection for them.

Beyond this kind of testimony there is another, more private kind—those passages in the book in which Agee writes of his personal sense of the realities around him. If we take from his statements of his intentions two key words, *actuality* and *divinity*, then these passages are meditations on the divinities of things. Here is the beginning of such a meditation, titled "On the Porch: 1": . . .

> Most human beings, most animals and birds who live in the sheltering ring of human influence, and a great portion of all the branded tribes of living in earth and air and water upon a half of the world, were stunned with sleep. That region of the earth on which we were at this time transient was some hours fallen beneath the fascination of the stone, steady shadow of the planet, and lay now listing toward the last depth; and now by a blockade of the sun were clearly disclosed those discharges of light which teach us what little we can learn of the stars and of the true nature of our surroundings. . . .

If, as Agee said, there are several sorts of truth, this is the kind that comes with night and an open sky; it sets the human subject in a huge, cosmic perspective. But the passage also has its roots in literature, and uses self-consciously the cadences and metaphors of poetry. It is in such passages that one is most conscious of Agee's youth, and of his youth naiveté, his taste for large and lyrical statements about art and life. The most highly colored prose is here, and Agee's critics have taken from these sections their examples of what they called his overwritten, inflated style. Certainly the book is written, some of it, in a high rhetorical style. So is *Moby Dick.* So is much of Faulkner. So is *King Lear,* for that matter. Twentieth-century America is embarrassed by the emotive use of powerful language; we are the heirs of Hemingway's Frederick Henry, who mistrusted words like *honor,* and only believed in the numbers of regiments and the names of battles. Agee uses that austere style at times, but he has also the high style that Hemingway was afraid of. This style is sometimes described as "poetic," but that term seems to be the wrong one for this kind of writing; it is not prose trying to be something else, but simply prose reaching to its rhetorical limits. Sometimes when Agee wrote in this style he failed, but those passages are *badly* written rather than *over*-written. Like most writers of high style, Agee loved words, and sometimes his love of words got in the way of his love of truth, but this will happen to any writer who tries to be true both to experience and to his medium at its richest.

Agee's two approaches to the problem of knowing, the descriptive and the personal methods, complement and extend each other. But we must also recognize a third approach, of a rather different sort: the *aesthetic.* Almost at the exact center of the book is a passage of some thirty pages titled "On the Porch: 2," in which Agee considers the aesthetic aspects of his work. . . . [He argues] that "everything in Nature, every most casual thing, has an inevitability and perfection which art as such can only approach, and shares in fact, not as art, but as the part of Nature that it is." This proposition—that the actual is not only different from, but superior to, the forms that man makes of the actual—is the basic aesthetic principle of the book. It underlies the use of the photographs as "Book

One,'' and the meticulous descriptions of seemingly trivial details of decoration, clothing, and the like. It sets aside art and all aesthetic intentions: the writer's aim is simply to render experience in words and pictures, so that it approaches as nearly as possible the mode of existence of the people and things that are the subject of the book.

This is a radical idea of what a literary work should be, and surely in the end an unworkable and self-defeating one (as perhaps Agee's inability to finish his book shows). But one can understand the instincts that brought him to such a position. In the presence of extreme, dignified human suffering, one night well feel that no words could express the quality of the actual. In the presence of such human experience, words can easily come to seem *mere* words, and art an idle and indulgent activity. Since not everyone can witness the actual lives of these people, the writer must put his testimony into words as best he can, but he will do so with a sense of inadequacy, and even of betrayal. (pp. 333-37)

But though the book is anti-art, it is also artful; that is, it is composed in intricate ways, on patterns that have analogies to works of art, and not actuality. There is, for example, the remark that the epigraphs are the themes of a sonata form. In a letter to his friend, Father Flye, Agee wrote that he wanted to "write symphonies," and the musical element in his work was always strong. *Let Us Now Praise Famous Men* was written to be read continuously, he said, "as music is listened to or a film watched," and these two forms of music and film with their variations, modulations, and repetitions are central to Agee's conception of the book's shape. And perhaps one should add that music had one further attraction for Agee, that a sonata cannot, by its nature, be imperative; musical form protected him from the pull toward propaganda. Agee's book has no argument, no narrative line, and no evident logic; it is one enormous *now,* a feeling, symphonically orchestrated, but conceptually undeveloped and unresolved, beginning with the immediacy of the photographs, and ending with a sentence that mixes the past and future tenses. In the body of the book the observations stand like a series of photographs, or like film clips, each one a few feet of sharply recorded motion—a car rolls through a small town, a storm comes up, and the images are recorded to stand, each separate and clear and isolated in space.

Time is not a significant dimension in this book. And so, though musical form is one suggestive analogy to its arrangement, the idea of *spatial* form is perhaps more important. The book resembles a collage, an arrangement of many diverse materials to make an integrated whole. In addition to Evans' photographs, it contains verse by Agee, a page from a third-grade geography textbook, Agee's answer to a *Partisan Review* questionnaire on "some questions which face American writers today," the 43rd Psalm, an article on Margaret Bourke-White from the *New York Post,* the Beatitudes, and a selection from Blake's "Proverbs of Hell." Agee regretted that he could not also include "fragments of cloth, bits of cotton, lumps of earth, records of speech, pieces of wood and iron, phials of odors, plates of food and of excrement."

One can see how Agee's actualizing aesthetic would lead to such a desire for *things.* But we must also recognize that *Let Us Now Praise Famous Men* is also a book of words. Whatever his assertions about the superiority of things, Agee was a writer in love with words and fascinated by the problems arising from the use of words. His heroes were the great word users, and James Joyce in particular appears in the book as an exemplary

artist, one who took seven years to record nineteen hours. Agee took one of his goals to be "the cleansing and rectification of language," and this concern linked him to another line of modern writers, the poets from Mallarmé to Eliot who were the purifiers of the dialect of the tribe.

The book also shows the influence of Joyce, and of other moderns like Faulkner and Dos Passos, in its formal complexity, in its discontinuities, its variations of style and tone. But perhaps its most modern quality of all is that it is about itself; it is a work of art concerned with the problems of creating a work of art; like Gide's *Counterfeiters,* Joyce's *A Portrait of the Artist as a Young Man,* Yeats's *Tower,* and Eliot's *Four Quartets,* it offers, as a primary experience, the experience of creating the work itself.

Agee called his book a failure, and did so with a kind of pride; failure, he said, was an obligation in such work. And his critics have accepted this judgment. But what does failure mean in such a book? Perhaps only that the book did not become the vast and complete record that Agee imagined. Or perhaps that it was written in words, and not in fragments of cloth and lumps of earth that he imagined to be truer to reality. But to fail in these terms is simply to fall short, in achievement, of the splendor of the conception, and in this sense every effort of the human mind fails.

The book was left unfinished, and it is hard to see what prodigy of human creation could have finished it. The unfinished state is, in fact, a significant part of its meaning—a symbol of the impossibility of adequately and completely expressing the predicaments of human divinity. I have not mentioned the ways in which *Let Us Now Praise Famous Men* is peculiarly American, and I am somewhat reluctant to, because I would not wish to suggest that it will not speak with an equal voice to all feeling men, but perhaps it *is* American in this: that it is naively and vastly ambitious in it goals. But I think it is American also in the eccentricity of its form, and in certain powerful feelings that it evokes—of human separateness and loneliness, and of distance and space. It is most a product of its origin in the way it celebrates whatever exists. One might return to the musical analogy, and say that Agee wrote, not a description, but a great Psalm, a hymn to actuality, on the theme that "everything that is is holy." (pp. 338-40)

Samuel Hynes, "James Agee: 'Let Us Now Praise Famous Men'," in Landmarks of American Writing, *edited by Hennig Cohen, Basic Books, Inc., Publishers, 1969, pp. 328-40.*

GENE W. RUOFF (essay date 1970)

[*In the following excerpt, Ruoff examines the themes and techniques of* A Death in the Family.]

How *A Death in the Family* reached us in its present state can only be guessed. Apparently the story proper was contained in a continuous manuscript, divided into chapters and three basic sections by Agee himself. It concerns four days in the life of the Follet family: three consecutive days relate Jay Follet's last evening at home, his departure to visit the bedside of his father, who has suffered a heart attack, and his family's discovery of and response to Jay's own death in an automobile accident on his way back home. Separated by a short but undetermined space of time, the final day of the novel concerns Jay's burial. The editors who prepared the manuscript for publication acknowledge in their prefatory note the wholeness of the narrative of Jay's death: "The ending of *A Death in the Family* had been reached sometime before Agee's death." Still, they felt that certain editorial decisions had to be made: "The only editorial problem involved the placing of several scenes outside the time span of the basic story. It was finally decided to print these in italics and to put them after Parts I and II." (p. 122)

The prose interpolations in *A Death in the Family,* all of which cover episodes in the life of Rufus Follet before his father's death, attempt to re-create the boy's sensory life in a manner close to that employed in *The Morning Watch*. Almost invariably they are more lyrically evocative and symbolically charged than the narrative into which they have been inserted. Read as a part of the novel, they move Rufus toward its center, turning the story of Jay's death into the central crisis of the boy's growing up. In reviewing the book, Leslie Fiedler noted its internal contradictions, sensing a not wholly constructive tension between the narrative of Jay's death and the larger family saga suggested by the italicized passages. Although Fiedler was divided in his response to the work, he seemed to value the lyrical passages more highly than the narrative core: "The point is, I think, that Agee's talent is peculiarly *visual,* that the world comes to him in sharp fragmented sights—all detailed foreground" [see *TCLC,* Vol. 1]. . . . If one agrees that description is Agee's greatest gift, *A Death in the Family* could hardly do without its added passages; as almost everyone has remarked, they contain some of the most brilliant writing in the book. (pp. 124-25)

A recently published prose fragment of Agee's . . . may point toward the ultimate form of *A Death in the Family:* "This book is chiefly a remembrance of my childhood, and a memorial to my father; and I find that I value my childhood and my father as they were, as well and as exactly as I can remember them, far beyond any transmutations of these matters I have made, or might ever make, into poetry or fiction." . . . Agee's renunciation of poeticizing or fictionalizing in his story is far removed from his shrill outcries against art in *Let Us Now Praise Famous Men*. It announces instead a dedication to an older, perhaps more difficult, kind of art: that which represents reality in terms of a continuous action rather than as the reflection of a sensibility.

Still, to speak of even the central account of *A Death in the Family* as a representation of an action requires some elaboration, because many of the novel's most sympathetic reviewers objected particularly to its lack of narrative movement. . . . What these critics seem to be expecting from any novel that is not overtly experimental is a narrative of character conflict and development, laced with motifs which converge in some final dramatic resolution: at best a well-made novel, at worst first-class melodrama. (pp. 125-26)

However, Agee was after something else in *A Death in the Family*. He wanted not the kind of action through which character is suddenly and dramatically changed and shaped, but the kind through which character is simply revealed. In his character portrayal he aims not at the eccentric but at the ethical: "that which reveals moral purpose, showing what kinds of things a man chooses or avoids." . . . Or, on a level less exalted but more in line with Agee's enthusiasms, the kind of action he found so characteristic of the silent movies he loved—Rufus' trip to the movies with his father begins *A Death in the Family*. Agee was struck with the way in which Charlie Chaplin's slightest, most individual movement could become a representation of general humanity: "At the end of *City Lights* the blind girl who has regained her sight, thanks to the Tramp,

sees him for the first time. She has imagined and anticipated him as princely, to say the least; and it has never seriously occurred to her that he is inadequate. She recognizes who he must be by his shy, confident, shining joy as he comes silently toward her. And he recognizes himself, for the first time, through the terrible changes in her face. The camera just exchanges a few quiet close-ups of the emotions which shift and intensify in each face. It is enough to shrivel the heart to see, and it is the greatest piece of acting and the highest moment in movies." . . . Agee's novel is filled with such quiet gestures of character revelation. Stopping off for a drink after the movies, for example, Jay lifts his son onto the bar: "'That's my boy,' he said warmly, 'Six years old, and he can already read like I couldn't read when I was twict his age.' Rufus felt a sudden hollowness in his voice, and all along the bar, and in his own heart. But how does he fight it, he thought. You don't brag about smartness if your son is brave." . . . Later in the night, when Jay is roused by his brother Ralph's drunken phone call to go to his father's bedside, his wife goes downstairs to fix a full breakfast for him: "Well, he thought, I can do *some*-thing for her. He put his things on the floor, smoothed the sheets, and punched the pillows. The sheets were still warm on her side. He drew the covers up to keep the warmth, then laid them open a few inches, so it would look inviting to get into. She'll be glad of that, he thought, very well pleased with the look of it." . . . The small episodes convey economically Jay's character and the nature of his relationship with his family; he is proud of his son but awkward in expressing it, because Rufus' accomplishments fall outside the accepted masculine values of his Tennessee heritage. Uneasy in the presence of Mary's quiet, automatic devotion, he attempts to compete with her in considerateness; his inordinate pride is not just in having done something for her, but in having done something she will interpret as an act of love.

Of course, the novel does not rest principally on subtle gestures of character revelation. Its major action portrays the responses of Jay's family, first to the fear, then to the fact of his death. The most agonizing section of the book is the period of suspension in time between Mary's receiving the terse phone call, telling her Jay has been involved in an accident but relating no details, and the return of Mary's brother Andrew with the news that he had been killed instantly. Mary is caught between two conflicting needs: she must hope for the best for everyone's sake, yet she must anticipate the worst in order to prepare herself for what she instinctively knows has happened: "'That's what I think,' Mary said, 'and that's what I'm ready for. But I'm not going to say it, or accept it, or do my husband any such dishonor or danger—not until I know beyond recall that it's so'." . . . Mary is joined in her vigil by her aunt Hannah, who is in some ways the most striking character in the novel. Throughout the wait, the burden of ethical decision is chiefly placed on Hannah: her every action must be weighed as to its effect on her niece. Her desire to reach out to help Mary is balanced by her knowledge that nothing she could do could help, that the best she can accomplish is to be there and to avoid hurting her. It is in the pain of Hannah's participation in Mary's emotions, feeling with and for her while at the same time weighing and judging the younger woman's actions by her own in a similar tragedy thirty years earlier, that we get the full sense of Agee's belief in the inherent goodness of humanity, a goodness which lies in nothing more than man's ability to act right in the fact of enormous pressure, or at least to want to act right. Although Hannah is afraid that Mary will fall into an unearned triumph of too-easy religiosity, towards which she has a natural tendency, she firmly keeps her fears unvoiced. Above all, Hannah's accomplishment as a human being is in her ability to forego lecturing on the basis of her own experience.

Hannah's impulses are not all noble: she is capable of a selfish exultation that someone else is now suffering what she has suffered. However, Agee will not allow her to be judged on her worst impulses. Throughout the novel he holds people responsible not for the possibilities for action they reject, but for the actions they undertake. Agee's belief in the sufficiency of functional goodness can hardly be over-emphasized. Readers miss the point who find in the obvious divisions between Mary and Jay—her orthodox piety, his non-belief; her urban refinement, his sometimes boisterous rusticity; her dislike of alcohol, his affection for it—indications of a marriage that would eventually have disintegrated. Whatever Mary's wistful hopes for Jay's conversion, whatever Jay's feelings of living under constraint, they had made the marriage work through the simple compromises, conscious and unconscious, that Agee establishes as the fundamental ground of human society.

In the long family conversation that follows Andrew's revelation of Jay's death, the family's unified spirit is earned rather than automatic, for its members are not in religious agreement. Joel, Mary's father, is a cynical humanist; Andrew tends to be a self-indulgent romantic agnostic; and Hannah's orthodoxy is far less securely optimistic than Mary's. The freakish cause of Jay's accident, a cotter pin lost from the steering assembly, with death itself resulting from one sharp blow to the chin, invites all manner of cheap irony and pious nonsense. The death can be viewed as anything from a malicious quirk of fate, one chance in a million, to a mercifully quick escape from lingering pain and invalidhood. Indeed, in the ensuing philosophical exchanges there is an occasional angry flurry. But basically the disagreements are muted by the individuals' awareness of responsibility to one another. In this section the work becomes a novel of ideas as well as human interaction, encompassing what Kenneth Seib calls, without exaggeration, "almost the entire range of human speculation about . . . that sense of the absolute which we must all confront sooner or later." . . . However, in marked contrast to common practice in novels of ideas, the concepts here are generated by the action; they never take over its direction, and the characters never become ciphers for philosophic positions. What is more unusual, though, the novel's ideas are not really placed in dramatic conflict. Because the characters are working toward the common goal of understanding and accepting the death of Jay, their views are more complementary than contradictory. Agee wrote in *Religion and the Intellectuals*, a forum in *Partisan Review*, . . . that his own beliefs were inconsistent: "I veer between belief in God, non-belief, and a kind of neutrality. In all three frames of mind I keep what I believe is meant by the religious consciousness." . . . (pp. 126-29)

Such a unity within diversity holds the family together when Mary senses a mystical visitation of Jay's spirit within the house. Both Hannah and Mary are convinced of Jay's actual presence. Mary to the point of speaking to her husband, while Andrew can only say, "'No, I had no idea *what* it was. But I know it was *something*'." . . . Even Mary's mother Catherine, who is so deaf the others must speak directly into what she fondly calls her good ear, is certain she heard footsteps. Although Joel himself is confused and embarrassed, he tries to understand: "The least I can do is accept the fact that three people had a hallucination, and honor their belief in it." . . . The quiet ease with which Agee introduces the supernatural

into the novel may reflect his reading of Charles Williams, which he mentioned to Father Flye in October 1952: "one of the very few contemporary religious writers who moves and interests me to read. . . . He takes the supernatural for granted, rather than semidoubtfully or on trust, let alone in any shading of agnosticism or atheism; and has a wonderful gift for conveying, and dramatizing, the 'borderline' states of mind or Being." . . . Jay's visitation evokes all these shades of response; Hannah particularly tries to understand the phenomenon in terms recalling Williams' characteristic descriptions of souls in mid-passage between the mortal and immortal regions, while Mary exhibits utter contentment in unrationalized experience.

The inclusiveness of Agee's religious values enables him to embrace even Father Jackson, the inhumanly frigid priest who begins his visit of consolation by lecturing the anxious and disturbed children, Rufus and Catherine, on the ill-breeding of staring at one's elders, and later infuriates Andrew by refusing to read the complete burial service over Jay's unbaptized corpse. When Father Jackson prays with Mary and Hannah, though, the ritualistic act becomes invested with a transcendent spirit apparent even to the uncomprehending, hostile ears of the children. . . . Although neither the children nor Andrew can disentangle their personal dislike for Father Jackson from their evaluation of him, Agee makes it clear that for Mary and Hannah the unworthiness of the priest does not hinder the effect of the sacraments. Agee seems to have reached such a point of toleration in his own religious views, when in his response to the *Partisan Review* forum he finds the institutionalism of the Father Jacksons as necessary as any other aspect of religion: "Prophets, institutionalists and the neutral mass are as mutually indispensable as they are inevitable. Christian values, social and otherwise, have endured (insofar as they have), thanks to the interaction upon them, and upon each other, of the three." . . . Within the novel, Agee accepts all humanly useful actions or attitudes as at least partial truths, perhaps even as parts of the same truth.

In terms of Agee's fictional achievement, to the extent that it is separable from his moral and philosophical achievement, his greatest triumph may lie in his presentation of the children of the household. They remain totally credible, bickering and fighting in the midst of events they only begin to understand. Agee's portrayal of himself as Rufus is almost ruthlessly exact: he wants to go to school on the day his father died, because he has a new yellow cap to wear and because having a dead father would make him important, just once, in the eyes of the older boys; he also wants his sister and him to be orphans, because, as he explains to his mother, they are something special: "'Like the Belgians,' he informed her. 'French. When you haven't got any daddy or momma because they're killed in the war you're an orphan and other children send you things and write you letters'." . . . Rufus never takes over the center of the novel; he grows up no more than is appropriate to his age and understanding. More importantly, Agee somehow manages to keep Rufus-Agee, the adult artist, from entering into his portrayal of the child. This, I suppose, is what he meant by having come to value his childhood as it was.

The novel's concentration on its central action may explain some of its seeming fictional shortcomings. There is no consistent point of view, because at different times different characters assume predominant roles. As a character Rufus is obviously an incompetent vehicle through which to view the events, and even the sensibility of an adult as centrally concerned as

Mary would distort them to some degree. Certain themes suggested early in the book, such as differences between Jay's and Mary's families, are dropped simply because subsequent events render them negligible. Background description of the characters is minimal, because everything really important about them is conveyed by their actions during the four days in question. The narrative itself is chronologically episodic rather than causal in structure, because that is the way in which the significance of the events is best revealed. Agee's fictional framework is the barest imaginable; only the content is rich, and the famous Agee prose rises as a tool to meet the richness of the revealed humanity.

In reviewing *A Death in the Family,* Dwight Macdonald commented that Agee needed a "sympathetically severe editor," . . . such as Thomas Wolfe had in Maxwell Perkins. Ironically, Agee had finally found such an editor within himself. His success in narrative control within his novel has, I think, been fully recognized only by his friend Robert Fitzgerald: "Jim arrived at his austere style fifty years and a torn world away from Edwardian Dublin and Trieste; if it took him twenty years longer than it took Joyce, who else arrived at all?" (pp. 129-32)

> Gene W. Ruoff, "'A Death in the Family': Agee's 'Unfinished' Novel," in The Fifties: Fiction, Poetry, Drama, *edited by Warren French, Everett/Edwards, Inc., 1970, pp. 121-32.*

ALFRED T. BARSON (essay date 1972)

[*In the following excerpt from his* A Way of Seeing: A Critical Study of James Agee, *Barson examines the themes of loneliness and contentment in* A Death in the Family.]

The characters of the hand-written draft [of *A Death in the Family*] are given the names of Agee's family; and in accompanying notes Agee writes that his intention is to tell of "my relation with my father and, through that, as thorough as possible an image of him: winding into other things on the way but never dwelling on them." Further down on this page he expanded the entry in what Victor Kramer thinks might have been Agee's outline for the book:

Detachedly:

A soft and somewhat precocious child. A middle-class religious mother. A father of country background. Two sets of relatives: hers middle class, northern born, more or less cultivated; his, of the deep mountain country.

Begin with the complete security and the simple pleasures and sensations.

Develop: the deficiency in the child which puts them at odds: the increasing need of the child for the father's approval.

Interrupt with the father's sudden death. Here either the whole family is involved, or it is told in terms of the child.

At end: the child is in a sense & degree doomed, to religion & to the middle class. The mother: to religiosity. New strains develop, or are hinted between her & her family.

More must be understood, however, in order to take Kramer's suggestion seriously. Foremost is the inescapable fact that the manuscript is far from finished. In May 1950 Agee wrote to Father Flye that he thought he could finish the book that summer. . . . That he repeated the same estimate five years later in his last letter to Father Flye and also nights before his death to his friend and publisher David McDowell, suggests that he got little further in the writing. Kramer and others have pointed out that, in addition to the incomplete state of the manuscript, the published version is in need of reediting. It is obvious that if the above note is taken as a possible outline for the novel, Agee had in mind much more than his relationship with his father. Indeed, he intended a history of the most formative years of his life, which would possibly explicate his "deficiency" or the manner in which he had "betrayed" his father. Other notes for the novel indicate that Agee was toying with a very complex plot, involving a network of misunderstandings involving every member of the family. Essentially the father, "at an uneasy time of his life," was trying to get ahead in his job. His purchase of an automobile—a chapter which Agee wrote but which was excluded from the published version—was symptomatic of his ambition. "He is progressive," Agee had noted. "In a sense it is this which kills him." Unfortunately, though, these notes can only suggest the broad outlines of Agee's ideas. Although they indicate the direction of his reaction to the contemporary world, as well as implying the values he sought to restore to consciousness through his art, they can inevitably be supported only by reference to unfinished or unpublished manuscripts or to his more explicit statements in forgotten issues of *Time.*

What remains and has been published is perhaps little more than half the novel Agee intended to write. The twenty chapters and six italicized interchapters ("several scenes outside the time span of the basic story," editor McDowell explains in his headnote) tell the story of Jay Follet's death. Much of the action is seen from the point of view of his six-year-old son, Rufus. But a great deal goes on outside the boy's perception or experience. The novel begins when he and his father spend an evening watching a double feature of Chaplin and William S. Hart movies. But after Rufus is put to bed, Jay is called home to his own father, who is thought to be dying. On the way back a cotter pin comes loose from the steering column of his car, and he is killed instantly. The remaining two parts of the novel concern the grief of Mary, his widow, and the funeral and burial—actions which swirl largely above Rufus' head.

As Agee saw it, his main problem in writing the story was to

> decide between a completely detached and deeply subjective treatment.
>
> I doubt if in complete detachment there is a story there. Rather, do the subjective, as detachedly as possible.

The outcome of these difficult instructions is remarkably similar to Agee's youthful ideal of abnormal sympathy and perfect balance. A good example of the result can be found in the shifting viewpoint Agee utilized in one of the best-known scenes of the novel, the seeming apparition of Jay's ghost to the family assembled in the Follet parlor:

> Can't eat your cake and have it, his father thought.
>
> Like slapping a child in the face, Andrew thought; he had been rougher than he had intended.

"But Andrew dear," Mary was about to say, but she caught herself. What a thing to argue about, she thought; and what a time to be wrangling about it!

Each of them realized that the others felt something of this; for a little while none of them had anything to say. Finally Andrew said, "I'm sorry." . . .

The subject of the passage is a remark about belief by Andrew, Mary's brother. There follows each character's reaction to the remark. This is a montage, a juxtaposition of viewpoints managed similarly to Joyce's technique in *Ulysses*. But Agee's style, unlike Joyce's, merges more than one subjective point of view and does not simply borrow from the film. Cinematic montage depends on the spatial relationship of visual details. Agee's shifting viewpoint can refer to visual details, but in this passage each element of response is a thoroughly subjective use of verbal expression: Mary's father, Joel, is given to cliché ("Can't eat your cake and have it"), Andrew to metaphor ("Like slapping a child"), Mary to half-thought ("But Andrew dear"), all followed by interior monologue ("What a thing to argue about"), and finally the authorial voice ("Each of them realized that the others felt something of this"). By detaching authorial control from the subjectivity of his characters, Agee has created a sense of presence rather than engaging in presentation.

This scene in which the family members grope to comfort one another also presents the essential drama of the novel, the interaction between loneliness and contentment. . . . Essentially loneliness is estrangement, and in *A Death in the Family* it is often treated as a state of moral susceptibility. Contentment, on the other hand, is the tacit assumption and sharing of certain values and is seen most often as a state of moral redemption. Andrew apologizes for his remark about belief because he has upset Mary. But he has also estranged himself from the group, and his apology brings him back into their common concern for Mary. Another example can be found in the scene where Joel and Catherine Lynch, Mary's parents, are waiting for news of Jay. Catherine announces that despite their prior feelings about Jay, they must now care for him and Mary in their trouble. "Certainly," Joel replies. Then he

> began to realize the emotion, and the loneliness behind the banality of what she had said; he was ashamed of himself to have answered as if it were merely banal. He wished he could think what to say that would make up for it. . . .

As Joel and Catherine act alone, the personal significance they attach to their words is not communicated, and the failure is apparent to each. But as they make a gesture toward one another, they restore the moral harmony.

> She felt his hand on her wrist and his head close to hers. She leaned towards him.
>
> "I understand, Catherine," he said.
>
> *What* does he mean that he understands, Catherine wondered. Something I failed to hear, no doubt, she thought, though their words had been so few that she could not imagine what. But she quickly decided not to exasperate him by a question; she was sure of his kind intention, and deeply touched by it.

(pp. 145-49)

Such individual instances of loneliness and contentment create a general pattern, the random acts of individuals brought together by human need. This pattern composes what Gerald Weales has called the power of the novel: "Agee's unwavering knowledge that each human being lives and moves in the loneliness of self, but that the family, when infused with love, can occasionally, almost accidentally, shore up that lonely self." Weales' criticism is valuable especially for the concept of "accidental compassion." For it is as if by accident that Joel places his hand upon Catherine's arm or that Hannah finds herself praying with Mary. Accidental compassion, furthermore, is part of Mary's religious faith. Religion is to her more than a ritual of comfort; it is the experience by which she endures her husband's death. Her prayer before sleep the night of Jay's death is, "If Thou, Lord, wilt be extreme to mark what is done amiss O Lord, who may abide it?" . . . Not only do the words bring the relief of tears in the realization of the emptiness of her life without Jay, but the accidental freedom with which she whispers them is dependent upon her belief that the trials of human life are insuperable and that God is therefore ultimately necessary. Similarly, it is an accident of compassion which is at the heart of Andrew's "conversion" in the closing pages of the novel. Agee's notes indicate his attempt to recall each detail of his father's funeral, "but mainly," he wrote, "I remember [my uncle's] needing to tell me about the butterfly." Not only is Andrew restored or "contented" by asking Rufus to share his thoughts, but the cause of his contentment is the accidental flight of a butterfly off Jay's coffin as it is lowered into the ground. The implication Andrew derives from the butterfly is that God has made a gesture concerning Jay to which he responds: "'If there are any such things as miracles,' his uncle said, as if someone were arguing with him, 'then that's surely miraculous'." . . . (p. 150)

Significantly, Jay is seldom susceptible to loneliness. For him, loneliness and contentment are one. Although Agee tells of the difficulties of Jay and Mary's marriage—his drinking, their religious differences, the history of their separate values—Jay is both a part of and apart from the world of the other characters. As Rufus perceives in the novel's first chapter, Jay "was more lonely than the contentment of this family love could help." However, in nature—the empty lot, the journey to his father's home, the visit to his great-grandmother's homestead—Jay is "on good terms with the loneliness . . . though he might be more homesick than ever, he was well." (pp. 150-51)

> And God knows he was lucky, so many ways, and God knows he was thankful. Everything was good and better than he cold have hoped for, better than he ever deserved; only, whatever it was and however good it was, it wasn't what you once had been, and had lost, and could never have again, and once in a while, once in a long time, you remembered, and knew how far you were away, and it hit you hard enough, that little while it lasted, to break your heart.
>
> He felt thirsty, and images of stealthiness and deceit, of openness, anger and pride, immediately possessed him, and immediately he fought them off. If ever I get drunk again, he told himself proudly, I'll kill myself. And there are plenty good reasons why I won't kill myself. So I won't even get drunk again.

(pp. 151-52)

The unresolved ironies of this monologue reveal the critical core of the novel. Jay's "plenty good reasons" rescue him from the temptations of the loneliness he feels because of the loss of his past, "what [he] once had been." . . . [The] search for the "what you once had been" is the object of many of Agee's fictional characters. Perhaps the question of exactly what Jay feels he has lost can never be answered. But remembering the significance of the Chaplin figure in "Scientists and Tramps," we may suspect that the loss is nothing so simple as the disappearing pristine innocence of an American Adam. Rather, the loss the characters feel seems part of a strategy to reveal what Agee considers the fundamental paradox of the human condition. Such was, for instance, the function of Irvine's loss in **"1928 Story"**: he believed in his adolescent confidence only insofar as Agee could exploit it as an illusion.

Agee's characterization of Rufus serves the same end. Though drawn along general lines, Rufus' delineation is specific enough to render a credible character. He is imitative of his parent's and elder's values. When he meets his Aunt Hannah to go shopping, he repeats the formula his mother had given him: "I'm *very glad* to come, Aunt Hannah, and thank you very much for thinking of me." . . . When choosing a hat, he picks the one he is sure will be approved. . . . But he can also be very discriminating. He knows why he appreciates his aunt: "of all grown people she was the most considerate," . . . and he knows that he dislikes Father Jackson, the priest who comes to pray at his father's funeral, for exactly the opposite reason. Rufus is likely to exhibit a very good mind discussing God with his mother . . . , or cunningly tormenting his baby sister . . . , or breaking his mother's rule in order to satisfy his curiosity about Negroes. . . . But his role in the novel seems greater than the portrayal of the young, sensitive son. In fact, Rufus' character is the clearest embodiment of the novel's theme of loneliness and contentment.

The interchapter which ends with Jay's monologue begins with Rufus' dream that turns into a nightmare. In the dream Rufus converses with darkness, which tells him it is a sheltering force; but soon darkness turns into a malevolent force. . . . The darkness is all that is unknown. The dream is of security and shelter, which brings with it a sense of personal identity. The nightmare, however, is that the dream is false—further, that the identity which security and shelter provide is an illusion. What Jay is yearning for is actually the identity of Rufus' dream. Yet the paradox is that while Rufus' dream compels belief, it is an unmistakable deceit.

The paradox of dream and nightmare, of desire and illusion, finally culminates in Rufus' feelings during his walk with his Uncle Andrew, following his father's burial. Rufus' initial reaction to Andrew's story about the butterfly is one of pride in sharing the confidence of his uncle, a source of contentment and security.

> He could see it very clearly, because his uncle saw it so clearly when he told about it, and what he saw made him feel that a special and good thing was happening. He felt that it was good for his father and that lying there in the darkness did not matter so much. . . .

But within the space of a moment Andrew reverses field. He is now condemning Father Jackson and God and Christianity, and by implication Rufus' aunt and his mother.

> They were standing at the edge of Fort Sanders and looking out across the waste of briers and of embanked clay, and Rufus was trying to hold his feelings intact. Everything had seemed so nearly all right, up to a minute ago, and now it was changed and confused. It was still all right, everything which had been, still was, he did not see how it could stop being, yet it was hard to remember it clearly and to remember how he had felt and why it had seemed all right, for since then his uncle had said so much. . . .

Hence the closing sentence of the novel—"But he did not ask, and his uncle did not speak except to say, after a few minutes, 'It's time to go home,' and all the way home they walked in silence" . . .—is actually Rufus' response to the central paradox of the novel. The contentment Rufus experiences as he is drawn into companionship with his uncle and which obliterates his fear of death and fear for his father's loneliness is, in fact, an illusion. Like the darkness which was first shelter then a monster, the "accident of compassion" is also deceptive. The novel ends, then, with Rufus "hovering over Cartesian vortices" as he tries to hold his feelings intact. (pp. 152-55)

> *Alfred T. Barson, in his* A Way of Seeing: A Critical Study of James Agee, *University of Massachusetts Press, 1972, 217 p.*

WILLIAM STOTT (essay date 1973)

[*Stott is an American critic and educator. In the following excerpt, he examines Agee's participation in the narrative of* Let Us Now Praise Famous Men *and discusses the purpose of the text's formlessness.*]

More than Agee's direct reporting of reality, it was his extraordinary participation in the narrative of *Let Us Now Praise Famous Men* that set the book apart from other documentary writing of the thirties. This aspect of the book drew far the most criticism. Agee was called to task for his "bad manners and exhibitionism," for "too many awarenesses on the subjective side," for a sincerity that was "too much, too prostrate." Even Lionel Trilling, who best perceived the book's excellence, thought Agee's autobiography and self-examination didn't succeed because too much of the reader's attention was taken up with subtracting Agee from his report [see Additional Bibliography]. Quite simply, *Let Us Now Praise Famous Men* was confessional in a way no documentary had been. In prior documentary writing—and in subsequent, down to the "new" or "personal" journalism of the sixties—confession was a strategy for telegraphing to the audience the feelings it should feel. The writer was an experiencer of a certain social condition, and his firsthand reactions were to guide the reader's own. The writer's personality figured in the report, if at all, in abbreviated form, as a type: usually the cool-headed fact-gatherer or the weeping Jeremiah. His complexities and passions, and the full story of how he got the story were left out of account.

Not with Agee. He exposed himself infinitely more than he did the tenants. He made public his tangled and often disreputable desires, his moral outrage at the "obscene and thoroughly terrifying" assignment he had taken on, and his (paradoxical) "self-nausea" at how poorly he was doing it. Like other documentary writers, he participated in the life he studied, tried to get "inside the subject." Yet simultaneously he confessed his distance from the tenants: showed how his participation came about and how thin it was. He participated, but he showed so *much* of the participation that he was seen to stand apart. He presented himself as he was: an actual man of complex personality in real relation with other actual inaccessible people—like George Gudger, whom he knew "only so far as I know him, and only in those terms in which I know him; and . . . that depends as fully on who I am as on who he is."

Agee used the reality of his relation with the tenants to prove *their* reality—not "as 'tenant' 'farmers,' as 'representatives' of [a] 'class,' as social integers in a criminal economy," but as humans. And he proved the relation's reality by laying bare his side of it.

He showed how hard he worked to make relation possible, to set people at their ease and encourage them to trust him. With a landowner, he was "even more easygoing, casual, and friendly than he was." With a Negro couple he had accidently terrified, he stood "shaking my head, and raising my hand palm outward," and smiling, so that "they should be restored, and should know that I was their friend." . . . His first night in the Gudger house he forced himself to eat a good deal more than he could hold so that he wouldn't seem to be eating to be polite. He found that George and Annie Mae were "quietly surprised and gratified in my appetite" and that the meal was the beginning of his "intimacy" with them.

He made it clear that he identified with these people in a deep, even reverent way very different both from the facile pity of most documentary and from the blunt opportunism of Franklin Roosevelt's remark quoted at the start of the inventory of the tenants' lives: "You are all farmers; I am a farmer myself." The Gudgers, though his exact contemporaries, seemed to Agee "not other than my own parents"; their house, "my right home, right earth, right blood, to which I would never have true right." At times he felt so close to the tenants he could "know almost their dreams" and, like Walt Whitman, "lie down inside each one." (pp. 298-300)

Agee makes plain to the reader why he worked at achieving intimacy with the tenants and why he so identified with them. He liked them. He took pleasure in the give-and-take, the easy tension, of being with them. He and Evans looked forward to their subtle negotiations with Bud Woods, who became "a sort of father to us" and who himself enjoyed the sessions and liked the young men long before he ceased mistrusting them. Agee valued the tenants' trust and affection. It was Mrs. Ricketts' "unforgiving face," her resentment of Evans and him the first afternoon, that more than anything made him choose this group of people to live with. "We shall have to return," he thought, "even in the face of causing further pain, until that mutual wounding shall have been won and healed, until she shall fear us no further, yet not in forgetfulness but through ultimate trust, through love." Evans has said that Agee made the tenants fall in love with him and that their love was reciprocated. Both facts are apparent in the book. . . . (pp. 300-01)

Agee divulged not only his love for the tenants but his carnal thoughts about their women. His extreme candor about sex and his sexual needs and fantasies troubled the original reviewers more than anything else. The "New Book Survey" in the *Library Journal* reported that **Let Us Now Praise Famous Men** had "beautiful, lyric prose of high merit," and, in the next sentence, "many objectionable passages and references"—shorthand for smut. Thirties documentary (and radical fiction, too) piously ignored human sexuality, except when it was degraded by economic need and, typically, a girl or woman sold her body to get food. Agee, quite against the temper of the

time, insisted on bringing into the open the sexual motive in normal behavior. He drove the car, and Emma sat beside him,

> her round sleeveless arms cramped a little in front of her. My own sleeves were rolled high, so that in the crowding our flesh touched. Each of us at the first few of these contacts drew quietly away, then later she relaxed her arms, and her body and thighs as well, and so did I, and for perhaps fifteen minutes we lay quietly and closely side to side, and intimately communicated also in our thoughts.

In such passages as this, Agee brilliantly disclosed the unacknowledged sexuality of everyday experience: the random small liaisons that happen all the time but that one doesn't talk about nor even, sometimes, realize. But he did something more: he verified the tenant woman's reality as a human, a woman, and not merely an integer in a criminal economy. To admit that such encounters can take place between a social "victim" and the reporter documenting his or her life is to bridge the social and economic gulf between them and severely weaken the idea that hardship is the *basic* fact of the victim's life. Cultivating real relation with the tenants meant that Agee had to go so far as to agree with Bud Woods, in the book's funniest moment, that there was a danger he, Agee, might be overcome with passion for Woods' slatternly wife, Ivy, and hence had better sleep under another roof.

Agee's recording the delicate dance of attraction between the tenant women and him is one of the book's triumphs. The same is not true, however, of his implicating them in sexual fantasies which seem to have been his alone. His suggestion that before returning to her husband Emma "could spend her last few days alive, having a gigantic good time in bed, with George, . . . and with Walker and me" is a huge presumption because Agee claims the others had the idea in mind ("this has a good many times in the past couple of days come very clearly through between all of us except the children") but gives no evidence to justify the claim. In the car Emma frankly relaxed her body against his; there is no comparable gesture of intimacy in the earlier scene. One appreciates why Evans would find the scene an embarrassment, since he is said to have been harboring a disreputable idea that in fact did not cross his mind.

This may be the chief problem in Agee's text: his confessions, sexual and otherwise, are occasionally forced on others. The problem is not his confessions about himself, his sexual exploits, his hunger for "a girl nearly new to me"; these are boastful and boyish, and entirely his business. (As a matter of fact, they are justified in the scheme of the work, a point argued later.) Neither is the problem the claims he makes about other people when these are confirmed by gestures of theirs which he reports. The problem is the humiliating things he imputes to others while giving the reader no reason to believe them true. For instance, did Annie Mae actually say, as Agee seems to imply, "Oh, thank God not one of you knows how everyone snickers at your father"? Or was it Sadie Ricketts? Or neither of them? Did Annie Mae really say, "I tell you *I* won't be sorry when I die. I wouldn't be sorry this minute if it wasn't for Louise and Squinchy-here"? Which of the tenants said, "I reckon we're just about the *meanest* people in this whole country"? Did any? Who said, "How did we get caught?" Wasn't it just Agee putting words in the tenants' mouths? "In what way were we trapped? where, our mistake? what, where, how, when, what way, might all these things have been different, if only we had done otherwise? if only we might have known."

Paul Goodman, reviewing *Let Us Now Praise Famous Men* in 1942, accused Agee of constantly reading himself into the tenants' lives, sometimes with "insufferable arrogance." In fact, though, Agee can do it without any arrogance whatever, provided the reader knows he is doing it. He can guess at the tenants' dreams or imagine—touchingly, plausibly—Louise's thoughts ("But I am young; and I am young, and strong, and in good health; and I am young") and the reader accepts his inventions as such, as the best hunches of a sensitive onlooker. Arrogance starts, however, when he fabricates and doesn't tell the reader—which he did, at least in part, in the "how were we caught" section. Agee elsewhere took such care to dignify the tenants that his handling of them here is incomprehensible. One doesn't doubt that the tenants felt such raw despair; indeed, Agee often alludes to it. What one *does* doubt is that they *told* him these things. Surely Annie Mae Gudger never spoke thus of her husband to James Agee: "He no longer cares for me, he just takes me when he wants me." That Agee would half pretend she had said it, rather than frankly acknowledge it a guess on his part, violates the fundamental insight of *Let Us Now Praise Famous Men;* it strips the tenants barer than they actually were. The sentence imposed on Annie Mae treats her as the captions treat the people in *You Have Seen Their Faces.*

Evans acknowledges that the "how were we caught" section makes him "squirm a little; I think it is a wrong note. Still, that's part of Agee's general psychological belief: give them everything; let's have the truth. He may have squirmed, too, and said, 'Well, squirm or no squirm this has got to go in.'" Certainly this impulse motivated Agee's confessions about himself. He went out of his way to expose what he called his "present immaturity": his erotic fixations, his guilt and death-longings, his hunger for "first" intimacies and apathy at subsequent. His telling these embarrassing facts is an important part of the book's strategy. He tells the truth about himself, humbles and even humiliates himself, so that he can uncondescendingly tell of the tenants' humiliation. He strips himself to have the right to report their nakedness. And there is a way in which the reader, who intrudes upon Agee as Agee intrudes upon the tenants, must also strip himself to look upon them. If he gets by the book's efforts to alienate and bore him, he must still pass the test of Agee's confessions. If these seem to him depraved and lunatic, as they did to several reviewers, and if he cannot recognize how similar compromising truths might be told about him, he will not see the tenants as Agee thought they truly were, as people like himself.

Through all his writing Agee was concerned to inculcate "a way of seeing" which might help in "restoring us toward sanity, good will, calm, acceptance, and joy." He was, as Evans insists, primarily a moralist. In *Let Us Now Praise Famous Men,* he sought to teach the educated thirties' reader how to feel and respond toward the underprivileged. This is the question with which the book permanently confronts its audience: how should we, relatively fortunate people, behave toward the unfortunate, the crippled, the deceived? And Agee's answer, which he puts into practice throughout the narrative, is as outrageous as it is Christian and simple: we should establish real relation; we should fall in love with them.

Lionel Trilling, while he thought Agee's argument "the most important moral effort" of his generation, believed there was a fault in its presentation. He felt Agee was suggesting that the poor and the damaged be loved *because of* their afflictions. He said Agee wrote of the tenants "as if there were no human unregenerateness in them, no flicker of malice or meanness,

no darkness or wildness of feeling, only a sure and simple virtue, the growth, we must suppose, of their hard, unlovely poverty." Trilling's criticism, which has been echoed by several recent scholars, is in part true. Agee believed that in poverty and suffering (and in failure, too) there was virtue. For him, the poor *were* blessed; they were the "famous men" whose children are within the covenant and whose seed shall remain forever. Writing in 1947 of Helen Levitt's photographs of slum-dwellers, he said: "This is the record of an ancient, primitive, transient, and immortal civilization, incomparably superior to our own." The idea wasn't put so baldly in *Let Us Now Praise Famous Men,* but no doubt Agee held it then. Nevertheless, he certainly did not claim the tenants free of human unregenerateness:

> In the people of [the rural South] you care most for, pretty nearly without exception you must reckon in traits, needs, diseases, and above all mere natural habits, differing from our own, of a casualness, apathy, self-interest, unconscious, offhand, and deliberated cruelty, in relation toward extra-human life and toward negroes, terrible enough to freeze your blood or to propel you toward murder; and . . . you must reckon them as "innocent" even of the worst of this.

To Agee, then, the tenants were "innocent" but not good.

Agee wanted to believe that a love relation between "the extremes of the race"—the educated and well-off, and the poor and ill-used—was possible and would redeem the world. . . . But as though embarrassed at the sentimentality of the idea, he hid it in grandiloquence and clouded allusion, and finally undercut it by implying that these boons would fall not to the tenants alone "but to us all," with the coming of the Messiah.

It was characteristic that Agee couldn't decide whether human or God's love would save the world. His text to *Let Us Now Praise Famous Men* is radically tentative, unfinished. The parts of it earliest composed were used unrevised, sometimes in quotation marks, with footnotes contradicting what the author formerly thought. (pp. 301-07)

Throughout the text Agee begins topics, breaks them off, reverts to earlier ones or shifts ahead (telling the reader not to be "puzzled by this, I'm writing in a continuum"), stops, often in self-disgust, and takes up the first topic once more. Over and over he redefines his theme, purpose, method, and starts again "a new and more succinct beginning." "I will be trying here to write nothing whatever which did not in physical actuality or in the mind happen or appear," he promises when the text is already half over. "These matters had in that time the extreme clearness, and edge, and honor, which I shall now try to give you," he says in the book's last sentence. These constant starts and abrupt revisions do two things: make the text disorderly and provide its fundamental order.

Agee was the first of many people who have tried to explain the ordering principle in *Let Us Now Praise Famous Men.* "The book as a whole," he said in the middle of the book, "will have a form and set of tones rather less like those of narrative than like those of music. That suits me, and I hope it turns out to be so." Evidently it didn't quite, for he appended a footnote comparing the forms of the text to those of movies and "improvisations and recordings of states of emotion" as well as music. When he finished the book, he tried writing a preface to explain its structure and found he couldn't: "For three or four months it has seemed to me that in twenty-five hundred words or so I could unify and make clear everything about this book that I wanted to or needed to. I have pretty well given that up now.''

Critics have sought to clarify the work by comparing it to *Moby Dick,* a Shakespearean five-act drama, and a Beethoven symphony—analogies which prove as unrevealing as they sound. Four scholars have found the key to the text, as they think it, in a distinction Agee tried to make among ''four planes'' of narration in the book. At least two of the planes are redundant, and all, as Agee conceded, are ''in strong conflict'' in many passages; but even *were* they always distinct, that would not explain why any one appeared at a certain moment and, hence, why the narrative has the curious shape it has. (pp. 307-08)

A better suggestion of the book's design has been made by Dwight Macdonald, who compared it to an anti-*Works and Days,* ''a chronicle of decay instead of growth, where the land does not nourish those who labor on it but destroys them.'' There is much of the black pastoral in *Let Us Now Praise Famous Men,* and surely Macdonald is right to define its form in terms of an anti-genre or (what is the same thing) a mixed genre. But when he says that ''Hesiod chronicled a way of life; Agee and Evans, a way of death,'' he overstates the morbidity of farm labor in the book. After all, Agee's final proof of the common humanity of tenant, journalist, and reader is that ''quite soon now . . . we shall all be drawn into the planet beside one another.'' To call the book an antipastoral ignores its religious dimension, and also—and much more serious— its fierce skepticism about its ability to communicate the reality it treats.

This urgent, at times tormented, straining to perceive and describe truly is the narrative's fundamental tone. On page after page Agee bemoans his incapacity:

> What's the use trying to say what I feel.

> The most I can do—the most I can hope to do—is to make a number of physical entities as plain and vivid as possible.

> Two essentials, I cannot hope to embody even mildly but must say only, what they are, and what they should be if they could be written.

> Let this all stand however it may: since I cannot make it the image it should be, let it stand as the image it is: I am speaking of my verbal part of this book as a whole.

He realized of course that to understand and convey ''the whole problem and nature of existence'' was ''beyond what I, or anyone else, is capable of.'' His attempt kept the text in continual revision, as he weighed each word to choose the one that least diminished the truth and struggled vainly toward a narrative structure that would make the ineffable clear. His manuscripts are full of paragraphs dropped and revived, uncertain commands to himself (''Better omit or put in as a postscript''), sections interpolated ''from a former preface'' or ''from an earlier draft towards a more whole attempt.'' The book's most important scene, the first meal with the Gudgers, is clumsily given as a flashback, a ''reversion,'' in a narrative that isn't taken up again. So miscellaneous is the text that Agee could find no better way to include large portions of it than to call them ''Notes,'' ''A Few Notes,'' ''Notes and Appendices.'' The whole odd arrangement of the chapters seems to have been decided on the spur of the moment, in pencil, on a

scrap of paper, with casual arrows shifting tens of thousands of words about.

And this lack of order *is* the order in the text: Agee's straining to communicate reality, and failing, and straining again give the narrative its form. It is a form we might call antidocumentary or metaphysical documentary or neo-Christian documentary, a form of repeated prefaces and incidental notes to a book that cannot be written, a form that must ''fail'' because, as Trilling said, ''failure alone can express the inexpressible.'' The form imitates the process of consciousness, wherein perception is sudden, inexplicable, quickly lost, and always beginning again. What one feels constantly behind the words on the page is a consciousness laboring toward the world, Nature, the truth. *Let Us Now Praise Famous Men* is a prologue, a ''preface or opening,'' to reality. The book's symbol might be the parenthesis Agee often left unclosed— (—open to the world. Or, even better, the punctuation mark he used to such fascinating excess and named a chapter for: the colon. Once, having summarized the tenant environment in a paragraph, he said, ''This is all one colon:'' and ended the sentence and paragraph thus, leaving two lines blank below. He may have been referring to his narrative, for in a sense *it* is all one colon that prefaces and points the reader to reality; a colon to a text that cannot be given.

The book's hero is, as Agee said, human consciousness, the instrument that tries the many soundings of reality and the source ''we have to thank for joy.'' Because Agee's consciousness is so forceful and rich, his most persuasive propaganda against the tenant system was exactly that it diminished consciousness, atrophied ''the use of the intelligence, of the intellect, and of the emotions.'' In tenant life ''a consciousness beyond that of the simplest child'' would result ''in a great deal of pain, not to say danger''; hence, the faculty had to be reduced or killed. This was the obscenity of tenant life. (pp. 309-11)

William Stott, ''The Text,'' in his Documentary Expression and Thirties America, *Oxford University Press, 1973, pp. 290-314.**

VICTOR A. KRAMER   (essay date 1975)

[*Kramer is an American critic and educator who has done extensive research into Agee's unpublished papers and is considered among the most influential scholars of Agee's life and works. In the following excerpt, he discusses Agee's intended focus in* The Morning Watch.]

Commentators on Agee's *The Morning Watch* . . . emphasize the growth into maturity of its twelve year old hero, Richard. But Agee's focus remains more specifically upon the immediacy of what is experienced, and less on change than is usually assumed. Agee's text, his working notes, excluded manuscript, and the biographical circumstances which contributed to the development of the novella all point toward an understanding of the book which recognizes the stasis which is the center of the work. This novella achieves success because of its focus upon a pinnacle of religious fervor which the reader senses must inevitably diminish. The book is about the hours of the Maundy Thursday vigil and morning of Good Friday when students at a rural boarding school are allowed to make visits before the exposed Blessed Sacrament in the Lady Chapel. Richard had been anticipating the vigil for months; he hoped to pray extremely well. Yet his hopes are not fulfilled, and the book is, in large part, a report of failure, while ironically he does experience genuine religious emotion. Throughout the hours portrayed Richard's mind is constantly distracted as he attempts to pray. After leaving the chapel, he and two other boys go for an early hour swim instead of reporting back to their dormitory. The swim, and other actions of Richard during the outing, are more distractions from his valiant effort to be religious. Nevertheless these hours include moments of high religious emotion; but hints that they inevitably pass are incorporated throughout the novella.

Throughout his fiction Agee was most interested in precisely focusing upon the intersections of space, time, and consciousness, and less so in constructing plots and developing character. Because of that interest his best writing is often based on personal remembrance. In all of his longer works of fiction Agee's characters remain almost static while a kaleidoscopic world is beheld by them. Thus, six year old Rufus in *A Death in the Family* does not change within that novel, and it would be a mistake to expect development in his characterization. Essentially he beholds events which might influence later development. Basically the same thing occurs in *The Morning Watch*, even though more change might be expected with a six year older protagonist. *The Morning Watch* resembles Agee's *Let Us Now Praise Famous Men* where the writer concentrates upon particularities remembered, often complex states of mind. This semi-autobiographical novella recalls the atmosphere of St. Andrew's, the boarding school near Sewanee, Tennessee, remembered by Agee from childhood. Real persons are the basis for much of its characterization. In the working notes a list of remembered names parallels a list of characters. One must assume that real events have had some bearing on the inception of this story.

Peter H. Ohlin, in *Agee* . . . , has suggested that Richard's gradual change in awareness about suffering and death is the theme of the book. This element is important; but equally important is the almost static quality of these hours, and Richard's mood. The novella suggests how an intensely religious emotion is felt, and how such a feeling is intruded upon by other awarenesses. This is presented from the point of view of the artist looking back upon his own precocious childhood, a time during which a twelve-year old could hardly perceive the complexity of what he was experiencing. Agee knew that religious emotion, for any person, was a combination of many different elements conjoined; but as one matures it becomes more difficult to reconcile religious feeling with other ways of feeling, thinking, and acting. (pp. 221-22)

We know . . . that Agee had been seriously thinking about religious questions during the years immediately preceding his decision to write *The Morning Watch*. It is often mistakenly assumed that he worked on the manuscript for *The Morning Watch* over a period of several years. In fact, the book was written with one spurt of energy during the spring of 1950. . . . Agee had spent "most of winter and spring" on his piece about John Huston. Then in a week the draft for the Maundy Thursday story was finished. The book is, therefore, the product of a period preceded by religious awareness; and a work which was written with relative speed. It seems to be an attempt artistically to recreate an earlier time of felt emotion.

The Morning Watch has been criticized because its ending is believed ineffective. Commentary often either expresses dissatisfaction with the lack of development in Richard's character, or explains his development in terms of the somewhat obvious symbolism incorporated into the work. Agee's emphasis, however, is upon the evocation of a particular fleeting

moment; and attention to the particularities of what Richard sees and imagines is the primary means of evoking what he feels. While what he experiences, both inside and outside the chapel does alter his consciousness, he feels at the end of his Good Friday's experience that he and his schoolmates remain "children."

As he planned his book, Agee noted that the focus was to be on religious emotion, yet mixed with the "beginning of intrusions of [a] sense of beauty and a sense of science," while the general "watershed" about which the story was to flow was to remain the "age of faith at its height." Essentially Richard's religious fervor is bounded by other experiences, and ultimately these hours will be lost. But during his watch the many forces at play within his mind are nearly balanced. Richard, of course, is not aware of all this. He is a rather bright boy who is attempting to feel religious.

Holy Weeks were special times for everyone at St. Andrew's. This time was so special that even Willard Rivenburg, the "great athlete" of St. Andrew's (who never even bothered to cross himself at crucial times in football games), was affected by the "stillness" which "came over everything." . . . For Richard the events of that week were the culmination of an elaborate series of attempts to foster religious emotion. His entire preceding year had been devoted to an intensification of religious fervor, and as this day arrives he is already near a high point of religious feeling. During the entire year preceding Holy Week Richard had, he thought, elaborately intensified his fervor. Denial and mortification had been practiced throughout that year, and even more so during the forty days of Lent. But just as his initial thoughts about the importance of his approaching watch are interrupted while he is still in bed, his attempt to cultivate religious emotion is doomed. As the narrative opens he lies awake waiting to be called by Father Whitman. He tries to meditate about Christ's Passion. But his attempts are broken by the happiness and blasphemy of other boys in the dormitory, and by his own mental distraction. (pp. 223-24)

Throughout the novella Richard's attempts to pray lead him through a series of distractions. Indeed there is hardly a thought which does not lead him quickly astray. At the end of his first half-hour in the chapel he realizes that mostly "his mind had been wandering: there had been scarcely one moment of prayer or of realization." . . . Much of the book devoted to Richard's attempts to pray is a record of his distracted mental state. While these hours are a high point of religious emotion, they are ironically a constant series of deviations from the path Richard desperately wants to follow. For instance, he is hardly in the chapel when its atmosphere of candles and flowers, which should allow him to think of God, drives his mind to remembrances of his father's funeral. (p. 225)

Richard wants desperately to maintain what he assumes to be a proper religious frame of mind. But Agee stresses that religious fervor is being infringed upon by other awarenesses. The working notes and excluded manuscript written in conjunction with the novella support a reading which emphasizes the futility of the young protagonist's attempt to sustain his religious feeling as it is intruded upon by all manner of things from sex to skepticism. In his working notes Agee asked himself what he hoped to accomplish. And his answers, as well as unused introductory and concluding passages, indicate that he felt his story should imply that innocence would yield to other ways of experiencing the world. Agee asked himself the following:

What really am I after in this story and is it worth doing? Religion at its deepest intensity or clarity of childhood faith and emotions; plus beginnings of a skeptical intellect and set of senses; how the senses themselves, and sexuality, feed the skeptical or non-religious or esthetic intellect; efforts at self-discipline. Religious-esthetic-biological experiences carrying with them above all, religious experience of an unusually fine kind, and the innocent certainty that it is doomed.

When for instance, Agee suggests Richard's attempts to feel religious are clouded by his remembrances of pious paintings, he implies that the young artist-to-be is distracted by the developing esthetic sense. . . . Agee noted that he wanted to do the book in terms of:

the watching in the chapel; wanderings of the mind and efforts at prayer; memories of the dead father; imagination of sex and sport; workings of guilt; excesses of religious intention and complications of guilt and pride; the excitement of . . . dawn . . . the locust hull; . . . the snake.

But then he asked:

Is [the snake] too obvious a symbol, and the locust? They seem so.
    Is this worth doing? I can't get any solid hold of it or confidence in it.
    A much gentler way of seeing and writing it? Or more casual? Mine is very dry and very literary.

These notes emphasize why there is little concern with characterization in the book. Agee wants to evoke "religious-esthetic-biological experiences." He even expresses doubt about his use of symbolism, the very element of the book most criticized. Richard Chase has argued that in place of "relaxed and perspicacious biography of spiritual change" the concluding parts of the book provide "spectacular semantic gestures" [see excerpt dated 1951]. (pp. 225-26)

Agee realized that perhaps too many elements in his narrative were too elaborately developed. In another of his working notes he suggested that he suspected "so many particularities. They drag, and they are dull. I keep working for the maximum number, an inch-by-inch account, when what I am after is the minimum in word and image, and a short handing of action." It must have been for such reasons he did rely upon the symbolism of the concluding section of the book. The shell which Richard finds, and with which he is fascinated, certainly connotes death and suffering. Yet Agee was doubtful about the effectiveness of that symbol. Its function in the narrative suggests a change in the boy's awareness about suffering; and his awareness will, importantly, provide a propensity for later development. But as the book closes Richard does not fully understand what the locust shell signifies, as he holds it "in exquisite protectiveness." . . . (pp. 226-27)

Richard senses all things fade. Yet he cannot fully realize that his religious emotion, which he has been desperately trying to enflame, will also fade. Almost immediately the boys go back to the school, and quickly as they are walking, Richard remembers with "surprise and shame" what day it is. He then continues thinking about the Passion.

Several crucial events occur to Richard in this last episode of the book. These experiences prepare him for later and inevitable change, but he does not mature during these few hours. More is expected of Richard than Agee ever hoped to handle, or could handle in a work of this scope, if we expected Richard to exhibit maturation. During these hours he is beginning to doubt the efficacy of formal religious practices. The novella concentrates on just the "beginnings of a skeptical intellect and set of senses." (p. 227)

When F. W. Dupee initially reviewed the novella he noted that the final scene at the Sand Cut was "not so well conceived" as the section set in the chapel, and he wondered if the "triumph in the chapel is not being capitalized on to an extent that is hardly legitimate." What should be emphasized is that the focus of the novella remains, even during the forbidden swim, on Richard's religious fervor. In that climactic scene, the dive and the attempt to stay under water an extremely long time is certainly an act of pride and a crucial step toward maturation; but it is also an act of religious devotion. The dive is symbolic of a rebirth after his failure to sustain the kind of emotion that he hoped for in the chapel. But Richard, as he dives, has "just time to dedicate within himself *for Thee!*," and his dive becomes an act of devotion. He prays "O Lord let me suffer with Thee this day," as his lungs are about to burst. . . . It is as if the religious emotion itself is near bursting. But it is important that the emotion does not collapse. Richard is still able, a moment later, to stand on the bank of the quarry and imagine what Jesus had suffered at that very moment.

The concluding section remains fundamentally built on the boy's intently religious attitudes during hours which remain very much part of a religious feast. However, Agee's fear that his method of writing was perhaps elaborate and too "literary" provides an insight into what he did accomplish—a sense of immediacy, and evocation of emotion, but emotion almost ready to disintegrate. In a related note he had written "R's waking emotion and the hollowness of the dormitory beds must be as nearly immediate and simultaneous as possible." Any indirection, abstraction, or use of symbols, unless very carefully integrated into the experience as a whole, would tend to detract from the immediacy of that moment.

No doubt Agee experienced difficulty deciding how the emphasis upon Richard's emotion would be best focused. There are several draft versions for alternate openings for the book. And, in addition, an introductory section and alternate ending were actually typed out. Whether these alternate passages were submitted to an editor is unknown; but it is clear that Agee was not sure how best to begin the novella.

The introductory manuscript is also about the difficulty of feeling religious emotion, but from the point of view of an adult. In the excluded passage Father Whitman, a priest who wakes the boys for their chapel visit, tries to feel, but cannot, the solemnity of the night. For him the meaning of the Passion is clear intellectually, but it is not something which he can feel. His disturbed thoughts provide insight into Richard's dilemma:

however clearly he realized it in his dull, tired mind, he could not realize it in his heart. . . .
I only want to be a religious, he told himself quietly. I haven't got it in me to be, and in twenty years of trying, none of that has changed.
(pp. 227-28)

The implication of Richard's incipient awareness, qualified by the opening description of Father Whitman, is that with maturity, religious emotion is complicated, and easily distracted. Throughout the novella Richard is not particularly aware of how his religious fervor functions. He cannot yet understand that religious emotion will not be forced. In the excluded passage the dull emotion of Father Whitman stands in contrast with the "sincerely devout" feelings of Richard. Father Whitman who has been a religious for twenty years, tries to meditate. He lies awake waiting to call the boys to their watch, but he realizes that Maundy Thursday and Good Friday have lost any special aura for him.

In conjunction with the unused introductory passage Agee's "possible addition" for the conclusion would also have slightly altered the book's emphasis. Agee suggested if the alternate opening was employed lines would "be added onto present ending, no new paragraph." These words were added to the working draft as well as typed in conjunction with the alternate opening for the work. On the last page of the narrative Richard approaches the school dormitory with his errant friends; he is carrying the locust shell which he had picked up in the woods, "his left hand sustaining, in exquisite protectiveness, the bodiless shell which rested against his heart." . . . The excluded ending added these phrases: ". . . and exactly as he had foreseen, there on the back steps was Father Whitman, and although his eyes too were just as Richard had foreseen, hard, sleepless, patient, eyes to be afraid of and ashamed before, it was not so very hard to meet them after all."

With a beginning which suggests the difficulty of sustaining religious fervor, and a conclusion which again returns to Father Whitman, the emphasis upon an "age of faith at its height," would have been more clearly evident. Throughout *The Morning Watch* Agee is most concerned with evoking the complex emotion of particular imagined moments, a high point in Richard's life. Agee is fascinated with the beauty of that time. The beauty is mostly in the immediacy. Richard is not aware of the vast differences between what he has attempted to experience and what actually has happened. Such a realization can only be made by a wiser person: Father Whitman or Agee, the artist, as he fictionalizes these moments. (p. 229)

> Victor A. Kramer, "'Religion at Its Deepest Intensity': The Stasis of Agee's 'The Morning Watch'," in Renascence, Vol. XXVII, No. 4, Summer, 1975, pp. 221-30.

GENEVIÈVE MOREAU (essay date 1977)

[*Moreau is a French critic. In the following excerpt from her biographical and critical study* The Restless Journey of James Agee, *she discusses Agee's perspective on art and its relationship to life, and comments on his ultimate achievement as an artist.*]

Among the crucial experiences of James Agee's artistic development, his stay in Alabama, which resulted in the composition of *Let Us Now Praise Famous Men,* appears to have been decisive. A confrontation with reality that abolished the separation between life and literature, setting in a new perspective the author's speculations on the artist's function and endeavor, it marks the beginning of a new orientation. In placing life above art, Agee became involved in bold and contradictory paths, where literature was experienced both as a necessity and as an impossibility.

Although Agee never expressed his views in a systematic fashion, they are affirmed throughout his work. Literature is seen

Agee in a scene from the film The Bride Comes to Yellow Sky, *which he scripted based on a story by Stephen Crane.* Time *Magazine.*

as an homage to life, a celebration. The artist must catalog the real with precision and fidelity, observe it with an attention that will illuminate its most obscure aspects. Language should follow the shape of reality; since words are inadequate, the writer has recourse to the use of sound, multiple meanings and symbols. Agee's writing attempts to deal with all the various aspects of life, although it cannot succeed in following all its intricacies.

Agee was subject to all the pitfalls of such an ambition: excess detail, lack of discrimination, tiresome inventories, a style that is ambiguous, sometimes ornate, distorted and rhetorical. Although he wanted to come to grips with life, he never completely freed himself from a certain preciousness acquired from his reading of the Elizabethans and his affinity for their writings. His language tended to become distant from its living sources.

It was because reality is born and reborn through language that Agee hesitated over the choice of a word and could not eliminate any of the alternatives. Agee wrote with the conviction that all literature is destined to fail to a greater or a lesser extent.

Music, photography and the motion picture were models Agee would always strive to equal. He tried by means of images to give his prose a sonority, a visual dimension and movement, to force the reader to respond to words with the spontaneity with which the ear perceives music, the eye a photograph or a film.

At times, by his own criteria, Agee succeeded in his literary task. His sentences unfold in an enchantment. The perfection he so ardently sought appears less often in the poetry of *Permit Me Voyage*, which contains too much technique and conscious refinement, than in the poetic prose of *Let Us Now Praise Famous Men* and of *A Death in the Family*.

Because poetry and existence were inseparable for Agee, his literary strivings reveal an extreme respect for life and the conviction that every being is also unique. His predilection for the ordinary was both a moral choice and an emotional involvement. Agee approached everyday, concrete reality with instinctive tenderness. He was so open to the emotions aroused in him by his perception of reality that he discovered a degree of passion that enabled him to perceive things "from within." He claimed the complicity of nature, of animals, and especially of the night, when the mystery of the world was intuitively revealed to him. In all, he brought to life a sacramental attention. Such a poetry, elaborated into a way of life, finds its basic laws in childhood. The qualities Agee claimed for the artist exist naturally in the child, whose capacity for wonder is still unrestrained. In his faith in innocence—that faith which is one of the Great American literary myths, from Mark Twain to J. D. Salinger—Agee retained his nostalgia for childhood; it offered him the means of revaluing a dehumanized world and of maintaining a state of grace. This is the source of his insistence on rediscovering who he had been. This also explains why writing seemed to him like a dreaded maturity. He undertook each new project to compensate for the absence of the work he despaired of writing, and if his literary production appears fragmentary and incomplete, it is partly a deliberate dispersion, explained by the very nature of his creative endeavor.

It is easy to see why Agee never belonged to any movement or literary school; yet his love of the land, his nostalgia for the past, his attachment to traditions, his sense of guilt and his obsession with sin and redemption undeniably link him with other Southerners. On these grounds it would perhaps be appropriate to place him among those writers whom Maxwell Geismar calls "the last of the Provincials."

Historically, Agee unquestionably belonged to the literary generation that was scarred by the Depression, tempted by political involvement and courted by journalism and movie making. He examined the problems of his time, sometimes preaching nonsubmission with Swiftian irony, urging a rebellion that would express itself not through acts of violence but through an obstinate adherence to a personal ideal. His work sprang from the old humanist tradition whose position was growing increasingly precarious. But although he was loyal to the past, he was also an innovator. His hatred of injustice, his religious sense of humanity as a mystical body, his contempt for bourgeois morality, made him sometimes appear as a liberator, even a revolutionary. In a satirical and impassioned explosion, he examined problems that are still those of America and of the world today: the exploitation of man by man, the individual reabsorbed or banished by society, crimes committed against or in the name of democracy and freedom. (pp. 269-72)

Both Agee's career—its gropings, failures and achievements—and his life, in its unrelenting quest and its sense of urgency, exemplify the fate of the American artist whose predicament it was to come to terms with himself as well as with a society that offered him constant pitfalls, compromises and denials of his talent.

Agee made the difficult journey through anger and rage to simplicity and love. He knew all the grace and terror of living and celebrated it in its magnificence and in its cruelty, leavening his observations with irony and humor. He saw the deep mysterious connection between ethics and aesthetics and emphatically asserted it in a work in which the most casual remark has the quality of true poetic utterance. (pp. 272-73)

> *Geneviève Moreau, in her* The Restless Journey of James Agee, *translated by Miriam Kleiger with Morty Schiff, William Morrow and Company, Inc., 1977, 320 p.*

LOUIS D. RUBIN, JR.   (essay date 1979)

[*Rubin is an American critic and educator who has written and edited numerous studies of Southern literature. In the following excerpt, he examines Agee's intent in* Let Us Now Praise Famous Men *to explore his own sensibility rather than produce a work of social documentary.*]

In the summer of 1936 Agee was delighted to receive an assignment from *Fortune* to go south with the photographer Walker Evans and "do a story on: sharecropper family (daily and yearly life): and also a study of Farm Economics in the South (impossible for me): and also on the several efforts to help the situation: i.e. Govt. and state work; theories and wishes of Southern liberals; whole story of the 2 Southern unions." It was, he added, the "best break I ever had on *Fortune*."

It was indeed a break; it was pivotal to his literary career. Though the articles he was hired to write proved unacceptable to *Fortune*, they developed into a book that some critics feel is almost a classic. In Geneviève Moreau's summation, *Let Us Now Praise Famous Men* "is an intense spiritual adventure, a search for innocence, and along the way all literature, all culture, is brought into question. It is an experimental, polyphonic work in which all the arts—literature, music, film—fuse. And though Agee repeatedly disavows its artistic purposes, it is as a work of art that *Famous Men* is ultimately valued."

What the assignment to go down to Alabama and write about sharecroppers did for Agee was to get him into the rural South, and into a confrontation with his own origins. For the downtrodden tenant farmers and sharecroppers of Alabama were his father's people. Though the Agees of the Tennessee hill country had not themselves descended from the mountains and into the squalor, deprivation and hard toil of the Gudgers, Ricketts and Woods whom Agee encountered in Alabama, James Agee discovered in the houses, lives and ways of these depressed agriculturalists of the rural South a concreteness and significance such as seemed otherwise missing from his adult life in the urban literary and journalistic world of the metropolis. Their lives seemed anchored in actuality. These people were *real*. As he prepared to spend a night in the rickety farmhouse with the Gudgers,

> the feeling increased itself upon me that at the end of a wandering and seeking, so long it had begun before I was born, I had apprehended and now sat at rest in my own home, between two who were my brother and sister, yet less that than something else; these, the wife my age exactly, the husband four years older, seemed not other than my own parents, in whose patience I was so different, so diverged, so strange as I was; and all that surrounded me, that si-

lently strove in through my senses and stretched me full, was familiar and dear to me as nothing else on earth, and as if well known in a deep past and long years lost; so that I could wish that all my chance life was in truth the betrayal, the curable delusion, that it seemed, and that this was my right home, right earth, right blood, to which I would never have true right. For half my blood is just this; and half my right of speech. . . .

(pp. 157-60)

It is because of this experience, reported retrospectively like the *madeleine* episode in Proust, that the involvement with the Gudgers in *Let Us Now Praise Famous Men* is artistically important to the author. The "half my blood" and "half my right of speech" are his father's family heritage. Hugh James Agee was killed in an automobile wreck when his son was six years old. James Agee's subsequent life—the years with his mother and her well-educated family of Northern antecedents, at Saint Andrews School in Sewanee, Tennessee, at Phillips Exeter, Harvard, and in New York City—had constituted a distancing from the social and cultural legacy of his birth and his childhood in Knoxville. Now, in a sharecropper's shack in Alabama, he is made aware of the extent to which that portion of his identity and his heritage had become obscured. But the memory of the past—"so keen, sad, and precious a nostalgia"—can give him renewed access to the circumstances of his own identity in time. *Let Us Now Praise Famous Men,* therefore, comprises the monument and record of James Agee's rediscovery of his Southern birthright. The writing of it would ultimately make possible for him the recreation of remembered experience that is *The Morning Watch* and, most important of all, *A Death in the Family.*

For that very reason, however, the sharecropper book is ineffective as a work of political and social reportage. For despite the extremely detailed portraiture of the sharecropping families, how they looked and talked, where they lived, what they ate, how they worked, how degraded their situation, Agee isn't really imaginatively concerned with them in their own right. It is *his experience there* that fascinates him. The tone painting, the evocations of scenery and circumstance, the continued questioning of his own motives, the expressions of outrage at those who dare to look down upon and pity the humanity of the sharecroppers, the apostrophes to human endurance constitute nothing more, and nothing less, than an exploration of his own sensibility.

Agee isn't interested in the Gudgers, but in how to think, feel and write about the Gudgers. Under the guise of declining to over-simplify and distort through imposition of any sort of formulaic, stereotyped presentation of sharecropping, Agee is recording his experience in Alabama. As one critic points out, the "lack of order is the order in the text: Agee's straining to communicate reality, and failing, and straining again to give the narrative its form. . . . The form imitates the process of consciousness wherein perception is sudden, inexplicable, quickly lost, and always beginning again. What one feels constantly behind the words on the page is a consciousness laboring toward the world, Nature, the truth." The inability to impose meaningful shape comes because the real meaning was *not* the Alabama experience as such, but his own alienation from what it represented, and how the alienation happened. The place to look for that was not in the details of sharecropper families in

Alabama, but in his memories of Knoxville, his childhood, his parents, his divided heritage—"the sources of life, whereto I have no rightful access, having paid no price beyond love and sorrow." Rightful repossession could come only through the resources of memory and understanding: the writing of *The Morning Watch* and *A Death in the Family,* an artistic travail which, pursued intermittently, occupied the remainder of his life.

That Agee declares that the usual ways of writing a book about sharecroppers won't work is quite correct; for he was not writing a book about sharecropping. Agee possessed a deceptive—deceptive to him—ability to engage himself thoroughly and completely in whatever topic came to hand or was assigned to him by an editor or a film maker. As a writer he could get involved in almost anything, and force his energies upon it, without any immediate insight into the relationship of the project at hand to any other aspects of his career or his work. It is the aptitude of the good journalist, the journeyman writer. But Agee was also an artist—an artist who was in search of his true subject, and who had not yet discovered it. In this instance his aptitude misled him, for what Agee was really drawn to wasn't sharecropping and sharecroppers but their symbolic relationship to his own imagination, something that he sensed was tied in with his memories and his origins, but without knowing quite why. So what he tried to do was to invest his portrayal of the sharecroppers with the imaginative dimensions of a significance that really belonged not to the sharecroppers but to the relationship with his past. Even so, it was not finally wasted. The discovery had been made that led ultimately to *A Death in the Family.* So we can only be grateful for the Alabama book. (pp. 160-62)

Louis D. Rubin, Jr., "Trouble on the Land: Southern Literature and the Great Depression," in Canadian Review of American Studies, Vol. 10, No. 2, Fall, 1979, pp. 153-74.**

DAVID WYATT (essay date 1980)

[*Wyatt is an American critic and educator. He writes in the introduction to his* Prodigal Sons: A Study in Authorship and Authority *that "the measure of a man finally became for Agee his power to generate a voice which could embody in fiction the invisible and previously unutterable life of the family." In the following excerpt from* Prodigal Sons, *Wyatt examines Agee's use of voice as a creative agent in* A Death in the Family.]

James Agee's *A Death in the Family* is haunted by the problem of inexpressibility. The writing of the novel constitutes a troubled passing of silence into voice. The unsaid and unheard define the sublime, even forbidden, origins of experience that the novelist must literally render prosaic. To speak or to hear is to fall. Yet a sense of personal urgency—that the time has come to "choose a name" for death—propels Agee into this autobiographical fiction to which we, as well, feel compelled to listen. In a shared anxiety over generating voice (writing) or attending to voice (reading), author and audience are bonded together into a relationship which parallels and illuminates those family bonds which are the origin and end of the story.

"Oh, it's just beyond words!" Mary, in one outburst, relegates the utterance of the story to where it *should* be. . . . She has been elected to speak, the coal has been put to her mouth. Trembling on the edge of voice, Mary must appeal to an audience she has not chosen. In the threat of being consumed by what she utters Mary experiences the dilemma of creation and selectivity which is Agee's. His autobiography befell him. But the telling of it is his choice. Every choice of words, every voicing in the novel, resonates with the author's anxiety over violating the silence of works already written by adding to them his own voice.

In Rufus's relationship to Jay we can discover the most crucial image of Agee's to his own past. The gap between father and son is not so much bridged as measured by voice. Only in silence do they come close:

> Rufus seldom had at all sharply the feeling that he and his father were estranged, yet they must have been, and he must have felt it, for always during these quiet moments on the rock a part of his sense of complete contentment lay in the feeling that they were reconciled, that there was really no division, no estrangement, or none so strong, anyhow, that it could mean much, by comparison with the unity that was so firm and assured, here.

It is the quietude of this moment which makes reconciliation possible. "There were no words, or even ideas, or formed emotions, of the kind that have been suggested here, no more in the man than in the boy child." At such times "silence was even more pleasurable" than speech, because speech bespeaks a distance between. Voice breaks this communion: with *"Well . . ."* the moment is over and the walk home resumes. Here voice registers a gap dividing generations even as it establishes an intimacy between them. Jay's interjection is both authoritative and gentle. If voice possesses both qualities, it is the most appropriate vehicle through which to realize life in a family. If the eye is democratic, voice is hierarchical. It asks us to acknowledge our place. Agee shares Milton's sense of the distancing power of authoritative voice. Leslie Brisman says of *Paradise Lost* that "voice is everywhere the emblem of the distance the recognition of which is creative, the failure of which is fall. Voice separates speaker from listener, author from image, in a way that distinguishes fertile brooding from the sterility of narcissistic self-confrontation." In order to escape from the sterility of isolated selfhood, each of Agee's characters is challenged to generate a voice in which he can brood upon the events befalling him. Yet because voice enforces acknowledgment of distance, and because Agee also wishes to create the impression of relaxed intimacy with his materials and among his characters, his narrative proceeds whenever possible through silence.

The act of writing the novel itself constitutes Agee's most ambitious generation of voice. When he admits to Father Flye that the book is autobiographical and that it leads up to the moment of his "father's burial," we can surmise that more than his biological parent is being buried in it. The story is not only about surviving one's creator; the act of telling it embodies Agee's will to assume a creator's role. If the book narrates Rufus's growing independence of his father, this act of narration accomplishes Agee's full assumption of imaginative independence from his literary fathers. It is his first major *fiction*. The separation anxiety implicit in such a project fittingly eventuates in a story about such separation. (pp. 101-03)

Agee's filial ambivalence emerges most dramatically in his closet drama **"Menalcas,"** where a king, after an incestuous marriage with his daughter, kills the son of that union. Alfred T. Barson concludes that it is the issue of creation itself which is here at stake: "Agee is describing the relationship between God and His creation and, on another level, the relationship between the artist and his art. In each instance there is an inability of the Creator to properly love His creation, to see it for what it is and to respect its essential otherness." In writing *A Death in the Family,* Agee simultaneously becomes a participant in both of these relationships while generating voice which respects the "otherness" of his characters and his creation. That the novel was nevertheless generated by guilt over asserting this distance as well as by pride in having attained it is supported by Victor Kramer's speculation that Agee intended to introduce it with "Dream Sequence." In this short story the dreamed murder of John the Baptist—the forerunner of the true creator—is confused with Agee's guilt over his dead father. . . . The decision not to use this as an opening for the novel suggests an editorial reluctance to include such a direct violation of the novel's seemingly benign casting of generational conflict. Yet the mere writing of the novel forced such a conflict upon Agee. J. Douglas Perry reminds us that "*A Death in the Family* is an epic about Agee's father and his father's people, his mother and her people. Agee is simultaneously Homer and Telemachus, bard and participant." To become the bard is to stop being the son. Agee's inability absolutely to assume either role is not only a measure of his humanity but the source of tension between creation and reception, voice and silence, which each of his characters recurrently experiences.

The dreamer concludes "Dream Sequence" by admitting that "all his life he had fiercely loathed authority and had as fiercely loved courage and mastery." The very harshness of this self-judgment seems to effect a softening in the speaker's attitudes, and he feels himself relaxed in his father's imagined presence: "And here he was, and all was well at last, and even though he was more rapidly fading, and most likely would never return, that was all right too." It is as if the decision to write his autobiographical novel, and the insight into its originating motives, together allay much of the conflict which generates the project. From the beginning of *A Death in the Family,* the father-son relationship seems anything but troubled. Agee presents the relationship between Rufus and Jay as remarkably quiet. Allen Shepherd remarks the atypicality of this project: "If it seems that *A Death in the Family* is an almost un-American novel in that it is about death, but not about violence, and about love, but not about sex, we may go two steps further and say that the novel is at least atypical in that it is about the achievement of identity, but not about alienation, and in that it is about a family, but not about a facilely allegorized Every-Family." The novel begins in a mood of passionate harmony, but in writing it Agee came to discover that a strong sense of alienation helps not only to create an artist's identity, but a son's. It is precisely at that moment when Rufus feels most alien from his father that he commits the act that initiates the search for his own independent identity. The task of the novelist and his boy-protagonist coalesce as Rufus gives voice to a knowledge of death: he "looked towards his father's face and, seeing the blue-dented chin thrust upward, and the way the flesh was sunken behind the bones of the jaw, first recognized in its specific weight the word, *dead*." To accept the weight of this word is to begin shouldering the consequences of one's mortality, one's original birth out of, and separation from, a mortal source. The assumption of voice here coincides with a distancing from the father achieved through a metonymy—Jay's sunken face—which empties him of further power to influence or enliven the son. It is remarkable that Rufus must learn the facts of death before the facts of life. In the face of

Catherine's impending birth his parents go to considerable trouble to prevent him from making *"see-oh-en-en-ee-see-tee-eye-oh-en-ess, between—between one thing and another."* Yet Rufus will be empowered by his experience of death to begin making his own connections, to grow up and become a father himself. The limited challenges one can impose upon the sexuality of a boy of six may account, however, for the generalized anxiety over generation that pervades the novel. Agee displaces such anxiety throughout into the one activity which for a writer constitutes the essence of identity: generating voice.

"We are talking now . . .": the novel opens with an acknowledgment of voice. Agee might not have chosen to begin in this way; the editors have nevertheless discovered a point of departure to which the action constantly recurs. A novel of a family talking, *A Death in the Family* turns upon moments when a voice chooses to break silence. This opening is appropriate insofar as it presents the beginning of the novel as depending upon the simultaneous decision to begin talking. There is no dramatic voice in "Knoxville: Summer 1915." The prelude is narrated, by the voice of a child that is also the voice of an elegist. Agee establishes no firm distance between these two voices, just as he blurs the distinction between narrator and reader through *"We."* All these identities diffuse here into a shared lyric experience. James Sonoski argues that "Agee's narrative techniques are designed to convey the distances between the voices in the novel and the way in which they are bridged." Yet this initial narrative voice, by retaining total possession of its story, prevents any other from distinguishing itself. Of the speakers in the family the narrator can only say that they have *"voices gentle and meaningless like the voices of sleeping birds."* Conversation among them is described, not enacted. If the prelude ends with the boy-elegist wondering who can *"ever tell me who I am,"* it may be because he has assumed so early and so absolutely the burden of narration. "If a premature assertion of the 'I' masks an anxiety about power of voice, then the listening relationship, in which one's own voice is silenced before voice more authoritative or more distinctly separated from the self, images the successful resolution of that anxiety." In the novel proper, Agee separates the voice of the boy from this more self-conscious adult intelligence to restore the gap between them which, if threatening to an independent "I," is also a primary force in determining its identity. It is inevitable that this restoration of authoritative voice does not fully resolve Rufus's temptation toward premature self-assertion, since the loss he experiences forces independence upon him. Giving voice to his identity remains for him an anxious task, compounded of both pride and shame. This is movingly illustrated during his encounter with the boys who tease him with the question *"What's your name?"* In suffering this challenge from a disbelieving audience to assert himself as the son of his father, Rufus is made to anticipate the situation in which he will have no other choice. What had been an anxiously obeyed prohibition from the living father—"Don't you brag"—becomes, after his death, a command that may be ignored.

If a listening relationship permits a lessening of separation anxiety, if "silence" is "less mistaken than trying to speak," this condition is most fully realized in Chapter 12, when Jay silently returns. Communication is here effected without speaking. Telepathy—what Joel calls "thought transference"—permits the family to feel Jay's *"presence"* without having to hear his voice. Except for Joel, who remains deaf to these unheard melodies, everyone present participates in this moment. That Catherine, normally unable to share easily in family conversation, *hears* Jay return only intensifies the sense of silence through which everyone else registers it. The attempt to articulate this experience serves to dispel it: "It just—means so much more than anything we can *say* about it." For Mary, speech succeeds not in reaching Jay but in "driving him away." Voice is here not so much a mediator as a threat to the purity of the immediate.

The mediating agent to which voice is all too often committed is the telephone. It breaks silence, like a "persistent insect," without allowing us to face each other. Telephoning parodies the distancing voice naturally establishes—"the voice seemed still to come from a great distance"—by creating the illusion that we are present to a voice from which we are actually absent. For Father Jackson, therefore, the telephone is the appropriate instrument of communication. When Hannah phones him all we or the children can hear is her voice, a premonition of his inability to speak to anyone. Yet in anyone's hands the telephone cannot but further the avoidance of love. Even the calls which send Jay after his father and Andrew after Jay reduce personal utterance to news. Aware that such communication imparts all the burden of knowledge with none of the release of confrontation, Andrew refuses to phone:

> he knew it was more than I could stand to *hear* over a phone, even from him, and so he didn't, and I'm infinitely grateful he didn't. He must have known that as time kept—wearing on in this terrible way, we'd draw our own conclusions and have time to—time. And that's best. He wanted to be with me when I heard. And that's right. So do I. Straight from his lips.

Straight from his lips: only the deepest love risks voicing itself without mediation. And only the strongest compassion would take upon itself this burden of saying. When Andrew finally arrives, Mary literally takes the words out of his mouth. "He's dead, Andrew, isn't he?" Here the breaking of silence becomes not a "sacrilege" but a restoration of presence, of the direct assumption of personal responsibility.

Once these words have been said, the telling of the whole story cannot be stopped. Agee even includes a character with limited powers of audition to ensure that "we can all hear." At the heart of this novel listens a deaf person. Catherine's presence sanctions the continued utterance of the unspeakable. The one pun in the novel—"grandmaphone"—ironically confuses Catherine with an instrument which preserves disembodied voice (gramophone) while meaning to link her with one (telephone) which conveys it. Yet Catherine's function as an embodied but defective listener is to reveal the inadequacy of anything but directly heard human voice. "Uncle Andrew says she's crazy even to try" to listen to or through anything else. She exists in relation to the bereaved family as the reader does to the authorial voice. Her malady forces what might otherwise be whispered, or left unsaid, into words. Narration becomes by virtue of her need to hear less a violation than a consideration. So must the story be told to the reader. We are "we." It is for us that Agee makes this personal tragedy audible. The reader's will to listen finds image in Catherine's trumpet: "It required immediate speech. That trumpet's like a pelican's mouth, he thought. Toss in a fish." Andrew's bitterness here partakes of the author's conflict between reluctance to speak any more than he must to keep the attention of his audience and his eagerness to speak so much as to capture it completely. Agee admits in a letter to Father Flye that a reader can completely consume, while being consumed by, a text: "I would suspect a chemical rule of reading as in 'influence,' 'imitation,' and 'plagiarism'; that in reading or in being influenced 'successfully' one does as much work as the authors did originally." The knowledge that in writing this novel of the death of his father Agee was himself fathering his own heirs accounts for much of the care he takes in generating, or in allowing his characters to generate, authoritative voice.

Ambivalence over whether to speak or remain silent resolves into a marriage of opposites in Joel and Catherine. He experiences language as a prison house. "He wished he could think what to say that would make up for it, but he could not think of what to say." She feels no anxiety over assuming voice: "He feels much more than he says, she comforted herself; but she wished that he might ever say what he felt." Catherine finds language a transparent medium. "I've always supposed, it was the business of *words*—to *communicate*—*clearly.*" Yet her theory is undercut by her practice, for the single most striking act of communication in the novel takes place wordlessly, between herself and Joel. It happens in Chapter 9, which intervenes between the sound of Andrew's arrival and his actual entrance, and where a temporary suspension of the plot gives us a picture of the married life that, for Jay and Mary, also might have been. At the same time, Catherine and Joel share similar, and then the same thoughts:

> She felt a moment of solemn and angry gratitude to have spent so many years, in such harmony, with a man so good, but that was beyond utterance. . . . he . . . felt a moment of incredulous and amused pride in her immense and unbreakable courage, and of proud gratitude, regardless of and including all regret, to have had so many years with such a woman; but that was beyond utterance.

It may be less important that these closing identical phrases again define the limits of voice than that they embody the wordless communion which the years of this long marriage have made possible. In such marriages silence is not an evasion but an expression of identity. On the night Jay leaves for the last time, he shares with Mary a similar moment of having "nothing to say." Once two voices achieve identity—grow up—through having been "influenced 'successfully'" by more authoritative ones, the testimony of their mature equality is silence.

If silence is the contrary of voice as well as its eventual fate, the negation of both is noise. A kind of Satanic force, its indulgence is a sin against the limits the novel sets for itself. However much Jay nods his "regret of the racket" his car makes, "the eyes which followed him could not forgive him his noise." Noise originates, in the first interpolated scene, from an unworthy and profane voice: "*An auto engine bore beyond the edge of audibility the furious expletives of its incompetence.*" The satiric personification of such racket suggests that Agee's anxiety over generating voice can diffuse into a more generalized one over creating *any* sound. That representing sound is for him a problem deeply implicated in the process of composition becomes clear in Jay's departure. The only experimental writing Agee ventures in the novel attempts to capture the noise of the car starting:

RHRHRHRHRHRH R
               H
            R
               H
            R
               H
                rh
                rh
                rh
                rh
                rh
                rh
                rh
                rh
             rh
             rh
              rh
C utta wawwwwk:
      Craaawwrk?
        Chiquawkwawh.
              wrrawkuhkuhk uh.
                Craarrawwk.
                  rwrwrk?
                      yrk.
                        rk:

This experience stimulates a response beyond the normal range of Agee's style. Such noise represents so wanton a violation of the silence which the author and his characters only carefully break as to drive Agee toward the limits of his art. It is too sheer a display of dissonance in a novel committed to assimilating all phenomena and relationships, however divergent, into an amassing harmony.

Father Jackson is the one character in the novel who most seems to deserve a similar kind of inhuman notation. Rufus and Catherine experience his voice as noise. If the novel's true test of maturity is whether one can speak to a child, the priest fails it. But then he does not speak, he is spoken:

> Father Jackson spoke almost wholly without emphasis and with only the subtlest coloring, as if the personal emotion, the coloring, were cast against the words from a distance, like echoes. He spoke as if all that he said were in every idea and in every syllable final, finished, perfected beyond disquisition long before he was born; and truth and eternity dwelt like clearest water in the rhythms of his language and in the contours of his voice; his voice accepted and bore this language like the bed of a brook.

Having wholly relinquished his voice to a higher power, Father Jackson cannot be expected to possess one of his own. His lack of a personal voice stands as emblem of his inability to beget anything truly original. He remains a perpetual son. This is, of course, Ralph's predicament, although he must admit the further mistake of having prematurely "fathered children." No more than the priest does he display a generating voice, a condition dramatized by Agee's reassumption of almost total narrative control during the chapter Ralph fills. It is clear from Ralph's few attempts to speak that his voice affects others like the sound of that "persistent insect" the telephone, of which Ralph is the novel's most impetuous and persistent user. Since "every tone his voice took, was controlled by his idea of what would make the best impression on others,'' Ralph experiences even his own voice, into the possession of which he has never entered, as an alien noise.

The redemption of noise is song. Song weaves voice and silence into a harmony in which the virtues of both are temporarily suspended. The novel begins by inducting us into a world in which every noise can modulate into music: *"First an insane noise of violence in the nozzle, then the still irregular sound of adjustment, then the smoothing into steadiness and a pitch as accurately tuned to the size and style of stream as any violin."* . . . Without creating anxiety, this music calls up a memory of generation, of the sounds which register the pulse and origin of our lives, *"the noises of the sea and of the blood her precocious grandchild."* Once the noises that keep time are admitted, the narrator (himself a precocious grandchild) hastens to quiet sound altogether as we hear *"the faint stinging bell; rises again, still fainter; fainting, lifting, lifts, faints forgone: forgotten. Now is the night one blue dew."* Silence prevails; we enter a *"Now"* world in which the family members can lie down together without anxiety. But the delicate balance of sound and silence which is song, and the harmony it celebrates, is shattered by the first phone call in the novel. It necessitates dialogue, the inevitable exchange of "furious and annihilating words." The experience of harmonizing song becomes a condition to which both characters and readers permanently long to return.

Andrew recovers song in Chapter 13. Agee inducts us into this episode in such a way that song emerges not as a fortuitous, but as a permanent (though perhaps unremembered), possession. As Andrew walks home with his parents he finds himself listening to the night: "Andrew could hear only their footsteps; his father and mother, he realized, could hear nothing even of that. How still we see thee lie." Here "O Little Town of Bethlehem" returns as the wonder of unexpected supply, as a voice which unwittingly, yet authentically, sings through us. As the lyrics of the song weave themselves more insistently into Andrew's meditation, Agee ensures that his moment of fully acknowledging their source will be simultaneous with the reader's. "*How still we see thee lie,* he heard his mind say. He said the words over, drily within himself, and heard the melody; a child's voice, his own, sang it in his mind." Here the lyrics are italicized, fully admitted to be of another voice. In Andrew's possession of a voice he is possessed by, the reader finds another image of his being "influenced 'successfully'" by the voice which authors the novel. In reading we are delivered up to being sung—to the authority of a voice which expresses us more authentically than we could alone—while seeming ourselves to sing. Agee realizes the definition of sublimity; the reader feels as if he had produced what he has heard. In its power to effect this sublime cancellation of "otherness" lies the consolation of fiction, of human song.

Jay makes this discovery while singing to Rufus. Song comforts not only by articulating an intimacy between father and son but by recovering a sense of the gap across which the generations have sung it and which it has helped to define and bridge. *"To the child it looked as if his father were gazing off into a great distance and, looking up into these eyes which looked so far away, he too looked far away."* As he keeps singing, the father hears the sound of his own mother's voice: "Don't you fret, Jay, don't you fret." The distance he gazes off into becomes filled with all those who have influenced him. . . . Singing voice has here helped to recall, notate, and preserve the sense of a line, of being not only a generator but generated.

It restores Jay to a sense of his own father, of his father's fathers, of his dependency upon them as well as his inevitable replacement of them. This is a vision of generations as a communal, not a competitive, labor. Each of us is but a refrain sounded again through our children. All of the anxiety in the novel over a creation independently creating is here fully acknowledged and momentarily dispelled as Jay simultaneously speaks as a father and listens as a son.

In *A Death in the Family* Agee risks generating voice. In doing so he supersedes the earlier limited claim he had made for his own language in *Let Us Now Praise Famous Men* that "words cannot embody; they can only describe." While attempting to father a novel of the death of his father Agee discovers the inadequacy of this theory in the face of his imagination and his experience. If this experience is to be represented, it must be through more than a mere way of seeing. A descriptive or cinematic mode—either documentary or screenplay—would have been an evasion of the challenge to bring his family to life. In order to recover the voices of his past Agee must discover his own. While still conflicted over assuming voice, Agee reveals it as the possession the use of which bespeaks the full acceptance of embodiment. As the most effective means of placing ourselves in the presence of another, even while it confirms the gap—generational or imaginative—across which one is speaking, voice must be generated by any author who wishes to "go back into those years" which send up the life of a family. This is the project of writing itself, the assumption of the burden of the past so that it can be reborn—given voice— in the present. (pp. 103-12)

> *David Wyatt, "Generating Voice in 'A Death in the Family',"* in his Prodigal Sons: A Study in Authorship and Authority, *The Johns Hopkins University Press, 1980, pp. 101-12.*

RICHARD H. KING (essay date 1980)

[*King is an American critic and educator. In the following excerpt, he discusses the aesthetic convictions that inform* Let Us Now Praise Famous Men.]

For Agee epistemology is aesthetics: to perceive is to perceive beauty. In *Famous Men* the aesthetic is founded upon two assumptions: first, the superiority of consciousness to imagination, and, second, the inadequacy of language for the task Agee sets himself. According to Agee, the camera and the "unassisted weaponless consciousness" are the means by which "immediacy" and "human actuality" can best be rendered. Since the connection between words and things is arbitrary, however, Agee questions the ability of words to convey what he wants about reality: "Words cannot embody; they can only describe." They are pointers, not the things themselves. Were it possible, Agee claims that he would have offered: "photographs; the rest would be fragments of cloth, bits of cotton, lumps of earth, records of speech, pieces of wood and iron, phials of odors, plates of food and of excrement . . . A piece of the body torn out by the roots might be more to the point." What Agee was attempting was an Emersonian vision, but one that denied itself the central romantic and modernist power: the imagination.

These notions need a bit of unpacking. At one level Agee located himself in a traditional American attitude of suspicion toward art and artifice. While artifice is a sign of corruption and decadence, the showing of function and display of craftsmanship are desirable. But though this suspicion of "artiness" was present in *Famous Men*, Agee meant more by his objection. A powerful motif running throughout *Famous Men* was the dangerous, explosive potential of art to change lives. The conventionally educated person emasculated art and rendered it thoroughly safe; but that was not a fault inherent in works of art as such.

Nor did Agee object to works of the imagination because they diverted political consciousness into safe channels. The arrangement of the elements in *Famous Men* suggests a Brechtian attempt at "alienation"—one is never allowed to settle into a conventional way of reading or ready set of responses. Excerpts from *King Lear* and Marx are followed by a page from an elementary school primer. But this alienating effect is also intended to distance the reader from conventional liberal or left-wing political responses. In an age that saw the flat-footed politicization of art, Agee stood Brecht on his head.

Agee objected most strenuously to the deification of the imagination because he felt that art obscured more than it clarified reality. Ultimately, art could not be taken seriously (rightly so by implication) because it involved a "willing suspension of disbelief." Over and against art stood reality or "nature," by which Agee seemed to refer to all that which is not consciously crafted for aesthetic effect; a meaning reminiscent of Emerson's in *Nature* where "nature" refers to all that is "NOT ME": "Everything in Nature, every most casual thing, has an inevitability and perfection which art as such can only approach . . . a contour map is at least as considerably an image of absolute 'beauty' as the counterpoints of Bach which it happens to resemble." And later: "It is simply impossible for anyone, no matter how high he may place it, to do art the simple but total honor of accepting and believing it in the terms which he accepts and honors breathing, lovemaking, the look of a newspaper, the street he walks through." In the final analysis, if art could not be taken literally, it could not be taken seriously. But if Agee's aesthetic registered the influence of a decade that had grown suspicious of the conversative implications of literary modernism and of a culture that was suspicious of artifice, he was too strongly influenced by modernism to have come to his view without considerable doubt and self-division. Using the techniques of literary modernism, he sought to forge a type of sophisticated realism that would in turn avoid the dangers involved in a naïve attempt to mirror reality. No matter how unfortunate we might judge his overly simple dichotomy between imagination and consciousness, art and reality, Agee had earned the right to this view.

The implications of Agee's privileging of reality over art were crucial in what followed in *Famous Men*. Agee's aesthetic of the "unassisted consciousness" is an example of what Jacques Derrida has called the "metaphysic of presence" which stands behind the Western philosophical and artistic tradition. That metaphysic holds that on principle unmediated access can be gained to God, Truth, the Good, the Absolute, Reality, or whatever might serve as the "god-term" in a religious or philosophical system. According to Derrida, such immediacy is impossible, and we find "only" traces of a former presence: absence is "already always there." By impliction we can never return to a time of unalienated origins, nor can we reach the end of history. That we only succeed in discovering the "trace" results not from insufficient rigor or faulty rationality, bad faith or moral shortcomings. It is in the nature of things. Furthermore, Derrida's critique of the metaphysic of presence speaks most clearly against the phenomenological effort to gain access to essences by bracketing normal assumptions and against the

anthropological nostalgia, running from Rousseau down through Lévi-Strauss, that seeks to discover man before his "fall" into written language. Agee's *Famous Men* bears a certain family resemblance to both such efforts. Also, Agee's suspicion of writing and his strong desire to present objects in their immediacy illustrate the valorization of visual over linguistic communication, and the demotion of "writing" to a necessary evil in communicating the truth about the lives he observed. The objects he wished to include in lieu of the text were not for him the signs of absence, but were marks of presence, of immediacy.

But Agee's aesthetic involved him in a crucial contradiction. He assumes, for instance, that actuality is "a universe luminous, spacious, incalculably rich and wonderful in each detail, as relaxed and natural to the human swimmer, as full of glory, as his breathing." Whether one traces this view to the Joycean epiphany in which beauty is "in" things rather than imposed upon them or invokes the Emersonian "transparent eyeball" which attempts to bring the "axis of vision" and the "axis of things" into congruence or claims with Blake that "everything that is is holy," Agee's notion of consciousness includes characteristics which are not deducible from the operations of the unassisted consciousness or from actuality itself. Moreover, with this theory of perception and of beauty, Agee has difficulties dealing with the existence of pain, suffering, or evil. If suffering is a "natural" phenomenon or evil is a part of perceived reality, then consciousness can hardly imply an aesthetic capacity for discrimination or a capacity for moral judgment. If everything that is is holy, then pain and suffering are illusory or, what is worse, potentially beautiful. Finally, Agee has it every way: truth is beauty is actuality is holiness, a thoroughly Emersonian notion.

There is yet another implication of Agee's aesthetic. If we follow Derrida's line of thought, we can see that Agee's efforts to empty his consciousness of imaginative artifice, to see things directly without mediation, inevitably must fail. Agee's frustration comes through in his constant moralizing throughout *Famous Men,* the double-binds he imposes on the reader (if you criticize the book, you are reading it the wrong way; if you like it, you are a philistine who fails to register its full power), and the violence he does against himself and his effort. He tries to establish his moral right, his epistemological purity, and his aesthetic immediacy by paradoxically confessing his failing in each of those realms. If I admit my faults, he seems to reason, I can achieve the proper vantage point, which is not a vantage point at all but the status of a "bodyless eye," a term reminiscent both of Emerson and of the aesthetics of the camera. But the problem is that he has transformed an ontological condition—that of our belatedness, our existence in a world of "traces" of absent presences—into a condition following from his (and our) failure. And we can see this in the language he uses to describe himself: he is a "spy," a sort of voyeur. But if he is going to capture the lives of the three families, he must necessarily intrude into and "violate" their lives. He is caught in a double-bind: not to violate is to forgo access to actuality; to enter their lives is to commit a moral fault.

At times in *Famous Men* Agee drops his impossible claims and allows the resulting complexity of interaction between himself and the families to emerge. One of the book's most powerful sections comes when Agee admits his sexual attraction to Emma Woods, speculates that she understands and reciprocates it, and writes of the resulting complications, hesitations—and communication. It is so powerful precisely because Agee represents himself as an embodied I not a "bodyless eye." And Emma emerges as fully human, a desiring subject whose desire is reciprocated, rather than as something "holy." It is not "immediacy" which is represented, for there is no such thing. Rather we grasp the mediations of time and place, education and status, culture and power, and sexual desire within which Agee, Evans, and the families are caught. But Agee rarely allows himself this freedom.

Here we must go back and take up the second central aspect of Agee's aesthetic—his theory of language and representation—and its relationship to Walker Evans's photographs. Evans, like Agee, was suspicious of artiness and commercialism and began his career by rejecting the former quality in Alfred Stieglitz and the latter tendency in the work of Edward Steichen. Though, according to John Szarkowski, Evans's work was informed by the notion that "nothing was to be imposed on experience; the truth was to be discovered, not constructed," his photographs are highly stylized and clearly posed. Unlike the photographs of Margaret Bourke-White, which are so obviously aimed at eliciting a stereotyped response from the viewer and are so artificially "natural" in their attempt to capture the subject in an "unguarded" moment, Evans's are stylized to the point of artlessness, or at least give the illusion of being so. They are "denotative" but only weakly "connotative"—or again not connotative in the expected ways. They don't do the thinking and feeling for the viewer, and are thus rarely "kitschy." As Susan Sontag has pointed out, Evans (like Agee) falls within the Whitman tradition which finds beauty or significance in the plain and commonplace, even in what is generally taken to be ugly or distasteful. The larger point here is that this is a cultural convention that makes use of artifice, device, and values of its own.

In a sense Evans's photographs work against the grain of Agee's prose. In their spare, austere, even classical quality, they come much closer to Agee's aesthetic than do the writer's romantic sensibility and literary style, which is dense, convoluted, and often extremely self-conscious and "written." Indeed, the last thing which could ever be said of Agee is the apt characterization Sontag gives of Evans's photography—"noble reticence."

There is yet another quality of photography that connects it with Agee's aesthetic and with his personal quest: it is an "elegiac art." It represents a past time and place that have been frozen and can be re-evoked in the present. At least with photography, the age of mechanical reproduction has served, contrary to Walter Benjamin's speculation, not to destroy the "aura," the sense of distance and even mystery, but to augment it. Photographs become icons that both imply and negate time. If we keep this in mind we can see why Agee was so fascinated by the camera: it could stop time. It returned an absence to presence, and this was what he was seeking in Alabama.

Unlike most books containing a text and images, the photographs, at least according to Agee, are "not illustrative" of the text, nor does the text serve as a relay point linking the pictures. Their arrangement does not tell a story. Very few of the photographs are referred to directly in the text; and as Agee would have it: "They, and the text, are coequal, mutually independent and fully collaborative." This is a case where Agee's intentions seem to be fully consonant with the effect of the text. And these intentions also illustrate another aspect of the book's strategy: the effort to involve the reader in the production of meaning rather than providing it for him.

But the photos also presented Agee with an insuperable challenge: how to do the same thing with words that Evans had done with the photographs? The fundamental problem facing Agee was that Evans's photographs are iconic or analogic messages, while human language is a digital mode of communication. Of course the photographs are not the objects they represent, but they stand in a "motivated" relation to those objects. One does not need a code to translate or transform the photograph into what it represents. By contrast, words, as Agee well recognized, have no connection by resemblance (of any sort) with what they stand for: the relationship is arbitrary or conventional. More specifically Agee notes that words can falsify through "inaccuracy of meaning" and "inaccuracy of emotion"; and they cannot "communicate simultaneity." Here Agee was onto what contemporary students of communication, such as Gregory Bateson, have emphasized: it is not just that the two modes communicate the same thing in different ways (one picture is worth a thousand words) but that they communicate different things in general (a thousand words still wouldn't necessarily communicate what a picture does). "Words," Agee writes, "like all else are limited by certain laws."

It is for this reason that Agee wanted to reject "naturalism." In his exhaustive description of a particular scene or experience the naturalistic writer conveys everything but what that scene is like. The description "gathers time and weightiness which the street [the scene described] does not of itself have; it sags with this length and weight." What is achieved is "the opposite pole from your intentions." Or to shift the metaphor, a naturalistic description resembles the situation of a person who in order to tell a joke must spend his time with an explanation "fifteen times the length of the joke." Agee leaves the matter unresolved, but adds that it is also a law of language that words attempt to be more than words. "Human beings may be more and more aware of being awake," that is, they use language according to its law of separation of word and thing, "but they are still incapable of not dreaming." Through our use of words we seek to bridge the gap between words and the objects they describe. Thus, Agee in *Famous Men* attempted to transcend the "languageness" of language via language, even though he knew the attempt would be futile. Where Faulkner attempted to overcome *time* by "saying it all in one sentence," Agee tried to overcome that mythical *space* between signifier and signified, between words and the objects they describe. Finally, the human capacity for language is a sign of that original separation from the source. The separation is a spatial one (in birth), but more importantly a temporal one involved in our being *in* time and being constituted by time. Agee's impossible aesthetic project, which pushed him to the limits of consciousness and language, mirrored his attempt to recover his own lost past, to overcome the spatial and temporal gap separating him from that still-point in his own life. (pp. 213-20)

Richard H. King, "From Theme to Setting: Thomas Wolfe, James Agee, Robert Penn Warren," in his A Southern Renaissance: The Cultural Awakening of the American South, 1930-1955, *Oxford University Press, 1980, pp. 194-241.**

EDMUND WHITE (essay date 1984)

[*White is an American novelist and nonfiction writer whose best-known works, among them* The Joy of Gay Sex *(1977),* States of Desire *(1980), and* A Boy's Own Story *(1983), treat homosexual life in America. In the following excerpt from a review of* Laurence Bergreen's *James Agee: A Life (1984), he discusses Agee's approach and technique, noting some of the outstanding passages from Agee's works.*]

This country has not produced very many Classical authors, those who seek out the normal, the eternal, the representative, and who suppress everything bizarre or accidental. To be sure, Large General Meanings have haunted American fiction from Hawthorne and Melville to Faulkner and Pynchon, but such intimations have usually been felt by Americans in the odd, the troubling, the unique. Few ordinary mortals are stigmatized with a scarlet letter, fewer still seek to avenge themselves on a white whale; the very intensity of scarlet and white crowd out the beiges, grays, and duns of everyday life.

But if most American writers have been Romantics, James Agee chose in his masterpiece, *A Death in the Family,* to represent his subject in its most generic, Classical aspect. Although the novel is closely based on an event out of his own childhood—his father's death in a car crash when Agee was only 6 years old—the book is not written exclusively from the point of view of the confused and bereaved little boy. There is none of the subjectivity, special pleading, or remembered anguish that one usually finds in fictionalized autobiography; nor is it primarily concerned with the child's awakening to adult realities. Instead, the tale reports the responses of each member of the family—the little boy and his sister, the widow Mary, her parents, her brother Andrew, and her aunt. No one is portrayed as a grotesque, nor does the tone ever turn Gothic. Everything, from the title to the level of diction to the selection of the smallest characteristic, radiates a quiet, noble glow. There are few interesting American novels that possess such composure; for a similar ambition and achievement one must turn to John Huston, the film director Agee so feverishly admired and with whom he collaborated in the making of *The African Queen.* (pp.25-6)

[When considering Agee's life, one may be] struck by the never expressed but ever immanent rage that Agee seemed to be feeling, especially in his epic bouts of self-destruction. The rage often pokes out in a weird word choice in the letters. Agee said feminists (whom he despised) were "hurt and dulled by the fractures and *foulnesses* of the love they experience" (emphasis mine). Of himself he said to his confessor and lifelong friend Father Flye, "I'm sometimes really forced to believe I have a *dirty* and unconquerable vein of melancholia in me" (emphasis mine). Again to Father Flye he complained of his suicidal impulses, saying, "I haven't enough good in me to realize the *filthiness* of this discontent" (emphasis mine).

This savage self-condemnation seems to me to be linked to a sort of intense, hushed voyeurism, an awed fascination with what adult men and women do behind closed doors. The pages in *A Death in the Family* that shine with radioactive beauty are those at the beginning that describe the intimacy between the wife and her husband, so soon to die. The masculinity of this adored man permeates the entire book, like strong scent burned into a sleeve. Again and again there is an almost liturgical return to a description of his dead body: "'I saw him—stripped—at the undertaker's,' Andrew said. 'Mary, there wasn't a mark on his body. Just that little cut on the chin. One little bruise on his lower lip. Not another mark on his body. He had the most magnificent physique I've ever seen in a human being.'" (p. 26)

The benign aspect of Agee's voyeurism was his compassion and curiosity. When doing the research for *Let Us Now Praise Famous Men,* Agee passed himself off as the son of poor farmers and lived in a vermin-infested shack with a sharecropper family for three weeks. In one sense this "research" was a shocking invasion of naïve people's privacy, even dig-

nity; in a more lasting sense, however, the book that emerged out of those three weeks has become one of the most memorable documents about American poverty ever written. . . .

Agee was only 45 when he died in 1955 of a coronary occlusion. . . . Despite the brevity of his life and his repeated blocks, he had done a great deal of work—endless and beautifully polished letters; a major body of film criticism published in *Time* and *The Nation;* numerous screenplays; two novels; a volume of short stories; a book of poems; and miscellaneous articles for *Fortune* and *Time.* (p. 27)

Agee at his best—in *A Death in the Family* or *The Letters of James Agee to Father Flye*—combined the fluency he cultivated as a journalist (and as a conversationalist) with a quirky integrity closer to the ideal he had learned at Harvard from I. A. Richards—the ideal of absolute fidelity to the rendered experience. It was this Agee who could write in *A Death in the Family:* "that darkness in which eternity lies bent and pale, a dead snake in a jar, and infinity is the sparkling of a wren blown out to sea." (p. 28)

> Edmund White, "Let Us Now Praise," in The New Republic, Vol. 191, No. 10, September 3, 1984, pp. 25-8.

ADDITIONAL BIBLIOGRAPHY

Bergreen, Laurence. *James Agee: A Life.* New York: E. P. Dutton, 1984, 467 p.
    Biography noted for its thorough research and objectivity.

Coles, Robert. "Childhood: James Agee's *A Death in the Family.*" In his *Irony in the Mind's Life: Essays on Novels by James Agee, Elizabeth Bowen, and George Eliot,* pp. 56-106. Charlottesville: University of Virginia Press, 1974.
    Examines the themes and techniques of *A Death in the Family,* focusing on the character Rufus and concluding with a discussion of current psychoanalytic approaches to childrearing.

Da Ponte, Durant. "James Agee: The Quest for Identity." In *Tennessee Studies in Literature,* Vol. VIII, edited by Richard Beale Davis, pp. 25-37. Knoxville: University of Tennessee Press, 1963.
    Discusses Agee's search for identity and the reflection in his fiction of his feelings of frustration and inadequacy.

Doty, Mark A. *Tell Me Who I Am: James Agee's Search for Selfhood.* Baton Rouge: Louisiana State University Press, 1981, 144 p.
    Examines Agee's personal life and the autobiographical aspects of his works, maintaining that Agee used fiction primarily as "a means . . . to explore his interior self."

Fultz, James R. "The Poetry and Danger of Childhood: James Agee's Film Adaptation of *The Night of the Hunter.*" *Western Humanities Review* XXXIV, No. 1 (Winter 1980): 90-8.*
    Considers Agee's scenario a faithful adaptation of Davis Grubb's novel, and speculates as to why the film has achieved the status of a minor classic while the novel has fallen into obscurity.

————. "Heartbreak at the Blue Hotel: James Agee's Scenario of Stephen Crane's Story." *The Midwest Quarterly* XXI, No. 4 (Summer 1980): 423-34.*
    Discusses Agee's film adaptation of Crane's "The Blue Hotel," commenting that "Agee's personal stamp is in nearly every line of the script, and there is in it a quality approaching nihilism, a repressed rage, a certain perversity which may be in Crane's story in a slightly different, less social and more metaphysical, form."

————. "High Jinks at Yellow Sky." *Literature/Film Quarterly* 11, No. 1 (1983): 46-55.*

Analysis of Agee's film adaptation of Stephen Crane's short story "The Bride Comes to Yellow Sky."

Hicks, Granville. "Suffering Face of the Rural South." *Saturday Review* XLII, No. 37 (10 September 1960): 19-20.
Review that considers *Let Us Now Praise Famous Men* "one of the extraordinary, one of the great books of our time."

————. Review of *The Collected Short Prose of James Agee,* by James Agee. *Saturday Review* LII, No. 9 (1 March 1969): 26.
Favorable review.

Huston, John. *An Open Book,* pp. 188ff. New York: Alfred A. Knopf, 1980.*
Recounts the collaboration between Agee and Huston on the screenplay for *The African Queen.*

Madden, David, ed. *Remembering James Agee.* Baton Rouge: Louisiana State University Press, 1974, 172 p.
Reminiscences by Father Flye, Robert Fitzgerald, Walker Evans, Dwight Macdonald, Whittaker Chambers, Mia Agee, and others.

Morris, Wright. "James Agee." In his *Earthly Delights, Unearthly Adornments: American Writers as Image-Makers,* pp. 155-61. New York: Harper & Row, 1978.
Examines Agee's reverent treatment of everyday life in *Let Us Now Praise Famous Men.*

Rupp, Richard H. "James Agee: The Elegies of Innocence." In his *Celebration in Postwar American Fiction 1945-1967,* pp. 99-111. Coral Gables, Fla.: University of Miami Press, 1970.
Contends that Agee attempted in his fiction to recapture his childhood, rejecting his adult life in favor of the lost innocence of his past.

Stanford, Donald E. "The Poetry of James Agee: The Art of Recovery." *The Southern Review* n.s. X, No. 2 (April 1974): xvi-xix.
Praises Agee's ability to transform the "solid plain [poetic] style of the sixteenth and early seventeenth centuries . . . into an effective medium for the twentieth century," and regrets his abandoning poetry for prose.

Taylor, Gordon O. "The Cruel Radiance of What Is: James Agee." In his *Chapters of Experience: Studies in 20th Century American Biography,* pp. 66-78. New York: St. Martin's Press, 1983.
Contends that *Let Us Now Praise Famous Men* is "an elaboration of the idea that to recognize the reality of his subjects' lives is necessarily to inquire into the reality of his own" and an attempt by Agee to "make their lives bespeak and symbolize his . . . and so to actualize himself along with them."

Trilling, Lionel. "Greatness with One Fault in It." *The Kenyon Review* IV, No. 1 (Winter 1942): 99-102.
One of the earliest favorable reviews of *Let Us Now Praise Famous Men.* Trilling considers the book "the most important moral effort of our American generation."

Young, Thomas Daniel. "The Contemporary Scene." In his *Tennessee Writers,* pp. 77-111. Knoxville: University of Tennessee Press, 1981.*
Critical summary of Agee's major works.

Wydeven, Joseph J. "Photography and Privacy: The Protests of Wright Morris and James Agee." *The Midwest Quarterly* XXIII, No. 1 (Autumn 1981): 103-15.*
Examines the conviction shared by Morris and Agee, and explored in *Let Us Now Praise Famous Men,* that the use of photography for artistic purposes is a potentially unethical invasion of the subjects' privacy.

Jean de Bosschère

1878-1953

(Also spelled Boschère) Belgian poet, novelist, short story writer, critic, diarist, editor, and illustrator.

Bosschère was the author of an elusive body of work that contains elements of symbolism, mysticism, imagism, and realism, yet remains independent of all literary trends and movements. In both poetry and prose, Bosschère's works exhibit an enigmatic series of paradoxes in which conflicting qualities—such as mysticism and nihilism, beauty and ugliness, simplicity and sophistication—intermingle, often mediated by subtle irony. Bosschère was also a distinguished illustrator of classic works of literature and provided each of his own works with illustrations that he considered equal in importance to their accompanying texts.

Commenting on his life, Bosschère wrote: "Not being born within the bosom of any religion, there was no rite and no baptism to protect me during the lonely, stormy years that constituted my youth, of which I have recounted a great part in *Marthe and the Madman*." The turbulence of his youth is perhaps more symbolically than literally rendered in the novel, which depicts a brother and sister who live as outcasts in a provincial town in Catholic Flanders and are persecuted as a result of their Judaism and Marthe's physical deformity. Marthe is ultimately driven to suicide, Pierre to madness and murder. Bosschère became interested in artistic creation at an early age, recalling that he had drawn "the episodes of a story . . . in a number of successive squares" before he was old enough to write. His first published works, primarily art history and criticism, earned him a modest reputation in his own country by the age of twenty. However, it was not until his emigration to England following the outbreak of World War I that he became known as a poet and illustrator. His poetry, which was published in both French and translated versions in English and American journals, was praised by England's leading Modernists, and Bosschère became a member of the literary circles surrounding T. S. Eliot and Ezra Pound. His poetry collection *La porte fermée (The Closed Door)*, published in 1917, has been cited as a probable influence on Eliot's poetry, with which it is often compared. In spite of his influence and popularity among the literary elite, however, Bosschère remained aloof from literary movements. He declared himself equally indifferent to both the critical and commercial success of his books, and in 1932 he wrote: "What I did never amounted to anything more than gratuitous solitary experiments. I mean that never, neither now nor in the past, did I think of publishing or showing them; only accident revealed my essays in the form of published books. . . . Thus I remained in the obscurity that I have loved since my childhood." Bosschère eventually left London for Paris, where he lived during the 1930s, and later withdrew to complete seclusion in a small town in central France. He died in 1953.

Critical reaction to both Bosschère's poetry and prose has been characterized by difficulty in reconciling the many paradoxical aspects of his writing. For example, while commentators often note the mystical qualities of Bosschère's works—his sense of the reality behind appearances and his sensitivity to the essential qualities of characters, objects, and situations—they dis-

Self portrait of Bosschere. From The World of Jean de Bosschère, by Samuel Putnam. The Fortune Press, 1932. Reproduced by permission of the publisher

agree as to the nature of this mysticism. Some critics regard Bosschère's vision of the world, particularly that conveyed in his early works, as essentially sympathetic to that of orthodox religion; others, however, observe cynical, sinister qualities in his works that suggest an attitude hostile to conventional conceptions of metaphysical reality. Similarly, Bosschère's use of common objects as symbols in works such as *Dolorine et les ombres* has led to his being identified with the Symbolist movement of the late nineteenth century. According to critics May Sinclair and René Taupin, however, Bosschère's works differ from those of the Symbolists in that his use of symbols does not represent a divine reality beyond that of the material world, but rather the sacredness of earthly life itself. This affirmation of corporeal existence is echoed in the theme of *Dolorine et les ombres,* which portrays a dreamer who brings about tragedy through his inability to recognize life's divinity. Critics also find disparity between the superficial beauty and simplicity of Bosschère's works and their underlying elements of tragedy, or even cruelty. Many of the poems in *The Closed Door,* for example, deal with simple themes in the form of parables, such as "Ulysse bâtit son lit" ("Ulysses Builds His Bed"), which concerns the reaction of a mob toward a superior individual. The poems are playful and seemingly naive on the surface; however, most commentators writing in English have agreed with the assessment of Conrad Aiken that "in reality they are masterpieces of ironic understatement and reveal upon closer scrutiny a series of profound spiritual or mental tragedies.'' In the later collections *L'obscur à Paris* and *Paris clair-obscur,* Bosschère's bleak vision of the world is no longer concealed beneath a pleasant surface. These works depict Paris as a nightmarish city inhabited by freaks, drunks, and madmen, and convey a sense of humanity's purposelessness and alienation. Mary and Benjamin Rountree have observed in these collections Bosschère's indignance at metaphysical injustice and his sense of ''the grotesquerie of human existence.'' Similarly, his friend Samuel Putnam wrote of the poet's philosophical outlook: ''As to M. de Bosschère's most mature poetic output, I am able to discover only a vast disillusionment.'' In addition to his poetry and poetic prose such as *Dolorine et les ombres,* Bosschère wrote works of fiction, including the novels *Marthe et l'enragé (Marthe and the Madman), The House of Forsaken Hope,* and *Satan l'obscur,* as well as a children's book entitled *The City Curious.* His nonfiction works include art history and criticism, a biographical and critical study of the Belgian poet Max Elskamp, and nature studies such as *La fleur et son parfum.*

Bosschère's illustrations, like his poetry and prose, frequently introduce elements of the fantastic and the grotesque into depictions of ostensibly commonplace or benign subjects, and they are often compared with the works of Aubrey Beardsley, whose illustrations emphasizing the erotic and the grotesque scandalized the English public of the 1890s. Most commentators agree, however, that Bosschère's angular figures seem more strongly influenced by the Flemish primitive painters than by Beardsley. Bosschère himself has stated that his illustrations are not intended to repeat or ''illustrate'' a character or situation already described in the text, but to express an emotion the book has prompted in the artist, ''even though it may be somewhat remote from the text, and born only of a reflex.'' Critical appraisal of Bosschère's drawings has been mixed: while some critics proclaim his works delightful in their originality, others are repelled by Bosschère's juxtaposition of beauty and morbidity. One critic has characterized Bosschère's illustrations as ''odious little drawings'' whose ''unpleasant prettiness . . . makes one think of poisoned comfits.''

Like his writings, Bosschère's illustrations have been most admired by those readers who have been intrigued by the enigmas and ambiguities of his work. Among these readers are some of the more prominent figures in modern literature, including Pound, Paul Valéry, and Antonin Artaud, who wrote of Bosschère: ''He established the trembling unity central to my life and my intellect.'' Thus, while Bosschère's once modest renown had faded into near anonymity by the time of his death, his works may yet be considered less a passing episode in the history of modern literature than a permanent, albeit obscure, region within it.

PRINCIPAL WORKS

Pierre Breughel l'enfer   (criticism)   1905
Béâle-Gryne   (prose)   1909
Dolorine et les ombres   (prose)   1911
Métiers divins   (poetry)   1913; also published as *Le bourg*
    (enlarged edition), 1922
    [*Twelve Occupations* (partial translation), 1916]
Max Elskamp   (biography and criticism)   1914
*The Closed Door   (poetry)   1917
Beasts and Men [compiler]   (folklore)   1918
Folk Tales of Flanders [compiler]   (folklore)   1918

The City Curious   (fairy tale)   1920
Weird Islands   (short stories)   1921
*Job le pauvre   (poetry)   1922
Marthe et l'enragé   (novel)   1927
    [*Marthe and the Madman,* 1928]
Les paons et autres merveilles   (nonfiction)   1933
    [*Peacocks, and Other Mysteries,* 1941]
Satan l'obscur   (novel)   1933
L'obscur à Paris   (prose poems)   1937
Le fleur et son parfum   (nonfiction)   1942
The House of Forsaken Hope   (novel)   1942
Paris clair-obscur   (prose poems)   1946
Jérôme Bosch et la fantastique   (criticism)   1962
Correspondance: Max Elskamp & Jean de Bosschère
    (letters)   1963
Fragments du journal d'un rebelle solitaire, 1946-1948
    (diaries)   1978

SELECTED WORKS ILLUSTRATED BY BOSSCHÈRE

Christmas Tales of Flanders   [compiled by André Ridder]
    1917
Gulliver's Travels   [by Jonathan Swift]   1920
The History of Don Quixote   [by Miguel de Cervantes]
    1922
The Fairies up to Date   [by Edward Anthony and Joseph
    Anthony]   1923
The Golden Asse   [by Lucius Apuleius]   1923
Uncanny Stories   [by May Sinclair]   1923
The First Temptation of Saint-Anthony   [by Gustave
    Flaubert]   1924
The Poems of Oscar Wilde   [by Oscar Wilde]   1927
Little Poems in Prose   [by Charles Baudelaire]   1928
The Decameron   [by Giovanni Boccaccio]   1930

**These works include the original French texts with accompanying
English translations.*

MAY SINCLAIR   (essay date 1917)

[*An English novelist, Sinclair was one of the first authors to incorporate the theories of modern psychology into fiction. In novels such as* The Divine Fire *(1904),* The Three Sisters *(1914), and* Mary Oliver *(1919), she utilized the psychoanalytic concepts of Sigmund Freud to explore the subtle consequences of sexual sublimation, while she rebelled against Victorian sexual and social values in her treatment of alcoholism, adultery, and other subjects previously considered unacceptable for women writers. Sinclair's works were highly praised by Bosschère, who wrote, ''Nowhere have I found a more convincing truth than in* Mary Oliver.*'' In the following excerpt from her introduction to* The Closed Door, *Sinclair discusses Bosschère's poetry and drawings. For a disagreement with Sinclair's assessment of Bosschère's poetry, see the first* Times Literary Supplement *excerpt dated 1917.*]

[M. de Bosschère] has been claimed as a mystic by the mystics, as a Catholic by the Catholics, and Francis Jammes very nearly mistook him for the chief mourner at the Pompes Funèbres of departed Symbolism. (pp. 1-2)

That was in March 1913. It would be interesting to know what M. Jammes thinks of his first impression and of his comparison now.

It was *Béâle-Gryne* and *Dolorine et les Ombres* that landed Jean de Bosschère among the Symbolists. I gather from its critics that *Béâle-Gryne* has something of that delicate, fastidious, subtle and persistent evasion of the actual which can only be called decadent when the bald or obvious statement of bald or obvious facts passes as the supreme achievement of maturity. To *Dolorine* I must return later on. It has given pause to more than one critic of M. de Bosschère. (p. 2)

It is the poet and draughtsman of the *Métiers Divins, Le Bourg,* and *The Closed Door,* with whom we have to do.

I do not know what it would be proper to call the *Métiers Divins* and *Le Bourg,* nor under what form they appear to their author. No descriptive title can be found for them among the convenient classifications of literature. They are not poems; but their prose is not the prose of prose. They are not *vers libres,* they are not parables, they are not proverbs. They are not what the "Imagists" have taught us to call "des Images." But they partake of the nature of the prose poem, the *vers libre,* the parable, the proverb and the "image." (pp. 2-3)

If you were to ask Jean de Bosschère what he thinks he is doing when he does this kind of thing, he might answer, like Théophile Gautier:

> "Moi, je fais émaux et camées" ["I am making enamels and cameos"].

But his *émaux et camées* are polished till they reflect the universe. He is a master of symbolisms and of sublimations. He has the mystic vision. He sees common things, the humblest inhabitants of space and time, *sub specie aeternitatis.* He is like his own looking-glass maker. He holds up his glass at an unexpected angle and shows you a surprising image of the world, a disconcerting image of your own face. And you see him peeping behind his looking-glass like a wise but slightly malevolent sorcerer and enjoying your bewilderment and your embarrassment.

The primrose by the river's brim is not a simple primrose by any means to him; it is always something more. (pp. 3-4)

You may call this sophistication, if you like, but it is really the ultimate naïveté of philosophy, the immediate innocence of spiritual science. It is that human vision which is the nearest we can get to divine wisdom.

For these poems of the *Métiers* and the *Bourg* are deceptive. You think that they are toys, quaint, grotesque, funnily-fashioned, fantastic in shape, well-mounted, solidly-made; and, though you admire the art and the artificer, you do not take him quite seriously at first. You think that he was playing when he made them, these diminutive images of every craft and every occupation of the Bourg, and that he made them for you to play with or to look at, to handle and throw aside.

Perhaps they *are* toys. For toys have an august history; they were once Lares and Penates; they were the sorcerer's dolls, and they were the watchers of the dead.

And you find that you are haunted by these images: they have the toy's stare of fixed, eternal wisdom; they watch and wait for you; they have the treacherous innocence, the sinister magic of the ancient toys. And the wisdom of their maker has something of the fixed, unearthly vigilance of the things that he has made. They are not really toys any more than the sorcerer's doll, or the image in the grave, or the quiet Lar sitting by the hearth is a toy. They are terrible engines of destruction for our sentimentalities, our irrelevances and insincerities, our imper-

tinent pretensions, our amazing levities and still more amazing gravities.

The Catholic mystics have claimed him as of their kindred; but there is no vague ecstasy, none of the "fliessende Licht der Gottheit" ["streaming light of the divinity"], about Jean de Bosschère. His "vision" is sharp and precise and pure as the outline of a privet leaf, or of a Dutch tulip. (pp. 4-5)

Sharpness, precision, purity, the cold clearness of crystal, the hardness of crystal, hardness attained by concentration, by sheer pressure of spiritual intensity—you will find all these qualities in the later work of Jean de Bosschère. They say he is obscure. It is the obscurity of crystal that shows dark when it is laid on darkness. Hold it to the light and you will see that it is all transparency.

But to appreciate this poet, you must bring to him something of his own. For, let there be no mistake, Jean de Bosschère has nothing in common with the Belgian poets who are best known and most honoured in this country. He has no well-known mark by which we can recognise him. There is not anything in the world of literature to which we can attach him. He slips through our fingers. He is aristocratic, fastidious, unbending. His art makes no appeal to our tendernesses, our prejudices, our picturesque emotions. He may be a mystic and a visionary, but his is not the mysticism and the vision we have been made familiar with through the poetry of Sir Rabindranath Tagore. Jean de Bosschère is not what we like a mystic and a visionary to be. He does not say the proper sort of consecrated things. He is not really what we like a foreigner to be. He is not innocent; he is not *naïf;* he is not spontaneous. He is deliberate, rather, and very sure. There is guile in his subtlety, and a little malice. And with all his simplicity he is not really simple. He is full of that profound and penetrating and complex irony which people hate.

"**Ulysses**" is full of it. (pp. 6-7)

I do not know whether many people will feel the cruel beauty, the cruel enchantment, of that poem. I do not know or want to know the secret of its preposterous charm. You cannot analyse it. The hard, unbreakable thing is a masterpiece of its kind, exquisite, final, complete.

You will find that unbending patrician quality of his in "**The Offering of Plebs.**"

> I want no heart that has loved,
> I want no friend who will be a heretic.
> There is the flesh and the dæmon of the mind;
> There are the trees and also the perfumes;
> There are shadows and memories,
> There are images and dreams;
> There is hope
> And sorrow;
> There is the thought that would be his
> And not mine,
> That would be in him like some foul foreign thing
> In a sealed-up chest.

That is the confession of the uncompromising lover of perfection. You have there the secret of his refusals and rejections. You understand that this poet will offer you nothing except on his own terms; you know precisely where he will fail you; and you know that if you are wise you will accept his terms. Then you will be rewarded by some rare concession to your humanity.

But it will be where you least look for it. You must not go out to look. You must not read a poem, say, like **"Homer Marsh Dwells in his House of Planks"** with any anticipation of concessions. It is a deceptive poem. Your first thought in your first reading will be, Surely he has abated his intransigeance: he has stooped to compromise. This is emotion. It bears some resemblance to the emotions that we know. If he can concede so much—

But no; there has been no compromise and no concession. It is the highly specialised performance of a spiritual being whose densest medium is several degrees subtler than ours.

Like Maupassant, Jean de Bosschère "hath a devil." When it condescends to deal in densities, it knocks you about with the elemental fury of a "Polter-geist." (pp. 8-9)

I said that I should have to go back to **Dolorine,** that strange work of which its author tells us in his "Argument" that it is not a novel, nor a story, nor a legend, nor a song, nor a thesis. . . . [It] is an inhabitant of more worlds than one.

It is M. de Bosschère's hybrid ranunculus and its predecessor [**Béâle-Gryne**] that have caused him to be labelled symbolist and romanticist and idealist, and decadent and mystic and New Catholic. We shall see how much he is any of these things.

This hybrid is a kind of novel written in a poetic shorthand. The method makes for much obscurity; it also makes for intensity, for sudden openings of beautiful light, and for a strange and subtle harmony. If it is not a thesis, it has a theme; that large and obvious theme which draws to it, fatally, by its very vastness, the young and ambitious writer: the tragedy of the dreamer at grips with Life, who cannot seize Life and hold it. Tristan Terne Soron, the artist in love with the Infinite and Ineffable, and Palamoune, the alchemist in search of the secret of Life, are the terrible Shadows that devour Life. Dolorine, the "mince petite vierge, chétive pleureuse" ["slight little maiden, pitiful mourner"], is the living woman who loves and is devoured by them. She is a work-girl: her mortal occupation is the making of paper flowers, but her *métier divin* ["divine calling"] is to live and love.

The note of the tragedy is struck in Tristan's speech to Dolorine in the Prologue: ". . . se vendre l'un à l'autre, se tisser, comme sparterie parfumée;—ah, se vendre, car sans cette monnaie que l'on frappe de soi-même, pas l'ivresse fatale de l'amour, sans cette monnaie que l'on frappe. Les marchands connaissent le prix, ce prix effroyable de la marchandise" [". . . to sell themselves to one another, to weave themselves like scented grasses;—ah, to sell themselves, for without this self-coined money, none of the fatal drunkenness of love, without this self-coined money. The merchants know the cost, the frightful cost, of these goods"].

Needless to say, it is Dolorine who knows, and who pays "le prix effroyable."

Now you can approach a theme like this in almost any attitude. And Jean de Bosschère is said to have approached it in the attitude of a symbolist. He himself repudiates that title and any other which would attach him to a school. He does not want to be attached—or to attach. I can't think of anything that would embarrass him more horribly than to learn that he had founded a school and that a body of young disciples were about to call on him with their respectful homage. But in **Dolorine** he distinctly shows a quality that causes him to be mistaken for a symbolist; a love of hieratic figures, a certain sacramental use of common objects, of the chaffinch in his "little wooden church" in the Maison Verte where Dolorine, Tristan and Pa-

lamoune live; the bread and fruit that Dolorine sets on the table, and the "Robe verte" [green dress"], the House itself. It is all faithfully in the manner of Claudel. No wonder if the hearts of the Catholics leaped up when they beheld the flowering of M. de Bosschère's mystic ranunculus. No wonder if they were annoyed when they found out that the *renoncule mystique* ["mystic ranunculus"] was, after all, a *renoncule scélérate* ["vile ranunculus"].

In Jean de Bosschère's language these things—the bird, the bread and fruit, the table, the green dress, the house, stand for something. Yet what they stand for is *themselves;* that is to say, their own mystic and eternal aspect as realities. Jean de Bosschère does not make use of symbols in the dilettante manner of the true *symboliste.* Or, rather, his is an inverted symbolism, a symbolism which is the opposite of Catholic, the opposite of Romantic, the opposite of the symbolism of Stephan Mallarmé. It is much more akin to the symbolism of Greek religion with its adoration of the magic *sacra* than to the Christian religion with its unholy repudiation of the earth. Jean de Bosschère's hieratic and romantic figures are not symbolic of a higher and diviner life than ours; they are symbolic of the divine beauty and the divine sorrow of our life itself. The bread and fruit are not symbols of a divine something which, so to speak, is not on the table, neither do they become divine by any process of transubstantiation; they *are* divine. And Tristan's tragedy is that he does not know this. The tragedy of all three is the unfaithfulness of Tristan and Palamoune to reality, their inability either to make their dream incarnate, or to recognise the divine dream already incarnate in the humble living things of earth. (pp. 9-12)

And Jean de Bosschère has worked out the tragedy in a way which shows how great a realist is in this poet who evades our efforts to label him. It closes in two acts of which you can hardly say whether it is the horror or the pity that is supreme. Dolorine brings forth an idiot child, a monster, as the fruit of her union with the half-hearted Tristan. The divided passion of the dreamer is fatal to the living offspring. Not with impunity are we unfaithful to the divinity of Life. The final act is the death of the child and its mother, told in the Epilogue. (p. 12)

This is not symbolism, it is not philosophy, it is not fantasy; it is as much a "slice of life" as a story of Maupassant or Tchehov; for such things happen. It is only the setting of the scene that is symbolic, only the poet's attitude that is philosophic, only the clothing of his figures that is fantastic.

When I began this Introduction I had only read the study of Max Elskamp, the **Métiers Divins,** the **Bourg,** and these poems of **The Closed Door.** I had not read **Dolorine et les Ombres,** and I was not going to read it, because, to tell the truth, I suspected in it a "symbolisme malsain" ["unwholesome symbolism"], and I had gathered that its author considered it negligible as a youthful indiscretion, and that I should do him no more injustice by neglecting **Dolorine** than would be done to Shelley by neglecting *Queen Mab* in an introduction to *The Cenci.* I was therefore inclined to leave **Dolorine** out altogether, or to be content with quoting one or two salient passages from Francis Jammes's review of it.

But in the genius of Jean de Bosschère there is a certain hard solidarity; a solidarity that comes from a clear and steady and all-round vision of life. Not necessarily of the meaning of life, but of the spectacle. Every poem that he has ever written is the expression of a very firm and definite attitude to *that.* So that in his work nothing is negligible, as I very soon found when I tried to make the *Métiers Divins* and the *Bourg* a jumping-off ground for an appreciation of *The Closed Door*. When I came to measure the distance beween the *Métiers* and those mature masterpieces, "The Doubter," "The Orchard," "The Blackbird and the Girl," and "The Old Woman," I found that the leap was beyond human power, and that there was no "take-off." There was no accounting for the breach in the continuity of Jean de Bosschère's genius. For there is very little—you might almost say there is nothing—in the *Bourg* or the *Métiers* to prepare you for those four poems.

For "Ulysses," for "The Offering of Plebs," for "Homer Marsh"—perhaps. But their meticulous fineness and finish, their clean intellectual chiselling, their thinness which is the thinness of transparent glass, and their hardness which is the hardness of crystal, all this is the work of a master craftsman, a consummate maker of *émaux et camées;* but, in all this diminutive perfection, there is no prophetic hint or sign of the bigness and thickness of the human tragedy of the four poems. It is the difference between an *objet d'art* and a live reality; between things wrought in gold and crystal and things woven from the twofold texture of life itself, of quivering spirit and quivering flesh. You cannot distinguish in them, any more than you can distinguish in the living creature, between lancinating thought and tortured nerve.

"Gridale," the first poem of the sequence called "Night," seems to me to mark the transition from the old perfection to the new. It is poignant, it is terribly human. But it is not perfect; it has the uncertainty, the lapses and exaggerated stresses of transition. (pp. 14-15)

Behind . . . grimness and . . . awful irony you discern the tragic horror of a spiritual maiming and a spiritual hunger unspeakable. But because the reality shadowed forth is so immense it does not quite get into the poem. At any rate, when Gridale goes out into the snow, and his wooden leg dots the way, till he drops at the end of the road with his brave song frozen on his lips, you feel, not the culmination of the tragedy, but an uncomfortable sense of the *"déjà vu,"* and of a too insistent punctuating of the agony. The wooden leg dots the way—and you resent its dotting.

In short, the wooden leg has been a false guide to Jean de Bosschère, and he has not yet found himself on that way.

It is all otherwise with the four poems that I have chosen as typical of his genius in its maturity.

"The Doubter" is a masterpiece of modern artistic portraiture. In a hundred and ninety-eight lines you are given all a man's inner life from babyhood to manhood. (pp. 16-17)

Jean de Bosschère is no longer the uncanny and unkind magician peering round the corner of the looking-glass; [in "The Doubter"] he has become a great humanist; he has thrown away his magic mirror with its images and laid his hands upon the naked truth. And the genius which has come to its own in this psychological tragedy is the same genius which conceived the pity and horror of "Dolorine et les Ombres." You gather that between the undeveloped and the mature work the poet has gone through a period of fastidious restraint. He has been a little afraid of himself. Hence the thinness and hardness of the *Métiers* and the *Bourg.*

The reality that he has made his peace with is sometimes the ugly reality of The Old Woman lying asleep in the grass in Greenwich Park. . . .

> Her white hair imitates the grasses
> In its rising and fall on her forehead.

> And the sun opens wider its wings;
> Her mouth half-opens;
> Black teeth beneath the golden rays.

Catholicism must now have about as much hope of capturing Jean de Bosschère as it had of holding François Villon four centuries ago. But this new grasp of grim and sordid things is not, after all, what we are to know and remember him by. If he has not written anything stronger than "The Doubter," nothing that he has written can be compared with "Homer Marsh Dwells in his House of Planks" for subtlety and spiritual value. Spiritual value—for in the finest works of this author each phrase stands for more than its mere face-value; and, if this is symbolism, he is a symbolist. For instance, a house is not only the thing of planks or bricks that a man builds on a piece of land, it is, like the Maison Verte in *Dolorine,* and like Ulysses's house of sycamore, essentially the thing that he builds *around himself:* it stands for the total of his nearest loves and interests; it is invested with his soul as much as it invests; it is as much the expression as the shelter and hiding-place of his secret life. So we know from the very title of this poem that the house of planks is more to Homer Marsh than any house he could have hired. It is part of his personality. The house is brought vividly home to you in one line. It is—

> . . . fixed to the mountain like the nose to the
>   steepness of a face;

fixed to the earth, and part of it as Homer himself is a part. (pp. 20-1)

But Homer imprudently detaches himself from this house and this bit of the earth which was his real self. He travels and leaves his house to Peter. (p. 21)

You think no harm can possibly come of this simple transaction. But you do not know Peter, nor Homer Marsh. You do not know Jean de Bosschère. (p. 22)

[Homer] returns to his house on the mountain. Everything is the same, carefully tended by Peter, yet everything is different.

> The fire smiles into Peter's eyes, and sings.
> The pots gaze at this friend with the bright eyes
> As friends gaze one at the other when there are too
>   many men.
> Not a speck of dust.
> How all these things seem to love one another! . . .

And, like a visitor taking his leave, Homer goes up his own path "towards the setting sun."

> In the hives
> The bees are angry.
> "Peter has taken the heart of my house."

That is all. It is quite clear, quite simple, altogether perfect. The tragedy of the destruction of a subtle relation between a man and the things that were once his. I do not know anything in the least like this masterpiece.

And in "The Orchard" we have the no less perfect expression of that other side there is to this poet—his mysticism, his sense of the Reality behind appearances. (pp. 22-3)

And so, after all, the mystics may claim him if they will. The approach of vision, the sense of the adorable Reality only half discerned, was never more accurately or precisely rendered. The effect is the more sure and certain because of his evident unawareness of what has happened to him: that the Closed Door is open and that it is no longer Night. (p. 24)

In the nature of the case this state of vision belongs rather to the poet than the painter; and we cannot hope to find it represented or even indicated in the drawings with which every work of Jean de Bosschère is illustrated. But, with this exception and one other that I shall make, his development as a draughtsman has followed his poetic genius in its choice of new paths and a new manner. The earlier drawings in dull orange and black which illustrate *Béâle-Gryne* and *Dolorine et les Ombres* suggest the golden stencilling of Crivelli, or the grave, attenuated slenderness of the figures in a Flemish altarpiece, say, of Memlinc or Van der Weyde. He has been compared (inevitably) with Aubrey Beardsley, the elaborately decorative Beardsley. The comparison is easy and obvious. Beardsley was, I believe, the first modern artist to see the value of the black background, and of the "massing of the blacks." But these things are tricks that any clever disciple of Beardsley could pick up and the individuality of every draughtsman must depend ultimately, not on the proportion of his blacks and whites, but on the forms of his masses and on his treatment of the line. The early Jean de Bosschère masses his blacks and revels in backgrounds as black as your hat; but his exquisite angularity, the straightness and stiffness of his figures, are reminiscent of the Flemish primitives rather than of Beardsley's fat and flowing curves. Sometimes, when he is romantic rather than hieratic, you might think of him as a sharp and delicate Beardsley, a Beardsley purged alike of splendid depravity and of all opulence of line. But, for all that, he is more like himself than anybody you can compare him with.

Even in the earliest work of all, in the illustrations to *Béâle-Gryne,* you will find here and there a figure, a ship, a house, drawn with the innocence and simplicity and the blunt firmness of an old Flemish woodcut.

But, in his "middle period," all that is far-fetched and decorative and exotic has disappeared, and what remains is as bare and straight and simple as a Flemish road with its two rows of poplars.

And he has worked for and achieved a greater strength, a greater simplicity and a greater originality, an intenser economy of effect. He deals now in strange curves that finish somewhere in mid-air, the junction of his lines takes place in the invisible; his figures are cut down to the barest essential. But the essential is always there. The uncanny humourist, the half-malign sorcerer, is at work in the drawings of the *Métiers* and the *Bourg.* He is at work with a certain triumphant frightfulness in **"Ulysses"** and **"The Offering of Plebs,"** and his own text justifies him. Impossible to believe that the same hand drew these unearthly designs and those of *Béâle-Gryne* and *Dolorine.* If you want to see how far in the direction of unconventionality this artist can go, take the illustration to **"The Blackbird and the Girl."** His problem was to draw a girl who was also somehow a flower. The artist doomed to convention would have drawn a girl growing out of a flower, or a flower growing out of a girl, or he would have stuck a girl's head on a stalk or something. Jean de Bosschère creates an entity with the essential nature and structure of a flower, and the essential nature and structure of a girl, a thing that is inwardly and truly both girl and flower. Monstrous yet gracile, She—or It—is blown to you across the page as a flower is blown on its stalk.

So far the draughtsman's evolution has followed the poet's, step by step. But a danger lies for him in the quest of originality, if his leaning to the bizarre and the grotesque should grow on him at the very moment when the poet's art is developing all in the direction of normal reality. It is the danger of divorce.

Now Jean de Bosschère cannot afford this divorce. He is not a poet who draws pictures for his poems nor a draughtsman who writes poems for his pictures, but an artist in whom poet and draughtsman are inseparably and inevitably one, who can no more help illustrating his own words than he can help writing them. His is so great a lover of perfection in fitness that, if he could, he would design the very type his books are set up in, he would print and bind them himself.

If you would ask the poet what his ideas about his *métier* are now, he would probably tell you something like this:

"As an artist I am no longer anything but a somewhat impersonal thing that thinks, apart from any idea of the utility of its thinking.

"I am aware that a certain state of grace, of cold lucidity, of absolute disinterestedness, is the indispensable condition of the creation of rare and beautiful work."

"A certain state of grace, of cold lucidity, of absolute disinterestedness": that is the root of the matter; and people who rebel against the immoral doctrine of art for art's sake would do well to note that one of its three conditions is a moral one.

I do not think that Jean de Bosschère will ever be a popular poet. I cannot see him falling from his "state of grace," melting, slackening, unbending and growing gradually facile and diffuse. I cannot see him doing any of the things that make poets popular. I cannot see him carried away on a surge of patriotism, and chanting the song of Belgium's liberation or celebrating the victories of the Allies once a month with punctual emotion. I cannot imagine him even listening with tolerable politeness while other people do these things. I cannot conceive him posturing in any proper attitude for a single instant. There is a sort of flavour that I own I don't like about the only War Poem he has ever written: **"Drum."** I may be wrong. But all I know is that those drums don't sound like drums to my barbaric ear. In fact, for anything that Jean de Bosschère has told us to the contrary, we should never know that there was a war going on at all.

And to me this silence of his is more impressive and poignant than most of the songs of the patriots. To have achieved, in the teeth of such overwhelming disaster, work of such beauty, of such finish, of such firmness and of such intransigent individuality, is to have kept his soul. (pp. 24-8)

May Sinclair, in an introduction to The Closed Door *by Jean de Bosschère, translated by F. S. Flint, John Lane Company, 1917, pp. 1-29.*

THE TIMES LITERARY SUPPLEMENT　(essay date 1917)

[*In the following excerpt, the critic disagrees with May Sinclair's evaluation of Bosschère's poetry in her introduction to* The Closed Door *(see excerpt dated 1917).*]

To us the most remarkable thing by far about this volume of M. de Bosschère's poems and drawings [*The Closed Door*] is Miss May Sinclair's introduction to it. Its dithyrambs have made us very uncomfortable. Here, says Miss Sinclair, we have a poet who is endowed "with that human vision which is the nearest we can get to divine vision." If this were all that we had to discover in the book we might have managed it. But it is not. M. de Bosschère "is full of that profound and penetrating and complex irony which people hate." He has "that unbending patrician quality"; he is "a spiritual being whose densest medium is several times subtler than ours." . . .

And as for his drawings, we are told that we might think of him "when he is romantic rather than hieratic" as a "sharp and delicate Beardsley purged alike of splendid depravity and of all opulence of line." Without pausing to wonder why, if depravity is splendid, it should be an advantage to be purged of it, we hasten to say that the reason why we have dwelt upon the introduction is that we wish it to stand plainly on record that there is evidence of the existence of a transcendental M. de Bosschère. On our own Bœotian soul this very superior person has left no impression, and since we consider it as dangerous to disagree with Miss Sinclair on literary matters as she finds it dangerous to disagree with Mr. Bertrand Russell on questions of metaphysics, it is due to her and to ourselves to make it clear that her enthusiastic praise has been given to a *Ding an sich* ["thing in itself"] of which no apprehension has been vouchsafed to us.

Our M. de Bosschère is an intelligent and irritating person who at his best can write a cynical parable after the manner of Oscar Wilde with a good deal less than Wilde's suave perfection. He is irritating not so much because he has a trick of saying commonplace things portentously, but because he is addicted to the ultra-modern habit of comparing large things to small. In the one poem which to us is thrilled with any presentiment of higher issues, **"Orchard,"** he tells us of

> Buttercups like the shavings of butter
> You eat with radishes.

It is hard to say whether this is more deplorable than Coningsby's dish of bacon and fried eggs "like a posy of primroses." They run each other very close. The chief difference is that Disraeli was a big man, whose lapses of taste are in the long run a minor affair, while if M. de Bosschère (*our* M. de Bosschère) falls he disappears and his work with him into a dark hole like the girl in his own parable of **"The Blackbird and the Girl."** Miss Sinclair assures us that the primrose by the river's brim is not a simple primrose by any means to him. But we still fail to see how it comes any nearer to being a primrose *sub specie aeternitatis* by being likened to a shaving of butter.

When these things are left on one side we have left the teller of parables. Homer Marsh gives his mountain home to Peter while he goes on a far journey; but when he returns, although he finds everything in the same place, his possessions smile upon Peter, not on him. And he goes up the path, towards the setting sun saying, "Peter has taken the heart of my house." **"Ulysses Builds his Bed"** is more cynical. The people resent his superiority, and when he has wholly compassed himself about with a strong wall he looks out, and

> He sees that the men are loaded with faggots,
> There is a funeral pile about his house;
> The women soak it with the oil of the lamps,
> And pour on it those of their toilet;
> The cooks the oil of the preserved fish;
> The wheelwrights the pitch of their carts;
> The boatman brings a cauldron of tar,
> And a captain, covered with Sioux medals
> Thrusts a torch's flame beneath the wood-pile.
> They roast Ulysses,
> For he is indeed theirs . . .

Whether this was worth doing we do not know, but we are inclined to allow that it has been well done. The subtleties have passed unobserved clean over our head. We are, however, quite certain that if they exist they are not in the verses themselves, which, whether in French or English, are straightforward to a degree and utterly devoid of musical resonance. In the rare cases where they are not straightforward they are unintelligible. The last poem in the book describes an old woman lying asleep on the grass at holiday-time in Greenwich Park. It ends thus:—

> But this woman here
> Is a sign of all the ages also.
> She is a carved pearl in a British Museum
>   showcase,
> A palustral fish-hook,
> And at the same time the delirium of the
>   Russian Ballet.
> Flesh without the thoughts that tear it,
> Flesh in the succulent desert of itself,
> A trepanned man eating a peach.
> The black, unlyrical love of beautiful beasts.

All Miss Sinclair's temerarious epithets crowd back into our mind. Yes, it must be. We have been left aside by the onward sweep of poetic evolution. In our stagnant backwater we murmur to ourselves, "L'idéalisme a cessé; le lyrisme est tari" ["Idealism is done with; lyricism has gone rotten"] with, as we think, a thousand times more justification than Fromentin. But that is our blindness. What seems to us a rather trivial adaptation of an attitude to life which Jules Laforgue grappled with and made creative is the work of "a spiritual being whose densest medium is several times subtler than ours." Well, well!

A review of "The Closed Door," in The Times Literary Supplement, *No. 817, September 13, 1917, p. 438.*

THE TIMES LITERARY SUPPLEMENT   (essay date 1917)

[*In the following excerpt from a review of seven books of fairy tales and legends, the critic discusses* Christmas Tales of Flanders.]

The stories [in **Christmas Tales of Flanders**] are sometimes abrupt in their inconclusiveness; homely and almost entirely unromantic. Sometimes a disagreeable hint of cynicism obtrudes itself; but this may have been left on our minds by the association with M. de Bosschère's illustrations; they are almost the only ones among these seven books which have any artistic pretensions—any, that is, worth considering—and of them all they are the most completely unsuited to their purpose. In the coloured plates prettiness and horror are strangely mingled and even the innocent acquires something oblique. Mr. de Bosschère's prettiness is not the inspired elegance of Aubrey Beardsley, who could endow inanimate objects with a disturbing beauty and wickedness; but there is something of Aubrey Beardsley's influence to be noticed in the coloured plates, as well as a medley of other suggestions—Flemish and Italian, Chinese and Japanese—and, more especially, the suggestion of the boulevard newspaper kiosk. "The Procession" is the least pretty of all these pretty plates; it is, in addition, an insolent little picture. Mr. de Bosschère reveals more genuine imagination in the black-and-white illustrations.

"Fairies, Goblins and Men," in The Times Literary Supplement, *No. 820, December 13, 1917, p. 621.*

CONRAD AIKEN   (essay date 1918)

[*An American man of letters best known for his poetry, Aiken was deeply influenced by the psychological and literary theories of*

Illustration entitled "Hoisting Themselves on Stilts" from Bosschère's Weird Islands. *Chapman & Hall, 1921. Reproduced by permission of the publisher.*

Sigmund Freud, Havelock Ellis, Edgar Allan Poe, and Henri Bergson, among others, and is considered a master of literary stream of consciousness. In reviews noted for their perceptiveness and barbed wit, Aiken exercised his theory that "criticism is really a branch of psychology." His critical position, according to Rufus A. Blanshard, "insists that the traditional notions of 'beauty' stand corrected by what we now know about the psychology of creation and consumption. Since a work of art is rooted in the personality, conscious and unconscious, of its creator, criticism should deal as much with those roots as with the finished flower." In the following excerpt, originally published in January, 1918, Aiken discusses themes and techniques in The Closed Door.]

From Mr. [T. S.] Eliot to M. Jean de Bosschère, the Flemish poet whose volume **The Closed Door** has now been translated into English by Mr. F. S. Flint, is a natural and easy step. It would appear, indeed, that Mr. Eliot has learned much from M. de Bosschère; certainly he is, in English, the closest parallel to him that we have. It is a kind of praise to say that in all likelihood Mr. Eliot's *Love Song of J. Alfred Prufrock* would not have been the remarkable thing it is if it had not been for the work of Jean de Bosschère: in several respects de Bosschère seems like a maturer and more powerful Eliot. What then is the work of M. de Bosschère?

To begin with, and without regard to the matter of classification, it must be emphatically said that this book has the clear, unforced, and captivating originality of genius. Whether, as

Miss Sinclair questions doubtfully in her introduction [see excerpt dated 1917], we call him mystic or symbolist or decadent—and all these terms have a certain aptness—is after all a secondary matter. These poems, in a colloquial but rich and careful free verse, occasionally using rhyme and a regular ictus, very frequently employing a melodic line which borders on the prosodic, seem at first glance to be half-whimsical and half-cerebral, seem to be in a key which is at once naive and gaily precious, with overtones of caricature; in reality they are masterpieces of ironic understatement and reveal upon closer scrutiny a series of profound spiritual or mental tragedies. The method of M. de Bosschère might be called symbolism if one were careful not to impute to him any delving into the esoteric; his themes are invariably very simple. One might call him a mystic, also, if one could conceive a negative mysticism of disbelief and disenchantment, a mysticism without vagueness, a mysticism of brilliantly colored but unsustaining certainties. But perhaps it would be more exact to say that he is merely a poet who happens to be highly developed on the cerebral side, as well as on the tactile, a poet for whom the most terrible and most beautiful realities are in the last analysis ideas, who sees that as in life the most vivid expression of ideas is in action, so in speech the most vivid expression of them is in parables. These poems, therefore, are parables. In **"Ulysse bâtit son lit"** we do not encounter merely the deliciously and fantastically matter-of-fact comedy, naive as a fairy story, which appears on the surface; we also hear in the midst of this gay cynicism the muffled crash of a remote disaster, and that disaster arises from the attitude of the animally selfish crowd towards the man of outstanding achievement. He refuses to be one of them, so they kill him. "They roast Ulysses, for he is theirs." Likewise, in **"Gridale,"** we do not witness a merely personal tragedy; the tragedy is universal. We see the crucifixion of the disillusioned questioner by the unthinking idolaters. In **"Doutes,"** under a surface apparently idiosyncratic in its narration of the humorously bitter discoveries and self-discoveries of a child, we have really an autobiography of disillusionment which is cosmic in its applicability. . . . Again, in **"Homer Marsh,"** we make the acquaintance of the gentle recluse who loves and is loved by his house, his fire, his kettle, his pipe and tobacco, his dog, his bees; but he goes away to travel, and lends his house to his friend Peter; and on his return finds to his bewilderment and despair that all these beloved things have curiously turned their affections to Peter. The tone is lyric, seductively playful and simple; the overtone is tragic. It is a translation into action of the profound fact that ideas, no matter how personal, cannot be property; that they are as precious and peculiar and inevitable in one case as in another, a natural action of forces universally at work.

It would be rash, however, to carry too far this notion of parables. Some of the poems in **The Closed Door** are so sensitively subjective, so essentially lyrical, so naturally mystic—in the sense that they make a clear melody of the sadness of the finite in the presence of the infinite, of the conscious in the presence of the unconscious—that one shrinks from dropping such a chain upon them. All one can say is that they are beautiful, that for all their cool and precise and colloquial preciosity, their sophisticated primitivism, they conceal an emotional power that is frightful, not to say heartrending. What is the secret of this amazing magic? It is not verbal merely, nor rhythmic; for it remains in translation. It springs from the ideas themselves: it is a playing of ideas against one another like notes in a harmony, ideas presented always visually, cool images in a kind of solitude. It is not that M. de Bosschère is altogether idiosyncratic in what he does, that he sees qualities that others do not see; but rather that he combines them unexpectedly, that he felicitously marries the lyrical to the matter-of-fact, the sad to the ironic, the innocent to the secular—the tender to the outrageous. He sees that truth is more complex and less sustaining than it is supposed to be, and he finds new images for it, images with the dew still on them. If novelty sometimes contributes to the freshness of the effect, it is by no means novelty alone: these novelties have meanings, unlike many of those factitiously achieved by some members of the Others group. This is a poet whose quaintness and whim and fantasy are always thought-wrinkled: they are hints of a world which the poet has found to be overwhelming in its complexity. Song is broken in upon by a doubting voice; flowers conceal a pit; pleasure serves a perhaps vile purpose; beauty may not be a delusion, but is it a snare? And what do thought and memory lead to? . . .

> Nevertheless he still believes,
> Ax in hand, this burlesque of a man still believes. . . .

Ax in hand! It is precisely such bizarre but significant imaginings that constitute the charm of this poet. And it is a part of his genius that, although hyperaesthetic, he is able to keep clearly in mind the objective value of such images, and to contrast them deliciously with the sentimental, or the decorative, or the impassioned. (pp. 138-41)

> *Conrad Aiken, ''Jean de Bosschère,'' in his* Collected Criticism, *Oxford University Press, 1968, pp. 136-41.*

POETRY (essay date 1918)

[In the following excerpt, the critic discusses the poems and drawings in The Closed Door.]

This Frenchman [De Bosschère], like certain modern poets of our own language, sees the characteristics, as of individual life, which lurk in inanimate objects and even in situations, as well as in living beings. He feels what might be called the soul of these. This form of vision is perhaps mysticism, but it is entirely apart from, though not contradictory to, theological mysticism. To one with a developed sensitiveness this form of individuality is a thing as real—in this world of illusions—as material appearances are. Much of Harold Monro's poetry is on this theme, and one may trace it in some poems of H. D., of Pound, Eliot, and others. One can find a slight similarity between Amy Lowell and Jean de Bosschère in the exaggerated form of the expression of their vision, though there is a heat and an artistic self-abnegation in the French poet which Miss Lowell does not attain, perhaps does not wish to attain.

''Homère Mare,'' for example, is a story-poem about the attachment of the human soul to the souls of his surroundings, and its estrangement from them. It has the serene, subdued beauty of a sunny pebbled road through a fair country.

''L'Offre de Plebs'' is probably the most beautiful poem in [*The Closed Door*]—one can hardly over-praise its peculiar beauty. The subject is sympathetic with the poet's temperament, and its gloom and playfulness express a depth of sensitiveness rarely reached. It is the perfect image of a mood—desire for solitude; and in spite of wistfulness it has no trace of sentimentality. . . . (pp. 48-9)

''Ulysse Bâtit son Lit'' is the expression of an individual soul in a small or large village—it might be in France, Argentina, or America, for it is everywhere the same. The poem is a perfect embodiment of the pettiness of the village spirit, which in this case resented a man's way of ''building'' his bed! God help these bed-builders of France, Argentina, or America!

The latter parts of the volume express more personal emotions and are less unlike the work of other poets. The themes of ''Doutes,'' ''Gridale,'' ''Verger,'' ''La Promesse du Merle,'' have been treated in poetry in various forms. ''Doutes'' and ''Gridale'' are in places rhetorical, but always lit with a weird and sometimes quaint fire which is the poet's own. (p. 50)

In [the poem ''La Promesse du Merle''], as well as in some of the others, the poetic height and depth of the emotion sometimes appear strained, but that depends on the temperament and even on the mood of the reader.

In the illustrations one can find the influence of Kandinsky's black-and-white—haunting patterns often like spilled and partly dried water. Also there may be a suggestion of Alfred Kubin—compare for instance Kubin's illustrations to his romance [*Die Andere Seite (The Other Side)*] with De Bosschère's at the end of ''Doutes.'' He is trying to escape Beardsley, and usually succeeds—indeed, he is on the whole self-expressive. One wishes that our American illustrators would give us, as intimately as these men, their own happy or sombre individualities. (p. 51)

> *M. M., ''Jean de Bosschère's Poems,'' in* Poetry, *Vol. XII, No. I, April, 1918, pp. 48-51.*

EZRA POUND (essay date 1918)

[Pound, an American poet and critic, is regarded as one of the most innovative and influential figures in twentieth-century Anglo-American poetry. He was instrumental in securing editorial and financial aid for T. S. Eliot, Wyndham Lewis, James Joyce, and William Carlos Williams, among other poets. His own Cantos *is among the most ambitious poetic cycles of the century, and his series of satirical poems* Hugh Selwyn Mauberley *is ranked with Eliot's* The Waste Land *as a significant attack upon the decadence of modern culture. Pound considered the United States a cultural wasteland, and for that reason, he spent most of his life in Europe. In the following excerpt, Pound reviews Bosschère's study of the Belgian poet Max Elskamp.]*

I confessed in my February essay [in the *Little Review*] my inability to make anything of Max Elskamp's poetry, and I have tacitly confessed my inability to find any formula for hawking De Bosschère's own verse to any public of my acquaintance; De Bosschère's study of Elskamp, however, requires no advocacy; I do not think it even requires to be a study of Max Elskamp; it drifts as quiet canal water; the protagonist may or not be a real man. (p. 5)

The further one penetrates into De Bosschère's delightful narrative the less real is the hero; the less he needs to be real. A phantom has been called out of De Foe's period, delightful phantom, taking on the reality of the fictitious; in the end the author has created a charming figure, but I am as far as ever from making head or tails of the verses attributed to this creation. I have had a few hours' delightful reading, I have loitered along slow canals, behind a small window sits Elskamp doing something I do not in the least understand.

So was I at the end of the first division ''Sur la Vie'' [''On the Life''] de Max Elskamp. The second division, concerned with ''Oeuvre et Vie'' [''Work and Life''], but raised again the questions that had faced me in reading Elskamp's printed work. He has an undercurrent, an element everywhere present, differentiating his poems from other men's poems. De Bosschère scarcely helps me to name it. The third division of the book, at first reading, nearly quenched the curiosity and the interest aroused by the first two thirds. On second reading I thought better of it. Elskamp, plunged in the middle ages, in what seems almost an atrophy, as much as an atavism, became a little more plausible. (pp. 6-7)

> Ezra Pound, "De Bosschère's Study of Elskamp," in The Little Review, *Vol. V., No. 6, October, 1918, pp. 5-8.*

F. S. FLINT (essay date 1919)

[*An English poet, translator, and critic, Flint influenced modern poetry through his work as the leading popularizer of French poets, poetic forms, and critical theories in British journals between 1909 and 1919. He was also a prominent member of the Imagist movement in poetry, and the poems in his collections* Cadences (1915) *and* Otherworld (1915) *are regarded among the finest and most typical of that movement, which advocated well-defined images rather than vague generalities in verse, as well as the elimination of rhyme and meter as "artificial and external additions to poetry." The master of ten languages, Flint was at one time considered England's foremost linguist; his numerous translations include Bosschère's* The Closed Door. *In the following excerpt, Flint comments on the poems in that collection.*]

M. Jean de Bosschère is [a] . . . Belgian poet—and artist (the word Belgian here is merely an indication of the territorial accident of birth), who fled from the German occupants of his country to England; but not until after he had lived some months with them in Brussels. He arrived in London with the manuscript, illustrated by himself, of his observations of the invaders. The British censors would not pass the book, because the drawings were too realistic; the Belgians did not appear heroic and beautiful in them! Perhaps, too, the censors did not understand M. de Bosschère's realism. But the incident is illuminating. M. de Bosschère does not see humanity as heroic or beautiful. . . . *La Porte fermée* [*The Closed Door*], which was conceived, written, and published in London, . . . is unique both in French poetry and in the series of M. de Bosschère's works. The poems in this book are in the French language; but they are, for the most part, of no country; they have a touch of the English spirit; there may be a strain of the Fleming in them; they are universal. Homère Mare is the simple man, who, tiring of his humble life, goes travelling, and loses his soul, which was in the pots and pans of his house, the flowers and the bee-hives of his garden. Ulysse is the hero who falls beneath the paws of the mob. Gridale is the martyr of his own idea. "L'Offre de Plebs" discusses friendship. "Doutes" is the cry of the unusual child on his discovery of the baseness and cowardice of humanity. "L'Homme de Quarante Ans" is the lament of middle-age at approaching death. Then there are the two exquisite meditations in a garden, "La Promesse du Merle" and "Verger"; an antiphony of maidenhood and spring, "Le Merle et la Jeune Fille," with its cruel, capricious ending, and three studies of Greenwich: "In the College," on the death of a little southern boy, "Tambours," a meditation on death, interrupted by the drums of the Boy Scouts, "les petits enfants de l'école du meurtre" ["little children of the school of murder"], and "La Vieille," who lies down in her black and jet on the grass of Greenwich Park beneath a sweltering sun. This list conveys nothing of the bite of M. de Bosschère's irony, when he is ironical; the depth of his sadness, when he is sad; the bitterness of his bitterness; the warmth and colour and harmony of his peace. He uses words as he uses black and

white, in black overpowering masses of unexpected incidence, when the mood is dark; in light, rhythmic, significant lines, when the mood is happy or ironical; and there is not a word or a line that is not M. de Bosschère's own peculiar property, having behind it, and pressing upon it with the force of their volume, a vast store of visual memories. (pp. 33-4)

> F. S. Flint, "Some Modern French Poets (A Commentary, with Specimens)," in The Monthly Chapbook, *n.s. Vol. 1, No. 4, October, 1919, pp. 1-40.**

THE TIMES LITERARY SUPPLEMENT (essay date 1920)

[*In the following excerpt, the critic reviews* The City Curious.]

In "**The City Curious**" we have an English and Continental blend. We take it that M. de Bosschère's original text has ironically supplied the amusing touch of Continental pomposity, and that [the translator] Miss Tennyson Jesse has embroidered upon the fantastic element. At any rate, this latter is slightly exaggerated, in a manner which is almost peculiar to English writers, whose fault too often lies in confusing invention with "letting oneself go." But to concoct a fairy tale on one's own is a thing difficult in the extreme, and this one is quite creditably carried through. Indeed, there was a moment, when the historian was presented to us studying a paper through a telescope, when we felt as though Lewis Carroll were speaking. M. de Bosschère has strewn the tale with a profusion of odious little drawings in which his morbidity is almost as obstinate as ever. The ugliness which he persistently seeks is curiously depraved in quality, and to this is sometimes added sheer silliness. It is purely silly, when you affect to draw a bird, to give it the long, naked torso of a centaur; or, when you represent a supposedly jolly mannikin, to draw the face of an embryo; or, to present a monster lifted, it would appear, from a Temptation of St. Anthony and call it a dolphin. All M. de Bosschère's luxuriance of line and pattern produces the oppression of nightmare. Now and again he permits himself to be quite normal. In the coloured plates prettiness is aimed at, with some success; but it is an unpleasant prettiness and makes one think of poisoned comfits. It is really ingenuous of M. de Bosschère and his admirers to imagine him as qualified to draw for children. We should hide all his pictures from them.

> "Some Fairy Tales," in The Times Literary Supplement, *No. 986, December 9, 1920, p. 830.**

JEAN DE BOSSCHÈRE (essay date 1932)

[*In the following excerpt, Bosschère discusses the relationship between his writing and his illustrations. At the beginning of this discussion he refers to a letter he received from Paul Valéry in which the eminent French poet wrote: "I thank you, Monsieur, for this double demonstration,* Béâle-Gryne, *graciously given by that ambiguous tool, the same curious pen which, page after page, leads the word to elude itself or sometimes directly to reveal, according to a different magic, a moment of allusions murmured from the other side."*]

Not being born within the bosom of any religion, there was no rite and no baptism to protect me during the lonely, stormy years that constituted my youth, of which I have recounted a great part in *Marthe and the Madman.*

Thanks, however, to one of the rare rays of good fortune, which found me in my isolation, the ceremony of baptism was performed upon me on the threshold of my conscious life, along the private path of correspondence: Paul Valéry consecrated me artist and writer. . . . (p. xi)

In 1909, this great writer recognised in me the worker in two professions that I then was, and have been without ostentation ever since.

Perhaps, there is a still older trace of my taste for these two professions. . . . I think I was five years old; the age at which all those who are going to draw consume much paper and many pencils. But what of those who are going to write? Upon the enormous sheet of paper which covered the table like a cloth, on which I was placed in the morning, and which was very much like a big book, I drew the episodes of a story that I invented in a number of successive squares, but at the same time I traced the indispensable text. This is the only kind of illustration that I admit, the most pure. (p. xii)

Since that time, I have never made a drawing that was not accompanied by some text, that is to say, which was not anecdotal, but *every* work is at a second, or several seconds, remove from an anecdote; the most abstract combination of lines is dependent on some anecdote, even when it appears to belong to nothing but geometry.

Afterwards, I never wrote or published a book of my own which did not contain both text and images. I say "images" and not illustrations for the reason that the latter would seem to give a secondary place to my drawings, whereas the text and the drawings have exactly the same weight of expression; they move together, they do not complete each other, but use a different language to the same end, and it would be difficult to say which is the more important. I have most nearly attained to what I am trying to do in *Job le Pauvre.*

But what I did never amounted to anything more than gratuitous solitary experiments. I mean that never, neither now nor in the past, did I think of publishing or showing them; only accident revealed my essays in the form of published books, or in the form of exhibitions for a few persons. Thus I remained in the obscurity that I have loved since my childhood, until the moment when one of my experiments had unhappy consequences; that is, when commercialized publishers began to exploit my aptitude for drawings. The result was a series of books from the classics illustrated by means of mechanical reproduction.

Now, if illustration, in the spirit in which it is generally conceived, is a blasphemy against thought, what can be said of the plates nearly always unsatisfactorily reproduced, because mechanically, that have been made after my original drawings, which already possessed the great fault of being pleasing to incompetent bibliophiles?

And it is this that is the burning core of the subject. The art of illustrating is commendable only at the moment that one forsakes it. To-day no one asks of it that it shall be photographic of the thoughts of the author of the book, nor that it shall consist of archaeological reconstructions. Such is not the artist's task.

Therefore, I believe that the only drawing one can put in the pages of a book, without betraying either the author or the reader, is the expression of an emotion, of an "idée-sentiment" ["idea-sensation"], that the book has given to the artist, even though it may be somewhat remote from the text, and born only of a reflex. The illustrator then becomes one of the passionate readers of the book, and the inspiration of the drawing possesses the same personal, artistic value as any other, es-

Illustration from Bosschère's Job le pauvre. *From* The World of Jean de Bosschère, *by Samuel Putnam. The Fortune Press, 1932. Reproduced by permission of the publisher.*

pecially where the creation of imaginative drawings is concerned. I believe that these latter have their true place in a book, which is a more personal thing than a picture. If the drawings for a book have a freedom, it is here that it is to be found. So far as I myself am concerned, I love them to the point of spiritual passion, and it should be remarked that, technically, such subjects as the erotic and the satanic, which ought to remain a mystery for nearly everyone, are better in an album than upon a wall, in a frame that is a part of the furniture.

It would please me very much to dwell upon this subject of the value of illustration as pure art. . . . I wish to state that every time a drawing is reproduced mechanically there is no question of art, but only a question of commerce; and it is comic to hear bibliophiles talking of progress, of the golden age, and of the decline of an illustrator, of whose work they have seen nothing but illustrations which are due to the industry of photographers.

It is not a discovery nor an original statement to say that wood-engraving, lithography, etching, all the processes of art by which a work passes directly from the hands of the artist into the hands of the public, without passing through any mechanical medium, that these engravings, if they show direct emotions and are not merely a repetition of the text, have the same value as a picture of the same artistic altitude and temperature.

In a book which is composed according to these principles, one finds, in addition to the text, some wood-engravings, lithographs or etchings, all vibrant from the hand of the artist.

For myself, I prefer etching, on acount of the variety of its means, and of the expressive shadings which it has at its command, on account of the prodigious magic that it holds, and also because of the secret alchemy of its elaborate technique; for it must not be forgotten that a great part of the value of a work comes from the passion that is put into its realisation. (pp. xii-xv)

I confess that I experience the joy of the cabalist, when the nitric acid mysteriously bites into the copper where I have traced my drawings in the wax. As the acid throws up its green bubbles I look through the window, and contemplate there before me, sometimes the dark forest of Fontainebleau, sometimes the shores of the Mediterranean, sometimes the roofs of Paris under which tragedies are unfolding equal to those that have been the material, the furnishing of all my life. (p. xvi)

Jean de Bosschère, in an introduction to The World of Jean de Bosschère: A Monograph *by Samuel Putnam, The Fortune Press, 1932, pp. xi-xvi.*

SAMUEL PUTNAM　(essay date 1932)

[*Putnam was a distinguished American biographer, editor, critic, and translator of works from French, Spanish, and Portuguese into English. Regarded among the most talented translators of his generation, he earned particular acclaim for his 1949 translation of Miguel Cervantes's* Don Quixote. *He is also known for* Paris Was Our Mistress *(1947), a highly praised portrait of the colorful inhabitants of Montparnasse in the 1920s and 1930s and an inquiry into the "Lost Generation" of expatriated American authors, and for* Marvelous Journey *(1948), a study of Brazilian literature. In* The World of Jean de Bosschère *Putnam, a friend of Bosschère, wrote the most comprehensive study in English of Bosschère's poetry, fiction, and artwork. In the following excerpt from that study, Putnam provides a survey of Bosschère's works from the beginning of his career to the 1928 publication of* Marthe and the Madman.]

I always have had a fondness for worlds, and a particular fondness for worlds that are round. It is, I discover, because Jean de Bosschère creates for me an autochthonous universe, one in which I am enabled to walk with the familiar realism of a dream, that I love him and am impelled to write about his work.

I love the world which Bosschère, the poet,—always the poet,—has created, and daily goes on creating, whether with pen or brush. I have come to love Bosschère, the painter, who is never more the painter than when the poet. In *Marthe et l'Enragé,* M. de Bosschère's first novel, I recognise the *début* of an important and quite unclassifiable novelist,—promisingly unclassifiable. There is, finally, the love I have for the ardent and caressing humility of a medieval craftsman which I find in the "noble and most blameworthy hands (*mes belles et très coupables mains*)"—the phrase is Baudelairean in its ring— of Jean de Bosschère turned illustrator, of Bosschère who, in electing the calling of an illustrator, with the humbleness before life and his media of a Cellini or a Michelangelo, has succeeded in creating *an art of illustration* of which he is the first, if not as yet the sole, exemplar.

All this, I am aware, sounds a bit lyric, and lyricism is a sin which the twentieth century finds it hard to forgive, especially our little reviewers, who must always be unearthing a "sig-nificance" of some sort,—social, psycho-analytic, God knows what,—in everything that is written or painted. This, however, happens to be my approach, essentially a personal one, to Bosschère, the only avenue by which it is possible for me to approach him, with that sincerity of love or hate which is the only criticism and the only excuse for writing.

Moreover, how draw near to any artist, except by crossing that moat which fends him, by way of that creative drawbridge which he chooses to let down? And Bosschère is never anything but lyric in intent. The one living artist, it may be, who, a certain critic remarks, has captured the magic of the fifteenth century and, blithely skipping some hundreds of years, has dropped the nightmare of the Flemish painters—of a Bosch or a Breughel—down into a world (a world of his own creation) in which the cathedral is the contemporary of the aeroplane. . . . (pp. 3-4)

Jean de Bosschère may be said to have begun his career as an archaeologist,—which, incidentally, is by no means a bad beginning for an illustrator. At the age of twenty, he already had made something of a reputation as a critic. Among his early works, we may notice one on *Edifices Anciens,* another on *La Sculpture Anversoise,* the volumes *Quinten Metsys,* etc. It is to be noted that, even in his books on archaeological subjects, the author included some of his own drawings.

But it was with *Béâle-Gryne,* published at Paris, in 1909, that M. de Bosschère won his first reputation as a poet, or at least, as the creator of a form for which poetry appeared to be the

Illustration from Béâle-Gryne.

only name. The present writer is unable to state whether or not the appearance of this work, beautifully printed by the Occident Press and illustrated by the author's own *images,* was a literary and artistic event; if it was not, it should have been, for it marked the arrival, not alone of a new and original talent, which is an event in any quarter of any century, but of a double talent, each half of which appeared to complement, rather than supplement, the other. Here was an artist telling a story which was not a story in the literary sense of the word, but rather a fairy tale for too-grown-ups, a monstrous and fantastic tale of some far-off world of the super-real—telling it with words and with pictures, and not with pictures to "illustrate" the words or words to "explain" the pictures; but where the words stopped, the pictures began, and where the pictures left off, the words once more took up the tale.

As for the *images,* some of them possessed the haunting quality of the Flemish primitives, while others displayed the clarity of a wood-cut, a clarity which would come as a surprise to those who know the artist of *The Closed Door* and *Job le Pauvre.* But on the whole, it may be said that the draughtsman's manner, his characteristic touch, which it seems he cannot lose, no matter how far afield he may wander, was already distinctly evolved. Indeed, it would seem that, after passing through what might be termed a breaking-up of line and colour, M. de Bosschère is coming back, in some of his latest work, to a matured version of that first "manner"; that this progress, in his painting as in his poetry—as we shall see, there is a certain parallelism between the two—is, and has been, toward a super-clear realism and a super-realistic clarity. (Not forgetting that a certain realism and a certain clarity are more incumbent upon the illustrator of other men's work than upon the poet drawing-in one of his own poems.)

As for the text—we will call it that, and avoid tedious refinements—of *Béâle-Gryne,* it was something quite new. The fact that it so successfully eludes all genres is, of itself, indicative. The careless might call this novel and apparently hybrid form the prose-poem; but if prose-poem it is, then there are no others like it. Not Baudelaire's, certainly; and I, for one, am not prepared to agree with Miss Sinclair, when she, in her introduction to *The Closed Door* [see excerpt dated 1917], remarks that "It was *Béâle-Gryne* and *Dolorine et les Ombres* that landed Jean de Bosschère among the Symbolists!" Such a classification is a tempting one, but one which inspection shows to be a trifle too facile, as Miss Sinclair herself admits. Something of Symbolism there undoubtedly is in *Béâle-Gryne,* just as there is something of Baudelaire (an "influence" which the critics seem to have overlooked); but the point is, there is so much more of Bosschère, and both M. de Bosschère and his works always strenuously resist pigeon-holing.

While Miss Sinclair informs us that she has not read *Béâle-Gryne,* she supplies us with what is, probably, as excellent a description as it would be possible to give of the intangible substance of this poetically substantial book:—

> I gather from its critics that *Béâle-Gryne* has something of that delicate, fastidious, subtle and persistent evasion of the actual which can only be called decadent when the bald or obvious statement of bald or obvious facts passes as the supreme achievement of maturity.

It is in its fastidiousness and its persistent evasion of the actual that the distinction of the work lies. When one reads the book, then turns to the title-page and notes the date,—1909!—one

experiences a slight shock. Here was a super-realism in full flower twenty years ago, a super-realism produced by no formula other than the ineluctable one of a profoundly personal genius. Here is the link between the last of the Symbolists and that after-war generation which is striving so painfully to achieve, or to retrieve, the alchemy and the transubstantiate mystery of existence. *Béâle-Gryne* may not be untouched by Symbolism; yet it would have been written, one feels, whether or not [Stéphane Mallarmé's] *L'Après-midi d'un faune* ever had seen the light. No need, either, to invoke a long since debauched Rimbaud (debauched by his own countrymen) and his *bateau ivre;* in these pages there stalks a new Drunkard, one who, encountering the disorder of his own soul, finds it not merely sacred, but—orderly! Here, in short, is the answer—one answer—to that first chapter of the Flemish Huysmans' *Là-Bas;* and back of it, beyond, stand the shades of Bosch and Brueghel, conjuring a shadowy Baudelairean monster, Ennui. (pp. 14-17)

It was two years later, in 1911, that *Dolorine et les Ombres* made its appearance. This work marks the maturation of the impulse that produced *Béâle-Gryne.* For it is a good deal more mature than the latter; more mature, not more delicately, more fragilely perfect in kind. *Béâle-Gryne* is youth, seeking and content with nothing short of perfection; *Dolorine* is the spontaneous and luxuriant flowering of an inevitable perfectedness, distinguished by a flawless fusion of feeling and expression. The prose of *Dolorine,*—for I, somehow, love to think of it as a piece of very rare and beautiful prose,—not infrequently attains a biblical elevation and simplicity. It is sometimes as beautiful, with the beauty that is akin to tears, as the *Book of Ruth* or the *Song of Songs.* (p. 20)

We have heard M. de Bosschère himself telling us what his book is not, and what it may be: a "hybrid buttercup." It has been referred to as "a kind of novel," as a "poetic shorthand," and its "obscurity" has been stressed.

As for the form, it is, simply, *Dolorine.* M. de Bosschère is one of those artists who know that each new and veritable work of art creates its own form, which it is the business of the critic to discover, that each new poem, picture, what not, if it be veridical, is nothing more nor less than the birth of a cosmos. (Let us take down our *Curiosités esthétiques* once more.) And so, *Dolorine* is not a poem, or a novel, or a kind of poem-novel; it is a world, a world that may only be called *Dolorine.*

As to the "shorthand," shall not each novel cosmogony have its language, which to us appears novel? If the idiom of one of M. de Bosschère's planets happens to fall upon our ears like a stellar Basque, this does not mean that the idiom in question is not, therefore, self-contained and self-complete.

Dolorine, with its tales of Tristan Terne Soron, the artist, Palamoune, the alchemist, and Dolorine, the paper-flower-girl, is, essentially, the tragedy of the Dreamer and Life. It is Tristan and Palamoune who are the "Shadows"; it is Dolorine who is devoured by the Shadows. Neither Dreamer nor Alchemist succeeds in capturing the meaning of life, though each, in his own way, ransacks infinity in his quest. The most they can do is to slay life, in the person of the girl,—the *"mince petite vierge, chétive pleureuse"* ["slight little maiden, pitiful mourner"],—who loves them. Tristan, being a dreamer, is half-hearted in his devotion to that earthly reality which Dolorine represents. The result is: a monster, an idiot child. The tale ends on a note of almost unbearable tragedy.

Such is the story, told with "hieratic figures" and "a certain sacramental use of common objects." It has led to the author being compared with Claudel, while others (Miss Sinclair among them) see in him a perduring realist. As for himself, this writer is not sure that he has, any longer, an idea of what the term "realism" means. If it means reality, is not that the thing which artist, poet, philosopher, madman,—all of us, even to the alderman and the mythical "man in the street,"—are after? But if it be taken to mean the visible, palpable, circumambient "reality" of a factual universe, then I am inclined to believe that M. de Bosschère's sympathies are with Tristan and Palamoune and their tragic destiny. For after all, Bosschère is the poet; and we shall see, a little later on, how to his eyes the poet and the world agree.

Nor can I discover any "obscurity" in *Dolorine*. "Obscurity" is another word, like "deformation" in painting, which has come to lose practically all connotation. The only obscurity I can see is that fatal barrier which speech always erects, when two ships attempt to hail each other upon an apparitional sea.

Certain of M. de Bosschère's critics have found in *Dolorine* an "unhealthy symbolism," and Miss Sinclair tells us that she was tempted, at first, to neglect the book "as a youthful indiscretion," like Shelley's *Queen Mab*.

> But in the genius of Jean de Bosschère there is a certain hard solidarity; a solidarity that comes from a clear and steady and all-round vision of life. Not necessarily of the meaning of life, but of the spectacle. Every poem that he has ever written is the expression of a very firm and definite attitude to *that*. So that in his work nothing is negligible. . . .

Nothing, indeed, is negligible, as one soon perceives who takes M. de Bosschère's work from its beginnings, or, at least, from *Béâle-Gryne,* and follows it through *Job le Pauvre* and *Marthe et l'Enragé.* The *roundedness* of the man, his very inability to escape from his own cosmology, give us confidence. His is a spherical world. (pp. 21-4)

The *Métiers Divins,* like the two preceding books, was illustrated by the author with drawings and woodcuts, chiefly the latter. Its creator, in a bibliography prepared for my own use, describes it as "a sort of song on the handicrafts, which shows his delight in handwork and fine technique." (pp. 28-9)

M. de Bosschère's early work is, unfortunately, hard to come upon (like most writers, the author himself is frequently to be found without a copy in a pinch) and for some time, being unable to lay hands upon either the *Métiers* or the *Twelve Occupations,* I was inclined to take Miss Sinclair's word for their "hard and thin" quality, an impression which the poet, characteristically, was at no pains to contradict. But having, of late, had a little better luck as a bookstall-forager, I find myself in disagreement. The *Métiers* have a hard quality, certainly; but that hardness—and even thinness, if you will—is an essential part of these little poems: they are nothing if not finely chiselled cameos; and is not a cameo usually hard? They, too, are not literary; they are the product of a manual-craftsman, of a poet who works with his own hands, and who loves the work of hands.

The following year, in 1914, came the critical study on Max Elskamp, the Flemish poet. This volume is worth reading, if only for the chapter on Elskamp's mysticism,—to see what, if any, light is shed on the "mysticism" of Jean de Bosschère.

Then came the war, and with it, early in 1915, the poet's flight from Belgium to London. He did not know it, but this was to mark, if not what one might call a turning-point, assuredly a new era and the dawn of new vistas in his creative life. . . . Jean de Bosschère might never have become the passionate and world-famous illustrator that he is to-day, had it not been for the British public and the British publisher. (pp. 29-30)

M. de Bosschère found, in John Lane, 1917, a publisher for what many, doubtless, would say is his greatest book thus far—I, personally, should hesitate between it and *Job le Pauvre,* though it and not *Job* might be my poetic choice in the end. *The Closed Door* is a miraculous volume. From the twelve poems it contains, it would be easy to pick anywhere from four to six that fall little short of the epic-in-miniature. I had thought I knew which ones I should select as my own choice, but when I look over the volume once more, I find that I am uncertain. Perhaps, the only two that I should, unquestioningly, rule out of the running are the ones entitled, respectively, "**In the College**" and "**Drums.**" The latter is a war-poem, the only one that Jean de Bosschère, the war-refugee, ever wrote, so far as I am aware; and I cannot help feeling that it does not succeed, that it does not carry over. As one of his critics [May Sinclair] has remarked, the poet's silence on the subject of war is "more impressive and poignant than most of the songs of the patriots."

But of the other poems in the volume, the ten others, not one is a little poem: "**Homer Marsh Dwells in His House of Planks**"; "**The Offering of Plebs**" (for which I do not care so much as for some of the others); "**Ulysses Builds His Bed**" (a right Ulyssean variation on the Ulysses theme); "**Gridale**" (strong and stark, possibly a bit too theatric); "**Doubts**" (a poem the greatness of which might be overlooked); "**The Blackbird's Promise**" (a poem the greatness of which could not be overlooked); "**The Orchard**" (which must be included in any selection); "**The Man of Forty**" (the greatest poem I know on the theme); "**The Blackbird and the Girl**" (a tragedy on a Greek vase); "**The Old Woman.**" (pp. 31-2)

In the course of his treatise [*L'Influence du symbolisme français sur la poésie américaine,* M. René] Taupin has no little to say regarding Bosschère, and the latter's influence upon the English and American Imagists. (p. 36)

M. Taupin believes that Bosschère is to be looked upon as "a true Imagist," and that he "will render immediately and strikingly evident the difference between a theoretic Imagist and a theoretic Symbolist." The critic then goes on to quote Miss Sinclair's dictum regarding Bosschère and the Greeks, the sacra, etc. . . . It was this attitude toward *the thing, the object,* according to the French scholar, that exerted so profound an influence over such men as Pound, Flint and Aldington, who

> restored to objects their poetic value, and created in America a new mode of viewing objects. It was love of all that falls within the sphere of the senses, of all that is alive, that they admired in Bosschère; and it is a well-known fact that there was a deep sympathy between the Belgian poet and the Imagist group. For the former, as for the latter, the natural object is always the adequate symbol. In his poetry, objects—the house, his door and his roof, the dining-room, his table, a hand at rest, some fruit on the buffet—all have their symbolical meaning. But what they symbolise is nothing other than their own existence. For Bosschère, they are alive; as for H. D. and the

Greeks, the mile-stone, the olive-trees, each blade of grass, each household god were all alive.

As for Flint, Bosschère's superb translator, "his own poetry has felt the influence."

Bosschère's most striking influence, however, was probably that which he exerted over T. S. Eliot. M. Taupin has this to say: "Like the Imagists, he (Eliot) has drawn upon Bosschère." (pp. 36-7)

Not long ago, a literary acquaintance asked me if I thought that breadth of canvas had anything to do with a writer's reputation, particularly his reputation with posterity. Upon reflecting but a moment, one is tempted to reply in the affirmative.... If Dante had written only sonnets, though equal in poetic quality to the *Divina Comedia,* would he be a world name?

This may be another disadvantage with which Jean de Bosschère has to contend. That delicacy and fastidiousness which are of the essence of his personality and his art have led him, always, to work within a smaller frame. Outside of *Marthe et l'Enragé,* which is a comparatively short novel as novels go, *Dolorine* bulks the largest of his creative work.

As we have seen, **The Closed Door** contains but a dozen of what hardly can be termed long poems, although ten of the twelve are possible masterpieces. **Job le Pauvre** is, if anything, an even thinner volume, in point of physical size, comprising as it does, without the translations, only some seventy-four pages of large type, generously displayed. It has, besides, a certain formlessness, which makes against it for the public eye. The barely perceptible division into fourteen poems does not take away from the fact that this is rather a poet's polished notebook than a book of poems.... [The] book should find a small but select audience; others will prefer the more looming dimensions of **The Closed Door**. It might even, almost, be said that these are poet's poems. (pp. 40-1)

The philosophy of **Job,** I think, may be said to be summed up in the lines:

> You have not known prayer in the name of bread
> You have not known that I am the poor man.

For Bosschère is a rather curious combination of aristocrat and humanitarian. He is the aristocratic democrat. His luminous sympathy with, rather than for, *le Pauvre* is evident (in **The Closed Door**) in such a poem as **"Homer Marsh Dwells in His House of Planks."** On the other hand, the poem which follows this, **"The Offering of Plebs,"** shows an utter disillusionment with the crowd and its gifts. Perhaps, Mr. Flint's "a misanthrope loving men but avoiding their contact" is not so bad a definition. As for any direct communion with the plebs, it would seem that M. de Bosschère's fastidiousness, that refusal to fall from a "state of grace" which Miss Sinclair, in her Introduction, prophesies, would shut him off from this. Yet, he cannot forget the implication of those *belles et très coupables mains.* It was Bosschère remembering this who wrote the *Métiers.* And he feels, likewise, that kinship which the poet always feels with *Job,*—Job, the enduring and perduring *poor man;* and **Job le Pauvre** is the expression of this feeling of kinship. (pp. 43-4)

[*Marthe et l'Enragé*] is a strange book. For myself, I am attracted by its unclassifiability, and I note that at least one French reviewer has had the same reaction. It is a poet's, rather than a novelist's, novel. Possibly, no better description could be given than to say, it is the sort of novel that one would expect Jean de Bosschère to write. And yet, it is not—precisely. It is hardly, at any rate, the novel that I should have anticipated from him. I am a little surprised, but not disappointed. On the contrary, I personally am delighted to see what a poet like M. de Bosschère can do, when he surrenders himself to a form and, working with all reverence within that form, still succeeds in achieving a new form.

For *Marthe* lacks the poetic formlessness—the word is a bad one, but I employ it from want of a better—of *Béâle-Gryne* and *Dolorine.* In it, the story emerges sharp and clear, from its setting of sombre shadows. This, I suppose, will not appear so strange to a critic who sees in Bosschère an essential and developing realist. Nevertheless, the effect of the whole is that of a symphony, rather than of a novel, an effect that is punctuated by the recurring thud of short staccato *refus de dire* paragraphs throughout the work. These paragraphs, by the way, are one of the few faults I would find with the book. They lend an unneeded emphasis; the symphonic effect is sufficiently evident without them. They are a trifle wearing on the nerves.

There is, as has been said, a story; but when the reader is through, it is not the story that remains with him, but an aroma, an atmosphere, a mood. For the chief thing the book does is to create an atmosphere, an atmosphere of spectral—one had almost said, of gruesome—melancholy. The tale is a bit horripilatory in spots, and its nocturnal reading is not to be recommended to the squeamish or the hypochondriac.

The central theme of *Marthe* is what might be termed an incest-motive, though "incest," too broad as well as too crude a term, fails to cover the psychologic refinements involved. The real romance of the book lies between Pierre and his sister, Marthe, not between Pierre and his sweetheart; and the tragedy lies in a harelip! Marthe, Marthe of the beautiful body, first curious about, then in love with love. The theme is one quite worthy of Jean de Bosschère's weird Flemish and, to lift M. Jaloux' phrase, "vaguely diabolic" genius, "ranging from the lyric to the grotesque." The tragedy culminates in a "bedroom scene"—but what a bedroom scene!—between brother and sister.

This is, it must be confessed, a situation which the Anglo-Saxon does not relish. Only the Russians, only a Dostoievsky, could have treated such an incident with the mastery exhibited by M. de Bosschère. To me, as the author handles it, the scene is not a "repulsive" one. It is too superbly tragic, too drenched with tears, for that. The brother is unable to live up to the dreadful duty his sister has forced upon him, the duty of showing her what it is, that beautiful and distant thing called love, the blossoming of which between her brother and Antoinette, the girl next door, she has had opportunity to observe. Pierre wishes to be faithful to the love he has for Marthe, to the close bond which has existed between them, but he is unable even—he lacks the courage or the presence of mind—to act a lie and deceive his sister. The strain is too much for Marthe; she loses consciousness. That is the scene, baldly retold; but no retelling can convey the power of the original, in its setting of horror and that horror which the reader senses is to come. The thing is not literature; it is life.

There is one other "incest scene" in contemporary French literature which comes irresistibly to my mind, and that is one to be found in Delteil's *On the River Amour (Sur le fleuve Amour)....* [Delteil's] scene is young and beautiful and poetic and fervent; but it is as different from Bosschère's as *A Midsummer Night's Dream* is from *King Lear*. There is, as a matter of fact, no little of Oberon and Titania's world even in this, it may be, the most human and "realistic" passage to be found in Delteil, just as there is a good deal of Hamlet and Lear's world in Bosschère's most elfin imaginings. By contrast with Delteil, the author of the passage in *Marthe* is a grim realist. It may be that, after all, this is the direction in which the poet of *Dolorine* and *Béâle-Gryne* is evolving, and that he has, instinctively or with a degree of consciousness, taken up the novel to express this side of his genius. And yet, there is, still, that vague and Flemish "diabolism," that sombre reverse of the mystic shield, which many critics have scented. For Jean de Bosschère is, and must be always, Jean de Bosschère. (pp. 45-8)

So much for Marthe. As for Pierre himself, prodded on by the cruelty of the world toward his beautiful sister of the harelip,— the barbaric cruelty of the world of children and, later, the ineffable cruelty of life,—he becomes *l'Enragé*, the Madman. In the end, following the scene in the bedroom, Marthe dies, apparently of self-starvation, while her brother becomes a murderer. For there are more stories than one in this story of Marthe. The relations between Marthe and Pierre are but one thread (one should not forget the scene between Pierre and Antoinette); at least two other characters are masterfully drawn.

For me, an atmosphere of even deeper tragedy than that surrounding Marthe and Pierre is created by the picture of the pagan family, exiles and pariahs in the little medieval town of Catholic Flanders, a tragedy poignantly emphasized by the mother's insane fear, when a younger daughter dies, lest the child's body be dug up from the community but prevailingly Catholic burying-ground. The town of Rupel finally becomes for the reader what it was for the members of this family, a haunting, inescapable incubus.

Such is *Marthe*, M. de Bosschère's first excursion into the field of the novel. M. Jaloux finds the book to be a little chaotic and uneven, but possessed of an extraordinary vitality. How much chaos and unevenness the jaded novel reader of to-day might forgive, to be able to get a little of that other attribute! M. Jaloux also finds the author of *Marthe* inclined, like Gide and Freud, to "tell all"; but he adds that, in the relations between Marthe and her brother, M. de Bosschère has done no little by creating a novel situation, one which, after all, hardly comes under the head of "incest," where Polti doubtless would classify it.

To sum up, it may be said that *Marthe* is like no other novel, but that it is a *good novel*,—as well as being grotesque, and fantastic, and poetic, and a number of other things. It is, in short, distinctly Bosschère-esque. (pp. 49-50)

We have considered first, the poet, since it was as a poet that Jean de Bosschère first won wider reputation. But in Bosschère, poet and painter are inseparable, quite. He himself has always, stubbornly, refused to recognise any cleavage. . . .

In the first place, no one who reads Bosschère can fail to note a remarkable, not to say startling, power of painting in words. (p. 59)

He is, it may be seen, a little intoxicated with colour. And his colours are seldom subdued; they are the lordly, the regal ones, the masters of the soul for good or ill. His are the primary and the impinging hues: scarlet, green, black, purple, mauve and violet. And yet, into what a delicate world he transforms them,

builds them up; a world of rose and grey, of "grey cloud and dew," a world "white and yellow as honey," a world of bronze dust and amber breezes. . . . (p. 62)

It all evolves into a very real world, the world of Jean de Bosschère. And, as may be perceived, the world of paint and words are one. . . . It is, essentially, a young universe that we behold emerging here, the universe of a young poet. . . . (pp. 63-4)

And yet, in many respects, this is the same mythic cosmos that we encounter in Bosschère the illustrator:

> Lastly, there passed a rich and white unicorn. It bore an amazon who carried a mystic candelabra. At one side, suiting its doleful voice to the beast's deadened pace, a barrel-organ whined its inveterate history. Round about, a stream of drakes whined interminably, in conformity with the deadened movements of the worthy beast and the toothless melodies of the death-rattling barrel-organ. The group belonged to a genre shy and rare.
>
> *Béâle-Gryne.*

It is, I know, the easy and the popular, the offhand course to refer this sort of thing to Beardsley and the now so thoroughly disreputable Nineties. Unfortunately, while this may be a convenient method of disposing of what is not to our palate, it is not good criticism in M. de Bosschère's case. . . . [He] owes a good deal more to his Flemish ancestry than he does to Beardsley, and he owes still more to his personal and invincible temperament. This was, in a manner, a "period." Bosschère, the poet, the painter in words, was to evolve into a painter of a different, a more realistic—if you prefer, a stronger; certainly a more mature sort. . . . (pp. 64-5)

In *The Closed Door*, as in *Job le Pauvre*, will be found likewise an evolution in the draughtsman's line and colour.

The poet, it devolves, has become a realist, at grips with life; *Béâle-Gryne* and *Dolorine* have become, apparently, more "unearthly" than ever, this unearthliness being no longer that of white unicorns bearing mystic candelabra—but—well, one must have a look at the illustrations in *The Closed Door*, and afterwards at those in *Job le Pauvre*, in order to be able to make out just what it is that is happening.

What is happening, as I see it, is simply this: the artist is feeling himself out, technically, as every artist must do when he reaches a certain stage of his career; and this feeling-out, for the artist, must be in the direction of a new and greater freedom. It is possible that M. de Bosschère was not uninfluenced by the spirit, if not by the letter, of what was happening round about him in the art world of Paris, where the phenomenon commonly and vaguely known as "modernism" was occurring. In the black-and-whites of *The Closed Door* you see it in the matter of line; in *Job* you see it in the employment that is made of coloured paper. But aside from voyagings and divagations in technique, it seems to me that the artist, especially of *The Closed Door*, is becoming, in spirit, more rather than less realistic.

Something, again, may depend upon one's definition of "realism." I am not aware, assuming that a "normal reality" is the goal of art,—and who knows what either the norm or the real is?—I am not aware that either the "bizarre" or the "grotesque" is incompatible with any reality with which I chance to be acquainted. In *Marthe et l'Enragé* we have the fruition of Bosschère the realist; and yet, is he a realist? How much of a realist? His Rupel is, obviously, not the Rupel of the Rupelians. The truth is, Jean de Bosschère has always been a realist, but he has never mistaken the commonplaces of his retina for reality. He has ever been the master, not the slave, of reality; he has been the true super-realist. Progress there most assuredly has been in the eighteen years between *Marthe* and *Béâle-Gryne,* the progress of a tree growing upward; and the tree never can become what it was not in the seed.

No, I feel that the poet and the painter have been, and must remain, essentially one; in this lies Jean de Bosschère's uniqueness. But surely, we may permit him his many-sidedness, and permit him to express now one side, now another—permit him to be, if and as he chooses, now the realist in words and the nonrealist in line and paint, now the realistic draughtsman and the unrealistic poet. For he is, when all is said, a poet; it all comes back to that:

> He sang his fill; there was an unprecedented peace, a second during which the world remained a blessed meadow, and no problem of any sort was raised.
>
> *Dolorine et les Ombres.*

—Not even the problem of "realism" or nonrealism. And it is as of a *prairie en bonheur* that I like to think of Jean de Bosschère's painting and poetry. (pp. 65-7)

> *Samuel Putnam, in his* The World of Jean de Bossch-*
> ère: A Monograph, *The Fortune Press, 1932, 160 p.*

MARY ROUNTREE AND BENJAMIN ROUNTREE (essay date 1979)

[*In the following excerpt, the critics examine the portrait of Paris presented in* L'obscur à Paris *and* Paris clair-obscur.]

The almost complete obscurity into which the name of Jean de Bosschère has passed mocks the promise and achievement that had, during his lifetime, won him the admiration and respect of an astonishing number of fellow artists, among them Eliot, Pound, Joyce, Edith Sitwell, Yeats, Rouault, Chirico, Ungaretti, Max Elskamp, Milosz, Gide, Claudel, Jammes, Audiberti, Jacques Rivière, Joë Bousquet, André Suarès, Max Jacob, Supervielle, Franz Hellens and Edmond Jaloux. When Bosschère died in 1953, he was practically unknown to the general reading public within France as well as without, this despite the fact that some had considered him worthy of the Nobel Prize of 1952. (p. 830)

Several collections of letters to Jean de Bosschère have been published in the years since his death, and all give impressive evidence of the stimulating influence of Bosschère's intellect. Younger disciples whose literary careers have far outdistanced Bosschère's own have not hesitated to acknowledge their debt to his artistic example. Antonin Artaud, for instance, places Bosschère at the very center of his own life and art: "Jean de Bosschère m'a fait. Je veux dire qu'il m'a montré combien lui et moi nous ressemblions et nous étions proches, et cette preuve au moment où je suis m'est plus précieuse que tout le reste. Il a établi l'unité tremblante, centrale, de ma vie et de mon intelligence" ["Jean de Bosschère has made me. I mean that he showed me how much we resembled each other and were kindred, and at the moment this proof is more precious to me than everything else. He established the trembling unity central to my life and my intellect"].

Illustration entitled "Strange-looking Creatures" from Bosschère's Weird Islands. *Chapman & Hall, 1921. Reproduced by permission of the publisher.*

A study of Bosschère's writings, particularly of his two remarkable volumes of *poèmes en prose* entitled *L'Obscur à Paris* and *Paris clair-obscur,* reveals the rare kind of vision and craftsmanship that could inspire a statement as generous as Artaud's. Published in 1937 and 1946 respectively, these two volumes grew out of Bosschère's experiences in Paris in the thirties when he lived there in almost poverty-stricken conditions.

Unlike Léon-Paul Fargue's lyrically ebullient portrait of Paris, the city which Bosschère saw and described in the prose poems of *L'Obscur à Paris* and *Paris clair-obscur* is essentially a place of nightmare, a dystopian vision peopled with grotesques, diseased minds and bodies, freaks, drunks, and lonely, frantic shadows of men and women. Dead dogs float down the Seine, and human beings find amusement most often in cruelty to others. As for other modern poets, notably Baudelaire and Eliot in *The Waste Land,* the city for Bosschère becomes a devastating metaphor of the human condition, of man's alienation and puny insignificance. If the despondently poor and the "poux métèques" ["foreign lice"] of his neighborhood arouse in him little if any sociological concern, they do, on the other hand, intensify his metaphysical outrage, his sense of the grotesquerie of human existence. The atmosphere he creates is claustrophobic, oppressive, relieved only infrequently by glimpses of light and beauty.

Like Baudelaire, Boschère explored a variety of tones in the prose poem, especially black humor, which is often disturbingly cruel in his two collections. But in its derisive response to horror and pain and in its fondness for perversely incongruous metaphors, Boschère's work more closely resembles that of Lautréamont than that of any other of his predecessors.

The *persona* of the poems is a splenetic *déraciné* ["displaced person"], rebellious, aloof, the quintessential stranger. Boschère achieves deep emotional resonance by an effectively sustained point of view: the fragile inner world of "l'obscur" ["darkness, mystery"] is constantly reshaped and dislocated by the outer world of the city, its faces and scenes internalized, and the subjective world of "l'obscur" is, in turn, externalized, projected outward onto the faces and scenes of the anonymous city. He moves through the streets always as an outsider and an observer, seeing reality as it is refracted through a tormented, introverted personality, in a disquieting state of mind often reminiscent of certain characters of Dostoevsky. (pp. 831-33)

Being both a painter and a sculptor as well as a poet, a combination not uncommon among the surrealists of his time, Boschère achieves a remarkably visual sense of place, a Chirico-like impression of the quality of light and shadow surrounding his lonely city dwellers. He catches eccentric details in the scenes he observes; objects and places assume an almost sentient presence, as in a sketch of his decrepit staircase of his seventh-floor room in a decaying building. He describes the staircase as "violemment personnel" ["violently personal"].... (p. 833)

His description of one of the slum areas surrounding Paris accumulates ugly, squalid detail in a relentlessly realistic fashion.... Other settings in the city reach a symbolic level of meaning, as, for example, the *métro* which translates Boschère's extreme introversion.... The subway satisfies his longing for a closed-circuit world and symbolizes his withdrawal into himself.

In his evocation of Paris and its creatures at night Boschère displays his finest poetic gifts. He illuminates the psychology of night people as they wander through the deserted streets of a large city curiously becalmed.... The isolation of the nighttime wanderer is broken only when "attentif, parfois il s'arrête, le pied sur un soupir tombé d'une fenêtre mal fermée" ["attentive, sometimes he stops, his foot standing on a sigh fallen from a poorly closed window"].... In this moment when two lives come tenuously together, Boschère captures the paradox of the modern city, where the presence of large masses of people serves only to increase the individual's awareness of his own estrangement.

A deserted Paris by night clarifies what Boschère considers the basic condition of modern man: his utter loneliness despite his deep desire and frequent opportunity to communicate. Throughout these prose poems the theme of man's alienation predominates. In some sketches it approaches a baldly editorial statement. From his room above, Boschère watches two men cross the street. They meet in the middle of the street and are so close to each other that they almost touch: instead they pass by, silently, without exchanging a glance, as if they were propelled on parallel rails.... In Boschère's city, impulses toward human contact and sympathy are stillborn.

Whereas for Eliot London is a wasteland of grimy streets, empty bottles, cardboard boxes, cigarette butts, and the pattern of modern life is reduced to a soulless, automatic ebb and flow, where city dwellers are damned to a bleak death in life, Boschère envisions the city not so much as a landscape of death in life as an embodiment of the afflicted, deformed modern consciousness. The grotesques, drunks, and madmen of *Paris clair-obscur* and *L'Obscur à Paris* are for him the natural inhabitants of a sick, decaying world.

In his descriptions of Paris and the people he observes on his long walks through the city, the word *leprous* recurs with such startling frequency that it ultimately conveys a sense of human isolation so acute that all men become "untouchables," corrupt and corrupting. At times Boschère seems to take perverse satisfaction in describing physical ugliness and the ravages of disease. In **"Le Rongeur maudit,"** for example, the subjects are a family of four, three of whom are afflicted with facial lupus. (pp. 833-34)

Even though this sketch is given over almost entirely to a grim contemplation of a hideous disease triumphing over its victims, its effects are somewhat attenuated by Boschère's compassion for them. In other vignettes, his revulsion against physical ugliness obscures any such emotion. Typical of these is his portrait of an undertaker lounging at the door of his "boutique aux cadavres" ["cadaver shop"]. The predatory stance of this man, who astutely located his business next to the morgue, arouses in Boschère a violent disgust which expresses itself in physical repulsion. The man reminds him of an over-ripe cheese—and worse.... (p. 835)

Most of Boschère's city scenes focus upon single individuals, or small, usually family, groups; and only rarely does he consider large masses of people. But one such scene deserves attention for its psychological penetration of a large crowd galvanized by the same emotions. It is a nocturnal carnival scene where a man in full evening dress stands perfectly immobile advertising a lottery. So convincing is his performance that the human being seems eerily to change into a thing as the crowd, initially amused, is little by little overcome by the uncomfortable impression that a genuine metamorphosis has taken place. The spectators feel themselves before "la contemplation d'un précipice, d'un abîme moral insondable" ["the contemplation of a precipice, of an unsoundable moral abyss"]. The menacing "thing" exerts a basilisk spell and his hypnotic eyes begin to terrify: "Ces yeux semblaient déjà avoir parcouru des zones sans fin de silence et d'immobilité effrayante" ["These eyes seemed to have already surveyed endless zones of silence and terrifying immobility"].... Though women weep and moan, the crowd, mesmerized by a kind of black magic, drinks in this "liqueur rare de la terreur" ["rare liqueur of terror"] and experiences a "délectable vertige" ["delightful giddiness"], as if in the presence of Satan himself. Such is their fascination that the mime's return to mobility, his return to being human, disconcerts them so profoundly that Boschère wonders that "nul ne jetât une seule pierre au fantôme quand il reprit l'usage de ses ressorts et alluma crapuleusement une cigarette tout à fait terrestre" ["no one threw a single rock at the phantom when he resumed movement and drunkenly lit a quite earthly cigarette"].... Through the dark satanic figure who reveals the human being as merely an object, the crowd experiences a terrifying illusion of death. This sort of recognition which dislocates man's usual perspective and shocks him out of his presumptuous complacency recurs repeatedly in Boschère's urban vignettes.

Boschère's city people, Goyaesque in their unsparingly realistic presentation, are, more often than not, deformed in body and soul. They appear morally stunted and crippled like the chronic drunkards around which some of the more painful sketches in these two volumes center. There is nothing picturesque or poetic about the lives of his *clochards* or *poivrots* [''bums or drunkards'']. At most, they are grimly humorous, like clumsy, brutal animals, in their grotesque postures and illusions. Excessive drinking for these people is merely one way of escaping from the blind alley of life, the futile, degraded impasse in which they find themselves.

Forms of escape and delusion pervade many of these character studies, but one particularly memorable vignette portrays the ultimate denial of reality: madness. The subject is a wildly derelict old woman who races perpetually through the streets, carrying all her possessions on her back. (pp. 835-36)

Boschère finds something majestic in her total abstraction from the tawdriness of the world surrounding her, and he surmises that she must be inwardly nourished by a glorious dream of grandeur. . . .

For these lonely figures clinging to any vestige of beauty for solace, Boschère feels compassion, admiration, and sometimes outrage at their capacity for self-delusion. Some of the most moving portraits are of old men in the city. One ragged old neighbor emerges from his shack every night to throw out table scraps to roaming alley cats. Often in Notre-Dame square in the early hours of dawn Boschère meets a yellow-skinned old pauper clad in filthy rags, too destitute even to feed the pigeons. Occasionally a slight smile moves across his face, a smile born of his deceptive belief that tomorrow will be better. He is, says Boschère, justifiably confused, like all men, by nature's daily renewal; each dawn seems to promise the old man a new life. . . . (p. 836)

This scene too illustrates the way in which man falls repeatedly victim to nature's sorcery, a theme which strikes darkly through many of these prose poems where Boschère's enigmatic attitude towards religion rises to the surface. Whether he is attracted to religion or repelled by it depends on whether he looks upon it as mysticism, which he considers a metaphysical reality, or as orthodoxy, which for him is a human illusion. (pp. 836-37)

Because of his sense of the dramatic, Boschère is able, within the severe economy of the *poème en prose,* to cast his characters, however humble, into situations, however insignificant, which suddenly reveal their innermost self, which give the reader the impression of plunging deeply into their consciousness. He explores admirably ambiguity, psychological nuance, the passage from one emotional or mental state to another. Even the most banal scene his thoroughly ironic vision charges with disturbing undercurrents of meaning, and he achieves a vivid narrative description through bold poetic imagery and striking juxtaposition.

Inherent in every scene lies an aspect of Boschère's moral and philosophical attitude. Indeed, he seems to be such an intimate part of his subject matter that one often feels that his situations and his characters, particularly the rebellious ones, have deep roots in Boschère himself. André Lebois singles out this anguished ''esprit de révolte'' [''rebellious spirit''] as the clearest evidence of Baudelaire's influence on these poems. Passing from the hands of atheistic parents into those of abstruse mystics, Boschère remained from early life profoundly isolated spiritually. Oppressed by apparently omnipresent evil and embittered by the unbreachable gulf separating reality from the absolute he sought, he approached eventually a kind of rejection of all matter found in the Albigensian heresy. It is this intense personal emotion, this unswerving conviction, which transforms reality in his work, lifts it to the level of poetic vision, and gives many of these prose poems a lasting value.

In revolt against metaphysical injustice, Boschère, often iden-

tifying himself with his characters, infuses into them a blasphemy, a burning hatred not entirely accounted for by the *données* [''given facts'']. The characters reach a truculence, an acidity reminiscent of Rimbaud, Lautréamont, and Blaise Cendrars, an explosive fury against what seems any man-made attempt to impose order on a diabolical creation.

Despite a few scenes of rather acrid farce, a few others of kindness, even tenderness, scenes not studied here, Boschère envelops the Paris of the thirties and, by implication, the world in general, in a somber vision indeed. All about him the failures and the hopeless stress the degradation of men and women. Imagery of the inhuman and monstrous, of disease and decay has justifiably led critics to assert his artistic kinship with his countrymen Bosch and Breughel. Physically repulsive, Boschère's people display a coarse nature that has tarnished all beauty, sullied all innocence.

When Boschère, after having written both poetry and novels, turned to the prose poem, it had already established itself as a poetic form of first importance; and Suzanne Bernard, historian and critic of the genre, on the basis of these two collections places Boschère among the most noteworthy of those poets creating and expanding a ''mythologie moderne'' of the city. While many of the conventions of city imagery, such as the lonely figure walking through a sleeping city, appear in Boschère's poems, he imbues them with his own anguished, sometimes morbid, perspective. His silent city where angry, tormented souls pace aimlessly in bleak solitude is sinister and threatening.

The city as symbol offered Boschère a powerful means of expressing his particular vision of modern man's purposeless, degraded existence in a universe blighted not only by man's own lust and animality but also by a deceptive god's capriciousness. Like his contemporaries, he views the city as a dark emblem of spiritual depletion, but his point of view strikes deeper, more pessimistic notes in its hallucinatory quality and its persistent, virtually unrelieved probing of ugliness and despair. Though Boschère has now receded to the periphery of the literary scene in which he played an important part in his own right and in the life and work of many of his contemporaries, *L'Obscur à Paris* and *Paris clair-obscur* still speak disturbingly to the concerns of the present-day reader. (pp. 837-38)

> *Mary Rountree and Benjamin Rountree, ''The City as Nightmare: Jean de Boschère's Paris of the Thirties,'' in* The French Review, *Vol. LII, No. 6, May, 1979, pp. 830-38.*

ADDITIONAL BIBLIOGRAPHY

Review of *The Closed Door,* by Jean de Bosschère. *The Athenaeum,* No. 4623 (November 1917): 594.
Maintains that ''M. de Bosschère's poems enshrine many unpalatable truths, but nevertheless are curiously fascinating.''

Bosschère, Jean de. Foreword to his *Weird Islands,* pp. v-vii. New York: Robert McBride & Co., 1922.
Discusses his use of drawings in *Weird Islands* to complement, rather than illustrate, the text.

Review of *The City Curious,* by Jean de Bosschère. *The Spectator* 125, No. 4823 (4 December 1920): 745-46.
Plot summary and favorable review.

Rachel Crothers

1878-1958

American dramatist.

Crothers was America's most prolific and popular woman dramatist during the first three decades of the twentieth century. In over thirty problem plays and social comedies she dramatized the conflicts resulting from rapidly-changing moral standards, focusing in particular upon the emerging role of women in society. Crothers observed, "With few exceptions, every one of my plays has been a social attitude toward women at the moment I wrote it." Today her plays are considered a valuable record of social change in the early twentieth century, as well as a significant contribution to the evolution of modern American drama.

Crothers was born in Bloomington, Illinois, to Dr. Eli Kirk Crothers and Marie Depew Crothers. When Crothers was five years old her mother completed medical school and established a practice in Bloomington, thus becoming the first woman doctor in central Illinois and setting an example for her daughter, whose plays were later peopled with intelligent, independent women much like her mother. Fascinated by the theater from childhood, Crothers later recalled that she consistently neglected her schoolwork in favor of theatrical pursuits, which included Sunday school skits and productions by the Bloomington Dramatic Club. Despite this alleged neglect of her studies, Crothers graduated from high school at the age of thirteen and enrolled in the New England School of Dramatic Instruction in Boston. Her avowed intent was to begin a career in New York's theatrical world, but Crothers's family disapproved of her aspirations and she soon returned to Bloomington to teach elocution. She eventually realized her dream, traveling to New York in 1896 or 1897 to seek work in the theater. When no job offers were forthcoming, she enrolled in the Stanhope-Wheatcroft School of Acting. "Not that I thought I needed it at all," she wrote, "but it would keep me in New York. I couldn't turn back." After her first term at Stanhope-Wheatcroft, Crothers was promoted from student to instructor and began coaching students in one-act plays that she wrote, directed, and staged. In 1897 she secured her first role as a supporting actress in a professional production, and she pursued a career as an actress for several seasons thereafter. At the same time, her Stanhope-Wheatcroft productions began to attract critical attention, and in 1902 Crothers finally achieved public recognition with *The Rector*, which was reviewed by the *New York Times*. Her first Broadway success followed in 1906 with *The Three of Us*, a four-act melodrama that was well received by both critics and audiences. After the success of *The Three of Us*, Crothers quickly rose to prominence as a playwright and director, contributing an average of one play a year to the Broadway stage for the next thirty years. She also became known as the theater's leading philanthropist through her establishment of the Stage Women's War Relief Fund during World War I, the United Theater Relief Committee during the Depression, and the American Theater Wing for War Relief during World War II. Crothers died in 1958.

Although virtually all of Crothers's major dramas deal with conflicts arising from changing social roles and moral stan-

dards, her career can be divided into three periods on the basis of her evolving approach to her subjects. In her earliest plays, written before World War I, Crothers most often portrayed a strong woman struggling for equality in a world dominated by men. In *The Three of Us* she introduced the character type of the independent heroine, which would appear in many of her subsequent plays, as well as one of her favorite themes, the double standard of sexual morality imposed upon women. The play's protagonist is the head of a household consisting of herself and two younger brothers, and she expects the respect accorded men in her position. When her reputation is questioned, she rebels against the demand of the play's male characters that she marry to save her honor, declaring: "My honor! Do you think it's in your hands? It's in my own and I'll take care of it. . . . I don't need you—either of you." Her assertion of independence is echoed by the heroine of *A Man's World*, who renounces her fiancé when he refuses to take responsibility for the child born of a past love affair on the grounds that only women should be held accountable for indiscretions. Eleanor Flexner praised *A Man's World* for tackling "the question of the double standard more intelligently and unequivocally than it had yet been treated by an American dramatist," and Arthur Hobson Quinn pronounced the play "one of the most significant dramas of the decade." *He and She*, Crothers's next important work, presents the conflict between a woman's career and her role as a wife and mother. The play concerns a woman whose artistic talent surpasses that of her husband and depicts the strife resulting from his insistence that she give up her career. She initially refuses his demand, resisting the argument that women are intended for domesticity. However, commentators note that the rebellious tone of *He and She,* like that of many of Crothers's dramas, is tempered by the play's ending: the heroine ultimately abandons her career and returns to full-time motherhood of her own accord for what she considers the good of her daughter. Radical on the surface, Crothers's plays most often conclude with an affirmation of traditional family values.

In Crothers's plays of the 1920s, her portrayal of women's struggle for equality became intertwined with an examination of the rebellion of Jazz-Age youth against their elders' rigid moral code. In *Mary the Third,* for example, Crothers presented the conflicting views of marriage held by three generations of women, focusing on the experimental approach taken by the youngest, who hopes to avoid the mistakes of her elders. During this period Crothers's plays were particularly timely, reflecting the growing affluence and sophistication of the post-World War I generation as well as America's increasing preoccupation with youth. During the 1930s, Crothers's plays began to depict the unexpected results of recent changes in moral standards and the newly-won freedom of women, expressing a cautious view of women's gains and reasserting the author's belief in traditional family values. In *When Ladies Meet,* which dramatizes the meeting between a man's wife and his mistress, she depicted the loneliness of both the married woman, whose marriage survives through her continual forgiveness of her husband's affairs, and the disillusionment of the mistress, whose naiveté is shattered by her lover's refusal to leave his wife for her. According to Eleanor Flexner, the play presents what was considered the predicament of the "modern woman": "Here is the successful, popular, intelligent, and independent woman who was the ideal of the first quarter of the century, obsessed with a horror of loneliness, with futility." *Susan and God,* Crothers's last professionally produced play, concerns a similarly dissatisfied woman who discovers a purpose in life upon her conversion to an evangelical religion. She intends to divorce her husband and become a full-time evangelist, but ultimately renounces the plan to seek fulfillment in her role as a wife and mother.

Although Crothers's dramas were overwhelmingly popular with audiences, critical opinion is divided as to their lasting value. Despite her concern with timely social issues, many critics dismiss her works as superficial and contend that Crothers sacrificed artistic values to commercial ends. Edmond M. Gagey, for example, maintains that Crothers "showed an unerring gift for selecting a timely subject, treating it with apparent daring, properly diluting it with sentimentality, and ending with the conventional—or at least the matinee audience—viewpoint." At the same time, however, her works are considered outstanding examples of the well-made play, and critics are almost unanimous in praising Crothers's careful construction, clever dialogue, and skillful characterization. In recent years Crothers's works have been the subject of renewed interest as important social documents examining the roles of women in modern American society.

(See also *Contemporary Authors,* Vol. 113 and *Dictionary of Literary Biography,* Vol. 7: *Twentieth-Century American Dramatists.*)

PRINCIPAL WORKS

Elizabeth (drama) 1899
The Rector (drama) 1902
The Three of Us (drama) 1906
A Man's World (drama) 1910
He and She (drama) 1911
Ourselves (drama) 1913
The Heart of Paddy Whack (drama) 1914
Old Lady 31 [adaptor; from the novel *Old Lady Number 31* by Louise Forsslund] (drama) 1916
A Little Journey (drama) 1918
39 East (drama) 1919
Everyday (drama) 1921
Nice People (drama) 1921
Mary the Third (drama) 1923
Expressing Willie (drama) 1924
A Lady's Virtue (drama) 1925
Let Us Be Gay (drama) 1929
As Husbands Go (drama) 1931
When Ladies Meet (drama) 1932
Susan and God (drama) 1937

WALTER PRICHARD EATON (essay date 1910)

[*In the following excerpt, Eaton reviews* A Man's World.]

"A Man's World," the newest play by Miss Rachel Crothers, author of "The Three of Us," fulfills the promise of that early piece, certainly much more than did her intervening work. . . . [By] its uncompromising allegiance to its premises (though the logical conclusion is not the happy ending dear to convention), its searching truth of feminine psychology, its air of quiet but studied realism, its obvious significance as a comment on the feminist movement of the day—a thoughtful, sympathetic, intelligent comment—it took its place as one of the most interesting native dramas brought to New York during the season. If the long arm of coincidence were not stretched so far to make the plot conform to the thesis of the play, "A Man's World" would be an important piece of stage literature. As matters stand, it is an interesting and at times a moving play, frankly and honestly written from a woman's point of view, but it just misses the masculinity of structure and the inevitableness of episode necessary to make it dramatic literature. It is, however, genuine work; it cannot be overlooked. This time Miss Crothers seems to have come back to stay.

Consider, first, Miss Crothers's daring in the choice of a theme and her greater daring in her solution of the problems that it raises. The theme is that ancient one so dear to dramatists and writers of fiction of all sorts—the double moral code. What the man demands of the woman who is his, she does not demand nor expect from him. Or, at any rate, if she vaguely expects it, she does not get it. The traditional treatment of the theme is to devise a situation in which the erring man is forgiven by the woman, who then in her turn asks forgiveness, only to be refused. That was the situation in "Tess," and that was the situation only a week earlier in Pinero's "Mid-Channel." But it is not the situation in Miss Crothers's play. The woman, it turns out, has done nothing whatever that needs forgiveness. She has a little theory—women do get such theories tenaciously into their heads nowadays—thus she does not care to have to forgive the man she loves for any unsavory episodes connected with "the living of a man's life." However, just such an occasion arises. The episode is particularly unsavory and she loves the man particularly hard. Yet she does not forgive him. She stands out partly from principle, if she is a woman. But chiefly there is that in her nature which will not permit her to forgive. So the bewildered and somewhat vexed man goes off forever as the curtain falls. This is a new twist to the old situation; this is the new woman, indeed; and this, a woman's play, faces the old problem without cant or sentimentality, and lands a good square blow.

The scene of **"A Man's World"** is laid "in an old New York house near Washington Square," and it is easy to surmise that the former "A Club," which inhabited lower Fifth Avenue, gave the suggestion of this home of men and women living a semi-Puritanical, semi-Bohemian life and earning their livings by writing novels about the East Side, painting miniatures, constructing "the great American drama," and otherwise serving the causes of sweetness and light. The most popular member of the household is Miss Ware, a novelist and worker among the East-Side girls, who has adopted a small boy called Kiddie. She says she took him under her wing in Paris, when his mother died, abandoned by the unknown father. But if Miss Ware is popular with the men, she does not escape the tongues of the women, and particularly that of a singer who is jealous of her. One of the men in the house—the only man successful from a worldly point of view—is Malcolm Gaskell, a newspaper editor. (Miss Crothers did not intend to be satiric.) The singer notes and broods over a resemblance to him in the face of the child, and puts the obvious construction upon it. Gradually— a little too gradually for dramatic purposes—the situation is forced. Gaskell is the first to suspect the gossip, believes that it does not concern him but only Miss Ware, and gives a great sigh of joy when she swears that the child is not hers. She tells how she took it from the dying mother and how from that day she has hated the father who let it come nameless into the world. But gradually the further revelation comes to both of them that Gaskell is the father. He does not so much ask forgiveness as he seems to demand it, or rather to expect it as a matter of course. But he does not get it. This may be a man's world, as he says, but Miss Ware cannot see it that way. Such is the main drift of the story: a long strain on coincidence, certainly, but carefully calculated to fit the thesis.

To sketch this skeleton, however, is only faintly to indicate the merit of Miss Crothers's drama. Her men, to be sure, did not always escape the charge of being dummies in trousers, but she filled her house of Bohemians with such truthful and appealing working women and set them in situations so admirably designed to bring out the pathos and social significance of their lot that they alone would make the play worth while. One of them, for instance, was a certain Clara Oaks. . . . Clara painted miniatures. She had come from the circles where daughters are supported in ease, but she was a poor relation, and, still further, had ideas of her own about supporting herself by "art." She was a weak and rather silly creature, plain of face and hopelessly without talent. The other artists gently "guyed" her through two acts. But in the third act, after she had held an exhibition of her work and nobody had come, she broke down, and there was no thought of "guying" any more. She became as pathetic a figure as the stage has seen in many a day. "I am one of those everlasting women," she wept, "that the world is full of, with nobody to take care of them, and who can't take care of themselves. I never had an offer of marriage. I'd marry anybody who would pay the bills. Any

little runt of a man can marry, and have a home and a family. Oh, oh, I want to be pretty and bad!" This poor little creature was painted so truthfully and played so poignantly by the actress that men and women alike in the audience were blinded by tears during her outbreak.

And so, later, when Miss Ware had explained to the jealous singer that Kiddie was not her child, and made the gossip believe it, the two of them discussed the peril of love and the power of man in words quite in keeping with their traits in the drama but also of penetrating insight and a kind of grim pathos. "You can't stir up any man's life," said the singer. "You're lucky if it looks right on top." And the novelist, the woman of dreams and theories, fought back the suggestion, till memory smote her of that resemblance of Kiddie to the man she loved. In some way unaccountable, that scene, as Miss Crothers has written it, seems far larger than the small room on the stage of the Comedy Theatre. Then and there these two characters speak indeed for themselves, but also for their sex. We may desire a more smooth, orderly and swift development of the narrative than Miss Crothers could compass, and a less strained plot, less warped to meet the requirements of the thesis, less obviously "doctored." We may condemn **"A Man's World"** pretty severely for these faults. But the fact remains that the play has something about it of passionate sincerity and feminine insight which redeems many faults and makes it significant, interesting, and at times deeply moving. (pp. 155-61)

Walter Prichard Eaton, "Miss Crothers Champions Her Sex," in his At the New Theatre and Others: The American Stage, Its Problems and Performances, 1908-1910, *Small, Maynard and Company Publishers, 1910, pp. 155-61.*

FRANCIS HACKETT (essay date 1916)

[*Hackett was a respected Irish-American biographer, novelist, and literary critic during the first half of the twentieth century. His reviews appeared in the* New Republic, *the* Saturday Review of Literature, *and other prominent American periodicals. In the following excerpt, originally published in the* New Republic *in 1916, Hackett reviews* Old Lady 31.]

It would be interesting to discover why Miss Rachel Crothers, who is a sensitive and knowing dramatist, decided to stoop to conquer. In spite of her stoop *Old Lady 31* is decidedly to be seen. From the point of view of a producer it is even quite courageous, but it makes concessions which, granting how intelligent Miss Crothers is, provoke a morbid curiosity.

Any one who has ever talked to a theatrical producer may imagine how *Old Lady 31* first hit that professional mind. Twelve old women on the stage for three acts, old women in the decrepitude of an old ladies' home. You can imagine this thought impinging on a Broadway mind. Nothing but old women—old women with their hair in nets, old women with high shell-combs, old women with shawls, old women with mittens, old women with caps—frumpy, toothless, deaf, quavering, senescent old things listening for the soundless footsteps of death. You may guess how this might strike a producer. Miss Crothers is an artist, with a strong sense of character. She could see it. But a producer! What do you see in the crystal, my dear? I see $42 in the house and ten old women on the stage. What do you see now, my dear? I seem to see twelve old women on the stage, and $18.75 in the house.

To produce *Old Lady 31* for Broadway was not considered possible until it was heavily "sugared up." After the fashion of sunshine biscuits and sunlight soap and sun-kist oranges, it was termed a "sunshine comedy," to begin with. That was undoubtedly supposed to remit some of the perils of asking Broadway to contemplate old age. It meant, in the sight of poverty and loneliness, the assurance of optimism which Broadway is supposed to crave. But the advertisement of optimism was not enough, the written bunkum of "wholesomeness" and sunshine. It had to be squirted into the play. And, in the prologue and also at the end, the syringe of sweetening was used.

The old couple Angie and Abe are leaving their sun-kist cottage—Angie to go to the old ladies' home, Abe to go to the poor farm. They have been married many, many years, but there are no children. "'Twan't to be." This is a real situation, one in which there is a great length of human retrospect, a definite pathos, a chance to reveal human nature and make the most of the drama to come. Well, Belasco couldn't have done a fouler deed. There was much excuse for the old lady's inevitable allusion to a lifetime of marriage without a single misunderstanding or a cross word. The couple next me held hands at this touching misrepresentation of intersexual experience, but I noticed he went out to smoke at the end of the first act and left her to boredom, just as usual. The rest of the prologue was a desperate effort to establish Angie's angelic character. She scrimped a little tobacco every day so that Abe might have a last smoke. "You beat all, mother." She regrets the poor auction at the end of their lifetime but rejoices that her old tea-strainer brought three cents more than it cost. Think of it, the good Lord letting fall that crumb of consolation. "Ain't the pansies sweet to-day? I'm out here talking things over with the pansies." Then a little sunshine philosophy. "That's what the pansies understand."

Few people know What Every Pansy Knows, of course, but is there anything more pestiferous in real life than these cooing human beings? Angie is to be the sweetest of old ladies. When she refers to her "bridal wreath" and blows a kiss to her old house, when she gives Abe a flower to press in his bible or plucks a bouquet for Abigail, she is to be the dearest old thing. It is a matter of scientific record, however, that mature women who live in the past to such degree as this, who hold conversation with the pansies at sixty and rejoice over a three-cent episode at an auction sale, are merely half-witted. If they had had less sentimentalism and more sense, there would have been absolutely no necessity for an auction. No sea-captain could have survived to old age with such a spouse. While he was at sea he might have gotten away with it. That is one of the attractions of life on the ocean wave. But if he had lived "to hum," as Miss Emma Dunn and Mr. Reginald Barlow so exultingly pronounced it, he would certainly have arisen one night while Angie slept, and tenderly extinguished her for ever under the tea-cosy, and then strode forth to take the good news to the sheriff.

So far *Old Lady 31* is sheer conformity to the professional idea of what Broadway wants. The minute we get to the old ladies' home, however, and have Miss Crothers reveal the human nature of the women in that home, there is that precious veracity which is bound to dominate a comedy audience. Louise Forsslund's book may have given Miss Crothers many pointers, but it is she alone who made possible for the stage the reality of these super-annuated types. The conventions of the stage required performers who were not actually as much "old ladies" as the title suggests. But this hardly interfered with one's sense of reality. One beheld, first, a rattlepate, spitfire, "gabby"

person rocking violently on the veranda, in conversation with an imposing and funereal doctor's widow, joined in a few minutes by a saturnine practical person, a Martha in a universe of Marys, a "grouch." Nothing could have been more humorous than this idiomatic talk on the veranda. It was soon enhanced by the addition of a coy, gurgling creature with Victorian curls. The kindliness with which these "inmates" were observed in all their foibles and sensitiveness and pettiness and magnanimity was not at all like the sentimentalism of the prologue. It had an artist's sagacity and penetration, and took the whole performance out of theatricality and back to the immense divertiveness of the world we know.

The pathos of the play is the separation of old Abe from Angie, at the door of the old ladies' home. Its inventiveness is shown in the successful revolutionary proposal to have a place made for Abe in the home, as *Old Lady 31*. Had Miss Crothers gone into the business of projecting this story without knowing and respecting her human material, it would have been a thin entertainment. But she had such a strong grasp of the characters she proposed to deal with that the new factor of a man in their communal life gave her just the chance she needed to exhibit their amusingness. Every kind of femininity comes out in the galvanizing presence of Abe, and every kind of masculinity is produced in Abe, and in the misogynistic Mike, by the presence of so many concentrating women. In all this part of *Old Lady 31,* the core of its drama, there are the qualities which make Miss Crothers a genuine contributor to American drama and America's capture of its own life.... [A] drama has been honestly placed in one of those neglected yet ramified areas of possibility which an integral group always provides, and not only has it been placed there with regard to its plausible occurrence but with regard to the fine interest of the group itself. By reason of her ability to appreciate such a group, to see its powerful interest regardless of the supposed needs of Broadway, Miss Crothers really equips herself extraordinarily to write genuine drama. And that one enjoys about *Old Lady 31.* But my enjoyment is marred by the stupid conventionality of the ending—Abe's windfall—and by the sunshine so assiduously poured in and about the character of Angie. Miss Crothers has integrity as a creator. It is worth fighting for, against Broadway and hell combined, and she has apparently not managed to plan for her integrity or to risk profit for it as much as she should. (pp. 221-25)

Francis Hackett, "Sunshine Comedy," in his Horizons: A Book of Criticism, *B. W. Huebsch, 1918, pp. 221-25.*

MARK VAN DOREN (essay date 1931)

[*Van Doren, the younger brother of Carl Van Doren, was one of America's most prolific and diverse writers of the twentieth century. His work includes poetry—for which he won the Pulitzer Prize in 1939—, novels, short stories, drama, criticism, social commentary, and the editing of a number of popular anthologies. He has written accomplished studies of Shakespeare, John Dryden, Nathaniel Hawthorne, and Henry David Thoreau, and served as the literary editor and film critic for the* Nation *during the 1920s and 1930s. Van Doren's criticism is aimed at the general reader, rather than the scholar or specialist, and is noted for its lively perception and wide interest. Like his poetry and fiction, his criticism consistently examines the inner, idealistic life of the individual. In the words of Carlos Baker, Van Doren brings to his best work "a warmth of epithet, a crisp precision of definition, and a luminousness of poetic insight." In the following excerpt, he reviews As Husbands Go.*]

The new comedy by Rachel Crothers, **"As Husbands Go"** . . . , will undoubtedly have the success that Miss Crothers usually has. It is full of clever lines, nice people, clear sentiments, and intelligent perceptions. But I fancy that it will go the way of its predecessors—out of the memory. Somehow or other the works of this gifted playwright are more ephemeral than they ought to be—or than they ought apparently to be, for the laws of forgetfulness are probably as just as they are inexorable. Pressed for a reason in the present case, I should perhaps say that Miss Crothers has everything a comic writer ought to have except a dash of madness in her laughter. She is too simply wise. She knows as much at the beginning of a play as she does at the end, and so the impression at the end is that she has done no more than work out certain details of truth. Her situation here is rich in possibilities, and it is easy to imagine a vulgar writer doing awful things with it. Two ladies of Iowa return from a summer in Paris during which they have fallen in love not only with Paris but with two European gentlemen. The gentlemen follow them home, and we are treated to the spectacle of Europe and America looking at each other. It is easy, as I have said, to imagine a vulgar writer taking sides. Miss Crothers does not take sides. But in the very levelness with which she scrutinizes the scene there is a lack of that passion which is quite as necessary in comedy as it is in tragedy, and which makes the best comedy one of the best things in the human world. (p. 338)

> *Mark Van Doren, "Barrie's Problem Play," in* The Nation, *Vol. CXXXII, No. 3429, March 25, 1931, pp. 336, 338.**

ARTHUR HOBSON QUINN (essay date 1936)

[*Quinn was an American educator, critic, and literary historian specializing in American drama. In the following excerpt from his highly acclaimed* History of the American Drama, *he surveys Crothers's early works.*]

It was only to be expected that the new spirit in drama would find its expression from the point of view of a woman. During the latter part of the Nineteenth Century, few women had followed the example of Mrs. Mowatt and Mrs. Howe, and those who did   need not detain us. They were usually romantic or farcical comedies and merely followed a mode of the time.

The work of Rachel Crothers, on the contrary, had from the beginning a quality of its own. Like Moody's, her plays have usually been a criticism of life, but unlike Moody she came to the drama not through the avenues of literature but through the definite training of the stage. She is, above all, a practical playwright, with a keen sense of what is theatrically effective. She directs her own plays and, with a feminine instinct for detail, presents a stage setting in which there is rarely a jarring note. Yet she has steadily declined to be merely entertaining, and in consequence her plays form a body of drama whose significance grows under inspection and whose unity of purpose becomes steadily more apparent. (p. 50)

Miss Crothers began her creative work with the writing and directing of one-act plays, and her first work to be professionally performed was a one-act comedy, **The Rector,** presented at the Madison Square Theatre in 1902. This is a treatment, with real insight, of a young clergyman who marries a pretty but not very practical girl, instead of the wife selected for him by his congregation. Her first long play, **The Three of Us** . . . , was laid in a mining camp in Nevada. If it is not as profound a study of the contrasted Eastern and Western types

as Moody gave us the same year in *The Great Divide,* it is a vivid and sympathetic presentation of a girl's character. Rhy MacChesney's determination to guide and protect her two younger brothers, even against their own ambitions and even at the risk of her own happiness, is appealing because it is carried out without heroics and because it celebrates the loyalty of thousands of women who, in the United States, play the dual rôle of sister and mother. But Rhy is not simply the self-immolating woman of European drama: she is also the head of the family and a woman of business. She is an active force, and when she has been put in a false position by giving her word to a clever schemer not to reveal certain information, she goes to his rooms at night and demands release from her promise. Much of the plot is conventional, it is true, but the characters are well drawn, and the preservation of the family of the MacChesneys kindles a responsive chord in anyone who sympathizes with youth fighting its battles against the world and its own inexperience.

The **Coming of Mrs. Patrick** . . . and **Myself Bettina** . . . showed no advance upon **The Three of Us,** but in her next play, **A Man's World** . . . , Miss Crothers produced one of the most significant dramas of the decade. With a few deft touches she establishes the atmosphere of a boarding house in lower New York. Around "Frank" Ware, a writer who is a woman of an independent but lovable nature, she places a well-drawn group of painters, writers and musicians, of whom Fritz Bahn, a violinist, Lione Brune, a singer, and Clara Oakes, a hapless miniature painter, are the most important. Frank Ware is bringing up "Kiddie," a boy of seven, whose mother had died in her house in Paris when the boy was born. Through her sympathy with this woman in her shame, Frank has become convinced that any scheme of things which permits the father of "Kiddie" to escape the consequences of his action is basically not fair, even if society has accepted the "double standard" of morality. So embittered is she that she fights against her growing love for Malcolm Gaskell, a vigorous personality who, unknown to himself and to her, is "Kiddie's" father. Miss Crothers's skill is shown in the way she makes every stroke count. In the second Act, laid in Clara's rooms, Lione, jealous of Fritz Bahn's love for Frank, points out in Clara's miniature of Kiddie his strong resemblance to Gaskell. It is a fine scene, in which is depicted the crystallization of rumor into suspicion. Moreover, Clara, the medium through which it is built up, is herself one of the best characters in the drama, and her outburst of grief at the failure of her pitiful exhibition and the uselessness of her life is truly pathetic, and made a deep impression on the stage. (pp. 51-2)

The height of the action comes in the third Act in two strong scenes. Lione tells Frank her belief in Gaskell's relation to Kiddie, and in the conversation of the two women Lione puts the conventional attitude clearly: "It's a man's world—that's the size of it. What's the use of knocking your head against things you can't change?" But Frank has a higher standard, and when Gaskell comes in to tell her he loves her, she questions him and finds he is really Kiddie's father. Skilfully Miss Crothers shifts the appeal from the general to the personal. Frank has been willing to love Gaskell without inquiring into his past. But when she finds out the truth she recoils. (p. 53)

Frank refuses to marry him, for she cannot make him see that he has committed any crime. To him, Kiddie's mother was an incident, and he runs true to form, being too honest to pretend to a remorse he does not feel. Miss Crothers had the courage to end her play logically, for Frank had been in love with an ideal of Gaskell rather than with Gaskell himself. *A Man's World* offers no solution for the situation it deplores, except the substitution of a career for a woman instead of the dependence upon marriage as her only resource. There is no railing at mankind, however, and it challenged Augustus Thomas' more profound analysis in his best play, *As a Man Thinks*, in which he definitely refers to *A Man's World*. It was not only her knowledge of feminine psychology that made the play important. When Fritz Bahn tells Lione, "Every woman keeps her own place in a man's heart," we realize that Miss Crothers knows both sides of the shield.

In *He and She*, . . . Miss Crothers dealt with a situation both modern and fundamental, the contest of husband and wife for supremacy and for the establishment of their respective spheres. Tom Herford and his wife Ann are both sculptors and have succeeded in keeping their professional and personal relations distinct until both enter an important competition. Her quick sympathy when she knows he has lost is sharply contrasted with his reaction when they learn a few moments later that Ann has won. He struggles bravely to rejoice with her, but he feels instinctively that her victory has brought about a crisis in their relations. Among the group gathered at their home to wait for the verdict, her father, his sister, and his assistant, Keith McKenzie, all show their disappointment, while the only one to rejoice is Ruth Creel, a representative of the girl who prefers her own career as an editor to the domination of the love of Keith. Then into this tense situation Millicent, the sixteen-year-old daughter of Tom and Ann, precipitates her love story with the chauffeur at her boarding school. This scene, in which Ann, with her heart full of the struggle between love and ambition, has to fight with all her skill to draw from Millicent the truth about her relations with the boy, is as quietly dramatic as anything Miss Crothers has done. Ann gives up her opportunity, although Tom tells her what will happen.

> *Tom:* You're cut up now—but if you should give this thing up—there'll be times when you'd eat your heart out to be at work on it—when the artist in you will *yell* to be let out. . . .

(pp. 53-5)

Miss Crothers reveals so sympathetically the man's point of view—that he must be the breadwinner and the head of the family, that the play on the stage secures the sympathy for Tom rather than Ann. . . . [The] dialogue is as fine as any she has written and her differentiation of the women like Ann and Ruth, as opposed to the domestic old-fashioned type like Daisy Herford, who frankly wants to be married, is complete. Perhaps the play is even yet ahead of its time, for the situation on which it is based does not occur as frequently as it undoubtedly will in the future. It was based, however, on an actual situation, in which the husband and wife were both skilled architects.

Ourselves . . . . is a powerful study of the responsibility which women of cultivation and refinement should assume for present moral conditions. Beatrice Barrington takes Molly from a reformatory into her own home and Molly develops an affair with Bob Barrington, Beatrice's brother. Molly delivers a curtain speech as she leaves the house of her benefactress:

> *Molly:* I'm goin' fast enough. I didn't ask to come. Lord knows I didn't want to. I don't know what you call good and bad—the way you see it—all I want is to get out. You happen to find out one little thing and act

like this when it's too late. Are you blind as bats? Don't you live in this world? Don't you know what is goin' on? If you feel like this about it, why don't you stop it? If this is the worst thing your men can do why do you let 'em? Why do you stand fer it and—and there wouldn't *be* any of us.

Young Wisdom . . . is a comedy dealing with an attempt at a trial marriage and the triumph of convention. In the same year she showed her versatility by writing a charming romantic comedy, *The Heart of Paddy Whack*, laid in Ireland about 1790. While the plot was conventional, Miss Crothers revealed her understanding of the imaginative quality in the Irish peasant, especially in the character of the boy Michael. In *Old Lady 31* . . . she took as a basis a novel by Louise Forsslund but enriched it by her additions. It is an appealing story of an old sea captain and his wife, who, through poor investments on his part, are brought to poverty. Rather than separate he secures admission to the Old Ladies' Home to which he has taken her and he becomes "Old Lady 31." The reaction of the women in the home, his rebellion and final capitulation and return, are dextrously managed to preserve the mellow fragrance of love in the twilight of two simple but gallant lives.

Miss Crothers's work was interrupted by her services as founder and president of the Stage Women's War Relief. But after a play, *Once Upon a Time*, hastily written for Chauncey Olcott and laid in a copper district in the Far West and in New York City, Miss Crothers wrote her striking comedy, *A Little Journey*. . . . It was not so much the unusual stage setting of the Pullman car, for that had been used before, but it was the natural way she made the various characters react to the situations. Julie Rutherford, a girl who has been brought up in luxury but is suddenly left with no alternative except a life with a distant brother who does not want her, loses her ticket and has to accept the help of Jim West, a Western type, who is much more real than the conventional cowboy so long in possession of the stage. Their rapidly growing love story is set against an amusing background of the various types which throng a sleeping car. The contrast of the first Act, with the characters' instinctive distrust of each other, and the second Act, with its note of temporary intimacy, is wrought in the spirit of true comedy. Then comes the sudden crash of an accident, and the lights go out. The third Act, on the hill top, in which the real natures of the characters emerge under stress, is a fitting conclusion. They do not all become heroic by any means, but the transition in Julie's nature is at least possible, and the assumption of half the group that the blow on her head has injured her reason is one of Miss Crothers's sure touches. In fact, the very skill with which the minor characters are drawn threatens to dwarf the interest of the main action, and this dramatic danger became more apparent in *39 East* . . . , in which one remembers much more clearly the boarding-house types than one does the love story which is intended to be the central motive.

After twenty years of playwriting, Miss Crothers showed the flexibility of her talent by treating with freshness and fidelity the problems of conduct presented by the younger generation after the war. The picture of Teddy Gloucester and her friends in *Nice People* . . . is accurate; we see vividly depicted the urge for pleasure at any cost and the shadow of boredom lurking over it all for the best of the group, while the others remain perfectly satisfied. The danger Teddy runs in her midnight escapade with Scottie Wilbur, both inflamed by liquor and passion, is indicated in a masterly scene in which the artistic reticence of the playwright scorns the details in which a Gorky or a Dreiser would have revelled. The polite unbelief of Teddy's friends in her story of the advent of Billy Wade and his midnight conversation with Teddy while Scottie lay in his drunken stupor on the couch, is also a clever touch. Miss Crothers does not make them all mere types—Eileen and Hallie are clearly differentiated; so are Trevor and Oliver. The defect with *Nice People* is that we cannot quite believe in Teddy's reformation, and her determination to give up the life she has lived and spend her days in the open air with Billy Wade is hardly convincing.

Nice People was a popular success; *Everyday* . . . was a failure, yet it was in some respects a more significant play. Miss Crothers laid the scene in the Middle West and depicted the rebellion of a girl who has been educated beyond the environment of her home and the tyranny of her father, who exercises a control over his wife almost beyond belief in this country. Yet the character of the mother . . . remains one of Miss Crothers's best creations. At the end the daughter goes out of the front door and leaves her mother to face her husband's wrath.

Undeterred by her failure in *Everyday*, Miss Crothers produced her sympathetic exposition of the present day youth in *Mary the Third*. . . . She shows us Mary the First in 1870 taking her mate by the lure of physical attraction; then she pictures Mary the Second in 1897 being taken by the man who among her lovers is the most insistent. And then, bringing these two women into the play as grandmother and mother, she reveals Mary the Third in 1923, mistress of a vocabulary that conceals nothing and with a determination to know the theory and practice of marriage, before which conventions fly. The periodic scenes are not mere preludes; every appeal to propriety from the horrified grandmother's lips sends the audience back to the memory of her conduct on the sofa in 1870! And the despair of the children when they overhear their father and mother strip their married life of its illusions is really a dramatic theme, which Miss Crothers published first as a one-act play. When the curtain fall on this second Act it seems impossible for the family life to go on, but Miss Crothers shows that the irresistible pressure of habit will bring the parents together again and that Mary the Third will choose her mate just as her mother did, because he needs her most—or she thinks he does. Human nature makes the ending of *Mary the Third* probable, but to call it a happy ending is to misunderstand a few essentials.

In 1924 Miss Crothers turned from the celebration and scrutiny of irrepressible youth to a satire of the cult of adult self-expression. As usual she was concerned not so much with novelty of plot, for the framework of *Expressing Willie* was not new. Minnie Whitcomb, a music teacher who comes from the Middle West, is a simple, natural girl. So is Mrs. Smith, who invites Minnie to visit her in order to counteract the influence upon Willie Smith, her son, of a group of ultra-modern people who live on the outskirts of art and of fashion. Willie has made money in tooth paste and his new friends are quite willing to share his hospitality and pretend that he is one of them. Modest despite his success in business, he stands in awe of them. But his mother, penetrating beneath their pretence, and desperate in her efforts to circumvent them, especially the widow Frances Sylvester, who has marked Willie for her own, sends for Minnie as a last hope. Minnie herself falls under their spell at first, but her love for Willie reacts in an unexpected way. Visiting him in his bedroom at night, she begs him in terms of the new psychology to express his real self and win Frances, the symbol

of all that is brilliant and desirable. When Frances herself arrives on the scene and Minnie takes refuge in the closet, it would seem as though Miss Crothers had deliberately chosen the most hopelessly ancient of devices to prove her originality. For the ensuing scene is high comedy and the artificial poseurs are routed by the alliance of a girl's unselfish love and a mother's shrewd wisdom, born of her devotion. Often have the love of a sweetheart and of a mother been pitted against each other on the stage. It remained for Miss Crothers to join them in a Holy Alliance against the powers of selfishness and pretence. . . . [To] Miss Crothers as playwright and director there rose from the critics who had been so often unaware of her achievement a veritable chorus of appreciation. How deft was her art can best be appreciated by a comparison of *Expressing Willie* with Booth Tarkington's *Country Cousin*.

In *A Lady's Virtue* . . . Miss Crothers produced a human and natural play, but was hampered by her yielding to the demands of the two actresses for whom the play was written. Her real interest lay in the character of the eternal courtesan, Madame Sisson, and her entrance into the Halstead family was delightful. But the part of Sally Halstead, the rather silly wife who has invited her to visit them, demanded more extended treatment than the plot would bear, and in consequence the playwright, yoking her wagon to two stars, failed to write a convincing play.

The first and the most lasting impression that the work of Rachel Crothers leaves is that of the craftsman. So easy is the flow of her dialogue that it is often unappreciated by the school of critics who are looking constantly for the unusual and the peculiar. Writing for a quarter of a century, she has had few stage failures, and to another school of critics this almost unvarying success seems suspicious. It must, they argue, be because of her acceptance of standards which have sent other playwrights to the wall. But meanwhile Miss Crothers has gone steadily about her own task, and has used the real talent that is hers for the entertainment of those who seek the playhouse for that purpose. It is talent rather than genius which is her portion and she is abundantly conscious of the fact. But instead of railing at conditions she cannot change, she has unfolded a panorama of characters and scenes which are aimed at audiences of intelligence who desire, however, no oversubtlety of motive or expression. So determined has she been not to become a "literary person" that it is remarkable how well her plays like *A Man's World, He and She,* or *Nice People* read in print. Without inventive power of the highest order, she is a keen observer of life, especially in the concrete, and her plays are filled with minor characters who indeed at times, notably in *39 East*, attract attention more easily than the major ones.

Her view of life is sane and progressive. She has a keen hatred for injustice and in her early plays, like *A Man's World* and *Ourselves*, she conducted a crusade for a more equitable adjustment of the claims of woman. Of late her ardor in this direction has cooled, and she has turned her scrutiny upon the failings of her own sex. With this diminution in intensity has come a greater subtlety, and a growth from the domestic comedy of *A Man's World* to the social comedy of *Expressing Willie*. This ability to progress, to keep abreast of the fashions of the theatre and the conditions of life, reveals the flexibility and adaptability which are her most characteristic traits. But the quality that lifts her work above the mass of modern playwriting is epitomized in a sentence in *Nice People:* "The vital things of character don't belong to anybody's day—they're eternal and fundamental." She has steadily declined to take the superficial currents of opinion seriously and she has in consequence been called conventional and conservative. But in the final judgment of the discriminating she will have her reward. (pp. 55-61)

Arthur Hobson Quinn, "Rachel Crothers and the Feminine Criticism of Life," in his A History of the American Drama, from the Civil War to the Present Day: Vol. II, 1936. Reprinted by Irving Publishers, Inc., 1979, pp. 50-61.

JOSEPH WOOD KRUTCH   (essay date 1937)

[*Krutch is widely regarded as one of America's most respected literary and drama critics. Noteworthy among his works are* The American Drama since 1918 *(1939), in which he analyzed the most important dramas of the 1920s and 1930s, and* "Modernism" in Modern Drama *(1953), in which he stressed the need for twentieth-century playwrights to infuse their works with traditional humanistic values. A conservative and idealistic thinker, he was a consistent proponent of human dignity and the preeminence of literary art. His literary criticism is characterized by such concerns: in* The Modern Temper *(1929) he argued that because scientific thought has denied human worth, tragedy had become obsolete, and in* The Measure of Man *(1954) he attacked modern culture for depriving humanity of the sense of individual responsibility necessary for making important decisions in an increasingly complex age. In the following excerpt, Krutch examines Crothers's dramatic technique in* Susan and God.]

Of Rachel Crothers we might say that if an Oxford movement had never existed it would have behooved her to invent one. In other words, that dubious religious awakening furnishes her with exactly the mild sort of problem she loves to treat, and she has not failed to seize the opportunity. An outbreak of emotional and complacent religiosity among the best people is in one respect like divorce in high places or the politer kinds of adultery. It poses, that is to say, a problem which is not exclusively one of morals or exclusively one of manners. It is difficult, indeed, to be quite sure where the one thing leaves off and the other begins, and consequently we can proceed as if there were no distinction at all which it is necessary to make. Of God's will as the subject of small talk at dinner one can say that it is blasphemous to begin with and, what is more, in doubtful taste. This, as a matter of fact, is precisely what, in substance, **"Susan and God"** . . . does say. God disapproves of such things, and so, when they recover from their surprise, will the best people.

If these remarks seem slightly condescending toward one of the most successful of living playwrights and toward a comedy which I should guess to be the first really substantial hit of the season, I can only reply that as far as they go they seem to me just, even if they do not tell the whole story. Miss Crothers does have a way of writing which frequently suggests a dramatization of one of the works of Mrs. Post. But she is also almost the only remaining composer of precisely the sort of thing which used to be called "a well-made play." We have plenty of skilful theatrical craftsmen of a different sort, but no one who can write in dramatic form exactly her kind of neat, careful, measured exposition and make it, while neither profound nor especially subtle, continuously if gently interesting as well as frequently witty.

The Susan at present in question is a spoiled and shallow woman who returns to her neglected husband and daughter, not because she intends to do her duty by them, but because dear Lady somebody or other in England has provided her with a new outlet for her egotism in the forms of a religion whose chief injunctions seem to be to confess and to meddle. The character is shrewdly drawn. . . . But I am not sure that the most amusing portrait is not really that of the awkward-age daughter, bursting with good health and defaced with spectacles and bridge work. At any rate that daughter is the occasion of the wittiest line of the play. She comes into her mother's bedroom proudly arrayed in a green chiffon negligee trimmed with fur, and she is crushed with the remark, "You look like a girl scout gone wrong." That has the sound of the ordinary wisecrack, but it is actually wit of a pretty high order for the simple reason that it expresses in the fewest possible words the essence of the incongruity in a situation which seems to the daughter herself thrilling and impressive.

Intellectually the great weakness of **"Susan and God"** is a last-act reformation for which nothing in the character of Susan has prepared anyone. In fact, every word she has uttered has tended to indicate that no possible conversion could be anything more than a conversion from one form of self-indulgence to another. Miss Crothers seems to have realized the difficulty and has tried to gloss it over by insisting that all the preparation for this sudden return to virtue and domesticity took place during the ten minutes between the second and third acts while the audience was in the lobby having its cigarette. The result is that while most of the play is a witty and not unpenetrating exposition of the character of a kind of rattle-brain to whom a fashionably exhibitionistic religion would make an irresistible appeal, the conclusion is neither more nor less than sloppy. But perhaps the author did not even expect us to take it seriously. (pp. 455-57)

Joseph Wood Krutch, "Religion in the Drawing-Room," in The Nation, Vol. 145, No. 17, October 23, 1937, pp. 455-57.*

ELEANOR FLEXNER   (essay date 1938)

[*Flexner has written widely on women in literature and politics. In the following excerpt, she discusses what she considers a decline in Crothers's artistry between 1909 and 1937.*]

Rachel Crothers has never found herself unable to keep in step with new trends in the theatre. For thirty-one years, with a few interruptions, she has been writing commercially successful plays and assimilating new manners and subject matter. Nevertheless, her work during the past two decades does not measure up to the promise of her earlier plays. By comparison with *A Man's World,* **When Ladies Meet** and **Susan and God** are unimpressive. Miss Crothers has come increasingly to sacrifice dramatic force and honesty of thought for sprightliness and well-turned phrases. In doing so she has followed a tendency which . . . is evident in the work of writers of comedy in general. More and more they have abdicated the realm of character development and conflict to toss back and forth ideas and arguments couched in witty speeches.

The measure of Miss Crothers' failure is best seen by examining *A Man's World,* which she wrote in 1909. While it is structurally a mass of devices which we now condemn as artificial and sentimental, it transcends hokum by the force of its ideas and the reality with which Miss Crothers invested her characters; she outdistanced the conventions of her craft in her thinking, and she embodied it in living human beings. She portrayed—remember, in the year 1909—a group of artists struggling for a precarious livelihood, in itself at that time a novel subject which she handled with directness and understanding, and she made her principal figure a woman bent on leading an independent life hampered by the conventions and gossip of a society which declared that if a woman wrote a good book it could be only because she got her ideas from a man or because she was in love. More important still, Miss Crothers tackled the question of the double standard more unequivocally and intelligently than it had yet been treated by an American dramatist, and—wonder of wonders—carried her thinking through to its logical conclusion despite the fact that it meant forfeiting the traditional reconciliation and happy ending.

A Man's World was followed by *He and She,* and *Ourselves,* both provocative pieces of work. Then suddenly came a series of sentimental, charming, and perfectly conventional character comedies: *The Heart of Paddy Whack, Old Lady 31, A Little Journey, 39 East,* coinciding with the war and postwar years when the general level of drama fell to a deplorable level. There were a few striking exceptions to the general rule— Augustus Thomas' *The Copperhead,* Jesse Lynch Williams' brilliant comedy, *Why Marry?*—and in Greenwich Village a young man was writing one-act plays about seamen, but the trend was away from realism, and Miss Crothers conformed.

During the season of 1919-20 came the first gun of a new dramatic revival: Eugene O'Neill's *Beyond the Horizon.* The following year there was nothing very iconoclastic about such offerings as *Rollo's Wild Oat* or *Just Suppose* or *The First Year* or *Enter Madame,* but there were also such novelties as *Miss Lulu Bett* and *The Emperor Jones* and Miss Crothers' *Nice People,* all radical departures in their several ways. Once again Miss Crothers was among the innovators.

And yet *Nice People,* by the standards of its time, is nothing like as forthright a play as *A Man's World* was in 1909. It is true that once again Miss Crothers has a significant theme: the conflict between the new moral standards of a postwar, jazz and booze-intoxicated younger generation and an older, more rigid code of behavior. She went even further, to examine the older generation's responsibility for the younger's warped sense of values. For you cannot, as Teddy Gloucester's aunt Margaret Rainsford points out, give a girl eighty dollars to throw away on one night's party, as well as three cars, a string of pearls, an allowance of twenty-four thousand dollars a year, and a small farm, and expect from her any great degree of self-restraint or seriousness.

But while Miss Crothers thus questions and evaluates the new standards and social relationships which followed the World War, her ideas are those which are to limit American comedy for the next decade. At one bound it has reached its apogee. Take the scene in which Mrs. Rainsford arraigns Teddy's smart, spoilt coterie of young people for their sins. One of them, Oliver Comstock, is congratulating Teddy on her courage in throwing up her old life and working on a farm instead:

> Oliver: It's a miracle, nothing less, what you've done.
>
> Teddy: Any of you could have done it if you had to.
>
> Mrs. Rainsford: Of course. You have more energy and daring and cleverness and intelligence for your age than any set of people in the world.
>
> Trevor: Mrs. Rainsford, I suspect you.

> Mrs. Rainsford: It's true, in spite of appearances. You have it all and you're throwing most of it away.
>
> Trevor: Am I included in this?
>
> Mrs. Rainsford: You haven't the faintest idea of your own importance.
>
> Teddy: You're not included in *that,* Trevor.
>
> Mrs. Rainsford: You're an institution—envied and limited—dreamed of and read about. In every city, every little town, all the way down, there's a set of you—and you might be an absolutely dynamic power for good.
>
> Oliver: Might be? What are we?
>
> Mrs. Rainsford: An equally great one for harm.

Miss Crothers is appealing here to the sense of responsibility, of *noblesse oblige,* of a privileged class, doubtless having in mind some such ideal as the British aristocracy and its tradition of "public service." Her inconsistency is that she has also gone to some pains to show that wealth is at the root of the evils she has been depicting—degeneration of values, lack of social responsibility. Such inconsistency recurs repeatedly in plays on the same subject: witness George Kelly's *Behold the Bridegroom,* Philip Barry's *Holiday* and *The Animal Kingdom,* S. N. Behrman's *Meteor* and *End of Summer.* All these writers apparently feel that if only the rich could be somewhat less rich, if along with their wealth they could develop ideals of frugality and abnegation, all would yet be well. They overlook the fact that the impulse towards wealth and the moral deterioration which accompanies it are indissolubly bound up with the primary motives of our social organism—profit, competition, *laissez faire,* and that one cannot distinguish between the end itself and the process which achieves it. It would be surprising if Teddy Gloucester and her friends were impelled by the sense of responsibility with which Mrs. Rainsford tries to imbue them; there is nothing in their background or in that of the parents who have accumulated the fortunes they now lavish on their children, to foster such a sense, excepting a superficial concept of charity and voluntary "social service" which provides a needed cushion of justification and self-righteousness to undue prosperity.

Thus Miss Crothers' social philosophy, and that of the majority of her contemporaries, amounts to nothing more than a code of breeding and good taste. Further they cannot go, for it would be flying in the face of values and ideals which they still personally accept and hold to be attainable, despite their profound dissatisfaction with certain phenomena which they observe and are totally unable to reconcile with their code of behavior.

In *Mary the Third* Miss Crothers was still dealing, however erratically, with a serious problem: the shifting moral code, specifically the question of divorce. She shows youth profoundly disquieted at the spectacle of its parents, who should provide it with a fixed code of moral values, trooping through the divorce courts. She shows the antagonism between youth experimenting with freedom in the search of more stable relationships, and an older generation trying to conceal its bankruptcy from its children. But her conclusions, even her line of reasoning, are lost in a jumble of bad craftsmanship inexcusable in a dramatist of her caliber and experience. Between 1925 and 1932 Miss Crothers confined herself to a series of comedies in which her talent for straight thinking and pungent characterization were less apparent than ever. Whether the milieu was a prosperous home in a Midwestern town, or New York Greenwich Village, or smart society at play on Long Island, her characters are pallid stencils of one another: the women lovely, alluring, smartly turned out "thoroughbreds," the men upstanding, affable American businessmen. One and all they are charming, commonplace, and completely lacking in individuality. In *When Ladies Meet,* however, we notice a very curious phenomenon. Like so many of her contemporaries, Miss Crothers has been forced to admit the fecklessness and bewilderment which have grown in certain circles of late years. This eventually leads the erstwhile author of *A Man's World* to an interesting position. Mary Howard is typical of Miss Crothers' latter-day heroines; she is beautiful, well groomed, and gracious. What interests us is her state of mind. Here is the successful, popular, intelligent, and *independent* woman who was the ideal of the first quarter of the century, obsessed with a horror of loneliness, with futility.

> Loneliness is something we can't help. If nothing comes that *completes* us—what can we do?— I haven't got anything that really *counts.* Nobody *belongs* to me—nobody whose very existence depends on me. I am completely and absolutely alone.

Jimmy Lee's verdict rings like a postscript from the unemancipated eighteen-nineties:

> Only a woman for a man—and a man for a woman—no matter how much of everything else we've got. It's true—and it's hell.

Thus the wheel is coming full circle. The modern woman who fought for and won the right to work on a basis of equality with men, the vote, moral as well as economic equality, a creative existence beyond the confines of her home, finds only dust and ashes now at the end of her struggle. Having broken her chains, fought with all her might and main *against being possessed,* dominated, owned by anything or anybody, she cries out herself for the possession of another human being, for someone to "belong" to her, someone "whose very existence depends on her." Here, obviously, is something different from emotional fulfillment as such. It is, of course a reversion with reservations. Feminine emancipation will not be completely discarded. Mary Howard will go on working, writing, no matter what ties she assumes. But this futility which she encounters at the end of her battle is a profoundly significant phenomenon today, and that it should emerge in the plays of that feminist among playwrights, Rachel Crothers, only makes it more so.

Miss Crothers has only twice attempted satire; neither time has she been completely successful, and in each case (fourteen years apart) she has almost duplicated her formula. In *Expressing Willie* . . . she ridiculed the current fad of seeing "greatness" in the most mediocre individuals and of cultivating the "expression" of that "greatness." Her mockery was delightful, and the device of allowing the sane and suppressed Minnie Whitcomb to triumph over her designing adversary by going her one better at "self-expression" and consequently emerging as a real personality, made for audience sympathy and hence good theatre. Yet *Expressing Willie* falls short of real satire because, unlike *Beggar on Horseback,* produced the same season, it never penetrates to the root of what it is mocking. Moreover, there is a dramatic contradiction in the fact that

if it had not been for the ridiculous fad we are laughing at, Minnie Whitcomb would never have asserted herself as she does, and hence the pursuit of "self-expression," if one is colorless and repressed, is apparently not quite as silly as Miss Crothers would have had us think. The dramatist is caught invalidating her own premise.

Precisely the same thing happens in *Susan and God* . . . , and once again lack of penetration blunts her satire. Susan Trexel and her husband are practically separated: Barrie is a drunkard, and Susan flits from one craze to another. Then she espouses "the new way to God"—a thinly veiled equivalent of Buchmanism—and sets about interfering in the lives of all her worldly friends with a view to reforming them. But her new gospel becomes a boomerang; her drunken husband overhears her saying that with God's help any man can make a fresh start. He demands not only God's help but hers, promising her the divorce she wants if he once breaks his word to stop drinking. Caught in the net of her own professions, she accepts the bargain, albeit unwillingly ("I wish I'd never heard of God!"). Actually it is affection for his daughter and the hope of winning back his wife's love which keep Barrie Trexel going straight until Susan herself realizes the extent of both her love and her obligations to her husband and child.

> I don't think God is something out there—to pray to. I think He's *here—in* us. And I don't believe He helps us one bit—till we dig and dig and dig—to get the rottenness out of us.

Now this is all very fine, but without her excursion into misguided piety Susan would in all probability never have acquired such insight. Yet Miss Crothers also shows us the less admirable results of "the new way to God"—hypocrisy, meddling, the evasion of immediate responsibilities for a "more glamorous mission." We are left of two minds as to whether it is thoroughly pernicious or admirable in its indirect results.

Her satire is further blunted by superficiality. Buchmanism is a spiritual and intellectual manifestation whose roots go deep into present-day life and whose implications are far-reaching. But Miss Crothers eschews any inquiry as to *why* it should take such hold among certain social groups, or mention of certain arresting recent developments in the movement, such as the endorsement, by some of its leaders, of fascist trends of thought. The only hint of more profound consideration is a remark by one of Susan's worldling friends:

> I don't think it makes much difference what it is as long as it's something to believe in or hang on to.

This is precisely the bankrupt frame of mind which leads, not only to Buchmanism but beyond it to more extreme ideologies, but Miss Crothers ignores or passes over the danger. The problem, as she sees it, is solely one of individual character, an approach which is certainly not that of the satirist, who must probe beyond the particular to the general. This ability Miss Crothers once possessed, and has now apparently lost. (pp. 239-48)

> *Eleanor Flexner, "Rachel Crothers," in her* American Playwrights, 1918-1938: The Theatre Retreats from Reality, *Simon & Schuster, 1938, pp. 239-48.*

JOSEPH MERSAND (essay date 1941)

[Mersand is an Austrian-born educator who has written and edited numerous works on American drama. In the following excerpt,

*he praises Crothers's dramatic skill and discusses her charac-
teristic themes.*]

Rachel Crothers has been writing successful plays for almost thirty-five years, which is a record unapproached in contemporary American drama. She has watched our drama grow and develop from the adolescent, diluted imitations of British and European successes to its world-acknowledged maturity. To that maturity she has made a significant contribution. Not only is she included in every history of the American drama, but some of her plays have found their way into anthologies, and she seems assured of her place in the pantheon of American dramatists. (p. 63)

Naturally, thirty-odd years at any profession or art would give anyone a certain degree of dexterity. Skill in dramatic craftsmanship Miss Crothers has shown since her first important play, *A Man's World*. . . . Few artists of our theatre know more about dramatic construction and technique. If Edith Wharton wrote a book on *The Art of Fiction*, would not an *Art of Drama* be welcome from Miss Crothers? Yet other distinctions are readily granted to her. Her understanding of the feminine character is unusually shrewd. All the great experts on the female of the species—W. L. George, John Erskine, John Langdon-Davies, Havelock Ellis, John Macy—could learn something from one of our most penetrating students of her own sex. And long before Clare Boothe shocked theatre-goers with her parasites of Park Avenue, Miss Crothers had delineated the predatory representatives of the species.

Since the greatness of any dramatist always depends on his insight into his characters and his ability to portray them so that the audience will accept them as living beings, it will readily be admitted that Miss Crothers is in the highest ranks of American dramatists. In the realm of ideas, too, she has revealed an unusually lucid mind, pointing out contemporary foibles and surveying critically our many imperfections. At a time when writers touched but hesitantly on such delicate subjects as the Double Standard, she wrote in *A Man's World* . . . , expressing an unusually bold viewpoint. Although her critics, like Eleanor Flexner in *American Playwrights, 1918-1938* [see excerpt dated 1938], may find fault with her ideas, they readily grant that she always has a clear idea and the power to present it so that all may understand it. In the realm of dramatic dialogue she has few peers and hardly any superiors. Her themes are always significant. A Crothers play is always built upon an idea that provokes extended discussion. Finally, she has demonstrated that the American drama can produce high comedy of the best traditional variety, that English drama has by no means a monopoly of that form, and that a play by an American can be a cultural experience while it entertains at the same time.

Her recent plays have been extremely successful, because she has insisted upon casting and participating in the direction. Her latest play, *Susan and God* . . . , was one of her greatest successes. Five years earlier, *When Ladies Meet* was given the kind of feminine reception which came later for Clare Boothe's *The Women*. *As Husbands Go* . . . and *Let Us Be Gay* . . . complete her hits of the past decade.

What does she like to write about? There are a few subjects which interest her very much. There are some themes which captivated dramatists of the past decade, which one will never find in a Crothers play. Social Significance, which seemed to be the be-all and end-all of the decade of the Thirties passed her by. With the wisdom she has exhibited from her earliest plays, she knew that social systems and ideologies come and go, but the ways of the human heart will always be dramatic material. Marriage, Divorce, Infidelity, Young Love, Psychoanalysis, the Double Standard, these are some of the topics that have interested her. It would be platitudinous to say that she is interested primarily in men and women as they are adjusted or maladjusted, usually in married life. Her characters are usually well-bred, well-read, and well-to-do. One cannot recall easily a poor person or a boor in all her plays. One will always find sparkling conversation that is always stimulating and quotable. Sometimes, as in *When Ladies Meet*, there are so many *bon mots* that few are remembered.

Although Miss Crothers has probably never formulated her theories of the functions and provinces of a dramatist, it is not difficult to perceive certain unifying threads which run throughout her plays. She is, for example, a critic of social behaviour. She follows the Ibsenian tradition in her early plays, such as *A Man's World*, which attacks a double standard of moral conduct. She dislikes the weaknesses of her own sex, whether it is their conceit, as in *Susan and God*; belated ideas of romance, as in *As Husbands Go*; false ideas of a career, as in *He and She*. She is for old-fashioned love as against cooked-up romance. She is for moderation in the younger generation. She thinks that a woman who makes a good wife has enough of a career to be satisfied.

Her plays of the last decade were all successful on the stage and are very readable. In *Susan and God* she satirized a flighty, affected American wife who left her dipsomaniac husband and went to England. There she imbibed a strong dose of person-

Rachel Crothers. Photo courtesy of the Billy Rose Theatre Collection, The New York Public Library at Lincoln Center, Astor, Lenox and Tilden Foundations.

alized religion in the Buchmanian vein and returned to America determined to convert her friends. When her husband begs her to save him, she consents hesitatingly, and discovers that she can live with him again, and preserve the household for her daughter's sake. The portrait was not too flattering, but it was vivid. . . . (pp. 64-7)

The problem of erring husbands is treated in **When Ladies Meet,** in which a philandering husband is confronted at last by his loyal wife and his newest flame, only to prove inadequate to either of them. In **Let Us Be Gay** and in **As Husbands Go** Miss Crothers turns the tables and criticizes the errant wives. In **Expressing Willie** . . . she pokes fun at the then widely discussed theory of psychoanalysis. In **Nice People** . . . she takes the younger generation to task for their post-war indiscretions. Thus it is seen that there is not a very wide range of subject matter in Miss Crothers' plays. One recalls Sir Walter Scott's remark about Jane Austen: "She possessed the exquisite touch which renders commonplace things interesting."

Perhaps marriage and divorce and infidelity are commonplace, particularly now when one out of every six marriages ends in divorce, but who of us has the right to say that there are subjects more vital than these? Take for example the many plays of social significance which were written in the Thirties. They were going to produce a new order in the theatre, in the social and economic systems, in the human heart. Have they succeeded in any way? Miss Crothers made no effort to move mountains. In fact she was quite content to move the human heart. At a time when most American dramatists were too weak to stand on their own feet she wrote as strong and as courageous a play as our drama had known up to 1909. During 1910-1920 when O'Neill was only beginning to write his one-acters, and before he had even seen his *Beyond the Horizon;* when Maxwell Anderson, Philip Barry, Robert Sherwood, were still in college; when Clifford Odets was only in high school, Rachel Crothers was writing with skill, good taste, and humor. In the last decade, when there was much tumult and shouting, all of which has already died, she persevered in her long-established manner, adding one popular success to another, finally **Susan and God,** in which all her strength and her few weaknesses were revealed.

Hardly any contemporary who wrote in the first decade of this century is active today. Is it not amazing that Miss Crothers' thirtieth play should be witnessed by the children of those young men and women who were thrilled by **A Man's World**? Her many admirers look forward expectantly to her newest play, knowing in advance that it will treat of the eternal verities with lucidity and with balance, with wit and with wisdom, with superb technical skill and yet with a naturalness which simulates life. Perhaps the most significant contribution from the point of view of longevity and consistency of effort to the American drama of our time has been made by Rachel Crothers. (pp. 67-9)

> *Joseph Mersand, "Rachel Crothers: First Lady among the Dramatists," in his* The Play's the Thing, *1941. Reprint by Kennikat Press, Inc., 1965, pp. 63-9.*

EDMOND M. GAGEY (essay date 1947)

[*In the following excerpt, Gagey discusses Crothers's later works.*]

No one was more skillful at straddling the current moral issues than Rachel Crothers, a prolific writer of sentimental and problem comedies. A keen and sagacious playwright, Miss Crothers

in her long and successful career showed an unerring gift for selecting a timely subject, treating it with apparent daring, properly diluted with sentimentality, and ending with the conventional—or at least the matinee audience—viewpoint. *Nice People* . . . represents one of her typical contributions to the drama of flaming youth. Teddy Gloucester, daughter of a Park Avenue millionaire, practices all the vices of the younger set—smokes, drinks, wears revealing evening dresses, and talks about sex. All this is profoundly disturbing to Teddy's aunt (the girl's mother is dead), who deplores "the emptiness—the soullessness of it all." When Teddy's father forbids her to keep a midnight date with Scottie Wilbur, man-about-town and expert dancer, she goes off to meet him anyway. The two eventually reach the Gloucester summer cottage on Long Island, with Scottie both bibulous and amorous and a big storm coming up. Teddy's reputation is saved, after a fashion, by the arrival of Billy Wade, an upright young stranger, who obligingly sleeps downstairs with Scottie while Teddy retires upstairs. Next morning Billy Wade departs and when Teddy's father and members of her fast set come in, they assume the worst. In a few hours the scandal has incredibly spread all over New York and Teddy has refused to marry Scottie, who is willing to do the right thing. Now honest Billy Wade reappears; in an unexpected bucolic twist Rachel Crothers has him and Teddy decide to turn the summer place into a farm. In the third act the reformed Teddy has become the ideal farm girl, devoted to her chickens and the mending of Billy's socks, but it is only with the greatest effort that she persuades the prim hero to marry her. He objects to her money. (pp. 188-89)

In 1923 Rachel Crothers returned to the flapper in **Mary the Third,** a considerably better play which shows the courtship of three generations of Marys. The youngest Mary, frank and modern, goes on an unchaperoned camping trip with another girl and three young men—two of them her suitors. She wants to find out what these boys are really like before rather than after marriage. Evading the issue as usual, the author has Mary suddenly feel her parents were right in forbidding the trip; she therefore pretends an attack of appendicitis. On the way home she accepts one of the suitors. Now unfortunately Mary and her brother overhear their parents quarreling and are shocked at the apparent hate between them. The children insist on a divorce and call their mother a kept woman because she is financially dependent on her husband. Mary also decides she will live with her fiancé in sin rather than wedlock, having discovered the horrors and hypocrisies of a respectable union. The parents separate temporarily, but when Mary sees how much her opinionated father really loves his wife, though he won't admit it, she sends him back to her and accepts her own suitor in marriage. The final scene parallels the words of the proposals to Mary the first and Mary the second, her mother and her grandmother, which are given in the play's two introductory scenes. Thus each Mary gets her man, though the methods may be different, and each feels hers will be the only lasting marriage in the world. While Miss Crothers played safe in her treatment of the flapper and free love, the play was moderately daring for its time and had the advantage of many amusing lines. (pp. 189-90)

Another Crothers play, **As Husband Go** . . . , came at a time when American matrons from the Middle West were making frequent pilgrimages to Europe. It takes occasion to contrast foreign men—attractive and romantic but frankly fortune-hunting—with the stodgy, dependable American husband, to the latter's glorification. With customary shrewdness the author makes the foreigners credible and not unsympathetic. Using the same formula of discussing a marital problem from a feminine angle with a seasoning of sentimentality, Miss Crothers in *When Ladies Meet* . . . contrives a meeting between wife and mistress in which the two women have an opportunity to understand each other's point of view, to the natural discomfiture of the husband. These two plays were interesting and workmanlike, but it was not until 1937, after more than thirty years of Broadway playwriting, that Rachel Crothers produced her finest work to date—*Susan and God*. Here, in spite of her usual conventional and not too convincing ending, she has a sound situation and excellent satire. To her fast and fashionable set in the country Susan Trexel—chic, attractive, gushing—returns from a long stay in England where she has been converted to Lady Wiggam's movement (not unlike the Oxford movement). Lady Wiggam has found God, says Susan, in a new way. It isn't necessary to change one's faith. "You can keep right on being what you *are*—an Episcopalian—or Ethiopian—or Catholic or Jew—or colored—or *anything*. It's just love—love—*love*—for other people—*not* for yourself." You need only to be "God-conscious" and have the courage to confess your sins publicly. For all her religious fervor Susan has had no thought since her return for her unhappy, inebriated husband Barrie and even less for her fifteen-year-old daughter Blossom, who has had practically no home but school, and whose only desire is not to be sent away again to camp ("If I get any more healthy, I'll die!") but to spend at least one summer with both her parents. Susan's friends decide to cure her of her evangelical fad by having one of them pretend conversion and make a ridiculous public confession. The deception begins successfully, but as Susan warms up to her subject Barrie and Blossom wander in unexpectedly. The husband, somewhat drunk, takes Susan's words about reformation seriously, and trapped by her own eloquence Susan cannot back out. The result is that she agrees not to divorce Barrie, as planned, but to spend the entire summer with him and Blossom at their country home. If he touches liquor during this time he must grant her the divorce she wants, and she also makes it clear they will live together merely as friends. Blossom is overjoyed, but the prospects are dreary to Susan. "I wish I'd never *heard* of God," she complains. Barrie lives up to all conditions and Blossom is deliriously happy, but by late August the husband finally realizes Susan's complete selfishness and the fact that she is through with him, drunk or sober. He then disappears on a two-day drinking bout, allowing Susan time to think matters over. The play ends—somewhat illogically in view of Susan's character—with complete reconciliation. . . . The satirical slant was a welcome change from Miss Crothers' normal sentimentality, though the play obviously is not without sentiment. (pp. 194-96)

> *Edmond M. Gagey, "Comedy—American Plan," in his* Revolution in American Drama, *Columbia University Press, 1947, pp. 175-231.**

YVONNE B. SHAFER (essay date 1974)

[*In the following excerpt, Shafer examines the feminist viewpoint presented in Crothers's works.*]

Considering the number of women writing for the American stage from Revolutionary times onward, it is surprising that a play advocating women's liberation didn't appear earlier. . . . The first woman playwright to deal with the subject was Rachel Crothers, and her plays were written with a "feminist viewpoint" and considered "in the vanguard of public opinion." (p. 95)

In *A Man's World,* as in many of her plays, the leading figure is an attractive, successful woman who feels a conflict between her career and romance. The woman in this case writes novels under the name Frank Ware, and has a great sympathy for women who encounter difficulties in the world, particularly women who have had romances, and possibly illegitimate children, and are considered "fallen women" by society. She is raising a child whose mother suffered in this way, and has a deep hatred for the unknown father. Although she is drawn to her publisher, Gaspell, she is not certain that she really knows him. She finds out that he is the father of the child, and in a very dramatic scene the differences in their moral outlooks are brought out, and they part. Gaskell admits he wouldn't marry her if she had been the child's unwed mother, but thinks she should marry him although he was the father. Condemning her outlooks and her writing, he says,

> Why this is a man's world. Women'll never change anything. . . . Women are only meant to be loved—and men have got to take care of them. That's the whole business. You'll acknowledge it someday—when you do love somebody.

Miss Crothers' criticism of the "double standard" made an impact on the public and prompted Augustus Thomas to write *As a Man Thinks* . . . as a conservative response to feminists. *A Man's World* established Miss Crothers as the chief spokesman for women in the theatre, a role which she maintained throughout the 20's and the 30's, although women's liberation was not always the central aspect of her plays. Despite the polemic quality of her plays, she was quite successful. Barrett Clark wrote,

> She was not a woman with a grievance who expected the public to condone poor play writing because her cause was just, but a skilled dramatist who knew that the best cause in the world could not be effectively pleaded unless the means of presenting it were acceptable to playgoers. Throughout her career . . . she has consistently borne in mind that though the theatre can be used to persuade, its function is not primarily hortatory.

Clark's point is demonstrated by the many amusing comedies Miss Crothers wrote which furnished vehicles for actresses such as Spring Byington and Gertrude Lawrence. These comedies frequently center around the difficulties of marriage. *Mary the Third* has an amusing structure, delightful staging, and some telling satire on women, along with sympathy for their problems. The first two scenes show a girl deciding to marry after being courted on a sofa which is in a sharp spot of light center stage. The first scene is in 1870 and the girl, Mary, is the mother of the second girl seen in 1897. Act I focuses on the third Mary (the grandchild of the first) and her conflicts with her mother and grandmother over morals and marriage. She would like to go camping for a couple of weeks with two young men she likes in order to see which one would make the best husband. She actually sets out on the trip in a speeding auto but secretly returns and discovers how unhappy her mother's marriage has been. Vowing that her life will be different from the first two Marys, she idealistically declaims,

> I shall have my own money. I'll *make* it. I shall live with a man because I love him and only as long as I love him. I shall be able to take

CROTHERS

TWENTIETH-CENTURY LITERARY CRITICISM, Vol. 19

care of myself and my children if necessary. Anything else gives the man a horrible advantage, of course. It makes the woman a kept woman. . . .

Despite this determination to be different, Mary the Third does just as her mother and grandmother did—she surrenders to the passion of the moment, and agrees to marry an attractive man in the usual "old blind accidental lottery."

Let Us Be Gay . . . again treats the problem of the double standard, but in a comic mood. A weekend in the country brings together several couples. A young girl and her fiance run into difficulties when they discuss morality, as she thinks she should widen her experiences before she settles down with one man. He objects strenuously, and presents the same idea that other men voice in Miss Crothers' plays:

> Bruce: When a man wants to marry—pick out a mother for his children, he wants the straightest, finest, cleanest thing in the world.
>
> Deidre: And if a girl wants the darling boy she marries to be the same thing—where the hell is she going to find him?
>
> Bruce: It's not the same thing at all for you and me.

The central figure is Kitty, who meets the husband she left when he had an affair with another woman. She has established a career for herself, and has tried to lead a gay, frivolous life to find out "What it was all about—to see why you did it." Now she is happy to go back to the stability of marriage although she certainly doesn't think it is perfect. It is interesting that she admits she has had affairs, and that the husband is still happy to get her back. Twenty years earlier in a similar situation in Pinero's *Mid-Channel* the wife was rejected and committed suicide.

The action in *When Ladies Meet* . . . builds to a fine scene between a publisher's wife and an attractive woman writer, the latest of a series of women her husband has promised to marry when he gets a divorce. Neither the wife nor the writer, Mary, realize who the other woman is, and the discussion of marriage, promiscuity, and other matters is frank, interesting, and amusing. One idea which certainly must have been ahead of its time was that women weren't really to be rejected by potential husbands if they weren't virgins. The publisher's wife says,

> Don't you think if a man *knows* in the first place a woman has had other men—if he loves her he doesn't give a damn—he just does? And if it's the real thing he wants to marry her. Why not?

When the ladies each realize who the other is, the play moves to a darker mood, and ends with another condemnation of the double standard. The wife realizes the other women were not tramps as she had always thought, but sympathetic, intelligent women like Mary, who also suffered from her husband's selfishness. Although she has condoned her husband's affairs for years, she now rejects him, and Mary, realizing her romance wasn't the unique, idealistic experience she had imagined, does the same.

Perhaps Miss Crothers' pessimistic appraisal of the difficulties faced by a career woman reflects her own experiences. The only play in which a woman tries to maintain a career and a marriage ends with a compromise between herself and her

husband which can hardly be called a happy ending. *He and She* . . . presents the difficulties of Ann and Tom Herford, both sculptors, and the problems which arise when they compete for a commission and she wins. Ann's father, husband, and friends (except another career woman) seem to think she has done something really rotten in competing and winning. In the end, problems with their child make her decide to devote her full attention to the girl and to ask the husband to execute her design. The ending seems weak since the problem of the child is somewhat contrived, and the outcome is ultimately unsatisfactory to everyone except the already spoiled daughter. Nonetheless, the dialogue is interesting and forcefully presents the point of view of the woman who wants a career. As in all Miss Crothers' plays, the minor characters are well developed, and help present all the points of view in the situation.

Rachel Crothers wrote almost thirty full-length plays, which were generally successful. Although there are some elements in them which are dated, many of them would play well today. She excelled as an actress, playwright, and director, and contributed to women's rights both by her life and her plays. (pp. 95-7)

> Yvonne B. Shafer, "The Liberated Woman in American Plays of the Past," in Players Magazine, *Vol. 49, Nos. 3 & 4, February-March & April-May, 1974, pp. 95-100.*

LOIS C. GOTTLIEB (essay date 1975)

[*Gottlieb is an American critic and educator whose works include the only book-length critical study of Crothers to date. In the following excerpt, she examines Crothers's treatment in* The Three of Us *of the dual standards of male and female morality prevalent in early twentieth-century America.*]

A Nevada mining camp in Crothers' *The Three of Us* is the appropriate setting for an unwomanly woman to be free of the restricting and artificial codes of behavior imposed on young ladies in the East. The woman, Rhy MacChesney, is twenty-five, single and the head of a household composed of two younger brothers. Rhy has kept the family surviving since the death of their father and mother almost ten years ago, but her funds are now running low. The author's stage directions emphasize the qualities in Rhy that have enabled her to keep the family together against great odds for such a long time: ". . . forceful and fearless as a young Amazon, with the courage of belief in herself, the audacity and innocence of youth which has never known anything but freedom—. . . . What she wears is very far from the fashion but has charm and individuality and leaves her free and unconscious of her strength and beauty as an animal." . . . Rhy explicitly rejects an image of woman which requires timid, passive behavior, fashionably impractical dress and coquettish relations with men because it would interfere with her life in the West.

She even rejects that staple of androcentric culture, the double standard. Crothers introduces the old situation of a woman discovered in distinctly compromising circumstances: she is unchaperoned in a man's room late at night. Crothers then manipulates this situation so that we question the assumptions beneath the negative moral judgment invariably drawn against the woman in order to see that the man might be condemned more justly.

An accumulation of accidents, secrets and eavesdropping causes Rhy to make an unchaperoned midnight visit to the home of Berresford, a wealthy unscrupulous and heretofore unsuccessful bidder for Rhy's favors. He tries to take advantage of her call. When Rhy rebuffs his advances, he informs her that she will have to become his mistress; her honor obviously has been compromised by her visit. Rhy has always believed that the double standard protected the honor of a "good" woman. She insists that only a worm like Berresford would use it to harm her. Then Townley, her poor but honest suitor, barges in, and he puts the inevitably negative judgment on Rhy's honor. Rhy is now caught between the crossfire of a bad man who uses the double standard to hold her in control for *his* benefit, and a good man who uses the double standard to hold her in control for *her* benefit—to keep her honor unstained. Rhy's patience with this dispute over her honor soon is exhausted, and she deflates the protective postures of both men: "Don't you dare to say you'll 'take care of it.' My honor! Do you think it's in your hands? It's in my own and I'll take care of it." . . .

Although Rhy asserts her independence from the double standard in this case, she continues to be limited by some of its restrictions. For example, she is unable to overcome the weakness ascribed to her sex when the situation involves Clem, the older of her two brothers. Clem is tired of being poor and under the domination of a woman. Rhy sees that he is headed for trouble, but she can not stop it. As she says, "He needs a man! I *am* womanish—but I try not to be." . . . The qualities of strength and perseverance which Clem admires in men are there in Rhy, but neither of them acknowledges her strength as effective in the family situation because she is a woman.

Rhy finally resolves her problems with Clem by providing him with the means to achieve manhood: defense of her honor and a male at the head of the family. In the first instance Rhy convinces Clem that she fears for her reputation because of the incident at Berresford's. Clem rises to this manly occasion and is punched in the eye defending Rhy's honor. In the second instance, Rhy and Townley plan to marry. There is little attempt to cover Rhy's domestic intention. Referring to Clem, she tells Townley in her "romantic" curtain line: "We must make a good man of him. I have you to help me." . . .

It is tempting to suggest that Crothers is using the double standard ironically. She shows us clearly that one of its functions is to assure even the most helpless man that someone is weaker than he is. But what today's reader discerns as irony, contemporary observers of the play declared "wholesome" and "heartwarming." The commentators who noted Rhy's criticism of the double standard saw no contradiction in her final action. Instead, they hailed Rhy's "womanly" nature as quick to respond to her brother's needs. Rhy's independence and energy have threatened the double standard only temporarily. These unfeminine qualities are eventually channeled into a socially acceptable outlet for woman, the family; and the strain on male-female relations is reduced. (pp. 443-45)

> Lois C. Gottlieb, "The Double Standard Debate in Early 20th-Century American Drama," in The Michigan Academician, *Vol. 7, No. 4, Spring, 1975, pp. 441-52.**

CYNTHIA SUTHERLAND (essay date 1978)

[*In the following excerpt, Sutherland examines how Crothers's dramas reflect the changing attitudes toward women between 1909 and 1932.*]

Ibsen's Nora shut the door of her "doll's house" in 1879. Among the generation of American women born in the 1870's

and 1880's, Zona Gale, Zoe Akins, and Susan Glaspell all won Pulitzer Prizes. Rachel Crothers, the successful dramatist who wrote more than three dozen plays, characterized her own work as "a sort of Comédie Humaine de la Femme." In an interview in 1931 she said: "With few exceptions, every one of my plays has been a social attitude toward women at the moment I wrote it. . . . I [do not] go out stalking the footsteps of women's progress. It is something that comes to me subconsciously. I may say that I sense the trend even before I have hearsay or direct knowledge of it." During the period in which most American playwrights confined their work to representations of the middle class, these women were distinctive because they created principal roles for female characters whose rhetoric thinly veiled a sense of uneasiness with what Eva Figes and others more recently have called "patriarchal attitudes." (p. 319)

Glaspell, Akins, Gale, and Crothers chronicled the increasingly noticeable effects of free love, trial marriage, the "double standard," career, divorce, and war on women's lives. Public rhetoric generally subsumed private sexual rhetoric in the theatre during this period, and dramatic discourse tended to mediate conflicting views of women's "legitimate" place in society more often than it intensified dispute. Although the sector of life subtended by domesticity was being steadily decreased by technological and economic developments in the early years of the century, feminist leaders, artists, and housewives shared the common inability to suggest an alternative social structure through which discontent might be alleviated. To the extent that female characters on the stage accepted the traditional sex role, a diminished state of consciousness manifested itself in language that avoided strong or forceful statements, evinced conformity, consisted of euphemism and question-begging, and celebrated the processes which safely domesticated erotic pleasure. (p. 320)

However, during the period before the thirty-sixth state ratified the Nineteenth Amendment in 1920, a significant number of plays did present exceptionally articulate female artists as figures incarnating the dilemma of people torn by the conflicting demands of sex role and career. In *A Man's World* . . . , Rachel Crothers's protagonist Frank Ware is a novelist who oversees a club for girls who "need another chance." She has published anonymously a defense of women's rights which even her friends—themselves painters, writers, and musicians—agree is much too good to have been written by a woman. After accidentally discovering that her fiancé, Malcolm Gaskell, has fathered her adopted seven-year-old son (the deserted mother had been her friend and died in childbirth), she renounces him. Avoiding a facile reconciliation, Crothers chose rather to stress Frank's abhorrence of her lover's complacent refusal to acknowledge responsibility for the deplorable consequences of his own sexual license. In the final curtain scene, their relationship is abruptly severed:

> Frank: Oh, I want to forgive you. . . . tell me you know it was wrong—that you'd give your life to make it right. Say that you know this thing is a crime.
>
> Gaskell: No! Don't try to hold me to account by a standard that doesn't exist. Don't measure me by your theories. If you love me you'll stand on that and forget everything else.
>
> Frank: I can't. I can't.

In *He and She* . . . , Crothers again explored the dilemma of a woman who must decide between sex role and career, in this instance, motherhood or sculpting. Ann Herford surrenders the commission she has won in a national competition to her husband, Tom, who has been openly skeptical that his wife could do "anything for a scheme as big" as the project required for the contest. When he wins only the second prize, his ego is badly shaken, and he retrenches to the familiar rhetorical stance of chief breadwinner. Reconciliation comes only after Ann abandons her prize in response to the needs of her teenage daughter. Crothers, although she shows a woman conceding final "victory" to her primary sex role, allows her character to voice bitterness and disappointment:

> Tom: . . . you've not only beaten me—you've won over the biggest men in the field—with your own brain and your own hands; in a fair, fine hard fight. . . . there'll be times when you['ll] eat your heart out to be at work on it—when the artist in you will *yell* to be let out.
>
> Ann: I know. . . . And I'll hate you because you're doing it—and I'll hate myself because I gave it up—and I'll almost—hate—her . . . my heart has almost burst with pride—not so much that *I* had done it—but for all women. . . . then the door opened—and Millicent [their daughter] came in. There isn't any choice Tom—she's part of my body—part of my soul.

Ann's uneasy capitulation to the obligations of motherhood is carefully orchestrated by the simplistic attitudes of two women who are in love with her husband's close friend, a partially caricatured "male chauvinist" hard-liner; one woman accepts a promotion in her job rather than tolerate what she views as his suffocating demands, the other chases him because she believes that "all the brains a woman's got [are]—to make a home—to bring up children—and to keep a man's love." That Tom and Ann might exchange roles, he taking over as parent temporarily while she carves her frieze, is outside the realm of dramatic choice, because, in Crothers's dialectical structure, the men and women are shown to be incapable of conceiving this as an alternative. General expectations that a shift towards a more egalitarian society would lead to personal and social enfranchisement in the progressive era as middle-class women moved in the direction of greater self-consciousness are clearly undercut in the endings of Crothers's plays. (pp. 321-22)

After World War I and the extension of the franchise, the momentum towards fully equal status for women slowed considerably. One of Rachel Crothers's characters sees herself as an exception to what was to become an increasingly regressive trend: "I haven't slipped back one inch since the war. Most women who sort of rose to something then have slumped into themselves again, but I've gone *on*. My life gets much fuller and wider all the time. There's no room for men. Why, *why* should I give up my own personal life—or let it be changed in the slightest degree for a man?" But the woman who speaks these somewhat fatuous lines will, during the course of the dramatic action, reveal her disingenuousness by seducing a member of the British upper class so that her "personal life" and career are, in fact, exchanged for marriage. (p. 325)

The plays that Crothers wrote in the 1920's signal her own ambivalence toward the contrived stance of young women whose gold-plated philosophy was an amalgam of "free-thinking" writers like Ellen Key, Mona Cairn, Havelock and Edith Ellis. Like Congreve's Millamant, they were choosing to "dwindle into a wife" rather than persevere in a search for practical alternatives. Crothers's formulaic plot for flappers continued to have the staple elements described by Clara Claibourne Park in her study of the young women in Shakespeare's comedies: "Invent a girl of charm and intellect; allow her ego a brief premarital flourishing; make clear that it is soon to subside into voluntarily-assumed subordination; make sure that it is mediated by love." But Crothers's perspective is ironic, because she juxtaposes romantic courtship and the harsh antagonisms that often grow between marriage partners. The plays she wrote during these years strongly emphasized deteriorating sexual relationships over a period of time, thus undermining the power of the traditional plot to sustain communal custom through ritual reenactment. In *Mary the Third* . . . , the playwright presented three generations of women in the throes of choosing mates. The grandmother, Mary the First, traps a mate with flirtation in 1870; the mother, Mary the Second, yields to the proposal of her most vigorous but most unsuitable lover in 1897. These two women are seen as mere anachronisms by Mary the Third, in 1923, who fecklessly flaunts convention by insisting that she will choose her mate only after going off to the country on an experimental trip with two men and another woman to "live naturally and freely for two weeks—doing a thing we know in the bottom of our souls is *right,* and knowing perfectly well the whole town is going to explode with horror." However, after only a few hours, Mary rationalizes her own lack of persistence, deciding to be "magnanimous" to the "deep prejudices" of her parents. She returns home. Fearful of being scolded, she and her brother hide and are horrified when they accidentally overhear their parents in a fight (reminiscent of Strindberg and foreshadowing Albee) that shaves off the thin skin concealing the bleeding tissue of their marriage. They hear their father tell their mother: "I'm flabbergasted at you. You seem to have lost what sense you did have. . . . I can't count on you. You aren't *there*. Sometimes I think you aren't the woman I married at all," and their mother's even more devastating reply: "And sometimes I think you're a man I *couldn't* have married. Sometimes I loathe everything you think and say and do. When you grind out that old stuff I could *shriek*. I can't breathe in the same room with you. The very sound of your voice drives me insane. When you tell me how right you are—I could strike you." The fate of the marriage of Mary the Second is left unresolved at the conclusion. Even though Mary the Third has seen her mother's agonized entrapment and recognized its partial basis in her inability to earn an independent income, the daughter herself yields to the pressures of convention and enters marriage knowing just as little about her future husband as her grandmother and mother had known of theirs. Self-deceived, she has only partly digested the teachings of those writers who had argued for new kinds of marriages: ". . . you *ought* to be able to [make your own living]. . . . I shall have my own money. I'll *make* it. I shall live with a man because I love him and only as long as I love him. I shall be able to take care of myself *and* my children if necessary. Anything else gives the man a horrible advantage, of course. It makes the woman a kept woman." . . . Significantly, Mary has rejected an intelligent suitor who has warned her that "unless we change the entire attitude of men and women towards each other—there won't be any marriage in the future" . . . , and disregarded the fact that she is as ill-trained to support herself as her mother had been.

Crothers's plays signal changes in the treatment of the "woman problem" in the theatre during the twenties. The dialectic between the "new woman" and her "old-fashioned" relatives increasingly undercut conventional comic endings as reconciliation with older patterns became a hollow act. In a series of skillfully constructed one-act plays, Crothers continued her mordant comment by creating the character of a successful but shallow politician, Nancy Marshall, whose words expose a growing "tokenism" in the feminist views of many of her contemporaries:

> We women must be considerate of each other. If I am nominated I'm going to be awfully strong for that. . . . Men have made a mess of it—that's all. The idea that there aren't enough houses in New York to go 'round. What nonsense! . . . All those awful people with money who never had any before in their lives ought not to be allowed to crowd other people out. It's Bolshevism—just Bolshevism. . . . And not enough school teachers to go 'round. . . . People ought simply to be made to teach school, whether they want to or not. . . . I can't teach school. God knows I'd be glad to—and just show them if my hands weren't so full now of—I'm going to have awful circles under my eyes from standing so long.

She contrasts her own knowledge of the nuances of political style with her female opponent's corpulent presence on the hustings: "She is so unpopular I should think she'd withdraw from sheer embarrassment . . . she is so unattractive. That's why the men have put her up . . . they're not afraid of her because they *know* she'll never get anywhere." . . . The sheer vacuousness of Nancy Marshall's political views elicits the response from her best friend that "Between you and her I'd vote for the best man going," and comes into sharp relief when compared to the comment of Mary Dewson, director of women's work for the Democratic party, after the election of 1932: ". . . we did not make the old-fashioned plea that our candidate was charming, . . . we appealed to the intelligence of the country's women."

In a one-act sequel, after the same friend calls her an "old maid," Nancy Marshall suddenly comprehends the real "importance of being a woman" and hastily puts on a proper gown for the purpose of attracting a proposal of marriage. The customary import of the courtship scene is compromised, because the gentleman of her choice has been rejected, in an earlier scene, by Patti Pitt, a young woman who sees herself as public property (she is an entertainer!), but who actually has meant it when she said "It's power, . . . I've got it and I mustn't throw it away. . . . Any woman can get married, but I have something more important to do." . . . The satiric treatment of both women by Crothers indicates that she was sensitive to the processes of rationalization used by women confronted by the choice between career and marriage, and had identified in those who opted for the latter an erosion of energy that was to continue to perpetuate, for a number of years in the theatre, the prominence of the "feminine mystique." (pp. 326-28)

[In a late play by Crothers, *When Ladies Meet*], the scenario of the struggle of female characters for economic and moral independence receives less emphasis than the failing and futile relationships all the women have with the men. Mary, a writer, and Claire, a wife, are both in love with the latter's philandering husband. Mary has continued to reject the persistent courtship of good-natured Jimmie, a friend who puts women "in pigeon holes and tab[s] them—[according to] a *man's* idea of women." Jimmie shrewdly arranges a meeting of mistress and wife at a mutual friend's country house. The play's title is drawn from a remarkable scene that occurs "when ladies meet" to discuss the fictional case in Mary's novel in which a mistress tells her lover's wife that she wants to live for a year with him on a trial basis. Claire's comments on the verisimilitude of Mary's novel barely conceal her response to her own situation:

> I suppose *any* married woman thinks the other woman ought to know enough not to believe a married man—if he's making love to her. . . . I happen to be married to a man who can no more help attracting women than he can help breathing. And of course each one thinks she is the love of his life and that he is going to divorce me. But he doesn't seem to . . . I can always tell when an affair is waning. He turns back to the old comfortable institution of marriage as naturally as a baby turns to the warm bottle. . . .

When her husband unexpectedly blunders into the room, fiction becomes reality—true to Claire's prediction—he begs to return, but she rejects him with a newly discovered decisiveness: "You can't conceive that I *could* stop loving you. It happened in just one second—I think—when I saw what you'd done to [Mary]. . . . I'm not going *home—now—or ever*." . . . Mary will continue to write and to live alone. The theme of the emotional consequences of both disintegrating marriages and the pursuit of careers had been introduced earlier in the play by their hostess, who diagnoses women's restlessness as due to a far-reaching lack of fulfillment in either institution: "Men mean a great deal more to women than women do to men. . . . I don't care *what* strong women—like Mary tell you about loving their work and their *freedom*—it's all *slush*. Women *have got to be loved*. That's why they're breaking out so. . . . They're daring to have lovers—good women—because they just *can't stand being alone*." (pp. 328-29)

Crothers had managed to write, on the average, a play a year since 1904. The incipient thirty-year-long quietism in feminist activities produced by apathy, factionalism, and personal loneliness is evident in the uneasy resignation of her later female characters. The playwright's response to a reporter, in 1941, revealed her final alienation from feminist causes and repeated her earlier assertion that her plays had mirrored, *mutatis mutandis*, the social evolution of sex roles: "What a picayune, self-conscious side all this woman business has to it. . . . I've been told that my plays are a long procession reflecting the changing attitudes of the world toward women. If they are, that was completely unconscious on my part. Any change like that, that gets on to the stage, has already happened in life. Even the most vulgar things, that people object to with so much excitement, wouldn't be in the theatre at all if they hadn't already become a part of life." (pp. 329-30)

> *Cynthia Sutherland, "American Women Playwrights as Mediators of the 'Woman Problem'," in* Modern Drama, *Vol. XXI, No. 3, September, 1978, pp. 319-36.**

LOIS C. GOTTLIEB   (essay date 1979)

[*In the following excerpt from her critical study* Rachel Crothers, *Gottlieb assesses Crothers's lasting achievement in American theater.*]

Crothers's career must be viewed in two parts: first her prewar years as a social-problem playwright; second, her postwar years as a writer of social comedies. In the early part of her career, Crothers was something of a curiosity: a woman playwright who was serious, who had ideas, and who was a social rebel. The realism of Crothers's early plays was highly praised, and she must be considered an important contributor to the arrival of modern drama on the American stage. As well, she helped to create an American drama out of American materials. She set her plays in the West, in New England, in a New York boardinghouse, and in the Bedford Reformatory, and she peopled them with characters of observable American manners and motives.

Women dramatists before the war were not scarce, but neither were they highly regarded. . . . Crothers fought against being denied serious consideration as a dramatist, or being left out of any phase of theater, because of her sex. Very early in her career, she became integrated into the production and management of her own plays. She represented in the theater "woman's progress" as defined by her times: she was succeeding in "the man's world," and she achieved her early reputation at least in part because of the oddity of her success.

In the latter part of her career, when she produced almost one new comedy a season for two decades, Crothers was accorded a status that bore little direct relationship to the quality or interest of her drama. She became known as America's foremost woman dramatist, America's most longlived and productive dramatist, and, finally, her comedies were perceived as social documents rather than as particular reflections of her times, shaped by an artistic vision and style. She was known for her sophisticated dramatic milieu, her skills in writing dialogue, crafting plots, and creating a thoroughly effective theatrical production. Her plays were typically peopled by glamorous, urban, upper-class characters, most of whom had a wide streak of Main Street piety and small-town prudery that eventually emerged from beneath their cosmopolitan features.

But what can be said in greater detail of Crothers's achievement in the American theater and what sources are available for measuring that achievement? Reviewing the critical reception of Crothers's plays has been one means of shedding light on various phases of her development, progress, and success in the theater. In the long run, however, attempts to describe Crothers's achievement with reference to the mountain of clippings of newspaper and journal articles, beginning as early as 1894, are diversionary; there is more material here for a history of American critical taste or of the conventions of the commercial theater.

As a gauge to Crothers's reputation, the reviews are informative to the degree that we discover that she was ahead of most of the critics and audiences in her prewar problem plays, but lagged behind some critics and a vocal segment of the playgoing population in the 1920s and 1930s. In the scattered references to Crothers's plays in treatments of early modern American drama, her reputation is usually downplayed because the dramas she wrote for the commercial theater are measured against criteria of the art theater, and these are criteria which Crothers's dramas fail to meet. (pp. 146-47)

[It is] in answer to the two questions of Crothers's relationship to the commercial theater and to feminism that some description of her achievement might be attempted and some refinement of her reputation proposed.

The commercial stage during Crothers's career became increasingly notorious for its play doctors and their wholesale rewriting of Broadway scripts, a practice which cast doubt on the integrity of all commercial playwrights. Indeed, Crothers indirectly criticized the play doctors by condemning the pressures on the commercial writer for box-office success, noting: "The greatest crime in the commercial theater is that its work is done too fast and under the financial pressure of try-outs and other heavy overhead expenses . . . if anything is seriously wrong with the structure of a play, you know that the solution is not going to be reached while that pressure is weighing down upon it." Crothers reacted angrily to the suggestion that managers influenced or compromised her scripts. On one occasion, she wrote to the editor of *Harpers Bazaar* of her outrage that "you should think any manager in the world has influenced my plays in any way whatsoever. Good, bad, or indifferent— such as they may be—they are deeply and utterly mine."

Nevertheless, the most frequently stated complaint about Crothers's plays, particularly her postwar social comedies, is that they represent the model of the successful, commercial play: ostensibly timely and with substance, but in reality, superficial, either defining too simply or resolving too easily a contemporary problem that could be, or should be, rendered with more complexity. Whether Crothers's treatment of social themes is so superficial as to permanently lower her reputation needs further debate. But the debate would be conducted on clearer grounds by separating the question of superficial or overly simple social analysis from the assumption that this aspect of Crothers's dramas was a direct result of crassly commercial motives and her overriding desire to please the lowest segment of her audience.

From the available evidence, Crothers's simplicity was a deliberate choice, reached on the basis of "failed experiments," such as *Young Wisdom*, and confirmed by the disastrous *Venus*, whose appeal was too dependent upon audience intelligence. Crothers avowed that directness and clarity were the theater's highest goals, and that theater moved people through their feelings, not through cerebral exercise. Indeed, Crothers wrote: "The playwright has no business to call upon his audience to wonder what he means—to weigh his dialogue with literature. A play means the objective representation of a phase of life. . . . Ibsen is the extreme—the last word in simplicity, the directness of playwriting. He has not a universal appeal because his stories—the questions of his life with which he deals—are grim dark tragedies, glimpses into horrible truths. But . . . it is his extremely simple treatment, the everyday dialogue of his living human beings which make his plays so playable."

Crothers's achievement as a feminist playwright is the second issue to discuss in an assessment of her general achievement as a dramatist. Crothers pursued the theme of woman's freedom, what she called woman's odyssey, for most of her career, portraying woman's adventures and tribulations in a country whose changing social and moral landscape profoundly affected woman's self-image and aspirations. Crothers's early plays challenge relations between the sexes on a personal as well as public level because her early women alter or reject their domestic roles and display a strength and ambition that contradict the presumed attributes of weakness and self-sacrifice in the feminine nature. What Crothers's later dramas portray is that woman's odyssey foundered on the rocks of fear—fear of freedom and fear of the loneliness that seemed inevitable in a world where men were not the central purpose of woman's life. Many of Crothers's later social comedies mock these fearful women, subtly, but with an unmistakable sense of authorial superiority, and they breathe an air of exasperation about the continuation of woman's struggle to freedom.

Nevertheless, woman is at the center of Crothers's dramas throughout her career. The question remains, however, whether Crothers was a "feminist" playwright. If that label means that Crothers wrote issue-oriented dramas, unequivocally supporting the wide range of feminist causes, then it would be inaccurate to call Crothers a feminist playwright. From a broader perspective, Crothers's plays are so obviously concerned with the impact of the woman question on the lives and relations of her characters that any other label but feminist seems inappropriate. Certainly, in the early part of her career, Crothers was especially interested in the character of the New Woman and in some of the issues of social and moral hygiene with which many women reformers allied themselves. Crothers's plays also continuously reflected the need of woman's economic independence, so that she was no longer demeaned by marriage as her only form of financial security, and so that she could regard herself as a dignified, adult, and purposeful member of the social world.

At the same time, many Crothers plays can be interpreted as arguments for a sexual status quo. They portray woman choosing to be the power behind some ordinary man; to cherish the sweetness of small domestic triumphs; to restrain her sexual desires in order to be pure for her impure man; to capitulate to the mindless swoon of romantic love; to accept even the most inadequate of marriages or mates as preferable to spinsterhood. These characters, however, seem less to argue against woman's freedom or against feminism in its broadest sense, and more to portray the reality that the New Woman had not emerged as the common type of femininity. Further, the number and frequency of domestic or capitulating women increase in Crothers's dramas after World War I, when feminism began to lose power as a movement for social change. While her women of the 1920s and 1930s are continuously entangled in the complexities of affairs and in the nets of love, one senses the author regarding this phenomenon as a fair target for comedy, a kind of reversal of the Shavian definition that love is a woman's overestimation of the difference between one man and another. Thus Crothers locates the greatest and most comic obstacle to modern woman's freedom and progress as her need for man.

No doubt, deeper probes could be sounded about the nature and expression of Crothers's feminism as it evolves through four decades of American social and theatrical history. It is clear, however, that her dramas are more closely tied to the central concerns of feminism and of modern American women than are those of her contemporaries. On the basis of her unique development of the theme of woman's odyssey and on the basis of her distinct achievement on the commercial stage, in both the early and later parts of her career, Crothers deserves regard and attention as an important contributor to the evolution of modern American drama and to the excellence of America's mainstream theater. (pp. 148-51)

> *Lois C. Gottlieb, in her* Rachel Crothers, *Twayne Publishers, 1979, 170 p.*

ADDITIONAL BIBLIOGRAPHY

Crothers, Rachel. "The Construction of a Play." In *The Art of Playwriting*, by Jesse Lynch Williams, Langdon Mitchell, Lord Dunsany, Gilbert Emery, and Rachel Crothers, pp. 115-34. Philadelphia: University of Pennsylvania Press, 1928.
    Reflections on the state of American theater, the technical aspects of playwriting, and Crothers's own beginnings as a dramatist.

Hamilton, Clayton. "Youth and Age in the Drama." In his *Problems of the Playwright*, pp. 77-88. New York: Henry Holt and Co., 1917.*
    Praises the treatment in *Old Lady 31* of old age, a subject traditionally avoided by American theater.

Hutchens, John. "Al Jolson and Others." *Theatre Arts Monthly* XV, No. 5 (May 1931): 366-74.*
    Favorable review of *As Husbands Go*.

Mantle, Burns. "Dramatists and Melodramatists." In his *American Playwrights of Today*, pp. 97-128. New York: Dodd, Mead & Co., 1929.*
    Brief biographical essay.

Mayorga, Margaret G. "The American Plays of Ideas." In her *Short History of the American Drama: Commentaries on Plays prior to 1920*, pp. 273-99. New York: Dodd, Mead & Co., 1940.*
    Briefly critiques Crothers's major works.

Nathan, George Jean. "*Susan and God:* December 13, 1943." In his *Theater Book of the Year: 1943-1944*, pp. 171-73. New York: Alfred A. Knopf, 1944.
    Review of the dedication of the New York City Center of Music and Drama. Nathan maintains that opening "a municipal theater with *Susan and God* is much like having launched one of the famous European municipal theatres not with Goethe's *Faust* or Molière's *Tartuffe* or Chekhov's *The Cherry Orchard* but with *Whose Wife Is Emily?*"

Woodbridge, Homer E. "Recent Plays of War and Love." *The Dial* LIX, No. 703 (14 October 1915): 325-28.*
    Considers *A Man's World* "well planned" but "in style and characterization . . . decidedly crude."

Jacques Futrelle

1875-1912

American short story writer and novelist.

Futrelle is remembered as the author of detective stories featuring Professor Augustus S. F. X. Van Dusen, also known as the Thinking Machine, a series character whom critics have found both remarkable and somewhat exasperating. Most notably in the anthology piece "The Problem of Cell 13," Professor Van Dusen achieves a superhuman—some have called it inhuman—level of logic and rationality. While this character conspicuously reveals Futrelle's familiarity with the works of Edgar Allan Poe and Arthur Conan Doyle, the stories involving the Thinking Machine in some ways differ significantly from the classic pattern of detective fiction and anticipate several modern developments in the genre.

Futrelle, whose ancestors were French Huguenots, was born in Pike County, Georgia. Prior to settling in the Boston area, where he was a member of the editorial staff of the Boston *American,* he had worked on a newspaper in Richmond, Virginia. Many of Futrelle's stories first appeared in the Boston *American,* including "The Problem of Cell 13." Published as a week-long serial, this puzzle of detection was turned into a contest for the newspaper's readers, who were challenged to submit solutions and compete for prize money. After several years with the *American,* Futrelle began to earn his living as a freelance fiction writer and wrote successfully in a variety of popular genres, including romances, westerns, and detective stories. However, Futrelle is remembered solely for his tales of the Thinking Machine. Critics speculate that he might have made a greater contribution to the evolving detective genre had his career not been cut short by his death on the *Titanic.*

In Futrelle's novel *The Chase of the Golden Plate,* Professor Van Dusen makes an appearance as an incidental character. His designation as the "Thinking Machine" derives from a later story involving a chess game between a master player and the professor, who has never played chess before but who asserts that by logic alone he will overcome his opponent's expertise. When the professor succeeds, the other player exclaims, "You are not a man; you are a brain-machine—a thinking machine." The logic and ingenuity of the Thinking Machine stories are regarded as their most outstanding qualities. Of these stories "The Problem of Cell 13," described by Howard Haycraft as an "unforgettable tour de force," is acclaimed as Futrelle's finest work. Critics cite the locked-room situation, the eccentric main character, and the inventive solution as the principal elements accounting for the story's classic status in the detective genre. Critical discussions of the Thinking Machine stories often focus on the professor himself, whose feats of logic are consistently astonishing, on occasion to the point of excess; as R. A. Whay has stated of Professor Van Dusen: "His invariable infallibility proves in the end a strain on the credulity." While critics have traditionally regarded the Thinking Machine as a coldly mechanical brain, in a recent essay Benedict Freedman argues that what accounts for his fascination is that this so-called perfect thinker in fact relies as much on intuition as deduction, and that he depends on insight into human character as much as reason, revealing himself to be a "likable human sort with loyal friends and a pleasant sense of humor."

Critics have compared the Thinking Machine with his literary predecessors, Poe's Auguste Dupin and Doyle's Sherlock Holmes, particularly because the professor shares their faith in the intellect and their superb deductive ability. However, while Futrelle indeed betrays an indebtedness to the works of Poe and Doyle in his emphasis on deductive reasoning, he also moved away from the traditional detective story by portraying more realistic and less violent crimes, as opposed to the exotic and often gruesome crimes that were a staple of nineteenth-century mystery writers. In this way Futrelle anticipated later developments in the detective story form, in addition to creating a character who, according to E. F. Bleiler, is "one of the best-imagined detectives" in American literature.

(See also *Contemporary Authors,* Vol. 113.)

PRINCIPAL WORKS

The Chase of the Golden Plate   (novel)   1906
The Thinking Machine   (short stories)   1907; also published as *The Problem of Cell 13,* 1918
The Simple Case of Susan   (novel)   1908; also published as *Lieutenant What's-His-Name* [enlarged edition; with May Futrelle], 1915.
The Thinking Machine on the Case   (short stories)   1908; also published as *The Professor on the Case,* 1909
The Diamond Master   (novel)   1909
Elusive Isabel   (novel)   1909; also published as *The Lady in the Case,* 1910
The High Hand   (novel)   1911; also published as *The Master Hand,* 1914
My Lady's Garter   (novel)   1912
Blind Man's Buff   (novel)   1914
Best "Thinking Machine" Detective Stories   (short stories) 1973
Great Cases of The Thinking Machine   (short stories) 1976

THE NEW YORK TIMES   (essay date 1907)

[*In the following excerpt, the critic reviews Futrelle's first collection of short stories,* The Thinking Machine.]

Jacques Futrelle's **"The Thinking Machine"** . . . is a reprint in book form of some serial yarns about the marvelous performances of Prof. Van Dusen. . . . The difference between Prof. Van Dusen and the ordinary man is the same as that between the ordinary man and the extraordinary woman. One by elaborate and minute analytical processes arrives at the conclusions which the other reaches by crosscuts not mathematically orthodox but perfectly adjusted to getting there.

The best story and the one which best illustrates the perverse ingenuity of the author who builds a mystery backward from an obvious solution into a something that is so fair an imitation of a blind maze that it may be mistaken at a casual glance for the real thing is furnished by the yarn called **"The Great Auto Mystery."** This yarn involves a beautiful blonde actress, a millionaire or two, a roadhouse, and a rather marrow-freezing experience with a corpse. There's another story about a lone house, hidden treasure, and a phosphorescent phantom—but the staginess of the phantom rather spoils it.

"The Thinking Machine," in The New York Times, *April 6, 1907, p. 202.*

THE NATION   (essay date 1907)

[*In the following excerpt, the critic contrasts the differing approaches to the detective story in Futrelle's* The Thinking Machine *and Arthur Morrison's* Martin Hewitt, Investigator *(1907).*]

The short detective story has become so thoroughly conventionalized within the last few years that it would be as unfair to accuse an author of imitating Sir Conan Doyle by describing the exploits of an unofficial detective of marked personal peculiarities, rapid and incisive deductive powers, as to accuse him of imitating Pinero by writing a play in three acts.

Mr. Futrelle has been bold enough to christen his elucidator in so many words the "Thinking Machine," mentioning only now and then his real name, Prof. Augustus S. F. X. Van Dusen, the scientific man who is consulted on occasions of great stress by Hutchinson Hatch, reporter, a journalistic counterpart of Dr. Watson. "Nothing is impossible," is Professor Van Dusen's dictum. "The mind is master of all things." Martin Hewitt, Mr. Morrison's detective on the other hand, always maintains, more modestly, that he has "no system beyond a judicious use of ordinary faculties."

The criminals with whom Prof. Van Dusen has to deal in the seven tales [of *The Thinking Machine*] are, perhaps, as modern a lot as fiction affords. They turn scientific knowledge to their own purposes in ways that are dark indeed; in fact, rather beyond the scope even of legitimate science. Mr. Morrison's criminals, equally ingenious, employ more familiar agencies for their nefarious business. Mr. Futrelle, it might be said in generalization, is the more fertile devising enigmas, Mr. Morrison in answering them without straining.

On this point, the detective story must be judged by canons of its own. It is the first duty of the writer to carry out his implied contract to provide for every problem a solution that shall be complete and adequate, with the minimum of evidence left in the detective's sole possession till the last moment. From this point of view, it is hard to justify the use of an actually false clue under any circumstances. The reader should have the chance to match his wits on even terms against the writer, who must give as much information as possible, without disclosing the final solution. Now Mr. Futrelle is guilty of keeping up suspense by false evidence. The whole mystery in one of these stories is sustained through twenty-six pages, on the supposition that a revolver shot fired in a certain direction struck nothing. It is only explained at the very end of the story that the constable merely missed his mark. The mistake might easily happen in an actual criminal case, but it does not properly belong in a detective story. For a narrative that complies with the same condition, giving substantially all the necessary clues before the final revelation comes, the first of the Martin Hewitt stories, "The Lenten Croft Robberies" may be cited.

A review of "The Thinking Machine," in The Nation, *Vol. LXXXIV, No. 2185, May 16, 1907, p. 457.*

RAFFORD PYKE   (essay date 1907)

[*In the following excerpt, Pyke contrasts Futrelle's stories in* The Thinking Machine *with Arthur Conan Doyle's Sherlock Holmes stories.*]

In sheer inventiveness and ingenuity [the stories in *The Thinking Machine*] at times surpass the now classical problems which interested the mind of Sherlock Holmes. "The Thinking Machine" is a name given to a certain Professor van Dusen, who is the incarnation of unemotional science. His logic is without a flaw; his mental processes are infallible. Sherlock Holmes was partly a man of action; but Professor van Dusen is wholly a man of thought. In this respect he resembles Mycroft Holmes, but without the amiable eccentricities of that cogitator. The problems that are given to him to solve are often, on the face of them, so impossible as to make the reader absolutely certain that they cannot in any way be mastered.

Take, for example the problem of Cell 13. Professor van Dusen consents to be placed in a certain cell of Chisholm Prison. The prison is built of granite. It is surrounded by a wall of solid masonry eighteen feet high and topped by a five-foot fence of steel rods. Armed guards are stationed in the yard both night and day, and electric lights dispel darkness as soon as the sun sets. Cell 13 is usually occupied by some person under sentence of death. Its walls are of solid masonry; its door is of chilled steel. Its window is a narrow slit. Outside the door are heavily barred gates, at which a sentinel is always watching.

Into this cell The Thinking Machine is thrust, after being thoroughly searched, and the doors are locked and barred upon him. The warden is especially warned to keep him in confinement, for The Thinking Machine has declared that within a week's time he will pass out of this dungeon unhindered and without the knowledge of his keepers. Here, surely, is a problem that seems insoluble, and the reader is quite as incredulous as are the friends of The Thinking Machine who arrange the test.

This story is perhaps the most absorbingly interesting and puzzling in the book; but the others are all extremely clever. If, after the reading is over, one still ranks them below the adventures of Sherlock Holmes, it is because the latter have greater realism and accord more closely with the conditions of actual life. Holmes sometimes makes mistakes, and this fact renders him more real as a human being. The incidents which befall him are also far more usual, and for that very reason are the more convincing. But *The Thinking Machine* is a book that will be read with avidity for its great cleverness; and other stories by the same author are certain to receive an appreciative welcome.

Rafford Pyke, "Mr. Futrelle's 'The Thinking Machine'," in The Bookman, *New York, Vol. XXV, June, 1907, p. 433.*

R. A. WHAY   (essay date 1908)

[*In the following excerpt, Whay reviews* The Thinking Machine on the Case, *the second series of stories featuring Professor Van Dusen.*]

For sheer ingenuity, the stories which Mr. Futrelle has built up about Professor Augustus Van Dusen, the Thinking Machine, are equalled by little, and surpassed by nothing in contemporary fiction. The soundest criticism that is to be brought against this second series of tales is that, as was the case with the first series, the invention is at times almost too clever. The deductions of the Thinking Machine are so swift and astonishing that the reader is often puzzled in following them. Mr. Sherlock Holmes had an uneven disposition and occasionally made mistakes. Professor Van Dusen is also more or less irritable, but his invariable infallibility proves in the end a strain on the credulity. Yet his exploits taken in homeopathic doses must appeal to the most jaded appetite. (p. 496)

Throughout the tales of *The Thinking Machine on the Case* the varied results of man's mechanical cunning play a prominent part. In the first story it is a motor boat carrying a dead man wearing a uniform that leads the authorities to think him a captain in the French navy, which crashes into a wharf in Boston Harbour. Another tale deals with the mysterious murder at his key board of the operator of the wireless of an ocean steamship. Of particular grimness is the story of **"The Crystal Gazer,"** which introduces an elaborate device by which the victim, peering into a crystal, sees what he takes to be a vision of his own murder. Again there is **"The Phantom Motor,"** which, night after night, enters one end of a short road lined on both sides by ten-foot walls, never comes out the other end, and cannot be found between. But what, above all, marks Mr. Futrelle's work in this as well as the earlier book, is not the cleverness of any particular tale, but rather the consistent excellence and fertility of invention of them all. (p. 497)

> *R. A. Whay, "Jacques Futrelle's 'The Thinking Machine',' in The Bookman, New York, Vol. XXVII, July, 1908, pp. 496-97.*

H. L. MENCKEN (essay date 1912)

[*From the era of World War I until the early years of the Great Depression, Mencken was one of the most influential figures in American letters. His strongly individualistic, irreverent outlook on life and his vigorous, invective-charged writing style helped establish the iconoclastic spirit of the Jazz Age and significantly shaped the direction of American literature. In the following excerpt, Mencken appraises the quality of Futrelle's work and summarizes Futrelle's brief writing career.*]

[*My Lady's Garter*] is the last novel that we shall ever have from Mr. Futrelle's pen, for he was one of the staunch fellows who helped the women and children into the Titanic's boats and then went down with the ship. A capital maker of galloping and unserious romances was lost in that memorable tragedy of the sea. He had a fine hand for devising astounding plots; he knew men and women; he wrote with plausibility and aplomb; and above all, he tempered the hot steel of derring-do in the oil of humor. It was as a humorist, indeed, that he made his first success. No doubt you remember the story—an extravagant and hilarious tale about a Kentuckian who bred a race horse with hind legs like a kangaroo's, and struck the bookmakers dead by running the beast a mile in 1.01. That story was a little masterpiece, perfectly planned and superbly written, and it made Mr. Futrelle a popular author over night. Then he tried the larger form of the light romance and succeeded again, but I doubt that he had got within sight of his best work when he died. *My Lady's Garter,* however, shows the way he was going. With its vixenish, red-haired heroine, its poetizing sub-hero, its sentimental villain and its five-thumbed detec-

tives, it assays a good deal more humor than sugar. There are still plenty of concessions, true enough, to the form and its conventions, but in most of them there are evidences of an effort to break away, and in the course of time, I have no doubt, Mr. Futrelle would have moulded that form into something better fitting his talents. His true field was humor: he had in him the making of a first rate satirist, a species of scrivener very rare among us—and it is a pity that he did not live long enough wholly to find himself. As it is, he left behind him three or four long stories of unusual ingenuity and charm, and a public which must sincerely mourn his passing. To die at thirty-seven in the full blush of health, with the door of opportunity wide open and skill just showing its quality—this, surely, was a fate too cruel for understanding.

> *H. L. Mencken, in a review of "My Lady's Garter," in The Smart Set, Vol. XXXVIII, No. 4, December, 1912, p. 158.*

HOWARD HAYCRAFT (essay date 1941)

[*Haycraft is an American editor and critic who, in addition to being the editor of several valuable reference works, has also edited a number of anthologies of detective stories and is the author of a literary history of the genre entitled* Murder for Pleasure: The Life and Times of the Detective Story *(1941). In the following excerpt from that study, Haycraft offers a brief survey appraisal of Futrelle's stories of the Thinking Machine.*]

The American detective story did not revert in important measure to the shorter form in which it was conceived by Poe, and which is still considered by many critics the theoretically perfect compass for its narration, until the appearance of Jacques Futrelle . . . , the creator of The Thinking Machine. (p. 85)

The Thinking Machine, Futrelle's amusing and believably eccentric contribution to the ranks of fictional sleuths, made a somewhat incidental first appearance in the closing chapters of an adventure novel, *The Chase of the Golden Plate*. . . . His complete name, we are told, was Augustus S. F. X. Van Dusen, Ph.D., LL.D., F.R.S., M.D., and M.D.S., and he was cast as a professor in an unnamed university near a large American city strongly resembling Boston. He wore a number eight hat, and his life was dedicated to the blunt proposition that two and two equal four—not sometimes but all of the time. Next to John Rhode's Dr. Priestley, he is probably the most truculent of all the detectives of fiction.

The best of the short stories in which The Thinking Machine performed his feats of mental wizardry were collected in two volumes: *The Thinking Machine* . . . and *The Thinking Machine on the Case*. . . . The first named was re-issued . . . as *The Problem of Cell 13,* the title of the first story in the book. This notable tale, found in many anthologies, is Futrelle's chief single claim to remembrance. Exemplifying detection-in-reverse (the theme is The Thinking Machine's attempt, on a wager, to escape from the death cell of a penitentiary), it is an unforgettable tour de force that no devotee should miss. Nearly all The Thinking Machine stories, for that matter, will stand rereading to-day. Except for occasional "dating" incidents inherent in the mise-en-scène, there is little in the writing to indicate their pre-war vintage. The concept of the problems is essentially fresh and modern, and the style is straightforward and agreeably free of the pomposity which characterized too much of the detective fiction of the time.

Had Jacques Futrelle lived beyond his thirty-seventh year, he might well have become one of the two or three leading names in the development of the American detective story. As it was, he brought to the genre a lightness of touch in advance of his time, and even by present-day standards his plots are still artful and his narratives readable. (pp. 85-7)

> Howard Haycraft, "America: 1890-1914 (The Romantic Era)," in his Murder for Pleasure: The Life and Times of the Detective Story, D. Appleton-Century Company Incorporated, 1941, pp. 83-102.*

HAROLD OREL   (essay date 1968)

[*The following excerpt is from Orel's essay "The American Detective-Hero," which traces the development of this popular figure from his creation in the stories of Edgar Allan Poe through the detectives in the fiction of Dashiel Hammett and Raymond Chandler, viewing Futrelle as an intermediate contributor to this evolution.*]

The American detective-hero had been completely characterized by 1845, the year in which the third and last of Poe's great stories about Monsieur Dupin was published. He was, and is, an ironic and occasionally saturnine sleuth, bookishly appreciative of the arts, given to epigrams, unastonished by human depravity, and convinced of the value of studying truth "in detail." The presence of a confidant is not really vital, and the narrator of Poe's tales is not clearly characterized. (p. 396)

[One contribution to the characterization, made prior to the fictions of Dashiel Hammett, was Jacques Futrelle's Thinking Machine,] who made his first appearance in a book dated 1907, and his second and last appear in a book dated 1908. (Futrelle, if he had not died aboard the *Titanic*, might have done more with him.) This brilliant scientist was "a wonderfully imposing structure," with a Ph.D., an LL.D., an F.R.S., an M.D., and an M.D.S., not to mention other recognitions of his ability from foreign educational and scientific institutions. He was not lovable. His brisk, contemptuous tone toward those who doubted his faith in human reason marked him as the logical—and ultimate—extension of Dupin, the thinking detective. We remember The Thinking Machine's sarcastic statement to an eminent Scotland Yard inspector, "You see, gentlemen of your profession use too little common sense. Remember that two and two always make four—not sometimes but all the time." A logician who believed that all things that start must go somewhere, he was able to escape from an escape-proof prison in that famous tale, **"The Problem of Cell 13,"** and to reclaim the Varron jewels from Bradlee Cunnyngham Leighton, the international thief. But in the stories that involve him action is not the primary element: rather, it is Futrelle's shining faith in the transcendance of human intellect. "Nothing is impossible," The Thinking Machine snapped angrily at a distinguished scientist on one occasion. "The mind is master of all things. When science fully recognizes that fact a great advance will have been made."

This kind of detective-hero is, to be sure, a special creation: nothing more can be done to characterize him. His confidence in intellectual processes now seems to be arrogant, even unfounded, but in the innocent years before World War I it cheered us on. A man who does not play chess, but who might defeat a chess champion simply "by the force of inevitable logic" becomes himself the logical result of generations of breeding, "the master mind." Perhaps it is not surprising that Futrelle should describe Professor S.F.X. Van Dusen, The Thinking

Machine, as not merely the owner of "a peculiar, almost grotesque, personality," but as "remotely German." (pp. 396-97)

The American detective began with Edgar Allan Poe's M. Dupin, an observer, a man who believed in the intellect. He developed into Jacques Futrelle's Thinking Machine—and later, when the postwar years made appropriate a new kind of culture symbol, he became an acting detective, like Dashiell Hammett's Sam Spade and Raymond Chandler's Philip Marlowe. . . .

And yet all our detective-heroes have this in common: they have little confidence in the police or in the formal machinery of the law. Their own justice—the justice of rugged individualists—is inevitably superior and more effective in identifying, and even punishing, the criminal. (p. 401)

> Harold Orel, "The American Detective-Hero," in Journal of Popular Culture, Vol. II, No. 3, Winter, 1968, pp. 395-403.

JULIAN SYMONS   (essay date 1972)

[*Symons is an English biographer and detective novelist who has received high praise for his works in both of these genres. His popular biographies of Charles Dickens, Thomas Carlyle, and his brother A. J. A. Symons are considered excellent introductions to those writers. Symons is better known, however, for such crime novels as The Immaterial Murder Case (1945), The 31st of February (1950), and The Progress of a Crime (1960). In the following excerpt, Symons briefly discusses the era during which Futrelle wrote and credits him with creating one of the most successful superhuman detectives to follow Sherlock Holmes.*]

In writing about most of Sherlock Holmes's immediate successors, one has to make a change of gear. The interest of their work lies in the ingenuity with which problems are propounded and solved, rather than in the ability to create credible characters or to write stories interesting as tales rather than as puzzles. The amount of talent working in this period gives it a good claim to be called the first Golden Age of the crime story, but it should be recognized that the metal is nine-carat quality where the best of the Holmes stories is almost pure gold. Yet for those prepared to accept these stories on their own level (as any addict should be) the variety of detectives and ideas offered in them gives enduring pleasure.

At the center of their work was the personality of the detective, who almost always appeared in several series of stories. A number of dichotomies mark these detectives, but the clearest division is between those in the Holmes category of Supermen with no emotional attachments and little interest in everyday life except insofar as it impinges on any particular problem, and the inconspicuous ordinary men who solve their cases by the application of common sense rather than by analytic deduction. The detectives in this second class are private investigators running their own agencies, because that was the fashion of the time, but they often look and sound like policemen. They are Lestrades and Gregsons removed from the official ranks and seen with a friendly eye instead of being made the butts of genius. The Superman is almost always given his accompanying Watson, who may do a lot of the humdrum investigation. The common-sense detective often works alone.

[One of the] . . . most successful Superman detectives of the period [was] Professor Augustus S. F. X. Van Dusen. . . . Van Dusen's principal appearance is in two collections of stories, **The Thinking Machine** . . . and **The Thinking Machine on the**

Case. . . . He carries Holmesian omniscience to the point of absurdity. He is introduced to us when he refers contemptuously to chess, saying that a thorough knowledge of the rules of logic is all that is necessary to become a master at the game, and that he could "take a few hours of competent instruction and defeat a man who has devoted his life to it." A game is arranged between the Professor and the world champion, Tschaikowsky. After a morning spent with an American chess master in learning the moves, the Professor plays the game. At the fifth move, Tschaikowsky stops smiling, and after the fourteenth, when Van Dusen says "Mate in fifteen moves," the world champion exclaims: *"Mon Dieu!"* (he is not one of those Russians who know no language but their own) and adds: "You are not a man; you are a brain—a machine—a thinking machine." From this time onward Professor Van Dusen is called the Thinking Machine. In appearance he is dwarfish, with a small white clean-shaven face, long white flexible hands, and a great domed head taking a size-eight hat, under which is a heavy shock of bushy yellow hair.

The whiff of absurdity is strong, but the Thinking Machine stories are almost all ingenious. The usual Futrelle story falls into two parts. In the first a mystery is shown to us, either by third-person narratives or as told to the Thinking Machine. His assistant, the reporter Hutchinson Hatch, does most of the legwork, and the Professor then solves the case. Among the best stories are: one in which poison is circulated through the application of a court plaster; another in which a man sees in a crystal ball the picture of his future murder in his own apartment some distance away (the basis of the trick is the creation of a duplicate room in the house where the victim sees the crystal ball); and a third in which a car disappears night after night in a lane which has a policeman at each end. The finest of all the Thinking Machine stories is **"The Problem of Cell 13,"** which begins with an assertion by the Professor that anything can be done by the power of thought. Told that nobody can think his way out of a cell, he replies that "a man can so apply his brain and ingenuity that he can leave a cell, which is the same thing." The story shows him doing just that, with some agreeable mystification in the course of it, and then explaining exactly how it was done. This story has become a classic anthology piece, rather at the expense of some of the others. Futrelle died when the *Titanic* went down. The evidence of his other books does not make it seem likely that his crime stories would have developed any depth of characterization, but within the limits of what he attempted he had a conspicuously original gift. (pp. 76-8)

> Julian Symons, *"The Short Story: The First Golden Age,"* in his Mortal Consequences: A History—From the Detective Story to the Crime Novel, *Harper & Row, Publishers, 1972, pp. 76-90.**

BENEDICT FREEDMAN   (essay date 1972)

[*In the following excerpt, Freedman asserts that in the Thinking Machine, Futrelle successfully blended two myths—the myth of the purely rational detective and that of the purely intuitive detective.*]

To every myth there is a counter-myth. The law of non-contradiction, supreme arbiter in logic and science, has no authority in the country of the imagination. Dreams, sleeping or waking, synthesize the irreconcilable, and the artist is most successful when injecting into an archetype the seed of its denial. No apotheosis without feet of clay. Jacques Futrelle so

dealt with the myth of the Thinking Machine. His delightful, intriguing, simply written story is ostensibly homage to the perennial ideal of perfect logical thinking, precise, flawless, ineluctable, all-encompassing, Plato's *dialectic*, Lully's *ratiocinator universalis*, Leibniz's *characteristica*, Poe's "analysis, *par excellence*," Watson's "assembled organic machine," Turing's Turing machine, Newell and Simon's General Problem Solver, the Pentagon's "failsafe" instant retaliation computer programs. Homage, but double-edged. For what makes Futrelle's story permanently readable is that he has introduced elements of doubt, even mockery, into his portrait of the perfect deductive thinker. He suggests, subtly, humorously, that ratiocination is not all, perhaps not even half. Buried at the core of thought are shadowy intuitions, wild surmises, paleolithic glimmerings, a noncognizable ooze contemptuously referred to as common sense. When Prof. Augustus S. F. X. Van Dusen has removed his size 8 hat, and the computing machine housed in his size 8 skull has processed the information, symbolized the data, chained the enthymemes, distributed the middle, and concluded apodictically, it is not some theorem of Boolean logic that solves the problem of cell 13 but such homely bits of folk wisdom as newspapermen will do anything for a story, or small boys for a ten-dollar bill. Van Dusen's deductive prestidigitation is magnificent. It rivals Dupin at his best and throws Holmes completely into the shade. But look closely. All the reasoning is in the air, the formidable escarps and ramparts of logic just cloud castles. What really holds up the plot is the not particularly esoteric observation that most people don't like handling dead rats.

The story is set up as an intellectual challenge, pure and simple. To support his contention that "the mind is the master of all things," the professor agrees to be shut up, without notice or chance for preparation, in the death cell of Chisholm prison, and "think" his way out. It is to the author's credit that he dispenses completely with the sensational elements even Poe deemed essential to the detective story. There is no murder. There is no crime. Not even a letter compromising a royal personage is at stake. The reader cannot for a moment become concerned about the fate of Prof. Van Dusen. Arrangements for the incarceration are made by two eminent scientists, and the warden is fully aware of the identity of his distinguished guest. If he fails, all it will cost the professor is an artichoke dinner and humbled pride. But Futrelle creates suspense and maintains it with great art, quite a feat in the absence of standard threats of death, dismemberment, and mesalliance. Futrelle's overall record on this score is noteworthy. In nineteen stories he resorts to murder only eight times, a bludgeoning average of .421, compared with Poe's .600 and Conan Doyle's .550. The Thinking Machine stories are dedicated to the proposition that the acrobatics of pure reasoning are interesting and dramatic in themselves. Reader, you who can't get out of a dress shirt, what would you do if locked up on death row with no weapons, no tools, no friends. Could you escape? If you put your mind to it? Of course you could! There is no problem without a solution, man is a reed but a thinking reed, and mind conquers all. But how? Well, more or less as Augustus S. F. X. Van Dusen does it, details to be worked out. And the reader is off on the delightful sport of solving the puzzle, second-guessing the size 8 brain, chuckling at the discomfiture of authority, and preening it over his awestruck friends at the artichoke dinner.

So iron bars do not make a cage, at least not to the cutting edge of pure intellect. But strictly speaking, the mind cannot of itself cut bars, elude guards, and vault walls. And the author has taken pains to establish the prison as a fortress worthy of its challenger. It is a "great, spreading structure of granite," surrounded by an eighteen foot masonry wall. Footholds? Not a chance. The author has made the wall perfectly smooth, inside and out, and if this were not enough, topped it with "a five-foot fence of steel rods, each terminating in a point." In any case, between the cell and the wall are seven locked doors or gates, six of them "solid steel." Guards abound, walls and floors are stone, the window bars new iron ("not a shadow of rust on them"), and arc lights keep the yard as brilliantly illuminated at night as by day. Having made the prison impregnable and the prisoner puny (Dr. Ransome notes "the pitiful, childlike physical weakness of the man"), the author is well aware that no solution involving cutting, blasting, tunneling, or scaling of battlements will be acceptable. Leaving in a coffin harks back to Edmond Dantes, bribery is only good for a false lead, disguise too hackneyed for more than humorous effect. While the well-trained detective story reader is counting the locked doors and making a note of the eighteen feet of masonry and five feet of palings in the same part of his memory where he logs Freeman Wills Crofts' timetables, both Futrelle and his hero have discarded literal escape. It follows that if the Thinking Machine cannot go forth into freedom, freedom must come to him. Corollary: help from outside. Presupposition: an information channel out. Plot necessity: an abandoned drainpipe. Loophole to be plugged: won't that be the first thing the guards investigate—a drain destined to be crammed with string, wires, money, and concentrated nitric acid in tin bottles? Plug: the dead rat.

All of this managed smoothly, in clear, readable prose, and with a nice eye to misdirection. Especially admirable is Futrelle's handling of the difficult question of confederates. When all is said and done, Van Dusen did not escape on brain power alone. He had considerable help. First, a rat to carry a ten dollar bill down the drain; then, a small boy to covet the ten dollars and discover the message wrapped in it; then, a newspaperman to read the message and covet a story; finally, a crew of workmen to pile into the prison grounds and create confusion galore. It might occur to the reader that if there is to be assistance on a large scale, why not from the beginning? Why bother with the drainpipe, the courier rats, the long thread of lisle unraveled from a stocking top? Might not the Thinking Machine have made his arrangements in advance and simply induced his colleagues to challenge him? Even a stray thought of this kind would destroy Futrelle's conclusion, so he carefully erases the possibility in the first scene. The Thinking Machine's animadversions on mind over matter are kept highly abstract, and it is Dr. Ransome who springs the prison test out of left field. Prof. Van Dusen reacts with surprise tinged with irascibility. A good touch. His annoyance removes any suspicion of a put-up job. The reader feels the problem is not only difficult, but fair. He is ready to count doors and visualize wiring diagrams.

But the ease and accuracy with which Futrelle putties up his joints are marks of professionalism, no more. What has kept **"The Problem of Cell 13"** alive and readable today is something deeper. Futrelle incarnated an idol of Western man, the Cartesian *cogito*. He habilitated him in the academic robes of Ph.D., LL.D., F.R.S., M.D., and M.D.S. He inserted the contents of encyclopedias into his brain and gave him the combinatorial powers of Babbage's Analytical Engine. Above all he bestowed on him the faith the nineteenth century inherited from the Enlightenment: that every problem has a solution. . . . It is the merit of Jacques Futrelle to have sensed, however obscurely, the tragic flaw in the Great Brain he created, a flaw

present in all conceptions of man as the rational animal, pure and simple, and the universe as the rational structure waiting to be rationally dissected. In the Van Dusen stories we have at once the *ne plus ultra* of mechanical reasoning and its hollowest fraud.

For scientific knowledge and logical deduction never of themselves solve human problems. Formalize, symbolize, analyze, categorize, normalize—at some point, and usually the crucial point, human judgment enters in. It is human judgment that frames the problem, selects the data to be attended to, chooses the theory to apply, evaluates the conclusions offered by the theory and, if need be, discards them. Each act of judgment is fallible. More often than not it finds its support in direct knowledge of other persons, anathema to S-R psychology and the logical positivists. When in another story the Thinking Machine argues as follows:

> "Finally, with my hand on her pulse—which was normal—I told her as brutally as I could that her husband had been murdered. Her pulse jumped frightfully. . . . Now if she had known her husband were dead—even if she had killed him—a mere statement of his death would not have caused that pulse,"

he appears to be proceeding according to the strict tenets of mechanistic psychology. He has administered a stimulus and drawn a conclusion from an incontrovertible objective response, which, in fact, may be quantified. The experimental animal's pulse rose from 72 to 120. But of course, neither Thinking Machine, author, nor reader is fooled. The whole chain of argument hangs on an intuitive peg, Van Dusen's appraisal of the woman's character, something he could never get from any schedule of measurements of vital parameters but only by knowing her. One can know a person and judge in a few minutes whether she could murder her husband without the slightest alterations in her heartbeat or, at the other extreme, whether she will have palpitations at the touch of a stranger's fingers, Ph.D., LL.D., F.R.S., M.D., M.D.S. though he is.

More than trust in his intuitive judgment is required for the Thinking Machine to work his ratiocinative marvels: there must be trust in other people, and trust in fate itself. Van Dusen may say at the outset that "Mind is master of all things." But in the end he acknowledges that he could not have escaped without Mr. Hatch, the newspaperman, and his extremely energetic physical activities on the outside. And when Mr. Fielding asks, "How did Mr. Hatch happen to come with the electricians?" the Thinking Machine replies, "His father is manager of the company." Which shows that God has also taken a hand to arrange things.

To the question, "What if there had been no old plumbing system" in the prison, the Thinking Machine responds confidently that there were other ways, and we believe him. What has been mechanically constructed by the hand of man ought to be mechanically analyzable by the brain of man. But Van Dusen gives an entirely different response to the question, "What if there had been no Mr. Hatch outside to help?" He says: "Every prisoner has one friend outside who would help him escape if he could." Here he is not appealing to his size 8 brain, to his thirty-five years of training in proving that two and two always equal four, or to the honorific strings of letters that flank his name on both sides. He rests his case on a humble item of human faith. No man is friendless. No man is alone.

As in all captivating works of art, ambiguity is much of what captivates. The Thinking Machine purports to be a logical robot; he is revealed as a likeable human sort with loyal friends and a pleasant sense of humor. No matter that his creator gives him thin shoulders, ''a perpetual, forbidding squint,'' thick spectacles, and bushy yellow hair; and sums him up as a ''peculiar, almost grotesque, personality.'' His actions belie the description, and the reader finds nothing grotesque or repellent about him. He is patient, suffers fools, is courteous to his guards, kind even to rats, and even at the moment of his final triumph considerate enough to remember his friend Ransome's predilection for artichokes. We come to like and admire the Thinking Machine, and very little of it is for his performance as universal cogitator. What strikes home are his insights into people and his faith in invincible human resourcefulness.

So Jacques Futrelle accomplished that most difficult of literary purposes, to blend two contradictory and deeply held myths in one convincing character. Either myth by itself leads to caricature. Pure problem-solving ingenuity is good only for the puzzle page of the Sunday paper. For all its dollops of local color, Poe's ''The Gold Bug'' is no story but an article on elementary cryptanalysis. At the other extreme, pure intuitive knowledge of human nature can easily become revolting, and Chesterton's Father Brown strays dangerously close to this pit. Prof. Van Dusen is an extraordinary thinking machine and so fulfills the perennial dream of man to understand and control his world. The hunched, slender professor with the yellow hair and crabbed voice is also a courageous, trusting human being, embodiment of the counter-myth of man as the child of faith and hope, with intimations of a wisdom beyond knowledge.

Did Futrelle do all this intentionally? That is another question. A writer is not obliged to have good diplomatic relations with his unconscious.... Did Futrelle sieze on the professor as a possible competitor to Sherlock, or more modestly, to Dr. Thorndyke? In any case, two volumes of Thinking Machine stories appeared, written in an honest, clear-cut style, and still worth reading. In his opening statement the author set his course. His hero was to be a Brain, nothing else. But the story itself changed that. The thinking machine became a thinking person. Writers learn to be humble before the words they put on paper. Splotches of ink, the words have the power to become a world in which the writer himself is a stranger. Does the artist make the work, or is he but an instrument in the hands of other forces? Here, however, we reach another myth and counter-myth. (pp. 79-84)

Benedict Freedman, ''The Thinking Machine,'' in The Mystery & Detection Annual, *edited by Donald K. Adams, Donald Adams, 1972, pp. 79-85.*

E. F. BLEILER   (essay date 1973)

[*Bleiler is an American editor, bibliographer, and critic prominent for his work in the genres of science fiction, fantasy, supernatural horror, and detective fiction. In the following excerpt, Bleiler examines Futrelle's place in the development of the detective story.*]

Just as there are poets who are known by a single poem, there are prose writers who are remembered only for a single story. Sometimes this is proper and suitable, but on other occasions both the author and the public are being poorly served. Jacques Futrelle, for instance, is familiar to almost everyone who reads detective stories as the author of **''The Problem of Cell 13,''** which is surely one of the dozen most famous detective stories

ever written. Yet it is not generally known that Futrelle wrote almost fifty other stories that continue the marvelous deductions of The Thinking Machine in his perpetual contest with the Impossible.

This situation is not entirely fair, for Futrelle at his best was an ingenious author who had many good, original ideas, a flair for contemporary dialogue, and (for us in the 1970's) a period flavor that evokes the dazzling, rootless world of the Edwardians. (p. v)

In several ways Futrelle anticipated later developments in the evolution of the mystery and detective form. Although to us, having lived through the hardboiled and the sexual schools, the Gibson-Girl types that appear in the earlier stories about The Thinking Machine may seem to be a concession to local fashion, there are other areas where Futrelle anticipated realism. The police in his stories are real detectives, such as Futrelle may have known from his newspaper work. They are neither strawmen nor idiots. Where they have limitations, these are such as might have been expected of a harness bull of the turn of the century. The crime reporter Hutchinson Hatch, too, knows exactly what he is doing when he gathers information for The Thinking Machine.

Futrelle, like R. A. Freeman in England a couple of years later, made an effort to be factually accurate, and the mechanisms that he invokes for crime are usually more solid than those of most of his contemporaries. (*Kidnapped Baby Blake*, of course, must be excepted from this statement and what follows!) It is here that Futrelle differs most markedly from the prevailing detective form of his day, the so-called school of Doyle. The essence of a typical British story of the period was a murder committed by outlandish means. Indian snakes that slide down bell cords, hallucinatory drugs (imaginary, of course), giant sea anemones, Oriental images with secret springs, obscure poisons (usually unreliably described) come immediately to mind. For Futrelle, on the other hand, mystery may surround the crime densely, but the means by which the crime has been committed are realistic. To put both approaches into a larger context: Futrelle's contemporaries usually applied the Romantic mode of exoticizing the rational; Futrelle used the Gothic mode of rationalizing the exotic. Futrelle's approach, of course, turned out to be the detective story of the following years.

Futrelle was writing detective stories of idea at a time when most of his colleagues were writing stories of incident or situation. Futrelle was not greatly concerned with action, nor with personalities (beyond the well-drawn Thinking Machine). He was greatly concerned, however, with evoking a plausible story out of a germ idea that involved special knowledge. Here, too, Futrelle was something of a pioneer, for while similar stories had appeared occasionally in the past, Futrelle was the first to create them consistently and systematically, and (at his best) to present them clearly and without encumbrance. About ten years earlier, it is true, M. D. Post had started his series of stories about Randolph Mason, where the point was quirks in the law that permitted a criminal to escape punishment; but it wasn't until later that Post achieved the capsulation that Futrelle demonstrated earlier.

The basic concept of the best of the stories about The Thinking Machine is the insoluble problem, the situation that is ''impossible''—to use the word that so infuriates Professor Van Dusen. A murder committed in a sealed room, an escape from an inescapable receptacle, a true vision in a crystal ball, a flawless charge of murder against a perfect alibi—these are typical. In each instance the Professor solves the problem by logical means, reducing the mystery into situations that yield to rationality.

The background out of which Futrelle built his stories is varied. He obviously was aware of British developments in the detective story, and he obviously knew Poe's work. It seems equally clear that he was immersed in the dime-novel phenomenon that was coming to a close around the first decade of the twentieth century. While his concept of a case is reminiscent of Great Britain, his use of dialogue parallels the dime novel at its best. He also seems to have borrowed one peculiar technique from the dime novel. The multimillion worders who wrote Nick Carter and Old King Brady, for example, simply sloughed off loose ends and inconsistencies by saying frankly, at the end of each story, that they did not know. Futrelle often uses the same technique although with him it creates an impression of verisimilitude. (pp. vi-viii)

It cannot be claimed that all of Futrelle's stories are on the same level of quality. Some are weak, perhaps because of haste, perhaps because of their destination in newspapers. His earlier stories, on the whole, where the situation of impossibility is sustained, are superior to the later, which sometimes are routine detective mysteries. But his better stories have a strange buoyant enthusiasm that carries them through. His narrative is fast, and The Thinking Machine is always wrapped in excitement. Historically, of course, Professor Van Dusen is an immensely important individual, for (with the exception of a few Sherlock Holmes stories) there is no other story from the earlier period of the detective story that has been reprinted and enjoyed more than "**The Problem of Cell 13.**" It is also quite possible that the Professor did much to establish for science fiction the image of the *savant manqué*. (p. viii)

In addition to the stories about The Thinking Machine Futrelle wrote a fair amount of other fiction. His books include [*The Simple Case of Susan*, a sentimental romance about confused identities; *The Diamond Master*, a mystery novel with an element of science fiction; *Elusive Isabel*, crime and impersonation in an embassy setting; *The High Hand*, a political novel; and two posthumous books, *My Lady's Garter*, burglary, impersonation and detection, and *Blind Man's Buff*, sentimental adventure in Paris, to a crime background.] . . . Of all these books, none is now worth reading except *The Diamond Master*, which displays craftsmanship and ingenuity and is in some ways his best work. Futrelle also wrote short stories featuring the detectives Fred Boyd, Dr. Spence, Garron and Louis Harding. Since most of his work first appeared in newspapers and magazines, it is almost certain that this listing is not complete. (p. ix)

> *E. F. Bleiler, in an introduction to* Best "Thinking Machine" Detective Stories *by Jacques Futrelle, edited by E. F. Bleiler, Dover Publications, Inc., 1973, pp. v-ix.*

E. F. BLEILER   (essay date 1976)

[In the following excerpt, Bleiler explains the differences between Futrelle's earlier and later stories about the Thinking Machine.]

Futrelle's earlier stories . . . [about The Thinking Machine] were concerned mostly with the word that The Thinking Machine dislikes so much: the Impossible. Impossible events and situations had to be shifted into the realm of possibility. A perfect alibi opposed to a perfect incrimination; a motor car that disappeared into thin air along a country road that was watched at both ends; a series of footprints that end in the middle of a snowfield—these were the situations of the earlier stories. In a sense these stories are quasi-scientific, in that an idea or fact serves as the basis for a story in some cases: the properties of illuminating gas, the optics of mirrors.

In the later stories . . . , Futrelle was much less concerned with the Impossible. Instead he delighted in positing a mystifying situation, out of which an explanatory story must develop. It is the role of The Thinking Machine to evoke such stories.

What is the crime that will explain a runaway speedboat with a corpse at the controls, a corpse dressed like a French admiral, with no easily perceived cause of death? Why does a young society burglar harass his victim by systematically destroying his overcoats? Why was an actor kidnaped and forced to enact a deathbed scene, and how can the incident be traced? Why does a young lady badger a surgeon into amputating a perfectly healthy finger?

This new direction in The Thinking Machine stories had obvious repercussions. It probably enabled Jacques Futrelle to sell his work to a wider market than the more scientific stories, since societal situations were more popular than germinal ideas. This redirection may be a gain for the modern reader, if he likes to examine the weird values of the denizens of the Gold Coast. In a larger sense, however, it was a loss, for it removed Futrelle's later work from the direct track of the evolving modern American detective story. By and large the detective story does not flourish in the Back Bay and on Beacon Hill.

Whether Futrelle might have returned to the mood of the Impossible stories, or turned in still another direction, is problematic, since his life ended abruptly. (p. vi)

> *E. F. Bleiler, in an introduction to* Great Cases of the Thinking Machine *by Jacques Futrelle, edited by E. F. Bleiler, Dover, Inc., 1976, pp. v-vii.*

W. E. DUDLEY   (essay date 1977)

[In the following excerpt, Dudley considers the probability that Futrelle imitated Arthur Conan Doyle's Sherlock Holmes stories.]

The Master [Sherlock Holmes] has inspired many imitators, and this, certainly, is not meant in any derogatory sense. In fact, it has been said that imitation is the most sincere form of appreciation. It is in that vein that we consider "The Thinking Machine," Professor Augustus S. F. X. Van Dusen, Ph.D., LL.D., F.R.S., M.D., and M.D.S.; "He was also some other things—just what he himself couldn't say—through recognition of his ability by various foreign educational and scientific institutions" ("**The Problem of Cell 13**"). . . .

Was Mr. Futrelle a student of the Canon [of Doyle's Sherlock Holmes stories]? Why, he must have been. How could any gentleman of letters fail to take note of those momentous events which were centred on Baker Street in the great metropolis of London? We *know* that the tales spun by Doctor Watson came to the attention of Mr. Futrelle. (p. 41)

What do we see of the Master in Professor Van Dusen? Well, consider the following:". . . For generations his ancestors had been noted in the sciences; he was the logical result, the master mind. First and above all he was a logician. At least thirty-five years of the half-century or so of his existence had been devoted exclusively to proving that two and two always equal four, except in unusual cases, where they equal three or five, as the case may be. He stood broadly on the general proposition that all things that start must go somewhere, and was able to bring the concentrated mental force of his forefathers to bear on a given problem. Incidentally it may be remarked that Professor Van Dusen wore a No. 8 hat" (**"The Problem of Cell 13"**).

Does that not ring bells? "From a drop of water . . . a logician could infer the possibility of an Atlantic or a Niagara without having seen or heard of one or the other . . ." (*A Study in Scarlet*).

"At least one famous name had been loaned to the proposed experiments, that of the distinguished scientist and logician, Professor Augustus S. F. X. Van Dusen—called The Thinking Machine . . .—[he] was a court of last appeal in the sciences . . ." (**"The Lost Radium"**).

Another bell rings: "Well, I have a trade of my own. I suppose I am the only one in the world. I'm a consulting detective, if you can understand what that is. Here in London we have lots of Government detectives and lots of private ones. When these fellows are at fault, they come to me, and I manage to put them on the right . . ." (*A Study in Scarlet*). (pp. 41-2)

Now we might consider the titles used by Futrelle. Is there, for instance, some connection between **"The Problem of Cell 13"** and "The Adventure of the Six Napoleons" plus *The Sign of the Four* and "The Adventure of the Three Garridebs?" One can only speculate.

And **"The Lost Radium"**?—how about "The Adventure of the Devil's Foot?" Ah, these are deep waters. . . .

"The Scarlet Thread" would seem to be an obvious reference to *A Study in Scarlet*. Here we may be dealing with the world's first true subliminal impression. . . .

As for **"The Brown Coat,"** what can we make of that? Why, there must be some kind of tie-in with "The Adventure of the Red Circle" and "The Yellow Face," and, of course, "The Five Orange Pips."

What about **"The Problem of the Stolen Rubens"?** We are certainly reminded of "The Problem of Thor Bridge," to say nothing of "The Final Problem." And, of course, we recall "The Adventure of the Beryl Coronet". By now we get the picture, the boy Futrelle and what he is reading: *Beeton's Christmas Annual* for 1887!

Think one moment of **"The Fatal Cipher,"** and right away it becomes *The Adventure of the Dancing Men*. Futrelle's life was short but how fortunate he was to spend it in that particular era. Just think, Futrelle was twenty years old in Vincent Starrett's magical year of 1895!

Let us conclude with one little telling piece of evidence that will forever link the creation of Futrelle to the Canon. In **"The Lost Radium"** we have this: "One ounce of radium! . . .—here in the *Yarvard* [italics supplied] laboratory . . ." And from "The Adventure of the Creeping Man" we glean this: "—you've heard of Presbury, of course, the famous *Camford* [italics supplied] physiologist?" Can there be any doubt? (pp. 42-3)

W. E. Dudley, "Ah, Yes, We Know 'the' Thinking Machine," in The Baker Street Journal, n.s. Vol. 27, No. 1, March, 1977, pp. 41-3.

ELLIOT L. GILBERT   (essay date 1977)

[*In the following excerpt, Gilbert examines the reasons for the exceptional popularity of "The Problem of Cell 13." He prefaces his comments with the following quote from W. H. Auden: "Each in the cell of himself is almost convinced of his freedom."*]

From the time of his birth in Georgia in 1875 to the moment of his death a scant 37 years later, Jacques Futrelle wrote only one detective story, **"The Problem of Cell 13"** featuring Augustus S. F. X. Van Dusen, the celebrated "Thinking Machine."

This statement is in fact not true, though many casual readers of detective fiction will think it is. During his brief career, Futrelle produced nearly 50 stories about the brilliant, cantankerous sleuth Van Dusen. . . . Rarely, however, are any of these other "Thinking Machine" tales reprinted in anthologies; for while no serious retrospective collection of mysteries fails to include one story by Jacques Futrelle, that story is invariably **"The Problem of Cell 13."** No wonder most readers suppose it is the only story Futrelle ever wrote.

Why this single piece of fiction should have overshadowed all the rest of its author's output is itself a problem worthy of the "Thinking Machine." We merely beg the question if we try to account for the popularity of the work by saying that it is the best of Futrelle's stories. What we want to know is *why* it is the best. Granted, the "impossible" challenge of the piece is irresistible; Van Dusen boasts that he can think his way out of the securest prison ever built and, when put to the test, brilliantly acquits himself by escaping on schedule from the death cell of a local penitentiary. But many of the other "Thinking Machine" stories present equally attractive "impossible" problems: the nearly magical concealment of a set of stolen jewels (**"The Missing Necklace"**), or the disappearance of an automobile from a road lined on both sides with stone walls (**"The Phantom Motor"**).

Perhaps there is some subtle resonance in **"The Problem of Cell 13"** to explain its extraordinary power over the reader's imagination. If so, a clue to the nature of that resonance may lie in certain striking parallels that exist between this first of the "Thinking Machine" tales and the first of Edgar Allan Poe's seminal detective stories, "The Murders in the Rue Morgue." At times Futrelle seems actually to be paying self-conscious tribute to Poe, especially in the choice of a name for his detective; Augustus Van Dusen and Auguste Dupin are similar enough to invite speculation. Both tales also deal with that most aboriginal of all detective fiction subjects, the locked room problem.

For Poe the locked room problem must be seen as the corollary of a general 19th-century preoccupation with solipsism. Romantic theoreticians, advocating as they did intense self-awareness, self-examination, and self-expression, were continually haunted by the prospect of such inwardness being carried too far, of the mind becoming irrevocably trapped in itself. Walter Pater, in his famous formulation of this vision, resorted naturally to the "locked room" metaphor when he characterized life as "the impression of the individual in his isolation, each mind keeping as a solitary prisoner its own dream of a world." Poe himself was as haunted by solipsistic images of dreams and prisons as any writer of his time, and in a story like "Murders in the Rue Morgue" he makes us see the world as the projection of a single obsessive consciousness: Dupin immured in the dark locked room of his apartment, that apartment virtually indistinguishable from the one in which the killing takes place, the murderous ape clearly invoked from the gloomiest recesses of the psyche. Still, the plain object of the story is to show the superiority of ratiocination over the terrors of solipsism; by solving the mystery of the Rue Morgue murders, detective Dupin also seems to demonstrate that it is possible for the imprisoned human consciousness to escape from the locked room of itself.

Poe's interest in the locked room problem also takes the form, in such tales as "The Black Cat," "The Cask of Amontillado," and "The Fall of the House of Usher," of an obsession with the theme of premature burial. There is hardly anything more representative or poignant in all of the writer's work than the terrible cry of Roderick Usher: "We have put her living into the tomb." The grave is the ultimate locked room, and in a theological age the problem of escape from that room would necessarily have a mystical solution; the events of the first Easter morning, for example, constitute one of the greatest of all locked room stories. However, a century in the process of abandoning theology requires a rational solution for its problems, and as a result 19th-century readers were treated to the ingenious semaphoric contrivances which Poe wanted installed over every grave to allow the prematurely buried to signal their readiness to return to the world; were treated, too, to the "death" of Sherlock Holmes followed by his surprising but entirely reasonable revival, and to the equally ratiocinative version of the rebirth myth in "The Resurrection of Father Brown."

Against this background, the extraordinary appeal of **"The Problem of Cell 13"** becomes clearer; for in this story, Jacques Futrelle offers nothing less than an ingenious rewriting of the Easter myth for the modern sensibility. The secular parody begins when Augustus S. F. X. Van Dusen (the name was first conceived for this particular tale and its middle initials both conceal and reveal the theological dimensions of the work) in the course of a meeting with some friends volunteers to enter a death cell—though guiltless of any crime—in order to demonstrate the possibility of escaping from it through the application of "brain and ingenuity." Coolly, Van Dusen predicts the exact day of that escape, and when his friends come for him at the prearranged time, they find the cell empty. Futrelle fills the story with many hints of its ritual significance. Van Dusen's incarceration mimics the suddenness and unpredictability of death:

> "I'd prefer that it begin tomorrow," said The Thinking Machine, "Because—"
>
> "No, now."

The sacrificial nature of the act is pointedly alluded to:

> "Are you sure you want to do this?"
>
> "Would you be convinced if I did not?" inquired The Thinking Machine.
>
> "No."
>
> "All right. I'll do it."

After his escape, Van Dusen is for a time seen as a mysterious extra person at the prison, duplicating an incident on the road to Emmaus. The Guard " 'only let in four electricians,' " the puzzled prison warden announces. " 'He let out two and says there are three left.' " " 'I was the odd one,' said The Thinking Machine."

> Who is the third who walks always
> beside you?
> When I count there is only you and I
> together. . .

begins T. S. Eliot's well-known version of the same event. Even the number 13 in the story is significant, the number rendered unlucky by the fact that there were 13 at table during the Last Supper.

Given the cleverness of detail in **"The Problem of Cell 13,"** here is resonance enough to account for the remarkable appeal of this first of the "Thinking Machine" stories. What Futrelle has done in his retelling of the Easter myth is to reconstruct a mystical tale for a rational age, making the gratifying point that human reason and human will are all that is needed to defeat even death. To the nervous and/or devout, such a solipsistic boast might seem the height of folly, a gratuitous asking for trouble. Augustus Van Dusen would no doubt have mocked such superstition; nevertheless, even as **"The Problem of Cell 13"** was first appearing in the pages of the *Boston American,* plans were being drawn for a certain trans-Atlantic liner also intended to demonstrate the triumph of human ingenuity over death, though fated instead to provide a monstrously ironic footnote to the Futrelle story. For when the *Titanic* sank on its maiden voyage, its hull crammed with watertight locked rooms, one of its passengers was the creator of Augustus S. F. X. Van Dusen. (pp. 33-4)

> *Elliot L. Gilbert, "Murder without Air," in* The New Republic, *Vol. 177, No. 5, July 30, 1977, pp. 33-4.*

ADDITIONAL BIBLIOGRAPHY

Barzun, Jacques, and Taylor, Wendell Hertig, eds. "Futrelle, Jacques (1875-1912)" and "Futrelle, Jacques." In their *A Catalogue of Crime,* p. 195, pp. 500-01. New York: Harper and Row, Publishers, 1971.
  Brief appraisals of Futrelle's work. The editors state that he "succeeded in giving entertainment, detection, and a touch of character well above the average set by the imitators of Conan Doyle. But Futrelle lacked the power to construct or characterize and too often neglected plausibility. His long stories are therefore unreadable. *The Chase of the Golden Plate* . . . revolts the reader's imagination and sense of truth in every part—dialogue, motive, and chase. *The Thinking Machine on the Case* . . . is a novel (*sic*) of looting and shooting, diamonds and suspicion, all equally absurd."

Moskowitz, Sam. "From Sherlock to Spaceships" and "Unexplained Phenomena." In his *Strange Horizons: A Spectrum of Science Fiction,* pp. 122-59, 218-48. New York: Charles Scribner's Sons, 1976.*
  Explains the differences between the detective story and science fiction and discusses the creation of learned detective heroes who used scientific means to solve crimes. Moskowitz considers this movement of the detective story into the science fiction form to be an important step, one that set into motion events which led to the increasing popularity of detective stories in America, and he cites Futrelle as one author who originated this trend with his story "The Flying Eye."

Murch, A. E. "The Early Twentieth Century." In her *The Development of the Detective Novel,* p. 205. Westport: Greenwood Press, Publishers, 1958.*
  Comments on the Thinking Machine stories and considers the status of Futrelle's detective in the genre. Murch states that "Van Dusen has a brilliant brain, but a brusque, unfriendly personality, a disregard of common courtesy to his associates, and indirectly to the reader, and he cannot be considered one of the popular detectives of fiction."

Review of *My Lady's Garter. The Nation* 95, No. 2464 (19 September 1912): 260.
  Points out a few good qualities in this novel but considers it of little value on the whole, calling it a "flimsy trifle."

Review of *The Diamond Master*. *New York Times Book Review* (11 December 1909): 783.

> Summary and review of *The Diamond Master*. The critic describes it as a "well-constructed and well-written story of mystery and action" and as a "breathlessly interesting tale."

"Futrelle Refused to Enter Lifeboat." *The New York Times* (19 April 1912): 6.

> Reports the circumstances surrounding Jacques Futrelle's death on the *Titanic* and the reunion of May Futrelle with family members following her rescue from one of the ship's lifeboats. Mrs. Futrelle is quoted as saying, "When the *Titanic* hit the iceberg there was the most appalling excitement, and who, after they have passed through such an experience could blame those poor people for the panic that overwhelmed some of them? . . . Jacques is dead, but he died like a hero, that I know."

"Jacques Futrelle's Last." *New York Times Book Review* (1 September 1912): 473.

> Summarizes Futrelle's posthumously published novel *My Lady's Garter*, stating that "it is written with dash and go and bubbling spirits, the author's attention—and the reader's too—all centered on the plot and the incidents, with none at all to spare for thought of probability or of literary quality."

Wells, Carolyn. *The Technique of the Mystery Story*. Springfield: Home Correspondence School, Publishers, 1913, p. 79ff.

> The first exhaustive study of the mystery story genre, with references to Futrelle throughout.

R(obert) B(ontine) Cunninghame Graham

1852-1936

(Born Robert Cunninghame Graham Bontine) Scottish short story and sketch writer, travel writer, essayist, critic, biographer, and historian.

Graham was one of the most remarkable personalities of the late Victorian and Edwardian eras. His tempestuous political career, as the first unofficial socialist in the English parliament, brought him as much fame—or notoriety—as his writings, which consisted for the most part of histories of the Spanish conquests in the New World and portraits of life in the uncivilized regions of South America as well as other places familiar to him from his travels. An aristocrat by birth, with a strain of Spanish blood inherited from his maternal grandmother, Graham was called "Don Roberto" by his friends and in the popular press, in recognition of his courageous nature, quixotic idealism, and cavalier good looks. In his lifetime he was a legendary character whose name evoked images of bold individualism and exotic adventure.

Graham was born in London in 1852. His father was a Scottish nobleman and a direct descendant of King Robert I of Scotland; his mother was the daughter of a Scottish seafarer and a Spanish heiress. The Grahams held title to the great estates of Gartmore and Ardoch in Perthshire, Scotland, and their ancestors included, in addition to the Scottish king, a colorful assortment of soldiers, heroes, and adventurers. As a young man, Graham attended preparatory school at Leamington and later the exclusive boy's school Harrow; however, though he excelled in athletics, his academic performance was disappointing. He later studied at schools in London and Brussels and privately in Switzerland with a tutor whose anti-racist views may have influenced Graham's own later thought. Throughout his childhood, Graham's family travelled extensively across Europe and the British Isles, and an enthusiasm for travel remained with Graham for the rest of his life. Many of his finest literary works, including *Mogreb-el-Acksa*, which is today regarded as a classic among travel books, were the products of his later wanderings.

When he was seventeen, Graham went to Argentina to learn cattle ranching in a venture that his father hoped would increase the family fortunes. On his arrival, Graham found the country in a state of civil war. His proposed partner had lost his ranch and cattle in the conflict, but was recovering his losses by traveling about the country selling hides and wools. Graham joined him and began a series of adventures that served as the basis for many of his later sketches. He met gauchos and revolutionaries, tried his hand at horse droving, cattle ranching, and surveying, and fought Indians. He learned to ride like a gaucho and acquired the love of horses that later led him to write such critically acclaimed sketches as "Calvary" and "Los Pingos," in which he unsentimentally protested the thoughtless cruelties to which horses and other animals were routinely subjected in so-called civilized societies. Graham was also struck by the omnipresence of death and violence as features of life on the South American plains. Later, in his South American stories and sketches, he sought to realistically portray the sudden and arbitrary manner in which life often ended in that environment.

Graham returned to Europe several times for visits during the next few years. On one of these occasions, he met and eloped with Gabriela de la Balmondière, much to the surprise of his family. She and Graham returned to America and lived for a time in Mexico and Texas. It was during this trip that Graham, in emulation of Bret Harte, made his first attempt at writing a magazine article based on his frontier experiences. In 1883 Graham's father died, and Graham returned to Scotland to succeed him as the laird of Gartmore. Graham also began to take an active interest in radical politics at this time, and in 1886 he was elected to parliament as the representative for the industrial district of North-West Lanark. Although he ran as a liberal, Graham supported numerous causes associated with socialism. He was an early advocate of the eight-hour working day, women's suffrage, and the nationalization of various industries. Graham's earliest published writings were the dozens of polemical articles that he wrote for various socialist and liberal publications, including William Morris's *Commonweal*, the *People's Press*, and the *Social Democrat*. His well-known essay "Bloody Niggers," an ironical denunciation of racism and imperialism and one of Graham's most direct statements of his skepticism concerning progress and religion, dates from this period. Although many of Graham's political ideas seemed radical to his contemporaries, Richard E. Haymaker noted in his 1967 study, *Prince-Errant and Evocator of Horizons*, that "nearly all of the programme he advocated has now, two generations later, been enacted into law."

Graham's parliamentary career ended in 1892 when he failed to win reelection. Afterward he resumed his interest in travel and began to give more serious attention to writing. His principal career, during the second half of his life, was that of a man of letters, although he remained vigorously active, even to the point of engaging in a special military assignment in South America at the outbreak of World War I, when he was sixty-two years old. Graham made his final trip to Argentina in 1936. As a life-long friend of the novelist W. H. Hudson, he had been approached to assist in the preparation of a Spanish edition of Hudson's writings. The long journey exhausted him, and he died of pneumonia in Buenos Aires at the age of eighty-four.

Graham's first book, *Notes on the District of Menteith,* appeared in 1895. It contained stories and anecdotes about the Menteith region of Scotland, the ancestral home of Graham's family. Whimsical in both tone and subject matter, reviewers found the book entertaining for its descriptions of local landmarks and characters and for Graham's claim to the throne of Scotland. Encouraged by this response, Graham began submitting stories and sketches to the *Saturday Review.* The following year a second volume appeared, containing sketches by both Graham and his wife Gabriela. Entitled *Father Archangel of Scotland, and Other Essays,* this was the first book in which Graham included sketches based on his travels in South America. Graham's short sketches appeared in numerous volumes over a period of forty years. Although his style and formal proficiency developed over this time, and although his later works reveal a less satiric, more sympathetic outlook than his earlier volumes, critics agree that his writings are, on the whole, extremely consistent in both style and theme. There are no radical changes in point of view, subject matter, or technique, and the autobiographical elements ever present in Graham's writings also further the impression that the early and the late works form a united whole. Graham was a campaigner for the underdog and an opponent of imperialism. He believed strongly that even the most primitive cultures should be respected and preserved, rather than extirpated in the name of progress. He was also suspicious of the idea of progress and of the materialistic values he associated with it, and whether he was writing about rural Scotland in a sketch such as "Heather Jock," or about the gauchos of Argentina in "A Vanishing Race," these concerns are always in evidence.

In 1898, Graham's literary reputation was firmly established by the publication of his most famous book, *Mogreb-el-Acksa,* which recounts Graham's journey across Morocco. Although it arose from the same tradition of Victorian travel fiction as A. W. Kinglake's *Eōthen* (1844) and Sir Richard Burton's *Pilgrimage to Al Madinah and Meccah* (1855-56), Graham's book differs from its predecessors in both positive and negative ways. Cedric Watt explains these differences in terms of Graham's relative lack of "belletristic elegance" in comparison to the works of Kinglake and Burton, and his lack of any systematic background knowledge of Arab culture. Nonetheless, Watt and many other critics believe that *Mogreb-el-Acksa* deserved its place among the classics of the travel genre. They observe that Graham's work is redeemed by his vitality of expression, his acute powers of observation, and his intelligent apprehension of the realities concealed below surface appearances and cultural differences. Moreover, the extent to which Graham's personality intrudes itself into his narrative, although

sometimes considered a fault of his writing, is also often thought to be an asset. His sense of irony, his struggles with the prejudices of his age—which he could not always transcend—his humanitarian sympathies, and his skepticism all combine in *Mogreb-el-Acksa* to create a vivid work of valuable cultural insight.

In addition to *Mogreb-el-Acksa* and his many volumes of sketches, Graham also wrote numerous historical works dealing with the Spanish conquest of South America, various odd episodes from South American history, and the lives of the Spanish conquerors. The best of these volumes include *A Vanished Arcadia, The Conquest of New Granada,* and *A Brazilian Mystic: Being the Life and Miracles of Antonio Conselheiro.* For all of their flaws, critics agree that these volumes still contain much of interest to readers today. Although Graham was not a professional historian and often made careless errors in the recording of historical detail, his first-hand knowledge of the countries of South America and his lively interest in character gave his histories an appeal often lacking in more scholarly accounts. Moreover, Graham's religious skepticism and sense of irony, as well as his love of adventure, made the conquests a rich subject for his exploration. Graham deeply felt the irony of using propagation of the Catholic faith as an excuse for conquest, adventurism, and exploitation; however, he could also admire the courage with which the conquistadores faced the hardships they encountered in the New World. In his histories, Graham defended the Spanish conquerors from the popular charge that they were worse than their modern English and American counterparts, but he also condemned them for their exploitation and slaughter of South American natives. Finding that Graham's broad sympathies and shifting point of view greatly enhance the interest of these works, Watt has stated: "If Cunninghame Graham were more consistent, he would be far less engaging."

Although his works were never widely popular and are often neglected today, Graham was greatly admired by many of his famous contemporaries, including Joseph Conrad, Ford Madox Ford, G. K. Chesterton, and George Bernard Shaw. Shaw's play *Captain Brassbound's Conversion* (1900) was inspired by *Mogreb-el-Acksa,* and Shaw also acknowledged that it was Graham's indignant retort to an angry parliament—"I never withdraw!"—that provided him with the basis for his dashing character Sergei Saranoff in *Arms and the Man* (1894). As Watt explains, Graham was "mythogenic: a generator and attractor of legends; a challenge to the artistic imagination." He was also a humanitarian and a visionary who relentlessly attacked the Kiplingesque ethnocentrism and imperialistic spirit of pre-war Britain. Graham believed strongly in respecting the integrity of other races and of native cultures, and the frequency with which these themes appear in his writings is often proffered by critics as an important reason why they were never more widely accepted by the British public, which was preoccupied at the time with Great Britain's efforts to seize a share of the wealth of Africa; however, this concern with cultural integrity explains Graham's interest and value for the contemporary reader.

PRINCIPAL WORKS

Notes on the District of Menteith, for Tourists and Others (nonfiction) 1895
Father Archangel of Scotland, and Other Essays [with Gabriela Cunninghame Graham] (essays) 1896
Mogreb-el-Acksa: A Journey in Morocco (nonfiction) 1898

The Ipané   (short stories, sketches, and essays)   1899
Thirteen Stories   (short stories and sketches)   1900
A Vanished Arcadia: Being Some Account of the Jesuits in Paraguay, 1607 to 1767   (history)   1901
Success   (short stories and sketches)   1902
Hernando de Soto: Together with an Account of One of His Captains, Gonçalo Silvestre   (history)   1903
Progress, and Other Sketches   (short stories and sketches) 1905
His People   (short stories and sketches)   1906
Faith   (short stories and sketches)   1909
Hope   (short stories and sketches)   1910
Charity   (short stories and sketches)   1912
A Hatchment   (short stories and sketches)   1913
Bernal Díaz del Castillo: Being Some Account of Him, Taken from His True History of the Conquest of New Spain   (biography)   1915
Brought Forward   (short stories and sketches)   1916
A Brazilian Mystic: Being the Life and Miracles of Antonio Conselheiro   (biography)   1920
Cartagena and the Banks of the Sinú   (history and nonfiction)   1920
The Conquest of New Granada: Being the Life of Gonzalo Jiménez de Quesada   (biography)   1922
The Conquest of the River Plate   (history)   1924
Doughty Deeds: An Account of the Life of Robert Graham of Gartmore, Poet and Politician, 1735-1797, Drawn from his Letter-Books and Correspondence   (biography) 1925
Pedro de Valdivia, Conqueror of Chile   (biography)   1926
Redeemed, and Other Sketches   (short stories and sketches) 1927
José Antonio Páez   (biography)   1929
The Horses of the Conquest   (history)   1930
Writ in Sand   (short stories and sketches)   1932
Portrait of a Dictator: Francisco Solano López (Paraguay, 1865-1870)   (biography)   1933
Mirages   (short stories and sketches)   1936

THE BOOKMAN, LONDON   (essay date 1896)

[*In the following excerpt, the critic reviews* Father Archangel of Scotland.]

All the papers collected [in *Father Archangel of Scotland* by G. and R. B. Cunninghame Graham] speak of Spain or Spanish America. They are travel impressions and character studies of exceptional interest, and, save where Mr. Cunninghame Graham becomes facetious, of great charm. Mrs. Graham preserves a calm demeanour throughout, writing of quiet, old-world, out-of-the-world things with a gentle sympathetic grace; and the same description intensified might serve for much of her husband's work, which is, however, varied by passages of great liveliness, uselessly angry outbursts, and foolish jokes. He feels strongly, is extremely sensitive to beauty and to the ugliness of modern life, hates shams, and hates solemnities. There a good many are with him. But he speaks as if he were alone, one solitary angry protester against a vulgar world, and wastes much breath in cheap sneers at what the better part of mankind are agreed in denouncing, if they cannot cure. It is only the ear of the better part he may hope to win; yet readers feel they are being snapped at every now and again, when Mr.

Graham is in a discursive humour. He is often in a discursive humour, and he rarely then says anything that is not either wild or trite, while otherwise his style and attitude have grace and beauty. Scots will prick up their ears at one passage—"No one in his wildest fits of patriotism ever talked of Merrie Scotland. . . . Loyal, abstemious, businesslike, haggis-eating, tender, disagreeable, true, a Scotsman may be, but merry never." Shades of Burns and Tam o' Shanter here protest; and some of Mr. Graham's own oratory gives his statement the lie. The mirth of Scots is mad and may be fearsome, but Mr. Graham must have kept poor company if he has not met with it. The commonplace political gibes and nearly all the modern allusions are irritating, and depreciate in a regretable way the value of a book which is otherwise delightful. **"The Horses of the Pampas," "A Jesuit," "De Heretico Comburendo"**—a description of Valladolid—some passages of **"In the Tarumensian Woods,"** and almost the whole of **"Father Archangel of Scotland"**—an account taken from a Spanish book of an attempt at the hard task of converting Aberdonians to the old Church—are excellent reading. Mr. Graham has nearly every talent wanted for the literary calling, save the contempt of making points cheaply. (pp. 26-7)

> A review of "Father Archangel of Scotland," in The Bookman, London, Vol. X, No. 55, April, 1896, pp. 26-7.

JOSEPH CONRAD   (letter date 1898)

[*Conrad is considered an innovator of novel structure as well as one of the finest stylists of modern English literature. In his preface to* The Nigger of the "Narcissus" *(1897), an essay that has been called his artistic credo, Conrad explained that "art itself may be defined as a single-minded attempt to render the highest kind of justice to the visible universe, by bringing to light the truth, manifold and one, underlying its every aspect. It is an attempt to find in its forms, in its colours, in its light, in its shadows, in the aspects of matter, and in the facts of life what of each is fundamental, what is enduring and essential—their one illuminating and convincing quality—the very truth of their existence. . . . My task which I am trying to achieve is, by the power of the written work, to make you feel—it is, before all, to make you see. That— and no more, and it is everything." Conrad was one of Graham's closest friends, and the two men corresponded for many years. In the following excerpt from one of Conrad's early letters to Graham, he praises* Mogreb-el-Acksa.]

I wrote to your mother about your book [*Mogreb-el-Acksa*]. I found it easier to speak to a third person—at first. I do not know what to tell you. If I tell you that You have surpassed my greatest expectations you may be offended—and this piece of paper is not big enough to explain how great my expectations were. Anyway they are left behind. I am ashamed of my moderation and now I am looking at the performance I ask myself what kind of friend was I not to foresee, not to understand that the book would just be *that*—no less. Well it is there—for our joy, for our thought, for our triumph. I am speaking of those who understand and love you. The preface is a gem—I knew it, I remembered it—and yet it came with a fresh force. To be understood is not everything—one must be understood as one would like to be. This probably you won't have.

Yes—the book is Art. Art without a trace of Art's theories in its incomparably effective execution. It isn't anybody's art— it is C-Graham's art. The individuality of the work imposes itself on the reader—from the first. Then come other things, skill, pathos, humour, wit, indignation. Above all a continuous feeling of delight; the persuasion that there one has got hold of a good thing. This should work for material success. Yet who knows! No doubt it is too good.

You haven't been careful in correcting your proofs. Are you too grand seigneur for that infect labour? Surely I, twenty others, would be only too proud to do it for you. Tenez vous le pour dit. [Take it as read.] I own I was exasperated by the errors. Twice the wretched printers perverted your meaning. It is twice too often. They should die! (pp. 110-11)

> *Joseph Conrad, in a letter to R. B. Cunninghame Graham on December 9, 1898, in his* Joseph Conrad's Letters to R. B. Cunninghame Graham, *edited by C. T. Watts, Cambridge at the University Press, 1969, pp. 110-11.*

BERNARD SHAW   (essay date 1900)

[*Shaw is generally considered the greatest and best-known dramatist to write in the English language since Shakespeare. Following the example of Henrik Ibsen, he succeeded in revolutionizing the English stage, disposing of the romantic conventions and devices of the "well-made play," and instituting the theater of ideas, grounded in realism. As Samuel Hynes has noted, Shaw was driven by a rage to better the world. A Fabian socialist, he wrote criticism that was often concerned with the humanitarian and political intent of the work under discussion. In the following excerpt, Shaw, who knew Graham well and sympathized with many of his political and social views, credits Graham's* Mogreb-el-Acksa *with providing the background for his play* Captain Brassbound's Conversion *(1900) and offers a character sketch of Graham himself.*]

I claim as a notable merit in the authorship of this play [*Captain Brassbound's Conversion*] that I have been intelligent enough to steal its scenery, its surroundings, its atmosphere, its geography, its knowledge of the east, its fascinating Cadis and Krooboys and Sheikhs and mud castles from an excellent book of philosophic travel and vivid adventure entitled *Mogreb-el-Acksa (Morocco the Most Holy)* by Cunninghame Graham. My own first hand knowledge of Morocco is based on a morning's walk through Tangier, and a cursory observation of the coast through a binocular from the deck of an Orient steamer, both later in date than the writing of the play.

Cunninghame Graham is the hero of his own book; but I have not made him the hero of my play, because so incredible a personage must have destroyed its likelihood—such as it is. There are moments when I do not myself believe in his existence. And yet he must be real; for I have seen him with these eyes; and I am one of the few men living who can decipher the curious alphabet in which he writes his private letters. The man is on public record too. The battle of Trafalgar Square, in which he personally and bodily assailed civilization as represented by the concentrated military and constabular forces of the capital of the world, can scarcely be forgotten by the more discreet spectators, of whom I was one. On that occasion civilization, qualitatively his inferior, was quantitatively so hugely in excess of him that it put him in prison, but had not sense enough to keep him there. Yet his getting out of prison was as nothing compared to his getting into the House of Commons. How he did it I know not; but the thing certainly happened, somehow. That he made pregnant utterances as a legislator may be taken as proved by the keen philosophy of the travels and tales he has since tossed to us; but the House, strong in stupidity, did not understand him until in an inspired moment he voiced a universal impulse by bluntly damning its hypocrisy. Of all the eloquence of that silly parliament, there

remains only one single damn. It has survived the front bench speeches of the eighties as the word of Cervantes survives the oraculations of the Dons and Deys who put him, too, in prison. The shocked House demanded that he should withdraw his cruel word. "I never withdraw," said he; and I promptly stole the potent phrase for the sake of its perfect style, and used it as a cockade for the Bulgarian hero of *Arms and the Man*. The theft prospered; and I naturally take the first opportunity of repeating it. In what other Lepantos besides Trafalgar Square Cunninghame Graham has fought, I cannot tell. He is a fascinating mystery to a sedentary person like myself. The horse, a dangerous animal whom, when I cannot avoid, I propitiate with apples and sugar, he bestrides and dominates fearlessly, yet with a true republican sense of the rights of the fourlegged fellowcreature whose martyrdom, and man's shame therein, he has told most powerfully in his **"Calvary,"** a tale with an edge that will cut the soft cruel hearts and strike fire from the hard kind ones. He handles the other lethal weapons as familiarly as the pen: medieval sword and modern Mauser are to him as umbrellas and kodaks are to me. His tales of adventure have the true Cervantes touch of the man who has been there— so refreshingly different from the scenes imagined by bloody-minded clerks who escape from their servitude into literature to tell us how men and cities are conceived in the counting house and the volunteer corps. He is, I understand, a Spanish hidalgo: hence the superbity of his portrait by Lavery (Velasquez being no longer available). He is, I know, a Scotch laird. How he contrives to be authentically the two things at the same time is no more intelligible to me than the fact that everything that has ever happened to him seems to have happened in Paraguay or Texas instead of in Spain or Scotland. He is, I regret to add, an impenitent and unashamed dandy: such boots, such a hat, would have dazzled D'Orsay himself. With that hat he once saluted me in Regent St. when I was walking with my mother. Her interest was instantly kindled; and the following conversation ensued. "Who is that?" "Cunninghame Graham." "Nonsense! Cunninghame Graham is one of your Socialists: that man is a gentleman." This is the punishment of vanity, a fault I have myself always avoided, as I find conceit less troublesome and much less expensive. Later on somebody told him of Tarudant, a city in Morocco in which no Christian had ever set foot. Concluding at once that it must be an exceptionally desirable place to live in, he took ship and horse; changed the hat for a turban; and made straight for the sacred city, via Mogador. How he fared, and how he fell into the hands of the Cadi of Kintafi, who rightly held that there was more danger to Islam in one Cunninghame Graham than in a thousand Christians, may be learnt from his account of it in *Mogreb-el-Acksa*, without which *Captain Brassbound's Conversion* would never have been written. (pp. 295-97)

> *Bernard Shaw, "'Captain Brassbound's Conversion': Sources of the Play," in his* Three Plays for Puritans, *Brentano's, 1906, pp. 295-301.*

THE ACADEMY   (essay date 1902)

[*In the following excerpt, the critic discusses the view of life expressed by Graham in* Success.]

It is perhaps not strange that the good old word humanity— Chaucer's humanitee—used in the sense of kindness for so many centuries—was found too delicate in constitution to bear all the alarming strain imposed in its use in modern civilisation, and that Society had to coin the chilly abstraction, humanitarianism, to help cope with our enterprising and greedy times.

"The Second Sally," from an illustrated edition of Don Quixote. *The illustrator, William Strang, used Graham as the model for the title character.*

Mr. Cunninghame Graham's *Success* makes us wish that the word humanist had a less restricted meaning to-day, and that it should henceforward denominate those writers in whose work breathes the spirit of a rare and fine humanity, writers who are not afraid of painting life as it is, and are not ashamed of presenting man with a finely humane ideal. We are aware that this heterogeneous modern Society of ours has a dislike for those ironists who touch even lightly on the raw places of civilisation, and a contempt for the philosophers who invite it to project its imagination for a moment beyond the limited horizon of its self-love. Nevertheless, the whole issue raised by *Success* is worth putting again and again—what does modern Society gain by its instinctive fear of the writers who show us things as they are?

For one thing, Society loses a good deal in misunderstanding all those significant writers who flatter it least. *Success* is an instance in point. Readers who come to this book will have to read it for its author's rare spirit, for its delicate wit and philosophy of life, and incidentally that implies that the reader will have to take a hammer to many imposing idols, and throw various fetishes into the street.

Some books offer us a great deal of gorgeous upholstery and no end of sham appearances, and the poor author has to inflate his spirit to bursting point to keep up the trick. Mr. Cunninghame Graham's sketches simply present casual but most significant snatches of life caught now here, now there, by his observant eye: life on the South American pampa, in a London prison, at a Spanish railway station, in an Ulster factory village, &c., and we see—oh, rare spectacle!—that to this traveller his fellows are really brother-men and that human life, whether it be manifesting its vagaries on the Hill of Golgotha or in the Old Kent Road, has the same sacred importance as a reality to be measured only by the measure of human sacrifice, suffering, or stupidity interwoven in it.

To his critical, kindling glance, the infinite variety of types and grades of mankind form a vast democratic family, no type better than another, but different, and the human specimens he sketches for us, whether they be Birmingham factory hands or Scotch Elders, Nonconformists, M.P.'s, or Parisian "horizontales," . . . all are the equal human children of that old bickering family of our crafty and plotting old mother Earth. It is indeed by this philosophic, this kindly, this ironic justice of his, while plunging us in *Success* into the daily accidental world of life just as it is, struggling, complex, prosaic, with the sun rising on the common old spectacle of man's incorrigible self-importance, of the strange and whimsical patterns of his diversity, of his weak humanity and stranger inhumanity towards his fellows that Mr. Cunninghame Graham strikes his own original note. And this note, though it seems satirical to say it, while aristocratic in tone, is too democratic in its broad charity and wide humanity to be loved of the democrats. And here comes in the fly in the average reader's ointment.

The fly in the reader's ointment in the case of Mr. Cunninghame Graham's writings is simply the place to which the author relegates "civilisation." Civilisation we know is "top dog" in the Anglo Saxon's world to day, and to the leader writers all the rest of the world is Barbarism, the bottom dog. But Mr. Cunninghame Graham, who is a keen critic of the facts of life, finds, like many travellers and artists before him, that if you gave civilised man more real freedom and enjoyment and took away much cant and half the "benefits" that stifle him, there would then be little to choose between him and the barbarian. There is nothing particularly startling in this doctrine (which is secretly held by perhaps most men in the City), but our author's artistic method is so individual as to raise blisters on the mind of every disciple of Progress. Whereas the artist *pur sang* [thoroughbred] in painting life strives to find the right perspective in which his subject reveals itself as a definite growth of character, soil and circumstance, and by showing us life's inevitability and by keeping us as mere spectators outside it, disarms us of our prejudices, Mr. Cunninghame Graham is always relating all species and types of human life together at his will and pleasure, relating us in Fleet Street, say, with the Gauchos in this sketch, or with the Arab tribesmen in that. His artistic method is a strange fusion of the artist's vision with the man of action's outlook, which often comes off brilliantly, as in **"The Gualichu Tree"** where there is a natural relation shown between civilised and uncivilised man, but often it is irritating, even inartistic, as in **"Los Sequidores"** where there is no relation shown. The method at times, though brilliant, is too inharmonious. As, however, the great general stream of the actual world's life to-day is the author's province, and as it is his special gift (and no other writer shows it) to shift and bring together the most diverse humours of life in a rapidly flashing spectacle, and to show us those relations and similarities which escape other minds, it would be folly to quarrel with the manner in which he gets his effects. To analyse the author's method, this brilliant style in which wit and philosophy and description blend into one pungent salt, is about as profitable as to analyse sea spray to show why it sparkles in the sunlight.

Some books have to be read for the pomp and show of things they place imposingly before us, and others have to be read simply for the spirit in which they analyse life. *Success* is one of the comparatively few books that fall naturally in the latter class. The author is a realist of the realists (you can feel the sharp edge and blunt outlines of material fact in his pages), and yet his vision of this world is half a poet's. His subtle compassion for his fellow men, his indignant tenderness for the weak, and his utter lack of sentimentality is, however, at the root of his charm. (pp. 436-37)

"An Ironist's Outlook," in The Academy, *Vol. LXIII, No. 1590, October 25, 1902, pp. 436-37.*

W. M. PARKER (essay date 1917)

[In the following excerpt, Parker praises the adventurous spirit of Graham's work.]

It has become generally recognized that the majority of widely-travelled people, if they are not out-and-out liars or something like strangers to the truth, are at least on familiar terms with exaggeration, or, as it is otherwise styled, the process of "drawing the long bow." Mr. Cunninghame Graham, as a scrupulous literary artist and a traveller combined, has proved by his unerring observation and verisimilitude of detail that he can convince even the most unbelieving trooper that ever walked God's earth. His imagination is at one and the same time iridescent and persuasive. Cunninghame Graham! What transports of delight in fresh, wild life that name conjures up!—scenes of

> Antres vast and deserts idle,
> Rough quarries, rocks, and hills whose heads
> touch heaven;

the grey ruggedness of Scotland, the sunny stretches of Spain, the cruel sand wastes of Morocco, and the arid pampas of South America. (pp. 197-98)

Mr. Cunninghame Graham's literary work has been characterized as that of the Scottish Maupassant. His style has a freshening touch of virility that strikes an unmistakable note of health. To employ the appropriate figurative lingo, he gives full rein to his vivid imagination yet with scarcely a hint anywhere of unbridled passions. He rarely mounts his high horse unless it be to pour scorn on some absurd modern social fetish. When he lingers for a while, on his travels, it is before the setting sun when, having raced the sun neck for neck, as it were, he alights from his saddle and settles himself to a well-earned smoke; and it is then that the vanished arcadias crowd into his reflections, and he sets him the pleasant task of inscribing nocturnes of regret over that past which lives on in the mind but which can never more be a reality. Most of these sobbing songs of long ago vent themselves in **"Scottish Stories"** where the eccentric old Scottish characters of a past generation are limned by an endearing hand. He has a deep and an abiding love for those old worthies, just as he has an attachment for some old, neglected haunt that tells its story in its moss-grown silence, and there are such unforgettable silences in **"A Princess," "A Braw Day,"** and **"Caistealna-Sithan"** where "crows winged their way, looking like notes of music on an old page of parchment, across the leaden sky." That is his reflective side only, because he has proved in one of his better-known sketches, **"Beattock for Moffat,"** that he has a sense for dramatic situation. He finds it, however, as difficult to pause for very long on these homely pictures as to resist the call of the wilds in South America, so that once more at the rising of the sun it is "boot, saddle, to horse, and away!" bounding over the windswept prairies.

To turn at random to any of his collected stories and sketches, to, say, **"Thirteen Stories"** or **"Success"** or **"Progress,"** produces a sensation of awe and obeisance before this high priest in the temple of Colour, "the soul's bridegroom," as a certain genius has happily phrased it. The man of letters stands out clearly in his pure, fastidious, restrained style and in his strict attention to the use of words, especially foreign words. The colour and atmosphere of the Argentine and the River Plate saturate his pages; and who is happier than he, this valiant horseman, mounted on a superb Barbary roan, riding over sierras and pampas. It is no "spavined" mare he rides. The sweet air seems to sing around him, the rhythmic cadence of the rider invades the very prose he writes, and the blood courses freer and fuller as the leagues upon leagues of ground are covered. As did noble, generous Cortes, he rides like a centaur, and his "prince of palfreys trots the air and makes the earth sing when he touches it—the basest horn of his hoof is more musical than the pipe of Hermes. . . . It is a beast for Perseus: he is pure air and fire. . . . In many of his South American sketches, and particularly in the ones called **"Success"** and that merciless piece of irony called **"Calvary,"** his attitude is the kind of full-blooded defiance in which that other modern Elizabethan, Henley, used to revel. Again his irony towards humanity finds outlet in his denunciation of missionaries sent out to convert the heathen of savage lands and in his contempt for the material success of modern civilization; the wonderful preface to **"Progress"** expresses his views on progress and success. "Failure alone is interesting." What is perhaps most striking in his best sketches, such as **"Success," "Los Seguidores," "From the Mouth of the Sahara,"** and **"La Tapera,"** is his suave melancholy that acts as a depression, a momentary relief, from his altitudes of virility. Equally interesting are the vivid pictures of this gringo's dealings with the gauchos. It is on his sagas of the saddle, rather than on his Scottish subjects, fraught though they be with an antique wistfulness, that Mr. Cunninghame Graham's fame is assured. On the saddle he is at home, and writing on equitation calls out his sympathies and literary powers. He stops to call your attention to the shyness of horses, of even wild horses that require to be caught with the lasso. He knows the use of bolas and of a hundred other kindred implements of sport and common usage in South American wild life. After an adventurous ride by tropical forests of lianas and ñandubays, sighting on the way ostriches and parroquets, tortoises and flamingoes, at the hot noontide he may draw up at a rancho to drink maté, while the burning sun shines down like brass. . . . The hush of nightfall on lonely spots; the tinkling of bells in the dusky distance; the first radiance of the dawn; here eating jerked beef and there riding "through forest, over baking plain, up mountain paths, . . . splashing through marshes, the water reaching up to the horse's girths"; the customs and superstitions of primitive foreign races; the unconventional peoples and surroundings he knows and loves so well; and, not least, the poignant sentiments of these uncivilised and ignorant races, whose failure and backwardness in the march of human progress are more interesting to him and better understood by him than the worshipped success of a boasted civilization—all these themes he treats with supreme mastery. Like his *confrère* in literature, Conrad, of whose unrivalled powers he was one of the first to take note, he is fascinated by mysterious waterways that seem to lose themselves in wending their courses and carrying men's secrets to the vast, open sea. (pp. 204-13)

Deplore it as we may well do, the fact remains that in his latest book, **"Brought Forward,"** he has made his farewell bow before the drop curtain, and present-day art is, indeed, the poorer for his departure from the arena of letters. He has bequeathed to this century artistic impressions of healthy, sane, open-air life on sierra and prairie and desert that will take their place side by side with the works of his two brother impressionists of elemental life—Joseph Conrad and W. H. Hudson. With the Scottish sketches in **"Brought Forward"** I have the feeling that somehow they never get under way, but his South American scenes have still the freshness and romance, as of yore. The most beautifully coloured sketches are **"El Tango Argentino,"** **"In a Backwater,"** **"El Masgad,"** and the sumptuous **"Feast Day in Santa Maria Mayor."** A lingering touch of regret, as of leaving a well-loved land, lends a sad, flickering hue to **"Bopicuá."** (pp. 213-15)

Mr. Cunninghame Graham's views are nothing if not healthily unconventional. One imagines him "swaggering" in the days of Elizabeth, decked in silk doublet and trunk hose, and beruffled, gracefully manipulating a rapier-thrust and footing it gaily in a galliard or a coranto—a Sir Philip Sidney to the life. His love of colours and conceits, of horsemanship and adventure, are essentially traits of the golden age of good Queen Bess. (pp. 218-19)

> *W. M. Parker, "A Modern Elizabethan: R. B. Cunninghame Graham," in his* Modern Scottish Writers, *1917. Reprint by Books for Libraries Press, 1968; distributed by Arno Press, Inc., pp. 197-219.*

THE ATHENAEUM (essay date 1920)

[*In the following excerpt, the critic finds fault with Graham's* A Brazilian Mystic.]

Imagine a remote upland region, where day and night alternately burn and freeze; cattle roam over a light soil, which changes with the seasons from choking dust to mud; the tropical forests, which crowd impenetrably on the lower slopes, are replaced here by scrub. This is the Brazilian Sertao, with a thinly-scattered, half-wild population of breeders and tenders of cattle. It is separated from the civilization of the coast by tracts of difficult country; inland, a range of mountains bars the way. In a lost corner of this far-off world, a desolate countryside backed by wild hills, there existed in 1893 a small village, named Canudos, nestling beside the reed-grown banks of a river.

In that year its stagnation was violently moved by the appearance of a band of fanatical wanderers, led by a gaunt, fiery-eyed, elderly man. Antonio Maciel, known as Conselheiro, the Councillor, having brought his followers so far, elected to dwell with them at Canudos. Within five years a city of some 15,000 inhabitants had sprung up in the wilderness, and had been swept out of existence again. In its flourishing time it was a labyrinth of reed-built hovels, dominated by a vast church of stone, never completed. In this Cyclopean fane Antonio preached his dangerous doctrine. The end of the world was at hand; the faithful must prepare for the new dispensation by repentence, prayer and fasting; they must resist to all extremity the decrees and forces of the Republic, in whose liberalism and innovations the visionary eye could easily discern the baleful characteristics of Antichrist's reign. This teaching was received with ecstatic fervour; Antonio's other-worldliness had caught the imagination of the dwellers of the Sertao. . . . The Republic, openly defied, sent, one after another, four expectations against Canudos. The approach to it was rendered difficult by the nature of the country; the town was fortified by a system of trenches; but the defenders were ill-armed, and it was thought at first that a small force would speedily settle the difficulty. The first expedition consisted of a hundred soldiers of the line and the ill-equipped militia of a small town. The last expedition, before it attained success, numbered over 10,000, with cavalry and artillery; the siege of the town lasted four months; in it perished the Councillor and all but an insignificant remnant of his followers.

Here was a theme for the flame and thunder of Carlyle's pen. Antonio Conselheiro was one of those who impress their fellows as standing in direct communication with the Divine, as being charged with a message from it. His message has no clear meaning for us; it led the faithful to disaster; but can it be held that his career and influence were of other than portentous and absorbing interest? In the process by which one man's faith becomes the life of ten thousand there is a mystery that touches nearly the quality of our humanity. "Every new opinion at its starting," says the Lecturer on Heroes, "is precisely in a *minority of one* . . . One man alone of the whole world believes it; there is one man against all men."

Mr. Cunninghame Graham gives us the story [in *A Brazilian Mystic: Being the Life and Miracles of Antonio Conselheiro*] with a certain graphic effect and some picturesque detail. Unfortunately, the picturesque detail is not chosen so as to throw light on the points that are most obscure and of deepest interest. The relation of the Councillor to his followers, his methods of organisation (which appear to have been so effective), his manner of life, especially during the sojourn at Canudos—these are but faintly presented. Insufficient records may be to blame, but more probably the historian neglected to investigate these points simply because they did not interest him. He enjoys the general aspect of the movement, the fighting, the wild setting of the incidents, the physical prowess of the Sertao horsemen; and we enjoy these with him. But to the inner significance of the events he brings nothing beyond a half-hearted rationalism, and a flimsy superfluous comparison of the Conselheiro following with early Christian sects.

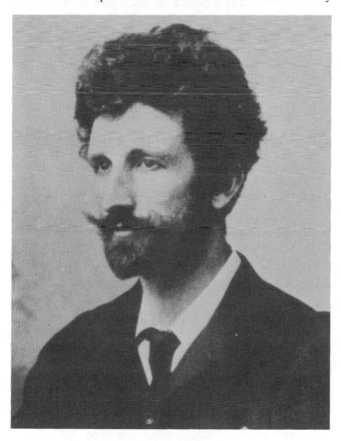

Graham as a young man.

It is a pity that the value of a book containing so notable a record should be impaired by grave defects of style and taste. Mr. Cunninghame Graham treats English syntax with a disregard which would appear slovenly in a private letter, and which at times involves simple statements in annoying obscurity. This confusion extends to the order in which he presents his subject, particularly in the Introduction. More serious is the frequent intrusion of commonplace reflections. Worst of all is an occasional pretentiousness, which cannot be too much deplored; it appears in peculiarly virulent concentration in the expression "Centaurs before the Lord" applied to expert horsemen, which occurs twice. When his narrative is running at full flood, these blemishes tend to disappear—. He has a gusto for adventure, a genuine appreciation of certain aspects of experience, of the movement, colour, freedom of open-air life. With the power he shows at times of swift and adequate narration, he might, had he undertaken his task more simply and humbly, have presented this tragic history with tenfold effect.

F. W. S., "A Voice in the Wilderness," in The Athenaeum, No. 4690, March 19, 1920, p. 368.

D. H. LAWRENCE (essay date 1922)

[Lawrence was an English novelist, poet, and essayist who is noted for his introduction of the themes of modern psychology to English fiction. In his lifetime he was a controversial figure, both for the explicit sexuality he portrayed in his novels and for his unconventional personal life. Much of the criticism of Lawrence's work concerns his highly individualistic moral system, which was based on absolute freedom of expression, particularly sexual expression. Human sexuality was for Lawrence a symbol of the Life Force, and is frequently pitted against modern industrial society, which he believed was dehumanizing. His most famous novel, Lady Chatterley's Lover (1928), was the subject of a landmark obscenity trial in Great Britain in 1960, which turned largely on the legitimacy of Lawrence's inclusion of hitherto forbidden sexual terms. In the following excerpt from a review of Pedro de Valdivia, Lawrence attacks Graham for what he perceives to be Graham's numerous failings as a biographer and translator.]

[Pedro de Valdivia] will have to go on the history shelf; it has no chance among the memoirs or the lives. There is precious little about Valdivia himself. There is, however, a rather scrappy chronicle of the early days of Chile, a meagre account of its conquest and settlement under Pedro de Valdivia.

Having read Mr. Graham's preface, we suddenly come upon another title-page, and another title—"Pedro de Valdivia, Conqueror of Chile. Being a Short Account of his Life, Together with his Five Letters to Charles V." So? We are to get Valdivia's own letters! Interminable epistles of a Conquistador, we know more or less what to expect. But let us look where they are.

It is a serious-looking book, with 220 large pages, and costing fifteen shillings net. The Short Account we find occupies the first 123 pages, the remaining 94 are occupied by the translation of the five letters. So! Nearly half the book is Valdivia's; Mr. Graham only translates him. And we shall have a lot of Your-Sacred-Majestys to listen to, that we may be sure of.

When we have read both the Short Account and the Letters, we are left in a state of irritation and disgust. Mr. Cunninghame Graham steals all his hero's gunpowder. He deliberately—or else with the absent-mindedness of mere egoism—picks all the plums out of Valdivia's cake, puts them in his own badly-kneaded dough, and then has the face to serve us up Valdivia whole, with the plums which we have already eaten sitting as large as life in their original position. Of course, all Valdivia's good bits in his own letters read like the shamelessest plagiarism. Haven't we just read them in Mr. Graham's Short Account? Why should we have to read them again? Why does that uninspired old Conquistador try to fob them off on us?

Poor Valdivia! That's what it is to be a Conquistador and a hero to Mr. Graham. He puts himself first, and you are so much wadding to fill out the pages.

The Spanish Conquistadores, famous for courage and endurance, are by now notorious for insentience and lack of imagination. Even Bernal Diaz, after a few hundred pages, makes one feel one could yell, he is so doggedly, courageously unimaginative, visionless, really sightless: sightless, that is, with the living eye of living discernment. Cortés, strong man as he is, is just as tough and visionless in his letters to His-Most-Sacred-Majesty. And Don Cunninghame, alas, struts feebly in the conquistadorial footsteps. Not only does he write without imagination, without imaginative insight or sympathy, without colour, and without real feeling, but he seems to pride himself on the fact. He is being conquistadorial.

We, however, refuse entirely to play the part of poor Indians. We are not frightened of old Dons in caracoling armchairs. We are not even amused by their pretence of being on horseback. A horse is a four-legged sensitive animal. What a pity the Indians felt so frightened of it! Anyhow, it is too late now for cavalierly conduct.

Mr. Graham's Preface sets the note in the very first words. It is a note of twaddling impertinence, and it runs through all the work.

> Commentators tell us (do they, though?) that most men are savages at heart, and give more admiration to the qualities of courage, patience in hardships, and contempt of death than they accord to the talents of the artist, man of science, or the statesman. (Funny sort of commentators Mr. Graham reads.)
>
> If this is true of men, they say it is doubly true of women, who would rather be roughly loved by a tall fellow of his hands (hands, forsooth!) even though their physical and moral cuticle (sic) suffer some slight abrasion, than inefficiently wooed by a philanthropist. (Ah, ladies, you who are inefficiently wooed by philanthropists, is there never a tall fellow of his hands about?)
>
> This may be so (continues Mr. Graham), and, if it is, certainly Pedro de Valdivia was an archetype (!!—) of all the elemental qualities nature implants in a man. (He usually had some common Spanish wench for his kept woman, though we are not told concerning her cuticle.)
>
> Brave to a fault (chants Mr. Graham), patient and enduring to an incredible degree, of hardships under which the bravest might have quailed (what's a quail got to do with it?), loyal to king and country (Flemish Charles V) and a stout man-at-arms, he had yet no inconsiderable talents of administration, talents not so conspicuous today among the Latin race. (Dear-dear!)

Thus—and I take all the above for granted—
etc.

Mr. Graham has shown us, not Valdivia, but himself. He lifts a swash-buckling fountain pen, and off he goes. The result is a shoddy, scrappy, and not very sincere piece of work. The Conquistadores were damned by their insensitiveness to life, which we call lack of imagination. And they let a new damnation into the America they conquered. But they couldn't help it. It was the educational result of Spanish struggle for existence against the infidel Moors. The Conquistadores were good enough instruments, but they were not good enough men for the miserable and melancholy work of conquering a continent. Yet, at least, they never felt themselves *too good* for their job, as some of the inky conquerors did even then, and do still.

Mr. Graham does not take Valdivia very seriously. He tells us almost nothing about him: save that he was born in Estremadura (who cares!) and had served in the Italian and German wars, had distinguished himself in the conquest of Venezuela, and, in 1532, accompanied Pizarro to Peru. Having thrown these few facts at us, off goes Mr. Graham to the much more alluring, because much better known, story of the Pizarros, and we wonder where Valdivia comes in. We proceed with Pizarro to Peru, and so, apparently, did Valdivia, and we read a little piece of the story even Prescott has already told us. Then we get a glimpse of Almagro crossing the Andes to Chile, and very impressive little quotations from Spanish writers. After which Valdivia begins to figure, in some unsubstantial remote regions with Indian names, as a mere shadow of a colonizer. We never see the country, we never meet the man, we get no feeling of the Indians. There is nothing dramatic, no Incas, no temples and treasures and tortures, only remote colonization going on in a sort of nowhere. Valdivia becomes a trifle more real when he comes again into Peru, to fight on the loyal side against Gonzalo Pizarro and old Carvajal, but this is Peruvian history, with nothing new to it. Valdivia returns to Chile and vague colonizing; there are vague mentions of the Magellan Straits; there is a Biobio River, but to one who has never been to Chile, it might just as well be Labrador. There is a bit of a breath of life in the extracts of Valdivia's own letters. And there are strings of names of men who are nothing but names, and continual mention of Indians who also remain merely nominal. Till the very last pages, when we do find out, after he is killed, that Valdivia was a big man, fat now he is elderly, of a hearty disposition, good-natured as far as he has enough imagination, and rather commonplace save for his energy as a colonizing instrument.

It is all thrown down, in bits and scraps, as Mr. Graham comes across it in Garcilaso's book, or in Gómara. And it is interlarded with Mr. Graham's own comments, of this nature: "Christians seemed to have deserved their name in those days, for faith and faith alone could have enabled them to endure such misery, and yet were always ready at the sentinel's alarm to buckle on their swords." Oh, what clichés! Faith in the proximity of gold, usually. "Cavalry in those days played the part now played by aeroplanes," says Mr. Graham suavely. He himself seems to have got into an aeroplane, by mistake, instead of onto a conquistadorial horse, for his misty bird's-eye views are just such confusion.

The method followed, for the most part, seems to be that of sequence of time. All the events of each year are blown together by Mr. Graham's qustiness, and you can sort them out. At the same time, great patches of Peruvian history suddenly float up out of nowhere, and at the end, when Valdivia is going to get killed by the Indians, suddenly we are swept away on a biographical carpet, and forced to follow the life of the poet Ercilla, who wrote his Araucana poem about Valdivia's Indians, but who never came to Chile till Valdivia was dead. After which, we are given a feeble account of a very striking incident, the death of Valdivia. And there the Short Account dies also, abruptly, and Chile is left to its fate.

Then follow the five letters. They are moderately interesting, the best, of course, belonging to Peruvian story, when Valdivia helped the mean La Gasca against Gonzalo Pizarro. For the rest, the "loyalty" seems a little overdone, and we are a little tired of the bluff, manly style of soldiers who have not imagination enough to see the things that really matter. Men of action are usually deadly failures in the long run. Their precious energy makes them uproot the tree of life, and leave it to wither, and their stupidity makes them proud of it. Even in Valdivia, and he seems to have been as human as any Conquistador, the stone blindness to any mystery or meaning in the Indians themselves, the utter unawareness of the fact that they might have a point of view, the abject insensitiveness to the strange, eerie atmosphere of that America he was proceeding to exploit and to ruin, puts him at a certain dull level of intelligence which we find rather nauseous. The world has suffered so cruelly from these automatic men of action. Valdivia was not usually cruel, it appears. But he cut off the hands and noses of two hundred "rebels," Indians who were fighting for their own freedom, and he feels very pleased about it. It served to cow the others. But imagine deliberately chopping off one slender brown Indian hand after another! Imagine taking a dark-eyed Indian by the hair, and cutting off his nose! Imagine seeing man after man, in the prime of life, with his mutilated face streaming blood, and his wrist-stump a fountain of blood, and tell me if the men of action don't need absolutely to be held in leash by the intelligent being who *can* see these things as monstrous, root cause of endless monstrosity! We, who suffer from the bright deeds of the men of action of the past, may well keep an eye on the "tall fellows of their hands" of our own day.

Prescott never went to Mexico nor to Peru, otherwise he would have sung a more scared tune. But Mr. Graham is supposed to know his South America. One would never believe it. The one thing he could have done, re-created the landscape of Chile for us, and made us feel those Araucanians as men of flesh and blood, he never does, not for a single second. He might as well never have left Scotland; better, for perhaps he would not have been so glib about unseen lands. All he can say of the Araucanians today is that they are "as hard-featured a race as any upon earth."

Mr. Graham is trivial and complacent. There is, in reality, a peculiar dread horror about the conquest of America, the story is always dreadful, more or less. Columbus, Pizarro, Cortés, Quesada, De Soto, the Conquistadores seem all like men of doom. Read a man like Adolf Bandelier, who knows the *inside* of his America, read his *Golden Man*—El Dorado—and feel the reverberation within reverberation of horror the Conquistadores left behind them.

Then we have Mr. Graham as a translator. In the innumerable and sometimes quite fatuous and irritating footnotes—they are sometimes interesting—our author often gives the original Spanish for the phrase he has translated. And even here he is peculiarly glib and unsatisfactory: "'God knows the trouble it cost,' he says pathetically." Valdivia is supposed to say this "pathetically." The footnote gives Valdivia's words: "*Un ber-*

gantin y el trabajo que costó, Dios lo sabe.''—"A brigantine, and the work it cost, God knows." Why *trouble* for *trabajo?* And why pathetically? Again, the proverb: *"A Dios rogando, y con la maza dando,"* is translated: "Praying to God, and battering with the mace." But why *battering* for *dando,* which means merely *donnant,* and might be rendered *smiting,* or *laying on,* but surely not *battering!. . .* These things are trifles, but they show the peculiar laziness or insensitiveness to language which is so great a vice in a translator.

The motto of the book is:
> *El más seguro don de la fortuna*
> *Es no lo haber tenido vez alguna,*

Mr. Graham puts it: "The best of fortune's gifts is never to have had good luck at all." Well, Ercilla may have meant this. The literal sense of the Spanish, anybody can make out: "The most sure gift of fortune, is not to have had it not once." Whether one would be justified in changing the "don de la fortuna" of the first line into "good luck" in the second is a point we must leave to Mr. Graham. Anyhow, he seems to have blest his own book in this equivocal fashion. (pp. 355-60)

> *D. H. Lawrence, " 'Pedro de Valdivia', by R. B. Cunninghame Graham," in his* Phoenix: The Posthumous Papers of D. H. Lawrence, *edited by Edward D. McDonald, 1936. Reprint by William Heinemann Ltd., 1961, pp. 355-60.*

LEONARD WOOLF   (essay date 1924)

[Woolf is best known as one of the leaders of the "Bloomsbury Group" of artists and thinkers, and as the husband of novelist Virginia Woolf, with whom he founded the famous Hogarth Press. The Bloomsbury Group, which was named after the section of London where the members lived and met, also included Clive and Vanessa Bell, John Maynard Keynes, Lytton Strachey, Virginia Woolf, Desmond MacCarthy, and several others. The group's weekly meetings were occasions for lively discussions of philosophy, literature, art, economics, politics, and life in general. Although the group observed no formal manifesto, Woolf and the others generally held to the tenets of philosopher G. E. Moore's Principia Ethica, *the essence of which is, in Moore's words, that "one's prime objects in life were love, the creation and enjoyment of aesthetic experience, and the pursuit of knowledge." A Fabian socialist during the World War I era, Woolf became a regular contributor to the socialist* New Statesman *and later served as literary editor of the* Nation *and the* Athenaeum, *in which much of his literary criticism is found. Throughout most of his life, Woolf also contributed essays on economics and politics to Britain's leading journals and acted as an advisor to the Labour Party. In the following excerpt, Woolf reviews Graham's* The Conquest of the River Plate, *noting both the accomplishments and the limitations of the work.]*

I was a little surprised the other day, reading a very critical review of Mr. Morley Roberts's book on W. H. Hudson, to see that the reviewer apparently implied that Mr. Cunninghame Graham was as a writer at least the equal of Hudson. It is no slight upon Mr. Graham to say that, despite the charm and finish of his books, I had never thought that they anywhere quite attained the level of "Far Away and Long Ago," or of isolated passages in some of Hudson's other books. When, therefore, I found a new book by Mr. Graham upon my table, **"The Conquest of the River Plate".** . . , I plunged eagerly into it in the hope that it would show me how much I had underrated Mr. Graham.

I cannot say that **"The Conquest of the River Plate"** has made me revise my opinion of the relative merits of Hudson and Mr. Graham. It is a fine book about a fine subject, but one cannot honestly say that it is anything more. The curse of journalistic criticism is that it tends to a sloppy or confused use of standards. There are, or have been, such things as great books and great writers, but they are extremely rare, and the critic of contemporary literature ought to make an effort to remember that a great prose writer is a man who writes great prose. It is arguable that Hudson never did write great prose, but, if he did not actually do so, he frequently trembles on the verge of doing so. But Mr. Graham never reaches that verge, and cannot, therefore, tremble on it. He is a competent writer, and he has a certain charm of personality which he often gets into his writing, but his sentences, and still more his paragraphs, never develop that fusion of thought, word, and rhythm which transmutes good writing into great prose. . . .

Most people think that the important thing is what a writer has to say, not how he says it. They may be right. At any rate, when I said that Mr. Graham's was a fine book on a fine subject, I was thinking of his subject and matter rather than of his prose style and the form of his sentences. The story of the conquest of the River Plate by the Spanish conquistadores of the sixteenth century is full of the kind of strange romance of which Mr. Graham is almost an ideal interpreter. Few books which I have read have succeeded in bringing more vividly before my mind the character of those brave and ruthless empire-builders, their terrible argosies, and the heroic meaninglessness of their lives and deaths. Perhaps the chief lesson of history is the futility of human endeavour, and, indeed, the human race would long ago have collectively committed suicide unless, unconsciously of course, it believed with Montaigne that it is not the end of the voyage but the voyage which matters.

> *Leonard Woolf, "The Romance of a Drowned Parrot," in* The Nation and the Athenaeum, *Vol. XXXV, No. 2, April 12, 1924, p. 51.*

HERBERT FAULKNER WEST   (essay date 1932)

[West was an American critic, publisher, and educator whose special areas of expertise were book collecting, nature writers, and Western philosophers. He has written or edited books on such authors as Stephen Crane and W. H. Hudson, as well as a major study of Graham's life and work entitled A Modern Conquistador: Robert Bontine Cunninghame Graham. *In the following excerpt from that study, West discusses Graham's stories in* The Ipané, Thirteen Stories, *and* Success.]

Of the fifteen sketches in **The Ipané,** four are about South America; one, southwest Texas; two are sea stories; two are about Morocco; three have Scotland for a background; one, Ireland; another describes the burial of William Morris; and the last was the now famous and immortal **"Niggers."** (p. 155)

The title story concerns the fortunes of one Hartogg and *The Ipané,* an iron ship which was a death trap, and which ran along the Brazilian coast. In this short story the author makes several digressions, which is his custom, and discusses the architecture of Asuncion, the morals of expatriate Englishmen, and other incidentals. There is in the story a relentless realism which has earned for Cunninghame Graham the title of the Scottish Maupassant. After the ship blows up and Hartogg is killed, the author writes, 'On the gun-deck of the Brazilian flagship the survivors were laid out, wrapped all in cotton-wool, livid and horrible, and looking like so many scalded pigs, and gasping their lives out tortured by mosquitoes and by heat'. There is no relief in the story. It is a perfect account of a horrible accident which the author once witnessed.

"**Un Pelado**" ("**A Poor Mexican**") is of particular interest, for it is based on an actual hanging Cunninghame Graham had witnessed and had written up for a Texas newspaper. This account, given in some detail, may be taken as an example of the genesis for a good many of the author's stories. (pp. 155-56)

José Maria Mendiola, a poor Mexican, had shot a shopkeeper named Hodges, 'a real white man, fresh coloured with the sandy hair and clear blue eyes which mark the man destined by Providence to keep a shop'. At the trial the Mexican had said that he had been swindled by Hodges and so shot him. Not a word did the Mexican understand of his trial and he went to his death stoically. His epitaph was spoken by an innocent bystander: 'No sense at all', said he, turning towards the nearest saloon, 'just didn't have no sense at all. Like killing a goat, didn't have sense enough to be afraid.' (p. 156)

These South American sketches are impregnated with the love of a man who looks back on his days riding the pampas as the happiest of his life. They are all strictly autobiographical. In his preface to his latest book (*The Horses of the Conquest . . .*), he writes: 'Over how many miles of pampa and of prairie, sabana, forest trails, and wild mountain paths, they (horses) have carried me, on journeys that to them could have no meaning, and that to me have been *the best remembered moments of my life*'. There is no writer better able to give a graphic picture of that vanishing life. There is no writer who has given such graphic pictures!

Of the two sea stories, "**S. S. Atlas**" and "**Bristol Fashion**," the former is autobiographical, and the latter, I imagine, is based upon some actual incident which the author had heard. The first tells of one of his trips from New York to Scotland, and then back again to the River Plate, on a tramp steamer in the late 'seventies. The crew got liquor and there was hell to pay. . . . The story smacks of the sea; the reader smells the dust-begrimed decks and the sickening smell of warm oil. It was this story which caused Conrad to write, 'If I could tell really what I feel for you, for your work and for the spirit that abides in the acts and the thoughts of your passages amongst this jumble of shadows and—well—filth which is called the earth, you would think it fulsome adulation'.

"**Bristol Fashion**" is one of Cunninghame Graham's stories that paints, without moralizing, the vileness, hypocrisy, and cruelty of man. It is a tale of the African coast and of Honest Tom Bilson. Some of his Krooboys steal a boat and escape from his ship. Later by disguising his ship to look like a Yankee barquentine he captures them again, knocks them unconscious, trusses them up, and sells them to a tribe of cannibals. Years later when Honest Tom was sitting around his respectable fireside he used to tell how he got the best of these niggers in 'true Bristol fashion'.

Cunninghame Graham knows the Scot well. He has told me with some conviction that he is not an Englishman but a Scotsman, and he believes that if Scotland had self-government it would be the most advanced government of Europe, possibly the world. Still he can write of the Scot, at the same time loving him, 'I know he prays to Gladstone and to Jehovah turn about, finds his amusement in comparing preachers, can read and write and cypher, buys newspapers, tells stories about ministers, drinks whisky, fornicates gravely, but without con-

viction, and generally disports himself after a fashion which would land a more imaginative and less practically constituted man within the precincts of a lunatic asylum before a week was out'.

In *The Ipané* there is a good example of Cunninghame Graham's skill in characterization when he describes one Mistress Campbell, a widow with four sons, who were 'well doing' lads—'that is, not given to drink, good workers, attenders at the church, and not of those who pass their "Sawbath" lounging about and spitting as they criticize mankind'. The widow's faith was great ('that first infirmity of uninstructed minds'), and her chief pride, after her sons, was centred in her cows, called in Salvagia 'Kye'. One day, her four sons were drowned in a pool known as Linn-a-Hamish. When Mistress Campbell heard of their fate, and the Celtic Coronach was wailed, she said nothing. 'She just gaed out and milked the kye.' It has been well said that the Scotch are a hardy race.

"**Snaekoll's Saga**," a story laid in Iceland, shows the curious range of Cunninghame Graham's imagination as well as his philosophy of futility. . . . This story has a touch of horror and artistry which ranks with the best of Maupassant.

The most famous piece of irony in this book was entitled "**Niggers**," which, Mr Edward Garnett suggests, 'gives the keynote to its author's genius, outlook and attitude to his fellows', and 'would confer immortality on him, with its fellow sketch "**Success**" (appearing in 1902), if he had written nothing more'. It is a bitter and ironic Genesis, and a satiric sketch of the rise of the Aryans, culminating in the now familiar Nordic myth. (pp. 158-61)

There is, to my knowledge, no more bitter and indignant denunciation of English Imperialism in all English literature. The British reviewers were, as Mr Garnett said, uncomfortably irritated by "**Niggers**." The readers of Conan Doyle, Lucas Malet, Anthony Hope, and other vendors of popular wares could not, with any stretch of the imagination, take kindly to *The Ipané*. Any writer who dares write what only a small intellectual minority feel, and who damns the hypocrisy of his fellows and his country with such intensity and clarity, must remain unpopular. But, "**Niggers**" was written thirty years or more ago, and, as Mr Garnett has pointed out . . . , is not heterodox to-day. No longer can England be imperialistic with any success, and the World War only gave proof of what such international mayhem will do. (pp. 162-63)

Most of the stories [in *Thirteen Stories*] reflect Cunninghame Graham's sardonic contempt for the human race, cruel, greedy, and acquisitive as it is. But there is a vitality, a virility throughout, a sort of physical gusto for life which checks, in part, the irony. There is also a melancholy feeling for the lost free days of the pampas, which never again could Cunninghame Graham know. Each sketch or story is a memoir.

The reader finds interspersed in the stories Cunninghame Graham's pungent remarks on religion, progress, civilization, women, cabbages and kings. He often expresses his feelings for animals, and of man's cruelty toward them, because everyone knows that animals have no souls and were created solely for the benefit of man, who, as all good Christians know, is the centre of the universe.

"**In a German Tramp**" the author has such touches as this, 'The captain spent his time in harbour fishing uninterestedly, catching great bearded spiky-finned sea monsters, which he left to die upon the deck. Not that he was hard-hearted, but merely unimaginative, after the way of those who, loving sport for the pleasure it affords themselves, hotly deny that it is cruel, or that it can occasion inconvenience to any participator in a business which they themselves enjoy. So the poor, innocent sea-monsters floundered in slimy agony upon the deck; the boarhound and the cats taking a share in martyring them, tearing and biting at them as they gasped their lives away; condemned to agony for some strange reason, or perhaps because, as every living thing is born to suffer, they were enduring but their fair proportion, as they happened to be fish. Pathetic but unwept, the tragedy of all the animals, and we but links in the same chain with them, look at it all as unconcerned as gods'. The naturalism of Mr George Santayana may be seen here.

It is also in this story that the author gives a masterly description of a Scottish professional religionist named Mr McKerrochar.

In the story "**The Gold Fish**" he tells of an Arabian runner who was given the task of carrying a crystal bowl with seven goldfish in it from Rabat to Tafilet. His orders were simple: not to break the bowl. The runner gets lost in the desert and later on, 'Under a stunted sandarac tree, the head turned to the east, his body lay, swollen and distorted by the pangs of thirst. . . . But the Khalifa's parting caution has been well obeyed, for by the tree, unbroken, the crystal bowl still glistened beautiful as gold, in the fierce rays of the Sahara sun'. (pp. 163-64)

"**The Hegira**" is a tale of old Mexico. This is a reminiscence of 1880. Man is depicted as cruel and bloodthirsty. This time the 'niggers' are Apache Indians. The author muses upon 'the tenacity of purpose, the futility of life, and the inexorable fate which mocks mankind, making all effort useless, whilst still urging us to strive'. It would seem as if Cunninghame Graham had been talking with Joseph Conrad, for I believe that this approximated his philosophy of life. Victory comes only in striving when one knows defeat is inevitable. Man is but a part of nature and suffers the same fate as any other part. He, in fact, suffers more, because his brain and nervous system have been more highly developed than any of his brother creatures of the jungle, plain or barnyard.

Sidi Bu Zibbala is a renegade Arab who changed his religion to Christianity. His reaction was much the same as the Jew, Heinrich Heine's. He was unhappy: 'I, Syrian, I say all the world dunghill. I try him, Syria, England, the Desert, and New York; I find him dung, so I come here and live here on this dunghill, and find it sweet when compared to places I have seen; and it is warm and dry'. His wife, disgusted too, hurls her English clothes overboard and becomes 'native' again. Cunninghame Graham has little sympathy with renegades or repentant sinners, believing a man should be true to himself cost what it may in public scorn or obloquy. A full-blooded sinner has more grace than a penitent, snivelling Calvinist. (p. 165)

"**Victory**," a short sketch, gives Cunninghame Graham's reaction to the battle of Santiago in the Spanish-American War, and 'how Cervera's Squadron met the fate which . . . God prepares for those who dare fight against superior odds'. In this story the author sheds a literary tear for the grandeur that was Spain. (He now writes to me after the recent revolution in Spain: 'Viva la Republica!') Spain's defeat symbolized the defeat of a country which for over seven hundred years had saved the southern half of Europe from the Moors. With his friend, Mr George Santayana, who declared his feelings in a poem 'Spain in America', Cunninghame Graham's sympathies

were with the underdog Spain. To them an old and honourable Latin culture was pitted against the ignorant and acquisitive Yankee. That the Yankee triumphed can be of no surprise to those who believe in the evolutionary beatitude: 'Blessed are the strong for they shall inherit the earth'. (p. 167)

The title essay [in *Success*] contains the author's philosophy of success and it is, paradoxically enough, a paean of failure. I wonder how many have read this volume which lies before me, and I wonder, too, what their thoughts of it were. Did the readers hurl it down in disgust cursing the author? Or did some of them feel a new comprehension, a sudden intuitive feeling, that here was a great mind uttering rare and magic words of truth? Quien sabe? ["Who knows?"] Here it lies, still giving solace to the weak! (p. 168)

This book contains all the qualities which make up Cunninghame Graham's chivalric and courageously honest attitude toward life. If Professor Miguel de Unamuno is looking for the return of Don Quixote he might find an incarnation by the Clyde, about twenty miles from Glasgow. 'Hoot awa', lads, hoot awa'!' There he will find an elderly hidalgo, 'the finest gentleman of all the realms of fact and fable, who still maintains in discourse with all whom he meets that the thing of which the world has most need is knights-errant, to do honour to women, to fight for the cause of the oppressed, and to right the wrong'.

Success is fleeting and most often to the vulgar. Our love and interest (except in America) is 'for those who fail, for those who have sunk still battling beneath the muddy waves of life. . . . The unlucky Stuarts, from the first poet king slain at the ball play, to the poor mildewed Cardinal of York, with all their faults, they leave the stolid Georges millions of miles behind, sunk in their pudding and prosperity. The prosperous Elizabeth, after a life of honours, unwillingly surrendering her cosmetics up to death in a state bed, and Mary, laying her head upon the block at Fotheringay after the nine and forty years of failure of her life (failure except of love), how many million miles, unfathomable seas, and sierras upon sierras separate them? . . . Failure alone can interest speculative minds'. . . . 'Nothing can stand against success and yet keep fresh.' Spain had been defeated by the rising Yankees, yet 'throughout all Europe, Spain alone still rears its head, the unspoiled race, content in philosophic guise to fail in all she does, and thus preserve the individual independence of her sons. Successful nations have to be content with their success, their citizens cannot be interesting. So many hundred feet of sanitary tubes a minute or an hour, etc. Yet those who fail, no matter how ingloriously, have their revenge on the successful few, by having kept themselves free from vulgarity, or by having died unknown. . . .' (pp. 169-70)

The vulgar, the popular, the democratic, the cheap, which Walt Whitman sang with such gusto, here is scorned by a mind aristocratic to the core. Here is a chivalric gesture for the failures, for those who die unsung, for those who wander the world, indifferent to the plaudits of the morons, and those material possessions which, when amassed, the world calls success. Would that America could read!

In five pages, the author, describing the funeral of Queen Victoria, satirizes the whole Victorian age. By harping constantly on the phrase that 'she was the Mother of her people, even the poorest of her people in the land', he brings forth the fact that appalling poverty engulfed the majority of her subjects. Throughout the five pages the irony of his own struggle in the House of Commons to get before the government an iota of representation for the thousands of poor and unemployed is apparent. Well the writer knew what class the government and the Queen had represented! The Forsytes mourned the most, for it was the passing of their age. Still the 'nobodies' kept their places while the cortège passed, chilled by the bitter wind, 'knowing their former ruler had been the Mother of them all'. (pp. 170-71)

> *Herbert Faulkner West, in his* A Modern Conquistador: Robert Bontine Cunninghame Graham, His Life and Works, *Cranley & Day, 1932, 288 p.*

JOHN GALSWORTHY   (essay date 1935)

[*Galsworthy was an English novelist who is best remembered today for a series of novels known collectively as* The Forsyte Saga *(1906-22). In the books of* The Forsyte Saga, *he employed a Victorian setting to explore the theme of the evil that can be brought about by ungovernable greed and acquisitiveness. In the following excerpt, Galsworthy praises Graham as a short story writer.*]

In these very few words I speak of Cunninghame Graham rather as writer, than as man. His peculiar and quite unique talent has been given so far as I know entirely to short stories, and one book of travels. I confine myself to his short stories, the more absorbing topic to a fellow-writer.

The short story is a form of fiction in which but few English have excelled, and none have reached the supereminence of de Maupassant or of Anton Tchehov. It is a form in which, for perfection, an almost superhuman repression of the writer's self must go hand in hand with something that one can only describe as essence of writer—a something unmistakable but impalpable, and not to be laid finger on. In the perfect short story one is unconscious of anything but a fragrant trifle, so focused and painted before our minds, that it is as actual, and yet as rounded, as deep in colour, as fine in texture as a flower, and which withal disengages a perfume from—who knows where, that makes it a carnation not a rose, a Maupassant and not a Tchehov.

Now Cunninghame Graham sometimes—as in **Hegira, A Hatchment,** and other stories—approaches this perfection. I am not sure that he ever quite reaches it, for a reason that, curiously, is his real strength as a writer. Very much of an artist, he is yet too much of a personality ever to be quite the pure artist; the individuality of the man will thrust its spear-head through the stuff of his creations. I may be wrong, but I cannot honestly recall any story of his in which his knight-errant philosophy does not here and there lift its head out of the fabric of his dreams, if not directly, then through implicit contrast, or in choice of subject. One can readily understand the queer potency which this particular quality gives to his tales, in an age and country very much surrendered to money and materialism. It is not that he is a romantic; on the contrary he is a realist with a steel-keen eye, and a power of colouring an exact picture hardly excelled. It is his clear, poignant realism that makes his philosophy ring out so convinced and convincing, and gives it the power to rip the gilding off the shoddy and snobbishness of our civilisation.

The bent of his soul, and the travels of his body have inclined him to those parts of the earth—the pampas, Morocco, Spain, Scotland—where there are still gleams at all events of a life more primitive, more aesthetically attractive, and probably saner than our own; and when, as in **Un Monsieur** and such

studies as **Appreciation,** he pitches on a purely 'civilised' setting, he rides home, indeed.

It is a rather strange thing, and a great tribute to his personality, that throughout what is really a sustained attack on certain habits of existence, and the bloated house they have succeeded in building for themselves, he never once gives the feeling of attacking for the sake of attacking. The assault is delivered, as it were, not by his reason and mind, but by his spirit and his nerves. As if, while he wrote, the music of our high civilisation would keep intruding its blusterous, rich, and flabby harmonies on his strange ears, so that he must leap from his chair, and, sitting down again, die, or insert in his screed the word 'accursed.'

And the real beauty of him is that the things of which he writes that word, directly or by implication, in a hundred tales, are really mean and sordid in that true sense of a word which has not, as so many journalists appear to imagine, any connection with absence of income, or presence of human nature in back streets.

With his style I personally have sometimes a fault or two to find, but I recognise in it to the full those qualities of colour, vibration, and sense of the right word that alone keep life beating in a tale. Without high power of expression philosophy is of little use to any artist, weighting his pockets till he is sitting in the road instead of riding along it with his head up, as this writer always does. He has a manner, and a way with him, valuable at a time when certain leading writers have little or none at all. And he has a passion for the thing seen, that brings into his work the constant flash of revelation. He makes us see what he sees, and what he sees is not merely the surface.

Withal he is a gallant foe of oppression, of cruelty, of smugness, and fatty degeneration; a real tonic salt to the life of an age that needs it. (pp. 192-94)

> *John Galsworthy, "Note on R. B. Cunninghame Graham," in his* Forsytes, Pendyces and Others, *Charles Scribner's Sons, 1935, pp. 192-94.*

EDWARD GARNETT   (essay date 1936)

[*Garnett was a prominent editor for several London publishing houses, and discovered or greatly influenced the work of many important English writers, including Joseph Conrad, John Galsworthy, and D. H. Lawrence. He also published several volumes of criticism, all of which are characterized by thorough research and sound critical judgments. Garnett was a personal friend of Graham's and often criticized and encouraged him in his work. In the following excerpt, he discusses the merit of Graham's sketches as well as their lack of popularity with the general public.*]

Graham's interest led him . . . into the field of South American history, a field of which English writers have surveyed only a corner or so; and in a series of studies—I. **The Conquest of the River Plate.** II. **A Vanished Arcadia.** III. **The Conquest of New Granada. IV. Hernando de Soto. V. Cartagena and the Banks of the Sinú.** VI. **A Brazilian Mystic.** VII. **Pedro de Valdivia.** VIII. **Bernal Diaz del Castillo.** IX. **José Antonio Paez.** X. **Portrait of a Dictator, F. S. Lopez**—he has brought to his subjects an intimate knowledge of the character and geography of the scenes and of the manners, outlook and material circumstances of his historical figures. Such a book as **The Conquest of New Granada** is indeed a rich mine of historical information, and every step in the career of the hero, Quesada, is annotated by Graham with circumstantial details which vivify the scenes and steep the whole picture in the living shades and tones of that vanished life. Nobody but Graham could have brought to life again with such colour and fullness the old Spanish chronicles of the conquest of the New World, for he writes as a man of action who has himself experienced many of the conditions he describes. In such reconstructions of the deeds of former generations, Graham's interest in practical matters, sense of human drama, keen eye for character and philosophic commentary combine to make a rich intriguing pattern as we see in *Doughty Deeds:* "An Account of the Life of [his ancestor] Robert Graham of Gartmore, Poet and Politician, 1735-1797, drawn from his Letter-books and Correspondence." This biography is a lesson in the art of clothing dry bones again with living flesh, and here Graham had the advantage, not only of intimate familiarity with the estate of Gartmore, its owners and the people round, but of having for subject a man even franker than himself in self-expression. And here I may touch on the matter of Graham's unpopularity as a writer. In a letter to me (15th January, 1900) he says: "I am afraid that the bar between me and the world is too heavy. You see, neither the Scotch nor the Spanish are a subjective people." He wrote of life as a Latin and with his piercing candour and ironical insight into the self-regarding motives of human nature, was devoid of moral "uplift" and sentimental camouflage. His first book, *Notes on the District of Menteith,* shows his wit and unconventionality, but his masterpiece of travel, *Mogreb-el-Acksa,* 1898, threw down the gage to the English public. It challenges all the Victorian shibboleths, especially that of the white man's burden and the cant that masked the propaganda of the Imperialists. As Conrad said, "From *Mogreb-el-Acksa* one experiences a continuous feeling of delight, the persuasion that we have got hold of a good thing. This should work for material success. Yet who knows.

"No doubt it is too good." It was. To repeat some words from my Introduction to an American edition, 1930: "The book is that rare thing, a spontaneous work of art. It is written with a verve and a brilliancy of tone that make it unique in English books of travel. . . . The incidents of travel and the many rencontres are lit up by the author's shrewd philosophy and his sarcastic appreciation of the wise and the worldly, of knaves and fools and of all the pitfalls that await our poor humanity combines with his gleaming irony to make a lively pattern on the page." Having corresponded with Graham in 1897, I suggested the following year that the sketches he was contributing to the *Saturday Review* should appear as No. I of The Overseas Library which I was then projecting, and *The Ipané* was published in 1899. It contained among others the immortal **"Niggers,"** and **"With the North-West Wind,"** a fine description of William Morris's funeral. In his next book, *Thirteen Stories,* the handling of the sketch was more assured, and indeed in brilliance and atmospheric strength Graham never surpassed that book's original quality. But it never "sold," as publishers put it. Nor did *Success,* the collection of sketches which at my request Graham brought together and published as No. IV of "The Greenback Library," 1902. And of the ten subsequent volumes of sketches, 1905-1936, only one, I believe, has reached a second edition. (pp. 126-27)

None the less Graham's best sketches should, I hold, occupy a permanent niche in English literature. One remembers how the British reader remained "incurious" about William Blake for long, long years. Authors possess their niches through their original qualities, and Graham's is secured, I believe, by his trenchant philosophy and his pulverizing contempt for worldly humbug. Dealing with the fundamentals of human nature his

great experience of all sorts and species of men, white, black, brown and coffee-coloured, gave him a more detached vision and more breadth of view than any of his English contemporaries. He was perhaps more "singular" as a man than his books, but the best of them breathe his unique spirit. Like the prince in the fairy tales he was accessible to all men yet stood aloof from them. He wrote only of individuals, not of types or classes of men, and though he rubbed shoulders with the governing classes and had many friends among them, he was spiritually apart from them, and as his books leave out of sight the great middle class it would be surprising if the latter had responded to them. To Conrad, Graham was essentially a *grand seigneur* [a great lord] and *un frondeur, cela vous est permis* [a censurer, if you like] whose idealistic lapses must be forgiven him. Thus Conrad writes (2nd February, 1899): "To me you are extremely real even when I perceive you clothed in your irremediable illusions." By this Conrad meant that Graham's readiness to address political meetings, called on behalf of suffering peoples and exploited minorities, was amateurish to one who knew that the revolutionary under-dog would prove no less tyrannical than his oppressor. (For this, see Conrad's brilliant prophecy of the Bolshevik tyranny of "a nation of slaves" in *Autocracy and War*.) (p. 128)

Graham's literary style is his own, clear and terse, often rhythmic in its restrained feeling and occasionally lapsing into blank verse. He had no power to create character and this, along with his lack of sentimental appeal and interest in the feminine world, was fatal in the ordinary reader's eyes. On the other hand, his gaucho life had trained and developed in him an extraordinarily keen eye for detail, and with sharp, unerring touches he could conjure up the living scene. See for example **"In a German Tramp."** As a good example of his all-comprehending gaze, I may instance **"Harboured,"** his valedictory sketch of Conrad's funeral. I was there and can testify to the truth and artistic harmony with which Graham has blended the effects of the Mass and the streets of Canterbury and at the grave where Conrad found his resting-place in Kentish earth. **"Harboured"** is a classic and for my part I do not see why it should not survive as does, say, a poem by Po-Chu-I. A work of art may be buried a thousand years, but when it is disinterred we see that it lives by its truth to art, to nature and to human feeling. So with the best of Graham's sketches, such as **"The Impenitent Thief," "Faith," "Reincarnation," "El Tango Argentino," "Beattock for Moffat," "War to the Knife,"** to name but half a dozen. So long as the circumstances of men's lives are comprehensible, I see no reason why posterity should not enjoy such sketches, if only there is enough artistic beauty to preserve their human interest. **"Niggers"** should live by its pillorying of the Englishman's attitude to natives. **"Success"** should last as long as English is read by the scorn with which it gives the lie to mankind's "fond adoration of accomplished facts." Only Graham could have written **"Success."** True what he says may be read between the lines of many great writers, but only Graham has stigmatized with such bold, freezing disdain mankind's idolatry of every man's god. (pp. 128-29)

Edward Garnett, "R. B. Cunninghame Graham: Man and Writer," in The London Mercury, *Vol. XXXIV, No. 200, June, 1936, pp. 125-29.*

G. K. CHESTERTON (essay date 1936)

[*Regarded as one of England's premier men of letters during the first half of the twentieth century, Chesterton is best known today as a colorful bon vivant, a witty essayist, and creator of the Father*

Brown mysteries and the fantasy The Man Who Was Thursday *(1908). Much of Chesterton's work reveals his childlike joie de vivre and reflects his pronounced Anglican and, later, Roman Catholic beliefs. His essays are characterized by their humor, frequent use of paradox, and chatty, rambling style. Chesterton was well-acquainted with Graham, and in the following excerpt from his autobiography, he recalls some characteristics of Graham as a politician.]*

I felt . . . [a] kinship with the sort of Scot who, even when he was interested in politics, would never really be allowed in practical politics. A splendid specimen of this type of man was Cunninghame Graham. No Cabinet Minister would ever admire his Parliamentary style; though he had a much better style than any Cabinet Minister. Nothing could prevent Balfour being Prime Minister or MacDonald being Prime Minister; but Cunninghame Graham achieved the adventure of being Cunninghame Graham. As Bernard Shaw remarked, it is an achievement so fantastic that it would never be believed in a romance. Nor can it be said in this case, that the Scots are in a conspiracy to praise each other; for I grieve to say that I heard one of these great statesmen deliver a speech full of the noblest ideals with Cunninghame Graham at my elbow, muttering in my ear in a soft but fierce fashion: "I never could stand a Protestant sermon."

There was a small row or scandal, connected with Cunninghame Graham and his candour in politics, which has always struck in my memory as a symbol. It explains why I, for one, have always got on much better with revolutionists than with reformers; even when I entirely disagreed with the revolutions or entirely agreed with the reforms. . . . I think the reason is that the revolutionists did, in a sense, judge the world; not justly like the saints; but independently like the saints. Whereas the reformers were so much a part of the world they reformed, that the worst of them tended to be snobs and even the best of them to be specialists. Some of the Liberal specialists, of the more frigid Cambridge type, did faintly irritate me; much more than any mere anarchist or atheist. They seemed so very negative and their criticism was a sort of nagging. One distinguished man, who happened to affect me in this way, was the late J. A. Hobson, not to be confounded with the S. G. Hobson whose excellent economic studies still enlighten our debates; but a most high-minded and public-spirited speaker and writer in his own right. I hesitate to name so honest and earnest a man in a critical spirit; but nobody who recalls, with whatever respect, that gaunt figure and keen and bitter countenance, will pretend that his own spirit was not supremely critical. He was one of the most independent and intelligent of the Liberal critics of Imperialism, and on that point I was wholly with the Liberals; I disliked Imperialism; and yet I almost liked it by the time that Hobson had finished speaking against it. And I remember one occasion when he took the chair at some meeting of or about Aborigines or the native races of the Empire; and he had Cunninghame Graham on his right, while I had the honour of sitting on the other side. Hobson made a very able political speech, but somehow it seemed to me to be a party speech; concerned more for Liberalism than Liberty. I may be wrong; anyhow, I missed something, as he picked holes in the British Empire until it consisted entirely of holes tied together with red tape. And then Cunninghame Graham began to speak; and I realised what was wanting. He painted a picture, a historical picture, like a pageant of Empires; talking of the Spanish Empire and the British Empire as things to be reviewed with an equal eye; as things which brave and brilliant men had often served with double or doubtful effects; he poured scorn on the provincial ignorance which supposes that Spanish Empire-

builders or proconsuls had all been vultures of rapine or vampires of superstition; he declared that many of the Spanish, like many of the English, had been rulers of whom any Empire might be proud. And then he traced such figures against the dark and tragic background of those ancient human populations which they had so often either served or conquered in vain.

Now in the course of this speech Cunninghame Graham had occasion to say in passing, touching some local riot and crime; "I have never been able to feel myself that tyrannicide, in certain circumstances, is intrinsically and inevitably indefensible." Will it be believed that there was immediately a horrible howling fuss about these words; that they were the only words of the speech that anybody bothered to remember; that these were only remembered as an execrable example of the frenzy of the foes of Empire; and that all the funny people on that platform were lumped together as gory regicides who went about drinking the blood of kings? And all the time, I had been saying to myself that Cunninghame Graham at least had been fair to Empires as Empires—whereas J. A. Hobson had not been fair to the British Empire at all. There was nothing particularly unprecedented or preposterous in what the Scottish Socialist had said about tyrannicide, though we may disagree with it for particular moral or religious reasons. He only said what practically all the great Pagans would have said; what all the admirers of Hermodius and Aristogiton would have said; what many Renaissance theorists, Catholic and non-Catholic, would have said; what all the great French Revolutionists would have said; what practically all the classic poets and tragedians down to modern times would have said. It was no more than was implied in a hundred sacred pictures of Judith or a hundred secular praises of Brutus. But Mr. Hobson would have been shocked, I fear, at the faintest suggestion of the killing of an evil king; but he was not in the least shocked at the implied impossibility of the power of a good king, or the modern ignorance of all that men have meant by kingship. (pp. 269-72)

> G. K. Chesterton, "Some Political Celebrities," in his Autobiography, *1936. Reprint by Hutchinson of London, 1969, pp. 266-82.**

PAUL BLOOMFIELD (essay date 1952)

[In the following excerpt, Bloomfield discusses the reasons for Graham's relative obscurity as a writer and notes the underlying humanitarianism evident in all of his works.]

Robert Bontine Cunninghame Graham . . . was the most adventurous spirit among British writers since Raleigh. Another superlative is called for. He has been the most neglected of the interesting writers in English who have 'flourished', as they say, during the last hundred years. It is a pity it should be so, though it has to be true of somebody. We shall have to try to understand why it is true of *him*, and we need not feel too much concern since, after all, the remedy is in posterity's hands.

I had to use 'British' when comparing Graham with Raleigh because he was three-quarters Scotch and one-quarter Spanish mixed with Italian, and for all his sturdy qualities had nothing of the English ironside phlegm. All four quarters were aristocratic; it is a point of some importance for an appreciation of his life and works. The writers of his own day with whom it is most natural to compare him, Samuel Butler, William Morris and George Bernard Shaw—the unconventional ones—also need to be contrasted with him, because they had not got, among their conspicuous traits, that *hidalguia,* that special

Graham in exotic garb.

feeling for the now demoded virtue of chivalry, which he infused into all his enterprises. I know that the young Morris had identified himself with Sir Palomides and that Samuel Butler had some important ideas about breeding, but the difference was that Graham *was* a *hidalgo*. Further, our nobleman, 'Don Roberto' to his friends, was a born guerrilla fighter—not, I mean, that he ever wanted to draw blood, but that what he liked was to campaign, in a civilian sense, with the 'small bodies' the dictionary speaks of when it defines 'guerrilla', adopted from the Spanish. On the pampa he rode with a knot of gauchos; in the House of Commons this Scotch laird *cum* Spanish grandee took his stand with the handful of pioneers of Labour or with Parnell and the awkward Irish; and when he set out for mysterious Tarudant in Morocco it was with a little guerrilla band, five in all, the other four consisting of Haj Mohammed es Swani el Bahri, 'a Moor of the Riff pirate breed', Hassan Suleiman Lutaif, a Syrian gentleman, Mohammed el Hosein, reputed slave-dealer, and Ali, a muleteer.

However, at bottom Graham was an independent even more than a guerrilla fighter. Hence the comparison with Morris, Butler and Shaw rather, say, than with W. H. Hudson and Charles Doughty, for 'independent' used like this suggests a touch of militancy (idealistic, of course) and Hudson and Doughty were patient men. In the Victorian era it was easier for a tramp than for a gentleman—unless he was a true solitary—to be independent, because social conventions were so binding, and

therefore at least we know that the men of some station who in those days showed sympathy for underdogs or rallied to unpromising causes were in earnest, not merely echoing the sentiments that have become obligatory for everybody, right, left or centre, or doing 'good' under the compulsion of social pressure. People were often reminded of Don Quixote when they saw Graham. There was more in it than appearances, as readers of his works soon find out. Not only the stories and sketches, the histories too are very personal—not biased: on the contrary, the personal element expresses itself in a passionate, unflagging effort to weigh the human worth of particular individuals with the utmost exactness in the scales of justice. Academic imaginations may well boggle at the majestic *naïveté* of such a thing. And the man who, after the adventures related in **Mogreb-el-Acksa,** went back to Morocco City with the idea of teaching the natives to limit their trade (which was to be conducted with the strictest honesty) to buying and selling only goods necessary for their established mode of life—that man may be called quixotic. What with one thing and another, Graham's friend and biographer, Tschiffely [see Additional Bibliography], could hardly have avoided calling him anything but 'Roberto' and 'Don Roberto' throughout his book; and although some people looked on him—and their reasons must be taken seriously—as a typical Scot, his own opinion was that 'unless I do not know even a little about myself, I have always felt that my outlook on most things in life has been, and is, Spanish'. (pp. 13-15)

I think it is obvious that his writing, which is nearly always about something that had happened to him or that he had observed, or relevant to a position he had occupied on the map, has an ingredient of healthy roughage mostly wanting in the English literature of his first fifty or sixty years. And yet he had illusions, not about men so much as about women, especially—it might be enough to say 'almost exclusively'—if they were prostitutes. He wrote a good deal, on the whole too sentimentally, about prostitutes. It is right for artists to side with society's victims, among whom they often figure themselves, but there is a difference, not in Graham's favour, between his affecting testimonial in **Charity** to the plump Gibraltese bawd Doña Ana and her big-hearted, all but vestal girls, and Maupassant's more artfully sympathetic *Maison Tellier*. Though I should not say that Chekhov's story *The Chorus Girl* was the perfect treatment of the theme of a good-natured tart in a fix between an elderly subscriber to her favours and his wife, it leaves Graham's **Un Monsieur** some way behind. Still, this is worth reading; when he makes his worst hash we can still taste the slice of life that went into the pot. But when he writes a small masterpiece—then he bears re-reading and is uncommonly good for reading aloud; then his story or sketch can jolt us out of complacency and in certain cases move us to tears as effectively as anything I know written in English in the last hundred years. Unluckily a significant fact about those prostitutes is that they led to Graham's books being neglected by the Edwardians, equally in the supposed interests of the morals of the Young Person and of the sensibilities of the prudish grown-ups for whom this country used to be justly famous and who as a class have withered almost away with such remarkable speed. (pp. 17-18)

[Graham's] dislike of established religions came out in cracks, not all as much to the point as this one: 'There are many people ear here who have "got religion" . . . and really seem as if they worshipped God for spite.' My feeling is that another reason, besides the harping on the virtues of *chinas, quitanderas, cocottes* and other loose ladies whom he came across, why his books did not go down very well is to be found in these digs at religion, sometimes at the Persons of the Trinity and the Madonna. A careless reader might therefore take him for irreligious. He would have to be a *very* careless reader, since how far Graham was from being anything of the sort there is conclusive evidence in print. *The Fourth Magus* to my mind is one of the most touching and beautiful religious stories ever written. As for Graham's own real position, not a very unusual one, he seems to me to have hit it off (I suppose quite unconsciously) in an admirable sentence about the hero of the story **"His People."** The returned native of Toledo goes into a church. 'Half furtively he dipped his hand into the holy water stoup and crossed himself, muttering it was a superstitious act, yet glad to yield to it, for a true Christian ought to testify, even though God for some mysterious purpose of His own has not vouchsafed him faith.' I can think of no secular writer who was more constantly and sensitively preoccupied with the rights and wrongs of human behaviour than Graham. (pp. 20-1)

Graham was one of the great horsemen of his day. He wrote well about horses; he avoided, in admirable stories like **"A Meeting"** or even in the earlier, very pathetic **"Calvary,"** striking sentimental chords in the way he was tempted to do by prostitutes and other victims of organized society, among whom horses must be included. . . . When I first read **"Calvary"** it seemed to me a little overdone. Surely, I thought, in London, among people as kind to animals as the English are, at the time Graham was writing of, horses were not being worked till they dropped. It is always a mistake to let oneself drift into these large, sanguine views of public benevolence. **"Calvary"** came out in *Thirteen Stories* in 1900. In March of last year (1951) I saw a newspaper paragraph headed 'Fifty Years Ago' which recalled that in March 1901 an *Evening News* reporter had in one morning counted eight fallen horses between Liverpool Street and St. Paul's; and that reminded me of the broken down cab-horses drawing the four wheelers of my childhood how it had made me shudder to use those old 'growlers'; and it also reminded me of the callous treatment I have seen cattle, pigs and hens get in country towns on market day *nowadays*. (pp. 21-2)

It is I think easy to form a just idea of [Graham's] political position. He was not a politician at all. When Burns was in the dock after the Trafalgar Square incident he spoke of himself as a Socialist, of Graham as 'a Social Reformer'. This was fair enough. Like Morris, who flared up impatiently if anyone catechized him about Marxist dogma, Graham in the 'eighties wanted (he would not have acknowledged this) a great discharge of evangelical lovingkindness—at once. He had much too much insight into human nature to believe for long that to abolish 'class' would mean an end of envy, greed and fear. About the Trade Union leaders, once they were prospering, Graham had rather the feeling that Milton expressed in his 'new presbyter is but old priest writ large', but this is not to suggest that Milton, solemnly trying to flatter one House of Commons into lifting the censorship of books, was the same kind of person as Graham trying to shame another House, and from inside, into *being good*. I do not agree with Tschiffely that Graham was only a Socialist of sorts till he began to think the movement might after all succeed, and only because he liked lost causes; I think it was not till he foresaw the probable success of the Left that he fully realized the intractability of the psychological problem—the existence in all of us of that 'new presbyter', biding his time. (p. 23)

What a relief—I am surely not only speaking for myself—to read the words of a man who spoke out like Graham. He had absolutely no diplomatic respect of persons. He was, of course, secure; but then secure people usually want to become still more secure. It is worth comparing his downrightness with the artful persiflage with which Shaw flattered when he appeared to be insulting his readers or audiences. But Graham's outbursts were more than mere impulsive tactlessness. There are passages in *Mogreb-el-Acksa* which are so amusing just because we know that what he is telling us about the little venal dodges and *cochonneries* practised on one another by the Moors might be an inside report on life among ourselves today. (pp. 23-4)

The relevance of this good man'e enviable life to our social development seems quite clear to me. His individualism depended on a core of integrity which some people—as many as possible—must have unless good-citizenship is to be equated with cipherdom. Anyhow, far as Graham was from being a Common Man, he was exceptionally full of Common Humanity.

In the main he wrote as if he were telling a true story, and as if—and it was the case—a warm-blooded, acute and well-disposed person were telling it. He was not one of those kind near-cynics (though he *was* a near-cynic) who come to see life all illusion. With my tendency to prefer a story about something to one not about anything much, however artfully presented, I am not very worried by his faults of carelessness. There is no doubt that his punctuation, not his strong point, is sometimes responsible for the muddle a sentence gets into, and for our breathlessness when a last comma is followed by a single word of one syllable. His spelling is variable. He constructs some of his stories awkwardly, and might with advantage have cut the preambles shorter. A tiresome habit he got into was colouring up his pictures with analogies: he abused the word 'like'—so many things reminded this much-travelled man of other things. In the histories many of the paragraphs are too short; he repeats himself; there is often no Contents page or no Index, sometimes neither. The proofs might to all intents and purposes never have been looked at. Both in the histories and the stories he is apt to bring up the same image again and again, for instance we are continually hearing about 'Trapalanda', a heathen heaven for men and horses which they approach in company with Christians, at any rate up to some parting of the ways, by a 'Via Crucis' or 'Via Dolorosa.'

Even I am a little dubious sometimes about his interjections, the more blasphemous ones, though 'blasphemous' is really much too strong; the important thing is that this assiduous chaperoning of his readers signifies an intense concern with the human reference of all he wrote, history and fiction, in so far as what he wrote ever was exactly fiction, and I believe this personal attention has some advantages that are denied to the more aloof 'scientific' historians and to followers in Flaubert's footsteps. There are perhaps times when Graham is too free with foreign words when English would do, but nobody knew better than he how useful outlandish idioms can be for shifting us from standpoints so familiar that they have bred insensibility to the psychological prospect. 'To jump behind a bush is better than the prayers of good men' is a stimulating change from 'Fear God and keep your powder dry'. If you are writing about Spaniards you are within your rights if you use Spanish sayings or words in Spanish with an untranslatable nuance.

The best of the stories and sketches are first rate. Reading a badly balanced selection one might get the idea that Graham was only interested in more or less primitive types. This would not be true. To be accepted wherever he went by the more rarefied members of society was part of his birthright, and how well he could hit them off can be seen in **"Fin de Race."** . . . One of the excellences of this narrative comes from Graham's refusal to embellish it, as he might have been tempted to do, by changing the names and stepping up the drama. As it stands it testifies, and in a sound literary way after all, in spite of the slapdash writing, to the feeling he had for life and character, the feeling, the respect, that humanize everything he wrote and make me, for one, prefer some of his most carelessly thrown-off trifles to anything but the best by many writers I can think of, with deservedly high—but not deservedly *higher*—reputations. He will come into his own, for 'God is not a bad man, after all', as so many of the obscure people who drift in and out of his stories are fond of saying. (pp. 26-7)

> *Paul Bloomfield, in an introduction to* The Essential R. B. Cunninghame Graham *by R. B. Cunninghame Graham, edited by Paul Bloomfield, Jonathan Cape, 1952, pp. 13-27.*

HUGH MacDIARMID (essay date 1952)

[*MacDiarmid was a respected Scottish poet, writer, editor, and translator. He was a Scottish nationalist who wrote many of his finest poems in the Scottish dialect, thus helping to raise that dialect "from the trough of banality into which it had sunk" in the early years of the twentieth century. MacDiarmid was also a socialist who rose to political prominence as the founder of the Scottish Nationalist Party. This party was the successor to the National Party of Scotland, which had been founded by Cunninghame Graham. In the following excerpt, MacDiarmid discusses Graham's relationship to Scottish life and literature of his day and concludes with an appreciation of Graham.*]

I was introduced to R. B. Cunninghame Graham by William Archer in London in the early 20s. My decision to make the Scottish Cause, cultural and political, my life-work dates from that moment. It is true I had been moving towards it before that—and along a similar path to his own, since I had been an active Socialist for over a dozen years. But unlike Cunninghame Graham I belonged to the working-class and through John Maclean had had a thorough indoctrination in Marxism. I doubt if Cunninghame Graham ever met John Maclean. If they had met it is unlikely they would have got on together, but, leaving such personal issues aside for the moment, it is unfortunate that Cunninghame Graham's Socialism was not based on an adequate theory of social causation. He was "one of these damned *aristos* who had embraced the cause of the people"—and as a consequence fell between two stools. He might have worked along with men like E. D. Morel, H. N. Brailsford, and Victor Grayson, but the future of the Labour and Socialist Movement lay with a very different type with whom he could not have worked and from whom he could not have disguised his contempt. He did not suffer fools gladly, and so far as the main and growing body of the Movement was concerned the hatred of intellectual distinction, the actual hostility to literature and the arts, and the fine presence of the man—a very peregrine—ensured that he would have no influence with them but be subjected to their vicious rancour. They knew—and could know—nothing of his writings; their pabulum was of a very different kind—and these two are mutually exclusive. Not only so, but a kind of Gresham's Law was operating—the level was already being dragged down by the worse element. The growth in electoral support of the Movement involved a progressive deterioration of mind and spirit. Though it was soon to command an overall majority of the voting electorate at successive general elections, the Labour

and Socialist Movement in Scotland was unaccompanied by any counterpart of the slightest consequence in literature and the arts and failed even to yield any book that influenced the general development of British, let alone European, Socialism, while the majority of the M.P.s it returned to Westminster were mentally negligible. Even when I met him first Cunninghame Graham was concerned with the failure of the Movement, in its concentration on what it conceived to be internationalism, to reckon with our intranational problems. He was soon to throw himself more and more actively into the Scottish Nationalist Movement which was now developing. . . . At that time the Scottish Nationalist Movement was largely led by writers—Lewis Spence, Neil M. Gunn, the Hon. Ruaraidh Erskine of Marr, William Gillies, Eric Linklater, and others, above all, a little later, Compton Mackenzie. Cunninghame Graham could get along well enough with men like these, but they were soon to give way, just as had happened in the Labour and Socialist Movement, to a gang of dullards with no cultural interests and certainly no personal intellectual or artistic gifts. Yet he kept up his interest and activity in the Scottish Cause to the end and one of the last times I met him we both spoke at an open-air meeting in the St. Rollox Division of Glasgow on a cold wet night. (pp. 9-10)

I am sure [Cunninghame Graham] could have said (if he had closely examined his mind and put aside for a moment his wonderful courtesy), of almost all those with whom he came into contact in the Scottish Labour and Socialist Movement, that (as Nicolas Berdyaev said of the exiled Social-Democrats with whom he had to associate in Vologda when he was exiled there): "I liked them; they were fine people, wholly devoted to their idea or ideals. Yet in their company the atmosphere became jejune and oppressive—an atmosphere which seemed to force one into a strait-jacket and made it impossible to breathe . . . Moreover I came into conflict with a phenomenon, long before it made its appearance in the open, which might be called their totalitarianism, and which demanded the unreserved subjugation of personal conscience to the conscience (if any) of the group or the collective."

What Cunninghame Graham really hated was the bourgeois spirit, and he knew well that the bourgeois spirit is "no mere sociological phenomenon characteristic of capitalist society (although there it is particularly prominent), but, in fact, may attend socialism and communism, Christianity and Atheism alike."

Mr. W. M. Parker, in the chapter he devotes to Cunninghame Graham in his *Modern Scottish Writers* [see excerpt dated 1917] . . . says: "In many of his South American sketches, and particularly in the ones called **'Success'** and that merciless piece of irony called **'Calvary,'** his attitude is the kind of full-blooded defiance in which that other modern Elizabethan, Henley, used to revel. Again his irony towards humanity finds outlet in his denunciation of missionaries sent out to convert the heathen of savage lands and in his contempt for the material success of modern civilisation; the wonderful preface to **'Progress'** expresses his views on progress and success. 'Failure alone is striking.' His friend Conrad called this 'the philosophy of unutterable scorn.'"

It was this irony and scorn towards humanity that caused him to be regarded in many quarters as anti-democratic. It is curious to reflect that in this he suffered in much the same way as another great Scottish writer (albeit of a very different order to Cunninghame Graham), namely Thomas Carlyle. I agree entirely with the late Professor Harold Laski when he said of the latter: "On the question of admitting Carlyle into the ranks of the Great Democrats there is likely to be a division of opinion. If democracy means (1) universal suffrage (2) *plus* the decision of all national questions by majority voting on that basis (3) *plus* the leadership of parliamentary orators, then Carlyle must be classed as an anti-democrat of the most pronounced and uncompromising type. But if the above system is not what 'the people' really desire, but only what they have been 'enchanted' (Carlyle's word) into believing they desire, their real and deeper demand being not for 'representative' self-government but for *good* government by competent rulers—does it not then follow that a prophet who voices this deeper thing would be a truer interpreter of the popular will than an advocate of the sort of democracy so bitterly denounced by Carlyle? And might we not on that ground acclaim him as the better democrat of the two? . . . [On] all *human* grounds Carlyle's claim to the democratic mind is fully as strong as, if not stronger than, that of many persons who, on the grounds of academic definition, claim to be better entitled to it."

I can certainly make a similar claim for Cunninghame Graham. . . . [He] would certainly have agreed with Carlyle that the people are (in the latter's phrases) "mostly fools" to the extent of being "mere mesmerized cattle" under the malign influence of the political cant and claptrap abundantly poured forth by "stump orators of every denomination, all intent on getting their votes." He would have been quite at one with Carlyle in not believing in democracy, conceived as a method of settling all questions by the counting of heads—a thing which Carlyle fiercely and continuously denounced as "the high way to anarchy and the Bottomless Pit." Nevertheless, Carlyle regarded his country and Europe generally—the Europe of his day—as irrevocably committed to Democracy of that sort. He called it "Shooting Niagara", not to be avoided when once you have got into the swirling current above the Falls, as England then was; and he predicted that the swift sequel of it would be a ruinous plunge into the whirlpools below, or, as we now call it, a world crisis. (pp. 12-14)

Cunninghame Graham would, I think, have shared that view. I am certain at all events he would have admired and greatly enjoyed Carlyle's expression of it. . . . [He] did not fall short of such expressions himself at times. I know that he hated commercialism so much that he was delighted and shouted his agreement and patted my shoulder once when I quoted to him from some unremembered source: "England can sink beneath the sea for all I care. Indeed, I wish it would. Forty-six million people with the obligation to export their pots and pans and cutlery and coal, or die . . . is that a life, is that something to be proud of? . . . England is the great anachronism, my friend; the Dodo who survived because twenty miles of sea protected it from a just retribution . . . No, wait! Wait! Of course we still have our culture, our ninety-nine ways of patting a ball about. If England sinks, how should we send a Test Team to Australia? Nevertheless, I prefer that solution to the new war which will soon come because we must sell our hideous eggcups in the Balkans." (p. 15)

But Cunninghame Graham's attributes were no asset among his countrymen but were generally resented as a sort of insult to their own irremediable mediocrity and lack of *panache*. . . . The "drift South," so far as Scots of outstanding brilliance are concerned, is not due only to ambition for professional and financial success. There is the need for the company of their own kind and these are seldom indeed to be found in Scotland. Scotland's "freemasonry of mediocrity" forces them out—and

in this process our Universities play their ignoble part. Witness their treatment of Carlyle, Stevenson, Thomas Davidson, and Sir Patrick Geddes—or the Scottish teaching profession's treatment of John Maclean and A. S. Neill. But, however stupid and spiteful and generally ill-conditioned the general attitude to brilliance, and more particularly to versatility (since to achieve distinction in any direction is hard enough, but to achieve it in several directions at once is not to be tolerated at all by the general run!) may be in Scotland, at least we do not have, what another Scottish writer (Mr. Cecil Gray) has called the "spirit of smug, pharisaical gentlemanliness, complicated with social snobbery, which permeates every aspect of English cultural life." . . . (pp. 16-17)

Yet Scotland has its own serious problems for any artist, different though they are from those encountered in England and under the English influence everywhere, and there is every justification to feel as, Miss Agnes Ethel Mackay tells us in her fine book on him, the Scottish Impressionist, Arthur Melville (1855-1904) felt; "Already he felt the restraint of his native city (Edinburgh). He needed a wider horizon and longed for the freedom of a larger outlook on art."

That is *au fond* [fundamentally] what has led so many Scottish artists and authors South and overseas. The need to escape from the intolerable anti-cultural, anti-intellectual atmosphere of their native country and go where they could find and fraternise with people of their own kind and enjoy the clash of like minds and the active co-operation and competition of men and women with similar creative abilities. And it operated in Cunninghame Graham's case as in that of so many others. It is only necessary to think of his best friends—men like Wilfred Scawen Blunt, Edward Garnett, W. H. Hudson, Joseph Conrad, Bernard Shaw. What had Scotland to offer in comparison?

It was Edinburgh that Arthur Melville rightly revolted from. Glasgow, however, rather than Edinburgh, concerned Cunninghame Graham, and I know that he saw it, as I did and do, in the words of Hölderlin I once adapted and quoted to him in this connection: "Barbarians of old, grown more barbarous still by their industry, their learning, even by their religion, impervious to every devout feeling, corrupt to the very core, insulting every well-fashioned spirit by the degree of their exaggeration and meanness, dull and discordant, like the fragments of a bowl thrown aside. . . . If only someone would tell this god-forsaken people that things are so imperfect amongst them only because they do not leave purity uncorrupted and sacred things untouched by their coarse hands; that nothing flourishes amongst them because they do not heed the roots of growth, divine nature; that amongst them life is empty and burdensome and too full of cold mute conflict, because they scorn the spirit, which infuses vigour and nobility into human activity and serenity into suffering and brings into cities and dwellings love and brotherhood."

While the living blood trickles away into the sand! I remember how horrified I was when I addressed the students supporting Cunninghame Graham's candidature for the Lord Rectorship of Glasgow University in October 1929, and found that they knew nothing or next to nothing of his writings. Even to this day he can have found only a pitiful handful of readers in the whole of Scotland. His books are not to be found in the majority of our public libraries. . . . Francis Parkman, the American historian, said that "one of the commonest disguises of envy is a preference for the inferior"—and modern Scotland has certainly rejected all the best work its sons have produced and acclaimed only what was comfortably low-brow enough. Thus

Cunninghame Graham has been rejected along with Norman Douglas, "Saki" (H. H. Munro), Francis Grierson and Richard Curle.... Yet it is writers like these, and not the popular writers, Kailyaird or otherwise, who are in keeping with and carrying forward and enriching our best national traditions, and in particular the tradition of the Wandering Scot, the combination of scholarship and adventure. (pp. 17-19)

Yet [Cunninghame Graham] remained caviare not only to the general but even to the small better reading public in Scotland, the reason being as I have suggested and as Mr. [William] Power somewhere said, that "the vein of cynical humanism that runs through all his books is as different as possible from the cosily insular sentiment of the Kailyairders [writers of a class of fiction which employs extensive use of the Scottish vernacular and generally deals with common life in Scotland]. It is the expression of the knightly sympathy with the underdog, and with the victims of fate or fortune, that made Cunninghame Graham a militant Socialist, and that drew him to the service of Scotland in her economic adversity and cultural strivings. For the blatantly selfish and self-satisfied type of vulgarian who was rampant in the days of her prosperity he has a withering contempt. The country of his Scots essays and sketches is a twilight Scotland, ennobled by tragedy and defeat. The Scotland of his dreams, which he is valiantly helping to create, is a Scotland nobly self-reliant and bravely idealistic, worthy of her own finest social and cultural traditions. His self-sacrificing devotion to her interests and prestige strikingly exemplifies the fact that national feeling is strongest in the cultured and travelled internationalist." (pp. 20-1)

There was nothing defeatist about Cunninghame Graham, but, as I remember someone saying, "Don Roberto has played many parts—so many that he is not to be identified with any one mode of living." By what category of his doings did the public know him best? 'Adventurer' suggests iself as a label, for it was not only in Spanish America that he welcomed hazardous experiences—in some of which the object was the making of money. But it must be discarded for the implication in it that he had his way to make. His was an assured position. While it pleased him to attribute certain actions and renunciations to his being without money, he could always have put a term to his impecuniosity if he saw fit.... "Politician" has to be rejected equally with "Adventurer"; his incursions into politics, though vigorous, were too desultory. Writer? He wrote many books, which certainly found favour with the elect, but he would have repudiated the designation. "Think," he wrote, "what an uneventful life a man who lives by literature condemns himself to pass. Others are preaching, praying, cheating and lying, fighting, exploring, inventing, risking their lives, and sailing on the sea. Whilst they are up and about the writer sits at his table cudgelling his brains!"

"In the many photographs included in Mr. [A. F.] Tschiffely's book [*Don Roberto, Being the Account of the Life and Works of R. B. Cunninghame Graham, 1852-1936*] he figures as so conscious of his superb appearance and as wearing his clothes with such an air that we are put in mind of the theatre; nevertheless we cannot do his ghost the wrong to consider 'Playactor,' for his label; he was too formidable. The obvious theatrical element in him is thus discounted by Mr. Tschiffely: 'His poses were so natural to him that on better acquaintance with the man they became part of him'; and with that hint we come to the compromise that Don Roberto in his long active life played—and perhaps overplayed—many parts, but that in all these parts he played that unique person himself. How did

he conceive this person? For his nearest approach to criticism, Mr. Tschiffely offers a caricature of his own in which Don Roberto figures as Don Quixote—without, however, satisfying us that there was any cause for which his hero would have exhibited himself on Rosinante as described by Cervantes. While there is nothing in his story as narrated to throw doubt on the sincerity of his championship of innumerable underdogs he presents himself primarily as a challenger of other top dogs. (pp. 21-2)

I have little fault to find with that. My own answer would be, I think, "Aristocrat." He sat lightly to life and to literature. As he says in **"Bopicuá"**: "It is not given to all men after a break of years to come back to the scenes of youth, and still find in them the same zest as of old. To return again to all the cares of life called civilised, with all its littlenesses, its newspapers all full of nothing, its sordid aims disguised under highsounding nicknames, its hideous riches and its sordid poverty, its want of human sympathy, and, above all, its barbarous war brought on by the folly of its rulers was not just at that moment an alluring thought, as I felt the little 'malacara' (white faced horse) that I rode twitching his bridle, striving to be off. When I had touched him with the spur he bounded forward and ... the place which for so many months had been part of my life sank out of sight, just as an island in the Tropics fades from view as the ship leaves it, as it were, hull down."

So Cunninghame Graham rides off, leaving us with the enigma of his personality unsolved, (and who after all wants a man reduced to a label?) with these characteristic words: " 'Tis meet and fitting to set free the horse or pen before death overtakes you, or before the gentle public turns its thumbs down and yells 'Away with him!' ... Hold it not up to me for egotism, O gentle reader, for I would have you know that hardly any of the horses I rode had shoes on them, and thus the tracks are faint."

Instead of wishing to reduce him to a label then, (I do not like "the last of the Caballeros" "a modern conquistador" or any of the other journalistic inventions), we may rejoice in the contradictions which were the man.... (pp. 22-3)

Hugh MacDiarmid, in his Cunninghame Graham: A Centenary Study, *Caledonian Press, 1952, 40 p.*

JESSIE KOCMANOVÁ   (essay date 1964)

[*In the following excerpt, Kocmanová examines Graham's works from a socialist perspective.*]

Robert Bontine Cunninghame Graham, who in appearance might well have sat for a portrait of Don Quixote, tilted not against windmills but against capitalism and the narrow hypocrisy of bourgeois society. In spite of the many tributes to his personality and genius from such writers as Bernard Shaw, Edward Garnett, Joseph Conrad, it is not unusual for his name to be missing from literary histories of his time. [L.] Cazamian, for example, does not mention him [in *A History of English Literature*], though he deals with far lesser writers of the period, nor does he appear in the *Concise Cambridge Bibliography* of English Literature. Doubtless as a result of his absence from these standard works, his name is not mentioned in the index to the Third Volume of the *History of English Literature* published for the Soviet Academy of Sciences, a work which has done much to rescue other undeservedly obscured reputations of this period of developing imperialism.

I would draw attention at the outset to what I think are the three main reasons for the general neglect of his work and personality.

The first is the fundamental reason, which has operated similarly in the case of other fine writers of the period of imperialism who have either been ignored or completely misrepresented. Cunninghame Graham in every word he wrote as an artist, and in his whole life, untiringly and without compromise attacked capitalism and bourgeois democracy, imperialism, colonialism and all they stand for. Any assessment of his work which ignores this aspect is bound to be inadequate.

Two further subsidiary reasons however contribute to present-day neglect. In his latter years, Cunninghame Graham, who had been a devoted socialist in the early days of the modern socialist movement in Britain, became disillusioned with the British Labour Party and—though a firm supporter of the Spanish Republic in the thirties—played little part in the progressive left-wing literary movement of the thirties in Britain. Already an old man in his eighties at this period, he devoted the last decades of his life to the newly-awakened cause of Scottish Nationalism. At this period, the attitude of British Marxists towards the fight within Britain for economic and cultural equality for all the nations of Britain, was not yet clearly worked out, and this weakness of theoretical equipment led at times to incomplete understanding of the aims of the most progressive of Scots Nationalists and consequently the latter remained isolated from the Communist Party. Although a large proportion of the Scottish Nationalist leadership of the thirties was out-and-out bourgeois, nevertheless there was nothing bourgeois in Cunninghame Graham's patriotism, which gave the lead to later socialist and communist elements in the Scottish Nationalist movement, above all to Hugh MacDiarmid and those who have followed him.

The third cause of neglect is the fact that Cunninghame Graham confined himself in imaginative literature to a single literary kind, which tends to appeal to the discriminating reader rather than to the widely popular audience, not because of any inherent lack of popular interest, but because when it reaches book form it is often less adequately advertised by publishing houses and less noticed by critics. This genre is that of the short tale which is rather an ironic commentary on life than a story. Graham never wrote a lengthy tale or a novel, probably because he was under no pressing necessity of earning a living and hence wrote only to please himself and was not open to the pressure of publishers, who prefer the securer market and more certain profits of the novel. That he was capable of the greater concentration and structural power demanded by a longer work is shown by the striking biographical and historical studies which he produced, and which have been almost completely neglected by critics.

Cunninghame Graham, though his name was well-known in the last decades of the nineteenth century, was appreciated as a writer—as was Joseph Conrad in his own lifetime—mostly by a small circle of friends and kindred spirits, themselves fine and perceptive critics or creative writers, such as Edward Garnett, W. H. Hudson, Morley Roberts, and Conrad himself. Graham was a prominent literary and public figure when Conrad was still making his way, and Conrad in fact owed a great debt to Graham's encouragement. Nevertheless Conrad's reputation has grown, while Cunninghame Graham's has faded and many of his works are out of print. A contributory cause is certainly the fact that Conrad, with the enthusiasm of his

friends and the need to earn a living to spur him on, proceeded to write a series of novels.

This matter of the literary genre is however not the basic cause of the neglect of Cunninghame Graham. We can see this when we contrast the total effect of his work in comparison with that of Conrad's. Conrad's reputation has never been so high as it is at the present day. Critical studies, biographical studies, volumes of letters, etc., continue yearly to be produced relating to Joseph Conrad. He has come to be seen as a master of prose style, vivid penetrating characterization, and daring artistic construction. It is above all as a master at revealing by means of subtle juxtaposition and contrasts fundamental problems of character and moral conduct that Conrad has been valued. Cunninghame Graham's mastery, though on a smaller scale, is of the same nature. Yet, in distinction to Conrad, there is little in Graham's trenchant condemnation of imperialism, which resounds and reechoes throughout his work, to commend him to the cynism and despair of so many twentieth-century critics. It is the general gloom and ironic despair of Conrad's outlook on life which has appealed to certain of the present generation of critics. Few have had such penetration as Arnold Kettle, who has pointed out that it is Conrad's power of laying bare the baseness and rottenness of capitalist and imperialist society, his concern for the moral integrity of the human protagonist of that situation, that is his first claim to greatness as a writer. In making this reassessment of Conrad, Kettle has shown the way to critics. However, an adequate reassessment of Graham's work, comparable to what has been done for Conrad, is still lacking. (pp. 14-16)

The titles of [Graham's collections of stories and sketches] are characteristically ironical. In 1902 appeared *Success*, followed in 1905 by *Progress*, and from 1909 to 1912 appeared *Faith, Hope* and *Charity*. These five volumes cover the period of Graham's most typical work, when he most clearly stood among the small group of anti-imperialist writers, whose claim to significance was only partly understood by Garnett. Graham, Conrad, Hudson, Blunt, even Galsworthy, were all critical of the complacent Victorian belief that the British Empire was a benevolent institution; but not all of them were hopeful that any action of theirs could in any way change the course of human events. The general attitude of these writers was well expressed by Blunt when he contrasted the old traditional conception of love of country with the chauvinistic "patriotism" of the imperialists.

None of them, however, had an identical outlook on the society of their time, though all were severely critical both in their considered opinions and in their artistic work. Blunt and Graham were both prepared to go to prison for their beliefs, while Hudson, Conrad and Gissing (who in respect of his antagonism to his age can in some ways be likened to the anti-imperialists), sacrificed financial success and health to their ideals of literary integrity. Blunt and Conrad both retained more of the "aristocratic" attitude to the rest of mankind, whereas Graham's sympathy with the downtrodden, outcast, defeated and humble extended almost to identification—there is in his stories no "distance" between the writer and the victim of society whom he depicts. Hudson was more of a pure romantic than either Graham or Conrad, much more of an escapist, even with something of 18th-century "sentiment" for the noble savage. Hudson, like Gissing, suffered severely from economic embarrassment, which in his case too led to a certain degree of self-pity and self-castigation—preventing him, for example, from accepting the generously extended invitations of Graham, and cutting him off, again like Gissing, from the society of his intellectual and artistic equals: "I was very sorry indeed not to be able to go; but I am unwell, out of sorts, also, in a sense, out of the world; certainly not fit to associate with those who are in it with something to live for, who have not yet lost all will and power to work and to play. To my sick soul your life seems almost too full, your activities too many and great, your range on this planet too wide." Along with this self-commiseration went a detachment from current reality, which led to his objecting to the ironic parallels and side-references to contemporary events which form one of Graham's most typical methodical devices. In a letter of 1904 referring to Graham's biography of Hernando de Soto, which Hudson praises highly, he adds however: "I would rather you had omitted some of your side-thrusts at our times."

Side-thrusts at the times, however, are one of the most effective and characteristic formal devices in Graham's work. The whole ironical point of an essay or sketch dealing with some apparently remote theme is frequently contained in the dying fall of a concluding sentence. But it would be wrong to consider these as merely side-thrusts. They arise from the deeply-rooted distaste and contempt for modern capitalist society which motivated all Graham's life and work. It is this distaste, combined with his capacity for infinite pity and his unchanging recognition of necessity and reality which forms the basis of his kinship with Conrad, although the artistic means which Conrad found for expressing his less explicit, less ideologically formulated distaste were much more oblique, though no less intimately bound up in the structure of his work.

Cunninghame Graham in point of time appeared earlier in print than Conrad, who published *Almayer's Folly* in 1895. By that time Hudson had been ten years in print (*The Purple Land*, 1885), while Graham was already known as a publicist. According to Herbert West, the first examples of his published prose (apart from some earlier South American journalism) were the three ironic letters of 1890 on United States persecution of the Sioux Indians, under the successive titles of **"But 'twas a famous victory,"** **"Ghosts Dancing,"** and **"Salvation by Starvation."** As West remarks, these letters are preludes to his later essays on **"Niggers"** and **"Success."**

In 1891 part of a speech he had made in the Commons on **"Economic Evolution"** was published as a penny pamphlet. This is not a political pamphlet in the ordinary sense of the word. We might consider it a nineteenth-century pendant to Goldsmith and Crabbe, with its contrast of the idyllic though stagnant life of an Irish village before the arrival of capitalist progress and after. Graham does not idealise the pastoral village of the past:

> Had there been but only more to eat, less rent
> to pay, one faith instead of two or three, no
> public house, and if the rain had cleared off
> now and then, the place would have been about
> as happy as it is possible for a place to be here
> in this vale of tears.

In terms which recall the peroration of Father Keegan in Shaw's *John Bull's Other Island* (1904), Graham goes on to contrast the life of the place after capital had arrived and built a factory.

The germ of all Graham's prose can in fact be found in his Parliamentary speeches and letters to the press. When the liberal reviews refused his sketches on the grounds of their "immorality," (for he did not hesitate to write of prostitution and other vices usually ignored or referred to euphemistically by

the Victorian press), he then published in the socialist paper *Justice*. Just as none of his professional political utterances were ever confined to platitudes (he was a public speaker calculated to make any chairman nervous), so his creative treatment of even the most exotic subjects never was remote from the pressing problems of his time.

There are several prevailing themes which Graham returned to again and again throughout his work, and as he said himself, his autobiography is to be looked for in his writings. Unlike most of his contemporaries, he never wrote for any other purpose than to please himself, express himself, or put a point of view before the public. This had doubtless harmful as well as beneficial results, for while it meant that he retained to the full his integrity as an artist, on the other hand he remained an amateur in the sense that he never came to grips with the paramount form which his own time demanded, namely the novel.

Cunninghame Graham was not of course the only artist of his time who preferred the short story. If with regard to his artistic method and emotional scope he can be compared with Conrad, within his own sphere of the short tale he challenges comparison with Kipling. Contemporary critical opinion is coming to realise that Kipling was a serious artist with a profounder and more sombre view of the life than of the boy-scout movement. And it is by virtue of his volumes of short stories, not by his attempted novels, that Kipling's claim to be a serious writer can best be supported. Like Graham's volumes, the volumes of Kipling's stories form a thematic whole, expressed by the title, and thus can better be judged as comprehensive works, than if they were mere random collections of different tales. The poems which Kipling interspersed between his tales serve the same purpose of summing-up or pointing the preceding tale as in Graham is rendered by the last paragraph or even last sentence of his sketches, which often turns away from the narrower subject of the tale to point a universal application.

Apart from their selected form, there is however little similarity either in method or in purpose between the two writers. Kipling above all tells a story; Graham prefers to suggest the story, while concentrating on the profounder aspects of character and fate. For Kipling, the hero is the little-known but faithful, dogged servant of imperialism, the son of Martha who does the work of the Empire even when the jelly-bellied flag-floppers desecrate his ideals with their loud-mouthed and tactless shouting of what he lets himself only whisper in his tight-lipped way.

The basis of the "work" of these bearers of the imperial burden, and the basis of their usefulness for the exploiters, is their sympathy for and understanding of the "lesser breeds" among whom they live. Kipling and his heroes are always trembling on the brink of the discovery that their whole way of life is a cowardly denial of this sympathy. Nevertheless, the decisive point of commitment is that however ill-rewarded and overworked, the son of Martha is the willing hireling of imperialism and colonialism who in the end betrays, like Kim, those for whom he feels love, kinship, understanding, but not respect.

Cunninghame Graham sees the life of colonial countries from an entirely different aspect. For him it is the outcast, the failure, the man who is defeated, who dies unknown in the desert or the pampas, whose fate typifies the fate of humanity:

> For those who fail, for those who have sunk
> still battling beneath the muddy waves of life,
> we keep our love, and that curiosity about their

lives which makes their memories green when the cheap gold is dusted over, which once we gave success . . . The unlucky Stuarts, from the first poet king slain at the ball play, to the poor mildewed Cardinal of York, with all their faults, they leave the stolid Georges millions of miles behind, sunk in their pudding and prosperity . . . Causes which hang in monumental mockery quite out of fashion, as that of Poland, still are more interesting than is the struggle between the English and the Germans, which shall sell gin and gunpowder to negroes on the Coast.

For Graham, the evil principle is greed, cunning, bourgeois prosperity, which makes men selfish, forgetful and cruel. Commerce and the bourgeois state are his enemies, and he fights them wherever he encounters them. However different and contrasted are his themes, the blighting effect of capitalism (or of earlier power-concentrating systems) is always present, whether emphasised or implicit. The correspondence between Graham and Conrad shows how close they were in their attitude to their own time. In a letter written before they had met, but after Graham had initiated their friendship by expressing his appreciation of Conrad's work, the latter speaks of his comprehension of Graham's attitude:

> If I've read you aright . . . you are a most hopeless idealist—your aspirations are irrealisable. You want from men faith, honour, fidelity to truth in themselves and others. You want them to have all this, to show it every day, to make out of these words their rules of life. The respectable classes which suspect you of such pernicious longings lock you up and would just as soon have you shot,—because your personality counts and you cannot deny that you are a dangerous man. What makes you dangerous is your unwarrantable belief that your desire may be realised. This is the only point of difference between us. I do not believe.

There follows a remarkable metaphor which we must regret Conrad never used in the symbolic structure of a novel or tale, when he speaks of the self-evolved knitting-machine, which ought to embroider, but only knits—"Its knits us in and it knits us out. It has knitted time, space, pain, death, corruption, despair and all the illusions,—and nothing matters. I'll admit however that to look at the remorseless process is sometimes amusing."

The apparently detached irony which renders Graham's criticism of society so biting, never ended in detached "amusement." Whatever was the scenic background of his work, he always plunged straight to his aim of laying open the corrupt heart of imperialism, the true "heart of darkness" of his time. (pp. 21-4)

Of the sketch **"Niggers"** Professor Herbert West wrote: "There is, to my knowledge, no more bitter and indignant denunciation of English Imperialism in all English. The British reviewers were uncomfortably irritated by **"Niggers"**. The readers of Conan Doyle, Lucas Mallet, Anthony Hope and other vendors of popular wares could not, with any stretch of imagination, take kindly to *The Ipané*. Any writer who dares write what only a small intellectual minority feel, or who damns the hy-

pocrisy of his fellows and his country with such intensity and clarity, must remain unpopular."

The form of this sketch is an elaborate description of the creation of the world:

> Jahve created all things, especially the world in which we live, and which is really the centre of the universe, in the same way as England is the centre of the planet, and as the Stock Exchange is the real centre of all England, despite the dreams of the astronomers and the economists.

At last, having created all minerals, plants and animals—enumerated with magnificent rhetorical elan—Jahve created man.

> This done, he needed rest again, and having set the sun and moon just in the right position to give light by day and night to England, he recollected that a week had passed.

The world now lay ready "for men to make it hideous and miserable." But obviously the creator cared little about any of his creatures, "except the people who inhabited the countries from which the Aryans came."

> Assyrians, Babylonians, Egyptians, Persians and the rest were no doubt useful and built pyramids, invented hanging gardens, erected towers, spoke the truth (if their historians lie not), drew a good bow, and rode like centaurs or like Gauchos. What did it matter when all is said and done? They were all "niggers", and whilst they fought and conquered, or were conquered, bit by bit the race which God had thought of from the first, slowly took shape.

Greece, Rome, medieval Europe flourish and decay:

> Thus through the mist of time, the Celtic-Saxon race emerged from heathendom and woad, and, in the fulness of the Creator's pleasure, became the tweed-clad Englishman. Much of the earth was his, and in the skies he had his mansion ready, well aired, with every appliance known to modern sanitary science waiting for him, and a large Bible on the chest of drawers in every room.

All the rest of mankind are "niggers", with one exception:

> Men of the Latin races, though not born free, can purchase freedom with a price, that is, if they conform to our ideas, are rich and wash, ride bicycles, and gamble on the Stock Exchange. If they are poor, then woe betide them, let them paint their faces white with all the ceruse that ever Venice furnished, to the black favour shall they come. A plague of pigments, blackness is in the heart, not in the face, and poverty no matter how it washes, still is black.

> Niggers are niggers, whether black or white.

This sketch, which echoes the arguments and at times even the language of the English translation of Marx's *Capital*, employs all Graham's power of picturesque description and invective to illustrate the materialist and dialectical conception of history. It is in fact a condensation of the opinions and arguments contained in one of Graham's rarest works, *The Imperial Kail-*

yard, a socialist pamphlet published in 1896, now out of print. The pamphlet deals with the inhuman treatment in South Africa of the Matabele tribes and employs savage irony similar to that in **"Niggers."** Naturally, in a topical pamphlet, the argument is more extended than in the sketch, in which we see to perfection the literary art of Graham, whereby he transformed and condensed a political argument into a piece of creative prose writing.

All Graham's collections of tales offer the same variety of scene and unity of viewpoint and tone. In the collection *Success*, the scene ranges from London at the height of Victorian prosperity to the Scottish Highlands and the wild regions of the River Plate, but throughout the writer contrasts those who have apparently failed, and yet remained true to some inner conviction, with the vulgarity of worldly success. The extremes of success and failure are summed up in the sketch **"Might, Majesty and Dominion,"** a description of the funeral of Queen Victoria.

We may contrast this description, written directly for the press at the time, with the same incident as Galsworthy describes it in his novel *In Chancery*. Galsworthy stresses the unity of the English people at this moment of summing-up:

> The Queen was dead, and the air of the greatest city upon earth grey with unshed tears . . . In silence, the long line wound in through the Park gate . . . And as it went by there came a murmuring groan from all the long line of those who watched . . . Tribute of an Age to its own death . . .

Graham however sees the fundamental contradictions behind the apparent unity. Thus after several pages in the manner of a *Times* obituary describing the material prosperity of Victoria's reign, with the recurring theme: "She was the mother of her people, yes, even of the meanest of her people in the land," the sketch ends as follows:

> Emperors and kings passed on, the martial pomp and majesty of glorious war clattering and clanking at their heels. The silent crowds stood reverently all dressed in black. At length, when the last soldier had ridden out of sight, the torrent of humanity broke into myriad waves, leaving upon the grass of the down-trodden park its scum of sandwich papers, which, like the foam of some great ocean, clung to the railings, round the roots of trees, was driven fitfully before the wind over the boot-stained grass, or trodden deep into the mud, or else swayed rhythmically to and fro as seaweed sways and moans in the slack water of a beach.
>
> At length they all dispersed, and a well-bred and well-fed dog or two roamed to and fro, sniffing disdainfully at the remains of the rejected food which the fallen papers held.
>
> Lastly, a man grown old in the long reign of the much-mourned ruler, whose funeral procession had just passed, stumbled about, slipping on the muddy grass, and taking up a paper from the mud fed ravenously on that which the two dogs had looked at with disdain.
>
> His hunger satisfied, he took up of the fragments that remained a pocketful, and then,

> whistling a snatch from a forgotten opera, slouched slowly onward and was swallowed by the gloom.

This sketch is one of the most finished pieces of prose by Graham. The measured fall of the first three and a half pages preserves perfectly the elegiac texture of an official funeral oration, and yet we are not unprepared for the final page just quoted, which turns the whole force of the previous pages upon the civilisation Graham is attacking. Two things prepare us: the several-times repeated sentence "She was the mother of her people, even the poorest of her people in the land," whose repetition does not become clearly ironical until in the concluding paragraphs we are confronted with one of those poorest; and occasional sentences of ironic intention, whose irony again does not fully break upon us until we read the final words of the essay. Such sentences, which never interrupt the elegiac cadence, are for example: "Great battleships, torpedo boats, submarine vessels, guns, rifles, stinkpot shells, and all the contrivances of those who think that the material progress of the Anglo-Saxon race should enter into the polity of savage states, as Latin used to enter schoolboys' minds, with blood." The final paragraphs are introduced by a sentence which sets the scene firmly in contrast to the solemn periods of the introduction: "So down the streets in the hard biting wind, right through the rows of dreary living-boxes which like a tunnel seemed to encase the assembled mass of men, her funeral procession passed."

In the first sentence of the concluding paragraphs above quoted, there can be little doubt that Graham intends to recall Kipling's "Recessional"—"The captains and the kings depart"—for the purpose of underlining the very different mood in which he ends his sketch. The concluding paragraphs are very closely-woven prose, where some words and phrases have the dual emotive significance we are more accustomed to find in poetry—for example the conjunction of the adjective "down-trodden" and the noun "scum," not in this case applied to the poor, but to the muddy grass, the unusual but vivid epithet "boot-stained," the ironic conjunction of "well-bred" and "well-fed" applied to the dogs. The "man grown old" we would naturally expect to be followed by the phrase "in the service of," but here we have merely "in the long reign," i.e. the reign which never touched him, of the monarch who was anything but a mother to the meanest of her people. Finally the suggestion of the indomitable courage and humour of the poor, "a snatch from a forgotten opera," is immediately contrasted with the hopeless prospect presented by the words: "slouched slowly onward."

The analysis of practically any paragraph or even sentence of Cunninghame Graham's will provide similar evidence of care and mastery in composition. His realistic method springs from the steadiness and lack of sentimentality of his vision, and from the fighting hardness of his blows at privilege and wealth, all the harder because artistically they are so selective.

Returning again to the question of the nature of Graham's realism and its partial kinship to the art of Joseph Conrad, while we pay tribute to the greater structural power and the subtle psychological analyses of Conrad, we may be sure that socialist art has also much to learn from the creative method of Graham. Conrad's experience of life, as well as his creative struggle for expression, had made him fundamentally a pessimist. It was above all the sincere conviction of Cunninghame Graham as man and artist that he respected and perhaps even envied. In 1899, when Graham tried to persuade Conrad to attend a peace meeting, instead of rending him with savage irony, which might well have been the fate of anyone else, Conrad wrote to explain and excuse himself, and vouchsafed a more open declaration of his view of politics than he afforded to most people: "I am not a peace man, not a democrat. (I don't know what the word means really.)" Graham knew well what the word meant and gave it its true expression in his art. For him it was never the democracy of the successful, the complacent, the bourgeois: it was the democracy of man the worker, man the failure, man the undefeated. (pp. 27-30)

> *Jessie Kocmanová, "R. B. Cunninghame Graham: A Little-Known Master of Realist Prose," in* Philologica Pragensia, *Vol. 7, No. 1, 1964, pp. 14-30.*

RICHARD E. HAYMAKER (essay date 1967)

[*In the following excerpt from his critical study of Graham's works, Haymaker discusses Graham's historical writings on the conquest of South America.*]

The segment of the past that appealed most to Cunninghame Graham's imagination (it will be remembered) was the conquista, "one of the greatest dramas, and certainly the greatest adventure in which the human race had engaged." Several small bands of men, after crossing an uncharted ocean in "crazy" cockleshells, wandered through vast mysterious continents rendered incalculably dangerous by miasmic jungles, bitterly cold heights and frequent ambushes by angry tribes, and in a few years, with the annexation of lands almost double the area of Europe, made their country, which for eight centuries had been but a cluster of small provinces absorbed in a struggle against a powerful enemy, into the greatest empire on earth. "What chiefly differentiate[d]" their wanderings from all others was "that the greater part of them were plunged into the unknown. Cortés had heard of Montezuma and his [kingdom], but by the vaguest rumours. . . . Pizarro and Almagro [hardly] knew . . . where they were going," and Quesada "fell upon his conquest by accident, just as a chance stroke with a pick sometimes reveals a rich lode in a mine." Indeed, the whole adventure had still more of the elements of "the books of chivalry that turned Don Quixote's brain". . . . Though many parts of this impossible achievement had of course been told to the English-speaking world, the telling had been strongly influenced by the *leyenda negra*—the "dogma . . . that we were never as those Spanish publicans." A more impartial account might be presented, so Graham thought, by one who was not weighed down with the aggressive Protestantism and racial pride inherent in the historiography of the days of Robertson and Prescott—some of it "the atavism of the time when Spain and England were rivals for the dominion of the seas"—and who understood more intimately and thoroughly the Spanish approach to life.

Though calling himself "a mere dabbler in the great mystery of history," he had most of the other qualifications necessary for such an undertaking. Familiarity with the general history of the *siglo de oro* [Golden Age], including some of the studies of the various Indian cultures, provided him with sufficient orientation. Writing largely from memory, he was liable to an occasional slip, but meticulousness in certain small matters, as well as some of the trappings of scholarship, seemed to him merely "an *ad captandum* appeal to the suffrages of those soft-headed creatures who are styled serious men." . . . Such precision is more the aim of the native historian. As indicated by his quarryings in the inexhaustible Archive of the Indies at Seville and by many of the quotations in his footnotes, Graham did, however, choose the hard, scholarly way of gathering his material, depending primarily upon the testimony of contemporary chroniclers and historians.

Aware that all histories contain subjective elements—something of the personality of the writer finding expression even in the process of selection and of arrangement—he brought to bear upon the records a critical intelligence. Thus Valdivia's assertion that fully twenty thousand Indians opposed his forces in a certain battle provokes this acid comment: "The historians of every war, even the latest, have been inclined to magnify the number of the defeated foe. It is a practice that does no great harm to anyone, and merely causes historians to be classed with politicians and with fishermen." (pp. 206-07)

Aware likewise that "all history is written to suit the conscience of the conquerors," he tells us that "had but a Mexican [or Incan or Chibchan or Guaraní or Araucanian] written upon the other side, the account no doubt would have been as different as that of Barbour in his *Bruce*, from the official chronicler of the English king." The country of each of these imaginary scribes was at peace with the world, and he and his compatriots "not only had no quarrel" with the invaders, "but never in their lives had heard the name, either of the Spaniards or of Spain." Thus when the Querandis were attacked for missing a day in supplying Buenos Aires with meat and fish, we are asked whether, if "an armed expedition of Indians [had] landed in Spain or England, . . . the inhabitants would have brought them provisions, without payment, for fourteen days." And when the conquistadores attempted to justify certain repressive actions by raising the charge of rebellion, we are told that as to whom "the Indians were to rebel against is not so clear." To the disinterested observer, as Graham keeps reminding us, they were really of the tribe of "filibusters, seeking to take away the patrimony of other men, to enslave them if they could. . . ."

In several ways he was himself peculiarly fitted to become a recorder of their deeds. Unlike Prescott and other arm-chair historians, he had felt on the skin and to the marrow many of the settings in which the action took place—some of them hardly touched by the passage of centuries. With a love perhaps even more keen than that of Parkman for the frontier life—"the 'lordliest . . . on earth'"—he had had many experiences similar to those of the conquistadores: shivering in front of a campfire or on tenterhooks at the thought of Indians creeping up in the darkness; marching through the night across unfamiliar country; suffering the pangs of hunger and of thirst; bivouacking alone, without even a fire, on a dry hummock in a swamp, holding his horse and listening to the wild beasts. . . . Consanguinity in spirit as well as in blood and long association with the descendants of these conquerors of half the globe gave him a certain intuitive insight into many of their responses to the situations that confronted them. There are, to be sure, pitfalls involved in such a fitness into which he occasionally stumbles—the intrusion of descriptions of the present appearance of a place and too great an identification with certain attitudes of this breed of men—but, in the main, it accounts for much of the vividness of his scenes, almost giving one the feeling that Graham himself was a member of the various expeditions.

Rarely has geography played so pronounced and romantic a part in history—at times a leading one—and hence the large space it occupies in his pages is fully justified. When his knowledge of it was slight, as in *Hernando de Soto* and *Pedro de*

Valdivia, the result is disappointing, but when intimate, as with those panoramas just presented—especially the rainforests of Colombia and Paraguay and the pampas of Argentina—the floral and faunal settings merely indicated in his sources are evoked with a sense of immediacy. Tempting though it must have been to such a lover and consummate interpreter of the wilderness, he does not luxuriate in landscape painting; rather, it is well interwoven with the action and often introduced with only a few strokes of the brush.

Most conspicuous amongst the animals—brought in by the Spaniards and so, in the beginning, few in number—are those prime favorites of Graham's: horses. Because of their importance in the conquista—now and then, as with Cortés and Quesada, deemed less expendable than men—they are frequently included in contemporary writings: their names, their colorings, their gear, their individual traits (occasionally more fully noted than those of their riders), and their exploits (preserved in the same heroic style). It pleased him that they inspired in many conquistadores a sense of comradeship, Díaz del Castillo speaking of them "as if they had been voluntary companions and sharers of the perils and the hardships of the campaign." . . . (pp. 208-10)

With the psychological and artistic skill evident in his sketches as well as his wide acquaintance with all sorts of persons, he was able to portray, briefly or at full length, many of the leading figures of the conquest. Extraordinarily alive, like Plutarch and Froissart, to the value of the small particularizing detail in revealing the real man and rendering him unforgettable, . . . he made skilful use of those found in his sources. Because of certain gaps in the available evidence, as in the early lives of most of the conquistadores, some of the lines of his portraiture are necessarily vague, but, with his knowledge of the hereditary and environmental influences that shaped them, he could, in the manner of a palaeontologist modelling an animal on the basis of a few fragments of bone, make the most of the merest hint. Doubtful of the value of exploring in the mysterious realm of motives and of long dissertations on character, he presented even his chief figures in much the same manner as those in his sketches: with the broad experience of the man of the world rather than the special techniques of the psychologist—an approach that deliberately by-passes some of the complexities of human nature. When the motive for a certain action was obscure enough to be subject to different interpretations—the obscurity often deepened by the explanation of the actor to others or to himself—he brought to bear upon it his shrewd insight into the primary impulses and patterns of conduct, directed by his large understanding of the conquistadorial temperament. . . . Since considerable independence of judgment was exercised and the artist is never entirely absent, many of his portraits show his own personal imprint. Painted usually with a Hals-like impressionism, they have more of the blush of life upon them than the more elaborate and "tighter" canvases of Prescott.

Much more interested in military and political than in social and economic matters, he became primarily a narrative historian. Though now avoided by most members of the guild as well as by artists in other fields because it seems to move largely on the surface of things, narration—along with melody in music or poetry, the most primitive and the most engaging form of expression—is, as exemplified by Macaulay and Parkman, the very blood and muscle of historical writing. Far from being superficial, it can interpret the motives of the actors and the deeper meaning of events—probably in the most reliable

sort of way, deeds making most explanations superfluous. . . . The narrative skill . . . [evident] in Graham's other writings was equal to the task: tracing the living stream of happenings through the dense flora of many documents, knowing which incidents merely to touch upon and which to present fully, fitting detail into the broad pattern, interpolating plausibly when testimony is lacking, and keeping everything flowing steadily like a river, with a varying pace and an epic sweep. (pp. 211-12)

At intervals in the flow of the narrative are many stirring dramatic episodes besides battles, such as Pizarro, like an old lion, fighting off assassins and, as he lay mortally wounded, dipping a finger in his blood and making a cross upon the stones; Soto, at full gallop, coming to a sudden halt just at the side of Atahualpa's chair flanked by a bodyguard of thirty thousand, his charger's hoofs cutting the grass "as a sharp skate cuts into ice"; the "thirty lances," on a cold windy day, crossing the flooded Río Ocholi under pressure by Indians on both sides; the converted witch-doctor, Oberá, who imagined "himself a David slaying the Spanish Philistines with sling and stone," leading a revolt in Santa Fé and Córdoba; and— "perhaps the strangest meeting . . . the world ever saw"— Quesada, Belalcázar and Federmann, each with the same number of men, "fate-led and brought together" from north, east, and south "by the invisible loadstone of chance" near the Chibchan capital in a *coup de théâtre* and, after some braving of each other in Homeric style, agreeing to present their claims of discovery to the Spanish court in person. (p. 213)

Though skilful in weaving landscapes and portraits into the ever-shifting sequence of events, as well as in alternating light and shade and in creating suspense, he was somewhat deficient, at least in comparison with, say, Prescott and even Parkman, in architectonic power. Some of this was of course due to the conditions of the realm in which he worked, for, unlike the novelist or the dramatist, the historian cannot create facts or events but only arrange the data provided by his various sources— the most intractable of material. More of it was due to the looseness of construction already indicated, most noticeable in the many repetitions not only within the volumes as a whole (understandable, since each was written independent of the others) but also within the individual volume. The locale or the theme gives a certain unity to *The Conquest of the River Plate, The Horses of the Conquest* and *A Vanished Arcadia,* and the focus on the central figure, generally more to *Bernal Diaz del Castillo, Hernando de Soto, The Conquest of New Granada,* and *Pedro de Valdivia;* but even with this latter group, the limitations of the verifiable evidence destroy the possibility of rendering the actual proportions of their lives. Construction is most taut in *The Conquest of New Granada.* . . . (pp. 214-15)

Although the style [of the histories] is inferior to that of his sketches (only in an occasional passage, such as several pampean and jungle landscapes and his leave-taking of Schmidel, does he become so poetically evocative), it is better than that of the majority of historians. It has, to be sure, most of the defects found in the sketches and at times, as in the latter part of *The Conquest of New Granada,* a certain flatness in diction and in rhythm, but, in the main, harmonizes well with its subject-matter. It is lucid in exposition; richly and subtly pigmented in local coloring; punctuated with arresting images and aphorisms and with quotations from his sources; and vigorous in scenes of action—often the passionate vigor of an eye-witness or participant. It can sustain the epic or heroic note over long stretches. Moreover, the style is profoundly revelatory of the personality of the author—passing events provoking eloquent commentary on a wide range of topics, in which especially noticeable are the mordancy of his humor and the compassion and tragic quality of his irony. Indeed, to use his phrase in regard to several of the chroniclers, he also could write *con el alma en la pluma* [with his soul in his pen].

Like most historians of the period, Graham saw the conquista largely through the eyes of the European. To a certain extent, as he himself realized, this was inevitable, for it is extremely difficult for the white man to get within the skin or skull of the Indian, and there are few contemporary records presenting his side of the conflict. Furthermore, though personally acquainted with some of their descendants, particularly amongst such nomadic or semi-nomadic tribes as the Pampas and the Guaranís, he was not well versed in pre-Columbian anthropology and archaeology, sciences which, however, had not then reached full maturity. The attention given to Chibchan and Guaraní culture in *The Conquest of New Granada* and *A Vanished Arcadia* does much to breed sympathy for their mode of living, but in such volumes as *Pedro de Valdivia,* the main section of *Hernando de Soto,* and even in *The Conquest of the River Plate,* the Indians have scarcely more than two-dimensional existence. Though not so effective as implicit interpretation through full descriptions of their cultural patterns or character sketches of their representative figures, his explicit refusal to demand of Indians, in the manner of Prescott, a higher standard of conduct than that of their adversaries and his emphasis upon their better qualities do much to counteract these deficiencies.

Among the better qualities emphasized are strength of arm and keenness of eye, valor and fortitude, devotion to leaders, and even occasional generosity and chivalry. The bows of the Aztecs, he tells us, were "so strong" that none of Cortés' men "could pull the string up to his ear"; the arrows of the Comanches and other Plains Indians had enough force behind them to pierce "helmets and breastplates made of Milan steel [like] paper or the thinnest silk"; and the sight of the Seminoles was so acute that "they were nearly always able, in the open, to see arrows coming [from the Spanish crossbows (which are considerably swifter than those from longbows)] and to avoid them." . . . As to the minds and souls of the generality of these so-called savages, Graham keeps reminding us, more than Prescott or Parkman could ever have brought themselves to do, that their minds were "quite as powerful . . . as [those of] any other race of men"—"their chieftains [usually showing themselves] far more reasonable in controversy than . . . their conquerors"—and, "by the tenets of the faith that we profess," their souls were "held quite as dearly, it may be, by the Creator . . . as even Englishmen."

Frequent tribute is paid to the achievements of the Aztec, Incan and Chibchan civilizations, some of them reminiscent of those of Babylonia and Egypt and some equal or superior to those of Europe: their love of flowers, music and the dance; their superb fabrics, giving dignity to their leaders and sumptuousness to their processions; their finely worked metals and precious stones; their intricate calendars, based upon a considerable knowledge of astronomy; the picture-writing of the Aztecs; the splendid irrigation and road systems of the Incas; and the great towns of the Aztecs and Incas, with their monumental stone edifices and sculpture. (The capital of Mexico, with its palaces, its teocallis on truncated pyramids, its great square, its canals and surrounding lagoons and mountains, impressed Cortés as the most beautiful city in the world.) Though "a

settled polity . . . was most patent in Peru"—an "imperialistic socialism," which "had practically stamped out poverty"—it was making considerable headway in New Granada and Mexico, and the life of all three, with its slow, spacious rhythms, possessed something of the appeal of Arcadia. Albeit vitiated by the large-scale sacrifice of human victims practiced by two of these civilizations, their religion was primarily a worship of nature—such higher deities as the sun and moon being "generally . . . an abstraction, a sort of summing up of the powers of nature, rather than [anything] finite"—and this kept them in relaxed harmony with the earth and its intricate web of life. Occasionally, some of the customs and arts of less civilized tribes, besides those of the Guaranís, come in for commendation, such as an Araucanian method of choosing a leader and the temple near Cofachiqui, whose "doors were guarded by six sculptured giants, so well carved [according to Garcilaso] 'that had they been in the most famous temples of Rome in its full power they had been held in admiration both for their perfection and their size.'"

Although some of the defects of the Indians (as indicated earlier) are noted, Graham was inclined to underestimate or ignore several of them, and in regard to their more dubious actions against the Spaniards, to tip the scales too readily on their side. Is not, for instance, the impression given of the Incan way of life too idyllic? Others, like John Collier and Siegfried Huber, seem more aware of the dangers of such totalitarianism, no matter how benevolent: the discouragement or suppression of individual initiative, the anthill mediocrity, the imposition of its culture on conquered peoples, and the perilousness of its equilibrium, all of which made development difficult and ultimate decadence or collapse inevitable. Did Atahualpa, as we are led to believe, go to the Spaniards at Cajamarca with peaceful intentions, and was he indeed "executed for crimes which it seems quite unlikely . . . he had committed"? A number of present-day historians are persuaded that, with the aid of Ruminagui, he was planning an encircling movement that would have cut them off from their ships, and that he gave the order himself for the smothering of his brother Huáscar. As to the massacre at Cholula, which Graham calls "perhaps the most atrocious deed of the whole Conquest . . . and . . . a stain upon the fame of all engaged in it," even so sympathetic a student of the Indians as Bandelier remarks, "From a military point of view the conduct of Cortés [was] entirely justified." The Spaniards did not kill as many Indians as has been reported and no more than necessary. It is of course true that, as Graham says, Cortés and others of his breed were hypocritical in dragging out the horror of human sacrifice to justify some of their worst atrocities, but even though it has been practiced since the dawn of history—in India, Assyria, Phoenicia, Greece, Rome, Germany, many parts of Africa and Polynesia, and elsewhere—and even though the Aztec and Chibchan rites did not involve any apparent cruelty for cruelty's sake or degrade the victims and the national character, is it not, along with cannibalism, so profoundly repugnant to our sensibilities (think of it, as many as eighty thousand, on a single occasion, having their chests slit open with a flint knife and their hearts, still beating, torn out!) as to disarm criticism somewhat of those who helped to eradicate it?

Along with most students of the early stages of this continental drift of history, Graham attributed the astonishingly swift subversion of the great Indian kingdoms to such factors as the cunning exploitation of their belief that the Spaniards were actually supernatural beings; the lack of aggressiveness on the part of the Chibchas as well as the Incas, the former being "so little warlike that when they fought and failed to get the upper hand, their practice was to supplicate the Sun to pardon them for having undertaken an unrighteous enterprise''; the concentration of too much authority (both secular and religious) in a single person, the seizure or slaying of whom was liable to paralyze the whole country; and the superior weaponry of their foes (armor that was proof against fire-hardened spears and obsidian swords, and portable arms that seemed to discharge thunderbolts) and higher level of military tactics, which had been learnt during centuries of guerrilla fighting in Spain and through added specialized training in the West Indies. More than other writers, he stressed, as might be expected, the enormous advantage given the Spaniards by the possession of horses, which, with their carnivorous reputation, hawk-bells jingling from their breastplates, and guns discharged from the saddle, were as terrifying as flame-breathing hippogryphs, and which provided [as they did the Aryans in India and the Kassites in Babylonia] an often crucial mobility. . . . A further factor for the easy defeat of the Indians, so we are frequently reminded, was the internal crises in all three major kingdoms, by which one faction could by played off against another, the ally of the Spanish galvanized with the hope of ascendency; but Graham should have stressed more the psychological obtuseness of their leaders (their failure to understand the ruling passions of the newcomers intensified the confusion) and the ripeness of all their civilizations for disintegration: the large dependence upon astrology and other forms of occultism to determine the course of action, the want of self-reliance and a sense of national solidarity on the part of the citizenry, and an inability to react creatively when confronted with a different way of doing things. Then, too, the diseases that the Spaniards brought with them, which, by their debilitating effect, often led to languor and thus to famine, probably played a bigger rôle than he realized. In short, most of the Indians, despite their great advantage in numbers and their valor in single combat, ''were as helpless as a flock of sheep before a pack of wolves.''

The treatment of the Indians after thay had been brought under the yoke outraged Graham more than it has most historians. Having seized all the precious metals and stones they could lay their hands on, and, like most soldiers (particularly from a country with a long tradition of warfare), looking upon manual work as degrading, the victors turned to economic expropriation and exploitation. (pp. 215-21)

This expropriation and exploitation (which [along with the vandalic melting down of *objets d'art* into ingots for easier transportation, the burning of quipus and pictographs, and the imposition of an ''entirely alien'' religion] trampled into dust with terrifying speed unique civilizations that had blossomed grandly for centuries) made Graham question at times the value of the conquista, in the North as well as in the South. ''Whether it was better that a whole polity, interesting by its growth, autochthonous and far removed from any other known to the older world, should be destroyed, and a fair country drenched in blood, in order that the cross [and industrialism] should rise triumphant over the foundations of the great Teocalli,'' he left ''to theologians to decide.'' As for himself, he was of the opinion that it might ''perhaps . . . have been as well for the Spaniards and the other European nations to have stayed at home and civilized themselves, a proceeding that they have delayed down to the present day.'' Unlike most subverted civilizations—the Egyptian, the Mesopotamian, the Greek, and the Roman—the Aztec, Incan, and Chibchan were given little opportunity to exercise a fertilizing influence upon that of their conquerors, and so the world became the poorer by the almost complete loss of a different rhythm of life and a different *Weltanschauung*. How much better it would have been, as Graham says, had the Spaniards conceived a way ''to take advantage of the picturesque idea'' that they were Children of the Sun, and borne ''themselves in a manner more befitting to their supposed lineage and state. The world might then have seen great Indian kingdoms in Peru and Mexico gradually inducted into European ideas, but with their own strange customs and religions still preserved.'' (pp. 221-22)

In the presentation of the conquistadores—far more successful than that of the Indians—Graham evinces a full awareness of their defects, especially their religious bigotry, their greed, their cruelty, and their perfidy. Impelled by a ''faith . . . pushed to the verge of madness,'' many of them—laymen as well as the ''good store of priests and friars'' who accompanied each of the expeditions—were all agog to wrestle ''with Lucifer to snatch the wildings from his claws.'' Those who resisted such snatching (the Christianity exemplified in their would-be saviours was scarcely reassuring) were dealt with in the summary manner that Santiago, on a white and rather long-backed charger, ''tramples down the Moors in many a Gothic statue over a church door in Spain.'' ''Missionaries and conquerors,'' so he informs us, are ''on the whole, more imbued with their own importance and sanctity, and less disposed to consider consequences, than almost any other classes of mankind. . . .'' (pp. 223-24)

The insatiable lust for gold (and gems), ''so inextricably mixed up'' with their missionary zeal ''that it is almost an impossibility to say where one . . . ended and the other . . . began,'' assumed such a fantastic power over these soldiers of fortune that the faintest rumor of its existence (often initiated or corroborated by the Indians in order to be rid of their odious presence) lured them on, like some ''yellow *ignus fatuus*,'' into the most treacherous of interiors. Seeing such frenzied questing for what was to them of little or no economic value, the natives came to the not altogether illogical conclusion that it was actually their god. (p. 224)

As . . . indicated in . . . the dragging out, when ready ''to commit some villainy,'' the horror of human sacrifice and of eating human flesh, the conquistadores were guilty of many acts of perfidy. When Cortés, in answer to a question, assured a *cacique* [chief] that he and his followers came ''from where the sun rises,'' Graham informs us that ''this was perhaps the first and the last time that he declared the truth to the poor Indians in the whole course of his life.'' At the beginning of an invasion, these crusaders usually proclaimed the defenders ''traitors and rebels'' to the king of Spain, and as soon as the natives had been induced to acknowledge him their ruler— even though, like Montezuma and Sagipá, having ''no real notion what [such an] assent involved''—they could henceforth ''represent themselves as acting legally.'' Yet even those who not only acknowledged vassalage but also became faithful allies were later—their invaluable services no longer needed—brought treacherously under the yoke of slavery. . . . Often the atrocities were committed to spread terror amongst their foes or, even in lands innocent of human sacrifice and cannibalism, to give vent to sheer malice, as when Soto, being denied thirty women slaves by a certain *cacique*, set fire to all the crops—''a method,'' says Graham, ''of bringing home the Christian faith and practice which never fails of arresting the attention of the sufferers. . . .''

With considerable persuasiveness, he extenuates, at least somewhat, most of these defects. Their bigotry, the result of an almost millennium-long response to the even more fanatical Moors—both looking upon their religion as "the sign of [racial and] national unity"—was a concomitant of "what appeared to them religious principles" and a "very real belief that they were introducing the true faith" to those wallowing in idolatries. "The Cross" was, indeed, "not a mere emblem of salvation, but a labarum that each man saw hung in the skies above his head." The lust for the yellow metal—a common human infirmity, partially immaterialized in them by being regarded as a means to power rather than something valuable in itself—provided a further, and probably the chief, incentive for a naturally home-loving people to erupt with such explosive force over half the earth. "All conquest is but robbery at best." Notoriously, perfidy is not limited to any particular country, and often success or failure for either side depended upon which could outwit the other. As for cruelty—"from the beginning of the world most conquests have been . . . pursued with violence and secured by cruelty." . . . Some of the worst cruelty—the terroristic sort practiced by Cortés and Pizarro—was done through strategic necessity. "When a European army finds itself beset by savages, and far removed from help, it must strike terror, so as to make its position safe." With such a keen delight in watching others break under pain, the Indians were surely their peers in cruelty. Those persons who have not seen what prisoners look like after dying at their hands, says Graham from personal experience, "need waste no time in racking their imagination, for the imagination of the Indians is sure to have outgone theirs at least a hundredfold."

The main reason the conquistadores were confident that, "in some strange mysterious fashion," even the "most tremendous" of their "crimes . . . were acceptable in the sight of the Great Power" (probably in accordance with the widespread but "mistaken view" that the means are justified by the ends) was that their spiritual leader and absolute master of the world, the Pope, had given a large portion of the newly discovered land to their king on the condition that it be Christianized, and this inevitably involved the introduction of "the blessings of the Spanish rule." Whenever a nation is convinced of having been given a divine mission to bring light to the dark places of the earth, "it sticks at nothing to enforce the truth as it conceives it." . . . (pp. 225-27)

The "conquistadores are to be judged," so Graham declares with a wisdom all too rare amongst historians, "not by the standards of our times, but by those of the days in which they lived." In sixteenth-century Europe, perfidy in politics was part of the facts of life (that of Cortés and Pizarro would surely have won the admiration of so realistic a philosopher as Machiavelli), and, as exemplified by the Inquisition and certain procedures in Geneva, "Christians of all denominations [showed] their love to one another by the rack and stake," heresy being regarded as a capital offense. "Elizabeth of England was [indeed] not a jot inferior to [the Duke of Alva] in her dealings with English Catholics," and, in Ireland, her lieutenants, using famine as well as the sword, laid waste every countryside they could not hold. "Personal slavery," which (it will be remembered) the Spanish Crown and Church attempted to restrict or mitigate and which, in such a country as Paraguay, was "never . . . so harsh as in the Dutch, the English or the French colonies," "seemed as natural" then "as wage slavery . . . to us," for it "was recognised by every European State." Besides being "cut off from everything that civilizes men" and often in desperate extremity amidst shrieking hordes, the Spaniards had another excuse for their cruelty: they had just emerged from a long struggle for their very existence with an enemy

whose ferocity, rapacity, and inventiveness in torturing is legendary. In sixteenth-century America, the Elizabethan adventurers acted in much the same manner; and, in the following century, the British colonists began a still more thorough extermination of the Indians, "thus at one blow solving the problem of their duty to an inferior race." Yet, even if the conquistadores are judged by the standards of his own times, Graham did not think they would fare badly. Many empire-builders from various non-Iberian countries of Europe, looking upon themselves as the instruments of progress rather than of God, were carrying fire and sword to innumerable unoffending and defenseless peoples in Asia and Africa. Disregarding the rights of the natives, they were committing the greatest enormities—smoking out Algerians in the caves of Mostagánem and massacring the men, women, and children of the Matabele in the Matoppo hills—and exterminating (rather than enslaving) large portions of Tasmanians, Australian blacks, and Maoris. In short, "that which the Spaniards did in the green tree three hundred years ago in [far-off] Mexico and in Peru, . . . all Europe does to-day in the dry tree of modern Christianity and in full view of an indifferent world." What more gruesome illustrations Graham might have chosen, had his generation been ours! (pp. 227-29)

Not only were the defects of the conquistadores extenuated in this fashion but their virtues, which were also exercised to a superlative degree, appealed so exhilaratingly to such a person as Graham that the ambivalence in his attitude toward these sons of St. James might best be described as a "reluctant admiration." Amongst the virtues—common even in the rank and file—was an impetuous and indomitable courage, capable of the most audacious deeds. (pp. 229-30)

As imperialists, they felt an intense pride in "broadening out the confines of the dominions of the crown of Spain" so as to include vast reaches in the New World and thereby become a veritable colossus in the Old. This sense of honor, as well as this "almost superstitious loyalty" and dreaming of *la gloire,* "redeemed [them] from vulgarity, that sin by which so many angels of more modern times have fallen into the pit."

As already indicated, the quality that shone brightest in Graham's sight—perhaps even more basic in their lives than any of the other virtues mentioned and certainly the most romantic—was the passion for adventure. Nourished on the exploits of Amadis and his fellow-heroes of the tales of chivalry and endowed with vaulting will and tireless energy, which could no longer find an outlet at home, they felt a compulsive urge to go half way round the globe, and, despite the occasionally almost limbo-like strangeness and the many perils, to keep plunging into the illimitable unknown and daring the impossible. "The fury of adventure" ran indeed more "in the blood of every Spaniard of the age" than in that of any other race." . . . (pp. 231-32)

Moreover, as "in all nationalities," there were some conquistadores, other than clergymen, who in their sense of justice and magnanimity toward their foes rose "superior to the spirit of [their] age" and who, in their writings, occasionally gave voice to the uneasy conscience of Spain. Among the latter were Cieza de León and Bachiller Enciso, both well versed in Indian customs and with a high regard for many of their traits of character, and among the former, Balboa, Alonso and Pedro de Heredia, Ferdermann, César, Garay, and Lorenzano de Aldana, the last, "in his will, [leaving] all his property to his Indians, in payment of their tribute in the future during their natural lives." When, in a desecrated burial-ground, *Cacique*

Capahá "gathered up with his own hands the relics of his ancestors," Soto, "who of all the *conquistadores* . . . was easiest to move by what he held to be a noble act, got off his horse" and embraced him, and, earlier, in order to insure fair play for Atahualpa, had offered "to answer with his own life for the Inca, should he be sent to Spain to stand . . . trial at the Emperor's Court." As is made plain in one of his recorded speeches, Quesada, who "comprehended his position in relation to the natives of the land more clearly than any other of the conquerors," tried to impress upon his troops that the Indians "are men like ourselves, if perhaps not so civilized, and every man likes to be treated with civility. . . . After all, even the ground we tread upon is theirs, by natural and divine right, and they allow us as a favour to be here, and owe us nothing." By far the most admirable of these true Children of the Sun—the only one "quite free from all taint of cruelty"— was Álvar Núñez, who, when, as one of the four survivors of the Narváez expedition, he reached Mexico with a large following of Indians, indignantly opposed their enslavement, and, instead, "sadly . . . dismissed them to their homes . . . with such presents as he could command," and who, as Governor of the River Plate, was so protective of the natives that (in the complaining words of Schmidel) "did but an Indian wench squeal, the soldier had to suffer for it." (pp. 233-34)

So strong was the personal essayist and the engaged man in Cunninghame Graham that throughout all his historical writings—in the main body of the text as well as in the footnotes— there is a frequent and considerable insertion of himself: his physical experiences in many lands, his reflections on a wide variety of subjects, and (as with Lord Acton) his moral judgments on men and events. Thus we are told how, on a sweltering day in a mission town of Paraguay, he once helped carry a Madonna weighing some five hundred pounds, what he thinks about such things as patriotism, the House of Commons, the peerage, bureaucrats, liberty, and logic—the sort of interludes for which Cieza de León and Garcilaso are commended—and, as we have been seeing, wherein he regards the conquistadores as having failed or been successful in living the good life, both as a group and as individuals. This procedure is, of course, eschewed by most contemporary historians, especially the academic, who, believing that *tout comprendre, tout pardonner* or that moral judgments, if rendered at all, should never be explicit, insist upon objective detachment. Such an attitude, so Graham feared, would lead, for example, even to the attributing of most of the greatness of Edward III of England to his "cheerful disregard of justice," and the conversion of the past into tomes "as dry as pemmican, and as indigestible." As in the sketches, the insertion of self does, it is true, have certain disadvantages: some of the comments may lose their appositeness when read in the context of a later generation, may also give a sense of special pleading rather than of judicial appraisal, or, like digressions in general, may snap the mood and therefore become irritating. On the other hand, it has, at least in this particular instance, certain advantages: the companionship of one who, with experiences and qualities similar to those of his heroes, keeps pointing out many correspondences between his own age and theirs, and who, as a choric character, involves us morally in the action, thus making the past seem more present and adding further dimensions, including depth, to our understanding of the events. It is this recurring personal note, more than anything else, that gives his life-histories their unique flavor. (pp. 249-50)

> *Richard E. Haymaker, in his* Prince-Errant and Evocator of Horizons: A Reading of R. B. Cunninghame Graham, *n.p., 1967, 374 p.*

JAMES STEEL SMITH (essay date 1969)

[*In the following excerpt, Smith examines Graham's short stories and sketches.*]

Graham should at last be given serious consideration as a writer of fiction. We shall find him not as remarkable a maker of short fiction as his contemporaries Joyce, D. H. Lawrence or Katherine Mansfield, but still a craftsman whose short romantic inventions have their own special qualities and which quite possibly could have more meaning for new readers today than they did for readers earlier in the century.

Without themselves seeming accidental or incomplete, Graham's tales leave one with an aftersense of fragmentation, a feeling that the scene or episode or persons described were fragments of something not given and to be guessed at. They are bright, vivid pieces, but their very vividness somehow suggests chipping, a breaking-off in such a way that the ragged edges, clear and hard, promise, without defining a larger reality—which, too, might be just a large, jagged fragment.

This sense of accidentality, incompleteness, fragmentation in Graham's work has two primary causes: 1) his making the core of a story explosive, unexplained, seemingly pointless violence or unrationalized, uncompensated loss, or both together, and 2) his choice of narrative modes that underline the elements of casual irrelevance and unreason in the events he describes.

The great majority of Cunninghame Graham stories are accounts of violent incidents or moments of irrevocable loss. Often much of the story presents the circumstances of the violence and loss, but seldom does it explain the violence or the loss. The whole impact of the story lies in the shattering, unexplained, and seemingly causeless. Indeed, the author's refusal to interpret his facts as conditioning circumstances perhaps achieves his point. Certainly, it accounts for the special impact of the violence and loss in his stories; it is as if he put up in a literary shooting gallery a rare vase and blasted it into fragments, without comment.

This sense of fragmentation in Graham's stories is further deepened by certain techniques he customarily adopted in the telling—his use of outsiders as observers and narrators of the action which they pass through or wander near, his creation of an unorganized cluster from a great number of miscellaneous, incidental facts, almost like an old man's reminiscing or a traveller's jottings, and the total suggestion of uncertainty, tentativeness, incompleteness. All of these techniques of a typical Cunninghame Graham story enable the author to express his sense of intellectual loneliness, his vagrancy of spirit.

Stories with such subjects and method might easily become empty, coldly mechanical, but they are saved from this by a romantic wealth of sensory detail and by an intense, almost painful humaneness, the author's obvious concern for his drifting men and animals; indeed, the contrast between this concern, this worried pity, and the brute violence and stark loss in his stories helps to create a peculiarly disturbing atmosphere throughout his fiction. Graham creates a world that would suggest the pointlessness of human feeling, but he keeps the latter very much alive in his accounts of that world.

Graham, rather than revealing the gathering of forces for violence or the consequent devastation, chooses usually to surprise us with a sudden explosion and then leave us only the barest hints of cause and effect. The greater part of **"Bismillah"** is an idyllic account of an Arab shepherd boy playing with a pet kid all day, but suddenly on the final page, without warning, Graham briefly describes the killing of the goat. . . . (pp. 61-2)

> The village elder felt its neck, and then drawing out a knife, after a pious "In the name of God," rapidly cut its throat. The kid uttered a little cry, and from its neck the blood spirted out in a stream upon the grass. One little jet fell on the boy's brown foot, and as he watched the last contortions of the dying kid with interest, but without feeling for his playmate's loss, dried in the warm sea breeze and looked as if a vein had been exposed. . . .

In "A Silhouette," one of his most effective stories, Graham first describes in a leisurely way the "quiet, but occasionally bloody, pastoral life" of two brothers who own a rancheria on the pampas. Then he introduces a band of roving, plundering gauchos, who encounter and pursue the brothers. One brother reaches the shelter of their rancheria; the other is caught and butchered. . . . (p. 63)

The callous hanging of a Mexican in Texas for killing a white man who had cheated him is described as swiftly, brutally, in "Un Pelada." In "Bristol Fashion" Honest Tom Bilson, who for much of his meandering account of his days as an African trader appears to be a rough but decent enough human being, suddenly reveals his pride at having evened his score with the Krooboys for having jumped ship: when, through trickery, he had gotten them back on board, he sold them to a cannibal tribe. The bloody sacking of a town frequently provides the central event for a Cunninghame Graham story—most powerfully, perhaps, in "Progress," the unsparing description of the brutal extinction of a village of religious fanatics by Mexican government troops, and in "On the Spur," in which a chieftain returns posthaste to his rebellious court at Marrakesh to destroy the opposition. In certain tales, like "El Tango Argentino" or "Heredity," a celebration produces a fatal stabbing; in these stories the writer does not prepare us for the violence; in fact, he keeps our attention away from the persons who will kill and be killed—then suddenly the whole crowded dance hall or bar becomes only two men involved in deadly combat; and, the killing done, the narration as abruptly stops.

One of Graham's finest stories, "The Grave of the Horseman," relies for its power on the way he peripherally hints violence in the first two-thirds of the tale and then in the swift climax reveals it directly. (p. 64)

These upsurgings of violence—often the sole unifying "subject" of a Graham story—effect not so much terror and pain as dismay at the unexplained cruelty and bloodletting, the irrelevancy of the act. His violence comes from nowhere and leads to nothing. It is an irrational force working beneath the surface—this surface most often the grasslands and peach groves of Paraguay, the stony deserts of Morocco, the ebullient merriment of carnival—and bursting out sporadically and inexplicably and then disappearing, for a while.

This discontinuity frequently has its source in Graham's focus on the loss, unexplained and unjustified, of something valued. A great many of his pieces are haunting, ironic accounts of human defeats—the loss of homeland, wives, self-respect, illusions, life; they remind one of Hardy's *Satires of Circumstance,* in their report of defeat without reason, their suggestion that victory would somehow not have made a difference. In his "Preface" to *Mirages* Cunninghame Graham, speaking of his own stories, acknowledges that "Virtue in them is quite

as rarely rewarded, as it is in real life, nor is vice especially triumphant. But then, although they tell us that death is the wages of the sinner, as far as I can see, it seems to be not very different for the saint". He much preferred, he confessed, writing about failure to writing about victory: "Failure alone is interesting. . . ." And it was from the failure itself, not the course of events leading to the defeat, that Graham made his story.

"Animula Vagula" is a cryptic account by an orchid-hunter—himself an expatriate—of how he found a dead Englishman, or American—he could not tell which—in a village up a jungle river; in the piece the author creates a sense of the lostness and aloneness of the unknown dead man. In "His People" a Spanish expatriate, after many years of successful toil in South America, at last gets back to Toledo; at first, he is happy to find the old buildings and streets still there, but then he discovers this continuity to be only on the surface—all his relatives and friends, "his people," are gone; his long-held hope proves to have been an illusion. Much the same story is told in "His Return" and in "Higginson's Dream." "Victory" impressionistically sketches in the despair of a Spaniard in an American hotel on receiving news of Cervera's defeat. Through the greater part of "El Jehad" an Arab, in his lonely wanderings, gradually builds a reputation as a prophet and at last calls for a Holy War, only to be faced down summarily by a French officer. In "Mirahuano" a Negro poet learns that, in spite of his talent, he is not accepted as poet or man by the white men and women and commits suicide; Graham restates the rejection through details about the disposal of the poet's body:

> His brothers in the Muses missed him from his accustomed haunts for two or three days, and then a countryman reported he had seen in the backwater of a stream an object which he had thought was a dead bullock or a cow. Wishing to secure the hide, he had lassoed it, and to his great astonishment he found it was the body of a negro, dressed in black clothes, as he said, just as good as those worn by the President. Being of a thrifty turn of mind, he had stripped them off and sold them at a pulperia, when he had dried them in the sun.
>
> It seemed to him fortuitous that a black rascal who in all his life had never done a stroke of work, but walked about just like a gentleman, making a lot of silly rhymes, at last should be of use to a white Christian such as he was himself, white, as the proverb says, on all four sides.
>
> He added, as he stood beside his half-wild colt, keeping a watchful eye upon its eye, and a firm hand upon its raw-hide halter, that as a negro's skin was of no value, he pushed the body back into the stream, and had no doubt that it would soon be eaten up by the caimans. . . .

In "A Wire-Walker" the narrator tells, in the course of a predominantly anti-woman discussion in a tropical bar, the story of a self-sacrificing woman acrobat—her loss of her husband to another woman, then her adopted child, and finally, in an acrobatic accident, her life. "Sor Candida and the Bird" tells slowly and quietly how Sister Candida, a Spanish nun, let a bird become the center of her love and how, in permitting her attention to be briefly diverted by a saint's parade on a hot summer's day, she let the bird die; a painful sense of the thinness and impermanency of human affections is left by this deftly told, unsentimental story.

Graham filled his tales with losers—beaten and dispossessed Indians, the uprooted of war in Paraguay and Uruguay, the fatally ill, prostitutes, expatriates who collect in hotels and at bars and campfires far from their native lands, the Westernized Arab who cannot fit back into Arab society. Their lives are isolated, incomplete. Graham's fictional society is an accumulation of splintered-off individuals, some occasionally heroic in their individualism, more of them pitiful in their loneness.

These two aspects of living—violence and incompleteness—that seem to have been Graham's constant concern partially account for the effect of shatteredness and discontinuity that characterizes his short fiction. But only partially. His way of shaping and placing and tilting his writing intensifies still more the reader's awareness of brokenness, fragmentation.

Graham very much favored the use of narrators to tell his story for him. An odd assortment of wanderers at a bar in the tropics, a consul in an Arab town, a retired sea captain, a muleteer snowbound with other travelers at a Spanish mountain inn, a lonely man talking about women to other lonely men on a hot night on a South American river—these were his favorite means for getting to the place of action, introducing his people, and raising uncertainties and making allegations. Such spokesmen could speak for themselves, or for the author if he made them enough like himself, restless, wandering, quixotically gallant, easily roused, somewhat self-dramatizing, worldly, sceptical. They could not observe or speak except through their kind of person; protagonists of other sorts could only be guessed about from the actions seen by the teller and as far as he could comprehend them. In **"The Captive"** the Belgian narrator, over the campfire, can describe only as an outsider the decision of a European girl raised among Southwest Indians to leave her liberator and lover and return to her Indian husband, children and captivity; the method and effect are twilight guesswork. In **"Charity"** a consul in a dreary, impoverished Arab town tells, as an only partly informed but curious outsider, about an Arab's kindness to a mother who had lost her boy in the plague; his speculations are broken up by sketchings of storm, Arab streets, a wedding party, all of which add to the tale's broken light. In such stories the reader is left with an obviously incomplete account, a report of one reporter.

Graham's narrators, moreover, by being themselves wanderers and, generally, addressing other wanderers, also give the tales a sense of process, becoming. The story is told from a moving point, as a kind of passing. One gets a feeling of having visited a foreign port with one of Graham's narrators, having seen a shocking or enigmatic incident and several intriguing persons, and then having to go back on board before he can investigate as much as he wants to. Whether or not he uses the indirect narrator, the entry into the essential story is usually indirect, wavering, suggestive of reminiscence, the groping into a bag of remembered pieces.

Probably too much has been made, by both Graham and his comtemporary commentators, of reminiscence as a base for his taletelling. Graham speaks of his tales variously as "the tales, essays or whimsy-whamsays in my little book" and as "the story of his [the author's] life." He has his narrator in **"Anastacio Lucena"** describe the "yarn" as "a memory, a recollection, for it is not a story, only a circumstance that I re-

member vividly, just as one never can forget an object seen in a flash of lightning" and then agrees when a listener suggests the term "impression" for it. [Edward] Garnett, in his introduction to *Thirty Tales and Sketches by R. B. Cunninghame Graham,* describes Graham's sketch method: "He paints men and their manners to the life, and he has a special sense for landscape. . . . His extraordinarily keen eye for detail makes his pictures accurate to a fault, for he is prone to crowd his canvas with too literal a record of things seen." William Spencer Child, in *The Contribution of Cunninghame Graham to the Literature of Travel,* holds that Cunninghame Graham often put into his writing "largely factual happenings with slight fictional modifications," and he suggests that much of his work is travel writing passing for fiction.

It cannot be denied that in some pieces the travel writer defeats, almost obliterates, the writer of fiction, and memory seems almost entirely to take over the author's intention. There are frequent passages of detailed description, especially in the tales of South America and Morocco, where one feels Graham simply wanted to record vivid memories of his early wanderings. . . . But in much of his writing this fund of remembered facts—personal adventures, firsthand observation of nature and society, traveler's gossip, family anecdotes—helps Graham, rather than hinders him, in creating fiction that is effective in its dilatoriness and indirection. The little travel talks, the botanical paragraphs (with their startling footnotes), the horse lore, the anecdotes within anecdotes, the South American historical background, the fond dwelling on architectural and costume detail all contribute to Graham's special quality as an imaginative writer—the awareness of the ambiguous and significant fragment, the simultaneously incidental and central.

His mode of indirectness, casualness and incompleteness is established in a variety of ways besides the use of narrators and the interspersal of recalled particulars, and generally his means are uncannily appropriate to the specific end. In **"A Meeting"** he beings by reminiscing, easily and slowly, about his ride across the plains of Paraguay after the civil wars. . . . After having stirred a sense of empty space, he mentions the occasional passing-by of women. . . . Then, going onward, the narrator is overwhelmed with the memories of a world almost emptied of human beings. . . .

> [T]he air of being in the grip of an all-powerful vegetation, reduced a man, travelling alone through the green solitude, to nothingness. One felt as if in all that wealth of vegetation and strange birds and beasts, one's horse were the one living thing that was of the same nature as oneself. . . .

Reportorially, flatly, he describes his stopping at a small ranch house and finding only one man there. The rancher suggests he let his horse free, that it will be a great treat for his own horse to have the company of another horse for a night. The two men talk ramblingly about the horses, the state of the countryside, politics, etc., while the horses play. The host recalls his own feelings on being released from prison and meeting his brother. In the morning the teller of the tale departs:

> As I rode out into the dewy trail a thick white mist enveloped everything. It blotted out the lonely clearing in the first few yards. It dulled the shrill, high neighings of the roan, who plunged and reared upon his rope. . . .

And one realizes that the title, "**Meeting**," did not summarize the whole story; there have been two meetings—one of them described in some detail, the other referred to only obliquely, here and there. One also senses that the two meetings were of the same kind.

A favorite Cunninghame Graham situation is the journey—in "**A Hegira**" the desperate flight of Indian prisoners from Mexico City to the American border, in "**Faith**" a woman's pilgrimage to Mecca to ask Mohammed that women have entry to paradise, in "**His Return**" an Arab's going back to his tribe, in "**Beattock for Moffat**" the death journey of a consumptive Scot from London to his home shire.

In each of these the author tells his tale in ways that intensify the sense of separation and distance and that are altogether appropriate to the particular journey. "**The Hegira**" first describes a miserable huddle of Indian prisoners at the Chapultepec Castle in Mexico City; then, in the author's reminiscence of his muletrain journey, we keep losing sight of them and picking up their trail northward; references to the fleeing Indians are interspersed with vivid accounts of the cities and the rugged mountains as the train moves north. The trail ends with a Texan's callous and proud account of how he slew the two remaining braves and squaw; the narrator sees for himself the newly dug grave and the Indians' whimpering dog. In "**Faith**" Graham rightly takes most of the narrative to describe the many places the woman pilgrim to Mecca passes, and the caravans moving by; the result is not simply a colorful Oriental pageant; it is rather, an intensification of the sense of insistent, faith-impelled movement. At the end the outcome of her journey is inconclusive, but the reader feels as though he has gone to the ends of the earth. Similarly, the slowness of the Arab warrior's return to his tribe in "**His Return**" sharpens the irony of his discovery that his native tents cannot be his final destination. In "**Beattock for Moffat**" the noting of the stops of the northbound train carrying the dying Scot back to Moffat makes very real his desperation for arrival, and its unlikelihood. This recording of stops and bypassed way-stations, especially within an awareness of impending death and the uncertainty of arrival, evokes a sense of universal passage, unwholeness. Things pass by. We pass them by. We do not really meet, and we go whirring further on into other neighborhoods.

Graham also sometimes brings his reader to this sense of bits-and-pieces by telling his tale as conjecture, leaving out what he does not know or else indicating where he is filling in from guess. In "**At Dalmary**," watching a Highland funeral, the author conjectures about the dead man and the living people of the clachan; in a scene of death he fabricates a life from pieces of fact and many hunches. The London grave of a Sioux chief stirred Graham to write a lyrical guess-piece, "**Long Wolf**," not fully enough formed perhaps to be separated from his sketches into a category of fiction. This sort of speculating, this "maybe it was like this," he used most effectively in "**A Princess**," a moving conjecture about the short life of a Polynesian princess buried in a gray, rainy graveyard on the east coast of Scotland. It is a little piece of fiction that hesitates short of the certainty of most fiction, and for that lack it is the more moving. Graham had more questions than answers about mankind's place and meaning, and luckily he permitted those uncertainties to develop not only his choices of subject and fictional situation but also his narrative techniques.

There was a danger here, of course, that this philosophical standoffishness could lead to a literary pose, a noncommital mechanicalness rather like that of Maugham. Occasionally he

succumbed, but in the great bulk of his short fiction he was prevented from doing this by two endowments: 1) a vivid sensory awareness and 2) the intensity of his humaneness, his indignation at suffering. Graham noted the details of his natural and manmade environment carefully and enthusiastically; he shared the naturalist's collecting-observing bent of his friend W. H. Hudson; he gathered a considerable lore of natural history, and sometimes he unloaded it rather abruptly and unreasonably. More often, though, he restrained his reference to nature, holding a nice balance between the general panoramic view of it and the close-at-hand particularizing, a balance congruent with his wry and tentative conception of existence. . . . [Graham's] lucid, evocative prose [is] . . . an apt vehicle for the romantic but somewhat distance-keeping mental stance of its author. It is not a showy or eccentric style. It is clear and flexible, somewhat colloquial but still a bit academic, capable of quick bluntness and of an occasional lyric sweetness. In its muted contrariety it is a very useful style for a writer who, like Graham, treats of far romantic scenes and often violent incidents. Grounded as it is in reported particulars, his writing creates a kind of acceptance that is necessary to effect ungrudging entry into his romantic world.

A second saving quality in Graham's writing is his humaneness, his capacity for sorrow and indignation at all suffering. His stories express his angry regret for the suffering of cart horses, game birds, hunted animals, blind and crippled men, Mexican revolutionaries, Apaches, prostitutes, expatriates, the scorned of all races, the Spanish soldiers in the Spanish-American War and the Boers in the Boer War, the poor, the ill, and many more categories of the hurt and the persecuted. He may express these feelings indirectly by describing the suffering, or he may sometimes permit himself or a spokesman to point out and condemn it. Fortunately, the latter direct expressions of feeling are rather infrequent, and indeed are not necessary, for Graham's anger and sorrow show through his prose clearly enough and give it a unifying vitality. He does not need didactic signals. There is never any doubt but that he is upset by all suffering and driven to indignation by cruelty or neglect, indeed by the whisper of force. He possessed the esthetic indignation of the eternal "anti," the artist easily pricked into reporting and protest by all injustices and oppressions, even by explainable pain.

Cunninghame Graham's fiction, filled as it is with fragments of violence and loss and moving as it does somewhere between acceptance and outrage, can seem remarkably like the fiction and drama of the absurd—particularly the latter of the past two decades. This is one reason for the present article; I feel that if we now turn again to look at this forgotten author and look at him free of such misleading labels as "Victorian" and "travel-writer," we will find his special literary voice persuasive and poignant. While not a major voice, it was an original one and one that will carry well into the contemporary ear if it can only reach it. Cunninghame Graham was a serious and full enough artist to bear rediscovery, and the consonance between the spirit of his art and the spirit of our time perhaps makes this present moment opportune for such rediscovery. (pp. 66-74)

> *James Steel Smith, "R. B. Cunninghame Graham as a Writer of Short Fiction," in* English Literature in Transition, *Vol. 12, No. 2, 1969, pp. 61-75.*

LAURENCE DAVIES   (essay date 1972)

[Davies is a leading scholar of Graham's life and works, and is the coauthor, with Cedric Watts, of Cunninghame Graham: A

Sketch for a portrait of Graham.

[Critical Biography (*see Additional Bibliography*). *In the following excerpt from his essay on Graham's South American sketches, Davies discusses the problems that confronted Graham in delineating a foreign culture for English readers.*]

How to be foreign but intelligible; how to convey a sense of apartness without losing the sense of relevance: these questions face any writer committed to the faithful treatment of an alien context. According to the anthropologist Frederick O. Gearing: "The opposite of being estranged is to find a people believable." Writers too must make the unfamiliar seem believable, understandable, without reduction to a universal blandness or insipidity. Joseph Conrad found that

> the mere fact of dealing with matters outside the general run of everyday experience laid me under the obligation of a more scrupulous fidelity to the truth of my own sensations. The problem was to make unfamiliar things credible. To do that I had to create for them . . . to envelop them in their proper atmosphere of actuality.

Not all writers want "the proper atmosphere of actuality." In *Rasselas*, Dr. Johnson's characters live in the world of fable and are subject to universal laws of human nature; there is very little to them that is specifically Abyssinian. Kafka's America is a land unvisited, peopled from dream, Dickens and Benjamin Franklin. The problem comes up when verisimilitude of milieu is important, when an author wants to profit from the unfamiliar without being taken over by it.

The more geographically and spiritually remote the setting, the more urgent the problem. R. B. Cunninghame Graham . . . the Scottish traveller, political activist and author, wrote essays,

sketches and short stories set in Africa and the Americas as well as in many of the countries of Europe. Of part Spanish ancestry, Graham was particularly concerned with Latin America. (pp. 253-54)

Graham was a dandy in both senses. He did not have to "please to live" and always claimed that he wrote only to please himself. Be that as it may, he kept an eye to the gallery, if only to taunt and provoke it. . . . For the moment, the important point is that he did not write primarily for Spanish-speaking readers. The imaginary privileged spectator, who is sometimes ignored and sometimes teased, is British. Deeply interested in and knowledgeable about South America, Graham had to accommodate ignorance a little if he was to communicate at all.

In the late nineteenth century, the educated Englishman probably knew more about South America than he did when Carlyle wrote his essay on Dr. Francia, ruler of Paraguay: "The heroes of South America have not yet succeeded in picturing any image of themselves, much less any true image of themselves, in the Cis-Atlantic mind or memory." From children's books like R. M. Ballantyne's and Mayne Reid's, to travel books, to serious histories like Prescott's, there was the opportunity to learn. But several things obstructed the view. The bigotry and rollicking xenophobia of books such as Kingsley's *Westward Ho!* infected responsible work as well; in many ways unfairly. Graham often accused even Prescott of anti-Catholic bias. Just as Graham was starting to write, the collapse of Baring Brothers, the London banking house, started the slow disengagement of British economic interests in the area. Literature does not necessarily follow trade, but there is no denying that a leisured Londoner of the nineties, if at all interested in life outside Europe, would have preferred to read about India or South Africa. South America had become the true *terra australis incognita*.

Graham therefore had to face the problem of credibility with which I started. . . . I shall discuss some of the South American sketches in order to show how Graham handled situations unfamiliar to his readers.

In a way the Moroccan sketches would serve just as well, but those set in South America are interesting for two additional reasons. Most of them were written between the late nineties and the First World War, many years after Graham's time in Argentina but before the wartime visit. Graham therefore relied heavily on his memory and in fact used the operation of memory as a major theme in his writings. Secondly, although Graham knew some Arabic, and although his Moroccan tales show the influence of the Moorish fable, his relations with Spanish and Latin American literature were closer and more conscious. Not long after his arrival in Argentina, the first part of *Martin Fierro* was published, and Graham several times describes campfire recitations both of Hernández' poem and Estanislao del Campo's *Fausto*. After leaving South America, Graham kept in touch with literary developments; the collection of books he willed to the London Library includes many Spanish and Portuguese titles from both old and new worlds. As a reviewer for the London *Saturday Review, Nation, English Review* and *Observer*, he dealt with travel and history books and translations from the Hispanic literatures. Graham then, although writing for a different readership, had the choice of whether or not to model himself on those Argentine and Uruguayan authors who dealt with the same locale. I hope to show that in fact his part diverged widely from that of the nineteenth-century classics.

Graham wrote no novels. Like Poe, he argued that short forms could better achieve unity and intensity. (pp. 254-56)

Very little of Graham's own work has anything resembling a plot. He shared with his friend Conrad the urge to "scrupulous fidelity to the truth" of his own sensations but was less ready to transmute his experience into fiction. Graham wrote comparatively few pure fictions; more often he conterpoints the memory of individual experience with elaborately detailed general descriptions. The method is not that of fiction, but neither is it the method of purely descriptive writing; the affinities, if anywhere, are with reflective poetry. He seeks to combine the suggestiveness and ambivalence of fiction with the authority and clarity of personal experience. Graham leaves much unsaid; he often works by indirect means.

"La Pulperia" is an example. It opens:

> It may have been the Flor de Mayo, Rosa del Sur, or Tres de Junio, or again but have been known as the Pulperia upon the Huesos, or the Esquina on the Napostá. But let its name have been what chance or the imagination of some Neapolitan or Basque had given it, I see it.

The choice of characteristic names links the specific and the general. Graham visualizes a particular pampa store, but it stands for hundreds of others. As in so many of his sketches, the function of memory will be central: resuscitating, focussing, elaborating. Most of **"La Pulperia"** is given over to description of the store and its activities. Objects are counted up: "ponchos from Leeds, ready-made calzoncillos, alpargatas, figs, sardines, bread". . . . Customs are explained in passing, against a strongly realized background: "Passing it [wine in a tin cup] round to the company, who touch it with their lips to show their breeding, I seem to feel the ceaseless little wind which always blows upon the southern plains, stirring the dust upon the pile of fleeces in the court". . . . It is all very carefully observed, but any sense of the place's individuality must come from Graham's own presence. In an orthodox short story, the *pulperia* would have one name, would have distinguishing features, and the author would be much less visible. Graham changes tense in the middle of the second paragraph as though his perception of his subject has changed. He asserts his opinions on the superiority of local over imported ploughs; he is ironic at the expense of European morality: "That which in Europe we call love . . . seems . . . to be in embryo [in Argentina], waiting for economic advancement to develop it". . . .

What we have so far is a travel essay. There is nothing much that is personal in the content, but everything personal in its presentation. The ending changes this situation entirely. Graham introduces an old gaucho who "stood dressed in his chiripa and poncho, like a mad prophet amongst the motley crew". . . . The veteran becomes drunk and absorbed in his past. A supporter of Rosas, the onetime *caudillo* [chief], he is enraged by Graham, who comes up to him yelling *vivas* for Urquiza, one of Rosas' old enemies. The gaucho is furious, foams at the mouth, sings obscene lampoons, drives his knife into the mud wall and collapses exhausted. The sketch ends abruptly, focussed on Graham:

> I . . . caught the infection, and getting on my horse, a half-wild "redomon," spurred him and set him plunging, and at each bound struck him with the flat edge of my facon, then shouting "Viva Rosas," galloped out furiously upon the plain.

This sketch then is not a short story, but neither is it simply a piece of description. The alien scene shares the centre of attention with Graham himself. The sketch is about a moment of rashness in Graham's youth. One might even say that the sketch is about the way objective memory may suddenly become personal.

"La Pulperia" is perhaps halfway in the spectrum between purely descriptive or discursive essays like **"The Lazo"** or **"The Bolas"** and apparent fictions such as **"Los Seguidores"** or **"A Silhouette."** In the fictions, there is no attempt at complexity of characterization. . . . In **"Los Seguidores,"** the brothers are distinguished as the sober one and the frivolous one but almost as a contrast in humours rather than character. In **"A Silhouette,"** character is even less important. Graham sacrifices individuality of character for individuality of moment. We are sufficiently prepared for the violent endings of both stories but prepared by the suggestions of environment rather than character. For example: "The cattle had become as fierce as buffaloes, and anyone who lost his horse had to make long detours, for to approach them was as dangerous as to come near a tiger or a lion." . . . As in **"La Pulperia,"** out of a background that is general and timeless, though definitely Argentine, there emerges a specific act of violence to nail the story down.

The execution at the end of **"A Silhouette"** is described all too vividly: "With a convulsive movement and a whistling sound, as when the air is suddenly let out of a pricked bladder, the blood gushed out, staining the grass and feet of the impassive gauchos who stood round". . . . Dialogue plays a minor part in such stories; it has a proverbial flavor to it, suggesting both moral locality and the universality of emotions. It is visual detail that is all-important. . . . Graham defines his position by reference to painting. Any complexity of tone in the two stories comes from the handling of visual motifs: the parallel of men and horses in **"Los Seguidores";** the contrast of motion at the beginning and stillness at the end of **"A Silhouette."** The very title **"A Silhouette"** is indicative; the characters' outlines are sharp, but their faces are dark. The story might almost have been written for the sake of the final tableau: "The horse snorted a little at the fresh-spilt blood, and then stood like a statue, outlined and motionless against the sky, in the full glare of the new-risen sun." . . .

Graham was well aware that sharply drawn background, the middle distance of the Venetian painter Basaiti, was essential to his technique. Defending what he had done in **"Victory"** (*Thirteen Stories*), he wrote to Garnett: "I wanted a heavy background, & I think if I had put them [the two main characters] in first, that they would have 'gone into' the background, as painters say. Again I am not a story teller, but an impressionist, & if I kept to the story & cut out my digressions & impressions nothing would be left."

The digressions, the impressions, the virtuoso shows of description, all call attention to the writer. Graham is very clearly present in his work, present as participator. He is a participator in the simple sense that some of the sketches involve him as a character, but more important is his participation as writer. On the face of it, many of Graham's ideas about writing belong to the central tradition of realism. The writer must and can only write about what he has seen and experienced. The writer must achieve a distance or detachment from what he creates. . . . [Graham wrote to Edward Garnett:]

> No one who is an artist *can* or should identify himself with his characters.

> [Chekhov is] extremely detached . . . but it is possible that we do not attach quite the same meaning to the word . . . you I know holding it to be a fault, & I as the highest praise.

> It is only human beings (& myself) I as you say patronise, not a class of them, which I stand outside of.

The last quotation indicates Graham's way. Patronizing is more active than detachment. Instead of concealing an inevitably subjective view of the world, Graham flaunts it. Detachment does not for him mean objectivity. He uses his patronizing self as a pivot. Graham tried to authenticate what he wrote about, tried to make it believable, by showing that he had been there. We are to accept what he saw as one man's view, but the limited view gives us our contact with the subject matter. Graham is his own chief character.

Graham's habit of indirection is important. We never know what or indeed whether anything will happen. This creates a tension between writer and reader different from that in most travel books—though perhaps it is significant that Graham's own travel book, *Mogreb-el-Acksa,* describes an attempted journey to a forbidden Moroccan city which never succeeded. Whether out of egotism or the desire to entertain, many travel writers make use of the interplay between the traveller and what he sees—Borrow's *Bible in Spain* is a good example— but the interplay is rarely ambiguous. We usually know where we are. In Graham's work, we don't; the sudden and violent endings, the flashes of vivid, often ironic detail are not explained or fitted into on orderly and logical progression. Cunninghame Graham deals in illogic, in the absurd, the incongruous and the inexplicable.

The personal involvement undoubtedly gets in the way. We are not always allowed to see for ourselves. There is no indifferent paring of fingernails for Graham. But the record of little-known and vanishing ways of life was only one of his objectives; the self-intrusion does not have to be seen as a conceited mannerism. Graham was a conscious artist. He indeed worried sometimes that he had intervened too little. About **"Cruz Alta",** . . . a long account of droving horses to Brazil, whose details he had checked with another member of the party, Graham wrote to Edward Garnett: "I abandoned myself *so entirely* to the flood of recollection, that when the thing was done it looked to me *too* simple." . . . This was fidelity to experience with a vengeance. The intrusion of the personal is a way of assimilating experience into the work of art. It is not a method suited to extensive development; it is bound to result infragmentation. Both Conrad and Graham reworked what they had seen and heard. Conrad sought objective structures, Graham subjective. Conrad was faithful to his own experience so that he could assure himself that nothing was contrived or false; Graham used his memory to authenticate and complicate what he reported from a special and limited point of view. These are two responses to the problem of credibility, two ways of being honest about the unfamiliar.

The elaborate descriptions of South American landscape make an interesting contrast with that absence of such detail which Borges has pointed out in *Martin Fierro.* According to Borges,

it is the foreigner who takes notice of local color; there are no camels in the Koran. The generalization is by no means universally valid; but the difference between a landscape which is taken for granted and a landscape which dominates is important for human scale. The domination of landscape in Graham suggests a world in which human decisions can effect little. The absence of landscape in Hernández suggests a world whose problems are caused and may be remedied by human action.

In the literature of the nineteenth-century Rio de la Plata, the moral perspectives are clear. Hernández, Echeverría, Mármol, Zorrilla de San Martín, Sarmiento, are in their various ways extensively partisan. Zorrilla's Christian triumphalism, Echeverría's and Mármol's metropolitanism, radically affect the alignment of their work. Hernández above all, with his dual moral purpose of teaching the gaucho and enlightening the city-bred, committed himself to showing the injustices inflicted on the country by a corrupt and unfeeling power structure. His remark that "all the world is a school" ("todo el mundo es escuela") epitomizes a common attitude to the moral and social value of experience. One looks at the world and learns and picks one's side.

Life in nineteenth-century Argentina and Uruguay made such commitment almost mandatory. To define oneself as Argentine meant establishing a position towards the history of a recently independent country. Moreover, once one determined to assert creole values over the Spanish-shadowed past and the French-and-English-shadowed present, there remained the question of which creole values to glorify. The cultural struggle of metropolis and provinces is likely to be bitter when, as in Argentina, the most distinctive features of national life are to be found in the depths of the country. In such an atmosphere, the dogma that he who is not for us is against us thrives and prospers.

Cunninghame Graham was a socialist and an enthusiastic believer in the international value of nationalism. In view of these clear allegiances, and in view of the partisan and didactic strain in Argentine literature, Graham's South American sketches seem remarkably reluctant to take sides. There are several possible reasons for his reluctance. Most simply, Graham's main experience of South America came before his interest in politics which, to judge by the letters quoted in Tschiffely's biography [see Additional Bibliography] developed in the early 1880s, during his stay in Texas. Secondly, in theory at least, Graham distinguished between art and life; social reform had no place in art. In an ironic frame of mind he wrote to Garnett apropos of Sir Walter Besant, an edifying popular novelist:

He at least, has striven to make us, more earnest, more healthy, & more English . . . for what is a problem for but to be solved.

In fact I look on all problems as a species of intellectual gymkhana. . . . You must not think we want any art here, as you say we want conduct, & we get it, together with spirituality. It is precisely that damned spirituality which is at the bottom of it all. . . .

Reacting from this kind of earnestness, Graham goes on to praise *Peer Gynt* and *Ubu Roi.*

Graham was not, in practice, as neutral as this last quotation might imply. Comparing himself with his friend the Argentine-born writer W. H. Hudson, Graham wrote: "He is incomparably better for he has no philosophy of things." Graham's comments and asides take positions, but the opinions are controlled by the situation. A typical Graham sketch intermingles his own ideas with the opening descriptions of setting; it is usually towards the end that he steps aside, leaving episodes and final details unaligned and unexplained. Graham envied Hudson his capacity for value-free observation; he realized that he himself was bound by nature to take sides but looked for ways of writing which made a strength of his weakness. The assertion of subjectivity, the admission that he relies on his memory, gives Graham's interjected opinions a qualified and less irritating status than those of an author who pretends to be omniscient. Graham does not pretend, though he is ready to show his special knowledge whenever necessary.

The argument that Graham remembered the Rio de la Plata in an apolitical way is weak in the face of his constant interest in developments there. Even when he was in Argentina, the transition from a pastoral to a mixed pastoral and agricultural economy had begun. Urquiza, the *caudillo* whose death is related in **"San Jose,"** had an interest in various railroad companies. Graham was in Argentina during Sarmiento's presidency, the Sarmiento who wanted to see a new Chicago arise in the pampas. Graham knew that he was commemorating a passing way of life. One of his first essays about the gaucho is called **"A Vanishing Race."**

It has several times been suggested that Graham wrote about South America chiefly to indulge in escapism and nostalgia. He undoubtedly looked back on his years there with affection. . . . But if the South American sketches present an attractive way of life, free, healthy and without hypocrisy, they also reveal the gauchos' casual attitude to violence which so shocked Hudson. Lack of hypocrisy may simply mean that men kill each other without apologizing: "looking down below the surface, all was as horrible as it is elsewhere, man preying on the animals, they on each other." Although a socialist, Graham's view of man is almost Hobbesian.

Graham's attitude to life of the pampas should be seen in its British context. He declared the "failure of civilisation to humanise," but a letter on Tolstoy (to Garnett, 27 March 1908) rejects any notion of a return to primitivism. . . .

> Though I deplore both **"Success"** & **"Progress"** as much as he does, I think it is no good to shut our eyes, & that *no one* . . . will now live on the land, who can get off it & that, unless they are Kirghiz or semi-wild people, that no scheme can be invented to make them do so . . . Nothing appears to me so false as the "back to the land" cry.

In terms of Sarmiento's choice, Civilisation or Barbarism, it is too late to choose. England is civilised, but still barbarous. The pampas exhibit man as naked animal in order to remind Europeans that they only allow barbarism to fester by dressing it up.

It may well be that Graham sought to shock his English readers, just as Kipling did at the other end of the political gamut. Kipling complained that English innocence underrated the heroes of colonial expansion; Graham that English innocence made false heroes of men like Cecil Rhodes. Kipling was out to prove that the work of Empire needs stern government, and Graham that stern Imperial government was not to be trusted. Kipling says "Men are wicked, therefore cherish social restraints"; Graham says "Men are wicked, and social restraints partake of their corruption." According to Graham social restraints—Factory Acts, for instance—may still be necessary,

but one must beware of the self-interest of those who enforce them.

I should emphasize that the sketches about South America are not intensively polemic. Graham draws his pessimistic conclusions elsewhere. But the pampas sketches form part of the same vision of human fallibility. There are moral perspectives in the South American work after all, but they are aligned for a universal and not a national point of view.

As far as is known, Graham wrote only one sketch in Spanish, and that for a Madrid periodical. But although written for Englishmen, or, if you like, for Graham's own diversion, a number of short pieces and nearly all his historical works had sufficient interest for South American readers to be translated. Borges lists Graham among the foreign writers who have succeeded in catching creole nuances. Histories of Argentine literature usually mention him only in passing. In such sketchily mapped territory, it is idle to talk about influences, but it might be possible to discuss resemblances.

I have suggested that Graham's work has an artistic energy and complexity which puts him aside from the *costumbrista* writers, the local colorists. And he does not associate himself with partisan literature. In a way, Graham anticipates Güiraldes.

Don Segundo Sombra and the corpus of Graham's work are both elegiac. They record an almost lost life. Both Güiraldes and Graham see the corrupting influence of modern life coming from the small towns as well as the cities. Unlike Hernández, neither of them sees the pampas from a purely gaucho point of view. Güiraldes' hero, although he is coming into his own inheritance, has to lean from Don Segundo. Graham tries to make the gaucho way of life credible to ignorant readers, using himself as intermediary. Güiraldes and Graham were conscious artists, perhaps even separated a little from the gauchos by their own self-awareness. Above all, both writers are concerned with the fact of violence: not Federalist violence, or Centralist violence, but human violence. Violence is not epic, as it is in *Martin Fierro*, the normal course of heroic action. In the world of Güiraldes and of Graham, violence is often in excess of a simple response to situation; it is either gratuitous or motivated by subconscious need. Young Cáceres must kill the bull at all costs.

We might take Güiraldes' statement of informed stoicism, proverbial in form, as an epigraph to Graham's work: "El que sabe de los males de esta tierra, por haberlos vivido, se ha templado para domarlos." [He who knows the ills of this country, because he has lived them, has stopped himself from curbing them.] Graham believed that it was essential to know the full range of human possibilities, best and worst, "los males de esta tierra." For this reason, he tried to interest British readers in the alien world of South America. He tried to make Argentina credible, in the sense with which I started out, by authenticating his material with his presence.

In doing do, he naturally ran the risk of himself being thought incredible. "There are moments," Shaw wrote, "when I do not myself believe in his existence." Graham's techniques were ultimately restricting. They were not suitable for large-scale treatment. Much more than Conrad, he was confined to writing about his own experience, although that experience was certainly varied. The author's intrusions may sometimes irritate rather than reverberate. But there is more method to Graham's art than at first appears. The generously cultivated amateur manner is a blind. Graham knew what he was doing, and within his limitations, he often did it well. (pp. 256-64)

Laurence Davies, "Cunninghame Graham's South American Sketches," in Comparative Literature Studies, Vol. IX, No. 3, September, 1972, pp. 253-65.

CEDRIC WATTS (essay date 1983)

[*Watts is an English critic. He is the coauthor, with Laurence Davies, of* Cunninghame Graham: A Critical Biography *(see Additional Bibliography), and the author of the study* R. B. Cunninghame Graham *(1983). In the following excerpt from the latter work, Watts summarizes Graham's value and interest as an author.*]

Cunninghame Graham is not a major author, and if we come to his work with the wrong expectations much of it can be seen as slight, bitty, thin, and repetitive: yarns, journalism, chat, and whimsy of the past. He was only marginally a writer of fictions: his concern for the sensed truth and his partly defensive, partly aggressive project to memorialize his own career meant that he either stayed within the bounds of what he had experienced or generally restricted invention to the locations he knew. If, however, we come to his work with the right expectations—a flexible cluster of criteria based on normal human curiosity and governed by common sense—we will find much to enjoy and something to learn. We move between relatively ephemeral, trivial material and, in contrast, pieces which linger in the imagination and bear rereading, the latter group including "The Gold Fish," for example, and "A Jesuit," "Christie Christison," "Might, Majesty, and Dominion," and "Animula Vagula." A work may ask to be treated as a tale or as an autobiographical recollection, as a travel essay or as a description of some bygone custom; often, the piece may prove to be a mixture of several of these.

As we look back from *Mirages* over the tales and essays of his previous forty years, we can readily see the continuities and the degree of evolution. The later work is technically more reliable and less erratic, better paced and balanced, although Cunninghame Graham was always capable of errors and lapses in spelling, punctuation, and syntax. (We often sense the amateurism of this "amateur of genius.") The later writer is more tolerant, more forgiving in outlook; the earlier satiric scorn and ironic indignation are muted. To the last, the better pieces maintain a blend of honest realism and stoical sympathy.

The thematic continuity between earlier and later work is extremely strong. . . . [Defense] of the underdog is the main preoccupation that links Graham the political campaigner with Graham the writer. In his tales, essays, biographies, and histories, as in his parliamentary speeches, he calls into question the belief in inevitable progress and faith in imperialism, and he sympathizes with the downtrodden and the victim, whether Maori, Zulu, Mescalero Indian, Aztec, or animal—horses on battlefields or elephants performing in circuses. Prostitutes, beggars, eccentrics: where he can speak up for them, he does; at best with a dry humor and a recognition that not all have hearts of gold.

As is natural to a man who lived an active life and preferred the sunny skies of Argentina and Morocco to the dank drizzle of Scotland, a strong element of cultural and chronological primitivism accompanies his criticism of civilization: his ideal world would be a preindustrial one of virile activity in an open, hot landscape, where men ride, work, drink, and occasionally fight, living for the moment and free from the urgings of con-

science and the claims of posterity. This puerile Arcadia is a familiar imaginative retreat for writers who know well those urgings and who nevertheless are too intelligently reflective ever to become domiciled in the primitive state that they commend. Graham recognized the irony. Near the end of his career he remarked: "I pray the empire builder . . . . . not to think I am enamoured of the noble savage . . . . . I know quite well that he uses no poison gas or bombs, simply because he has not got them, and is constrained to do his level best with poisoned arrows. . . . ." (pp. 114-15)

In this matter, as in others, his work is ambiguous and tends toward paradox. He looks on the primitive sometimes with admiration, sometimes with equanimity, and sometimes with distaste, depending on its nature, his vantage-point, and his polemical purposes. With religion, as we have noted, he has a perennial concern, and can look variously with scorn, sympathy, and approval at particular manifestations of it. Scottish missionaries he can see as misguided exporters of a dismal, life-denying creed to regions happier and better without it; Jesuits he can often admire for their heroism and paternalism in South America; gnostic fanaticism, as of Antonio Conselheiro, he can regard as a mental disease yet also as an idealism that lifts men from the mundane. Cunninghame Graham was a romantic and a skeptic: his spiritual forebears included both Shelley and Voltaire. In racial matters, he sometimes endorses the prejudices of his day, as in some patronizing or mocking reference to Jew or Negro (in "Rothenberger's Wedding," for instance); but he can also, at his best, challenge or transcend that prejudice, as we saw in the case of "Mirahuano." His attitude to women may here and there be the rather dominative one that fits the conventional posture of the "virile man of action"; but on numerous occasions he challenges sexual chauvinism and exposes its callousness.

Cunninghame Graham was a man of paradoxes, expressing more overtly the complexities that can be found in many people who live with sufficient fullness in any cultural phase. In this century, steadily increasing critical interest has been drawn to such paradoxicality in individuals and their works: therefore Graham may attract and reward new attention.

A central paradox is that which he poses eloquently in the late essay "Mirage":

> So it may well be after all that the world of the mirage is the real world, and that the world we live in is a mirage. Mankind has always loved to be deceived, to hug illusions to its heart, to fight for them and to commit its direst follies in the name of common sense. . . . .
>
> When, therefore, fellow Hadgi, the mirage spreads its lake before you, do not allow your horse to put his foot in it or it will vanish from your sight.
>
> Behind the mantling vapour rise castles, towers, cathedrals, lines of aerial telegraphs stretching up to the moon, palaces, fantastic ruins, galleons and galleasses that sail bedecked with flags.
>
> All these exist in the mind's eye, the only field of vision where there is no astigmatism.
>
> Rein up your horse, before his feet destroy and bring them back again to earth. Why peer behind the veil to see life's desert all befouled

with camels' dung, littered with empty sardine tins and broken bottles, and strewed as thick as leaves in Vallombrosa with greasy, sandwich papers?

At any cost preserve your mirage intact and beautiful. If riding in the desert you behold it slowly taking shape, turn and sit sideways in your saddle, pouring a libation of tobacco smoke towards your Mecca and muttering a prayer. . . . .

The passage is "dated"; stylistically slightly archaic for the time of writing, too. It is redolent of late-nineteenth-century romanticism by its stance, argument, tone, and phrasing ("fellow Hadgi [pilgrim] . . . . . Why peer behind the veil . . . . .?"), which recall Fitzgerald's *Omar Khayyám* or early Yeats and the Aesthetic prose of the 1890s. At a casual glance it might pass for a wistful reverie by Arthur Symons or Richard le Gallienne, although the quirky Miltonic allusion ("leaves in Vallombrosa") offers a warning. What gives the passage its paradoxical edge is suggested by the reference to "life's desert all befouled with camels' dung, littered with empty sardine tins and broken bottles, and strewed . . . . . with greasy, sandwich papers." The essay purports to commend illusion, dream, and ideality; but these mundane references remind us that again and again Graham had been concerned with drawing attention to precisely those sardine tins, those broken bottles, those greasy sandwich papers. In all his best work, the mundane realist controls the aspiring romantic. This passage reveals, in addition, a further and greater tension.

It has recently been argued, by Professor A. D. Nuttall in *A Common Sky,* that the reason modern writers and critics place such high value on the concrete and particular in depictions of life is that they are responding to a solipsistic fear. The solipsist holds that the individual self constitutes the sole verifiable reality; our sense of an outside world is unverifiable and may be deceptive and delusive. Nuttall argues that although common sense revolts against such a notion, it is tenacious and hard to exorcise; it generates anxieties. "It is strange how many modern writers betray real anxiety in their efforts to give a rich, felt 'substance' to the things they describe. . . . . Perhaps, in short, the romantic and post-romantic stress on 'impact' is *compensatory.*" "If a man feels the real world slipping from him, he tightens his grip on it."

For us the application is clear. Cunninghame Graham's work, as we have seen, from time to time expresses radically skeptical and even solipsistic notions ("It may well be . . . . . that the world we live in is a mirage"), and there is something akin to a compensatory anxiety in his determination to render the concreteness of the world. "We all must put our finger in the Saviour's wounds, before we can believe," he says; and he delights when the senses seem unexpectedly to provide incontrovertible guarantee of remembered reality, with a scent of mimosa suddenly recalling the River Plate, the sight of green turtle-fat evoking the Indians of Bahía Blanca, and the smell of oranges summoning the forests of Paraguay. So an ontological fear may well reinforce his memorializing concern: he is striving to give fixity as well as durability to his remembered world.

Another paradoxical feature of his outlook . . . is the tendency for his defense of the underdog to extend itself from political into aesthetic regions, to the point where he argues that the impoverished and amateurish work may actually be more effective than the opulent and professional. In "**A Repertory**

Theatre," the amateur production of a Spanish play seems to him more evocative than a professional treatment could be; in "**Miss Christian Jean**," clumsy paintings stimulate his imagination as proficient ones do not; in "**Euphrasia**," the poorly carved cross and cheap iron railings make the war memorial the more poignant; and among the chroniclers, it is the ex-soldier Bernal Díaz, with his honest, unpolished comments, who for Graham brings the Conquest most immediately to life. This has obvious relevance to our judgment of Graham's own pages. Cunninghame Graham's quirky awkwardnesses of style and narration, his inconsequentialities and digressions, his love of a gratuitous footnote about a horse or a Spanish phrase: all these features can, where the material purports to be autobiographical, serve as warrants of authenticity. Faults may become merits. The more Graham presents himself as a traveler and man of action turned only late to writing, the more the quirks and flaws provide confirmation. We make allowances for the lapses, and when a tale succeeds, we may give extra credit for the overcoming of conspicuous difficulties.

It is also the case that his huge and largely autobiographical output permits us to know him so fully and intimately that to be critically severe to Graham would seem as unjust as to be harsh to an old and close friend. He helped underdogs; today he himself is an underdog who deserves a little help. Much modern literary criticism perversely strives to isolate from their authors the works under discussion. With Graham's work, this is impossible. Among real-life characters, he was and is one of the most interesting; and the ample collection of tales, essays, biographies, and histories constitutes a large part of his masterpiece, warts and all: the living Cunninghame Graham. (pp. 115-18)

> *Cedric Watts, in his* R. B. Cunninghame Graham,
> *Twayne Publishers, 1983, 135 p.*

ADDITIONAL BIBLIOGRAPHY

Dobie, J. Frank. "The Gauchos and Horses of Hudson and Graham." In his *Prefaces,* pp. 187-200. Boston: Little, Brown and Co., 1975.*
    Comparison of Graham's and W. H. Hudson's respective portrayals of life on the South American pampas.

Harris, Frank. "Cunninghame Graham." In his *Contemporary Portraits, third series,* pp. 45-60. New York: Privately printed, 1920.
    Reminiscence of Graham which includes a discussion of his parliamentary career. Harris also focuses on Graham's adventurousness and love of sport and examines the way in which these traits helped to shape Graham's writings. Harris calls Graham "an amateur of genius."

Macauley, Robie. "Stranger, Tread Light." *The Kenyon Review* XVII, No. 2 (Spring 1955): 280-90.
    Discusses Graham as a writer of "epitaphs." Macauley states that Graham's portraits have a peculiar finality about them: they summarize "all of the salient things" that Graham saw about his subjects—"their particular quarrel with life, or their particular failure, or their particular compromise"—and each is an "acute summing up."

MacShane, Frank. "R. B. Cunninghame Graham." *The South Atlantic Quarterly* LXVIII (1969): 198-207.
    Discussion of Graham's work in relation to his times. MacShane discusses which features of Graham's prose set him apart and made him seem a rebel against the materialistic tendencies of the age.

Meyers, Jeffrey. "Robert Bontine Cunninghame Graham." In his *A Fever at the Core: The Idealist in Politics*, pp. 39-48. New York: Barnes and Noble, 1976.

Recapitulation of Graham's political career which also includes a brief discussion of his writings. Meyers stresses the visionary nature of many of Graham's political ideas.

Stallman, Robert Wooster. "Robert Cunninghame Graham's South American Sketches." *Hispania* XXVII, No. 1 (February 1945): 69-75.

Discussion of Graham's place in the "art-for-art's-sake" era. Stallman states that unlike other authors of the 1890s, Graham's escape to a "vanishing Arcadia" was not a fiction, but an actual journey to a real place in South America.

Tschiffely, A. F. *Don Roberto: Being the Account of the Life and Works of R. B. Cunninghame Graham 1852-1936*. London: William Heinemann, 1937, 458 p.

Biographical work that gives a colorful account of Graham's years in South America. Tschiffely's book is augmented with many interesting photographs, though critics have noted that he sometimes failed to carefully verify his facts.

Walker, John. "Oscar Wilde and Cunninghame Graham." *Notes and Queries* n.s. 23, No. 2 (February 1976): pp. 73-4.*

Discussion of a previously unpublished letter from Oscar Wilde to Cunninghame Graham. Walker suggests a probable date for the writing of the undated letter and explains its significance in terms of the personal philosophy and literary tastes of both men.

————. Introduction to *The South American Sketches of R. B. Cunninghame Graham*, by R. B. Cunninghame Graham, edited by John Walker, pp. 3-19. Norman: University of Oklahoma Press, 1978.

Discusses Graham's characteristic themes and techniques.

————. "Introduction: Cunninghame Graham and Scotland." In *The Scottish Sketches of R. B. Cunninghame Graham*, by R. B. Cunninghame Graham, edited by John Walker, pp. 1-15. Edinburgh: Scottish Academic Press, 1982.

Biographical and critical essay with emphasis on Graham's writings about Scotland.

Watts, Cedric T. "A Letter from W. B. Yeats to R. B. Cunninghame Graham." *Review of English Studies* n.s. XVIII, No. 71 (1967): 292-3.*

Previously unpublished letter which documents that Graham knew Yeats, if only as a business acquaintance. The letter is a polite rejection of a play that Graham submitted to the Abbey Theater. Yeats's letter explains that the play, which deals with miraculous subject matter, would be a "dangerous play for a theater managed by Protestants for a largely Catholic audience."

————, and Davies, Laurence. *Cunninghame Graham: A Critical Biography*. Cambridge: Cambridge University Press, 1979, 333 p.

Comprehensive study of Graham's writings, travels, and political career.

John (Henry) Gray

1866-1934

English poet, short story and novella writer, dramatist, critic, essayist, and translator.

Gray was one of the most elusive and fascinating figures associated with the Decadent movement of the 1890s, and his poetry collection *Silverpoints* is among the essential works of that era. A well-known member of Oscar Wilde's social circle, he was rumored to have been the model for the title character of Wilde's notorious novel *The Picture of Dorian Gray*. Gray was also a talented translator as well as a poet. Along with Arthur Symons, he was among the first in England to perceive the significance of the French Symbolist movement for modern poetry, and he included translations from the works of such poets as Paul Verlaine and Stéphane Mallarmé in *Silverpoints*. For this reason, Gray is often credited with introducing contemporary French poetry to English readers.

Gray was born in London in 1866, the oldest of the eight children of John and Hannah Gray. His father was a carpenter and a dockyard laborer. Since Gray's parents were Nonconformists (dissenters from the official Church of England), he was sent to a Wesleyan day school. He was later awarded a scholarship to the Roan Grammar School, where he was regarded as an excellent student. However, he was forced to quit school at the age of fifteen in order to help support his brothers and sisters, working for a time as a metal-turner at the Woolwich Arsenal, but continuing to study in his free hours. He taught himself Latin, French, and German. He also studied music, drawing, and painting, and eventually was promoted to a position in the drawing office of the arsenal. Gray's studious habits were again rewarded when, at the age of eighteen, he passed the examinations for the Civil Service. He was given a job in the General Post Office, but later earned a promotion to the position of librarian in the Foreign Office. Gray's work in the Foreign Office was not demanding, and he was able, for the first time, to devote much of his time to literature. He began to write numerous essays and poems, as well as to prepare translations of various French and German works. He was soon also spending his free time mingling in the fashionable life of literary London, attending the theatrical premieres of all the season's promising new works and frequenting the music halls—a favorite haunt of many of the literary figures of the fin de siècle. He soon became well-known to the members of the Rhymers' Club, an informal group of young poets that included William Butler Yeats, Lionel Johnson, and Ernest Dowson, and was a frequent guest at their meetings in the Cheshire Cheese Tavern. He was often seen at Wilde's favorite haunt, the Café Royal.

Although the exact date of Gray's first meeting with Wilde is not known, and in spite of Wilde's public assertions that he did not meet Gray until 1892, two years after *Dorian Gray* first appeared in serial form, scholars of this period believe that the two actually met in 1889 through their mutual acquaintance Charles Ricketts, the publisher of the *Dial* and the designer of Gray's *Silverpoints*. In evidence critics note that numerous documents dating from the period reveal that by 1891 Gray was known as "Dorian" throughout London literary circles. Moreover, although it can never be proved conclusively

that Gray was the model for Wilde's protagonist in *Dorian Gray*, critics cite many details in the novel—including the coincidence of Dorian's surname, his youth, good looks, and initial innocence—that suggest a connection. Moreover, it was in 1892 that Gray began writing "The Person in Question," a short story in which an aging doppelgänger suddenly appears to a young aesthete, illustrating for him the likely course of his future. The thematic similarities between "The Person in Question" and *Dorian Gray*, the autobiographical tone of Gray's story, and the fact that Gray suppressed it until long after his death, all suggest that Gray was indeed the prototype for Wilde's decadent hero. Although Gray greatly admired Wilde and was at one time proud of their friendship, Wilde's increasingly indiscreet behavior and his blatantly homosexual liaison with Lord Alfred Douglas appears to have alarmed Gray. As it became increasingly apparent that a scandal was imminent, Gray withdrew from Wilde's circle. Moreover, critics believe that it may have been the spectacle of Wilde's decline that precipitated in Gray a spiritual crisis that made him decide to alter his life.

While the publication of *Silverpoints* in 1893 brought Gray to the brink of literary fame, his personal unhappiness eventually led him to abandon London literary society. Gray had converted to Catholicism in 1890 and, as the 1896 publication of *Spiritual Poems* attests, became increasingly more devoted to a religious way of life. Both he and André Raffalovich, a Jewish convert and prosperous financier, were instrumental in the conversion of the artist Aubrey Beardsley while he was dying of tuberculosis, and Gray's edition of *The Last Letters of Aubrey Beardsley* (1904) was one of his last literary projects before a silence of twenty years. In 1898, Gray entered Scots College in Rome to study for the priesthood. He spent the remainder of his life as a priest in Edinburgh, Scotland, and, as numerous reminiscences avow, Gray was an exemplary cleric with a reputation for self-sacrifice in the service of the poor. He himself lived quite comfortably during these years: Raffalovich had also moved to Edinburgh in 1905, and there financed the erection of St. Peter's Church, where Gray was appointed rector. Gray and Raffalovich had known each other since 1892, and their much-chronicled friendship, often characterized as formal but profound, ended only with their deaths in 1934.

While Gray published several collections of poetry at various stages of his life, the volume which is considered his most important, and the one with which his name is most readily associated, is *Silverpoints*. Gray's first collection, *Silverpoints* was published at a time when the Decadent movement in English letters was approaching its peak of notoriety: Wilde's novel *The Picture of Dorian Gray* had recently appeared, Aubrey Beardsley's drawings and illustrations had begun to attract notice in books and magazines, and many of the characteristic poets of the period—including Arthur Symons, Ernest Dowson, and Lionel Johnson—were producing works whose shared traits formed what has come to be considered the fin-de-siècle style. For several reasons Gray's *Silverpoints* is recognized as the epitome of this style. The publishers of this collection were John Lane and Elkin Mathews, whose company the Bodley Head also published the *Yellow Book* and whose *Keynote* series of fiction and poetry included numerous titles, often illustrated, by authors who were attacked in the English press as "decadent." In addition, the volume was designed to be of visual as well as literary interest, an ornate and ostentatiously delicate artifact which is still admired for its affected craftsmanship. Further identifying his collection with the Decadent sensibility, Gray included among his own poems several translations from the works of Charles Baudelaire, Arthur Rimbaud, Mallarmé, and Verlaine, thus establishing an alliance with a recent school of French poets who were labelled by critics, or who labelled themselves, as Decadents. Gray's own poems in *Silverpoints* repeatedly display the influence of his French models: ingenious prosodic devices, perverse or openly pathological poetic themes, and an underlying Catholic worldview. Characteristic of the Decadent school, Gray's poems in *Silverpoints* are of blatantly narrow interest, directed toward fellow initiates receptive to unusual nuances of aesthetic and spiritual experience. Representing the thematic poles of bizarre sensuality and orthodox religious piety are the poems "The Barber" and "A Crucifix," the first an exotic vignette which more than one critic has called surrealistic for its hallucinatory effect and obscure sadism, and the second a reverent description of the eponymous sacred object. While Gray's early poems have often been noticed by critics for their technical accomplishments and profound expression of essential Decadent themes, the significance of *Silverpoints* is considered as much cultural as literary: nearly a century after its publication, this volume continues to serve as one of the most conspicuous emblems of the cult of Decadence that flourished during the 1890s.

After the publication of *Silverpoints*, Gray produced several other collections of verse throughout the 1890s. These volumes, the most prominent being *Spiritual Poems*, explicitly reflected Gray's transition from fin-de-siècle aesthete to devout Christian. Gray wrote and published very little during the more than twenty years following his ordination as priest in 1901. In 1926, he published *The Long Road*, a reflective and autobiographical allegory in which, as Gray wrote to his sister, "the Road symbolizes life, and its monotony only is varied with the excursion of the excursionist's own invention. . . ." A few years later, Gray began writing essays for *Blackfriars*, a monthly magazine of the Dominican order, and in 1931 he published *Poems*. In this last collection of poems, according to critics, Gray most clearly demonstrates his alertness to twentieth-century poetic trends and confirms his development from a prototype of the 1890s Decadent to a modern artist with a mature and individual voice. Gray's last work of fiction, *Park: A Fantastic Story*, is considered his most important. Described by Brocard Sewell as "part science-fiction, part novel of ideas," *Park* has as its protagonist a priest in his sixties who seems to be a fictional persona of Gray himself and shares many of his traits and habits. While on one of his frequent walks, Reverend Mungo Park finds himself in a future England in which the former Anglo-Saxon population has degenerated to a race of backward subterranean creatures and the rulers are a superior civilization of Roman Catholic blacks. Critics have traced the origin of *Park*'s storyline to Gray's longstanding interest in and identification with black people and to his speculations on the conversion of black Africans to the Catholic Church. In addition, critics have found that *Park* reflects the influences of such earlier futuristic novels as William Morris's *News from Nowhere* (1890) and H. G. Wells's *The Time Machine* (1895). With the exception of *Silverpoints*, *Park* is the only work of Gray's to receive significant critical favor. Bernard Bergonzi has called the novella a "curiously timeless work" which "deserves a niche in the history of modern English fiction."

While many of the authors and artists associated with the Decadent movement converted to Catholicism at some point in their lives, Gray is an exceptional case of one whose brief career among the dandified sect of the 1890s evolved into a successful vocation in the Catholic Church. Perhaps the sincerity of his conversion is best evidenced by his later attempts to destroy copies of *Silverpoints* whenever he found them and to forbid the reprinting of this rare collection. Nevertheless, it is largely this work which accounts for Gray's importance in literary history as one of the most prominent and gifted authors of the fin-de-siècle period.

PRINCIPAL WORKS

Silverpoints (poetry) 1893
The Blackmailers (drama) 1894
The Blue Calendar, 1895 (poetry) 1894
The Blue Calendar, 1896 (poetry) 1895
The Blue Calendar, 1897 (poetry) 1896
Spiritual Poems (poetry) 1896
The Fourth and Last Blue Calendar, 1898 (poetry) 1897
Ad Matrem (poetry) 1904
Verses for Tableaux Vivants (poetry) 1905
Vivis (poetry) 1922
Saint Peter's Hymns (poetry) 1925
The Long Road (poetry) 1926
Poems (poetry) 1931
Park: A Fantastic Story (novella) 1932
*The Person in Question (short story) 1958

*The work was written around 1892.

[FRANK HARRIS]   (essay date 1893)

[Harris was a highly controversial English editor, critic, and biographer who is best known as the author of a maliciously inaccurate biography of Oscar Wilde, a dubious life of Bernard Shaw, and a massive autobiography which portrays Edwardian life primarily as a background for Harris's near-Olympian sexual adventures. A man frequently referred to in colorfully insulting terms by major critics, he was by most accounts a remarkable liar and braggart, traits which deeply color the quality of his works and their critical reception. His greatest accomplishments were achieved as editor of the Fortnightly Review, Pearson's Magazine, *the* Evening News, *and the* Saturday Review *of London. As editor of the* Saturday Review *he helped launch the careers of Shaw and H. G. Wells, hiring them as drama critic and literary critic, respectively, during the mid-1890s. Shaw later wrote that Harris "had no quality of editorship except the supreme one of knowing good work from bad, and not being afraid of it." Harris's fame as a critic rests primarily upon his five-volume* Contemporary Portraits *(1915-30), which contain essays marked by the author's characteristically vigorous style and patronizing tone. The following review of* Silverpoints *was published anonymously by Harris in the* Saturday Review.]*

The English people and its mouthpiece, the old-fashioned critic (if he is still alive), have lost an emotion in life that can never return—the capacity for being shocked. The shockers and the shocked both enjoyed it immensely; but the fun of the thing has gone, along with the age of chivalry, Macaulay's schoolboy, and the father who really consigned Mr. Swinburne's early volumes to the flames. Mr. John Gray has, therefore, come a little late. *Silverpoints*, indeed, is dressed in all the form and art of modern book production. The print is in the italic type of the "Aldines," and the cover is a singularly beautiful design by Mr. C. Ricketts; while the contents are "in the movement," and as modern and decadent as they can be. Still we cannot help feeling that the hope is forlorn. It would not be very hard for any one who has read those much-talked-of *Décadents* and *Symbolistes* to bring all kinds of charges against Mr. Gray on the score of plagiarism. He has studied MM. Verlaine and Mallarmé to some tune as well as the smaller fry, Moréas, Laforge and the rest. He has assimilated some of their spirit without any ill result. He is really original, and must pay the penalty for this, greater in England than in any other country, as a first class misdemeanant in literature. A great many people will be repelled, and the irreverent will laugh. When Mr. John Gray imitates, he is perfectly frank and says so. Master Builder Verlaine is freely quoted and Baudelaire is cruelly mangled. That he has a poetic gift, any one who will take the trouble to read *Silverpoints* carefully (we do not say that it is worth reading) will find out for himself. Mr. John Gray writes before he has learnt to speak. He would sing before he is rid of stammering, and he strikes beautiful chords on dumb pianos. In groping about for the colour and symbolism of adjectives he has forgotten their original use. He is the lame man running before he can walk. In a very striking and original poem, however, entitled **"The Barber,"** Mr. John Gray reveals that he is a poet, though he is so anxious to be mistaken for a *poseur*. It is the only piece that comes up to the binding. For the rest, with the exception of a few lines here and there, the verse is very foolish and affected, and sad stuff at the best. Careful of accent and careless of accidence, Mr. John Gray has thrown down a bomb into poetical dovecots that turns out on inspection to be merely a squib.

[Frank Harris], in a review of "Silverpoints," in The Saturday Review, *London, Vol. LXXV, No. 1958, May 6, 1893, p. 493.*

CLEMENT SCOTT   (essay date 1894)

[In the following review of a performance of The Blackmailers, *Scott attacks the play and its collaborators Gray and André Raffalovich.]*

I may be very stupid, but I do not quite understand the assumed position of the young authors of **"The Blackmailers,"** two able and enthusiastic young men, fond of the stage, students of dramatic literature in all countries, but who, having written a play on a disagreeable subject, turn round and say, "It is no child of mine." Mr. John Gray and Mr. André Raffalovich clearly believed in the subject of **"The Blackmailers,"** or they would not have written it. They certainly had faith in its success, or they would not have taken a theatre in which to produce it. They evidently had confidence in their judgment, or they would not have asked their friends to come and see it. I cannot conceive they would have been so unwise as to leave their poor play alone at rehearsals unattended; nor do I understand the position of an author who, having taken and paid for a theatre in order to show his own work, in which he believed, allows any stage manager or director in existence to alter the motive or the fabric of the play. Suggestions at rehearsal from practical people are of the greatest possible value. They often help a play on to success. But no stage manager or director is ever permitted to change the tone, style, or dramatic method of a play. That would be intolerable. It must stand or fall by

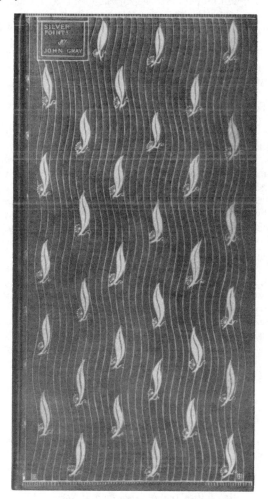

Cover of Gray's Silverpoints, *designed by Charles Ricketts.*

the author's intention, and it frequently fails because the author's ideas are not in the least carried out by the actors and actresses. On the other hand, more often than not, clever actors and actresses help the lame dog of an author over the stile. What I should like to know is in what respect the play as it was written and intended to be acted by the authors differs from the play that we all saw produced. . . . Apart from the subject, which I consider essentially disagreeable, and unnaturally forced for the purposes of the stage, it was the character of the hero that fogged me completely. What was he, this young Blackmailer? A good man, a weak man, or a detestable scoundrel? I could not make him out. He started full of virtuous sentiment; he tried hard to struggle against and resist temptation; he argued with and lectured a young friend as if he were his own tutor at the University or the head master of a public school; he became the catspaw of a scoundrel, but he ever refused to pick the chestnuts out of the fire. Then all on a sudden this much-tempted youth and hater of blackmailing in any form turns out the most outrageous rascal who ever appeared in dramatic print. Out at elbows as he is, with cash and credit gone, threatened with a criminal prosecution on the instant, his family comes very nobly to his assistance. Men in this predicament are generally allowed to sink without a helping hand. But when the family offer to get this reprobate out of his hobble and send him off to the Colonies, what does he do? He turns round like a cur and snaps at the assisting fingers. He bullies and blackguards a venerable old gentleman whose grey hairs should at least be respected, he insults his uncles, his cousins, and his aunts, and, worst of all, he turns round and grossly insults his own mother, whose one sin has been her leniency towards this cub. Having grossly insulted his family, and by inexcusable cruelty brought tears into his mother's eyes, he thinks he will commit suicide. But he is too much of a coward for that, and sneaks off to Paris to cheat and blackmail more people, rather glorying in his power of imitating the criminal classes. The play ends with the mother's regret that such a blackguard should disgrace humanity. Well, it is not a cheerful subject, however we consider it. There may be University and public-school men who would blackmail innocent women and blackguard their own mothers. But they are in a hopeless minority, and it is scarcely worth while to write plays in order to advertise such abnormal cases of depravity. At any rate, this is not holding the mirror up to nature. It is showing an unnatural monster in a very dirty and dusty looking-glass. It will be a grievous thing if our clever young men who would and could write well for the stage are led away into the fool's paradise full of faddists and eccentrics. The public has not called for this kind of work, and does not want it. They want pictures of men and women, not monsters. The public taste is not diseased, it is healthy; and, in my humble opinion, the men and women who waste their talent over "**Mrs. Lessinghams**" and "**Blackmailers,**" and these kind of people, waste their time also, and the time of the public, which is worse. (pp. 766, 768)

> Clement Scott, "The Playhouses," in The Illustrated
> London News, *Vol. 104, No. 2878, June 16, 1894,*
> *pp. 766, 768.**

OSBERT BURDETT   (essay date 1925)

[*In the following excerpt from his* The Beardsley Period, *a study of 1890s authors and artists, Burdett discusses Gray's early poems.*]

John Gray, the author of **Silverpoints** and **Spiritual Poems,** has several literary affiliations with the [other poets of the Beards-

ley Period]. . . . Altogether, in appearance, inspiration, intention, style and subject [*Silverpoints*] is a very characteristic volume. The verse is that of an accomplished craftsman, very much in his own movement, who can write but cannot sing. It is the curiosities of the pen, not the subtleties of the heart, that he reveals, seeking to intensify the convention then in fashion. Both Ernest Dowson and John Gray translated Verlaine's *Spleen.* Dowson's version sings itself charmingly into English, and becomes an English lyric on the way. Gray's rendering halts; even his original verses seem to shun a smooth rhythm, as if, in this poem, to remind us that the vital objection to translations is that they usually rob us of our English. Indeed, the sense is apt to be at the mercy of Gray's interlaced little metres. He is often condensed or obscure, but always scholarly in manner. Domination is a word of five syllables to him, and when he rhymes heart and spikenard we know that the flaw seemed lovely to himself. He does not hesitate to distribute the word sun-beam between two lines, or to begin a line with the last word of a sentence, though he does not approach Gerard Manley Hopkins in these devices. Carelessness can never accomplish experiments like these, which are the careful licences of the craftsman. "**The Barber,**" a poem not far in feeling from Beardsley's ballad, describes a dream that in any preceding decade would have been remembered differently. The two opening stanzas from the lines "**To E.M.G.**" show John Gray at his best:

> Lean back, and press the pillows deep,
>   Heart's dear demesne, dear Daintiness;
> Close your tired eyes, but not to sleep . . .
>   How very pale your pallor is!
>
> You smile, your cheek's voluptuous line
>   Melts in your dimple's saucy cave.
> Your hairbraids seem a wilful vine,
>   Scorning to imitate a wave.

The skill is undeniable, but does it touch anything deeper than critical interest and curiosity? Perhaps it was because Gray was doubtful of this that he left poetry for the priesthood. (pp. 165-67)

> Osbert Burdett, "The Poetry of the Period," in his
> The Beardsley Period: An Essay in Perspective, *Boni*
> *and Liveright, 1925, pp. 154-92.**

BROCARD SEWELL, O. Carm.   (essay date 1965-66)

[*Sewell is an English critic and biographer whose special interest is in English authors of the late Victorian and Edwardian periods, especially such Roman Catholic authors as Frederick Rolfe and Arthur Machen. In his autobiography,* My Dear Time's Waste *(1966), Sewell details his own conversion to Catholicism and his entry into the priesthood. Of his literary interests he has stated: "As a very young man, working in Hilary Pepler's private press at Ditchling, I often heard mention of Father John Gray of Edinburgh, a poet, who was said to have been closely associated in earlier life with Oscar Wilde and other fin-de-siècle writers. . . . Interest in John Gray led to interest in other 1890s figures, notably André Raffalovich, Olive Constance, Arthur Symons, and others, and late survivors from the nineties, such as E. H. Visiak, Arthur Machen, and Montague Summers. . . . As a biographer I am chiefly concerned with the preservation of the memory of men and women reckoned as minor figures of their era, but who seem to be men and women whose personalities and achievements deserve greater recognition and appreciation." In the following excerpt, Sewell comments on the novella* Park.]

A writer in *Two Friends* [see Sewell entry in Additional Bibliography] has asked: 'Is *Park* the most *priestly* novel in the English language?', and he goes on to say that 'There have been other and more prolific priest-novelists: Wiseman and Newman, Robert Hugh Benson, Canon William Barry, 'John Ayscough' (Monsignor Bickerstaffe-Drew). Archbishop David Mathew has published three beautifully written novels: *In Vallombrosa*, *Steam Packet*, and *The Mango on the Mango Tree*. But *Park* is perhaps the only English novel which could only have been written by a priest.' *Park* is not a story of church life, or a tract. In form it is a dream; and the haunting clarity of ordered dream is caught in prose of deceptive simplicity which reveals to the careful reader many facets of the author's complex and enigmatical personality.

The story's hero, Dr Mungo Park, is a priest and a seminary professor (of moral theology). In fact, as Miss Alexandra Zaina has observed in an essay on John Gray's prose in *Two Friends*, Park 'is Gray himself, much addicted to walking, and accurately described down to a missing tooth.' Older worshippers at St Peter's church, Morningside, Edinburgh, remember the impressive reverence with which Canon Gray used to pronounce the words ET INCARNATUS EST in the Creed. Somewhere in the novel Park is present at a pontifical high mass: 'One feature affected him deeply, the genuflection at the words Et incarnatus est; but it always did.' The Canon once amazed the guests at André Raffalovich's Sunday luncheon table by observing: 'Sunday is a miserable day;' to which he added: 'It's a miserable life altogether.' An echo of these sentiments will be found in *Park*. At the luncheon these words were received in stunned silence; after which, as his Dominican friend Fr Edwin Essex has recorded, someone said quietly: 'But dear Canon, think of the joy you give to others'; at which he shook his head and left them to sort out what he really meant.

A very old friend of John Gray's, one of his converts, who had received some of his rare confidences, told a strange story which is recorded in *Two Friends*. One morning at about the time of the Oscar Wilde scandals John Gray, then a civil servant at the Foreign Office and a noted young poet and man about town, was walking up Coventry Street, near Leicester Square, when a stranger approached him and imparted to him some information which was utterly devastating. He made his way to the nearby church of Notre Dame de France, and knelt in prayer before the image of the Blessed Virgin. A few minutes later, as it seemed to him, he noticed that it was dark; and an old lady bearing keys came up to him and told him that she was going to lock up. It was night, and he had been on his knees all day.

The late William Muir was an old and sick man when he told this story, and because his memory was at times confused I did not feel that this recollection could be accepted as a fact. Later, I discovered the following passage in *Park,* which makes one wonder.

> Park served private masses (in the cathedral) all night. At one of them his fellow-server was the prince. At some time or other a stranger found him and rescued him with the brief words Come on. He then first realized his fatigue, if not exhaustion. For four hours his poor wrung heart had been filled with the love of Christ.

The author of *Park* takes for granted in his readers a certain familiarity with the texts and ceremonies of public worship in the Latin rite. This is a difficulty for some, but not a serious

one, I think. Most of these brief allusions or quotations can be understood from the context, or could be elucidated by inquiry of any instructed Catholic. (pp. 216-17)

Part of the fascination of the book lies in its descriptions of the Cotswold scenery which Gray knew so well from his yearly walking-holidays. The region is described as John Gray saw it—and he was a man who really *saw* things—yet as existing in a totally different era and civilisation.

> He made to put on his shoes. Cuan did it for him, and laced them. He walked towards one of the panels of the room; the man slid it open and he passed out of doors. He could not see the horses, but there was Cotswold, earth and sky; the familiar golden soil and cool green, the coloured pattern of fields, crop, stubble, grazing, early ploughing; hedges of quick, draped with clematis and tangled with black bryony. The eastern sky was a dense formation of thin, horizontal clouds. . . .

Park abounds in terse apothegms, as did Canon Gray's conversation, the fruit of his experience of life and his meditations.

> Remember every human being is unique; & the duration of time is best regarded as one second.

> For men of every position and every origin there is only one way to peace: purification of the heart and the proper direction of the energies.

The more one reads *Park* the more one finds in it. Some believe that *Park* can never be a popular book; as Mr Walter Shewring has said, 'it has the dryness of a patrician wine'. But popularity is relative. If David Jones's *In Parenthesis* can go into paperback, why not *Park*? (pp. 217-18)

> *Brocard Sewell, O. Carm., "On Re-reading 'Park',"*
> in The Aylesford Review, *Vol. VII, No. 4, Winter,*
> *1965 - Spring, 1966, pp. 215-18.*

MORAY McLAREN (essay date 1966)

[*In the following review of a new edition of* Park, *McLaren praises the novella as a minor classic.*]

Those familiar with the nineties know the name of John Gray (then a youthful layman) as the author of that strangely evocative "slim volume" of poems, *Silverpoints*. They may recall, too, that he is mentioned in *De Profundis* when Wilde bewails the fact that he had not remained friends with such people as John Gray instead of becoming infatuated with poor Alfred Douglas.

Edinburgh people of my generation will recall him as an elderly priest and constant attender at those unique literary salons of the 1920s and early 30s held by his friend André Raffalovich. They will recall, too, his economy of speech. He seldom said anything, but when he did every word was of memorable value.

By that time the highly self-disciplined and religiously rigid Canon Gray had all but given up writing. His extremely rare appearances in print, whether in verse (**The Long Road**) or in prose, as in [**Park**] . . . , all came out in guardedly limited editions. His words on the printed page were as arresting as his occasional verbal utterances. Gray said and wrote little, but even from the days of *Silverpoints* (a volume he tried to recall and destroy) his economy in words was strangely effective.

André Raffalovich, from a painting by A. Dampier May, 1886.

Though a product of the nineties he owed nothing to any other author of that or (I think) any other period.

It is this that makes **Park** as fascinating reading today as it was when it came out. Its prose has the effect of timelessness. No one would claim that it is a great work, but it is unique. Its appeal will inevitably not be large, but its resurrection even in this limited form is to be welcomed surely even by those who never knew John Gray or to whom his name is but a recondite memory.

The fantasy concerns a dream, but a dream with the alarming factuality of atmosphere of what one can only describe as a benevolent nightmare. Mungo Park, a priest in his sixties, is on a walking tour in the Cotswolds. Between Burford and Oxford the illusion of death and the projection of his sentient being into the remote future seizes him. The England in which he finds himself *looks* not very different from the England in which he had lived, but the inhabitants are changed. The English have gone and their place taken by Catholic negroes who are rulers over a kind of powerful theocracy. They accept Fr. Park's inexplicable reappearance from the remote past in their midst. On the whole they treat him well, accept the fact that he is a priest, and initiate him into something of their language and customs. He comes to the end of his walk believing (so it is hinted) that he is dying again—but he is only back in our "present."

What makes this nightmare fantasy credible is the extreme economy of the style in description and above all in dialogue.

There are practically no descriptions save of the familiar English landscape; and conversations are as laconic as they so often are in dreams. One believes that one is reading the account of a dream that has been actually dreamt.

But, of course, it was nothing of the kind; it was an effort of Gray's imagination, a work of art. Not an ambitious work of art, but, I repeat, unique. It ought not to be forgotten. (pp. 1356-57)

Moray McLaren, ''A Fantastic Story,'' in The Tablet, Vol. 220, No. 6602, December 3, 1966, pp. 1356-57.

BERNARD BERGONZI   (essay date 1966)

[*An English novelist, scholar, and critic, Bergonzi has written extensively on the works of H. G. Wells, T. S. Eliot, and other major figures in twentieth-century literature. In the following excerpt, originally published in 1966 as an introduction to* Park, *Bergonzi offers a survey of Gray's poetry and prose.*]

John Gray was once regarded as an archetypal young man of the 1890s. He was a friend of Oscar Wilde's, and was indeed rumoured to be the original of Wilde's Dorian Gray, though he denied it. He was a frequenter of some rather hot-house literary and theatrical *salons,* and his two books of poems, **Silverpoints** . . . and **Spiritual Poems** . . . , both designed by Charles Ricketts, were slender monuments of *fin de siècle* preciosity in book production. Ada Leverson remarked of **Silverpoints:** 'I remember looking at the poems of John Gray (then considered the incomparable poet of the age), when I saw the tiniest rivulet of text meandering through the very largest meadow of margin. I suggested to Oscar Wilde that he should go a step further than these minor poets; that he should publish a book *all* margin; full of beautiful unwritten thoughts. . . .' Gray was not, perhaps, considered quite so 'incomparable' a poet as Ada Leverson suggested: Lionel Johnson dismissed him as 'a sometimes beautiful oddity' and Yeats does not mention him in the *Autobiographies.* He remains a rather shadowy figure in the annals of the period.

Like Lionel Johnson, Ernest Dowson and Aubrey Beardsley, Gray was a convert to Catholicism; and his beliefs were reflected in **Spiritual Poems,** 'chiefly done out of several languages'. But Gray was significantly unlike many of his contemporaries in refusing to complete the pattern by dying young. In 1898 he made a radical break with the London fashionable world and literary scene, leaving it for good to become a student for the Catholic priesthood at the Scots College in Rome. . . . (p. 114)

[In] becoming a priest Gray did not feel any need to abandon completely his literary activities, though for many years he wrote only a few hymns and devotional verses. But towards the end of his life he published two more books of poems— mostly secular in content—**The Long Road** . . . and **Poems** . . . , followed in 1932 by a novel, **Park.** As a writer, and particularly as a poet, Gray, in his long if not highly productive literary career, showed an interesting blend of continuity and innovation. Several of the poems in **Silverpoints** can be dismissed as no more than elegant and decorative exercises in the customary idioms of the nineties, though all are marked with an unusual degree of verbal fastidiousness. A poem such as **'Les Demoiselles de Sauve',** to take a typical example, is like a skilful attempt at a verbal equivalent of a Beardsley drawing. But some of Gray's early poems show an unexpected degree

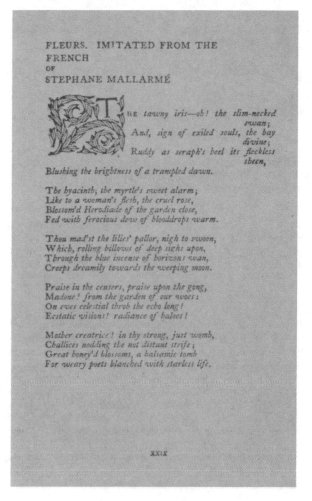

A page from Silverpoints.

of originality, as for instance **'Song of the Seedling'**, which attempts an empathetic penetration into vegetable life:

> Rain drops patter above my head—
>> Drip, drip, drip.
> To moisten the mould where my roots are fed—
>> Sip, sip, sip.
> No thought have I of the legged thing,
>> Of the worm no fear,
>> When the goal is near;
> Every moment my life has run,
> The livelong day I've not ceased to sing;
>> I must reach the sun, the sun.

This offers curious anticipations of some poems on similar themes by the late Theodore Roethke.

One of the oddest, and most successful, poems in *Silverpoints* is called simply **'Poem'**. Its way of shedding a sinister and bizarre light on an ordinary scene may recall that Gray was an early admirer—and translator—of Rimbaud and other French symbolists:

> Geranium, houseleek, laid in oblong beds
> On the trim grass. The daisies' leprous stain
> Is fresh. Each night the daisies burst again,
> Though every day the gardener crops their heads. . . .

In this sonnet one sees, I think, some of Gray's typical qualities as a poet: a laconic precision of language, an unusual, carefully manipulated verse movement, and a certain oddity of phrasing—as in 'the daisies' leprous stain'—which is Gray's most obviously ninety-ish trait.

In Gray's later poetry these qualities are substantially unchanged, though he had in the meantime become aware of the changes in poetic attitude associated with Pound and Eliot. There is a slightly strident air of modernity, for instance, in the final stanzas of **'Audi Alteram Partem'**, from *Poems* . . . :

> Unwinding its concentric crawl,
> a needle scrapes your epiderm,
> methodically as the firm's
> unnumbered patents foolproof all.
>
> Pay the price. Prolong the search
> for, right or wrong, what pleases us.
> Listen, the patriarch of Uz
> Is singing in the Temple church.

The last two lines seem to contain a distinct echo from Eliot's 'Sweeney among the Nightingales'. And one sees in the rhyme of 'us/Uz', recalling the 'burns/Burns' of **'Poem'**, that Gray preserved a taste for *rime riche* over a period of nearly forty years. Gray's essential gifts are very apparent in another late poem, **'Evening'**. Its terse but suggestive understatements and deliberate bareness combine effectively with a wavering but beautifully controlled movement (though I find the descent into conventional 'poetic' imagery in the final stanza rather a disappointment. . . . (pp. 115-17)

During the nineties Gray contributed a few short stories to the periodicals of the time; an interesting story called **'The Person in Question'**, a treatment of the *Doppelgänger* theme with a certain flavour of *Dorian Gray* about it, was first published a few years ago in a limited edition. But it was not until he wrote *Park* in the last years of his life that Gray fully displayed his remarkable talent as a prose writer: *Park,* it seems to me, is Gray's most sustained imaginative achievement, and a work that deserves a niche in the history of modern English fiction. Subtitled 'a fantastic story', *Park* is a curiously timeless work; though in one sense it looks back to a utopian romance like William Morris's *News from Nowhere,* and has clear affinities with H. G. Wells's *Time Machine* and other fantastic tales of the nineties, it is also reminiscent of the more sophisticated forms of present-day science fiction. This timeless quality is particularly evident in the style, on which much of the novel's claim to distinction must rest, a dry, mannered and deliberately understated mode of narration which recalls the laconic precision of the best of Gray's verse.

The eponymous hero of the book, the Revd. Mungo Park, is a Catholic priest of sixty who undisguisedly seems to embody many of Gray's own attributes. He is a professor of moral theology in a seminary who is spending a holiday on a solitary walking tour in the Cotswolds. On the road from Burford to Oxford he undergoes some kind of alarming experience whose nature is not revealed; but we are abruptly shown its effect on Park in the opening Paragraph:

> Mungo Park walked on in the belief, absurd as he knew it to be, that he had died. There are catastrophes (so he assured himself) where the victim need not add to his perplexity the pain of suspending his judgment. And this hypothesis was some relief to him here and now—if,

as in his anguish he thought, it *is* here & *is*
now. He dismissed as impertinent his own critical question: when did it happen and where
and how?

Park discovers that he is not dead, but he is in a transformed
England which affords him many surprises, and quite a few
puzzles. The original inhabitants have all disappeared, and the
country is now run by a theocracy of Catholic Negroes—an
aristocratic and highly cultivated race. Park is well treated by
them—after an initial unfortunate incident when he is peppered
in the legs with gunshot by an irresponsible gamekeeper—but
they regard him with a good deal of wariness, as he cannot
give what they would regard as a satisfactory account of his
origins. At first Park has to communicate with the Wapami,
as this new ruling race is called, in Latin, but eventually he is
able to learn something of their language; his principal frustration stems from his inability to practise his priestly office.
The Wapami do, indeed, suspect that he is a priest, like many
of themselves, but since he is unable to produce any tangible
proof of his ordination he is not permitted to function. A principal cause of difficulty between Park and his hosts is that they
employ a different system of arithmetical notation from the
decimal method, so that they do not accept that Park is telling
the truth, or even talking sense, when he insists that he is fifty-
nine years old. Eventually, since they cannot account for him,
nor he for himself, he is given the status of one officially 'dead',
which means that he has freedom of movement though subject
to certain legal disabilities; Park is now known as Drak. and
has a companion among the Wapami called Dlar (formerly
Dom Egid Reni of Reni), who is also legally a 'dead man',
since he was once condemned to death for an unnamed offence
and then reprieved.

Park makes a variety of discoveries about this new world, like
the original Mungo Park, the late eighteenth-century Scot who
also made explorations among Negroes, though those were
savages whilst the Wapami are an eminently civilised race.
The Wapami are organised as a feudal society leading a generally pastoral existence, though (as in *News from Nowhere*)
there seems to be a certain amount of technological organisation
behind the scenes. (pp. 118-20)

[Park] contains immediate echoes of the fantastic fiction of the
1880s and 1890s. The division of the story between the Wapami
on the earth and the vanquished white race living beneath
recalls Wells's *The Time Machine*, though Gray does not attempt the unmitigated horror of Wells's story. Again, the notion of a cataclysm that has overthrown traditional society,
replacing it with a utopian or pastoral order, is manifest in
such works as *News from Nowhere* or Richard Jefferies's *After
London*. And the theme of a race living permanently below
the ground has come into greater prominence in the science
fiction of our own day, reflecting a preoccupation with nuclear
war, as, for instance, in James Blish's *A Case of Conscience*
where it is the threat, which did not materialise, of war which
has driven city populations underground, where they have lost
the desire to emerge (this, too, is a novel which has a Catholic
priest as its hero). Gray was original, however, in reversing
the customary racial paradigm and making the black races
superior to the white. Gray's sister wrote of him that he 'was
deeply interested in the black man (he was a keen anthropologist) and used to say, although he was a white man he was
black inside, and foretold in a general way that the black man
would rule'.

Like all good writers of fantasy, Gray sustains his imaginative
world by preserving an air of absolute matter-of-factness; we
are given plausible-sounding details of the vocabulary and
grammar of Bapama (the Wapami language), and occasional
footnotes remind us of the difference between Wapami nu-
meration and our own. If the story seems obscure in places on
a first reading, it is because Gray presents his narrative solely
through the dramatised consciousness of Mungo Park, and events
are presented as they impinge upon his sensibility, not in the
order which would best form a coherent objective picture of
what is happening. Gray displays a Jamesian austerity in sup-
pressing overt authorial comment, but through the eyes of Park
he occasionally offers some haunting, strongly visual descriptive passages, as in the account of Ini'in's garden, which is an
imagist poem in prose. . . . (pp. 121-22)

Much of the book's singular flavour is found in the numerous
conversations, laconic yet mannered, which in their glancing
obliquity have a slight hint of the dialogue of Ivy Compton-
Burnett. (p. 122)

Like most modern fantasies that dramatise the problem of loss
of identity, *Park* can be called Kafka-esque. But there is little
sense of existential anguish in Gray's narrative . . . ; one has
rather the calm air of a scholastic disputation perceived with
the weird consistency of a dream. (And a dream-narrative is
what, ultimately, *Park* turns out to be.) *Park* is a puzzling
story, but without deep mythic power; one recalls *Alice in
Wonderland* rather than *The Castle*. It is both Gray's strength
and weakness as a writer that he is above all a stylist; his effects
are, as it were, on the surface, and though there are hints of
symbolic overtones, I do not think one could usefully subject
Park to a large-scale symbolic explication. But the surface of
Park is of an unusually fascinating kind: Gray had a remarkable
feeling for words, and a very curious imagination, and in this
novel he achieved a unique and satisfying fusion of these qualities. (p. 123)

> *Bernard Bergonzi, "John Gray," in his* The Turn
> of a Century: Essays on Victorian and Modern En-
> glish Literature, *Barnes & Noble Books, 1973, pp.
> 114-23.*

GEOFFREY GRIGSON (essay date 1967)

[*Grigson is an English poet and critic. He is often associated with
a group of poets, including Louis MacNeice, Stephen Spender,
and W. H. Auden, who came to prominence in the 1930s and who
published their work in Grigson's poetry journal* New Verse. *This
journal was among the most influential of the 1930s, both for the
quality of its content and for the outspoken critical opinions of
its editor. Grigson urged his contemporaries to avoid obscurity
of both thought and language in their writing and to strive for
precise observations precisely expressed. "Report well," Grigson
has advised the modern poet. "Begin with objects and events; a
stone begets vision, and there's nothing to tell except truth, which
'can never be told so as to be understood and not be believed,'
and there is no other way of telling it." In the following excerpt
from a review of* Two Friends, *edited by Brocard Sewell (see
Additional Bibliography), Grigson summarizes Gray's career and
comments on what he considers Gray's poetic masterpiece, "The
Flying Fish."*]

Reasons for reading about John Gray are because one knew
him (which I didn't) or knew of him in the legendary era of
his Roman Catholic priesthood in Edinburgh, with his odd other
half of the legend, André Raffalovich, living nearby in wealthy
aesthetic pietism; because one admires some of his writings

(which I do); and because he exemplifies a double problem, of life, and of 'modernism' in literature growing out of the equally queer stuff of 'decadence'. (p. 177)

In 1893 Wilde paid for the printing of Gray's first poems, *Silverpoints*, widest margins, binding and typography by Ricketts, period confections (including translations from Verlaine, Rimbaud, etc.) not without rhythmic and verbal intimations of a reality which would be long delayed.

After *Silverpoints*, he wrote affected religious poems; also—with Raffalovich—an Ibsenish-ninetyish play about blackmail in society. Then 1895, the Wilde Year, during which 'every suitcase in London was packed for instant flight'. The trial made Raffalovich write a book on homosexuality, and he, too, now became a Catholic. Gray also left the Foreign Office, and became a candidate for orders, not long before Pierre Louÿs married a different bride, the poet Heredia's daughter. . . . Both had retreated out of decadence, and their youth, renunciators, far from Wilde's London or Louÿs's Paris. (p. 178)

In another way there was no retreat, but an advance out of soft into hard language. Small books came out rather privately, and two of them matter. About *Park* . . . , an admirably written story of cultured, philosophic (Catholic) Negroes who have conquered England and breed horses on Cotswold, while the English live a mass rodent life in Tube tunnels, contributors [to *Two Friends*] have something to say. About the poems in *The Long Road* . . . little is said, and in nineteen pages on Gray [see excerpt dated 1961], Mr Iain Fletcher does not even mention Gray's long, hard, sharp, strange single masterpiece, **'The Flying Fish'**, one of the good 'modern' poems of our century. This is a critical feat like assessing Eliot without 'The Waste Land' or Coleridge without 'The Ancient Mariner'.

In this poem held tightly together in rhyming quatrains by its tone, which is quizzing, inconsequent and consequent, by its scenery and geography, mid-oriental without being specific and yet precise (reminding one of a story by Conrad placed where Chinese and Malaysian meet), by its mineral or consonantal collection of words, its slightly ironic, archaic 'modernism', one is without preamble put into the company of Hang the buccaneer:

> Myself am Hang, the buccaneer,
> whom children love and brave men fear,
> master of courage, come what come,
> master of craft and called Sea-scum.
>
> Student of wisdom and waterways,
> course of moons and the birth of days:
> to him in whose heart all things be,
> I bring my story from the sea.

Hang quickly introduces himself, his guise on the quay of the merchants, Hang undisguised on his pirate junk and in his palace and his gardens in the island sea.

> So cotton rags lays Hang aside;
> Lays bare the sailor's gristly hide;
> he wraps his body in vests of silk,
> ilk is as beautiful as ilk.

He enumerates, leaving the description of himself, the six strange birds which fly in the farthest sea:

> I mind the fifth, I forget the fourth,
> save that it comes from east and north;
> the fifth is an orange white-billed duck;
> he diveth for fish like the god of Luck;

> He hath never a foot on which to stand,
> for water yields and he loves not land.
> This is the end of many words,
> save one, concerning marvellous birds.

Save one: Hang, having dealt with marvellous birds, now enumerates marvellous fish, beginning with the dolphin and the swordfish; and ending with that one he hasn't mentioned, since 'The last strange fish is the last strange bird'—the Flying Fish, whose bitter enemies are the other five fowl and the other five fishes:

> In sea and sky he hath no peace,
> for the five strange fish are his enemies,
> And the five strange fowls keep watch for him,
> they know him well by his crystal gleam.
>
> Oftwhiles, sir Sage, on my junk's white deck,
> have I seen this fish-bird come to wreck;
> oftwhiles (fair deck) 'twixt bow and poop,
> have I seen that piteous sky fish stoop.
>
> Scaled bird, how his snout and gills dilate,
> all quivering and roseate!
> He pants in crystal and mother-of-pearl,
> while his body shrinks and his pinions furl.
>
> His beauty passes like bubbles blown;
> the white bright bird is a fish of stone.
> The bird so fair, for its putrid sake,
> is flung to the dogs in the junk's white wake.

The sage, in the second part, interprets the Flying Fish as a symbol of aspiration born of fear; though the Fish remains and does not lose its shining solidity in the abstract.

In the throbbing heart of this farthest sea the fish says, in his own iridescent heart, how splendid are his eyes, how his back 'has the secret of every shell': it is the ugly birds who devise his ill.

Not wishing to be a son of air, he wishes nevertheless to be rid of water:

> All his hope is a fear-whipped whim,
> all directions are one to him.
> There are seekers of wisdom no less absurd,
> Son Hang, than thy fish that would be a bird.

Texture, tone, movement—though one may see the poem as a distanced image of Gray's own life, all lives of aspiration—sufficiently mark **'The Flying Fish'** and on this level make it entirely acceptable and memorable. On the interior level, or in its entirety, one sees how the poem relates to the image of *Park;* but in that novel no dead-fish-and-bird is flung contemptuously to the congers: a dream instead is realized, the ugly have retreated into their holes, even if the vision in the end is withdrawn.

Otherwise John Gray is a poet—so far as we have all his poems?—of now and then sparkling oddments or images:

> You see fleet and fair
> gazelles by hippogriffins torn,
> a wild curvetting unicorn
> across a cherry-coloured morn.

But enough of him there is to establish an individuality of style and imagination. . . . Like Ivor Gurney he is one of the half-hidden poets who cannot be left out of this century's account. (pp. 179-82)

Geoffrey Grigson, "Dorian Gray: John Gray," in his The Contrary View: Glimpses of Fudge and Gold, *Rowman and Littlefield, 1974, pp. 177-82.*

JAMES G. NELSON   (essay date 1971)

[Nelson is an American critic and educator. In the following excerpt, he discusses Gray's translations in Silverpoints.*]*

Even more than [Arthur] Symons' *Silhouettes,* John Gray's *Silverpoints* expressed the French poetic idiom in English. Not since John Payne's *Songs of Life and Death,* published in 1877, had England produced a book of verse so wholly French in its orientation. (p. 198)

Gray's attentiveness to French poetry and French literary customs of the day is most apparent in his translations—or what he preferred to call "imitations"—of Baudelaire, Verlaine, and others. But it can also be seen in his practice in *Silverpoints* of dedicating each of his poems to an individual—**"Heart's Desmesne"** to Verlaine, **"Mishka"** to Henri Teixeira de Mattos, **"Summer Past"** to Wilde, **"On a Picture"** to Pierre Louÿs— and his use of epigraphs from the French symbolists. Gray chose the epigraph to the volume ". . . *en composant des acrostiches indolents"* from Verlaine's "Langueur"; and he links two companion poems, the "Did we not, Darling, you and I" and the "Lean back, and press the pillow deep" by two epigraphs from Jules Laforgue's "IX" from *Derniers Vers,* an ironic poem about love.

It is in his twelve "imitations" that one is best able to judge Gray's sensitivity to and affinity for French symbolist poetry. Although he takes great liberties at times with the originals by altering words and shifting the emphasis so as to create effective English poems to his own taste, on the whole he captures the French remarkably well. For instance, Gray develops *"Le Chevalier Malheur"* in a slightly different way from Verlaine by not telling us that the knight is kind until we see that he has renewed the speaker's heart. Verlaine begins the poem, *"Bon chevalier masqué,"* but Gray opens with "Grim visor'd cavalier." Gray describes the lance, which Verlaine does not characterize, as "unpitying." By omitting a line in which Verlaine has the knight say *"Tandis qu'il attestait sa loi d'une voix dure,"* he retains the original impression of his mysterious silence. Verlaine's closing line, *"Au moins, prudence! Car c'est bon pour une fois"* was spoken to him by a policeman the day he was released from prison. Gray alters the tone and impact when he says in less familiar and more explicit words, "Once only can the miracle avail.—Be wise!"

Although Gray loses some of the richness of imagery and meaning in his rendering of Mallarmé's *"Les Fleurs,"* considering how difficult Mallarmé is to translate, Gray's *"Fleurs"* is good. Gray omits the first stanza, in which Mallarmé uses compressed imagery to describe a former relationship between the stars, representing the absolute, and the earth. Gray, by his addition of "starless" to the last line of the poem, "For weary poets blanched with starless life," may allude to this symbolism of stars to indicate man's separation from the absolute. Gray's line, "Blushing the brightness of a trampled dawn," imitating *"Que rougit la pudeur des aurores foulées"* shows how successfully Gray can recreate Mallarmé's words. He loses, however, the impression of light in *"le myrte à l'adorable éclair"* and *"un sang farouche et radieux"* and omits the sobbing of the lilies. In the last stanza he alters the image: *"Calices balançant la future fiole, / De grandes fleurs avec la balsamique Mort"* to "Chalices nodding the not distant

strife; / Great honey'd blossoms, a balsamic tomb." Mallarmé's figure of death pouring from the flowers is superior to Gray's tombs.

Of Gray's several excellent translations of Baudelaire, *"A Une Madone"* is the freest. Although Gray retains the sadism in this poem, he makes the man and the woman less fierce than they are in Baudelaire. He omits the only reference to the man's physical desire, four lines beginning: *"Ta Robe, ce sera mon Désir, frémissant. . . ."* He also leaves out the content of the line describing the hatred which the serpent jealousy breeds in him: *"Ce monstre tout gonflé de haine et de crachats."* By changing *"En Vapeurs montera mon Esprit orageux"* to "So shall my soul in plaintive fumes arise," he continues to soften the picture of the speaker. Gray's lover is a "Torturer filled with pain" as Baudelaire's is a *"Bourreau plein de remords"*; but Gray's is "sick with fear" at the same time as Baudelaire's is *"comme un jongleur insensible."* The niche in which Mary is to stand is *"d'azur et d'or tout émaillée"* in Baudelaire but "with mercy stained, and streaked with gold" in Gray. Baudelaire says, in an image of shoes, that the speaker's *"Respect"* will be *"humiliés"* by Mary's feet. Gray omits the idea of humiliation. Gray's Mary will "smile supreme" when she crushes the serpent, but Baudelaire's *"railles."* Where Baudelaire describes Mary as a *"sommet blanc et neigeux,"* Gray speaks of her "pitying eyes."

Gray's care in retaining the basic shape and movement of the French poems in his imitations, his painstaking efforts, for instance, to arrange the phrases within his stanzas in much the same order the French writers used, and his attempts to recreate the patterns of sound in the French poems as far as possible by substituting equivalent patterns in English, suggest a very serious and purposeful desire to convey an accurate impression of French symbolist poetry to the English reader. Under Gray's sensitive touch, the imitations, harmonizing with his original poems in themes and in style, form a fitting close to *Silverpoints.* (pp. 206-07)

James G. Nelson, "The Bodley Head Poets: Poisonous Honey and English Blossoms," in his The Early Nineties: A View from the Bodley Head, Cambridge, Mass.: Harvard University Press, 1971, pp. 184-220.*

JAMES G. NELSON   (essay date 1974)

[In the following excerpt, Nelson explains the aesthetic tradition in English literature which culminated in the poetry of the 1890s and considers Gray's Silverpoints *in the poetic context of this era.]*

The poetry of the nineties in England never has been sufficiently valued by students and critics of literature. Of the several reasons one legitimately might advance to explain the lack of interest in such poets of the period as Ernest Dowson, Lionel Johnson, John Gray, Arthur Symons, even the early W. B. Yeats, is the failure on the part of readers to understand the nature of the experience conveyed in the poems. In this essay I should like to explore briefly a sampling of poems from the canon of Gray, Dowson, and Johnson—poets I consider typical of the aesthetic milieu of the nineties—in an effort to arrive at a better understanding of the aesthetic experience so central to the nineties poetic tradition.

The most interesting poets of the nineties are a part of an aesthetic tradition which extends from the Romantics, especially John Keats, through Dante Gabriel Rossetti and other

Pre-Raphaelite poets into the so-called decadent nineties. Although the aesthetic pronouncements of John Ruskin and Matthew Arnold in such influential works as *Modern Painters*, vol. II, The *Stones of Venice,* the essays in *Culture and Anarchy,* and those such as "The Study of Poetry," were influential so far as the aestheticism of the nineties is concerned, it was the works of Walter Pater, especially the Pater of the early essays—the "Wordsworth" and those collected in *The Renaissance*—which were crucial in the development of the aesthetic stance of the nineties poets.

However, important to both the aestheticism of Ruskin, Arnold, and Pater was the concept of "coming to life," of, as Pater stated it in its extremest form, burning "always with this hard, gemlike flame." Culture and art were, in particular, a means of rising above the low-pulsed, death-in-life condition of narrow-minded Puritanism and Philistinism which characterized Victorian society. Through what Arnold called "curiosity," that "desire after the things of the mind simply for their own sakes and for the pleasure of seeing them as they are," one could live a truly vital, more intensely satisfying life. And although in "Sweetness and Light," Arnold subordinated this desire "'to render an intelligent being yet more intelligent'" to what he called "the moral and social passion for doing good," the poets of the nineties, sickened and repelled by the materialism and vulgarity of late Victorian society, largely ignored Arnold's "moral and social passion."

Instead, they sought through a highly personal, eccentric pursuit of art and culture to attain what Pater called "this fruit of a quickened, multiplied consciousness," . . . a heightened sense of aesthetic awareness by being present "at the focus where the greatest number of vital forces unite in their purest energy." . . . Rather than seeking a multiplied consciousness, an Hellenic breadth of view through an involvement with life, an altruistic effort to share one's "passion" with others, the nineties poets, attentive to the life styles of such figures as Rossetti and Pater as well as to the aesthetic views conveyed in their writings, retreated into a realm of art and personal emotions which served as the sole source of intensity and life. Their moments of intense perception, of vital awareness resulting from an often fleeting encounter with beauty, became the center of many of their poems. (pp. 223-24)

Such a moment of perception is Keatsian, one might say, in its intensity, in its ecstatic sense of being alive. These moments of "coming to life" through an encounter with beauty are crucial to one's understanding of the essential nature of the aesthetic experience embodied in much of the best poetry of the nineties. Intensity is at the very heart of the aesthetic process of burning "always with this hard, gemlike flame." (p. 224)

Often in the poetry of Keats, Rossetti, and the poets of the nineties as well as in Pater's own portrait of "Lady Lisa," concrete beauty is manifest in terms of a beautiful woman, often a "femme fatale"; the experience of the vital moment being seen as the result of an encounter of a mentally prepared, "sensitized" person with the woman. For instance, in Keats's "Lamia," Lycius, having "grown wearied of their Corinth talk," has separated from his companions. As he walks alone through the evening landscape, "his phantasy" is "lost, where reason fades, / In the calm'd twilight of Platonic shades" (II. 232-36). At the delicious sound of Lamia's voice, he turns: "And soon his eyes had drunk her beauty up, / Leaving no drop in the bewildering cup, / And still the cup was full." . . . (p. 225)

This prototypical encounter with beauty remained a favorite means of conveying the nineties' experience with beauty, but, oftentimes, as in the poetry of John Gray, with some distinctly "modern" and "decadent" touches which are alien to the poems of Keats. For instance, in **"Mishka"** . . . , Gray conveys the typical moment of aesthetically satisfying, erotically intense pleasure through an hallucinatory state in which images blend into one another. **"Mishka,"** reminiscent in many respects of the *symboliste* mode in vogue at the time in France, features a bear who is a mingling of the human and the animal in the sense that he is also a "poet," has fists, and appears "white like a hunter's son." In stanzas two and three, Mishka encounters the *femme fatale* who appropriately enough for a bear appears as the "honey-child," that is, a bee. Surrealistically monstrous in form, the honey-child summons the bear:

> Mishka! Mishka, as turned to stone,
> Hears no word else, nor in anywise
> Can see aught save the monster's eyes.

Fascinated, Mishka follows the bee "into her lair / Dragged in the net of her yellow hair"—a sequence of events which suggests that the bee not only faintly is associated with Arnold's "sweetness" or beauty but also with her Swiftian opposite, the spider. Her thighs each a "mound of honey, the exotic bee, her hips vibrating, sings Mishka into an Edenic realm which serves as the counterpart of Lamia's "purple-lined palace of sweet sin." Although there are, as in Keats, ominous signs and sounds—the monstrous form of the bee, the scream of "a far bird-note" and "the triple coil" of the honey-child's hair which is "wound" round Mishka's throat—the bear, who has now succumbed to the blandishments of the paradise as his enchantress strokes "his limbs with a humming sound," maintains his intense, pleasurable state of sensuous ecstasy, Gray concluding his poem with two quiet "correspondences":

> The honey-child is an olive tree,
> The voice of birds and the voice of flowers,
> Each of them all and all the hours,
> The honey-child is a wingèd bee
> her touch is a perfume, a melody.

That Gray concludes his poem with no impulse, as was habitual in the case of Keats, to awaken his dreamer, suggests, perhaps, that the aesthetic experience has, indeed, become an end in itself, a moment of life in the midst of death one wishes at all costs to sustain.

A far more sinister moment of aesthetically generated intensity is objectified in Gray's Swinburnesque **"The Barber,"** a poem in which the poet draws on the profession which throughout history—especially in decadent societies—has dealt in the most extreme form of artifice, that of improving on nature through the use of cosmetics, wigs, masks, and strange dyes. A forerunner of Aubrey Beardsley's barber, Carrousel, Gray's artificer is a symbol of the decadent artist whose love of *maquillage* leads to madness. Dreaming that he was a barber beneath whose hands went "oh! manes extravagant" and "many a mask / Of many a pleasant girl," the poet in his strangely beautiful yet terrible world of sleep runs the gamut of decadent moods, devices, and motifs.

Like a master of all the plastic arts, he dreams of transforming with ecstatic joy his pleasant clientele—

> I moulded with my hands
> The mobile breasts, the valley; and the waist

I touched; and pigments reverently placed
Upon their thighs in sapient spots and stains,
Beryls and crysolites and diaphanes,
And gems whose hot harsh names are never said.
I was a masseur; and my fingers bled
With wonder as I touched their awful limbs.

Shifting abruptly to the present tense in what becomes increasingly an hallucinatory situation beyond the control of the dreamer, the poet-barber beholds the last of his "pale mistresses," his ultimate *objets d'art,* come to life in a nightmare of intensely realized surrealistic buffoonery:

So, at the sound, the blood of me stood cold.
Thy chaste hair ripened into sullen gold.
The throat, the shoulders, swelled and were uncouth.
The breasts rose up and offered each a mouth.
And on the belly pallid blushes crept,
That maddened me, until I laughed and wept.

Although **"Mishka"** and **"The Barber"** follow the paradigmatic form of such poems of Keats as "La Belle Dame sans Merci" and "Lamia," what happens after the encounter with beauty differs significantly. Whereas in Keats the intensely pleasurable encounter leads to an awakening which is rude and often shattering, in Gray the encounter, whatever its outcome, avoids a return to reality. With the exception of his "To Autumn," Keats's poetic objectifications of intense experience led him into the process of conceptualization or thought, to what Keats himself called philosophizing. If much of his early poetry is free from this process, it is so because as he suggests in the "Epistle to John Hamilton Reynolds," he "dare not yet" at so early a stage in his poetic apprenticeship "philosophise" [sic]. . . . In other words, in his mature poetry Keats's encounter with beauty leads beyond pure feeling and emotion, the aesthetic experience, itself, to thought and a heightened awareness of the meaning of reality, ugly, and aesthetically unsatisfying though it be. Gray, especially in poems like **"Mishka"** and **"The Barber"** values the emotion, the mood, the psychological state resulting from the moment of encounter for its own sake.

In his notable contribution to what had by the nineties become a veritable "tradition" of poems on paintings, appropriately entitled **"On a Picture,"** Gray effectively demonstrates how the contemplation of beauty can give rise to intensity of feeling and simultaneously create a mood which is aesthetically pleasurable and salutary in and of itself. A verse portrait of John Everett Millais' famous Pre-Raphaelite painting of Ophelia, **"On a Picture"** conveys a calm but intensely felt response to the death of a beautiful woman which enables the observer to loose himself from the world and, like Ophelia, drift silently, painlessly into an eternal state of "noble sloth." The persona views Ophelia as an embodiment of ultimate stasis, a moment beyond time when death as well as all forms of beauty embalmed in art are intensely inviting and most to be desired. Although Ophelia's "maidly hands look up, in noble sloth / To take the blossoms of her scattered wreath,"

No weakest ripple lives to kiss her throat,
Nor dies in meshes of untangled hair;
No movement stirs the floor of river moss.

Until some furtive glimmer gleam across
Voluptuous mouth, where even teeth are bare,
And gild the broidery of her petticoat. . . .

The nature of the aesthetic experience herein revealed not only involves the sterile, passive contemplation of beauty one associates with the Paterian culture-observer, but also the morbidly erotic element which gives the aestheticism of the nineties its decadent flavor. (pp. 225-27)

James G. Nelson, *"The Nature of Aesthetic Experience in the Poetry of the Nineties: Ernest Dowson, Lionel Johnson, and John Gray,"* in English Literature in Transition, *Vol. 17, No. 4, 1974, pp. 223-32.**

CHRISTOPHER S. NASSAAR (essay date 1974)

[*In the following excerpt from his* Into the Demon Universe, *a study of Oscar Wilde, Nassaar uses Gray's "Poem" as an illustration of what he considers the evil nature of the poet of* Silverpoints.]

John Gray, in the poems that make up his volume of decadent verse, *Silverpoints* . . . , has for one of his main themes the identification and celebration of the evil within the human soul. Here is one of the best of his poems, titled simply **"Poem"**:

Geranium, houseleek, laid in oblong beds
On the trim grass. The daisies' leprous stain
Is fresh. Each night the daisies burst again,
Though every day the gardener crops their heads.

A wistful child, in foul unwholesome shreds,
Recalls some legend of a daisy chain
That makes a pretty necklace. She would fain
Make one, and wear it, if she had some threads.

Sun, leprous flowers, foul child. The asphalt burns.
The garrulous sparrows perch on metal Burns.
Sing! Sing! they say, and flutter with their wings.
He does not sing, he only wonders why
He is sitting there. The sparrows sing. And I
Yield to the strait allure of simple things.

In the first stanza, nature is represented as evil. The gardener attempts to suppress and control the evil daisies, but every night they burst again and their leprous stain remains fresh. In the second stanza, a child recalls some vague, romantic legend about daisies—Wordsworth's "To the Daisy" poems come to mind here—but the child, ironically, is foul and yearns to make "a pretty necklace" of the leprous flowers, and wear it around her neck. In the third stanza, the life-giving sun, leprous flowers, and foul child unite to form an unholy trinity. The sun is scorching and it makes the asphalt—a symbol of civilization—burn with its oppressive heat. The metal statue of Burns is totally out of place in this un-Romantic setting, but the garrulous sparrows, symbols of uncontrolled nature, are quite at home, and they sing as they perch on the silent statue of the Romantic poet.

This garden setting is entirely in accord with the evil nature of John Gray, and he ends his poem by yielding happily "to the strait allure of simple things." In **"Poem,"** Gray celebrates evil, locates it both within himself and in the outside world, and embraces it. Almost a century before, Wordsworth had "heard a thousand blended notes, / While in a grove I sate reclined," and had said that "To her fair works did Nature link / The human soul that through me ran." Gray's human soul links with a nature that is the antithesis of Wordsworth's—a nature thrilling with evil beauty. (pp. 60-2)

Christopher S. Nassaar, *"The Darkening Lens,"* in his Into the Demon Universe: A Literary Exploration of Oscar Wilde, *Yale University Press, 1974, pp. 37-72.**

LINDA C. DOWLING (essay date 1977)

[*In the following excerpt, Dowling analyzes* Silverpoints *as a critique of the fin-de-siècle poetic style.*]

Published after frustrating delay in March of 1893, John Gray's *Silverpoints* at once became an icon of the *fin de siècle*. Its fastidious italic type, unusual dimensions (11 x 22 cm), and gold-stippled binding (designed by Charles Ricketts) seemed to express the attempt in the period to develop a new aesthetic. (p. 159)

[A] tone of ironic dismissal is heard in contemporary reviews of the book. Frank Harris finds only one poem (**"The Barber"**) to come up to the binding; for the rest, "Mr. John Gray has thrown down a bomb into poetical dovecots that turns out on inspection to be merely a squib" [see excerpt dated 1893]. Richard Le Gallienne, in his usual breathless prose, declares the format of the volume to be "of a far-sought deliciousness," but is relieved to report that "Mr. Gray cannot accomplish that gloating abstraction from the larger life of humanity which marks the decadent." As the nineties receded, commentators tended to treat *Silverpoints* more seriously, but they continued to treat it as an icon, a two-dimensional symbol of *fin de siècle* dandyism and daintiness. In their attempt to dismiss French Decadence as adolescent posturing without true disciples in England, Harris and Le Gallienne skimmed the poems and pronounced them not decadent. Modern critics have passed over the poems and studied Gray's life instead. The third dimension of *Silverpoints*—its poetry—has been, until very recently, all but ignored.

Gray's plight, of course, is one shared by Wilde, Johnson, Beardsley, and other artists of the period. To a certain extent, a disproportionate emphasis on lives rather than works is part of the price for their common concern with fashioning a self, with what Yeats called the perfection of the life. Like Yeats, Gray was powerfully influenced by Wilde and Wilde's ideas, and what glimpses one gets of this rather obscure young man suggest that he, too, tried to create a suitable persona for himself. The "mask" Gray chose was an imitation of Wilde's own, as we see in his speech **"The Modern Actor"**: there he ends his impressionistic description of a play with a personification of its spirit, a creature who "lurks and listens—a very young and beautiful man, with long grey hair—or speeds to and forth with such rapidity that the *lines of his loveliness* are lost, and he seems a *poisonous scarlet mist*!" To John Gray, a carpenter's son from Woolwich who by his talent for languages rose to become a librarian in the Foreign Office, the glamorous Wilde was "my loved master."

But though—or perhaps because—he studied Wilde and dressed the part of the exquisite young dandy, Gray did not achieve any particularly distinctive personality. Possessing neither the flair for self-advertisement of a Symons or a Le Gallienne nor the compelling presence of a Yeats or a Johnson, he was often overlooked: the newspapers complained that his speech before the Playgoers' Club was barely audible; the biographers of the nineties record none of his *mots*, merely his presence at the Crown or the Cheshire Cheese; and Michael Orme remembers that wherever Gray went, he was usually mistaken for the actor Gordon Craig. We find a more memorable version of this obscure yet polished persona—remote, impersonal, fastidious, and faintly mocking—when we turn to Gray's poems. Indeed,

it is in the poetic speakers of *Silverpoints* that this elusive figure of the nineties creates his most distinctive self, embodying a poetic perspective which not only differed remarkably from those of his fellow Rhymers but which significantly extended the range of the late-Romantic aesthetic idiom.

Though the Rhymers' Club was hardly a monolithic organization—the only thing that could be said of all its members, grumbled Yeats, was that they were too many—modern critics have perceived certain shared formal characteristics and themes in the work of its members. As Yeats himself remarked, the poetry of Symons, Johnson, Dowson, and the early Yeats is the poetry of longing and complaint. Deliberately limited in scope and emotional tonality, it celebrates the beauty and peace of the ideal or dream world even while lamenting the tragic evanescence of any human vision of it. Some of Gray's poems—**"Complaint"** and **"Summer Past,"** for example—have obvious affinities with this poetry of nuance and regret, but most of the poems in *Silverpoints* avoid the mode of *la chanson grise* and range eclectically from a mannered imitation of Elizabethan love sonnets (**"Lady Evelyn," "A Halting Sonnet"**) to a sort of prediction of modernist Imagism (**"Poem"**). The collection's tone of dandiacal aloofness, its avoidance of statement or commitment, and (to borrow Pound's splendid image) its Sargasso Sea eclecticism, all locate *Silverpoints* within the poetic tradition of the *fin de siècle*.

Like his friend Aubrey Beardsley, however, Gray was at the same time making an original contribution to that literary movement, for Gray like Beardsley is a critic of the styles he adopts. Just as Beardsley's designs for the J. M. Dent *Morte D'Arthur* constitute a satiric critique of Pre-Raphaelite art, so the poems of *Silverpoints* reflect critically on the assumptions nineties poets inherited from Aestheticism, for Gray's major concern was to confront the pretensions of a newly autonomous Art with those of a newly devalued Nature. In this context John Gray can be seen as participating in an essentially internal critique of Aestheticism, one conducted by men utterly indifferent to the jibes of a Gilbert or a Du Maurier. The process of self-conscious revaluation may be said to have begun with Pater's suppression of the Conclusion to *The Renaissance* and to have ended with Pound's *Mauberley*.

Modern critics have typically taken the strictures of Yeats and Pound on the attitudinizing, the rhetorical "stilts," and the "muzziness" of nineties verse as the beginning of the modernist direction in poetry. But in doing so they have overlooked the participation of the *fin de siècle* writers themselves in the process of self-criticism. In the same way, the myth of the "tragic generation" has tended to emphasize the doomed sincerity of nineties artists while ignoring the playfulness and self-parody that inform their work. Wilde's *Importance of Being Earnest*, Beerbohm's "Defense of Cosmetics," and Johnson's "A Decadent's Lyric" are not peripheral ironies operating at the expense of the *fin de siècle* movement in literature; they lie at the center of its aesthetic. Like the adventures of Adoré Floupette in France a few years before, they indicate the crucial function in late-Romantic literature of self-parody as criticism.

Borrowed from the ironic mode of Flaubert, Baudelaire, and Laforgue, tha dandiacal stance of passionate, analytical detachment is the characteristic posture taken before aesthetic experience by Gray's poetic speakers. In **"Les Demoiselles de Sauve,"** for example, the speaker observes three self-conscious ladies who, passing elegantly through a crutched-up old orchard, pose three late-Romantic attitudes toward nature—Whistlerian ("pale blossoms, looking on proud Jacqueline, /

Blush to the colour of her fingertips''), Symbolist (''high-crested Berthe discerns, with slant, clinched eyes, / Amid the leaves pink faces of the skies''), and Paterian (''Ysabeau . . . presses, voluptuous, to her bursting lips, / With backward stoop, a bunch of eglantine''). But oblivious to any reality beyond self, the demoiselles de Sauve—daughters of the artifice that long ago in another garden undid nature—are not safe in the wild; they and the attitudes they embody are trespassing in nature, as Gray indicates:

> Courtly ladies through the orchard pass;
> Bow low, as in lords' halls; and springtime grass
> Tangles a snare to catch the tapering toe.

This is nature watching art's narcissistic absorption in itself. And even as the tangled complexities of the orchard are treated as a mere backdrop by the artificial ladies, nature is poised to revenge herself by entrapping art's mincing pretensions and overthrowing its careful form.

Throughout *Silverpoints* Gray dramatizes his sense of the dangerous limitations of late-Romantic Aestheticism by pitting its inflated notion of Art against a subtly rebellious nature. Plants, in particular, are endowed with identities and experiences of their own, as when, in **"Song of the Seedling,"** Gray allows us to participate empathetically in organic process:

> Rain drops patter above my head—
>   Drip, drip, drip.
> To moisten the mould where my roots are fed—
>   Sip, sip, sip.

Whether they inhabit a Blakean world of innocence and energy, as here, or the snarled jungle of Darwinian conflict we find in **"The Vines"**—

> Bramble clutches for his bride,
> Woodbine, with her gummy hands,
> All his horny claws expands,
> She has withered in his grasp

—natural objects in *Silverpoints* possess an extraordinary degree of will and consciousness. Gray's lyrics, like many of the poems Yeats wrote during the same period, are remarkable for their vivid and oftentimes disturbing sense of nature's separate life. Even apparently conventional personification contributes to this effect, for images like ''Woodbine, with her gummy hands'' distance nature, rendering her less familiar, not more. Gray's characterization of the unknowable, independent life of seed, shoot, and flower is another expression of his sense of the alienation of nature from the not-nature that is, Yeats tells us, art. Similarly, though their rococo delicacy may disguise it, the decorously courting flowers of Gray's **"Crocuses in Grass"** foretoken both Pound's ''gilded phaloi of the crocuses . . . thrusting at the spring air'' and the tumescent vegetation of Lawrence.

The poems of *Silverpoints* suggest that it is too late for the late-Romantic artist to assume a Wordsworthian posture before nature; nature has become alien and unknowable. If, like the speaker of **"Wings in the Dark,"** he sets out in pursuit of nature, he will return with little more than his own metaphors. His boat transformed into a Pegasus, the speaker of that poem finds that the fish he hunts may be imagined—

> Low on the mud the darkling fishes grope,
> Cautious to stir, staring with jewel eyes;
> Dogs of the sea, the savage congers mope,
> Winding their sulky march Meander-wise

—but the imagination cannot light the way to grasp the thing itself. The approach, if it is to be managed at all, will be by indirection and darkness:

> Suddenly all is light and life and flight,
> Upon the sandy bottom, agate strewn.
> The fishers mumble, waiting till the night
> Urge on the clouds, and cover up the moon.

Even if, like the speaker of **"Summer Past,"** the artist suspects there is murmurous communication within nature herself—

> The great trees condescend to cast a pearl
> Down to the myrtles, and the proud leaves curl
>   In ecstasy

—he will eventually learn that human consciousness is forever cut off from this secret language. The artist must face the unresponsive blank of nature's physical qualities—''the sheen / Of restless green''—or artificially superimpose human significance upon this blank—the moss-gods, naiads, and holy trees of the speaker's quest, which are ''song-set'' because they have been placed in nature by the poetic imagination.

At the same time, the two dream-vision poems of *Silverpoints* suggest that art itself is scarcely more comprehensible. **"The Barber"** presents a parable of the artist who, powerless to control his creations, becomes their prey. As the barber's timid ministrations give way to erotic manipulation, his clients change, growing monstrous and finally ravenous for their creator:

> Thy chaste hair ripened into sullen gold.
> The throat, the shoulders, swelled and were uncouth.
> The breasts rose up and offered each a mouth.

Like the repulsive flowers bred by Des Esseintes, the art object, now coloring and shaping itself, has reversed roles and begun to act on the artist.

Gray, whose gentle mockery of his hero resembles that of Huysmans, delicately parodies in the poem **"Mishka"** the effect of fatal knowledge on the artist. Mishka, a bear and ''poet among the beasts,'' is rapt away from his hibernating world by a dream of a honey-child and is granted knowledge of all things by her kiss. Slyly readmitted to Eden by his betrayer, the bear now knows only Edenic things. This finally means knowing only his Eve, for as the external world contracts, she swells to replace it, blurring its outlines:

> The honey-child is an olive tree,
> The voice of birds and the voice of flowers,
> Each of them all and all the hours,
> The honey-child is a wingèd bee,
> Her touch is a perfume, a melody.

Drugged with sensuality, without will or consciousness, Mishka has become the beast among poets.

The *femmes fatales* of the dream-visions present another troubling aspect of the problematic world of *Silverpoints*. Ensnared in their coiling tresses, bear and barber learn that knowledge of art is for the artist a complicated matter: if he attempts to use it, it will betray him, and if he allows it to use him, he betrays himself. Nor is it easier to settle the rival claims of art and nature, for when art imitates nature's fluid transformations of form and color, it becomes, like the barber's mistress, loathsome. But if the artist spurns these subtle living modulations, he is paralyzed and impoverished—as Mishka, fast in the embrace of the honey-child, does not see

> The shadows lie mauven beneath the trees,
> And purple stains, where the finches pass,
> Leap in the stalks of the deep, rank grass.

All the poems of *Silverpoints* involve speakers or protagonists whose selves are considerably less substantial than the art or nature they confront. Gray's most distinctive persona, for example, is the melancholy corpse of "Jules Laforgue," who laments to the lover mouldering beside him that "none esteem how our black lips are blackening." Perhaps this sense of their own impermanence and insubstantiality is why the speakers of **"Poem"** and **"On a Picture"** seek to merge themselves with the flux of nature or the fixity of art. Yet yielding himself to both experimentally means the artist need not commit himself to either, as we see in Gray's **"Poem"**:

> Geranium, houseleek, laid in oblong beds
> On the trim grass. The daisies' leprous stain
> Is fresh. Each night the daisies burst again,
> Though every day the gardener crops their heads.
>
> A wistful child, in foul unwholesome shreds,
> Recalls some legend of a daisy chain
> That makes a pretty necklace. She would fain
> Make one, and wear it, if she had some threads,
>
> Sun, leprous flowers, foul child. The asphalt burns.
> The garrulous sparrows perch on metal Burns.
> Sing! sing! they say, and flutter with their wings.
> He does not sing, he only wonders why
> He is sitting there. The sparrows sing. And I
> Yield to the strait allure of simple things.

Set, like so many of the poems in *Silverpoints,* in territory claimed by both art and nature, the poem subtly relates the artist's discovery of his role to an abdication of self. Thus the speaker, initially repelled by the crude banality of city garden and city child, finally yields to them. The leprous daisies and foul child are both expressions of the sordid and ceaseless assertiveness of natural process. But the little girl, like the decapitating gardener, is an artist figure, powerless to control nature's antipathy to the reductiveness of art. The speaker's recognition of his symbolic kinship with her comes with his vision of another artist—Burns. Imprisoned in ceremonial bronze, the onetime poet of upland moor and brawling tavernside is now mocked by the rank vitality and expressiveness of nature. As everything moves and sings around him, the poet remains silent and self-contained, fixed by art. Recognizing a comic embodiment of his own self-repressed isolation, the speaker abandons his detachment and submerges himself in the mere flux of nature.

The sources for Gray's splenetic irony may be found in Baudelaire, in *la névrose* of the Goncourts, and in the *maladie fin de siècle* of Huysmans, whose famous hero at one point must stimulate his jaded appetite for experience with a fetid cheese and onion sandwich purchased from another foul child. Similarly, the dandiacal speaker's revulsion from the teeming squalor before him suggests the nausea of the twentieth-century existentialist at the pulpy mindlessness of nature, just as the speaker's decision to yield himself to process looks forward to the choices of the existentialist self. As structure and title suggest, **"Poem"** is about the limitations, the poverty of art. Laid out in the trim oblong of the sonnet form, the poem, whose burns / Burns rhyme mocks the Promethean fires of Romantic poetry, and whose reiterated "sing" suggests the insistence on lyricism of its aesthetic, manages one of the elocutionary disappearances of the poet that Mallarmé had called for. Fleeing from the archaizing ("some legend"), the hand-me-down investitures ("unwholesome shreds"), all the threadbare conventions of Romantic verse, the speaker willingly resigns his chances for the heavy celebrity of official art in favor of the problematical freedom, anonymity, and severity of post-Romantic expression.

If Gray's **"Poem"** shows us, in the embarrassed stolidity of sparrow-fretted Burns, art as seen by nature, his **"On a Picture"** shows us nature as seen by art, specifically, as seen by the art of John Everett Millais, whose famous *Ophelia* (1852) this poem describes. Her passionless face as inexpressive as the unravelled garland beside her, the girl, like the speaker of **"Poem,"** seems to have abandoned herself to the strait allure of flux:

> Not pale, as one in sleep or holier death,
> Nor illcontent the lady seems, nor loth
> To lie in shadow of shrill river growth.

Poised between earth and sky, life and death, Ophelia is, in her "noble sloth," the image of art's transcendence of flux—not merely because she is dreamily indifferent to the shrill impingement of nature, but because nature's teeming energy itself has been stilled:

> No weakest ripple lives to kiss her throat,
> Nor dies in meshes of untangled hair;
> No movement stirs the floor of river moss.

Just as the speaker seems about to conclude his meditation on the calm nullity of art, however, he breaks off as if anticipating some motion from without:

> Until some furtive glimmer gleam across
> Voluptuous mouth, where even teeth are bare,
> And gild the broidery of her petticoat.

A poem about a picture about a heroine of drama, Gray's deceptively fragmentary lyric is a sonnet celebrating the inward-looking stasis and cool self-sufficiency of art even while hoping for its violation by nature.

At the same time, by invoking both a specific Pre-Raphaelite canvas and the Pre-Raphaelite custom of writing sonnets on paintings, Gray is able to step outside the frame, as it were, to examine a particular view of art whose influence on *fin de siècle* artists was more pervasive than that of the Symbolists. The "longing for pattern, for pre-Raphaelitism, for an art allied to poetry" that held the young W. B. Yeats mesmerized before Millais' *Ophelia* was the desire to free beauty from everything except its old abounding nonchalant reverie of death. To the critical Hamlet lingering outside the picture, however, this floating image of a beauty enhanced by madness and approaching death will remain incomplete "until . . ."—but the rest is silence; neither the time nor the nature of art's transformation can be expressed.

Beyond this, **"On a Picture"** can be read as a kind of epitome of the volume in which it appears. All the themes which most concern Gray are here—the tension between nature, envious of art's calm perfection, and art, in love with nature's fluid fecundity; the parasitic dependence of "Aesthetic" Art upon the art that feeds it; the drifting, dying shapelessness of contemporary art forms; and finally, the inability of the late-Romantic artist to achieve wholeness and authenticity in his work.

The movement which began with the Pre-Raphaelites, the poem suggests, is at once still in process and yet somehow frozen. It has become the fashion to see the resolution of this paralysis in the modernism of Yeats, Eliot, Joyce, and Pound, and to view the eclecticism and experimentation of the nineties—even though their contribution to modernism is clear—as a kind of desperate floundering after faith.

The biographical impulse which has dominated commentary on the *fin de siècle* has encouraged this view. Yet whether it is the brilliant mythopoeia of Yeats, the lurid press-agentry of Symons, or, more recently, the gossiping debunkery of Rupert Croft-Cooke, biographical emphasis has narrowed our vision and distracted criticism from its true object, the literature of the period. Though we may reasonably view John Gray and his book in the context of the "tragic generation," we are finally compelled to recognize that the significance of *Silverpoints* lies beyond the studied, enigmatic career of its author or the fastidiousness of its binding. For if we judged John Gray's book by its cover, we might say merely that *Silverpoints* endorses a delicate and self-conscious art. But for all the meticulous rhyme schemes and subtly calculated play of rhythm and assonance in the poems those covers enclose, their variousness and obscurity, their self-irony and parody of each other, and, most of all, their presentation of the late-Romantic artist's struggle with a comically conscious and recalcitrant nature, all suggest a certain final skepticism about the power, or even the point, of Aestheticism's Art. (pp. 160-69)

> Linda C. Dowling, "Nature and Decadence: John Gray's 'Silverpoints'," in Victorian Poetry, *Vol. 15, No. 2, Summer, 1977, pp. 159-69.*

[GARY H. PATERSON]   (essay date 1979)

[*In the following excerpt, Paterson demonstrates how aspects of the decadent style of* Silverpoints *are effectively utilized in Gray's religious verse.*]

The 1890s saw the attraction to Catholicism—serious or otherwise—of a surprising number of writers associated with the decadence in England. There was, however, probably no more meaningful conversion—either in a religious or a worldly sense—than that of John Gray.

Physically attractive, graceful in manners, a writer of delicacy and promise (although without aristocratic pedigree), Gray not surprisingly found himself close to the centre of the artistic limelight in the beginning of the decade—as protégé of Oscar Wilde. The metamorphosis from dandy-minion and creator of effete and scandalous verse to the punctilious and slightly distant Canon Gray of St. Peter's, Edinburgh, is rather difficult to imagine. And yet, in the crucial years of the early 1890s, the two extremes of decadence and religious fervour do seem to coexist in his life as well as his art. (p. 89)

Although John Gray's connection with the Decadence during the early nineties was certainly more than flirtation, he had already been received into the Roman Catholic Church in 1890. His biographers have been hard-pressed to reconcile the recently converted Gray with the very secular, sometimes irreverently sinister poetry of *Silverpoints.* Fr. Brocard Sewell comments as follows: "Probably he had fallen away from the first fervour of his conversion to Catholicism, and a second, more effectual 'conversion' had followed four years later."

Ultimately, it is not the biographical problem that concerns us here, but the fact remains that although Gray's two volumes,

Silverpoints . . . and *Spiritual Poems* . . . would seem to indicate the direction of his tastes, there are poems in the former of a distinctly religious flavour while the latter contains several religious poems which embody important decadent attitudes. It is my contention that the religious poetry composed in the "decadent" style is more strikingly successful than his more conventional and straightforward expression of religious emotion to be found either in *Spiritual Poems* or *Ad Matrem.*

In *Silverpoints,* following a poetic description of Parsifal's adoration of the consecrated Wine in an imitation of Verlaine, Gray included a poem dedicated to Ernest Dowson called **"A Crucifix"**. . . . On a careful reading of this poem, several aspects of decadence become manifest. The compelling atmosphere as we are led along the aisle to where the crucifix stands is a mixture of artifice and life-like reality leading to a highly personal, intensely experienced aesthetic moment. The windows, though *painted* orange, blue, and *gold,* admit smiling mystic sunbeams. The crucifix itself is artificial, "tinted", "adorned with gold and green" and yet so life-like as to express "the last convulsion of the lingering breath."

Recognizing the close connection between artificiality and the life-like is an important clue to an understanding of Gray's intent. One of the qualities noticed by critics of John Gray is his ability to express the intensely perceived aesthetic moment. His description of Ophelia in **"On a Picture"** "demonstrates how the contemplation of beauty can give rise to intensity of feeling." Similarly, the experience in **"A Crucifix"** is nothing if not intense. The mannered artificiality of "long fluted golden tongues of sombre sheen" gives way to the dying words of Christ and the wild rhythms of "Bleed, bleed the feet, the broken side, the hands." Here Gray has used the aesthetic experience not as an end in itself, but as a vehicle for the statement of Christ's message in the poem. The elaborate and self-conscious conclusion is also appropriate to the dandified and exquisite artifice of the preceding verse.

"Saint Sebastian" is a poem in *Spiritual Poems* which delicately describes a painting of the saint *in extremis* and creates an aesthetic moment much the same as **"A Crucifix"**. Carefully, elaborately, the scene is gathered together beginning with the fragments of a downward staircase revealing steps "Each ever mauver than its fellow mauve". . . . In the following stanzas . . . , Gray describes the emotions of what seem to be the faithful who await the death of St. Sebastian "in a hush so still, / The stair they stand on scarcely knows the throes / Of their unanimous breathing". . . . Immediately, the emotional involvement of the spectator is emphasized. The poem then moves in a sometimes surprisingly "modern" choice of phrase into a description of the landscape:

> Earth is a landscape, where an orange grove
> Has all the seeming of a labyrinth,
> Even as orange as the heaven is mauve;
> The sun is gold as heaven is hyacinth,
> As glowing as a founder's open stove. . . .

With the mention of "an insolent pavilion" . . . at the right and "lilac clusters, heavily drooping" . . . against the tent walls, the scene then turns from "mauve heaven and orange earth" . . . to a vision of the inferno, where "knotty limbs are fierce with scarlet stuff" . . . and "rank hair veils . . . ears, which hearken not". . . .

From this vision of sin and the picture of the captain ready to fire his darts, the scene changes along with the stanza form—to a more excited five lines of trochaic trimeter. The saint is "pale", burning with love, dripping blood which engenders bright carnations. Conventional description is vitalized by the feverish pathos in "Pale Sebastian's feet / Clutch the ground for strength" . . . or,

> Eyes reluctant turn
> From the wicked crew;
> Eyes with love which burn
> For the ill they do,
> Heavenward must turn. . . .

The final stanza, however, dissolves the idealized picture that has been created. Sebastian is human; his human skin "Cannot choose but shrink". . . . Even though a saint, he is ashamed of his human failings; on the brink of martyrdom he is not forgetful of what he is.

The poem, which really attempts to include too much, does manage to present a kind of microcosm of the situation of man and the problem of evil. Sebastian, whose eyes are never far from heaven and eternity, is nevertheless tied to a body and flesh that "cannot choose but shrink". As such, he is exposed to the evils of the world and the future denizens of hell; his own feet are also firmly planted in the ground. The role of the spectators, the faithful, is really ours: we wait, like them, for "The holy hour" . . . when "more than earthly night shall night be dark". . . .

The link between human and divine recognized in the aesthetic moment of **"A Crucifix"** is again envisioned here in the figure of Sebastian, who becomes a Christ-figure in the final lines of the poem. In both poems the theme of the Incarnation is conveyed through distinctly decadent poetic imagery.

A comparison with some of the inferior religious verse of either *Silverpoints* or *Spiritual Poems,* such as **"Mon Dieu M'A Dit"** or the poem in *terza rima* beginning, "Lord, if thou art not present, where shall I / Sick find thee absent?" will show that John Gray is most confident and most successful when he fashions his theme to suit the ornate decorative style characteristic of the decadence. In doing so, he moves beyond *l'art pour l'art* in presenting traditional religious themes in a striking and attractive manner. (pp. 89-94)

[*Gary H. Paterson*], *"Spiritual Decadence? Some Religious Poetry of John Gray," in* The Antigonish Review, *No. 39, Autumn, 1979, pp. 89-95.*

RUTH Z. TEMPLE (essay date 1981)

[*Temple is an American critic and educator specializing in English literature of the late-Victorian and Edwardian periods. Her critical history* The Critic's Alchemy: A Study of the Introduction of French Symbolism into England *(1953) is among the most infor-*

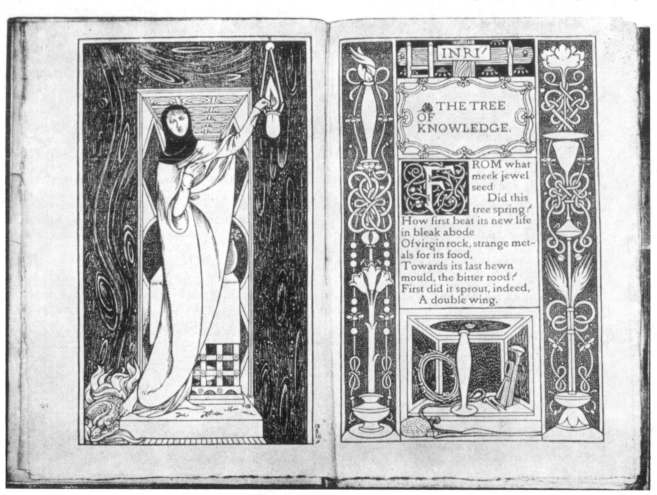

Page decorations by Charles Ricketts for Gray's Spiritual Poems.

mative and illuminating works on fin-de-siècle writing. In the following excerpt, Temple discusses Gray's fiction and criticism.]

When in 1928 A. J. A. Symons brought out *An Anthology of 'Nineties' Verse,* Charles Ricketts wrote Fr Gray: "I thought you and Michael Field came out very well in the Verse of the Nineties. I found Dowson and Francis Thompson below their reputation." Nearly a century has now elapsed since the nineties and it is surely time for a judicious reappraisal of all those minor authors who comprised the fin-de-siècle. I find myself in agreement with Ricketts in his rating of the four poets here represented, even though the poems of Gray in that collection are not among his best. But Gray was a prose writer too, and a final estimate must take account of that portion of his work.

The range of subject and manner in [Gray's] prose pieces is remarkable. The most dated is one of the latest to be published, **"The Beauties of Nature"** . . . , its import obscure, its tone and taste uncertain, its language lush, its manner pseudo-smart, after Wilde. It is a sort of parable. The other prose allegory is one of Gray's most delightful compositions and the first published: **"The Great Worm,"** a fantastic fairy tale with a symbolic meaning laid on in a sort of postscript, which appeared in the first issue of Ricketts's decorative journal *The Dial.* . . . It is Gray's nearest approach to the stylistic elegance of Beardsley but has a more relaxed charm.

> He did not snort lightning, and none but honeyed words ever left his gentle lips. He came into the city one day, choosing his steps most carefully, so as not to derange public edifices, and threading himself through triumphal arches with marvellous dexterity. He inquired his way to the palace; and, when he reached it, he found, as will readily be believed, that the entrance was too small to admit him. Not being pressed for time, he stretched himself out the full length of the terrace, with a part of his tail hanging over the battlements.
>
> Meanwhile, the traffic of the city had adroitly diverted itself into suburbs.

Here are imagination, invention, visual imagery, the inconsequence of the dream—and none of the sentimentality that disfigures the unchildlike fairy tales of Wilde. (pp. 49-50)

Quite other modes are illustrated in five stories which appeared in successive issues of *The Butterfly,* . . . from the unsuccessful realism of **"Old Gough"** through historical romance *à la Salammbô* to the understated ferocity of **"The Loves of the Age of Stone,"** a little masterpiece. Neither William Golding nor Henry Treece has conveyed with more economical intensity the "social" behavior of the savage. This and **"Light,"** which appeared in *The Pageant,* . . . seem to me Gray's most interesting published stories. **"Light"** is a study of religious conversion. It has what none of the others has, psychological penetration and the expert evocation of supernatural states of mind like those described in *Spiritual Poems.* Indeed in the story Gray made thematic use of his translation, from that book, of Jacopone da Todi's "Excellent Way." The convert is an ordinary woman in humble life, a Non-conformist. Implausible as the event is, Gray has made it plausible, and the sequence of the heroine's emotional experiences is expertly created. Some of the descriptions are reminiscent of certain passages in *Ecstasy,* the novel by Louis Couperus translated by Gray and Teixeira de Mattos.

Another "inner" tale is **"The Person in Question."** That it was not published in Gray's lifetime may support the conjecture that it has autobiographical significance. It does have, as Bernard Bergonzi has recently noted, a flavor of *Dorian Gray* [see excerpt dated 1966]. As **"Light"** suggests the author's acquaintance with the psychological phenomena of religious conversion, so this story persuasively reveals the state of soul of a young man who despairs of his future when it is symbolically forecast for him by the appearance of a double—himself but older, and curiously repellent. (p. 51)

If I have devoted what may seem a disproportionate amount of space to Gray's early prose pieces, this is because they are uncollected, unanthologized, and almost entirely ignored. Bergonzi, in his otherwise excellent introduction to the new edition of Canon Gray's *Park,* finds that not until that late work did Gray show talent as a prose writer. But the qualities Bergonzi finds in *Park* are already in the stories: "a dry, mannered and deliberately understated mode of narration which recalls the laconic precision of the best of Gray's verse." Exactly so. Gray's stories are, most of them, the stories of a poet. That is not to say that they are written in "poetic" prose. On the contrary, with one or two exceptions, they have a sobriety and sureness of tone and taste, an assimilation of form to content, that is in the best prose tradition of the nineties. Nevertheless, they bespeak a poet's talents: deficient in characterization, they excel in creation of mood and picture and of mood through picture. What they do is indeed best expressed in Gray's account of the Sensitivist school which serves as translator's note in *Ecstasy.* . . .

> the word being understood to apply to the method of their literary art, to their manner of seeing and making seen. . . . A person, say, gets a visual impression; a Sensitivist would describe what he exactly saw, and not what his intellect, going upon his past experience, would tell him he saw. . . . Reflection will show at once the intelligence of this distinction of sense and intellect, and a novel of the sensitivist school will show its utility. Most people, knowing that water is transparent, look *through* it: they see water green, brown, or whatever it may be in its density. Some, with a quicker sense, look at its surface, and almost always see beautiful colour.

(p. 52)

This sounds very like the program of the Impressionists. And indeed, of all the terms in current use for the distinctive art of the fin-de-siècle, impressionism seems most useful.

Gray's ear is much less sensitive than Dowson's, and lyric grace is rare in his poetry. He is very far from practicing Verlaine's prescription, "De la musique encore et toujours." Oddly enough, he comes closest to it in his translations, those, for example, of Verlaine, where his cadences, though not the echo of the original, nevertheless compose a graceful English poem; those, also, of Spanish and Italian religious poets in *Spiritual Poems.* **"Sound,"** rejected from *Silverpoints,* does not convey sounds but only the idea of various instruments.

Rare, too, are verbal felicities, the magic of a memorable phrase. There is often a curious uncertainty about Gray's diction in verse. Frequently an adjective will start from its context, so inappropriate are its connotations, as in the line "To lie in shadow of *shrill* river growth" (**"On a Picture"**) where the tone of the whole poem is languorous and this one discordant word only puzzles. Or, in "**Sound,**" "And *creeping* morning's rapture trills," where both sound and sense of *creeping* falsify the "rapture." This kind of thing betrays a want of poetic tact. Gray does claim, in the same translator's note (in *Ecstasy*), the artist's right "to throw over . . . a considerable portion of the tyranny of the grammar book; to use the word that best conveys the impression desired, although such have not the sanction of custom." Of course this describes what Mallarmé did, what Mallarmé finds Maeterlinck doing in *La Princesse Maleine:* "Ce sont des mots à côté, tous déviés un peu, qui pour leur rencontre font entrer un spectre." But like all experimental methods this one must justify itself by success. I do not think Gray has this way with words—the apparition does not enter to effect the resemblance to Mallarmé's that has been alleged.

Indeed the English Decadence did not emulate Mallarmé in his effort to give a purer sense to common words. That endeavor remained for a later poetic generation. Instead, trademarks of decadent verse are imprecision of language, a kind of verbal blur, together with the use of concrete words for emblematic effect, not for image. Here Swinburne excelled the minor poets. "Pale beyond porch and portal," "the lilies and langours of virtue"—these are the authentic, the essential Decadence; the echoes and imitators are as inferior as Pope's imitators were to Pope.

Gray's much reprinted "**Heart's Demesne**" and "**Complaint,**" with "**The Barber**" (*Silverpoints*) have the nineties languor, the sadistic-erotic overtones in would-be imitation of Baudelaire, all these expressed in a lush Swinburnian vocabulary heavily freighted with what has been called old guard language: it will neither surrender nor die (it has done both now, and nothing so dates a poem). "**Complaint**" is an exceedingly inept poem, full of padding (one of Gray's common faults) and nonsense:

> in my heart a flame
> Burns tireless, 'neath a silver vine.
> And round entwine
> Its purple girth
> All things of fragrance and of worth.

Much better, though disfigured by imprecise language and sentimentalism, is "**Battledore**", . . . a descriptive poem in the pseudo-medieval manner of Pre-Raphaelitism:

> The weary Lady Constance yields
> Unto a great desire.

(The great desire is to join the sisters in their game of battledore.) Nevertheless the poem shows skill in the evocation of lively motion in a vivid scene.

Gray, like Gautier and Beardsley, was acutely conscious of the visual world. This is the first excellence of his verse.

Several of his poems are explicit descriptions of pictures: "**A Crucifix**," "**On a Picture**," in *Silverpoints*, and in *Spiritual Poems* "**Saint Sebastian**". . . . And actually most of his poems, except the religious ones, are pictures. In "**Poem**" (*Silverpoints*), a poor child, leprous daisies, and sparrows are juxtaposed in a scene unfortunately marred by the intrusion of the child's thoughts and the observer's obscure comment. "**The Forge**" . . . is a *chose vue*—John Gray would really as a boy have seen a working forge. It is described in appropriately pedestrian rhythms which forecast the relaxed prose cadences of Fr Gray's poems of observation.

> Half shapes of light leap higher than man's height
> Out from the blackness and as soon subside,
> Flame-flesh-shapes, sweat-stamped clinging cotton
>   swathed,
> In violent action, following the guide
> Of the smith's gesture bidding where to smite.

Here, too, Gray cannot resist the sentimental comment of the implied spectator: the smith is "maimed in his poor hands" and crooked for (a good line, however): "It bends a man to make no matter what." At the opposite extreme is "**The Flying Fish**", . . . with its sing-song ballad stanza and couplet rhyme, its brilliant images and imaginative range, swinging along at an intoxicating pace to its symbolic climax. (pp. 52-5)

The meaning of "**The Flying Fish**" is possibly like that of "**Mishka**" (*Silverpoints*) and "**The Great Worm**": the poet (flying fish, bear and dragon-worm), mild, harmless, handsome, simple and spontaneous creature that he is, is an anomaly in the real world, doomed to be a sacrifice to his vision of the ideal. But Gray was no *Symboliste,* and we need not belabor his poems to make them yield multiple meanings. In this, too, he is of his period. As he wrote in an obituary of Aubrey Beardsley . . . , "C'est le symbole même qui intéresse l'artiste, et non pas ce qu'il symbolise." ["It is the symbol itself that interests the artist, and not that which it symbolizes."] (p. 55)

It is in his religious verse, some original and some translated, that, I think, Gray achieves his real distinction. Not in all, alas. One sort, the pseudo-childlike, using ballad stanza and the simplest diction as in "**The Ox**" . . . and in most of the *Blue Calendars*, is rarely successful and often lamentable. The ox says:

> I hold it for a solemn troth
>   I shall no more be sacrificed.
> For when to prophethood He groweth
>   I cease to symbolise the Christ.

Dowson's somewhat ambiguous praise of *The Blue Calendars* sent him in 1895 is apt indeed: "it reminds me of the deliciously quaint sign of a cabaret in Montmartre 'Le Moyen-Age-fin-de-siècle.'" (The Age of Faith was a less fortunate influence on the Decadence than was Watteau.) But even with the poem of short line and simple diction he has an occasional success. "**On the Holy Trinity**" (deservedly reprinted in *The Oxford Book of Mystical Verse*) achieves with its original rhyme scheme and cadence an authentic medieval flavor.

> The triple crown
> Hath deep renown;
> Ring without clasp
> No sense can grasp.
> It is a depth without a floor.
> Is rest, is grace,
> Shape, form and space;
> The source, the ring
> Of everything;
> A point which never moveth more.

(pp. 56-7)

More impressive are Gray's devotional poems in the baroque manner. "**The Tree of Knowledge**," also reprinted in *The Oxford Book*, and the two translations from Jacopone da Todi all use a complex stanzaic structure and intricate rhyme scheme, and the last, "In Foco l'amor mi mise," is a *tour de force* of sustained cadence woven through stanzas of feminine rhyme.

> My heart was broke asunder:
> Earthward my body sprawling

The arrow of Love's wonder
From out the crossbow falling,
Like to a shaft of thunder
Made war of peace, enthralling
My life for passion's plunder.
Love setteth me a-burning. . . .

Perhaps in these poems Gray came closest to what he craved as "the impossible in poetry"—"something to be got from words and images quite exterior to words and thought" (Preface to *Spiritual Poems*).

Testifying to the strong religious current of the decade, Arthur Machen writes in 1902 that Catholic dogma is:

> merely the witness, under a special symbolism, of the enduring facts of human nature and the universe; it is merely the Voice which tells us distinctly that man is *not* the creature of the drawing room and the Stock Exchange, but a lonely Awful soul confronted by the Source of all Souls.

He concludes, therefore, that to make literature one has to be "subconsciously Catholic." Gray had, no doubt, to be consciously Catholic, and we owe his best poetry to the fervor which in the end deprived us of a poet.

It is for his spiritual poems that Gray deserves the title of "incomparable poet of the age"—and I have not forgotten Francis Thompson. In other respects, he is strictly "comparable": a prose writer of some distinction, certainly superior to Dowson (one regrets the translation of *Adolphe* he proposed but did not execute—this to have been illustrated by Beardsley!); an impressionist in the nineties manner in secular verse, though of wider range than many contemporaries; a sensitive translator like Arthur Symons of the new French poetry. That the immortality of John Gray the minor nineties poet should be entrusted to *The Oxford Book of Mystical Verse* is probably more nearly poetic justice than the world usually provides.

Celebration of the Holy Mysteries yields in the priest's last two collections of verse to celebration of landscape, and in the interval between *Silverpoints* . . . and *The Long Road* . . . Gray's style has come fully into the twentieth century. Of the nineties poet, disciple of Gautier, there is left "the man for whom the visible world exists." But stanzaic and metric patterns are now loose and variable, relaxed to follow the flow of narrative. Eliot and Pound have been writing not unheeded by Canon Gray, though he leaves to them irony and the urban scene. An occasional dissonant syllable or eccentric word is, of course, not learned from the moderns—these devices were in the early Gray's poetic manner. And from his early poetry survives the taste for a felicitous and eloquent close. "The Swan," following "Leda" in the two-part sequence . . . concludes (anticipating Yeats):

Till sudden lightnings split
The burning sky, and empty it;
And raucously as eagles cry
An eagle screamed across the sky.

Now, from "Andante" (*Poems* . . .), "like planets on a starry night / all those spirits gaze." Or, from "Aqueducts," an ambitious and accomplished poem on how and why they are built: "when the perfected instrument at length / stalks the descending hills and strides the plain." Ricketts, to whom Fr Gray sent the late poems, found the diction of these poems

"throughout crisp clean and delicate, passing at times into beauty." It is an apt judgment.

The title poem of the small collection **The Long Road** and "Ode" from *Poems* are both the fruit of Fr Gray's many miles and hours of walking. The eye moves along a hedge, dissecting its multiple structure: the gaze shapes contours of hills and valleys—the gaze of a draftsman, not a painter. **"Ode"** is, I think, the best of the poems as it is certainly the most various. The natural phenomenon celebrated is a stream, traced from its birth in mountain mist through phases of brook, river, and nasty urban polluted marsh to its imminent renascence:

While windmills still gesticulate,
    dim, motionless, the river seems to wait
        upon the first salt kisses of the ocean's lips;
        where a white pharos herds the ships.

"The Long Road" might serve as preface to *Park*, an involuntary time-traveller's tale and Gray's last and longest published work. The poet's persona is a traveller who savors the passing scene but not his accommodations along the way. . . . The character Park, on the contrary, has been translated into a realm where nature is its well known satisfactory self but the accommodations have been transformed—answering to the hedonistic day-dreams of a wayfarer who at normal nightfall must put up at an "abysmal inn." And like the poem, *Park* is confidential—providing insight into Gray's perception of himself which is perhaps more exactly Gray's self-constructed mask, a self or mask curiously at variance with the portrait of the compassionate artist-priest drawn in the letters to that fellow artist Michael [Field]. "[A] certain reticence . . . and traces of inhibition in your mind and texture"—these are the traits Charles Ricketts complained of in the poems sent him. He hopes that his friend will write more, "with greater confidence in the value of your impulse to write." To the memory of this other fellow artist, link between the nineties and the priestly vocation, designer of his first books, Gray dedicated his **Poems**. Ricketts would have enjoyed *Park* but perhaps found there the same "reticence in mind and texture."

In that "fantastic story," as it is subtitled, a priest walking in the Cotswolds finds himself suddenly in a civilization aeons later though the landscape is unchanged. The narrator-traveller is named Mungo Park, surely after the eighteenth-century Scotsman who made two difficult journeys into Africa in search of the sources of the Niger.

Park has all the merits of Gray's early prose; the writing is spare, simple, its rhythm disciplined. Through extreme economy in narration and description—ellipsis, juxtaposition instead of smooth transition—the reader is forced to collaborate as in the *nouveau roman* of the 1950s. Though there are analogies with Wells's *Time Machine*, Gray's vision is original: a future where a black race dwells sparsely and securely in an unspoiled Cotswold countryside traversed by nothing more advanced than horses, undisturbed by a white populace teeming below ground where they perpetuate the repellent urban technology of our century—such as subways. Fr Gray had an interest in archaeology and an admiration for the black race. His sister remembers that he used to say he was black inside and foretold that "the black man would rule." His early ironic story "The Advantages of Civilization" . . . anticipates the vision of *Park*. There a visiting Fijian "Bishop," fruit of the civilizing efforts of a Methodist Missionary Society, proves on an excursion to the British Museum to know more about art and history than his white entertainment committee. What we conclude about the author of *Park* (since Park is Gray, from his priestly calling to his age, sixty, his build, his addiction to walking, and even his four missing teeth) is his intense devotion to the land and, no less, to the ritual splendor of church ceremonies, these being a daily feature of life in a regime where the state is the church and the church is Roman Catholic.

Park is modest, humorous—more courageous and steadfast of spirit than he knows. He is an oddly engaging anti-hero. The world he is plunged into is in many ways congenial: a priestly world, hierarchical, ceremonious, inscrutable, rigidly ordered. And the priest adapts to it rather easily, learning something of the language (which, of course, the author has constructed)—with his equals he communicates in Latin which is still the language of what is still the Catholic Church—taking direction, asking only a few discreet questions, conforming to the Rule which he can only gradually and imperfectly ascertain, relying, above all, on Divine help to preserve his serenity. Always he takes comfort in the beauty around him, from the familiar natural scene and the simple suitable clothing provided him to the splendor of Church vestments and interior design and the elegance of the books he is given. Park responds to the kind of beauty Gray loved and has Gray's skill in conveying it. . . . Most often the elements of landscape and of habitation are reduced to linear effects and expressed with a draftsman's precision that conveys to the reader concept rather than image. We are reminded of Gray's early training—and of the method of Robbe-Grillet, who had the same sort of training.

The paraphernalia of the Church that had been Gray's steady preoccupation perhaps since his student days in Rome distract Park when he is first allowed to officiate at a service, and there is in this passage a hint of that special importance of the Mass for Gray that he had testified to in a letter . . . :

> The procession formed. Park, with his restless, distracted habit, had begun by noticing the types, the linen, the vestments, the processional cross, the candlestick he himself carried; until, moved with contrition, he said to himself: There is nothing more beautiful nor more terrible than the mass; and, with eyes downcast, he went about his business as an acolyte. . . .

There is even a reminiscence of the nineties Gray in the satirical treatment of his one reception by ladies, the ladies of the Court. . . . Women are almost absent from Park's scene and there is no evidence whatever of family life. The land of the Wampami might be a vast monastic community, hierarchical, ceremonious, inscrutable, rigidly ordered. If we ask: how explain this white priest's relative indifference to the obviously subjugated hordes of his own race below the pleasant surface?—they repelled Park and even frightened him on his conducted tours below—well, Fr Gray showed no sign of fellow-feeling with the masses. He hated parties (one compensation of Lent is no parties), except children's parties; he was uncomfortable in groups. His ministry to individuals, whether his intellectual equals or the poor, is quite another thing. (pp. 57-63)

Park may be an allegory of Gray's own life as he perceived it, both in its provisions and its deprivations, a life of ritual, of sensory beauty and inexplicable demands, of comradeship; a life, finally, of accommodation in an alien world, to a rule imposed, and accepted because it comes—everything comes—from God. It is not the priest's province to rebel. (p. 63)

Pierre Louÿs' long ago response to the news that his friend had chosen to become a priest was incredulity: how could he submit to a rule? In the willing submission to that rule lay the beginning of salvation. The energy, determination, and steadiness of purpose that had shaped John Gray's worldly and literary success in the nineties were the means whereby Fr Gray pursued his priestly calling. But that he had undergone transformation, had, in effect, been called, his letters and his religious poems leave no doubt. Unlike the minor artists of the nineties who could not keep their footing on the tightrope in the storm of life, Fr Gray survived the nineties—he himself believed—through the intervention of Divine Grace. The great artist of that age who survived it to become a poet of our language saw the necessity of choice.

> The intellect of man is forced to choose
> Perfection of the life or of the work,
> And if it take the second must refuse
> A heavenly mansion, raging in the dark.

Yeats, for the world's blessing, chose perfection of the work. Canon Gray, who had made the other choice, is assured of a heavenly mansion. His earthly monument, a monument moreover to a life-long friendship, is St Peter's Church. His best epitaph is his own: "Memento Mei" (*Vivis*).

> Earth bore me; and, God helping me
> betimes, I had some little worth;
> (how small he knoweth) and upon
> my errantry set forth at birth;

Canon John Gray, circa 1931.

humbled, triumphant, bore my load
of scars, and burst my road to earth

quia pulvis sum.

(pp. 63-4)

*Ruth Z. Temple, "The Other Choice: The Worlds of
John Gray, Poet and Priest," in* Bulletin of Research
in the Humanities, *Vol. 84, No. 1, Spring, 1981, pp.
16-64.*

G. A. CEVASCO (essay date 1982)

[*Cevasco is an American critic and educator specializing in the
Aesthetic and Decadent movements of the late nineteenth century.
His* John Gray *is the most extensive and informative study of
Gray's life and works. In the following excerpt from that study,
Cevasco discusses Gray's early poetry and criticism and the later
novella* Park.]

Like all aspiring young authors, Gray was anxious to see his
name in print. His first opportunity came in 1889. Early in
that year, he was invited by Charles Shannon, printer and
lithographer, and Charles Ricketts, artist, author, and book
designer, to contribute to a periodical they were starting [the
Dial]. (p. 25)

In his first piece for the *Dial* (1889), **"Les Goncourts,"** Gray
did not confine his remarks to the novels of Edmond and Jules
de Goncourt; instead, he ranged freely over their entire vision
of art and life. To begin with, he considered their concept of
the true artist: "always an abnormal creature, a being with an
overdeveloped brain, or diseased nerves." Since a good writer
is more than "a literary grocer," he must of necessity give
vent to his own personality in all that he does. An artist's
greatness, the Goncourts held, springs from his very being,
from his unique personality "that discovers new motives, and . . .
an earnestness with which to carry them out."

Once this concept of the artist is fully understood, Gray agreed,
the sensitive reader has a better chance of dealing with the
exacerbated consciousness responsible for the eccentric style
of the Goncourts; for "never was great work more destitute of
charm for the vulgar than that of MM. Edmond and Jules de
Goncourt." If the novels of the Goncourts were beyond certain
readers, and even if those readers form a majority, the defect
should be sought in the limitations of the readers, not in the
novelists' works of art. The Goncourts, it had to be understood,
were far too advanced for the multitude. In short, Gray admired
the style of the Goncourts for its implied protests against vulgarity. Their willingness to experiment, to violate all conventionality, Gray believed, would be beneficial for English art
and literature.

During the last years of the Victorian period, most creative
writers were searching for freedom from the trammels of tradition. A regeneration, Gray proposed, required an end to all
hostility to the modernity of French art and letters; it demanded
as well a new respect on the part of the British public for the
artist and his aspirations. "It is quite the rule," Gray maintained, "that the really great only gain their place after fierce
struggling; for apart from the actual work, they have to create
a taste for it, a task generally tedious in proportion to its worth."

What Gray especially admired about the Goncourts was their
neurotic sensibility, their idiosyncratic prose, the haunting melody that sounded throughout all they wrote. Their style was
such that Gray, consciously or unconsciously, imitated it
throughout his own essay. Impressed with the meticulousness

of everything the Goncourts had written, Gray paid lavish attention to his choice of words. He favored strong and strained
expressions. At times he even convoluted his syntax, just as
the Goncourts had done.

When Gray expatiated on the Philistinism of the British public,
for example, he wrote: "And what shall we, we English, say?
we the chosen? we who understand so well that a book, to be
good, must recount a series of good actions? we who like the
shadow thrown across the hero's path only for the pleasure of
seeing it swept away again? who feel impatient if the wedding
is delayed? Germinie Lacerteux was not married to Coriolis?
Put it away! Dear me! if Freddie should get hold of it! Shocking
blemishes, happily so soon discovered. Let us beware of the
glittering poison."

Gray's writing in the style of the Goncourts added a special
touch to his essay, but for him to cover as much as he tried
to is a different matter. Inexperienced as a critic, he scattered
his best points and failed to develop a central theme. On the
positive side, he did distinguish clearly the art of the Goncourts
from the realism of Balzac and the naturalism of Zola; moreover, he weighed the contributions of the Goncourts to the
novel. He wrote extravagantly of the literary achievements of
the Goncourts and also praised them as "literary men influencing the manner of seeing, not thinking, of contemporary
painters." It was the Goncourts, Gray emphasized, who made
much of the youthfulness in the art of the century, who wrote
appreciatively of the Japanese prints that were beginning to
influence the best of modern art.

Despite certain shortcomings, **"Les Goncourts"** is an important bit of criticism. Foremost, in focusing on the work of the
Goncourts as he did, Gray properly stressed the value of what
was being done by French writers; and he did so ten full years
before Arthur Symons published his *Symbolist Movement in
Literature* (1899), the first book published in England to introduce such French authors as Huysmans, Mallarmé, Verlaine, and Rimbaud to English readers. Then, too, as an enthusiastic disciple of the Goncourts, Gray, in attacking those
who adhered to insular standards, helped foment the aesthetic
protest that would so concern artists and writers during the
nineties.

As a young, eager poet, Gray was receptive to what was being
accomplished by writers on the other side of the channel. His
interest was more than simple Francophilia, for the more he
read the Goncourts, Baudelaire, Mallarmé, Verlaine, and
Huysmans the more convinced he became that France was more
aesthetically advanced than England. His enthusiasm would
lead him to begin his own personal attempt to domesticate
French art—an attempt that would lead him four years later to
publish his *Silverpoints*. (pp. 26-8)

During the years that Gray was contributing to the *Dial* he was
also translating and editing quite extensively and submitting
creative material to such periodicals as the *Butterfly,* the *Pageant,* and *La Revue Blanche.* . . .

The most important prose work that Gray wrote during this
period of his life is a story that he did not publish. Its exact
date of composition is not known, but internal evidence suggests that it was written early in the nineties, probably late in
1892. The story is **"The Person in Question,"** one of Gray's
most successful pieces of fiction. . . .

Why had a typed manuscript certified by Gray to be "a true
copy" never before been published? That Gray preserved the

work among his private papers for more than forty years rules out any supposition that he may have withheld the story for literary reasons. Why had he hidden it away? Did he hope for its posthumous publication? It would seem that Gray did not publish the story during his lifetime because it would serve to link him to Wilde. Indeed, **"The Person in Question"** has much in common with *The Picture of Dorian Gray.*

In Wilde's novel, the hero's portrait becomes a faithful record of his sins and iniquities, while his person remains young and unsullied. In Gray's story, the narrator perceives a pitiful portrait of himself, of his empty vain life, in a future period in which all he has to look forward to is old age and regret. The perception of Gray's narrator is Gray's own vision of himself in his declining years, aimlessly doing the same things of which he had already grown tired. Such a revelation, Gray's insight into himself, accounts for his choosing the path to Rome.

At the time that Gray wrote **"The Person in Question,"** it is apparent, he had an obvious dread of continuing in his dissolute ways, of drifting into an even more meaningless old age, of living his whole life without purpose or direction. It follows that his story is more than just another amiable bit of fiction. The work is highly autobiographical, virtually confessional, and is, in essence, an imaginative handling of the doppelgänger theme with a certain flavor of *Dorian Gray* about it. Little wonder that **"The Person in Question"** entices and baffles, reveals and conceals, suggests and recommends all sorts of meanings.

The story begins at the Café Royal. Here, one day in late August or early September, the narrator confronts the person in question. He cannot recall the exact day, but he remembers that it was miserably hot. During lunch he overhears a soft voice coming from someone sitting at a neighboring table. Anyone else might have thought the voice that of an individual slightly intoxicated or half asleep; the narrator recognizes its pitch as similar to the timbre of his own voice.

Curious, the young boulevardier turns to look at the individual from whom the disturbing voice has come. "I knew the person knew I looked at him, though he seemed not to notice; but I stared steadily. I am not particular on this point; I know when I am at liberty to stare, not to mention the fact that people stare at me enough, people, too, who know better."

The narrator observes a figure about his own proportions, even like him in face, except that this mysterious individual is at least twenty-five years older and has a straggly beard. An exact likeness between them is obscured by the added years and beard. Perplexed, the narrator pauses to consider what he at first supposes to be merely an apparition. Coincidences can only reach a certain point within safe and normal limits, he reasons, and he remains baffled by the distinct gestures and turns of phrase of the older man.

Except for age and a certain repulsiveness, the person in question is twin to the narrator. "Yet, though his voice, manner, and sequence of acts were my own, his movements did not follow mine seriatim. I took trouble and arranged tests to be sure of this." The person begins to follow the narrator through the streets, to cafés, to the theater and social gatherings. Week after week, whenever he dines in public he comes across the person in question.

After at first being amused by his doppelgänger, the narrator grows anxious. The person is not an apparition, and the character fears that "in some near or remote sense *he is myself.*"

Finally, the narrator comes to feel a solicitude for and dependence upon his other self.

One day, several months later, the person in question does not make his usual appearances. His absence disturbs the narrator, who sulks about, more anxious and confused than before. To distract himself, he goes to an exhibition. In his wandering about the fairground, he unexpectedly meets the person at a roller coaster. He is aghast that the person is seated on the coaster beside a strange woman. A sudden waft of her cheap perfume across the still, dusty air makes the narrator turn his head with revulsion and hate. Realization that the woman drenched in *foin coupé* is a common streetwalker causes him to recoil in shock. Horrified almost to the point of hysteria, he flees the exhibition. A few days later, however, he begins roving the streets in a desperate search for the mysterious stranger.

"I have never seen him since. Days and evenings and nights I passed, haggard, looking for him. My senses grew painfully keen as I strained sight and hearing for a trace of him. I could not bear to be in a place where there was a door, and a possibility of his entering behind me. I would even snuffle at times, in my despair, for a waft of the dreadful scent, that *foin coupé.*" At night the narrator is unable to sleep. In complete agony he keeps berating himself: "What shall I do? What shall I do?"

"What shall I do, indeed? That is the tragedy of my life now: what shall I do? I am so broken in health that I have every cause for concern." Whatever the cost, the narrator vows, "I must find him, or know why I ever saw him, who he was, and something about him." But the story concludes with the full fury of such unanswered questions still tormenting the narrator.

In the same way that his narrator is tormented by the enigma of the person in question, Gray was tormented by the fragmentation of his own personality. Just as the narrator grapples with his doppelgänger, Gray tried to grapple with the duality of his own life. The more he played the part of a Dorian Gray, the less the role meant to him. What should he do?

Toward the end of 1892, Gray began to realize that a break with Wilde was imminent. In the same year, Gray had been introduced to André Raffalovich by Arthur Symons. The close friendship that sprung up between Gray and Raffalovich was of no particular concern to Wilde. He had already taken up with Lord Alfred Douglas and was beginning to experience success as a playwright.

How Gray regarded Douglas, how Douglas in turn looked upon Gray, how Raffalovich looked upon Wilde and Wilde in turn regarded Raffalovich, and how all four principals may have interacted with each other is too complex a problem to pursue here. How others looked upon the four figures is likewise too involved an issue for present analysis. What is germane, however, is a comment Arthur Symons made in one of his essays about the habitués of the Café Royal—the very place where Gray's narrator first meets his doppelgänger—and the air of unreality that surrounded Wilde and Gray.

"Nor must I omit to mention Oscar Wilde, an apparition; sometimes with John Gray, another apparition," Symons wrote. The fact that Wilde and Gray struck Symons as apparitions is noteworthy inasmuch as both wrote about apparitions of sorts themselves, Wilde in his *Dorian Gray* and John Gray in **"The Person in Question."** *The Picture of Dorian Gray* was of course well known to Symons, but there is little chance that he knew of **"The Person in Question."**

Whatever part Gray plays in Wilde's *Dorian Gray*, the figure of Wilde, to some extent at least, can be discerned in **"The Person in Question."** When Gray wrote his story, Wilde, nearing forty, had grown fat and foolish. More than likely, Wilde had begun to appear morally repulsive to Gray. The narrator's disgust with the person in question when he discovers him with the harlot at the exhibition is Gray's perception of himself becoming another Wilde—not the witty Wilde who was able to charm everyone he met, but the Wilde who had taken up with roughs, renters, and stable boys. If Wilde enjoyed "feasting with panthers," that was his concern; but Gray wanted no part of such a life-style. Dealing with the turpitude of his own life was difficult enough for Gray.

The person in question, it becomes increasingly obvious, is Gray's future self, the pathetic image of a dandy grown old. In *Dorian Gray,* the dandy remains young and handsome while his portrait grows old and ugly. In **"The Person in Question,"** the narrator is allowed to see himself as he will be in twenty-five years, an effete, blighted, depraved individual. Gray could relish playing the role of a young and adventurous Dorian, but he could not deal with the prospect of his growing older into a morally bankrupt Oscar Wilde.

Though **"The Person in Question"** was not a major effort on Gray's part, he must have had some regard for the piece to have preserved it for so many years among his private papers and manuscripts. Having put so much of himself into the story, he could hardly dismiss it as just another literary exercise. Unfortunately, neither he nor any of his close friends who may have read **"The Person in Question"** expressed any critical judgments on the work. Had any such judgments been rendered, the uniqueness of Gray's handling of the doppelgänger would undoubtedly have been singled out as the one factor that sets the story apart. Other nineteenth-century writers had used the theme quite often, few to the same degree or as effectively as had Gray.

Readers who know of Gray, Wilde, and the autobiographical nature of **"The Person in Question"** can appreciate the story more fully than a reader who may simply happen upon it. The echoing question that brings the story to its close—"What shall I do? What shall I do?"—is especially meaningful to anyone knowledgeable of Gray's contemplation of suicide at the time he was writing the story. But even a reader unacquainted with the confessional aspects of the story can still appreciate its fine use of language, its tension, suspense, and highly emotional ending. Finally, to label **"The Person in Question"** a most compelling work of fiction, one that makes excellent use of the doppelgänger theme, is hardly an exaggeration. (pp. 34-9)

Early in 1892, after translating several works of the French Symbolists and writing poems of his own in their manner, Gray gave some thought to gathering the best of his efforts into an anthology of sorts. (p. 46)

To keep his first book of poetry selective and memorable, Gray limited the volume to twenty-nine poems. Sixteen of the total number were original; thirteen, translations. Among the translations are seven "Imitations" from Verlaine, three from Baudelaire, two from Rimbaud, and one from Mallarmé. And as had Verlaine before him, Gray dedicated particular poems to friends and acquaintances, to a prominent actress, and even to a genuine princess. Oscar Wilde, Ernest Dowson, Frank Harris, Jules La Forgue, Pierre Louÿs, and Verlaine were among the men of letters so honored. The actress was Ellen Terry, whom

Gray greatly admired, the member of royalty, Princess de Monaco.

For an epigraph, Gray chose the words "... *en composant des acrostiches indolents.*" Those familiar with French poetry recognized the letters *P.V.* appended to the epigraph as the initials of Paul Verlaine. Readers of Verlaine may even have recalled the poem from which the words were taken—*"Langueur."* Gray's choice of such an unusual inscription is a clear indication that he approved of the decadent languor of Verlaine's poetry, and that he too, like Verlaine, would create, poetically, an atmosphere of dreamlike sloth. Gray's "indolent acrostics" would be crafted, furthermore, with all the care and ingenuity that Verlaine exercised in the writing of his verse.

That general sense of languor that Gray aimed for pervades most of the poems in *Silverpoints,* but in subject matter and style they run a wide gamut. To categorize them is difficult. Some celebrate evil; a few are devotional. Indolent languor is offset by intense passion in those poems that treat of venereal themes. As though to steep the emotions in all that is sensuous and sensual, Gray mingled images of honey and roses, purple breasts and golden hair, founts of pleasure and tears of pain throughout the lines of those poems that explore unchecked nature and depraved beauty. In the more delicate and less decadent works, there is a denial of the grossness of matter and a glorification of the spirit.

Several of the poems, moreover, can be read as self-conscious critiques of inherited aesthetic assumptions about autonomous art and impoverished nature. Then, there are two or three poems that are definite prototypes of Imagism. Others proclaim the beauty and peace of an ideal world even while lamenting that such are beyond human attainment. The few sonnets are mannered imitations of Elizabethan love verse. In short, the poems in *Silverpoints* fly off in all different directions, but their unique point of convergence is a dandiacal aloofness: in their dreamlike mood they avoid clear statement, commitments of any kind or degree.

In common with other poets of the fin de siècle, Gray had a gift of epithet, of rhythm, of symbol, of color. But his perspectives were highly individual. His original poems are marked by singularity and subtlety. In his so-called "Imitations," Gray had the ability to reproduce with surprising exactitude the rhythms and most complex measures of his models. Most of his English renditions of difficult French poems are more than masterpieces of technique, however; for, more often than not, he could capture the spirit of the original and transmute it into striking English verse. At times, his translations convey the chief characteristics of the original; other times, Gray's individuality breaks through. And that is why he preferred to place the term "Imitated from the French" at the head of his renditions from the works of Verlaine, Baudelaire, Rimbaud, and Mallarmé—the poets he most admired. (pp. 50-2)

Toward the end of 1930, Gray began work on a novella, *Park: A Fantastic Story.* Unlike **"The Person in Question,"** his other important work of fiction—which he had written some forty years before but never published—*Park* was a work that Gray was determined to see in print. (p. 122)

Though the book was not meant for the crass reader, there was concern over how even its select readers and perceptive critics might respond. To appreciate, one must understand, but to what extent would those few readers drawn to *Park* understand and appreciate?

The title of Gray's novella provided no difficulty, coming as it does from the name of its protagonist, Dr. Mungo Park, a priest and seminary professor of moral theology. In many ways, however, Reverend Park is Reverend Gray himself, and much that Gray recounts under the guise of fiction is autobiography. Not only are both in their early sixties, but Park's character embodies several of Gray's own attributes. Physically, they are the same man, athletic and well proportioned, balding slightly, and even missing four teeth. More important, the eponymous hero of the work is spiritually and psychologically akin to Gray himself.

Like his fictional counterpart, Gray loved to go on long walking tours, and one of his favorite spots was the Cotswolds, the locale of the novella. One day, when out walking along the Oxford road near Burford, Park undergoes a paranormal experience. He has a sudden illusion of death. When did it happen and how, he wonders. Bringing his emotions under control, he hypothesizes about life and death. He concludes that he cannot be dead, that somehow his sentient being has been transported into the remote future. His stick still hangs on his wrist, and he can hear his watch ticking. He verifies that his many pockets still hold his map, handkerchief, pencil, knife, keys, and rosary.

Park comes to realize that somehow he is now in another dimension of time. The place is still the Cotswold Hills of southwestern England, but the populace has changed. A highly cultivated race of blacks, the Wampani, have taken over the country. The original Anglo-Saxon inhabitants are now living a troglodytic existence beneath the surface of the earth. (p. 123)

After spending an indefinite amount of time among the Wampani, at the end of the story Park again—as he did at the beginning—fears that he may be dying. "He moved along the top edge of the valley, gently rocked in his spirit by the circumstances: the light and loneliness; when it struck him that something was going a bit too far. He thought he would sit down, or perhaps lie down. He had sometimes foolish apprehensions about his heart. He heard a long musical note, which made him think he was ill. He had an illusion of false memory. . . . He or another said: I am afraid he is dead."

When at last he opens his eyes, he is back in the world of reality: "It was the most lovely of spring days; and he walked on slowly, recovering his soul. What a world! The hedges were still white with fruit trees in flower and the ground was wild with celandine, wood anemone, violets, some primroses. . . . It affected him as the natural scene did under that sort of restorative fatigue." Just as he had walked into a dream world, he now walked out of it. And so Park continues his walk and arrives in Malmesbury in time for tea.

Perplexed about his paranormal experience, his reverie, Park consults his physician. Likewise perplexed by what he hears but wishing to put Park at rest, the physician explains: "You were asleep . . . ; it was not a faint. It was a short, deep sleep; and what you experienced was a waking state." As difficult as it is for Park to believe that he has been in a short sleep and has had a long dream, he cannot refute his physician. To reassure Park, the physician adds that though the period of slumber was brief, Park's dream was simply—in the last words of the novel—"somewhat more elaborate than usual."

Different works that Gray had read contributed in their own way to *Park*. He had of course read a great deal of travel and utopian literature, as well as a great deal of fantastic fiction. His reading of such futuristic works as Morris's *News from Nowhere,* Wells's *The Time Machine,* and E. M. Forster's "The Machine Stops" probably made the strongest impression upon his imagination.

Like *News from Nowhere, Park* depicts a feudal society showing the kind of pastoral utopian existence that Morris so favored. *The Time Machine* looks far into a future in which all humanity is divided into two groups, as it is in *Park,* though Wells's concentration upon stunted, brutish creatures who live underground and feed upon aesthetic, childlike individuals must have been repellent to Gray. Like *The Time Machine,* "The Machine Stops" is yet another story set in a future period in which all life has withdrawn below the surface of the earth; from this work of Forster's, Gray could have borrowed the "strange speaking room" in which Park finds himself, a room with apparatus foreshadowing the wonders of television.

Mungo Park's *Travels in the Interior of Africa* (1799) also influenced Gray. The name of the Scottish explorer suggested to Gray the name he would give the protagonist of his novella; yet when the fictional Park is asked the origin of his curious appellation by the Wampani, he responds facetiously that *Mungo* is the name of a little-known saint and that *Park* in his language signifies an enclosed recreational property. Of greater importance is the fact that Gray knew the explorer had encountered blacks in Africa. Blacks were simple savages to the original Mungo Park, but the fictional Park discovers that the blacks in the England of the future are eminently civilized men.

There are several reasons why Gray reversed the customary racial stereotype. One can be found in a statement made by his sister, Sister Mary Raphael. She recalled that when her brother was a young man, he was deeply interested in the black man, that he used to say that "although he was a white man he was black inside," and that he foretold in a general way that some day the black man would rule. When Gray first developed such admiration for the black race that he preferred to think of himself as a black man at heart, Sister Mary Raphael unfortunately failed to specify; but it is noteworthy that in his novella, Gray has one character say to Park: "Drak, your skin is white, more's the pity; but you are black inside."

An additional reason for Gray's interest in blacks is that his younger brother Alexander, who served in the British army, married a black woman, and their son was later educated by Dominicans in England. Finally, when Gray was at The Scots College he encountered black seminarians who were in Rome preparing for the priesthood. The occasional black among so many white students prompted Gray to reflect upon the future of the church in Africa and what kind of Catholics blacks might ultimately become.

Befitting its subject matter, *Park* has a quality of the poetic and the timeless. There are few lengthy descriptive passages in the work, other than those that dwell on the Cotswold landscape. Gray paints the Cotswolds in the diction and imagery of the poet, focusing on "earth and sky; the familiar golden soil and cool green, the coloured patterns of fields, crop, stubble, grazing, early plowing; hedges of quick, draped with clematis and tangled with black bryony. The eastern sky was a dense formation of thin, horizontal clouds."

Having the Cotswold earth and sky for backdrop gives the story an element of reality. Gray also carefully worked out such factors as language, costumes, diet, architecture, interior design, and even a televisionlike "speaking room" in order to bestow touches of reality upon the narrative. The dialogue, however, often creates a different impression.

Descriptions of the Cotswolds and casual references to the plausibility of the Wampani are handled in a mannered, deliberately understated fashion that slows down the pace. The dialogue, on the other hand, speeds up the story. The result: a counterpointing of visual and aural effects. Then, to connote the timelessness he sought, Gray omitted quotation marks from the many conversations in which Park so frequently engages. (pp. 126-29)

The oneiric nature of much of the dialogue almost makes it seem that Gray is at times simply recounting puzzling episodes from his more unusual dreams; but, then, as has so often been said, the artist dreams while he is awake. *Park* is a sustained effort of Gray's imagination, the result of his creative mind, a work of art but a piece of fantasy as well. And once *Park* is categorized as a fantasy, it is tempting to search for some hidden meaning in Park's dream, some involved allegory behind Gray's surface narrative.

Like any work of art worth thinking about seriously, *Park* might be interpreted in a number of ways. Was he, for example, pondering the high-low dualism of human life in his depiction of the two groups of individuals Park encounters? Bernard Bergonzi, who has made a special study of *Park*, does not believe it fruitful to delve into any of the philosophical complexities the novella presents. That the work may have symbolical overtones, he readily admits. But in his opinion, the chief effects of *Park* are to be found on the surface. As Bergonzi reads *Park*, it is essentially a dramatization of "the problem of the loss of identity . . . but without deep mythic power" [see excerpt dated 1966].

Alexandra Zaina, another Gray specialist [see her essay in *Two Friends*, ed. Brocard Sewell], is also of the opinion that despite symbolic overtones *Park* does not have any special esoteric dimensions; yet she admits to being troubled by a feeling that the story may have unsuspected levels of meaning. She questions, for example, the purpose of a map made up of straight lines, ragged forms, and unknown signs which a Monsignor Villa Gracil shows Park, forcing him—and the reader—to piece together anew the geography of England. She also wonders if there might be a code which would make the names of Drak, Dlar, and such other characters as Svillig, Ini'in, Villa Gracil more intelligible.

An onomastic study of the names of various characters, regrettably, does not indicate any discernible pattern. Proceeding from the known to the unknown reveals nothing. That Drak is Park, Gray informs the reader. Another character, A Ra, who dedicates an oratory to St. Sebastian, is clearly André Raffalovich. Other names, however, are not so obvious; indeed, they are impossible to decipher. They could represent various individuals Gray knew, but, lacking clues, the reader remains baffled. If there is some special meaning to place names, or the blacks being labeled Wampani and their language being designated Bapama, Gray does not even hint an explanation.

After speculating upon such questions and not arriving at satisfactory answers, critics are forced to conclude that we may never fathom completely all that is implicit in *Park*. The novella remains something of a verbal curiosity. There is no key that will open the narrative to a particular meaning. If there were, Gray has failed to give reasonable hints. At best, he parceled out what he may have intended into disparate elements. There is no disagreeing with Brocard Sewell's contention that *Park* cannot be categorized or classified: "it is part science-fiction, part novel of ideas."

Despite its troublesome ambiguities, *Park* has drawn its share of critics. A critic for the *Times Literary Supplement* was not especially satisfied with the novella. Reading with a captious eye, he dismissed the work as "the kind of thing art for art's sake comes to in the long run." That the novella might appeal to some readers depended upon whether one took to Gray's style: "a blend of Firbankian preciosity with a sort of avuncular sacerdotal jollity." *Park* had certain qualities, he conceded; but it was on the whole "undisciplined and self-indulgent." A critic for the *Manchester Guardian* preferred to discuss *Park* as science fiction. Now and then, he pointed out, the novella even attained to the superior qualities found in Kafka and Firbank.

John Pope-Hennessy, who reviewed *Park* for *Blackfriars*, was more enthusiastic. *Park,* he proposed, has "a distinctive quality" which makes it "a remarkable and sometimes beautiful book." Among several critics who agree with Pope-Hennessy is Brocard Sewell. "*Park* is a small masterpiece," he contends. "Its prose is pure." Alexandra Zaina also rates *Park* the most important of Gray's prose writings: "a minor masterpiece." *Park* is proof enough for her that Gray was "far more than a fossilized survival of an earlier day."

Bernard Bergonzi goes even further. Willing to concede that *Park* reveals some of its author's weaknesses, Bergonzi feels that the novella is nonetheless Gray's most sustained imaginative achievement. He recommends that this "curiously timeless work . . . deserves a niche in the history of modern English fiction." Bergonzi especially admires the novella for its "mannered and deliberately understated mode of narration . . . which recalls the laconic precision of the best of Gray's verse."

Park, nevertheless, has never been—nor will it likely ever be—a popular book. Its subjectivity of treatment so limits appeal that only two editions of the novella have ever been published. At the moment there is little demand for a third printing. Popularity is relative at best, and Gray never sought mass appeal; still, he may have wished that this unusual piece of fiction had the quality to attract a larger share of readers than it has.

Fully aware of the rather restrictive nature of *Park*, one critic was moved to remark that the work "has the dryness of a patrician wine." His apt metaphor is perhaps the best critical summation of *Park*—its brilliant style, its overall quality, its limited appeal. (pp. 129-32)

There are so many contradictions about Gray, the man, the priest, that any attempt to sum up his life is fraught with the danger of oversimplification. To evaluate him as a poet, fiction writer, and essayist is no less difficult. Practically every book written about the nineties mentions his name, but allusions to him or his work are often so casual that he would seem to be at best an insignificant figure. The same critics who too quickly consign him to a literary limbo are usually those least familiar with his poetry. To know his poetry is not to admire it, necessarily, but some knowledge of his creativity allows for more objective criticism.

To think of Gray only as a nineties' poet, furthermore, is not quite proper. Gray's gifts, as Ian Fletcher has pointed out, survived into the twentieth century and were fulfilled. Fletcher's admiration for Gray the poet has encouraged him to collect all of Gray's verse and to plan for its eventual publication. Only after all his poetry is collected in one volume, Fletcher maintains, will readers and critics be able to deal with "a quietly compelling identity," to formulate a clearer idea of Gray's achievement.

Much of the poetry that Gray wrote in the twenties and thirties, especially that found in *The Long Road* and *Poems,* . . . compares favorably with that written by some of the better-known so-called moderns. That Gray had his own individualized styles, and cannot be conveniently categorized, is to his credit.

Several Grays followed one another through the decades. The poet who wrote *Silverpoints,* for example, does not at all resemble the poet who composed *The Blue Calendars;* nor does he closely approximate the poet who decade after decade seemed to find another voice. Oversimplification is so often falsification that to label him with one catch term or another is misleading. Geoffrey Grigson, nevertheless, likes to think of Gray as "less of a naturalist in the weak Georgian sense than a fantast in search of a hard style."

In addition to one or two admirable short stories, Gray the writer of fiction did complete two noteworthy novellas. Neither **"The Person in Question"** nor *Park* has attracted more than a handful of readers, however. Nor is it likely that Gray will be remembered for his essays. His dramas do not stand a good chance of ever being republished. Much of what Gray wrote will remain curiosity pieces. All that being said, it is amazing how many of Gray's poems and examples of his prose have been published since his death in 1934. Dozens of his poems have been reprinted in anthologies and journals. (pp. 137-39)

The few critics who have focused on the lasting quality of the best of Gray's work have good reasons for their views; still, what Gray's reputation may be fifty years from now, even they are not willing to conjecture. A fair-minded estimate allows the inference that Gray will not be soon forgotten, that his life, works, and influence will continue to attract more and more scholars.

The critic Geoffrey Grigson may overstate his case a bit when he writes glowingly of some of Gray's poems, especially **"The Flying Fish,"** which he labels "one of the good 'modern' poems of our century"; but there is no refuting his judgment that Gray is "one of the half-hidden poets who cannot be left out of this century's account." Every indication is that the memory of John Gray will more than merely linger–it should increase. (p. 139)

> *G. A. Cevasco, in his* John Gray, *Twayne Publishers, 1982, 156 p.*

ADDITIONAL BIBLIOGRAPHY

Cevasco, G. A. "John Gray (1866-1934): A Primary Bibliography and an Annotated Bibliography of Writings about Him." *English Literature in Transition* 19, No. 1 (1976): 49-63.
    Most complete bibliography of primary and secondary works.

Fletcher, Iain. "Amendments and Additions to a Bibliography of John Gray." *English Literature in Transition* 22, No. 1 (1979): 62-7.
    Additions of both primary and secondary works.

"Brotherhood of the Bard." *The Graphic* XLVII, No. 1219 (8 April 1893): 383.
    Passing comment on *Silverpoints,* stating of Gray "that if he would abandon the affectations of contemporary French verse, he might write excellent English poetry."

O'Brien, Mrs. William. "Friends for Eternity: André Raffalovich and John Gray." *The Irish Monthly* LXII, No. 737 (November 1934): 699-706.*
    Sympathetic account of their personal and literary friendship.

Sewell, Brocard, ed. *Two Friends: John Gray & André Raffalovich.* Aylesford, Eng.: Saint Albert's Press, 1963, 193 p.*
    Biographical and critical essays. Contributors include Sewell, Iain Fletcher, Alexandra Zaina, Patricio Gannon, and John Gawsworth.

Tindall, William York. "The Forest of Symbols." In his *Forces in Modern British Literature, 1885-1946,* pp. 224-82. New York: Alfred A. Knopf, 1949.*
    Brief consideration of Gray's importance among fin-de-siècle poets.

O. Henry

1862-1910

(Pseudonym of William Sidney Porter) American short story writer, journalist, and novelist.

O. Henry is perhaps the most popular and widely known American short story writer of the twentieth century. During the eight-year period that he lived and wrote in New York City, the short story form was at the height of its popularity, and dozens of periodicals featuring short fiction competed for the works of celebrated authors. It was against this background that O. Henry quickly rose to the position of the most sought-after and acclaimed American short story writer by virtue of his distinctive works: typically brief stories, characterized by familiar, conversational openings, circumlocutory dialogue, plots hinging on improbable coincidence, and variations on the surprise or twist ending. The highly ironic, sentimental, or unexpected story conclusion has been so closely identified with O. Henry that his name has become synonymous with fiction of this kind.

O. Henry was born William Sidney Porter, the second son of Dr. and Mrs. Algernon Sidney Porter of Greensboro, North Carolina. Following Mrs. Porter's death when O. Henry was three, Dr. Porter moved with his children into his mother's house, where the boys' grandmother and an aunt undertook their education and upbringing. As a teenager, O. Henry helped support his family by working as a pharmacist's assistant in an uncle's drugstore, and he obtained his pharmacist's license in 1881. Never in robust health, O. Henry worried particularly about contracting pneumonia, which had been the cause of his mother's early death. When at nineteen he developed a persistent cough, he sought the more beneficial climate of southwest Texas, where he worked on a cattle ranch owned by family friends. His health improved after several years, and at twenty-two he moved to Austin, where he met his first wife and found work as a bank teller. In 1894 he purchased a weekly humor paper, retitled it *The Rolling Stone,* and supplied virtually all of the paper's content. When the paper failed after a year's publication, he continued to submit humorous stories and articles to other newspapers. Also in 1894, O. Henry was dismissed from his bank post because of shortages in his accounts. When the case was reinvestigated in 1895, and embezzlement charges seemed imminent, he fled Austin for Houston and later New Orleans, sailing from there to Honduras. In 1897, after learning that his wife was seriously ill, he returned to Austin and surrendered to authorities. After his wife's death he was convicted of embezzlement and sentenced to five years in the Federal Penitentiary in Ohio, where he was assigned to the prison pharmacy's twelve-hour midnight shift. His duties included prescribing and administering medication and tending to injured prisoners. O. Henry had made his first professional story sale to a magazine shortly before his conviction, and he continued to submit short stories for publication, based on his experiences in the southwest, in Central America, and in prison, using his in-laws' Pittsburgh address as a screen for his actual circumstances.

O. Henry's criminal conviction and prison term was for some time the most uncertain and controversial aspect of his life. One of his biographers, Al Jennings, who was in the penitentiary with O. Henry, recounts that the writer's greatest fear was that he would be recognized and greeted by a former inmate while in the company of others. Many of O. Henry's closest acquaintances never knew that he had spent time in prison, and he often juggled dates to account for the years spent in prison. As a result there was some initial uncertainty about several important dates in his life, but biographers now believe that they have established an accurate chronology. It was common for early biographical essays to hotly debate the question of his innocence or guilt. Most modern biographers conclude that while O. Henry may have been technically guilty of embezzlement, he was almost certainly following the extremely lax bookkeeping policies of the Austin bank.

Obtaining an early release after serving three years of his sentence, O. Henry lived for a short time with his wife's parents, but moved to New York City in the spring of 1902 at the urging of *Ainslee's Magazine* editors Gilman Hall and Richard Duffy, who had been printing his stories and were confident that he could make a successful career writing for New York magazines. O. Henry began publishing stories in numerous periodicals under pseudonyms that included variations of his real name. He quickly gained fame under his most often-used pen name, O. Henry. A contract with the New York *Sunday World* for a weekly short story provided him with a steady income, while the *World*'s circulation of nearly one-half million assured

Culver Pictures, Inc.

him a wide readership. O. Henry's remuneration from the *World*—one hundred dollars per story—was liberal for the time, and he also supplemented his income by selling stories to other magazines that were anxious to print his popular works. However, he was financially irresponsible and continually in debt. He loved to sit for hours in restaurants and bars, observing the other patrons and constructing instantaneous fictions about them, and then leave a tip that often exceeded his bill. He was also lavish in the handouts he dispensed to panhandlers and prostitutes who, he claimed, often provided him with the germ of a story whereby he more than recouped his initial investment. Increasingly, he turned out stories in haste to honor the generous advances he received from editors.

Biographer Richard O'Connor has written that "the year 1904 . . . was easily the busiest and most productive of [O. Henry's] career. As the price for his stories went up, he simply produced less. But that vintage year . . . saw him at the peak of his creative power." Since his arrival in New York two years earlier, O. Henry had been steadily gaining not only in popularity but also in critical regard as an important literary figure. In 1904, *McClure's Magazine* editor Witter Bynner suggested assembling O. Henry's stories with Central American settings as a novel under the title *Cabbages and Kings*. His first short story collection, *The Four Million*, followed two years later, and his works, rescued from the impermanence of periodical publication, became more widely known. Further compilations of his stories appeared yearly thereafter and for several years after his death, which was caused by a variety of health problems, including diabetes and cirrhosis of the liver exacerbated by alcoholism.

O. Henry's fame rests upon the type of short story he wrote and not upon the distinction of any individual work. The archetypal O. Henry story is described by his biographer and critic Eugene Current-García as possessing several unmistakable characteristics: "the chatty, shortcut opening; the catchy, piquant descriptive phrasing; the confidential, reminiscent narrator; the chance meeting of old pals; and half a dozen or more variations of the surprise ending." His stories are often divided into five distinct groups according to their settings: the American South, the West, Central America, prison, and New York. By far the best known and most often reprinted are the stories set in New York City. These one hundred and forty stories, making up nearly half of his total output, capture the essence of early twentieth-century city life, and include the frequently anthologized "Gift of the Magi," "The Furnished Room," "A Municipal Report," "The Skylight Room," and "An Unfinished Story." Commonly recurring themes in O. Henry's short stories are those of deception, mistaken identity, the effects of coincidence, the inexorable nature of fate, and the resolution of seemingly insurmountable difficulties separating two lovers. In the stories that revolve around deliberate deception, O. Henry often used a plot contrivance that he called "turning the tables on Haroun Al-Raschid," the caliph from *The Arabian Nights' Entertainments* who disguised himself to mingle with the common people. In O. Henry's stories it is the common people—the clerks, salespeople, factory and office workers—who save assiduously for the infrequent evenings when they can dress in their finest and mix with the rich and powerful. A favorite device of O. Henry was to depict a poor working man or woman whose potentially romantic encounters come to nothing because of the ridiculous poses they feel obliged to adopt while pretending to be wealthy. Although plot resolutions of O. Henry stories often depend on improbable coincidence, some critics assert that the wealth of detail concerning characters and settings makes the stories appear naturalistic despite the sometimes fantastic plots.

During the last decade of his life and for about a decade following his death, O. Henry was the most popular and widely read American short story writer. He was commonly regarded as the modern American master of the short story form, ranked with Edgar Allan Poe, Nathaniel Hawthorne, and Bret Harte. His works were considered models of the genre and his short story techniques were taught in college writing courses. The growing tide of favorable assessments culminated in C. Alphonso Smith's *O. Henry Biography,* published in 1916. At about this time, however, O. Henry's critical reputation began to undergo reevaluation. Critics began to question the validity of the excessive praise that O. Henry had garnered in the previous two decades, and some—most notably Katharine Fullerton Gerould and Fred Lewis Pattee—dismissed his work as facile, anecdotal, journalistic, and of little lasting literary value. Gerould went so far as to denounce O. Henry's pervasive influence on the modern short story as "pernicious," while Pattee questioned the moral basis of the works, writing that O. Henry's nonjudgmental portrayals of criminals amounted to an endorsement of lawless behavior. Other critics noted how quickly O. Henry stories seemed to date, and his trademark surprise endings were called overly sentimental and predictable.

Concurrent with the growth of negative criticism in the United States came the first translations of O. Henry's stories and the beginning of his great renown abroad. He underwent a particular vogue in Russia, where he remains one of a very few American writers who is both popular with readers and sanctioned by the Soviet government. With the advent of experimental literary forms in American literature in the 1920s and 1930s, O. Henry's critical reputation reached its lowest point. The tendency of literary critics—when they mentioned O. Henry at all—was to relegate him to a minor place in American literary history. In the 1960s, however, another reevaluation began to take place, inspired largely by the fact that despite his decline in critical standing, O. Henry had always retained popularity with readers. Critics continue to reassess O. Henry's contribution to literature, with most maintaining that his characteristically brief, humorous, sometimes sentimental stories have earned him a permanent place as a skilled and inventive story writer who profoundly influenced the course of the American short story for half a century.

(See also *TCLC,* Vol. 1; *Contemporary Authors,* Vol. 104; *Dictionary of Literary Biography,* Vol. 12: *American Realists and Naturalists;* and *Yesterday's Authors of Books for Children,* Vol. 2)

PRINCIPAL WORKS

Cabbages and Kings (novel) 1904
The Four Million (short stories) 1906
Heart of the West (short stories) 1907
The Trimmed Lamp (short stories) 1907
The Gentle Grafter (short stories) 1908
The Voice of the City (short stories) 1908
Options (short stories) 1909
Roads of Destiny (short stories) 1909
Strictly Business (short stories) 1910
Whirligigs (short stories) 1910
Sixes and Sevens (short stories) 1911
Rolling Stones (short stories) 1912

Waifs and Strays (short stories) 1917
O. Henryana (sketches and poetry) 1920
Letters to Lithopolis (letters) 1922
Postscripts (humor) 1923
O. Henry Encore (humor) 1939
The Complete Works of O. Henry. 2 vols. (short stories
    and novel) 1953

STANHOPE SEARLES   (essay date 1905)

[*In the following excerpt, Searles reviews O. Henry's first book,*
Cabbages and Kings.]

With his stories of life in the Central American republics Mr.
Henry is seriously threatening the supremacy of Mr. Richard
Harding Davis in a field in which for several years the more
widely known writer has been absolutely alone. There is no
resemblance whatever between *Soldiers of Fortune* and *Cap-*
tain Macklin and *Cabbages and Kings* as stories, but in their
point of view and general impressions of the strange countries
about which they write the two authors are much alike. One
of Mr. Henry's absconding Latin-American presidents might
readily be fitted, orders, uniform, accent, braggadocio and all,
into any chapter of *Soldiers of Fortune*. . . . The American
Consul, the gentlemanly adventurer clamouring for a concession, the fakirs and hucksters of the United States, of France
and Germany and England, the exiled bank presidents under
a cloud, the promoters of revolutions and the derelict drunkards—these people you find in O. Henry's pages and they
are much the same as in the pages of Mr. Davis. They are
portrayed with much humour and sympathy and keenness, and
behind them you are made to see that wonderful background
of white beach and waving palm trees and sunshine and flowers
and fruit and dirt and discomfort; you are made to feel all the
heat and disorder and squalor, and to understand with perfect
sympathy the American or European who looks out over the
dancing blue waters and longs wistfully for "God's Country."

Cabbages and Kings is a book of very unusual interest and
cleverness. The general popularity will necessarily be limited
by the fact that it is essentially a man's book—above all the
kind of man who at some time of his life has felt the nostalgia
strong upon him and yearned to slake his thirst with the drinks
of home. At first sight the book seems to be merely a strung-
together series of sketches, introducing various characters and
episodes, each to be read for its own sake, and having little
connection with those which precede and follow it. It is not
until the very end that the reader realises that there has been
an actual mystery throughout. . . . Then for the first time are
understood countless allusions and innuendoes, and certain
characters of whom it was impossible entirely to approve stand
out in a more favourable light. A number of the chapters might
be taken bodily from the book and held up as admirable examples of short-story telling. (pp. 561-62)

> Stanhope Searles, "O. Henry's 'Cabbages and
> Kings'," in The Bookman, *New York, Vol. XX, No.*
> *6, February, 1905, pp. 561-62.*

NICHOLAS VACHEL LINDSAY   (poem date 1912)

[*An American poet and essayist, Lindsay is remembered for his*
strongly rhythmic popular poetry. Many of his best poems were

CABBAGES
AND KINGS

BY

O. HENRY

NEW YORK
McCLURE, PHILLIPS & CO.
MCMIV

Title page of O. Henry's first book.

written to commemorate such figures as William Booth, the foun-
der of the Salvation Army, and John Chapman, the American folk
hero Johnny Appleseed. In the following poem, Lindsay pays
tribute to O. Henry.]

THE KNIGHT IN DISGUISE

[Concerning O. Henry (Sidney Porter)]

> *"He could not forget that he was a Sid-*
>   *ney."*

Is this Sir Philip Sidney, this loud clown,
The darling of the glad and gaping town?

This is that dubious hero of the press
Whose slangy tongue and insolent address
Were spiced to rouse on Sunday afternoon
The man with yellow journals round him
    strewn.
We laughed and dozed, then roused and read
    again,
And vowed O. Henry funniest of men.
He always worked a triple-hinged surprise
To end the scene and make one rub his eyes.

He comes with vaudeville, with stare and leer.
He comes with magephone and specious cheer.

His troupe, too fat or short or long or lean,
Step from the pages of the magazine
With slapstick or sombrero or with cane:
The rube, the cowboy or the masher vain.
They over-act each part. But at the height
Of banter and of canter and delight
The masks fall off for one queer instant there
And show real faces: faces full of care
And desperate longing: love that's hot or
    cold;
And subtle thoughts, and countenances bold.
The masks go back. 'Tis one more joke.
    Laugh on!
The goodly grown-up company is gone.

No doubt had he occasion to address
The brilliant court of purple-clad Queen Bess,
He would have wrought for them the best he
    knew
And led more loftily his actor-crew.
How coolly he misquoted. 'Twas his art—
Slave-scholar, who misquoted—from the heart.
So when we slapped his back with friendly roar
Æsop awaited him without the door,—
Æsop the Greek, who made dull masters laugh
With little tales of *fox* and *dog* and *calf*.
And be it said, mid these his pranks so odd
With something nigh to chivalry he trod
And oft the drear and driven would defend—
The little shopgirls' knight unto the end.
Yea, he had passed, ere we could understand
The blade of Sidney glimmered in his hand.
Yea, ere we knew, Sir Philip's sword was drawn
With valiant cut and thrust, and he was gone.

                  (pp. 52-4)

Nicholas Vachel Lindsay, "The Knight in Disguise,"
in his General William Booth Enters into Heaven and
Other Poems, *Mitchell Kennerley, 1913, pp. 52-4.*

HYDER E. ROLLINS (essay date 1914)

[*Rollins was an American educator, editor, and critic. In the
following excerpt, he discusses some characteristics of O. Henry's
short stories.*]

All critics, so far as I know, class O. Henry's stories as hyphenated, capitalized "Short-Stories"; but if they hold to the hide-bound *a priori* rules which require a short-story to fulfil the three classic unities, to deal with one character only, and to show rigid compression and condensation of details, they are hoist with their own petard. For O. Henry gleefully breaks every rule and heartily enjoys the critics' discomfiture. The only thing that may be confidently postulated of his stories is that they usually produce a single effect on the mind of the reader. This alone, it would seem, is enough to make a short story a "short-story": most certainly it was the ideal that Poe had in mind. O. Henry recognized no rigid, unalterable laws of structure: the story was the thing, and there was a best method of telling each story. Indeed he declared: "Rule I of story-writing is to write stories that please yourself. There is no rule 2. In writing, forget the public. I get a story thoroughly in mind before I sit down at my table. Then I write it out quickly, and without revising it, send it to my publishers. In this way I am able to judge my work almost as the public

judges it. I've seen stories in type that I didn't at first blush recognize as my own."

The elucidation was unnecessary, for his stories plainly evince such workmanship. That O. Henry was a technical artist, few will deny: even his mannerisms, such as his interpolative comments on plot-structure and his pseudo-moralizing divagations, cannot debar his narratives from the short-story class. Nevertheless, it is to be regretted that he took so many liberties, for his mannerisms may soon cease to amuse, and they are likely to lower his rank in literature. (p. 223)

It was quite usual for him to ramble carelessly afield, making sundry vague remarks about the attitude of the Columbia College professors towards grammar and the plagiarism he is contemplating, and then to lament that, in thus sparring for an opening, he has forgotten to follow Aristotle's directions! Or to open a story with the casual remark that "It was a day in March," and to advise: "Never, never begin a story this way when you write one. No opening could possibly be worse. It is unimaginative, flat, dry and likely to consist of mere wind." In later stories, such as "The Unprofitable Servant," he makes no 'bones' of confessing that he wrote thus in order "to swell the number of words" for which he was paid. Indisputably this is attractive, though one feels that it is unwarranted, that the author has taken an undue advantage to secure humor. The truth is O. Henry failed to take himself and his art seriously. He strove only to arrest the momentary attention of the rapidly moving mass of readers. And in his stories the first sentence, which is customarily some such remark as "No, bumptious reader, this is not a continuation of the Elsie series," invariably does this. Furthermore, since the preconceived effect that his stories attempt to produce is usually one of surprise or humor, his introductions always aid in producing this effect.

There is little skirmishing in the body of his stories: it progresses rapidly, and shows a rigid economy of words. O. Henry's mania for suppression of detail comes nearer to equalling that of "Guy de Mopassong" (as he calls him) and of other French writers than does that of any other American writer, not excepting Poe. He had a distinct aim, and he wrote every word with this aim in view. His stories are customarily short: not many run over three thousand words, and the majority contain about two thousand. (pp. 223-24)

Yet, paradoxical as it may seem, nearly every one of his stories contains one or more digressions, which always seem necessary, and which remind one forcibly of Thackeray. (pp. 224-25)

His conclusions—they are O. Henry's and no one else's. Children play "crack-the-whip," not for the fun of the long preliminary run, but for the excitement of the final sharp twist that throws them off their feet. So adults read O. Henry, impatiently glancing at the swiftly moving details in pleased expectancy of a surprising ending. The conclusion is an enigma: the author has your nerves all a-quiver until the last sentence. There are few explanations, the surprise comes quickly, and the story is finished. O. Henry is as much a master of the unexpected ending as Frank Stockton was of the insolvable ending, and one must admire his skill. For although these endings are unexpected, the author never makes any statement in the body that can be held against him. On the contrary, the body is a careful preparation for the dénouement, even if the most searching reader can seldom detect it. . . . But the continued use of the unexpected ending grows tiresome, and when one sits down and reads all or the greater part of the two hundred and forty-eight short stories, he feels that the biggest surprise

O. Henry could have given him would have been a natural, expected ending. But it should be added that his surprise endings have none of the brutal cynicism which distinguishes de Maupassant's ''Necklace'' and Mérimée's ''Mateo Falcone''; his endings, on the other hand, are genuinely humorous, genuinely sympathetic, and genuinely human.

For the sake of vividness the majority of the short stories are told in the first person. Either a character who participated in the action is the narrator; or an outsider tells the story as a participant told it to him; or the story is told apparently in the third person until the author intrudes with his own comments and makes it a first-person narrative. At other times the strict third-person narrative is used; but in whatever way the stories are told, O. Henry is always talking, always explaining his views.

Stages of plot as definite as those in the Shakesperean drama may be located in most of his stories, and they are well adapted for dramatization, as the recent success of *Alias Jimmy Valentine, A Double-Dyed Deceiver,* and others show. This goes to prove that even though O. Henry pokes fun at all rules, he obeys them in the fundamental particulars. He is a clever architectonist in spite of himself. While he prided himself upon his disregard of conventional rules and upon his originality, his technique (if one ignores his manneristic digressions) conforms closely to the very rules that he affected to despise. (pp. 225-26)

Life is a mixture of smiles and sniffles and sobs, with the sniffles predominating, declared O. Henry in **''The Gift of the Magi.''** The petty joys, the petty pretentions, the petty worries of his people confirm the statement; but he also has the idea that life is one constant surprise, that the unexpected continually happens. He is, then, a pure romanticist who strives earnestly for realistic effects. (p. 228)

[O. Henry's characters] are described by their actions, or by brief, trenchant sentences that are hurled at our heads, as ''He wore heliotrope socks, but he looked like Napoleon.'' O. Henry uses rapid suggestive—never detailed circumstantial—description that is highly colored by bold figures of speech. Where many writers would waste three hundred words in a vain attempt to catalogue features so as to put an image of a character in one's mind, O. Henry can in twenty five words paint a clear, unforgettable picture. No other writer has excelled him in the use of suggestive description. Sometimes his characters are described by their unusual surroundings. But since he seldom assumes complete omniscience, it is rare that he attempts any psychological analysis.

Subjectivity of delineation makes our author's characters interesting chiefly as they reveal his views of life, and interest in characters is overshadowed by interest in plots. But for briskness, sympathy, and humor of characterization, O. Henry has few peers.

Just as his plots and his characters are humorous in conception and in treatment, so the most striking trait of O. Henry as a stylist is humor. In most instances his fun bubbles out spontaneously, but *The Gentle Grafter* bids somewhat too plainly for laughter. His stories show few pathetic-comic mixtures, for he recognizes no pathos save that of monotony, of degradation, of lost ambition, which is inherent in the lives of people; but they do show mixtures of sentiment and humor that verge on the ridiculous. Some of his means for securing humorous effects have already been noted: other and less satisfactory means used to attain this result are a continual juggling of words, execrable punning, and a superabundance of faulty literary allusions.

Humor lightens even the brief descriptions that are scattered through his stories. There is little more tendency to adjectivity in his descriptions of objects than there is in his descriptions of persons. The force and vividness of his descriptions are due rather to unusual words, to an abundance of verbs that suggest sound and movement, to numerous and striking similes and metaphors. (pp. 229-30)

About O. Henry's diction let me explain in the apt words of one of his characters: ''That man had a vocabulary of about 10,000 words and synonyms, which arrayed themselves into contraband sophistries and parables when they came out.'' His vocabulary, which is really very large, is a servant, not a master. He had absolutely no respect for conventional usage. Words must be coined to express his thought, or the usual meaning of words must be distorted; O. Henry did both without compunction. In addition to this maltreatment of words (and in the mouths of his low characters it becomes mere punning), his vocabulary was stretched by an appalling number of slang words and slang phrases. There can be little doubt that it is the presence of slang that makes O. Henry appeal so strongly to the general reading public to-day; for the public is drawn to a writer who scorns academic niceties of speech and strikes out on a new path, untrammelled by convention. There is no doubt, further, that in his unexcelled mastery of slang our author was quite effective. But taste changes and, what is more pertinent, slang itself changes, so that his constant use of slang will some day count heavily against him.

Henry Ward Beecher, who is reported to have said that when the English language got in his way it didn't stand a chance, had a worthy disciple in O. Henry. For the latter not only made a servant of words, but he also made a servant of grammar and rhetoric. It is amusing when he writes a sentence abounding in pronouns, becomes confused, and cries in parentheses, ''Confound the English language,'' but it is also cheap. Like Mr. Kipling he affects the verbless and fragmentary sentence, often with good results; and his paragraphs often lack ease of movement, composed as they are of intentionally jerky sentences. That O. Henry's piquant audacities of style are attractive is indisputable, but they are certain to lose their piquancy and to lower his rank in literature.

On the other hand, his stories have the absolute harmony of tone so essential to the short-story writer. Harmony is felt even in **''Let Me Feel Your Pulse,''** a short story that opens with broad burlesque and ends in the subtly allegorical. There is, also, a nice proportion, an artistic condensation of details, and a vividness of style that call to mind Poe in America, Mr. Kipling in England, and de Maupassant in France.

Many of his stories are marred by local and contemporaneous allusions that in a few years will be pointless and vague. . . . However pleasing such allusions may be when they are penned, they fail to interest succeeding generations. The slanginess of his style, too, is certain to render him distasteful, perhaps unintelligible, to future readers, just as it has already hindered the translation of his stories into foreign languages. Slang is ephemeral. It will make one a writer for the hour, not a writer for all time. Realizing this, O. Henry had planned a series of new stories. ''I want to show the public,'' he said, ''that I can write something new—new for me, I mean—a story without slang, a straightforward dramatic plot treated in a way that will come nearer my ideal of real story-writing.'' **''The Dream,''** which was to be the first of the new series, was broken off in the middle of a sentence by his death. In its incomplete form it appeared in the September, 1910, *Cosmopolitan,*—a more pathetic "unfinished story" than that of Dulcie.

If necessary, O. Henry's claim to permanence in American literature could be based, like Poe's, on his mastery of the short-story form, for in this respect no other American writer has excelled him. But he has other admirable traits: his frank individuality, his genuine democracy, his whole-souled optimism, his perennial humor, his sympathetic treatment of characteristic American life are irresistible.

For several years O. Henry has been the most popular short-story writer in America, and the "four million" have cried for more stories. It would be absurd to say that the inherent value of his work was not primarily the cause of his popularity, for although slangy mannerisms might attract readers, the latter will not be held if there is not something worth while in the stories themselves; and it seems improbable that the public will soon change from an enthusiastic to a Laodicean temper. To judge O. Henry as if he were a novelist is unfair. He wrote only short stories. He should be judged only by the short-story standard. And although I cannot consider O. Henry great, because of the limitations previously mentioned, yet I do believe that he will always be counted as one of the best American writers of the short story. (pp. 230-32)

> *Hyder E. Rollins, "O. Henry," in* The Sewanee Review, *Vol. XXII, No. 2, Spring, 1914, pp. 213-32.*

KATHARINE FULLERTON GEROULD (INTERVIEW WITH JOYCE KILMER) (interview date 1916)

[Kilmer was an American journalist and poet who is chiefly remembered as the author of the much-anthologized poem "Trees." In the following excerpt, he interviews Gerould, who was a novelist, short story writer, and journalist. Gerould's remarks about O. Henry's influence on the modern short story elicited comment in the Bookman *(see excerpt dated 1916).]*

O. Henry has been called many things. Some people have called him the twentieth century Balzac. Some have called him the American Maupassant. Katharine Fullerton Gerould has a new name for him. She calls him a Pernicious Influence.

And the author of "Vain Oblations" and "The Great Tradition" was not in a sternly critical mood. . . . Mrs. Gerould was at peace with all the world—but, nevertheless, she called O. Henry a pernicious influence.

Now, the traditional way for a contemporary short story writer to refer to O. Henry is blushingly to disclaim the inheritance of his mantle. And Mrs. Gerould, in spite of the fans which her extraordinarily vivid articles about the Hawaiian Islands have brought her, is above all things a writer of short stories—in the opinion of some critics the foremost living writer of short stories in English. Therefore, her opinions on the craft of short story writing have authority. I asked her why she characterized O. Henry in this unusual way.

"Well," she answered, with a smile, "I hear O. Henry is being used in the schools and the colleges. I hear that he is held up as a model by critics and professors of English. The effect of this must be pernicious. It cannot but be pernicious to spread the idea that O. Henry is a master of the short story. O. Henry did not write the short story. O. Henry wrote the expanded anecdote."

"What is the difference between them?" I asked.

"It's hard to define the difference," Mrs. Gerould replied, "but it's impossible to confuse the two forms. In a short story there are situation, suspense, and climax. O. Henry gives the reader climax—nothing else!

"O. Henry takes one incident and sets it down. What he gives us isn't a big enough piece of life to have any associations—though in other hands, those of Kipling, for example, it would have all its tentacles out, so to speak, and would seem to be actually related to life.

"In a short story you should get life in the round, as you do in Maupassant's short stories. From seeing how people act in certain circumstances which are described you should be able to imagine how they would act in any other circumstance.

"It's not a matter of length. In the very shortest of Maupassant's stories you find the people etched in so clearly that you know them; you know how they would act whatever extraneous conditions might enter. But you do not find this to be the case in O. Henry's stories; you know how the people acted in one set of circumstances, but you have no idea how they would act at any other time.

"Therefore, in this respect it seems to me that Maupassant has moral significance, and O. Henry has none. I might say that the O. Henry stories are concrete—there is nothing fluid or lifelike about them. And this is due to the fact that I mentioned—that you are told how the characters acted, and not made to understand how they always would act.

"The really great short story writers make us know their characters, make us know how they would act in any conceivable circumstances. . . .

"But O. Henry will continue to be read," said Mrs. Gerould, "because he is always so sentimental. And of course people adore to be told that there are no moral hierarchies. Nevertheless, he is not the real thing, and his influence is most pernicious. . . .

"In the modern short story the bad influence of O. Henry is to be seen in the treatment of material. In concrete incident the short story is better than it used to be, but it shows lamentable moral unconscientiousness. The author does not stand his short story up and relate it to life as he used to. O. Henry has taught him that this sort of labor is unnecessary.

"The modern short story is better technically than its predecessor of fifteen years ago, but poorer intellectually. The modern short story writer sits down at his desk with nothing in his head but the idea of a man slipping on a banana peel—a concrete incident. . . .

"But that seems to satisfy people. Anything visually exciting and dramatically emotional will go down. But you can't blame O. Henry entirely. It's the American taste, I suppose. The movies satisfy people—we all go to the movies and enjoy them—and if the movies give us what we want, then why should the short story writers bother their heads to give us anything more than incidents?"

> *Katharine Fullerton Gerould, in an interview with Joyce Kilmer, in* The New York Times Magazine, *July 23, 1916, p. 12.*

THE BOOKMAN, NEW YORK   (essay date 1916)

[*In the following excerpt, the critic challenges Katharine Fullerton Gerould's remarks about O. Henry (see excerpt dated 1916).*]

In the magazine section of the New York *Times* for July 23d there appeared an interview with Katharine Fullerton Gerould, written by Joyce Kilmer, which has elicited considerable comment. What Mrs. Gerould had to say concerned the short story in general, and the inevitable limitations of the American novel. But the impression that most readers of the interview took away was one of disparagement of the work of O. Henry, which, we think, was not just what Mrs. Gerould meant. (p. 31)

Now we are not quite ready to believe that Mrs. Gerould thinks that a liking for O. Henry is in itself pernicious, or that the use of his stories in colleges and schools is likely to work much harm. We prefer to think that she considers the danger may lurk in accepting O. Henry as the one master, and his form as the one form, to the exclusion of everyone else. Read and admire O. Henry as much as you like provided you do not forget that before O. Henry were Poe, and de Maupassant, and Bret Harte, for original as Porter was, he had read widely of the works of other men and occasionally showed himself subject to their influence. Mrs. Gerould holds up Maupassant by way of contrast. Was there ever a tale more in the vein of Maupassant than O. Henry's **"The Furnished Room"? "Thimble, Thimble"** was, to use Porter's own words, "borrowed from *The Lady or the Tiger* of the late Frank R. Stockton." Again Mrs. Gerould contends that in the very shortest of Maupassant's stories you find the people etched in so clearly that you know them; you know how they would act whatever extraneous conditions might enter. "But," she says, "you do not find this to be the case in O. Henry's stories; you know how the people acted in one set of circumstances, but you have no idea how they would act at any other time."

If we were inclined to be impolite we should say that Mrs. Gerould invites the suspicion that her knowledge of neither Maupassant nor O. Henry is profound. In other words she seems to have forgotten all but the very best of Maupassant and merely to have nibbled here and there at O. Henry. There are certain of de Maupassant's stories—"Les Bijoux," "La Parure," "Le Pardon,"—we might extend the list to include twenty or thirty titles—which have everything that the short story should have. In a few hundred words Maupassant not only builded up a vast tragic edifice, but so drew the characters that they can never be forgotten. But on the other hand there are scores of his tales which are nothing more than expanded anecdotes. The O. Henry short story, Mrs. Gerould is quoted as saying, has neither situation nor suspense—only climax. How about **"A Municipal Report"**? Are there not situation and suspense there? And does not the figure of the grim old negro servitor, sprung from a race of Zulu kings, stand out in the memory? Certainly there were situation and suspense in **"A Retrieved Reformation,"** from which story of perhaps twenty-five hundred words was made the play called *Alias Jimmy Valentine.* Has Mrs. Gerould read **"A Black Jack Bargainer,"** or **"Mammon and the Archer,"** or **"The Defeat of the City,"** or **"The Fifth Wheel,"** or **"The Shamrock and the Palm,"** or **"The Gift of the Magi,"** or **"The Duplicity of Hargraves,"** or **"Next to Reading Matter,"** or **"The Last Leaf,"** the last two suggestive respectively of Cyrano de Bergerac and an episode in Murger's *Scènes de la Vie de Bohême?* With full recognition of the decided talent of the author of *Vain Oblations* we contend that Mr. Kilmer's interview shows Mrs.

Gerould as a person given to the expression of snapshot judgments or of certain very definite limitations. (pp. 32-3)

"Strange Opinions," in The Bookman, *New York, Vol. XLIV, No. 1, September, 1916, pp. 31-3.*

C. ALPHONSO SMITH   (essay date 1916)

[*Smith was an American critic and the author of the earliest book-length biography of O. Henry, which contained the first published revelation of O. Henry's prison term and provoked severe criticism for making this detail known. In the following excerpt, Smith examines some of the predominant themes in O. Henry's fiction.*]

Every one who has heard O. Henry's stories talked about or has talked about them himself will recall or admit the frequent recurrence of some such expression as, "I can't remember the name of the story but the *point* is this." Then will follow the special bit of philosophy, the striking trait of human nature, the new aspect of an old truth, the novel revelation of character, the wider meaning given to a current saying, or whatever else it may be that constitutes the point or underlying theme of the story. Of no other stories is it said or could it be said so frequently, "The point is this," because no other writer of stories has, I think, touched upon such an array of interesting themes.

Most of those who have commented upon O. Henry's work have singled out his technique, especially his unexpected endings, as his distinctive contribution to the American short story. (p. 203)

The unexpected ending, however, is not, even technically, the main point in the structural excellence of a short story. Skill here marks only the convergence and culmination of structural excellencies that have stamped the story from the beginning. The crack of the whip at the end is a mechanical feat as compared with the skilful manipulation that made it possible. Walter Pater speaks somewhere—and O. Henry's best stories are perfect illustrations—of "that architectural conception of the work which perceives the end in the beginning and never loses sight of it, and in every part is conscious of all the rest, till the last sentence does but, with undiminished vigor, unfold and justify the first." In fact, it is not the surprise at the end that reveals the technical mastery of O. Henry or of Poe or of De Maupassant. It is rather the instantly succeeding second surprise that there should have been a first surprise: it is the clash of the unexpected but inevitable.

It is not technique, however, that has given O. Henry his wide and widening vogue. Technique starts no after-tones. It flashes and is gone. It makes no pathways for reflection. If a story leaves a residuum, it is a residuum of theme, bared and vivified by technique but not created by it. It is O. Henry's distinction that he has enlarged the area of the American short story by enriching and diversifying its social themes. In his hands the short story has become the organ of a social consciousness more varied and multiform than it had ever expressed before. . . . Whether in North Carolina or Texas or Latin America or New York an instant responsiveness to the humour or the pathos or the mere human interest of men and women playing their part in the drama of life was always his distinguishing characteristic. It was not merely that he observed closely. Beneath the power to observe and the skill to reproduce lay a passionate interest in social phenomena which with him no other interest ever equalled or ever threatened to replace.

Man in solitude made little appeal to O. Henry, though he had seen much of solitude himself. But man in society, his "humours" in the old sense, his whims and vagaries, his tragedies and comedies and tragi-comedies, his conflicts with individual and institutional forces, his complex motives, the good underlying the evil, the ideal lurking potent but unsuspected within—whatever entered as an essential factor into the social life of men and women wrought a sort of spell upon O. Henry and found increasing expression in his art. It was not startling plots that he sought: it was human nature themes, themes beckoning to him from the life about him but not yet wrought into short story form.

Take the theme that O. Henry calls "turning the tables on Haroun al Raschid." It emerges first in **"While the Auto Waits,"** published in May, 1903, a month after **"A Retrieved Reformation."** . . . O. Henry had discovered a little unexploited corner of human nature which he was further to develop and diversify in **"The Caliph and the Cad,"** **"The Caliph, Cupid, and the Clock,"** **"Lost on Dress Parade,"** and **"Transients in Arcadia."**

The psychology is sound. Shakespeare would have sanctioned it. . . . If Haroun al Raschid found it diverting to wander incognito among his poor subjects, why should not "the humble and poverty-stricken" of this more modern and self-expressive age play the ultra-rich once in a while? They do, but they had lacked a spokesman till O. Henry appeared for them. He, by the way, goes with them in spirit and they all return to their tasks happy and refreshed. They have given their imagination a surf bath.

Habit is another favourite theme. A man believes that he has conquered a certain deeply rooted habit, or hopes he has. By a decisive act or experience he puts a certain stage of his life, as he thinks, behind him. O. Henry is not greatly interested in how he does this: he may change from a drifting tramp to a daring desperado; he may marry; he may undergo an emotional reformation which seems to run a line of cleavage between the old life and the new; a woman may bid farewell to her position as cashier in a downtown restaurant and enter the ranks of the most exclusive society.

But, however the break with the past comes about, O. Henry is profoundly interested in the possibilities of relapse. Such stories, to mention them in the order of their writing, as **"The Passing of Black Eagle,"** **"A Comedy in Rubber,"** **"From the Cabby's Seat,"** **"The Pendulum,"** **"The Romance of a Busy Broker,"** **"The Ferry of Unfulfilment,"** **"The Girl and the Habit,"** and **"The Harbinger"** would form an interesting pendant to William James's epochal essay on habit. Indeed I have often wondered whether the great psychologist's fondness for O. Henry was not due, in part at least, to the freshness and variety of the story teller's illustrations of mental traits and mental whimsies. No one, at any rate, can read the stories mentioned without concluding that O. Henry had at least one conviction about habit. It is that when the old environment comes back the old habit is pretty sure to come with it.

Of these particular stories, **"The Pendulum"** makes unquestionably the deepest impression. O. Henry at first called it "Katy of Frogmore Flats" but reconsidered and gave it its present name, thus indicating that the story is a dramatization of the measured to-and-fro, the monotonous *tick-tock* of a life dominated by routine. **"The Pendulum"** should be read along with the story by De Maupassant called "An Artist." Each has habit as its central theme, and the two reveal the most characteristic differences of their authors. In the setting, the tone, the story proper, the conversations, the characters, the attitude of the author to his work, there is hardly an element of the modern short story that is not sharply contrasted in these two little masterpieces, neither of which numbers two thousand words. (pp. 204-09)

"What's around the corner" seems at first glance too vague or too inclusive to be labelled a distinctive theme. But it was distinctive with O. Henry, distinctive in his conduct, distinctive in his art. What was at first felt to be an innate impulse, potent but indefinable, came later to be resolutely probed for short story material. "At every corner," he writes [in **"The Green Door"**], "handkerchiefs drop, fingers beckon, eyes besiege, and the lost, the lonely, the rapturous, the mysterious, the perilous, changing clues of adventure are slipped into our fingers. But few of us are willing to hold and follow them. We are grown stiff with the ramrod of convention down our backs. We pass on; and some day we come, at the end of a very dull life, to reflect that our romance has been a pallid thing of a marriage or two, a satin rosette kept in a safe deposit drawer, and a lifelong feud with a steam radiator."

From **"The Enchanted Kiss,"** written in prison, to **"The Venturers,"** written a year before his death, one may trace the footprints of characters who, in dream or vision, in sportive fancy or earnest resolve, traverse the far boundaries of life, couching their lances for routine in all of its shapes, seeking "a subject without a predicate, a road without an end, a question without an answer, a cause without an effect, a gulf stream in life's ocean." Fate, destiny, romance, adventure, the lure of divergent roads, the gleam of mysterious signals, the beckonings of the Big City—these are the signs to be followed. They may lead you astray but you will at least have had the zest of pursuit without the satiety of conquest. (pp. 209-10)

In **"The Complete Life of John Hopkins,"** fate and destiny give place to pure romance. . . .

John Hopkins experienced poverty, love, and war between the lighting and relighting of a five-cent cigar. But they were thrust upon him. He was no true adventurer. The first true adventurer is Rudolf Steiner of **"The Green Door."** (p. 213)

But the venturer is a finer fellow than the adventurer, and in **"The Venturers"** O. Henry tilts for the last time at a theme which, if health had not failed, says Mr. Gilman Hall, would have drawn from him many more stories. In a little backless notebook which O. Henry used in New York I find the jotting from which **"The Venturers"** grew. . . . **"The Venturers"** harks back to this entry, the last in the book: "Followers of chance—Two knights-errant—One leaves girl and other marries her for what may be 'around the corner.'" (pp. 214-15)

In fact, the central idea of **"The Venturers,"** the revolt against the calculable, seems at times to run away with the story itself. Ives marries Miss Marsden at last because he became convinced that marriage is the greatest "venture" of all. But what convinced him? The expository part of the narrative has put the emphasis elsewhere. The centre of the story seems not quite in the middle.

Another theme, one that O. Henry has almost pre-empted, is the shop-girl. (p. 216)

Certainly no other American writer has so identified himself with the life problems of the shop-girl in New York as has O. Henry. In his thinking she was an inseparable part of the larger life of the city. She belonged to the class that he thought of as under a strain and his interest in her welfare grew with his knowledge of the conditions surrounding her. . . . It has been said that O. Henry laughs with the shop-girl rather than at her, but the truth is that he does not laugh at all when she is his theme; he smiles here and there but the smile is at the humours of life itself rather than at the shop-girl in particular. (p. 217)

But the shop-girl is a part of a larger theme and that theme is the city. (p. 226)

A city was to O. Henry not merely a collective entity, not merely an individuality; certainly not a municipality: it was a personality. (p. 227)

His Latin American stories may serve as illustrations. They deal sparingly with native characters. O. Henry evidently felt some hesitation here, for in his rapid journey from Honduras around both coasts of South America the unit of progress was the coastal town. There was little time to study native character as he studied it on his own soil. The city, therefore, rather than the citizen, is made prominent. An American doctor, for example, who has travelled widely in Latin America, considers O. Henry's description of Espiritu unequalled in accuracy and vividness as a sketch of the typical Latin American coastal town. Certainly no one of his Latin American character portraits is as detailed or as intimate. (pp. 228-29)

But it is in his references to American cities that O. Henry's feeling for the city as a unit is best revealed. It has been said of George Eliot that her passion for individualizing was so great that a character is rarely introduced in her stories, even if he only says "Breakfast is served," without being separated in some way from the other characters. The same may be said of O. Henry's mention of American towns and cities. Sometimes the differentiation is diffused through the story from beginning to end. Sometimes it is summarized in a phrase or paragraph. (p. 229)

Nowhere does O. Henry's insight into human nature, his breadth and depth, his pervasive humour, or his essential Americanism show more clearly than in such stories as **"The Duplicity of Hargraves," "The Champion of the Weather," "New York by Campfire Light," "The Pride of the Cities," "From Each According to His Ability," "The Rose of Dixie," "The Discounters of Money," "Thimble, Thimble,"** and **"Best-Seller."** In each of these he stages a contrast between the North and the South or the North and the West.

The task was not an original one but he did it in an original way. Since 1870 American literature has abounded in short stories, novels, and plays that are geographical not only in *locale* but in spirit and content. (p. 238)

Before the advent of O. Henry, however, short story writers had fought shy of essaying such a contrast within the narrow limits of a single story, a contrast for which the drama and the novel seemed better fitted. Bret Harte and Hamlin Garland, Sarah Orne Jewett and Mrs. Wilkins-Freeman, Thomas Nelson Page and Joel Chandler Harris, and a score of others had proved that the short story could be made to represent as large a territory as the novel. But as an instructed delegate each short story preferred to speak for only one constituency. When it tried to represent two at the same time, there was apt to be a glorification of the one and a caricature of the other.

It is one of O. Henry's distinctions that he is fair to both. . . . O. Henry is "genial and equal-handed" not only in the characteristics selected but in the way he pits characteristic against characteristic, foible against foible, an excess against a defect,

then again a defect against an excess. Art and heart are so blended in these contrasts, wide and liberal observation is so allied to shrewd but kindly insight, that the reader hardly realizes the breadth of the theme or the sureness of the author's footing.

O. Henry was not a propagandist, but one cannot re-read these stories without feeling that here as elsewhere the story teller is much more than a mere entertainer. He has suggested a nationalism in which North, West, and South are to play their necessary parts. It is not a question of surrender or abdication; it is a question rather of give and take. (pp. 240-41)

But each theme that has been mentioned is but an illustration of that larger quest in which all of O. Henry's stories find their common meeting-place—the search for those common traits and common impulses which together form a sort of common denominator of our common humanity. Many of his two hundred and fifty stories are impossible; none, rightly considered, are improbable. They are so rooted in the common soil of our common nature that even when dogs or monuments do the talking we do the thinking. The theme divisions that we have attempted to make are, after all, only sub-divisions. The ultimate theme is your nature and mine.

It is too soon to attempt to assign O. Henry a comparative rank among his predecessors. We may attempt, however, to place him if not to weigh him. (p. 243)

A glance through O. Henry's pages shows that his familiarity with the different sections of the United States was greater than that of [Washington Irving, Edgar Allan Poe, Nathaniel Hawthorn, or Bret Harte]. He had lived in every part of the country that may be called distinctive except New England, but he has not pre-empted any locality. His stories take place in Latin America, in the South, in the West, and in the North. He always protested against having his stories interpreted as mere studies in localism. There was not one of his New York stories, he said, in which the place was essential to the underlying truth or to the human interest back of it. Nor was his technique distinctive. It is essentially the technique of Poe which became later the technique of De Maupassant but was modified by O. Henry to meet new needs and to subserve diverse purposes. O. Henry has humanized the short story. (p. 245)

> *C. Alphonso Smith, in his* O. Henry Biography, *Doubleday, Page & Company, 1916, 258 p.*

CARL VAN DOREN   (essay date 1917)

[*Van Doren is considered one of the most perceptive critics of the first half of the twentieth century. He worked for many years as a professor of English at Columbia University and served as literary editor and critic for* The Nation *and* The Century *during the 1920s. A founder of the Literary Guild and author or editor of several American literary histories, Van Doren was also a critically acclaimed historian and biographer. Howard Moss wrote of him: "His virtues, honesty, clarity and tolerance, are rare. His vices, occasional dullness and a somewhat monotonous rhetoric, are merely, in most places, the reverse coin of his excellence." In the following excerpt, Van Doren discusses the essential traits of O. Henry's fiction.*]

Mature when he found himself, allowed less than ten years of working life, O. Henry exhibited in his twelve volumes only one method, varied as his management of it was. His earlier stories, indeed, were written with a more careful finish than he found in demand upon Broadway, but his falling off in finish was in the interest of a quality which ruled his art. For

O. Henry as a young man in Austin, Texas.

O. Henry, among the fiction writers of his generation, was the raconteur. He is said on sound authority to have composed many of his stories to the last detail before writing a word. Whether or not this was his general practice, the fact remains that he was the literary quintessence of a type which flourishes in America, the man whom easy social boundaries have allowed to slip through all grades of experience and who finds himself called upon to render an account of his adventures to that very large body of his countrymen who stay at home and have yet the sharpest hunger for unusual incident and character. Such a man is not at all the instinctive autobiographer, whose capital is his own deeds and emotions. He is nearer the actor than the historian. His methods must be swift and easy, not too subtle. Even though he take the gravest topic, he must handle it a moment, lightly, and then be up and away to outrun boredom. Occasionally he may be sentimental, but he must insulate his sentiment with laughter. He must be colloquial, tactful, full of memories, inventive, pungent, surprising. He may speak as if he has been in every action he tells of, but he must speak as if the action no longer weighs upon him, as if his philosophy has conquered his past and made it all into material for art or mirth. (p. 250)

His method developed, so far as it can be said to have developed at all, chiefly in the direction of greater freedom for himself behind the raconteur. As he became more assured of his audience, he kept less out of sight. "Don't lose heart," he sud-

denly exclaimed in the midst of **"A Night in New Arabia,"** "because the story seems to be degenerating into a sort of moral essay for intellectual readers. There will be dialogue and stage business pretty soon." And again in **"Tommy's Burglar":** "The burglar got into the house without much difficulty; because we must have action and not too much description in a 2,000-word story." These are the perilous flippancies of a man among friends. But though O. Henry accepted more and more the insouciance of Broadway, he did not really give up his own secrets or visit his emotions upon the world. . . . The subtler moods, about which one learns either from others or from oneself, only by long brooding, O. Henry left untouched, partly because they are subtle and partly because they are private.

"If I could have a thousand years—just one little thousand years—more of life, I might, in that time, draw near enough to true Romance to touch the hem of her robe." These words [from the story **"He Also Serves"**] illuminate the mood and substance of O. Henry. The object of his vision was not history or morals, as with Hawthorne, or the world of dreams, as with Poe, but what he called adventure. "The true adventurer," he said in **"The Green Door,"** "goes forth aimless and uncalculating to meet and greet unknown fate." One need not be a hero or a philosopher to adventure thus. It is enough to keep an open and hopeful mind, a vigilant eye, and an unfading gusto for the prizes one takes on such a hunt. Like a scientist, the adventurer desires to find his facts in reality, but he wants to meet them at a time when the meeting will seem to have the significance of art. O. Henry was an adventurer of this type and a connoisseur of adventure whose restless avidity in exploring his field of romance appears in the astounding riches of his invention and illustration.

The first impression, indeed, which one is likely to take from a volume of his stories is of his high-spirited profusion. Images, turns, strange conceits, fantastic foolishness pour in upon him like a flood. He is gay, irresponsible, impudent, hoaxing; no writer in the language seems clever immediately after one has been reading O. Henry. Much of his ingenuity is verbal, but it seems almost exhaustless. (pp. 251-52)

[An] irrepressible opulence shows in his plots. Not ignorance of the austere bounds of probability but chuckling unconcern for the timid conventions of realism lies behind his romancing. Some have found in O. Henry's capricious plots the defect of the recluse who writes about a world of other men. There is no reason, however, to think that he regarded his strange tales as normal. He wrote to please himself and the magazines that paid him.

"A Night in New Arabia" thoroughly illustrates the point. Old Jacob Spraggins, a retired malefactor with a conscience which impels him to charity, has a daughter Celia, who loves the grocer's boy. This, of course, is only a new version of the case in [the early fourteenth-century metrical romance] *The Squire of Low Degree.* And O. Henry, like the nameless medieval poet, takes the wish of his readers for a guide. After a period of suspense much briefer than the Squire's seven years in Lombardy, the grocer's boy, having suddenly been made rich and worthy by certain expiatory thousands from his sweetheart's father, is made richer by the girl herself. Such an outcome is quite in the popular tradition; so is Celia's stooping to a parlor maid's cap and apron to conquer the modesty which she knew would never aspire to an heiress. Moreover, as the title of the story makes clear, O. Henry was deliberately parodying, with the sympathy of knowledge, *The Arabian Nights.*

Indeed, that great fountain head of romance comes to one's mind again and again in a reading of O. Henry. Not only verbal reminiscences, which abound, and the atmosphere of the swarming city suggest it, but a certain popular quality in the plots, as if not a man but a generation had invented them. They seem too varied to have come from one head, and their bewildering conclusions, no matter by what breathless route arrived at, generally fulfill the desires of a whole populace.

This quality of fulfillment, of course, lies at the very heart of popular romance. It is the supernatural providence of the world of fiction, and the changes which have come over the fashions in heroes and manners have not essentially altered it. Heracles, happening by, wrests Alcestis from the death that has been decreed; St. George appears just at the moment of despair and defends the English against the horrible Saracens; exactly at the right instant, in **"The Church with an Overshot Wheel,"** the stream of flour sifts down through the gallery floor and reveals the lost Aglaia to her father. Deity, saint, coincidence,—something must furnish the element of wonder and the desired miracle. One should not be misled by the fact that new names have been given to the mysterious agent. Named or nameless, it has existed and exists to accomplish in art the defeated aspirations of reality. It is O. Henry's most powerful aid, brilliant in his endings, everywhere pervasive. His strong virtue was the genius to select from the apparent plane of fact whatever might bear testimony to the presence in life of this fiery spirit of romance. By this he spoke to the public with something of the authority of a priest of their well-trusted providence.

It would be easy, smiling at the thought of O. Henry in the rôle of priest, to dismiss him with the sharp charge of having suited the public, if that charge were a final condemnation. One must admit outright that his taste was often bad. . . . It has been urged that his bad taste, which was largely verbal, must be excused because slang was his normal idiom. . . . The fact that he wrote as he talked may explain why he wrote as he did, but it cannot justify his bad taste any more than it can avert its chief penalty, which is that in twenty years much of his work must appear tawdry or unintelligible. That price he paid for certain easily bought roars from his generation.

Thus in language, as in plots, it appears that he was close to the general audience which took his art for its amusement. And the evidences of that kinship have led many persons into cant about his universal humanity. As a matter of fact, it was his curious search for romance, quite as much as his humanity, which took him into every hole and cranny of the world he worked in. He was no indiscriminate lover of the human race, swollen to quick tears and tenderness at the mere proximity of a crowd. He was not even a hail fellow, back-clapping and vociferous, but shy, chary of intimates, too much an ironist for general embraces. His whole life was a spectatorship. He was often obliged to deny what was said of him as soon as he took the public fancy, that he had been engaged in every calling he wrote about. Nor should critics who thus complimented him on his experience at the expense of his insight, have needed the facts of his career to obviate such a judgment. His work alone carries the proof that he was a spectator. Few workers could have mastered the details of so many crafts as he learned how to use, in fiction, by his observant loafing. Moreover, when one comes to think of it, almost all his stories have at least one end in the street or some public place, where he might have seen it and deduced the rest. And, finally, there was in his temper a certain balance arising out of a philosophy which,

whether natural or deliberate, is invariably a detached philosophy, a spectator's reading of life.

With his wide, serious, shrewd experience, O. Henry was destined to clearness of vision. He had need of it, indeed, in the kaleidoscopic world which he dominated, for he was dealing with that uncharted thing which his generation called "real life." But he had no delusion regarding the value of promiscuous experiments in it. "Nearly everybody nowadays," he said, "knows too much—oh, so much too much—of real life." Nor did he mistake reality. Human beings naturally joined in orderly existence, he knew to be something real. He had been made too conscious of the social order ever to forget it. Again and again he expressed a sense of the instability of the spaces which lie outside human laws. (pp. 253-56)

To appreciate reality as he did is to be a moralist. Perhaps it is with surprise that one first realizes how thoroughly, in the midst of his world of gay and fascinating romance, under his sparkle and foam of cleverness, O. Henry exhibits the rules by which men live together. After half a dozen volumes one thinks less than at first of the crackle of the endings; they seem but the mannerism of a technique, like the resounding last lines of sonnets. Gradually then emerges O. Henry's true humanity, as skilled in detecting the real motives of men as in perceiving the romantic possibilities of their lives. Above all, it is intelligent. Except when he is farcical, and so legally without the law, he is almost unerring in the disposition of his sympathies. . . . He did not stop thinking to feel. Consequently he kept much of the improbability of his plots out of his characters, who, through the most bewildering dances of fortune, maintain a proportion and consistency which could have been imparted to them only by a mind conscious of some kind of order in human conduct. This order, his system of morality, pervades O. Henry's whole universe. It is not always according to statutes—in **"A Municipal Report,"** one of his truest stories, he condones a murder—and it is not always austere. Indeed, its basis seems to be largely the instinct for fair play which exists in all popular codes. It rounds out his plots with poetic, which is popular, justice. It makes him condemn certain offenders, outspokenly, beyond the need of art, that no one may miss the moral. But it does not afflict him with sentimentalism, mob judgment, or limp concession to popular prejudices. Stoutly as he stood by the world which he represented in his art, he preferred its sense to its nonsense when it came to judging life. Just as, in his invention, he sums up and a little transcends the romantic majority of the people, so, in his reading of life, he speaks for the undeceived minority of sensible men.

This is solid ground. But as the favored story teller of that substantial public which keeps alive public art O. Henry does not speak for too narrow a minority, for those rectangular realists, for example, who think they follow Mr. Bernard Shaw. This is to say, O. Henry was sensible but not speculative. To all appearances, he cared little for general ideas. Skeptical in religion, he rarely talked skepticism; sociology he avoided; his discussions of life seldom took him beyond the province of daily conduct. He was as content to handle the world before him as his more cosmopolitan, if less humane, contemporary, Mr. Kipling. And yet O. Henry's stories are alive with the sense of irony, of the constant meddling of the "little cherub who sits up aloft." One thinks of Mr. Hardy in this connection, and there opens up a world of contrast between the art of the populace and an art which has speculation at its roots. The irony of O. Henry is as impudent as Swift's, sometimes as cruel as that of Mr. Hardy, but it is too gaily, too briefly dealt with to become a real menace to the happiness of an irrepressible comic scene. The grinding spirit of irony which allows comedy to call tragedy cousin, O. Henry never took with full seriousness. Unlike Mr. Hardy, he never hunted for an agent, long and broodingly behind the ironic fortune which taunts human effort, never found a systematic malice, a diabolical providence, to which to ascribe all the acts of irony. Like the public he represented, he had comedy's short memory, which soon forgets the first biting impertinences of fate and greets new ones with a laugh. His comedy had and took no time to build up a principle that might account for the hostile facts it met. Satisfied that there lay in each of them a little mirth, this comedy gathered such mirth where it found it, used it, flippant and prodigal, in the day's business, and pushed on to new enjoyment. Mr. Hardy's tragedy, following, gleaning, storing up, has the later and the impressive word. But the comedy of O. Henry, for all it speaks so lightly, has passed, it must still be remembered, with keen and open eyes, along the same highway. (pp. 256-59)

> *Carl Van Doren, "O. Henry," in* The Texas Review, *Vol. II, No. 3, January, 1917, pp. 248-59.*

[FRED LEWIS PATTEE]　(essay date 1917)

[*Pattee was an American literary critic and historian who, in such works as* A History of American Literature, with a View to the Fundamental Principles Underlying its Development *(1896) and* The First Century of American Literature *(1935), called for the recognition of American literature as distinct from English literature. In the following excerpt, Pattee attacks the popular American literature of his time as epitomized by the works of O. Henry.*]

After thirty years of pretty continuous reading in American literature I can say that never has the published output been so clever, so sparkling, so arresting as at the present moment, and never has it been so shallow and inconsequential. Literature that has any excellencies save the mechanical ones connected with the modern art of "putting it over" seems to be disappearing. In place of the great still books of the earlier periods, more and more are we getting literary journalism,—clever and animated little scraps in the place of fiction, sparkling shallowness, ephemeral smartness for the pulp-paper magazine and the Sunday Supplement.

This is a terrible indictment of a generation, especially if one will admit—and who will not?—that the soul of an epoch is to be found in its written product. Is the indictment too strong? For an answer we can do no better than study what undoubtedly is the leading literary success of the generation, the author who in the last seven years, according to the statement of his publishers, has sold one million, eight hundred thousand copies of his stories,—O. Henry, already crowned, it would seem, as an American classic.

Never has there been in America a literary arrival more startling and more complete than his. He appeared with the suddenness of a comet. Hardly had we learned of his existence and his name before he seemed to be filling the whole east. He was one William Sydney Porter we were told, a southerner who had seen rough life in the south-west, in Honduras, in South America,—tramp, cow-boy, adventurer, crude realist, who was bringing exotic atmospheres and breezy sections of life in uncharted regions west and south of the Caribbean. Then suddenly we found him acclaimed—strange metamorphosis!—interpreter of New York City, Scheherazade of "little old Bagdad on the Hudson," first licensed revealer of the real heart of the modern Babylon of the west, and then, before we could rub our eyes, we were told that he was dead. From *Cabbages and Kings,* his first book, to the end in 1910, was six years,—six years and ten volumes. Two posthumous issues there were, then a set of twelve, advertised everywhere as by "the Yankee de Maupassant," and sold beyond belief.

But the mere selling of almost two million copies is not the remarkable thing about O. Henry: he has been given a place beside the masters. Editors of college texts are including his work among the classics. A recent book of selections from the work of the world's greatest short story writers includes only five Americans: Irving, Hawthorne, Poe, Bunner, O. Henry. (pp. 374-75)

Manifestly, to study the work of this modern crowned classic is to study the minds of those who crowned him. Through the works of O. Henry one may estimate O. Henry's period, for a people and a generation are to be judged by what they enjoy, by what they teach in their schools and crown in their academies. Success like his means imitators, a literary school, a standard of measurement.

The first approach to the man—the only approach until recently—must be through the twelve volumes of his writings. Read all of them if you would know him, but beware: they are intoxicating. One emerges from the twelfth book of the strange Harlequin epic completely upset, unable for a time rightly to evaluate, condemning, yet inclined by some strange wizardry to praise. Where else may one find such a melange,—stories bedeviled and poured into bomb-shells; traversities and extravaganzas; rollicking farce often as vulgarly grotesque as the picture supplement of the Sunday edition; short stories violating every canon of the text-book, yet so brilliant as to tempt one to form a new decalogue of the art; sketches, philosophizings, burlesque hilarious? What spirits! what eager zest in life! what curiosity! what boyish delight in the human show! one must go back to Dickens to match it. Not a dull page, not a sentence that does not rebound upon you like a boy's laugh, or startle you, or challenge you, or prod you unawares. It is strong meat prepared for jaded palates: there are no delicate flavors, no subtle spiceries, no refined and exquisite essences of style. Its tones are loud, its humor is exaggerated, its situations and characters extremes. It is pitched for men, for healthy, elemental men: men of the bar-room and the frontier.... And yet, for all that, and notwithstanding the fact that the stories record life on isolated masculine ranches, in vice-reeking tropic towns, and the unspeakable areas of New York City, at every point that touches the feminine—paradox again!—the work is as clean as Emerson's. Not a page in the twelve volumes that may not be read aloud in the family circle.

Before one has spent an hour with the volumes, one is conscious of a strange duality in the work, one that must have had its origin in the man himself. It is as if a Hawthorne had sold his pen to Momus. There are paragraphs where the style attains a distinction rare anywhere in literature; one might cull extracts that would imply marvellous wholes. We realize that we are dealing with no uncouth ranchman who has literary aspirations, who writes in slang for want of legitimate vocabulary. We are in the hands of one who has read widely and well, one who has a vocabulary, not including his slang, which may be called unique, which may be compared indeed with that of a Pater or a James. His biographer records that for years the dictionary was his favorite reading, that he pored over it as one pores over a romance, and his reader may well believe it. (pp. 375-77)

[The] comic device most affected by O. Henry, one that may be called his most prominent mannerism, is a variety of euphemism, the translating of simple words and phrases into resounding and inflated circumlocutions. So completely did this take hold of him that one finds it in almost every paragraph; all his characters speak in it as a kind of dialect. A waiter becomes "a friendly devil in a cabbage-scented hell;" a tramp is "a knight on a restless tour of the cities;" a remark about the weather is "a pleasant reference to meteorological conditions." Instead of saying that Mr. Brunelli fell in love with Katy, he says: "Mr. Brunelli, being impressionable and a Latin, fell to conjugating the verb *amare* with Katy in the objective case." A little of this is laughable, but O. Henry wears it threadbare. The plain statement, The woman looked over at him hoping he would invite her to a champagne dinner, becomes, "She turned languishing eyes upon him as a hopeful source of lobsters and the delectable, ascendant globules of effervescence." It is too much.

His humor is more forced, more deliberately artificial, than that of Mark Twain. It is the humor of one who is *trying* to be humorous. He is brilliant rather than droll. He makes use constantly of incongruous mixtures for the last outrageous ingredient of which you feel he must have ransacked his whole experience. . . . Everywhere incongruous association: . . . "He had gout very bad in one foot, a house near Gramercy Park, half a million dollars, and a daughter." It is as if he had paraphrased Sterne's dictum into "If I knew my reader could guess what is coming in the next sentence or even in the next phrase I would change it instantly."

But it is not with the literary comedians that O. Henry is being classed by the reading public who have crowned him: it is as a serious contributor to American fiction, as a short story writer *sui generis*, the creator of a new genre, a genius, an "American de Maupassant." Conservative criticism as always has been inclined to wait: a comet be it ever so brilliant fades if you give it time, but the hand of the critic of O. Henry has been forced. It becomes impossible to ignore the voices of the times that greet us everywhere,—in university and public library, in home and club and barber shop, in the work of even the critics themselves. What of O. Henry as the writer of American short stories? (pp. 382-83)

It seems that **"Whistling Dick's Christmas Stocking,"** which was published in *McClure's Magazine* in December, 1899, the story that first introduced him to northern readers, was the beginning of his work, and as we read we feel it was by no accident that it was accepted and published by the magazine which was among the earliest to popularize its subscription price and journalize its literary content.

The story was in the new field of fiction which had been opened by Kipling. Beginning with the closing years of the century had come the demand for the concrete, for exciting stories by writers who had been a part of what they wrote,—Jack London from Alaska, [Richard Harding] Davis from South America, and the like. A fiction writer to hold his readers must have had an unusual experience in a new and picturesque area. . . . The new tale with the strange name of O. Henry instantly gained a hearing because of the strangeness and freshness of its content. It seemed to deal realistically with the winter exodus of tramps to New Orleans, and it was told apparently by one who had himself been a tramp and who spoke with authority.

The story discloses much. It tells us for one thing that the transition from Sydney Porter, the Texas newspaper paragra-

pher, to O. Henry the short story writer, came through the medium of Bret Harte's California tales. Like Harte's work, it is a story of sentiment, theatric rather than realistic, theatric even to the point of falsehood. . . . Like Harte's work too, the tale is a dramatized paradox. . . . Even the style reveals the influence of Harte. (pp. 383-84)

This same attitude toward life and material we find in **"An Afternoon Miracle," "The Sphynx Apple," "Christmas by Injunction,"** indeed in all his stories of the south-west. All were molded by Harte as Harte was molded by Dickens. The West is used as startling and picturesque background; the characters are the conventional types of western melodrama: desperadoes, cowboys, train-robbers, sheep-men, miners,—all perfect in theatric make-up, and extreme always in word and action. Like Harte, the writer had no real love for the West, and he never worked with conviction and sympathy to show the soul of it. Here and there a glow of insight and sympathy may hover over the studies that he made of his native South, but one finds it rarely in others of the two hundred and fifty stories that make up his set of books; certainly one finds it not at all in the fifty-seven that deal with the south-west. By a change of some two hundred words any one of them could be transferred to the East, and lose nothing of its value. By the changing of half a dozen names, for instance, **"The Indian Summer of Dry Valley Johnson"** could be laid in Hoboken, New Jersey, and gain thereby. Johnson could just as well be a milkman from Geneva, New York.

The external manner of Harte he outgrew, but never did he free himself of the less obvious characteristic that renders the work of both men inferior when compared with absolute standards: neither had a philosophy of life and a moral standpoint. Of the two Harte is the greater, for Harte's work is single—never does he give us the serious mixed cheaply with buffoonery,—and once or twice does he make us feel an individual human soul, but even Harte must be classed with those who have debauched American literature, since he worked the surface of life with theatric intent and always without moral background.

In the second group of O. Henry's stories fall the South American studies and *The Gentle Grafter* series that fill two whole books and overflow into other volumes of his set. Despite much splendid description and here and there real skill in reproducing the atmosphere and the spirit of the tropics, *Cabbages and Kings* must be dismissed in its author's own terms as mere "tropic vaudeville," extravaganza of the newspaper comic-column type. In *The Gentle Grafter* series, moreover, we have what is undoubtedly literature at its very worst. It may be possible that the series rests on fact; a prototype for Jeff Peters undoubtedly there was,—a certain voluble convict in the Ohio prison who told the writer all these adventures; but for all that, the tales are false. They are not life: they are *opéra bouffe*. The characters are no more flesh and blood than are Punch and Judy. They talk a dialect unknown outside of the comic theater. Sophomores at dinner may occasionally use circumlocution for humorous effect, but here everybody is sophomoric and supersophomoric; they never speak save in words sesquipedalian. . . . An Irishman in the heart of the forest bids the first man he has seen for months to dismount from his mule in terms like these: "Segregate yourself from your pseudo-equine quadruped." This is not an occasional pleasantry for humorous effect: it is the everyday language of all the characters. It is not slang, for slang is the actual words of actual men, and since the world began no one ever talked like this. It is an argot deliberately manufactured for the burlesque stage.

Art is truth,—truth to facts and truth to the presumption fundamental, at least in civilized lands, that truth is superior to falsehood and right superior to wrong, and that crime is never to be condoned. Despite the freedom of his pages from salacious stain, O. Henry must be classed as immoral, not because he uses picaresque material, or because he records the success of villainy, but because he sympathizes with his law-breakers, laughs at their impish tricks indulgently, and condones their schemes for duping the unwary. It does not excuse Jeff Peters to explain that he fleeces only those who have fleece to spare, or those rich ones who enjoy an occasional fleecing because it affords them a new sensation. *The Gentle Grafter* is cloth of the same loom that wove *Raffles* and all the others on that shelf of books that are the shame of American literature. The taint extends through all of O. Henry's work. He had no moral foundations. At heart he was with his bibulous rascals: train robbers, tramps, desperadoes, confidence men, sponges and all his other evaders and breakers of the law. He chuckled over their low ideals and their vulgar philosophy like one who sides naturally against law and order and soberness. (pp. 385-87)

The last period of O. Henry's life began in 1904 when he was engaged by the New York *World* to furnish a story each week for its Sunday Supplement. He had been in the city for two years, and had constantly written stories of life in the southwest and in Central America. He had studied the demands of the time. . . . He had gained in ease, in constructive art, in brilliancy of diction and of figure of speech. Now with the beginning of his contract with the *World* came the culmination of his later manner, that manner by many considered to be the real O. Henry. Seldom now did he attempt ambitious plot stories like **"A Black Jack Bargainer"** and **"Georgia's Ruling."** Often his weekly contribution to the *World* cannot be called a story at all. It was a sketch, an expanded "paragraph," an elaborated anecdote, a study, a "story" in the newspaper sense of the word. (pp. 387-88)

The requirements of the newspaper "story" are exacting. It must be vivid, unusual, unhackneyed, and it must have in it the modern quality of "go." It is an improvisation by one who through long practice has gained the mastery of his pen, and by one, moreover, who has been in living contact with that which he would portray. It is written in heat, excitedly, to be read with excitement and then thrown away. There must be no waste material in it, no "blue pencil stuff," and there must be "a punch in every line." The result is a brilliant *tour de force* called forth by the demand of the times for sensation, for newness, for fresh devices to gain, if only for an instant, the jaded attention of a public supersaturated with sensation.

Complaint has come that one does not remember the stories of O. Henry. Neither does one remember the newspaper "stories" he reads from morning to morning, brilliant though they may be. The trouble comes from the fact that the writer is concerned solely with his reader. Anything to catch the reader. It is a catering to the *blasé*, a mixing of condiments for palates gross with sensation. The essence of the art is the exploiting of the unexpected,—the startling comparison, manner, climax. Everywhere paradox, incongruity, electric flash-lights, "go"— New York City, ragtime, Coney Island, the Follies,—twentieth century America at full strain.

O. Henry lacks repose, and art is serene. He moves us tremendously, but never does he lift us. One cannot take seriously even his seriousness. How can one approach in the spirit of serious art a story with the title **"Psyche and the Pskyscraper,"** or one that opens like this:

THE

FOUR MILLION

BY

O. HENRY

Author of
Cabbages and Kings

NEW YORK
McCLURE, PHILLIPS & CO.
MCMVI

Title page of O. Henry's first collection of New York stories

The Poet Longfellow—or was it Confucius, the inventor of Wisdom?—remarked:

> Life is real, life is earnest;
> And things are not what they seem.

(pp. 388-89)

It is all fortissimo, all in capital letters. He slaps his reader on the back and laughs loudly as if he were in a bar-room. Never the finer subtleties of suggested effect, never the unsuspected though real and moving moral background, seldom the softer tones that touch the deeper life and move the soul, rare indeed the moments when the reader feels a sudden tightening of the throat and a quickening of the pulse. It is the humor of a comic journalist—an enormously clever and witty journalist we must admit—rather than the insight of a serious portrayer of human life; it is the day's work of a trained special reporter eager that his "stories" shall please his unpleasable chief and his capricious public long ago out-wearied with being pleased.

On the mechanical side of short story construction O. Henry was skilful even to genius. He had the unusual power of gripping his reader's attention and compelling him to go on to the end. Moreover, he was possessed of originality, finesse, brilliancy of style and diction, and that sense of form which can turn every element of the seemingly careless narrative to one startling focus. It is this architectonic perfection that has endeared him to the makers of hand books and correspondence courses. He began at the end and worked backward. Skilfully in the earlier stages of the story he furnishes materials for a solution; the reader falls into the trap, sees through the whole plot, and is about to turn to the next tale when the last sentence comes like a blow. Study the mechanism of such tales as *Girl*, "The Pendulum," "The Marry Month of May" and the like. One may detect instantly the germ of the story. (pp. 389-90)

Brilliant as this all may be, however, one must not forget that it concerns only the externals of art. His failures were at vital points. A short story must have characterization, and O. Henry's pen turned automatically to caricature. . . . A short story should be true: exaggeration is not truth. A short story should leave sharp cut and indelible the impress of a vital moment in the history of an individual soul. It should "take you by the throat like a quinsy" and not because of a situation, but because of a glimpse into a heart. O. Henry, however, deals not with souls but with types, symbols, stock figures of comedy. His point of view is that of the humorist who works with abstractions: the mother-in-law, the tramp, the fat man, the maiden lady. As a result he leaves no residuum. He amuses, he diverts, he startles, and we close his book and forget.

But his shop girls, are they not individuals? Are they not true? Do they not move us? Moved undoubtedly we are, but not because we enter the tragedy of any individual shop girl. His sermon like "An Unfinished Story" on the pernicious system that creates the type moves us even to anger, but we shed no tears over any individual. The atmosphere is too artificial for any real emotion. It is a tract, a sermon in motley, not a short story. One feels that the constructive art of a piece as brilliant as even "A Lickpenny Lover" overshadows all else within it. It is based upon an untruth: the form of the lover's proposal had to be carefully fabricated so as to make possible the final sentence which is the cause of the whole tale, and one knows that no rational man ever so worded a proposal, and that no lover as ardent could have failed to make clear his position. It smells of the footlights; it was deliberately manufactured not to interpret life, but to give a sensation.

In much of his later work he impresses us as a raconteur rather than as a weaver of that severe literary form, the short story. One feels almost the physical presence of the man as one opens a story like this: "Suppose you should be walking down Broadway after dinner, with ten minutes allotted to the consummation of your cigar while you are choosing between a diverting tragedy and something serious in the way of vaudeville. Suddenly a hand is laid on your arm." . . . One has the impression of a man blinking at ease over his cigar in the hotel lobby. His stories are brief—two thousand five hundred words the later ones average—and they follow each other breathlessly. He is familiar with his reader, asks his advice on points of diction and grammar, winks jovially, slaps him on the back and laughs aloud: "There now! it's over. Hardly had time to yawn, did you?" "Young lady, you would have liked that grocer's young man yourself." "It began way up in Sullivan County, where so many rivers and so much trouble begins—or began; how would you say that?" He opens like a responder to a toast at a banquet, with a theory or an attitude toward a phase of life, then he illustrates it with a special case holding the point of the story skilfully to the end, to bring it out with dramatic suddenness as he takes his seat amid tumultuous applause. Many of his stories, even as Mrs. Gerould has declared [see excerpt dated 1916], are mere anecdotes.

This then is O. Henry. Never a writer so whimsical. By his own confession *Cabbages and Kings* is "tropic vaudeville," and the book is not widely different from all that he wrote. He was contemporary with the ten-cent magazine; it made him

and it ruined him. He drifted with the tide, writing always that which would be best paid for. A few times he tried to break away as in "Roads of Destiny" with its Hawthorne suggestions and "The Church with an Overshot Wheel," but it was only fitfully that he even struggled to escape the vaudeville world. "The Enchanted Kiss," an absinthe dream with parts as lurid and as brilliant as anything in DeQuincey, came at the very beginning of his work. The ephemeral press had laid its hands upon him and he gave it its full demands. (pp. 390-93)

We may explain him best, perhaps, in terms of his own story "The Lost Blend": a flask of coarse western humor,—John Phoenix, Artemus Ward; a full measure of Bret Harte,—sentiment, theatric posing, melodrama; a dash of de Maupassant,—constructive art, finesse; a brimming beaker of journalistic flashiness, bubbles, tang, and then—insipid indeed all the blend without this—two bottles of the Apollinaris of O. Henry's peculiar individuality, and lo! the blend that is intoxicating a generation,—"elixir of battle, money, and high life."

Exhilarating surely, but a dangerous beverage for steady consumption. Sadly does it befuddle the head, the heart, the soul. It begets dislike of mental effort, and dependence solely upon thrill and picturesque movement. It is akin to the moving pictures, where thinking and imagination die. (pp. 393-94)

Are we not arriving at a period of ephemeral literary art, a shallow period without moral background and without philosophy of life, a period, dominated by the pulp-wood journal, a period, in short, in which an O. Henry is the crowned literary classic? (p. 394)

[*Fred Lewis Pattee*], *"The Journalization of American Literature," in* The Unpopular Review, *Vol. VII, No. 14, April-June, 1917, pp. 374-94.**

YEVGENY ZAMYATIN (essay date 1923)

[Zamyatin is considered one of the most influential Russian fiction writers and critics of the decade following the Bolshevik revolution. During this period, he urged young writers to remain independent of political pressures and to create a new reality through experimentation with form and language. Zamyatin consistently employed new techniques in his art, and his work is recognized for its arresting language, fantastic imagery, and ironic viewpoint. He wrote that true art is created by rebels and heretics, not by men obedient to official demands. Critics have also commented on the courage and integrity of his philosophy, as demonstrated in his essays, his stories, and especially in My (*written in 1920, but never published in the Soviet Union; published in English as* We, *1924). We has been called the forerunner of the contemporary anti-utopian novel, as well as a significant influence on Aldous Huxley's* Brave New World *(1932) and George Orwell's* Nineteen Eighty-four *(1949). In the following excerpt from the introduction to a 1923 Soviet edition of O. Henry's short stories, Zamyatin examines some reasons for O. Henry's popularity with Russian readers.]*

Advertisements shout; varicolored lights blink, in windows, on walls, in the sky; trains clatter somewhere in the air overhead; floors madly climb on floors, each on the other's shoulders—the tenth, the fifteenth, the twentieth. It is London, Paris, Berlin, wound up ten times more feverishly: it is America.

At top speed, by telephone, by telegraph, one must make millions, swallow something on the run in a bar, and then—a ten minute rest over a book in a flying coach. Ten minutes, no more, and in those ten minutes one must have something complete, whole, something that will fly as fast as the one-hundred-mile-an-hour train, that will make one forget the train, the clatter, the whistles, everything.

This demand was met by O. Henry (William Sidney Porter . . .). His short, sharp, quick stories hold a condensed America. Jack London is the American steppe, its snowy plains, its oceans and tropical islands; O. Henry is the American city. It does not matter that London wrote *Martin Eden* and urban stories; and it does not matter that O. Henry wrote a book of the steppes, **The Heart of the West,** and a novel, **Cabbages and Kings,** depicting the life of some South American province. Jack London is still, first and foremost, the Klondike, and O. Henry is New York.

It is wrong to say that the cinema was invented by Edison: the cinema was invented by Edison and O. Henry. In the cinema, the most important thing is motion, motion at any cost. And in O. Henry's stories the most important thing is dynamics, motion; hence his faults and his virtues.

The reader who finds himself in O. Henry's cinema will come out of it refreshed by laughter: O. Henry is invariably witty, amusing, youthfully gay—like A. Chekhonte who had not yet grown into Anton Chekhov. But occasionally his comic effects are overdrawn, far-fetched, somewhat crude. The feelings of the movie public must be touched sometimes: O. Henry stages charming four-page dramas for it. Once in a while these dramas are sentimental and cinematically edifying. But this happens seldom. O. Henry may wax emotional for a second, but immediately he rushes on again, mocking, laughing, light. A quick tongue, a quick wit, quick feelings—every muscle is in motion, very much as in the case of another American national favorite, Charlie Chaplin.

What does Charlie Chaplin believe in? What is Charlie Chaplin's philosophy? Probably nothing; probably none: there is no time. And the same is true of O. Henry, and of millions of New Yorkers. O. Henry begins one of his stories, **"The Higher Pragmatism,"** punning and playing with the sound of the words: "The ancients are discredited; Plato is boiler-plate; Aristotle is tottering; Marcus Aurelius is reeling; . . . Solomon is too solemn; you couldn't get anything out of Epictetus with a pick." And this is, perhaps, one of the few occasions when O. Henry speaks seriously. As a rule, when he is not afflicted with sentimentality, he laughs and jests. Even through his makeup, we occasionally catch a glimpse of the inimitable Charlie Chaplin. Smiling, he starves; smiling, he goes to prison; and he probably dies with a smile. Perhaps his only philosophy is that life must be conquered with a smile. O. Henry is one of those Anglo-Saxons who sang hymns on the *Titanic* as it was slowly sinking. He probably understood, or, at least, sensed remotely, that the huge, comfortable *Titanic* of nineteenth-century civilization had struck an iceberg and was majestically sinking to the bottom. But O. Henry was at home on his ship; he would not abandon it. With jests on his lips—sometimes frivolous, sometimes tinged with bitterness—he would die courageously, like Spengler's "Faustian" man.

This ineradicable, resilient vitality had been bred into O. Henry by his whole life: the hammer tempers the steel. He himself had lived in the shabby furnished rooms where he often brings his reader. He himself spent nights on park benches. He is the New York bohemian, the romantic American tramp. His biography would probably make an excellent motion picture: O. Henry the salesman in a tobacco shop; O. Henry the clerk behind a drugstore counter; O. Henry over a ledger in a business office; O. Henry the member of a gang of railway thieves in South America; O. Henry in prison for three years. And, after prison, not the "Ballad of Reading Gaol," but gay, light stories, splashed with laughter. The blow that broke the pampered, delicate Wilde struck the first creative spark from O. Henry.

Want, and the fever of the huge American city, drove him, whipped him on. He wrote too much—some years as many as fifty or sixty stories. This is why his work is uneven. True, even among his weakest lines there will be an occasional glint of true O. Henry gold. But then, the same carbon produces both coal and graphite and diamonds. At any rate, O. Henry has produced diamonds, and this brings him into the vicinity of such masters of the short story as Chekhov and Maupassant. And it must be said that O. Henry's technique—at least in his best works—is sharper, bolder, and more modern than that of many short-story writers who have already assumed their place as classics.

A pungent language, glittering with an eccentric and unexpected symbolism, is the first thing that captures the attention of O. Henry's reader. And this is not the dead, mechanical eccentricity found in the symbols of the Imagists. In O. Henry the image is always *internally* linked to the basic tonality of his character, incident, or entire story. This is why all his epithets or images, even when seemingly incongruous or far-fetched, are convincing and hypnotic. The housekeeper of a rooming house (in the story **"The Furnished Room"**) has a "throat lined with fur." At first the image is difficult to assimilate; but as the story proceeds, it is varied, becoming sharpened with each variation. Now it is simply a "furry throat," or "she said in her furriest tones"—and the cloying figure of the housekeeper, never described in detail as it would have been by the old narrative method, is etched in the imagination of the reader.

O. Henry achieves especially striking effects by employing the device which can most accurately be described as that of the *integrating image* (in analyzing literary prose we are compelled to create our terminology afresh). Thus, in the story **"The Defeat of the City,"** Miss Alicia Van Der Pool is "cool, white and inaccessible as the Matterhorn." The Matterhorn—the basic image—is developed as the story goes on; it becomes ramified and embraces almost the entire story broadly and integrally: "The social Alps that ranged about her . . . reached only to her knees." And Robert Walmsley attains this Matterhorn. But, even if he has found that the traveler who reaches the mountaintop finds the highest peaks swathed in a thick veil of cloud and snow, he manages to conceal his chills. "Robert Walmsley was proud of his wife; although while one of his hands shook his guests' the other held tightly to his alpenstock and thermometer."

Similarly, the story **"Squaring the Circle"** is permeated with the integrating image: nature is a circle, the city a square. In **"A Comedy in Rubber,"** the image is of the rubbernecks as a special tribe, and so on.

O. Henry's kind of story approaches most closely the *skaz* form (to this day, one of the favorite forms in the Russian short story): the free, spontaneous language of speech, digressions, purely American coinages of the street variety, which cannot be found in any dictionary. His, however, is not that ultimate, complete *skaz* form from which the author is absent, in which the author is but another character, and even the author's comments are given in a language close to that of the milieu depicted.

But all these are the static aspects of a work of art. The urban reader, who grew up in the mad whirl of the modern city, cannot be satisfied with only the static elements; he demands the dynamics of plot. Hence all that yellow sea of criminal and detective literature, usually crude and unartistic verbally. In O. Henry, brilliant language is usually combined with dynamic plot. His favorite compositional device is the surprise ending. Sometimes the effect of surprise is achieved by the author with the aid of what may be called the *false denouement:* in the plot syllogism, the reader is deliberately led to the wrong conclusion, and then, somewhere at the end, there is a sudden sharp turn, and an altogether different denouement reveals itself (in the stories, **"The Rathskeller and the Rose," "Squaring the Circle," "The Hiding of Black Bill"**). Very complex and subtle compositional methods may be found in O. Henry's novel, *Cabbages and Kings.*

Unfortunately, the composition of O. Henry's stories, especially in the endings, suffers from sameness. The chronic surprise loses its point; the surprise is expected, and the exception becomes the rule. The reader has much the same feeling as he experiences under Wilde's shower of paradoxes: in the end he sees that each paradox is but a truism turned inside out.

However, Tolstoy's Nekhludov did not love Katyusha Maslova a whit less because her eyes were just a little crossed. And his faults did not prevent O. Henry from becoming one of the most beloved writers of America and England. (pp. 291-95)

> Yevgeny Zamyatin, *"O. Henry,"* in his A Soviet Heretic: Essays, *edited and translated by Mirra Ginsburg, The University of Chicago Press, 1970, pp. 291-95.*

B. M. EJXENBAUM   (essay date 1925)

[*Ejxenbaum was a major Russian critic whose unwillingness to espouse the Party line in literary matters caused him to be ostracized by the Soviet literary establishment. A central figure in the Formalist literary movement from its inception until the Soviet condemnation of Formalism in the 1930s, Ejxenbaum was also a member of The Society for the Study of Poetic Language, a group which maintained that literary criticism should focus on the specific, intrinsic characteristics of verbal art, or "concrete poetics." During the purges of nonconformist factions in literature in Soviet Russia in the 1940s, the public "confessions of ideological error" that Ejxenbaum was constrained to make were so obviously ironical that he was denied "rehabilitated" status, and until the gradual loosening of strict governmental controls over literature in the late 1950s, he found it virtually impossible to publish. He was in the process of reestablishing himself as a literary critic concerned with problems of concrete poetics when he died in 1959. In the following excerpt, originally published in the Russian periodical Zvezda in 1925, Ejxenbaum provides a formalistic analysis of the style and structure of O. Henry's short stories.*]

For some reason [Russian readers] were completely unaware of O. Henry's name until 1923, although he had died back in 1910 and during the years preceding his death was one of the most popular and beloved authors in America. During the years O. Henry was publishing in his own country (1904-1910) his stories would hardly have attracted the Russian reader's attention. Their success in our day is all the more characteristic and significant: they obviously satisfy some literary need. Of course, for us O. Henry is only a foreign guest artist, but one who has appeared on call, by invitation, not accidentally. (pp. 1-2)

The short story generally has made its appearance in Russian literature only from time to time, as if by chance and solely for the purpose of providing a transition to the novel, which we here are accustomed to consider the higher or more dignified species of fiction. In American fiction the cultivation of the short story runs throughout the 19th century, not, of course, as an orderly, consecutive evolution, but as a process of incessantly elaborating the various possibilities of the genre. (p. 2)

It goes from Washington Irving, himself still tied to the traditions of manners-and-morals sketch writing in England, to Edgar Allan Poe, to Nathaniel Hawthorne; after them come Bret Harte, Henry James and, later, Mark Twain, Jack London and, finally, O. Henry (I have listed, of course, only the most prominent names). O. Henry had good reason to begin one of his stories (**"The Girl and the Habit"**) with complaints against the critics' constant reproaches for his imitating this or that writer. . . . The short story is the one fundamental and self-contained genre in American prose fiction, and the stories of O. Henry certainly made their appearance in consequence of the prolonged and incessant cultivation of the genre.

On Russian soil O. Henry showed up minus those national and historical connections and we of course regard him as something else again than do the Americans. . . . Thus, literature coming from another country undergoes a curious and often far from invalid refraction when it passes through local national traditions. O. Henry in Russia is preeminently the author of "picaresque" stories and clever anecdotes with surprise endings—what for the American reader apparently seems a secondary or traditional feature. It is enough to compare Russian and American editions of O. Henry's "Selected Works." Of the 33 stories in a Russian edition and the 25 in an American one only five coincide. "Picaresque" stories and stories with humorous plots predominate in the Russian edition, while primarily sentimental "slice-of-life" stories are collected in the American one, with only those of the "picaresque" stories admitted which show the criminal repenting or on his way to reform. The stories about which American critics and readers rave pass unnoticed in Russia or cause disappointment. Tender stories about New York shopgirls have more appeal for the American reader. . . . American critics have been trying to "elevate" O. Henry (as the Russian critics have Cexov) to the level of classical traditions. They eloquently argue a resemblance between O. Henry and, for instance, Shakespeare on the basis of their common sympathies and frame of mind. (pp. 2-3)

The real O. Henry is found in an irony pervading all his stories, in a keen feeling for form and traditions. Americans cannot help wanting to prove a resemblance in outlook between O. Henry and Shakespeare—it is their way of expressing "national pride." As for the Russian reader, he, in this instance, does not care about comparisons. He reads O. Henry because it is entertaining to read him and he appreciates in O. Henry what is so lacking in our own literature—dexterity of construction, cleverness of plot situations and denouements, compactness and swiftness of action. Torn from their national traditions, the stories of O. Henry, as is true of the works of any writer on foreign soil, give us the feeling of being a finished, complete genre, and they contrast in our minds with that fluidity and vagueness now so evident in our literature. (pp. 3-4)

However consistent and homogeneous—and, in many people's opinion, even monotonous—O. Henry's work might appear, there are noticeable vacillations, transitions and a certain evolution to it. Sentimental stories—stories about New York shop girls or others of the type of **"Georgia's Ruling"**—predominate in the years immediately following his imprisonment (though they do also appear later). Generally speaking, the comic or satiric and the sentimental do very often go together in the poetics of one and the same writer in just their function of correlated contrasts; this is what we find in the work of Sterne, of Dickens and, to some extent, in the work of Gogol'. In O. Henry this combination stands out with particular relief owing to the fact that his basic orientation toward the anecdote with its unexpected and comically resolved ending is so extremely well-defined. His sentimental slice-of-life pieces, therefore, give the impression of experiments—so much the more because they are all of them, in terms of technique and language, much weaker than the others. Usually they are drawn-out, wishy-washy, with endings which disappoint the reader and leave him feeling unsatisfied. The stories lack compactness, the language is without wit, the structure without dynamism. American critics, it is true, would seem ready to place these stories higher than all the others, but that is an evaluation with which we find it difficult to agree. An American, in his leisure time at home, readily gives himself over to sentimental and religious-moralistic reflections and likes to have appropriate reading. That is his custom, his tradition, a feature of national history conditioned by the peculiarities of his way of life and civilization. (pp. 10-11)

[The] construction of the story from beginning to end (rather, it would be better to say in this case—from end to beginning) had already formed in O. Henry's mind before he sat down to write, which is, of course, a very characteristic feature both for the short story . . . and for O. Henry. What he did at his desk was to work out the details of language and narration. What sort of work was that, what principles guided him, what procedures did he use? The basic principle was to get rid of stylistic clichés, to come to grips with "bookishness," with the slick "middle" style and to subject the "high" style to irony. This opened the way for his extensive use of slang in crime stories, his express avoidance of "artiness," his unfailingly down-grading images, their humor stemming from their oddity and unexpectedness, and so on. Frequently we find in O. Henry an attitude of outright irony toward one or another literary style, an irony which has the effect of bringing his own principles into the open. . . .

At those points in his stories where the need to advance the narrative or tradition would have made a special description requisite, O. Henry turns the occasion to literary irony. Where another story writer would have used the opportunity to wax eloquent or to transmit detailed information about his characters—their personalities, outward appearances, dress, past history,—O. Henry is either exceedingly terse or ironic: "Old Jacob Spraggins came home at 9:30 P.M., in his motor car. The make of it you will have to surmise sorrowfully; I am giving you unsubsidized fiction; had it been a street car I could have told you its voltage and the number of flat wheels it had." . . . There you have a typical O. Henry twist. (p. 14)

The parodic device of substituting the language of an official report for literary description . . . is systematically employed in the story **"A Municipal Report."** The story is, in the broad, a polemic—an answer to Frank Norris's assertion that only three cities in the United States were "story cities"—New York, New Orleans and San Francisco, whereas Chicago, Buffalo or Nashville held out nothing for a story writer. The story takes place, as a matter of fact, in Nashville, but instead of describing the city, O. Henry interpolates into the text quo-

tations from a guidebook which clash with the style of the usual literary description. The very fact of inserting such quotations carries with it the character of parody. The narrator arrives in the city on a train: "All I could see through the streaming windows were two rows of dim houses. The city has an area of 10 square miles; 181 miles of streets, of which 137 miles are paved; a system of waterworks that cost $2,000,000, with 77 miles of mains.". . . Further on, in a conversation between the narrator and one of the characters: "'Your town,' I said, as I began to make ready to depart (which is the time for smooth generalities), 'seems to be a quiet, sedate place. A home town, I should say, where few things out of the ordinary ever happen.' It carries on an extensive trade in stoves and hollow ware with the West and South, and its flouring mills have a daily capacity of more than 2,000 barrels.". . .

It is an interesting fact that this parodic or playful use of quotation—one of O. Henry's most constant stylistic devices—was noted long ago by American critics. O. Henry quotes Tennyson, Spenser and others, informing their words with new meaning, inventing puns, deliberately misquoting parts, and so on. Russian readers unfortunately miss all of this as they also do, for the most part, those instances of play on words in O. Henry's crime stories which are motivated by the speaker's illiteracy (for example, confusion of scientific words as in the case of "hypodermical" instead of "hypothetical"). (p. 15)

The general observation should be made that O. Henry's basic stylistic device (shown both in his dialogues and in the plot construction itself) is the confrontation of very remote, seemingly unrelated and, for that reason, surprising words, ideas, subjects or feelings. Surprise, as a device of parody, thus serves as the organizing principle of the sentence itself. It is no accident that he goes out of his way to avoid orderly and scrupulous descriptions and that his heroes sometimes speak in a completely erratic way; the verbiage in these instances is motivated by a special set of circumstances or causes.

O. Henry has provided us a sort of treatise on how characters should speak when undergoing emotional stress. This "treatise" is the story **"Proof of the Pudding,"** a story which brings us back to the old genre of "conversations" between the editor or journalist and the writer. O. Henry was altogether very apt to express himself ironically with regard to editors and editorial boards. . . . [In **"A Technical Error"**] we read: "Sam Durkee had a girl. (If it were an all-fiction magazine that I expected to sell this story to, I should say, "Mr. Durkee rejoiced in a fiancée')." In **"Proof of the Pudding"** the editor and the story writer meet in a city park. The editor has persistently rejected the writer's manuscripts because the latter followed the French and not the English manner in his stories. They join in a theoretical dispute. The editor reproaches the writer for spoiling his pieces at their very point of climax: "But you spoil every dénouement by those flat, drab, obliterating strokes of your brush that I have so often complained of. If you would rise to the literary pinnacle of your dramatic scenes, and paint them in the high colors that art requires, the postman would leave fewer bulky, self-addressed envelopes at your door." (pp. 15-16)

The editor is indignant because the heroine in one of the stories they are discussing, after having discovered from a letter that her husband had run off with a manicurist, says: "''Well, what do you think of that!'': absurdly inappropriate words. . . . No human being ever uttered banal colloquialisms when confronted by sudden tragedy.'''. . . The writer argues to the contrary that "'. . . no man or woman ever spouts "high-falutin" talk when they go up against a real climax. They talk naturally and a little worse.' " . . . The special humor of the story consists in the fact that, immediately after their conversation, both simultaneously find themselves in identical "dramatic predicaments." Having failed to resolve their argument, they go off to the writer's apartment where they find a letter from which they learn that their wives have left them. Their response "in practice" turns out to be the opposite of what each had expounded in theory. . . . The ironic meaning of the story is wholly directed against references to "real life," where things are always supposedly "not that way," the sort of references with which, one must suppose, editors had regaled O. Henry and brought him to a state of exasperation; in real life, it turns out, anything goes.

It is highly characteristic of O. Henry's general parodic bent that he frequently takes problems having to do with literary practice itself as themes for his stories, making theoretical and ironic comments on matters of style and now and again having his say about editors, publishers, reader demands and so on and so forth. Some of his stories remind one of the once very popular sonnet parodies where the subject matter was the process of composing a sonnet itself. These pieces disclose a very keen awareness on O. Henry's part of forms and traditions and confirm the view of his work as a sort of culmination point reached by the American short story of the nineteenth century. He was a writer of fiction no less than he was critic and theorist,—a feature very characteristic of our age which has completely dissociated itself from the naïve notion that writing is an "unconscious" process in which all depends on "inspiration" and "having it inside one." We haven't had a parodist with so subtle a knowledge of his craft, so inclined time and again to initiate the reader into its mysteries, probably since the time of Laurence Sterne.

However, first a few words more about O. Henry's style. His narration is invariably ironic or playful. His writing is studded with metaphors but only for the purpose of disconcerting or amusing the reader with the unexpectedness of the comparisons made—a surprise of a literary nature: their material is not traditional and usually runs counter to the "literary norm," downgrading the object of comparison and upsetting the stylistic inertia. This applies with particular frequency to descriptive passages about which, as we have seen above, O. Henry maintained an invariably ironic attitude. . . . Naturally enough, in the narrative and descriptive passages of his stories, O. Henry more often than not enters into conversation with his reader, making no point of arousing in him an illusion of direct contact or of reality but rather forever emphasizing his role as the writer and, therefore, conducting the story not from the standpoint of an impersonal commentator but from that of his own person. He brings in an outside narrator (as in his crime stories) in those cases where there is occasion for using slang, for playing on words, or the like.

Given such a system of narration, dialogue stands out with particular relief and takes on a substantial share of the effect of plot and style. The terseness of the narrative and descriptive commentary is naturally compensated for by the dynamism and concreteness of speech in the dialogues. The conversations of the characters in O. Henry stories always have a direct connection with the plot and with the role the character in question plays in it; they are rich in intonations, fast-moving and often devious or ambiguous in some special way. Sometimes a whole dialogue will be built on an incomplete utterance or on mutual misunderstanding with implications, in certain cases, not only for style but for the plot, as well. (pp. 16-17)

[In] O. Henry's hands the short story undergoes regeneration, becoming a unique composite of literary feuilleton and comedy or vaudeville dialogue. (p. 18)

Unexpectedness of ending is the most striking and consistently commented on feature of [O. Henry's] stories, the unexpectedness, moreover, being almost invariably of the "happy ending" variety. . . . [The] O. Henry story is parodic or ironic through and through—not only where the author himself interferes with the story in progress but also where nothing of the sort takes place. His stories are parodies on a certain, commonly accepted short story logic, on the usual plot syllogism. By itself, the surprise effect is a common feature of both the novel and the short story, and the American short story in particular. But for O. Henry this quality of the unexpected constitutes the very heart of the construction and bears a perfectly specific character. His endings are not merely a surprise or contrary to expectation, they appear in a sort of lateral way, as if popping out from around the corner; and it is only then that the reader realizes that certain details here and there had hinted at the possibility of such an ending. This is the surprise of parody, a trick surprise which plays on the reader's literary expectations, throwing him off center and very nearly mocking him. Frequently, the story is so constructed that it is not clear until the very end where the riddle actually lies or what, in general, all the events portend,—the ending not only serves as the dénouement but also discloses the true nature of the intrigue, the real meaning of all that has occurred. Therefore it often happens in O. Henry that not only the reader but also one of the characters in the story is fooled. 'It takes a thief to rob a thief'—that's the situation typical for O. Henry's system (*cf.*, **"The Ethics of Pig,"** **"The Man Higher Up"**). He does not even set out "false tracks," as is commonly done in mystery stories, but operates with the help of ambiguities, half-statements or barely noticeable details which turn out at the end to have been highly significant. . . . (pp. 21-2)

No wonder "crime" material should have come in so handy for O. Henry. It was, of course, not so much a matter of the crooks in themselves but, rather, the fact that the "picaresque" story supplies excellent motivation for his plot devices. His crooks are not so much of American as of Arabian-Spanish-French origin, their tradition going back to the early "picaresque" stories and novels. What he had to have, for the most part, was motivation via some piece of trickery or cleverness or via a misunderstanding of the kind that supplied the basis for the well-known and truly typical O. Henry story, **"The Gift of the Magi"** (the husband sells his watch to buy his wife a set of combs while his wife sells her hair to buy him a watch chain). This amounts almost to a plot scheme in pure form, a kind of algebraic problem under the signs of which one could substitute any other facts one likes.

The principle of the surprise dénouement by itself makes it obligatory that the dénouement be a happy or even comic one. So it was in Puškin's *Belkin Tales* (parodies fundamentally) and so it is with O. Henry (compare Puškin's *"Grobovščik"* [The Coffinmaker] and O. Henry's **"The Head-Hunter"**). In the affairs of everyday life, we are very much accustomed to surprise of a tragic nature, but, at the same time, it brings in its wake an outcry against fate. In art, there is no one against whom to cry out. No one forces the writer to vie with fate, even if it be on paper. A tragic dénouement requires special motivation (guilt, nemesis and "character" are the usual ones in tragedy), and that is why it is more natural in a psychological novel than in a short story of action. The reader has first to come to terms with the tragic dénouement, to understand its logical necessity, and for that reason it must be carefully prepared so that the force of it does not strike on the *result* (in other words, does not come at the very ending) but on the *progression* toward the ending. Happy endings in O. Henry stories, as in *Belkin Tales,* are by no means a response to the pressure of the American reading public's "demands," as is customarily claimed, but the natural outcome of the principle of the surprise dénouement, a principle incompatible in a story of action with detailed motivation. And it is also for this reason that tragic endings are so rare and so paradoxical on the screen,—psychological motivation is altogether too foreign to the nature of the motion picture. In the O. Henry short story, with its parodic focus on the finale, a tragic outcome is possible only in the case of a *double* dénouement, as in **"The Caballero's Way,"** where Tonia is killed but, on the other hand, the Kid remains alive and celebrates his revenge. To put it more strongly, O. Henry's stories are so far from any psychology, any ambition to foster in the reader an illusion of reality and bring him into contact with his heroes as people, that the very categories of the tragic and the comic can be said to be inapplicable to his works.

O. Henry, as a general rule, does not address himself to his readers' emotions,—his stories are intellectual and literary through and through. Stories in which he tries to introduce an emotional tone, in the effort, perhaps, to attune himself to the tastes of his editors and the reading public, inevitably take on a sentimental character and simply fall out of his system. He has no "characters," no heroes; he works on the imagination of his readers by picking out and juxtaposing incisive and unexpected particulars which, by reason of their being very concrete, are striking. In this way, he compensates, as it were, for the schematic structuralism of his stories (a device connected with the art of parody: *cf.* details in Sterne). No wonder that the structures of his stories were habitually fully formed in his mind, as [his friend and biographer Al] Jennings bears witness, and no wonder that he could so easily change the facts,—he thought in schemes, in formulas, like an expert theoretician. The work went into details of language and delineation. That explains the impression of a certain monotony about which O. Henry's Russian readers often remark. Despite his popularity and his supposed lightness and readability, O. Henry is a very complex and subtle writer. He is so good at deceiving his reader that the latter more often than not even fails to notice where it is the author has led him to,—into what milieu of literary parody, irony and play on form he has turned up in O. Henry's company. (pp. 22-3)

> *B. M. Ejxenbaum, in his* O. Henry and the Theory of the Short Story, *translated by I. R. Titunik, Ann Arbor: Dept. of Slavic Languages and Literatures, University of Michigan, 1968, 41 p.*

CLEANTH BROOKS, JR. AND ROBERT PENN WARREN (essay date 1943)

[*Brooks and Warren are considered two of the most prominent figures of the school of New Criticism, an influential movement in American criticism that also included Allen Tate and R. P. Blackmur. Although the various New Critics did not subscribe to a single set of principles, all believed that a work of literature had to be examined as an object in itself through a process of close analysis of symbol, image, and metaphor. For the New Critics, a literary work was not a manifestation of ethics, sociology, or psychology, and could not be evaluated in the general terms of any nonliterary discipline. In the following excerpt, Brooks*

and Warren closely examine the plot of the story "The Furnished Room."]

[O. Henry's **"The Furnished Room"**] is obviously divided into two parts. The first part, which ends with the death of the lodger, concerns his failure in the search for his sweetheart and the motivation of his suicide; the second part concerns the revelation, by the landlady to her crony, that his sweetheart had, a week earlier, committed suicide in the same room. What acounts for the fact that O. Henry felt it necessary to treat the story in this fashion? What holds the two parts of the story together? To discover the answers to these two related questions, let us consider the story itself.

The most interesting question has to do with the young man's motivation. In one sense, O. Henry has deliberately made the problem of his motivation more difficult by withholding the information that the sweetheart is dead. The young man does not know that she is dead; indeed, in the room, he gets, with the scent of mignonette, a renewed hope. Why then, under these circumstances, does he commit suicide? Presumably, the explanation is this: he has been searching fruitlessly for five months; he is, we are told, tired—and, we assume, not only momentarily tired physically, but spiritually weary. Indeed, we are told: "He was sure that since her disappearance from home this great water-girt city held her somewhere, but it was like a monstrous quicksand, shifting its particles constantly, with no foundation, its upper granules of today buried tomorrow in ooze and slime." But we are not supposed to believe, even so, that he would have necessarily turned on the gas this particular evening, except as a despairing reaction from the hope which has been raised by the scent of mignonette. This is the author's account of the motivation of the suicide. But is the motivation, as presented, really convincing? That will depend on the character of the man. What sort of man is he? Actually, O. Henry has told us very little about him except that he is young, has searched for his sweetheart for five months, and is tired. Especially does the question of the man's character, and state of mind, come up in the incident in which he notices the odor of mignonette. Did he really smell it? Did he merely imagine that he smelled it? "And he breathed the breath of the house . . . a cold, musty effluvium . . . mingled with the reeking exhalations of linoleum and mildewed and rotten woodwork. . . . Then, suddenly, as he rested there, the room was filled with the strong, sweet odor of mignonette. It came as upon a single buffet of wind. . . . The rich odor clung to him and wrapped him around."

The suddenness with which he notices the odor, the power of the odor, the fact that he can find no source for the odor, and finally the complete disappearance of the odor, all tend to imply that he merely imagines it. But over against this view, we have the testimony of the landlady that the sweetheart had actually occupied the room. This question is important, for it is crucial for the young man's lapse into acute despair. If the odor is real, the author must convince his reader that it exists; if it is imaginary, the author must convince his reader that the psychological condition of the young man will account for its apparent existence. These are the tests which the reader must apply to the situation. We have already pointed out that there is some evidence on both sides of the question. The reader must, of course, decide for himself which explanation must be taken, and more importantly, whether the explanation is convincing, and renders the action credible. The author, however, seems to weight the evidence toward the presence of the real odor. If this is the case, how are we to account for the fact that the search reveals no source of it, especially since the odor is so overpoweringly strong? Or, perhaps the author has in mind some idea that the odor provokes a mystical communion between the two lovers. But this does not relieve the fiction writer from the necessity for furnishing some sort of specific clue to his meaning. (Moreover, if we are to take the whole experience as an hallucination, the author is certainly not relieved from providing some clear motivation for the event.)

To sum up: it is obvious enough, from the detailed description of the room, that O. Henry is trying to suggest a ground for the man's experience in the nature of the room itself. That is, the room in its disorder, its squalor, its musty smell, its rubbish and debris of nameless lives, reflects the great city, or the world, in which his sweetheart has been lost, and in which all humanity seems to become degraded and brutalized. It is easy enough to see why O. Henry should want to suggest the contrast between what the sordid surroundings mean to the hero and what the odor of mignonette means to him. As the girl is lost somewhere in the great city, so the odor is lost somewhere in the room. After the young man is told that the girl has not been there, and after he has been unable to find the source of the odor, the room itself is supposed to become a sort of overwhelming symbol for the futility of his effort. This intention on the part of the author may be sound enough, but the fact that we see what the intention is does not mean that the intention has been carried out. The whole effect of the story depends on the incident of the odor, and we have seen that the handling of this detail is confused.

Assuming that this objection is valid, the basic remedy suggests itself at once. The author needed to go back and fill in the character of the young man much more fully. The reader might then have been able to follow the processes of his mind as he goes through his crucial experience, and the specific nature of his response to the odor would have been clarified. But O. Henry chooses an easier solution. Resting upon his rather thin and sketchy characterization of the young man, the author chooses to give a turn to the plot by a last-minute surprise. In the second part of the story the landlady tells her crony that she has lied to the young man about the girl.

What is the effect of this revelation? It is intended, obviously, to underline the "irony of fate," to illustrate the hard-heartedness of the city in which the young man finds himself, to justify the young man's overwhelming sense that the girl has been in the room, and, all in all, to pull the story together. For the sympathetic reader this conclusion is supposed to suggest that the bonds of love stretch across the confusion and squalor of the great city, and that, in a sense, the young man has finally succeeded in his search, for the lovers are at last united in death. The young man finds, as it were, the proper room in the great city in which to die.

But is the story really pulled together? The end of the story depends on the lie. But are the lives of the lovers altered by the lie? Does the lie cause the death of the young man? It is conceivable that, had the landlady told the truth, the shock of the information might have saved the young man from suicide, but this is the merest speculation. The character, as given in the story, commits suicide in despair when the landlady tells him that the girl has not been there; the landlady's telling him that the girl is irretrievably lost, is dead, would presumably have had the same effect.

Actually, is there any point in the lie except to trick the reader—to provide the illusion of a meaningful ending? Whatever irony

lies in the ending is based on a far-fetched coincidence, and does not depend on the fact that the woman said one thing rather than another. (Readers who are inclined to accept the conclusion of the story as meaningful might try reconstructing the story with the young man's calling at the door, finding with horror that his sweetheart has committed suicide there a week before, renting the room, and turning on the gas. We would then still have the ironical coincidence and a sort of union of the lovers, but the story would seem very tame and flat.) O. Henry, by withholding certain information and thus surprising us with it at the end, has simply tried to give the reader the illusion that the information was meaningful. The irony, in the story as we have it, simply resides in a trick played on the reader rather than in a trick which fate has played on the young man.

Readers who feel that the end of this story is a shabby trick will be able to point out other symptoms of cheapness: the general thinness of characterization, the cluttered and sometimes mawkish description, the wheedling tone taken by the author, and the obvious play for emotional sympathy in such writing as the following: "Oh, God! whence that odor, and since when have odors had a voice to call?" In other words, we can readily surmise that the trickery involved in the surprise ending may be an attempt to compensate for defects within the body of the story itself.

But a trick of plot does not make a story. A surprise ending may appear in a very good story, but only if the surprise has been prepared for so that, upon second thought, the reader realizes that it is, after all, a logical and meaningful development from what has gone before, and not merely a device employed by the author to give him an easy way out of his difficulties. The same principle applies to *coincidence* . . . in general. Coincidences do occur in real life, sometimes quite startling ones, and in one sense every story is based on a coincidence—namely, that the particular events happen to occur together, that such and such characters happen to meet, for example. But since fiction is concerned with a logic of character and action, coincidence, in so far as it is purely illogical, has little place in fiction. Truth can afford to be stranger than fiction, because truth is "true"—is acceptable on its own merits—but the happenings of fiction, as we have seen, must justify themselves in terms of logical connection with other elements in fiction and in terms of meaningfulness. (pp. 114-18)

Cleanth Brooks, Jr. and Robert Penn Warren, "How Plot Reveals," in their Understanding Fiction, *Appleton-Century-Crofts, Inc., 1943, pp. 108-83.**

GRANVILLE HICKS (essay date 1953)

[*Hicks was an American literary critic whose famous study* The Great Tradition: An Interpretation of American Literature since the Civil War *(1933) established him as the foremost advocate of Marxist critical thought in Depression-era America. Throughout the 1930s, he argued for a more socially engaged brand of literature and severely criticized such writers as Henry James, Mark Twain, and Edith Wharton, who he believed failed to confront the realities of their society and, instead, took refuge in their own work. Hicks was shocked by the effects of the Great Depression and believed that events demanded a new commitment on the part of writers to clearly understand and express their times. In Marxist terms this meant that all American artists should comprehend the growth of capitalism and its negative side effects, such as war, periodic depressions, and the exploitation and alienation of the working class. Thus the question Hicks posed was always the same: to what degree did an artist come to terms with the economic conditions of the time and the social consequences of those conditions? He believed that it was the task of American literature to provide an extremely critical examination of the capitalist system itself and of what he considered its inherently repressive nature. After 1939, Hicks sharply denounced communist ideology, which he called a "hopelessly narrow way of judging literature," and in his later years adopted a less ideological posture in critical matters. In the following excerpt, Hicks reminisces about his youthful enthusiasm for the stories of O. Henry and his later disillusionment with them.]*

Thirty-four years ago, when I was a freshman in college and was asked to write a theme on my favorite author, I unhesitatingly named O. Henry. During the preceding twelve months I had gone through every volume in the collected works, and it seemed to me that reading matter had never given me more pleasure. I wasn't prepared to argue that O. Henry was the greatest author who ever lived, but he was my favorite.

Less than a year later I was wondering what in the world I had seen in his stories, and the question has been bothering me ever since. In the intervening years I have read some of the stories now and then as I have run across them in anthologies, but there has never been a suggestion of the old spell. Now, reading through all of them again, I have found no magic, but I think I have caught some hint of the way in which the magic operated thirty-five years ago.

I was reading O. Henry at the right time and place—in a small town and within a decade of his death—and, what is more important, at the right age, for I was still in my teens. To me the stories were full of the glamour of the big city, which I had never seen, and the strangeness of far-off places. They brought me a world of sophistication, populated with gentlemanly cynics and honorable rascals; and the slangy, hyperbolic, pun-strewn style seemed to me the acme of wit. Finally, they were romantic, and the fact that the romances took place not in Zenda or Graustark, regions of which I was growing tired, but in city boarding houses and Texas restaurants made me feel that life was worth living.

All these things counted heavily, but I am afraid, as I look back, that what counted most was the trick ending. I could not, of course, have read many O. Henry stories without learning that I was going to be tricked, but I still was all eagerness to see how, this time, it was going to be done. The magic, in short, was that of a first-rate prestidigitator—no more and no less—and I loved it. Then all of a sudden—I think it was when I discovered Sherwood Anderson's "Winesburg, Ohio"—I lost my taste for sleight-of-hand.

It was true in my time, and it continued to be true for some time thereafter, that most literate young people succumbed for a while to the O. Henry fever. And there must still be willing readers. . . . His work has survived, but his reputation and his influence have not. Many journalists have borrowed from his style, and through the decades countless derivative stories have been published, but the prestige of his kind of story has declined, and it must be years and years since an O. Henry Prize was given to an O. Henry story. The central tradition of the American short story has, fortunately, moved in a different direction.

O. Henry was a culmination rather than a source. His humor was basically the familiar humor of the tall tale; he had learned exaggeration from Davy Crockett and his descendants, the comic distortion of the language from Artemus Ward and Josh Billings and the art of the inverted axiom from Mark Twain. Mark Twain had also taught him something about the trick ending, and so had Bret Harte, Frank Stockton, Ambrose Bierce and many writers who have been forgotten.

Among his American contemporaries his chief instructor was Richard Harding Davis, whom he often satirized, and perhaps he was also acquainted with an author who, at close range, looked like Davis—Stephen Crane. Overseas there was the surpassing brilliance of Rudyard Kipling, sometimes acknowledged in the tales, and he knew Maupassant at what now appears to be his worst.

O. Henry was shaped in the age of Victoria, and a Victorian he remained to the end. Vagabond, embezzler, alcoholic and philanderer he might be, but, like the Pirates of Penzance, with all his faults he loved his Queen—or, at any rate, paid tribute to the standards associated with her name. He wrote more than 250 stories without a single situation that his contemporaries could call even remotely risqué.

In **"An Unfinished Story"** he admitted that underpaid shop girls might sometimes yield to temptation, but that was as far as he would go. Most of his rascals are perfect gentlemen in their relations with women, and if they are not, their indiscretions are veiled from the reader. . . .

Victorianism, however, was the least of his faults. If there had existed in his time, as there does now, a kind of unwritten law against the abuse of coincidence, O. Henry would have had to go out of business. Nor was it merely probability that was sacrificed for the sake of the trick ending; whatever understanding he had of human beings and the life they lead was thrust to one side whenever it threatened to interfere with the game he was playing with his readers. . . .

Yet the magic power of the stories, in the right circumstances, cannot be denied and has to be explained. Perhaps the explanation lies in the fact that they were strong magic for O. Henry himself. Despite his chatty style, he was one of the least personal of writers, and he never could have written the autobiographical novel that he often talked about. He was protecting, not revealing, himself in what he wrote.

He was creating a world for O. Henry, a world in which an unconventional way of life could be reconciled with great respect for convention, in which the golden hearts of ne'er-do-wells and rogues were exposed for all to see, in which romance was ever present but only in acceptable guises. The hand of fate—and it seems likely that at bottom he was gripped by a determinism as black as Mark Twain's—could be manipulated to achieve pleasant comedy and a miraculous succession of happy endings.

He wrote what he thought the public wanted, and his guesses were excellent, but he also wrote to please himself. Otherwise there would be no understanding the vitality that produced so many stories, and so many that are good by O. Henry standards, in not much more than ten years. . . .

He was, indeed, a master of make-believe and therefore in his own way a myth-maker. If he was, like his Jeff Peters, an adept at the shell game, he gave his readers the illusion that they were the ones who were bound to win, that they were the happy beneficiaries of fate. He knew a lot about illusions, including the fact that he needed them.

Granville Hicks, "A Sleight-of-Hand Master," in The New York Times Book Review, *December 27, 1953, p. 5.*

V. S. PRITCHETT (essay date 1957)

[Pritchett is a highly esteemed English novelist, short story writer, and critic. Considered one of the modern masters of the short story, he is also considered one of the world's most respected and well-read literary critics. Pritchett writes in the conversational tone of the familiar essay, a method by which he approaches literature from the viewpoint of a lettered but not overly scholarly reader. A twentieth-century successor to such early nineteenth-century essayist-critics as William Hazlitt and Charles Lamb, Pritchett employs much the same critical method: his own experience, judgment, and sense of literary art are emphasized, rather than a codified critical doctrine derived from a school of psychological or philosophical speculation. His criticism is often described as fair, reliable, and insightful. In the following excerpt, Pritchett discusses the relationship between O. Henry and his fiction.]

O. Henry is one of the many casualties of American literature. Original, inventive and prolific in his short stories, he is one of those writers of whom the critics say: Could have done better if he had tried. In his life and in his work there is a failure of the sense of responsibility. Chekhov's beginnings were just as difficult and commonplace as the American's. Like O. Henry, he began by writing crude comic sketches for popular papers, and had to be fished out of vulgar employ by discerning editors; but whereas O. Henry perfected only his craft, Chekhov (like all great artists) strenuously perfected himself as a means of seeing and feeling his subjects. Chekhov grew; O. Henry copied himself. Chekhov was concerned to write less and better. O. Henry certainly worked hard, but rather in the Puritan way that finds in work of any kind a drugging or redemption in itself. The result is that behind the laughter of O. Henry's caricatures and the wit of his invention, there is a sensation of moral exhaustion and personal lassitude.

O. Henry was a modest, fastidious, impenetrable character. He was enclosed, furtive and evasive. The fact is he was shut in by an amiable and undisquieting alcoholism; his secret was that he had served a prison sentence of three years for embezzlement. These two matters were symptoms rather than causes of much earlier cooling-off from life. (p. 697)

Mr Gerald Langford's new biography *Alias O. Henry,* [see Additional Bibliography], goes thoroughly into [the confusing story of O. Henry's embezzlement conviction]. He finds it just as hard to make up his mind about O. Henry's guilt or innocence as others have done. O. Henry himself was evasive and self-contradictory; protesting his innocence, and yet clearly having no notion that what he was ready to admit displayed some kind of guilt. His attitude was ambiguous; and this ambiguity provides half the comedy of his tales of grafters and frauds. When the man becomes the artist, we see him converting what is a painful failure to face reality into low garrulous poetry of cunning and trickery. He becomes a fabulist. This is among the oldest delights of popular story-telling. O. Henry's enormous success with the great public does not depend on his shallowness and sentimentality, but on his sharing the common pleasure in watching people do each other down, in the out-smarting of the market. In his life, after he came out of gaol, O. Henry added incompetence to innocence. He shared Balzac's need of debt as a stimulus to work. He borrowed money incorrigibly and continuously, even when he was highly paid; he spent it or, rather, gave it away, absurdly. There are stories of him giving tips in restaurants many times larger than the bills. There is a drifting, indifferent quality in this carelessness. He was not the arrogant borrower; he was cringing, promising, sentimental, almost sobbing. We have the

William Porter (O. Henry) in his teller's cage at the First National Bank of Austin.

impression of a gentle, dandyish, pleasantly pickled man stuck in a dream and who soothed himself, when he woke up, by occasional fits of theatrical sentimentality.

O. Henry's earliest stories were written in prison. He emerged with a natural feeling for the lonely, the underdog and the rogue; also with a desire, not for security and affection, but for anonymity. For many writers the edge and freedom of the anonymous life have been indispensable. The security of his second marriage was intolerable to him. He was just the man to be lost with advantage in the streets of New York. He became domesticated to the backrooms of small hotels, the pavements, doorways, cheap bars, park seats of the city. He was a dedicated night wanderer—the habit was partly responsible for the breakdown of his second marriage. He hated literary society, preferring to talk with the shop girls, tarts, bar props and others who gave him his material. He was protected by his fastidiousness and by his work from the waste of literary Bohemianism. But, as Mr Langford says, when he attacked the sterility of literary company, he was not altogether sincere. Literary society is often sterile and too much of it is fatal, above all to short-story writers who use up their material more quickly than any other kind of writer. O. Henry needed the streets and the bars. But literary society of the right kind might have given O. Henry the impetus to go beyond the commonplace limitations of his work, to resist the downhill tendency of his talent. Occasional stories, like *An Unfinished Story* or *A Municipal Report,* show how it was well within his powers to go deeper than contrivance and anecdotal trickery. Clearly he felt exposed without them, but he could have been given the courage.

The sudden extinction of O. Henry's fame after 1910 is saddening but natural. By the Twenties a major literary movement had begun in the United States, and O. Henry was lost in the journalistic and characterless period that preceded it. He belongs to the vernacular tradition, though H. L. Mencken thought he perverted it with false and ornate Broadway-ese. Yet the hostile critics, I think, are merely copying each other when they damn O. Henry for his use of coincidence and for snap-endings that trick the reader. (The trick was, in any case, part of the gaiety.) The hostile forget that O. Henry's virtue is his speed of narrative; it moves forward freely; it jumps with confidence. He is economical and at home in his tale.

This technical proficiency of O. Henry's is in itself delightful because it has the attraction of daring and impudence. His gaudy phraseology, his colliding metaphors, his brilliant malapropisms are not always in excess. We can at once picture the woman in *Telemachus, Friend* who would have 'tempted an anchovy to forget his vows' and who had an air of welcome about her that 'seemed to mitigate her vicinity'; we see her, after supper, when her two lovers find her, 'with a fresh pink dress on and cool enough to handle'. The low comedy of courtship is a traditional subject, and in handling it O. Henry brought the American talent for using metaphors grotesquely wide of the mark. He had the important comic gift of capping a good joke with an even more powerful riposte to it. In *Telemachus, Friend,* for example, we are not only told the wrong method of seizing a lady's hand—'Some men grab it so much like they was going to set a dislocation of the shoulder'—but we are told the right method which begins with splendid sentences, straight out of the Mark Twain tradition:

> I'll tell you the right way. Did you ever see a man sneak out of the backyard and pick up a rock to throw at a tom-cat that was sitting on a fence looking at him. He pretends he hasn't got a thing in his hand, and that the cat don't see him and that he don't see the cat.

A great deal of O. Henry is hilarious, school-boy stuff on the surface. He has not the polish or the maturity of a writer like W. W. Jacobs, but he has a far greater range. He has the blessed American gifts of economy and boldness in comic writing; the gift also of bouncing the reader. When we object to his exaggeration and caricature, we should discriminate. The impulse is fundamental to American folk comedy and corresponds to the native and traditional sense of the tall and fabulous. Much of American comedy consists of bluffing and counter-bluffing fantasy: the duke and king episode in *Huckleberry Finn,* for example. This quality comes out very strongly in O. Henry's Texan stories which—after excepting his masterpiece *The Municipal Report*—seem to me his richest. . . .

Mr Langford makes much of O. Henry's statement (made in his last year when he was planning to write a novel) that writers do not tell the truth. It is inferred that O. Henry was beginning to see through the haze in which he lived his stunned life and was about to face realities he had avoided. He was infantile about money, he was puritanical about sex: he disliked being compared with Maupassant who was a 'filthy writer'. We cannot imagine what O. Henry's 'truth' would have been, but we can guess that it would have been the end of him as a comic writer. It is fatal for the comics to resolve their problems; their only salvation lies in improving their jokes. Only serious writers seem to be able to get away, sometimes, with living above their moral means. It is unjust, but there it is. (p. 698)

> *V. S. Pritchett, "O. Henry," in* New Statesman, *Vol. LIV, No. 1393, November 23, 1957, pp. 697-98.*

DONALD F. PEEL   (essay date 1961)

[*In the following excerpt, Peel examines and defends O. Henry's use of the surprise ending.*]

Probably the best known feature of O. Henry's writings is the "surprise ending." (p. 7)

Some writers seem to think that using the surprise ending is playing some kind of a trick on the reader. . . . This is surprising criticism. What kind of plot would one have if it were not premeditated? The surprise ending, after all, is only the climax of the story placed at the end of the story. O. Henry used it to achieve the greatest possible climax, as will be shown later. If the reader is "tricked," it is usually because he tells the story himself and supplies a conventional ending.

One critic [H. C. Schweikert, in *Short Stories* (1913)] points out that O. Henry often uses coincidences that in a lesser writer would be "bunk." One of his most famous stories, **"The Furnished Room,"** rests on an almost incredible coincidence, yet most critics do not notice this. **"The Church with an Overshot Wheel"** and **"The Higher Abdication"** both rest on the coincidence of a child, lost from home at an early age, returning to that home by chance in later life, and being recognized by its remembrance of an object. . . . [Many] of his methods seem cheap or brassy today. However, O. Henry is not responsible for the change in tastes.

The surprise ending was not a new device in fiction when Porter began using it. Examples of it could probably be found in all the types of short fiction that preceded the American short story. (pp. 7-8)

Yet, in spite of its long history and the approval of the reading public, the critics have a tendency to look down on the "surprise ending." . . .

[Berg Esenwein, in *Writing the Short Story* (1908),] asserts that it is the easiest kind of plot from which to write a story.

One question is, does the surprise ending have a legitimate place in the short story? Also, has O. Henry's use of the surprise ending done anything to change that status?

It should be kept in mind that the short story is fiction; it is not reporting a news event; it is not even a "human interest" news report; it is not a "column" in the newspaper sense of that word. The short story may be based on a news report, but it must be more than reporting. It must be an artistic presentation of the facts if it be based on facts, not a *sine qua non.* This assumption rests on the definition of the short story:

> A short story is a narrative presenting characters in a struggle or complication having a definite outcome. . . . Most critics insist that a short story shall have unity of action, unity of tone, and shall produce a single effect.
> [Blanche Colton Williams, *Short Stories for College Classes*].
> (pp. 8-9)

As the painter selects what he puts on canvas, so the fiction writer selects details to produce a single effect and a definite outcome. The reporter is not concerned with a single effect, or with a definite outcome, for life itself often does not provide a definite outcome to a struggle or complication. So the fiction writer must part company with the reporter. It might be argued that the photographer can affect the degree of reality which he records by use of equipment—filters, lens—or by darkroom technique, and that the reporter can vary his reporting by slanting. And so they may; but, as they do so, they move from the realm of fact into the realm of art.

The definite outcome is, or should be, the climax of the story. There is no universal rule as to where this climax should be placed. It could be at the beginning, in the middle, or at the end of the story. Generally it is towards the end of the story, and this climactic ending is what makes the story. As to the exact place—who could assign one? Some of the correspondence schools have tried to reduce writing to an exact science, but such it will never be. Art is more than mechanics. It is for the individual author to determine where the climax will be the most effective, not for the critic to set an arbitrary rule. If the artist, the author, finds that his most effective writing comes from placing the climax in a surprise ending or in a culminating sentence, he is guilty of no literary, no artistic, no ethical, no moral error. The surprise ending, after all, is no more than a climax to the story, placed at the end.

The surprise ending, however, should be distinguished from the culminating sentence. The surprise ending sums up and finishes the story, but details may follow. The culminating sentence is a "punch" line which ends the story immediately. In **"Gift of the Magi"** the surprise ending comes when Jim reveals that he has sold his watch to buy Della her present; then O. Henry goes on to add that of all who give gifts, these are the wisest. (This added moral is a favorite device of his.) In **"Romance of a Busy Baker,"** a culminating sentence sums up the whole story: "We were married last evening at 8 o'clock in the Little Church around the Corner." If there is anything of the vaudeville in O. Henry's stories as Pattee suggests [see excerpt dated 1917], it is more with the culminating sentence than in the surprise ending. Since the technique is similar for both, the term "surprise ending" will be used to include both, with the reservation that there is a distinction. (pp. 10-11)

A valid surprise ending . . . should be plausible. Though it may be unnatural, in the sense that it seldom occurs in real life, it must seem natural to the reader. It should depend on the shifts and twists of human agents. Changes in circumstances should be intrinsic to the story.

On the other hand, the ending should not depend on arbitrary arrangement of external circumstances. One of O. Henry's weaknesses is the use of coincidences that seem almost incredible. . . . **"The Furnished Room"** has already been cited as an example. It is almost incredible that in a city of four million people a young man should come by chance to the same room in which his lost love had committed suicide. **"The Higher Abdication"** has another coincidence: A bum climbs into a wagon and goes to sleep. While sleeping he is driven to a ranch. It turns out that he is the son of the owner of the ranch who was lost or stolen from home at the age of two. **"The Church with an Overshot"** depends upon a similar coincidence. A little girl is lost from home at the age of four. She returns at the age of twenty and is recognized because she recognizes an old song her father sang when she was a child. Another of his famous stories, **"The Third Ingredient,"** rests upon a far-fetched coincidence. A young man rescues a girl who has jumped off a ferry boat. Out of all the rooming houses in New York he comes by accident to the one in which she lives.

There are other reasons for the failure of the surprise ending. One of the devices of O. Henry to achieve the surprise ending is the story within the story. The surprise ending comes at the external story's ending and is too often an inconsequential or trivial statement. As in the **"Halberdier of the Little Rheinschloss,"** the story begins with the question of why a cigar case was broken; this leads to another story which has no connection with the first; the surprise ending comes in the explanation of the cigar case which is completely inconsequential. A surprise ending that leaves the basic conflict unsolved may be regarded a failure. **"Hearts and Crosses"** is such a story; the husband and wife are brought back together by the birth of their child, but the conflict between them is not thereby solved, only delayed to a future date.

The surprise ending must be nearly the same as the single effect. When a story becomes too involved for a single effect, a surprise ending is almost impossible. In **"An Afternoon Miracle,"** O. Henry uses two involved stories, and tries to bring them together in a "surprise ending." First, there is a story about the hero, Bob Buckley, and his pursuit of an outlaw; then there is an account of the heroine, snake charmer Alvarita, who is in pursuit of one of her snakes. When hero and heroine get together, the "surprise ending" is that she screams at the sight of a caterpillar. This climax is rather a letdown after Bob Buckley has a barefisted fight with a knife-wielding outlaw. (pp. 11-13)

The surprise ending was the method of writing that O. Henry found to be most effective. He sacrificed reality no more than any artist must sacrifice reality. That one form of writing—realism, naturalism, surrealism—is closer to reality than another is at best a matter of opinion. (pp. 16-17)

One outstanding characteristic of O. Henry's work of which critics have taken little note is his use of the technique of "after the thunder, the still, small voice." This is the adding of a moral after the punch line or surprise ending, which we have already noted. O. Henry's stories are often didactic in this fashion. Its use in **"Gift of the Magi"** has already been noted.

Another favorite technique of O. Henry is that of storyteller. Someone has said that it is the old American game of "tell me another" or "I'll top that." Most of the stories in *The Gentle Grafter* are of this nature. He uses this method often to provide a surprise ending.

Besides these there are perhaps four main methods that O. Henry uses to bring about a surprise ending:

a. The withholding of information. An example of this is **"The Double Dyed Deceiver"** where we are not told the identity of the youth the Llano Kid murdered until the end of the story. The revealing of this information provides the surprise. There is a similar usage in **"A Municipal Report,"** and many other stories.

b. The angle of narration. This is not so much the withholding of information, as the telling of the story so that the information is not necessary until the denouement. This is the method used in **"Gift of the Magi"**—**"The Love-Philtre of Ikey Schoenstein,"** and **"The Romance of a Busy Broker,"** among others.

c. Attempts to mislead. This is the old method of letting the reader tell the story. . . . If the surprise ending could ever be called a "trick plot" it is in this usage. Yet, the author does not mislead the reader so much as the reader misleads himself. In **"October and June"** O. Henry uses a conventional situation of a difference in age between a man and a woman. The reader assumes that the man is the older and is surprised (or should be) to learn that it is the other way around. In **"Girl"** a conventional situation is used: a wealthy man is pursuing a girl;

the reader assumes that he wants to marry her; actually he wants to hire her to be his cook.

d. The misunderstanding. This is an old device in fiction. A typical O. Henry example is **"Hygeia at the Solito,"** in which a wealthy cattleman takes a sick man home to his ranch to recuperate; a doctor apparently examines the man and pronounces him well; the rancher puts him to work; the man does recover from his illness, and it turns out that the doctor examined the wrong man.

Possibly, there are other methods that could be mentioned, but most of O. Henry's stories could be classified under these headings. O. Henry found the surprise ending in use in fiction, made it his own, and passed it on to become one of the most popular short story devices.

The statement, in one form or another, has been made by critics that O. Henry was willing to sacrifice anything, even truth, for the sake of the surprise ending. The question of truth in fiction is one that has long vexed critics perhaps even before the Puritans charged that fiction was "lies." Porter was aware of the problem; he opens **"The World and the Door"** (*Whirligigs*) with the comment:

> As for the adage quoted above [truth is stranger than fiction], I take pleasure in puncturing it by affirming that I read in a purely fictional story the other day the line: "Be it so," said the policeman. "Nothing so strange has yet cropped out in Truth" [the capital 'T' is Porter's].

This comment, of course, does not answer the question as to what is truth in fiction. Pattee's explanation as to O. Henry's failing is that he does not present "humanity as humanity actually is." This statement provides us with a guide that we can use in reaching a working definition. Pattee seems to suggest that there is a distinction between *fact*, *truth*, and *opinion*. *Fact* can be defined in terms of its roots; that is, a *fact* is something that is done (a definition preserved in "an accessory after the fact"), a deed. A *truth,* on the other hand, is a generalization deduced from a fact or facts, and is to be distinguished from *true.* Thus, "God exists" is a truth but not a fact; "God created the heavens and the earth," is a *fact,* a *true* statement but not a *truth.*

According to these definitions, fiction may contain *truth* even though it is not *fact*. For example, in fiction, a writer may put a rocket ship in orbit around Mars. Since what he writes is admittedly fiction no demand should be made that he treat of *fact*. As to truth, having his rocket ship in orbit, the writer must then make his characters act in accordance with known laws of human nature. (pp. 17-19)

Does O. Henry make his characters act in accordance with known laws of human nature? In **"Gift of the Magi"** Della and Jim each sacrifice a prized personal possession to give a gift to the other; this surely is in accord with the known actions of people in love. In **"A Municipal Report"** a man conceals what might have been evidence of a murder; considering the character drawn of the murdered man, the *persona* might well act as O. Henry alleges. Then there is Dulcie of **"An Unfinished Story"**; she spends her last fifty cents for an imitation lace collar to wear on her first date. True to human nature? Instances of such observation of human nature might be multiplied. (p. 20)

O. Henry's stories possess truth and reality (not *realism* by the technical definitions of that term). The story **"The Third Ingredient"** rests on a highly improbable coincidence, but truth does not depend on probability. *Truth* rests on the question: Do the characters in the writer's universe, i.e. the story in question, act as people have acted in the universe which the reader knows? And for **"The Third Ingredient"** the answer must be yes.

Hetty, the lead, when fired from her job goes home and in a matter-of-fact way begins to prepare lunch. She finds a girl preparing potatoes and invites her to contribute them to the beef stew; later she meets a young man who has an onion to contribute and invites him to join. Surely nothing in this violates human conduct. The story revolves around a young artist (miniature painter, more accurately) who has been rescued from a suicide attempt. She and her rescuer have fallen in love at first sight; this is not unusual psychology. Now granted that in a city of four million people it is improbable that these two people should be brought back together, the question is: if they could be brought back together, would they still have this feeling of love? Records show that it is quite possible that the feeling would continue. The question of how long it would continue is not relevant since O. Henry does not attempt to answer that phase of the problem. O. Henry then does remain true to human nature. (p. 22)

William Sidney Porter was aware of his faults. He did protest the debasing of art and of literature. The artist, according to O. Henry's concept, has a responsibility to society and to his ideals.

The artist fulfills his responsibility to society by living up to his highest ideals. He has, according to Porter, no right to produce work simply because it will sell nor should he attempt to sell work for any reason other than its artistic excellence. Thus in **Heart of the West** he portrays a young cowpuncher as riding his horse through a picture he has painted rather than to allow the state legislature to purchase it for the deeds of his father (the cowpuncher's father.)

An analysis of O. Henry's work will show that the writer did not always fulfill the critic's demands. Much of his work does not meet the highest standards of artistic excellence. Yet O. Henry should not be written off for this failure, anymore than Arnold and Wordsworth should be for their respective failures to live up to their respective written creeds. Much that O. Henry did write is of the highest quality.

Nor can O. Henry be summed up simply as a humorist. His best work is too profound for such a simple description; his best work has that mingling of comedy and tragedy that is the mark of great art.

Another reason for considering him as a great writer is that many of the objections to his work are not based on valid critical studies, but are rather expressions of the reaction against form and mechanics that began in the 'teens and which continues to a certain extent to the present time. Such transitory standards should not weigh heavily in judging an artist's work.

Therefore it seems likely that for his mastery of the surprise ending and for his insight into human nature William Sidney Porter will continue to rank as one of the masters of the short story. (pp. 23-4)

Donald F. Peel, "A Critical Study of the Short Stories of O. Henry," in The Northwest Missouri State

College Studies, *Vol. XXV, No. 4, November 1, 1961, pp. 3-24.*

ROMAN SAMARIN   (essay date 1962)

[*In the following excerpt, a Soviet critic offers an appreciation of O. Henry.*]

There are writers whom we love especially because they are so warmhearted, candid and humane.

Such an author was O. Henry—William Sidney Porter . . .—a "really remarkable writer and great realist," as A. V. Lunacharsky characterized him in his day. O. Henry belongs to the scintillating pleiad of American authors who came to the fore at the turn of the century. Their works give powerful and expressive reflection to the turbulent, dynamic epoch when the United States became—as O. Henry derisively dubbed her—the greatest hard-currency and gold-reserve power in the world.

After a difficult, deprived youth and after being thrown into jail on an unproved charge of embezzling funds (his literary career practically began in prison), O. Henry knew all too well what lay behind the sumptuously advertised showcase of American democracy. In "New Baghdad," as he was wont to call New York, if you wanted to save your skin, you had to beware of the fellow on the neighboring bench or behind the counter, in the next room or in the house across the street, on the nearest corner or in a passing cab. In short, you had to be on guard against anybody sitting, drinking, sleeping, walking or riding next to you.

It would seem that O. Henry, past master of the humorous short story, could hardly describe anything so ruthlessly. If we are to believe his other stories, in that mad monotonous struggle for existence waged in the "New Baghdad" of his day there could also be spots of good luck. But O. Henry mocked at them. Even when giving his short stories a happy ending, he derided the American philistine who demanded that he concede that much to him.

Some critics say that O. Henry saw in art a means of creating soothing illusions; they refer to his **"Last Leaf"** as a case in point. A girl artist, dying of pneumonia, luckless, untalented but sweet, apathetically awaits the day when the last leaf falls from the old ivy vine climbing up the wall opposite her window. The doctor had given her to understand she would live no longer than that. . . . The days pass, but the leaf keeps glowing in its bright autumn colors against the dreary gray of the brick wall. The girl conquers her disease. We know, however, that the leaf she has been gazing at was not the one that had long been blown away by the autumn wind, but the one that had been skillfully painted on the wall by the old artist living downstairs. His art had saved her life. That is the power of illusion, you might say: the real purpose of art is gently and wisely to delude and sooth the suffering heart.

But the old artist paid a price for saving the girl. He contracted pneumonia during the cold wet night he had painted his masterpiece, and died. Consequently, the meaning of art lies not in creating an illusion, but in serving man, as the forsaken artist showed. There was a moment in his life when he was really great—because he saved another.

In serving man and fulfilling the writer's duties as he understood them, O. Henry drew a broad panorama of American life at the turn of our century, leaving behind him a unique portrait gallery of American types of his time.

The Big City in his panorama stands aggressively in the fore. He once remarked that he had written of the things the giant city had whispered, trumpeted and shouted to him. In his short stories you can hear that music: the blatant voices of hired newspaper writers and advertising agencies that shape the minds of the philistines, the bawling of hard-boiled politicians and demagogues, the whispers and complaints of those who have been dumped to the bottom of society or are docilely dragging out a drab existence in the hope of somehow making ends meet. O. Henry's stories often mention those vain naive hopes, the dreams that never come true. Even if they do, the very incredibility of the fact only confirms the illusory quality of the dreams.

The voice of the Big City resounds in dozens of his stories—ominous and sad, inviting and revolting, lofty and banal, evil and lyrical. It was O. Henry who perceived the nocturnal outlines of a large American city as a broken chain of buildings capped with clouds and tinted by the night lights and cold mists in gray, dull brown, ash, pale lilac, gray-brown and sky-blue. What a wealth of tones his sharp eye caught, what a gloomy and grand phantasmagoria of big city lights he created! And somewhere amid that gloomy grandeur, all alone amid many people—for that is the law of the capitalist city—was a girl with a warm heart, bravely fighting for her life, unwilling to submit to the deadly power of the city. The descriptions of cities in O. Henry's stories are done with remarkable artistry, signifying the introduction of a powerful theme into American literature.

In depicting the Big City in all its frightening grandeur and cynicism, O. Henry did not yield to the demands of the rapacious laws of the society of his time. He made the reader see the cruel senselessness, inhumaneness and abnormality of the life his heroes led. He gave a general idea of the absurdity of the system under which dire poverty was the source of the amassing of fantastic wealth, and under which the rich became slaves of their millions and lost all human semblance. For O. Henry they were leaches who sucked their capital out of the poor, to whom they paid a pittance so that they might keep body and soul together and help the rich make their millions. . . .

On the other hand, he had many warm words for those who stood behind the counters of other people's shops and slaved at other people's factories.

He wrote a great deal about the dangerous life of cowboys, stockbreeders and farmers of the West. Their images, akin to the heroes of Jack London's stories, are painted in the somewhat conventional tones of the romanticism of the Far West. There on the plains and along the great rivers whose beauty O. Henry could convey with as much skill as his grand cityscapes, on little ranches and farms lived the real people, those who were neither lured nor subjugated by the stone labyrinths of the Yellow Devil.

O. Henry's humor—from the most tender manifestation to the boldest caricature—was characteristic of his perception of American life. Some American critics like to see nothing but the humorist in him, the "great consoler," entertainer and jester. But his laughter was not merely humorous, no matter how diverse its nuances. O. Henry was also a satirist. His "Businessmen," for instance, featuring the different types of American "caliphs," is deeply satirical.

His satirist's talent was especially manifested in **"Cabbages and Kings."** How topical today is that story of the small South

American republic Anchuria, ruled by the Yankees. A man from the States boasts about the role he plays in Anchuria: "My job is private secretary to the president of this republic, and my duties are to run it. I'm not headlined, but I'm the mustard in the salad dressing just the same. There isn't a law goes before Congress, there isn't a concession granted, there isn't an import duty levied but that H. P. Mellinger he cooks and seasons it."

This is O. Henry's satire. And it is just as pointed and cutting in our day. Of course, **"Cabbages and Kings"** was written in another vein than that of Mark Twain's splendid pamphlets directed against the evils perpetrated by U.S. imperialism in China and the Philippines. But O. Henry's satire also testifies to the splendid heights reached by progressive American literature in those years, to the presence of unique talent in it.

In the mid-20th century we have not forgotten our charming and clever friend O. Henry, with whom we find it so pleasant to laugh and muse over the imposing and tragic subjects he touched upon in his books.

O. Henry liked to call his readers his kith and kin. We have nothing against being his relatives, and think of him with deep feeling and gratitude as we mark the centenary of his birth. He is very dear to us. (pp. 55-8)

> Roman Samarin, "O. Henry—'A Really Remarkable Writer' (On the Centenary of O. Henry's Birth)," in The Soviet Review, Vol. 3, No. 12, December, 1962, pp. 55-8.

EUGENE CURRENT-GARCÍA (essay date 1965)

[*An American critic and educator, Current-García is the author of* O. Henry (William Sydney Porter), *a thorough biographical and critical study that includes an examination of O. Henry's regional background and its influence on his works. In the following excerpt, Current-García discusses some technical aspects of O. Henry's short stories.*]

[A] strong reaction against O. Henry's popularity and influence . . . set in during the debunking period of World War I after the first wave of critical enthusiasm for O. Henry's writings was spent. Critics like Pattee [see excerpt dated 1917] and N. Bryllion Fagin roundly denounced these stories on the grounds of superficiality and falseness; they could not forgive O. Henry's failure, as they saw it, to take himself and his art seriously because they felt that the very brilliance of his technical skill, so misapplied, wrought great mischief upon the corpus of the American short story as a whole. (p. 135)

The problem presented by O. Henry, however, was more readily dismissed than analyzed. Primarily, it was the problem of technique—one analogous to that with which Poe in the preceding century had baffled his contemporary critics. How should one approach, explain, and judge the elements which, in combination, resulted in that "unmistakable charm of a master trickster"? What criteria should be applied? Poe's critics likewise had accused him of playing fast and loose with his materials, of sacrificing truth and reality for the sake of achieving sensational effects; but they recognized that he too was a master craftsman whose technical dexterity enabled him to achieve the precise literary effects which he deliberately intended to produce. The American critics' tendency to deplore technique, or at least to relegate it to a subordinate role while focusing their attention on the artist's alleged "content," can thus be seen at work in Pattee's attack on O. Henry just as strongly as it originally operated against Poe. (pp. 135-36)

To condemn O. Henry's stories *in toto* for not being realistic and serious, for depending too heavily on coincidence, and for playing to the gallery is an evasion of the critic's responsibility—unless it can be shown that these characteristics invariably result in badly written stories. This, O. Henry's severest critics have seldom been willing to do. His intention rather than his achievement has been the object of their censure, and the result is that O. Henry criticism over the past five decades has swung from the one extreme of thoughtless adulation to the opposite one of hasty and ill-considered dismissal, based too cavalierly upon the examination of individual stories. . . . (p. 137)

One way to account for [his] . . . mysterious afflatus is to recognize that at the core of O. Henry's being lies an element of surprise or wonder, as though everything his eye lighted on were sufficient cause for startled pleasure. Van Wyck Brooks has noted that New York City seemed to belong to O. Henry because of "the fresh curiosity with which he approached it, his feeling of wonder about it . . . which made for a literary virtue transcending his occasional cheapness and coarseness, his sometimes unbearable jocularity and meretricious effects" [see *TCLC*, Vol. 1]. No shrewder observation of O. Henry's art has been made, but it might also be extended to cover not only his New York stories but his entire approach to the problem of fiction. For the element of surprise is the keynote of his technique as well.

The most obvious technical manifestation of O. Henry's delight in the unexpected is, of course, in his famous surprise endings; for scarcely a single story among his nearly three hundred fails to meet his specifications for a conclusion other than the one the reader is apparently being prepared for. In sheer quantity O. Henry's surprise endings are therefore impressive, though qualitatively too many of them are so patently contrived that the sophisticated reader soon tires of the guessing contest which their anticipated discovery interposes between himself and the author. Invariably the result of some trick of reversal based on essential information withheld or only partially disclosed, the surprise ending was a well-worn device long before O. Henry's day; it entered the short story with the emergence of the form itself and was developed at the hands of many writers from Washington Irving on. Nor did O. Henry add any significant features to it which had not already been employed by writers like Poe, Bret Harte, Stockton, Bierce, Aldrich, and others. In its various forms, the surprise ending included the hoax and the practical joke, the anti-conventional or distorted revelation of events, the paradoxical or antithetical disclosure, the manipulation of psychological concepts, the double reversal, the problem close—all of which had been worked with varying success by O. Henry's predecessors and contemporaries. He, however, paid them the sincere flattery of imitating all their methods, using at least seven different variants of the surprise ending, the most nearly original of which were those disclosing sudden proof of the tyranny of habit or of environment, as in **"The Girl and the Habit"** and in **"The Lickpenny Lover."**

Any list of plot summaries would immediately show that most if not all of these surprise endings that O. Henry contrived were based on sheer coincidence, the plausibility of which is unacceptable to those who seek in fiction a reasonable reflection of events in actual life. This is the source of much of the adverse criticism leveled at O. Henry by critics nurtured in the Realistic tradition, and insofar as his stories violate a cardinal principle of fiction expressed by Melville—that "it should present another world, and yet one to which we feel the tie"—their criticism is valid. But there is another side even to this coin. Many of his stories, as H. E. Rollins noted, are as brilliantly contrived for achieving the single effect as those of Poe and de Maupassant, and O. Henry's so-called surprise endings are logically prepared for within the framework of the narrative; so that his technique does decidedly conform to the rules "that he affected to despise" [see excerpt dated 1914]. (pp. 137-39)

Compression . . . applied to seemingly realistic dialogue and to descriptive phraseology containing the unlooked-for term constantly operates in O. Henry's stories to produce fresh surprises and incidental delights. In many of his Western and Central American stories, for example, his liberal use of the Spanish-American vernacular, gracefully inserted into specific names for things and people and into many common colloquial expressions, again serves this dual purpose by conveying both a subtle flavor of the place itself and a humorous (or violent) turn of the story. The whole tone of humorous exoticism in **Cabbages and Kings** is set in the brief glimpse of a native messenger boy dashing down Coralio's "grass-grown" street, shrieking: " '*Busca el Señor* Goodwin. *Ha venido un telégrafo por él!*' " . . . . (pp. 141-42)

While the precise effect of these dialectal contributions cannot be scientifically assayed in any given story, it is nevertheless plain that over the whole stretch of O. Henry's writings his facility in rendering the speech patterns and rhythms of incidental common folk adds much to the vivacity, variety, and interest of his stories. This fact is demonstrable not only in his Western tales but also in those of other settings; for comparative analysis has shown that he employed with astonishing accuracy at least five different native American dialects along with as many foreign ones. Besides Texas cowpoke language, these include the colloquial speech of Cumberland Mountain whites, as well as the mixtures of Spanish-English, German-English, French-English, and Italian-English. (pp. 142-43)

[The] broadly democratic appeal found in O. Henry's stories [is due to] the fact that he succeeded in making all his romanticized types seem important—even the dregs of humanity—by portraying them sympathetically and humorously through their own language. As a stylist, in fact, his most striking trait is humor; and once again, it is worth noting that O. Henry's humor is his own, a unique quality, not a mere shadow of Twain's or Stockton's or that of any of their predecessors. Rather, as [Gerald] Langford has mentioned [see Additional Bibliography], it is closer in both flavor and technique to the humor of later writers like Dorothy Parker, Robert Benchley, James Thurber, and E. B. White (or, he might have added, S. J. Perelman); that is, an intellectualized humor based on a fondness for and a firm grasp of odd, esoteric, yet precise terminology.

Humor resulting from clever turns of phrase, from unusual and unexpected word combinations and distortions—the humor of surprise—is thus central to O. Henry's technique. Puns, coinages, sophistries, slang, malapropisms of various kinds are all among the standard logomachic devices he used over and over again to keep his readers on the *qui vive*. He usually concentrated them in his opening passages but he also sprinkled them liberally throughout his stories. (pp. 143-44)

[Quoted sample passages] still give but a hint of the elaborate word-play that O. Henry's ingenuity contrived in order to spice his tales and keep his readers chuckling. Like Shakespeare and

Sheridan, he enjoyed tampering with standard idioms, both English and foreign, so as to produce both pure and antithetical malapropisms, blundering misquotations, and word-mutilations and distortions, often brilliantly original in conception. One student has noted hundreds of these, of which the following are a brief sampling:

> "I reckon in New York you get to be a conniseer; and when you go around with the '*demitasse*,' you are naturally bound to buy 'em stylish grub."
>
> . . . .
>
> "I never saw a man eat with so much earnestness—not hastily like a grammarian or one of the canal, slow and appreciating like a anaconda, or a real '*vive bonjour*.' "
>
> . . . .
>
> What's this? Horse with the heaves [*hors d'oeuvres*]?"
>
> (p. 145)

Still further examples of O. Henry's artistry with words may be seen in his numerous literary allusions, chiefly to well-known Shakespearean plays and the ancient Classics as well as to his favorite *Arabian Nights;* but occasionally he alludes also to the writings of standard modern authors. His purpose again here is generally humorous; for as one writer has noted, in most of the hundred or so extended allusions to Shakespeare found in his stories, "he shows a tendency to word-play or to an unexpected turn similar to that manifest in the plots of his stories" [see Gates entry in Additional Bibliography]. (p. 146)

Thanks to another scholar's labor, there is even more abundant evidence of O. Henry's use of the ancient Classics; for a total of some 450 "clearly recognizable allusions" to them have been spotted in his various writings [see Echols entry in Additional Bibliography]. Curiously enough, most of these allusions reflect a serious intent on O. Henry's part; and they indicate that, even though frankly appealing to a mass audience, he could still take for granted that many of his readers would recognize and appreciate his references to Homer, Cicero, Caesar, and to other Greek and Latin poets. Still, in at least seventy-five separate instances his purpose in making them was clearly humorous; and his methods were primarily those of punning and word mutilation. (p. 147)

Unfortunately, when such word-play loses much of whatever freshness it once possessed, it becomes sadly dated, if not downright cheap and tawdry; for O. Henry with the punning bit firmly between his teeth was not noted for restraint. Some of his misused or garbled Latin phrases—such as "adjourn sine qua non," "requiescat in hoc signo," "requiescat in pieces," "sine qua grata," "non compis vocis," etc.—no longer sound as funny as they once did, possibly because the original phrases themselves have become virtually standard English or because too many other jokesters have similarly garbled them. And yet, many of his linguistic capers still sound both apt and witty to the tolerant ear of a Classics specialist:

> A newspaper office is a "sanctum asinorum," and by the same token the office of a public stenographer is a "sanctum Remingtorium." Two fugitives alight from a train in Arizona, happy to return once more to "terra cotta," perhaps true in that climate.
>
> (p. 148)

It is left to O. Henry to provide the translation to end all translations of Caesar's opening lines: "Omnes Gallia in tres partes divisa est: we will need all of our gall in devising means to tree them parties" [Edward C. Echols].

Besides these deliberately ludicrous examples of O. Henry's tampering with the Classics, however, the same writer has shown that much oftener he employed classical allusions for a serious and significant purpose: "The 375 serious allusions in his short stories vary from the obvious and usual to references which assume a rather advanced classical knowledge for full comprehension." . . . Some of the ways in which the Classics are thus widely used in O. Henry's stories are in the names of places, institutions, and persons—often with symbolic overtones, as in the Hotel Lotus, the *Minerva Magazine,* Caligula Polk, Aglaia, Artemisia, etc. Other uses are made of them as symbols of the cultured individual, or as figurative comparisons to heighten personal descriptions, as in the quite effective portrait of Ida Bates, the young typist at the Hotel Acropolis who "was a hold-over from the Greek classics. There wasn't a flaw in her looks. . . . I saw her turn pink, perfect statue that she was—a miracle that I share with Pygmalion only." Many other classical comparisons appear in references to the weather, the social and economic competition prevalent in New York, the political solidarity of the South, the carnival gaiety of New York night life, the Western landscape at different seasons and times of day, the composition of literature and song, and, inevitably, the swift passage of time. From a classicist's point of view, many of O. Henry's serious classical allusions are both apt and pointed; often they are subtle as well in conveying complex moods and attitudes through the medium of a single sharp image, as in the glimpse of young Mary Ann Adrian cowering in her parents' rigid Calvinistic church beneath the disapproving glare of the congregation—"a hundred-eyed Cerberus that watched the gates through which her sins were fast thrusting her."

It may be doubted whether a great many of O. Henry's vast audience ever possessed a sufficiently broad classical background to appreciate as fully as he did the aptness of his allusions. But what they could appreciate and readily respond to was his lightness of touch in making them, to his easy assumption that he and his reader together stood on the same ground, sharing the same point of view, and that only a matter of chance therefore caused him rather than his reader to think of the appropriate comparison first. This, too, was part of the charm of the master trickster, capable of selecting repeatedly the unexpected word or phrase, which yet seemed in its context the inevitable choice to fit the occasion. . . . (pp. 148-50)

As a rhetorician, O. Henry is often at his best in descriptive passages . . . , lightly sketching in the vivid yet characteristic details . . .—and relating them to their temporal and spatial environment, often with a pun or *double-entendre* half concealed in the texture of his prose. (p. 150)

Whether serious or in a jesting mood—but often both by rapid turns—O. Henry's sheer love of words may break loose unexpectedly at any moment into colorful passages which, even though not wholly germane to his plot, nevertheless seize the reader's attention and achieve Conrad's stated purpose of making him *see, hear,* and *feel* the life relived on the printed page. Rhythm, movement, the right collocation of vowels and consonants, sound and sight images—all coalesce in these passages to produce a significant bit of experience. And even though

they are rarely sustained beyond a page or so . . . , there are a great many of them. (p. 151)

This is where [O. Henry's] art of compression and subtle joinery comes into play to justify and support the daring self-assurance with which he tosses together ingredients of a seemingly indissoluble nature, only to surprise the reader with a blend that is both light and satisfying and that possesses its own independent, distinctive characteristics. Much of his successful craftsmanship, as well as his popularity, rests on his sureness of touch, his confidence that the very process by which he makes a tale unfold will keep his reader on the alert for new surprises—will keep him, in fact, diverted and puzzled fully as much by the sleight-of-hand movements of the performing artist as he is by the substance of the story itself. Thus, scarcely has the story got under way than the reader has become an unwitting participant in its development: he supplies its unwritten portions, fills in its gaps and swift transitions, looks ahead in an effort to anticipate its forthcoming twists, turns, and outcome. Though possibly unexpressed, the question in the reader's mind "How will he pull this one off?" becomes no less important than "What happens next?"

To test the assertion just made, one need only examine closely the structural pattern of a typical O. Henry story—not necessarily one of his better-known ones—and note one's own reaction to it on a first reading. **"The Poet and the Peasant,"** for example, combines a number of his favorite ingredients, devices, and situations. The story opens as a first-person narrative, the speaker telling of "a poet friend of mine" who wrote a nature poem recently and submitted it to an editor. Having spent his entire life in close contact with nature, he had produced "a living pastoral"; yet the editor rejected it as being too artificial. And so while lunching together, "several of us," the narrator continues, indignantly condemned the editor. Among the group was Conant, a successful, city-bred fiction writer, who despised "bucolic scenes"; he, however, wrote another poem called "The Doe and the Brook," described by the narrator as "a fine specimen of the kind of work you would expect from a poet who had strayed with Amaryllis only as far as the florist's windows, and whose sole ornithological discussion had been carried on with a waiter." . . . He signed it, "and we sent it to the same editor."

At this point the reader's curiosity has been thoroughly whetted; his only concern is to learn the fate of the second poem. But O. Henry coyly turns the whole matter aside with his offhand remark: "But this has very little to do with the story." Yet the next sentence raises the possibility that Conant's poem does have something to do with the story, for it reveals that "just as the editor was reading the first line of the poem, on the next morning, a being stumbled off the West Shore ferryboat, and loped slowly up Forty-second Street." Now follows a fairly detailed, ludicrous description of a typical young rustic carrying a battered valise; he is so obviously the hayseed, however, that—although passersby smile knowingly at first sight of him—they quickly decide upon closer scrutiny that his antics and manner, like his appearance, are too patently overdone to be real. A confidence man, Bunco Harry, even sidles up to advise him quietly, as he stands gawking into a jeweler's window, that his make-up is "too thick." Nothing the innocent young rube can say to justify his identity can convince the swindler that he is not also a crook in disguise; and, while Bunco Harry tolerantly invites him to have a drink, he cannily declines the young man's offer "to play a game or two of seven-up."

By now the reader is puzzled as to whether any relationship exists between the poet and this peasant, but the problem of Haylocks has already begun to complicate his puzzlement. It is now a question of finding out what lies in store for him, besides that of linking him up somehow with Conant. In rapid order everyone he meets suspects him of chicanery: Bunco Harry is convinced that the $950 he flashes in a roll as big as a teacup is counterfeit; the bartender and other assorted hoodlums take him for a poorly disguised detective; a second bartender to whom he entrusts the valise knows without opening it that the only nine-fifty in it is "a ninety-eight cent Waterbury that's stopped at ten minutes to ten." Everyone on Broadway sardonically regards him as "the oldest of 'gags' that the city must endure." Even the newsboy spurns his proffered twenty-dollar "yellow back" as stage money; and a gambling-house steerer whom he appeals to for guidance toward a sporting house angrily accuses him of being a police decoy. At each turn of events the irony of Haylocks' predicament receives a further complicating, humorous twist; and the reader wonders how many more variations of it the author will be able to crowd into his swift-moving narrative before it grows tedious.

Thoroughly rebuffed by "the great city that is so swift to detect artificialities," Haylocks now decides that his difficulties have been due to his clothes, which make him look like a hayseed; he therefore spends part of his fortune for a complete outfit (brilliantly described by O. Henry in four compact sentences); then, resplendantly, he sets forth once again down Broadway "with the easy and graceful tread of a millionaire." And within a few minutes he is spotted by a trio of hold-up men, who size him up immediately as "the juiciest jay" they have encountered in months. O. Henry wastes no further words explaining what happens next: his narrator simply indicates that at half-past eleven "a man galloped into West Forty-seventh Street Police Station" to report breathlessly that he has been robbed of $950, his entire share of his grandmother's farm. At this point the story of Haylocks (or Jabez Bulltongue, the name he gives the desk sergeant) ends, and with no further transition, the narrator proceeds, in four more short paragraphs, to wrap up also the unfinished account of Conant and the story as a whole.

Conant's poem, "The Doe and the Brook," of course, receives high praise from the editor as "'the work of one whose life has been heart to heart with Nature,'" its finished artistry forcibly reminding him of a homely comparison—"'it was as if a wild, free child of the woods and fields were to don the garb of fashion and walk down Broadway. Beneath the apparel the man would show.'" . . . Conant himself laconically accepts both the praise and his check, and O. Henry ironically offers the reader his choice of mixed morals suggested by the story: either "'Stay on the Farm'" or "'Don't Write Poetry.'" Only the naïve reader, however, will fail to recognize that neither of these touches the underlying meaning of the story, which has to do with the age-old theme of appearance versus reality, as well as with the basic human tendency to rely on snap judgments derived from an inadequate interpretation of the former. Granted that O. Henry's flimsy little tale offers no very profound commentary on these matters, is it after all just an idle piece of jugglery, devoid of art and perhaps even of truth . . .? Is it mere pointless prestidigitation, designed to flatter and cajole the unthinking masses? If so, one might still bear in mind the import of Anatole France's "Jongleur de Notre Dame," the hero of which found favor in the Virgin Mother's eyes by performing humbly the one skill he possessed. For if O. Henry's story is jugglery of the same sort, it is at least

unpretentious in its appeal to a mass audience; moreover, its essential cleverness is artfully concealed beneath a surface level of pseudo-cleverness sufficient to delight the many who read on the run.

On the one level **"The Poet and the Peasant,"** like so many other O. Henry stories, is simply an entertaining bit of fluff. Its power to divert and amuse springs from a series of obvious related ironies; from O. Henry's absurdly comic portrayal of the young Ulsterman, and from his narrator's slangy insouciance in juxtaposing the two seemingly unrelated accounts, welding them together as though there were nothing out of the ordinary in doing so, and applying two different idioms to his two groups of characters. All this superficial trickery provides ample entertainment for the typical O. Henry fan. But beneath this surface level there is suggested also a cluster of related truths about art and life, about knowledge and ignorance, and about human fallibility in distinguishing the genuine from the spurious. That O. Henry's technique enabled him to compress so much within the compass of a Sunday supplement page—and with such seeming artlessness—is the true measure of his artistry. (pp. 152-55)

> *Eugene Current-García, in his* O. Henry (William Sydney Porter), *Twayne Publishers, Inc., 1965, 192 p.*

GEORGE MONTEIRO (essay date 1973-74)

[*Monteiro is an American critic, translator, poet, and editor. In the following excerpt, he examines the different ways that O. Henry and Ernest Hemingway used surprise endings in their short stories.*]

Literary historians and critics today mention Ernest Hemingway and O. Henry in the same breath only to contrast their stories, particularly the endings of those stories, and they do so, invariably, to O. Henry's disadvantage. While O. Henry is customarily offered up as the facile contriver of ingenious plots, Hemingway is invoked as the architect of the virtually plotless story. O. Henry's stories work toward surprising, sometimes astonishing endings—so runs the argument—but Hemingway's stories often seem to stop without really finishing. Indeed, so evidently radical was Hemingway's departure from the received conventions of the short story, that on one occasion his friends Scott Fitzgerald and Christian Gauss actually accused him of having constructed in "Big Two-Hearted River" a story "in which nothing happened."

Hemingway himself had something to do with the terms of the comparison of his stories with those of O. Henry. To his Shandyean interlocutor in *Death in the Afternoon* he explained that as for himself it had been a long time since he had "added the wow to the end of a story." If he did not have his predecessor precisely in mind, he was at least referring to his predecessor's kind of story. In short, although he had once been an imitator of O. Henry's work [as Hemingway critic Charles A. Fenton maintains in *The Apprenticeship of Ernest Hemingway: The Early Years* (1954)], Hemingway would now have us believe that he had long since elected to compose what he took to be a different, less traditional kind of story than the one advocated by the day's "handbooks" on short story writing.

Critics have so totally accepted Hemingway's word that he spurned the surprise ending that they have failed to acknowledge that Hemingway was wont to employ his own brand of the surprise ending. On first look, the ending of the typical

Hemingway story may appear to be radically muted, its effect more oblique than that of the typical O. Henry story. But like O. Henry's, those endings are unexpected and highly ironic. One need look only at "A Clean, Well-Lighted Place" with the older waiter's dismissal of his despair as "probably only insomnia," "Indian Camp" with the child's conviction that as for himself, despite the suicide he has just witnessed, he will never die, and the revelation in "A Canary for One" that the American couple, who have just been subjected to a long disquisition on the superiority of American husbands, are about to get a divorce—one need only sample Hemingway's characteristic endings to see that in his own way Hemingway was as addicted to the "wow" as was O. Henry. What he did do, in reality, was adapt the surprise ending to his own quite different view of human experience. (pp. 296-97)

A New York story about artists, [O. Henry's] **"The Last Leaf"** turns on the idea of heroic sacrifice. The aging artist Behrman's sacrifice of his life in order to paint a life-sustaining image of a leaf on the wall opposite the window of a dying young woman is the stuff of open-faced sentimentality. At the cost of life the old artist paints the masterpiece he has talked about for a lifetime. But Behrman as a character has no depth, no complexity, nor is he intended to have any. Neither, for that matter, do the story's other principals, the two young girls who share the flat above Behrman's. But then the author does not intend anyone to take on life at the expense of the plot. His total interest is in the turn his incident takes. His characters are counters to be maneuvered toward the surprising irony which scoops out the plot. Evidently the characters have been invented to serve the pure plot line of the incident the author has devised. Recognizing this, we must agree that they serve their function well. They say their lines but never get in the way of the action. There is no evidence in **"The Last Leaf"** that O. Henry was interested in what Henry James once called the prime function of fiction: to convey "A direct impression of life." What interests O. Henry is an action which surprisingly and ironically reveals a moment in which death and sacrifice work ironically to sustain youth and life. In fact, O. Henry moves quickly through the exposition necessary to crack out his denouement. One even senses that the author is impatient to get the preliminary terms of his story squared away so that he can uncover his particular irony. As a result, there is one ironic moment in the story and that one is, in characteristic O. Henry fashion, saved for the end. The dying girl has been deceived into choosing life over death and it has been a failed artist who has at last found an occasion and a purpose worthy of his modest art. The irony remains locked in the incident. Above all, it is not adequate to suggest that O. Henry's vision of life is ironic. Indeed, despite O. Henry's use of the universal themes of sacrifice and death, the story offers us no sense of universal fate or timeless psychology. The author's vision of human experience never breaks out of the incident which he has devised. Only the sentimentality of the surprisingly happy ending remains. It is of course a tribute to O. Henry's inventiveness that for multitudes of readers that has sufficed. (pp. 297-98)

Most readers will agree that Hemingway's ["The Snows of Kilimanjaro"] is a more complex performance than O. Henry's **"The Last Leaf."** Its mosaic of retrospectives and its shifts between Harry's inner reality and the outward reality he shares with his wife have no parallel in O. Henry's story. Nevertheless, the stories deal with the same basic situation: a disabled artist facing death. And both stories depend upon a "wow" ending. Indeed, the fate of Hemingway's hero, complete with the presentation of his apocalyptic translation to the "House

of God" at the top of Kilimanjaro, succeeded by his wife's shrieking recognition that—all-too-naturalistically—Harry is dead, provides us with Hemingway's complicated version of the surprise ending. If we do not know whether or not Harry has undergone an eleventh-hour redemption, we have nevertheless had the surprise of learning of his death even as we have first experienced his "rescue." Hemingway's "second" ending exactly reverses that of O. Henry's story **"The Last Leaf"** but only after his "first" ending has paralleled it.

That O. Henry himself was one of the writers Hemingway had in mind when writing "Snows" is suggested by the exchange between the husband and wife. "You can't die if you don't give up," encourages the rich woman; to which the writer replies, "Where did you read that? You're such a bloody fool."... As the doctor in **"Last Leaf"** says, "She has one chance in—let us say, ten.... And that chance is for her to want to live ... [W]henever my patient begins to count the carriages in her funeral procession I subtract 50 per cent, from the curative powers of medicines."

While subscribing implicitly to the critical theories of Edgar Poe and following the sometime practice of Nathaniel Hawthorne in that he would invent the incidents which would convey the single, predetermined effect of his tale, O. Henry works out everything toward his "wow" ending; but Hemingway tries to make every detail of the story release that "wow" gradually.... In O. Henry's **"The Last Leaf"** we are left with an incident which concludes ironically; in Hemingway's "The Snows of Kilimanjaro" we are left with a chapter in the author's assessment of the ironic nature of human experience. The difference, of course, is one of total outlook. Fascinated by the small ironies of human experience, O. Henry heightened the drama of life to an artificially precise final effect, but Hemingway, seeing the whole of human life as itself inherently and inescapably ironic, worked to move the reader toward his own discovery that irony is at the core of human experience. Despite the essential differences, however, and all public disclaimers notwithstanding, in practice Hemingway never did forsake the "wow" or surprise ending. He merely moved it around a bit. (pp. 300-02)

George Monteiro, "Hemingway, O. Henry, and the Surprise Ending," in Prairie Schooner, *Vol. XLVII, No. 4, Winter, 1973-74, pp. 296-302.*

WALTER EVANS (essay date 1981)

[*In the following excerpt, Evans uses a close examination of the short story "A Municipal Report" to demonstrate that in many respects O. Henry's works foreshadowed the techniques of postmodernist fiction.*]

What can be said for O. Henry? In the face of modern critics' alternate heated denunciation and glacial indifference to his work can a contemporary construct any reasonable case for O. Henry's significance in the Postmodern era? The case now extant certainly does more harm than good; a few critics have rather fruitlessly explored most conventional avenues of literary appreciation seeking to praise O. Henry in the ways they praise other writers. But since, on the whole, his work won't really support much informed praise of characterization, setting, theme, influence—or even trick endings—modern criticism has wasted very little approval on O. Henry.

Yet, surprisingly enough, a remarkably strong case for O. Henry's significance exists if one cares to make it. As a first step one need do little more than call to mind many of America's most imaginative and talented contemporary writers: Nabokov, Barth, Barthelme, Coover, Gass, and the many other Postmoderns artistically heir to such innovators as Laurence Sterne and James Joyce. The characteristics by which such writers identify themselves, the patterns according to which they construct their works, and the standards by which they prefer to be judged could not more harmoniously blend with the O. Henry canon.

How are we to understand the term Postmodern? I employ it here as the least restrictive and dogmatic of several terms commonly applied to contemporary American avant-garde fiction. (p. 101)

I don't wish to be misunderstood as implying that Postmodernist writers restrict themselves to some dogmatic party line, but prominent among the tendencies which do seem to characterize many of their fictions are:

- a pervasive and intense self consciousness;
- a fondness for significant allusions, often copious or extended, to art/literature which exist in the "real" world;
- innovative structural patterns irrelevant to "plot" in the traditional sense;
- deliberate use of stereotypes, particularly of character;
- style marked by evident artificiality and verbal play ("linguistic foregrounding");
- metafictional references to storytelling;
- toyings with "reality" as in the imposture motif, determinism, coincidence;
- and parody.

Enough, for now, about Postmodernism. What about O. Henry? Critics like to praise originality as long as the work in question is not too original. It would appear that, as far as his current reputation is concerned, O. Henry made the mistake of writing too innovatively half a century too soon. We may condemn him on traditional grounds, but must—or so it seems to me—praise him on Postmodernist grounds. Perhaps the best test case for O. Henry's significance in Postmodern terms can be made on the basis of **"A Municipal Report,"** a story frequently reprinted even today, and in 1914 chosen in a *New York Times* poll as the best American short story ever written. I don't personally endorse the poll's results, but certainly few more innovative, more technically fascinating short stories have ever been written.

In O. Henry's first, most immediate, and most modest challenge to tradition, **"A Municipal Report"** commences with two epigraphs. Some earlier writers favored similar beginnings. Poe, for instance, was fond of prepping his reader with brief quotations from other writers—fond enough to fabricate them (as in "Ligeia") when he couldn't locate precisely the phrase he desired. But O. Henry prefaced **"A Municipal Report"** quite uniquely, so far as I know, in a couple of respects. For one thing, he employed two epigraphs rather than one:

> The cities are full of pride,
> Challenging each to each—
> This from her mountainside.
> That from her burthened beach.
>
> R. Kipling
>
> Fancy a novel about Chicago or Buffalo, let us say, or Nashville, Tennessee! There are just three big cities in the United States that are "story cities"—New York, of course, New Orleans, and, best of the lot, San Francisco.
>
> Frank Norris

The first of the epigraphs, Kipling's, functions rather as one might expect—as a thematic prologue. But the second, by Norris, operates like none other I can recall in a short story—quite literally as a "challenge" to be accepted. The implied conflict between Kipling and Norris, O. Henry proceeds to elaborate in his first two paragraphs, declaring: "it is a bold and rash deed to challenge in one sentence history, romance, and Rand and McNally."

Does all this really matter?

It seems to me absolutely fundamental—for at one sweep he immediately indicates that the narrative to follow functions as a kind of demonstration rather than as a purer fiction, rather than as an essentially mimetic fiction, rather than primarily as a rendering of human experience. O. Henry immediately follows his acknowledgment of Norris's challenge to a Nashville setting with the word: "Nashville." O. Henry thus unambiguously prepares us to identify the story's stimulus as rhetorical.

The story's rhetorical focus (more what one expects of an essay than of a short story), indicated with these contradictory epigraphs, O. Henry then underlines in the first couple of pages with references to a wide variety of writers and literary works. Kipling he quotes somewhat incorrectly: "East is east and west is San Francisco." *The Arabian Nights* (by all accounts O. Henry's favorite book, as it seems to be John Barth's) he alludes to in describing San Francisco as "the Bagdad of the New World." The Old Testament provides a reference to Adam and Eve; Shakespeare supplies "'tis enough—'twill serve" (from Mercutio's death speech in *Romeo and Juliet*); a reference to Sidney Carton calls up Dickens's own tale of two cities, neither of them on Norris's list—nor do Norris's cities figure prominently in the Bible, *the Arabian Nights,* works of Kipling, Shakespeare, or any of the other writers the story mentions with almost Nabokovian enthusiasm: Irving, Tennyson, Lamb, Chaucer, Hazlitt, Marcus Aurelius, Montaigne, and Hood. Thus, with his copious literary references and allusions, throughout **"A Municipal Report,"** O. Henry constantly foregrounds the rhetorical dimension of the fiction he's creating before our very eyes.

So much, for now, for the epigraphs and allusions. Much more impressive, daring, and original is a pattern not of allusion but of quotation which he employs to rhetorically structure the piece, or at least one dimension of the piece. In fact, O. Henry creates in **"A Municipal Report"** a unique contrapuntal pattern of coordinated structures: one a tale of selfless devotion, pitiful pride, and justifiable homicide; the other O. Henry's self-conscious reaction to Norris's challenge. The latter dimension, that dominating the story's title, O. Henry repeatedly reintroduces to the reader's mind by a series of quotations, presumably from some Rand McNally guide to American cities:

> Nashville—A city, port of delivery, and the capital of the State of Tennessee, is on the Cumberland River and on the N.C. & St. L. and the L. & N. railroads. This city is regarded as the most important educational centre in the South.

Throughout the first two-thirds of his story O. Henry scatters five similar quotations. This first, referring to the river, the railroads, and education, O. Henry immediately exploits by discussing the area's moisture, his arrival by train, and the commencement of his education regarding the city itself. The second quotation, decribing Nashville's "undulating grounds" and streets and lights, O. Henry counterpoints by describing a nighttime cab ride through the hilly streets, meanwhile mentioning many of the area's lights. The next quotation, referring to a local Civil War battle, prefaces a paragraph of military metaphors (involving "marksmanship" and "battle" and "enemy" etc.), introducing the hotel cuspidors and the associated character who later turns out to be the villain, a vainglorious professional Southerner, Major Wentworth Caswell. After suffering interminable delay at the bar because of Caswell's disquisitions on the Civil War and on genealogy, the narrator escapes to his lonely room where, as he removes a shoe and drops it on the floor, he determines that Nashville must be a colorless city, "Just a good, ordinary, hum-drum, business town."

The next guidebook quotation identifies Nashville as a manufacturing and business center—specifically mentioning shoes and boots, thus keying the transition. The general topic of the quotation—business—appears in the next paragraph when the narrator identifies his "own business," arranging for a Miss Azalea Adair to write regularly for a Northern literary magazine. A Negro cabman dressed in tatters drives the narrator the mile and a half over "uneven brick paving" to his "business" destination, Miss Adair's home.

The subsequent quotation appropriately describes Nashville's linear dimensions, miles of streets, paved and unpaved, and waterworks. Arriving at their destination the cabman charges two dollars rather than the fifty cents he deserves: "I *has* to have two dollars to-night and business is mighty po'." . . . The narrator identifies himself (to cabman and reader) as a Southerner who feels compelled to pay because of "inheritance." Inside, he meets Miss Azalea Adair, fifty years old, impoverished, "a descendant of the cavaliers." She charms him too much for talk of business and he makes an appointment to see her again the next afternoon, incidentally remarking (again O. Henry prods Norris, though so far the latter seems to have been correct) that in her hometown "few things out of the ordinary ever happen." . . .

The last quotation describes Nashville's extensive trade in shoes, hollow ware, and flour. Moments later Miss Adair rings for an unshod Negro girl and, handing her one of the very torn dollar bills the narrator only minutes before gave the cabman, orders the girl "to Mr. Baker's store on the corner" to buy tea and sugar cakes.

Interpolating in every few pages of narrative such radically alien material as these quotations strikes me as absolutely unique in two respects: the quotations' mere presence and their function. (pp. 102-05)

O. Henry's interpolated material (1) appears to have only the most marginal relevance, and (2) appears not in a body but scattered throughout the story.

So much for their presence: I know of no short story writer before O. Henry who has done anything like it. Barthelme comes later.

Now, how do these interpolations function? In at least three crucial ways. First, rhetorically the quotations guard in the reader's consciousness Norris's city challenge which O. Henry accepts so enthusiastically in producing **"A Municipal Report."** The quotations remind us again and again that we are experiencing a rhetorical construct; they repeatedly puncture the pure narrative dream, the mimetic illusion, the willing suspension of disbelief so much more important to every earlier American short story I can recall.

Second, the interpolations function as a structuring device, introducing the motifs of imagery and the details of setting and physical action which undergird the first two-thirds of the story. O. Henry cleverly and imaginatively matches our progress through the story to our progress through the quotations: (1) railroads, water, and education; (2) hills and streetlights; (3) Civil War battle experiences; (4) business; (5) extent of the city and its streets; (6) the trade in shoes, hollow ware, and flour. Significantly, when the "plot" really begins to develop in the last third of the story the quotations disappear and the structuring principle reverts to a traditional tactic, causal action.

Third, and not at all obvious, is the possibility that O. Henry means to imply (tweaking Norris's nose, as it were) that O. Henry himself, as writer, has been no closer to Nashville than an almanac or encyclopedia or city guide could take him. Absolutely nothing in the story seems in the least specific to Nashville. The streets, hotel, hills, run-down mansion could exist with perfectly equal credibility in dozens of American cities—only the drizzle he describes so vigorously lends the fictional city anything approaching unique personality. . . . The quotations function as do no other elements of the story: to endorse the title, **"A Municipal Report,"** and make the story seem uniquely Nashvillian. Yet a close reader can hardly avoid two conclusions: (1) almanac quotations from a regionful of cities could have set the scene with equal effect. (2) O. Henry not only realizes the fact, but rubs in it both Norris's nose and the reader's.

The setting of **"A Municipal Report"** leads to another interesting aspect of O. Henry's work; the intense avoidance of realism. In his case the opposite of realism is not dreamlike imagination or fantasy but pure artifice, though some might prefer the term artificiality. It may be that O. Henry's writing skills were too limited for him ever to rise above stereotypes of setting, character, and dialogue. On the other hand, few marks of a writer's skill matter more than his ability to disguise or triumph over his inevitable limitations. In describing the characters of **"A Municipal Report,"** as in many of his other stories, O. Henry didn't merely imply stereotypes; he insisted on explicitly pointing out to the reader that the stereotypes are stereotypes, the cliches cliches. The narrator says of Major Caswell, for example, "I knew him for a type the moment my eyes suffered from the sight of him." . . . O. Henry more subtly—but hardly less pointedly—indicates cliche elements of Miss Azalea Adair's personality by describing her "reception room." . . . (pp. 105-07)

O. Henry deserves no credit for relying on types, but he reveals creditable ingenuity in admitting their existence to the reader; he both solicits and merits the respect we pay to the successful puppeteer or muppeteer or magician or "illusionist." O. Henry doesn't really ask us to suspend our disbelief (as we never believe that doves turn to silk scarves) so much as to appreciate the skill and artifice of the acknowledged illusion. As with **"The Gift of the Magi,"** we are charmed not because we believe, but because the artifice could not be more perfectly, more delightfully artificial.

His self-conscious narrative style convinces as little as his self-conscious characters, but shares the same energetic, almost narcissistic striving for effect that pleases so much when it succeeds. (p. 107)

The following sentence is not a mistake. In **"A Municipal Report"** as in many of his best stories, O. Henry's style achieves the same emphatic lack of naturalism, of realism, of credibility as his characters and his plots. O. Henry's charm, more than that, O. Henry's best claim to genius, lies in his self-conscious artificiality. From the first page to the last of "**A Municipal Report**" he charms the reader (one who reads him without prejudice) with rhetorical games ("East is east and west is San Francisco"), often not dissimilar to those of such writers as Sterne and Joyce, games in America wrongly traced back no earlier than Nabokov and the Postmoderns.

Inspired verbal play O. Henry demonstrated from his earliest fictions. Humor in his early *Rolling Stone* pieces, the humor magazine he edited in Austin, often involved fractured quotes, malaprops, spoonerisms, outrageous puns, and imaginative respellings. The style owes more to regional humorists like Charles Farrar Browne (of Artemus Ward), David Locke (of Petroleum V. Nasby), and Henry Shaw (of Josh Billings) than to the genius of Joyce (who after all came after O. Henry, not the other way around). But no American prose writer—certainly no previous short story writer—devoted more energy to verbal play, or derived more success from it. (pp. 107-08)

The self-conscious, rather Barthian or Borgesian references to story-telling in "**The Gift of the Magi**" and elsewhere in his canon abound in "**A Municipal Report**" as well, but here their context more than ever emphasizes their "deconstructive" function of playfully calling into question the basic concepts of traditional fiction. . . . O. Henry plays a variety of Borgesian epistemological games in asides to the reader.

"I must tell you how I came to be in Nashville, and I assure you the digression brings as much tedium to me as it does to you.". . . In the first place, direct addresses to the reader in the second person seem far less common in short stories than in long. More interesting, however, is the reference to a "digression," for in fact—in traditional short story terms—"**A Municipal Report**" so far consists of nothing *but* digressions. The narrator here promises exposition which a reader hungering for traditional fiction (assuming such a reader is still reading) must regard at this point as an unexpected treasure trove. On one level O. Henry is simply teasing. On another, however, the comments *are* digressions, for O. Henry and the sympathetic reader are most concerned with his jazzlike improvisations and experiments with traditional formal expectations. The exposition here introduced *is* a digression in that in a sense it is merely a sop to convention, essentially distinct from the story's technically innovative heart and soul. (pp. 108-09)

[Another] comment mentions "the story that is so long in coming, because you can hardly expect anything to happen in Nashville.". . . Here, as at numerous points in "**A Municipal Report**," O. Henry refers to his story as a "story" and recalls the Norris challenge. The excitement O. Henry cultivates, the suspense for which he intrigues, the interest and anticipation he creates focus not on any of the characters or their situations so much as they focus on O. Henry's ability (so far in serious doubt for a traditional reader) to tell a story, to vanquish Norris. The few critics who have written on the story seem not quite to understand what O. Henry was about, but they intuitively show more respect for the challenge and response than for the characters—as did O. Henry himself in a precis describing the story for an editor before he wrote it: "The whole scheme is to show that an absolutely prosaic and conventional town (such as Nashville) can equal San Francisco, Bagdad or Paris when it comes to a human story.". . . (p. 109)

Long ago "appearance versus reality" sank to a critical bromide on a level with Christ figures; even accepting the concept's critical vulgarization, certainly the theme of illusion, a toying with reality, functions much more significantly in the work of such Postmodernists as Nabokov and Borges than in that of most earlier twentieth-century American writers. No question intrigued O. Henry more, in Gerald Langford's terms, than "the situation of the imposter or wearer of a disguise.". . . Eugene Current-Garcia endorses the theme's significance: "without doubt the theme of pretense—the desire to pose for what one is not, if only for a few moments and regardless of the price exacted—is the most persistent one in O. Henry's writing; for it crops up again and again in nearly all his stories from the earliest to the last few he left unfinished at his death.". . . Most of *The Gentle Grafter* stories involve con men; many other stories involve impoverished scions masquerading as wealthy aristocrats ("**The Renaissance at Charleroi**"), ordinary Americans as sophisticates ("**A Cosmopolite in a Cafe**"), rivals in love as trusted confidants ("**The Love-Philtre of Ikey Schoenstein**"), cowards as desperadoes ("**The Passing of Black Eagle**"), criminals as solid citizens ("**A Retrieved Reformation**"). The list of impostures he develops extends almost endlessly.

In "**A Municipal Report**" the imposture motif involves Miss Azalea Adair's valiant, heartrending, and childishly futile pretense of maintaining the elite standard of living she'd formerly been accustomed to. Caswell also pretends he's well-to-do and living on an "inheritance." A more significant imposture involves Old Caesar's unsuccessful attempts to pass himself off as a selfish uninvolved cabdriver rather than a selflessly loyal retainer, and his more successful attempt (only the narrator and the reader find him out) to conceal his final identity as murderer. Significantly, the narrator guards Old Caesar's secret guilt as zealously as O. Henry's friends guarded his own background of embezzlement, conviction, and imprisonment.

Only one theme rivals imposture in O. Henry's work: "the idea of fate as the one unavoidable reality of life" (Langford . . .), the idea "that destiny or fate imposes inescapable roles on the individual" (Current Garcia . . .). One can easily link the notions of fate and the paradoxical fitness of O. Henry's routine trick endings. I find equally interesting, however, O. Henry's emphatically pronounced fondness for a rather ordinary story, "**Roads of Destiny**," which consists of one beginning and three alternate endings: in each the poet David Mignot dies shot by the pistol of the Marquis de Beaupertuys. Gerald Langford's biography cogently develops the theme of fatalism through O. Henry's life. . . , certainly after the prison term, but most impressively before. Nabokov, of course, repeatedly plays with the concept, in "Signs and Symbols," for example; and in stories like "The Garden of Forking Paths," Borges invokes fate and determinism with a profound artistry. O. Henry undeniably equals them in sincerity and commitment to the premise.

Coincidence, often outrageous coincidence, functions significantly in the great majority of O. Henry's stories, much as in the stories of many contemporary avant-garde writers. It may sound strange to relate coincidence and fate, but Nabokov, Borges, and other Postmodernists constantly juxtapose the two (as in the stories mentioned above). The world "juxtapose" may betray deeper links, however, for in O. Henry as in the Postmodernists and others, coincidence normally functions as an agent of fate. What other agent but fated coincidence selected Old Caesar as the narrator's cabman? What other agent determined that the hotel boor, the narrator's first Nashville acquaintance, would be the villainous husband of the woman he sought? What other agent chose such a fortuitous moment for rigor mortis to allow Caswell's dead hand to release the button torn from Caesar's coat, a moment when the narrator—the only man who would immediately recognize it, understand its significance, and desire to protect its owner—could conceal it from prying eyes?

Parody also distinguishes the Postmodernists, and few writers have parodied others—or themselves—more enthusiastically and repeatedly than O. Henry. Among his earliest ventures were the burlesques and satires of his *Rolling Stone*. Later and more successfully, he parodied popular romantic fiction in **"Best-Seller,"** crime stories in **"Tommy's Burglar,"** his own work in **"A Dinner at ———"** which he subtitled, "The Adventures of an Author with His Own Hero," anticipating Pirandello (*Six Characters in Search of an Author*). He wrote many other parodies, and the mass of his stories contain at least moments of self-mockery. (pp. 110-11)

We have identified in O. Henry's work a great variety of the characteristics identified with Postmodernism: a pervasive self-consciousness, fondness for allusions, innovative structural pattern, deliberate use of stereotypes, style marked by evident artificiality and verbal play ("linguistic foregrounding"), metafictional references to storytelling, toyings with "reality" as in the imposture motif, determinism, coincidence, and finally parody. But apart from the criteria of Postmodernism as evidenced in **"A Municipal Report,"** do grounds for honest praise of O. Henry exist? I think so—in two very important areas.

For one thing, the works of O. Henry have entered the American imagination on the most fundamental level. He generated material which has since become almost folklore. Like a great many other Americans, long before I'd ever read any of his stories I'd absorbed by osmosis story patterns he created: the tramp who vainly seeks imprisonment so he can spend a comfortable winter, then decides to reform at the very moment he's arrested for loitering (**"The Cop and the Anthem"**). . . ; the husband who sells his prized watch to buy his wife some expensive combs, while she has cut and sold her hair to buy him a watch fob—the story of **"The Gift of the Magi,"** like so many of his others, is more familiar to Americans and holds more genuine mythic value than almost any forgotten tales of Greeks or Romans or Norsemen.

Undeniably, O. Henry has become a permanent part of the American imagination, one good reason to value him. Another is his originality. No one reading an O. Henry story could reasonably mistake it for a story by any other writer. Poe's definitive essay on the tale (in his 1842 review of *Twice-Told Tales*) proclaims "invention, creation, imagination, originality" to be a single trait, a "trait which, in the literature of fiction, is positively worth all the rest." From the beginnings through Barthelme, America has never produced a more unique fiction writer than O. Henry.

O. Henry published **"A Municipal Report"** six months before his death at the age of 47. In those last few months of his life he often spoke of great work he intended to do, work which would tower over anything he had yet produced. I doubt now, as I have always doubted, that O. Henry could produce anything we could value by the conventional standards which critics like Brooks and Warren have taught us to honor. The standards by which Nabokov and Barth and Gass and Coover and Barthelme are honored differ radically from Brooks and War-

ren's, however, and by these O. Henry had it in him, I think, to produce work of genius.

"A Municipal Report" seems to me close to such work, but even if it falls short, it is a fascinating and incredibly innovative short story. O. Henry himself once seemed to me a formerly overrated and now justly forgotten hack. On a closer look he seems a neglected, prescient, pre-modern master of Postmodern fiction. (pp. 111-13)

Walter Evans, "'A Municipal Report': O. Henry and Postmodernism," in Tennessee Studies in Literature, *Vol. XXVI, 1981, pp. 101-16.*

ADDITIONAL BIBLIOGRAPHY

Abrams, Fred. "The Pseudonym 'O. Henry': A New Perspective." *Studies in Short Fiction* 15, No. 3 (Summer 1978): 327-29.
  Examines a number of theories about the origin of O. Henry's pen name.

Arnett, Ethel Stephens. *O. Henry from Polecat Creek*. Greensboro, N. C.: Piedmont Press, 1962, 240 p.
  Account of O. Henry's boyhood and youth.

Boyd, David. "O. Henry's Road of Destiny." *Americana Illustrated* XXXI, No. 4 (1937): 579-608.
  Romanticized account of O. Henry's life prior to his major success as a writer.

Brown, Deming. "O. Henry in Russia." *The Russian Review* 12, No. 4 (October 1953): 253-58.
  Discusses the reasons for O. Henry's popularity with Russian readers.

Cannell, Margaret. "O. Henry's Linguistic Unconventionalities." *American Speech* XII, No. 4 (December 1937): 275-83.
  Lively examination of O. Henry's unconventional, idiomatic use of language that, the critic maintains, is responsible for the widespread use of colloquialisms in modern fiction.

Clarkson, Paul S. "A Decomposition of *Cabbages and Kings*." *American Literature* 7, No. 2 (May 1935): 195-202.
  Traces the previous publications of the short stories that were gathered together as the chapters of the novel *Cabbages and Kings* and the ways in which O. Henry constructed a unifying plot.

Courtney, Luther W. "O. Henry's Case Reconsidered." *American Literature* 14, No. 4 (January 1943): 361-71.
  Reexamination of O. Henry's 1898 conviction on embezzlement charges, concluding that he was technically guilty.

Davis, Robert H., and Maurice, Arthur B. *The Caliph of Bagdad: Being Arabian Nights Flashes of the Life, Letters, and Work of O. Henry*. New York: D. Appleton and Co., 1931, 411 p.
  Thorough biography quoting extensively from the letters and memoirs of friends, family members, and acquaintances of O. Henry as well as from his own letters.

Echols, Edward C. "O. Henry's 'Shaker of Attic Salt': Part I" and "O. Henry and the Classics: Part II." *The Classical Journal* 43, No. 8 (May 1948): 488-89: 44, No. 3 (December 1948): 209-10.
  Demonstrates that O. Henry utilized an extensive background in classical literature for both serious and comic purposes in his stories.

Fenton, James. "Set Form." *New Statesman* 88, No. 2259 (5 July 1974): 22.
  Maintains that O. Henry produced awkwardly contrived stories and considers the famous surprise endings to be merely feeble devices.

Gallegly, Joseph. *From Alamo Plaza to Jack Harris's Saloon: O. Henry and the Southwest He Knew*. Paris: Mouton, 1970, 213 p.
Historical study of the social conditions prevailing in the areas of the American Southwest where O. Henry spent much of his early life. The critic includes some critical commentary on the stories that have southwestern settings.

Gates, William Bran. "O. Henry and Shakspere." *The Shakespeare Bulletin* XIX, No. 1 (January 1944): 20-5.
Provides numerous examples of passages from O. Henry's stories that echo, reflect, or parody passages from Shakespeare's plays.

Green, Benny. "Oh, Henry!" *The Spectator* 232, No. 7617 (22 June 1974): 772.
Comments on the enduring popularity of O. Henry.

Harris, Richard C. *William Sydney Porter (O. Henry): A Reference Guide*. Boston: G. K. Hall, 1980, 229 p.
Comprehensive annotated bibliography of writings about O. Henry.

Henderson, Archibald. "O. Henry after a Decade." *The Southern Review* I, No. 4 (May 1920): 15-18.
A favorable reconsideration of O. Henry's place in literature ten years after his death.

Jennings, Al. *Through the Shadows with O. Henry*. New York: H. K. Fly Co., 1921, 320 p.
Autobiographical account by the former cowboy and train robber who claims to have known O. Henry while both were fugitives in Honduras, and who later was incarcerated in the Federal Penitentiary in Ohio with O. Henry. According to O. Henry biographer Gerald Langford, discrepencies of date and wildly improbable adventures that parallel O. Henry stories make Jennings's account somewhat suspect.

Knight, Jesse F. "O. Henry: Some Thoughts on the Urban Romantist." *The Romantist*, No. 3 (1979): 33-7.
Characterizes O. Henry as a Romantist whose stories recreate the innocence of the American spirit during the time of great hope and promise at the beginning of the twentieth century.

Langford, Gerald. *Alias O. Henry: A Biography of William Sidney Porter*. New York: Macmillan Co., 1957, 294 p.
Biography attempting to provide a complete and dispassionate examination of O. Henry's life by avoiding the romanticizing of many earlier biographical accounts that contributed to the "O. Henry legend" without shedding real light on O. Henry's elusive personality.

Long, E. Hudson. *O. Henry: American Regionalist*. Austin: Steck-Vaughn Co., 1971, 43 p.
Biographical study, relating some incidents from O. Henry's life to aspects of his works.

Marks, Patricia. "O. Henry and Dickens: Elsie in the Bleak House of Moral Decay." *English Language Notes* XII, No. 1 (September 1974): 35-7.*
Demonstrates O. Henry's indebtedness to the scene of Jo's death in Dickens's *Bleak House* for the conclusion of his story "Elsie in New York."

McCreery, David J. "Imitating Life: O. Henry's 'The Shamrock and the Palm'." *Mississippi Quarterly* XXXIV, No. 2 (Spring 1981): 113-21.
Examines a historical incident of impressment into forced labor on a Guatemalan railroad from which O. Henry borrowed details for his story "The Shamrock and the Palm."

Mencken, H. L. "In Praise of a Poet." *The Smart Set* 31, No. 1 (May 1910): 153-60.*
Praises the "extraordinary and often painful vivacity" of the "amazingly ingenious" stories in *Strictly Business* and *Options*, but notes that O. Henry's stories all "suffer vastly from sameness."

O'Connor, Richard. *O. Henry: The Legendary Life of William S. Porter*. Garden City, N.Y.: Doubleday & Co., 1970, 252 p.
Thorough critical and biographical study.

O'Faolain, Sean. "On Subject." In his *The Short Story*, pp. 171-92. New York: Devin-Adair Co., 1951.*
Uses O. Henry's "The Gift of the Magi" as an example of a short story that, relying wholly on an anecdote, does not offer the exploration of human nature that is essential to good fiction.

Sartin, Howard. "Margaret and 'The Unknown Quantity'." *Southern Humanities Review* X, No. 1 (Winter 1976): 1-18.
Examination of O. Henry's daughter Margaret's efforts to prove her father innocent of embezzlement charges.

Sinclair, Upton. *Bill Porter: A Drama of O. Henry in Prison*. Pasedena, Calif.: Privately printed, 1925, 58 p.
A fictional exploration of O. Henry's mental state while imprisoned and an examination of the ways authors reshape their own experiences in literature.

Williams, Blanche Colton. "William Sidney Porter ('O. Henry')." In her *Our Short Story Writers*, pp. 200-22. New York: Dodd, Mead, and Co., 1941.
Favorable overview of O. Henry's career.

Woollcott, Alexander. "O. Henry, Playwright." *The Bookman* LVI, No. 2 (October 1922): 152-57.
Account of O. Henry's unfulfilled intention to write a play based on his short story "The World and the Door" after the great popular success of the dramatized version of another of his stories to which he had relinquished the rights.

James Weldon Johnson

1871-1938

American novelist, poet, autobiographer, historian, and critic.

Johnson is regarded as an important black American author whose novel *The Autobiography of an Ex-Colored Man* anticipated the work of later writers, such as Ralph Ellison, concerned with the nature of racial identity. While contemporaries considered Johnson's novel an accurate sociological document revealing the lives of black Americans, it is studied today as a complex work providing an ambiguous psychological study of its anonymous title character. As a poet, Johnson is best known for *God's Trombones,* a collection of seven poems that captures the rhythmic and spiritual essence of traditional black sermons. Although literature for Johnson was only one aspect of an active and varied professional life, he produced highly accomplished works in several literary genres, including the novel, conventional and experimental poetry, popular songs, literary and social criticism, and autobiography.

Johnson was born in Jacksonville, Florida, where his father worked as headwaiter at a luxury resort hotel and his mother taught grammar school. Throughout his life Johnson was influenced by his family's adoption of American middle-class ideals as a means to racial equality. Considered a good student at Jacksonville's Straton Grammar School, he showed early virtuosity in both music and literature, but because secondary education was not available to black students, he was sent to a preparatory school at Atlanta University in Georgia. He remained at the university as an undergraduate, and during this period composed lampoons of teachers and fellow students, in addition to what he called "rather ardent love poems." Johnson graduated in 1894 and was recommended for, and received, a scholarship to Harvard University medical school; however, he turned down this offer in order to return to Straton Grammar School as its principal. His employment of subtle but persistent changes at the school resulted in an enlarged curriculum which included the teaching of Spanish, and, by adding a grade level each year, accreditation through the secondary level. Although he continued to teach for several years, Johnson simultaneously pursued other careers: as a lawyer with a private practice; as founder of the *Daily American,* believed to have been the first black daily newspaper in the country; and as lyricist for Cole and Johnson Brothers songwriters. With his younger brother Rosamond and his song-and-dance partner Bob Cole, Johnson wrote successful popular songs and later acted as road manager of the group when it toured the United States and Europe.

In 1906 Rosamond Johnson and Cole decided to produce their own musical, and Johnson, apprehensive about prospects for the group's future, abandoned his show business activities to accept a position in the U.S. Consular Service, which he was offered in recognition of his work with the Colored Republican Club during Theodore Roosevelt's successful presidential campaign. He began service at a small post in Venezuela, and it was at this time that he wrote most of *The Autobiography of an Ex-Colored Man,* which he had begun in New York. Later he was advanced to a post in Nicaragua, where he completed the novel. In 1913, when a new Democratic administration refused to send him to a more desirable location, Johnson resigned his post and spent the next year traveling between

New York, where he hoped to find work, and Jacksonville, where he was settling the estate of his late father. When "Fifty Years," a poem commemorating the Emancipation Proclamation, appeared in the *New York Times* in January 1913, Johnson's literary reputation soared and the work's popularity influenced publishers of the *New York Age* to hire him as an editorial writer in 1914. His popular column in this newspaper was conciliatory toward the opposing political factions aligned with either Booker T. Washington—who emphasized industrial education and repudiated political agitation for black Americans—and W. E. B. Du Bois, whose militant leadership challenged and eventually usurped that of Washington. Johnson also candidly stated his belief that the black press should serve as an instrument of propaganda and used his column to attack Jim Crow laws at home and American policies abroad in such occupied lands as Haiti. In 1916 he joined the National Association for the Advancement of Colored People and served as the organization's executive secretary from 1920 to 1930, during a time when the NAACP gained enormous influence among black people and wielded power on Capitol Hill. During these years Johnson published the poetry collections *Fifty Years, and Other Poems* and *God's Trombones,* as well as writing the historical study *Black Manhattan* and editing the works of lesser-known black poets in an anthology titled *The Book of American Negro Poetry.* In 1931, he returned to teaching as professor of creative literature at Fisk University in Nashville, Tennessee, a position that was created for him. Johnson died in 1938 in an automobile accident.

Despite Johnson's contemporary celebrity as a diplomat and political activist, he is best known today as an important forerunner of the revival in black literature known as the Harlem Renaissance. Johnson's first work, *The Autobiography of an Ex-Colored Man*, was published anonymously in 1912. While Johnson's anonymity served the practical purpose of dissociating him from a potentially controversial work, this strategy also lent verisimilitude to the fictional narrator, who claimed a secret identity was essential to his survival. Most critics accepted the novel as an authentic autobiography but an inartistic one, finding interest primarily in the work's detailed delineation of class stratification and other aspects of black American culture—a subject that would be sensationalized in Harlem Renaissance literature. Edmund Wilson, for example, argued that the literary value of *The Autobiography* did not equal its value as a "human and sociological document." Modern critical reassessments recognize the novel as a complex work in which understanding the narrator is central to understanding the work as a whole. The narrator, whose father was white, is "legally" a black man who has successfully passed as a white businessman and who considers his impersonation a practical joke on white America. Since early childhood, the narrator had invariably fled confrontation with the social consequences of his racial identity, often turning the "joke" upon himself. For example, after years of taunting the "niggers" in school, he is told abruptly by a teacher that he is black. While throughout the major part of the novel the narrator speaks abstractly about his racial pride and the work he intends to do on the behalf of other black people, his squeamish reaction to the squalid life of rural black America, and his condemnation of the behavior he found there as offensively unrefined, reveal his essentially middle-class white sensibility. Because the story is plotless, the picaresque "hero" is free to comment upon what he observes in the American North and South. However, critics have questioned the reliability of his perceptions of his environment and reactions to it. His over-sensitivity to pain and fear, Marvin P. Garrett and Nicolas Canaday have argued, is a result of insecurities that will not allow the narrator to face his identity. Similarly, Ladell Payne compares the narrator to the ten-dollar gold piece in which his father had drilled a hole in order to place it around his son's neck, a memento "which proclaims its value yet is absolutely worthless because much of its substance is gone." Maurice O'Sullivan posits that Johnson's preoccupation with the contradictions in his narrator are rooted in the "double consciousness" theory of Du Bois and Alain Locke, which recognizes the psychological tension in personalities who have no clear identification as either black or white; thus, according to O'Sullivan, the novel ultimately offers no resolution, but only the possibilities for both tragedy and pathos.

God's Trombones is considered Johnson's most artistically successful work, and one which Locke contends achieves epic proportions. Locke, like Richard A. Long, notes the assertion of black pride throughout the work, and the rejection of American and European standards and perspectives. Familiar biblical imagery of old-time Southern preachers is echoed rhythmically through repetition, alliteration, and other devices designed to induce "hypnotic grandeur." *God's Trombones* sustains the rhythm as well as the speech patterns of black preachers without using limiting conventional dialect, an accomplishment Payne regarded as "one of [Johnson's] greatest skills as an artist."

Later critics, however, have considered the collection "tame" and less potent than the sermons it imitates, mirroring Harriet Monroe's early assertion that in poems like "The Creation," Johnson "should have let himself go more rashly" in his interpretations. Nevertheless, *God's Trombones* remains an impressive poetic achievement for its translation of the rhythms and metaphors of black preachers into literary language rather than the minstrel show dialect often used by poets of the time.

Johnson's relatively small literary production has had a great influence on later generations of writers. *The Autobiography of an Ex-Colored Man* moved the black novel beyond simplistic autobiographies and sentimental apologies for the "tragic mulatto," and his poetry emphasized the black American's contributions to folk literature. Biographer Eugene Levy states that "Johnson took what he considered the raw material of folk art and transformed it into an artistic form to which readers of the era could favorably respond."

(See also *TCLC*, Vol. 3 and *Contemporary Authors*, Vol. 104.)

PRINCIPAL WORKS

The Autobiography of an Ex-Colored Man   (novel)   1912
Fifty Years, and Other Poems   (poetry)   1917
The Book of American Negro Poetry [editor]   (poetry)
   1922
God's Trombones   (poetry)   1927
Black Manhattan   (history)   1930
Along This Way: The Autobiography of James Weldon Johnson   (autobiography)   1933
Saint Peter Relates an Incident: Selected Poems   (poetry)
   1935

H. L. MENCKEN   (essay date 1917)

[*From the era of World War I until the early years of the Great Depression, Mencken was one of the most influential figures in American letters. In his literary criticism, Mencken encouraged American writers to shun the anglophilic, moralistic bent of the nineteenth century and to practice realism, an artistic call-to-arms that is most fully developed in his essay* "Puritanism as a Literary Force," *one of the seminal essays in modern literary criticism. Another important polemic,* "The Sahara of the Bozart"—*considered a powerful catalyst in spurring realism in Southern literature—attacked the paucity of beaux arts in Southern culture as well as the tendency in the region's literature toward romanticizing the Old South as a land of latter-day knights and fair ladies. In the following excerpt, Mencken discusses* The Autobiography of an Ex-Colored Man.]

[In] *The Autobiography of an Ex-Colored Man*, . . . all the author seeks to do is to tell his own story, with certain generalizations by the way. He is, like most Afro-Americans of any intelligence, chiefly white and of good blood; more, he is so nearly pure white that, in the end, he marries a white wife and passes over from the one race into the other. The value of his tale lies in the accuracy of its details—its pictures of the social life of the negro, North and South. He distinguishes three classes, (*a*) the tough niggeroes, (*b*) the order of niggero servants, dependent on the whites, and (*c*) the new order of well-to-do, industrious, self-respecting and aspiring niggeroes. It is the misfortune of the South that the first class is still numerous, and that the second is shrinking. It is the double misfortune of the South that the white Southerners still exhibit a vain and passionate intolerance of the third class. The brunette Napoleon (or Rockefeller, or Roosevelt, or Garranza, or Garrison), when he comes, will come out of Class III. . . . The anonymous author handles the question of miscegenation somewhat gingerly, though it is, in a sense, the main matter of his book. Interbreeding is going out of fashion in the South; it is no longer customary down there for every gentleman to have his xanthous mistress. But that is not because the Southerners have re-enacted the seventh commandment, but because the more sightly yellow girls have improved in education and aspiration and self-respect, and are thus less willing to enter into concubinage. A compensatory movement, not to be mentioned in a family magazine, shows itself in the North. You will find some notice of it in the present work. . . . (pp. 141-42)

H. L. Mencken, "Si Mutare Potest Aethiops Pellum Suam . . . ," in The Smart Set, *Vol. LIII, No. 1, September, 1917, pp. 138-44.**

WALTER F. WHITE (essay date 1922)

[*White was an American essayist, novelist, non-fiction writer, and autobiographer whose novels* The Fire in the Flint *(1924) and* Flight *(1926) provided revolutionary depictions of middle-class black Americans and the effects of racism on their lives. An influential civil rights activist who gained national attention as an investigator of lynchings for the National Association for the Advancement of Colored People, White became the organization's executive secretary after Johnson resigned the post. In fictional and nonfictional works, White analyzed the underlying causes of lynching and documented the successes and failures of the civil rights movement from the early 1920s through the mid-1950s. In the following excerpt, White praises Johnson's anthology* The Book of American Negro Poetry.]

It is but natural that in the revival of poetry during the past decade in the United States the Negro, with his wealth of emotionalism, his imaginative and creative gifts, his abundance of experience, and his vividness of expression, should play his part. There is no racial group in America which has a larger share of that sense of rhythmic values from which poetry is formed; nor of that gift of imaginative creativeness, of being able to shake off mere mortal inhibitions and prohibitions and to soar into regions of pure fancy. It is of this gift that the "spirituals" or jubilee songs were born. . . . He is yet largely propagandist and he voices more frequently than is consistent with accepted literary standards his bitter and vehement denunciation of lynching, of the denial of opportunity, of the proscriptions of race prejudice. This is unfortunate, in a sense, yet it is a natural reaction. When Carl Sandburg or Amy Lowell or Edgar Lee Masters begin to write they have only the problems of ordinary mortals to contend with. But when an American Negro undertakes to express his emotions in verse or prose or music or sculpture or painting he has the additional burden of a prejudice which baffles and confronts him every minute of his waking hours. . . .

In Mr. Johnson's book [*The Book of American Negro Poetry*] we have a valuable anthology of the work of thirty-one Negro poets, several of them very able ones, prefaced by an essay by Mr. Johnson, who is himself a well-known poet. . . .

Mr. Johnson's book has its chief value—and this is said in no disparagement of the work of the poets he quotes—in an admirable and well-written preface of some forty pages on The Creative Genius of the American Negro. In this he establishes in a manner that has not been done before the rightful place

which the Negro occupies in American literature, and his contributions in folk-songs, ragtime, and folk-dances. It will be surprising to many persons to know that the first woman poet in America to publish a volume of her works, except one, was a colored woman, Phillis Wheatley, born in Africa and brought to America as a slave. It will be interesting to know that more than one hundred Negro poets of more or less merit have published volumes of their verse ranging from pamphlets to substantial volumes. Equally surprising and interesting to the uninformed will seem the merit and value of much of the poetry that these colored writers have produced. Mr. Johnson has rendered a genuinely valuable service in thus presenting for the first time the work of these little known writers. . . . Those who know Mr. Johnson's own verse need not be told of the high place that his work holds in this collection. (p. 694)

Walter F. White, "Negro Poets," in The Nation, *Vol. CXIV, No. 2970, June 7, 1922, pp. 694-95.**

JAMES WELDON JOHNSON (essay date 1927)

[*In the following excerpt from his introduction to* God's Trombones, *Johnson explains his poetic style in this collection as a derivation from the sermons of Southern black preachers.*]

A good deal has been written on the folk creations of the American Negro: his music, sacred and secular; his plantation tales, and his dances; but that there are folk sermons, as well, is a fact that has passed unnoticed. I remember hearing in my boyhood sermons that were current, sermons that passed with only slight modifications from preacher to preacher and from locality to locality. Such sermons were, "The Valley of Dry Bones," which was based on the vision of the prophet in the 37th chapter of Ezekiel; the "Train Sermon," in which both God and the devil were pictured as running trains, one loaded with saints, that pulled up in heaven, and the other with sinners, that dumped its load in hell; the "Heavenly March," which gave in detail the journey of the faithful from earth, on up through the pearly gates to the great white throne. Then there was a stereotyped sermon which had no definite subject, and which was quite generally preached; it began with the Creation, went on to the fall of man, rambled through the trials and tribulations of the Hebrew Children, came down to the redemption by Christ, and ended with the Judgment Day and a warning and an exhortation to sinners. (pp. 1-2)

The old-time Negro preacher has not yet been given the niche in which he properly belongs. He has been portrayed only as a semi-comic figure. He had, it is true, his comic aspects, but on the whole he was an important figure, and at bottom a vital factor. It was through him that the people of diverse languages and customs who were brought here from diverse parts of Africa and thrown into slavery were given their first sense of unity and solidarity. He was the first shepherd of this bewildered flock. His power for good or ill was very great. It was the old-time preacher who for generations was the mainspring of hope and inspiration for the Negro in America. (pp. 2-3)

The old-time preacher was generally a man far above the average in intelligence; he was, not infrequently, a man of positive genius. The earliest of these preachers must have virtually committed many parts of the Bible to memory through hearing the scriptures read or preached from in the white churches which the slaves attended. They were the first of the slaves to learn to read, and their reading was confined to the Bible, and specifically to the more dramatic passages of the Old Testament. A text served mainly as a starting point and often had no relation to the development of the sermon. (p. 4)

The old-time Negro preacher of parts was above all an orator, and in good measure an actor. He knew the secret of oratory, that at bottom it is a progression of rhythmic words more than it is anything else. Indeed, I have witnessed congregations moved to ecstasy by the rhythmic intoning of sheer incoherencies. He was a master of all the modes of eloquence. He often possessed a voice that was a marvelous instrument, a voice he could modulate from a sepulchral whisper to a crashing thunder clap. His discourse was generally kept at a high pitch of fervency, but occasionally he dropped into colloquialisms and, less often, into humor. He preached a personal and anthropomorphic God, a sure-enough heaven and a red-hot hell. His imagination was bold and unfettered. He had the power to sweep his hearers before him; and so himself was often swept away. At such times his language was not prose but poetry. (p. 5)

At first thought, Negro dialect would appear to be the precise medium for these old-time sermons; however, . . . the poems [in *God's Trombones*] are not written in dialect. My reason for not using the dialect is double. First, although the dialect is the exact instrument for voicing certain traditional phases of Negro life, it is, and perhaps by that very exactness, a quite limited instrument. Indeed, it is an instrument with but two complete stops, pathos and humor. This limitation is not due to any defect of the dialect as dialect, but to the mould of convention in which Negro dialect in the United States has been set, to the fixing effects of its long association with the Negro only as a happy-go-lucky or a forlorn figure. The Aframerican poet might in time be able to break this mould of convention and write poetry in dialect without feeling that his first line will put the reader in a frame of mind which demands that the poem be either funny or sad, but I doubt that he will make the effort to do it; he does not consider it worth the while. . . . The passing of dialect as a medium for Negro poetry will be an actual loss, for in it many beautiful things can be done, and done best; however, in my opinion, *traditional* Negro dialect as a form for Aframerican poets is absolutely dead. The Negro poet in the United States, for poetry which he wishes to give a distinctively racial tone and color, needs now an instrument of greater range than dialect; that is, if he is to do more than sound the small notes of sentimentality. I said something on this point in **The Book of American Negro Poetry,** and because I cannot say it better, I quote: "What the colored poet in the United States needs to do is something like what Synge did for the Irish; he needs to find a form that will express the racial spirit by symbols from within rather than by symbols from without—such as the mere mutilation of English spelling and pronunciation. He needs a form that is freer and larger than dialect, but which will still hold the racial flavor." . . . (pp. 7-8)

The second part of my reason for not writing these poems in dialect is the weightier. The old-time Negro preachers, though they actually used dialect in their ordinary intercourse, stepped out from its narrow confines when they preached. They were all saturated with the sublime phraseology of the Hebrew prophets and steeped in the idioms of King James English, so when they preached and warmed to their work they spoke another language, a language far removed from traditional Negro dialect. It was really a fusion of Negro idioms with Bible English; and in this there may have been, after all, some kinship with the innate grandiloquence of their old African tongues. To place

in the mouths of the talented old-time Negro preachers a language that is a literary imitation of Mississippi cotton-field dialect is sheer burlesque.

Gross exaggeration of the use of big words by these preachers, in fact by Negroes in general, has been commonly made; the laugh being at the exhibition of ignorance involved. What is the basis of this fondness for big words? Is the predilection due, as is supposed, to ignorance desiring to parade itself as knowledge? Not at all. The old-time Negro preacher loved the sonorous, mouth-filling, ear-filling phrase because it gratified a highly developed sense of sound and rhythm in himself and his hearers.

I claim no more for these poems than that I have written them after the manner of the primitive sermons. (pp. 9-10)

James Weldon Johnson, in a preface to his God's Trombones: Seven Negro Sermons in Verse, *1927. Reprint by The Viking Press, 1969, pp. 1-11.*

HARRIET MONROE   (essay date 1927)

[*As the founder and editor of* Poetry, *Monroe was a key figure in the American "poetry renaissance" that took place in the early twentieth century.* Poetry *was the first periodical devoted primarily to the works of new poets and to poetry criticism, and from 1912 until her death Monroe maintained an editorial policy of*

Johnson as a child.

printing *"the best English verse which is being written today, regardless of where, by whom, or under what theory of art it is written."* In the following excerpt, Monroe praises God's Trombones.]

For some time Mr. Johnson has been known as a leader among the American Negro poets, and as by all odds their best editor. His *Book of American Negro Poetry,* and his two books of *Spirituals,* with their prefaces, are monuments of patient and sympathetic scholarship and of devotion to his race in its highest achievements.

The present volume [*God's Trombones,*] is his own highest achievement as a poet. The author says modestly in his excellent preface [see excerpt dated 1927]:

> I claim no more for these poems than that I have written them after the manner of the primitive sermons.

But it is something of an achievement to suggest, as he does, the spirit and rhythm of those sermons, and to do it without the help of dialect or of antiphonal repetitions. There may be two opinions about the tradition of dialect; at least Mr. Johnson makes a very good argument against it in his preface, and gets on very well without it.

With the old-time Negro, religion was a grand adventure. It exalted him into rapture, and his imagination lavished gymnastic figures upon it. Here, for example, are two stanzas from *The Creation:*

> Then God himself stepped down—
> And the sun was on his right hand,
> And the moon was on his left;
> The stars were clustered about his head,
> And the earth was under his feet.
> And God walked, and where he trod
> His footsteps hollowed the valleys out
> And bulged the mountains up.
>
> Then he stopped and looked and saw
> That the earth was hot and barren.
> So God stepped over to the edge of the world
> And he spat out the seven seas;
> He batted his eyes, and the lightning flashed;
> He clapped his hands, and the thunders rolled,
> And the waters above the earth came down,
> The cooling waters came down.

We have space for only a hint of the book's quality. Mr. Johnson does not claim to have originated the sermons; like Joel Chandler Harris he has set down what he heard—the essence of it; and he is entitled to credit of the same kind. Hardly to the same degree, however, as the authenticity is less complete, the art less perfect. I wish he could have let himself go a little more rashly; for the creation myth, as I heard Lucine Finch repeat her old mammy's version, was more powerfully poetic than Mr. Johnson's.

However, we should be grateful for this book. As the author says:

> The old-time Negro preacher is rapidly passing, and I have here tried sincerely to fix something of him.

(pp. 291-93)

Harriet Monroe, "Negro Sermons," in Poetry, *Vol. XXX, No. V, August, 1927, pp. 291-93.*

ALAIN LOCKE   (essay date 1927)

[*Locke was an American essayist, critic, editor, and educator whose works concentrate on black culture. With the publication of his* The New Negro *(1925), he became a recognized authority on black cultural achievements in America, especially during the Harlem Renaissance. Locke's career was based on the hope that knowledge of the art and culture of black Americans would be used as an "internal instrument of group inspiration and morale and as an external weapon of recognition and prestige." In the following excerpt, Locke discusses the literary and cultural significance of the folk sermons in* God's Trombones.]

The subject matter of [*God's Trombones: Seven Negro Sermons in Verse*]—the bardic role of the ante-bellum Negro preacher, clothed even in his literacy with the inspiration of faith and swaying his audiences with epic power and conviction, conjures up a background that would dwarf any but a major poet's voice and stature. In a flash of inspiration several years ago Mr. Johnson gave us what still remains perhaps the best of these folk-pictures in **"The Creation,"** which now in beautiful and elaborate format, is given to us with six companion poems and an essay on the originating genius, the old-time Negro shorter. The essay has the advantage of the commentator, and at this perspective Mr. Johnson offers us a vivid view of these "shepherds of the people." They and their flock will some day be the epic background and tradition of the Negro poet if ever Negro poetry becomes what it can become—a spiritual world and sun instead of remaining just a satellite of American verse in general.

What Mr. Johnson felt by instinct in **"The Creation,"** he now puts explicitly before the reader, and his fellow artists, the inspiring thought that there is an epic background here in the humble past of the Negro which, if treated with dignity and reverence, will be a rich and fair new province of poetry. It is not too much to say, in spite of the actual accomplishment of one of the most distructive of the year's volumes in verse, the real and final significance of Mr. Johnson's work will be this prophetic vision and influence pointing to what is yet to come.

The problem of the actual writing of these folk sermons is admittedly difficult: complete identification with the themes and idioms of a by-gone generation, a thoroughly incandescent revitalizing of its mood and faith, are perhaps impossible. At this late distance rhetoric must come to the rescue of a lapsing diction and poetic fictions re-kindle the primitive imagination. It is a question of Ossian all over again. The comparison with genuine folk-poetry is constantly in mind and the poet judged by the hard epic standard of objectivity, impersonality and the extent to which he approximates the primitive originals or reproduces their authentic quality. That Mr. Johnson succeeds as often as he does in passages of really fervid and simple folk poetry is great credit to his artistry. At least three of these poems in my judgment have this quality and are really great. **"The Creation," "Judgment Day,"** and in the main **"Go, Down Death."** To proclaim too enthusiastically the perfection of poems like the last-mentioned is to forget, in an age of personalism, the touch and tang of epic poetry. These are folk-things, and the epic standard must apply.

But especially after one has heard these poems read aloud or almost chanted in keeping with the rhapsodic fervor of the originals, one's ear does learn to discriminate and appreciate the true epic quality. (pp. 473-74)

*Alain Locke, "The Negro Poet and His Tradition,"
in* Survey, *Vol. LVIII, No. 9, August 1, 1927, pp.
473-74.*

ZONA GALE (essay date 1934)

[*Gale was an American novelist, short story writer, dramatist,
and essayist. A leader in the American "revolt from the village"
movement, she depicted in her novel* Miss Lulu Bett (1920) *a
woman's escape from the drudgery and dullness of small-town
life. Gale's dramatization of the novel won the Pulitzer Prize in
1921. Her later fiction was neither popular nor critically favored,
displaying as it did her growing mysticism, embodied in her motto,
"Life is something more than that which we believe it to be." In
the following excerpt, Gale praises Johnson's autobiography* Along
This Way.]

The minute record of a human being's life, set down by himself,
may be a fascinating form of literature. This is chiefly true
when the human being is aware; and thus able to observe in
retrospect and to interpret creatively all that has befallen him,
and his relationship to events and to his fellows. It is to this
creative interpretation, plus the power of almost "total recall,"
as Mrs. William Vaughn Moody named it, that *Along This
Way* owes its singular interest. There are other factors, but it
is from the stark picture of James Weldon Johnson, aware and
sensitive and able to interpret, who has here written his autobiography, that the major interest of the book derives.

Born in Nassau, with a background which he paints in a few
colorful pages, Mr. Johnson follows the fortunes of his family
to Jacksonville, Florida, where he lived his boyhood. His picture of his parents, of his mother, Helen Louise Johnson, teacher,
and his father, James Johnson, head-waiter at a great hotel—
which the little boy thought that his father owned—and later
a minister, (though not, as he said, "by trade")—these and
the portraits of his grand-parents are those of sturdy and definite
personalities, with a sharp sense of righteousness, and a liking
for good literature and for well-ordered surroundings. . . .

The child's goings and comings, by "the fence of the barking
dog" and to the church and the store, are built up in straight,
clear narrative, on to the night when he fell asleep at the revival
meeting and refused to be awakened until he had been carried
home, and then, in explanation, claimed to have had a vision,
describing and embellishing a picture of heaven which he had
seen in a book. This vision he was obliged to repeat to others,
"to my inward shame," and finally he was taken into the
church as the result of it. At school he announced himself an
agnostic. These experiences, he writes, led to "as nearly an
emotional and intellectual a balance as I have reached."

All the Jacksonville boyhood, with its well-scaled narrative,
its clear vignettes of persons, and its portrait of the city of that
day, is given a thrilling interest as recorded by one retroactively
conscious of his environment. Music, clothes, food, baseball,
religion; the boy's jobs as brick-carrier and cart driver; love;
the learning of Spanish—are all living experience. . . .

[It] must be remembered that James Weldon Johnson is a Negro, and that his encounters with and his reactions to the white
race form one of the spiritually invigorating phases of this story.
Not, of course, the main phase—one of the values of the recital
is in the autonomy of the narrator, the integrity of his individual
contests and controls. But with that individual growth runs
along many a social import of high value, such as his reactions
to education, to religion and to race. His respect for and devotion to the Negro equals his respect for and devotion to the

cause of the white, the brown or the red race—and this is a
very great deal to say of a member of any race. . . .

It is to be seen, from one so emancipated, so able to evaluate
the human being in terms of humanity, that an estimate of the
American white's problem in relation to the Negro, and of the
Negro's attitude to the white majority's social interpretations
in the matter, is of the very greatest moment. And that estimate,
indeed, is implicit in the text, rather than in any utterance. One
would say that it's suggested solution is made from the viewpoint of omniscience, as imagined by every highly-evolved
religion or philosophy: *More light for every creature. And woe
be unto those who withhold it.* This, the alleged slogan of
civilization, is one which this autobiographer applies indifferently to all problems. If one wishes to make any exceptions
whatever, it is with no instance from him. His humor is implicit
in his text, too. Regarded with question in a restaurant, this
Ph.D. begins to speak Spanish, and at once quiets the questioning. Mr. Johnson's conclusion is that any Negro will do,
save a Negro who is an American citizen. Asked to move into
a "Jim Crow" car, this Phi Beta Kappa requests that the law
be kept further and that two white men then sitting in the "Jim
Crow" be moved into the first class car. This cannot reasonably
be refused, but the men prove to be a manaic and his keeper,
and the maniac's first act, in Mr. Johnson's vacated seat, is
to thrust his manacled hands through the glass of the window.
(p. 20)

Fine studies of Rosamond Johnson, of Grace Nail, his wife,
and of innumerable interesting personalities met in his work
and in his attendance at the Institute of Pacific Relations, add
to the color and interest of the volume. The treatment of lynching is as restrained as a handling of that savage subject can
well be. Mr. Johnson's last word is: ". . . man must continue
to hope and struggle on; each day, if he would not be lost, he
must with renewed courage take a fresh hold on life and face
with fortitude the turns of circumstance. To do this, he needs
to be able at times to touch God; let the idea of God mean to
him whatever it may."

One likes to recall Carl Van Doren's wise and thrilling word
about this autobiography: that "it is a book which any man
might be proud to have written about a life which any man
might be proud to have lived." (p. 21)

> *Zona Gale, "An Autobiography of Distinction," in*
> The World Tomorrow, *Vol. XVII, No. 1, January 4,
> 1934, pp. 20-1.*

DAVID LITTLEJOHN (essay date 1966)

[*Littlejohn is an American critic, novelist, and journalist whose
critical studies include works about André Gide and Samuel Johnson. In the following excerpt, he discusses the strengths and shortcomings of Johnson's poetry and his novel* The Autobiography of
an Ex-Colored Man.]

Negroes in America have been writing and publishing as long
as white masters, slave owners and publishers, have allowed
them to do so. . . . From Phillis Wheatley to the Harlem Renaissance of the 1920's, few colored Americans had the training or the leisure to write, and their scattered efforts were at
best mediocre. These efforts took the form, most often, of
either Old Black Joe dialect tales or poorer imitations of poor
white models: genteel fictions, village librarian's verse. (p. 22)

Two poets of the pre-Renaissance period stand slightly apart—Paul Dunbar and James Weldon Johnson—if only for their celebrity. (p. 23)

James Weldon Johnson . . . , a contemporary of Dunbar's, outlived him to become one of the most distinguished Negro Americans of his time: a lyricist for Broadway shows, U.S. Consul in Venezuela and Nicaragua, a teacher, attorney, novelist, poet, editor, professor, and executive secretary of the NAACP. His autobiography, *Along This Way*, is one of the more dependable and readable of Negro leaders' autobiographies. His noteworthy "serious" poems are black propaganda pieces in nineteenth-century rhetoric, on the "This Land Is Our Land" theme; they include, in **"Brothers,"** . . . what may be the first outspoken dramatization of a lynching in verse.

His claim to a degree of poetic celebrity, however, rests on *God's Trombones* and **"St. Peter Relates an Incident,"** both written well after the end of the period in question, though still obviously the work of an older writer. The former, a collection of seven imitations of Negro sermons, once appeared striking and original; but so many examples of the colored preacher's sermon have appeared since (Faulkner's, Ellison's, Baldwin's, Ossie Davis', etc.), examples more compulsive, more stirring and effective, that Johnson's versions may read today like tame, overcivilized outlines, without the real spirit, the crescendo rhythms, the extraordinary imagery one associates with the genre. Although **"The Creation"** is the best known, **"Judgment Day"** strikes me as the best, the most rhapsodic and rolling. Certain sequences of others are effective—the Flood in **"Noah Built an Ark,"** Pharoah's Army in **"Let My People Go,"** the nailing on the cross in **"The Crucifixion"**—

> Jesus, my lamb-like Jesus,
> Shivering as the nails go through his hands;
> Jesus, my lamb-like Jesus,
> Shivering as the nails go through his feet.
> Jesus, my darling Jesus,
> Groaning as the Roman spear plunged in his
>   side;
> Jesus, my darling Jesus,
> Groaning as the blood came spurting from
>   his wound.
> Oh, look how they done my Jesus.

But the collection as a whole still seems slightly anthropological-condescending, a book of imitations far less potent than their originals. . . . (pp.24-5)

J. W. Johnson's *The Autobiography of an Ex-Colored Man* . . . is more a social phenomenon than a novel, and its notoriety—some of which has endured—is the combined product of its once-daring title, its anonymous publication (which led readers to presume it factual for fifteen years), and the novelty of its "outspoken" message to 1912 America. It reveals itself today as an utterly artless, unstructured, unselective sequence of Negro-life episodes, written in a style as flat and directionless as the floor of an enormous room. The climactic episodes, moreover—the hero's high life in Bohemian New York as a ragtime pianist, his European tour with a millionaire patron—betray only adolescent fantasies beneath the dull surface of prose. More interesting is what Johnson reveals, of America and himself, between the lines of plot. His essayette digressions, for example, offer a fair view of the antediluvian race relations in America during this period, albeit a view peculiarly fogged by his own prejudices: W. E. B. DuBois is a far more dependable authority. The prejudices themselves, though, the self-reve-

lation, may have for some white readers still a strangely pathetic appeal. He—the "hero," if not Johnson—is a pure example of the self-styled "better class of Negroes," a member of DuBois' "Talented Tenth," who hoped in these distant, deluded years to effect a liaison with "the better class of whites," and to detach himself utterly from the despised lower Negro classes. (p. 26)

Along with this class consciousness goes a dilettantish championing of the popular Negro arts, reminiscent of the detached folklorist's interest one feels in *God's Trombones*. His hero lists, in fact, the Uncle Remus stories, the Jubilee songs, ragtime, and the cake-walk as the four great cultural contributions of the American Negro, and paragraphs of his prose are devoted to the latter two. *The Autobiography* is anything but a "good" book; but, for all the naïveté, the snobbery, the fantasy, and the flatness, it does afford a unique and perhaps useful portrait of a period and a type. (p. 27)

> *David Littlejohn. "Before 'Native Son': The Dark Ages," in his* Black on White: A Critical Survey of Writing by American Negroes, *The Viking Press, 1966, pp. 21-38.**

RICHARD A. LONG   (essay date 1971)

[*Long is an American essayist, dramatist, editor, and poet whose work has been primarily concerned with black literature and culture in America and Africa. His essays have appeared in numerous magazines and journals, and he has coedited* Negritude: Essays and Studies *(1967) and* Afro-American Writing: An Anthology of Prose and Poetry *(1972). In the following excerpt, Long discusses the stylistic and thematic divisions of Johnson's poetry.*]

The verse output of James Weldon Johnson falls into four groups: lyrics in standard English, poems in the dialect tradition, folk-inspired free verse, and a long satirical poem. The first two groups are contemporary and were published in the volume *Fifty Years and Other Poems*. . . . The prayer and seven Negro sermons of the third group constitute *God's Trombones*. . . . The last group is represented by the poem **"St. Peter Relates An Incident of the Resurrection Day,"** privately printed in 1930, and republished with a selection of earlier poems in 1935.

The early poetry of Johnson belongs to the late nineteenth century tradition of sentimental poetry in so far as its techniques and verse forms are concerned, seldom rising above the mediocrity characteristic of American poetry in the period 1890-1910, during which it was written for the most part. In purpose, however, Johnson's early verse was a species of propaganda, designed sometimes overtly, sometimes obliquely, to advance to a reading public the merits and the grievances of blacks. In this sense the poetry of Johnson is an integral part of a coherent strain in the poetry of Afro-Americans beginning with Phillis Wheatley. . . . (p. 374)

More particularly, we may note the relationship of Johnson's early poetry to that of Paul Lawrence Dunbar, his much admired friend and contemporary. Though they were about the same age, Dunbar was by far the more precocious, and his virtuosity had an obvious impact on Johnson, though little of Dunbar's verse bears any obvious burden of racial protest, in spite of the real personal suffering Dunbar underwent because of misunderstanding and neglect that he ascribed to his color.

Another factor of importance in the early verse of Johnson is his composition of verses to be set to music by his brother

J. Rosamond Johnson; the search for euphony and piquancy and the use of devices such as internal rhyme betrays the hand of the librettist.

The division of Johnson's poetry into standard lyrics and dialect verse, as in the case of Dunbar's poetry, reflects a self-conscious distinction made by the author himself. Johnson's first collection of his poetry, which appeared eleven years after Dunbar's death, presents forty-eight standard poems, followed by a segregated group of sixteen "Jingles and Croons." The dialect poems reflect of course a literary tradition of their own since in point of fact the themes and forms of such dialect poetry as was written by Dunbar and Johnson and many others reflect no tradition of the folk who used "dialect." In point of fact, it is useful to remember that the dialect poets learned mainly from their predecessors and employ for the most part uniform grammatical and orthographic conventions which suggest that they did not consciously seek to represent any individual or regional dialect. Johnson himself gives a brief account of the dialect literary tradition in his introductions to Dunbar and other dialect poets in **The Book of American Negro Poetry**. . . . (pp. 374-75)

One of Johnson's dialect poems, because of its popular musical setting, is widely known and thought by many to be a genuine folk-product. The low-key sentimentality of **"Sence You Went Away"** is nevertheless that of the stage and not of real life. The last stanza will illustrate the point:

> Seems lak to me I jes can't he'p but sigh,
> Seems lak to me ma th'oat keeps gittin' dry,
> Seems lak to me a tear stays in ma eye,
>   Sence you went away.

The other dialect poems in Johnson's first collection which should be classified among the "croons" are **"My Lady's Lips Are Like De Honey," "Nobody's Lookin' But de Owl and de Moon," "You's Sweet to Yo' Mammy Jes de Same," "A Banjo Song."** The titles are sufficiently indicative of their range and content. The "jingles" are frequently in the form of dramatic monologue, and while they (partly because of their later publication), have never become platform rivals to Dunbar's monologues, **"Tunk (A Lecture on Modern Education)"** and **"The Rivals"** can challenge comparison. The first is an exhortation to a truant schoolboy in which the light duties of white folks in offices are contrasted with the labors of black folks in the fields. The second is an old man's reminiscences of a crucial episode in the courtship of his wife. Both poems are written in long line rhyming couplets, Johnson's preferred verse form for his dialect verse, though a variety of stanza forms and rhyme schemes is employed, some with great versatility as the refrain from **"Brer Rabbit, You's de Cutes' of 'Em All"** illustrates:

> Brer Wolf am mighty cunnin',
> Brer Fox am mighty sly,
> Brer Terrapin an' 'Possum—kinder small;
> Brer Lion's mighty vicious,
> Brer B'ar he's sorter 'spi'cious,
> Brer Rabbit, you's de cutes' of 'em all.

Of the standard poems of Johnson collected in **Fifty Years,** at least ten are more or less overtly on the race problem and among these are several of Johnson's most important poems. In contrast, the more generalized poems have hardly more than a passing interest except for a group of six poems **"Down by the Carib Sea"** in which Johnson treats images from his Latin-American experience as a U.S. consul in Venezuela and Nic-

aragua. Unfortunately, even here, conventionality of diction vitiates what might have been a poetic expression of enduring interest and value.

The group of ten race poems includes three of the "appeal" genre in which the black poet addresses his white compatriots and invites an improvement in their attitudes toward the blacks. This genre of Afro-American poetry runs from Phillis Wheatley to Gwendolyn Brooks, and may be said to have been already conventional when Johnson essayed it, though the sincerity with which he takes up the form cannot be doubted. In the short poem **"To America"** he asks:

> How would you have us, as we are?
> Or sinking 'neath the load we bear?
>
> • • • • •
>
> Strong willing sinews in your wings?
> Or tightening chains about your feet?
>   (pp. 375-76)

Another genre in the race poems is that of pointing out the virtuous black and inviting sympathy and understanding. **"The Black Mammy"** and **"The Color Sergeant"** illustrate this genre. The theme of the Black Mammy who has nursed with tenderness the white child who may some day strike down her own black child has its own kind of immortality, combining as it does the mawkishness of mother love with America's quaint racial customs. **"The Color Sergeant"** is based on a real incident in the Spanish-American War and may be said to prefigure the Dorie Miller and similar poems of succeeding wars.

A lynching poem is called **"Brothers"** and is a stilted dramatic exchange between a lynch victim and the mob who burn him alive. The division of objects from the ashes is intended perhaps to recall the casting of lots for Christ's clothes:

> You take that bone, and you this tooth, the chain—
> Let us divide its links; this skull, of course
> In fair division, to the leader comes.
>   (p. 376)

In two of the race poems Johnson addresses black people specifically. One of these is the famous ode to the dead creators of the spirituals, **"O Black and Unknown Bards."** The harmony and dignity of the poem are fully deserving of the praise it has received. The poet marvels continually:

> There is a wide, wide wonder in it all,
> That from degraded rest and service toil
> The fiery spirit of the seer should call
> These simple children of the sun and soil.

But his conclusion seems timid and apologetic,

> You sang far better than you knew; the songs
> That for your listeners' hungry hearts sufficed
> Still live,—but more than this to you belongs:
> You sang a race from wood and stone to Christ.
>   (p. 377)

The second decade of the twentieth century was a period of innovation and change in American poetry. The establishment of **Poetry Magazine,** the Imagist manifesto, the appearance of Frost, Masters, Sandburg, Lindsay and Pound all bespeak the new spirit. The annual anthologies of Magazine verse edited by William Stanley Braithwaite beginning in 1913 which were one of the chief forums of the new spirit despite Braithwaite's own conservatism were surely well-perused by his friend James Weldon Johnson. Accordingly, it is not surprising to find a sudden modification in Johnson's poetic practice develop during this decade, for his poem **"The Creation"** precedes by almost a decade its publication with companion pieces in *God's Trombones* in 1927. (p. 378)

"The Creation" was conceived, as it were, in the heat of the moment. Only gradually did Johnson develop the series of poems which constitute the seven sermons and the opening prayer in *God's Trombones*. The principles he employed in writing these poems, based closely on the practice of the folk preacher, are explained in the Preface [see excerpt dated 1927]. (pp. 378-79)

The medium Johnson chose for the sermon poems is a cadenced free verse which very effectively reflects the rhythmical speech of the folk preacher. Johnson uses the dash to indicate "a certain sort of pause that is marked by a quick intaking and an audible expulsion of the breath. . . ." (p. 379)

"Listen, Lord," "The Creation," "Go Down Death," and **"The Crucifixion"** are generally of a more exalted interest than the other pieces, but all of them capture effectively the imagery, the intensity, the sly humor, and the hypnotic grandeur of the black sermon tradition. In **"Listen, Lord"** the blessing of God is invoked on the preacher in these terms

> Put his eye to the telescope of eternity,
> And let him look upon the paper walls of time.
> Lord, turpentine his imagination,
> Put perpetual motion in his arms,
> Fill him full of the dynamite of thy power,
> Anoint him all over with the oil of thy salvation,
> And set his tongue on fire.
>
> (pp. 379-80)

The general technique developed by Johnson for *God's Trombones* constitutes a giant leap from his archaizing early poetry. Unfortunately the many pressures of his life as a public man and as a cultural mentor prevented him from utilizing his new freedom in a substantial body of work, though the continuing popularity of *God's Trombones* since its initial publication and its appeal to a broad stratum of readers have given this slim volume an importance in American poetry enjoyed by few other works of comparable scope.

A special irony of Johnson's creations is that they have often themselves reentered the folk stream they were intended to fix and commemorate, and have in turn sustained through countless recitations the continuation of a living tradition.

While Johnson expressed no overt ideological objectives concerning his verse sermons, it is significant that they were not offered either in the spirit of his early standard verse or of his "jingles and croons." The sermons are an assertion of black pride and black dignity with no reference to perspectives and standards of others.

A further direction in his poetic practice was revealed by Johnson in the long satirical poem **"St. Peter Relates an Incident of the Resurrection Day."** (pp. 380-81)

The poem, arranged in six sections of varying length, presents St. Peter, long after Resurrection Day, recounting to some of the heavenly host the unburying of the Unknown Soldier. The discovery that the man who had been honored by generations of Americans in his magnificent tomb was black is the O'Henryesque reversal in the poem. The limpidity of Johnson's handling of the theme in quatrains of rhyming couplets, a favorite meter for narration and monologue with him in his earlier verse,

is illustrated by his description of the reaction to the Klan's suggestion that the soldier be reburied:

> The scheme involved within the Klan's suggestion
> Gave rise to a rather nice metaphysical question:
> Could he be forced again through death's dark portal,
> Since now his body and soul were both immortal?
>
> (p. 381)

An untitled envoy, the last poem in *Fifty Years and Other Poems*, contains the following lines, central to its thought:

> . . . if injustice, brutishness and wrong
> Should make a blasting trumpet of my song;
> O God, give beauty and strength—truth to my words. . . .

Eighteen years later a revised and now titled **"Envoy"** closes the second and final selection of Johnson poems:

> . . . if injustice, brutishness, and wrong
> Stir me to make a weapon of my song;
> O God, give beauty, truth, strength to my words.

In this revision two important points are presented in capsule. Johnson continued to revise and modify his poems, a fact which should be taken account of in any future study devoted primarily to the texts. The second point is that Johnson's conception of the function of the poet, the black poet particularly, had evolved from the apologetic tradition, in which racial justice is implored and in which an attempt to show the worthiness

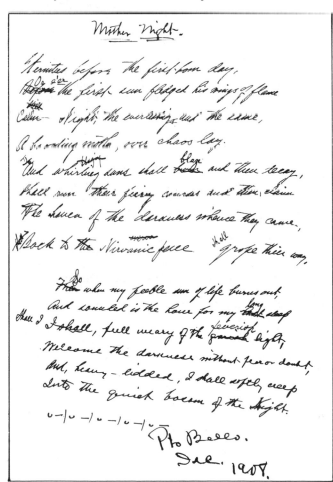

Holograph copy of Johnson's poem "Mother Night."

of blacks is made by showing their conformism, to a militant posture, in which the poet uses his talent as a weapon with concern only for beauty, truth and strength. In both phases, Johnson was a poet who recognized the propriety of propaganda. His earlier concern was with influencing opinion ("a blasting trumpet"); his later concern was asserting the verities, with a willingness "to make a weapon of my song." (p. 382)

> Richard A. Long, "A Weapon of My Song: The Poetry of James Weldon Johnson," in PHYLON: The Atlanta University Review of Race and Culture, *Vol. XXXII, No. 4, fourth quarter (Winter), 1971, pp. 374-82.*

MARVIN P. GARRETT (essay date 1971)

[*In the following excerpt, Garrett discusses* The Autobiography of an Ex-Colored Man *as a novel in which Johnson's ironic intent is made evident through the recollections of a "morally obtuse and self-centered" narrator.*]

In the second chapter of James Weldon Johnson's **The Autobiography of an Ex-Colored Man,** the unnamed narrator discourses upon the lasting effects of remembered tragedies:

> In the life of everyone there is a limited number of unhappy experiences which are not written upon the memory, but stamped there with a die; and in long years after, they can be called up in detail, and every emotion that was stirred by them can be lived through anew; these are the tragedies of life. We may grow to include some of them among the trivial incidents of childhood—a broken toy, a promise made to us that was not kept, a harsh, heart-piercing word—but these, too, as well as the bitter experiences of mature years, are the tragedies of life. . . .

The narrator's recollections represent the key to the novel's narrative design, becoming the primary means by which Johnson directs irony at his narrator. The author's treatment of early recollections closely parallels Alfred Adler's theories on the subject. Adler states that the early recollections of an individual, whether fancied or real, are a source of insight into that person's behavior pattern. Placing great importance upon man's cognitive activities, he emphasizes that an individual's response to the world depends upon his conception of it. Applying these principles in his analysis of neurotic behavior, Adler describes the neurotic's conception of the world as only partially valid, noting that the reasons he offers to explain his behavior, while often "good" reasons, are never "sufficient" ones. Although Johnson's novel is not a source for Adler's theories, the psychiatrist's remarks provide an excellent perspective from which to consider Johnson's psychological portrait. To explore the ironic design of **The Autobiography of an Ex-Colored Man** is to investigate the complex feelings and behavior patterns which emerge from the apparently digressive recollections of Johnson's protagonist. (pp. 5-6)

The narrator's weakness, his continual failure to struggle vigorously against obstacles, indicates that he is more pathetic than tragic. Although he endeavors to deceive both himself and the reader by presenting himself as a victim of a hostile environment, his efforts to place the blame for his dissatisfied state of being entirely upon society represent only a partial truth, the evasions of a character whose insufficiencies are the primary object of the novel's ironic mode.

In his definition of "structural irony," M. H. Abrams notes that the term is distinguished by its employment of a structural device which sustains duplicity of meaning. Johnson achieves his ironic effect by using the early recollections as a device which reveals the fallibility of the narrator. Extreme sensitivity to pain and excessive concern with security and self-protection are the most prominent patterns in the narrator's earliest recollections. For example, upon recalling a childhood incident in which he pulled up some bottles which were hedging a garden, he emphasizes the "terrific spanking" he received for his misdeed, indicating that pain is the force that stamped this trivial childhood incident in the narrator's memory. . . . Similarly, the wash tubs where, when young, he was "scrubbed until his skin hurt" are also seared into the protagonist's memory because of their connection with pain. . . . He vows that he can remember to this day the pain caused by the soap getting into his eyes. Such extreme sensitivity to pain, such excessive concern with self-protection, results in the narrator's adoption of behavior patterns affording the least discomfort to his tender ego.

The narrator's attempts to repress guilt, to justify his mode of existence, grow directly out of his egocentric desire to avoid pain. Avoidance of self-reproach is exhibited in the early childhood recollection in which the protagonist, unaware that he is partially black, joins his white schoolmates in stoning the "niggers." When reprimanded for his actions by his mother, he reveals his hierarchy of values, a hierarchy in which security and self-protection rank above moral principles and sympathy for the suffering of others. Betraying his self-centered, self-pitying character, he responds to his mother's harsh reprimand by attempting to evade responsibility for his actions: "I did hang my head in shame, not because she had convinced me that I had done wrong, but because I was hurt by the first sharp word she had ever given me." . . . Similarly, when the narrator receives a piano from his father, he feels "almost remorseful" that he had not displayed more affection for his father during a recent visit. The pain that he "almost" feels vanishes, however, as he realizes his "feeling of disappointment that the piano [is] not a grand." . . . Perhaps the most arresting example of the process by which the narrator represses feelings of remorse occurs in the opening pages of the novel: ". . . I suffer a vague feeling of unsatisfaction, of regret, of almost remorse, from which I am seeking relief, and of which I shall speak in the last paragraph of this account." . . . The sequence of words, "unsatisfaction," "regret," and "remorse" represents a movement toward an increasingly self-reproachful attitude by the protagonist. The word "unsatisfaction" merely indicates "a lack of satisfaction and fulfillment," a "negation of the state of pleasure." "Regret," somewhat more forceful, emphasizes the "feelings of sorrow over something left undone, even the things left undone by oneself." The word "remorse," the most painfully self-reproachful term, is defined as "deep torturing guilt felt for one's actions." The impact of the guilt and the pain is blunted, however, just as in the episode with his father by the qualifying word "almost." Thus every movement toward self-awareness by the narrator is only partially achieved, thwarted by his cowardly retreat before the painful truth.

The narrator continually attempts to place the blame for his condition outside himself, but such efforts are merely another element in his elaborate scheme to deceive himself and others. The protagonist's incredible hypocrisy is most tellingly revealed in his recollections about his school days. Characterizing the behavior of other students as "dishonest," he defends his own devious actions as examples of his "cleverness" and his "sly sense of humor." . . . (pp. 6-8)

Just as the protagonist's recollections demonstrate his reluctance to undergo the pain of honest self-analysis, these same recollections reveal how he attempts to deal with the distortions created within him by his excessive pride and fear. His recollections of his early childhood depict a protected world in which he acted like a "perfect little aristocrat" and was treated like a "pampered pet dog." . . . The protagonist's inordinate fascination with his own beauty illustrates the egocentric vision which results from such a protected existence. . . . His self-love leads him to seek excessive security in an effort to avoid any painful situations and his pride is so entangled with feelings of insecurity that fear becomes the predominant response adopted in every situation encountered. Recalling his return to school after the ugly incident in which he discovers that he is not white, the narrator expresses, in a rare moment of honest self-analysis, the distortions he himself has created.

Valuing security above all else, the protagonist seeks to exercise control over others because he feels secure only when in a dominant position. Yet, paradoxically, he asserts his power in a passive and safe manner. The narrator's "inability" to play accompaniment in a musical duet is a fine example of this behavior: "I have never been a good accompanist because my ideas of interpretation were always too strongly individual. I constantly forced my *accelerandos* and *rubatos* upon the soloist, often throwing the duet entirely out of gear." . . . This assertion of "individuality" by the narrator is actually an attempt by him to dominate the situation albeit passively. The intricate relationship between the protagonist's feelings of weakness and his need to dominate is illustrated by his friendship with "Red." Fear is the force which motivates the narrator to use "Red" as a device for self-protection: "The friend I bound to me with hooks of steel. . . . I had been quick enough to see that a big, strong boy was a friend to be desired at a public school." . . . The protagonist's admiration of power leads him to select the Old Testament figures of Samson and David as childhood heroes, figures which serve the ironic function of emphasizing his weaknesses. While David and Samson represent power, they also are remembered for their heroic struggles against overwhelming odds. The narrator's association with these figures only increases the irony at his expense, for his life is most conspicuous for its marked absence of struggle against obstacles. Yet the irony is less damaging from those he admires than from one he rejects. The protagonist's misconception of power as a means of self-aggrandizement, his acute misunderstanding of the self-possibility of growth in suffering are nowhere better illustrated than in his recollection of his youthful consideration and dismissal of Christ as a hero: "I became interested in the life of Christ, but became impatient and disappointed when I found that, notwithstanding the great power he possessed, he did not make use of it when, in my judgment, he most needed to do so." . . . (pp. 9-10)

The behavior pattern most frequently adopted by the protagonist, despite his admiration of power, is that of flight, foreshadowed in an early recollection of his childhood attempt to feed bread and molasses to a cow. When the cow moves to accept his offer, he jerks back "in half fright," his typical response in difficult situations throughout his life. . . . Later, when the narrator's money is stolen on his way to Atlanta University, his wounded pride and embarrassment override his determination to achieve his educational goal and he flees to Jacksonville, Florida, where he works in a cigar factory. While

there, he becomes involved with a schoolteacher and his admiration for her leads him to contemplate marriage. When his factory shuts down, however, rather than seek employment in the same town or a nearby area, as do most of his fellow-employees, he is seized by "a desire like a fever" and forsakes his growing commitment to the schoolteacher by fleeing to New York to seek his fortune.

The protagonist's excessive concern with self-protection, his instinctive response to danger, supports the suggestion made by Johnson's brother that the author should choose the more concise title of *The Chameleon* rather than the title Johnson eventually selected. While the title favored by Johnson's brother does emphasize that the changes undergone by the narrator stem from his inordinate need for self-protection, Johnson's title places greater significance upon the loss of identity which results from his fear-ridden existence. . . . A stunning illustration of the narrator's selfishness and loss of moral concern occurs in the scene in which he witnesses the burning of the Negro by the white mob. Ironically his racial ambiguity affords him the opportunity to experience the pain of the horrible burning, to view "what he did not want to see." As in the earlier killing of the white woman, his response to the scene is self-interested: "A great wave of humiliation and shame sweep over me. Shame that I belonged to a race that could be so dealt with." . . . Unable to feel sympathy for the white woman killed by her black lover or the black man burned by the white mob, unable to identify with either the black race or the white race, unable to empathize with the suffering of others, he isolates himself from more than a race or country—he separates himself from the community of suffering human beings.

The quiet self-destruction of the protagonist is conveyed through Johnson's manipulation of the fire-fever image pattern. Employing the positive associations of fire and fever, intense passion and artistic creativity, concomitant with their negative connotations of destruction and disease, Johnson depicts the gradual decline in the narrator's character. In his youth, the protagonist's highly emotional nature finds its outlet in a "feverish interest and excitement" in books . . . and in his passion for music which he always plays "with feeling." . . . Another instance of the connection of the narrator's emotional being with fire is his infatuation for his duct partner, a feeling which he describes as having "fired [his] imagination and heart with passion." . . . Yet, even in his early years, the protagonist is reluctant to reveal his emotions because it is so painful for him. Gradually, he forsakes his artistic ideals for a more judicious and materialistic existence, a process of deterioration exemplified by his abandonment of his desire to be a black musician and his decision to seek success as a white business man. The narrator's abandonment of art as an outlet for his emotions results in a transfer of his passion to an unhealthy desire to possess money. Images of fire and fever, once associated with the protagonist's artistic creativity, become agents of destruction which consume his identity as a black man and an artist. The land through which he travels on his way to Atlanta University is described as "burnt up," . . . suggesting the destructive nature of the journey. The excursion results in the narrator's loss of his money and in his cancellation of his plans to attend college. Similarly, because he is seized by a "desire like a fever," . . . the protagonist forsakes the Jacksonville schoolteacher to go to New York where he indulges in gambling, foreshadowing his eventual capitulation to materialism.

Although afflicted with "money fever," the narrator's writing of his autobiography results in his partial enlightenment. But

Johnson's irony is relentless and even the narrator's partial awakening becomes the object of irony. In his realization of the possibility that he may have erred in pursuing a life of wealth and security, he contrasts his state of being with that of Booker T. Washington whom he describes as "making history and a race." . . . Johnson's irony is indeed savage here, for the narrator's life only serves to belie Washington's position that material success is the key to social and psychological success for the Negro. Despite his material advancement, the protagonist remains in an "unsatisfied" condition at the novel's conclusion. (pp. 10-13)

Any critical approach to the novel which fails to recognize how intimately its construction contributes to the ironic design must remain incomplete. *The Autobiography of an Ex-Colored Man* is interesting, then, not merely for its "panoramic view of Negro life," but for the subtlety of its ironic presentation of a morally obtuse and self-centered character. (p. 14)

> Marvin P. Garrett, "Early Recollections and Structural Irony in 'The Autobiography of an Ex-Colored Man'," in Critique: Studies in Modern Fiction, *Vol. XIII, No. 2, 1971, pp. 5-14.*

HOUSTON A. BAKER, JR. (essay date 1973)

[*A poet and educator, Baker has contributed critical interpretations of black literature to anthologies and periodicals, including* Phylon, Black World, *and the* Virginia Quarterly Review. *In addition, he is the editor of critical volumes on African, Caribbean, and black American literature. In the following excerpt, Baker examines* The Autobiography of an Ex-Colored Man *in relation to the Southern literary tradition of tragic novels involving mulatto characters.*]

The Autobiography of an Ex-Colored Man, like Frederick Douglass's *Narrative of the Life of Frederick Douglass* (1845) and William Wells Brown's *Narrative of William Wells Brown, a Fugitive Slave* (1847), opens with a first-person narrator who belongs to the literary class known (since the days of the abolitionist movement) as the "tragic mulatto." Neither Douglass nor Brown can say with certainty when he was born, and each has heard rumors that his father was a white man. Johnson's narrator has only the vaguest memories of the time and place of his birth, and his father is recalled as the white man who came to his mother's small house several times a week. The setting is the rural South, complete with the white aristocrat and his black mistress. While this certainly fits one turn-of-the-century literary perspective, Johnson's narrator handles the situation with a telling irony more characteristic of Douglass or Brown than of the Plantation Tradition. When he decides to marry a white woman, the aristocrat must send his mistress away. This situation has a direct parallel in the relationship between the heroine and her lover in William Wells Brown's *Clotel* (1854), but the invective and polemicism (not to mention the maudlin sentimentality) that surround the departure in Brown's novel are almost totally absent in Johnson's. The narrator's simple and detached description in *The Autobiography of an Ex-Colored Man* offers an astute and ironical commentary on the South:

> I remember distinctly the last time this tall man came to the little house in Georgia; that evening before I went to bed he took me up in his arms and squeezed me very tightly; my mother stood behind his chair wiping tears from her eyes. I remember how I sat upon his knee and watched

him laboriously drill a hole through a ten-dollar gold piece, and then tie the coin around my neck with a string. I have worn that gold piece around my neck the greater part of my life, and still possess it, but more than once I have wished that some other way had been found of attaching it to me besides putting a hole through it.

The gold piece is not only worthless, but also serves as a symbol of the commercial transactions to which black Americans were prey during the days of American slavery. The skillful mood-building and the undercurrent of criticism that characterize the opening scenes run through the novel; and the narrator maintains his state of clinical detachment to the last. (pp. 435-36)

He quickly learns to play the piano by listening to his mother's renderings of old Southern songs and is designated by the local newspaper as an "infant prodigy." He also has keen reading abilities and absorbs instruction and entertainment from books unknown to his peers. In a sense, the progression of his musical tastes is the reverse of his literary development. In music he moves from the songs of his mother's heritage to the Western classics; while in reading he moves from the Bible through *Uncle Tom's Cabin* and the works of Alexander Dumas and Frederick Douglass. The protagonist's reading constitutes a type of abolitionist history, since he overcomes the lure of Western Christianity, acquires enlightenment from the work of Harriet Beecher Stowe, resolves to be a race man at a commencement speech on Toussaint L'Ouverture, and ends with the adoption of one of the greatest black abolitionists as his hero. The narrator has been forced toward this moral and intellectual awakening by a classroom incident in which the teacher asked all of the white children to stand up and abruptly told him that he did not belong among them. . . . Johnson's protagonist retreats into a world of books and music and becomes aware of what Du Bois calls the "double consciousness" that fragments the black self. . . . (pp. 437-38)

Johnson had read and been greatly impressed by Du Bois's work [*The Souls of Black Folk*], and it is not surprising that the mulatto status and the varying musical inclinations of his narrator act as symbolic projections of a double consciousness. The narrator modulates between the black world and the white (often with less than equanimity) and seems torn between the early melodies of his mother and the Chopinesque style that wins his white beloved. In a sense, *The Autobiography of an Ex-Colored Man* is a fictional rendering of *The Souls of Black Folk,* for Johnson's narrator not only stresses his bifurcated vision, but also his intellectual genius. He maintains an open, critical attitude toward the many sides of black American culture, condemns in unequivocal terms the limitations of the black situation, and assiduously records his movement from a naïve provincialism toward a broad cosmopolitanism. The narrator, in short, is a black man of culture recording the situations and attitudes that have succeeded in driving him underground, to a position the larger society might define as criminal. . . . *The Autobiography of an Ex-Colored Man* is both the history and the confession of one of the "talented tenth" (that class of college-bred black Americans in whom Du Bois placed so much faith); it offers the rehearsal of a "soul on ice" who draws substance from a world that could not recognize his true character nor sympathize with his longings. Each of its episodes is an effort at personal definition and a partial summing up of the black American past.

The narrator goes South to attend a black college established by the Freedmen's Bureau and Northern philanthropy; he circulates among the Southern black folk, and discovers (in the manner of Booker T. Washington) the value of a trade for an ambitious black man. He (like the more than two million blacks who left the South between 1890 and 1920) is driven by economic conditions to migrate to the North again, and he chooses to work out his destiny in New York. Quickly throwing off the pursuit of "useful work," he becomes involved in the underworld of black urban life (which had not yet moved uptown to Harlem), and he is one of the earliest recorders of the new black urban condition:

> New York City is the most fatally fascinating thing in America. She sits like a great witch at the gate of the country, showing her alluring white face and hiding her crooked hands and feet under the folds of her wide garments— constantly enticing thousands from far within, and tempting those who come across the seas to go no further. And all these become the victims of her caprice.

After such a description, it is not surprising to find the narrator caught in a dissipating ritual of gambling, late hours, and heady pleasures. But there is also insight. He describes one aspect of the city life of his day—the successful black jockeys, the black entertainers who acted on the minstrel stage while they possessed the talent of fine tragedians, the affluent hustlers and the badman heroes who brought white society slumming. Moreover, it is at this period in his wanderings that he recognizes the greatness of black musicians, those "unknown bards" who originated rag-time and jazz and found them copied by white musicians who made a fortune. After an encounter with a black badman (in which a wealthy white woman plays a significant rôle), the narrator goes to Europe with a decadent American millionaire who has found release from ennui in his music. He thus becomes one of the first fictional, black artistic exiles. . . . Finally, however, the pull of his heritage, his ambition to be an influential black American, and an ironic incident in which he witnesses a European musician turn the raw material of rag-time into classical harmonies lead him to return to the United States. . . . [He] overcomes the temptation to remain in exile and refuses to attend his patron's siren song on the intractability of the American racial problem.

The last quarter of *The Autobiography of an Ex-Colored Man* concerns the narrator's attempt to become a transcriber of cultural values; like the speaker in Jean Toomer's "Song of the Son," he returns to the South to gather the seeds of his heritage. . . . He sets out to collect the folk songs of his mother's people and to transcribe them into the written, Western forms that will preserve them and insure their universal recognition. There is an implicit optimism at this point in the novel, since the narrator is now an educated and traveled man (having made the "grand tour" and acquired one or two foreign languages) who seems capable of realizing his early ambitions; he has come full circle, returning to the land of his birth dedicated to an enterprise that will raise its "forgotten man" from a position that was occupied by his own mother. Unlike Du Bois, however, who could call for the recognition of *The Souls of Black Folk* in his "After-Thought," the narrator never has the opportunity to complete his task. The chattel principle (a fundamental assumption of the American slave system) drives him from the South. The principle—which asserts that blacks are property to be worked, whipped, and herded about at will— was reinforced by the Dred Scott decision (1857) handed down by Chief Justice Roger B. Taney and the Supreme Court itself,

and the informing force of *The Autobiography of an Ex-Colored Man* derives from its presence as the *sine qua non* in black-white relationships in America. The protagonist witnesses the burning alive of a black man and is overcome with humiliation that he is a member of a group that the country at large considers beneath the status of animals. . . . His reaction is as bitter and telling as the reflections of his early hero—Frederick Douglass—on the same situation: "they [professing Christians who own slaves and support slavery] would be shocked at the proposition of fellowshipping a *sheep*-stealer; and at the same time they hug to their communion a *man*-stealer, and brand me with being an infidel, if I find fault with them for it."

The Autobiography of an Ex-Colored Man, in its treatment of the chattel principle, moves toward the category of the protest novel, and its denunciation of Southern inhumanity is particularly effective since the lynching scene climaxes the novel and brings to an end the narrator's hopes for the art of his people. The process of culture building and broad humanistic development comes to an abrupt halt as the narrator is forced to take the lesser course: he joins the vast white American fraternity that considers money-making the acme of human virtue. It is not surprising, therefore, that the novel concludes with stock situations: the tragic mulatto passing for white and chuckling at the great joke he is playing on society; his sudden depression (with shades of Charles Chesnutt's *The House Behind the Cedars* and William Dean Howells's *An Imperative Duty*) when he falls in love with a white woman; *amor vincit omnia* as the white, blond, and blue-eyed ideal accepts his proposal; and the resultant happiness of brighter mulattoes and more money in the family. Yet the overall tragic dimensions of the narrative are heightened by the protagonist's realization that he has sold his birthright for what might be (and his employment of hackneyed literary conventions supports his suspicions) "a mess of pottage." He has rendered his confession as a lesson to those who will follow, and his story—which celebrates black folk culture and depicts the tragic dilemma of the black situation— concludes with the narrator in a somewhat static condition of endless self-recrimination. In his rôle as an artist—an individual who sees, evaluates, and records—however, there resides an influential and seminal dynamism. (pp. 438-42)

> *Houston A. Baker, Jr., "A Forgotten Prototype: 'The Autobiography of an Ex-Colored Man' and 'Invisible Man'," in* The Virginia Quarterly Review, *Vol. 49, No. 3 (Summer, 1973), pp. 433-49.**

ROGER ROSENBLATT (essay date 1974)

[*Rosenblatt is an American journalist, essayist, and author who has worked as literary editor and columnist for the* New Republic *and as editorial writer and columnist for the* Washington Post. *In the following excerpt, he discusses* The Autobiography of an Ex-Colored Man *and its affinities with and differences from novels in the "tragic mulatto" tradition.*]

It is extraordinary that a novel as complicated as *The Autobiography of an Ex-Colored Man* was produced as early as 1912. This was a time when most black authors were engaged in creating stereotypes of black characters in order to counteract other stereotypes which white authors, such as Thomas Dixon, had set before the public. The prevalent theme in black fiction was middle-class upward mobility. The new stereotypes of this post-Reconstruction literature substituted a protest against repression and the caste system for a protest against slavery, yet their ideals were far from egalitarian. Generally these novels were not only anti-Semitic and anti-foreigner; they were anti "low" blacks as well. This attitude was, of course, an apology to the white readers for being black, and the so-called tragic mulatto heroes of the period attained their tragic proportions not because they were caught in the middle, between the black and white worlds, but because they had not quite entered the white one. (p. 174)

Judged by normal literary standards, the *Autobiography* was a misfit in its era; and yet it is composed of most of the same ingredients as the popular fiction that was produced around it. Except for the final paragraphs of the novel, in which the narrator expresses regret, or more accurately, allows for the possibility of regret, for his decision to pass for white, his story presents the classic "tragic mulatto" situation with all the standard elements. The hero of the narrative tells us at the start that he is writing his autobiography out of a "vague feeling of unsatisfaction, or regret, of almost remorse, from which I am seeking relief." . . . (pp. 174-75)

With the exception of this belated expression of doubt, the *Autobiography* can pass for a typical period piece. Throughout the novel there is immense importance attached to breeding and heredity. It is suggested that if the hero of the narrative possesses superior qualities of mind and character, these must be traced to the white side of his parentage: "'Well, mother, am I white? Are you white?' She answered tremblingly: 'No, I am not white, but you—your father is one of the greatest men in the country—the best blood of the South is in you—'". . . . It never occurs to the narrator that his father is in any way to blame for his difficulties. Both his father and benefactor are frankly admired for the aristocratic distance they maintain in their social relations.

The hero also shows contempt for dialect as opposed to proper English. He notes class distinctions among other blacks in order to demonstrate to the middle-class white reader, whose feelings he anticipates, that he fully shares his reader's notion of what constitutes class superiority. . . . Moreover, he uses a customary divide-and-conquer strategy with his white readers, aiming all the anti-white sentiment expressly at Southern whites, thus fostering an attitude with which the Northern readership cannot help but be pleased. In a long passage on the backwardness of Southern whites he intimates the suggestion that blacks and Northern whites join forces in the name of enlightenment and modernity.

Not only is there nothing in the plot or tone of the *Autobiography* that would have disturbed its audience; there is nothing associated with its author's life or reputation to indicate anything unusual in the book. Johnson issued the *Autobiography* anonymously, and waited fifteen years before affixing his name to the second edition, but by the time of that edition he was a well-known lawyer and had held positions as a career diplomat under Teddy Roosevelt and Wilson. No one would have judged so established a figure and the author of so gentle a race poem as **"O Black and Unknown Bards"** as capable of producing protest literature. Indeed, by post-Wrightian standards the *Autobiography* is not protest literature at all, but neither is it the apologetic literature it appears to be. In a sense, the novel, like its hero, passes for white, yet, also like its hero, it quietly indicts the white nation, North and South, by its existence. (pp. 176-78)

Autobiography is to a large extent a novel of education. As such, it suggests not only that the hero has learned something by the end of it, principally by way of surviving a number of crises, but that he has also dealt with his growing pains with

sufficient perspective to relate the meaning of his story to us. He must have achieved an ordered and relatively complete understanding of his life in order to communicate and interpret it; yet as he tells his story he has to feign a narrative innocence or else reduce his tale to a series of axioms. Since he is a first-person narrator, his vision must always seem to be restricted to the present moment, without predictions of future actions. Nor can anything occur in the novel unless he learns of it himself. He presents us with the same problem as Bob in *If He Hollers:* Is he reliable? To what exent does his reliability or the lack of it shape the book?

The Ex-Colored Man introduces himself to us with this opening:

> I know that in writing the following pages I am divulging the great secret of my life, the secret which for some years I have guarded far more carefully than any of my earthly possessions; and it is a curious study to me to analyse the motives which prompt me to do it. I feel that I am led by the same impulse which forces the un-found-out criminal to take somebody into his confidence, although he knows that the act is likely, even almost certain, to lead to his undoing. I know that I am playing with fire, and I feel the thrill which accompanies that most fascinating pastime; and, back of it all, I think I find a sort of savage and diabolical desire to go gather up all the little tragedies of my life, and turn them into a practical joke on society. . . .

By this brief introduction he defines himself in all his ambiguities. He alludes to his blackness as a guarded secret, placing it in the category either of the best of his earthly possessions or of an extra-terrestrial gift. In either case he gives the impression of being possessed by his possession rather than of being in control of it. Still, although this secret is clearly his own and belongs to him, he refers to himself as a criminal for being in possession of it. On the other hand, he feels the thrill and fascination of being able to divulge it, not out of a desire to unburden his guilty conscience, but out of a feeling of power. He claims that by divulging his secret he will effect his own ruin, and yet he compares his announced confession to a pastime. And finally, when his reader appreciates that he has built his opening statement to a high pitch of excitement, mounting "thrill" upon "impulse," "fire" upon "thrill," and topping all with "a savage and diabolical desire," he then turns around one more time by reducing this accumulated passion to "little tragedies" and "a practical joke."

What Johnson has done in this first paragraph is to equip his narrator with all the unresolved tensions and vacillations which characterize the entire story. The paragraph consists of three declarative sentences that begin with the assertions "I know," "I feel," "I know." Yet within each of these declarations the narrator reveals that he is not an assertive man. As soon as he has decided to make his bold confession, he simultaneously decides to analyze his motives, and in analyzing those motives he only "thinks" that he finds something "savage and diabolical." The truth is that there is nothing savage or diabolical either about his motives or about his manner of describing them. He claims to risk his "undoing," to be "playing with fire," but it is clear that the narrator has strategically protected himself, even while divulging this "greatest secret"; for by saying that he fully expects the worst once his confession is made, he has actually gained the "confidence" of his ally, ourselves. He knows that no decent reader-confessor would ever turn traitor on a privileged communication. He also knows that once it is revealed that the secret he has been guarding is not some heinous crime, but merely skin color, his ally will be so relieved that he will open his heart to this "criminal" forever. (pp. 178-80)

Although the heroes of his childhood are David and Samson, those noted for courage against great odds, the Ex-Coloed Man is always searching for more favorable odds, in fact, the sure things. He seeks the easy ways. In the matter of his education he chooses the black college over Harvard or Yale, yet it takes only one set-back to dissuade him from college altogether.

In situations which require action, he steps aside. He confesses that as a boy he preferred to "hide" in his books. After having been robbed of his tuition money, he makes no complaint, nor does he try to retrieve the money. After a shooting in the night club, in which he is circumstantially implicated, he cannot even stomach reading a newspaper account of the event. When he spies his long-lost father in a box at a European opera house, and considers the life to which his father has subjected him, he is caught between weeping and cursing, and does neither. As he witnesses the burning of a fellow black man at the stake, his only response is shame. (p. 181)

Music . . . reveals him. He starts out playing classical piano, then picks up rag. At the same time he feels that rag music is too closely associated with blacks, so he begins to study ways in which classical music may be played like rag. Then he develops his own style in which rag is played classically, shifting continually as he goes from culture to culture, color to color, until eventually he gives up music completely. In point of fact he was never really choosing beween black and white music, though he claimed that as his dilemma. He knew from the start that he primarily sought the admiration of a white audience, and the kind of rag he invents is black music filtered through meshes of traditional [white] taste.

He chooses his friends by their appearance of respectability, avoiding contact with blacks generally, except for those who share his own theories of class stratification. When he has the choice of leading or being led, he always picks the latter, as when he set sail for New York, and merely "cast his lot" with those bound for the same destination. A drifter by nature though not an indiscriminate one, he functions as the accompanist on the piano to singers who lead him. And when the strange white benefactor is looking for a companion on his European tour, there is the Ex-Colored Man, ready to be patronized. His final choice is to be black or white, and he makes it with little difficulty.

Each of these choices, of course, defines him. The decisions she makes concerning his education all point to acquiring the kind of education which will not identify him with a particular people. In various choices of taking action he will not make a move if he risks being singled out or conspicuous. Nor will he venture into romance if there is a chance of his appearing foolish or noticeable. He will not be associated with a specific kind of music, and he will be very careful about the choice of his friends because he does not wish to be connected with a particular kind of people. He will refuse opportunities for leadership out of the fear of becoming prominent. Most significantly, he will choose the absence of color over color because to be colored is to be different, to stand out.

Each of his choices defines him, and each is the wrong choice. Through all of them he reveals himself to be the thoroughly adaptable man, accommodating, at one remove from experience, parasitic and shifty, smooth in self-defense, polished in making the kind of confessions for which there are no penalties; in sum, a fake. Because of all of these things he is not to be trusted, and this is essential to know. It means that his opinions are not to be trusted, his information and tastes are not to be trusted, and most important, neither is his self-esteem or exoneration.

What Johnson did with his Ex-Colored Man was to create a man so completely and obviously out of things (which is why he is identified by being formerly, not presently, something), that he becomes, through his own words, his harshest critic. The Ex-Colored Man is the epitome of the adaptable man. As such he indicts himself, and at the same time his existence indicts the world that encourages or necessitates his adaptability. Like his white benefactor, he is, at the end of his story, as alone as a man can be. He tried to beat the system by disappearing into it, and the success of his strategy may be measured by the absoluteness of the nothing he became. (pp. 182-84)

> *Roger Rosenblatt, "The Hero Vanishes," in his* Black Fiction, *Cambridge, Mass.; Harvard University Press, 1974, pp. 159-200.**

LADELL PAYNE (essay date 1979)

[*In the following excerpt, Payne compares the themes and techniques of* The Autobiography of an Ex-Colored Man *to earlier, contemporary, and later works in Southern literature.*]

Johnson is a recognizable part of a Southern literary movement that includes both blacks and whites. As had Charles Waddell Chesnutt, . . . James Weldon Johnson drew upon both Negro folklore and his own experiences as a Southern black for the subject matter of his writing. Chesnutt presented Negro folk tales in his conjure stories; Johnson collected spirituals and in *God's Trombones* preserved the cadences of the Negro folk sermon. But Johnson was a more restrained, conscious artist than was Chesnutt. Like Joel Chandler Harris, Chesnutt used dialect extensively in his conjure stories and, when depicting the speech of uneducated blacks, in his novels; Johnson avoided dialect because he felt it was looked upon almost exclusively as a source either of pathos or of humor and these were not the effects he was after. Yet in works such as *God's Trombones,* Johnson clearly suggests Southern Negro church speech through his reproduction of the Southern black minister's characteristic rhetorical devices—the repetitions, the alliterations, the pauses, the echoes from the King James Bible, the folk images—all of which show that he was as conscious of dialectical nuances as was Twain in writing *Adventures of Huckleberry Finn* or Faulkner in writing the Rev'un Shegog's Easter sermon in *The Sound and the Fury.* Johnson's ability to create the effect of dialect without using its typical spellings or illiteracies is one of his greatest skills as an artist.

Johnson's fiction evidences a similar skill. Like earlier Southern writers black and white—Cable, Twain, Chesnutt—Johnson dramatizes the theme of the tragic mulatto. As with Chesnutt's protagonists in *The House Behind the Cedars* and *The Marrow of Tradition,* the central issue confronting the hero of *The Autobiography of an Ex-Coloured Man* is his identity in a society where racial caste determines who one is. But here the similarity ends. In spirit and in form, Johnson's work is much

Songwriters Bob Cole, James and Rosamond Johnson.

closer to Ellison's *Invisible Man* than it is to anything by Chesnutt.

The ex-coloured man, like Ellison's protagonist, is the novel's nameless narrator. Referred to throughout as "I," he is never named because to do so would reveal his identity to the white world within which he lives. While Johnson's purpose is to lend verisimilitude to his narrative, his effect is similar to Ellison's: neither protagonist has an identity. The invisible man's identity is denied him by a society which will not see him as he is; the ex-coloured man finally denies his own identity as a black when he elects to "pass" and become "white." Like Ellison's novel, Johnson's is organized in picaresque fashion around the experiences and perceptions of the narrator. Even the judgment the ex-coloured man passes on himself and society suggests the ironic vision of the invisible man: ". . . back of it all [the decision to write an autobiography], I think I find a sort of savage and diabolical desire to gather up all the little tragedies of my life, and turn them into a practical joke on society." . . . (pp. 44-6)

He is splendidly happy until one day when he is about ten years old his teacher identifies him as Negro before the class. Like many other Southern protagonists, black and white, he is shattered by a knowledge he cannot comprehend. In Faulkner's *Absalom, Absalom!* (1936), Mr. Compson imagines Charles Etienne De Saint Velery Bon, when he is told "that he was, must be, a negro," looking at himself in "the shard of broken mirror" during "hours of amazed and tearless grief . . . ex-

amining [him]self . . . with quiet and incredulous incomprehension." In Johnson's 1912 novel, the protagonist rushes to his room and goes quickly to his looking glass. . . .

> How long I stood there gazing at my image I do not know. . . . I ran downstairs and rushed to where my mother was sitting. . . . I buried my head in her lap and blurted out: "Mother, mother, tell me, am I a nigger?" . . .

He is, in effect, asking his mother *who he is*. She answers that he is neither a "nigger" nor white; her refusal even to name his father makes his identity even more equivocal. Nameless, raceless, fatherless, like the Joe Christmas of Faulkner's *Light in August*, he is a person without a definable self. And also like Joe, he assumes a racial identity based, as Cleanth Brooks has pointed out, on a state of mind rather than on the possession of Negro genes. . . . (pp. 46-7)

In *Absalom, Absalom!* when Charles Bon learns that he is a Negro, he revenges himself upon Thomas Sutpen (the father who has rejected him) by destroying Sutpen's "Design." Tainted with only the suspicion that he is part Negro, Joe Christmas defies and defiles God and the society which have made him. In contrast, the ex-coloured man accepts the place society allots him. He compensates, however, by withdrawing into his books and music. Like Chesnutt's John Walden in *The House Behind the Cedars*, Johnson's protagonist gains such solace as he can from his reading. But instead of the Southern favorites Sir

Walter Scott and Bulwer-Lytton, it is the northern Harriet Beecher Stowe who shows him his "exact relation to the world in general." Even granting Stowe's excesses, *Uncle Tom's Cabin* would appear to offer more realistic guidance to any nineteenth-century American, white or black, than either *Ivanhoe* or the *Last of the Barons.* After he learns about slavery from *Uncle Tom's Cabin,* he can talk with his mother freely about the past and about his white aristocratic father. As with Robert Penn Warren's Jack Burden in *All the King's Men,* knowledge of the past helps to define the present. The definition of self gained from indirect and partial knowledge leads to a desire for a fuller, first-hand knowledge. His mother's tales of time past and the "old folks" cause the narrator to want to see the South. And while his South is perhaps not the dark Helen of his blood (as it was for the Eugene Gant of *Look Homeward, Angel*), it is the land of his birth and holds a "peculiar fascination . . . over [his] imagination." . . .

Music offers a means of both social and economic survival. His early recitals give him status in the community. On the one occasion when his father visits them in Connecticut, the twelve-year-old narrator stirs parental pride so much by playing a Chopin waltz that his father sends him a new upright piano. It is with his ability to play and give lessons on the piano that he supports himself during a portion of his adult life.

Given some measure of self-definition by his reading, his music, and his discussions with his mother, the narrator becomes not only reconciled to but proud of his race. He begins to dream of "bringing glory and honour to the Negro race." He wants "to be a great man, a great coloured man." As high school comes to an end, he plans to enter Harvard or Yale. But with the death of his mother and no help from his father, the narrator decides to use such money as he has to attend Atlanta University.

The narrator's first trip South is disappointing. Instead of the luxuriant, romantic South of his imagination, he finds red earth covered by tough, scrawny grass, straggling roads, and cottages of unpainted pine. . . . Instead of being inspired to admiration by Stowean darkies, he is repelled by the unkempt, shambling, slouching, loud Negroes whom he meets; he is attracted only by their dialect and hearty laughter. Like Ellison's invisible man and almost all of Chesnutt's protagonists, Johnson's narrator has not only accepted the white man's stereotype of the black, but also the white man's judgment of him. And like the invisible man who wants to reject his Southern heritage by having a Yankee breakfast but then affirms it when he buys a yam from a sidewalk vendor, Johnson's protagonist finds a valid basis for identifying himself with the South when he eats a breakfast of Southern fried chicken, boiled hominy, and biscuits, thus realizing at least "one of [his] dreams of Southern life."

Robbed of his savings by a black train porter, the narrator cannot attend Johnson's alma mater. He goes instead to Johnson's hometown where he lands a job in a tobacco factory and teaches music in his spare time. Like Wolfe's Altamont, Faulkner's Jefferson, or Twain's St. Petersburg, Johnson's Jacksonville is the place of his youth; the life he describes is the life he knew as a boy growing up in the South. (pp. 47-9)

[A] rejection of the traditional Southern racial caste system is one of the characteristics which separate modern writers such as Twain, Faulkner, Styron, McCullers, and Warren from the white culture which produced them. Unlike the Southern white writers, however, who in some measure elect to stand outside

their culture, the black Johnson is an unwilling outcast from full participation in all aspects of Southern life. He is both a part of Southern society and apart from it. While I cannot prove cause and effect, the result seems to be a curious coupling of the life and works of the old-fashioned Southern man of letters with that of the Southern writer since Twain who questions and rejects some of the traditional values of Southern life. (p. 50)

Johnson does not dramatize either the enraged or the subservient black in his novel. His true interest and subject matter is the independent Negro middle-class; that is, his own class. His narrator's entrance into the freemasonry of the race is actually his entry into respectable Negro society. Through his narrator, Johnson becomes an apologist for this group, commenting approvingly on its social excursions, public balls, church socials, and music. Indeed, the narrator is about to take a permanent place within the Jacksonville black community when the cigar factory [where he works] is closed.

The factory shut-down, like the death of the narrator's mother or the loss of his savings, is another of the obviously fortuitous accidents by which Johnson moves his narrator along on his semi-picaresque journey. The narrator quickly gives up his plan to marry a young school teacher, raise a family, and live respectably in Jacksonville for the rest of his life. Instead, he goes north to New York where he enters the world of pool playing, gambling, and jazz. He becomes a rag-time pianist and supports himself by playing at black clubs and white social gatherings. He leaves this milieu as quickly as he enters it; serving as a *deus ex machina,* a white patron who likes him and his playing takes him to Paris.

He spends his time there studying French, seeing the sights, and attending the opera. Like a latter-day Moll Flanders discovering one of her former husbands in prison, the narrator suddenly discovers that he is sitting by his father and half-sister during a performance of Gounod's "Faust." Already attracted to the beautiful girl next to him, the narrator experiences an almost overwhelming sense of affection for a sister he cannot approach. He wants to fall worshipfully at her feet, but cannot because of the blood tie; he wants to touch her hand and call her sister, but he knows he cannot reveal himself in this way. Almost suffocating, he leaves the theater and gets drunk. The situation is comparable to that of Charles Bon when he finds himself in his father's Mississippi home courting his own half-sister. Faulkner, however, universalizes Charles Bon's plight to the point of tragedy by forcing Quentin Compson, Shreve McCannon, and the reader to project themselves into Bon's mind as each tries to recreate the past. Johnson, on the other hand, merely states that his narrator's plight is "a real tragedy." With Gounod's music playing softly in the background, the effect appropriately enough is merely pathetic, not tragic. Although the result is a lesser achievement by a lesser artist than Faulkner, the black-white blood tie and the hints at incest in both *Absalom* and the *Autobiography* certainly suggest parallel visions of the actual relationship between Southern blacks and whites.

While in Europe, the narrator sees a way to fulfill his childhood ambition of becoming a great coloured man. He decides to return home, "to go back into the very heart of the South," and transform Negro folk materials into classical forms that would both reveal their worth and help preserve them. When the narrator's patron learns of this purpose, he tries to persuade the narrator that his intention is quixotic. The patron, who throughout the novel has been described as a man trying to escape, to bridge over, or to blot out time, argues that since evil is a force which cannot be annihilated, the best one can do is seek such personal happiness as one can find. . . . As an ironic commentary on his own attempt to escape both personal misery and time, this hedonistic patron eventually commits suicide.

In contrast to his patron's self-destructive hedonism is the benevolent theism of the ex-slave whom the narrator meets on his return voyage to New York. The ex-slave's present status as a free, cultured man, a physician graduated from Howard University, is visible proof that the condition of the race is not hopeless. His faith that "there is a principle of right in the world, which finally prevails," and "a merciful justice-loving god in heaven" sustains his belief that racial justice will eventually prevail. It also philosophically justifies the narrator's plan to return to his people. (pp. 51-2)

Some of Johnson's comments about Southern whites also suggest at least a sympathy for stereotypical Southern whites and their attitudes. More, he sees a fundamental similarity between white and black Southerners in that both defend their vices as well as their virtues. While on the train from Nashville to Atlanta, Johnson's narrator observes a Jewish businessman, a university professor from Ohio, an old Union veteran, and a Texas cotton planter as they begin to converse. The narrator comments that Southerners are more unreservedly gregarious than Northerners, that they not only must talk, but must express their opinions. Whether or not this is true, it is certainly a Southern notion. And after listening to a discussion of race in which the Texan takes an ignorantly bigoted position, the narrator admits to feeling:

> a certain sort of admiration for the man who could not be swayed from what he felt he held as his principles. . . . all along, in spite of myself, I have been compelled to accord the same kind of admiration to the Southern white man for the manner in which he defends not only his virtues, but his vices. He knows that, judged by a high standard, he is narrow and prejudiced, that he is guilty of unfairness, oppression, and cruelty, but this he defends as stoutly as he would his better qualities. This same spirit obtains in a great degree among the blacks; they too defend their faults and failings. . . . It is the spirit of the South to defend everything belonging to it. . . .
>
> (p. 53)

Through his narrator, Johnson even accepts the conventional view of most white Southerners that whereas Northern whites love the Negro as an abstraction, a race, but have no particular liking for individual Negroes, Southern whites despise the Negro race, but have a strong affection for its individual members.

Once more in the South, the narrator begins to gather the Negro folk materials he intends to preserve and publish, including folk songs and sermons collected at Negro revival meetings; that is, the same materials Johnson himself collected and published ten to fifteen years later in *The Book of American Negro Spirituals* and *God's Trombones*. Indeed, the narrator's depiction of a black preacher's sermon includes the line, "Young man, your arm's too short to box with God!" Johnson used the same line to begin his verse sermon **"The Prodigal Son"** in *God's Trombones*. The point is not that Johnson repeated himself (so did Faulkner and Wolfe, among others), nor that

his imagination rendered the same subject matter into both prose and poetry (as did the imaginations of other failed Southern poets), but that Johnson saw in Southern evangelical black Protestantism a major portion both of the source and embodiment of Southern black culture. Obviously Southern white protestantism has not been so exclusively wedded to white folk culture as the church has been to the total black experience. But the church, especially in the rural South, remains the single most important source of community identity for white and black Southerner alike. The importance of their churches in the community and their common evangelical Protestantism are qualities shared by Southern blacks and whites identifying both as Southerners in contrast to people whose roots are in other regions of our nation.

At the very time he is collecting materials which affirm the cultural value of his race, the narrator sees a Negro lynched. He is filled with humiliation and shame at belonging to a race which could be so treated. He decides that "to forsake one's race to better one's condition [is] no less worthy an action than to forsake one's country for the same purpose." He returns to New York and becomes a successful white man. No longer an artist or collector of folk culture, he becomes the prototypical white American businessman. . . . He falls in love with and courts "the most dazzlingly white thing" he had ever seen. Although she knows he is an "ex-coloured man," she marries him and bears him a son and a daughter.

Yet despite "making it," he looks upon himself with some ironic detachment. He sees his very existence as a practical joke played on white society. And although he professes to love a lily-white wife, his marriage simply extends the joke. But Johnson clearly intends that the joke is also on the narrator. When his wife dies, his sole ambition is to keep his children untainted by his race. And when he sees Booker T. Washington in New York, he feels like a coward, a deserter, a traitor to his people. He sees that Washington and others are men making history while he is "an ordinarily successful white man who has made a little money." He has become the thing suggested by his white father's first gift to him: a ten-dollar gold piece with a hole drilled in it. He is like a coin which proclaims its value yet is absolutely worthless because much of its substance is gone. (pp. 53-5)

> Ladell Payne, "Themes and Cadences: James Weldon Johnson's Novel," in The Southern Literary Journal, Vol. XI, No. 2, Spring, 1979, pp. 43-55.

MAURICE J. O'SULLIVAN, JR. (essay date 1979)

[*In the following excerpt, O'Sullivan contends that the conflicts and contradictions within the narrator cause* The Autobiography of an Ex-Colored Man *to waver between pathos and tragedy, and ultimately to remain unresolved.*]

Near the end of James Weldon Johnson's *The Autobiography of an Ex-Coloured Man,* the narrator, whose name we never learn, reflects on his economic and social success in passing as a white: "The anomaly of my social position often appealed strongly to my sense of humour." Although his sense of humor is rarely in evidence in the book, the Ex-Coloured Man's preoccupation with anomalies provides much of the justification for the many critics who question his reliability as a narrator. In fact, the protagonist's willingness to exist in a state where he remains acutely conscious of the contradictions between what he understands himself to be and what others see him as is a primary reason for much of the modern condemnation of him, which ranges rather narrowly from viewing him as an "ironic" figure [see excerpt dated 1971 in *TCLC,* Vol. 3] or a "morally obtuse and self-centered character" [see excerpt dated 1971] to Roger Rosenblatt's final unsympathetic judgment: "He tried to beat the system by disappearing into it, and the success of his strategy may be measured by the absoluteness of the nothing he became" [see excerpt dated 1974].

But there is very little of the absolute about Johnson's novel, and lack of sympathy for the narrator is not quite the reaction towards which Johnson seems to be working. Eugene Levy has shown that, given "the consistency between Johnson's views as expressed in *The Autobiography* and those he expressed elsewhere," he would hardly have been using his main character's opinions to make him ironic. Moreover, in a letter to George Towns, Johnson himself suggested that he had tried to avoid a negative impression of his protagonist:

> The form of the story was for a long time a problem to me, but I finally decided that a direct, almost naive, narrative style would best suit the purpose of the book. It was my object to put before the reader certain facts without having him feel that the narrator himself was prejudiced. I feel that I have fairly well succeeded.

The narrator's allusion to his sense of humor provides a more telling clue to Johnson's purpose; it becomes the speaker's way of acknowledging a gap between the reality of his present and the illusions of his youth, between his consciousness and his social behavior. And just as the Ex-Coloured Man turns from attempts at reconciliation, on the one hand, and rejection, on the other, the ambivalence of a smile, Johnson offers his audience the possiblity of leaving the book with similarly unreconciled feelings.

Much of the Ex-Coloured Man's ambivalence stems from sources explored by Johnson's two great contemporaries, W. E. B. DuBois and Alain Locke. But where DuBois and Locke found in the double consciousness a possible source of future strength in, as DuBois writes, its "longing to attain self-conscious manhood, to merge [the] double self into a better and truer self," Johnson found such doubleness fundamentally destructive and belittling, even to the point where he makes his narrator belittle his own destruction. Yet Johnson also recognizes the power of such a division to create sympathy for a character caught within it. In the midst of struggling between ideals and disillusionment, between self-dramatization and objective analysis, between principles and irresolution, the Ex-Coloured Man provides us with a richly complex image to which Johnson encourages us to respond with equal complexity.

Our ambivalence toward the narrator begins in the opening paragraph of his book:

> I know that in writing the following pages I am divulging the great secret of my life, the secret which for some years I have guarded far more carefully than any of my earthly possessions; and it is a curious study to me to analyse the motives which prompt me to do it. I feel that I am led by the same impulse which forces the un-found-out criminal to take somebody into his confidence, although he knows that the act is likely, even almost certain, to lead to his undoing. I know that I am playing with fire, and I feel the thrill which accompanies that

most fascinating pastime; and, back of it all, I think I find a sort of savage and diabolical desire to gather up all the little tragedies of my life, and turn them into a practical joke on society. . . .

Although Rosenblatt has nicely pointed out how the contradictions and reductionist rhetoric here uncover the "unresolved tensions and vacillations which characterize the entire story," his detailed discussion of the paragraph reflects both the complexity and appeal of the character it reveals, a man either unable or unwilling to translate his contradictions into the kind of paradoxes with which readers feel safe. In the image of his diabolical playing with fire, for example, the narrator promises us both Satan and Prometheus. But he provides us with neither. Instead we find a character who, unlike Satan, lacks force of will and, unlike Prometheus, acts solely for himself. He is a rebel violating the most sacred taboos of his time, but a rebel who sees himself as more confidence man than revolutionary.

At the heart of the book, the tensions between the narrator's potential, implied through self-dramatization, and his actions, asserted through the reductionist rhetoric, fascinate and repel. However, the very techniques that establish these tensions disguise them. In fact, while the Ex-Coloured Man leads us to accept his suggestion that passing was betrayal, he discourages us from judging him. His final admission of failure, sharply contrasted with the "small but gallant band of coloured men who are publicly fighting the cause of their race" . . . , balances sympathy against scorn without allowing either emotion to dominate. By offering himself to us as both a modern Hamlet finally achieving a private anagnorisis and a Felix Krull exploring and rationalizing all perspectives, he allows us the possibility of not choosing either.

Much of the problem in sorting out our responses to the work and its hero arises from the shifts in direction Johnson gives his narrator. Whenever we approach the Ex-Coloured Man's experiences too closely, he diverts us. On his second night in New York, for example, he and three companions from Jacksonville, all of whom have come to New York to find work, disagree on what to do after the narrator has lost money at a gambling club: . . .

> I lived to learn that in the world of sport all men win alike, but lose differently; and so gamblers are rated, not by the way in which they win, but by the way in which they lose. Some men lose with a careless smile, recognizing that losing is a part of the game; others curse their luck and rail at fortune; and others, still, lose sadly; after each such experience they are swept by a wave of reform; they resolve to stop gambling and be good. When in this frame of mind it would take very little persuasion to lead them into a prayer-meeting. Those in the first class are looked upon with admiration; those in the second class are merely commonplace; while those in the third are regarded with contempt. I believe these distinctions hold good in all the ventures of life. . . .

Here in a nicely structured moral point our attention is shifted from experience to sermon. The narrator presents his companions' argument, interprets it, and then reflects on it. But as we follow this process, we should remember the context in which he preaches. The other men, who have come to town to find jobs, wasted the previous night at the club and woke too late to start looking. Yet we smile condescendingly at what appears to be their resolve to stop gambling, go home, and be good. Rather than see the narrator as a negative influence, distracting his friends from their responsibilities, we are led to look upon his careless smile with admiration and their resolutions with contempt. Such manipulation implies a need to manipulate just as the objectivity of so much of his style, its lack of immediacy, implies a need to get outside himself and frame his experiences. His model might very well be the man who became his patron—a jaded ironist (and possibly another black who has successfully passed) who enjoys watching life from a distance.... But while the patron chooses merely to observe, the narrator, as the writing of his autobiography shows, cannot be satisfied with such a passive role. He must reexamine and, through his manipulations, recreate.

Because the Ex-Coloured Man's attempts at recreating his life reflect the ambivalence of his attitude toward it, the structure of his work inevitably suffers. Although he speaks of the two great tragedies of his life, for example, as the deaths of his mother and wife, he shows himself responding more profoundly to two other events: his discovery of his blackness and the lynching he witnesses. The first two experiences are human ones, transcending any suggestion of race except the fact that, given the racial nature of his situation and its effectiveness in inhibiting his ability to develop relationships with other people, these events isolate him more fully. The other two events are uniquely black experiences that make his life what it is. His discovery of his blackness leads to his uncertainty as to who—or what—he is and the lynching motivates him to pass as a white.

Whether or not this is a conscious attempt at misdirection, either by Johnson or by his protagonist, it does underline the narrator's unreliability, a characteristic closely related to his irresolution. Few readers still see the narrator as a "soul struggling toward greater personal freedom and responsibility." Instead most critics have focused on lack of resolution as the key to the Ex-Coloured Man's movements. Given a choice, he always opts for the easiest alternative. When his mother dies, he chooses a Southern black school over Harvard; when he is robbed, he leaves Atlanta rather than seek help; when he discovers the thief, he chooses to laugh rather than accuse. But at the same time that he avoids confronting crises, he vitiates criticism by arguing for principles that create an aura of almost Victorian morality around him. For example, he manages to admit guilt without accepting responsibility for it while explaining how he helped a schoolmate:

> I began my third term, and the days ran along as I have already indicated. I had been promoted twice, and had managed each time to pull "Red" along with me. I think the teachers came to consider me the only hope of his ever getting through school, and I believe they secretly conspired with me to bring about the desired end. At any rate, I know it became easier in each succeeding examination for me not only to assist "Red," but absolutely to do his work. It is strange how in some things honest people can be dishonest without the slightest compunction. I knew boys at school who were too honourable to tell a fib even when one would have been just the right thing, but could not resist the temptation to assist or receive assis-

tance in an examination. I have long considered it the highest proof of honesty in a man to hand his street-car fare to the conductor who had overlooked it. . . .

After suggesting that he was merely cooperating with his teachers, the narrator discusses such a firm set of values that by the end of the paragraph he leaves us with the impression of bedrock rectitude. But the contradiction between these principles, nurtured in a romantic acceptance of his mother's world, and his actual behavior suggests that even in this final recreation of his life he is unable or unwilling to synthesize the two. And thus he ends his paragraph with a rather curious *non sequitur*.

The conflict between his principles and practices continues throughout the novel, reaching its zenith when he chooses to reveal his heritage to his white fiancée. As she touches him to acknowledge her love for him, he acts, according to his lights, nobly:

> I understood, and could scarcely resist the longing to take her in my arms; but I remembered, remembered that which has been the sacrifical altar of so much happiness—Duty; and bending over her hand in mine, I said: "Yes, I love you; but there is something more, too, that I must tell you." . . .

But duty's call was not always so loud. Only two pages earlier its voice merely whispered when he encountered a black friend from his past:

> One Saturday afternoon, in early June, I was coming up Fifth Avenue, and at the corner of Twenty-third Street I met her. She had been shopping. We stopped to chat for a moment, and I suggested that we spend half an hour at the Eden Musée. We were standing leaning on the rail in front of a group of figures, more interested in what we had to say to each other than in the group, when my attention became fixed on a man who stood at my side studying his catalogue. It took me only an instant to recognize in him my old friend "Shiny". My first impulse was to change my position at once. As quick as a flash I considered all the risks I might run in speaking to him, and most especially the delicate question of introducing him to her. I confess that in my embarrassment and confusion I felt small and mean. But before I could decide what to do, he looked round at me and, after an instant, quietly asked: "Pardon me; but isn't this—?" The nobler part in me responded to the sound of his voice and I took his hand in a hearty clasp. Whatever fears I had felt were quickly banished, for he seemed, at a glance, to divine my situation, and let drop no word that would have aroused suspicion as to the truth. . . .

And with his first fiancée, a black woman in Jacksonville, duty appears to have been mute, for the protagonist apparently abandons her without a word.

The most notable image of the narrator's irresolution is his passing, which is not taken as a willed, conscious act but accepted as the inevitable result of not acting: "I finally made up my mind that I would neither disclaim the black race nor claim the white race; but that I would change my name, raise a moustache, and let the world take me for what it would; that it was not necessary for me to go about with a label of inferiority pasted across my forehead." . . . Since we see little of his wife's character in the book, we suspect that he has fallen in love with an image rather than a person. His first description of her, for example, concentrates on the external: "[S]he was almost tall and quite slender, with lustrous yellow hair and eyes so blue as to appear almost black. She was as white as a lily, and she was dressed in white. Indeed, she seemed to me the most dazzlingly white thing I had ever seen." . . . Our suspicions that her whiteness has a good deal to do with his response are strengthened when he sees her again and describes her in terms that might strike the reader as somewhat less than ideal: "Never did she appear more beautiful; and yet, it may have been my fancy, she seemed a trifle paler, and there was a suggestion of haggardness in her countenance. But that only heightened her beauty . . .". . . . His submission to whiteness is almost total during their courtship and the early years of their marriage. It becomes total when the wife he worships dies during her second delivery. His description of their children suggests that he has transferred his devotions:

> First there came to us a little girl, with hair and eyes dark like mine, but who is growing to have ways like her mother. Two years later there came a boy, who has my temperament, but is fair like his mother, a little golden-headed god, with a face and head that would have delighted the heart of an old Italian master. And this boy, with his mother's eyes and features, occupies an inner sanctuary of my heart, for it was for him that she gave all; and that is the second sacred sorrow of my life. . . .

There is none of the traditionally strong father-daughter love here. Nor is there any of the usual tension between a father and the child responsible for the loss of his mate. But what is most noteworthy about the Ex-Coloured Man's affection for his son is that the boy resembles the mother in looks rather than personality; it was her image the narrator worshipped, not her character.

This combination of the narrator's passing and his worship of the son-wife image is the culmination of a whitening process that pervades his book. He begins by thinking himself white. Even when he discovers that he is black, his blackness serves more as an affliction than an identity. His patron, recognizing that he has never fully assumed that identity, warns him of the dangers of trying to after the narrator reveals his plans to leave Europe and return to the States to explore the black American South: "This idea you have of making a Negro out of yourself is nothing more than a sentiment; and you do not realize the fearful import of what you intend to do." . . . Such a contradiction of intention is apparent in the novel as early as the Ex-Coloured Man's first awareness of his blackness. From that point on he seeks to achieve salvation by making black conform to white or at least by making black respectable according to white standards. After hearing his black classmate Shiny speak on Toussaint L'Ouverture, for example, his response was to begin "to form wild dreams of bringing glory and honour to the Negro race." . . . Even in these admittedly unrealistic dreams he already believes that glory and honor cannot be found in the race and its traditions but must be brought to them. (pp. 60-8)

But what if the narrator's essential self is ambivalent in its duality, unable to be either black or white, constantly seeing the white self from a black perspective and the black self from a white perspective? The experiences must then occur in much the same way that images are reflected by the distorting mirrors of a fun house. And if this is so the control so evident in the narrator's prose is neither an attempt to show a successful synthesis nor an attempt to disguise the true self. Rather it is an acknowledgment of the need for control to survive by a character who has given up all hope of prevailing. The Ex-Coloured Man's prose would thus reflect his life, which has been a series of not quite uncontrollable experiences. This is probably nowhere so clear as in an allusion to the diabolically playful image of his opening paragraph. While attending a performance of *Faust* at the Paris Opera, he sees his natural father:

> I sat through the opera until I could stand it no longer. I felt that I was suffocating. Valentine's love seemed like mockery, and I felt an almost uncontrollable impulse to rise and scream to the audience: "Here, here in your very midst, is a tragedy, a real tragedy!" This impulse grew so strong that I became afraid of myself, and in the darkness of one of the scenes I stumbled out of the theatre. . . .

As always the impulse proves not uncontrollable but merely "almost uncontrollable," and so the Ex-Coloured Man can stumble out. Unlike Faust he will choose to sell his soul not for knowledge, love, or power but only, as he tells us on his last page, for a "mess of pottage." Even in an ideal environment, physically removed from American racism and surrounded by the music he loves, he refuses to confront his past and connect it with his present. At the heart of his refusal is fear, fear of self. But it is not so much the fear of self-actualization, the motive he suggests in this passage, as the fear of self knowledge. Once again the narrator has chosen to stumble about in his darkness. What we are left with at the end of his autobiography is not a synthesis of—or even a choice between—Faust and Esau, the overreacher challenging the cosmos and the devout son hustled by his trickster brother, but a juxtaposition of the two. By offering the possibility of both tragedy and pathos, both souls and pottage, James Weldon Johnson has refused both us and his narrator the solace of resolution. (pp. 69-70)

Maurice J. O'Sullivan, Jr., "Of Souls and Pottage: James Weldon Johnson's 'The Autobiography of an Ex-Coloured Man'," in CLA Journal, Vol. XXIII, No. 1, September, 1979, pp. 60-70.

NICHOLAS CANADAY (essay date 1980)

[*In the following excerpt, Canaday discusses* The Autobiography of an Ex-Colored Man *in relation to biographies and fictional biographies that form the greater part of early black American literature.*]

To place James Weldon Johnson's *The Autobiography of an Ex-Coloured Man* within the context of the black autobiography is to reinforce the ironic interpretation of that work, for Johnson's novel is an ironic black autobiography. As a student of black literature, historian, and compiler of anthologies, Johnson was very much aware of the tradition of black prose in the nineteenth century. It begins, of course, with the slave narratives and proceeds through the autobiographies of the long years before the turn of the century. (p. 76)

While choosing the title of the novel, Johnson no doubt realized that his work would be thought of, at least by some readers, within the framework established by the black autobiographies of the past. When first published anonymously in 1912, the book was in fact received as an autobiography, but of course at face value as that of a Negro passing for white who was unwilling to reveal his name. Since the "colored" man has abandoned his race, as even the title announces, for some readers the title reverberates ironically with the well known attitudes of all the proud black autobiographical accounts that tell of growth into a new identity.

Anonymity, in fact, is a strategy that emerges as a function of the character of Johnson's narrator. Besides the fact that he refuses to reveal his own name, he will not mention the name of the Georgia town in which he was born, nor any names, places, or dates by which he or those who are part of his story may be identified. He is not seeking recognition; he is fleeing from it. In the traditional black autobiography people are identified because the author seeks to give them credit for aiding or inspiring him and because they will take pride in reading about his achievements. Because of fear and shame—not confidence and pride—anonymity is a major motif in Johnson's novel.

The tone reflects these elements. In the context of the black autobiography this tone is unique: it speaks in the beginning of "a vague feeling of unsatisfaction, of regret, of almost remorse, from which I am seeking relief. . . ." This pervasive mood of sadness is in contrast to the usual tone in black autobiography of determination and confidence, sometimes even triumph. Such books were written primarily to leave a record of success and a story of a life to be emulated. Johnson's ironic narrative is an object lesson, too, but a sad one, a lesson in failure.

The fact is that Johnson's narrator—and here the author's deliberate irony is apparent—was never really a "colored" man as Johnson used the term. This black autobiography goes from white to white with a very superficial playing of the role of colored in between. His "faint recollection" . . . of the place of his birth, Georgia, seems a dim racial memory. His roots are not in the black world at all: "I have only a faint recollection of the place of my birth. At times I can close my eyes and call up in a dreamlike way things that seem to have happened ages ago in some other world." . . . Conscious memory in fact begins for the narrator in his boyhood in Connecticut, and his life there as a child is very untypical of the black experience. It is as though he were middle class and white: his house, his schooling, a financial support from an absent father. These conditions are the basis for the traumatic shock that occurs when his teacher in school reveals that he is considered a Negro, and on that day, in his words, he made a "transition from one world into another." . . . The best description of that new world is DuBois' concept of "twoness"—a condition that haunts him for the rest of his life and affects every decision he makes. . . . The ambivalence of being both American and black is, of course, never resolved by the narrator until at the end when he repudiates his black heritage altogether. Thus during the main action of the novel he is condemned to be neither white nor black, and at the end he sees this in tragic recognition: "Sometimes it seems to me that I have never really been a Negro, that I have been only a priviledged spectator of their

inner life." . . . More accurately, what he has in fact seen has been his own version of the inner life of black folk.

The unknown white father in the tradition of the black autobiography is a figure typically referred to as a member of an oppressing and exploiting caste, who rather casually takes a black woman and then discards her. Either he completely lacks concern for his progeny, or he punishes them for reminding him of his guilt. Johnson's novel presents the reader with what are in effect two white fathers of the narrator. The biological father, despite the mother's pathetic devotion to him, gives him only a ten dollar gold piece that cannot be spent because it has a hole in it and, on the last occasion they meet, a piano. The father, according to the sentimental mother, was supposed to have used his influence to have helped the narrator get started in the world, but that prospect is inevitably betrayed. The narrator's surrogate father, his millionaire patron, develops in him a fine appreciation for comfortable living—it turns into a love of luxury—and encourages the nervous sensuality he has learned from his mother. Just as his mother had been ashamed of their Negro heritage, so the patron urges him to give up his race. The patron strongly insists that the narrator has no responsibility to anyone but himself. . . . In the end the resigned cynicism of his white patron combines with an overwhelming sense of reserve taught him by his mother to produce the narrator's final decision to become white forever.

Yet neither of these white fathers was really a sufficient, strong model. As the narrator moves through the early part of his life—spoiled, rather indolent, accustomed to pleasant surroundings—it becomes clear that what he lacks is a firm principle in his life. Neither parent has evidenced any such conviction, and without the ballast of any settled values his actions spring only from nervous impetuousness, fear, and shame. Not only is he impressed with the shallow and selfish arguments of his white patron, but he even admires such an ignorant and biased person as the Texan whom he hears on the train mouthing standard racist arguments about Negroes: As a matter of fact, the narrator judges the Texan's opponent in the debate, the college professor from Ohio, as a "pitiable character" . . . , even though the professor has shown courage as well as intelligence in his statements. The only plausible explanation for the narrator's admiration for the Texan is that the narrator is unduly impressed with the force and conviction of the man, however wrong-headed his cause.

Force and conviction are typically absent in the narrator of this novel; fear and shame are present. In the tradition of the black autobiography shame is expressed for one reason: failure to meet one's obligations to the black community. Such shameful behavior can take the form of exploitation of other blacks or even betrayal. More often it simply is a failure to cooperate in some mutual endeavor. In Johnson's *The Autobiography of an Ex-Coloured Man* the narrator feels shame for the wrong reasons. A sense of it is expressed when he sees "those lazy, loafing, good-for-nothing darkies" . . . , as his physician friend calls them, on the streets of Washington. This view reflects basically a white sensibility and the narrator's own class bias. More serious is his shame when he views the lynching that finally drives him out of the South permanently. He expresses horror rather than terror because he has no fear for himself as a victim, and shame rather than anger because of what it takes to be his own disgrace. . . . His fear is that he will be revealed as a Negro and his shame made public. Thus he adds at the moment he makes his decision to leave his race that "it was not discouragement or fear or search for a larger field of action and opportunity that was driving me out of the Negro race,'' but that ''it was shame, unbearable shame.'' . . . (pp. 76-9)

Once the traditional narrator is free and ready to begin a new life it is usual for him to take a new name. . . . A new name is the requisite label for a new identity, and taking a new name in self-baptism is an act of will that symbolizes dedication and determination. In Johnson's novel, on the contrary, the taking of a new name at the end of the story represents surrender. It is a name that the narrator will not even mention, certainly not a proud proclamation of a new identity. (p. 80)

> *Nicholas Canaday, '' 'The Autobiography of an Ex-Coloured Man' and the Tradition of Black Auto-biography,'' in* Obsidian: Black Literature in Review, *Vol. 6, Nos. 1 & 2, Spring & Summer, 1980, pp. 76-81.*

ADDITIONAL BIBLIOGRAPHY

Adelman, Lynn. ''A Study of James Weldon Johnson.'' *The Journal of Negro History* LII, No. 2 (April 1967): 128-45.
  Biographical sketch tracing Johnson's early life and various careers.

Anderson, Jervis. *This Was Harlem: 1900-1950*, pp. 15ff. New York: Farrar Straus Giroux, 1982.*
  History of Harlem which includes references to Johnson's literary and political influence during the Harlem Renaissance.

''The Poems of James Weldon Johnson.'' *Boston Evening Transcript*, section 2 (12 December 1917): 9.
  Positive review of Johnson's *Fifty Years, and Other Poems*.

Brawley, Benjamin. ''James Weldon Johnson.'' In his *The Negro in Literature and Art in the United States*, pp. 97-104. New York: Duffield & Co., 1930.
  Biographical sketch.

Bronz, Stephen H. ''James Weldon Johnson.'' In his *Roots of Negro Racial Consciousness: The 1920's, Three Harlem Renaissance Authors*, pp. 18-46. New York: Libra Publishers, 1964.
  Biographical and critical discussion. Bronz regards Johnson as the ''one-man symbol of the New Negro,'' and examines his early life for influences that led to Johnson's later success and versatility. Johnson's poetry, essays, and other works, which Bronz considers essentially polemical, are briefly discussed.

Carroll, Richard A. ''Black Racial Spirit: An Analysis of James Weldon Johnson's Critical Perspective.'' *Phylon* XXXII, No. 4 (Winter 1971): 344-64.
  Assessment of Johnson as a literary critic. Carroll contends that although Johnson's criticism is largely dismissed today, his basic critical philosophy is rooted in a belief in the uniqueness of black people, and therefore of the black artist, and that Johnson remains a ''worthy progenitor of the proponents of the black aesthetics'' of contemporary times.

Chamberlain, John. ''The Negro on Manhattan Island.'' *The New York Times Book Review* (27 July 1930): 5.
  Review of Johnson's history *Black Manhattan*. Chamberlain notes that the work contains a historical depth beyond its title.

Du Bois, W. E. B. ''Whither Bound, Negroes?'' *New York Herald Tribune Books* (18 November 1934): 4.
  Discussion of Johnson's *Negro Americans, What Now?* in which Du Bois rebuts what he regards as Johnson's superficial handling of economic and racial solutions to problems of black people in America.

Gibbs, William E. ''James Weldon Johnson: A Black Perspective on 'Big Stick' Diplomacy.'' *Diplomatic History* 8, No. 4 (Fall 1984): 329-47.
  Examines Johnson's role as U.S. consul in Venezuela and Nicaragua, and his subsequent efforts before and after the First World War to expose—in print, propaganda abroad, and through the NAACP—the diplomatic consequences of American racial arrogance in South America and the Caribbean, and the relationship between Jim Crow laws in the United States and the ''ugly American'' policies in other countries populated by black people.

Greene, J. Lee. ''The Pain and the Beauty: The South, the Black Writer, and Conventions of the Picaresque.'' In *The American South: Portrait of a Culture*, edited by Louis D. Rubin, Jr., pp. 264-88. Baton Rouge: Louisiana State University Press, 1980.*
  Compares and contrasts significant works in the development of Southern black literature. *The Autobiography of an Ex-Colored Man*, Jean Toomer's *Cane*, Ralph Ellison's *Invisible Man*, and Ernest Gaines's *The Autobiography of Miss Jane Pittman* are used as representative works by black authors which treat the South favorably.

Huggins, Nathan Irvin. *Harlem Renaissance*, pp. 5ff. New York: Oxford University Press, 1971.
  Includes numerous references to Johnson's political and literary activities during this historic era.

Kostelanetz, Richard. ''The Politics of Passing: The Fiction of James Weldon Johnson.'' *Negro American Literature Forum* 3, No. 1 (Spring 1969): 22-4, 29.
  Discusses the theme of racial ''passing'' presented in *The Autobiography of an Ex-Colored Man*. Examining the novel in a historical context, Kostelanetz considers it superior to earlier works treating the dilemma of passing because of Johnson's unsentimentality and his ''masterful'' exploration of the problem.

Levy, Eugene. *James Weldon Johnson: Black Leader, Black Voice.* Chicago and London: University of Chicago Press, 1973, 380 p.
  Biography. The work also includes a bibliography of works by and about Johnson.

Margolies, Edward. ''The First Forty Years: 1900-1940.'' In his *Native Sons: A Critical Study of Twentieth-Century Negro American Authors*, pp. 21-46. Philadelphia and New York: J. B. Lippincott, Co., 1968.*
  Examines *The Autobiography of an Ex-Colored Man*, which Margolies calls ''by far the best novel produced by a Negro prior to the 1920's.''

Skerrett, Joseph T., Jr. ''Irony and Symbolic Action in James Weldon Johnson's *The Autobiography of an Ex-Colored Man*.'' *American Quarterly* 32, No. 5 (Winter 1980): 540-58.
  Examines critical controversy surrounding the reliability of the protagonist of *The Autobiography*. By comparing the perspective established in the novel to that of Johnson's autobiography *Along This Way* and his essays, Skerrett attempts to establish the extent to which the fictional opinions in the novel express Johnson's own.

Stepto, Robert B. ''Lost in a Quest: James Weldon Johnson's *The Autobiography of an Ex-Colored Man*.'' In his *From Behind the Veil: A Study of Afro-American Narrative*, pp. 95-127. Urbana: University of Illinois Press, 1979.
  Places *The Autobiography* in the historical context of slave narratives and early black autobiographies, particularly Booker T. Washington's *Up From Slavery* and W. E. B. Du Bois's *The Souls of Black Folk*, in order to highlight the modernity of Johnson's perspective. Stepto calls *The Autobiography* the single work that ushered in the modern black American novel.

White, Walter. ''Negro Spirituals.'' *The Bookman*, New York LXII, No. 4 (December 1925): 490-02.*
  Review comparing Johnson's *The Book of American Negro Spirituals* with other contemporary texts of the time on the subject.

Lionel (Pigot) Johnson

1867-1902

English poet, critic, essayist, and short story writer.

Johnson was one of the principal members of the group of English artists and writers that William Butler Yeats described as the "tragic generation" of the 1890s. This group, which included such celebrated figures as Aubrey Beardsley, Oscar Wilde, Ernest Dowson, and Arthur Symons, is often noted for its high incidence of poverty, sickness, alcoholism, homosexuality, and mental illness, and many of those associated with it died at an early age. The lives and careers of the "tragic generation" span the fin-de-siècle period—an era of controversy and transition in all of the arts during which the Decadent movement in art and literature flourished. This movement, influenced by the French Decadents and Symbolists and by Walter Pater's doctrine of "art for art's sake," is characterized by experimentation with new aesthetic theories and an eagerness to deal artistically with all of human experience, including those subjects proscribed by Victorian mores. Although Johnson's personal characteristics, social connections, and poetic themes lead many critics to number him among the Decadents, others question the validity of this assumption, arguing that Johnson's works do not sufficiently reflect the thematic and stylistic features that characterize Decadent literature.

Johnson was born at Broadstairs in Kent. His family was of predominantly Welsh origins, although one of Johnson's distant ancestors was an Irish yeoman who had fought against the Catholics in the uprising led by the revolutionist Wolfe Tone in 1798. Johnson emphasized this connection when his friendship with Yeats and the other writers of the Irish Renaissance led him to take an interest in Irish literature and politics, and he took pride in considering himself an Irishman. Johnson's father was an officer in the English military, as were the other men in Johnson's family, and Johnson's upbringing reflected the conservatism of military life and the values of a protestant middle class. Even as a schoolboy Johnson found this atmosphere uncongenial. In his *Winchester Letters,* written at Winchester College when he was sixteen, Johnson denigrated his family and its cultural limitations by referring to his home as "philistia"; he also expressed an interest in converting to Catholicism, a desire which his family found objectionable. While at Winchester he won the school prizes for both prose and verse, and was named the editor of the school magazine, the *Wykehamist.* In 1885 he won a scholarship to New College, Oxford. In later years, Johnson remembered both Winchester and Oxford in poems which associate these institutions with both the classical tradition and the contemplative, scholarly life that he loved. It was while he was at Oxford that Johnson began taking a nightly glass of whiskey as a remedy for insomnia. Drinking gradually became habitual with Johnson, however, and his visitors at school noted that he kept a large bottle of whiskey on hand at all times.

Following his graduation from Oxford in 1890, Johnson moved to London to pursue a literary career. In the same year he also took the step that he had been contemplating since his days at Winchester and converted to Catholicism. The ritual and antiquity of the Catholic Church apparently held a strong fascination for Johnson, who was devoted to all that was traditional

in both culture and religion; it was this aspect of his adopted faith that Johnson most often commemorated in his religious verse, most notably in his poem "The Church of a Dream." Because of the mysterious allure the Catholic Church was known to hold for many of the Decadents, some critics, including the American philosopher George Santayana (who knew Johnson at Oxford), have questioned the sincerity of his religious convictions; others, including the Catholic writers Wilfrid Meynell and Katharine Tynan, have commended Johnson for his devoutness and defended him from the charge that he had adopted Catholicism only as part of an elaborate pose. Regardless of his motives, Johnson's embracement of Ireland as his homeland and Catholicism as his religion provided him with a useful mythology on which he based much of his poetry and prose.

In London, Johnson supported himself by writing critical articles for various papers and magazines, including the *Academy,* the *Spectator,* the *Athenaeum,* and the *Daily Chronicle.* Soon after his arrival in London he also joined the Rhymers' Club, a group of young Irish, Welsh, and English poets who met on an irregular basis at the Cheshire Cheese tavern in Fleet Street to read their verses and discuss poetry. The Rhymers included Yeats, Symons, Dowson, and others whose works were influenced by the French Symbolist movement. Generally, as Norman Alford describes them, the Rhymers were "anti-idealistic, opposed to generalization that could be explained or debated," and "in reaction against the intrusion, as they saw it, into Victorian poetry of what Yeats called 'impurities'—curiosities about science, about history, about religion." Although Johnson was often vigorously opposed to such "impurities," his own verse reflects many of these concerns. A number of Johnson's verses appeared for the first time in the two anthologies produced by the Rhymers: *The Book of the Rhymers' Club* and *The Second Book of the Rhymers' Club.*

During his years in London, Johnson's alcoholism grew worse and led to eviction from his lodgings on several occasions. His health declined, and his biographers report that as a result of his alcoholism he suffered a series of strokes that caused partial paralysis. His death in 1902 at the age of thirty-four was probably the result of a stroke, although the exact cause has remained a mystery. This was due in part to the protectiveness of his family, and in part to the myth-making propensities of Ezra Pound, who, as the editor of Johnson's *Collected Poems,* reported in his introduction to that volume that Johnson was killed in a fall from a high stool in a tavern.

Johnson's first book was *The Art of Thomas Hardy.* This study of Hardy's fiction was well received by critics and helped to establish Johnson's literary reputation. Reviewers were quick to draw comparisons between Johnson's critical style and that of such noted authors as Matthew Arnold and Walter Pater. In discussing Johnson's book, Edmund K. Chambers commended him for his lucidity and insight, and more recent critics have also been favorably impressed by Johnson's ability to combine the personal note of impressionistic criticism with traditional scholarship, leading to sound judgments on abstract and general questions of literary form. Johnson's other critical writings are collected in his *Reviews and Critical Papers* and *Post Liminium,* both of which were published posthumously. While Johnson had no specially developed critical theory to advance, the overall fairness, erudition, and high quality of his critical writings continue to elicit the admiration of critics.

Johnson is perhaps best remembered today for his poetry, most of which was published in *Poems* and *Ireland, with Other Poems.* The first of these collections is generally considered by critics to be superior to the second, which contains a number of poems withheld from the earlier volume. Although Johnson's poems are similar in some important features to those of the English Decadents, in other ways they elude precise classification. Critics have often noted the sense of loneliness and inner conflict in Johnson's more personal poems, most prominently "The Dark Angel," which describes an irresistable recurring temptation that poisons the poet's existence, and "Mystic and Cavalier," which begins with Johnson's famous line, "Go from me: I am one of those, who fall." Some critics, including Iain Fletcher, believe that Johnson was very likely expressing his own emotional struggles with alcoholism and homosexuality in lyrics such as these. These aspects of Johnson's verse, as well as his personal connections with many prominent figures in the Decadent movement, have often led critics to regard him as a Decadent poet. However, when Johnson's poetry is considered separately from the details of his biography, such a judgment cannot be made with the same certainty. Although Johnson's poems are often austere and melancholy, reflecting both his isolation from the world and intense inner conflicts, they also contain many elements that set them apart from the verses of such Decadents as Symons and Dowson. As Yeats has noted, in addition to moods of "temptation and defeat," Johnson's poetry "conveys an emotion of joy, of intellectual clearness, of hard energy; he gave

us his triumph." Ezra Pound has also remarked upon the sense of intellectual precision and mastery of classical form that distinguishes Johnson's verse from the poetry of disorder and dissolution so characteristic of the fin de siècle. Moreover, as Fletcher and John R. Reed have both explained, Johnson's style and technique have more in common with Matthew Arnold than with Symons or Dowson. Reed writes that Johnson's poems "do not express dissolution in their form or exploit tantalization in their syntax. Even while treating nihilism, Johnson's poetry seeks the security of solid form. It does not participate in decay; word meanings do not slide from one suggestion to another. Instead it is a bulwark against decay and no sly undercurrent cancels it." However, many critics disagree with the attempt to limit the definition of Decadence to a consideration of literary style alone. They argue that the Decadent movement was also a social phenomenon, and that those writers whose lives reflect their involvement in that phenomenon and whose writings express themes commonly associated with the Decadent philosophy, ought to be numbered among the Decadents.

Under this broader definition, Johnson may be considered a Decadent. His poetic themes do commonly touch upon such typically Decadent concerns as the yearning for respite from unappealing mundane existence, regret over vanished beauty, and the conflict between the flesh and the spirit. Until a more widely accepted definition of Decadent literature can be arrived at by critics, it is likely that the controversy over how to classify Johnson's work will continue. Meanwhile, most critics agree that even though Johnson lacked the range of expression necessary to a major poet, he was nonetheless one of the most important writers of the fin de siècle.

(See also *Dictionary of Literary Biography*, Vol. 19: *British Poets, 1880-1914.*)

PRINCIPAL WORKS

The Art of Thomas Hardy (criticism) 1894
Poems (poetry) 1895
Ireland, with Other Poems (poetry) 1897
Post Liminium (essays and criticism) 1911
The Poetical Works of Lionel Johnson (poetry) 1915
Some Winchester Letters of Lionel Johnson (letters) 1919
Reviews and Critical Papers (criticism) 1921
The Complete Poems of Lionel Johnson (poetry) 1953
Some Letters of Lionel Johnson (letters) 1955

EDMUND K. CHAMBERS (essay date 1894)

[*Chambers was an English essayist and critic noted for his work in the field of Shakespearean scholarship. His studies occupy a transitional position in Shakespearean criticism, one which connects the biographical sketches and character analyses of the nineteenth century with the historical, technical, and textual criticism of the twentieth century. In general, Chambers is noted for his conservative approach to literary studies and his critical exactness. In the following excerpt from a review of Johnson's study* The Art of Thomas Hardy, *Chambers praises Johnson as a literary critic.*]

I have read Mr. Johnson's essay [*The Art of Thomas Hardy*] with great and increasing admiration. It is, indeed, an admirable book: admirable in temper, admirable in felicity; revealing to us, one would gladly think, a new master in this most difficult art of criticism, one whose writings may stand on our shelves beside the golden volumes of Arnold and of Pater. The lucidity of Arnold, the luminosity of Pater—how rare they are, and how desirable; how the insight and the scholarship of which they were born put to shame the incomplete equipment of the modern critic. For, indeed, criticism is "in a parlous state, shepherd"; through those who, when they are not running a tilt for the latest formula from France, are most often intent on using the books they profess to interpret as mirrors to convey to us some choice reflections of their own personalities. Certainly the personality of the artist must always be an important element in every form of art: the adventures of a soul moving amongst masterpieces, is an adequate definition of criticism; but here, as elsewhere, the value of an impression depends entirely upon who is impressed; nor may we call the individual likings and dislikings of the man in the street criticism, but only the likings and dislikings of him who is by nature a critic. And the nature of a critic does not consist merely in a pretty turn for epigram, nor in a naive capacity for self-revelation; although many authoritative judgments have been built on such slender foundations, so that you shall hear a man discourse of tragedy, who has never learnt Greek.

Not so did Arnold or Pater approach his sort, not so does Mr. Johnson. In his book, as in their books, you snuff at once the "ampler other and diviner air": the wide and sane judgment, the large sweep and amplitude of outlook, these are notes of his work throughout. It is the manner of the scholar and the thinker, of one who has conversed long and intimately with fair dreams and great civilities: *Omne immensum peragravit mente animoque.* Nor in all his journeyings has he ever been a mere Dryasdust, an amorist of barren knowledge, seeking only to "properly base Oun": always his spirit has been finely touched to the central elements of life, to its sad and joyous harmonies; so that his eyes have been purged with euphrasy and rue—euphrasy of insight and rue of experience—and he can see and speak to us of things as they indeed are, *sub specie aeternitatis,* in their true colours and real proportions. Such, one thinks, is the education of the genuine critic, and to that large fellowship Mr. Johnson has shown himself, by this his first book, to belong.

In a prefatory chapter of exceeding interest, Mr. Johnson lays down some of the principles of his literary faith, declaring there his "loyalty to the broad and high traditions of literature; to those humanities which inform with the breath of life the labours of the servants, and the achievements of the masters of that fine art." By no means a *laudator temporis acti,* fully in sympathy with all that is vital and fruitful in the literary tendencies of his own day, he would yet lay stress upon what is too often forgotten, that extravagance is no sign-manual of genius, and that reverence for the great traditions of the past, fidelity to its indwelling spirit, are still, as they have always been, indispensable conditions to the highest flights of literary perfection. And in this lies his admiration for Mr. Hardy: that, modern as are the emotional and intellectual problems with which his novels deal, subtle and psychological his interests, original and audacious the methods he applies; none the less, by his sincerity, by his grandeur of conception, by his constant worship of the "fair humanities," he is a worker in the direct line of the great masters. Mr. Hardy writes of Wessex and of Wessex folk, a land and a people left behind in the breathless sweep forwards of civilisation, "a very old, aged" country, with manners and thoughts of an historic, almost primeval,

simplicity. Writing of this, he can adhere with minute and loving fidelity to the actual materials before him: he can transcribe this life in all its quaintness, with all its tribal peculiarities; he can show it shot across with countless threads of influence from the greater world outside, influences that complicate its emotions and perplex its philosophies; and doing all this, he can be neither provincal nor eccentric; because of his touch upon the central truths of life, its large outlines and ruling passions, whereby man is sib to man all the world over.

I have left myself but little room to say anything of Mr. Johnson's style: of its dignity, its restraint, its capacities for stately imagery and rhythmical modulation. . . .

To me the great charm of Mr. Johnson's writing lies in the inconceivable magic of his quotations and allusions. His reading has been very wide, and he uses it with a consummate art. His chapters are starred with the great sayings of the poets and sages he loves, each bringing with it a trail of associations, with incommunicable richness of effect. . . .

I close Mr. Johnson's book with a feeling of profound gratitude to him, with a sense that he has given me a new work of art for my contemplation and consolation.

> *Edmund K. Chambers, in a review of "The Art of Thomas Hardy," in* The Academy, *Vol. XLVI, No. 1172, October 20, 1894, p. 297.*

ERNEST RHYS (essay date 1895)

[*Rhys was an English poet, novelist, editor, and critic. He is perhaps best known for his work as the editor of Everyman's Library, a literary series of over one thousand volumes. Although his editorial achievements tend to overshadow his other works, Rhys was also a poet and novelist whose works reflect the influence of the writers of the Celtic Revival. He was well acquainted with Johnson and along with W. B. Yeats and T. W. Rolleston was a founder of the Rhymers' Club. In the following excerpt, Rhys comments on Johnson's* Poems.]

In his *Poems* Mr. Lionel Johnson is likely to suffer at the hands of most readers, because he is known to them as a critic first and a poet afterwards. They will turn to him for certain ascertained qualities, and will not fail to find them—the academic note, the accent of the inveterate bookman, the classic predilection, and the rest. And if we have any complaint to make of Mr. Johnson, it is that he has, of malice prepense apparently, played too much into the hands of his prejudging critics. For it is where he is most himself, most impulsive and original, and least reminiscent and theoretic, that he is most convincing. One such poem as that entitled "**To Morfydd,**" the second in the book, is worth many experiments in the use of curious metres to which Mr. Johnson is given, and which rather remind one at times of the metrical excesses imposed by Gabriel Harvey long ago upon Spenser. (p. 343)

The refrain of ["**To Morfydd**"] was taken down, we believe, from the lips of an old Welsh woman; and so far it goes to prove our case, that Mr. Johnson's writing is best when it touches life. Fortunately, although there are many pieces in the book whose spirit is purely literary, there is a quantum of others which may fairly be put in the same category with "**Morfydd.**" Others, again, have something of both qualities, as the delightful dedicatory poem, "**To Winchester,**" which has all the mingled reminiscent charm, spirit of old association, and emotion, both historic and human, essential to the "making" of such things. . . . Winchester and Oxford account for much that is telling and excellent in these poems, and for something too, no doubt, of any excess they may have of academic qualities. But here Mr. Johnson's range by no means ends. One interesting feature about his work, which remains to be traced, is that, with all his classic sympathies, he has been led on so far in other and Celtic fields. Some of the most distinctive numbers in his books are those treating of Wales and Ireland. . . . Of this world we hear much in his pages. Even in the heart of the England which he celebrates like a lover in so many of his poems, he has all the longing of the Celt for other and westward places. This is the motive of the two striking stanzas, **"Desideria,"** inscribed to Mrs. Hinkson, of which we quote the second:

> In hunger of the heart I loathe
> These happy fields: I turn with tears
> Of love and longing, far away:
> To where the heathered Hill of Howth
> Stands guardian with the Golden Spears,
> Above the blue of Dublin Bay.

Of a part with his love for Ireland, we may consider perhaps the strong Catholic sentiment running through his later poems; for Mr. Johnson is another in that remarkable band of poets who have served a Roman Church and an English Muse. (pp. 343-44)

Ernest Rhys, "Mr. Lionel Johnson's 'Poems'," in The Bookman, *New York, Vol. 1, No. 5, June, 1895, pp. 343-44.*

W. B. YEATS (essay date 1898)

[*The leading figure of the Irish Renaissance and a major twentieth-century poet, Yeats was also an active critic of his contemporaries' works. As a critic he judged the works of others according to his own poetic values of sincerity, passion, and vital imagination. One of the three founders of the Rhymers' Club, the others being Ernest Rhys and T. W. Rolleston, Yeats was a friend of Johnson and recorded his memories of Johnson in his* Autobiographies *(see Additional Bibliography). In the following excerpt from* The Bookman, *Yeats reviews the poems in Johnson's second collection,* Ireland, with Other Poems.]

Arthur Hallam distinguishes in the opening of his essay on Tennyson between what he calls "the aesthetic school of poetry," founded by Keats and Shelley, and the various popular schools. "The aesthetic school" is, he says, the work of men whose "fine organs" have "trembled with emotion, at colours and sounds and movements unperceived by duller temperaments," "a poetry of sensation rather than of reflection," "a sort of magic producing a number of impressions too multiplied, too minute, and too diversified to allow of our tracing them to their causes, because just such was the effect, even so boundless and so bewildering, produced on their imaginations by the real appearance of nature." Because this school demands the most close attention from readers whose organs are less fine, it will always, he says, be unpopular compared to the schools that "mix up" with poetry all manner of anecdotes and opinions and moral maxims. This little known and profound essay defines more perfectly than any other criticism in English the issues in that war of schools which is troubling all the arts, and gradually teaching us to rank such "reflections" of the mind as rhetorical and didactic verse, painted anecdotes, pictures "complicated with ideas" that are not pictorial ideas, below poetry and painting that mirror the "mutliplied" and "minute" and "diversified" "sensation" of the body and the

soul. Mr. Johnson, like Wordsworth and Coleridge, has sometimes written in the manner of the "popular schools," and "mixed up" with poetry religious and political opinions, and though such poetry has its uses everywhere, and in Ireland, for which Mr. Johnson has written many verses, and where opinion is still unformed, its great uses, one must leave it out when one measures the poetical importance of his poetry. I find poetry that is "a sort of magic," in **"Poems,"** published in 1895, and in the present book, **"Ireland"** . . . , and the most unpopular "sort of magic," for it mirrors a temperament so cold, so austere, so indifferent to our pains and pleasures, so wrapped up in one lonely and monotonous mood that one comes from it wearied and exalted, as though one has posed for some noble action, in a strange *tableau vivant*, that casts its painful stillness upon the mind instead of upon the body. Had I not got Mr. Johnson's first book when I was far from books, I might have laid it down scarcely begun, I found the beginning so hard, and have lost much high pleasure, many fine exaltations; and though I have kept his new book as long as I could before reviewing it, I do not know if I admire the first book more merely because I have had longer to make its sensations my own sensations. In a poem that changes a didactic opinion to a sensation of the soul, Mr. Johnson sings the ideal of his imagination and his verse.

> White clouds embrace the dewy fields
>   Storms lingering mist and breath:
> And hottest heavens to hot earth yield
>   Drops from the fire of death.
>
> *Come!* sigh the shrouding airs of earth:
>   *Be with the burning night;*
> *Learn what her heart of flame is worth,*
>   *And eyes of glowing light.*
>
> I come not. Off, odorous airs!
>   Rose-scented winds, away!
> Let passions garnish her wild lairs,
>   Hold her fierce holiday.
>
> I will not feel her dreamy toils
>   Glide over heart and eyes:
> My thoughts shall never be her spoils,
>   Nor grow sad memories.
>
> Mine be all proud and lonely scorn,
>   Keeping the crystal law
> And pure air of the eternal morn:
>   And passion, but of awe.

Poetry written out of this ideal can never be easy to read, and Mr. Johnson never forgets his ideal. He utters the sensations of souls too ascetic with a Christian asceticism to know strong passions, violent sensations, too stoical with a pagan stoicism to wholly lose themselves in any Christian ecstasy. He has made for himself a twilight world where all the colours are like the colours in the rainbow, that is cast by the moon, and all the people as far from modern tumults as the people upon fading and dropping tapestries. His delight is in "the courtesy of saints," "the courtesy of knights," "the courtesy of love," in "saints in golden vesture," in the "murmuring" of "holy Latin immemorial," in "black armour, falling lace, and altar lights at dawn," in "rosaries blanched in Alban air," in all "memorial melancholy" things. He is the poet of those peaceful, unhappy souls who, in the symbolism of a living Irish visionary, are compelled to inhabit when they die a shadowy island paradise in the West, where the moon always shines, and a mist is always on the face of the moon, and a music of many sighs always in the air, because they renounced the joy of the world without accepting the joy of God.

The poems, which are not pure poetry according to Arthur Hallam's definition, will, I think, have their uses in Catholic anthologies, and in those Irish paper-covered books of more or less political poetry which are the only imaginative reading of so many young men in Ireland. "Parnell," "Ways of War," "Ireland's Dead," "The Red Wind," "Ireland," "Christmas and Ireland," "Ninety-Eight," "To the Dead of '98," and "Right and Might," even when they are not, as they are sometimes, sensations of the body and the soul, will become part of the ritual of that revolt of Celtic Ireland which is, according to one's point of view, the Celt's futile revolt against the despotism of fact or his necessary revolt against a political and moral materialism. The very ignorance of literature, among their Irish readers, will make the formal nobility of their style seem the more impressive, the more miraculous. (pp. 155-56)

> *W. B. Yeats, "Mr. Lionel Johnson's Poems," in* The Bookman, *London, Vol. XIII, No. 77, February, 1898, pp. 155-56.*

LOUISE IMOGEN GUINEY (essay date 1902)

[*Guiney was an American poet, essayist, and critic who won recognition for her delicate, Old English-style ballads and poems written in the manner of the seventeenth-century Cavalier poets. Guiney's poetry reflects both her reverence for the Catholic tradition and her deep religious faith; her critical efforts were often directed toward restoring the reputation of literary figures whose works had faded from the public's memory. Guiney was a close friend of Johnson, as well as the editor of a selection of his poetry. In the following excerpt, she praises Johnson's poetry and criticism.*]

An early death has lately robbed the world of letters in England of its one critic of the first rank in this generation. Poet-minds of the Arnold breed, with what may be called the hush of scholarship laid upon their full energies and animations, must necessarily grow rarer and rarer, in a world ever more noisy and more superficial. They cannot expect now the fostering cloistral conditions which were finally disturbed by the great Revolution. Yet they still find themselves here, in a state of royal dispossession, and live on as they can. Of these was Lionel Johnson. In criticism, though he seemed to care so little about acknowledging, preserving, and collecting what he wrote, he was nobly able to "beat his music out;" his potential success lay there, perhaps, rather than in the exercise of his singularly lovely and austere poetic gift. But this is not saying that he was more critic than poet. On the contrary, he was all poet; and the application of the poet's touchstone to human affairs, whether in art or in ethics, was the very thing which gave its extraordinary elasticity and balance to his prose work. Being what he was, a selfless intelligence, to him right judgments came easy, and to set them down, at the eligible moment, was mere play. He had lived more or less alone from his boyhood, but alone with eternal thoughts and classic books. Whenever he spoke, there was authority in the speech coloured by companionship with the great of his own election: with Plato; Lucretius and Virgil; Augustine; Shakespeare. His capacity for admiration was immense, although in his choice of things admirable he was quite uncompromising. Beyond that beautiful inward exaction, "the chastity of honour," he was naturally inclined to the charities of interpretation. He gave them, but he asked them not, and would not thank you for your casual approval, except by his all-understanding smile. Neither van-

ity, ambition, nor envy ever so much as breathed upon him, and, scholar that he was, he had none of the limitations common to scholars, for he was without fear and without prejudice.

A striking feature in the make-up of his mind was its interplay and counterpoise of contrasts. Full of worship and wonder (and a certain devout sense of indebtedness kept him, as by a strict rubric of his own, an allusive and a quoting writer), he was also full of an almost fierce uninfluenced independence. Not wholly blest is the poet who has historic knowledge of his own craft; for to him nothing is sayable which has already been well said. Lionel Johnson, even as a beginner, was of so jealous an integrity that his youthful numbers are in their detail rather scandalously free from *parentalia*. Yet by some supernatural little joke, his most famous line,—

> Lonely unto the Lone I go,

had been anticipated by Plotinus. With a great vocabulary, his game was always to pack close, and thin out, his words. Impersonal as Pan's pipe to the audience of *The Anti-Jacobin* or *The Academy*, he became intensely subjective the moment he reached his fatherland of poesy. His utterance, as daring in its opposite way as Mr. John Davidson's, has laid bare some of the deepest secrets of the spirit. And side by side with them lie etched on the page the most delicate little landscapes, each as happily conceived as if "the inner eye" and "the eye on the object," of both of which Wordsworth speaks, were one and the same.

One might have thought, misled by Lionel Johnson's strongly philosophic fibre, his habits of a recluse simplicity, his faith in minorities, his patrician old-fashioned tastes, that he would have ranged himself with the abstract critics, with Joubert and Vauvenargues, rather than with Sainte-Beuve. But it was another of his surprising excellencies that he was never out of tune with cosmic externals, and the aspirations of to-day. Into these his brain had a sort of detached angelic insight. His earliest book, written while he was very young, was not about some subtlety of Attic thought: it was a masterly exposition of *The Art of Thomas Hardy*. This same relevance and relativity of our friend, this open dealing with the nearest interest, was his strength; he not only did not shrink from contemporary life, but bathed in the apprehension of it as joyously as in a mountain stream. How significant, how full of fresh force, have been his many unsigned reviews! Nothing so broad, so sure, so penetrating, has been said, in little, of such very modern men as Renan and William Morris.

It is perhaps less than exact to claim that Lionel Johnson had no prejudices. All his humilities and tolerances did not hinder his humorous depreciation of the Teutonic intellect; and he liked well King Charles II.'s word for it: "foggy." Heine, that "Parisianized Jew," was his only love made in Germany. Nonscientific, anti-mathematical, he was a genuine Oxonian; a recruit, as it were, for transcendentalism and the White Rose. . . . Culture in him, it is true to say, was not miscellaneous information; as in Newman's perfect definition, it was "the command over his own faculties, and the instinctive just estimate of things as they pass." (pp. 7-11)

His non-professorial conception of the function of a man of letters (only it was one of the thousand subjects on which he was sparing of speech, perhaps deterred by the insincerities all about him) amounted to this: that he was glad to be a bond-slave to his own discipline; that there should be no limit to the constraints and the labour self-imposed; that in pursuit of the best, he would never count cost, never lower a pennon, never bow the knee to Baal. It was not his isolated position, nor his exemption from the corroding breath of poverty, which made it easy for such an one to hold his ground; for nothing can make easy that strenuous and entire consecration of a soul to what it is given to do. It extended to the utmost detail of composition. The proud melancholy charm of his finest stanzas rests upon the severest adherence to the laws and by-laws of rhythm; in no page of his was there ever a rhetorical trick or an underbred rhyme. Excess and show were foreign to him. Here was a poet who liked the campaign better than Capua. He sought out voluntarily never, indeed, the fantastic, but the difficult way. If he could but work out his idea in music, he preferred to do so with divers painstakings which less scrupulous vassals of the Muse would as soon practice as fasting and praying. To one who looks well into the structure of his poems, they are like the roof of Milan Cathedral, "gone to seed with pinnacles," full of voweled surprises and exquisitely devotional elaborations, given in the zest of service, and meant either to be searched for or else hidden. Yet they have the grace to appear much simpler than they are. The groundwork, at least, is always simple: his usual metre is iambic or trochaic, and the English alexandrine he made his own. The shortcoming of his verse lies in its Latin strictness and asceticism, somewhat repellent to any readers but those of his own temper. Its emotional glow is a shade too moral, and it is only after a league of stately pacing that fancy is let go with a looser rein. (pp. 12-13)

With all his deference, his dominant compassion, his grasp of the spiritual and the unseen, his feet stood foursquare upon rock. He was a tower of wholesomeness in the decadence which his short life spanned. He was no pendant, and no prig. Never poet cared so little to "publish his wistfulness abroad," and here was one gentle critic, at least, whose head was as clear as any barbarian's concerning the things he would adore, and the things he would burn. He suffered indeed, but he won manifold golden comfort from the mercies of God, from human excellence, the arts, and the stretches of meadow, sky, and sea. Sky and sea! they were sacrament and symbol, meat and drink, to him. To illustrate both his truth of perception when dealing with the magic of the natural world and his rapturous sense of union with it, take certain lines, written at Cadgwith in 1892, "Winds rush and waters roll"; an Oxford poem of 1889, "Going down the forest side"; and one (with its lovely opening anticipation of Tennyson), dating from Falmouth Harbour, as long ago as 1887, "I have passed over the rough sea, And over the white harbour bar."

Surely no pity need be wasted upon one who resolved himself into so glorious a harmony with all creation and with the mysteries of our mortal being. To be happy is a feat, nowadays, nothing less than heroic. Lionel Johnson, after all and in spite of all, dared to be happy. As he never worried himself about awards, the question of his to-morrow's station and his measure of fame need not obtrude upon a mere character-study. Memorable and exhilarating has been the ten years' spectacle of him in unexhausted free play, now with his harp, now with his blunted rapier, under the steady dominion of a genius so wise and so ripe that one knows not where in living companies to look for its parallel. (pp. 22-3)

Louise Imogen Guiney, in an introduction to Some Poems of Lionel Johnson *by Lionel Johnson, edited by Louise Imogen Guiney, Elkin Mathews, 1912, pp. 7-23.*

PAUL ELMER MORE (essay date 1904)

[*More was an American critic who, along with Irving Babbitt, formulated the doctrines of New Humanism in early twentieth-century American thought. The New Humanists were strict moralists who adhered to traditional conservative values in reaction to an age of scientific and artistic self-expression. In regard to literature, they believed that the aesthetic qualities of a work of art should be subordinate to its moral and ethical purpose. More was particularly opposed to Naturalism, which he believed accentuated the animal nature of humans, and to any literature, such as Romanticism, that broke with established classical tradition. His importance as a critic derives from the rigid coherence of his ideology, which polarized American critics into hostile opponents of his work (Van Wyck Brooks, Edmund Wilson, H. L. Mencken) or devoted supporters (Norman Foerster, Stuart Sherman, and, to a lesser degree, T. S. Eliot). He is especially esteemed for the philosophical and literary erudition of his multi-volumed* Shelburne Essays *(1904-21). In the following excerpt, More praises Johnson's poetry.*]

Mr. Johnson's death last year (1902), at the early age of thirty-five, was an irreparable loss to modern English literature, and took away from the little band of Gaelic enthusiasts the one writer who held his genius in perfect control. There is something pathetically aloof in the fragmentary story of his life as it reaches us through his friends. (p. 185)

It is one of the pitiably sad and still heroic chapters of our literary annals. "With all his deference," writes Miss Guiney [see excerpt dated 1902], "his dominant compassion, his grasp of the spiritual and the unseen, his feet stood foursquare upon rock. He was a tower of wholesomeness in the decadence which his short life spanned. He was no pedant and no prig. Hesitations are gracious when they are unaffected, but thanks are due for the one among gentler critics of our passing hour who cared little to 'publish his wistfulness abroad.'" There lies the difference. From the wistfulness, I had almost said the sickliness, of Mr. Yeats who seeks relief in wasteful revery, we pass to the sternly idealised sorrow of Lionel Johnson, well knit with intellectual fibre, and we understand that imperious victory in defeat which Milton personified in his Satan, thinking more of his own state, one feels, than of the fallen angel; we are made aware for the moment of that hidden spirit within us which triumphs in failure—the unconquerable will, and what is else not to be overcome. It is good to read such poetry; there is a fountain in it of consolation—and which of us in our passage through the world does not need consolation?—and we drink from it the refreshment of a great courage. If I were asked to name the ode written in recent years which exhibits the whitest heat of poetical emotion expressed in language of the most perfect and classical restraint, which conforms most nearly to the great models of old, I should without hesitation name Mr. Johnson's *Ireland*. (pp. 187-88)

One needs no drop of Irish blood in his veins to feel the exaltation and minstrelsy of the poet's mood. One feels, too, the strange mingling of passion and aloofness, of melancholy and triumph, that speaks in almost every poem of his two slender volumes. I have contrasted his art with that of Mr. Yeats; there is a certain fitness in quoting the living poet's appreciation of his fallen compeer. Lionel Johnson, he writes, "has made a world full of altar lights and golden vestures and murmured Latin and incense clouds and autumn winds and dead leaves, where one wanders, remembering martyrdoms and courtesies that the world has forgotten. His ecstasy is the ecstasy of combat, not of submission to the Divine will; and even when he remembers that 'the old Saints prevail,' he sees the 'one ancient Priest' who alone offers the Sacrifice, and remembers the loneliness of the Saints. Had he not this ecstasy of combat, he would be the poet of those peaceful and unhappy souls, who, in the symbolism of a living Irish visionary, are compelled to inhabit when they die a shadowy island Paradise in the West.'' It is this ''ecstasy of combat,'' this triumph of defeat I choose to call it, that, in my judgment, marks Mr. Johnson as the one great, shall I say, and genuinely significant poet of the present Gaelic movement. (pp. 189-90)

> Paul Elmer More, ''Two Poets of the Irish Move-
> ment,'' in his Shelburne Essays, first series, G. P.
> Putnam's Sons, 1904, pp. 177-92.*

KATHARINE TYNAN (essay date 1907)

[*Tynan was an English poet, novelist, and critic. She was also closely associated with most of the members of the Celtic Revival, and was herself the author of over one hundred novels and numerous poetry collections. Although her literary output was extensive, today she is remembered primarily for her religious verses, which are noted for their delicacy and the sincerity of their sentiments. Tynan was a close friend of Johnson, and in the following excerpt she appraises his work as a critic and poet.*]

When I knew [Lionel Johnson] first, his two volumes of poems were yet to come. So also was his **Art of Thomas Hardy,** surely a stupendous and exhaustive piece of criticism. One knew his poems in the two volumes collected by the Rhymers' Club, and his criticisms in *The Speaker, The Anti-Jacobin* (during its too brief revival by Mr Frederick Greenwood), *The Outlook, The Academy, The Daily Chronicle* and elsewhere. We used to hail him in those days as the heaven-born critic who should make criticism one of the arts, as it has been in France, as it rarely is in England. He always wrote beautifully, in a clear, lambent, cultivated style, with perfect knowledge, with perfect sympathy, with the generosity which the critic, of all men, most needs when he has first the critical faculty. His intellect and his knowledge in a sense overdominated his poetry. It smacks so much of scholarship at times as to be over-deliberate, over-informed. Except at its very best it lacks the passion, the impulse, the rush of inspired poetry. I recall only one poem which has throughout the white light of poetry, the movement and the energy. That is the poem, **''To Morfydd,''** in which for once Lionel Johnson stood side by side with the Celtic poets he admired so passionately. It haunts one's memory with a sense of whiteness and brightness long after one has read it. (pp. 328-29)

When I first knew Lionel Johnson, he was about twenty-four, but he knew so many things concerning the art and literature of all the ages that one had a feeling he must have lived before to have learned so much. He was so steeped in the great poetry and literature of the world that his own poetry had a strange air of maturity irreconcilable with his years. It was almost too serious, too stately for the work of a very young man. There was something of the enchantment of the ages about it, something of the golden light which for the imaginative hangs over his own Oxford, his own Winchester. Full of singular felicities, ripe, polished, weighty with thought, one had to know this sage of the early 'twenties to realize how a youth could produce such work. An occasional critic was not kind to Lionel Johnson. One could imagine how some people not knowing him might be repelled by the almost unnatural air of wisdom, as of all the ages, which was in his work as in himself. It might have been said of him that he *built* the lofty rhyme. It was built steadily, perfectly: the one thing it nearly always lacked was

unpremeditation. But how lofty the rhyme he built one realizes afresh looking over [**Poems,**] the first of the slender grey volumes which bore his name. (p. 330)

It was said of his poetry that it was not musical. Perhaps it was not often lyrical, but it had the music of a Nocturne, of a Fugue. What could be more stately, more measured, like a high-hearted Funeral March, than [**''The Last Music''**]? . . . Again, the Winchester poem which concludes his second volume surely sings itself. One loves the melody of it, the colour, the gracious Latinity. It is a delightful poem with its succession of great names, fragrant with the very air of Winchester, of Oxford. (pp. 341-42)

The poem has the magical charm which lies over **''Thyrsis''** and **''The Scholar-Gipsy,''** where the very names are sweet to one's ear, as though they came out of Fairyland. Lionel loved Arnold, and well he might, for they were something of born brothers. Lionel was a person of passionate adherences. Where he loved and trusted, he loved and trusted entirely. He had no misgivings. Winchester, Oxford, Ireland, Wales, Cornwall; he loved them as he loved his friends, entirely. Those two books of his are a rosary of friendship, for every poem has its dedication.

Though he died midway of his life and his work, who shall say that it was not a singularly happy life? He was so sure of the kingdom of heaven. He was born out of his due place and time. He ought to have been in a medieval monastery or in a college of pre-Reformation Oxford. One could imagine his little head bent over an illuminated folio. Well, he made his illuminations. These two volumes of poetry set holy heads against a background of pale gold. His second book, **Ireland,** is full of his passionate patriotism to the Island of Sorrows, his passionate sonship towards the Mother of God. What a solace this chivalrous and passionate devotion towards the Lady of Heaven must have been to him in the growing solitariness and weakness of the last years! The second book, in poetical achievement, is not equal to the first. Perhaps he grew a less-exacting critic towards himself. He told us that he wrote reams of poetry in those years when illness had laid him low and he grew more and more aloof, closing his doors upon even his best friends. After his death his family failed to find the poems. Remembering how he wrote them—on backs of old letters, on bills, in the fly-leaves of books—one wonders! In one of my own books, which I bought back after the dispersion of his library, I found two new poems written. How many then are scattered up and down the world in the many, many books he owned? (pp. 343-44)

> Katharine Tynan, ''A Catholic Poet,'' in Dublin Re-
> view, Vol. 142, No. 283, fourth quarter, 1907, pp.
> 327-44.

JOYCE KILMER (essay date 1912)

[*An American poet and critic, Kilmer is best known for his popular, sentimental poem ''Trees.'' In the following excerpt, he discusses Johnson's Catholicism and its influence on his critical writings in* Post Liminium.]

Louise Imogen Guiney wrote soon after [Lionel Johnson's] death these words: ''Snow-souled and fire-hearted, sentient and apprehensive, Lionel Johnson, after all, and in spite of all, dared to be happy.'' And a brave happiness, a joyous appreciation of physical and spiritual life, shows in all [the] essays and critical papers which Mr. Thomas Wittemore has collected under the title **"Post Liminium."**

This wholesome optimism, separating him as it did from the morbid pessimism which certain of his contemporaries borrowed from the Decadents of France, served also to distinguish him from his associates in the Irish literary revival. To this movement he gave his enthusiastic support. His lecture on **"Poetry and Patriotism in Ireland,"** and the many poems which testify his passionate devotion for the country of his ancestors are known to all who have hailed the rebirth of Gaelic culture. But he never was enamored of mountains of mist, of still pools reflecting the shadows of dead gods. For one thing he had a chivalrous faith, which is not as a rule characteristic of the Neo-Celt. Ireland was to him above all things Mother of Saints, the steadfast defender of the religion which glorified his life. So when he wrote of the heroes who died for Ireland's freedom, he did not describe them as dwelling with Cuchullain and Finn in some vague land of clouds. Instead he called them "high heaven's inheritors" and said:

> For their loyal love, no less
>   Than the stress of death sufficed
> Now with Christ in blessedness,
>   Triumph they imparadised.

This is typical of his attitude toward life. Sane but never commonplace, religious but never pietistic, he shared the common sense of the mystics and the mirthfulness of the saints.

Lionel Johnson never carried out his intention of following **"The Art of Thomas Hardy"** with a similar study of Walter Pater. But in the book before us are included four brief papers on the work of his beloved tutor. These are not only the affectionate tributes of a disciple, they are sound criticism and accurate interpretation. Pater's name has been attached to ideas utterly alien to his philosophy. He has been claimed as the sponsor of a grotesque Hedonism which would have disgusted him. It is good to read his pupil's concise summing up of that much misunderstood book, "Marius the Epicurean," and to notice his insistence on Pater's "elegant severity," on his intellectual and moral scrupulousness.

Recently an English critic has said that Pater found beauty but did not know what to do with it. This is a fine phrase, but it does not bear close scrutiny. For Pater did at least one useful thing with the beauty that he found, he shared it. And from Lionel Johnson got his direct and finished manner, his rich scholarship, and his discerning appreciation of classical art. Traces of Pater's influence are evident in much of Johnson's prose. But there is one poem which is particularly interesting in its display of the poet in his two-fold nature. To the classicist, Aquinum is the home of Juvenal. To the simple Christian, it is the home of the Angelic Doctor. Lionel Johnson, classicist and Christian, hails it in honor of both its sons,

> O little Latin town! rejoice,
> Who has such motherhood as this.

His knowledge is too sure for him to yield to a sentimental mock-paganism, and he writes,

> Ah, Juvenal! thy trumpet sound:
>   Woe for all the fallen soul of Rome!
> But the high saint, whose music found
>   The Altar its eternal home,
> Sang: Lauda Sion! heavenward bound.

(pp. 469-70)

A good example of the effectiveness of Johnson's humor and common sense is found in his comments on the "Journal and Letters of Marie Bashkirtseff." This book had been hailed with delight by some of the "realists" of the day, who applauded its rather vulgar frankness and its rather hysterical eroticism. It is easy to imagine how such a work would impress the fastidious senses of an intellectual aristocrat like Lionel Johnson. His impulse would be either to ignore it or to bury it under a mass of angry scorn. But Johnson is too angry to ignore the book, too wise to blurt out his anger. He starts his criticism with an amusing but destructive parody. . . . Then, having skillfully enlisted ridicule on his side, he goes on first to an ironic praise of the Journal, then briefly to a serious analysis of its evil tendencies. And then, and not before, he is ready to let loose his wrath against the book, its author, and its admirers. "Such souls are merely miserable, pitiable: not admirable, not estimable. . . . Some lovers of extravagance and of perversion may enjoy these dismal pages, with all their outcries and affectations: to those who love the natural beauty of the natural mind, and to those who know the strength and sternness of a real sorrow, these pages must seem false and wretched, and the liking for them a melancholy sign of disordered times."

If any proof were needed of Johnson's freedom from narrow prejudice, it would be found in his delightful appreciation of George Borrow. Borrow, the vagabond, the gypsy, the stanch foe of Popery, to whom every Jesuit was a criminal conspiring to overthrow the House of Hanover—how does he impress this ardent Roman Catholic? Here are his words: "You may prefer Popish priests to Protestant pugilists; you may loathe philology and ale; you may feel for the tragic house of Stuart; you may take no personal interest in East Anglia, Wales, or Spain, and but little in gypsies: yet, if by natural grace you have it in you to love Borrow's genius, you can forgive him all." And then follows eloquent praise of "Lavengro," "The Romany Rye," and the rest, written with convincing enthusiasm.

No, his tastes were not restricted by artificial boundaries. There was nothing provincal or narrow about his outlook. The essays in this collection range from Charlotte Brontë to Izaak Walton, from Lord Byron to Cardinal Newman, from Boswell to Leonardo da Vinci. But always, whether his subject be Blake or Burke, Savonarola or Matthew Arnold, he writes with a quiet splendor, in a style scholarly but not pedantic, painting vivid pictures, making acute criticisms, never hurrying and never posing. All is written so smoothly that no single phrase stands out as of surpassing excellence; there are no epigrams surrounded by dullness. All of the papers, slight as they are in intent, (most of them were written for the public press,) have the careful finish which Pater taught to be necessary to all written thought, and all of them show that blend of erudition, spirituality, and humor which is Lionel Johnson's peculiar power.

The essay on **"Coventry Patmore's Genius"** and that called **"The Soul of Sacred Poetry"** are of especial interest because the theories discussed in them have so direct a bearing upon Lionel Johnson's own work as a poet.

In Patmore's poems he finds a proud isolation from the world, a mystical aloofness. He speaks of his fastidiousness, of the "insolent" beauty of his work. But while he recognizes the value of this quality, he speaks with greater delight of Patmore's reverence for humanity, "whence he inferred, wherein he discerned, divinity," and of the wholesome activities of his vigorous life. And he writes "Like almost all the greater saints of the Church, he loved laughter and epigram, and truth fortified with jesting; he prized the discipline of sorrow, but he loathed melancholy."

In **"The Soul of Sacred Poetry"** Lionel Johnson places next in importance to "a precise faith, ardent at the heart and rich with the blood of life," that reverent familiarity, that devout audacity, which "stirs the imagination to mystical journeyings in heavenly places." He would have the poet of sacred things shrink from no intimate expression of intimate emotion. How far from his ideal are the rhymed sermons which serve as hymns among the more rationalistic of our denominations! And how excellently he is in accord with the frank expressions of joyous piety which have come down to us in the old carols. This was the way of those Cornish peasants, who in all reverence and love called the Virgin "Aunt Mary." . . .

Not in vain do we seek for this reverent familiarity with divine things in his own verse. Religion was for him an essential complement of life. It enters his poems as it enters his thoughts, simply and naturally. In the poems of Francis Thompson there is frequently something overwhelming. He is august and sacrificial. But Johnson is close to humanity. A poem by Francis Thompson comes into one's consciousness like a Cardinal in all his pomp. But a poem by Lionel Johnson comes like a friendly parish priest, an approachable human creature, and touched, nevertheless, by a ray of the splendor of God. (p. 470)

Joyce Kilmer, "Lionel Johnson," in The New York Times Review, *September 1, 1912, pp. 469-70.*

MILTON BRONNER (essay date 1912)

[*In the following excerpt, Bronner discusses Johnson's literary criticism.*]

Serenity, gravity—these terms might well apply to all [Lionel Johnson] ever wrote. Johnson might be careless with his own life, he was never careless with his work. In the hurly-burly of the world he might become convivial, but his art was to him a temple of rest and a haven of peace; it was a shrine to be approached with due ceremonial and on bended knees and with bowed head. It demanded of him and received the best that was in him,—all his reverence for the old established masters, all his emulation of their ways, all his care for polish and truth and beauty. So that we are loath to think the time may ever come when there will not be a small corner reserved for a tablet whereon will be inscribed words in memory of this genuine poet and even more genuine critic. (pp. 179-80)

For the most part Johnson's poetry largely conforms to Wordsworth's definition of poetry as "emotion remembered in tranquility." When Johnson sings of Ireland's wrong, his heart has ceased to be disturbed in its beat. When he sighs over some "church of a dream," be sure there are no longer tears in his eyes, for, to quote his friend Yeat's beautiful words:

"He has made a world full of altar lights and golden vestures, and murmured Latin and incense clouds, and autumn winds and dead leaves, where one wanders remembering martyrdoms and courtesies that the world has forgotten."

When Johnson died in 1902 one of his best friends said that in him England had lost her one critic of the first rank in this generation [see Guiney excerpt dated 1902]. Many references were made to his relations with his tutor and friend, Walter Pater, and he was spoken of as if he were a minor replica of that master. The truth is that he was more of an Arnold than a Pater, an Arnold without a theory that he sought to impose

upon his generation, but like him in his ready composition of critical essays and his polish in verse. This is not to deny that he was profoundly influenced by the work and the teachings of Pater. In his generation, the latter exercised great sway over many and especially over Wilde, Johnson and Arthur Symons. Now while Johnson more than the other two approximated the master in his grave, careful, musical prose, he did not follow him in his various studies of the arts and in fiction as Symons did. Perhaps Johnson could best be described as a minor Arnold-cum-Pater. His is essentially a literature of the Oxford closes and of the library, not of life.

The Oxford closes—they stood for his long dreams about books and about the great issues of living and dying. He brooded over the works of genius until in the words of Sir Joshua Reynolds, whom he loved to quote, he felt "warmed by the contact and formed the artist-like mind." To use his own fine phrase, he found a "living soul in old books, not antiquarian dust." He was endlessly citing from memory passages from men like Sidney, Milton, Bacon, Augustine, Cardinal Newman, and the great Latins. Nevertheless, he was not unaware of the danger of too much study of the classics and sounded—as much for himself as for others—the note of warning that too great a delight in the ancients is responsible for a dislike of contemporary art. Therefore he strove to read the works of the men of his own time, too, to estimate them fairly, and to take such joy as he could in them, measuring their worth by the foot-rule the great men of the past had bequeathed. Armed thus, he was the champion of no school, the partisan of no particular literary quarrel. Indeed, as he said: "Extremes are just now in fashion and favour, with this unfortunate result: that catholicity of taste is set down as the sign of lukewarmness and of half-heartedness. . . . We are so violent in these days; and, to our irreparable loss, there is no Arnold left to charm us into serenity."

But that happens to be precisely what he tried to do: he attempted to charm the thoughtful public back into serenity with his quiet, sane criticism, with essays of a scholar in the humanities who displayed always something of the grace and gravity and suavity we associate with Oxford dons and Roman Catholic prelates from the ancient University of Louvain. (pp. 181-82)

[With] a modest competence enabling him to pick and choose, it is needless to say that when Johnson became a critical reviewer, he employed an unusual discretion in selecting the subjects for his pen. Designed mainly for the newspapers of the day, nevertheless, as now gathered into the volume ***Post Liminium***, they show a finished art that would seem to assure them a wider audience than that of the fleeting hour. A mere glance at the table of contents shows us that he never wrote about any books toward which he felt indifference. There was either strong attraction or something of repulsion. It might be the attraction of men of his church like Savonarola, Saint Francis, Pascal, Erasmus, Henry Vaughn, Thomas à Kempis, and Cardinal Newman; or personal heroes like Pater and Hardy; or sceptics like Lucretius, Renan and Lucian. But whether there was attraction or repulsion, there was always courtesy—as to a living person encountered—tolerance, broadmindedness. There was also applied the touchstone which, employed by the real critic, constitutes in itself almost an act of artistic creation, an act which makes something that is by way of being literature. In these stray essays gathered from dusty newspaper and magazine files, we find matter written carefully, conservatively, judiciously. We are told that often editors, who expected a certain review, were in despair because of its non-appearance until almost at the last ultimate moment, but we are also assured that the "copy" was such—in its beautiful clear handwriting, its careful punctuation, its air of finality—that the pages could be rushed to the printer without use of the blue pencil. And it was criticism in its infinite variety, whether of praise or blame, excoriation or mere parody. The grave, serene poet was capable of expressing any mood a given book evoked in him.

Pater always aroused his enthusiasm and called forth his best. His four notes on this writer are indisputable evidence of the fact that he perhaps meditated writing a book on Pater, even as he had done on Hardy. Nowhere in his own work or in the reviews by other men, will you find lovelier little notes of appreciation than in these Pater essays. (pp. 182-83)

When he praises, he does so liberally and generously, striking out sentences of memorable beauty as he goes. This, for instance, in an article on Charlotte Bronte. "She had faced tragedy and walked with sorrow; she had known the special pang of desiderium, of the vain backward look that rests wistfully upon graves."

In his poems you will find no indication of a sense of humour, but in his essays on authors you will find plenteous evidence. The Bashkirtseff nine days' wonder aroused in him only the spirit of parody, while Mr. W. H. Mallock's ingenious rendition of Lucretius into Fitzgerald's *Omar* quatrains led him smilingly to remark that it was "a valorous attempt to bridle Behemoth, to put a hook in the nostrils of Leviathan."

There is a certain school of showy critics, somewhat in vogue to-day, who attempt to attract attention by holding a thesis always contrary to what the world generally accepts as established, and by stating it in terse epigrammatic sentences. Johnson, too, could at times achieve this terseness, if not the showy contrariety, as in this tribute to one of the masters: "—the contempt of Swift, the pensive serenity of Addison, the simple tenderness of Steele. Combine the three, and there is Thackeray: too clearsighted to accept delusions, too reverent to despair, too kindly to be always glad."

Or consider this realism which occurs in a passage on writers of sacred poetry, in which he tells us they must have a mingling of mysticism and reverence, with a familiarity that sometimes shocks timid souls; in this passage he is telling us how really great writers of sacred verse contemplate sacred things:

> Take the Nativity. Here is an hour-old baby lying, perhaps crying, upon a stable litter, in a small Jewish village, at a certain definite date. This wretched baby could abolish time and space, for it is God. Take the Crucifixion. Here is a worn-out man, dying upon a gibbet, amid sneers and jeers, in the company of two common thieves. This miserable man could make the earth stand still, for He is God.
>
> (p. 183)

> It is held upon all hands that to write about the works of a living writer is a difficult and a delicate thing: I have felt the inevitable difficulty; I have tried to preserve the becoming delicacy. Throughout these essays upon the works of Mr. Hardy, there will be found, I trust, no discourtesy in my censure: I trust still more, no impertinence in my praise.

In this old-fashioned manner of high courtesy Johnson began the preface to what is in so many aspects his most memorable and most finished piece of work, ***The Art of Thomas Hardy***. It was in some ways a pioneer book. To begin with, in those days—it was written in 1892 and published in 1894—it was a rather new thing in England to print a critical survey of the work of an author still living and writing. The fashion, even then common on the continent and especially in France, has since then been adopted in the English-speaking countries countries with the result that Meredith, Henry James, Barrie, Kipling, Hewlett, Shaw, and many more have seen in print books devoted to their output. But this Johnson volume was a pioneer in another way too. It marked the beginning of the really critical appreciation of Hardy's work; it focussed upon him the attention of those whose opinion was worth while; and suddenly literary England, once for all, woke up to the fact that in Hardy it possessed an authentic master of fictional art.

This in itself was no mean achievement for a lad of twenty-five, but even to-day the book stands as the best criticism we have of Hardy, for this youth—himself a literary creator—saw behind the processes of creative art, comprehended its difficulties, understood the necessity of making the right and honest choice of matter and manner, preached fidelity to the old, established masters and the old, established canons, and insisted that the real artist must have a clear understanding of the age in which he lives.

The book was thus rich and full, because all the best of what he had lived and thought and dreamed was put into it. To write about Hardy, we feel sure, was not the result of a sudden resolve. We are convinced that as boy and man he had long read and loved the Hardy novels. As a schoolboy at Winchester and later as a student at Oxford, it is certain that he made many pedestrian trips through the Wessex country. The man who once boasted that he knew every inch of Welsh soil could doubtless have repeated the assertion about Dorset. In this book we catch glimpses of him in the land of Hardy, studying its hills and streams, idling in its towns and villages, sitting in the simple old inns, and listening with delighted ears to the talk of the peasant folk.

The fruit of all this love of the Hardy books was a sane appreciation of them. He did not set himself up as a critical schoolmaster, giving marks and credits. "I cannot understand," said he, "why your soldier and your saint should be remembered for their victories, and pardoned for their faults; whilst your artist of a thousand conquests must have ever rehearsed against him the tale of his failures and of his faults."

Not only did he appreciate Hardy, but he brought to the work an open mind and this was no mean feat for a devout Catholic, confronted by such an author as his hero. Johnson differed radically in beliefs with Hardy the positivist and disagreed with him about the meaning of the universe. Hardy's thoughts about human progress, about the testimony of physical science, about the sanctions of natural and social ethics were all more or less alien to Johnson, but he managed whole-heartedly to admire Hardy's fidelity to his vision of what is the truth, even as he managed to understand the attitude of Lucretius.

Now there are two kinds of books of criticism which really count,—the provocative and the contemplative. The one whets your appetite for knowledge of authors to you unknown; the other, of service after you have read an author's works, fixes and confirms and elaborates your ideas concerning a writer who is worth while. Johnson's "Hardy" belongs to the latter class. It presupposes a full knowledge of the Wessex novels. It presumes that you greatly admire them. It is filled with long quotations of favourite passages which you can thus savour afresh, while he descants upon their beauties, their rightness of vision, their minute observation, and their fidelity to truth. Johnson insisted that the novelist's art is a serious art and found in Hardy's best books a decided effect of gravity, seriousness, and deliberation. They are faithful to the spirit of the age and to the spirit of the country. Their dignity comes from their preoccupation with dignified men and women, conscious of the great verities, life and death, love and hate. Their solidity comes also in part from the novelist's grave and deliberate style, a sustained equability which reminded his young critic of the best and wisest of the Latins. Using something of this gravity himself, Johnson related in a passage of memorable beauty the chief characteristics of the Hardy novels.

Now, next to the way in which Hardy treats of life and death and of the great human passions, Johnson appreciated best his Wessex folk, the genuine peasant class, rooted to the soil. He pointed out that when Hardy strayed away from Wessex his hand lost its cunning and that even in Wessex, when he would fain portray the so-called "better classes," there was something lacking. The people he understands best and paints best are the masses:

"Read a page of rustic talk in Mr. Hardy," says Johnson, "and you will think of Shakespeare: listen to an hour of rustic talk in Wessex, and you will think of Mr. Hardy."

Nor is this exaggerated praise. There is no man whose rustic clowns are so faithful to the reality and who yet have so much in common with the pantaloons of the great Elizabethan dramas. In fact, as Mr. Hewlett said at a later date, speaking of Hardy's poems: "He is the peasant articulate, informed by Art and Thought."

Now just because this book was avowedly an appreciation, it must not be inferred that Johnson did nothing but render praise. We have already observed that he felt Hardy lost his mastery when he left Wessex sights and scenes. He was also not blind to certain extravagances in some of the novels, certain audacities of situations, touches of vulgarity, humour that was not far from bad nature, too much insistence upon coincidences in time and place. The critic found fault with Hardy's use of the split infinitive, his imperfect punctuation—concerning which Johnson himself was a pedant, notably in the use of the colon, about which he had many a hard-fought battle with the printers. Johnson criticised Hardy's vocabulary with its sometimes undue parade and pomp, its use of erudite terms, its phraseology culled from the arts, its expressions taken from the physical sciences.

He was equally critical in his choice of the Hardy novels he deemed best worth considering. *The Return of the Native, The Woodlanders, The Mayor of Casterbridge,* and *Far From the Madding Crowd* were the ones he considered most characteristic and most nearly perfect. He sturdily resisted the worldwide praise of *Tess.* He yielded to none in his appreciation of certain great qualities in the book, but there was that about him in his devotion to religion which for once forbade his holding the critical balances evenly. It was that which made him exclaim passionately concerning *Tess:* "The novels which 'vindicate the ways of God to man' are indeed wearisome; but fully as wearisome are those which vindicate the ways of man to God."

For once the religionist could not abide the ways of the sceptic and pessimist. For once he lost his temper. But it was the only time. Small enough lapse in a book composed in so modest a spirit that he could write: "It amply contents me to dream, that some gentle scholar of an hundred years hence, turning over the worn volumes upon bookstalls yet unmade, may give his pence for my book, may read it at his leisure, and may feel kindly toward me."

From his ivory tower the lonely, frail, wistful, young poet sent but few hostages to Time, but we are fain to think the future lover of Hardy as a long-established classic will always want on the shelf, with the great novels, that exposition of their art which was at once a genuine criticism of literature and a real revelation of the critic's own charming personality. (pp. 183-85)

> Milton Bronner, "The Art of Lionel Johnson," in The Bookman, *New York, Vol. XXXVI, No. 2, October, 1912, pp. 179-85.*

DIXON SCOTT (essay date 1912)

[*In the following excerpt, originally published in the* Manchester Guardian *in 1912, Scott discusses Johnson's essays in* Post Liminium.]

There were both disorder and defiance in Lionel Johnson's brief life, but to read this wise collection [*Post Liminium*] is to wonder whether all the rebelliousness may not have been a sort of twisted barrier, behind which, as in a secret garden, he could grow the white flowers of an austere and untroubled art. A shining rectitude lies on all these pages, and a noble quiet; the reader walks unwearied in the high, clear, windless atmosphere of reverie. Merely reviews, for the most part—done for different dailies and weeklies, and mostly anonymous—there is not one of them with an anxious or excessive line, and few that fail to achieve, in addition, what one of his own shining phrases calls "the severe beauty of a starry night." And it is scholar's script too—its aloofness fortified by knowledge, quickened by golden comparisons, and continually ennobled by the presence of royal phrases from the saints and the singers—from Crashaw, Aquinas, à Kempis—Milton's Latin, Lucian's Greek. Simply as a concourse of these things the book is a delight, and Johnson's own periods move among their "crested and prevailing" visitors with an air as composed and highbred as their own. Just a little *too* composed, perhaps. In a slight sleekness here and there—something almost complacent—one may detect a weakness; it is sometimes as though an everyday idea, caught conversationally, had been brushed and laundered and then sent out again as literature. Yet this may be as much the fault of the matter as of the method. It is of books he is speaking—often of the very noblest books—and he does his Erasmus or his "Fioretti" or his "Marius" the honour of approaching them with ceremony—if he does not seem to bow it is because he will not stoop. And even when the elegance seems least appropriate it does not do to call it snobbishness. When he turns, for instance, in his essay on Pater to speak of the plain facts of his master's career and says—

> Fifty-five years of life, some thirty of literary labour: it affords room for production in goodly quantity when, as in this case, there are also leisure, felicitous circumstances, scant hindrance from the pressure of the world—

we may check at the stilted "scant" and the "goodly," suspecting a mere perfumed pedantry; but to have dropped the mantle for a moment there might have meant fumblings and an irreverent awkwardness a line or two later when he enters on an utterance like this:—

> In all this mode of seeing things and of undergo-
> ing their influence, the inflowing of their spirit,
> there is a mysticism not unlike Swedenborg's
> doctrine of celestial correspondence; or that
> mystical interpretation of nature so necessary
> to Newman, as when he says of the angels,
> "Every breath of air and ray of light and heat,
> every beautiful prospect is, as it were, the skirts
> of their garments, the waving of the robes of
> those whose faces see God in Heaven"; a sac-
> ramental and symbolic theory of the universe,
> which *Spiritus intus alit;* whereby, as Mr. Pater
> has it, "all the acts and accidents of daily life
> borrow a sacred colour and significance." A
> perpetual wondering joy in the messages brought
> by beautiful things, through their visible forms,
> was a kind of worship to him; he had a Fran-
> ciscan poetry in the almost childlike freshness
> of his delight in them; though "refining upon
> his pleasure," as Crashaw put it, he carefully
> sought out the precise secret of the delight.

There indeed the vestments are fitting, and the thought rises level with its companions, and the serene lapse of the clauses that surround the quotations has a movement almost as lovely as that of the messengers they bear. It is true that it has nothing of the sudden, carbonic brilliance of essential thought set free by hard cutting. This is manifestly the beauty that is gained by delicate accretions—clause silting subtly over clause, film upon film, until the whole substance is a cloudy shimmer and the germ has grown into a gem. But then that is how pearls, true pearls, always *are* made. And when an artist offers you pearls it is foolish to ask for a stone.

Was that sharp division between his art and his life, then, a wholly good thing for the latter—a way of working off any wilfulness externally, leaving the rest free to blossom undis-turbed? We once heard the purest artist living—an old friend of Johnson's—Yeats himself urge that it was so. "Beauty is the spoil and the monument of such battles" was one of his high phrases. Yet it is a proposition one wants not to accept. And there *is* a certain paleness in this prose—and the paleness is the price of its purity. For after all there are only two ways in which a writer can make such critical work independently and indestructibly vital—and Johnson held back from both. Life in the rough, on the other hand, whose strong intrusion can cross-fertilize criticism, he coldly and relentlessly locked out. There are only two places where the lines tremble—and that is because they are scorning the tremors of others—the nerves of Marie Bashkirtseff, the noisiness of Byron. ("He did one thing well: he rid the world of a cad—by dying as a soldier.") In the essay on Izaak Walton the word "river" never once occurs; in that on Stevenson one-third deals with Addison; in that on Savonarola we hear of "thunders of thought and flames of desire"—but never once see the dire glare in the central piazza of the City of the Lilies. His figures of speech are never human figures; his metaphors are always august—even Nature herself only enters obliquely, thrown back by the mirrors of the poets. We were once told that this Johnson knew Boswell's *Life* by heart; but he was not sealed of the tribe of Sam. Even when he turns to praise his London it is still life at one remove that we get—life carefully filtered through earlier letters before judged fit for his own. . . . (pp. 233-36)

It is the noise of London heard through closed shutters, as in his room at Clifford's Inn. And then, on the other hand, he was insufficiently the renunciant. He was too temperate an ascetic. A man may brood above a single book until it becomes a door opening upon the infinite—can concentrate on his book-ish essay till it becomes fuller of stir and vitality than the crowded streets he disdains. Pater could do that—Mr. Yeats can do that—so could Francis Thompson and Symons. But Johnson—no. After building those barriers against life he had perhaps too little energy. A sense of space and wide issues haunts this work—but it is gained by material devices, by a beautiful tangling of his topic among other topics—by extend-ing, not by transforming it. He thrust his delicate hands into the air about him, into Apollo's garden, brought them back laden with lovely rumours and echoes; but the effect is still finite. Instead of the original flower we have a wonderful clus-ter exquisitely arranged. But there has been no passionate dis-tillation of the celestial honey hidden in the first.

But come!—do let us be proportionate. These things were only meant for journalism, and here we are testing them with re-agents as drastic as those which he applied to the high masters. It is wonderful that they withstand them so well—and, for other reviewers, a model and a reproof; but it is not fair. And then, too, there is always his poetry—where, perhaps, the consecration was completed and the grail achieved. It is needful to remember that, in order to complete the picture. This prose of his was perhaps just an interspace, a compromise, a dim and subdued half world. Clifford's Inn sounds cloistered—but how far away is the snarl of Fleet Street? Life to a man like Johnson may well have seemed a rather hellish business; his poetry is purely paradisal and here, in these pages, we are perhaps watching his beautiful spirit pacing coldly in the pur-gatory of its choice. (pp. 236-37)

> *Dixon Scott, "Lionel Johnson's Prose," in his* Men
> of Letters, *edited by A. St. John Adcock, Hodder and
> Stoughton, 1923, pp. 233-37.*

EZRA POUND   (essay date 1915)

[*An American poet and critic, Pound is regarded as one of the
most innovative and influential figures in twentieth-century Anglo-
American poetry. He was instrumental in obtaining editorial and
financial assistance for T. S. Eliot, Wyndham Lewis, James Joyce,
and William Carlos Williams, among other poets. His own* Cantos
(1917-68) *is among the most ambitious poetic cycles of the century, and his series of satirical poems* Hugh Selwyn Mauberley
(1920) *is ranked with Eliot's* The Waste Land (1922) *as a significant attack upon the decadence of modern culture. Pound
considered the United States a cultural wasteland, and for that
reason spent most of his life in Europe. In the following excerpt
from his preface to* The Poetical Works of Lionel Johnson, *Pound
discusses the extent to which Johnson's poetry remains acceptable
to readers and critics of generations succeeding that of the 1890s.
In an unexcerpted portion of this preface, Pound states: "I think
I have been chosen to write this* Preface *largely because I am
known to hold theories which some people think new, and which
several people know to be hostile to much that hitherto had been
accepted as 'classic' in English poetry; that is to say, I reverence
Dante and Villon and Catullus; for Milton and Victorianism and
for the softness of the 'nineties' I have different degrees of antipathy or even contempt. Mr. Elkin Mathews (the publisher of* The
Poetical Works of Lionel Johnson) *wanted, I think, some definite
proof that Lionel Johnson was still respected by a generation, or,
if you will, by a clique, of younger poets who scoff at most things
of his time."*]

A traditionalist of traditionalists, [Lionel Johnson's] poems are criticism for the most part. One might almost say they are literary criticism in verse, for that is the impression which they leave, if one have laid them by for long enough to have an impression of the book as a whole, and not a confusion, not the many little contradictory impressions of individual poems. I am accustomed to meeting his friends, and his friends, with sole exception of Mr Yeats, seem to regard him as a prose writer who inadvertently strayed into verse. His language is formal. It has an old-fashioned kind of precision that is very different from the sort of precision now sought, yet, in the dozen places where this stately and meticulous speech is moved by unwonted passion, Lionel Johnson has left poems as beautiful as any in English. . . . Now Lionel Johnson cannot be shown to be in accord with our present doctrines and ambitions. His language is a bookish dialect, or rather it is not a dialect, it is a curial speech and our aim is natural speech, the language as spoken. We desire the words of poetry to follow the natural order. We would write nothing that we might not say actually in life—under emotion. Johnson's verse is full of inversions, but no one has written purer Imagisme than he has, in the line

> Clear lie the fields, and fade into blue air.

It has a beauty like the Chinese.

Having held out for a uniform standard of appreciation, having insisted that one should weigh Theocritus and one's neighbour in one balance I cannot, for the sake even of courtesy, cast that standard aside. I do not, however, contradict it when I say that the natural speech of one decade is not the natural speech of another. In 1590 it was the fashion of the court to parley Euphues. Shakespeare's characters use a florid speech to show their good breeding, and 'Multitudinous seas incarnadine' probably got as much applause *quia* magniloquent as a witticism of Wilde's *quia* witty. In 1600 people were interested in painted speech. It was vital. It was part of the time. For a later age it is rank affectation. Some say the 'nineties' spoke as they wrote. I have heard it said that 'A generation of men came down from Oxford resolved to talk as prose had been written'. They had, presumably, the conviction that the speech of life and of poetry should be the same. They were quixotic. They loved the speech of books and proposed to make daily speech copy it.

Men of the Renaissance had done something like this. They wrote excellent Latin, but daily speech did not follow it. Lorenzo Valla wrote invectively as Johnson might have written elegiacally, 'linguam latinam magnum sacramentum est.' And, indeed, Johnson wrote Latin, as beautifully as Flaminius, so far did his reverence lead him.

> Defecit inter tenebris cor triste.

He would have been content always writing Latin, I think, but failing that, he set himself the task of bringing into English all that he could of the fineness of Latinity. He wrote an English that had grown out of Latin. He, at his worst, approached the Miltonian quagmire; the old error of supposing that an uninflected language can be written according to rules of order fit for an inflected speech and for that only.

Yet, because he is never florid, one remembers his work, or one thinks of his work in one's memory as if it were speech in unruffled order. One does this in spite of his inversion, in spite of the few treasured archaisms, in spite of his 'spelling it *chaunted*'.One thinks that he had read and admired Gautier, or that at least, he had derived similar ambitions from some

traditional source. One thinks that his poems are in short hard sentences. The reality is that they are full of definite statement. For better or worse they are doctrinal and nearly always dogmatic. He had the blessed habit of knowing his own mind, and this was rare among writers of his decade.

The 'nineties' have chiefly gone out because of their muzziness, because of a softness derived, I think, not from books but from impressionist painting. They riot with half decayed fruit.

The impression of Lionel Johnson's verse is that of small slabs of ivory, firmly combined and contrived. There is a constant feeling of neatness, a sense of inherited order. Above all he respected his art.

From the Elizabethans to Swinburne, through all that vast hiatus, English poetry had been the bear-garden of doctrinaires. It had been the 'vehicle' of opinion. For Swinburne it was at least the art of musical wording. For Johnson it was the art of good writing. The last is a rare thing in England.

I think we respect Johnson to-day, in part for his hardness, in part for his hatred of amateurishness. His sense of criticism is to be gathered from his own prose. . . . (pp. 361-63)

He never pardoned in himself a fault which he would have detected, and perhaps even have condoned, in another. . . . Johnson is not the first poet of the 'nineties' to reach one. . . . Johnson's poems were almost the last to catch one's attention. Their appeal is not so much to the fluffy, unsorted imagination of adolescence as to more hardened passion and intellect of early middle-age. I cannot speak of more than that. They hold their own now, not perhaps as a whole, but because of certain passages, because of that effect of neatness and hardness.

In the midst of enthusiasms one thinks perhaps that, if Gautier had not written, Johnson's work might even take its place in Weltliteratur, that it might stand for this clearness and neatness. In English literature it has some such place, with the writings of Arnold and of Christina Rossetti. His attitude toward the past was pragmatical. He seemed to regard what had been as good, or as, at least, bearable. His taste was catholic. There is no use regretting this fault. He had its virtues. The **'Post Liminium'** is a complete world of culture; his own, wrought out of worthy things. His mind was openly receptive. This gentleness sets him apart from our decade. But if he was traditionalist, he was so in the finest sense of that term. He really knew the tradition, the narrow tradition, that is, of English, Latin, and Greek. This intelligent acquaintance with the past differentiates him from the traditionalists of his time, and of ours.

He would, for instance, have welcomed good *vers libre;* he would have known how the Greeks had used it. You could have discussed with him any and every serious problem of technique, and this is certainly a distinction among 'the poets of England'. He might have differed from your views of good writing but he would have believed in good writing. His hatred of slovenliness would have equalled your own. (pp. 367-68)

[His] language is, in a sense, *of* his time, though it would never have deigned to be the common speech. It was part of his fear of life, a fear that he was not afraid of, but which he openly acknowledged (*Nihilism*):

> I shall be calm soon, with the calm death brings.
> The skies are grey there, without any star.

His sense of traditional book-speech and his sense of traditional form combine to make him somewhat unreadable. He falls into stanza poems, that is to say into vain repetitions and weak-enings of the original statement. For instance, the complete poem

> Man is a shadow's dream!
> Opulent Pindar saith:
> Yet man may win a gleam
> Of glory, before death.

is carried on into a series of strophes and is probably weakened by quoting 'golden Shakespear' in the second of them. The inversions do not lend it vitality. The beautiful poem beginning **'In Merioneth'** is to my sense complete without the last stanza, though I dare say our fashion is no more permanent than his fashion, but we are done with imaginative reason—at least for our time. Poetry is concerned with statement, not with arguments and conversions. This is no more than saying of Johnson what one must say of all save the greatest poets; that a part of his work is transient. *Pars labitinam vitabit* (pp. 368-69)

> Ezra Pound, "Lionel Johnson," in his Literary Essays of Ezra Pound, edited by T. S. Eliot, New Directions, 1954, pp. 361-70.

ROBERT SHAFER (essay date 1921)

[*Shafer is an American critic and editor. In the following excerpt, he discusses Johnson's criticism collected in* Reviews and Critical Papers.]

Lionel Johnson's critical writings can hardly find a place amongst our greatest criticism; and yet, judged by the severest standards, they rank high, having a permanent value. Their value might have been greater, one supposes, had Johnson been given the necessary time for polishing and welding his thoughts about literary art, or his judgments upon books as they came to him from the press. (p. 9)

[The essays in **Reviews and Critical Papers**] show clearly Johnson's excellence as a critic of literature. They are written vividly, in a style pointed by the freshness of his thought and the reality of his interest rather than by any meretricious playing with words or other kind of cheap cleverness. Without any of the heaviness of Dr Samuel Johnson's rhetoric, the younger Johnson's style shows a profitable study of his great predecessor's manner of talking and writing; as when he speaks of finding in some Irishmen "a certain amiable narrowness, . . . a conservatism rather obstinate than strong, less resolute than stubborn," or observes that "a militant faith is one thing, and an irritable fussiness another." Johnson has been very generally regarded as a disciple of Walter Pater, and he has himself expressed, in both prose and verse, a depth of friendly and reverent feeling for Pater that implies at least the warm sentiment of discipleship. One can indeed trace an indebtedness in some peculiarities of style, though Johnson's style is in general no more like Pater's than it is like Samuel Johnson's; but with this, actual relationship between the two men ends. Each took his literary art with a great and becoming seriousness, it is true, but it needs only a moment's reflection to see that the ends each sought to serve—the ideas each attempted to express artistically—were not only different, but deeply opposed to each other. Pater's constant attempt was to replace what he took to be the worn-out and discredited view-point of the Christian world with the Epicurean creed of sensation as the end of life, whereas Lionel Johnson was never so deceived by the intellectual fashions of the moment, but steadfastly held

before his readers the spiritual and moral ideals of traditional Christianity.

More important than style, then, the great thing shown in these reviews is what we may call, simply, Johnson's good sense. We see everywhere the activity of the judging faculty, the balancing or weighing of the qualities a writer has, the pronouncement of a verdict upon the book in hand. The verdict is always acute; at times it is unusually expressive in a very few words; as when he says of Byron, he "could shout magnificently, laugh splendidly, thunder tumultuously; but he could not sing"; and "stanza upon stanza of *Childe Harold* reads like the finest things in Irish or American oratory, grandoise and sweeping." Or hear him upon Boswell, anticipating some recent defenders of that gentleman: "A very quaint man, a very ludicrous man, but certainly a great man: causes and effects must be commensurable, and the Boswell of *Boswell's Johnson,* that splendid and unique creation, cannot have been no more than a prying, impertinent, besotted, brainless busy-body, a meddling, mannerless, self-important little chatterer, with a big note-book and a good memory. Men 'don't do such things' as write masterpieces without a master's ability."

Johnson's, moreover, was a learned good sense; his judgment was informed, disciplined by intimate, repeated contact with the enduring things in the classical and modern literatures. His learning was great, and it was real in that he had made the spirit of great men his own, yet it did not sit heavily upon him. He was a scholar to some purpose, not from mere acquisitiveness. He was thus not drawn into the past by his protracted studies; he rather drew the best things of the past into himself, for enlightenment, while remaining ever a true son of his own day, fully alive to the interests, the problems, the hopes and fears of his generation. In consequence there was no pedantry or, in the popular sense of the word, "academic" flavour in his evaluations of current literature. He was able to enter into the spirit of the writers of the hour, but thanks to his disciplined judgment he entered with his eyes open and knew what he saw. It is a rare accomplishment; it operated to give meaning, weight, authority to Johnson's always polite and friendly words.

His type of criticism had its opponents in his day, and of course has them still. With those opponents sensible men will agree that a significant criticism of literature is no dead mechanic exercise, but no less must sensible men assert against them that criticism worth the reading is something other than the mere variegated record of "the soul's impressions," however delicate. Here there can be no real controversy, but the use of a critic's obviously necessary standards is neither easy nor mechanical. Without singularly keen perceptions and unfailing tact the critic may as easily as other men, to put it plainly, make a fool of himself and stultify his work. Lionel Johnson did neither. His reviews are impressive witness to the correctness, and hence the usefulness, of this sturdy type of criticism. His verdicts wear well—are in the main as good to-day as when he wrote them—and testify that in some regions at least men can, if they will, find permanent truth.

Johnson's taste and tact were of course not free from limitation. But both, evidently, were not assumed, like "company manners," for the public performance. Both were real and of his very nature—not "created," but merely developed and deepened by his long studies and voluntary companionship with

> . . . thoughts and things of an eternal fashion:
> The majesty and dignity
> Of everlasting verity.

He proved, then, a severe yet sympathetic judge of literary form or style; he had as well a lively and true sense for what may be called the personal or individual note in literature, a matter of course closely connected with style, but much larger and the fundamental quality opposing humane letters to the exact sciences; and he had also no mean capacity in sound judgment of thought and morals in their more abstract aspects. No critic has possessed all three of these kinds of sensibility, or perception, in equal degree; and very generally a man who possesses the first and second kinds is found to have little talent for the third. Johnson, certainly, was more at home—more interested and interesting—in the realms of style and personality in literature; yet not his least claim to our concern is his competency, his so general soundness, in the field of the more generalised or abstract criticism. Miss Guiney has spoken of his "strongly philosophic fibre" [see excerpt dated 1902]. Everyone may not be able to discern this, but everyone who knows Lionel Johnson will see what she meant. For Johnson, though in no sense a philosopher, was a man, not only in the sphere of literary art, of sound principles firmly grasped and clearly understood.

It is a nice question how in these days of narrow training rather than of education, when intellectual provincialism is enjoying an unacknowledged but almost perfect triumph, Johnson came to acquire and retain a view-point so sound and so well rounded. He learned something beyond doubt from Samuel Johnson, and he got more, very probably, just from the saving grace of his own nature. Moreover, even yet there is less sheer tyranny of popular opinion in England than in America. But our guess is that a chief influence saving him from the mental and moral confusion on every side was his entry into the Roman Catholic Church. He was received into that Church, not in extreme youth as a matter of family tradition, but—as result of his own questionings and thought—in 1891 after he had come down from Oxford. It is not meant, of course, that Johnson's mere subscription to the dogma of the Roman Catholic Church, whatever it may have done for him spiritually, worked in him any miracle intellectually. The important thing, from our present viewpoint, is the larger meaning of such an act as a very definite spiritual affirmation, made deliberately. It is true, the mere knowledge that one has made oneself a corporate part of this ancient depositary of Christian faith must fortify one inwardly; but in addition the definite spiritual affirmation itself—disposing once and for all of so much!—provides a unique foundation on which to base a life. That act of faith—and of course, for the personal result in this life, it need not be one so trying to the present-day mind as was Johnson's—becomes a point of orientation for all human affairs. And for a man of Lionel Johnson's open-eyed, independent intelligence such definite faith in the spiritual nature and destiny of humanity means, not the stagnation and deadening of thought, but merely a fruitful guidance of it that assures for one's thinking, force, consistency, and the unplumbed strength of traditionary wisdom. There should be nothing strange in this; and there will be nothing strange to anyone who knows the lives of, for instance, such men as Milton or Samuel Johnson. Their conduct of life, so much happier than Lionel Johnson's in the practical matters of day to day, was based upon unquestioning religious faith which served, exactly in the manner here indicated, as the starting-point for vigorous, fruitful and permanently significant lives.

Here, too, in [his] slight reviews, Lionel Johnson points, not so stridently as implicitly, a lesson for the present day. This is not the place to enlarge upon our multiform modern con-

fusion, where impudent shams and old delusions run their way practically unchecked through our praised enlightenment, and where so-called scientists easily impose deadening superstitions upon the multitude; but it is evident the time has come when men must realise anew the permanent place of faith in human life, and must choose with opened eyes between the two faiths possible—for there is no more "proof" with one than with the other—between faith in a mechanical universe, with all its impossibilities, and faith in our spiritual nature and divine destiny, with all its difficulties. These reviews, it is thought, have a present interest from their subject-matter; they have some permanent interest from Lionel Johnson's clear and spirited manner of judging literary and human values, from his unswerving insistence upon the reality and meaning of our better selves. (pp. 11-16)

> Robert Shafer, in an introduction to Reviews and Critical Papers *by Lionel Johnson, edited by Robert Shafer, E. P. Dutton & Company, 1921, pp. 9-16.*

ERNEST BOYD (essay date 1922)

[*An Irish-American writer and translator, Boyd was a prominent literary critic known for his erudite, honest, and often satirical critiques. In the candidly wrought essays which form his important studies of Irish literature,* Ireland's Literary Renaissance *(1916) and* The Contemporary Dramas of Ireland *(1917), Boyd evaluated Irish literary works apart from English literature. He was also a respected translator, especially of French and German works, and his* Studies in Ten Literatures *(1925) demonstrates his knowledge of modern foreign literature. In the following excerpt, Boyd examines Johnson's place among the poets of the Irish Literary Renaissance.*]

Lionel Johnson cannot be considered an Irish poet in the sense that Yeats is. His English birth and Oxford education left such an imprint upon him that he was in the same position as his older Irish friends [John Todhunter and T. W. Rolleston] of the Rhymers' Club; they could but partially recapture the tradition which had been reborn to displace in Irish literature the tradition in which they had developed. Alone amongst his compatriots in this group Yeats consistently preserved his nationality, as all his poems in the two books of the Rhymers' Club testify. With the exception of Johnson's beautiful *Celtic Speech,* none of the other Irish contributions shows any decidedly national characteristics. (p. 189)

Without insisting upon the question of relative merit, we may try to estimate that portion [of Johnson's poetry] which belongs to the history of the Irish Literary Revival.

The best of the poems illustrating this side of Lionel Johnson's talent have been published in a selection made by W. B. Yeats, entitled *Twenty-one Poems,* which appeared in 1904. What differentiates these verses from those of the author's contemporaries is a certain classic hardness of outline, and a restraint not usually found in the loose reveries and wistful outpourings of the Irish muse. Johnson's Greek and Latin studies, his admiration for Pater, who was his tutor, could not but influence his own writing. Whether the theme be English or Celtic, there is always an aloofness in the passion of the poet; he does not abandon himself utterly to his mood. It was easier for Johnson to be reserved than it was for most of the Irish poets. Classical education, for instance, has rarely been their lot. They have approached the literatures of Greece and Rome, not as disciples of Pater, but as children seeking a new field of romance and adventure. Nothing would be more different, did we possess them, than the impression of a man like Johnson and those of

Yeats or A. E., on reading Homer. But more important, as enabling Johnson to exercise the classic virtue of restraint, is the fact that he wrote of Ireland from the head more than from the heart. His conversion to the political tradition of Ireland must necessarily have been largely a matter of intellectual conviction. The Irish strain in his blood was of the slightest, and a generation or two of highly Anglicised forbears, one of whom helped to crush the Rebellion in 1798, did not tend to strengthen his sense of Irish nationality. In view of these facts, Johnson's enthusiasm for Ireland may be described as that of a convert. His intellect was stirred before his heart, otherwise it could be difficult to account for what must have seemed an apostasy. Not by emotion, but by argument, can the de-nationalised Irishman be restored to his country, for the former would appeal precisely to those instincts which he lacks. It need not surprise us, therefore, if Johnson's poems, arising out of a thought, possess qualities not commonly found in the verse of his contemporaries, which are inspired by an emotion.

A further point of dissimilarity between Johnson and the Irish poets with whom he was associated is the strongly marked note of Catholicism which characterises so many of his poems. Whether he joined the Catholic Church in the hope of thereby accentuating his newly-found Irish nationality, or whether he wished to be in the literary fashion of France, as were so many of the English "decadents" of the Eighteen Nineties, we cannot tell. It is possible he may have been prompted by mixed motives, in which literary, social, and even spiritual, considerations played a part. Be that as it may, Johnson's Catholicism constitutes him the only poet of the Revival, apart from Katharine Tynan, whose religion has coloured his work. But here, again, his English education and training produced effects which distinguish him from the Irish Catholic. English Catholicism is, by comparison with that of Ireland, intellectual. If, by chance, an Irish poet gives expression to Catholicism, it is either in the instinctive, wild, half-Pagan fashion of the *Religious Songs of Connacht,* or after the simple, tenderly devout manner of Katharine Tynan. . . . The intellectual fibre, the stern asceticism of [Johnson's] religious poetry, is quite unknown to the few Irish poets of any importance who have written out of a like inspiration.

The statement that the Irish element in Johnson's work is the fruit of intellectual rather than emotional patriotism must not be taken to imply that it is weak and colourless. Putting the question on the lowest level we might say that the convert or proselyte frequently surpasses in zeal the older brethren in the faith. Perhaps, indeed, there was something of that enthusiasm in Johnson's adoption of Ireland. In his verse this ardour often resulted in impassioned lines of intense feeling and great beauty. *Celtic Speech, Ways of War* and *Ireland,* to name but three, are unsurpassed by none, and equalled by few, of his contemporaries. For perfection of form and depth of emotion these poems are noteworthy. As a master of words and technique Johnson ranks with Yeats, but he had more scrupulous regard for classical tradition, as was natural, given the circumstances of his early life. Indeed, so far as such a slight contribution to Anglo-Irish poetry permits the comparison, one might say that Johnson is Yeats with an English classical education and the Oxford manner. For all the difference between their lives and education, Yeats and Johnson are curiously alike. Both, each according to his literary tradition, have a jealous care for the art of verse, both have something aloof in their manner, as of men who live remote from the passions of the common world. Subsequent events have eliminated much of this inhumanity from Yeats's work, but while Johnson was living the two must have been very similar in this respect, except that Yeats came more in contact with humanity. He had neither the instincts of a scholar nor the habits of a recluse which heightened the austere, ascetic traits in his friend's work.

In their literary theories they were as one, so far as Ireland is concerned. Johnson's *Poetry and Patriotism in Ireland,* the only lecture of his to the Irish Literary Society that has been preserved, reads like a pronouncement of Yeats's. The arguments are the same, only the voice and manner are different. In pleading for a wider conception of national literature than that accepted from the poets of *The Nation,* Johnson defines the aims of the Revival as Yeats has done. But, as one might expect from the delicate critic of Thomas Hardy, there is more catholic understanding of literature in general, and above all, a greater precision of thought and language than are usual in Yeats's criticism. We may note also an accuracy of allusion and quotation whose absence has so constantly irritated or amused readers of Yeats's essays. As a worker in the early days of the Irish Literary Society, Johnson was a valuable second to Yeats, whose ideals and ideas he fully understood and supported. His broad culture and thorough literary education gave him an influence which must have been valuable to Yeats, who was almost alone in his concern for the general standards of literature. It must always be uncertain whether Johnson, if he had lived, would have continued to identify himself increasingly with the literature he was helping to foster. If one may judge by the somewhat analogous cases of his fellow Rhymers, Todhunter and Rolleston, he would not. The prior claims of literary interests and associations already formed would probably have drawn him. It is significant that the volume of critical essays, *Post Liminium,* contains but two dealing with Irish literature, one of them being the lecture just referred to, and the other a very journalistic sketch of Mangan. This fact does not suggest a deep interest in the work to which a part of him contributed. But with this part we may be satisfied, both because of the quality of the contribution, which compensates for the absence of quantity, and because of the act of contribution itself, which was a testimony to the strength of the cause. It is to the credit of the Revival that it should have attracted and influenced a writer who had every temptation to consecrate himself entirely to English literature, where his fame was well on the way to being established. (pp. 190-94)

> Ernest Boyd, "The Revival of Poetry: Lionel Johnson, Nora Hopper, Ethna Carbery and Others," in his Ireland's Literary Renaissance, *revised edition, Alfred A. Knopf, 1922, pp. 188-211.**

GEORGE SANTAYANA   (essay date 1945)

[*Santayana was a Spanish-born philosopher, poet, novelist, and literary critic who was for the most part educated in the United States, taking his undergraduate and graduate degrees at Harvard where he later taught philosophy. His earliest published works were the poems of* Sonnets, and Other Verses *(1894). Although Santayana is regarded as no more than a fair poet, his facility with language is one of the distinguishing features of his later philosophical works. Written in an elegant, nontechnical prose, Santayana's major philosophical work of his early career is the five-volume* Life of Reason *(1905-06). These volumes reflect their author's materialist viewpoint applied to such areas as society, religion, art, and science and, along with* Scepticism and Animal Faith *(1923) and the four-volume* Realms of Being *(1927-40), put forth the view that while reason undermines belief in anything whatever, an irrational animal faith suggests the existence of a "realm of essences" which leads to the human search for knowl-*

edge. Late in his life Santayana stated that "reason and ideals arise in doing something that at bottom there is no reason for doing." "Chaos," he wrote earlier, "is perhaps at the bottom of everything." Santayana knew Johnson in his undergraduate days at Oxford, and in the following excerpt from a book of reminiscences he discusses Johnson's Catholic faith as reflected in his poetry.]

[Lionel Johnson was] in his first year at New College. He had rooms at the top of the new buildings overlooking Holywell. Over the roofs of the low houses opposite, the trees in the Parks were visible in places, as well as the country beyond: and pointing to the distant horizon Lionel Johnson said sadly: "Everything above that line is right, everything below it is wrong." These were almost the first words he spoke to me, and they formed an admirable preface to a religious conversion. (pp. 54-5)

Lionel Johnson lived only in his upper storey, in a loggia open to the sky; and he forgot that he had climbed there up a long flight of flinty steps, and that his *campanile* rested on the vulgar earth. The absence of all foundations, of all concreteness, of all distinction between fiction and truth, makes his poetry indigestible. I see that it is genuine poetry—an irresponsible flux of impassioned words: and his religion too was genuine religion, if we admit that religion must be essentially histrionic. Let everything that comes, it says, be to thee an Angel of the Lord; embroider upon it in that sense, and let the vulgar world recede into a distant background for an endless flapping of angelic wings and chanting of angelic voices. The age had given Lionel Johnson enough verbal culture and knowledge of literature to raise his effusions in that angelic choir to a certain level of refinement and fancy; but he was not a traditional Catholic, accepting good-naturedly a supernatural economy that happened to prevail in the universe, as political and domestic economy prevail in one's earthly fortunes. Nor was he a philosopher, enduring the truth. He was a spiritual rebel, a spiritual waif who couldn't endure the truth, but demanded a lovelier fiction to revel in, invented or accepted it, and called it revelation. In part like Shelley, in part like Rimbaud, he despised the world and adored the unreal.

Had that first saying of his to me, that everything above the horizon was right and everything below it wrong, represented his primary and constant mind, he might have become a monk as he had intended; because that is the foundation of Christianity. There is a divine world *surrounding us;* but there is sin and damnation *in us.* Lionel Johnson never seemed to me to feel this as, for instance, St. Paul and St. Augustine felt it. What he felt was rather the opposite, that everything within him was right, and everything outside wrong; and if he made an exception of the blank sky, this was only because he could fill it at will with his poetry. In other words, he was a transcendentalist and a humanist; for that reason he seemed a prophet to [Lord Francis] Russell; and at bottom nothing could be more contrary to Christian humility and to Catholic discipline. (pp. 56-7)

Nor do I profess to have fathomed his Celtic inspiration or his Celtic Catholicism. He says in his lines on *Wales:*

No alien hearts may know that magic, which acquaints
Thy heart with splendid passion, a great fire of dreams;

and I am willing to believe him. But to my prosaic apprehension he remains a child of premature genius and perpetual immaturity; and I cannot forget what Oscar Wilde is reported to have said of him, that any morning at eleven o'clock you might see him come out very drunk from the Café Royal, and hail the first passing perambulator. Yet I should be the last to deride the haze in which he lived, on the ground that Bacchus had something to do with it. Bacchus too was a god; and the material occasion of inspiration makes no difference if the spirit is thereby really liberated. Lionel Johnson lived in the spirit; but to my sense his spirituality was that of a transcendental poet, not that of a saint. His mind was subjective in its presuppositions or in the absence of all presuppositions; so that after reading him through you are aware of a great wind of passionate language, but not of what was said or of what it all was about. And this vagueness was hardly due to absorption in something higher, because it did not liberate him from everything lower. So at least he tells us in *The Dark Angel.*

> Because of thee, no thought, no thing
> Abides for me undesecrate . . .
> Of two defeats, of two despairs;
> Less dread, a change to drifting dust,
> Than thine eternity of cares.

And if we ask what the alternative to these two despairs may be, and what will issue from the triumph that he still hopes for, we find nothing positive, nothing specific, but only transcendental spirit, still open to every thought and to every torment:

> Lonely, unto the Lone I go;
> Divine, to the Divinity.

These words are the words of Plotinus and of Christian mystics; but here we do not feel them to be backed by either the Platonic or the Christian scheme of the universe: they are floating words. Even the firmness and constructive power of the Catholic faith could not *naturalise* Lionel Johnson in the Catholic world. The same emotional absolutism, the same hatred of everything not plastic to the fancy, which drove him from Victorian England into Celtic poetry and Catholic supernaturalism, kept him from accepting definition and limitation even there; he could not deny himself other dreams. As he writes in *Gwynedd:*

> We will not wander from this land; [Wales]
>   Here distress
> Dreams, and delight dreams: dreaming, we can fill
> All solitary haunts with prophecy,
> All heights with holiness and mystery;
> Our hearts with understanding, and our will
> With love of nature's law and loveliness.

The last two lines may seem to contradict what I am saying but I quote them in order to be fair. Understanding, with love of nature's law, if it were real understanding of the true law of nature, would stop all that dreaming, or reduce it to wasted time and gratuitous trouble, as he himself says in *The Dark Angel,* already quoted:

> Because of thee, the land of dreams
> Becomes a gathering-place of fears:
> Until tormented slumber seems
> One vehemence of useless tears.

But the word nature, in a Celtic poet, does not mean what it meant to Lucretius, nor understanding what it meant to Aristotle, nor law what it meant to Newton. These words mean rather landscape, divination, and magic; as, in the line about Wales, where he says he will not leave *this land,* he means the *soul* of this land, which is the land of dreams.

The passionate need of sinking into these dreams, and defying the false world that pretended to be more real, seems to me to have been the secret of Lionel Johnson in all his phases. It was what made him a pagan or a Buddhist at Winchester, a Baudelairean Catholic at Oxford, and a Fenian conspirator in London. In his verse he could modulate those dreams lyrically, but not logically, morally, and historically as the Church had modulated her original inspirations; and he dared to take them, as the Church did hers, for revelations of the truth. But his dreams had no such application to the facts and sorrows of life as had the Christian faith. Their passion remained dreamy, weak and verbal, and he perished not a martyr to his inspiration, but a victim of it. (pp. 59-62)

> *George Santayana, "Russell," in his* The Middle Span: Persons and Places, Vol. II, *Charles Scribner's Sons, 1945, pp. 44-75.*

IAIN FLETCHER (essay date 1951)

[*Fletcher is an English poet and critic who is known for his critical studies of such noted late-Victorian authors as George Meredith, Algernon Swinburne, and Walter Pater. In the following excerpt, he discusses the manner in which the contradictory influences of the classic tradition and the aesthetic movement helped to shape Johnson's poetry.*]

In poetry, the first influence to which Johnson submits may be termed the 'classical' tradition in English, as specially represented by Gray, Arnold, and Bridges perhaps. The emphasis, in this tradition, falls on sanity, proportion and *ordonnance*, qualities constantly lauded in Johnson's criticism. A further characteristic here is reverence for authority—like the Scots notion of the *makar*, let us say—an honouring and partial imitation of one's predecessors. It is so in Arnold, in Gray's *Progress of Poesy*, in Johnson's formal elegies. And this involves too, the habit—so frequent in Latin verse, particularly after Pontanus—of silently assuming the phrases, sometimes the sentences even, of earlier writers. This is natural where stress lies on the *organic* quality of tradition and where 'the pleasures of memory' is an essential element in aesthetic, the pleasing strangeness of the old jewel skilfully adapted to its new setting. Continuous in Gray, it occurs also in Arnold. Johnson quotes *ad nauseam* in his criticism, while his verse refers often enough to literary figures, favoured passages and even to theological *minutiae*. Analogous is the reverence for institutions as well as for Classical literature: Johnson has poems on *Winchester, Oxford, The Classics*, on Virgil and Lucretius among poets, Sertorius and the Emperor Julian among historical personages—both representatives of a defeated order and thus temperamentally sympathetic. 'Plain in thy neatness'— this tradition distrusts the ornate; is severe in its choice of epithet, though lavish enough with the devices of rhetoric. Johnson's florid early poetry shows rather the lax influence of the Preraphaelites, while in his last phase he seems also to react away from the 'dry beauty', Pater's phrase, of this tradition. Classical objectivity implies a hard, clarified surface, often originating, as in Gautier, from just this preoccupation with style, though Johnson's poetry has none of the rich concrete quality of Gautier.

The other, contradictory influence is the Aesthetic Movement. His introspectiveness, his sustained melancholia, his sense of spiritual isolation, even the 'triumphant niceties' of ritual and puncuation are all characteristic. It is in the subject matter of certain poems that this influence works most strongly, where the theme centres round the conflict between the demands of the religious and the aesthetic life. In *To a Passionist* . . . the two orders of experience are contrasted, but not reconciled: *et purpureos in flores, Tua vulnera formasti.* In *Pax Christi,* though, written on the day he was received, there is hope that sensuous beauty may be somehow sacramentalized through the Church. To the year before his submission belong *Men of Assisi,* and the rather fine *Men of Aquino,* where a vague reconciliation is attempted. The theme reappears on a different level in *A Friend* . . . , human and divine values being radically contrasted. In *The Church of a Dream* and *The Age of a Dream,* the *milieu* is too remote to bear on the problem directly. In *Propheta Gentium* . . . there is a conflation: Master Vergil is honoured and the good pagan redeemed, when his art lies at the service of the Messiah.

The language of Johnson's poems shows both influences. *Fin de siècle* epithets occur, such as 'wan', 'stilly', 'dim' or 'pale'— 'a pale and lonely way'; 'gray' used as synonymic of pensive and solitary, part of the pronounced colour sense of the period. One thinks immediately of Dowson here, and it is difficult to decide whether he influenced Johnson or *vice versa*. Another characteristic in common is that of writing sonnets in Alexandrines.

Where epithet occurs, though, it is generally more precise, less vague and delicate. Johnson's conscious placing of the individual word suggests the writer of prose, for the poet works rather in terms of word-clusters, in images and metaphors, though this is less true of poets with little visual imagination. Certainly there is no attempt at ambiguity, at deliberate enrichment by ambivalence of mood and expression. Discussing the 'pleasing strangeness' of Pater's diction, Johnson remarks: ". . . as language loses its 'uncharted freedom', becoming fixed and formal, literary artists are increasingly forced to this 'strangeness,' which is to be had far less by a *bizarre* vocabulary that by a sensitiveness to the value, the precise value, of common words in their precise significance. *Mystery, economy, pagan, cordial, mortified,* to use such words, with just a hint of their first meanings, is for the scholarly writer and reader a delicate pleasure. . . ." This is applied specifically to prose; none the less in his own verse Johnson uses just such words with what seems to be a similar intention. There is an obvious contrast here with Wilde's well known description of the prose of *A Rebours,* to which the adjective 'bizarre' becomes immediately applicable.

Johnson's most favoured rhetorical figure is simple repetition, *anaphora:*

> And therefore, on a night of heavenly fire;
> And therefore, on a windy night of noon.

Master words are often repeated to arrive at a cumulative effect as in *By the Statue of King Charles* with its reiteration of 'stars', 'night' and 'skies'. One of the features of Arnold's verse had been repetition which only serves the purpose of maintaining that unemphatic note he aimed at. Johnson follows him in this irritating habit: "Well fare she, well! As perfect beauty fares" (*Oxford*); "I cannot, cannot tread your sterner way" (*To the Saints*), where the effect is merely petulant. *Nihilism* provides an example of the use and misuse of this device. "Man's life, my life: of life I am afraid." Here the effect is cumulative. In "Only the rest! the rest! Only the gloom, soft and long gloom", the repetition of 'rest' makes merely for collapse in rhythm, disastrous with a poet so deficient in metaphor, one who must depend so largely on aural effects as Johnson.

Arnold again must bear responsibility for the profusion of interjection and exclamation: "Ah!" to say nothing of "Oh!", though the effect is happy enough in the second part of *In Memory.* There is a continuous distinction between the "Oh!" of apostrophisation and the "O" of the direct vocative. But, as with his frequent use of repetition, this is requiring the reader to do the work of the poet. The poet is evading the problem of creating through his language the sense of exaltation or of address, is relying rather on indicating the fact by technical devices.

Johnson's prosodic virtuosity is natural. Like many late Victorian poets he felt the necessity for poetic innovation. His manipulation of metre is generally careful, but never daring. There is nothing of that exquiste licence, the last flower of knowledge, the knowledge of where to transgress. The six-syllabled three-stressed quatrains of *By the Statue of King Charles, Parnel, The Red Wind,* predominate in the volume of 1895; but his preference later is for the metre of *Walter Pater, De Profundis* and *Vita Venturi Saeculi,* which accords with a more hieratic diction. The earlier of the two poems called *A Friend* illustrates an ability to vary accent. His metrical diversity is not accompanied by architectonic skill. Too often he writes the stanza, even by the line, only in a few durable poems is there any sense of *flow.* To rhyming words he devotes little attention. In *The Troopship* the same rhyme is repeated in the course of successive quatrains. He never thinks to vary monorhymes with double rhymes except where a definite metrical pattern has been adopted. The ear becomes tired of his Preraphaelite trick of pairing unstressed endings, particularly those in 'y' and 'al'—verity, majesty, immortality, augural, memorial, vesperal. Of whole poems perhaps the most felicitous metrically is *Dead,* with its searching hesitant movement, together with the third section of *Sancta Sylvarum,* which has the very winged quality of those pursuing fawns it describes; in Johnson its speed and lightness are unique.

Le Gallienne, in his reader's report, defines the essential limitation of Johnson's verse, its singular barrenness of 'metaphor and fancy', and its consequent monotony. He has no gift 'for the striking line and of lyric passion.' He recurs constantly to single words which are substituted for metaphors as repetition is substituted for passionate utterance. Such words as 'vesperal', 'courtesy', 'immemorial', 'Hesperian', 'sternness', 'chivalry', possess for him a special emotional significance. Whereas in prose such epithets are sufficient to carry the weight of exposition, in poetry it is not with exposition that we are primarily concerned. This limitation is the more felt, accompanied as it is by such a slender response to things visible. One does, naturally, come upon *choses vues:*

> My step fills as I go,
> Shy rabbits with quick fears:
> I see the sunlight glow
> Red through the startled ears. . . .

and this response is evident too in the opening of *Heddon's Mouth, Gwynedd, A Cornish Night,* and in the first stanza of *Windermere,* with its almost imagistic clarity. But his eye, though, stays for a moment only on the composition of the scene before him for, all too soon, the weight of the past, its learning, its many vivid associations, begin to blur the present. In his later poetry almost all reference vanishes to the firm world of objects. Such poems as *Before the Cloister* and *De Profundis*—their author's own preference among the poems of *Ireland*—are compacted almost entirely of style alone. Such poetry wavers "from phantom to phantom of feeling, without

a shred of fine matter, all a-tremble with unfelt emotion, all made up of a few properties shaken together into rhyme and pretty coloured words". Mr. Santayana's conclusion is hardly less severe. "The absence of all foundations, of all concreteness, of all distinction between fiction and truth, makes his poetry indigestible" [see excerpt dated 1945].

But in accepting these verdicts we are in danger of refusing to distinguish Johnson's positive quality. Having elaborately played Devil's Advocate, let it be confessed that I belong to that 'certain class of mind', Le Gallienne's term, which finds in this poetry the quality of its defects. To this class of mind aural is at least as important as visual beauty; a sense of style diffused over a whole poem preferable above fine lines. Modern taste tends to reject work like Johnson's, responding as it does to predominant effects of colour rather than to effects of form. In painting the seduction of colour; the evaluation of poetry in terms of the vigour and evocative force of its images, these are natural enough in our present age. A society which has lost its hierarchic pattern, has lost its forms of encounter and address, its dignity of choice, measures the past in the twilight of its own limitations, judging it admirable only where it mirrors some foreshadowing disorder. A moral centre, a sense of style, a concern with human obligation at its noblest, these, where it is most typical, are the attributes of Johnson's verse. The sanctity of scholarship, the beauty of there past, the sense of piety towards institutions, now that the response to these things has faded, such Byzantine virtues have their place. While in the more personal poems, the frigid grace is heightened by allusion to the 'romantic agony' and the very muted quality of the communication, the inability or refusal to 'speak out', has of itself a curious discreet charm. *Morfydd, The Dark Angel, The Precept of Silence, Mystic and Cavalier* here and in two or three of the Latin poems is the essence of his achievement. All his life he seems to have been haunted by that Old Testament phrase 'And there is sorrow on the sea'. His insensitivity to the external world derives from this passion of elemental forces being more real to him than the pathos of tangible objects. This is the sea of Arnold's dying faith; even more it is 'the unplumb'd, salt estranging sea' of a desparing solitariness of spirit. And these elemental energies contract with the inorganic society of the industrial Northern world around him, where man is divided from man, and from himself. The void that separates us from each other: that is Johnson's theme: "I know you: solitary griefs . . ." "A man like other men: yet, am I like them then?" "But in the lonely hours I learn . . ." The lonely hours in which he hears even more clearly the dark angel 'ever on the wing'. (pp. xxxv-xli)

> *Iain Fletcher, in an introduction to* The Complete Poems of Lionel Johnson *by Lionel Johnson, edited by Iain Fletcher, The Unicorn Press, 1953, pp. xi-xliv.*

A. BRONSON FELDMAN (essay date 1953)

[*In the following excerpt, Feldman discusses the technical and emotional qualities of Johnson's poems.*]

Whenever I think of Lionel Johnson my memory echoes the response of Hamlet to Horatio's outcry on the weird event at Elsinore. You recall the outcry: "O day and night, but this is wondrous strange!" Then the Prince's response: "And therefore, as a stranger, give it welcome." There is a manifestation of the soul of Lionel Johnson in the valiant intelligence of that line. For young Johnson was distinguished among the geniuses of England and his century by the way he always welcomed the stranger in thought and art. For readiness and breadth of mental hospitality he had few equals in the literature of his time. In the handful of rare volumes bequeathed to us by the untimely silenced youth there are more things heavenly and earthly than were dreamt of in the philosophy of most of his fellow Victorians. (p. 140)

Johnson existed just to read and to write. Yet there was almost nothing of the bookworm, the pedant, in his blood; no critic could complain that his writings were mere results of a *cacoethes scribendi*. The generosity of his mind to fresh experience, the clarity of his outlook on the world, enabled Johnson to find distinctions between reality and misfortunes and less luminous intellect would have found only a terrific mixture of fantasy and fact. In short, Johnson was not simply a reader and a writer: he was a *seer*. The books he loved held faithful mirrors up to nature. His own books possess a wealth of truth.

Lionel Johnson is chiefly remembered today for his poetry. . . . The principles of poetry that he cherished are briefly noted in his Winchester correspondence. He insisted that "Art is intensely scientific, poetry has laws." These laws compelled the true artist to maintain strict forms and modes of communicating his emotions. Of course the artist revealed his mastery by the skill with which he concealed his travails over structure and design. Johnson was pitiless to poets who made design and structure their primary concern. To his religion of literature devotion to the letter and the line was nothing but deadly. The first requirement of a poem for him was "the necessary foundation of natural instinct," that is, passion. The phrase occurs in a criticism of Thomas Lovell Beddoes, a criticism of wonderful acuteness, coming from a lad of seventeen. He voiced his theory of art in the following outburst:

"There is nothing on earth—perhaps not even music, not even painting—of equal divinity with a single line of pure word-music, a single thought caught from passing emotions and changing aspects, and fashioned into the beauty of a phrase—there is nothing equally sovereign with poetry."

Naturally, for such a rhapsodist, the quintessence of poetry was to be discovered in the lyric. At bottom Johnson agreed with the doctrine of Poe that there could be no such thing as a long poem, since a poem had to be a work of ecstasy. And Johnson would have agreed with Poe's hostility to the "heresy of the didactic." Still, the English poet would have protested that a real poet was also a teacher. He wanted to instruct the people in religion, in ethics, and the pursuit of beauty. Yeats failed to see the difference between Johnson's doctrine that poets were teachers and the dogma that literature must be didactic. The two friends fought many a wit-combat over the matter, without converting each other. When the Irish bard could bring himself, for instance, to praise Walt Whitman, it was exclusively for the sake of the American's utterance of pain or bliss. Johnson, on the other hand, admired Whitman because the Yankee singer "takes this world and shows that nothing is common or unclean." Johnson loved Goethe's *Faust* because at the end the hero begins to drain waste lands, to serve humanity instead of self. The boy Johnson even hoped to reach "ignorant peasantry, vulgar bourgeois, and ridiculous aristocrats," with his songs! *Mirabile dictu*, in a manner he succeeded, as I shall try to demonstrate.

His verse lures curiosity by its combination of traditional metres with extraordinary rime patterns, archaic vocabulary with the boldest modern imagery. He spells chant "Chaunt" and uses the word "lets" meaning hindrances, as well as "conceits,"

in the sense of Shakespeare's age. Without a tremor Lionel executed the inversion "Sleep they well" in his lyric "**Trentals**," and the inversion "Snows the land cover" in his carol for Christmas. His feeling for melody went unoffended by the startling pentameter with which he broke the organ rhythms of his blank verse monolog "**Julian at Eleusis**":

> Chance and change; change and chance! strange chance, hard change.

Gerard Manley Hopkins never dared dissonance like this. Many of Johnson's lines appear to defy scansion in the same way. But every variation of his metre was deliberate, and he sometimes gave the impression of working for nothing more than the "virtuoso bliss" of inventing new rhythms, new stanzas. He became radiantly happy, he said, at the discovery of a new form of verse. It is the imagery of Johnson, however, that endears him to those who care for poetry in our day—those who care for articulate, rhythmic, magical beauty, I mean, not the lovers of extravagant, soliloquacious unprose. Johnson's princely taste, his graceful scholarship, saved him from the follies of "free," or libertine, anarchic verse. Thus his finest lines and phrases have the marmoreal spell of the Greek immortals. He has also left us phrases and lines of a burning modernity. There is an Aeschylean splendor in the couplet,

> Armored he rides, his head
> Bare to the stars of dawn.

depicting the statue of the martyred King Charles I at Charing Cross. In the same volume containing these two Hellenic lines we encounter a couplet that must have inspired T. S. Eliot in the making of his "Hollow Men." This is the couplet:

> And this is Death's dreamland to me,
> Led hither by a star. . . .

Compare Eliot's poem with its lines about "death's dream kingdom" visioned "Under the twinkle of a fading star." Johnson's influence on Eliot is considerable, but greater by far on Eliot's teacher, Ezra Pound, who has often acknowledged the spell of Lionel on his poetry. Pound contributed a eulogy as preface to the *Poetical Works* of Johnson . . . [see excerpt dated 1915], and wrote a line of pity and praise for him in *Hugh Selwyn Mauberley*. . . . Worthy of note is the echo of some cadences in Johsnon's lyric, "**Mystic and Cavalier**," which may be clearly heard in Pound's poem, "A Virginal." The parallel is unmistakable. Here are two lines from the latter:

> No, no! Go from me. I have left her lately . . .
> For my surrounding air has a new lightness . . .

And here are four lines from Johnson's lyric:

> Go from me: I am one of those, who fall.
> What! hath no cold wind swept your heart at all,
> In my sad company? . . .
> Yours are the victories of light . . .

On the other hand, the finger and voice of Yeats are plainly discernible in page after page of Johnson's songs about Ireland, and his songs for her saints. It was through the power that he wielded in the destinies of Yeats, Pound, and Eliot, that Johnson succeeded in reaching the minds of the "ignorant peasantry, vulgar bourgeois, and ridiculous aristocrats,"—not to mention the desperate proletarians—whom he desired as audience for his art.

The majority of Johnson's poems are revisited, even by admirers, with reluctance, because of the chill that lingers in them, indeed the odor of death. We can cheerfully bear what Louise Imogen Guiney called his "Latin strictness and asceticism" [see excerpt dated 1902], when the ascetic severity is felt as passionate self-defense against the temptation to wrong and violence. But we cannot long bear the breath of winter that streams from so many of his songs, in particular the love songs. "Latin strictness" alone will not account for the icy sterility in them. Their very titles communicate their bleakness: **"A Burden of Easter Vigil," "A Death," "At the Burial of Cardinal Manning," "Dead"** (there are two lyrics with this title), **"Ireland's Dead," "Light! For the Stars Are Pale," "Morning Twilight," "The Dark Angel," "The Darkness," "The Gloom"** . . . Yeats informs us that his friend's best poetry is "natural and impassioned," but the passions that usually prevail are sorrow and remorse; the singer is forever grieving. He envied Heinrich Heine his glory of being able to laugh in pain. His nickname for Heine was "laughing Christ." The sources of the English poet's woe have been lost under the reticence of his childhood friends. All we know of them is that he frequently wandered away from his father's house, where the genial currents of his soul were frozen, and spent hours in churchyards, "and even, when possible, vaults and charnelhouses," in order to commune with their phantoms, "to force the paraphernalia of death to unfold their secret." Perhaps it was the passion for consorting with ghosts that induced the dominance of white among the colors in Johnson's poetry, a dominance that has attracted the attention of several critics, particularly the historian of Johnson's era, Holbrook Jackson. Psychoanalytic materialism would probably trace the poet's sentiment for whiteness to his mother's bosom, or at least the gown in which she came to his cradle at night. Starvation for maternal love surely promoted his conversion to the motherchurch of Rome. The flame of his favorite color fused in his imagination the starkness of death and the purity of life. Thinking of white, he could feel his soul sheltered under the wings of the "White Angels Around Christ," glowing tranquil under the "Light from the Light of Light."

Johnson was not without the gift of laughter, but he exhibited it more in his prose than in his verse. He contributed an excellent prose satire on decadent poetry to the first number of *The Pageant*, a satire entitled **"Incurable,"** which contains a delicious parody of the kind of songs on sex and suicide that Ernest Dowson and Arthur Symons were making fashionable in the 1890s. Here is a quatrain from the parody:

> Her body music is: and ah!
> The accords of lute and viola
> When she and I
> Play on live limbs love's opera.

The sole poem in his published works that shows us a jolly soul is the sonnet on Samuel Johnson. . . . A verse eulogy of Charles Lamb says much about joy and merriment but is actually a celebration of saintliness. When Johnson sings of sitting in fancy at the table of the Vicar of Wakefield, or listening to Tobias Smollett's chapters of "Matthew Bramble's pleasant wrath," or pronounces his happiness in the humors of Sir Roger de Coverley, and other amusing gentlemen of the eighteenth century, we are more impressed with the picture of the solitary poet in his library than with the evocation of the comic figures he reads about. There is certainly no joy in the lines he dedicated to the joys of the grape, **"Vinum Daemonum"**—no joy at all, only a delirium and repressed tears.

It is a relief to turn from Johnson's sad failures in poetry to his sad triumphs. Unquestionably he donated to England a few

of her deathless lyrics. The song **"To Morfydd"** with its haunting refrain,

> Oh! what are the winds?
> And what are the waters?
> Mine are your eyes!

will live forever, even though its students have learned from Yeats that Johnson lied about its creation, claiming that he obtained the magic tercet from a Welsh ballad. Yeats explains the falsehood as the result of an irresistible wish of the poet to hide the fact that he shared in the primitive Gaelic emotion. Equally permanent are the verses **"By the Statue of King Charles at Charing Cross,"** which will always move us, including our remorseless democrats, with its perfect Dantesque cadences:

> Ye, when the city sleeps;
> When all the cries are still:
> The stars and heavenly deeps
> Work out a perfect will.

If this quatrain reminds us of Dante's line, *"In la sua volontade e nostra pace,"* it is only to endow the words of Johnson with another radiance. Likewise, when we recall a great song by Goethe in reading Johnson's piece, **"The Precept of Silence,"** concerning the knowledge of divine powers attained through hunger and loneliness, we are not disturbed by thoughts of plagiarism; we sense an exaltation by thoughts of an emotion all men have known. At Johnson's best his songs always recall the lyrics of past masters. But the recollection is not merely of literature but of life. His songs only seem to be made of ink; the truth is they are made of blood. (pp. 147-53)

> *A. Bronson Feldman, "The Art of Lionel Johnson," in* Poet Lore, *Vol. LVII, No. 2, Summer, 1953, pp. 140-60.*

BARBARA CHARLESWORTH (essay date 1965)

[*In the following excerpt, Charlesworth discusses Johnson's aristocratic and solitary temperament and its expression in both his life and works.*]

[The] world in which Johnson lived, spiritually and physically, was gray, relieved only by gold, the color he associated with fantasy. In a room which had curtains of gray corduroy hung over the doors, the windows, and the bookcases, Johnson slept all day and read during the night. Yeats asked him whether his schedule did not separate him from men and women; he replied, "In my library I have all the knowledge of the world I need." (p. 82)

Vicisti et vivimus ["conquered yet alive"] was the motto of his family, one that Johnson thought peculiarly appropriate to himself, and so it was, for among the essential qualities in his character were a sense of defeated aristocracy and a contempt far more genuine than Wilde's for the world around him. It was this aristocratic remoteness, this dandyism, in Johnson that most deeply impressed Yeats; it is also the characteristic which Yeats most often associates with all "the tragic generation" who liked to murmur, "as for living—our servants will do that for us."

Johnson's sense of aristocracy was based not on family but on learning, an aristocracy of culture. On the very simplest level his attitude reveals itself in what Katherine Tynan calls "a little haughtiness towards the men who lacked Latin and Greek." Now Yeats was among those with that unfortunate deficiency, and one has the impression that Johnson's aloof manner at times made Yeats feel gauche and uncomfortable; for instance, Yeats' tendency to seize impetuously upon ideas and work them out, his desire to talk to other Rhymers about the world "as a bundle of fragments," met only with Johnson's freezing silence. For what, in Johnson's mind, was the use of noisy opinions, of ideas which were to be put into action? Ignoring that part of Arnold's theory of culture which reflected a hope for social melioration, Johnson envisioned the man of culture as one who stood aside completely from a world intent on its own destruction, a world not worth saving. (pp. 88-9)

In a paragraph about Pascal Johnson shows by his quotation of Newman's motto—"cor ad cor loquitur" ["heart speaks to heart"]—that he associates Newman as well as Arnold and Pater with a tradition of aristocratic temper, almost of hauteur:

> A lover of superiorities, he [Pascal] has pity for their opposites, but mere contempt for the meagre and the middling.... France has no writer, certainly no lay writer who resembles him in his superb austerity: *"on mourra seul"* ["one dies alone"], he said, and in truth he both was and is a man of isolation, dwelling apart.... He is one of the voices which at rare intervals come from the heart of a man, and go to the hearts of men: *cor ad cor loquitur,* and deep answers deep.

A similar hauteur may have been one of the elements which turned Johnson toward Roman Catholicism. For, as Newman pointed out in "The Second Spring," Catholicism in England was associated with two groups: Irish immigrants, "coming and going at harvest time, or a colony of them lodged in a miserable quarter of the vast metropolis," and a few members of the very good old families, "an elderly person, seen walking in the streets, grave and solitary, and strange, though noble in bearing, and said to be of good family and a 'Roman Catholic.'" Both of these groups were free in Johnson's mind from any connection with Philistia—and indeed, his discovery of Irish ancestry was, in Santayana's opinion, another of Johnson's ways of rejecting the Philistine world. But besides its connections with aristocrat and peasant and its remoteness from the middle classes, Roman Catholicism may well have had a link in Johnson's mind with intellectual superiority and wideness of culture; at least one sees it allied to both in works as widely different as "Bishop Blougram's Apology" and Harold Frederic's *The Damnation of Theron Ware.* If Johnson read the latter work, he would have found a reflection of his own feelings in its presentation of the Irish priest, Father Forbes, and the Irish (and aristocratic) girl, Celia Madden, as the two people of greatest polish and intellectual culture in an otherwise narrowly provincial, deeply Philistine small town.

While he approves of its cultured flexibility on the one hand, Johnson is also proud of a deliberately outmoded dignity in Catholicism; in fact, a modern Catholic might almost be alarmed by his pleasure in connecting the Church with the old, the outworn, the cast-off, as it appears in his poem **"The Church of a Dream."** The poem was written in 1890, only a year before Johnson's conversion to Catholicism, so that its intention, one gathers, was to praise.... Thus Johnson's acceptance of the Catholic faith, however genuine it may have been, did not really serve as a bond between him and the rest of the world; on the contrary, he made his religion into yet another protective wall. Nevertheless, the very care that Johnson took in using his religion, his culture, even the daily routine of his life, to separate himself from the world argues for the possibility that in his heart he wished for acceptance. His frailty, his short stature, his bookishness, may have set him apart in a family whose men were all expected to be good soldiers, strong believers, and good sports; he, in return, rejected all his family's values; yet did so with a hidden emotion which suggests that secretly the value must still have meant a good deal to him.

Lionel Johnson was not a man to take even his closest friends into his confidence; it must, therefore, be mainly his reading of Johnson's poetry that makes Yeats say, "much falling he / Brooded upon sanctity." Yet even those lines, though beautifully succinct and delicate, especially in their echo of Johnson's "Go from me: I am one of those, who fall"—the line that Yeats intuitively knows as the best expression of Johnson's spirit—do not, save for that echo, state the truth of the matter in all its negation: Johnson brooded not on sanctity but on sin. His poetry is much more concerned with damnation than with beatitude.... Very often, God seems remote to Johnson, or if He be near, He comes in vengeance not in love.... **"The Dark Angel"** tries to reach a ... more hopeful solution; yet again most of the poem is taken up with terrible internal conflict of which the resolution is simply imposed by a change from Manichean to Neoplatonic theology:

> Dark Angel, with thine aching lust!
> Of two defeats, of two despairs:
> Less dread, a change to drifting dust,
> Than thine eternity of cares.
>
> Do what thou wilt, thou shalt not so,
> Dark Angel! triumph over me:
> *Lonely, unto the Lone I go;*
> *Divine, to the Divinity.*

Johnson does not believe that he will change to drifting dust, although he wishes perhaps that he did, for a complete materialism would offer him escape; he accepts instead the complete spiritualism of Neoplatonic thought because, paradoxically, it offers a similar escape from all personality and with it all sense of sin.

What ... his central poems show is that Johnson, who had of his own will turned away from society, found himself separated as well from a sustaining belief in the presence of God. His attitude to life removed him from society, his conscience and his fear of death made him feel very far from God. As a result, he was left in that state of mind which Eliot describes in "The Waste Land." After the Thunder's word "Dhayadhvam"—sympathize—Eliot describes the fate of the man who has not done so:

> I have heard the key
> Turn in the door once and turn once only
> We think of the key, each in his prison
> Thinking of the key, each confirms a prison.

As it happens, Johnson once used that very image in one of his letters to Russell: "You must forgive my silence, if speech pleases better in this hollow prison vault of a world, where we fumble and grope in the dark to find the keys."

From this loneliness, alcohol served as one escape; his books served as another. For although they could not really help him to "find" himself, Johnson discovered that he could lose himself in books. In his library he could forget the society of his own time, forget frustration, bad conscience, failed hopes, forget loneliness—his books made for him "the good place." Indeed Wilde's prophecy that certain elect spirits would in time seek their impressions not from actual life but from art had its fulfillment in Johnson almost as soon as it was made. For Johnson's "moments" were different from those described by Pater, in that they did not arise from immediate, strong sensory impressions: they were moments of sensuous, emotional, and spiritual culmination lived vicariously, at one remove from the experience itself. Other men's moments swept Johnson out of himself: "Take me with you in spirit, Ancients of Art, the crowned, the sceptred, whose voices this night chaunt a *gloria in excelsis,* flooding the soul with a passion of joy and awe."

Books carried Johnson to the past, especially the past of England in the eighteenth century, "the enchanted, the golden, the incomparable age." . . . Johnson did not read of the past in order to achieve a better understanding of the present; he did so to escape the present. In **"Oxford Nights,"** after describing his pleasure in works of the eighteenth century—books read at night while all the rest of Oxford sleeps—Johnson continues:

> Dream, who love dreams! forget all grief:
> Find, in sleep's nothingness, relief:
> Better my dreams! Dear, human books,
> What kindly voices, winning looks!
> Enchaunt me with your spells of art,
> And draw me homeward to your heart:
> Till weariness and things unkind
> Seem but a vain and passing wind.

Even the Rhymers' Club served Johnson as an elaborate daydream. Arthur Symons thought of the Club's meetings as pale and ineffectual imitations of Bohemian gatherings in the Latin Quarter, but to Johnson they were re-enactments of the Friday meetings of Samuel Johnson's Club. If they were subdued and gray re-enactments, so much the better; the mind might then be freer to envisage the past and to enjoy its melancholy difference from the present. (pp. 89-93)

Related to Johnson's flight to the literary past is his constant returning to his own youth, not the childhood spent with his family—not even were he to simplify it by dreams would he be part of that world—but his youth at Winchester:

> A place of friends! a place of books
> A place of good things olden!
> With these delights, the years were golden;
>   And life wore sunny looks. . . .

The mourning of youth and its recollection as a period without struggle, without consciousness of self within or responsibility without, is a major theme in Johnson's poems. . . . (p. 94)

And yet, according to the pattern set by Rossetti's artistic isolation and by Pater's cultured retirement in Oxford, a total rejection of life could appear almost noble. Thus when Johnson describes J. C. Mangan's life as one of "dreams and misery, and madness, yet of a self-pity which does not disgust us, and of a weakness which is innocent," when he says that Mangan's was "the haunted enchanted life of one drifting through his days in other days and other worlds, golden and immortal," he intends a high compliment—the compliment of identification, and the recognition as well that Mangan is living by the code: in artistic terms he has kept himself unspotted from the world. And Johnson's air of high lineage may well have come from his interior sense that he too was doing so: Newman's gentleman, Arnold's man of culture, Rossetti's true artist, Pater's scholar, Wilde's individualist, each represents a very different vision of the good life; nevertheless, out of each of them

it is possible to extract a single common element: an isolated pursuit of and pleasure in a beauty which the mass of men cannot enjoy or even undnerstand, a beauty caught momentarily in one's own fantasies. Johnson extracted that element and lived by it to his great unhappiness.

Lord Francis Russell, describing Johnson's influence upon him, writes: "He taught me a lesson I have never forgotten, and that is that all the supposedly real things of life, that is to say the external things, the physical things, the humours, the happenings, disgraces, successes, failures are in themselves the merest phantoms and illusions, and that the only realities are within one's own mind and spirit. " Finding nothing in society which he could "love or believe in," Johnson turned his gaze upon himself, but that created "a torment of perpetual self-consciousness" from which he had to escape if he were not to end in "an unnatural state of mind." His escape was fantasy, and so, paradoxically, the "realities of his own mind and spirit" became illusions, daydreams which eventually destroyed what had been a clear mind, a disciplined intelligence. (p. 95)

> *Barbara Charlesworth, "Lionel Johnson," in her* Dark Passages: The Decadent Consciousness in Victorian Literature, *The University of Wisconsin Press, 1965, pp. 81-95.*

DEREK STANFORD (essay date 1970)

[*Stanford is an English literary critic, poet, and biographer known for his insightful studies of nineteenth- and twentieth-century authors. His special area of critical interest is the art and literature of the 1890s. In the following excerpt, Stanford discusses Johnson's literary criticism in relation to the Decadent movement of the 1890s.*]

The charge of decadence levelled at Johnson—decadence as referring, not to some defect of constitution, but the elaborate and conscious espousal of a cult of the abnormal in literature—is easily answered from his own writings.

No nineteenth-century critic held in higher honour literary craftmanship than did Johnson; but artistry, as he understood it (the consummate means to the worthy end), and verbal virtuosity as the aesthetes pursued it (a self-regarding preciousness) were quite antithetical notions. 'Style,' he wrote, in an essay on Kipling, 'the perfection of workmanship, we cannot do without that; but still less can we endure the dexterous and polished imitation of that.'

Of the literary psychology behind the 'decadence', Johnson had much that was pertinent to say. 'There are plenty of reasons,' he declared, 'why literature should be in a somewhat unsatisfactory state: but the chief reason is surely too much ignorance of the past, an unreflecting concentration upon the present, and a morbid haste to anticipate the future. Able men commit follies of taste in style and idea which are incompatible with a willing study of the old masters, and of the old writers who came worthily after them. Many a dull book written a hundred years ago, is better reading than many a popular book of our time: for its faults are faults on the right side. There are living today [1891] men capable of the finest work, but lacking humility, patience, reverence, three forms of one inestimable spirit.'

In the same essay he speaks of the young 'decadent' poet who refuses to refuel himself from the wells of tradition as 'my friend of self-sustaining and self-devouring genius'—a statement pre-dating T. S. Eliot's counsel concerning the 'nearly indispensable nature of "the historical sense" for anyone who would continue to be a poet beyond his twenty-fifth year'.

To the 'decadent contention of the essential amorality of the masterpiece', Johnson replied that 'So long as art proceeds from, and appeals to, men of a whole and harmonious nature, art must express that wholeness and that harmony: an artist is forbidden by the facts of his natural structure to dissociate his ethics from his aesthetics: as well might he try to live by bread alone, without exercising reason, or by reason alone, not eating bread.'

It was, no doubt, these elements of traditionalism, of intellectual moralism and formal discipline, which led Paul Elmer More, one year after Johnson's death, to speak of him as 'the one writer' among 'the little band of Gaelic enthusiasts . . . who held his genius in perfect control' [see excerpt dated 1903].

But though the elaboration of Johnson's principles as a critic (best seen in the first chapter of his book on Thomas Hardy), show him as far removed from the chief artistic concerns of the Decadents and the Symbolists, by friendship and by background influence he was near enough to them for his judgment not to spring from misunderstanding. There was, for example, Johnson's great and abiding admiration for Pater whose *Marius the Epicurean* he described as 'a book to love and worship'. 'It is Johnson's opinion,' writes Barbara Charlesworth, 'that Pater's scholarship, taste and prose style made him the final authority and arbiter of critical taste for his time.'

But if Johnson was aware of Pater's points of strength, he must have registered likewise his near scepticism and the melancholy fascination which he felt for philosophies of flux. As it was, Johnson possessed an antidote to the dark side of Pater in another author—*an author of belief*. 'Certainly, to the present writer,' he confessed, 'the thirty-six volumes of Newman, from the most splendid and familiar passages down to their slightest and most occasional note, are better known than anything else in any literature and language.'

'This is an age,' wrote Johnson, 'of greater sensiblity, more governed by the emotions and desires, than any other; literature abounds with sick and morbid beauty; everywhere men are drifting from one philosophy of doubt to another, aware of their own futility, and tired of all thought and action. . . . To such an age comes Newman, and sets forth a solution and a cure. Not, as some have said, an anodyne or opiate; because Newman's method has a logical consistency, though it may not be the logic of the sciences.'

It was Pater, one may say, who provided Johnson with the key to an understanding of his contemporaries; but it was Newman who imparted to him the means of rightly assessing them. (pp. 193-95)

There is no better brief assessment of Lionel Johnson's colleagues and contemporaries than the notes which he sent in 1895 to Katherine Tynan for a talk she was to give in Ireland on the younger British poets. . . . If he is severe on Arthur Symons—whose amoral impressionism he disliked and whose verse declarations of free-love he parodied in *A Decadent's Lyric*—he is equally critical of William Watson's pseudo-traditionalism, which one might think would have met with his approval: 'An almost unfailing dignity of *external* manners; and always an attempt at *internal* gravity and greatness. . . . An understudy, as actors say, of the great man . . . capable of deceiving you for a time by his air of being the true master

instead of a very serious and accomplished substitute. . . . Read Wordsworth's *Ode to Duty*, and Watson vanishes.'

Johnson's significance as a critic might be considered under three heads: historical, theological, and intrinsic. For literary history, his importance resides largely in his opposing the currents of relaxed thought and style in the verse and prose of the 'nineties, and in resisting the fashionable 'decadent' flux. Because of his more intellectual cast of mind he saw the connection between a fluid phenomenalism ('"the flowing philosophers" to whom life is a drifting and a change') and sensationalism, and firmly repudiated them both.

The value and importance of Johnson for a Christian criticism of literature is that he pre-eminently possessed the gift of imaginative charity to supplement and, at times, temper the hard-cutting-edges of dogma. In this light, he has a good claim to be considered as the first Catholic critic of the nineteenth century writing in England.

Thirdly, his value lies in the potentially perennial pleasure which his writings open to us: their felicity of composition, their genial and courteous reflectiveness, the relish in literary good manners which they so readily attest. 'To have committed regularly to paper a criticism of literature so eminently literative in itself, is to have fulfilled, in a way quite other than its author intended, what Oscar Wilde campaigned for in his phrase "the critic as artist".' (pp. 195-96)

> *Derek Stanford, in an introduction to "Friends that Fail Not," in* Critics of the 'Nineties, *edited by Derek Stanford, 1970. Reprint by Roy Publishers Inc., 1971, pp. 191-96.*

GARY H. PATERSON   (essay date 1973)

[*In the following excerpt, Paterson discusses the importance of religious thought in Johnson's life and writings.*]

While at Oxford in the 1880's, the philosopher George Santayana received the following letter of introduction about one of his younger contemporaries: "[Johnson] is the man I most admire and—in the world, knows every book that is, transcendentalist, genius, and is called affected. The way for you to treat him is to take no notice when he tries (as he will) to shock you. If he discourses, listen: it will be worthwhile." From the memoirs of people who knew him while at Oxford and, indeed, much later in the nineties, one gathers that the first impression of Lionel Johnson is the shock of discovering such tremendous erudition in such a delicately youthful looking person. (p. 95)

The description of Johnson as transcendentalist in the extract quoted provides a clue to his aesthetic interests. "Transcendental" is not exactly, perhaps, the correct word to describe Johnson's temperament as it is expressed in his writings; rather, "mystical"—the mixture, as he once indicated in an article, of Celtic idealism and Germanic metaphysics that are combined in the English people—might be more appropriate. The strain of mysticism, he said, has produced "a literature full of strangeness and propensity, of thought quivering with emotion", a description that adequately describes some of Johnson's best poetry.

To be sure, it has been argued that Johnson's art is anything but emotional. Ezra Pound once wrote that the impression of Johnson's verse "is that of small slabs of ivory, firmly combined and contrived. There is a constant feeling of neatness, a sense of inherited order. Above all he respected his art'' [see excerpt dated 1915]. Even his speech, according to his contemporary, Arthur Waugh, was carefully, unemotionally ordered: "Certainly he was the first man of my own age that I encountered who picked his words, and talked with any sense of form." And yet, in spite of all this classical reserve there is, especially in his religious poetry, a deep sense of loneliness in the struggles of this life, which is expressed in terms of the most poignant emotionalism. A famous example will suffice here:

> I fight thee, in the Holy Name!
> Yet, what thou dost, is what God saith:
> Tempter! should I escape thy flame,
> Thou wilt have helped my soul from Death.

Johnson's transcendentalism, idealism, mysticism, anti-materialism—the terms do converge, perhaps—is one valid approach to his religious attitudes. He shared the decadents' hatred of mammonism, progress, action, and philistia, returning in a kind of dream-like escape via literature and art to the Middle Ages and, more particularly, to the eighteenth century. But, as will be shown, there were other influences at work upon him, notably Arnold's humanism and theory of culture, and the writings of Newman and Pater.

The first substantial record of Lionel Johnson's thoughts appears in the volume of letters published in 1919 called *Some Winchester Letters of Lionel Johnson.* These letters, written between 1883 and 1885, while Johnson was between the ages of sixteen and eighteen, illustrate the variety of influences and currents of thought that were the substance of undergraduate discussion at that time. It might be argued that the letters, due to Johnson's age, ought not to be weighed too heavily, and indeed the capriciousness of his opinions from letter to letter indicates the flexibility of his mind. On the other hand, several themes recur—notably, his desire to become a priest and his admiration for the humanity of such figures as Christ, Shelley, Browning, and Whitman.

What one notices most immediately in the *Winchester Letters,* however, is the trait of Johnson's that had impressed Lord Russell in his letter to Santayana—"transcendentalism". Early letters show that in Johnson's attraction to Buddhism, there is a concern for the needs of humanity and the necessity of finding a religion in which there is the sense of sharing or communion among its members. A typical letter to Russell, written 14 October 1883, points out the tension in Johnson between his own attraction to "idealistic" and "popular" religion:

> To come to the real subject. I quite feel the sense of power and nobility in the Buddhist system; but it revolts me. I could not find any rest in a religion that required arithmetic and scientific knowledge. I have read carefully the first eight chapters of Sinnett's *Esoteric Buddhism* . . . My position of mind with regard to them is this; I quite believe that the Powers, etc., they assume are real, that their lives are high in ideal; but that religion must be popular, not scientific. Were I alone in the world such a life of abnegation and purity and absorption of self into duty would be the ideal for me; but think of the people you meet every day, and then of that system! . . . I have an idea that religion must vary under various circumstances; let the East keep its lofty ideals, and

the West a simpler Christianity. I hate the very thought of degrees in religious questions; I hate the idea of anyone patronizing me, whether the head of the adepts, or an Evangelical parson. I have nothing to say against the religion of Buddha; it is an extremely noble one; but, as I said before, it repels, chills me. I would rather be a Roman Catholic.

Even after his felicitous discovery of Nirvana, Johnson's opinions remain essentially unchanged. His concern for humanity is particularly significant in these letters and his delight in a religion that can be shared by many people as they worship together is mentioned several times.

It is not surprising, therefore, that he expresses his admiration for the humanism of Matthew Arnold. Early in the *Winchester Letters* (7 October 1883), he declares his ambition "to turn out a kind of Matthew Arnold in a more professedly 'religious' way; *i.e.,* combine the position of a man of letters with that of a quasi-religious lecturer." For a time, while he was in a mood of despondency in his search for a satisfactory form of religion, he looked to Arnold for light, albeit insufficient: "In the meantime, what Matthew Arnold calls 'morality' and 'conduct' will be a half-guide."

The humanism of Arnold and of Whitman, who is often revered in the latter pages of the *Winchester Letters,* along with Shelley, were important influences upon the young Lionel Johnson. He recognized the need for some communication outside the self, some connexion with society. On 15 May 1885, he wrote to Russell, "I am very self-confident and independent of others' opinions; but I cannot live without their companionship and love. Isolation is easy enough: but it is not good to be alone." But Johnson was no social prophet in the sense that Carlyle and Ruskin were. The concern for humanity in his early letters is manifest and remained throughout his life, but it was a concern that did not find expression in practical courses and systematic schemes for social reform. What appears far more often—and this is the impression that is most commonly associated with Johnson—is his yearning to be far from the bustle of London, alone in his rooms heavily hung with gray corduroy, with his books and dreams of an imagined past.

In matters of religion, one finds in the *Winchester Letters* that fundamentally, Johnson puts his faith in Christianity rather than in agnosticism or paganism, for in the Christian Church he finds an attempt to affirm once again the state of harmony in the world that had been broken by the Fall. To J. H. Badley, he writes as follows:

> Mankind by nature (i.e., in Eden—vide Genesis) was harmonious: harmony was broken by discord, 'that harmony might be prized': hence the social aims and propaganda of love, either red dabbled with blood or thin with ghostly dearth, fade away, pass into the past: but the great unity of Christianity is the return to that state wherin life was one orchestra of sympathies, near to the feet of God: or, before love met with ugliness.

The *Winchester Letters* show Johnson to be ill at ease with the middle-class Anglicanism he had inherited from his parents and, while he turns now to Buddhism, now to agnosticism, one notices a sympathy for and attraction toward the Roman Church. On 19 May 1884, he writes, "I will be—no! am now— a priest because I take the priesthood for my office in the world . . . And truly so: for my own nature leads me thitherward almost to Ultramontanism.''

The submission to Rome, however, did not come for another six years. In the meantime, he consolidated his religious opinions and attitudes toward the Catholic Church. In *Bishop Blougram's Apology,* by his great favourite, Browning, he found little to quarrel with. The intensity of individual worship was attractive to his mystical tendencies as evidenced by the following: ''Do realize the 'beauty of holiness' in the Catholic sense: the beauty of ecstatic worship: you will find it one of the nearest approaches permitted to the ideal Beauty of Plato.''

The mention of ''intensity of individual worship'' leads very naturally to the next great influence upon Johnson's religious attitudes, the person and writings of Walter Pater. On 15 March 1885, Johnson wrote to Lord Francis Russell, ''I am revelling in Pater's book: full of the most perfect literary quality, and infinitely wise and true and beautiful.'' *Marius the Epicurean* remained a favourite of Johnson's throughout his life. In an article Johnson described Pater's method of ''didacticism'' as follows:

> Little incidents and contrasts, touched with the deftest tact, convey the 'moral'. Marius is not, in fact, converted, though his death was 'full of grace'. Yet the sweetness and greatness of Christianity steal over him, as over the reader, as though the writer 'willed' if almost without words; whilst it is through his austere delicacy in using them that the miracle is worked upon us.

While he is praising Pater here, his use of the words ''sweetness'' and ''delicacy'' offers a clue to what Johnson finds appealing in Pater's portrayal of early Christianity. ''Sweetness'' suggests feeling, and more particularly pleasurable sensation, which is an important part in Johnson's attraction to Catholicism. Like Pater, Lionel Johnson found immense satisfaction in the pictorial and sensory aspects of the Catholic ritual. To Campbell Dodgson, on 15 April 1889 (two years before his conversion), we have the following: ''On Passion Sunday I saw the mass of Deposition at the Pro-Cathedral: a lovely sight, with the immense blaze of wax tapers and a crowd of bishops.''

But Pater's influence upon Johnson was much deeper than merely the appreciation of the sensory elements of ritual. In Pater's wrtings, which might have been interpreted by some as mere encouragement to sensationalism, Johnson found a key to transcendentalism:

> In all this mode of seeing things, and of undergoing their influence, the inflowing of their spirit, there is a mysticism not unlike Swedenborg's doctrine of 'celestial correspondence': or that mystical interpretation of nature so necessary to Newman; as when he says of the angels: 'Every breath of air and ray of light and heat, every beautiful prospect is, as it were, the skirts of their garments, the waving of the robes of those whose faces see God in Heaven': so to speak, a sacramental and symbolic theory of the universe, which *Spiritus intus alit:* whereby, as Mr. Pater has it, 'all the acts and accidents of daily life borrow a sacred colour and significance.'

Lionel Johnson was quick to notice the more austere side of Pater and his notion of *ascesis.* In an article entitled ''Mr. Pater and His Public'', he describes this tendency as follows:

> The athlete, whether of Greek games or of philosophic study, or of religious passion, or of artistic devotion, was ever an image dear to Mr. Pater; asceticism, in its literal and widest sense, the pruning away of superfluities, the just development or training of essentials, the duty of absolute discipline, appealed to him as a thing of price in this very various world.

Submission or the attempt at submission to rigorous discipline was closely bound up with Johnson's daily life from the days of the *Winchester Letters* to his death. The accounts of his struggles to maintain a nightly fast and vigil lest he succumb to the urge to drink from the ever-present whiskey bottle at his bedside have been told to us by Iain Fletcher. Much of Johnson's religious poetry is concerned with his struggle against the two-fold Dark Angel in his life, alcoholism and homosexuality. The search for some kind of ordering influence in his life, especially when it came from Pater—whose notions of Beauty and Art he admired so much—were particularly appealing to Lionel Johnson's temperament. It should be noticed, finally, that in the many-faceted personality of his master, in the subtle humour of his writing, Johnson found in Pater, in the company of Newman and Arnold, ''the secret of that ideal delicacy and graciousness, to which 'that sweet city with her dreaming spires' can minister so well.''

The influence of Newman is fundamental in the religious life of Lionel Johnson. Although he is seldom mentioned by name in the *Winchester Letters* and in other letters after 1885, there is much in the tone of Johnson's writing, in his discussions about Catholicism *vs.* Anglicanism, in his attitude toward the Roman Church that derives from Newman. In the introduction of his edition of Johnson's letters, Rev. Raymond Roseliep writes as follows concerning the relation of Pater and Newman to Johnson's Catholicism:

> But it was Pateresque 'ritual' that above all gave Johnson a compass to direct the needs of his own temperament: and though ritual to the master meant a system of thought, to the disciple it was a way of life. That way of life he rooted sincerely in Newman's sterner dogma, which was eventually to give him security in the faith Newman himself had freely chosen.

The ''sterner dogma'' of Newman is also associated in Johnson with ''strictness of conscience''. Comparing Socrates with Newman, Johnson writes, in an article on Pater, '''I want to make you anxious about our souls,' was the appeal of Cardinal Newman to his hearers. 'I want to make you interested in your souls,' was the appeal of Socrates.''

In his essay on Newman, Johnson attempted to examine the personality of Newman by suggesting that he possessed psychological insight together with definite and rigid moral principles: again the notion of the strict conscience is suggested. By combining the moral certainties of Newman's faith with the discipline of Pater's *ascesis,* Johnson was able to achieve, in theory at least, some ordering element in his life.

A more significant debt to Newman was Johnson's reliance, for the most part, upon Newman's arguments for the validity of the Catholic Church as opposed to the Anglican. Like Newman, Johnson argued that one must look to the primitive Christian Church to find valid orders and the true Apostolic succession and that if the early heresies were not valid, then neither could the Anglican Church be so considered. (pp. 95-102)

In an important and lengthy letter to Campbell Dodgson written on 30 August 1888, significantly enough, three years before his conversion, Johnson bases his arguments on behalf of the Catholic faith on Newman's reasoning. His remarks were made in answer to Dodgson's suggestion that "if the Anglican Church is a true portion of the Roman Catholic . . . no member of it can be justified in leaving it". Johnson retorts by upholding the view that the Catholic Church must be seen in its totality, that corruptions set in within the primitive Christian Church, that the Nestorians, Arians, Donatists, and Monophysites possessed orders as valid as the Anglicans. The letter, which should be quoted at length, is an extremely important one for several reasons. It illustrates the place of Newman in the consolidation of Johnson's religious beliefs in the years preceding his conversion; it proves that Johnson's attraction to thè Church was not merely emotional or part of a pose, but rather, a definitely sincere and reasoned attempt to reach out for truth in the matter of religion. His final settlement in Rome rests, as he admits, upon an admission of faith and an acceptance of the Roman supremacy as "dogma second only to the Holy Eucharist". (p. 103)

Johnson's religion was definitely a central part of his life. He was not, as Santayana has pointed out, "a traditional Catholic, accepting goodnaturedly a supernatural economy that happened to prevail in the universe, as political and domestic economy prevail in one's earthly fortunes." Of all the aesthetes who dallied with religion in the 'nineties, Johnson was—with the possible exception of John Gray—the most intellectually precise in his religious attitudes. It is ironical that such a mind could produce some of the most emotionally expressive religious poetry of the decade. (p. 106)

> Gary H. Paterson, "The Religious Thought of Lionel Johnson," in The Antigonish Review, No. 13, Spring, 1973, pp. 95-109.

JAMES G. NELSON (essay date 1974)

[*Nelson is an American critic and educator. In the following excerpt, he discusses the ways in which Johnson's life and work exemplify an aesthetic experience of the type that Walter Pater described as born of "impassioned contemplation" and detachment from the world.*]

[One] kind of aesthetic experience which is encountered in the poetry of the nineties derives its specific nature from the writings and life-style of Pater. In his essays, imaginary portraits, and the novel, *Marius the Epicurean*, Pater seems to sanction a life of detachment, a life lived within a hieratic circle of *objets d'art*, books, paintings, etc.—a life consecrated to what he called in his "Wordsworth" essay "Impassioned contemplation." The Paterian aesthete or culture-observer who emerged was at times like Wilde's Lord Henry [in *The Picture of Dorian Gray*] who from his own cooly aloof sphere of observation relished what Professor De Laura (in reference to the Paterian aesthete) has termed the "aesthetic patterning in the life of the world about him," a world which for a time has its focus the beautiful and fascinating Dorian Gray. Others locked themselves away in rooms and protected themselves from the world by windows and walls draped as in the case of Lionel Johnson with gray corduroy curtains. Detached and set apart, they sought

Holograph of the first page of the manuscript of Johnson's last poem, "Walter Pater," completed a few days before his death.

to attain their moments of impassioned contemplation through an intimacy with the thoughts and ideas of the great minds of antiquity, and the actions of the great and lofty souls of the past.

In appearance a delicate, handsome boy of fifteen, Johnson shied away from what seemed to him the crass and feverish world of his day, losing himself in books, a small group of literary friends, and his dreams of more comely ages—the Athens of Plato, the world of the medieval church, the reign of Charles I. In answer to Yeats's question of why he kept aloof from men and women, Johnson replied, "In my library I have all the knowledge of the world that I need." Shut away in his rooms, Johnson existed in a realm apart—a calm, serene atmosphere befitting one who entertained of a night such revered personages as Plato. Fearful not only of the world but also of his own weaknesses, Johnson created for his edification images of order and strength, proof against the assaults of whatever made for disorder and imperfection. Like Arnold, he idolized the great men of the past who in the midst of a world frightening and disheartening in its turmoil and disharmony remained calm and serene in their steadiness of purpose.

The aesthetically edifying experience of impassioned contemplation is beautifully exemplified in several of Johnson's finest and most characteristic poems such as **"Plato in London,"** in which the poet invited Plato into the cloistered atmosphere of his own room. Like a priest ministering before the altar, Johnson invokes the philosopher divine. . . . Essentially a poem in which the poet plays off London, a modern Sodom and Gomorrah, against images of order—Athens, Plato's "own city of high things," and "the calm stars, in their living skies"—and reason—Plato who "shows to us, and brings, / Truth of fine gold"—**"Plato in London"** expresses Johnson's sense of an order inherent in the universe which denies the "noise and glare" of the world. His sense of reverence for Plato reflects his devotion to those who were able to "possess their souls" (as Arnold expressed it) and create for themselves a reasonable, serene, and comely life. . . . That Johnson found comfort and joy in such images, whether they be men of the past like Plato or men of the present like Newman and Pater, is further borne out by his portrait of Charles I in his most famous poem, **"By the Statue of King Charles at Charing Cross."** Left alone with his thoughts and night, the poet meditates upon the martyred king who had come to be revered as a saint by Johnson and the ardent advocates of the Anglo-Catholic movement. An alienated artist figure who, like Rossetti's James I, was thrust into a life of action against his will, Johnson's Charles rises above the "world" through the cultivation of his aesthetic temperament. Alone and aloof, "the fair and fatal king" rides on through "London's gloom," bringing grace to those who faint from weariness, "vexed in the world's employ." Through "the splendid silence" of the night, "the saddest of all kings / Crowned, and again discrowned," Charles emerges as the very image of the "Passionate tragedy" of those who in the cause of art, beauty, and high-mindedness are martyred by the world. Arnoldian in its elegiac tone, **"By the Statue of King Charles"** represents Johnson at his best. Like the face of Charles, his verse is often "stern / With sweet austerity," conveying as it does a quiet and solemn intensity of vision and emotion, the fruits of his moments of impassioned contemplation. (pp. 229-31)

James G. Nelson, "The Nature of Aesthetic Experience in the Poetry of the Nineties: Ernest Dowson, Lionel Johnson, and John Gray," in English Literature in Transition, *Vol. 17, No. 4, 1974, pp. 223-32.*

NORMAN ALFORD (essay date 1980)

[*Alford is an English fiction writer and critic. In the following excerpt from his book-length study of the poets of the Rhymers' Club, he examines Johnson's poetry and criticism.*]

At the age of sixteen and a half, Lionel Johnson wrote from Winchester College to Francis Russell (later 2nd Earl Russell) who anonymously edited the letters from which I quote:

College,
October 7, 1883.

. . . I have not the smallest wish to go into the Church; but my choice of a career is limited to that and literature; to tell you the truth, I should like to burst upon the astonished world as a poet; there you have the height of my ambition. Somewhat conceited, is it not? but the amount of poetry, if I may use the word, that I have already perpetrated, would fill a respectable volume. I should like to turn out a kind of Matthew Arnold in a more professedly 'religious' way; i.e., combine the position of a man of letters with that of a quasi-religious lecturer. The only reason I should have for taking Orders

would be the intense desire of getting hold of some of the rotten old pulpits occupied by dotards and exploding some more sensible and higher doctrines than any I have yet heard; but the explosion might bring the Church down about my ears. People of a certain class might accept from a 'priest' teaching they would reject from a layman. Still, I never really think the Church will be my destination.

Why do people want dogmas, and refuse to live without abstruse creeds? and why do they want to know everything, when they are quite as happy in reverent ignorance? I never felt the want of definite creeds, or of an anthropomorphic Saviour; I don't understand the need of them. If you want a powerful anti-clerical defense of the Godhead of Jesus, read Browning's 'Christmas Eve and Easter Day'; it is quite plain, and very powerfully put; the best thing about it being, that it leaves you to think what you like, without inflicting Church doctrine upon you . . .

This letter, the first in the collection referred to, is as representative as any. Johnson never really changed his point of view. He did indeed, in later life, 'combine the position of a man of letters with that of a quasi-religious lecturer'—that was precisely the role which he was to fulfil for the remainder of his days. Reading the letters we observe his constant demand for some form of transcendentalism—does it matter what form it takes? To Johnson, of course, it did seem to matter. His reverence for Arnold influenced his thought and his verse permanently. But his desire to be 'a kind of Matthew Arnold in a more professedly "religious" way' betrayed his separateness from Arnold. With Arnold, culture, as T. S. Eliot has written, tended to usurp the place of religion. Johnson wished to put the religion back by means of what, copying Orwell's term, we may call 'double-think.' Far from reconciling Christianity with 'Aestheticism,' Johnson made one subserve the other according to his fancy or state of mind at the time. This conflict, leading as it did to moral tensions, appeared in his personal poems such as **'Dark Angel'**; it explained the contrast between, say, **'A Dream of Youth'** and **'Dominica in Palmis,'** and was most explicit, perhaps, in **'To a Passionist'**. . . . (pp. 107-08)

The emergence of the latent conflicts in the poet, between aestheticism and Christianity and morality gave rise to some of the most striking poems of his entire work. One might say that the repressed youth of Winchester and Oxford had very little to write *about*. The inspiration was essentially bookish. That is not, of course, a condemnation or even a necessarily pejorative reflection but is an explanation of why much minor verse *is* minor verse. Johnson's 'personal' poetry is the more moving, then, because it is expressing such an internal conflict. Weygandt wrote that Johnson's verse had 'the dignity and sonorousness of Browne, the tenderness of Otway, the melancholy and evening light of Collins.' But he also wrote:

In body Lionel Johnson was never more than a child, and there is, I think, something of that hardness of heart and narrowness of sympathy which lack of knowledge of the world preserves in children.

Of the Rhymers, Johnson seems to have possessed the most acute mind. It is in the choice of application of his powers that he seems fallible. I can see Mr. Iain Fletcher's point that there was no-one, in the 'nineties, able 'to make an intellectual situation of which the creative power might profitably avail itself' [see excerpt dated 1951]. This was the major function which Arnold had believed that critics should fulfil. To propose Pater for the role, as one might, is to invite the question: Did he create an *intellectual* situation? With regard to Pater's disciple, Johnson, I agree with Mr. Fletcher when he says: 'With him an unco-ordinated mental curiosity usurps the place of "a conscience in intellectual matters."'' For example we may take Johnson's periodical pieces, collected in *Post Liminium,* which range from Boswell to Pater, from Parnell to Marie Bashkirtseff. Such a range would be admirable if some kind of connection were discoverable between the various pieces or if some common pattern of experience enabled the illumination of one writer by another. But there is little or no connection.

One cannot say that Johnson influenced the world of letters in any major way by his criticism, as one can say, for example, of Arnold that he countered the eccentricity and insularity of the English genius, encouraging restraint; or, of T. S. Eliot, that he initiated a revaluation of writers by a careful analysis of the exact sense of their works and of the relation between the form and the content. Arnold had insisted that for true appreciation of art it is necessary 'to get one's self out of the way.' Art is not a substitute for life but a means to a fuller understanding of it. The Pateran Aesthetes obliterated the distinction between art and life:

> . . . They wanted life to be art—in other words, they wanted a life purged of all its coarse, vulgar, trivial elements. Accordingly they turned away in life from all its inartistic elements. Where the poet's primary impulse may be said to be a 'religious' one, the attempt to grapple with experience and to find other and significance in it, and his artistic impulse only secondary, a continuation of the same impulse—the desire to embody and transmit his vision—the aesthetes made a religion out of art. They inverted the order of the creative mind and relegated the dynamic 'religious' principle to the periphery, where it became immobilized and nullified.
> [D. S. Savage, "The Aestheticism of W. B. Yeats."]

This attitude involved,

> . . . that relativity in religion and morals, that distillation of intellectual essences into tenuous sentiment—even the most intractably logical subject might be dissipated into pure feeling—so characteristic of all Pater's writing.
> [Iain Fletcher]

In Johnson's poetry, the subjectivity of the poet is such that he often fails to communicate with the reader. The rhetoric is that of the closet drama which takes place within the solitary's skull—all excitement within but odd and disquieting, often merely dull, in the form in which it is communicated. As Santayana wrote, '. . . after reading him through you are aware of a great wind of passionate language, but not of what was said or of what it was all about. . . . [The] absence of all foundations, of all concreteness, of all distinction between fiction and truth, makes his poetry indigestible' [see excerpt dated 1945].

The quality above all which makes some of his poems memorable is their music. They remind us of the importance which the Rhymers attached to reading verse aloud. We shall search in vain for compression, for the striking image or confrontation in his verse. At his best there is a rain-washed clarity of description and statement, often descending to the merely prosaic but, when successful, impressive in its neatness and grace. **'Dead'** is, I think, a fine example of prosodic virtuosity and illustrates the qualities I have been describing:

> In Merioneth, over the sad moor
>   Drives the rain, the cold wind blows:
> Past the ruinous church door,
> The poor procession without music goes.
> Lonely she wandered out her hour, and died.
>   Now the mournful curlew cries
>   Over her, laid down beside
> Death's lonely people: lightly down she lies.
> In Merioneth, the wind lives and wails,
>   On from hill to lonely hill:
>   Down the loud, triumphant gales,
> A spirit cries *Be strong!* and cries *Be still!*
>
> (pp. 116-18)

Born in happier days Johnson might have lived to a serene age, fulfilling his chosen function. The ideals he cherished, however, took no account of times and seasons, of the new industrial society, of the increasing democratization of the people. With a little more humour and common humanity he might have effected some kind of compromise with the modern world. Perhaps it is to his refusal or inability to be aware of it that we owe his verse. But the classical virtues of wholeness, sanity, harmony were not only in the mind and were certainly not the perquisite of small communities of recluses. At best the 'nineties could produce excellent imitations—but the spirit of Johnson was in conflict, not in harmony—he was indeed 'the victim of his own inspiration.' (pp. 119-20)

> *Norman Alford, "Lionel Johnson," in his* The Rhymers' Club, *Cormorant Press, 1980, pp. 107-20.*

R. K. R. THORNTON (essay date 1983)

[*In the following excerpt, Thornton discusses Johnson in the context of the Decadent movement of the 1890s.*]

[Three traditions]—Celticism, Catholicism and the Classics—are the subject and part of the nature of many of [Johnson's] best poems, and they are his props when inspiration fails. If at times the poems read like hollow exercises, they are never less than skilful, and at his best his work rises to an austere perfection. The purity of this perfection lies to a large extent in Johnson's abandoning argument for sound, preferring what Yeats calls 'pure poetry' to a poetry of discursiveness and argument about history and politics. When Yeats describes in *Autobiographies* how Johnson and Horne 'imposed their personalities' on the Rhymers' Club, he makes a comment that is echoed more than once in his work: 'I saw . . . that Swinburne in one way, Browning in another, and Tennyson in a third, had filled their work with what I called 'impurities,' curiosities about politics, about science, about history, about religion; and that we must create once more the pure work.' Johnson uses the same antithesis in his impressive speech on **'Poetry and Patriotism in Ireland'** which is printed in *Post Liminium* . . . ; the poet writes, let us say, dreams and all manner of imaginative things, in plaintive, lovely cadences, about the faeries, or about the mysteries of the world, birth and life and death, writing out of the depths of his own nature; and lo! instead of being grateful, we abuse him for not writing historical ballads, valiant and national, upon Patrick Sarsfield or Owen Roe.

It is his own poetry that he is describing.

Other writers escaped 'impurities' and 'curiosities' in impressionistic visual detail. Indeed when Pound wrote that Johnson could not be shown to be 'in accord with our present [1915] doctrines and ambitions' he admitted that 'no one has written purer Imagisme than he has in the line "Clear lie the fields, and fade into blue air' [see excerpt dated 1915]. But the colour of such lines, or indeed whole poems like **'In England'** . . . is not what we come to expect from Johnson; he evokes a mood and a music, and if it is colourless and cold it is because he restrains his use of description, limits to a small range his similes and metaphors, and concerns himself with music both as subject and principle of construction. When Johnson writes of Byron, another essay from *Post Liminium,* he prefers Byron the satirist as many modern critics do, but denies that the satire is poetry.

> Byron could shout magnificently, laugh splendidly, thunder tumultuously; but he could not sing. There was something in him of Achilles, nothing whatever of Apollo. Think only of these mighty masters of passion, Aeschylus, Lucretius, Dante, Milton, Hugo; what sweetness proceeding from what strength! They are filled with a lyrical loveliness, the very magic of music, the beauty almost unbearable. By the side of these Byron is but a brazen noise.

'Pure poetry' and music are obviously the same thing. . . . Johnson makes another contrast of the architectural power of design in Hardy's novels with the music which is more proper to poetry: 'music is wont to leave but a vague sense of airy charm. That flying, elusive delight has its place in literature: but only, I think, in verse'. . . . (pp. 119-20)

It is of course no surprise that Johnson should aim for the pure poetry of music; he knew his contemporary French poetry and Verlaine's demand for 'De la musique avant toute chose' ['music above all else'] and more important for such a disciple, he knew his Pater and the claim that 'All art constantly aspires towards the condition of music.' But it is his first and foremost interest. When in **'The Dark Angel'** Johnson finds that because of his sinister enemy 'no thought, no thing / Abides for me undesecrate', the first thing he mentions is the bringing down of the uncontaminated quality of music to a sensual level:

> When music sounds, then changest thou
> Its silvery to a sultry fire.

'The Last Music' is a good example of Johnson's practice of capturing the vague charm and elusive delight, creating the decorous and sorrowful music rather than describing it. It is a poem which . . . has another poem behind it, . . . Robert Bridges's 'Elegy on a Lady whom Grief for the Death of her Betrothed Killed', of which Johnson had written in the *Century Guild Hobby Horse* for 1891 that 'Arnold, we find, is not the only poet of our day, who without a specious resemblance can use the ancient symbols and imageries for the stately expression

of sorrow'. But where Bridges's poem has descriptive detail and a narrative line which seems to cry out for illustration by some late Pre-Raphaelite, Johnson has no narrative and his indefinite epithets merely create a mood, almost totally unpictorial. . . . The poetry moves by an intertwining of two sets of ideas, that of music, breath, wind, and life, with that of silence, calm, and death, and achieves a balance between them not by a paradoxical reconciliation but by a continued acceptance of the restfulness of death and a vocabulary which animates the dead woman. She rests and sleeps, just as Bridges's lady goes to her lover. The whole effect is a gentle melancholy of reverence. (pp. 120-22)

[The] whole poem revolves around the idea of music which grows nearer and nearer to silence.

Repetition is the most noticeable feature of many of Johnson's poems, his **'By the Statue of King Charles at Charing Cross'**, **'To Morfydd'**, or **'The Church of a Dream'**, for example. Take the last poem. . . . Not only do we have the repetition of words, the 'Saints', 'long', 'golden vesture', 'clouds' and so on, but also a repetitive syntax that builds up the picture out of small sections some adding to, some modifying what has gone before: 'In gray, sweet incense clouds; blue sweet clouds mystical'. The effect is in a way Biblical, or at least ritualistic, not inappropriate both for the subject and for the writer who was to be for the Rhymers' Club, says Yeats, 'our critic, and above all our theologian'. . . . Indeed, Johnson's poems are sometimes cast in the form of prayers, poems like **'Guardian Angels'**, **'Friends'**, the third **'Cadgwith'** poem, or the poem **'To Leo XIII'** which strikingly recalls Hopkins's prayers for the return of England to Rome; and Johnson was in the habit of writing Latin prayers in his copies of books that had some connection with his friends. Clearly he could have been influenced by Biblical and ecclesiastical repetitions, and he could also have found examples in the medieval Latin lyrics that he knew, since his nine Latin poems show the same marked rhymes and balanced construction.

More important even than this repetition of words or motifs within the framework of a poem is his repetition of words or concepts throughout his work. One needs no concordance to see which words are frequently and deliberatley repeated: death (or dead), silence, star, moon, white, rose, music, wind, water, sea, sky, sun, dream, night, calm, fire, flame, earth, light, and soul. One can perhaps best see the importance of these words by looking at **'The Dark Angel'** and noting in what things he delights, how they are tainted and how Johnson overcomes the tempter in a heroic renunciation (more hoped for then achieved) which is firmly founded in Revelation. . . . There is a finely grandiloquent ascetic idealism [in **'The Dark Angel'**] balancing the fear of worldly corruption; and Johnson's favourite words fall fairly neatly into the two sides of the Decadent dilemma, worldly things and eternal things, with words like 'music' mediating between the two. Some of the words having a place in both groups, worldly in their literal sense, eternal in a symbolic one.

The things which stand for earthly life are traditionally those natural delights which are also changeable, emphasizing the mutability of things, sea, wind, night and day, weathers and seasons. Johnson took a great delight in the natural world in his younger days, as one can see from his description of sunrise and sunset seen from the top of Snowdon, though even there his habit of mind is to connect the night with the old myths of battle in the heavens; but nature is more a symbol than a vividly realized subject. At times nature is a consoling influence; as in the first **'Cadgwith'** poem:

> Winds rush and waters roll:
> Their strength, their beauty, brings
> Into mine heart the whole
> Magnificence of things. . . .

But the opposite is usually the case, where things eternal scorn (to use Yeats's phrase) common bird and petal, and Johnson laments the gulf between the world and one's ideals. Writing more typically of elemental forces rather than tangible objects, Johnson contrasts the impermanence of winds and waters to the stability of the stars, and sees the moon and stars relieving the blackness of night and all darkness, real and symbolic.

The moon and the stars, 'the fires of God' as Johnson calls them in one poem with a hint of Hopkins which merely emphasizes the difference between the exactly-focussing Jesuit and the Decadent who turns away from the world, mark the point where the first group of words merges into the second, where earthly becomes heavenly and spiritual. Death, as with Dowson, always hurrying near Johnson's mind, also marks the change from worldly delights to those white pure things to which he is drawn in his finest moments, where he sees the soul, perfected and made white, living eternally in the radiance of God; though the difficulties and dangers of the getting there are as important as the arrival for his verse. (pp. 122-26)

An awareness of Johnson's typical themes and movement is a great help in understanding all his poetry, but particularly those more mysterious poems which he does so well, where a vague but powerful sense of sin and threat radiates from some haunted face. **'A Stranger'** and **'Quisque Suos Manes'** are two such, which in fact clarify each other, and there are interesting comparisons to be made with Dowson's poems of division, particularly 'To One in Bedlam'. Johnson's stranger is somehow wilder and more separate than Dowson's madman. . . . There is none of the calm, sad security of Dowson's nuns, much more the haunted isolation of Johnson himelf as he separates the passing image from the essence and concentrates, with varying degrees of success, on the essence, which lives in the 'measureless consummation that he dreamed'. (pp. 127-28)

Again, the basic pattern of permanence against impermanence lies behind poems like **'To Morfydd'**, whose music has been praised, but whose meaning has been ignored:

> A voice on the winds,
> A voice by the waters,
>   Wanders and cries:
> *Oh! what are the winds?*
> *And what are the waters?*
>   *Mine are your eyes!* . . .

What Yeats called 'his only love song, his incomparable *Morfydd*' . . . is in fact no more a conventional love song than any other of Johnson's poems. It is a sort of Celtic 'Cynara,' longing for the eyes past change beyond the changeful world, and hearing hints of eternal music across the 'estranging sea' which also kept Arnold conscious of being alone. The companion poems of three and four years later, **'To Morfydd Dead'**, long for death to join him to her so that they can 'wander through the night, / Star and star', but the complex cross rhyming and sound patterning—perhaps imitated from Welsh verse—the formal and inverted syntax which provide the elegant charm of the poems, and the passionate decorum of their idealism is more in evidence than any tangible Morfydd.

The tension between real and ideal can at times be resolved with what seems a too easy choice, but in poems like **'Magic'** the choice seems not only difficult but also heroic and right. . . . The choice of images [in **'Magic'**] is not based on their pictorial quality but on their significance; the viol, the harp, the tabour, are not parts of a procession which we visualize but shorthand for a state of mind; 'Their fancies lie on flowers' does not ask for a literal imagining, and although the scornful 'ye / Lead Love in triumph through the dancing city' is clear, it is not pictorial. A comparison with Dowson's 'Cynara' reveals the same antitheses and indicates the more tangible physical realities in Dowson, but even in Dowson's poem the kisses, the wine, the dancing, the roses are much more disembodied than they might at first appear. Johnson's poem stands up well to such a comparison, since it is phrased with a fine delicacy of touch, balancing long and short words, long line against short line, developed argument against brief assertion, in musical and stately cadences. It was perhaps this poem that Yeats remembered in 'The Grey Rock' when he addressed his 'Companions of the Cheshire Cheese':

> you may think I waste my breath
> Pretending that there can be passion
> That has more life in it than death.

Johnson did indeed have a passionate yearning for eternity.

It would be a mistake to leave Johnson seeming quite as detached as I have suggested. He had, among his unworldly passions, other loves, as he wrote in **'To the Saints'**:

> Here upon earth a many loves I know,—
> Of friends, and of a country wed to woe;
> Of the high Muses; of wild wind, pure snow;
>
> Of heartening sun, exhilarating sea.

To his love of literature, Ireland and nature, one must add therefore his love of friends, for he had something of Yeats's genius for friendship and his consciousness that 'my glory was I had such friends'. His two poems called **'A Friend'**, his poems **'In Memory'** of Malise Archibald Cunningham-Grahame, his **'To a Spanish Friend'**, his **'To a Belgian Friend'** with its echo of the syntax and form of Dowson's 'Nuns', his **'Counsel'**, **'To Certain Friends'**, **'Friends'**, the over-protesting **'De Amicitia'**, and all those collected and uncollected prayers for his friends and dedicatory verses he was in the habit of making, as well as the dedications of individual poems, all these testify to the importance friendship had for Johnson, and his increasing conviction of its eternity. As he says at the end of **'Friends'**, 'Heaven were no Heaven, my friends away' and his hatred is reserved for one, perhaps Wilde to whom he had introduced Lord Alfred Douglas, who had taken not only his friend but his friend's purity, creating yet another of Johnson's haunted sinners. . . . Perhaps Johnson was conscious of his own tendencies here, but friendship extends through all his other affections and beliefs and welds them into a whole.

'Why should men', asks Yeats after a passage about Johnson, 'live lives of such disorder and seek to rediscover in verse the syntax of impulsive common life? Was it that we lived in what is called "an age of transition" and so lacked coherence, or did we but pursue antithesis?' . . . Whatever the reason, it was certainly in verse that Johnson discovered the syntax; Celticism gave him a tradition of failure in battle with the compensation of serving a lofty cause, Catholicism gave him a religion which reconciled the aesthetic and the moral, literature gave him a tradition which reincarnated the dead authors into their own and he hoped his eternity, and friendship gave this disturbingly solitary man his link with his fellows. He urges friends, admired authors, saints and patriots, all towards his own ideal of white perfection won from struggle, and is haunted by his failure to achieve it. His lines in memory of Ernest Dowson, undistingiushed though they are, bring together many of the different strands: he refers to Dowson's short story 'The Dying of Francis Donne' by quoting its epigraph, he remembers the ceremonial and ritual appropriate to his Church and his fellow Catholic, and he sees death as powerless against friendship, as it had always been against faith, love, literature, and music. His passionate ideal and the struggle against himself to realize it are both the cause and subject of his best work.

How is it then that an unsensational, rather scholarly poet who is at times visionary, at times occasional, should come to be considered not only as a Decadent but as characteristic of the period? It is surely that he has that longing for the ideal, and the sadness at its impossibility, that love which is powerful but also sterile, that assumption that eternity is gained by being assumed into art, that consciousness of technique, that awareness of artistic inspiration rather than the inspiration of life, that leaning towards music as technique and image, that feeling for formality and tradition, his Catholicism—'that too was a tradition' says Yeats in *The Oxford Book of Modern Verse*. Perhaps most important of all he could fit with little adaptation into the myth of the period, the myth of failure where poets were defeated in their desire to resolve the conflicting elements of their Decadent dilemma. Yeats is right to leave us with a picture of him moving towards that 'measureless consummation that he dreamed.'

Johnson was not a narrow traditionalist in theory nor out of key with his time. In his book on Hardy, he wrote that

> the supreme duties of the artist towards his art, as of all workmen toward their work, are two in number, but of one kind: a duty of reverence, of fidelity, of understanding, toward the old, great masters; and a duty of reverence, of fidelity, of understanding, toward the living age and the living artists.

Yet it is harder to find things about contemporary poetry that he admired than to find things he disliked. His critical eye was too keen to let him fall in unwittingly with any school of writing. Comparing the authors of the past with a modern in **'Friends that Fail Not,'** Johnson mocks the modern who could 'compose a "lyrical note" upon "world-weariness," and an "aquarelle" or "pastel" upon "Pimlico at twilight"', adding a little later that 'He has caught the gray and vanishing soul of a tragic impression. If my friend is not of this pallid school, he will probably belong to the school of fresh and vigorous Blood.' He likewise mocked the Aesthetic school, saying of the phrase 'Art for Art's sake' that 'I have spent years in trying to understand what is meant by that imbecile phrase.'

With an intimacy with the literary styles of his day and an eye acute enough to parody them, he remained aloof from their extremes. His poetry lacks the colour of his impressionist contemporaries, as it lacks romantic colour. It endures for its music, clarity, and intellectual hardness, its self-conscious literariness and its order. The strength and tragedy of some of his best poetry lie in the eternal battle of desire and indulgence. He said in **The Art of Thomas Hardy** that

> It is in the conflict of will with will, and of force with force, that Tragedy finds a voice:

men battling with the winds and waves, or with the passions and desires; men played upon by the powers of nature, or by the powers known to science, or with the powers known to conscience: an eternal warfare, and no illusion of battles in the clouds.

Out of this he created his image. (pp. 129-33)

> *R. K. R. Thornton, "Lionel Johnson," in his* The Decadent Dilemma, *Edward Arnold, 1983, pp. 108-33.*

ADDITIONAL BIBLIOGRAPHY

Alexander, Calvert. "Lionel Johnson." In his *The Catholic Literary Revival*, pp. 129-39. Port Washington, N.Y.: Kennikat Press, 1935.
> Discussion of the literary influences that led Johnson to convert to Catholicism, and of the manner in which his religion influenced his poetry.

Burdett, Osbert. "The Prose Writers." In his *The Beardsley Period: An Essay in Perspective*, pp. 193-247. New York: Boni and Liveright, 1925.*
> Discussion of Johnson's literary criticism, with particular emphasis on his study *The Art of Thomas Hardy*.

Chislett, William, Jr. "Lionel Johnson: The Classicist as Celt." In his *Moderns and Near Moderns*, pp. 148-52. Freeport, N.Y.: Books for Libraries Press, 1928.
> Examination of Johnson's attitude toward the Celtic Revival movement. Chislett notes that Johnson argued against narrow-minded provincialism in favor of "wise generosity," as well as openness to "all excellence" and "literary catholicity."

Colby, Elbridge. "The Poetry and Prose of Lionel Johnson: Parts I and II." *The Catholic World* XCVI, No. 576 (March 1913): 721-32; XCVII, No. 577 (April 1913): 52-63.
> Discussion of Johnson's poetry and its place among the works of the Celtic revival. Colby finds Johnson's poems more hopeful and optimistic than those of the other Celtic poets and attributes this to his Catholicism. In part II, Johnson's critical writings are discussed. Colby argues that Johnson's approach to criticism, although "deep and scholarly," was too academic and impersonal.

Croft-Cooke, Rupert. "Wilde, Lionel Johnson, Ernest Dowson, and Count Stenbock." In his *Feasting with Panthers*, pp. 227-92. New York: Holt, Rinehart and Winston, 1967.*
> Discussion of Johnson's place among the writers of the nineties. Croft-Cooke's study includes details of Johnson's literary friendships and interesting biographical notes.

Dowling, Linda C. "Pursuing Antithesis: Lionel Johnson on Hardy." *English Language Notes* XII, No. 4 (June 1975): 287-92.
> Discussion of Johnson's study *The Art of Thomas Hardy*. Dowling suggests that Johnson employed a Yeatsian "mask"—that is, the image of Samuel Johnson, whom he wished to emulate—in writing *The Art of Thomas Hardy*.

Evans, Ifor. "Oscar Wilde, Ernest Dowson, Lionel Johnson and the Poetry of the Eighteen-Nineties." In his *English Poetry in the Later Nineteenth Century*, pp. 390-420. London: Methuen and Co., 1966.*
> Discussion of Johnson's relationship to the members of the Decadent movement. Evans maintains that Johnson stands apart from the other decadents because of the nature of the influences that shaped his poetry.

Fletcher, Iain. "The Dark Angel." In *Interpretations: Essays on Twelve English Poems*, edited by John Wain, pp. 155-78. London: Routledge and Kegan Paul, 1955.

Close reading of one of Johnson's best-known poems. Fletcher identifies many of the poem's more remote and difficult allusions and analyzes its meaning as he points out its technical strengths and weaknesses.

Gannon, Patricio. Preface to *The Poets of the Rhymers' Club,* edited by Patricio Gannon, pp. 11-21. Buenos Aires: Colombo, 1953.*
Discussion of the influence of the French Symbolist movement on the poets of the Rhymers' Club.

Gould, Warwick. "'Lionel Johnson Comes the First to Mind': Sources for Owen Aherne." In *Yeats and the Occult,* edited by George Mills Harper, pp. 255-84. London: Macmillan Press, 1975.
Study of Yeats's sources for his fictional character Owen Aherne in his *The Tables of the Law.* Gould draws comparisons between Yeats's portrait of Johnson in his *Autobiographies* and Aherne's characateristics, which also correspond closely to Johnson's self-portraits in his story "Mors Janua Vitae" and the poem "Mystic and Cavalier."

Harris, Frank. "Lionel Johnson and Hubert Crackanthorpe." In his *Contemporary Portraits, second series,* pp. 179-91. New York: privately published, 1919.*
Personal reminiscence of Johnson and a brief discussion of his works. Harris remembers Johnson as a gifted critic and a "skilled craftsman in poetry."

Hind, C. Lewis. "Lionel Johnson." In his *More Authors and I,* pp. 174-79. New York: Dodd, Mead and Co., 1922.
Discussion of Johnson's literary criticism. Hind notes Johnson's unfailing fairness as a critic, even to authors with whom he was not at all sympathetic.

Meynell, Wilfrid. Preface to *The Religious Poems of Lionel Johnson,* by Lionel Johnson, pp. v-xi. London: Elkin Mathews, 1916.
Discussion of the influence of Catholicism on Johnson's poetry.

Muddiman, Bernard. *The Men of the Nineties,* pp. 80ff. London: Henry Danielson, 1920.
Discussion of the characteristic features of art in England during the 1890s, with biographical and critical comments on the chief figures of the era. References to Johnson appear throughout.

Nelson, James G. *The Early Nineties: A View from the Bodley Head,* pp. 13ff. Cambridge, Mass.: Harvard University Press, 1971.
Uses John Lane's publishing company the Bodley Head as a focal point for discussing the diverse influences that contributed to the spirit and ideals of the nineties. Nelson discusses Johnson's contributions to the Rhymers' Club anthologies.

O'Brien, Edward J. "Lionel Johnson: *Post Liminium.*" *Poet Lore* XXVI, No. III (Summer 1915): 405-08.
Examination of Johnson's essays in his *Post Liminium* collection. O'Brien comments favorably on the clarity and simplicity of Johnson's style.

Paterson, Gary H. "Light and Darkness, Sound and Silence in Lionel Johnson's Poetry." *The Antigonish Review* XI, No. 45 (Spring 1981): 93-103.
Discussion of the symbolic significance of certain recurring motifs in Johnson's poetry. Paterson enumerates the moods and ideas that Johnson commonly associates with these images.

Plarr, Victor. "The Art of Lionel Johnson." *The Poetry Review* 1, No. 6 (June 1912): 252-63.
Reminiscence of Johnson and a laudatory appraisal of his criticism and poetry by a former member of the Rhymers' Club.

Reed, John. "Decadent Poetry." In his *Decadent Style,* pp. 72-127. Athens: Ohio University Press, 1985.*
Finds that, despite a temperament and lifestyle that conformed to the pattern of an 1890s Decadent, in his poetry Johnson does not display the stylistic qualities peculiar to Decadent verse.

Rutenberg, Daniel. "Crisscrossing the Bar: Tennyson and Lionel Johnson on Death." *Victorian Poetry* 10, No. 2 (Summer 1972): 179-80.*
Comparison of Tennyson's and Johnson's attitudes toward death as they are revealed in Tennyson's poem "Crossing the Bar" and Johnson's poem "Falmouth Harbor," two works that employ the same central metaphor.

Shuster, George N. "Ruskin, Pater and the Pre-Raphaelites." In his *The Catholic Spirit in Modern English Literature,* pp. 166-86. Freeport, N.Y.: Books for Libraries Press, 1922.*
Analysis of the influence of Walter Pater and the Catholic church on the writings and the viewpoint of Johnson and others.

Stanford, Derek. Introduction to *Three Poets of the Rhymers' Club,* edited by Derek Stanford, pp. 11-37. Cheadle, England: Carcanet Press, 1974.*
Biographical and critical discussion. Stanford notes the manner in which the tragic aspects of Johnson's life and personality are reflected in his verse.

Tynan, Katharine. "Lionel Johnson: Wykehamist." *The Catholic World* CXIII, No. 676 (July 1921): 507-13.
Discussion of Johnson's religious attitudes by his close friend, the poet Katharine Tynan. Tynan's article is based on personal reminiscences of Johnson, as well as on his *Winchester Letters.*

Waugh, Arthur. "Lionel Johnson." In his *Tradition and Change,* pp. 98-107. London: Chapman and Hall, 1919.
Reminiscence of Johnson at Oxford and an examination of the traditionalist elements in his poetry. Waugh observes that the preponderance of such elements in the poetry of a young man whose generation was overwhelmingly concerned with emancipation is suggestive of the isolation of Johnson's life.

Weygandt, Cornelius. "Lionel Johnson, English Irishman." In his *Tuesdays at Ten,* pp. 67-71. Philadelphia: University of Pennsylvania Press, 1928.
Discusses the influence of Winchester College, classical literature, the Celtic Renaissance, and Catholicism on Johnson's poetry.

Whittemore, Thomas. "Preface." In *Post Liminium: Essays and Critical Papers,* by Lionel Johnson, edited by Thomas Whittemore, pp. vii-xi. London: Elkin Mathews, 1909.
Biographical and critical discussion of Johnson's career.

Yeats, William Butler. "The Tragic Generation." In his *Autobiographies,* pp. 185-223. London: Macmillan and Co., 1955.
Personal reminiscence of Johnson. Yeats discusses Johnson's profound learning, his rejection of the world, and his alcoholism.

Ludwig Lewisohn

1883-1955

American critic, novelist, short story writer, autobiographer, dramatist, essayist, and translator.

During the 1920s and 1930s, Lewisohn was considered a significant figure in American letters, particularly for his autobiographies *Up Stream* and *Mid-Channel* and for his autobiographical novels *The Case of Mr. Crump* and *The Island Within*. He was also a prominent literary critic who introduced American readers to little-known European authors and who was an early follower of the psychoanalytic school of criticism. Both as a fiction and nonfiction writer, Lewisohn sought to expose and revile what he considered a repressive puritanism in American life and literature, focusing in his novels on overtly sexual themes and insisting in much of his criticism on the covert sexual origins of literary expression. However, due to the changing literary trends and social mores of the twentieth century, Lewisohn's works appear dated to contemporary readers. In addition, the controversies engendered by Lewisohn's fervent advocacy of Judaism have also contributed to the decline of his reputation. But despite this decline, perhaps in some ways because of it, Lewisohn has retained the interest of scholars specializing in the development of modern American fiction and criticism, as well as historians of Jewish thought in America.

An only child, Lewisohn was born in Berlin. While his family had enjoyed a modest but comfortable living in Germany, increasing financial hardship led them to seek new opportunities in the United States when Lewisohn was seven. The Lewisohns settled in Charleston, South Carolina, in a predominantly Protestant community. Although they had long been assimilated in European culture—thinking of themselves as Germans first and Jews second—and retained few Jewish customs in their new environment, they were ostracized by their Christian neighbors. Anxious for his son's acceptance, Lewisohn's father enrolled him in a Methodist Sunday school, while his mother, a rabbi's daughter who refused to abandon all ancestral tradition, remained Lewisohn's spiritual link to his Jewish heritage. As enthusiasts of culture and classical literature, both parents encouraged Lewisohn's love of reading and literary aspirations. He attended public schools in Charleston, where he supplemented his native fluency in German with Latin and French, and where he was exposed to the sphere of Southern Christian gentility against which he later rebelled in writings denouncing Puritan traditions.

During his years at the College of Charleston, Lewisohn excelled in his studies, although he was barred from many activities with his fellow students. After an unprecedented early election to the college's literary and debating society, he invited further alienation from his peers by introducing topics, such as sexuality and racial issues, which were socially objectionable at that time. In 1901 Lewisohn left Charleston with a Master of Arts for postgraduate studies at Columbia University. Despite the unrelieved isolation he had previously known, he remained steadfast in his identification with Anglo-American cultural traditions and was confident that he would attain a college professorship, his ethnic background notwithstanding. While attending graduate school, Lewisohn read extensively

in modern German literature. The realistic nature and tolerant spirit of that nation's literature was a strong contrast to current American literature and proved to be an important influence on Lewisohn's fiction. Lewisohn attributed the differences between German and American literature to what he deemed the central weakness of the Anglo-American mind, a ''moral illusionism'' anchored firmly in the Puritan ethic, with which he was becoming increasingly disenchanted. He received a second master's degree in 1903, earning his way by tutoring, for despite excellent grades he was unable to obtain a fellowship or scholarship. Lewisohn was also unsuccessful in securing a teaching appointment and was candidly informed by one of Columbia's advisors that this was because he was Jewish. This episode, as he recalled in *Up Stream*, forced Lewisohn to acknowledge the anti-Semitism that he had attempted to ignore for years. Relinquishing his remaining identification with Anglo-American values, Lewisohn abandoned the pursuit of his doctorate and, as he was then convinced, the hope of a university career.

With the assistance of a sympathetic instructor from Columbia, Lewisohn worked for a brief time as a reader for a New York publisher, a position he regarded as drudgery, considering fellow employees as ''slaves in soul'' and the free-lance writing he did salvation. In 1906 he married an English divorcée twenty years his senior with grown children; this union served as the basis for *The Case of Mr. Crump* and other works dealing with marital discord. Desperate for funds after leaving the publishing firm, Lewisohn produced several potboiling serials, which he later admitted inspired extreme self-disgust. The first novel that he considered a serious work, *The Broken Snare,* was concerned with extramarital relationships and was recommended for publication by Theodore Dreiser. Although published in 1908, the controversial novel was neither favorably reviewed by most critics nor well received by the general public. Again aided by his friend from Columbia, he was referred to and refused by several universities where teaching positions were open, but was finally offered an instructorship in German at the University of Wisconsin in 1910; he remained for one year, then left to teach German at Ohio State University for the next six years. During this period, Lewisohn's identification with Judaism was far less pronounced than was his affinity for German ideals, which he found embodied in a literature revealing "the widest moral and intellectual liberty and tireless spiritual stirring." In 1917, in the face of mounting anti-German sentiment inspired by World War I, Lewisohn left Ohio State after his espousal of German culture drew attacks from the university community.

Lewisohn accepted the post of drama critic for the *Nation* in 1919, retaining it for a year but remaining the periodical's associate editor until 1924. Around 1921 he met Thelma Spear, a young singer. Their relationship continued over the next sixteen years, inspiring a great deal of adverse publicity and, due to Lewisohn's propensity to discuss his personal life in his writings, incurring threats of libel suits from his wife. Unable to get a divorce in the state of New York and fearing prosecution, Lewisohn and Spear left the United States in 1924 for more than a decade abroad. An extended stay in Palestine intensified his growing interest in Jewish causes, and his studies in Vienna of Sigmund Freud's theories inspired his later psychoanalytic approach to literary criticism. Lewisohn's second novel, *The Case of Mr. Crump,* was published in Paris because American publishers considered its subject matter provocative; although it was much-praised in Europe and by a few Americans, among them Dreiser and Sinclair Lewis, its entry into the United States was forbidden and its American publication deferred until 1947.

Lewisohn finally obtained a divorce from his wife and, having also discontinued his involvement with Spear, remarried in 1940. The scandals inspired by his personal life, coupled with his ready adoption of unpopular or seemingly fanatic points of view, had already begun to contribute to declining sales of his books and diminished stature as a literary authority. He once angrily protested that his exclusion from the *Oxford Companion to American Literature* was "a son-of-a-bitch's trick, attributable to the most brutal malice." To supplement his income, Lewisohn lectured to interested Jewish groups. He divorced his second wife, married again in 1944, and, in 1948, was appointed a professor of Comparative Literature at Brandeis University, his first teaching post in thirty years, where he taught until his death in 1955.

The Case of Mr. Crump is considered by many critics to be Lewisohn's best novel and a laudable example of American Naturalistic fiction of the 1920s for its uninhibited treatment of its subject. In a postscript to the novel, Lewisohn affirmed that "in the present state of public opinion in America and of a man's professional and economic dependence on that opinion, the wife holds dice so heavily loaded from the beginning that

any vulgar and unscrupulous woman may unresistingly ruin any man whom, by any means, she can lure or force into a marriage ceremony." A "thesis" novel based on Lewisohn's experiences during his first marriage, *The Case of Mr. Crump* addresses the subject of marital discord in a way that recurs less forcefully in his other early works: an unwary youth, raised in puritanical surroundings, becomes trapped in an unhappy marriage from which there is generally no recourse but violence. Lewisohn's call for sexual harmony in marriage, and his promotion of social and cultural changes he deemed essential to such harmony, punctuate the plot of the novel. Many critics believe that, because Lewisohn's experience colored his attitude toward marriage so adversely and immutably, his portrayals of married couples are largely stereotypes meant to demonstrate a thesis. More often, however, Lewisohn's novel has been praised for both its narrative artistry and its thematic force. In his 1982 study of Lewisohn, Seymour Lainott reiterated the high approbation the novel received upon its initial appearance: "*Mr. Crump* impresses not because of its thesis but because it is a ripe work of fiction: dense in detail, expertly organized, effective in dialogue . . . and in characterization."

Lewisohn was equally fervent about the danger of absolute ethnic assimilation into a cultural mainstream. His own sense of displacement had always been acute, and he believed that only self-destruction could be wrought by the loss of one's identity. *The Island Within,* after recording the ancestral history and emigration to America of Arthur Levy's family, finally focuses on the inner conflicts of the protagonist who, unlike the assimilated Jews around him, is drawn inevitably to the wellspring of his own heritage. Lewisohn's autobiographical works were also firmly grounded in his personal philosophy, as evidenced by his condemnation in *Up Stream* of Puritanism in American life and literature, as well as his inveighing, in *Mid-Channel,* against Pauline Christianity. The highly personal nature of Lewisohn's fiction and autobiographical writings is also characteristic of his literary criticism. While many of Lewisohn's critical analyses have been considered astute, he has often been castigated for allowing his strong biases to interfere with his evaluations of literature. In such works as *The Spirit of Modern German Literature, The Poets of Modern France,* and *The Creative Life,* Lewisohn emphasized the artist's individuality and asserted that the greatest works of literature invariably have their origins in the human need for self-expression. *Expression in America,* his most controversial critical work, chronicles the literary struggle against, or acquiescence to, those forces in American culture that Lewisohn felt stultified creativity. In *Expression in America,* he also made extensive use of psychoanalytic interpretation, an approach which many commentators, even those who advocate the application of psychoanalysis to literary criticism, have found weakens rather than supports Lewisohn's otherwise sound arguments.

Lewisohn is frequently criticized for the radical partisanship of his literary and social criticism, which occasionally clouds his judgment, and for his inability to create credible characters in his fiction. Lionel Trilling has observed that Lewisohn "often catches admirably the temper of a group of people, but individuals he seems to see in the patterns laid down by popular or artistic tradition. And it is exactly the novelist's function to break up these patterns." Some critics have noted that even Lewisohn's Jewish characters, who are central to his fiction, are no more animated than talmudic mosaics. Nonetheless, Lewisohn's contribution to American letters, from his literary analyses to sociological discourses, has been significant, and most commentators concur with Carl Van Doren that Lewisohn "touches nothing that he does not enlarge. Nor is this because he puffs up his theme from within or rounds it out with dropsical additions. Rather, it is because he sees each character and each situation as items in a general pattern which is bounded by nothing less than time and space."

(See also *Contemporary Authors*, Vol. 107 and *Dictionary of Literary Biography*, Vol. 4: *American Writers in Paris, 1920-1939;* Vol. 9: *American Novelists, 1910-1945;* and Vol. 28: *Twentieth-Century American-Jewish Fiction Writers*.)

PRINCIPAL WORKS

The Broken Snare   (novel)   1908
The Modern Drama   (criticism)   1915
The Spirit of Modern German Literature   (criticism)   1916
The Poets of Modern France   (criticism and translation) 1918
The Drama and the Stage   (criticism)   1922
Up Stream: An American Chronicle   (autobiography)   1922
Don Juan   (novel)   1923
The Creative Life   (criticism)   1924
Israel   (nonfiction)   1925
The Case of Mr. Crump   (novel)   1926; also published as *The Tyranny of Sex* (abridged edition), 1947
Cities and Men   (criticism)   1927
The Island Within   (novel)   1928
Adam   (drama) [first publication]   1929
Mid-Channel: An American Chronicle   (autobiography) 1929
Stephen Escott   (novel)   1930
The Last Days of Shylock   (novel)   1931
Expression in America   (criticism)   1932, also published as *The Story of American Literature* [enlarged edition], 1939
This People   (novellas)   1933
An Altar in the Fields   (novel)   1934
The Permanent Horizon: A New Search for Old Truths (nonfiction)   1934
Trumpet of Jubilee   (novel)   1937
The Answer   (nonfiction)   1939
Haven [with Edna Manley Lewisohn]   (autobiography) 1940
The American Jew: Character and Destiny   (nonfiction) 1950
The Magic Word: Studies in the Nature of Poetry (criticism)   1950
In a Summer Season   (novel)   1955

WILLIAM MORTON PAYNE   (essay date 1908)

[*The longtime literary editor for several Chicago publications, Payne reviewed books for twenty-three years at* The Dial, *one of America's most influential journals of literature and opinion in the early twentieth century. In the following excerpt, Payne favorably reviews* The Broken Snare.]

It is not often that we come upon a novel written with the conscious artistic purpose of Mr. Lewisohn's **"The Broken Snare,"** in which the imperative demands of technique—both verbal and architectonic—are never ignored, and which yet has no lack of rich human substance. The author has taken Flaubert for his model, and has shown himself a not unworthy disciple of the master. More than most works of fiction, this is the story of a man and a woman, to the exclusion of all other personalities; of their love and its consequences, to the exclusion of all other interests. The woman is an ardent creature, cramped by the conditions of a peculiarly mean and sordid existence; the man has the artist's temperament, and what he imagines to be deep convictions concerning the futility of the marriage-bond. The two agree to join their lives without the usual legal proceedings, and set out for a honeymoon in the South. For a short time all is idyllic with them, and then the inevitable break comes, to which we are led through the gradual stages of sub-conscious unrest, growing irritation, jarring mutual revelations of character, and the clash of fundamentally opposed ideals. Then there is separation, and a long term of suffering for both; finally, the sex-duel sees the woman the victor, the man's intellectual pride is abased, and they are reunited upon the terms that have been decreed by the wisdom of the ages as the only possible foundation for the family and for human society. It will thus be seen that the book, despite its boldness of speech and conception, is ethically wholesome. It does not seek by means of false sentiment to incline us to the acceptance of evil, and its moral emphasis is not misplaced. It is not a book for the young person to read, but it is one from which the mature mind can get nothing but good, and one which offers a singular satisfaction to the artistic perceptions.

> *William Morton Payne, in a review of "The Broken Snare," in* The Dial, *Vol. XLV, No. 537, November 1, 1908, p. 295.*

H. L. MENCKEN   (essay date 1922)

[*From the era of World War I until the early years of the Great Depression, Mencken was one of the most influential figures in American letters. His strongly individualistic, irreverent outlook on life and his vigorous, invective-charged writing style helped establish the iconoclastic spirit of the Jazz Age and significantly shaped the direction of American literature. As a social and literary critic—the roles for which he is best known—Mencken was the scourge of evangelical Christianity, public service organizations, literary censorship, boosterism, provincialism, democracy, all advocates of personal or social improvement, and every other facet of American life that he perceived as humbug. In his literary criticism, Mencken encouraged American writers to shun the anglophilic, moralistic bent of the nineteenth century and to practice realism, an artistic call-to-arms that is most fully developed in his essay "Puritanism as a Literary Force" (1917), one of the seminal essays in modern literary criticism. A man who was widely renowned or feared during his lifetime as a would-be destroyer of established American values, Mencken once wrote: "All of my work, barring a few obvious burlesques, is based upon three fundamental ideas. 1. That knowledge is better than ignorance; 2. That it is better to tell the truth than to lie; and 3. That it is better to be free than to be a slave." In the following excerpt, Mencken applauds Lewisohn for debunking several American myths in* Up Stream.]

The Young Intellectual, as everyone knows, is having a rheumatic time of it in the Republic. His groans and protests, indeed, fill the land, and whenever he can raise the money without security he takes ship for foreign parts, there to immerse himself in sneers. He is the Hamlet of our time and nation. But does the name of Hamlet exhaust the whole tale of human suffering and disaster? I doubt it. There have been men as hard beset by fate, and even men worse beset: Lazarus, Job, Werther, Tadeusz Kosciuszko, William Jennings Bryan. They have a brother in one whose inner agonies seem to be little suspected: the 100 per cent American. If he is mentioned, it is simply to mock him. Yet there must be pains running up and down his vertebrae, in these days of wholesale Katzen-jammer, that are certainly as poignant as any felt by the Young Intellectual. With every new dawn comes a new cackle in derision of him, a new blasting of his patriotic hopes, a new outrage upon his delicacies. I confine myself, in example, to onslaughts purely literary, and in that field to a salient few. First "Jurgen," with its appalling chapter upon life in hell. Then "Main Street." Then "Three Soldiers." Now Ludwig Lewisohn's **"Up Stream."** And on some near tomorrow John Kenneth Turner's staggering history of the American share in the war.

The Lewisohn book lacks the rattle and glitter of "Three Soldiers," and is hence less likely to arrest the attention and arouse the ire of the New York *Times*, the American Legion, the Rotary Club, the Sulgrave Foundation, the Ku Klux Klan, and other such eminent agencies of correct thought. But it is far more searching and profound, and a far mellower and nobler piece of writing, and so I incline to think that in the long run it is likely to leave deeper and more florid scars. All that "Three Soldiers" says, in brief, is that war is a rough and dirty business, and that it is intensely unpleasant to be thrust unwillingly into a trench, and hoofed by cads in epaulets. The news is not actually new; many a man of logical talents, I daresay, reached it a priori and without any experience of army life. But **"Up Stream"** says something that is far less obvious, and says it with almost irresistible persuasiveness: to wit, that the brand of Americanism which is now officially and semi-officially on tap, and which countless evangelists strive to force down the gullets of groaning wops, bohunks, polacks, greasers, heinies, squareheads, and kikes, is indistinguishable both microscopi-cally and macroscopically from numskullery and bounderism—that it is intolerably ignorant, cowardly, servile, and disgusting, and that the measure of an immigrant's dignity as a man is to be taken by noting the energy and diligence with which he resists being physicked with it. If he submits docilely, with tears in his eyes, then some foreign principality has lost either an imbecile or a rascal. But if he gags heroically, biting both the doctor and the policeman, then the American Republic has gained a man.

Let me hasten to add that Lewisohn himself is no such laudable Berserker; in his own chronicle he appears less as hero than as betrayed innocent. A German Jew of sound and civilized stock, he was brought to the United States as a child, and experienced in his youth the harsh pressures which play upon the immigrant, here as everywhere. Those pressures are partly economic: it is hard to make a living in a strange land, with new concepts of labor and barter to master, and a new language, and new and disconcerting prejudices. But they are also partly social: the immigrant is not only poor, but also lonesome. No wonder he so eagerly falls a prey to cultural temptations—to the lure of ideas and customs that, at all events, promise him decent human companionship! No wonder the prairie States produce Germans and Scandinavians who are Prohibitionists! No wonder the Jews of the towns turn Episcopalian! Where Mr. Lewisohn lived, in some backwater of the South, the decent whites were all Methodists. In his groping teens, cut off from his heritage and still too feeble to stand alone, he succumbed easily to that bizarre revelation. At fifteen or sixteen young Ludwig confessed his sins, renounced Moses, threw away his phylacteries, and joined the Epworth League!

His story thereafter is a story of gradual recovery from that supreme storm of spiritual measles—with a dash of major sur-gery at the end. The Epworth League, of course, could not hold him long—else there would have been no book of his to review today. Inside the plaster Methodist, it soon appeared, there was a very real poet, and this poet presently broke out. What was ahead for him? Great joy, to be sure, but also dif-ficulty and disillusion—poverty, the iron face of prejudice, struggle, heartburning, doubt, dismay. It was the Jew rather than the German who had all these dragons to face. In college, at the univerisity, above all when the time came to make a living, there was an ominous hemming and hawing. Certain very attractive teaching posts, it appeared, went only to flat or concave noses; certain great seminaries had an immovable pas-sion for Nordic blonds. But I doubt that this stone wall really gave the young scholar as much pause as he now thinks it did. He was rebuffed and humiliated, but not everywhere. Finally, he found a comfortable berth in a fresh-water State university, and there he roosted when I first knew him—writing books, acquiring an audience, developing a style, studying and teach-ing, getting shelter and enough to eat. A happy enough life—for a man interested in prosody. A far, far lift above the in-tellectual sewers of the South, and the puerile concerns of the Epworth League.

Then came the war, and catastrophe. It was now the German, not the Jew, who went upon the chopping block. The story, as told, is full of hesitations and restraints; there runs through it an obvious effort to avoid bitterness. But what an experience it must have been, what a colossal disillusionment!—old friends turned into treacherous and shameful enemies overnight; the hard work of years requited with denial and contumely; the air full of threats, ominous whispers, extravagant accusations; in-credible poltroonery everywhere; all the normal decencies and amenities of life sacrificed to an ignoble and idiotic hate! Lew-isohn, as I say, holds down the soft pedal; he is plainly trying to be magnanimous. But what he fails to tell may be supplied out of the common history of that time. It is a history that must be written some day, and to the last detail. No man who had a hand in the making of it should be forgotten. For two long years it was a humiliation to be an American, and for one of them it was a downright disgrace.

But there were compensations, and one of them is before us: Lewisohn was cured. The danger that menaced him before the hurricane was not that he was a Jew, but that he was a typical American pedagogue, and likely to remain one. Given time enough and ease enough, and he might have become the exact counterpart of the poor dolts whose craven swineries he now so pityingly describes—pathetic vacuums whose place in the world, by a fine irony, is now fixed by his pages. He escaped that depressing fate. He came out of the spiritual stockyards a dubious American, if current standards count for anything, but a fine artist. His skill now shines forth from his book. It is of capital value as document, pure and simple; it displays its facts adroitly and it carries conviction. But it is of even greater value as—I almost said a work of imagination. It has color, charm, grace, finish, eloquence. It is the book of a man who knows how to write English. (pp. 434, 436)

H. L. Mencken, "Dream and Awakening," in The Nation, *Vol. CXIV, No. 2962, April 12, 1922, pp. 434, 436.*

LUDWIG LEWISOHN (essay date 1923)

[*In the following excerpt, Lewisohn explains his standards and values as a literary critic.*]

I have a very thoughtful friend who is always pointing out what seems to him a discrepancy in my activities. He says that I am a radical in my notions about life and a classicist in my notions about literature. My answer is that he is quite right, that I accept the imputation and glory in it, provided, of course, that I am permitted to define my terms.

A radical is one who inists that men shall live by the use of reason. (He means it. He does not stop using his reason when he is suddenly confronted by some particularly hoary and disreputable prejudice, taboo, superstition. It is at that point that he insists all the more on using his reason. Even at the risk of hurting someone's feelings. For by sparing this, for the moment, imaginary antagonist's feelings our radical gives that antagonist the continued privilege of spreading ruin and feeling righteous.)

A classicist is one who has accepted the teaching of the history of literature that the fundamental character of art-form is determined by the medium and the nature of man. (Art is communication. It must be intelligible. Therefore it must be articulate. There are irreducible minima of articulate intelligibility. Where these do not exist art has not yet begun to be. Gertrude Stein has not transcended the traditions of art. She has not yet reached them. *Note:* If terms and the things they stand for are to mean anything and we are to have poetry and prose then the *fundamentum differentionis* is the presence in poetry of a perceptible recurrence of similar rhythm-groups. . . . No, this is not pedantic. It is only exact.)

I am, then, a radical and a classicist. And, humble as I am, I am in amazingly good company—Plato, Euripides, Montaigne, Milton, Shelley, Goethe, Nietzsche. . . .

I knew from the beginning that I would please no one. While I was a university teacher my colleagues thought me dangerous, subversive, prone to defend the new, the revolutionary in life and letters. Now, on the other hand, my past is thrown up at me. Among dramatic critics I am thought of as academic. When I write fiction I am told that I am a licentious fellow. It is all inevitable enough; it is often amusing. There is nothing for me to do but serenely to accept the penalties of my position. For the plain truth is this: People in our time and country are not accustomed to have those who think know anything and they are even less accustomed to having one who knows try to think. The radicals have read nothing written before 1900; the university men vote the Republican ticket and walk humbly in the sight of their trustees and their God. . . .

So much for my central position which I felt it more or less of a duty to define. Now for the more strictly personal, indefinable, elusive things. For criticism, too, is art. . . .

It is borne in upon me more and more that I am something of a simpleton. I can grasp everything in Plato and in the second part of "Faust." What I read there corresponds to my experience of both the soul and the world. I cannot understand even one-half of what is written in, let me say, the prose of Mrs. Virginia Woolf or the verse of Mr. D. H. Lawrence. I keep wondering whether others do or whether they don't care. When I don't want to understand I listen to music. When I read literature I insist on understanding. Do my friends deceive themselves? Or do I deceive myself into thinking they deceive themselves in order to save my vanity as a man and a critic? At all events I am more and more tempted to flee from the works of the very subtle and the neo-mystical to works that I can understand. Mr. Lawrence's poetry can drive me as far back as Pope and Horace; the new mystics—including such

great writers as Jacob Wassermann—as far back as Swift and Hume. It is hopeless. I can't get away from my combination—radical and classicist.

As a simple person I should possess the immunities of my temper and my limitations. I don't. I am often told that I am too intricate and profound. Or else that I ape intricacy and profundity. In brief, I am known here and there as a vicious "highbrow." And that is always, I observe, when I say things that seem obvious and plain and incontrovertible to me. Here are some of them:

If a book or a play isn't, in the ultimate sense, a work of art—isn't the translation of first-hand experience into creative form and vision—it isn't worth reviewing.

But if it is—then it is inviolable. The critic shouldn't tinker, advise, or, in the ordinary sense, find fault. For, in that ordinary sense, a work of art has no faults. Works of art differ as faces differ in beauty, intelligence, significance. But each human face is that face. Each authentic work of art is that work of art. It has grown in its author's mind and soul as a child grows in its mother's womb. I do not wish to reduce that truth to the absurd. Nearly every truth can be so reduced. But before every work of art, however humble, I try to be passive, to discover what the author willed to do, to project. . . . I don't talk past books or plays or poems. People are constantly talking past my own books. They establish no inner contact with them. They read as they run and then tell what *they* think, what they would have done, what they would have had me do. If I have one aim as a critic it is that no author shall accuse me of that carelessness, arrogance, impertinence. If I cannot get under the skin of a work of art I leave it alone.

If I err, if I do not always follow my own counsel perfectly, it is because, as time goes on, I care less and less for art in its more abstract forms and more and more for life. I am too preoccupied to be held by anything that approaches the decorative. It is the remediable moral suffering in the world that crowds my vision—the remediable moral suffering, remediable by a little hard thinking, a little tolerance, a little more goodness, a little less righteousness. If I write a criticism it is to further that supreme end; if I write a novel it is to further the same end. Is that bad criticism and bad art? It may be because I am a bad critic and a bad artist. It is not because my method and my aim are at fault. For the same aim and method were and are the aim and the method of Isaiah and Euripides, Hauptmann and Shaw. The greatest art has always sought to lessen the evils that are under the sun. But I am only I and this city is only this city and the great choices being taken from me I have a little choice left. If that little choice is indeed all I have I do not hesitate. Shall I be a fairly accomplished aesthete or a pamphleteer? A pamphleteer, by all means. Even a pamphleteer needn't write ill. Lessing was one, Swift another. (pp. 583-84)

Ludwig Lewisohn, "Ludwig Lewisohn," in The Nation, *Vol. CXVII, No. 3046, November 21, 1923, pp. 583-84.*

THOMAS MANN   (essay date 1926)

[*Mann was a German novelist, short story and novella writer, essayist, and critic who singlehandedly raised the German novel to an international stature which it had not enjoyed since the time of the Romantics. Like his contemporaries Joyce and Proust, Mann keenly reflected the intellectual currents of his age, particularly the belief that European realism was no longer viable for the inhabitants of a sophisticated and complex century. Yet, while Joyce and Proust expressed this predicament through the form of their writing, Mann maintained the outward convention of realistic fiction, emphasizing an ironic vision of life and a deep, often humorous, sympathy for humanity. In his introduction to the 1926 edition of* The Case of Mr. Crump, *Mann praises Lewisohn's novel and applauds the motives behind its creation.*]

According to its form [*The Case of Mr. Crump*] is a novel. It operates with fictive personages, narrates their actions, expresses their relations in dialogue and points these in such a manner that the absorbed and fearful reader perceives on every page the development of that criminal catastrophe which is the book's disastrous ending. It is, then, fiction, well and astutely composed, utilizing all the methods of modern technique, a work of art, in a word, in so far as it preserves its coolness of tone, keeps its distance, permits things to speak for themselves and sustains that severe and curbed and almost serene silence which is peculiar to all art and especially to the art of speech, and leaves it to the reader or beholder to draw his own conclusions. But simultaneously and at every moment the book is both more and less than a novel; it is life, it is concrete and undreamed reality and its artistic silence seems in more than one passage desperately like a cry. There is about the book something stripped and naked and so terribly immediate that it seems at every moment to negate its own form from within and to be ready to shatter that form. This circumstance will depress the book's value in the eyes of those who still demand a purely aesthetic impression. But one cannot fail to observe the book's indifference—an indifference that belongs to our time—toward such disapproval; its voluntary renunciation of mere aesthetic distinction, its readiness to make far-reaching aesthetic sacrifices in the service of documentary vigor. And it is notable that this indifference, this readiness and this renunciation are transformed unawares into artistic values of an ethical order and by a moral means elevate and ennoble the book again as a work of art—a process that illustrates the human oneness of the ethical and aesthetic categories by means of a most moving example.

We have here, then, a novelistic document of life, of the *inferno* of a marriage. That word exhausts the book's horrifying and infuriating subject matter—a marriage that should never have been contracted nor would have been save for the man's weakness and youthful inexperience—a marriage which, under the protection of cruel social hypocrisy and of a cruel social fear for the abstract institution, becomes an *inferno*—first through the scandalous legal advantages possessed by the woman as such, finally and hopelessly through the passional crime that brings to ruin the gifted and promising protagonist.

It is American conditions that are delineated. Lewisohn is an American. He lives in Paris, since he cannot well live in America, where this book of his has been forbidden too. It was forbidden the mails in the name of that national morality, which plays so horrifying a part in the story, and has appeared only in a limited edition printed in France. And it is well that it has now been translated and may freely circulate among us. For there is no doubt that it genuinely enriches our store of foreign literary goods. The author declares that the book arose from his determination to tell "as well and as entertainingly as he could the true story of Herbert Crump." One must grant him that his power to stir and entertain us is very great. His book stands in the very forefront of modern epic narrative. His style is manly, sincere, precise and strong; there is in it a high determination after compact and direct truth and one is impressed and enchanted at once. At times he has the dry and

desperate humor of Strindberg, as the subject itself leads one to be frequently reminded of Strindberg. The characters are human beings—even the woman, Anne Crump, remains human in all her repulsiveness. And this is meritorious. For without the corrective of creative justice and insight, the author's feeling of solidarity with his hero might easily have made of the woman a mere demon.

Finally the publication of this book is to be welcomed because it may thus extend its influence back across the ocean and contribute to that Europeanization of America that should be the counterpart of our much discussed Americanization and which is indeed the aim of the best Americans of our time. Among these, though living in temporary exile, Lewisohn must be numbered. These men, Lewisohn, Mencken, Sinclair Lewis, Judge Lindsay, the groups that gather about the *American Mercury* and the *Nation*, are striving to transform the handsome, energetic children of American civilization into beings of a ripe and adult culture. We Europeans, in the meantime, have no right proudly and indifferently to disregard such problems as that in this book merely because our social morality is a trifle more mature. The world has become small and intimate and there has arisen a common responsibility which only the malignant reactionary dare repudiate. Lewisohn declares at the close of his story that he desired to appeal "to the heart of mankind itself." He shall not have made, nor would I willingly suffer him to have made, this appeal in vain. (pp. vii-viii)

> *Thomas Mann, in a preface to* The Case of Mr. Crump *by Ludwig Lewisohn, 1926. Reprint by Farrar, Straus & Giroux, 1965, pp. vii-viii.*

JOSEPH WARREN BEACH   (essay date 1926)

[*Beach was an American critic and educator who specialized in American literature and English literature of the Romantic and Victorian eras. Of his work, Beach noted: "I do not aim so much to render final judgments and deliver certificates of greatness, which is something manifestly impossible and a trifle ridiculous, as to analyze and interpret stories and poems as expressions of our humanity and as effective works of art." In the following excerpt, Beach examines* Up Stream.]

With regard to *Up Stream*, I am of a . . . divided mind. It is of course an important book, but I do not feel sure as to the degree of its importance. It is a very serious arraignment of race prejudice and of Puritanism, of an indubitable sincerity and power. The picture of the author's parents isolated and spiritually obstructed by their double handicap of German and Jew is both touching and beautiful in its spirit, as is his account of his own enthusiastic espousal of Saxon poetry and culture. And it may well be that I put an extravagant valuation on manner in writing as opposed to matter. I have failed to find in this volume passages that seem to me capable of being put alongside of passages from the finest prose-writers—Rémy de Gourmont, say, or Bernard Shaw.

There is better writing, if I am not mistaken, in his more recent volume of criticism, *The Creative Life*. There is, for example, the admirable passage in which he tells how he has fallen between the two stools of the academic and the journalistic, and has consequently failed to please either his university colleagues or his free-lance rivals in New York. "I knew from the beginning that I would please no one." And there are occasional sayings of aphoristic fineness reminding one of his master, Goethe: "A people that crushes the creative will has only an Egyptian future and will leave as its chief monument a tomb reared by a slave.''

It is not in *Up Stream* his occasional betrayal that he was not born to the English idiom that bothers me. I am afraid we shall have to reconcile ourselves to the occasional misfit of a preposition so long as we have the privilege of welcoming writers whose parents spoke a foreign language. They bring us matters so much more important than precision in the use of English prepositions. And I do not suppose I should hold it against Mr. Lewisohn that he shows no sense of humor. Depth and intensity of feeling are of course more important than the ability to treat a serious matter lightly. And yet somehow I cannot persuade myself that the pages of Mr. Lewisohn on prohibition and its allies make as good reading as Mr. Mencken's. I admire the spirit of humanity in which they are written; I admire the intensity of feeling, and warm to the man who has such warmth himself. But I cannot help marking the phrases of railing emphasis, as I shall italicize them in the passage I quote, and I feel that the phrases, if not the feelings they express, betray a lack of some of the elements of good sense. Of prohibition he says:

> Each time the question came up I found my Anglo-American friends succumbing a little more and a little less willing to protest against the *raucous propaganda*. It became in the end almost ''bad form.'' In the first place, twenty-one states were already dry—even Michigan. So the *terrible fatalism* of democracy, inherent in its worship of majority opinion and its fundamental rejection of qualitative distinctions, was making itself felt more and more. If a disease spreads, expose yourself to it. Why should you want something better than others? I found my acquaintance almost *so sodden in their folly*. Furthermore—it was a question of morals and they had an *unconquerable hesitation toward taking a negative attitude* [here the overheated pen slips and blots the page with obscurity] on a question of morals. Even those who were not at all fanatical and themselves drank were willing to let things take *their evil course:* ''It does nobody any good; it does some people harm; I mustn't be selfish. . . .'' They looked at me with estranged eyes when I said: ''I'd be willing to take an oath never to touch fermented liquor again if only I could save our people from *the infamy of prohibition*.''
>
> (pp. 215-18)

Here is a fine indignation. Here are even fine strokes; but they are fine in proportion as the author turns his sarcasm in the direction of ironic description rather than in that of invective and epithet. One is tempted to say of such writing, ''There is something Prussian about this, something over-blunt and rigid, something military. There are moments when Mr. Lewisohn is in danger of classifying himself with the fanatics whom he opposes.'' Mr. Lewisohn has given perhaps in *The Creative Life* the clue to his comparative failure to make literature. He says that, as time goes on, he cares less and less for art in its abstract forms and more and more for life. And when he speaks of life, he means, so far as the artist is concerned, propaganda, or—less invidiously—the turning of art to the service of human causes. He is confronted with a choice between being an aesthete and a pamphleteer, and he chooses the latter. ''A pam-

phleteer, by all means. Even a pamphleteer needn't write ill. Lessing was one, Swift another'' [see excerpt dated 1923].

Those are noble models, but dangerous to cite. For it is doubtful whether either one was primarily a pamphleteer; and in any case they were writers who did not allow their devotion to a cause to interfere with the purity of their writing. Swift wrote his *Modest Proposal* out of an indignation as well grounded as Mr. Lewisohn's, but he did not allow a pebble of ill-directed sarcasm to trouble the surface of his terrible irony. And he produced a work of art the like of which we have never conceived in cause-ridden America. (pp. 218-20)

But for all that one cannot but regard *Up Stream* as no mean augury for the future of American prose. (p. 224)

> Joseph Warren Beach, ''Auguries,'' in his The Outlook for American Prose, 1926. Reprint by Kennikat Press, 1968, pp. 202-82.*

THEODORE DREISER   (letter date 1927)

[*Considered among America's foremost novelists, Dreiser was one of the principal American exponents of literary Naturalism. He is known primarily for his novels* Sister Carrie (1901), An American Tragedy (1926), *and the Frank Cowperwood trilogy (1912-47), in each of which the author presented his vision of life as a meaningless series of chemical reactions and animal impulses while he expressed a sense of sentimentality and pity for humanity's lot. Deeply concerned with the human condition but contemptuous of traditional social, political, and religious remedies, Dreiser associated for many years with the American socialist and communist movements, an interest reflected in much of his writing after 1925. In the following letter, Dreiser comments on the manuscript of* The Case of Mr. Crump, *which Lewisohn had asked him to review.*]

My dear Lewisohn:

Having just finished a careful reading and examination of *The Case of Mister Crump*, and before venturing an opinion or criticism, may I ask you one or two questions—questions which I would ask you to ponder long and seriously before you answer me.

First, do you believe that you are far enough removed, in time, from the actual events about which this book is written, to approach them with the clear, uncolored, unemotional viewpoint which any writer must have when fictionizing that which lies nearest his heart? Do you think you have brooded long enough about those years of your life, which you have dramatized here, to be able to set them down without bitterness, without hate, and without distortion? Personally I don't believe you have. When you let such lines as ''That foul and treacherous old hag would try to drag him into her own slime'' . . . mar the perspective of true psychologizing, you are too close to your emotions, to honestly portray any character.

Do you not think it wiser to let the years mellow your viewpoint? For it is obvious—far too obvious—that you have suffered keenly throughout the years of your first marital existence, and that self-evident fact is embittering the tone of your work. It is hard for any of us to stand on the sidelines and view ourselves with impartiality, but is that not necessary in transcribing our temperaments to fiction? And can that fiction have real power—real force—reality itself, until we have reached that stage of objectiveness which gives us an honest, or at least unbiased, viewpoint.

Strindberg was many years removed from his suffering before he wrote *The Confessions of a Fool*—I myself waited eight years before *The "Genius"*—and here you are, only barely four years away from the strife which so embittered you, trying to review it calmly. I don't think it can be done. And until it can be done, you are not qualified to attempt this kind of thing.

For instance, on p. 137, you state casually enough, "their long talks out in the open resulted in their most harmonious moods. Such hours were the only truly pleasant ones that Herbert could recall out of their long companionships, the only ones without a bitter or an acrid aftertaste." That sentence in itself seems to justify at least the incipiency of the relationship, and had you given this early phase of it its true color, as it was to you in those days, you would have at least justified yourself for the entanglement which followed. For every contact must have a first justification. You cannot deny it, and you cannot evade it. This is only a hint of the quality which I believe you will be able to infuse into the book if you will wait a little while and then rewrite it.

Of the writing, the vivid, incisive style, I have only praise—its intensity—its facility—its compelling interest, are undeniable. I quarrel only with the harshness, the vulgarity, the bitterness, the one-sided-ness, the psychological astigmatism, which transfuses it. This eradicated, I think the work will prove arresting to many—very many. And I would be among the first to endorse it as you now desire me to do. As it stands I cannot honestly say more than I have said in this letter & that, of course, is not what you want. If you think I am entirely wrong will you tell me just where[?] (pp.451-53)

> *Theodore Dreiser, in a letter to Ludwig Lewisohn on January 6, 1927, in his* Letters of Theodore Dreiser: A Selection, Vol. 2, *edited by Robert H. Elias, University of Pennsylvania Press, 1959, pp. 451-53.*

JOSEPH WOOD KRUTCH   (essay date 1927)

[*Krutch is widely regarded as one of America's most respected literary and drama critics. Noteworthy among his works are* The American Drama since 1918 *(1939), which analyzes the most important dramas of the 1920s and 1930s, and "Modernism" in* Modern Drama *(1953), in which he stressed the need for twentieth-century playwrights to infuse their works with traditional humanistic values. A conservative and idealistic thinker, he was a consistent proponent of human dignity and the preeminence of literary art. His literary criticism is characterized by such concerns: in* The Modern Temper *(1929) he argued that because scientific thought has denied human worth, tragedy had become obsolete, and in* The Measure of Man *(1954) he attacked modern culture for depriving humanity of the sense of individual responsibility necessary for making important decisions in an increasingly complex age. The following excerpt is from Krutch's review of* The Case of Mr. Crump.]

Mr. Lewisohn's hideously powerful novel [*The Case of Mr. Crump*] is a story of the unequal conflict between a creative artist and the vulgar entanglements of his disordered life. Herbert Crump, a promising young composer, comes from his quiet home in a little Southern city to the sordid loneliness of a New York boarding house and there, in the bleakness of his spirits and without realizing the extent to which he is committing himself, drifts into an alliance with a vulgar woman standing upon the brink of middle age. (p. 149)

It is upon the portrait, physical and spiritual, of Mrs. Crump that the novelist centers his effort, and it is indeed her book. Beginning with a description in a tone of half-detached irony

of her and her antecedents, it gradually increases in power and ferocity as it describes the increasing sluttishness of her personal habits and the increasing meanness of her soul. No disgusting detail of her physical decline is omitted and no aspect of the tortuous process of her mind is left unanalyzed, until she at last stands forth a figure at once monstrous yet credible. In spite of the increasingly preposterous disparity between their ages and the violent incompatibility of their temperament she clings to him for various reasons—because she needs his meager earnings for the support of herself and her family, because she needs his growing fame for her position in life, and because she needs his body for the satisfaction of the last desperate flicker of her passions. Yet these reasons are not the only or the worst ones. There is, in addition, a dumb, relentless possessiveness, a stubborn unreachable inexorability, a determination to revenge herself upon her husband for the unhappiness of her life, which is terrifying in its intensity. To him her malignity, so impersonal and incalculable, becomes almost a symbol of that mysterious evil of the universe which nothing can reach or placate, and through him she becomes, for the reader also, sinister in her inhumanity. Without that touch of almost insane malignity she would be, for all her meanness, grotesquely pitiful, but because of it pity is drowned in fear.

By reason of its bitterness, its frankness, and its almost brutal directness, Mr. Lewisohn's book challenges comparison with various other ultra-modern novels, but it is set apart from them all by two faiths—the one artistic, the other moral—that its author has managed to retain. Unlike so many of his fellows he still believes in the power of standard English, composed with complete, syntactically clear sentences and arranged in orderly paragraphs, to express the full force of whatever thoughts or feelings the most chaotic situation can call forth, and unlike so many more others he still retains a perhaps romantic faith in the ultimate importance of certain fixed values in the world of ethics. Because of the first his novel has a beauty of form which only throws into sharper relief the hideousness of its material, and because of the second it gives the effect not of complete futility but of something won in a battle of good against evil.

When Crump, goaded at last to madness, struck his wife down and saw that she was dead a certain calmness came over him:

> Quietly he went to the window and opened it and looked up at the stars. If the universe was a mere mechanism and we but accidental crawlers on this planet's crust, neither deeds done nor undone mattered and love and hate and cruelty and mercy and rancor and justice were indistinguishably one. But if this were not so, if—were it only by a slow process of becoming—the universe strove, like man himself, for values beyond the dust, then he had helped to reestablish the shaken moral equilibrium of the world, to save cosmos from chaos, to make justice prevail.

A little earlier he had wondered at this tendency of his "to ally his small troubles to the eternal nature of things and to drag the universe into his tiny conflicts." He had amusedly considered how difficult it was for a man, riding in the smoker of a Pullman car and dressed in a Kuppenheimer suit, to conceive himself as the protagonist in the universal drama. Yet it is just this power to project himself upon the universe, to see his struggle as the struggle of evil against good, which sets the spiritual tone of the book. Perhaps it is merely a romantic delusion, but, delusion or not, it is still capable of an effectiveness in art, for it gives to the hero his dignity and lends to his story something of the elevation of tragedy. Perhaps Mr. Lewisohn is the only man alive capable of writing such a book and capable at the same time of maintaining that the world which it describes is something more than sound and fury. (pp. 149-50)

Joseph Wood Krutch, "Significant Ugliness," in The Nation, *Vol. CXXIV, No. 3214, February 9, 1927, pp. 149-50.*

CARL VAN DOREN (essay date 1932)

[*Van Doren is considered one of the most perceptive critics of the first half of the twentieth century. He worked for many years as a professor of English at Columbia University and served during the 1920s as a critic and literary editor for* The Nation *and* The Century. *A founder of the Literary Guild and author or editor of several American literary histories, Van Doren was also a critically acclaimed historian and biographer. Howard Moss wrote of him: "His virtues, honesty, clarity and tolerance are rare. His vices, occasional dullness and a somewhat monotonous rhetoric, are merely, in most places, the reverse coin of his excellence." In the following excerpt, Van Doren considers the importance of* Expression in America *to the development of American literary criticism.*]

The canon of American literature refuses to stay fixed. Thirty, even twenty, years ago it seemed to many observers that the end of a literary epoch had been reached and that the elder classics were secure on solid thrones. Bearded and benevolent, the faces of Bryant, Longfellow, Whittier, Lowell, Holmes, and sometimes (rather oddly) Whitman, looked down unchallenged from the walls of schoolrooms. Emerson was the American philosopher, Irving the American essayist, Cooper the American romancer, Hawthorne the American explorer of the soul, Poe the American unhappy poet (unhappy on account of his bad habits), Thoreau the American hermit, Mark Twain the American humorist (barely a man of letters), Henry James the American expatriate, and Howells the American Academy. Here were fifteen apostles set in a rigid eminence, braced by minor figures grouped more randomly about them.

Where is that accepted canon now? Emerson and Hawthorne and Thoreau, risen dramatically above Bryant, Longfellow, Whittier, Holmes, and Lowell, stand in the rarer company of Poe and Whitman. Irving and Howells have shrunk and faded. Cooper has scarcely held his own. Mark Twain seems a great man of letters as well as a great man. Henry James seems a brilliant artist whatever nation he belongs to. Herman Melville has thrust himself by main strength, and Emily Dickinson has gently slipped, into the canon. Several writers of the past forty years now mingle on virtually even terms with the sacred band.

There is no use trying to calculate how much the rank of some of these elder classics was due to the vested interest of publishers who had issued collected editions, or of teachers in schools and colleges who knew how to "teach" Longfellow but not Emily Dickinson, Howells but not Dreiser, Irving but not Mencken. Vested interests were not all. A good many men and women taught to read in the nineteenth century could not endure to read about the twentieth when they saw it bared in literature. Patriotism and propriety had a hand. So, of course, had the natural inertia with which each age resists the age that follows it. But all these vested interests, this provincialism and patriotism and propriety and inertia, have been threatened. They would be overwhelmed if they were aware of their defeat

by the rush with which the literature of the United States has advanced in two or three decades from a point of relative inferiority to a point where it is on the whole equaled only by the literature of Germany among its present contemporaries.

No doubt a good many years will have to pass before the traditional canon is thoroughly revised and Americans are ready to distinguish between their major and their minor prophets. Not much help can be expected from the American Academy or from the universities. They will do no more than wait till the work has been done by actual workers. Then they will hold on to the revised canon with stubborn opposition to any further changes which some later age may have to insist upon.

When the new canon has been arrived at, and before it has in turn been superseded, Ludwig Lewisohn will be seen to have done as much for the revision as any single man. His **"Expression in America"** is a critical milestone. He has done what was most needed to be done. Detaching himself from the more myopic controversies which go on in the United States, he has from the distance of his exile looked back with a commanding eye. His point of view is high as well as distant. He has not even mentioned the numerous ephemerides with which most historians of American literature clutter their pages. He has put down the previously mighty and exalted the previously humble without self-conscious argument. And this he has done not in literary contentiousness but in obedience to the most rigorous and lofty principles by which the whole course of American literature has ever been estimated.

Literature he regards as "the fullest and most continuous expression of the totality of man's life." It is "part of the biologic process. Man is, to put it on the humblest plane, a speaking and singing animal." Literature may formerly have been "an elegant diversion or an illustration of the foreknown and fixed," but it has become "moral research, a road to salvation, the bread of life." Ancient authority having disappeared, literature "must teach and deliver in a new and flexible sense or it is meaningless. Scripture, I may repeat, having become literature, it was necessary for literature to become scripture." The man of letters cannot be overlooked or undervalued. He "lives with the highest awareness his day in human history; unconsciously or consciously he shapes his experience into a work which implies such a universe as he dreams or can endure, or else implies the repudiation of the world and the triumph, however pessimistic, of man's spirit over the hostile gods." The man of letters, having this responsibility, must be held strictly to account. "Nothing avails except stringent veracity or the sovereign creative imagination."

Other historians of American literature might perhaps have agreed with these strong doctrines if they had heard of them. In a sense, all general statements are true. It is the application of them to special instances that matters. Mr. Lewisohn has not held back his hand when it comes to his applications. On many points he may be disagreed with. He is, after all, himself only one man with passions, susceptibilities, prejudices. But he has here freed himself as far as it is perhaps possible from idiosyncrasies of taste and opinion. He has with astounding learning and sympathy brought the whole of American literature before the bar of his own judgment, and there has handed down his verdicts with the most scrupulous judicial austerity.

Mr. Lewisohn admits so little divorce between literature and life that his book is naturally more than a study of the literary production of the United States. "All men," he quotes from Emerson, "live by truth and stand in need of expression. . . .

The man is only half himself, the other half is his expression.''
''Expression in America'' amounts consequently to a kind of
spiritual history. Here, studied with a force and range and point
and beauty rarely found in literary historians, are the successive
steps which the United States has taken in the process of becoming aware of itself, of overcoming its hesitant, polite beginnings at self-expression, of admitting to the record the world
of consciousness outside the genteel tradition, of engaging in
a violent critical debate between decorum and candor, of at
last standing up among the literary nations of the earth. The
book, incidentally a superb history of American literature, is
primarily a moral epic of America. It could hardly have been
written before 1929. As much as any single book is likely soon
to do, it sums up the intellectual achievements of the United
States in a time of drastic change.

If Mr. Lewisohn is proved by events to have been a bad prophet,
it will be because his country either could not or would not
hold itself up to the level of his prophetic demands. They are
simply the true demands of great literature anywhere. Without
attention to them the United States will not have a great literature or recognize it when it has come. (pp. 429-30)

> Carl Van Doren, ''Toward a New Canon,'' in The
> Nation, *Vol. CXXXIV, No. 3484, April 13, 1932, pp.
> 429-30.*

GRANVILLE HICKS (essay date 1932)

[*Hicks was an American literary critic whose famous study* The
Great Tradition: An Interpretation of American Literature since
the Civil War *(1933) established him as the foremost advocate of
Marxist critical thought in Depression-era America. Throughout
the 1930s, he argued for a more socially engaged brand of literature and severely criticized such writers as Henry James, Mark
Twain, and Edith Wharton, who he believed failed to confront
the realities of their society and, instead, took refuge in their own
work. Hicks was shocked by the effects of the Great Depression
and believed that events demanded a new commitment on the part
of writers to clearly understand and express their times. In Marxist
terms this meant that all American artists should comprehend the
growth of capitalism and its negative side effects, such as war,
periodic depressions, and the exploitation and alienation of the
working class. Thus the question Hicks posed was always the
same: to what degree did an artist come to terms with the economic
condition of the time and the social consequences of those conditions? Hicks believed that it was the task of American literature
to provide an extremely critical examination of the capitalist system itself and of what he considered its inherently repressive
nature. After 1939, Hicks sharply denounced communist ideology,
which he called a ''hopelessly narrow way of judging literature,'' and in his later years adopted a less ideological posture in
critical matters. In the following excerpt, Hicks assesses the virtues and shortcomings of* Expression in America.]

Hitherto even our best histories of American literature have
been faintly suggestive of the scrapbook and the filing cabinet.
Mr. Lewisohn writes as if no one had ever written of these
American authors before, as if he had read their books just
yesterday and was eager to tell us what he thought about them.
He writes freshly and personally and very well indeed. He
writes out of a full knowledge of his field, and he has in addition
such a vivid awareness of the literature of other countries as
puts the professional scholar to shame. His book [**''Expression
in America''**] is better than his principles, and there is not an
author he mentions about whom he does not say something
fruitful. (p. 240)

But of course this is not merely the record of the adventures
of a soul among masterpieces and near-masterpieces. It is not
merely an account of what books Lewisohn enjoys, but also
an account of how they came to be written. ''It was equally
inevitable,'' he writes, with that touch of pompousness that
invades his style whenever he mentions the subject, ''that I
use the organon or method of knowledge associated with the
venerated name of Sigmund Freud.'' Hence we find scattered
about the book such phrases as ''defensive rationalization,''
''psychical and physical masochist,'' ''compensatory fantasy,'' ''feigned substitute for the mother-womb,'' ''*Schuld-
gefühl*,'' ''unconscious homo-erotic wishes,'' and ''homosexual's atavistic subconscious memories of the men's house in
primitive societies.'' We learn that Poe suffered from ''a trauma
sustained in infancy,'' that Emerson, Thoreau and James had
little sexual vitality, that Hawthorne and Melville had mother
fixations, that Howells was repressed, and that entire literary
movements may be explained on the basis of ''group neuroses.''

It is needless to say that any method which may provide insight
into human conduct should not be disregarded. Though we
may wish Freud could give us more, we must gratefully accept
whatever it is he can give. But we cannot be satisfied, as
Lewisohn sometimes is, with the mere juggling of words, and
we cannot escape the realization that at best the Freudian method
can explain but a small portion of the mental processes whence
literature springs. Lewisohn, for example, makes a virtue of
saying frankly that Whitman was a homosexual, but he does
not show how his homosexuality influenced ''Leaves of Grass.''
Emerson's low sexual vitality may or may not be an explanation
of certain of his weaknesses; it obviously does not explain his
central strength. If the excellence of ''The Scarlet Letter'' is
due to Hawthorne's ''happy and harmonious union with Sophia
Peabody,'' why is ''The House of the Seven Gables'' ''all
texture, all atmosphere, quite without bone or muscle''? Why
should a ''powerful mother fixation'' make Melville a weak,
petulant writer and Moody a strong and noble one? Because,
says Lewisohn, Moody ''reacted creatively and not neuroti-
cally.'' Words, words!

This reliance on Freudianism, even when its weaknesses are
patent, is all the more striking because of Lewisohn's rejection
of all explanations of literary activity in terms of environmental
forces. ''In the study and interpretation of the arts,'' he writes,
''we can dismiss in respect of the individual's possibility of
expression and his special approach to it, the pressure of environment.'' Again: ''Of environment the influence is so doubtful
and confusing in all but superficial matters as to be negligible.''
Can he mean this? Can he mean what he says in the preface,
that the experience of the modern poet is ''wholly individual''
and takes shape ''under the informing law of the individual
creative mind''?

One asks if Lewisohn can mean this, not only because he has
argued so vehemently in his novels that the individual develops
fully only as part of a cultural unit, but also because so much
that he says in this book contradicts the extreme individualism
of the passages just quoted. He points out in one place, for
example, that the collective culture of his time and place is the
writer's necessary material, whether he revolts against it or
accepts it. In another he says that the artist is ''part of the
collectivity even as rebel and revolutionary; he is mouthpiece
first of his clan and race and city, next of all mankind.'' But
are not clan and race and city parts of a man's environment?
If he is their mouthpiece, is he not vitally influenced by them?

And if he is mouthpiece for his clan, race and city, is he not also mouthpiece for his class?

Moreover, Mr. Lewisohn does refer from time to time to the influence of political and economic forces on literature. He heads a chapter, for example, "Demos Speaks." He mentions Mark Twain's indebtedness to the frontier and the influence on Howells of the section and class in which he was born. He explains the conflict between Babbitt and Spingarn in sociological terms; he shows how More's critical views are associated with political conservatism; he asserts that economic security is a foe to critical excellence. It is true that he recognizes his inconsistency and tries to save himself by saying, "The environment, age, country, culture, climate, has everything to do with determining the existence and entire character of the work of both the bard and, above all, the artificer." But, even granting that Lewisohn is right in believing the creative spirit unique, which is obviously not the case, we may point out that he has himself used sociological explanations in dealing with "essential expressions of the spirit of man."

One does not object, of course, to these sociological explanations; one only wishes there were more of them. If Lewisohn had been willing to pay a little more attention to economic forces, as they shape the ideologies of the various classes, he might have explained the peculiar dominance of Puritanism in America and the survival of many Puritan qualities. He might have shown why the genteel tradition arose and why it has persisted. He could have found a much better interpretation than Freud can give him of the weaknesses of Emerson and Thoreau, and he could have discovered in Whitman's class background a better clue to his virtues and defects than he was able to discover in his homosexuality. He could have dealt far more cogently with those two paradoxical persons, Henry Adams and Henry James, and he could have avoided the confusion that permeates his discussion of contemporary literature.

It is apparent that Lewisohn went out of his way, just as far out as he possibly could, to avoid coming to grips with the problem of class alignments and their influence on literature. He regards himself as a complete individualist and declares that "all creative spirits are necessarily heretics." Why he holds this opinion can easily be seen by anyone who has read **"Up Stream"** and **"Mid-Channel."** Though by birth, culture and training a member of the bourgeoisie, Lewisohn was, on racial grounds, repudiated by the bourgeoisie of America. He became, of necessity, heretic and rebel. Yet, as his novels so clearly show, he was not satisfied with his individualism; he wanted to belong to something. But he was not willling to face the fact that there is only one alternative to belonging to the bourgeoisie.

So he has been divided. On the one side there is his individualism, which expresses itself both in a noble love of liberty and in a petulant contempt for instrumentalism as a philosophy, behaviorism as a psychology and communism as a form of social organization, as well as for any explanation of literature in terms of social forces. On the other side there is his insistence that individualism is not enough, his scorn for "the rebel who has nothing but his rebellion," his recognition that "liberty means a new principle of action." He knows that individualism is petering out as a literary force, and his whole discussion of the writers whom he groups in the chapter called "Beyond Naturalism"—Cabell, Cather, O'Neill and the like—is a record of his failure as well as theirs. Yet he cannot, at this late date and isolated as he is from the American scene, take the step that would genuinely liberate him.

It is sad to note even in this book evidences that Lewisohn's individualism not only involves him in contradictions, but actually is cutting away the man's integrity. His humanitarian zeal, once so strong and admirable, withers away: like so many good liberals, he is moved to attack one social evil in America and one only, prohibition. He is taking refuge also, one notices, in metaphysical vagaries. He believes in reconciliation to "the suffering but not overwhelmed spirit of man," whatever that may mean, in "inherent values," in an "absolute" liberty of life and art. He says in one place that religion is necessary to art and in another indicates that it is dying. He is suspiciously impressed by the new physics as well as the new psychology. What else could one expect? Here as everywhere we find evidences of the breakdown of liberalism and individualism. But these lamentable symptoms, after all, concern us less at the moment than the fact that, if individualism is declining, here is surely one of the glories of its twilight. (pp. 240-41)

> *Granville Hicks, "The Sunset Glow of Individualism," in* The New Republic, *Vol. LXX, No. 906, April 13, 1932, pp. 240-41.*

DOROTHEA BRANDE   (essay date 1933)

[*Brande was an American editor, novelist, and critic. In the following excerpt, she attacks Lewisohn's reading of American literature in* Expression in America.]

Not long ago in actual years a number of the young writers of these states became simultaneously agitated about the dearth of genius and the poverty of art in our country. With praiseworthy earnestness they set about altering conditions so that genius might flourish here. It was not the first period in the history of the world which had produced no genius of the first order for some two or three hundred years; men of major genius do not arise according to any predictable periodicity. Nevertheless, since it seemed to her young literati so humiliating a fact that America had not made her addition to the roster of the world's great names, although she had celebrated the fourth centenary of Columbus's landing in the closing years of the nineteenth century, with an enterprise which was truly even though somewhat ludicrously American, they set about enriching America's soil so that any seed of genius might take root and flourish in it.

That their ideas had the stale novelty which characterizes most current critical and educational thought, that with the sole addition of the vocabulary of the "new psychologists" the set of notions with which we were so impressively presented were the off-scourings of the unsound romantic French, German, and English ideas of the century and a half before, were facts which were not apparent to the intellectual parvenus who made up the reading-public of these young men. An enormous acclaim greeted the efforts of Mr. Van Wyck Brooks to find "a usable past" for those of our generation, of Mr. Randolph Bourne to arouse an intellectual revolution, and of Mr. John Dewey to establish subjectivism from kindergarten to college.

This wild acclaim of silly notions was not surprising. By following their recommendations one could appear a full-grown critic with no further preparation for the task than a set of opinions, impulsively arrived at, put down in a psycho-analytical jargon which was already at the disposal of any newspaper-reader. Overnight we had a whole school of new critics applauding, further, and recommending each other's work. No one who was alive in the twenties is likely ever to forget the stirring days of our "Intellectual Renaissance". But the American genius yet tarried.

By the thirties those rousing days had begun to appear a little tarnished. Mr. Bourne was forgotten, Mr. Brooks was silent, Mr. Dewey was being taken more seriously by newspaper readers than by philosophers. *The American Mercury* had not its old bracing tone, although Mr. Mencken continued in its pages to appreciate music justly and severely, while trying to foist off on those who looked to him for literary judgements the *Poet and Peasant* of Mr. James Branch Cabell, the *Main Street, Babbitt,* and *Arrowsmith* of America's literary Bizet.

The palmy days of the "Renaissance" were over, but each publishing season sees attempts to galvanize it into life again. One of the most notable of these attempts here concerns us, in the nature of a second wind for one of those who shaped the earlier period: Mr. Ludwig Lewisohn's *Expression in America,* published last year, and its companion anthology, *Creative America,* just issued. The earlier book was heralded with something like hysteria—doubtless aggravated by nostalgia. Six hundred pages devoted to the literary history of our country! Explaining to us the reasons for our literary poverty; heartening us by calling to our attention tenuous excellences which we had, in our despair, overlooked; ending on a high note of hope! And in words which (although barbarous) we could all understand! Mr. William Soskin declared that "The shrill voices of the literary faddists fade into an embarrassed silence as Lewisohn booms forth his literary judgements. *Expression in America* is the most important book on American art offered to the American people in a number of years". Mr. Seldes "cannot think at the moment of a story of American literature which comes within a hundred miles of this in stature and scope". It was "the best and most interesting book of criticism of American writing" Mr. Franklin P. Adams had ever read. Mr. Rascoe will turn over the book to his son "with the suggestion that he can toss all the other books on American literature into the ash can", and Mrs. Paterson finds it "the finest volume of American criticism to date, stimulating, admirable, even noble". Mr. Charles Hanson Towne would have us thank Mr. Lewisohn on our knees.

It would be a naïve soul today who could be misled by this "Brekekekex" of the newspaper critics into believing that Mr. Lewisohn's book would truly lead him forth into new and starry adventure. But not the wariest could expect the overflowing absurdity of *Expression in America* and *Creative America.* From misquotation to misquotation, over error after error, through misapprehension simple and misapprehension compound, Mr. Lewisohn flits on, intent on his "revaluation of the past in the terms of the present", using for that purpose "the organon or method of knowledge associated with the venerated name of Sigmund Freud". Yes, that is the treat the critics had in store for us when they sent us breathless to this epoch-making book! At last, at last, a history of American literature written in that bastard jargon which is the language neither of criticism nor of the psychiatric clinic, but a dreadful compound which will not even exist for "revaluation" by a Lewisohn of the future.

It is impossible to discuss soberly tomes based on the fallacy that the "modern man" must have the art of the past "revaluated" for him before it can be absorbed or appreciated. If such were truly the case there could be no enduring work of art, and the word "genius" would be meaningless. Nevertheless the books are significant, and their reception is significant. Are true scholarship, true criticism, true—although the very word is in disrepute—nationalism in so grave a state of decline

that there is no one to rise and say, not indeed to Mr. Lewisohn and his upholders, but to the young men and women who are forming their tastes and opinions today, "Do not accept this book; its judgements are eccentric and personal; its scholarship is faulty; its author is incapable of comprehending your people"?

It seems that today such words cannot be said. The critic who utters them, no matter how soberly and advisedly, will be called a sneerer, a conservative, an anti-Semite—as though stupidities of the sort that abound in *Expression in America* were never written except by the members of Mr. Lewisohn's race. That they come to us oftenest and in their most extreme form from Jewish writers cannot be denied; unhappily, whatever their origin, they have penetrated the ideas of every race within our borders. By some incomprehensible rule of contemporary sportsmanship, we must be supinely complaisant while a Mr. Lewisohn reiterates his nonsense, and often offensive nonsense, about America and Americans. We may not protest. . . . (pp. 189-93)

It would not be true to say that no illumination came to me in the days spent in reading these two volumes. I had, indeed, an experience so sharp, so vivid, so personal that if I were able to convey it well it must surely wring approval from Mr. Lewisohn himself. Undoubtedly I shall fail, but I must try:

In the pages devoted to excerpts from his own work in *Creative America,* Mr. Lewisohn quotes from *The Case of Mr. Crump* a chapter which he entitles "A Musician's Childhood". Herbert, the hero, is a boy growing up in the South. "Sunday afternoons were quiet and drowsy", and every Sunday the boy listens to a chant which comes from the Afro-American church across the way. (p. 196)

Here Mr. Lewisohn gives two lines of music.

"The chant must not be lost"! That "chant" which filtered into the knowledge of Mr. Lewisohn and Mr. Lewisohn's little hero through the hymn-singing Negroes on Sunday afternoons was in no danger of being lost. It will never be lost while any descendant of a New Englander lives. Mr. Lewisohn need not preserve it for us, though we thank him for recognizing its beauty. . . . We will gladly let it furnish his hero "with the ground-work of the thematic material of the tone-poem 'Renunciation' with its motto from Goethe, 'Entsagen, sollst du, sollst entsagen'". But must we pretend that we are hearing it for the first time, or hearing it aright, when we meet it in this twice-corrupted form?

As in those bombastic, presumptuous sentences about the "Negro chant", so again and again in these two books: here are volumes condescendingly filled with the words of our people, purporting to bring to us an unappreciated treasure. These words, these ideas, filtered through an alien mind, do certainly still bear upon them some trace of their original intent, do remotely testify, for all the warping, distorting, and falsifying of their meaning, to the early presence in this country of a strong and intelligent race. *Entbehren sollst du: sollst entbehren.* Mr. Lewisohn was moved. Here, too, he would preserve for us, and for more recent comers to our shores, what was never in danger of dying out. Although he did not understand it, although it comes almost unrecognizably back to us, he was instant to serve us, so that our literature "might not be lost". But there are those of us to whom his service is supererogatory, for there are still men and women in America who learned to read in their fathers' libraries, as they had from their mothers the true air of "By cool Siloam's shady rill". (pp. 197-98)

Dorothea Brande, "Mr. Lewisohn Interprets America," in The American Review, *Vol. II, No. 2, December, 1933, pp. 189-98.*

ADOLPH GILLIS (essay date 1933)

[*In the following excerpt, Gillis summarizes Lewisohn's importance as an author.*]

Lewisohn has always been, in his life and in his works, a peculiarly American phenomenon; and all the more so, strangely enough, because he has been opposed to many things universally regarded as American. This may be a paradox, but then so is Lewisohn. He is, for example, a traditionalist; and yet he is also a rebel.

The truth is that he has been too self-contained to be completely the child of his age; too intent despite the difficulties of modern life which have certainly beset him as sorely as his fellows, upon following an inner light. When we pierce, if we can, to the core of Lewisohn, we find the most uncompromising—and also, it must be said, the most humane—egoism left in the world today. For Lewisohn, despite the terrible doom upon the individual pronounced by modern thought, still cherishes a faith in human freedom; and it is this faith and its summons to unremitting battle, which has kept his work so passionately alive.

It would be a mistake, however, to suppose that Lewisohn has not shared the disenchantment which has produced a Spengler and a Krutch. He has known their sense of futility; but he has outgrown it, as he has outgrown his youth. Long ago, as a boy of twenty at Charleston College, Lewisohn wrote his master's thesis on Matthew Arnold, whose gloom is assuredly as noble as the pessimism now in fashion. There is evident in this essay of the literary novice a shrewd understanding of the modern elegiac note; but there is evident, too, what so many of our Cassandras lack, an acceptance of the self-responsibility which loss of faith only the more imperatively enjoins. "Sink in thyself!" sang Arnold. "There ask what ails thee, at that shrine!" And Lewisohn, "sunk in himself" these thirty years since, has looked at life from the perfectionism of an aristocrat, shocked at its numberless evils, and yet—and this is significant—never recoiling from them, never once despairing of their ultimate defeat. Disillusionment is simply not in him. Rather, life has held for him the ecstasy of a cause; the dissident in him has found in it a sufficient measure for his powers. And that is his answer to the prophets of doom—the sheer desperateness of man's battle calls for courage, indeed makes life itself worth living.

But there are some who deny the efficacy of his doctrine and point to certain limitations in Lewisohn's temper that sharply circumscribe his greatness. He has no humor; he is too self-engrossed; he is not really a creative writer but a critic—these, to take them all at once, are the arrows directed against him, whose barbs, sad to say, are not always free from venom. But, to consider these charges in the order of their naming, asking humor from Lewisohn is asking the unthinkable. With such a man, whose vision of the world is often somber, we may question the fidelity of his picture but we cannot compel him to laugh. American literature has too long resounded with the hollow merriment that betrayed the spiritual emptiness beneath. More than anything else it has needed not merely noisy laughter nor a delicate and all-forgiving gentility but rather straightforward speech with the merciful asepsis of its message.

Little need be said on the other two counts; they refute themselves after but a moment's reflection. If Lewisohn's novels—*The Case of Mr. Crump, The Island Within, The Last Days of Shylock*—are not specimens of a creativeness beyond the technically critical, then error must be allowed to sin in peace. For, indeed, these novels and others reveal in high degree what Lewisohn has himself so sternly exacted of his "poets," that they body forth an honest vision, and in the flame of man's suffering light up the vast theater of the world. Who will deny this virtue in Lewisohn? Will it be those who dislike the emphasis of his voice? If so, we must remind them of Anatole France's pertinent saying: "All who flatter themselves that they do not write themselves into their work are the dupes of the most fallacious illusion." How much more compelling, therefore, is the urge to self-recording in the case of a man whose artistic impulse and creative self-justification make him the symbol of a larger life and, as in *Up Stream* and *Mid-Channel,* announce him, to put it bluntly, as both herald and prophet of his day!

He stands out at last, both as man and artist, distinguishable above the welter of contemporary letters, still a champion of good—and nearly always lost—causes. That is why for him, as some have failed to understand, "the life of the mind is so much an affair of the passions." Truly so: there is no schism for him between truth and conduct, between the ideal and reality. There is only the battle between. And in waging that battle, in book after book, Lewisohn—one of the most thorough-going libertarians in letters today—shows no sign of the creative drought which in the clamor and restlessness of our era has overtaken so many a figure in American literature. The reason is not far to seek. In an age of skepticism, Lewisohn believes; in an age of inertia, he fights on. That, as we have said before, gives his work vitality while at the same time it challenges our respect. (pp. 105-10)

Adolph Gillis, in his Ludwig Lewisohn: The Artist and His Message, *Duffield and Green, 1933, 110 p.*

ERNEST SUTHERLAND BATES (essay date 1934)

[*In the following excerpt, Bates contends that both Lewisohn's fiction and nonfiction betray a development from an enlightened intellectual to a sectarian fanatic.*]

Eight years ago literary America was agog over the news that another masterpiece had been refused the use of the United States mails—those being the days when John Sumner and the Federal Post Office were still acting as effective publicity agents for radical sex literature. The particular masterpiece was a novel, **"The Case of Mr. Crump,"** published in Paris and written by Ludwig Lewisohn, one of our leading expatriates in that legendary paradise of good, dead Americans. (p. 441)

[The] interest of the book was not centered in its hero. The delicately artistic Crump, always blameless in his conscious motivation, unable because of his very nobility to make head against the animal cunning of his wife, and altogether too good for this wicked world, would very soon have become tiresome had he not been over-shadowed by Mrs. Crump. The strength of the work lay entirely in its depiction of her personality. Here was a virago who combined the vices of all the detestable women one has ever met; not to be encountered whole in any land on earth, degenerate actuality never producing such perfection of evil in a single person, but seemingly more real than the half-fulfilled creatures about us, a Platonic essence incarnated in repellent flesh, a Mars of women, hateful to gods and men—hateful not merely because she was stripped by the author of every shred of moral decency but because she was also rendered disgusting by her filthiness of speech and manners and by an accumulation of bodily infirmities, such as snoring, wheezing, belching, and retching, repeated page after page until the woman was transformed into a kind of pervasive stink, unendurable but inescapable. All this accomplished in the coolest behavioristic manner, devoid of adjectives, inspired by a loathing so intense that it hypnotized author and reader into simply gazing upon the detestable object without breath or desire for comment.

American literature has not been rich in works born of hatred, our authors either lacking the emotion or lacking the courage to express it. Mr. Lewisohn, as Thomas Mann in a judicious introduction to the volume pointed out [see excerpt dated 1926], was conforming to a European pattern, but he bettered the instruction he had received, evincing a degree of creative malice beyond the reach of even such masters as Swift, Byron, or Strindberg.

The book, of course, has the defects of its qualities. Very early the reader discovers that the author is not going to permit Mrs. Crump, by any chance, to perform even the smallest act of ordinary human decency such as occasionally adorns the life of even the most reprobate of mortals. Mrs. Crump is incapable of saying "Good morning" or "It's a pleasant day" without an interested motive. Moreover, this motive is imputed, not shown directly; we are not taken into her own consciousness; the method of presentation is pictorial. Crump's inner righteousness, on the other hand, is fully and lovingly revealed. The book is precisely such a one as Crump himself would have written had he possessed the genius of Mr. Lewisohn.

So it came as no great surprise when Mr. Lewisohn some years later, in his second autobiography, "**Mid-Channel**," virtually admitted his own spiritual identity with Mr. Crump. Certain incidents of the novel had already appeared, with very different implications, in "**Up Stream**," and the sweet and gentle "Mary" of that volume, her husband's helper and inspirer, author of "Humble Folk," to which he contributed a eulogistic introduction, had been developed by Mr. Crump's imagination into the self-righteous and revengeful Elise of "**Don Juan**," and finally into the amazing Mrs. Crump who bore no resemblance to the Mary in whom she had originated. Similar though less complete was the transformation of the author of "**Up Stream**" into the Lucien Curtis of "**Don Juan**" and then into Herbert Crump, the formerly integrated Mr. Lewisohn becoming eventually a divided personality, Mr. Crump-Lewisohn, whose self-contradictory drives were destined to lead him into strange attitudes and thoughts still stranger. (pp. 441-42)

Rankling memories of social injustice, the consciousness of unrecognized abilities, the sense of being enslaved by one's inferiors were at last beginning to bear their bitter fruit in exacerbated egotism, a persecution complex, and a tendency to regard the suffering personal self as a crucified Messiah. Mr. Lewisohn, or Mr. Crump-Lewisohn as he was now about to become, was too angry to be able to detect his real enemies in the industrial leaders of an economic system responsible for both the war and the intolerance from which he had suffered. Instead of being led to an analysis of the causes of the situation, he was hypnotized by the personal suffering. For this his domestic difficulties, following close upon the final events recounted in "**Up Stream**," were no doubt largely responsible.

These inspired his next volume "**Don Juan**," a much milder preliminary version of "**The Case of Mr. Crump**." "**Don Juan**,"

besides being a plea for freer divorce, which was entirely consistent with Mr. Lewisohn's earlier philosophy, introduced a new note in its violent attack upon the conception of marriage as "comradeship," its hero, the author's obvious mouthpiece, demanding "mistress and madonna; the one to love and serve him, the other for him to love and serve." This demand for a return to the age of chivalry, which was, incidentally, a return to the ideals of Charleston, South Carolina, as known in youth, was the first of the compensatory devices adopted by Mr. Crump. Accused of not being sufficiently American, he would be that best of Americans, "a Southern gentleman," regardless of the fact that this traditional Southern gentleman had already been ridiculed out of existence by Southern writers themselves.

Then followed the flight to Europe, and a new discovery. After being an incarnation of the national genius and of the Southern gentleman, Mr.Crump-Lewisohn decided that he was neither the one nor the other but rather an incarnation of the Jewish genius. Those fools, derided in "**Up Stream**," who had urged that he could not be a good American because he was a Jew, had after all been right. For the much-persecuted Jews had, alone of peoples, been consistently devoted to the life of the intellect and to purely spiritual attainments, all other nations having resorted to the rule of force. Therefore he would devote his pen to the cause of Zionism, the establishment of a purely spiritual political state in Palestine—since Great Britain, in harmony with its own national genius, was willing to assume responsibility for whatever exercise of force might prove necessary to maintain that state. "**Israel**," the resultant work, was a remarkable union of bad arguments with genuinely moving passion and such splendor of description that a non-Jew in reading it was likely to be filled with envy for those not like himself precluded by a luckless Gentile inheritance from participating in such an inspired movement. And by those who regard the treatment of the Jew as the worst blot on "Christian" civilization, the somewhat hectic theses of "**Israel**" can readily be pardoned. Having propounded them and done his duty by Zionism, the author settled down to live comfortably in Paris and write "**The Case of Mr. Crump**."

This adventure in Judaism, however, though to Mr. Crump merely a temporary satisfaction of personal and emotional needs, was really much more than that to the other member of their strange partnership, Mr. Lewisohn finding in the sufferings of his race a deep and abiding stimulus to his powerful, and, at its best, profoundly sympathetic and clear-sighted, imagination. For once thrusting Mr. Crump aside, Mr. Lewisohn in "**The Island Within**" produced another great novel, less intense than its predecessor but far saner, in characterization the fullest and in content the richest of any of his works.

Dealing primarily with four generations of a single Jewish family in Poland, Germany, and the United States it traced the subtle interplay of environment, heredity, and personality with marvelous acumen. True, at one point, the inevitable Mr. Crump snatched the pen and almost ruined the work by trying to turn it into a tract against mixed marriages, but fortunately Mr. Lewisohn snatched the pen back again in the nick of time to write the powerful closing section, supposed to be found in an old manuscript, on the massacre of the Jews at Mainz during the first crusade. Had he written nothing but that single chapter, it alone would have entitled Mr. Lewisohn to literary immortality.

Meanwhile, unfortunately, Mr. Crump was busily endeavoring to stamp his own fretful personality upon the mind of his age. One may in charity pass swiftly over these efforts of misdirected talent—"**Mid-Channel,**" the whining autobiographical sequel to "**Up Stream,**" and "**Stephen Escott,**" a resurrection of the Southern gentleman, in which the hero, supposedly with the reader's sympathy, murders his wife because she won't be a madonna, and "**The Golden Vase,**" a romantic idealization of post-middle-age philandering. In all these, Mr. Lewisohn still struggled, though unsuccessfully, against the Crumpish influence, and in the single instance of his brilliant tour-de-force, "**The Last Days of Shylock,**" he momentarily escaped into clarity. But after each even partial defeat, the lowering Crump has come back with renewed energy, and there can now be no doubt that his has been the final victory.

"**An Altar in the Fields,**" the Crump-Lewisohn novel of the present year, was written entirely by Crump. It purports to deal with two Americans, Dick Belden and Rose Trezevant, who meet in a literary boarding-house in Greenwich Village. Belden, a "very advanced" young author from Iowa, murmurs, on first seeing the romantically named heroine, "She's certainly durned good-looking"; a little later, he blushes "inwardly" on finding that he has noticed her "high firm bosom." Has no one borne the news to Paris that very advanced young Iowans no longer say "durn" or blush, even inwardly, at noting the quality of "bosoms"? The wonder grows when one learns that this young Iowan has already been in New York for three years at the time of this morally unsettling experience, enjoying at least a speaking acquaintance with editors who greet him, on his entering the office, with such words as these: "I don't remember anything today . . . I got home from a party at four o'clock in the morning . . . When the mists cleared . . . I knew that I had all but—all but, mind you—fornicated more or less in public, more or less under Janie's nose last night," and who then call up their wives and explain ". . . Yes, I expect you to overlook it . . . Christ, no, I made no date with the slut, I barely know who she is . . ." Are such frank and simple manners, in the presence of comparative strangers, really characteristic of New York editors, or are they only characteristic of New York editors as seen, somewhat too hopefully, from the left bank of the Seine? The truth is that Crump at the very outset has fallen a victim to mythology, first to the myth of the blushful countryman, then to the myth of the degraded urbanite, both of them antiquated before the Lewisohn family ever left Berlin.

Dick and Rose are happily married, but she tries to get on the stage and poor Dick can't work on his novel for thinking of the dreadful men she must be meeting. They quarrel and she returns to her parents, and Dick still can't write because he keeps thinking of how unhappy they both are. They are reconciled and go to Paris, and Dick can write less than ever because he wants a child and his wife won't consent to have one. Then a wise Jewish physician takes them to the Sahara Desert and there, in the passionate garden of Allah dedicated to Robert Hichens, the wife accepts her husband's embraces without benefit of birth control. They return to America and buy a farm in Connecticut. Rose, happily pregnant, has given up all thoughts of the stage, and at last, thank God, Dick can write.

How, it may be asked, if Mr. Crump-Lewisohn has so completely forgotten the America he once knew as this fantastic story would indicate, was he able, quite recently, to bring out so creditable an "Anthology of American Literature" [as "**Creative America**"]; how was he able, only two years ago, to write so good a book as "**Expression in America**"? There is a double answer. In the first place, Mr. Crump-Lewisohn has not entirely forgotten Mr. Lewisohn's clear insight into the elements of verbal beauty, and wherever it is a question purely of technique, as it often is in these two volumes, his judgment jis still, perhaps, more nearly infallible than that of any other contemporary writer. In the second place, wherever it is not a question of technique but of understanding American culture, "**Expression in America**" and the "**Anthology**" based on it are, as a matter of fact, quite inadequate.

The inadequacy springs from an attempt to write a history of American literature from a completely unhistorical point of view. Environmental influences, the author writes, "are so doubtful and confusing in all but superficial matters as to be negligible," adding the dictum that "personalities create cultural changes." If one asks why certain types of personality, such as the American big business man, appear in particular eras, he receives the reply: "Why they are born at certain times . . . is a mystery. That it is the will of God, is, properly interpreted, not the least rational of answers to this as to other ultimate mysteries." Having thus rejected environmental explanations in favor of the will of God, Mr. Crump-Lewisohn proceeds to over-emphasize a single environmental influence, that of sex-repression, to the neglect of all others, thus being led to confuse colonial Puritanism with the much more lasting Methodism that followed it, to misunderstand the pioneer, and to avoid any serious discussion of the effect of modern industry on modern culture—in other words, to misinterpret every phase of American life from the beginning.

Furthermore, "**Expression in America**" represents, in large part, a direct repudiation of Mr. Lewisohn's earlier critical position, and is, in essence, a surrender to the academicism that the author still affects to despise. Thus he denies to Melville the rank of "even a minor master" on the ground that his work does not vindicate "the moral order" of the universe; and he prefers Mark Twain to Whitman as an artist because he was not a homosexual. Stuart Sherman in his most didactic vein was not so moralistic or confused as Mr. Crump-Lewisohn. We are told that Mark Twain "had no philosophy, no values," that he was "adolescent in intellect" with "the ideas of a village agnostic," and that in his work "we find the crudest and most shallow treatment of the most intricate matters," and then we are assured that "all this, be it emphatically noted, does not count against Mark Twain; it counts for him," because it shows that he was "the average American of his time."

O Mr. Crump, Mr. Crump, what have you done with Mr. Lewisohn? Could you not have reread the essay on tragedy in "**The Modern Drama**" before writing your nonsense on Melville, could you not have looked into "**Up Stream**" to learn whether one becomes a great artist merely by being an average American?

No, Crump could not have done either, because he is convinced that he is a far better man than Mr. Lewisohn ever was, being not merely critic and novelist but priest and philosopher as well. In various recent essays, announced for publication in a single volume, accurately entitled "Toward Religion," Crump has developed his romantic pseudo-mysticism—which bears the same relation to genuine mystical experience that the yearnings of impotence bear to the ecstasies of fruition—into a pseudo-philosophy of the "Form-Urge," a semi-divine spiritual principle supposed to reside in nature and in all men but to be particularly transmitted through biological heredity to the leisure-loving members of the middle class, as distinguished from the aristocratic lovers of power at the top and the dull mass of slaves at the bottom, "though fairly constantly recruited" from the latter. Is this incredible even from Crump? (pp. 446-49)

Heil Hitler! For the mad Nordic myth is twin brother to this new mysticism of the blood, likewise masquerading as biological science, which pretends to find the rule of the middle class established in the constitution of the universe. Heil Astor, Vanderbilt, and Gould! Heil Daniel Drew! Heil, Rockefeller, Morgan, Henry Ford! For with all these men their sacred property has been the symbol of their character. Heil Kreuger, and Heil Insull! For with them, most surely, property was the outward embodiment of an inward vision.

The case of Mr. Lewisohn has proved to be a case of protracted suicide, or, more accurately, a case of the supplanting of a given character by its opposite within a single organism. One of the finest intellects of our time strove to master its environment and failed—as what artist will not fail in a business-ridden society that has no place for him? Subtly within the personality arose a counter-force, creating first the subjective consolations of megalomania, then a refusal to acknowledge the nature of the environment, and finally, made possible to a proud spirit by this refusal, a submission to the environment when renamed "the ultimate mystery," "the form-urge," "the will of God." (p. 450)

Ernest Sutherland Bates, "Lewisohn into Crump," in American Mercury, Vol. XXXI, No. 124, April, 1934, pp. 441-50.

REINHOLD NIEBUHR (essay date 1934)

[*Niebuhr is considered one of the most important and influential Protestant theologians in twentieth-century America. The author of such works as* The Children of Light and the Children of Darkness *(1944) and* Christian Realism and Political Problems *(1953), he persistently stressed the reality of original sin and emphasized the tragic condition of fallen humanity, opposing the secular and liberal Christian tendency toward discounting sin in favor of economic and political explanations of human misery. Niebuhr saw the problem of modern humanity as one in which an overwhelming sense of confusion and meaninglessness have been brought on by technocracy and the resulting rush for power. He saw the task of modern Christianity to be that of ministering to both the worldly as well as the spiritual needs of humankind. In the following review of* The Permanent Horizon, *Niebuhr observes a prevalent theme in this collection of essays.*]

Mr. Lewisohn's latest volume ["**The Permanent Horizon**"] is not his most important one. It embodies a series of essays on various subjects which achieve cohesion through their common polemic against all forms of modernism, liberal and radical. The author states his thesis in the words:

> It is the purpose of this book by a tentative reexamination of human instincts and human experience, to help to reestablish the character of the classical or permanent man. Reason leads neither to "machinism" nor to economic determinism; the developed and disciplined religious instinct does not lead to hate, obscurantism, and tyranny. It is still possible to make true reasons and the will of God prevail.

Mr. Lewisohn is thus unequivocally arrayed with the classicists against various forms of modernism, whether the mechanism of urban life, the sex ethics of Mr. Bertrand Russell, or the political theories of the Communists.

In this conflict Mr. Lewisohn is both a doughty and a vulnerable combatant. He is a formidable foe because he has a very sane and wise insight into the interior problems of the human spirit and a true understanding of the organic relations of life which modernists fail so frequently to comprehend. But his position is vulnerable because he is still too much the liberal individualist and moralist either to do justice to the merits of radical politics or to restore classical religion without doing violence to it. Radical politics and classical religion have one thing in common—their appreciation of the vast forces and destinies which transcend the power and yet determine the fate of the individual. His individual, for all his insistence upon the organic relation of the individual to his historic culture, is essentially discrete and omnipotent. He calls upon him to be converted and to save civilizaion by his change of heart. "Cannot," he asks, "a planned and ordered society be built by the cooperation of free personalitites, by free men taking counsel together?" That question betrays a rather naive individualistic view of the realities of politics. May it not be possible that the freest and most moral individual Mr. Lewisohn could conceive would still be under the compulsion of class interests (largely unconscious) to oppose the project of a planned society? Let him read Mr. Hoover's recent defense of liberty!

The same erroneous individualism and moralism expresses itself in the chapter entitled "A Bourgeois Takes His Stand." Mr. Lewisohn does not like the Communist practice of casting the bourgeoisie in the role of the devil. He counters by drawing a touching picture of their angelic virtues. "The bourgeois desires security, dignity, privacy, liberation from sordid care for the sake of cultural disinterestedness. If he does not desire the last for himself he desires it, or at least in many cases creates it, for his children"; or again, "the bourgeois, the disinterested property-owning man of the ages, capable of disinterestedness because he owns property." Forgetting that the middle classes are historically not middle between poverty and wealth but between aristocracy and proletariat he declares that "by virtue of his middle station he [the middle-class man] has always been nearer the center of both nature and human nature. So, too, he has in practice if not in theory held to the right uses and the permanent meaning of property." He even allows himself a palpable falsification of history when he declares, speaking of German politics, that "when in a given election the Nazis lost, the Communists gained and vice versa; the numerical strength of the parties of the middle remained fairly constant." The real fact is that Communists gained at the expense of the Socialists as German desperation increased, while the fascists wiped out the parties of the middle, a fact which reveals what becomes of the disinterestedness of the man of property, of even a little property, in the hour of political crisis.

Mr. Lewisohn's picture of the man of property may fit a very few individuals. It does not fit the men for whom property is primarily a source of power, our financial and industrial oligarchs. (For some curious reason oligarchs cease to be bourgeois in Mr. Lewisohn's statement of his case.) It does not fit those for whom property is primarily a source of privilege and enjoyment and who have precious little interest in "cultural disinterestedness." It does not even fit the desperate lower middle classes, who try frantically to preserve their individual liberties and their property against the inexorable forces of a collectivist civilization (whether capitalist or Communist) and become the pitiful victims of the capitalists in their efforts to escape communism. Even if Mr. Lewisohn's picture of bourgeois man were a true one, as it may be in the case of a few middle-class professionals, it would still fail to do justice to political realities. The individual disinterestedness of high-minded men is no guaranty of the disinterestedness of their collective behavior, when group clashes with group in economic and social conflict.

Mr. Lewisohn's individualism and moralism betray him as much when he is interpreting religion as when he is refuting radicalism. "The universe exists," he says, "only as it exists in the human consciousness. Were man obliterated there would not only be chaos but there would be void." Yet he believes that "spiritual health can be gained only by the 'voluntary affirmation of the obligatory'—what our grandfathers called and often practiced with so much dignity and beauty as submission to the will of God." Here the thought of the modernist and the classicist are in obvious conflict. The obligatory can only be spoken of as the "will of God" if one can believe that life, and all its systems and opportunities, have meaning and purpose transcending our purposes and independent of our ability to comprehend the meaning. If man himself creates the universe in his imagination, it becomes a chaos the moment its stubborn facts and inexorable forces outrage and frustrate his individual needs and purposes.

Mr. Lewisohn is, in short, a modernist who is too wise to accept some of the credulities and absurdities of modernism but too individualistic and moralistic either to understand classical religion or to do justice to political radicalism. (pp. 455-56)

Reinhold Niebuhr, "'A Bourgeois Takes His Stand'," in The Nation, *Vol. CXXXIX, No. 3615, October 17, 1934, pp. 455-56.*

ROBERT SHAFER (essay date 1935)

[*In the following excerpt, Shafer attacks Lewisohn for employing Freudian psychoanalytic theories in his works of literary criticism.*]

[Dr. Ludwig Lewisohn is] a very able man who could have exerted a powerful influence in favour of straight thinking and significant criticism if he had ever fairly set about it. "To a philosophic eye," wrote Gibbon, "the vices of the clergy are far less dangerous than their virtues." And similarly it is because such men as Mr. Wilson, Mr. Max Eastman, and Dr. Lewisohn are setting an example of shoddy work and slapdash thinking that the [vicious] tendency I speak of has become important.

In the Preface to *Expression in America* Dr. Lewisohn states that he has inevitably used "the organon or method of knowledge associated with the venerated name of Sigmund Freud"; because, he adds, "the portrayer of any aspect of human life or civilization who does not do so to-day will soon be like some mariner of old who, refusing to acknowledge the invention of mathematical instruments because their precision was not yet perfect, still stubbornly sailed his vessel by the stars." This is more emphatic than illuminating, but illumination comes from the body of the book. At the beginning of its eighth section we read:

> The nineteenth century was the century of easy solutions and of eternal truths that lasted ten years. There is a deep human pathos in this circumstance. For one kind of intelligible universe men desired at once to substitute another equally intelligible and stable in order to have a rest, however bleak, for their souls. It is now clear, tragically clear, if one likes, that the nine-

teenth century succeeded solely in asking the pertinent and crucial questions. All its answers were absurdly premature; all its solutions are strewn like withered leaves on an autumnal road. The disillusion, be it remarked, is not with science as an organon; it is with a type of mind that jumped to conclusions suiting its inner climate and then sought to impose its special interpretation, its sombre subjective poetry, upon the world as truth and fact.

This diatribe issues in the characterization of some of the work of Dr. John B. Watson as "grotesque drivel," and of the behaviouristic psychology as degenerate "mechanistic dogmatism"—"a superstition as empty and as rigid as any previous superstition that ever plagued the mind." The Freudian psychology, on the other hand, though it is certainly as naturalistic as the variety thus denounced, Dr. Lewisohn enthusiastically accepts, because it "approaches profoundly suggestive explanations" of human experience. In other words, Dr. Lewisohn's attitude is somewhat similar to Coleridge's towards Christianity. The Freudian psychology "finds" him, or comes home to him, as behaviourism, for example, evidently fails to come home to him. I wish there were more evidence to offer on this particular question; but I can only record that Dr. Lewisohn does not, as might be supposed from his words quoted above, merely accept psychoanalysis as a useful "method of investigation, an impartial instrument like, say, the infinitesimal calculus" [Freud, *The Future of an Illusion*]. As such, it has, beyond question, proved valuable in the treatment of mental disease; though its employment is an extremely delicate matter, involving of necessity, I believe, the physician's inculcation of naturalistic philosophical assumptions. This may shed some light on it; but, in any case, Dr. Lewisohn obviously assumes that the Freudian psychology, which has been elaborated from a basis of psycho-analytical investigation, is a body of valid scientific knowledge, doubtless incomplete, perhaps subject to modification in detail, but not conjectural, not a "merely tentative grouping of ideas for the purpose of testing theories," and not, like everything of the sort bequeathed us by the last century, "absurdly premature."

From the wealth of matter in *Expression in America* illustrating the consequences of this assumption, I choose two typical "explanations," both of which happen to be concerned with criticism:

> Poe's critical theory is a defensive rationalization of his instinctive and inevitable practice, a justification, a glorification of his own lack of passion, humanity, ethical perception, continuity of power, imaginative sympathy, knowledge of man and of human life—of all the capacities and qualities, in brief, that give substance and import to a writer. Poe, like all persons whose inner self-esteem is abnormally low, needed to build a legend of greatness for himself. He made his own limitations the laws of art. . . . The childish confusion at the heart of his critical theory is to be found in his use of the word truth. He uses that word as though it meant proposition, scientific statement, maxim or saw. With these forms of intellectual expression literature has in fact little to do. But Poe pretended to himself, for unconscious reasons of his own, that he was fighting a mean

didacticism, when he was declaiming against the necessary and eternal content of literature, which he himself was incapable of achieving. . . .

The second "explanation" may be given at once: . . .

> Howells, like his age, was acutely and negatively sex-conscious. We have no need to be always protesting against that which does not trouble us. . . . Tradition and authentic personal report have it that as he grew older he grew ever sourer and more intolerant on this subject, . . . falling into a kind of negative frenzy at the slightest suggestion of man's mammalian nature and hence as obsessed by sex as a fighting prohibitionist is by alcohol. . . . Howells' avoidance of human passion in his works is clamorous in its significant and sultry silence. Nor is tradition wholly ignorant of the aging novelist's uneasy and unconsciously guilty methods of sublimation.

> (pp. 40-4)

It is no part of my purpose in this place to comment generally on Dr. Lewisohn's interpretations of Poe and Howells. They invite such comment, because they are open to serious question at a number of points. Their drift, however, if we pass by details, is towards something familiar enough and scarcely doubtful. We did not have to await the Freudian psychology for the discovery that man is a limited, conditioned creature, whose thought is dependent upon his capacities, including his capacity for experience. But Dr. Lewisohn, of course, has more than this to say; and the remarkable thing which calls for special notice is his conclusion in each case that the critical theory under examination has no validity, because of the conditions back of it. The Freudian psychology, in other words, does not simply "explain" Poe and Howells—it explains them away—after which Dr. Lewisohn rescues what he thinks serviceable in the work of each.

In the case of Poe we are definitely informed that the mental condition out of which his work issued was pathological. Not only his criticism, but his tales and poems also, are the products of a diseased mind; though Poe did have "rare and brief" "moments of insight, however troubled." Yet Howells is explained away in terms not different from those which serve for Poe, while it is not pretended that his was really a diseased mind. There are, to be sure, hints looking in this direction, dropped quite after the manner of gossipers who take pains to assure one that they could say more if they would; but on the other hand a great deal is said to show that Howells's mind was of a type common, or indeed practically universal, in his age and country. And, moreover, the process of compensatory or defensive "rationalization" of which Poe and Howells were the victims is detected by Dr. Lewisohn repeatedly in Americans of every generation, and not only in literary people, but in whole sections of the population.

How, indeed, could it be otherwise? Zeal for law and order, we are told, is simply the expression of an unconscious desire to commit crimes which, nevertheless, one is "ethically inhibited from committing." The Puritans of early New England ferociously punished those who disobeyed their regulations because only such punishment could express the "smothered rebellion" of their "natural passions." "The conventional gloating of the 'pure' over the 'impure'" is the expression of

envy, which, when it is otherwise impotent, vents itself in cruelty. The more "pure" one is, in other words, the more "violently sex-conscious" one really is. If one says that another person is "sex-obsessed," one really "bears witness to one's own obsession and to the agonized cry of one's soul: What I dare not do, you shall not do!" In fact, Dr. Lewisohn says, "this process of ambivalence, of simultaneous attraction and repulsion, of desire and fear, must be understood by any one who wishes to penetrate to the true character of men and their ways." And elsewhere he explains "the true character of men and their ways" when he remarks that our "ambivalence" "pollutes and sickens the soul from age to age."

How, I may repeat, could it be otherwise? If things are thus with humanity, the wells of thought are indeed poisoned; and, of course, once the process of "ambivalence" has been discovered through the analysis of mentally diseased people, it can be seen wherever one may choose to look. Nothing would be easier than to exhibit the "fierce ambivalence" which animates Dr. Lewisohn himself, because no one writes with more constant personal reference than he, so that the data in his case are not only abundant, but perfectly transparent. To follow his example, however, would chiefly gratify ribald spirits; and it is more to the present purpose to notice that, according to Dr. Lewisohn and Dr. Freud, there are some instances in which reason really is reason. Examples are to be found even in America, and include, amongst others, Mr. Van Wyck Brooks, Dr. Joseph Wood Krutch, and Dr. Lewisohn. But here arises a difficulty. What is reason?

Dr. Lewisohn is perfectly frank and very insistent in asserting that he is wholly reasonable. Hence I suppose, if he is correct concerning himself, we may discover the nature of reason from its operation in him. But how, on the basis of the Freudian psychology, can he know whether he is correct about himself or not? I am unable to see the slightest possibility of his knowing this, or of our knowing it. If, however, we proceed to contemplate the operations of what we may provisionally call Dr. Lewisohn's "reason," what do we find? I cannot, of course, give anything like a complete report in small space. I can only present a few instances showing the *way* in which Dr. Lewisohn's "reason" works. It tells him, then, that there is an "enormous . . . cleavage between the past and the present," that real change is the rule, that discontinuity marks our world, and that man "has undergone changes which have transmuted the very groundwork of his character and outlook." Yet at the same time it tells him that there are "changeless elements" in man, in nature, and in human life; that "sound literature" has a "changeless character," and so "speaks permanently to men," because men have "eternally" the same "preoccupations"; and that "the effects demanded of literature have not changed in their *essence* from Isaiah and Euripides to, let us say, Dreiser and Shaw." Nevertheless, "there are no external or fixed standards by which either genius may be known from without or creative activity guided from within." Genius, in fact, "creates values as it goes along," working wholly from within; and what genius creates is inherently moral, beautiful, universal in significance, and imperishable. Criticism, however, "is the disengaging and weighing of these values into which men transmute their experience and from which alone experience derives both its *meaning* and its *form*." Criticism thus demands complete detachment, in order that the critic may "hold the balance utterly level." But that education is to be condemned "by which the gentleman withdraws himself from the mob." Still, it is true that "the minority that carries on a national culture is small," and that "the principles of the majority of men are mean and superstitious and barbarous.'' For this reason, doubt-less, ''all creative spirits are necessarily heretics.'' Yet ''it is indeed quite open to question whether the greatest works of the human imagination have not been produced when the artist identified himself largely with the collective culture and tra-dition of his folk.'' And the real explanation of art is to be found in the truth that ''the creative and the procreative instinct are one.''

This collocation of passages, which might be greatly extended, shows how easy it would be to make Dr. Lewisohn's ''reason'' look ridiculous. He has impetuously said his say as he has gone creatively and rapidly along, trusting his genius. When occa-sionally he thinks of his ''reason,'' he is apt to regard it as something supernal; but he is actually guided by his passions, and does not even attempt consistently to ''rationalize'' them. In complete accord, like Mr. Edmund Wilson, with a familiar modern belief, he takes it for a certainty that if he can just be fully enough himself, without let or hindrance, he will strike a vein of fundamental reality uniting him with what is similarly real in all other men. This is the ground of his opposition to all standards, of whatever kind—an opposition which, with other of his ''certainties,'' allies him in his own despite with aesthetic critics whom he has venomously attacked. This, too, explains how he could write, in 1924, that ''the function—perhaps the chief function—of the American critic'' ''must be'' the effort to make a larger number of people understand why artists and writers, or all ''creators,'' of necessity lead irregular lives. And this, finally, accounts for his easy confi-dence that the terrors of the Freudian psychology could be invoked against others without recoil upon himself. He stood, like his venerated master, beyond the fateful circle. The Freud-ian psychology, in other words, was to be welcomed as a useful servant. Through it he could deliver knock-out blows, without taking the trouble to argue any question on its merits. I do not mean that this has been his conscious attitude. His truly mon-umental self-righteousness is, I am sure, genuine. But he is very easily satisfied when he wants to believe anything; and I do not see how, if he had deliberately tried, he could have made it more evident that in reality he has simply used the Freudian psychology as a bludgeon, for his own purposes. And I do not see, in addition, how Dr. Lewisohn could have made it more evident that this fancied resource has in fact weakened and vitiated his work, encouraging him to write confusedly, thoughtlessly, and yet violently. (pp. 45-50)

> *Robert Shafer, ''Criticism,'' in his* Paul Elmer More
> and American Criticism, *Yale University Press, 1935,*
> *pp. 1-58.**

OSCAR CARGILL   (essay date 1941)

[*An American educator, historian, and literary critic, Cargill edited critical editions of the works of such major American au-thors as Henry James, Walt Whitman, Frank Norris, and Thomas Wolfe. In the following excerpt, Cargill provides a general es-timate of Lewisohn's fiction and nonfiction.*]

Lewisohn has written his autobiography in *Up Stream* . . . and *Mid-Channel*. . . . The first is undeniably an important book, both a moving human document and a fearless tract for racial equality. One is stirred to indignation that a man must suffer so much humiliation and injustice as is painfully set down in *Up Stream* merely because his blood is not that of the dominant stock in America. One does not believe, of course, that Lew-isohn was always so discriminated against as he thinks he was.

For example, we doubt if ''Brewer'' of Columbia hated him because he felt in him ''the implacable foe of the New England dominance over our national life'' or because he was a Jew. But that Lewisohn had sufficient reason in other instances to see malice behind any choice that involved himself is sufficient commentary on the existing racial prejudice to disturb any liberal American. And the record of national hostility during the war-hysteria to all things German—even in our universi-ties—is mortifying, so painful, in fact, that the revert to it only under the moral compulsion that the memory will do us good. *Up Stream* is the perfect antidote, with its broad cosmopolitan reference and its passion for universal culture, for 100% Amer-icanism.

How, then, shall we view *Mid-Channel* which is the direct antithesis of *Up Stream*? In the earlier book Lewisohn had insisted that he could take no refuge in the spirit or traditions of his own people. ''My psychical life,'' he says, ''was Aryan through and through.'' After this was written, however, he sep-arated from his Gentile wife and took a Jewish mate; further, he made an intense study of the cultural traditions of the Jews, learning Hebrew and Yiddish of which he had hitherto been ignorant, and he consorted with leaders of his race in Germany, among whom the Zionists made the strongest impression on him. The result was a trip to Palestine and a conversion to Zionism, which he preached in *Israel* . . . and to which he recurs more movingly in *Mid-Channel*. Assimilationism was the impractical ideal of the nineteenth century Jew; nationalism is the practical ideal of the twentieth century leader of his race, according to Lewisohn. That is, the national race consciousness which he finds objectionable in Americans in *Up Stream* he now advocates breeding among his own people. Furthermore, though Lewisohn derides ''German-Jews'' and ''American-Jews'' and declares himself for ''Jewish-Jews,'' it is not at all clear on just what model he would form his people. Who are the Jewish-Jews? Certainly not the bourgeois-Zionistic rabble of Jerusalem today, who no more resemble the ancient He brews, to whom Lewisohn reverts, than a lyric by Irving Berlin resembles a psalm of David. Is Mr. Lewisohn a Jewish-Jew? Nonsense. Mr. Lewisohn is an American, and there is no evi-dence in *Mid-Channel* that all his reading of the Torah and the Prophets has changed him one iota from the sort of person he was in *Up Stream* when he could see no Jewish elements in his own psyche. *Mid-Channel* is not only unconvincing because of its twentieth century nationalism, but also because it is too apologetic in regard to the broken marriage. The author's self-pity and his excuses are tedious, and his new assumption that he is an introvert is contradicted by his reporting on what is about him. There is a moving passage in *Mid-Channel* on the St. Valentine's day massacre of the Jews in Strassburg, in 1349, and some good satirical writing on wealthy Jewish ladies who make it a principle to receive in their salons only such Jews as do *not* associate with Jews, but that is all.

As narratives, Mr. Lewisohn's autobiographical studies are better reading than his fiction and, we are inclined to think, more important. . . . In all his novels he carries a heavy burden of expository matter and his tendency has been to reduce dia-logue and action appreciably with each new book. *The Island Within* . . . , Lewisohn's best novel, devotes more than a hundred pages to the ancestry of his hero before he himself is introduced. This antecedent material tells the story of the sufferings of a Jewish family in Europe from 1840 to the Great War, yet as a representation of persecution it is far less effective than sim-ilar material in Abraham Cahan's *The Rise of David Levinsky*. Cahan has felt his experience, while Mr. Lewisohn's is obviously a piece of reconstruction. When he finally gets down to his study of Arthur Levy, son of an American furniture manufacturer, who is driven from a medical internship in a public sanitarium, because he cannot stand the abuse accorded Jewish patients, into psychoanalysis as a career, Lewisohn becomes really effective. Doctor Levy's infatuation with Elizabeth Knight, daughter of a Methodist minister, leads to a hasty marriage when she becomes pregnant, though Mr. Lewisohn takes pains that the doctor should declare his intentions before Elizabeth can reveal her condition. After the birth of their son, a fine Jewish boy in appearance, Doctor Levy and his wife drift apart. She scores her first success as a writer by pillaging his special knowledge of psychoanalysis for magazine articles, then discovers a knack for writing stuff that publishers snap up. Lewisohn makes it clear that Elizabeth is in no sense an artist and intimates her writing is a form of sex release—a necessary gratification since she is inhibited towards her husband because he is a Jew. Eventually, they part peacefully enough. She completes the book which will outsell all her others, and he, after identifying himself again with his people through volunteering his services to the Beth Yehuda Hospital, is induced to go on a mission in their behalf in Rumania. Elizabeth agrees to alimony only for the support of the boy.

Artistically considered, the novel is weakened at the end by the introduction of a long manuscript on a massacre in 1096 of the Jews of Worms which Arthur Levy reads prior to accepting the mission to Rumania. The remorseless drawing of Elizabeth could be more cheerfully applauded if Arthur Levy were less of a saint. Small episodes in *The Island Within* are much better handled than those which advance the plot: the futile effort of Elizabeth to get a good room for herself and her son under the name of Levy in an Adirondack hotel, and Arthur's success in reconciling his sister and her husband after their marriage has gone awry. Of course, *The Island Within* raises the issue of whether or not happiness is possible in an exogamic marriage. Lewisohn is plainly convinced that it is not. We would agree, if the persons involved were so differently endowed as to sensibility and intellect as were Arthur and Elizabeth—but this is not a fair case. They could hardly have made a go of it were they of the same race. Special pleading spoils the case. On the other hand, Mr. Lewisohn convinces us that there is less psychological strain and soul-searing for the weak in the harbors provided by racial colonies within the large cities. Further, we like his idea that the culture of any racial group is worth perpetuating.

Stephen Escott . . . , which followed *The Island Within,* is by no means so earnest a book, but it displays a wit and sardonic humor, lacking in Lewisohn's earlier novels and not recaptured in *The Last Days of Shylock* . . . , *The Golden Vase* . . . , or in *An Altar in the Fields.* . . . The two great defects of *Stephen Escott* are its lack of unity and its narrative method. The book has three parts, though organized as five; we follow Stephen through a precipitate marriage to a "pure" Wisconsin girl to his blessed release after too many years through the death of his wife from uremic poisoning; next, we find him in France trying to make up for years of sex-starvation with a rich woman who lives wholly for her sensations; when that episode comes to an end, we follow him back to America where he is a mere spectator, while his law-partner, an able and brilliant Jew, works to free the protagonist in a love-murder from a sadistic district attorney. Each unit in this novel would make a whole, or all of them might have been harmoniously joined had Lewisohn been able to make more of his theme of the broadening effect upon a rather narrow Yankee mind of a partnership with a

Jewish intelligence. There is some great stuff in *Stephen Escott*—especially the portrait of Dorothy Escott, but the novel reminds one more of an overturned basket of vegetables than a horn of plenty. Lamentable, moreover, is the prosy expository method.

Marred, too, in the telling, is *Trumpet of Jubilee* . . . , a story of a Jewish refugee woman and her son, Gina and Gabriel Weiss, who fled the Third Reich, after the murder of Kurt, Gina's husband, to seek hospice with relatives in a small town in the American mid-West. Anti-semitism in Germany raises a righteous wrath, but when Mr. Lewisohn makes Gina's American cousin Julian go mad, for not much other reason than his opposition to Zionism, and when he presents the now mature Gabriel as a splendid knight in shining armor fighting for Zionism and British imperialism (in a war which he placed in the late 'forties), we simply have to surrender our critical faculties to coast along. *Trumpet of Jubilee* is a very strange book.

With the exaggeration of sex in the 'twenties it was inevitable that someone should write a history of American letters from the Freudian point of view. Freudian studies of individual authors had filled the magazines and two interesting books, one by [Harvey] O'Higgins and one by D. H. Lawrence, before Ludwig Lewisohn completed his *Expression in America* in 1932, which he had begun in 1927. Despite the fact that Mr. Lewisohn had had a seminar in American literature with Professor Trent when he was at Columbia years before, the greatest weakness of *Expression in America* is the author's obvious unfamiliarity with his material. It is irritating to have him call Emerson's "Hamatreya," "*Mama*treya," and Sarah Orne Jewett's "Marsh Rosemary," "*March Rosary.*" Yet we could dismiss little slips of this sort, even though numerous, did the author show a general familiarity with historical material. Such a section, however, as the second in his volume entitled "The Polite Writers," allegedly treating "that entire group of writers, from Longfellow to Brander Matthews," demonstrates Lewisohn's unfitness for his task, since it betrays not only an abysmal ignorance of the authors cited, but also an unwillingness to examine the material. It is nothing more than a wild harange against a number of people in no sense related (Joaquin Miller is lumped with Longfellow, Sill, and Lanier) whom Mr. Lewisohn suspects of perpetuating the "Puritan" tradition, which he believes to have been stultifying. We do not know what the "Puritan" tradition was since the author dismisses the colonial writers with a wave of his hand. If the force of Puritanism was as evil as he thinks it, it deserved a more adequate study than he has accorded it.

Although *Expression in America* is valueless as an historical study, it is at times stimulating as social and literary criticism. There is, for example, a good passage on the German pietists and poets of Pennsylvania in colonial days. The attack upon Franklin's "venery for health" is soundly indignant, but strange from the lips of the castigator of Puritanism. There is pertinency in his observation that genteel Boston of 1884 "was so disgustingly 'pure' because it was so violently sex conscious," and his citation of the blushes of Irene when Silas Lapham indicated where her bedroom would be in their new house is apt. One is delighted with his insistence that Howells, so generally neglected or derided in the 'twenties, is important: ". . . the more one reads him the surer one is that in the fine sense of Jules Lemaître, he exists—he and his works, and can never wholly fade from the cultural landscape." The high-water mark of the book is the tenth section, "The Great Critical Debate," dealing with the battle-royal between Babbitt and More on the one side and Mencken and his constituency on the other. Here Lewisohn draws upon a wide reading in comparative literature to enforce his points, and his page is rich and nourishing. More of this and less dogmatism, and *Expression in America* would have been a great book. (pp. 729-35)

> Oscar Cargill, "The Freudians," in his Intellectual America: Ideas on the March, *The Macmillan Company, 1941, pp. 537-763.* *

ALFRED KAZIN (essay date 1942)

[*A highly respected American literary critic, Kazin is best known for his essay collections* The Inmost Leaf *(1955) and* Contemporaries *(1962), and particularly for* On Native Grounds *(1942), a study of American prose writing since the era of William Dean Howells. Having studied the works of "the critics who were the best writers—from Sainte-Beuve and Matthew Arnold to Edmund Wilson and Van Wyck Brooks" as an aid to his own critical understanding, Kazin has found that "criticism focussed many—if by no means all—of my own urges as a writer: to show literature as a deed in human history, and to find in each writer the uniqueness of the gift, of the essential vision, through which I hoped to penetrate into the mystery and sacredness of the individual soul." In the following excerpt, Kazin considers Lewisohn's works within the intellectual context of the 1920s.*]

[The] passion with which [Ludwig Lewisohn] insisted upon the elementary facts of the creative process singled him out immediately at a time when cynicism and apathy could so easily be taken for the tragic sense. This is not to say that he was averse to the extravagances and inanities of contemporary critical thought. On the contrary, he was the most frenzied apostle of them, since he carried the postwar discovery of sex and the growingly bitter calumny of the past to the point of self-ridicule. But Lewisohn was never a "simple" figure, and his worst qualities represented the exaggerations of a mind which was in itself indispensable to the growth of a mature criticism in America. Few critics in America have ever, indeed, had so moving an ideal of the critic's function or kept to it so stubbornly. It was merely unfortunate that the very intensity with which he insisted with an almost religious conviction upon the nobility of art and the universal significance of creative expression—"Art is the life-process in its totality"—tricked him into saying too much.

The climate of opinion in the twenties was largely responsible, for it was deceptively friendly to Lewisohn. Criticism in the twenties—and not only then—needed to be told that it had "neither passion nor vision." Our critics "are very able, very honest, very well-informed, and very witty. But, to put it mildly and yet correctly, they don't care enough." Lewisohn told them—rather often. Inevitably, he conceived a function for his criticism that was oracular rather than didactic. More strikingly than any other in a generation of critics who wished to write like artists, he was a tormented and imaginative writer who carried over into his criticism the tensions of his novels. At the same time he was an oversensitive alien who had been lacerated by Know-Nothingism in the Middle West during the war, a Jew who raised the immemorial loneliness of the Jewish mind to a historical principle, and a humorless lover-hero of the Freudian epoch who translated his domestic difficulties into pompous dicta for everyone at large. As the future was to prove, Lewisohn's criticism was thus not merely creative, but also a form of martyrology.

The extent to which Lewisohn interpreted his temperamental qualities as absolutes, and his personal prejudices and superstitions as critical dicta, was unique only in its frankness; but the imperturbable gravity and messianic confidence with which he refused ever to look beyond his own ideas were extraordinary. When the war was over and Oswald Garrison Villard called him from his unhappy university experiences in the Middle West to review plays for the *Nation*, Lewisohn took his liberation as a call to arms. Two liberations—Lewisohn's and that of American literature—had plainly coalesced; and with his passionate devotion to Goethe, his superior scholarship, his lofty taste, he instinctively took 20 Vesey Street for Weimar and "the unthinking herd" for a race of doltish Eckermanns. Born a German and a Jew, he had been educated in a genteel Southern Episcopalian environment which gave him his florid style but cheated him, as he was later to feel, of his true heritage. He was an exile and unwanted; and with his sensibility, a self-indulgent rhetoric formed by passionate reading in the English romantic poets, and the Latinisms of Southern gentility, it was inevitable that he should remember his unhappiness bitterly and phrase it grandly. When he was refused a fellowship at Columbia in his youth, it was because "they"—the Calvinist enemies of freedom and truth—"felt in me the implacable foe of the New England dominance over our national life." "I was beaten, broken, breadless," he wrote in his autobiography. "I was a scholar and forbidden to teach, an artist and forbidden to write. Liberty, opportunity. The words had nothing friendly to my ear." Compelled to teach German rather than English literature, his isolation during the war confirmed in him the sense of a spiritual mission in America. Later his unhappy marital experiences proved to him that the artist had no freedom in America and that "the Nordic Protestant masses" had no conscience and no delicacy; "they know only superstition or a whip."

To a literary generation which saw all the wisdom of life in the passion for individual freedom and a hatred of provincialism, Lewisohn's passionate interpretation of his sufferings became the emblem of its own purpose. His conception of art as autobiography became infectious at a time when to regard oneself as an artist was to talk of oneself as a victim. Where the ego had once been a figure of speech, it was now a banner, and Lewisohn's esthetic gave the self-conscious individualism of the day a new solidity and impressiveness. For with all his faults, he was no mere rhapsodist, no secondhand Rousseau. He had greater cultivation than any of his fellow critics save Van Wyck Brooks; he knew the principal European literature at first hand, and not merely for the purposes of quotation; he was devastatingly, irrepressibly in earnest. The Hebraic genius which he was so sentimentally to misinterpret did reveal its scriptural attributes in him. He believed, as very few students of literature in America have ever believed, with a sense of pressing, driving, irresistible need, in the highest purpose of expression.

It is in *The Drama and the Stage,* a selection from his drama reviews published in the *Nation*, that Lewisohn's exciting contribution to the postwar renaissance is seen at its best. He did not delude himself that the new American theater on Broadway that emerged in the wake of the early experimental theaters was as sustained and imaginative as the great experiments in the modern drama at the Théâtre Libre in Paris and the Freie Bühne in Berlin.

> No one can understand the theatre who sees it too intently from within; no one can serve it

who does not, as it is today, hold it a little cheap. . . . Revolving stages, subtle lights, elaborate scenes are in their right order beautiful and useful things. They become a menace when they cause it to be forgotten that the platform is the platform of the eternal poet struggling with the mysteries of earth. This is not fine language; it is the plain and sober truth. But who will admit it?

Who did, indeed? Lewisohn's style, usually a little too oily, always too intent upon the rolling period, the ceremonious, vaguely celestial epithet, had not yet expanded into the purely magisterial splendors of *Expression in America.* Nor did it conceal his sober good sense and salutary passion for that conception of criticism as spiritual scrutiny which Jules Lemaître would have understood, but never George Jean Nathan; Alfred Kerr, but never Percy Hammond. Nathan, he remarked,

> wants to sit quietly in his aloof and faun-like elegance and glance at the exquisite form and glow of the petals and forget annoying things. . . . Never was the theatre less likely than today to become a gentleman's Paradise. . . . We must cast in our lot with the world process and seek to bring the gravest and most stirring of the arts nearer in its true character to an ever-increasing number of men.

In those first great days of liberal criticism Lewisohn was more than a working critic; he was a force for progress. He aimed his reviews at the public, "the contented middle classes . . . who will endure physical but not moral suspense." He corrected superficial journalists and told them to read the *Poetics.* He satirized academic snobs given to desiccated piety to the past by reminding them of the contemporary and topical problems discussed in the Greek and Elizabethan theaters. He kept himself aloof from dramatic shoptalk and the jargon of the Broadway reviewers. "You do not understand the theatre," he had a manager say in an imaginary dialogue. "And you," Lewisohn replied "wearily," "understand nothing else." And that was certainly true. Yet Lewisohn's criticism soon began to defeat its own purpose. Over and again he wrote in the *Nation* that "the poet, the experiencing one, is a poet at every moment, in every relation. He cannot become an average man at a feast or in a church or in a jury box. His vision is his constant self. His material is not stone or iron or market values or laws; it is love and aspiration and ecstasy. His business is with fundamentals." But the lofty tones, at first so portentous, soon lost their flavor and became a mechanical rhetoric of exaltation. It was true, as Carl Van Doren said in one of those necessary tributes to Lewisohn that are now never heard at all, that Lewisohn's merit always lay in his power to enlarge and elevate the matters before him; but Lewisohn's conception of those "matters" became increasingly patronizing and even irresponsible. His own master, Goethe, had said it best: *Im Anfang war die Tat.* As Lewisohn became fixed in his special enmity to the American scene, he increasingly showed a curious disinclination to look at Fact and a positive incapacity to look at the objects of his criticism fairly and dispassionately. Criticism was expression; it was autobiography, usually Lewisohn's own; it was lyrical, confessional, religious, "scriptural." But was not a critic's first duty to the simple homely truth?

In his own mind, and in his eloquent declamations on the high duty and austere function of criticism, Lewisohn agreed that it was. No critic in America save Paul Elmer More had gone so studiously to the whole history of criticism for guidance. No critic had ever insisted so strenuously on the need of precise study of the basic facts underlying a philosophy, an art, a spiritual vocation. Abstractly, indeed, Lewisohn was the most admirable of critics: a naturalist of great imaginative perception and with a salutary insistence on form; a scholar of great sensibility and seemingly the very type of the discerning and generous critical intelligence. In practice, for all his contempt for impressionism and the empirical methods of most American critics, he began more and more to write the history of literature as the history of Ludwig Lewisohn. By one of those summary psychic equations and emotional transferences that contribute so much to imaginative art but can corrupt the necessary poise of criticism, Lewisohn solemnly reasoned out his critical position to a point where he could evaluate literature in America solely in terms of his own character, his own sense of race, his own vicissitudes, and his own private aspirations as citizen, lover, and artist. He had begun, quite properly, by treating his European education and sense of "difference" as a personal advantage. His service, frequently valuable, was to leaven the lump, to talk the language of Goethe and Sainte-Beuve to the parochial, the superficial, and the complacent. Yet it is not too much to say that Lewisohn ended by defrauding himself, and the process was all the more gross because it rested on a lofty idealism and superior pretensions.

Out of the code of what Lewisohn repeatedly called "selfhood"—the artist against the world—he came to interpret almost sadistically the basic qualities of the literature he sought so passionately to elevate. It was not enough for him to write in his autobiography that "the Jewish problem is the decisive problem of Western civilization. By its solution this world of the West will stand or fall, choose death or life." Nor was it enough to say, as many were eager to agree, that "the relations between the sexes constitute the deepest and sorest problem of American life." For Lewisohn did not stop there. If he did not, like Mencken, consciously exploit the foibles of the postwar period, he became intoxicated with them. Where Mencken continued to proclaim his most egregious convictions on the level of pure comedy, Lewisohn began to write criticism at the heroic pitch of Wagnerian Volk metaphysics. In a world of intellectuals who adhered to nothing but themselves, he had suddenly recovered his race, his natal Hebraic culture, his place in the Judaic tradition. In a world of skeptics who chafed under their own skepticism, he had found a Moses in Freud and the whole meaning of life—not merely a method—in Vienna.

Lewisohn had, then, at least two seeming advantages over his rootless and empirical fellow critics when he sat down to compose the interpretation of American literature he had planned ever since he had been a graduate student at Columbia in 1904; and to them he now added a spiritual exaltation of psychoanalysis. For most of his contemporaries literary psychoanalysis was an interesting postwar experiment, a dissection of dead authors who could not defend themselves for the titillation of contemporaries who would not object. For Lewisohn it was a method of salvation. "Is it not but natural," wrote a friendly psychoanalyst, "that he use this science as a yardstick to measure the shortcomings of American literature? What applied to himself, and he often insisted that his case was a paradigm for the world, must equally apply to others. Psychoanalysis gave him his freedom for objectified creation; can it not provide the insight into what hampered or made for success of other contributors to American literature?" Since Lewisohn's "healingprocess" was now complete, his study of the American tradition became, quite deliberately, a vindication of his talent and his due, a reversal of traditional standards. Where he had been the victim of the Gentiles, he was now their arbiter; and his creed was monstrous in its simplicity: "If ever there was a civilization in which evil, in the utterly questionable sense of sin, has been emphasized to a destructive and corrupting extent, it was and is America."

"Historic explanations are not statements of cause," Lewisohn had written in *Mid-Channel,* one of his autobiographies. "They are only rationalizations after the fact." In this light his *Expression in America* was truly, as Ernest Sutherland Bates said, an attempt to write a history of American literature from a completely unhistorical point of view. For Lewisohn felt no need to examine individual types and particular works disinterestedly or in the light of contemporary philosophies, social compulsions, the climate of opinion, the complexities of the national culture, the weaknesses of mortal flesh: he *knew.* For all his power, his sensibility to esthetic quality, he promptly revealed that he had very little curiosity—a critic's most obvious excuse for existence—about minds different from his own. With his thesis and his nostalgic idealization of an abstract European standard which Americans could never, never hope to emulate, he refused to understand, and lacked even the will to investigate, anything upon which his ubiquitous and tireless "selfhood" could not fasten. What had ailed American writing from its dark colonial infancy on had been the baneful influence of the Puritan mind and the Calvinist tradition of repression. How could one doubt it in the face of what he himself had suffered, in the face of Prohibition, John S. Sumner's snoopers, the Anti-Saloon League mind, and the pious banalities of Professor Stuart Sherman?

It has to be said of Lewisohn, of course, that he could be incandescent even when he was irrelevant and moving even when he was wrong. Yet it is indisputable that the man who wrote of Emerson and Thoreau "That they were chilled undersexed valetudinarians, deprived of helpful and sympathetic social and intellectual atmosphere, renders their achievements only the more remarkable," lacked something indispensable to the comprehension of the American imagination. Emerson, it may be, would have understood Lewisohn as he would not have understood some other critics of the day, and Lewisohn did appreciate a basic quality in Emerson that Irving Babbitt never did when he wrote that the professors so given to celebrating Emerson would have been shocked to see his ideas in practice. It was this Hebraic humanism in Lewisohn, the belief he held, with Willam Blake, that "truth cannot be uttered so as to be understood and not be believed," that enabled him to appreciate Paul Elmer More's quality at a time when the modernists and traditionalists merely suspected each other.

Lewisohn was, indeed, one of the few critics of the day who talked good sense during the New Humanist controversy. No one in the liberal camp saw so clearly into the superficial estheticism of the twenties and inveighed so passionately against its nihilism. Yet for all his frequent brilliance of judgment, his own esthetic was not a directive. One could understand, even if one could not approve, the lofty neo-Goethean patronizing of Mark Twain as "our one American example of the bardic type of artist and sayer . . . one whom the common people can understand because he is theirs." Common people, forsooth! But what was one to say of a student of American literature who could in all sobriety declare that a "thousand *voluntary* delusions and repressions still afflicted" American writing after the Civil War? Or that "Franklin's eighteenth-century shop-

keeping attitude toward the moral life . . . has survived in America and in America alone"? His highest praise, always, was "not ignoble." Not ignoble! It was the pure distillation of his fear of the enemy—Mencken's "booboisie" armed with pitchforks against truth and expression—and of his contempt for him. (pp. 273-80)

> *Alfred Kazin, "Liberals and New Humanists," in his* On Native Grounds: An Interpretation of Modern American Prose Literature, *1942. Reprint by Harcourt Brace Jovanovich, Inc., 1963, pp. 265-311.**

LESLIE FIEDLER   (essay date 1959)

> [*Fiedler is a controversial and provocative American critic. While he has also written novels and short stories, his personal philosophy and insights are thought to be most effectively expressed in his literary criticism. Emphasizing the psychological, sociological, and ethical context of works, Fiedler often views literature as the mirror of a society's consciousness. Similarly, he believes that the conventions and values of a society are powerful determinants of the direction taken by its authors' works. The most notable instance of Fiedler's critical stance is his reading of American literature, and therefore American society, as demonstrating an infantile flight from* "adult heterosexual love." *This idea is developed in his most important work,* Love and Death in the American Novel *(1960), along with the theory that American literature is essentially an extension of the Gothic novel. Although Fiedler has been criticized for what are considered eccentric pronouncements on literature, he is also highly valued for his adventuresome and eclectic approach, which complements the predominantly academic tenor of contemporary criticism. In the following excerpt from* The Jew in the American Novel, *Fiedler compares the use of eroticism in novels by Lewisohn and Ben Hecht.*]

In Ludwig Lewisohn and Ben Hecht, the two most admired Jewish novelists of the twenties, the erotic theme is [stated] . . . in exaggerated, almost hysterical tones. There is something about their work not merely brash and provocative (this they intended), but vulgar and crude; and it becomes hard to remember that they seemed once the most promising of young novelists, before one was translated into a prophet of the new Zion and the other into a maker of successful movies. "More gross talent than net accomplishment," a disgruntled critic finally said of Hecht, and the phrase will do for Lewisohn, too. They chose to begin with such different masks, the professor and the reporter, that it is difficult to see how much they had in common, how both contrived sexual melodramas to project the plight of the Jew in the Jazz Age. A pair of titles, however, Lewisohn's *Don Juan* (1923) and Hecht's *A Jew in Love* (1931), frame the period and define its chief concern.

Unlike [Abraham] Cahan, who preceded them, and the Proletarian novelists, who were to follow them, Lewisohn and Hecht are hostile to Marxism; and the Marxists (most of them Jewish, of course) who appear in their books are portrayed as self-deceivers, attempting to conceal their personal anguish behind an artificial fog of socialist cant. The secular Jewish prophet honored by Hecht and Lewisohn is not Marx but Freud; and the secular religion to which they respond is what they call Freudianism, though, like many intellectuals in their time, they were not quite sure where Freud ends and D. H. Lawrence begins. Psychoanalysis seemed to them primarily one more device for mocking the middle class, one more source for arguments in defense of sexual emancipation. Beyond this, their interest remained superficial. Lewisohn's novel, *The Island Within,* contains what is probably the most unconvincing psychoanalyst in literature and manages to tuck away an utterly improbable description of an analysis, somewhere between its "epical" beginning and the little sermon on mixed marriages with which it ends.

Their common devotion to Eros and to Freud as his prophet, Lewisohn and Hecht develop in quite different ways. Lewisohn sets his in a context of belated German Romanticism, from which he derives a mystique of passion somehow synthesized with internationalism, pacifism, and a Crocean commitment to art. Hecht, on the other hand, adjusts his to a provincial version of *symbolisme,* which means for him a dedication to disorder and cynicism in art and life. Celebrated in his day as a new American Huysmans, he has become for us undistinguishable from the pressroom heroes of his *Front Page,* flip hard-guys to whom whiskey is the Muse and Chicago the Earthly Paradise. Lewisohn typically identifies himself with his protagonists, harried by women and bourgeois taboos, but pledged to fight for freedom with the sole weapon of art; Hecht presumably separates himself from the scoundrels who are the heroes of his books, though he covertly sympathizes with their amoral contempt for decency and tenderness.

The leading characters of both, though presumably intellectuals, are notable not for their ideas but for their efforts, successful or baffled, to find in themselves the demonic, impulsive sources of life. In this they are the authentic products of their age, though uneasy projections of their Jewish authors. What has a Jew to do finally with the primitivism and phallic mysticism which possessed the era? Only when he revolts not merely against philistinism but against his own most authentic traditions can he espouse such a cause. It is illuminating to remember that writers like D. H. Lawrence and Sherwood Anderson, the real high priests of the erotic religion, portrayed Jews in their fiction as natural enemies of the primitive ideal, antitypes of the passionate hero: cold, cerebral, incapable of the dark surrender of the self.

It is true enough that when Lewisohn uses **Don Juan** as a book title, he does so ironically and that he somehow feels obliged to pretend (however unconvincingly) that his protagonist is not a Jew; but he is all the while *living* the role in his own much-publicized life. In the news and gossip columns as well as in the pages of his novels, Lewisohn concentrated on justifying his love life—with time off for belaboring the poor women who failed him and the divorce laws which hampered his style. The only subject to which Lewisohn responds in his fiction with real fervor, the single spring of his creative work, is his own sex life desperately projected as typical.

The Island Within, his attempt at a major novel, opens with a manifesto declaring his epic ambitions and defending them against the proponents of the novel of sensibility, just then replacing the older, objective form. His declared intent is esthetically reactionary enough, but he cannot abide even by that; before the book is half over, he has abandoned the broad-canvas portrayal of three generations of Jewish life in Poland and Germany for a more intimate evocation of modern marital difficulties, for his usual blend of self-pity and editorial. No sooner has he reached America, than he heads for the bedroom, the old battle ground on which the sensitive Jew, a psychoanalyst this time, still struggles with the *shikse* (in the teeth of public opinion and benighted law) for the possession of his own soul. (pp. 79-81)

Lewisohn is explicit, however pat and superficial, and in **The Island Within** (actually published three years before *A Jew in*

Love) he gives to the erotic-assimilationist novel its final form. Arthur Levy, the protagonist of Lewisohn's novel, never abandons his vocation as a lover; he merely transfers his desire from the representative of an alien world to the symbol of his own people, thus reinforcing a battered Romantic faith in sexual passion with an equally Romantic commitment to Zionism. As he has earlier combined the advocacy of sexual freedom with a vaguely internationalist humanism, so now he combines it with a revived Judaism, adapted to the modern scientific mind.

He pretends, indeed, to find in the Jewish tradition sanctions for his view of love. Is not Jewish divorce, he asks rhetorically, easier than Christian? Were not the Jews always skeptical about the notion of marriage as a sacrament? Have Jewish women historically not represented a *tertium quid:* neither servile like the slavewomen of the Anglo-Saxon world before modern times, nor hopelessly lost like the "emancipated" Gentile women of the current era? Have they not remained at the heart of the tradition the Jewish intellectual has temporarily abandoned, waiting to bestow on him when he returns the warm fulfillment he has vainly sought in strangers? We have come full circle from Cahan's view of ghetto Judaism as a castrating force.

But Lewisohn is prepared to go even further than this, from a defense of Zion as the true Eros, to an attack on the Gentile woman as the false Aphrodite. It has all been the fault of the *shikse* and of the Jewish intellectual only so far as he has become her victim. It is no longer the Gentile world which rejects the Jew in Lewisohn's fiction (that world is, indeed, eager to draw him in and suck him dry), but the Jew who rejects it—even as Arthur Levy rejects the hope of assimilation and sets out at his story's end back to Europe, back to his people's past, to investigate the plight of his fellow Jews in Rumania.

We have reached at last the reverse of Harland-Luska's theory in *The Yoke of the Thorah;* Jessica has yielded to Delilah. Not by rejecting the Gentile girl for the Jewish one but by preferring her, the sensitive Jew commits spiritual suicide. The *shikse* represents no longer the promise of fulfillment, of a blending of cultures, but only the threat of death, of the loss of identity. The reversal, however, like the original thesis, remains a little too pat, more suited for sermonizing than poetry; at any rate, in neither case did the authors make of their themes moving and memorable fictions. Yet with Lewisohn's establishment of the antistereotype in its classic form something has been accomplished, that is to say, the last possibility of the erotic-assimilationist novel has been exahusted. His novel rests like a melancholy capstone on the whole period which reaches from the eighties to the dying twenties, a monument to an unsuccessful quest by whose example later writers have profited. After **The Island Within,** the Jewish-American novelist knew at least one direction in which he could not go. (pp. 82-4)

Leslie Fiedler, "The Jew in the American Novel,"
in his The Collected Essays of Leslie Fiedler, Vol.
II, *Stein and Day Publishers, 1971, pp. 65-117.**

LOUIS FRAIBERG (essay date 1960)

[*Fraiberg is an American critic and educator who has done extensive work to promote the use of psychoanalysis in literary criticism. In the following excerpt, he discusses Lewisohn's role in the development of psychoanalytic criticism in America.*]

Ludwig Lewisohn begins *The Story of American Literature* with a statement of purpose in the light of which the book deserves to be judged. In it his emphasis, as is proper, is upon his critical thesis, but he relies so heavily in its development upon certain psychoanalytic ideas that I must direct the major part of my attention to these at the risk of seeming to slight what is actually more important. He is attempting "a portrait of the American spirit seen and delineated, as the human spirit is itself best seen, in and through its mood of articulateness, of creative expression." The vicissitudes of that spirit are understood by him largely in terms of a moral struggle in which the impulse to the free expression of American experience in literature collided with the powerful inhibiting influence of the Puritan tradition. In Lewisohn's view, Puritanism triumphed throughout nearly all of our national history, to our great loss. "To it, rather than to the harsh but not ignoble struggles of the wilderness and the frontier, is to be attributed all that is unlovely and cruel and grotesque in the life of the American people." Its doctrine of grace for the few and damnation for the many imposed an artificial dichotomy upon everyday living in which the satisfaction of normal appetites was regarded as sinful, and the only acceptable kind of conduct was based upon their suppression, since it was necessary to curb one's worldly desires in order to seek salvation. This denial of natural behavior had its reflections in the writings which Lewisohn chose to study in his book.

As long as the Puritan influence was dominant, runs his claim, it was impossible for our literary men to write about the realities of human experience. They were confined to themes unrelated to the actualities of American life and therefore removed from that passion and urgency which alone can produce great literature. The intellectual revolution of the nineteenth century cracked the shell of the complete and perfect universe postulated by the theocrats and their descendants, and at last permitted a direct view of things as they are. Its literary outcome was the rise of realism and naturalism. A new type of reader also arose, "one to whom literature [is] no longer an elegant diversion or an illustration of the foreknown and fixed, but moral research, a road to salvation, the bread of life." The modern writer addresses himself to this reader, and he writes not of man's relation to God and eternity but of human experience and his kinship through it with his fellows. For an understanding of that experience and its expression in literature Lewisohn calls psychoanalysis to his aid:

> It was . . . inevitable that I use the organon or method of knowledge associated with the venerated name of Sigmund Freud. The portrayer of any aspect of human life or civilization who does not do so today will soon be like some mariner of old who, refusing to acknowledge the invention of mathematical instruments because their precision was not yet perfect, still stubbornly sailed his vessel by the stars.

His recognition that psychoanalysis was not a complete and closed system marks a more mature comprehension of it than was shown by either Brooks or Krutch, and this is further borne out by his specific applications of it to the work of individual writers. Nor does he fall into the error of basing his whole argument upon it. To him it is a tool, a means toward an end. His reliance is first upon his critical judgment; psychoanalysis is a secondary, though valuable, help.

The first important place where it is of assistance to him is in his examination of the Puritan character and the characters of Puritan writers. In the pervasive conviction of sin that discolored everyday life, in the hysteria of many sermons, in the guilt which was so great that it could not be borne and had to be projected onto heretics and witches he sees a pathology not only personal but moral. The ruling delusion of the time, epitomized by Edwards' famous sermon, "Sinners in the Hands of an Angry God," generated the fear that justified the forcible saving of men from the consequences in eternity of their own actions by temporal punishments inflicted with a cruelty which was matched only by the righteousness of the responsible authorities.

Psychoanalysis has something to say here about sex and sadism, and Lewisohn says it. Edwards and Mather were sick souls. The violence of their expressed religious feelings was a measure of the dammed-up sexuality which could find an outlet only in the perverted forms of aggression against others and symbolic mortification of their own flesh. For this combination of spiritual self-torture and the physical punishment of nonconformists they found justification in the age-old rationalization of those who scourge the helpless. "To excommunicate an heretic . . . is not to persecute; that is, it is not to punish an innocent, but a culpable and damnable person, and that not for conscience, but for persisting in error against light of conscience." From excommunication to hanging is but a step for such a mind. This was the mentality that regulated daily conduct for the colonists and that, according to Lewisohn's view, stifled any possibility of true literary expression.

Psychoanalysis supports his depiction of the Puritan character, as far as it goes, although a more thoroughgoing examination based on an appreciation of psychoanalytic ego psychology would reveal some things to be said on the positive side. There was a strength, a channeling of energy into work, which was well adapted to the needs of the country, a moral earnestness which might have been carried too far but could not have been wholly destructive—in short, the story has at least two sides. All that we are given, however, is the overwhelming impression that there lay like a blight upon the young nation "the undying Puritan conviction that man and nature and man's instincts are from the beginning evil and without hope." We are presumably meant to conclude that pathology ruled the colonies. Lewisohn's evidence from their own writings demonstrates plainly that certain of the powerful Puritans could not handle their sexual feelings in what we would consider normal ways and that this influenced their actions as public figures. What he does not quite succeed in establishing, at least on psychoanalytic grounds, is any connection between this situation and the inability to write literature.

I believe, nonetheless, that his case is sound, although not for the reasons he gives. If the authorities regard human experience as evil, then it is perfectly natural for them to refuse to tolerate—let alone to encourage—its expression in literature. But for this knowledge one does not need psychoanalytic support. Furthermore, even the psychoanalysis of 1932, the year of Lewisohn's book, gives no ground for such an idea. An inhibition of sexuality and its conversion into symptomatic behavior may be connected with the production of literature, or it may not. And it makes no difference whether we are dealing here with good writing or bad. The choice of writing as a profession and the writer's attainments therein have not been shown to be correlated with a specific type of personality or a specific frustration. The whole field of vocational choice is only beginning to be explored by psychoanalysis; not much is known about it yet from this standpoint. It is questionable whether simple generalizations like those assumed by Lewisohn were valid and whether they affected the quality of the work under discussion. His critical estimate of the Puritan influence is a reasonable one, though somewhat one-sided, but his psychoanalytic "foundation" for it is extremely shaky.

As he carries the story forward from the colonial period, those inheritors of a watered-down Puritan tradition, the Polite Writers, get short shrift at Lewisohn's hands. For him, Irving is the typical example of the kind of mind that, lacking the Puritans' conviction, nevertheless languidly follows in their footsteps. To such men human experiences no longer seem actively evil but merely beneath the notice of the genteel. The passionate wrestling with sin has dwindled to a pretense that what really counts is conformity to the manners of polite society. A stringent code of ethics has given way to rules of etiquette. Consequently, literature can deal only with an unrealistic idealization of human beings which keeps silent about the "major and intenser experiences of life." This affected other writers of the time as well. Lowell, for instance, failed in criticism "through the ancestral Puritan aversion from dealing with ultimate questions in any field except theology and politics." Holmes managed to salvage some honor for a few remarks indicating that his scientific training gave him a hostility to Calvinism, but that is not enough in Lewisohn's eyes to redeem his failure to face reality. On the other hand, P. T. Barnum produced literature in his autobiography, crude and vulgar though it was, because he "wrote out what he thought and saw and dreamed and knew."

We begin here to see the bias of the book emerging. Literature must touch life, not celebrate that which attempts to evade life, as Lewisohn defines it. What cannot be seen so readily is how psychoanalysis supports this thesis or why its support should seem necessary to a literary critic. There seems also to be emerging the implication that technical quality is somehow irrelevant. The worth of writing in this view could depend upon its theme, its fidelity to reality, its concreteness and therefore its power to move the reader, and not on style, skill or polish. I shall not debate this critical position but only point out that psychoanalysis offers very little here to Lewisohn, except peripherally. It does not evaluate literature as literature; that is the function of the critic and the aesthetician. It merely provides certain incomplete bits of information about the place of literature in human life. He who draws conclusions from its store of facts does so on his own responsiblity and at his own peril. Lewisohn seems to be overly ambitious for psychoanalysis, and tries to press it into service beyond the point where a cautious psychoanalyst would go.

Things become slightly better in the book as the Transcendentalist Revolt brings the emergence of the individual, although not yet the artist of reality whom Lewisohn admires. Its outstanding figures, Emerson and Thoreau, lack fire, but this is a constitutional deficiency and not the outcome of a struggle to contain fiery natures. They are not prisoners of the bleak Puritan tradition; they are simply cold. It is not depreciating the power of their intellects to say that their "light was almost polar. It gave no warmth." Such personalities could write only upon "nature and metaphysics and morals" rather than on subjects closer to the human heart, for only upon the first of these could they muster up the equivalent of strong feelings. Lewisohn believes he has psychoanalytic warrant for his contention that the sexual deficiency in both Emerson and Thoreau directly prevented them from treating realistic themes. Emerson's was an attenuated nature, and this thinness could not

express what it did not feel. His instincts, says Lewisohn, were trustworthy, even to the extent of understanding his own "lack of intensity, of severity, of absorption in the concrete coil of things." What he wrote under their prompting is worth preserving; the remainder ought to be rejected as old-maidish and therefore of relatively little literary worth. Here again Lewisohn goes beyond psychoanalysis while leaving the impression that he has scientific backing. In point of fact, he is functioning as a critic whose thesis is being satisfactorily developed but who imagines that he needs extra assistance. When closely examined, the outside help proves to be mostly irrelevant, and the original chain of reasoning is not strengthened thereby.

Thoreau is something else again. His bachelorhood is not of the mind alone; he is actively un-sexual. His aversion to marriage is shown by extracts from the Journals and letters. Introducing these Lewisohn remarks: "Yes, excellent reader, I have to 'drag in' sex here as I shall do again and again. God dragged it in from the beginning of things. . . ." This patronizing air is understandable considering the kind of audience he felt himself to be addressing, but it reveals little about the problem. Lewisohn repeatedly states that Thoreau is a great writer and just as often says that he is a defective man. There is an unexplained gap here. If there is a relationship between a man's sexuality and the quality of his writing, as Lewisohn evidently believes, then we are left with a mystery, since the gap has not been bridged by psychoanalysis, and Lewisohn does not bridge it by criticism. He says only: "That they [Thoreau and Emerson] were chilled undersexed valetudinarians, deprived of helpful and sympathetic social and intellectual atmosphere, renders their achievements only the more remarkable." Here again he is too ambitious for psychoanalysis.

He attempts to make it serve his critical ideas in his analysis of *Walden*, a discussion which illuminates Lewisohn more than it does Thoreau. The book is praised as the record of one who practiced what he preached, who followed his own private convictions, who did not conform. It is praised for style, for social analysis, for prophetic insights. There is no doubt that Lewisohn regards it as one of the masterpieces of American literature. And yet:

> Unfortunately *Walden* contains a chapter called, "Higher Laws" which, in the accustomed Puritan way, blunts all the arrows, retracts all the brave and lofty sayings of the earlier and later chapters and makes it necessary for Thoreau to be saved, as by fire, for our uses and the uses of posterity. That chapter is full of the Puritan's cheap unfairness to the senses, his complete unwillingness to bring the whole of human nature under creative and significant control. "There is never an instant's truce between vice and virtue. . . . We are conscious of an animal in us, which awakens in proportion as our higher nature slumbers." Ah, no, good Puritan. *We* are not; you are. We are not conscious of any inner division and have long integrated all aspects of our nature upon the highest or, rather, the most significant and fruitful plane that is attainable by us. . . .

Lewisohn here elevates the principle of harmony to a position of the greatest importance in literature, and he makes it dependent upon the writer's honest view of his own nature. The rub lies in his equation of literary value with sensuality which, in spite of his disclaimer, he seems to regard highly for itself and not merely as something integrated into "the total harmony of life." It would appear that in his enthusiasm for the discovery of sensual (including sexual) values, which he has made with the help of psychoanalysis, he has overstated his case. His contention that literature is the less worthy as it stays away from matters which many people do not wish to discuss is at least debatable. Nor have I found any basis in psychoanalytic writings for this position. To state it simply, the value of literature does not depend upon the frankness with which it treats sexual or economic or philosophical problems but rather upon its ability to express and communicate human experience. There is no reason to assume that this does not inlcude Thoreau's un-sexual, un-sensual, transcendental experiences.

Another major group of nineteenth-century American writers is likewise depreciated by him on the ground that their artistic vision did not reveal to them the world as it is, or even a portion of reality which they then took for the whole, but rather a world of shapes and fancies drawn from their imagination. Poe, Hawthorne and Melville are the "troubled romancers" who were so ensnared in their unconscious conflicts that they could not partake of real experience and consequently could not portray it in their writings. What they did, therefore, was to invent private worlds onto which the inner drama could be projected without regard for externals. Art, says Lewisohn, is "first of all [the artist's] personal substitute for lacks and defeats that are otherwise unsupportable." According to this theory the genesis of art lies in emotional unbalance, and it consists of an attempt to make the artist whole. There is a certain amount of justification for this attitude in the psychoanalytic theories of the restitutive function of art, but stated in such blanket terms as he uses, it can have relatively little validity. It is not enough to know that a country is mountainous; we need to know the location of the passes, their accessibility and under what conditions they may be used. (pp. 145-52)

Lewisohn emphasizes psychic rather than literary factors. His evaluation of Hawthorne is based upon what he sees of the author's motivation—almost obsessive guilt—and a repeated insistence upon the role played by psychic determinism in the choice of the theme and its treatment. There is nothing wrong with this as far as it goes, but it does not go far enough. What we have here is the beginning of psychoanalytic understanding, but it is a beginning beyond which Lewisohn does not advance. Having shown that Hawthorne clothed his guilt feelings in literary forms and was compelled to use certain symbols he is led to the final conclusion of this position. If a work of art can be "explained" (except for the fact of genius) by the writer's psychic needs, then it follows that *The Scarlet Letter* is successful because it reflects or is the result of some successful psychic integration. And so we read:

> It is but sober truth that we owe Hawthorne's one thoroughly achieved book and unique masterpiece "The Scarlet Letter" to his happy and harmonious union with Sophia Peabody. . . . He is at last able in those earlier years of his marriage really to project, truly to create, to send forth into the world a work separate from himself, living with a life of its own and therefore easing him of a portion of his inner burden. This book, alone among his books, moreover, deals with central things—with normal guilt, with genuine passion, with the operations of recognizable minds.

Such a one-to-one correlation between life and work is difficult to establish and so general that from a psychoanalytic standpoint it is, even though valid, not very valuable, since it tells us nothing that we did not already know without the help of psychoanalysis. Nor is Lewisohn satisfied wth the mere statement that an author puts himself into his work (for that is what it amounts to); a few pages later he tries to extend the insight. But there he becomes once more the critic and passes from the application of psychoanalysis to his own critical judgment:

> Nor will work which thus speaks permanently to men ever be without that beauty of form which is the precipitate of its spirit, which is indeed part of and inseparable from substance, which constitutes in the last analysis, the *act* of artistic communication.

Up to a certain point psychoanalysis serves him. It helps him see the author's gross motivation—plus a few specific insights here and there—and choice of themes; it shows him the universal meaning of some rather common and obvious symbols; it enables him to see the universality of the author's appeal in so far as the work arouses psychic echoes in the reader. But it does not give him clues to what present-day psychoanalysis finds to be of importance: the specificity of not only theme but treatment, not only problem but language, not only symbol but beauty. Lewisohn sees art largely as the struggle of a gifted neurotic. He lacks sufficient knowledge of psychoanalysis to carry the conception further, to explore the ways in which artistic activity is different from daily actions of other kinds, to examine the product as an independent entity as well as a neurotic residue, to understand the role of the ego as well as that of the id. (pp. 154-55)

Psychoanalysis grows more complex every year, but Lewisohn evidently did not advance beyond its threshold. It is true that he asks some of "the pertinent and crucial questions" and that this is no mean achievement. We need to know, however, not merely that a writer's inner life appears disguised in his writings but how it does and what we may reasonably conclude therefrom. We need to know in what ways the writer is affected by the "national neurosis" and whether his writing attacks or supports it. We need to know if science can tell us what constitutes genius, beauty, and artistic (as distinct from emotional) appeal. And we need to know the ways in which science looks at intellectual, moral and artistic movements. To this last Lewisohn has made a limited contribution, one which has the merit of possessing a degree of accuracy, sense and good will but which nevertheless suffers from vagueness outside its area of competence, from limited scope and from the innocent expectation that it can accomplish more than its resources actually allow. . . . He has read parts of psychoanalysis and understood parts of what he has read. Then he has behaved as though he has read and understood all of it.

Lewisohn is encouraged by what he knows of psychoanalysis to assert his conviction that art is best considered from the standpoint of its human origins and human uses. "Art is social and moral and religious and metaphysical, not because it has to be made so, but because man is so and because the artist is a man." We need not adopt a philosophical or religious system as the basis for a theory of art. If anything, it would seem rather that these ought to be derived from an adequate comprehension of human nature, and to this, he holds, psychoanalysis is making the most significant contributions. Its importance in Lewisohn's scheme of things is thus very great but only as a means to an end, and this is the role it plays in his criticism. He abhors fixed and closed systems of knowledge and conduct, particularly those which some people feel constrained to impose upon others. His plea is for the development of an ethic and an aesthetic which shall grow out of the true nature of humanity as it is being increasingly revealed by the discoveries of science and the untrammeled operation of free minds. Art must be permitted to emerge by the free choice of the artist among models as well as materials, but his exprssion must be in accord with his inner nature and not with a received standard external to his own perceptions. The classics, for instance, are not to be regarded "as norms of practice but as examples of the creative spirit in action."

From this man-centered viewpoint, and particularly from the assumption that what is "natural" is good, it is easy to understand Lewisohn's enthusiasm for psychoanalysis. He sees it as a kind of twentieth-century justification for attitudes much like those of Rousseau, a position which is not wholly supported by its clinical findings. He sees it also as an aspect of the movement in modern thought toward realism and naturalism as well as of the literature that these may ultimately lead to. In his view, therefore, it has importance not so much for its scientific usefulness as for the encouragement it offers to those who think as he does. Science is thereby subordinated to ethics, surely a possible and reasonable procedure, but one which, in the wrong hands, can lead to disaster, as we have seen in our time. Whether its service to literature is necessarily thus enhanced may also be questioned. Lewisohn is on safer ground in his insistence upon a moral reference for art. He has not succeeded, despite his good will, in establishing a workable relationship between art and psychoanalysis. (pp. 158-60)

> *Louis Fraiberg, "Ludwig Lewisohn and the Puritan Inhibition of American Literature," in his* Psychoanalysis & American Literary Criticism, *Wayne State University Press, 1960, pp. 145-60.*

DAVID F. SINGER (essay date 1965)

[In the following excerpt, Singer explores the reasons for Lewisohn's embracement of Judaism.]

The return to the fold of Jewish intellectuals who had lapsed into Western culture has been a noteworthy phenomenon in modern Jewish history. European Jewry can point to a number of its sons who overcame a background of estrangement and were able to find their way toward integration in the people and ethos of Israel. The religious development of Franz Rosenzweig is a classic case in point. Such occurrences in American Jewry were, for a while, virtually non-existent. The spiritual pilgrimage of Ludwig Lewisohn from alienation to affirmation, therefore, stands out as an early phenomenon of special importance in American Jewish experience. (p. 319)

For many intellectuals the First World War was a rude awakening from the nineteeth-century dream of human perfectibility and the progress of mankind. The undercurrent of violence which had lurked beneath the apparent prosperity and rationality of the Victorian reign of peace had, at long last, come to the surface. Social critics, turning their attention to every aspect of American life, found it to be, in the words of Ezra Pound, "an old bitch gone in the teeth / a botched civilization."

Ludwig Lewisohn was one of the many critics who turned the spotlight on American civilization. Like Mencken, Anderson, and Lewis, he denounced the "booboisie," the materialism, and the cultural sterility of American life, and that blend of prudery, commercialism, and sanctimoniousness which was summed up in the term "Puritanism." Lewisohn differed, however, from his fellow critics in two fundamental ways. As a Jewish immigrant, he viewed America from a different perspective than native Americans like Lewis and Anderson, who had their roots in and were a product of America. Of even greater significance are the facts that Lewisohn's outlook was molded by his experiences in pre-World War I America and that his criticism was based on a sense of his Jewishness. Secondly, much of the criticism of the 1920's was nihilistic in its tendencies, in that it became fashionable to damn America and everything American indiscriminately. Intellectuals had no desire to improve society, and thus their attacks were not undertaken in behalf of some alternative ideal. The critics of the Jazz Age "felt superior to other men, had no desire to reform them, and rejoiced in their separateness." Lewisohn's criticism, on the other hand, was constructive in that he had a vision of a better society and a program of action to achieve it.

Lewisohn's examination of American life served as the starting point for what came to be in its final formulation a schema describing the historical development of Western civilization. Central to this schema are the strains of pagan, Christian, and Jewish ways of life. Western history was for Lewisohn the history of the interaction of these three *Weltanschauungen* with one another. He contended that the strain of Christianity must be held responsible for the failure of Western man to achieve peace and stability, whereas a new synthesis of the Hebraic and pagan mentalities he held out as man's hope for salvation.

The pagan way of life, which is the oldest of the three, is usually identified by Lewisohn with Greek thought. He often uses the term "Hellenism" in referring to it. The pagan, according to Lewisohn, accepts man and the universe as given. He views nature as implacable and fortunate as "mad and blind and brutal." . . . As a consequence of their acceptance of man and nature as they are, the Greeks laid the foundations for science. Given an irrational universe, the aim of paganism was to "understand the nature of things as far as the mind of man will reach and thus subdue his fear." . . . Thus, Hellenism, our heritage from classical antiquity, is identified by Lewisohn with "the fearless mind, the scientific temper." . . . At times he refers to it as "knowledge," . . . "nature," . . . and "science." (pp. 319-21)

Sensing the indifference of the universe toward man's aspirations, paganism attempted to instill in man a stoical attitude toward life. Men were admonished to curb their desires and to face age, death, and the malevolence of nature with serenity. The pagan acceptance of an indifferent universe was strikingly expressed in the advice of a Greek poet to "refrain from asking what tomorrow will bring forth and count as gain whatever days Chance gives." . . . In a world where chance ruled, it was imperative that man live for the moment.

Paganism's fundamental weakness, Lewisohn claimed, was that it ignored the fact and the problem of human suffering. It accepted pain as incurable and sufferng as the very essence of the fabric of life. It offered humanity no consolation. Man had to make the best of what was at most a precarious existence. This fatal weakness left paganism defenseless against a rising Christianity which sought to fill the spiritual void. (p. 321)

While Lewisohn's attitude toward Jesus is on the whole sympathetic, for Paul he has only contempt. To Lewisohn's mind it was Paul's philosophy as embodied in Christianity which was to blame for the failure of that movement to serve as the guide to the good life for man. What Paul had done, Lewisohn claimed, was to transform the pagan acceptance of man and nature into a complete repudiation of the natural world. For truth Paul substituted vision, for reason faith. If the end of history was at hand, what mattered "nature which was about to be shriveled up like a scroll or man who was an immediate candidate for heaven or hell?" . . .

The world did not, however, pass away, and from the repudiation of nature and reason there sprang that "incurable antinomy and dualism at the heart of Christianity." . . . It was this dualism which Lewisohn emphasizes as a source of Christianity's failure to humanize life. For war, cruelty, and injustice, and all the passions of the natural man continued, but Christianity, "declaring all these purely evil and wholly damned," . . . was unable to deal with them. Because it rejected the natural world, Christianity had to endure its repaganization. Thus, the most provocative point of Lewisohn's discussion is that Christianity "lost the world by repudiating the world." . . . (p. 322)

The source of Lewisohn's concept of the dualism of Christianity becomes clear when we examine the course of his own alienation from American society. In attempting to discover the reason for Western man's failure to achieve a peaceful and secure life, Lewisohn projected his own experiences into a universal conception of history. (p. 323)

Two factors, both of a personal nature, made his encounter with anti-Semitism excruciating. The first of these was Lewisohn's egotism. Even a superficial reading of Lewisohn's autobiographical works will make the reader aware that he is dealing with a man who is extremely conscious of his abilities. Lewisohn was a quiet and withdrawn youth and withal possessed of a Faustian passion for knowledge and reading. Looking back on his early years he recalled how he came on the idea of a literary career: "I realized the meaning suddenly of that constant scribbling which I had been impelled to during the preceeding months. I had a gift for literature! I knew it now; I never doubted it again. My fate had found me." . . . (pp. 323-24)

Of even greater significance was Lewisohn's extremely close emotional attachment to his mother. The Lewisohn family, because of financial reversals, had been forced to abandon their upper-middle-class life in Berlin and to emigrate to America. The loss of status took a great emotional toll from Ludwig's parents. His father and especially his mother now centered all their hopes and ambitions on their child. . . . There was thus more at stake in Lewisohn's encounter with anti-Semitism than the quest for personal success: it meant tragic suffering for his family. . . .

When, in 1922, in *Up Stream,* Lewisohn first took America to task for its failures, he laid the blame on that intellectual whipping boy of the 1920's, Puritanism. To it he attributed the "duality" of the American mind. This duality could be traced to the puritanical law code which dominated American life. (p. 324)

When, in 1929, in *Mid-Channel,* Lewisohn argued that it was the dualism of Pauline Christianity which was responsible for the failure of the West, he was elevating American Puritanism to a universal level.

It was clear, Lewisohn argued, that Christianity was failing as a humanizing agent, and that it was helpless in dealing with the barbarism which dominated the West. The very concept of human progress itself would become meaningless unless the Western world established a new moral order.

This new order of society, Lewisohn proposed, was to be achieved through a "new synthesis of Hellenism and Hebraism, of science and conduct, of nature and spirit." . . . Lewisohn accepted the modern scientific spirit as a means of improving the material life of man. He was, however, only too well aware of the potential threat which a belief in secular progress posed for Western man. It is in his critique of what he refered to as "secularist, mechanical meliorism" . . . that Lewisohn is most profound and perhaps most relevant to our times. The First World War had awakened him to the fact that science could be a tool of destruction as well as an instrument of progress. The War had demonstrated that the average man was "a more powerful barbarian for the tools that science put into his hands." . . . (p. 325)

Lewisohn was particularly scornful of Jewish liberals, radicals, and socialists who, in spite of the moral bankruptcy of secular meliorism, continued to worship it as man's hope for the future. "We have forgotten or repressed the past. We have been inattentive to history . . . and our dreadful and sinful forgetfulness or repression did not even cease when out of the center of Europe came the pagan fury which destroyed one-third of the living Jewish people and when out of the East of Europe came that answering fury, which is in the process of destroying another three million." . . . These Jews had closed their eyes to the fact that science could work for man's betterment only if it operated within a spiritual framework. What was needed was an all-pervasive ethos which would provide a hierarchy of values within which science and social meliorism could function. This ethos Lewisohn found in Judaism.

Forged into a consciousness of his Jewishness by a society which would not forget his origins, Lewisohn began a period of study which led to a complete affirmation of Judaism. "The spirit and history of my people came flooding into my mind and heart in stronger and more brimming waves. It became literally unimaginable to me that I had been or seemed to have been so alienated and estranged." . . . Lewisohn's conception of the meaning of the Jewish heritage was not static but grew ever more deep and sophisticated as he studied and mastered the language, history, and literature of his people. (p. 326)

Having traced the source of Western man's difficulties to the dualism of Pauline asceticism, it was only natural that Lewisohn, in presenting the Jewish heritage, would emphasize its realistic approach to human life. Judaism, Lewisohn believed, neither accepts nor repudiates without discrimination the natural man and his world. It "holds to the middle path of civilized reality between pagan self-destructiveness and Christian asceticism." . . . It is a realistic ethos which seeks to sanctify the natural world, the raw material from which a new life is to be wrought. One of Lewisohn's favorite examples of Judaism's "sanctification" of human life, of its desire to curb and guide rather than to destroy, was the Rabbinic view of marriage. Rejecting both the Christian view of celibacy and paganism's undue preoccupation with sex, Judaism sought in marriage to make human love the central force of life. Ever conscious, however, of his own experiences, Lewisohn was quick to add that the Jewish sages were well aware of "the actual difficulties of human relationships." . . . (pp. 326-27)

Lewisohn places great emphasis on the point that Judaism is unascetic in its entirety. It is eminently concerned with the "actual world" . . . and from prophetic times has attempted to "regulate the means by which justice may be expressed in human society." . . . The human ideal is the man of wisdom, and the goal of wisdom is to establish "peace through love." . . . Since Judaism does not believe man to be corrupt it does not desire a metaphysical salvation but only that man be righteous. Thus the Jewish sages always return to the deed, the human act that works to establish peace among men. The Hebraic ethical tradition sought to attain, through the sanctification of the natural world, peace for all men.

This initial formulation of the Jewish heritage, in which Lewisohn emphasizes what he viewed as the fundamentally different approaches of Judaism and Christianity to man and the world, tends on the whole, like his portrayal of Christianity, to be narrow and distorted. Lewisohn, in an obvious attempt to present Judaism in a light that will be most aceptable to modern man, completely ignores a whole dimension of Judaism. In endeavoring to discredit the stereotype of Judaism as a formal legalism, he turns it into a pure humanism. To claim that "Jewish teaching has nothing to say of faith" . . . is to divest Judaism of its theological content. To ignore the Jew's commitment to the laws of the Torah and to quote a Talmudic statement that "to derogate from the Torah is often in its interest" . . . as typical of Rabbinic thought is simply intellectual dishonesty. Lewisohn was too well-versed in Judaic studies to have overlooked a whole dimension of Hebraic belief and practice. Desiring to make the Jewish heritage palatable to modern man in a secular world, he transformed a theistic religion into humanistic ethics. (p. 327)

In Judaism's affirmation of the Oneness and Uniqueness of God and in its negation of the idolatries of the world, be they the "nationalistic state of modern times," . . . or the "idols of Hitler or Stalin," . . . was to be found that hierarchy of values which could serve as a guide for the social order. The history of the Jewish people was the history of the martyrdom of a nation which ". . . died in order that from this world of power, war, force, hate, there might not disappear one 'kingdom of priests,' one 'holy nation,' one people that had forever exchanged the edge of the sword for the witness of the spirit." . . . The ethical values of the Torah were not mere social constructs. They were rungs of the ladder of a "hierarchy of moral values" . . . and were ultimately derived from "that supreme moral discovery of the Jewish spirit—the imaginative identification of the self with all other selves that fill the world." . . . Here was a spiritual framework which could give direction and meaning to man's attempts at human betterment.

For the Jew the implications of Lewisohn's visions were clear. As the bearers of the Hebraic tradition they were "now, as ever, the people chosen for the redemption both of ourselves and of the world. . . ." . . . It was their duty to resist assimilation and to Judaize the "civilizations of their homeland in proportion to their numbers and ability." . . . The Jew would thus exchange "cultural parasitism" . . . for cultural creativeness. If they attempted to obliterate their separateness, Jews not only "betrayed themselves but presented, in measure of their power, the redemption of the world." . . . (pp. 328-29)

This is the spiritual voyage of Ludwig Lewisohn. He had come to America as a pilgrim seeking salvation and had found misery. Though cruelly hurt in his youth, he never lost faith in man's potentiality for the good. While his fellow critics of the 1920's could only scoff at man and society, he criticized constructively and formulated a blueprint for achieving the good society. In returning to the Jewish heritage, Lewisohn had found his happiness in being more rather than less himself. (p. 329)

> David F. Singer, "Ludwig Lewisohn: A Paradigm of American-Jewish Return," in Judaism, Vol. 14, No. 3, Summer, 1965, pp. 319-29.

STANLEY F. CHYET (essay date 1968)

[Chyet is an American historian, biographer, and critic. In the following excerpt, he offers a reevaluation of The Island Within.]

The Island Within is not lacking in dissonance. Lewisohn was in love when he published it in 1928—he had fallen in love with a woman [Thelma Spear] and with a heritage—but alas, for all his expectations, his love for the woman would pass before long into contention and ruin. His love for the heritage, and the people of the heritage, would live and strengthen itself and become "the ultimate existential reality of [his] life and being." This passionate attachment to Jewishness is not so easily explained—this attachment which had had to contend with a notion of Judaism as an "archaic orientalism." *The Island Within* does not completely wipe away the long years when Lewisohn was all but totally incapable of any construction of himself as *homo judaicus*, a man aware, he would say later, that "his ultimate self is Jewish and that his creativity and that deepest self are *one*." No, *The Island Within* does not completely wipe away the long years when he had valued nothing Jewish in himself—when to be a "Pan-Angle" or a Southern Methodist or an "Aryan" bespoke the selfhood he had hungered to claim. Always, of course, there had been a Jew in him; and a struggle on that score, but he would not know it in its fullness until long after, even long after *The Island Within*. For the echoes of the struggle still sound within the pages of his first Jewish novel. The field is not yet cleared of battle; the Jew in him, the particular Jew he would be, has not tasted victory entire, only seen it aglimmer in the distance.

As a novel, *The Island Within* is scarcely flawless, and I suppose it fair to say that no one who reads it with care can dismiss as entirely groundless Leslie Fiedler's caustic description of it as a "blend of self-pity and editorial." If that were all one could say of it . . . but, *pace* Fiedler, it is an unforgettably beautiful book, one in which Lewisohn's *spiritus rector*, Matthew Arnold, would have recognized a high seriousness, a book rich in melancholic sensibilities and a probing of the tragic dimensions and riddles of the Jewish inheritance. And it is an honest book—is that among its limitations?—making no pretense to ultimate wisdom, offering no fulsome solutions to the heart-wounding fret at its core. For all its air of treatise—a word which Lewisohn himself applies to it—the book is a curiously unideological expression. Certainly Lewisohn is eager to urge on the Jewish reader his conviction as to "the security and, yes, the human dignity, that a tradition lent to the freest minds." Certainly he wants the Jew who denies his Jewishness to "put away a pretense—a stubborn, hard, protective pretense" and to "possess the knowledge that he stood by birth at the human centre of things." Still, Arthur Levy, the novel's protagonist who finds his way back to Jewish pride, "didn't, *of course*, care about myth or ritual or dogma. *He never would*." I have added the italics and am reminded of that delicate passage in *Mid-Channel* where Lewisohn speaks of his expatriate quarters in Paris as "a Jewish house, wherein appropriate symbolical tokens . . . of our history and its memories and its pieties are plain for all men to see"—and yet, he goes on to say, he is at pains "to avoid over-emphasis and even the shadow of going beyond our needs and convictions. So we have placed no *mezuzah* at our door.'' Pride, Jewish pride, speaks forth from *The Island Within,* but it is a fragile, careful pride, one, still aborning, of touch and discovery. And question. Absent is the assertive religious commitment for which Lewisohn would in later years—depending on the reader's own aspiration—be acclaimed or contemned.

''The concrete, closely considered,'' Lewisohn had once declared, ''is more far-reaching in its significance than the broadest generalization.'' *The Island Within* validates the insight. Sculpted by the experience of the Gilded Age and World War I and the 20's, it addresses itself with undiminished power and relevance to the experience of the 60's. To be sure, such a novel would not be written today. In diction, in structure, in tone, it is at variance with what generally emerges as the temper of contemporary fiction, but these, it seems to me, are matters of technique, not spirit, not meaning. In sensitivity, in ability to move the reader and introduce him to the peculiar ambiguities of American Jewish life, in these respects Lewisohn's novel has lost nothing with age. His own characterization of it holds true: ''a story not poor, perhaps, in the significant elements that make up the fate of man.'' I am tempted to omit the ''perhaps,'' for in essence the experience Lewisohn reveals and reflects upon is not one we of the 60's are entitled to brand alien. *The Island Within* stands in a sort of ancestral relationship, it might be said, to the work of later writers, Malamud and Bellow and even Philip Roth and Fiedler.

Mutatis mutandis, Arthur Levy is no stranger to us. Indeed, is it hyperbole to suggest that his tribe has undergone a prodigy of increase? At the least, we American Jews today harbor within our ranks more than a negligible minority of young people—and their elders?—who more or less self-consciously regard their ancestral heritage as something to be treated with as much indifference as boldness or decency will allow. There is, of course, among many of us a current enthusiasm for the State of Israel. I am grateful for this, but I recognize that even this represents something of a turning away from the Jewish past. It is Israel's secular modernity, her military and technological prowess, that feeds our pride and commands our esteem. Israel as a spiritual entity, a projection of Jewish history, a fountainhead of Jewishness, is far less able to excite us. It is with the Army of Israel, and with the Hebrew University, and with the Haifa Technion, that most of us feel connection—but the Hechal Shlomo, Israel's rabbinical establishment, is something else again. I do not cite all this as invidious or blameworthy, but merely to adumbrate the degree to which we continue to inhabit Arthur Levy's world, that world at odds with ''myth or ritual or dogma.'' And do we not also share with Arthur Levy a troubling question: ''Where would be the spiritual dwelling-place of his boy?'' Where, in truth?

One final and quite personal word. When I knew Ludwig Lewisohn—it was on the Brandeis University campus during the late 40's and early 50's—he was in his last years. He was gentler, sweeter, it is my impression, than he had been at earlier stages of his life. For that, doubtless, age and honors were responsible, and I believe, too, his devoted Louise deserves no small share of credit. I was enormously impressed by him, and inspired by him, and I loved him—for his sadness, his aristocracy, the *m'kor chayyim,* the spring of life, I touched in him. Already there is far too much of myself in this paragraph, but I would have the reader indulge me this once and know my debt to this man. I think I am not the only one to owe him much. He made a Jew of me—he, his work, and

particularly this book, *The Island Within.* He made me prize what, it is true, was mine by birthright, but it was through my discovery of him that I began to care about that birthright. Even before I knew him in person, he had made a Jew of me, this book his instrument—and it may be, I allow myself to hope, his book will prove as fruitful in the future as it has proven in the past. If the reader takes these words as my *kaddish* for Lewisohn, I shall not complain. (pp. xii-xv)

> *Stanley F. Chyet, in an introduction to* The Island Within *by Ludwig Lewisohn, The Jewish Publication Society of America, 1968, pp. ix-xv.*

JERROLD HIRSCH   (essay date 1980)

[*In the following excerpt, Hirsch offers a reconsideration of Lewisohn's critical ideas in* Expression in America.]

Ludwig Lewisohn. Ludwig *who?* It is a question that contemporary Americans can pose without fear of embarrassment. The Twayne United States Series, now 258 volumes, has a book on Zane Grey and Paddy Chayefsky, but not on Lewisohn. Yet in the 1920s Lewisohn was a widely read and admired literary critic. His work both as translator and critic helped introduce Americans to the work of the French symbolist poets and modern German novelists and dramatists. His books on modern drama and his column in the *Nation* gave critical support to naturalist playwrights and aimed to develop an audience that would regard the theater not as a diversion but as a forum for the exploration of the human dilemma. The various selections Lewisohn put together in *A Book of Modern Criticism* . . . included the work of foreign writers as well as Americans. It was designed to show rebellious American writers and critics that they were not alone, and to provide them with ammunition in their battle against the literary status-quo.

Criticism, Lewisohn claimed, was a form of *creative expression.* And because he was also a novelist (though he wanted to be remembered for his novels, today they are no better known than his criticism is), his claims did not seem simply the attempt of a critic to gain equal status with poets and novelists. The publication of *Expression in America* . . . , a study of American literature, was greeted as a literary event. It seemed to many the capstone of the work of an influential and illuminating critic. His anthology, *Creative America* . . . , was based on the critical principles he had developed in *Expression in America.* Today, *Expression in America* is out of print. It is forgotten. So, too, is Lewisohn.

Strictly speaking this is not true. There are pieces on Lewisohn's childhood in South Carolina, his role in introducing modern German literature to American audiences, his anticommunism and on his Zionist activities and writings. His work is briefly noted, sometimes only footnoted, in surveys of American literary criticism; it makes a useful exhibit in studies of the impact of Freud on American novelists and critics; it can be used to support a thesis about the end of American innocence, or the impact of ethnicity on American culture. Unpublished dissertations treat Lewisohn as a Jewish novelist, as an intellectual trying to reconcile his Jewish and American identities, and as a literary critic.

All these writings are helpful and sometimes illuminating, but all also indicate that as a critical force, as someone who influences our view of authors and their works, Lewisohn is dead. And this is the tacit, if not explicit, assumption underlying whatever discussion of Lewisohn there is. Thus the dissertation on Lewisohn's literary criticism is based on a conclusion it never tries to prove: while Lewisohn's fight for free expression and his anti-provincialism were worthy of praise his literary criticism is valuable to us only as a reflection of an exciting and intellectually significant period in American literary history.

Maybe so. And if so the treatment Lewisohn has received is adequate: that is, it might be further developed and given more dimension, but it will remain an aspect of American literary history rather than a part of a living American literature. But the case against Lewisohn needs to be proved, not assumed. It has not even been argued in a long time.

The question is one that Lewisohn himself thought was central to the study of American writing: in *Expression in America* he referred to how Goethe once remarked of a poet: "He can help us no longer." Goethe's comment provided Lewisohn with a principle:

> It is the mark of the essential poet that he continues to help us across the ages and across revolutions in morals, religions, economic systems. That a given writer was fashionable in his own day or brilliantly entertained his generation continues to be interesting to the antiquarian study of that day and that generation. In the history of literature conceived of as the ultimate articulateness and intercommunication of man concerning himself and his fate the works of such writers have no place. . . .

The fundamental question about Lewisohn, then, is, can he still help us? Has he something to say about literature, about American writing that endures? Do his remarks on individual authors elucidate their particular qualities? Can Lewisohn's voice enrich our appreciation of our literature? My own answer to these questions is a qualified yes. But the first task is to reopen the discussion.

One way to do that is to look at what reviewers wrote about the book and thus have a sense of what they thought noteworthy about *Expression in America*. What qualities did they praise? Which did they find objectionable? Many praised his style and his elevated view of literature. Some attacked Lewisohn's criticism of the Puritans, and his use of Freudian analysis. Marxist critics thought he ignored the class basis of art and did not understand the modern state. And those writers interested in a pure aestheticism, a formalistic criticism and art, found no inspiration in *Expression in America*. Literary historians questioned the validity of Lewisohn's method. (pp. 98-9)

Taken together the reviews of *Expression in America* touched on many of the critical issues. They did not, however, adequately explore Lewisohn's view of literature, the role of the artist and the relationship between experience and expression. Lewisohn's attack on Puritanism, his use of Freudian analysis and his ahistorical approach need to be examined in the larger context of his ideas about literature and expression in this country. Then one can argue about those views and whether Lewisohn's approach helps us better understand the works of individual authors and the spirit of American literature.

The reviewer's job, however, was to *introduce* a new work. This they did. With time more probing studies should have appeared, and *Expression in America*'s qualities and place in our literature should have become clearer. The problem was that such studies were not forthcoming. Kazin's view of Lewisohn in *On Native Ground* [see excerpt dated 1942] . . . could have marked a beginning, but it ony served to close a discussion that had never really developed.

Though *Expression in America* went through several printings and was issued in a Modern Library edition in 1937, and in a 1939 edition, with a new chapter surveying the writings of the '30s, it never had the critical influence its initial reception promised. Many writers of the '30s were more interested in Marx than Freud. From this perspective Lewisohn's study seemed an "escape into the perfumed galleries of religio-freudianism." Marx not Freud was the true science: "With all his talk of science, it's plain that Lewisohn's misty and emotional philosophizing reflected a wholly unscientific, a non-materialist, conception of the history of science." The Marxist critics of the '30s, who so assuredly dismissed writers whose viewpoints differed from theirs, now seem as distant, if not more so, than the writers they tried verbally to guillotine. Yet in the '30s, in the middle of the Great Depression, one did not have to be a Marxist to be more concerned with a radical than a tragic view of life. Lewisohn claimed to be concerned with the eternal spirit of man. He could seem elevated. He could also seem hopelessly abstract.

During the '30s some writers continued to explore formal aesthetic problems. They denied that the life of the author was of any value in discussing literature. Their "new criticism" eventually had a tremendous vogue. They had no use for Lewisohn's concern with the relationship between life and literature. Therefore he could not help them.

Lewisohn thought his criticism would endure, would make a difference, because it was based on principles that transcended the trends of the moment. He strove for a stance that was Olympian and above the battle. He took sides and offered judgments and interpretations but he no longer saw himself as a partisan in the literary battles of the moment. After all he stood with, or rather tried to stand with, such eminent literary figures as Goethe, Matthew Arnold and Sainte-Beuve. They were as important to him as the Puritans and Freud.

While Lewisohn had joined H. L. Mencken and other critics of the '20s in playing "the liberating game of baiting the Puritans," he finally concluded that this "game" could provide a critic with neither a philosophy nor a method. In *Mid-Channel* . . . , one of his autobiographical works, he wrote:

> Most of my contemporaries and I have a dreadful secret. It is this: Our intellect is the creature of a reaction against something limited and changeable and even perishable. . . . Mencken, Lewis, Anderson, Masters, even Cabell with his escape into romantic irony—how will their work look in a hundred years? The truculent go-getter and the tyrannical Methodist will not last forever. Human types come and go. . . . The human adventure is an eternal thing. Of this overwhelming fact, I find no hint in all our writing.

Although Lewisohn's view of Puritanism was a central aspect of *Expression in America* his aim was not to bait conventional Americans but to interpret and judge the national literature. Lewisohn argued that the function of literature was to offer an expression of life, a creative insight into the nature and meaning of the human adventure. His perspective was cosmopolitan. He intended to assess the contribution of American writers to world literature. In *The Spirit of Modern German Literature* . . .

he had proudly denied that he was a "narrow specialist. Period by period, I know English literature rather better than German, and French reasonably well. Nor have I myself much respect for any criticism that is not intelligently aware of at least two literatures besides the one under discussion." And while he intended *Expression in America* to be cosmopolitan and erudite, he also aimed it, not at specialists but at thoughtful readers: "Whenever thoughtful people gather today in the Western World, their talk, leaving sooner or later the vexing questions of war and peace, or food and oil, drifts toward books." . . . The success of his book offered some evidence to support his thesis. . . . (pp. 101-02)

Expression in America was offered as fulfillment, as triumph. This partly accounts for a style that was sometimes magisterial, sometimes passionate, sometimes foolish and at times all of these. Whether one found Lewisohn's writing elevated or merely inflated depended to a large extent on whether one shared his views. However, he could seem convincing because he wrote in such an authoritative tone. His style demanded assent. Thus, when Lewisohn was not convincingly authoritative he appeared arrogant, pompous or merley foolish. His style was such that if one disagreed with him one immediately began to wonder if the Emperor really wore any clothes. (p. 103)

Lewisohn's style also reflected his rejection of impressionistic criticism. He offered *Expression in America,* not as a personal and evocative record of his impressions of the great writers, but as an assessment of American writing against standards he thought valid. He had definite ideas about the purpose of literature, the role of the artist, the relationship between experience and expression, form and content. While his vision was fundamentally romantic and presupposed an agnostic and relativistic outlook, his attitude toward the forms in which "the poet" could express himself was traditional.

For Lewisohn the purpose of literature was neither aesthetic nor didactic—"an elegant diversion or an illustration of the foreknown and the fixed," . . . but the search for moral values. The modern reader no longer lived in a "fixed and finished world," for

> Sometime near the middle of the nineteenth century an old crack in that rigid shell which was supposed to represent the universe suddenly burst, and vistas opened racing into the infinite past and the infinite future. Space joined time in being unimaginable. Authoritative wisdom became dust. . . .

In this situation literature was taking over the function of religion. Modern readers sought in literature what they had once found in religion: *"scripture had become literature and literature scripture."* . . . In a world in which knowledge could no longer be "assumed to be closed; final and infallible," . . . literature was "moral research, a road to salvation, the bread of life." . . . (p. 104)

Creative literature, Lewisohn thought, had a central role to play in modern life. He assumed literature could save the world. Both these assumptions have been denied—often by creative writers. Lewisohn's expectations were boundless. Today we have lowered our expectations. Still, Lewisohn's faith in the ability of the artist to give creative form and meaning to experience is an affirmation of life. At times Lewisohn could express this faith with poetic power. (p. 105)

Expression in America chronicled the literary fight against those forces in American culture that had led to a divorce between experience and expression. Those writers who advanced the cause were to be celebrated. Some had tried and failed. The reasons for their defeat were to be explained. Others had not tried. They were to be dismissed.

It was the Puritan heritage that kept American writers from integrating experience and expression: "Men wrote not what they thought or believed or experienced but what, according to Puritan business morality, a good and respectable man ought to experience and to believe." . . . Where Lewisohn found only "moral pathology" and "hard depravity," other scholars have found that the Puritans struggled nobly, intelligently and sometimes eloquently, not only with the Puritan problems but with fundamental human dilemmas. Thus, as one critic had noted, in Lewisohn's version of American history the "dramatis personae seem actors on an empty stage haunted by vague luring shadows of Puritanism in the wings."

Lewisohn had no sense of history. He had instead a definition of what constituted literature and a formula to explain why, with a few exceptions, American writers had not produced "literature" until his own time. He claimed that by the pre-world War I period American writers had finally succeeded in reintegrating experience and expression. It was the naturalist writers who "reconquered life for art, reintegrated experience with expression and were the liberators of our cultural life." . . . Lewisohn's view of experience was static and vague. He would no doubt argue that he was interested in those eternally human aspects of individual experience. He had argued like Goethe that the general was rooted in the particular. Yet, he had no feeling for, or interest in, the particular experience of writers; he ignored the impact of public events on private lives. And notwithstanding his own erudition and the value he assigned books, his view of experience was surprisingly anti-intellectual. Part of an author's experience is the ideas of his time, his relationships with his contemporaries, and the books he reads. These aspects of experience Lewisohn minimized or ignored. Some writers succeeded in integrating experience and expression because they were geniuses. . . . (pp. 106-07)

In each period of American history Lewisohn picked out those writers who he thought contributed to a reintegration of experience and expression—Emerson, Thoreau, Whitman, some local color writers, the natualists—until he could stop and say the revolt had succeeded. Here was the great tradition of which contemporary American writers could claim they were a part. Lewisohn intended his version of the history of American literature to offer creative sustenance to writers and readers. He argued that his goal was not to set the work in its time, determine influences and examine other matters that he thought would concern only literary scholars. Lewisohn claimed his method allowed him to separate the wheat from the chaff. Yet, his method often failed. For example, Lewisohn did not understand that part of what is valuable to us in the writing of Emerson and Thoreau is that they are not our historical contemporaries. One needs to understand what they considered central issues before one can determine whether they continue to have relevance. Lewisohn simply dismissed their talk of oversoul, of Swedenborgianism and related topics. He discussed their work without ever discussing their view of nature. (p. 107)

In place of historical understanding Lewisohn offered Freudian analysis. He assumed, as did others influenced by Freud, that this method was neither culturally nor historically bound. Lewisohn used Freudianism as a weapon in the fight for realistic and naturalistic expression. It proved the scientific evidence that Puritan inhibition was unnatural. American writing had suffered too long from "enormous antecedent exclusions." . . . The national literature was not a realistic expression of experience. Individual writers failed to fully reflect their experience because of their Puritan inhibitions and their neuroses. Instead there too often had been a flight into fantasy. Freud, Lewisohn thought, had shown that "sex, contrary to the common uninstructed opinion, is not peripheral and localized, but pervasive." . . .

Lewisohn's use of Freud weakened rather than strengthened the book. He created false dichotomies: "Was it the quality of American life or was it wholly their own natures which drove these three [Poe, Hawthorne, Melville] into expression that has the structure of a neurosis?" . . . His inquiry might have had more productive results, if he had not phrased it in either or terms. Nor is his definition and analysis of the writers' alleged neuroses illuminating or convincing. It is curious that he never used Freudian theory to analyse the work of art itself. His descriptions and conclusions about an author's character were stated with an ease and severity that had not been won from materials. . . . (p. 108)

In time the conception of American literature as a revolt against Puritan inhibitions was bound to seem a "formula" that had served its purpose. It sustained those writers and critics who fought for a "free modern literature in America." It was inevitable that later scholars, such as Alfred Kazin, would argue "that a kind of historical complacency had settled upon our studies of [modern American] literature, and that while the usual explanation of it as a revolt against gentility and repression had the root of the matter in it, it did not tell us enough and had even become a litany." Kazin argued that modern American literature was roted in the industrial transformation of America in the post-Civil War years—urbanization, the new immigration, the railroads, the populist revolt, the Progressive movement. While it was exactly these aspects of the American experience that Lewisohn ignored, he did not commit the most serious errors Kazin catalogued. He did not simply tell of freedom won. He did try to answer "whether literature came with the freedom." (p. 109)

For Lewisohn, then, the story of American literature was neither a record of final triumph nor simply a recounting of successive revolts. Rather, Lewisohn wrote the history of American literature as if it was the story of Goethe's Faust. Goethe wrote the first half of Faust when he was a young man and the second part when he was much older. In the first part Goethe removes Faust from a life of scholastic devotion into a world of broader and more varied experience. Faust throws off traditional bounds. It is in the second half of the play that Faust strives to reconcile his newly found freedom with a search for order, for enduring principles. In Lewisohn's version of American literary history the first half of Faust had been written. The question was whether the story of American writing would parallel the story of Faust. Would there be a second act? This is still a relevant question.

Lewisohn offered a noble view of literature's importance to modern man. He had a critical standard. He made it explicit and he defended it eloquently. His weaknesses, however, are glaring. He made no effort to reconcile historical objectivity and private taste. His description of Puritanism lacked any historical depth. His use of Freudianism was seldom helpful. Puritanism and Freudianism could not bear the analytical weight

Lewisohn gave to them. And thus his accounts of some writers now appears prejudiced and inadequate. Yet, many of his statements were perceptive and challenging. . . .

Our problems are no longer with Puritan inhibition preventing the expression of experience. Only pornographers any longer complain about the repressive force of Puritanism. We have ample avenues of expression. Our problem is determining who and what merits our attention and respect. . . . Today Lewisohn's account of American literature reads best, not as a history of the efforts of successive generations of writers to reintegrate experience and expression, but as a defense of the value of literature itself and a belief in the continuing relevance of our classic American writers. (p. 114)

> *Jerrold Hirsch, "Ludwig Lewisohn: Can He Still Help Us? A Reconsideration of 'Expression in America'," in* Seasonal "Authors" for a New Season: The Search for Standards in Popular Writing, *edited by Louis Filler, Bowling Green University Popular Press, 1980, pp. 98-116.*

SEYMOUR LAINOFF (essay date 1982)

[Lainoff is an American critic and educator who has written extensively on American literature and literary figures. In the following excerpt, he offers a survey of Lewisohn's literary criticism.]

Though many of [Lewisohn's] novels, especially those of love and marriage, have no lasting merit—the thesis rendered threadbare and the material insufficiently dramatized, his critical writings, in various degrees, nearly all have value.

His early criticisms from the academy were clear, informative, and well expressed. His journalism for the *Nation* applied high standards to literature and drama, purgative without being small-spirited. His *Cities and Men* were his ripest studies, and in his relaxed moments in *Expression in America* he provided first-rate analyses. He is on weakest grounds when he is most combative, forgetting to keep "his eye on the object" (in Matthew Arnold's phrase) and letting the personal tensions of his novels enter into his critical writings. The best examples of this tendency are the anti-puritanical and Freudian sections of *Expression in America*. Lewisohn is at his best as a critic, which is often, when he is least tendentious. (p. 65)

Lewisohn's best critical study, in his pre-*Nation* days, was *The Spirit of Modern German Literature* . . . , first delivered as lectures at the University of Wisconsin at the invitation of Professor A. R. Hohlfeld, Chairman of the German Department. One feels it was written *con amore;* the book is rich in content, the product of his many years of reading and teaching German literature. It is, to a large degree, introductory, and devotes space to a summary of novels and other works; indeed, many of the authors taken up are still unknown to the American reading public. But it serves as more than a helpful manual; it also signifies Lewisohn's beginning to turn critically from a flexible and idealistic Naturalism to an emphasis on creative expression, the expressiveness of the individual artist.

Lewisohn begins by asserting that the perennial source of art is the "struggling, agonizing human soul"; literature grows out of "the impassioned experience of life." However, modern German literature began in a quest for doctrinal Naturalism, though Naturalism in Germany had idealistic ends. The early German Naturalists, culminating in Hauptmann, were confirmed meliorists, lacking the pessimism of Naturalists in other countries. After an initial subjection to a doctrinaire Natural-ism, German writers affected a "self-contained mastery of their medium".... They were liberated from Emile Zola into more free forms. (pp. 69-70)

[After] discussing the Naturalists, Lewisohn turns with special animation to the literature expressive of personality: Richard Dehmel, Rainer M. Rilke, Stefan George, Hugo von Hof-mannstahl in poetry, Hesse and Ricarda Huch in fiction. He finally discourses, at some length, on Nietzshe and Goethe, representatives of the tradition of striving (*Streben*) for the higher self. Of Nietzshe, he concludes: "It is clear, then, that even if we strip Nietzsche's work of its questionable meta-physics, and even discount the doctrine of the superman, there is left the noblest and austerest summons to freedom, fortitude and greatness in the personal life that ours, or indeed, any age has known—there is left the inspired philosophic vision of . . . free creative personality . . .".... (pp. 70-1)

We see, from this quotation, that *The Spirit of Modern German Literature* holds simultaneously the earlier critical credo Lew-isohn espoused, that of an expressive Naturalism, with a new emphasis on the creative personality that Lewisohn would stress in his years as an editor for the *Nation*. Goethe, for Lewisohn, mirrors both tendencies at once—an objective rendering of nature and the aspirations for superior accomplishment dem-onstrated by *Faust*. The spirit of modern German literature, therefore, is twofold: "for in it we find on the one hand, naturalism, cultivation of science, social organization for the collective welfare and practical efficiency . . . and on the other hand we find: an individualistic humanism, the cult of beauty . . . and a tireless spiritual striving." . . .

One of the most pleasing of Lewisohn's critical works, *The Spirit of Modern German Literature*, lacks the magisterial au-thority of the later *Cities and Men* and parts of *Expression in America;* it also, however, to the reader's relief, avoids the combativeness, personal intrusiveness, and Freudian misread ings of some of his later criticism. (p. 71)

[*Poets of Modern France*] consists of seventy pages of discus sion mostly of French Symbolist poets and ninety pages of his original translations of French short poems. . . . His aim here, as in his two earlier critical works, is partially pedagogical. His discussion, brief as it is, had few precedents in America, the most notable of which, Amy Lowell's *Six French Poets* (1915), was narrower in scope.

He begins with a new note in his criticism, one that will sound and resound later: "The struggle of man, however blind and stumbling, however checked by tribal rage and tribal terror, is toward self-hood." For the first time an autobiographical im-pulse asserts itself in the criticism. His unpopular position of neutrality during the War, his subsequent isolation and his need to achieve self-hood, will lead to *Up Stream*, upon which he would soon be at work. In *Poets of Modern France* the chords of resistance and self-assertion are struck. Lewisohn seems to link, in part, his own travails with the *Symbolistes*, who sought a "new freedom and a new music." Citing Remy de Gourmont, he avers that a poet must create his own aesthetic. (pp. 71-2)

The Creative Life . . . chiefly derives from columns written for magazines; Chapter 1 and the first section of Chapter 4 first appeared in the Literary Review of the *New York Evening Post*. The book puts forth a theory of literature, as against the prac-tical criticism evidenced in Lewisohn's earlier work. Lewisohn here does not vary radically from the premises underlying *The Spirit of Modern German Literature*, but his emphasis falls more

on the creative sources of art rather than on the mimetic ap-proach implicit in a doctrine of Naturalism.

In his prologue he declares himself a radical in life, a classicist in literature. A "radical" as he employs the term would more properly be defined as a "liberal" today; a "radical" in his use wishes to do away with "hoary prejudices" and to re-mediate "moral suffering." A "classicist" might be more accurately defined as a "conservative," and Lewisohn seizes the chance to state that he finds Joyce and Woolf unintelligible; he also cannot understand the viewpoint of such "mystics" as Jacob Wasserman (whom he translated). Strangely, Lewisohn, so responsive to experiment in French and German and in European drama, was unsympathetic to literary innovations in English. He particularly disliked D. H. Lawrence, who was achieving more successfully in some of his novels what Lew-isohn was trying to do; even Amy Lowell and the Imagists he found too unconventional for his taste.

In any event, literature, no matter how personal to the artist, has to have an ultimate social purpose: ". . . as time goes on, I care less and less for art in its most abstract forms and more and more for life. I am too preoccupied to be held by anything that approaches the decorative."

Clearly, Lewisohn's approach to art is experiential, i.e., the writer derives his subject matter from his own experiences or autobiography. The creative mind builds on experience and "gives the vision of that experience to mankind." Interpreting experience in a fresh or original way must bring the artist into opposition with the solid citizenry, who have compartment-alized experience to avoid surprise.

Contradictions appear between Lewisohn's theoretical state-ments and his expressions of literary preference. Although he states that artists are all romantics at heart, for "the Universe, as William James finely said, is as wild as a hawk's wing," his personal predilection in English literature is the eighteenth century; the work of criticism he especially admires is Samuel Johnson's *Lives of the Poets*. Although he advocates experi-ment in fiction ("Liberation can obey no law but an inherent one . . ."), he feels most at home with the realistic, even plum pudding, novel: Butler's *Way of All Flesh*, Maugham's *Of Human Bondage*, Galsworthy's *Forsythe Saga*. Among Amer-ican writers he praises Edith Wharton, Sinclair Lewis, and Theodore Dreiser. A romantic idealist in theory, he is a realist by inclination. As said before, he is more pliant in judging Continental literature. Much of the book is devoted to an attack on "ancestral pieties,"a view characteristic of the 1920s and ironic in light of his later conversion to traditional Judaism.

The essential inconsistency of the work—his defense of the creative mind together with his lack of sensitivity to many of the creative currents in this period—mar the work and make it less useful than *Drama and the Stage* and *The Spirit of Modern German Literature*. One passage from *The Creative Life* about American literature, concerned with Emerson, Thoreau, and Whitman, he would have done well to keep in mind when writing *Expression in America*. He speaks of a need to reev-aluate American literature and recognize its progressive prom-ises: "We have a national past to cultivate, a past dedicated to freedom, to the right of revolution, to the creative life in its widest and fullest sense."

Cities and Men . . . is possibly the best of Lewisohn's critical books, with effective travel sketches of European cities and mature literary studies of writers to whom he responded most in his literary career. If the reader were asked to recommend one of Lewisohn's books of criticism above the rest, this is the book he might select.

The first chapter, "Culture and Barbarism: An Irrelevant Introduction," attempts to reconcile the disparities of *The Creative Life.* Whether the attempt grew from further introspection or from the suggestion of others, one cannot ascertain. Lewisohn was sensitive to what he believed was informed criticism from those around him.

Here again he defends "subjective" literature agaisnt so-called "objective" standards. "Why do the critics distrust the modern autobiographical instinct . . .?" Lewisohn cites writers, such as Tolstoy, whose works were "one long confession." Of course, though art derives from life, art diverges from life because of its form and interpretive qualities. "When the work is finished . . . it has become transposed into another and more intelligible world; it has become detached from the world of mere reality. . . ." He goes further, moreover, by embracing Mann and Dreiser as "subjective" writers. Even Samuel Johnson speaks in the "eternal individual human voice." Autobiography is not inconsistent with realism and Naturalism, for realism and Naturalism find their source in personal pain. Thus Lewisohn strives to unify the sometimes inconsistent strands of expressiveness and Naturalism in his outlook.

The real barbarism in literature is the pseudoclassical which disguises past paganism and historical cruelties as forms of tradition and order. *Cities and Men,* written in Europe, records Lewisohn's discovery of aspects of historical experience even more disturbing than the provincial rigidities of American life. He saw beautiful, now decadent, cities that glorified past wars and organized peacetime savagery. The art that glorifies a wicked past, he concluded, is a bad art; only the voice of reason and humanity deserves to be heeded. "Men read epic and ballad and classical tragedy or see cathedrals of the Middle Ages and admire ferocity in war and the obedience of henchmen and uninquiring faith in baseless myth. They read Amos and Socrates, Montaigne and Goethe and Whitman, and they are set free for the pursuit of goodness and truth." . . . (pp. 81-4)

Looking back to Matthew Arnold, Lewisohn sees the ultimate distinction between good and bad art as that between an art that promotes culture and an art that sustains barbarism. During his years on the *Nation* an opponent of Humanism, Lewisohn is now shaping a humanism of his own. It is needless to harp on inconsistencies. As is well-known, even critics of the highest order—a Plato, a Wordsworth, a Coleridge—are sometimes inconsistent and also subject to change. Critics of a lesser order, like Lewisohn, are even more rarely of one piece. Lewisohn began as an exponent of a nondoctrinaire naturalism, which never lost its attraction for him, then advocated an art of personal experience, and then propounded a new humanism. Strangely, while beginning his first chapter with a defense of expressiveness which embraces realism and Naturalism as well, at the end of the chapter he almost abandons the autonomy of art altogether, subordinating art to the realm of reason, humanity, and wholeness of personality. (p. 84)

Lewisohn's major critical work of the 1930s was *Expression in America* . . . , a literary history of the United States that employed eclectically critical approaches derived from the anti-Puritan rebellion of the early twenties, the Naturalism of Dreiser and the Europeans, the discoveries of Freud, and the Humanism evident in *Cities and Men.* Lewisohn seemed to assemble all his critical resources, past and present, to undertake his most ambitious critical enterprise.

Subsequent to *Expression in America,* upon which he had been working intermittently for some five years, Lewisohn turned increasingly as critic to a stress on symbol and myth; he paid tribute to Otto Rank, the psychoanalyst, for leading him in this direction, though most readers have followed the same route through the works of Ernst Cassirer, Suzanne Langer, and Northrop Frye. Lewisohn's work most concerned with "word" and "myth" was the late *The Magic Word.* . . . Clearly, Lewisohn did not remain steadfast with one critical theory for thirty years, but responded, in his own fashion—often reinforced by his evolving atittudes and needs outside of criticism—to the shifting cultural trends of succeeding decades.

Expression in America, Lewisohn's personal history of American literature, appeared in 1932. . . . In the preface he stated that his interest in American literature had taken hold when he was a member of a seminar conducted by Professor Trent at Columbia University; the plan for the book took shape in 1927. He thought of this long study, over 600 pages in length, as the culmination of his critical endeavors.

Undoubtedly, the book has merit, written at the height of Lewisohn's confidence in his critical abilities. Precise and lucid in style, it is eminently readable. . . . (pp. 91-2)

But the work falls in esteem when one compares it, for example, with D. H. Lawrence's *Studies in Classic American Literature* (1923), another original approach to American writing. Lewisohn lacked Lawrence's gifted set of values on love and life generally and Lawrence's sense of the mythic relevance of American classics.

Critical ingenuity or originality must be based ultimately on a philosophical core; in contrast to Lawrence's rich store of values, Lewisohn applied an eclectic group of criteria consisting of a primitive Freudianism, Arnold's notion that literature serves as a surrogate for moral or scriptural traditions, and a liberal rationalism and progressivism opposed to aristocratic or reactionary tendencies. Many of his judgments derive from the now outworn prejudices of his day, the anti-puritanical sentiments of his contemporaries and their aversion to American literature before Whitman. The final result mixes invigorating statements with eccentricities. To one commencing a study of American literature, *Expression in America* is unreliable; the professional scholar must carefully sift the good from the bad. It is lively and sometimes exceptional, but also at times marred or outdated.

It is often classified as an illustration of Freudian criticism; certainly Lewisohn states his Freudian views openly in his preface: "It was equally inevitable that I use the organon or method of knowledge associated with the venerated name of Sigmund Freud." Several of his definitions of literature suggest Freudian derivation: literature as a personal expression originating in a neurosis or compensaing for it. Many of his most flagrant judgments are Freudian. His forerunners in this school of criticism were F. D. Prescott's *The Poetic Mind* (1920), Van Wyck Brooks's *The Ordeal of Mark Twain* (1920), and J. W. Krutch's *Edgar Allan Poe* (1926). Louis Fraiberg, in *Psychoanalysis and American Literary Criticism,* thinks these early psychological critics approached their subjects too naively.

But Lewisohn's preface also incorporates the views of the later Matthew Arnold, as exemplified in "The Study of Poetry" (1880). Literature, in Arnold's elevated view, provides a substitute for religious codes now in decline. Lewisohn writes: ". . . literature was no longer an elegant diversion or an illustration of the foreknown or fixed but moral research, a road to salvation, the bread of life." . . . The last part of the work, especially, including the long last chapter inveighing against the chaos of modern literature, owes more to Arnold than to Freud. Lewisohn's growing emphasis on spiritual values in literature might account as well for his later change of title, dropping the more Freudian *Expression in America* for the more neutral *Story of American Literature.* (pp. 92-3)

In his preface to *Art and Artist,* a selection from Otto Rank's writings on art translated from the German in 1932, Lewisohn sees Rank breaking new ground in discovering the sources of art. Rank abandons all approaches that seem indebted to nineteenth-century mechanism. Consequently, Lewisohn seems less sympathetic than he had been to Naturalism and Freudian principles, as they were commonly applied to literary criticism.

Freud had correctly shifted attention from the nineteenth-century view of a universe governed by scientific principles as the source of art to the human psyche; but even Freud had encouraged certain rigid concepts, thought Lewisohn, that owed their existence to nineteenth-century mechanism. One such concept was that art is the sublimation of sexual instincts, a view too partial to do justice to the total scope of man's creativity. Rank, on the other hand, sees man as the creator of his universe through art, myth, science, and religion. Rank based his conclusions on studies of anthropological and psychological materials; Ernest Cassirer, whom Lewisohn never mentions though his later statements bear similarities to Cassirer's, based his conclusions on neo-Kantian grounds.

To the reader of Lewisohn's work, the most significant implication of Lewisohn's preface is his unstated, but inevitable abandonment of the idea of the "Creative Eros" as the source of art—the idea upon which his short novel *The Golden Vase* was predicated. Lewisohn writes of Rank: "Thus he destroys the facile notion of art as a by-product of the sexual instinct."

All art, Lewisohn asserts, is "creative and self-representative," a free spiritual activity tending to liberate the artist from the biological and material and from the collective culture of his age. The personality of the artist is autonomous, an example of man's ability to elevate himself to the level of vision.

The Magic Word: Studies in the Nature of Poetry . . . , Lewisohn's last critical work, consists of an introduction, a chapter called "The Magic Word," which incorporates a theory of poetic diction, and separate chapters on Homer, Shakespeare, and Goethe. The section on Shakespeare is so wrong-headed it almost ruins the book.

The introduction states that poetry and literature originate in word and myth. Western criticism, which Lewisohn all too succinctly summarizes, has paid scant attention to the "word" or poetic diction. Exceptions, he continues, are the moderns Valéry and Rilke. "Is it not strange, since words are the materials of human expression, its very substance and texture, the stuff of which it is made, that no one apparently has sought the secret of the character of literature in *them,* in the nature of language itself and as such?" Lewisohn implies a greater originality adhering to his discussion than is deserved. Certainly, in the nineteenth century "words" were not neglected. One thinks immediately of chapter 14 of *Biographia Literaria* (1817), in which Coleridge amends Wordworth's conception of poetic diction; of the section on language in Emerson's *Nature* (1836), whch proffers a symbolic theory of expression; and of "The Hero as Poet," in *On Heroes, Hero-Worship, and the Heroic in History* (1840), in which Carlyle echoes

much of what Lewisohn tries to communicate: the poet as the mythmaker of his age and the word as symbolic and musical vehicle. In dismissing his predecssors as nonexistent, Lewisohn was perfunctory and neglectful.

The second chapter, "The Magic Word," is better. Lewisohn cites the verses in *Genesis* that remind us that, though God created all living things, man was assigned the task of naming them—a kind of second creation. Man's first utterances were both the cry (*Anruf*) and the call (*Zuruf*), both exclamation and symbol. Archibald MacLeish's statement, therefore, that a "poem must not mean but be," is inaccurate; a poem both *is* and *means* simultaneously. Examining words for identical objects in different language families, Lewisohn concludes that these words are so disparate it is apparent that symbolic meanings outweigh the imitative in importance.

The French *symbolistes,* beginning with Mallarmé, demonstrated a heightened consciousness of words in poetry, but invented nothing new. Lewisohn praises Mallarmé, Valéry, and Rilke, but years had not softened his hostility to contemporary American poets: "Among Americans, the angry repudiation of this country, which set in with Ezra Pound—their tragic alienation, their spiritual homelessness, in both the world and the universe—produced the opaque and tortured and helplessly cacophonous work of the neo-esthetes from Wallace Stevens to, let us say, Delmore Schwartz." . . . Lewisohn has retained this damaging blind spot to the last.

Along with the "word" we find the "myth," which, resembling a dream, symbolically bodies forth a total picture of life. Myths express "the realities of the soul." In his discussion of myth Lewisohn often seems to adopt the commonplaces of the 1940s and 1950s that he found compatible with his own views. The successors to the great myths of the past have been reduced in scope in modern times because of the bleakness of our spiritual landscape. Myths cannot grow in the desperate "twilight region" of modern life. (pp. 102-04)

The Magic Word, like *Expression in America,* is a work of mixed merit. The book displays extensive learning, though with serious lacunae, a fine use of poetic lines as touchstones (always one of Lewisohn's strengths), and a mature eloquence only occasionally marred by self-consciousness or the wish to dazzle. It presents Lewisohn entering new critical areas during the post-World War II period. (p. 106)

> *Seymour Lainoff, in his* Ludwig Lewisohn, *Twayne Publishers, 1982, 148 p.*

ADDITIONAL BIBLIOGRAPHY

"Ludwig Lewisohn: In Memoriam." *American Jewish Archives* XVII, No. 2 (November 1965): 109-13.
  Presents a personal tribute to Lewisohn as an artist and dedicated Jew.

Analyticus [pseudonym of James Waterman Wise]. "Ludwig Lewisohn." In his *Jews Are Like That!,* pp. 109-26. New York: Brentano's, 1928.
  Traces the development of Lewisohn's Jewish identity and its implications for all Jews.

Ascherson, Neal. "Ill Mated." *New Statesman* 97, No. 2509 (20 April 1979): 560-61.

Illustrates the reversal of critical attitudes toward the main characters in *The Case of Mr. Crump* that has occurred since its publication.

Bragman, Louis J. "The Case of Ludwig Lewisohn: A Contribution to the Psychology of Creative Genius." *The American Journal of Psychiatry* XI, No. 2 (September 1931): 319-31.
  Intimately links the focus of Lewisohn's works with his personal life.

Chamberlain, John. "Ludwig Lewisohn in Mid-Stream." *The New York Times Book Review* (28 April 1929): 5.
  Praises Lewisohn's efforts to enrich his intellectual milieu.

De Voto, Bernard. "Jewry in America." *The Saturday Review of Literature* IV, No. 41 (5 May 1928): 840.
  Explores *The Island Within* as an epic work.

Edman, Irwin. "Odyssey." *The Menorah Journal* XIV, No. 5 (May 1928): 508-11.
  Praises Lewisohn's eloquence as a novelist and lucidity as a social commentator in *The Island Within*.

Hicks, Granville. "A Daniel for Shylock." *The Nation* CXXXII, No. 3424 (18 February 1931): 187-88.
  Finds *The Last Days of Shylock* to be a valuable work despite problems generated by its characterization.

Hindus, Milton. "Ludwig Lewisohn: From Assimilation to Zionism." *Jewish Frontier* XXXI, No. 1 (February 1964): 22-30.
  Surveys Lewisohn's major works as unvarnished appraisals of American experience.

Hoffman, Frederick J. "Further Interpretations." In his *Freudianism and the Literary Mind*, pp. 277-308. Baton Rouge: Louisiana State University Press, 1945.
  Portrays Lewisohn as a crusader against both moral repression and its amoral countermovement.

Krutch, Joseph Wood. "Great Men of the Past Seen as Contemporaries." *New York Herald Tribune Books* 8, No. 27 (13 March 1932): 1.
  Asserts Lewisohn's relevance in his approach to literature as both critic and historian.

Le Gallienne, Richard. "A Radical Praises the American Classics." *The Literary Digest International Book Review* II, No. 10 (September 1924): 709-10.
  Endorses Lewisohn's struggle against literary iconoclasm.

Lowell, Amy. "The Case of Modern Poetry Versus Professor Lewisohn." *The Bookman*, New York XLVIII, No. 5 (January 1919): 558-66.
  Finds Lewisohn's treatment of modern poets to be based entirely on personal taste.

Melnick, Ralph. "Oedipus in Charleston: Ludwig Lewisohn's Search for the Muse." In *Studies in American Jewish Literature*, No. 3, edited by Daniel Walden, pp. 68-84. Albany: State University of New York Press, 1983.
  Examines the formative forces, particularly his mother's influence, that shaped Lewisohn's life and work.

Mencken, H. L. "Portrait of a Lady." *The American Mercury* 10, No. 39 (March 1927): 379-80.
  Offers high praise for *The Case of Mr. Crump*.

Mezvinsky, Norton. "The Jewish Thought of Ludwig Lewisohn." *The Chicago Jewish Forum* 16, No. 2 (Winter 1957-1958): 77-82.
  Traces the progression of Lewisohn's Jewish philosophy in conjunction with the unfolding of his artistic career.

Sherman, Stuart P. "Is There Anything To Be Said for Literary Tradition?" *The Bookman*, New York LII, No. 2 (October 1920): 108-12.
  Scourges Lewisohn for what he perceives as a cavalier rejection of literary and critical traditions.

Sutton, Walter. "Early Psychological Criticism." In his *Modern American Criticism*, pp. 6-25. Englewood Cliffs, N.J.: Prentice-Hall, 1963.
  Finds Lewisohn's Freudian interpretations of literature to be relevant, although inadequately used as critical tools.

Trilling, Lionel. "Flawed Instruments." In his *Speaking of Literature and Society*, pp. 21-6. New York: Harcourt Brace Jovanovich, 1980.
  Contends that Lewisohn's artistic insufficiencies invalidate his sound moral precepts.

Rainer Maria Rilke

1875-1926

German poet, novelist, dramatist, biographer, and short story writer.

The following entry presents criticism of Rilke's novel *Die Aufzeichnungen des Malte Laurids Brigge (The Notebooks of Malte Laurids Brigge)*. For a complete discussion of Rilke's career, see *TCLC*, Volumes 1 and 6.

The Notebooks of Malte Laurids Brigge is considered Rilke's most significant prose work as well as a seminal work of modern literature. Concerned with the delineation of a hypersensitive and artistic temperament, *Malte* takes the form of the journal of a young writer who presents in graphic prose his lurid perceptions of life in modern Paris and his dreamlike memories of childhood. While *Malte* is most often referred to as a novel, critics recognize that Rilke's work belongs as much to the realms of philosophy, psychology, and poetry as it does to fiction.

Rilke began *Malte* in 1904 during his first extended visit to France and continued to work on the manuscript for the next six years. Containing a considerable amount of material taken from his own letters and diaries from 1902 to 1910, Rilke's narrative condenses incidents from this time period to occupy one year of the protagonist's life. Malte Laurids Brigge is a twenty-eight-year-old aspiring poet who is the last descendant of an aristocratic Danish family. After moving to Paris to study and seek the autonomy he believes necessary to become an artist, he experiences a growing sense of anxiety and exhaustion. Malte's perceptions of Paris and his experiences there become nightmarish ordeals which he transcribes in his diary. Malte declares that he is "learning to see," but because of his fear and heightened distress, Paris appears to his eyes as a series of grotesque and macabre images, reinforcing his sense of life as a pageant of suffering and evil and driving him into further emotional isolation. The passages which relate Malte's day-to-day experiences in Paris convey the impression that his acute sensibilities are being constantly assaulted by the sights, sounds, and smells of the city, a condition he finds harrowing and repulsive. Juxtaposed with Malte's detailing of his immediate impressions are reflective passages concentrating on his past, especially his childhood spent at ancestral estates in Denmark. Critics find that these sections of the novel dealing with Malte's past serve a two-fold purpose: to help him come to terms with the repressed pain of his unhappy childhood and to provide a psychological escape from the terrors of his daily life in Paris. After his initial confrontation with the difficulties and failures of the personal relationships throughout his life, he begins to consider his past in a larger context, so that the idiosyncrasies and tragedies of historical figures become equated with his own personality. This process enables Malte to shift his focus from one of egotistical self-absorption to one that is artistic and universal.

Prominent among the thematic concerns of *Malte Laurids Brigge* are questions regarding God, love, and death. Malte's obsession with death is introduced in the first sentence: "So, then people do come here in order to live; I would sooner have thought one died here." *Here* refers to Paris, where Malte

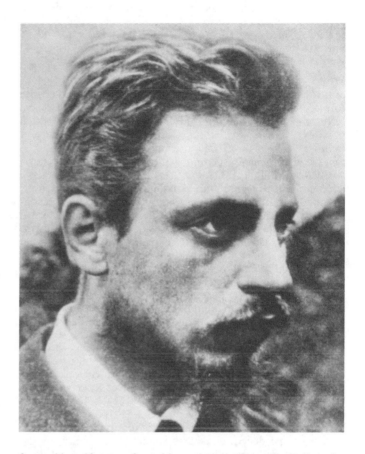

forces himself to confront his enormous fears, including the fear of death, which obstructs his ability to "see" life—a prerequisite to artistic expression. As Malte is exposed to life in Paris, he is reciprocally reminded of death. Early in the notebook he describes the oldest hospital in Paris, Hôtel-Dieu, as a death factory where individual deaths are meaningless and people do not know how to die properly. The presence of death in the streets of Paris so overwhelms Malte that it colors his sense of reality with nightmarish hues of decay and putrefaction. For example, he peers into a child's face and sees not youth and life, but a fat, greenish face with an eruption on the forehead. When he finds the reality of death and disease overpowering, Malte seeks refuge in childhood memories of his grandfather's death which, by contrast, he saw as dramatic and noble. Love, another prevalent theme, is especially important in the second half of the novel, in which Malte maintains that the act of loving is infinitely preferable to the state of being loved, which must be avoided in order to preserve one's individuality. According to Theodore Ziolkowski, "If we reduce Rilke's theory of love to its simplest form, we can say that he regards love in the conventional sense as a threat to be survived, because ordinary love tends to focus upon a specific object, demanding that it remain constant. Being loved thus restricts the freedom of the individual to develop in his own direction. To *love*, on the other hand, is a timeless activity. . . ." At the end of the novel, Rilke uses his own version of the Prodigal Son parable to illustrate this theory. Malte identifies himself with the young man who flees those who love him out of fear that their love will restrict and distort his growth. While the Biblical protagonist makes a moral journey from transgression to repentance in order to experience the fullness of God's paternal love and forgiveness, the return home of Rilke's prodigal is conditional and precarious—"We know not whether he remained." In the view of most critics, Malte's is a frigid, if not essentially faithless, vision of a vague and unloving God who is merely a "direction" rather than an object of love.

While *Malte* has often been praised for its thematic depth, critics have been less certain in their evaluations of its artistic form. Some have found unifying patterns in the work, but most have pronounced it a confusing assemblage of fragments and possibly a failure as a work of art. Resembling a variety of familiar genres—novel, autobiography, diary, and prose poetry—*The Notebooks of Malte Laurids Brigge* belongs exclusively to none of them, nor does it succeed in creating an artistic structure unique to itself. To a limited extent *Malte* functions as a traditional bildungsroman, because after a painful reconstruction of his childhood and education in the harsh, urban world, the protagonist undergoes considerable personal growth. Nevertheless, as David H. Miles explains, "Malte's obsession with the concept of a 'personal death'—his existential memento mori—would seem directly to contradict the bildungsroman's traditional romantic interest in the art of living." Because of the central character's pervasive sense of isolation, repulsion, and angst, the work is often compared to Fedor Dostoevski's *Notes from Underground* or, more recently, Jean-Paul Sartre's *Nausea*. Even though *Malte* contains numerous passages which were borrowed nearly verbatim from Rilke's letters and journals, critics invariably shun a strictly biographical reading, maintaining that although Rilke shared much of Malte's perception and temperament, Malte is not Rilke. Rilke stated that through the creation of a character who was the incarnation of his repressions and fears, he hoped to exorcise them from himself, while practicing the aesthetic discipline and distance required to produce a work of literature. Commentary on the novel is divided over whether or not he was successful, with some critics charging that it is a structurally incoherent work, and others contending that its impressionistic, mosaic-like quality perfectly correlates with Malte's inner experience.

In spite of, or perhaps because of, its ambiguous form and intent, many critics have called *Malte* one of the most important works in modern literature. More than a mere cathartic exercise, *Malte* is a remarkable achievement which challenges both writers and readers. According to William H. Gass, "Rilke succeeded in furthering the art of fiction so far as to make its continued practice forbidding if not impossible. From its readers . . . *Malte* requires a wholly different dedication; it requires a *gaze*. Paradoxically, it is just such difficulties which drive us on, so that the novel has become more beguilingly daunting for every age of its existence."

(See also *Contemporary Authors*, Vol. 104).

RAINER MARIA RILKE   (letter date 1911)

[*In the following letter to Lou Andreas-Salomé—a Russian-born German novelist and critic whom Rilke met in 1897 and with whom he made two visits to Russia, where they met Leo Tolstoy—Rilke discusses his relationship to his character Malte Laurids Brigge.*]

You see, I am still in a hurry to get to myself, I still presume that this theme can be of interest; would you like to go into it once more? Please, please, do, I will help you, as best I can, perhaps I'll be bad at it,—in that case there is a point of departure: *Malte Laurids Brigge*. I need no answers to my books, that you know,—but now I deeply need to know what impression this book made on you. Our good Ellen Key naturally confused me promptly with Malte and gave me up; yet no one but you, dear Lou, can distinguish and indicate whether and how much he resembles me. Whether he, who is of course in part made out of my dangers, goes under in it, in a sense to spare me the going under, or whether with these journals I have really got for fair into the current that is tearing me away and driving me across. Can you understand that after this book I have been left behind just like a survivor, helpless in my inmost soul, no longer to be used? The nearer I came to the end of writing it, the more strongly did I feel that it would be an indescribable division, a high watershed, as I kept telling myself; but now it turns out that all the water has flowed off toward the old side and I am going down into an aridity that will not change. And if it were merely that: but the other fellow, the one who went under, has somehow used me up, carried on the immense expenditure of his going under with the strength and materials of my life, there is nothing that was not in his hands, in his heart, he appropriated everything with the intensity of his despair; scarcely does a thing seem new to me before I discover the break in it, the rough place where he tore himself off. Perhaps this book had to be written as one sets a mine; perhaps I should have jumped way away from it the moment it was finished. But I suppose I still cling too much to possession and cannot achieve measureless poverty, much as that is probably my crucial task. My ambition was such that I put my entire capital into a lost cause, but on the other hand its values could become visible only in this loss, and that is why, I remember, Malte Laurids appeared to me for the longest time not so much as a going under, rather as a singularly dark ascension into a remote neglected part of heaven. (pp. 32-3)

> *Rainer Maria Rilke, in a letter to Lou Andreas-Salomé on December 28, 1911, in his* Letters of Rainer Maria Rilke: 1910-1926, Vol. 2, *translated by Jane Bannard Greene and M. D. Herter Norton, W. W. Norton & Company Inc., 1948, pp. 32-5.*

RAINER MARIA RILKE   (letter date 1915)

[*In the following letter to a correspondent identified with the initials L. H., Rilke explains the expression of human suffering in* Malte.]

What is expressed in the suffering that is written into *Malte Laurids Brigge* (forgive me if I mention this book again when we have just discussed it) is really only *this*, with every means and always anew and by every manifestation this, *This:* how is it possible to live when after all the elements of this life are utterly incomprehensible to us? If we are continually inadequate in love, uncertain in decision and impotent in the face of death, how is it possible to exist? In this book, achieved under the deepest obligation, I did not manage to express all of my astonishment over the fact that men have had for thousands of years to deal with life (not to mention God), and yet towards these first most immediate problems—strictly speaking, these only problems (for what else have we to do, today still and for how long to come?)—they remain such helpless novices, so between fright and subterfuge, so miserable. Isn't that incomprehensible? My astonishment over this fact, whenever I yield to it, drives me first into the greatest dismay and then into a sort of horror, but behind the horror again there is something else and again something else, something so intensive that I cannot tell by the feeling whether it is white-hot or icy. I tried once before, years ago, to write about Malte, to someone who had been frightened by the book, that I myself sometimes thought of it as a hollow form, a negative mold, all the grooves and indentations of which are agony, disconsolations and most painful insights, but the casting from which, were it possible to make one (as with a bronze the positive figure one would get out of it), would perhaps be happiness, assent,—most perfect and most certain bliss. Who knows, I ask myself, whether we do not always approach the gods so to speak from behind, separated from their sublimely radiant fact through nothing but themselves, quite near to the expression we yearn for, only just standing behind it—but what does that mean save that our countenance and the divine face are looking out in the same direction, are at one; and this being so, how are we to approach the god from the space that lies in front of him? (pp. 146-47)

Rainer Maria Rilke, in a letter to L. H. on November 8, 1915, in his Letters of Rainer Maria Rilke: 1910-1926, Vol. 2, *translated by Jane Bannard Greene and M. D. Herter Norton, W. W. Norton & Company Inc., 1948, pp. 146-51.*

FEDERICO OLIVERO (essay date 1929)

[*In the following excerpt, Olivero offers a general discussion of* Malte.]

Die Aufzeichnungen des Malte Laurids Brigge is the story of a mind told in a kind of visionary recitative,—a series of subtle psychological notations and of scenes of refined realism which remind us of Jacobsen. This autobiographic, and therefore lyrical, novel—written by a Danish student in Paris,—lyrical in its substance and often in its expression,—is at the same time the fragment of an existence and a commentary on life.

It includes the intimate history of Malte from infancy to maturity, from the first dreams to the highest forms of thought, that is to say, to the revelation that the supreme, the only and true love is in God.

Malte, who is a descendant of a noble family in Denmark, lives in poverty and solitude in a foreign country, and notes the memories of the past and the impressions of his surroundings in this diary. Rilke's lyrical spirit is often revealed in passages of fine poetry, in rare images, in portraits of scenes and personages and in his evocations of states of mind. But the mind of Rilke arises clear before us from his poetry, but not from these pages, where it appears to be veiled; his spirit is not so strongly impressed on this prose as it is on his lyrical poetry.

The uncertain figure of Abelone gives us the characteristics of the work; although largely founded on truth, neither the personality of the leading characters, nor the figures of the other characters stand out clearly in these pages; the lyrical and poetical nature of Rilke's mind does not know how to create a real figure,—like [Jacobsen's] Frau Marie Grubbe or Niels Lyhne. There is no organic construction in this work, but a wandering uncertainty in the course of the real or spiritual events; nor is there any dramatic contrast. The figures appear

on his scene without prominence, like bleak clouds which appear on a sky darkened by mists, without taking any definite forms. These minds are in close contact with mystery, but far off real life. And all the figures—be they of dead or living persons—appear from the mist of memory.

The book is made up of notations of spiritual events in an unquiet soul in spiritual solitude and in the tortures of doubt, the abstruse bitter fruit of his intellectual pride, which the author does not wish to admit. He is overwhelmed by the passion for analysis of himself, and casts a shade on all the work like the melancholy of a long nightmare, through which his existence appears like a sad vision. In some passages, on account of the extremely minute selection and description of particulars, and the excessive insistence on every gradation of sensation and emotion, the impression of the scene escapes us;—of this prolixity, which lessens his power to produce vivid effects, and which is strangely contrary to the thrilling conciseness of his lyrical poetry, an example can be seen in the pages where he describes the waiting room in the hospital.

The elements of disintegration, which destroy the real life of Malte, are reflected in the style, and in the writer's analytical manner of observing and portraying, which reduces the scene to a hazy dream. Malte lives in spiritual indecision, passing through life as a somnambulist, as if existence held him in a painful spell which he cannot break. Sorrow makes his senses sharper, and from time to time he sees a sorrowful reality. He loves the poor, the blind newspaper-seller, the beggar and the sick; he lingers in the hospitals and loves suffering things; Paris, where he lives, seems to him to be 'a city built to die in'; even the air is sorrowful. He seeks for the old curiosity shops, as a refuge, and the sumptuous melancholy of the gardens, the Tuileries, the Luxembourg Gardens, and the quiet of the Librairie Nationale. His oldest recollections are noted, since Rilke's aim is, above all, to make his first impressions live again; the delicate, sensitive son speaks of his forefathers: the Brigge, the Brahe, the Gyldenlöve and the Grubbe families,—and of the castles of Ulsgaard and Urnekloster; he remembers his childhood; the first part of the book is woven with memories, fancies and childish fears, and with recollections of his ancestors.

The picture of Malte is not a mask of the author, but a portrait of his soul; and we perceive the solitary and desolate mind behind his eyes and in the looks of all his characters. Like Rilke, Malte is a student of art; he attempts to write dramas and dreams of composing poetry. Malte is twenty-eight years old and has written a study on Carpaccio and a drama, and thinks of writing lyrical poems; but the idea that poetry is the fruit of long experience, and of an entire lifetime, restrains him. Events—the few that there are—and personages—are harmonized together so as to give a single tonality to the picture. But [G.] Bianquis rightly observes: 'There is no unity, only the unity of emotion;—and a few great topics: solitude, sorrow, poverty and death'. The work in his unity of sentiment and style is exquisite, and finished in its details; but there is no action, it is the picture of a psychological state, of an attitude of the mind towards life.

In the descriptions, as in the landscapes of Whistler, the colour is laid in thin layers, in shadings which produce a singular intensity of effect; in this way his figures assume a spiritual character—almost spectral—and at the same time they are vividly true and yet unsubstantial as apparitions. The entire composition is filled with a painful rapture and everything tends to bring the principal theme to light: the aspiration from the deepest solitude to the search for the only companion, God. As Ellen Key remarks: 'All the strength is concentrated in this uttermost branch of his family tree in one thought: to search for God'.

Malte is a work which determines the unconscious purpose of all his work as a writer: the portrait of his soul; the book gives new features to this picture; a sense of fear,—for example,—of innate terror, which is unknown to his verses, and which dominates here; the book is everywhere instinct with a sense of an anguish which rises mysteriously from the darkest depths of the spirit,—a melancholy haze of thought and sentiment, as if a dark and pearly sky were curved over his interior landscape and filled the atmosphere with its weariness—an overcast sky without a glimpse of blue.

He carries out his work with singular patience of execution, very accurately and skilfully, discovering the relations between the emotions and suitable terms to express them;—with the eye of a painter ready to observe colours and lines, he aims at a form strictly modelled on reality.

The substance of the book is made up of memories—or dreams of memories—rather than real recollections; Malte really lives the existence of a visionary, a long 'rêverie' which is broken suddenly and brutally from time to time by flashes of painful reality. And the resulting note is one of sadness, of a gloomy greyness through which luminous spectres wander. (pp. 246-50)

> *Federico Olivero, in his* Rainer Maria Rilke: A Study in Poetry and Mysticism, *W. Heffer & Sons, Ltd., 1931, 301 p.*

BABETTE DEUTSCH   (essay date 1930)

[*Deutsch was an American poet, fiction writer, translator, and critic. Her poetry has often been praised for both its intellectual and emotional qualities as well as its technical accomplishment. Similarly respected, her literary criticism is concerned with poets*

Holograph copy of the first page of The Notebooks of Malte Laurids Brigge.

of the twentieth century. Among the works she has translated is Poems from the Book of Hours *(1941; rev. ed. 1969), a selection from Rilke's* Das Stundenbuch. *The following excerpt is from Deutsch's review of the first English translation of* Malte, *which was published in the United States as* The Journal of My Other Self.]

The author of this fantastic book [*The Journal of My Other Self*] was a member of the Austrian aristocracy who rejected the military career traditional with his family, to pursue his studies in philosophy. He attended the universities of Prague, Munich and Berlin and traveled about in Russia, Italy and France. For a time he was secretary to Rodin. It was during a prolonged stay in Paris that he wrote the present volume.

The reason for mentioning these facts of his private history is that this book, ostensibly the journal of a Danish mystic, Malte Laurids Brigge, who, having fallen upon evil days, has come to Paris to die or perhaps to go mad, is apparently the journal of Rainer Maria Rilke himself, with just sufficient distortions of detail to give it the fictive character desired by the author. The opulent arrogant charm of life in a noble house that is the background of Malte's childhood must have been known to Rilke through his own childhood experiences. The odd characters whom Malte encounters and who might easily have walked out of a novel by Dostoevsky were presumably drawn from acquaintances Rilke made in Russia. The familiarity with the corners and byways of Paris he probably obtained during his period in Rodin's service.

One wishes that the poet had thrown off all disguises and written this piece of prose frankly in the first person. As it is, the book confuses the reader by carrying him from Paris to Denmark and back again, introducing all manner of people who seem to have no excuse for being except the author's wish to present yet another kind of strangeness, and concluding with a fresh interpretation of the story of the Prodigal Son which seems related only casually, if at all, to the opening section of the book. Indeed, the *Journal* appears to have neither a beginning, a middle nor an end. Time, which obsesses Rilke (since Malte is, after all, Rilke's *alter ego*), moves backward or stands still as the author pleases. What memory evokes is sometimes clearer and more vibrant than the current of immediate experience. There is, of course, no reason to object to this kind of treatment—is it not the very essence of Proust? The difference between Proust's work and this slight book is that whereas the author of *Remembrances of Things Past* manages to build a harmonious and complicated design with his many diverse fragments, Rilke's effect is of something haphazard, distracted and often irritating.

The value of the book, which must not be denied, is in the extreme subtlety of emotion which the author reveals in exploring common events. He unites to the mystic's alert reverence, the psychologist's sensitive curiosity. He is thereby able to give the essential quality of a given moment, distinct as an odor (he had evidently a sharp sense of smell and often used olfactory images).

The best of the book is of one nature with Rilke's poetry, which registers a quivering responsiveness, and is at once mystical and sensual.

> *Babette Deutsch, "'Be Not Afraid, God'," in* New York Herald Tribune Books, *December 14, 1930, p. 7.*

HENRY HAZLITT (essay date 1930)

[*Hazlitt was an American editor, journalist, and literary critic. The following excerpt is from his review of the American edition of the first translation of* Malte.]

[*The Journal of My Other Self*] is a strange work: an autobiography, a journal, but never chronological. It reaches back from the present to memories of earliest childhood; moves forward again, then back. It makes no distinction between the inner and the outer worlds; the reader must divine for himself how much of what is set down is imagined and how much remembered, where reality ends and hallucination begins. There is no building toward a climax, no progression, no transition; episode and reverie succeed each other without warning. Separated events are constantly narrated as if the writer were resuming a prior narrative, and as if the reader already knew the necessary facts. The book passes through the mind like a series of uneasy dreams. Nothing, so to speak, is seen on all sides or in full daylight, but in a half-darkness illuminated by fitful flashes of lightning. And many of the scenes are as vivid and unforgettable as only objects caught in such a light can be.

I cannot guess to what extent this is the journal of a person imagined by Rilke, and to what extent it is a true spiritual autobiography. A sympathetic reader might call the narrator a mystic; others will call him simply a neurotic, a sick body in a sick soul. Nearly everything comes to him in terms of the horrible, the terrifying, the disgusting. "People come here, then, to live?" he begins. "I should rather have thought that they came here to die." And he is talking of Paris. He describes a pilgrimage through the houses:

> There were the midday meals and the sicknesses and the exhalations and the smoke of years, and the sweat that breaks out under the armpits and makes the garments heavy, and the stale breath of mouths, and the oily odor of perspiring feet.

I spare you more and worse. He goes into the street. There is a carnival, and laughter. Laughter? "Laughter bubbled from their mouths like matter from open sores." More than once he has seen a ghost, and he is obsessed by the subject of death. We carry our deaths within us, he thinks, as a fruit bears its kernel. Our deaths resemble us. There was the death of his grandfather, old Chamberlain Brigge, which was two months long, which shouted, groaned, and roared so loud that the villagers rose from their beds as if there were a thunderstorm. There was the death of his father, and the doctor who came to perforate the heart for "certainty," while the young son looked on:

> He carefully withdrew the instrument, and there was left something resembling a mouth, from which twice in succession blood escaped, as if it were pronouncing a word in two syllables.

Gruesome episodes are followed by accounts of wild childhood fears; by descriptions of nervous convulsions in others, in which the narrator seems to enter the very body of the person he is describing; by pure bravura passages, which even in translation are often hauntingly melodious, and by touches of grim humor, as in the account of Felix Arvers, who delayed his death to correct a nun's pronunciation of "corridor," or of Nikolai Kusmitch, who became so sensitive that he could feel time blowing past his ears, and was nauseated by the motion of the earth turning on its axis.

The reader will find in this book faint suggestions of Poe, of Amiel, of Baudelaire, of the Hamsun of "Hunger," even of Proust (though the *Journal* was first published in 1910, three years before "Swann's Way"). I put down these names merely to indicate certain kinships, not strong resemblances or sources of influence. *The Journal of My Other Self* is too original and personal to fit into any established genre.

> *Henry Hazlitt, "Rainer Maria Rilke," in* The Nation, *Vol. CXXXI, No. 3415, December 17, 1930, p. 679.*

WILLIAM ROSE (essay date 1938)

[*In the following excerpt, Rose examines the conception of death in* Malte.]

In approaching the study of a poet from whose mind the question of death was never absent, it is natural to seek for morbid elements both in his ideas and in his poetry. It may be said at once that Rilke's conception of death as deduced from his poetry is not morbid, but when we look at his most important work in prose, *Die Aufzeichnungen des Malte Laurids Brigge*, we see that it is pervaded by apprehension and abounds in descriptions of the macabre. Shortly after his last sojourn in Paris and a year before his death, Rilke wrote to his friend and translator Maurice Betz to explain why he had left suddenly without having come to say good-bye: "Le sort a quelquefois de ces trous où l'on disparaît; le mien s'appelle malaise, maladie . . . que sais-je" ["The turns of fate sometimes lead to gaps into which one disappears; mine is called malaise, malady . . . I don't know"]. This *malaise* is seen in its most extreme form in *Malte*.

Malte is the study of a mind in the thrall of an 'anxiety neurosis,' and to understand its relation to Rilke's personal experience, for it contains much of an autobiographical nature, we must go back to his first visit to Paris in 1902. When Rilke first thought of going to Paris he wrote that he would find solitude there. He was feeling deeply the failure of a play which he had had produced in Berlin. He was conscious of his mission as a poet, but felt that he was not understood by the public, and our inkling of his state of mind at this time is substantiated by the evidence he has given us of the effect upon him of his first experience of Paris. This evidence we find both in *Malte* and in his letters, some of which, in fact, he used as material for the book.

His first impression was coloured by the numerous hospitals. ". . . Man fühlt auf einmal, dass es in dieser weiten Stadt Heere von Kranken gibt, Armeen von Sterbenden, Völker von Toten" ["You feel all at once that in this vast city there are multitudes of sick, armies of dying, nations of dead"]. He had never felt that in any other town, and he says it was strange that he felt it just in Paris where the life urge was stronger than elsewhere. It was not life, for life is something calm, spacious, simple. The life urge is hurry and pursuit, the urge to possess life at once, wholly, concentrated in an hour. Of this Paris was full and that was why it was in such close proximity to death. Again he says that Paris seemed to him to be rushing along like a star that had lost its way, heading for some fearful collision. (pp. 70-2)

Malte is from the north, a Dane, the last surviving member of an ancient noble family, living alone in a room in Paris. The book is an amalgam of observation and introspection, the association of ideas leading Rilke constantly to hover between the depiction of actual experience and the revelation of inmost thoughts and feelings. It consists mainly of descriptions of Malte's reactions to Paris and reminiscences of his boyhood, his mind being haunted by ghosts of the past, and in the accounts of his early life in an old ancestral mansion ghosts actually appear and are taken as a matter of course. There is even the ghost of a house which had been burnt down, but which both the boy and his mother are convinced can still be seen. This absorption of Malte in his childhood, with all the uncanny details that surge up in his memory, has a bearing on a matter which may be of profound significance for an understanding of Rilke's psychology. . . . [In] some of Rilke's poetry a connection appears between the two terminal experiences of birth and death. We are told that Rilke was born prematurely. He came into the world two months too soon, and it is possible that this congenital defect influenced his future mentality, that he never overcame psychologically the original shock of birth. His shrinking from the roughness of life, his withdrawal into a world of his own, the nostalgia which found its expression in a restless search for contact with God and an understanding of the problem of death, are susceptible of a psycho-analytical interpretation which is beyond the scope of this essay. Some light is thrown on this aspect of his psychology by the passage in *Malte* which relates how the child would pretend to be a girl, to whom he gave the name Sophie, and would tell his mother about the misdeeds of a certain naughty boy named Malte. And Rilke's biographer, his son-in-law, tells us that the poet himself was brought up like a girl until his fifth year, being dressed in girl's clothes, wearing long hair, and playing with dolls, and that he was kept aloof from children of his own age. He even once came into his mother's room pretending to be a girl, and announced his intention of staying with her since René (this was his original name: he changed it to Rainer later on) was a good-for-nothing and had been sent away. If there is anything in the suggestion that Rilke was from the first incompletely adapted to life, there can be little doubt that his early upbringing fostered a disinclination to face the world.

The most striking example of the atmosphere which pervades the book is the passage in which Malte describes how, as he lay in bed, old fears of his childhood returned—the fear that a thread of wool frayed from the edge of his blanket might be hard and sharp like a steel needle; that a button on his nightshirt was larger than his head and heavy; that a breadcrumb falling from his bed would turn to glass and smash when it reached the floor, and that with it everything would be smashed for ever; that the edge of an opened letter was tabu, something that nobody must see, something indescribably valuable, for which nowhere in the room was safe; that he might swallow a piece of coal in his sleep; that a number in his mind would grow till there was no more room for it inside him; that he was lying on grey granite; that he might scream and bring a crowd of people who would break open the door; that he might betray himself and say things he was afraid of; that he might not be able to say anything since everything is unutterable. He concludes by saying that he had prayed for his childhood and it had returned, but he felt that it was still as oppressive as it had been in reality and that he had not benefited by growing older.

Malte's realisation that he "had not benefited by growing older" summarises in one pregnant sentence the theme of the book— the maladjustment to life of an artist, the last descendant of a decaying race. We think of Thomas Mann's *Buddenbrooks* and of the interest which the novelist shares with the poet not only in the phenomenon of decay, but in death and the manner of dying. A certain taste for the macabre, which is noticeable

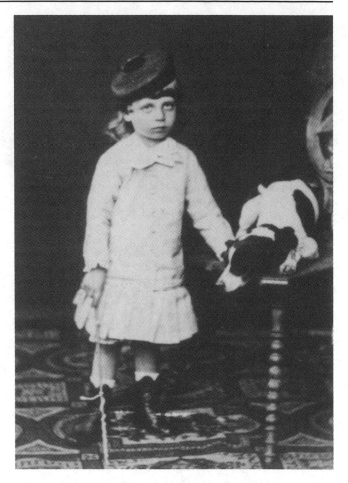

Rilke, in girls' clothing, at age four.

occasionally in Rilke's poems, reappears in *Malte*, both in the description of horrors and in the accounts of the way people die. We have seen what he thought of the commonplace or impersonal deaths in the Paris hospitals. In the long-drawnout end of Malte's grandfather, the masterful old Kammerherr Brigge, which was difficult and awe-inspiring, Rilke describes a 'personal' death almost as though it were a banshee that dominated the house and the whole countryside during the days and nights that the old man lay dying. . . . Malte talks too of the death of his grandmother, his father and mother, and many others; of his fear at the sudden death of a girl who sat opposite him in a tram at Naples, of his fear at the death of his dog, of his fear when the flies came into his room in autumn after the first night-frosts and slowly died all over the room, of the nights when he would sit up oppressed by fear and cling to the thought that sitting was at least something one did when one was alive—that dead men do not sit.

We see Rilke a prey to a deep-seated fear of both visible and invisible terrors. The book is to a great extent a looking back on childhood, and he was able to write it by a process of intense introspection which put the rational and the irrational on the same plane. The characters that appear in it, those of the past and those of the present, are as real to Malte as his own actual experiences and impressions. As Rilke said in a letter to his Polish translator, they are symbols of Malte's own distress, and his relation to them is conditioned by the fact that the intensity of their lives displays the same rate of vibration as his own. Life is always withdrawing into a state of invisibility, and Malte can only achieve contact with it by conjuring up phenomena and scenes which he finds either in memories of his childhood, in his Parisian environment, or in reminiscences of his reading. All these varieties of experience possess the same validity for him, they are all equally present and permanent. Past fears, present terrors and presentiments of the future are all equally real.

However much Rilke may later have achieved a more balanced relation to life, *Malte* is the creation of a mind that was at the time full of morbid fears. Even in his letters at this period we find him complaining, for example, with reference to a train journey between the French frontier and Turin that the high mountains made the way seem like a tunnel. . . . He had never been to London, but the very thought of it was appalling. . . . Both in the **Stunden-Buch** and in **Malte** he declares that it is the cities which make it impossible for men's lives to come to fruition, and that by the inhibiting of their lives their deaths too are inhibited.

Rilke once thought of undergoing psycho-analytical treatment, so he must have realised the neurotic element in his make-up. . . . Profoundly uneasy as he was, however, about his physical and nervous condition, he fought shy of the prospect of being left with what he called a 'disinfected soul.' He said that psycho-analysis could only help him if he were to make up his mind to give up writing. Then he could have the devils driven out of him, since devils are only a disturbing factor in a bourgeois existence, and if his angels happened to be driven out as well, then that too would have to be regarded as a simplification and he would console himself with the thought that in his next profession, if any, he would have no use for them anyway. He very soon decided, however, not to submit to treatment. He said that he was not going to risk the possibility of his angels being given a fright.

To say that Rilke gave full vent in this book to the fears which haunted him is not completely to identify him with Malte Laurids Brigge. We are, however, justified in suggesting that in the creation of a fictional character he was able to allow freer rein to his apprehensions and obsessions than was possible in his lyrical utterances or his letters. Rilke is not Malte, but there is more than sufficient evidence of the important autobiographical element. It is not only of Malte's distress that the characters in the book are symbols. The whole uneasy atmosphere of the book bears witness to Rilke's own brooding mind, and no German author has given us in fiction form a more ruthless self-revelation since that most remarkable book of the eighteenth century, *Anton Reiser*. (pp. 73-80)

> William Rose, "Rilke and the Conception of Death," in Rainer Maria Rilke: Aspects of His Mind and Poetry, *edited by William Rose and G. Craig Houston, Sidgwick & Jackson, Ltd., 1938, pp. 41-84.*

E. M. BUTLER (essay date 1941)

[*Butler was an English critic and novelist. In the following excerpt, she discusses Rilke's fictional alter ego in* Malte *as a "literary scapegoat."*]

The hero of **The Notebooks of Malte Laurids Brigge** is one of those poetical scapegoats of which Werther is the great prototype. Both Goethe and Rilke (and how many other poets?) put all their emotional and mental torments upon the head of a creature made in their own likeness, and sent him away into

the wilderness, bearing all their iniquities 'unto a land not inhabited'. The parallel holds in another respect. The suicide of Jerusalem, and the death of the young Norwegian Sigbjörn Obstfelder, provided the two high priests of poetry with the second victim, whose blood had to drench the altar. These are modern instances of art arising from ritual, and still impregnated with its magical function. Ceremonial purification became poetic catharsis in *The Sorrows of Werther,* and the sacrificial victim was transformed into the hero of an immortal novel. For if the emotional need for a scapegoat was the same which was felt in Aaron's day, the mind and the heart, the sins and the sufferings of the victim became the focus of interest for Goethe even before the self-purification had begun to take effect. The relation between art and autobiography, between confession and creation in *Werther,* a difficult critical problem, is actually the relation between ritual and art; certainly the novel was due to an instinct for purification, as much as to the creative impulse.

Read in this fashion, and we have Rilke's authority for doing so, **Malte Laurids Brigge** loses much of its incoherent character, although the transformation into art is by no means so complete as in *Werther.* Quite apart from the style, whose laboured irony, mannered prose and purple patches compare ill as a confessional medium with Goethe's lyrical, spontaneous and natural language, Rilke somehow fails to convince the reader of Malte's separate reality. Poetry and truth, far from being inextricably mingled, relieve each other throughout the book whenever it suits the author. Straight autobiography alternates with pure fiction; at times too Malte leads Rilke's life; at others Rilke leads Malte's; and these fourfold changes are not aesthetically fused. Malte's poetical existence often hangs by a hair; nevertheless, it can be saved by accepting him as Rilke's double and scapegoat; whereas all is lost aesthetically if one attempts to make either the author or his hero responsible for the book as a whole. It is extraordinarily miscellaneous. Goethe used real letters in *Werther* and copied out a whole passage he had earlier translated from Ossian, perhaps instinctively impelled by the guiding ritualistic motive to attach to his literary scape-goat something that had belonged to himself. Rilke positively plundered his own correspondence as well as paraphrasing many of his poems. Indeed, if he were not known to be a highly conscientious artist, one would accuse him outright of book-making. For, although the letters and passages from letters he incorporated in **Malte Laurids Brigge** were written with this end in view, the reminiscences from Jacobsen, Bang, Hofmannsthal, and André Gide seem almost like plagiarism with their strong verbal similarities. So that, what with these passages and the pages devoted to renderings of Froissart, Commynes and other writers, an investigation of the sources of **Malte Laurids Brigge** is not unlike retrieving objects from a magpie's nest. But they were assimilated to an extent that made them completely Rilkean, even the doctrine of nonpossessive love which he owed to Gide. As for the pages on French history in the fourteenth and fifteenth centuries, he treated them as he had treated the torso of Apollo in **New Poems**, as material for his art; and the fragmentary nature of the confessions is compensated for completely by the all-pervading colouring of fear. This gives emotional unity to the book, and is the decisive factor in its aesthetic effect. (pp. 204-06)

I agree entirely with Edmond Jaloux in his acute remark that **Malte Laurids Brigge** might have been written by one of Dostoyevski's characters, but not by the novelist himself. The vast canvas, the abysmal knowledge of the human heart owned by the Russian writer were not within Rilke's scope. The haunted mind, the panic fears, the egocentric torments of Malte are saturated with nordic gloom; Jacobsen and not Dostoyevski is the prevailing influence in these confessions.

The impression of reading *Malte Laurids Brigge* is almost identical with the one produced by [Jacobsen's] *Niels Lyhne, Marie Grubbe* and *Mogens*—a general feeling of minute observation and meticulous description; of delicate lights and shades; of highly sophisticated, even decadent, emotions. The historical learning behind *Marie Grubbe* is reflected in Rilke's accounts of French history; the number of curious deaths described is also in the tradition of Jacobsen. Rilke even borrowed the phrase 'he died his hard death' and applied this comment on Niels Lyhne's end to the appalling demise of Christoph Detlev Brigge; and he further filled the gallery at Urnekloster with portraits of persons in *Marie Grubbe*. By making his scapegoat an aristocratic young Dane, he proclaimed his kinship with the north rather than with the east of Europe. Dostoyevski was hardly more than a room-neighbour, a disturbing and problematical influence, which only made matters worse for Malte, and which was eventually removed.

And indeed, as the book draws to a close, Malte's isolation becomes such, that one cannot imagine it being broken, even by the presence of someone next door. More and more his mind was thrown back upon itself; after he had recollected his childhood and early youth, he had no other occupation than to revive memories of life from books, since of personal life there was none: it had been swallowed up by fear. Lovers and death rose to confront him from the printed page: unhappy lovers, unthinkably ghastly and brutal deaths. The illusion of love could not protect him from the onslaught of death; he tried to exorcise it in the parable of the prodigal son; then he crumpled up and disappeared. He left a silence behind him which seems still to be ringing with his terrified outcries. The scapegoat had been driven forth into the wilderness; but one has the uneasy impression that he might return again; and that the ritual act of purification lacked some essential feature.

Rilke's prolonged monologue with his own reflexion in *Malte Laurids Brigge* is not great art. The scapegoat Malte is not an aesthetic creation, but a pallid looking-glass image, mutely repeating Rilke's gestures and expressions. He disappeared or 'went under' when the latter finally moved away from the mirror. His existence in the world of art is tenuous; the part he played in his author's life was of greater importance.

The novel obviously marks a crisis in Rilke's attitude to God, a crisis which might be hailed as the loss of a delusion, or deplored as the loss of an ideal. The future artist-god had never been more than a sublime hypothesis, deriving from Rilke's belief in the creative and transforming powers of art. Metaphysically he had represented a goal to which to approximate, although so remote, such aeons removed from us in time, as to be practicably unattainable. Nevertheless, Rilke had believed him to be capable of mythological treatment; and it had been his supreme ambition to represent this divinity in his works, much as the Hindus portray the next and final avatar of Vishnu, the god Kalki on his milk-white steed. But either Rilke's inspiration was at fault, or his conception of the deity. He could be invoked, he could be sought; but ransack the apparent world for similes as Rilke might, he could not represent him, not even when he identified him with death, which proved to be merely begging the question. Death was just as nebulous and amorphous and resisted aesthetic creation quite as stubbornly as the 'Russian' God. Incapable of representing his godhead, Rilke began to transform life into art. What he learnt during

the process is what every artist has to face sooner or later, the realisation that life is much more creative than art. So that his mythological dream, the apotheosis of art, appeared to be founded on a delusion. Either art was not as creative as he had thought, or he was not such a great artist. Both these doubts were paralysing, and quite sufficient to account for the terrible apprehension present in every line of *Malte Laurids Brigge*. For this scepticism struck at the roots of his reason and justification for existence. Either he was the prophet of a new religion, or he was nobody and nothing.

Rilke had been hoist with his own petard. He had used in a private and narrow sense a word with the widest and most colossal connotations. It was steeped in unfathomable mystery, heavy with antiquity, and shining with the resplendent visions of the mightiest minds in the world. The word was too much for him, for the word was God. It had been a double-edged tool from the very start; for Rilke could no more free himself from its magical power than the most superstitious savage. Again and again he had involuntarily used it in a purely religious sense; and he had now come to the parting of the ways. He must abandon this term (that is to say he must abandon God), and create his artistic mythology by other means. He must find an adequate substitute for the emergent aesthetic deity. (pp. 210-12)

> *E. M. Butler, in her* Rainer Maria Rilke, *The Macmillan Company, 1941, 437 p.*

W. L. GRAFF (essay date 1956)

[*In the following excerpt, Graff examines the significance of death in* Malte.]

It was in Paris that Rilke was concerned with death in its ugliest forms, trying desperately to discover some hidden sweetness in it. All the negative elements of his own existence became magnified as he saw them reflected in the faces of haggard women, of girls cheated out of youth and love, of starving students, of beggars and cripples, of sick people driving in taxicabs at a few pennies an hour to wholesale death in the hospitals. The mouldy odor of all the secretions of poverty—of its births, its lusts and its deaths—well-nigh smothered him at the sight of a demolished tenement. . . . To be strictly exact, the thick daubs of this picture belong to the poet's pseudonym, Malte. But all we have to do is to step back and look at it from some distance, and the Rilkean physiognomy appears true to life. His letters of the period, in fact his whole work, substantiate it. After all, what else could be expected of such a hypersensitive soul as we have found Rilke to be. Married scarcely over a year, unaccustomed yet to the unexpected taste of fatherhood and of a home of his own, he had been forced by economic difficulties to leave wife and child on the heath of Worpswede or in the care of relatives. Alone, with only the burning flame of poetic aspiration in his heart, he was compelled to live frugally in a poorly furnished room, walled in among neighbors whose mysterious coming and going echoed faintly in his solitude. And outside, the hum of the city, hard and heavy with the weight of human suffering borne by a light-hearted race. . . . Paris meant for Rilke both the hope of fulfilment of his artistic dreams and the descent into the depths of human woe and death.

In the Malte *Notebook* death, together with all infirmities of flesh and soul, in the crucible for purification. But the partly purified product is no longer associated with Malte. It appears in the lonely, self-contained things of the *New Poems*, only to be thrown back into the alembic of the *Elegies* and to emerge crystalline and transparent in the *Sonnets*. In his Malte-moods Rilke fingered human misery and death in all their sinuous folds with that same passion for form which moved Rodin in his search for the *modelé*. By itself the *Notebook* is only the negative cast: it must be read with that understanding.

Malte revels in the ghastliest manifestations of human wretchedness with a determination that has every symptom of mad morbidity, and yet he is conscious of the fact that with all his dread he is "like one who stands on the threshold of something great." . . . As far as Rilke himself is concerned it all is like a mud bath designed to bring health and strength. The death of Malte's grandfather, Christoph Detlev Brigge, is something that engulfs with fierce voracity all that used to come under the equally autocratic sway of the chamberlain's robust personality. . . . It would be a childish simplification if we classified this death as the biological outcome of dropsy, just as Rilke on his deathbed would have repudiated the suggestion that the meaning of his own death could be exhaustively diagnosed as leukemia. Similarly the life of Malte's father was so perforated with the fear of death that he carried in his briefcase the story of King Christian IV who, three hours before dying, asked his doctor: "Oh doctor, doctor, what is your name?" and answered his own question with the clear voice of agony: "Death, Death." . . . No wonder that the father's will contained a clause ordering his doctor to pierce his heart in order to make quite sure that he would not be buried alive. And Malte, his son, insisted upon being present at the awful operation. . . . And when Malte's dog died, its hard, strange look accused its master of having allowed death to come. . . . Also the attitude of the living toward death is a matter of insistent curiosity on the part of both Malte and Rilke. Malte's grandmother Margaret was so possessed with self-asserting vitality that she resented all rivalry and looked upon life and death as a competitive sport in which she was always to come out on top. She even could not bear the indiscretion of her own daughter who was bold enough to die before her. . . . Malte remembers a fat girl dying suddenly in a streetcar in Naples. In a frantic effort to scare death away, the mother disarranged her daughter's clothes, poured something into her mouth, shook her body shouting her name and finally slapped her face. . . . Such is our obstinacy in refusing to grant death its turn to live.

In the prose of Malte's *Notebook* a great variety of deaths and of fears are microscopically scrutinized and elaborately worked out, in keeping with Rilke's will to defeat death by facing it and giving it form. (pp. 245-47)

> W. L. Graff, in his Rainer Maria Rilke: Creative Anguish of a Modern Poet, *Princeton University Press, 1956, 353 p.*

NORBERT FUERST   (essay date 1958)

[*Fuerst is an American educator who has written extensively on Rilke. In the following excerpt, he examines the prominent themes in* Malte.]

Malte Laurids Brigge is a magnificent failure. It is certainly not a novel in the American or English sense. It is far from being a *roman* in the French or in the Russian sense, though we think of the Russian *roman* at first when we approach *Malte*. It is called the Papers, or Notebooks, or Journals of M. L. Brigge, but the loose leaves of this fragmentary journal are not interspersed with realistic incidents, which, by their insignificance, make a book so lifelike. No detail here wakens us out

of the nightmare. No ray penetrates through the mental darkness. We walk, with the book, through splendid days and starlit nights, but we walk like the blind. We are shown treasures of love and pity, but we recognize them in the distortions in which the insane may recognize things.

Malte Laurids Brigge is a young Dane in Paris. He is worn out by the artificial life of that city and choked by the preponderance of death. He learns to experience all the shades of fear. He writes down in his journal the deaths of people he knew at home—great, meaningful, and private deaths, each crowning an entire life. He looks back on his own life and on his work, for he is a writer. He speaks with contemptuous criticism of his own works. The realization that he himself has not done anything important makes him doubt the importance of other works. The discovery of the huge misunderstanding hidden under the name of Paris opens his eyes to the sum total of falseness, neglect, and superficiality of which culture is composed. He begins to dig at what lies deepest in his soul— impressions of his childhood and youth. He brings it to light and it is: ghosts, death, sickness, fright, misery, impotence, failures—a life torn on all sides by frustrations. The streets of Paris and the countryside of Denmark arise by turns; but the châteaux of his childhood harbor only the fearful forebodings of the dreadful realities which he faces now, as the neighbor of a million woes.

At the end of the first part of the book the figure of a girl begins to emerge; she continues to grow luminous in the ever-darkening perspectives of the tale. It is the figure of Abelone, Malte's early love. The second part begins with her and with the theme of love, only to fall back into the desolation of scenes of death and mental or bodily ill. All the dreary shadows stalking through the book are outlined in the clearest language and seen with the eyes of a painter. Nobody knows where the stories begin, but each ends sharply, almost with a detonation. Again and again, the *Journal* harks back to the theme of love, to the accusation that men have never known how to love, that men have only been the loved ones. The names of famous women glitter on the pages. Malte is forgotten. His journal is now occupied with saints and Christ and God.

The Notebooks of Malte Laurids Brigge were supposed to be the coherent formulation of the insights which were formulated disjointedly in the *New Poems*. The German readers of Rilke almost unanimously rejected his new statements in favor of the *Book of Hours*. . . . It is still necessary today to defend Rilke's progress in *New Poems* and *Malte*, because some of his best critics think he was on the wrong road. He was never so much at peace with his conscience. Within a few years he created the bulk of his work. . . . This was the result not of overstrained effort but, as Rilke claimed, of the right attitude. After all, his intransigence was only wisdom. Every tendency can find fulfilment only in absoluteness. Whenever one activity is fully developed, the other activities become subservient to it. *Malte* contains the application of this to literature or poetry, and *Malte* proves that not the full but only the atrophied application can be called aestheticism.

Malte begins with the actual situation of Rilke in Paris in 1902, when it meant for him "the revelation of perdition," but after three paragraphs the poet grants the "education" which Paris has to bestow: "I learn to see." The next key words are "I am afraid" . . . ; and they are echoed in "I have done something against my fear" . . . , that is, he has described the death of the Chamberlain. That is what Rilke calls somewhere else "Dinge machen aus Angst" ("to create things out of fear").

Small wonder that it leads to the celebrated passage on poetics. . . . "There is so little to verses, if you write them when young. You should wait, gathering essence and sweetness for a whole life. . . . For verses are not sentiments, as people think; they are experiences. . . . Only when the memories have become fused with our blood, undistiguishable from ourselves, only then it may happen that in a rare hour a verse rises from their midst." But this famous page is only the preamble to some pages of never-quoted, because nearly ludicrous, questions. These (seven) questions state the problems, that is, the subjects, treated in Rilke's poetry:

> Is it possible
> . . . that nothing important has yet been realized?
> . . . that mankind has remained on the surface of life?
> . . . that all of history has been misunderstood?
> . . . that people try to relive something dead and gone?
> . . . that mankind explores something that has never been?
> . . . that we still use plurals, though only individuals remain?
> . . . that people think "God" is something they have in common?

The questions mean only one thing: that to every age and to every artist all the important problems of mankind are unsolved and new. Art knows no "progress," it cannot learn (like science) from a former epoch. It begins anew with every artist. Young Malte knows only one reply to his ingenuous questions, to sit down and write. The *Notebooks* were to present *his* solutions to his problems. They do so, without being more coherent than the *New Poems*. Here, too, we have to do with independent, isolated poems, only they are prose poems.

The prose poems immediately following upon Malte's "poetics" have one common theme, fear. Most of them have also a countertheme, poetry. . . . After reading Rilke's letters to Lou [Andreas-Salomé] we know that fears of poverty, sickness, and insanity actually pursued him. He could silence them only by expressing them, "making things out of his fears." This is the origin of many of the *New Poems* and most of the *Malte* poems. (pp. 85-9)

Rilke's poems—in verse or in prose—are not expressions of a superior detachment; they owe a great deal of their dynamics to the fact that they represent struggles, barely victorious struggles, precarious and hard-won victories. They are frequently enactments of crises. Their insistent treatment of human suffering does not spring from Christian charity but from pain in his own flesh and his own mind.

Two years after the completion of *Malte,* Rilke was still much perplexed about his partial identity with Malte. In a letter of December 28, 1911, he writes: "No one but you, dear Lou, can distinguish and prove whether and how far he resembles me. Whether he, who is in part made out of *my* dangers, perishes in them in order to save *me* from doing it. . . . Can you understand that I live as the survivor of this book, completely helpless, unoccupied and not occupiable. . . . The Other One, dead one, used me up. He squandered the forms and objects of my life on his expensive perdition. Nothing is left that was not in his hands and heart. With the fervor of his despair he appropriated everything" [see excerpt dated 1911].

The dark chapters of *Malte* were neither vicarious experiences nor hallucinations but real and crude sufferings: sickness, poverty, and humiliation. Malte's sufferings are Rilke's, especially from 1902 to 1906; and Malte's antidotes are Rilke's, espe-

Lou Andreas-Salomé. Reproduced by permission of Herrn Thomas Pfeiffer.

cially from 1906 to 1910. One theme is his recurrent sicknesses (at least once a year) and the fear of suffering them while alone in a huge and strange metropolis. One variation was the humiliation that he felt when he was forced, every year, to take refuge with the parents of the wife whom he could not support. Another variation was the humiliation of living from stipend to stipend (and later from hospitality to hospitality), never really earning his living; of alternating between short-term invitations to castles and long-term sentences served in dingy student hotels; of being sensitive to everything socially refined, but being miserably dependent and shamefully impotent in the economic world. The poignancy of many pages in the first half of *Malte* is due to the pangs with which Rilke felt the mortifications of his life, especially in the years 1902 to 1906. The fearful passages of the second half are more far-fetched for the simple reason that from 1908 on, Anton Kippenberg, of the Insel-Verlag, put Rilke's life on a more secure and more self-supporting basis. Also, from about the same time Rilke was taken as an equal into the circle of the countesses and baronesses Schwerin-Uexüll-Rabenau-Fähndrich, which was a prelude to his still firmer foothold in the circle of the princess of Thurn and Taxis. The frightened, frustrated, morally sick and mortally afraid Brigge, twitching under every humiliation, is a faithful replica of the frustrated Rilke at the age of thirty.

Thus *Malte* is the book of squirming exegesis of the period 1902-10. In all its artificiality it is full of life, or rather of the impossibility of life. In the least elusive reference to the book . . . [see excerpt dated 1915] Rilke has said as much: "What has been suffered through in *Malte* is again and again this one thing: how is it possible to live while the elements of life are out of our grasp? While we are inadequate in love, uncertain in decision, and incapable in death—how is it possible to exist?" There, evidently, he is translating the difficulties of his existence into the problem of existence itself, into a classical and simple formulation of the existential problem.

The *Notebooks* are an intense, if incoherent, effort to elaborate Rilke's private philosophy. Many of the individual prose-poems are of a superb beauty and force. (The overrefined ones are in the second volume, the most brittle near the end.) But as a whole the book is inconclusive; it seems to end with many question marks. There is only continual waiting in his "long, quiet, aimless work toward loving God"; and there are incalculable difficulties in the fact that "he was now very hard to love" and uncertainty without end in the fact that God "did not yet want to love him." But from the rising claims which the themes of love and of God make in *Malte* we may infer that Rilke's period of wholehearted service to art was drawing to a close and that a turn towards the very "life" which he had opposed was imminent. (pp. 92-4)

> Norbert Fuerst, in his Phases of Rilke, *Indiana University Press, 1958, 209 p.*

FRANK WOOD (essay date 1958)

[*In the following excerpt, Wood discusses the structure of* Malte *and its central themes of childhood, love, and death.*]

In *The Notebooks of Malte Laurids Brigge,* begun in 1904 and published in 1910, Rilke imaginatively records a poet's experience against the background of his culture. The work therefore provides a parallel to, and summary of, many aspects of *New Poems,* in much the same way as the Rodin essays accompany **The Book of Images,** or *Stories about God* complete **The Book of Hours.** It would be oversimplification to say that such parallelism falls into a neat pattern of question and response, though it does illuminate the dialectical play of Rilke's thinking, so fundamental in all he wrote. The *Notebooks* are a kind of inventory-taking, while serving at the same time as a springboard into the future. (p. 95)

Despite the many possible analogies this work is extremely difficult to place within a definite literary pattern or tradition. The fact that it is at the same time all things, and yet not strictly one, is tantamount to saying that it is not completely achieved as a work of art. The poet himself referred to its casual growth and lack of organization, at times labeling it a mere "mosaic" constructed of loose notes and letters lying in a bureau drawer. (pp. 95-6)

A certain amount of parallelism can be worked out between the first and second halves of the book. The Prodigal Son theme at the end is anticipated in Malte's Paris exile and recurrent nostalgia for home, the historical deaths balanced by the graphic description of the old Chamberlain's death. But a coherent pattern is nowhere worked out, and one is more aware of the dissimilarities between the two sections, beginning with the tapestry description of Our Lady of the Unicorn in the Castle of Boussac, which announces a conspicuous change in pace and style. The contrapuntal development of the first part is sharp and clean (in painting one would speak of impressionistic *pointilisme*). Not only is the diction forceful because of the author's firsthand experience of Paris scenes and his memories of Sweden and Prague; death, the master of the revels, actually engenders the laconic, thrusting style with its ironic understatements and various rhetorical devices. In complete reversal of the usual procedure, this most curious of prose works begins with dying and ends with rejection of possessive love. Whatever happens within these pages happens with and beyond

death. Only on such a premise does Malte have the courage to start all over and make a clean breast of things, arraigning his age in a series of challenging questions that admit of but one answer.

> Is it possible that despite discoveries and progress, despite culture, religion and world-wisdom, one has remained on the surface of life? Is it possible that one has even covered this surface, which might still have been something, with an incredibly uninteresting stuff which makes it look like the drawing-room furniture during summer holidays?
>
> Yes, it is possible. . . .
>
> Is it possible that all these people know with perfect accuracy a past that has never existed? Is it possible that all realities are nothing to them; that their life is running down, unconnected with anything, like a clock in an empty room—?
>
> Yes, it is possible. . . .

In the second part the distance of author from subject is greater; the protagonist is no longer *in* the events described but rather reflects back *on* them (witness the marginal notations toward the end). The episode of the newspaper vendor, for example, is handled quite differently from the St. Vitus victim and other destitutes in Part I. The historical deaths retold from Froissart seem remote and cold compared with the old Chamberlain's end. Time and place are less clearly focused as the central figure, drawing the summary of his experience, weaves the formerly isolated events into a personal philosophy. Abelone and the Prodigal Son are raised to the rank of the mythical.

Generically, the *Notebooks* present a variety of literary patterns and models, such as autobiography in the style of the older German *Bildungs-Roman;* the novel of education; real or imaginary correspondence and, finally, a daily record or journal. Yet if they actually fit into none of these categories, the main flaw lies in the author's conception of the titular hero. Here unity and clarity are not always achieved. Rilke's earliest plan for the work envisaged a central character participating (*à la* Gide) in a fictitious dialogue concerning a young Dane who had died, leaving behind a bundle of manuscripts. Quite in keeping with the "anonymous" quality of his poetic universe Rilke often had a flair, like the German romanticists and Kierkegaard, for the use of the pseudonym. The first written entry, dated September 11, rue Toullier, reveals the planned dialogue become a monologue, and Rilke writing about himself, perhaps utilizing his recorded notes of Paris shortly after his arrival. Malte is conceived as a poet, but not until three years later, after a period of intense poetic experimentation and several travels, does the author get down to his conception of Malte as a person distinct from himself, a kind of mirror in which to see reflected the unbearable experience he was not yet strong enough to realize, in many ways a Malte realized through the medium of Cézanne. So absorbed did the author become with his character in the final stages of writing that the latter "grew beyond" the experiences to which he had predestined him, constraining his maker "to hold himself back" from new ones. Malte becomes more and more detached from his creator; in dissatisfaction with his own fictitious living he seems to draw dangerously on the poet's own life. The old romantic *Doppelgänger* motif is largely at the bottom of Rilke's later description of Malte to his French translator as "the companion of so many nights, my friend and confidant. He accompanied me to Venice, he was myself as I wandered about in Paris streets, he stopped with me under the shade of the Allyscamps, together we met the shepherds in the Baux. In Kopenhagen, on the Langelinie, I saw him, we met each other in the Taxus avenues of Fredensborg, he still remembers the overly-sweet fragrance of phlox in summer, his youth was mine,'' but, as he significantly concludes, ''he was my own ego and yet another.''

It is impossible to avoid mention of Goethe's *Werther* as a forerunner of the *Notebooks,* though the dissimilarities are greater than the likeness. Both Werther and Malte are ''scapegoats'' loaded with their particular burden of sin. But whereas Goethe, as Butler points out, achieves ''a relationship between art and autobiography, between confession and creation,'' with Rilke ''poetry and truth, far from being inextricably mingled, relieve each other throughout the book whenever it suits the author'' [see excerpt dated 1941]. Hence the emotions to be cast out— fear and love—still raise their problematical heads in the end. (pp. 98-100)

Whatever real unity the *Notebooks* achieve is made possible by the interweaving of theme and motif that holds the loose structure together. Whether the locale be Paris or Denmark or a stylized Prague, the impinging present or the rediscovered past, separation in time and experience is acutally no separation at all. Malte's childhood in retrospect and Malte's maturity in the present are so similar in quality and substance that a comparison of the Denmark-Prague-Paris motifs adds up to the same problem-clusters (Rilke will later speak of the great ''question dynasties'') of childhood, love, and death, all rooted in the dark soil of ''dread.'' The Schulin and Mathilde Brahe episodes, for example, symbolize from one direction the same blending of real and unreal that is accomplished from another in the description of dismantled Paris houses. (p. 102)

The theme of childhood, the matrix from which all Rilkean conceptions of poetry spring, is not thoroughly assimilated and comprehended by the central character; indeed, it could hardly be otherwise since he is caught in the unsolved conflict of truth with fiction, biography with imaginative construction. In describing this past the author does indeed move between the two poles of dread and charm, with inevitable forays into the sentimental and bathetic. Four years after Malte's appearance Rilke was still writing of this ''boundless childhood'' of which ''so much will of course never accumulate again, even if one were to have decades more to achieve under the most unspeakable sufferings and most incomprehensible blisses.'' The overwhelming burden of this past is succinctly stated in four lines, after the lengthy anxiety manifestations of the preceding sections: ''I asked for my childhood and it has come back, and I feel that it is just as difficult as it was before, and that it has been useless to grow older.'' And one recalls the famous birthday passage, a preliminary draft of **''The Death of a Boy''** poem of 1915, with its caustic examples of adult obtuseness: ''and one saw even at a distance that it was a joy for somebody quite different, a totally alien joy.''

Childhood may be the beginning of wisdom, but the character Malte begins with dying. At times within eyesight of the goal, his strength is insufficient to the task and he becomes the passive victim, not the active hero. Not yet had Rilke discovered the formula to convert such defeat into the symbolic transcendence of the *Sonnets to Orpheus:*

> Despite my fear I am yet like one standing
> before something great, and I remember that it

was often like that in me before I began to write. But this time I shall be written. I am the impression that will change. Ah, but a little more, and I could understand all this and approve it. Only a step, and my deep misery would be beatitude. But I cannot take that step; I have fallen and cannot pick myself up again, because I am broken.

Some light is thrown on this fearful hesitancy by Malte's heavy dependence on historical and literary references in his attempts to communicate the tensions existent between past and present, living and dying. His education and his experience of life were seemingly too indirect, too much derived from secondary sources. Hence his book is weighted with descriptions of *objets d'art,* memoirs of historic personages, and accounts of families that read like chronicles. The first and second parts nicely balance each other with a passage in each touching upon the relevance of literature to experience. Malte in Paris, after all human aid has failed, notes that he has ''prayed,'' but, significantly, his prayers are fragments of Baudelaire and the Book of Job (we recall that **The Book of Hours** was originally conceived as ''prayers''). The passage in the second part projects Malte as a young boy, and is concerned with the relationship of literature to life as seen from the childhood perspective. (pp. 103-04)

References to death in the first half of the book are generally ironic, emphatic through pithy understatement, even spiced with sardonic humor. Indeed, the whole spiritual landscape of [Thomas Mann's] *The Magic Mountain* is compressed into one line: ''In sanatoria, where people die so willingly and with so much gratitude to doctors and nurses, they die from one of the deaths attached to the institution; that is favorably regarded.'' Reflections on the theme in the second half are sober and branch off into metaphysics: ''Sometimes I reflect on how heaven came to be and death: through our having distanced what is most precious to us, because there was still so much else to do beforehand and because it was not secure with us busy people . . .''

In **The Book of Hours** there is apprehension of physical death rooted in a more or less physical dread. In the **Notebooks,** along with many repulsive naturalistic details, the theme is handled much more expansively and subtly, set off against ''something else'' where it does not have to stand alone in a void. The *real* death of the Chamberlain not only requires feverish movement and a sense of space; it also involves the intimate aspects of an entire community's living: its daily occupations and births, its nights and animal world. What lends the subject a poignant force is its location in a definite social milieu, the twilight realm of Paris *misère,* and the equally twilight regions of history and family anecdote. (pp. 105-06)

In the second half there is more integration between the themes of death and love, since the latter, for Rilke, can only be fully grasped if the death reference is included. By contrast with the earlier descriptions death is here raised to the plane of the mythical, the historical. The reconstructed ''inner'' destinies of the False Dmitri, Charles the Bold of Burgundy, and Charles VI of France are symbolical projections of Malte's own feelings into the turbulent lives he has read about, chiefly in Froissart. To the charge of obscurity Rilke later replied that factual ''identification'' was not necessary, that the reader would still derive enough from ''the tension of these anonymities.'' The resultant atmosphere is one of horror, wonder, and admiration, strained through reflection and meditation. He contrasts the immense and unsuspected potentialities of his characters' "inner realms" with what ordinarily passes for "objective" history. (p. 106)

Upon the realm of death follows that of love, or rather both are interwoven. Since love, for Rilke, is a direction and not a goal, the passages dealing with this theme are necessarily symbolical projections, blueprints of the poetic imagination rather than of everyday reality. Whereas death, experienced to the hilt in Malte's early Paris days, is a fact, an already assimilated ingredient of what he lived through, love is a mystical possibility, a potentiality existing only in faint, fluttering outline. The wavering uncertainty again arises from the conflict between fiction and life, for surely personal guilt feelings are in some measure responsible for the "women-in-love" passage in the *Notebooks:*

> For centuries now, they [the women] have performed the whole of love; they have always played the full dialogue, both parts. For the man has only imitated them, and badly. And has made their learning difficult with his inattentiveness, with his negligence, with his jealousy, which was also a sort of negligence. And they have nevertheless perservered day and night, and have increased in love and misery. And from among them, under the stress of endless needs, have gone forth those powerful lovers who, while they called him, surpassed their man; who grew beyond him when he did not return, like Gaspara Stampa or like the Portuguese nun, who never desisted until their torture turned into a bitter, icy splendor that was no longer to be restrained.

Abelone, Malte's childhood friend, is a fictitious sister of these historical personages, and when she passes from the scene singing "because I never held you close, I told you forever," she supplies us with a key to the Prodigal Son theme that follows. Malte wonders why Abelone "did not use the calories of her magnificent feeling on God," adding "but could her truthful heart be deceived about God's being only a direction of love, and not an object of love? Didn't she know that she need fear no return from him . . .? Abelone and the Prodigal are in similar case. The Prodigal realizes that only One may love him, "but He was not yet willing."

The genesis of the Prodigal Son parable may be traced to the poet's personal conflicts in the early Prague years. . . . "After scarcely a year," he informed a friend in 1897, "I tore myself away against the advice of everybody by an act of violence, and have, since that time, been declared a kind of Prodigal Son." The conception of the False Dmitri in the *Notebooks* incidentally derives from a similar source, for his is "the strength of all those who have gone away." In his own personal life, in his relations with others, Rilke more than once envisages variations of the Prodigal Son theme, as when he observes that "A togetherness between two people is an impossibility. . . . But, once the realisation is accepted that even between the *closest* human beings infinite distances continue to exist, a wonderful living side by side can grow up, if they succeed in loving the distance between them . . ." A personal confession, of course, is not to be confused with art creation like the *Notebooks* passage, though taken together, the two certainly admit of contradictions, a vicious circle of reasoning. The emphasis on "distance" at least points a finger in the direction of the Prodigal Son.

Thus Rilke was already attracted to the parable before he came across Gide's version (*Le Retour de l'Enfant Perdu*, 1907), which doubtless lent some impetus to his own interpretation. The two versions, however, have little in common, except here and there a tone, a certain quality of mind. Gide's work is built around a sequence of dramatic dialogues; Rilke treats the original Biblical story in the style of the historical vignettes that immediately precede it. Gide emphasizes the Prodigal's return as a result of failure, induced by despair and doubt, to go far enough to seize his freedom, which his younger brother may conquer in his stead. The return of Rilke's Prodigal is simply that of one "who did not want to be loved" and, confronted by his forgiving parents, had only "the gesture of supplication with which he threw himself at their feet, imploring them not to love." It is, in fact, neither story, legend, nor parable, but a symbolic representation of the unrequited-love theme. In a marginal note to the Abelone passage Rilke states this theme with an aphoristic concision, which only loses its tense sharpness in some of the late poems: "To be loved means to be consumed. To love is to give light with inexhaustible oil. To be loved is to pass away, to love is to endure." (pp. 107-09)

The *Notebooks* have frequently been supposed to conclude in tragedy, though Malte's death or even ultimate disaster is nowhere explicitly made clear. The tragedy is neither conclusive nor inevitable in the parable of the Prodigal Son. The poet himself, to a certain extent, fathered the sinister interpretation in a [1907] letter to his wife during the Cézanne phase: "For Cézanne is nothing else but the first primitive and bare achievement of that which in M. L. was not yet achieved. Brigge's death: that was Cézanne's life, the life of his last thirty years." . . . At any rate, it can hardly be a question here of a literal death. Malte may "die" figuratively to his past, and we may even feel that he is incapable of ever coming to terms immediately with the forces of his immense solitude. Certainly it is no death implemented by a brace of pistols or even by the quiet disintegration of so many symbolists at the turn of the century. A critic like Angelloz reaps positive consolation from the book's conclusion: "Malte represents humanity on its march towards God, man in his realisations, his successive sublimations, and 'eternal return' whose goal is: to give birth to him who wishes to love. From death to love and from love to God, such appears to us to be the profound meaning of the *Notebooks*."

Such a judgment errs too much in the other direction, though clearly the work is not merely a private record of a single artistic existence but that of an entire generation, the so-called *décadents* around 1900. It should therefore be read not only as a psychological history of a weak descendant of an old Danish family, who may or may not perish, but also as a warning to the aesthetic types of the day to persist and thus rise above the impact of experience as a part of their artistic obligation. The Kalckreuth *Requiem*, written during these years, particularly emphasizes that not victory but surviving is everything. This is what Rilke meant later by saying that his book should be read "against the grain."

Butler's ingenious theory that Malte Laurids Brigge represents the failure of Rilke's hypothetical artist-god (cf. *The Book of Hours*) and a move in the direction of the transformation of life into art in an attempt to find an adequate substitute, while extremely interesting, does less than justice to its artistic importance. Though no one would claim the *Notebooks* to be a completely achieved work of art, Malte's story nonetheless provides a valuable commentary on the Paris poetry and that yet to come, interpreting and enlarging still nuclear ideas. More than that, Malte allows us an inside view, as the poetry itself rarely does, into the poetic mind in process, with all its variety and even confusion. It may well be that such interior exploration is the chief value of this most unusual novel. As Fritz Martini correctly points out in his recent close analysis of Rilke's method in the *Notebooks,* Rilke substitutes for the traditonal novel form an associatively constructed sheaf of momentary impressions and fragmentary allusions, which seem almost to have been picked at random. But Rilke's ''impressions'' are not arbitrarily selected, nor do they operate merely on the surface as in so much impressionistic writing; they are rigidly determined by the author's peculiarly individual experience and by the complex of themes and motifs that weave through all his work. So far at times is Rilke from narrating objectively that, as in the case of some of the historical vignettes, for example, the problem of narration becomes itself the theme. Reflecting back upon himself, the author uses his material merely to probe into the still undivulged meanings of inner experience. As Martini phrases it, Rilke's language tends, as commonly since Nietzsche, toward expression as a means of aesthetic or ontological evaluation.

But if confusion is undeniably there, it is because, in Malte's words, ''Fate loves to invent patterns and designs. Its difficulty lies in complexity. But the life itself is difficult because of its simplicity.'' Without the *Notebooks* behind him, the poet would hardly have ventured to cross the Duino threshold in 1912. (pp. 114-16)

> *Frank Wood, in his* Rainer Maria Rilke: The Ring of Forms, *University of Minnesota Press, 1958, 240 p.*

RONALD GRAY   (essay date 1965)

[*Gray is an English critic who has written extensively on German authors. In the following excerpt, he focuses on several crucial ambiguities in* Malte.]

Die Aufzeichnungen des Malte Laurids Brigge, written between 1904 and 1910, is almost the equivalent of Rilke's diary during those years. (p. 263)

From the beginning, Malte is determined to reject no experience of that overwhelming power, both within and outside himself, threatening his own and every other existence, which he calls 'das Große'. In fact he deliberately sets out to experience this power, believing, like Rilke himself, that he is one of those who are sent out, not in order to proclaim heaven to men, but 'to be among human kind, to see everything, to reject nothing, not one of the thousand transformations in which the uttermost extreme disguises and blackens and makes itself unrecognisable'. And again like Rilke, he is one of those who 'go about with a desire to comprehend all things, and who (still not yet understanding) make the excessively great [das Übergroße] into an activity of the heart, that it may not destroy us'. The greatness, or excessive greatness, of which Rilke speaks here is above all the fact of death and annihilation. Malte seeks it in the memories of his childhood, when his own shadow, cast by his bedside light, would loom up behind him, threatening him with extinction. He recalls it in the death of his grandfather, Kammerherr Brigge, 'the great death' whose immense dimensions were fully apparent to the old man, and which bore no relationship to those 'little deaths' experienced by men who regard their end with as little emotion as they do their life. He recalls also people he has seen on the streets, a man seized with a fit, as though 'the greatness' were bursting out of him and destroying him. There are also scenes from

Malte's present life: his entry into a hospital, where the same childhood experience sweeps over him again; the day when he sees a wall horrifying in its ugliness, and feels the wall present with its horror as an aspect of himself. All this Malte describes with a vividness and sensitivity which, it seems, can only lead to madness. In fact, while Rilke was still writing the book, he observed to a friend that if it was ever completed it would be the account of a man for whom the trial of facing the greatness of suffering was too immense. For unlike Kafka, with whom some similarities will be noticed here, there is no question for Malte of this suffering ever being seen as good. He attempts rather to take the facts of death and suffering into himself without hope of release or victory or transformation: to make them into an 'activity of the heart' as they are an 'activity' of the external world, and thereby establish an identity between his own life and that of the whole.

In so far as there is progression in the *Notebooks,* it is towards a containing of these terrors, a living in equanimity with the certainty of extinction. Significantly, however, this comes about in association with a decreasing concern with Malte's day-to-day experiences and encounters, and his own personal memories. Towards the end of the first half of the book, and increasingly in the second half, the diary-entries refer to people and events of which Malte has no direct knowledge, and which evidently represent Rilke's own reflections on his reading at the time. The reality of the environment yields place to literary sources, and sections are now devoted to thoughts evoked by Michelet's *History of France,* by accounts of Cézanne, Beethoven, Ibsen, Sappho and others. The main impressions to be had from these are twofold. There are further reflections on men who are represented as having lived the same kind of life in the past as Malte is living now. There are also reflections on women whose lives present a kind of solution for his fears. These predominate more and more, and all point towards that ideal repleteness which Rilke was later to stress as one aspect of the *Elegies* and *Sonnets.* The lives of women such as Gaspara Stampa, Marianna Alcoforado, Louïze Labé are all drawn upon for examples of a love which endures in spite of the complete absence and indifference of the lover. They are women who so little needed any return of their love that at length their isolation became their fulfilment: 'who did not desist until their torment was reversed into an austere, icy glory that could no longer be restrained'. It is this reversal of suffering into glory that Malte himself, near the end, seems to attain or foreshadow. The attainment of these women is the projected image of his own desired condition. Like Bettina von Arnim, the unrequited lover of Goethe, each of them 'spread out into the whole from the very beginning, as though she were past her death'; each of them 'lay down outstretched in Being, belonging to it, and whatever took place in her was eternal in all Nature'. They thus needed no requital, for like Rilke's Angels they were at one with the whole of Being, they had that 'stärkeres Dasein' ['stronger being'] that the Angels possessed, and lived on as though already in death.

With the last two sections of the book, Malte seems very close to the realization of a similar condition in himself. If the book has a pattern, it is one that leads towards this new development, whereby the suffering endured in the earlier part is taken up, 'reversed' into the austere glory of self-fulfilment. Once again, the reflections on which this discerning of a pattern might be based are concerned not with Malte's personal experiences, but rather with his reinterpretation of an old and long familiar story, the parable of the Prodigal Son. They are, then, not so much a realization of the new condition by Malte himself as an imaginative account of how the condition would reveal itself in another. These considerations put aside, however, there remains the essentially literary question, in what sense these final sections may be regarded as a climax, in what way they affect the structure of the work as a whole. That Rilke was disposed, on at least one occasion, to see a climax in the last pages, may reasonably be concluded from his letter to his publisher, written when the book was just completed: 'Poor Malte begins so deep in misery and reaches, if you want to be particular about it, as far as eternal bliss; he is a heart that spans a whole octave; after him very nearly every song is possible.' On this reading, the *Notebooks* reveal the progression through which Malte comes, like the Christ of Rilke's poems, to a complete possession of suffering, and thereby, on these terms, to perfect fulfilment.

The parable of the Prodigal, however, as Malte retells it, no longer has the import it has in the Gospels. It has an interpretation evidently influenced by André Gide's *Retour de l'Enfant Prodigue*, in which the prodigal comes home not to be received with love and feast-making, but to encourage his younger brother to do as he himself has done. Life in the wilderness, hazardous as it is, is preferred to the humdrum pleasures of conventional society. Malte's prodigal is conceived in similar terms, in so far as he also can find no share in the society to which he returns. His story is, Malte is persuaded, 'the legend of one . . . who did not wish to be loved'. He has learned during his absence to maintain the 'inner indifference of his heart', so that he acts now freely, in his own right, and is no longer beholden to the love which his relatives attempt to bestow on him. He has also learned 'never to love, so as never to bring another into the horrible situation of being loved'. For in the Nietzschean terms in which Rilke is surely writing here, to love is to express the will to power over another; it is a means of subduing the other to one's own desires, a form of that subtle 'Christian' undermining of the other which Nietzsche abhorred. The return of the prodigal is therefore descibed in these terms:

> Those who have told the story usually try at this point to remind us of the house, as it used to be: for there only a little time has passed, a little recorded time, anyone in the house could tell you just how much. The dogs have grown old, but are still alive. Report has it that one of them set up a howl. The whole daily round is interrupted. Faces appear at the windows, faces grown old and matured, with a touching resemblance. And in one quite old face recognition suddenly pales through. Recognition? No more than that?—Forgiveness. Forgiveness of what?—Love. My God. Love.

> He for his part had ceased to think of it, busy as he had been: to think that it could still exist. Understandably, of all that then ensued this alone was handed down by tradition: the gesture, the astonishing gesture, never before beheld, the gesture of entreaty with which he flung himself at their feet, imploring them not to love. Taken aback and hesitant they lifted him up into their arms. They interpreted his impetuous act in their own fashion, forgiving him. It must have been an indescribable liberation for him that all misunderstood him so, despite the desperate unambiguousness of his bearing. He probably felt able to stay. For he perceived

more and more each day that the love of which they were so vain, and in which they gave each other such secret encouragement, had no concern with him. He was almost obliged to smile as they exerted themselves and made it the more clear, how little they meant it for him.

> What did they know of him? He was terribly hard to love now, and he felt that One alone could still do so. But He did not wish to as yet.

In these sentences, concluding the *Notebooks,* Malte portrays through the reinterpretation something of himself. The prodigal has reached that state of total indifference in love, which is one of the ideals set out in the earlier part of the book. He does not need the offer of human contact made by his father's people; he has come to terms with his loneliness in a way unimaginable by them, he is complete within himself. In terms of the Nietzschean 'reversal of values', he has reached a summit of his experience, a state which Rilke describes as reaching as far as eternal bliss. On the other hand, in traditional terms Malte could hardly be worse placed than in this lack of contact with other men. A somewhat supercilious tone towards the 'bien pensant' well-wishers, a perverse pleasure at their misunderstanding, and a touch of smug self-praise are the qualities most likely to be seen from this older viewpoint. And apart from such contrasting interpretations, there must remain a sense of unease at this as a portrayal of bliss. It does not have the feeling of blissfulness about it, rather of a cold indifference stemming from a psychic defect, and on this account the *Notebooks* seem to end on an uncertain note.

This is, or can be, a purely literary question. The pattern of the *Notebooks* as a whole depends on the interpretation of this final passage: if it is a climax, the book will be seen progressing upwards towards it; if it is a final defeat the book trends 'downward' in that direction. Either way, Malte seems to have come to terms with suffering not so much by enduring it as by cutting himself off from contact with all others. But does Rilke present this as an ideal or as a deplored end? His own comments at different times, both while the book was being written and afterwards, are inconclusive, and in part this was due to his own uncertainty as to the extent to which Malte's life could be identified with his own. . . . [The] earliest passages of the book are direct transcripts of some of Rilke's personal diary-entries and letters. By the time the book was finished, however, Rilke could speak of having diverged from his 'alter ego', much as Goethe had from Werther: Malte had 'developed into a figure, completely distinct from myself, which acquired a particular existence of its own and which interested me the more strongly, the more it differed from me'. By this account, Malte was a sheerly literary character through whom Rilke explored the possibilities of a situation, without committing himself to the ideas expressed. He did in fact intend, in the middle of writing the book, that Malte should die at the end, and had he done so, the work would have remained quite certainly a work of literature in which the consequences of a given course of life were followed through to their inevitable outcome. The question of an author's self-identification with his characters is, however, a delicate one. Rilke was decidedly more involved in Malte's explorations than his avowal of a distinction would lead one to suppose, even to the point of foreseeing his own early death: 'Sometimes it seems to me', he wrote of the book while still at work on it, 'that I could die, once it is finished.' And when it was in fact finished, he was to make clear, only a few months after his disclaimer, how much Malte's attitude had been his own all along: 'I am somewhat horrified when I think of the high-handedness [die Gewaltsamkeit] I have shown in Malte Laurids, how I had gone on with him in a deliberately consistent despair [konsequente Verzweiflung] till I was beyond everything, beyond even death in a sense, so that nothing more was possible, not even dying.' This would make of the *Notebooks* much more of a personal statement by Rilke, a continued publication of what might still have gone into his own private diaries, a nonfictional statement of views which he held himself. At the same time, the passage reveals another part of Rilke's self that stands opposed to what he has accomplished. He is a little horrified; he speaks of his own high-handedness: he may well mean to imply that he was aware of some falsity in the attitude represented by Malte, that he had in some way done violence to the truth of life as he knew it to be. Within a week of making this self-accusation, indeed, he uses much stronger terms. 'As for myself, I breathe again whenever I think that this book is in existence; it had to be, I was so indescribably under obligation to write it, no question of choice. But now I feel a little like Raskolnikov after the deed, I don't know at all what is to come now, and I am even a little horrified when I reflect that I have written this book; with what strength, I ask myself, with what right, I might almost ask.' The suggestive overtones of these final questions, the feeling of having been not only high-handed but almost murderous, reveal Rilke's sense of an evil deed accomplished. Far from having brought Malte to span a whole octave between deepest misery and eternal bliss, he seems to perceive here how Malte's final isolation and repleteness cuts him off from all living contacts and is . . . more akin to a state of damnation. His attitude towards his own work in the year that it was completed was thus ambiguous and vacillating, and it is not surprising if these qualities are read out of the book itself. In later years . . . there were occasions when he was obliged to forbid young people to read *Malte*. Its purport was too difficult to grasp, and only an extremely careful reading would distil the true sense: 'For this book, which seems to have its issue in the proof that life is impossible, must be read so to speak against the current. If it does contain bitter reproaches, they are not at all aimed at life. On the contrary, they are a statement that, for want of strength, through distractions and inherited misconceptions, we lose almost entirely the countless earthly riches that were intended for us.' In other words, the book must be read resistingly, not in sympathy with the views Malte expresses, but with a constant determination in the reader to maintain from his own resources an awareness of the 'earthly riches' that the book does little or nothing to foster. This too is of course a possible mode of reading, though the reader may be tempted to reply as Goethe did to an interlocutor, 'Don't tell me about your doubts, tell me about your beliefs. I have enough doubts of my own.' At the same time, to read in this fashion is to resist one of the ideals which Rilke was still proclaiming at Muzot, at the time when he wrote his corrective. The state of pure Being, hinted at in Malte's portrayal of Bettina von Arnim 'as though she were past her death', like Rilke's own experience of inhabiting his own body like a ghost, is that of Malte himself in the final pages, so far as one can judge, and it is also the state of the angelic beings as they are depicted in the First Duino Elegy.

The final lines of the *Notebooks* contain one further ambiguity. Hitherto, Malte has spoken of God as 'a direction of love, not love's object'; in tune with his own desire not to be loved, he has said 'no return of love need be feared from Him'. The love of God, as he conceives it, and as many Christian mystics have conceived it, is inspired with the purpose of schooling human

beings to the point of exerting a godlike love themselves: 'quietly postponing the pleasure so that we, slowly learning, may give vent to our whole heart'. For in thus giving full vent to human aspirations, the 'direction of love' will be realized at its fullest intensity. The outcome of this belief, however, as it is seen in the final passage, looks more contemptuous than loving; if Malte does love these people it is quite intransitively. And the last two sentences of the book appear to recognize this inadequacy: 'He was terribly hard to love now, and he felt that One alone could still do so. But He did not wish to as yet.' In one sense, the words may be taken as indicating the final postponement of reciprocal love, as though Malte had expressed his aspirations so intensely that no return was needed, and it was no doubt this sense that Rilke had in mind when he spoke of Malte reaching to eternal bliss. On the other hand, the words also imply a love in the more usual, transitive sense of the word: one which can surmount even the greatest obstacles. As so often happens in the novels of Thomas Mann, there is reintroduced here at the end a meaning of the word 'love' which is quite unconnected with the meaning it has acquired during the course of the work. In so far as this second sense is taken, Malte appears as the deliberate self-excluder from love, the man who realizes in himself the state which some theologians have regarded as the self-imposed punishment of the unbeliever. The last words of all, 'But He did not wish to as yet', thus give a curiously vacillating quality to the ending. Malte must both welcome this seeming denial, since to do so must on his terms enhance his spiritual status, and at the same time fear it and long for it to come to an end. The 'as yet' betrays this yearning in its paradoxical intensity: like the sustained 'cello-note in Mann's *Doktor Faustus* it echoes on with a hope beyond hopelessness.

There does not seem to be any way out from this dilemma except in the abandonment of self-enclosing isolation as an ideal. The self-enclosing may have wide bounds; it may, as Rilke believed, establish a sense of enclosing far more than is normally meant by 'the self'; yet it leads inexorably back to acceptance of an unredeemed world, not to the vision of a new earth. Since the world so accepted remains with its dualities, the acceptance itself remains ambiguous, and it is never really apparent whether it is acceptance or not. . . . (pp. 263-71)

Ronald Gray, " 'Malte Laurids Brigge'; 'The Duino Elegies'," in his The German Tradition in Literature: 1871-1945, *Cambridge at the University Press, 1965, pp. 263-77.*

DAVID H. MILES (essay date 1974)

[*Miles is an American educator and critic specializing in German literature. In the following excerpt, he places Malte in the tradition of the German bildungsroman ("development novel"), viewing it as a modern counterpart to Johann Wolfgang von Goethe's* Wilhelm Meisters Lehrjahre *(1795-96; Wilhelm Meister's Apprenticeship) and Gottfried Keller's* Der grüne Heinrich *(1880; Green Henry).*]

To include Rilke's sole novel, *Die Aufzeichnungen des Malte Laurids Brigge* . . . , in a consideration of the German Bildungsroman may appear at first a misplaced judgment; the Danish poet seems to be less a descendant of Wilhelm Meister or Heinrich Lee than of Dostoevsky's Underground Man—transported from Petersburg to the fifth floor of a shabby Parisian hotel. At an age—twenty-eight—when Wilhelm had already married into an established social order and Heinrich had taken up service in an established political order, Malte, landing in

Paris alone, experiences a virtual breakdown on all levels of existence—within and without himself, psychological as well as social. And if this were not enough to discount the work from the normal tradition of the Bildungsroman, the form certainly would, for the entire "novel" consists of Malte's confessional journals written during the year in Paris. The work dispenses completely with the nineteenth-century fiction of the narrator easing the reader into a comfortable, imaginary world.

Yet in many ways *Malte,* rather than such other modern novels as [Hermann Hesse's] *The Glass Bead Game* and [Thomas Mann's] *The Magic Mountain,* is the most logical and at the same time most radical development of the Bildungsroman in the twentieth century. The journal form, for instance, surprises us less when we compare its function to the role of the "Confessions" in *Wilhelm Meister* or the autobiography in *Der grüne Heinrich.* For Malte's *Bildung,* like that of Wilhelm's aunt-in-law and Heinrich in Munich, arises directly from the therapeutic act of writing itself. His self may not "grow," but it *is* gradually recovered and restored in a psychological sense. Moreover, Malte's image as hero is not as far removed from that of the standard *Bildungsheld* as one might at first suppose; recalling Goethe's strictures on the model hero of the genre (in *Wilhelm Meister . . .*), we see that Malte fulfills perfectly—indeed almost pathologically—the requirement that the hero be more a man of "viewpoints" than of "actions," of "events" rather than "deeds." Malte's life, as far as we can reconstruct it from the scattered entries in his diary, follows precisely the pattern common to the nineteenth-century Bildungsroman, at least up until his year in Paris: beginning with a secluded childhood spent on landed estates in Denmark and followed by several years of formal schooling at a military academy, his "education" had been completed by an extensive *Bildungsreise* ["educational tour"] through Russia, Italy, and France.

Once we have accepted *Malte* as a legitimate heir to the Bildungsroman tradition, we can observe a number of fascinating and striking developments at work in it, particularly when we hold it up to *Wilhelm Meister* for the sake of contrast. In Goethe's novel, for example, the lack of a national theater provided young Wilhelm with material upon which to found his romantic dreams of acting and founding a theater company; for Malte, however, the lack of such a theater can only serve to remind him of the progressive secularization and fragmentation of culture that has taken place since the time of the classical theater of antiquity. "Let us be honest about it," he writes, "we have no theater, any more than we have a God: for that, community is necessary." . . . Moreover, Malte's traumatic childhood experience of depersonalization while playing with masks in front of a mirror . . . his horrifying recognition of the tenuousness of the self, in effect—contrasts sharply and tragically with Wilhelm's wistful memories of childhood days spent playing with puppets. The theme of the guiding institution, of the secret society of enlightened tutors, has also undergone a radical change; Heinrich Lee's *departure* from the count's castle had already sounded a note of revolt against the Goethean ideals of the Tower Society, and Malte simply moves further along the very same path. In fact, the pattern of his experiences traces a curve diametrically opposed to that of Wilhelm: beginning on the country estates of his childhood (the name "Urne-kloster" ["urn-cloister"] itself is symbolic, and the paintings there function for him in a sense as a "Hall of the Past"), his path leads him directly to the lonely crowd of the modern metropolis. The anonymity of a

Parisian hotel has replaced the sacred Tower Society, and the only higher order left is that of the private self.

This isolation leads in turn to a radical revision of the concepts of love and death in the novel. Traditionally, the hero of the Bildungsroman has ripened via a series of amorous exploits ranging from the sensual to the sublime. Malte, however, aside from a passing Platonic fancy for his aunt Abelone and a friendship with his cousin Erik, loves no one; his goal, in fact, is to sublimate his earthly passions into an "intransitive" love, directed only toward an infinite God (as in the parable of the Prodigal Son with which the novel concludes . . .). Like the great saintlike lovers of history—the forsaken women whom he eulogizes in his diary—Malte would become an *unloved* lover, for to be loved by anyone, even by Christ (whom Malte terms a "Facilitation of God"), is to halt one's growth, to become, as he puts it, a stigmatized nun, a mere object of passion. "To be loved," Malte realizes, "is to be consumed," whereas "to love is to endure." . . . What Malte is suggesting here is very similar to what Sartre would later refer to, in a different context, as *mauvaise foi* ["bad faith"], and what Frisch would term *Bildnis* ("graven image")—namely, that life must avoid stereotypes if it is to remain free and allow for growth. In a sense, Malte's commitment to this unceasing inner activity of perception provides an analogue to the doctrine of ceaseless *physical* activity in *Wilhelm Meister;* in both novels there lives the notion that commitment to any *one* goal can seriously endanger the process of growth.

Malte's obsession with the concept of a "personal death"—his existential memento mori—would seem directly to contradict the Bildungsroman's traditional romantic interest in the art of living. Yet one must also remember that a constant criticism leveled at the genre is precisely that it has been overly concerned with the romantic, uncommitted years of youth rather than the later realities of maturity and death. . . . In his visions of a "proper death" as one that has developed organically out of one's own way of life, Rilke is merely extending Goethe's organic view of life to include its fulfillment in death as well. Whereas the concept of death in *Wilhelm Meister* is at best ambiguous (Mignon's death is likened to a fruit containing a hidden worm, and yet at the same time there are strong hints of immortality), in *Malte* death is the final fruit of life itself, rather than a passage to another realm. Beyond the affirmation of a this-worldly life, however, there is the important point that only through an imaginative projection into death itself can we see our development as an organic whole. Thus Malte, realizing that "all our insights occur *after* the event," finds his greatest admiration for the romantic writer Bettina von Arnim, who, in her letters, "from the very beginning worked things through as if she were after her death. Everywhere she put herself deep into existence"; . . . italics mine). It is the same mystic capability, one might add, that we find in Keats, who, shortly before his death, stated that he felt as if he were *after* his death already. In attempting to project himself into that sphere where life and death are viewed as one, Malte himself would also become capable of a love that, like Bettina's, would be equal to all and would require no response. . . . (pp. 986-88)

The most central theme of *Malte,* however, is that of memory. "I have prayed for my childhood," Malte writes, "and it has come back." . . . The great "sickness" from which he must recover is precisely the intolerable burden of this unresolved past: "Here and there on my quilt lie lost things from my childhood and are like new," he notes, "all forgotten anxieties are here again.'' . . . And again, in the concluding parable, it is the unfulfilled, unconfronted (''ungetan'') childhood of the Prodigal Son, Malte's double, that causes him to return: ''To take all this upon himself once more, and this time in reality, was the reason why he . . . returned.'' . . . To shoulder the past again, to affirm that his childhood and youth could not have been otherwise, is Malte's supreme task.

Although the conclusion of *Malte* is open, we sense that the work suggests not only the hero's survival but his active development as well. From an overweaning preoccupation with fear and sickness in the first half of the novel, Malte moves in the second half to questions of love and God. Whereas the first part (framed by accounts of the agonizing death of Malte's grandfather) consists largely of Parisian experiences and of recollections of Malte's childhood, the second moves on to reflect upon the ''childhood'' of the world itself—in particular upon the late Christian Middle Ages and Greek antiquity. Moreover, a private, esthetic solution in the first half (''I think I should begin working on something, now that I am learning to see'' . . .) contrasts sharply with a collective, ethical—almost religious—resolve in the second half: ''Couldn't we try to develop ourselves a little, and slowly take upon ourselves our share of work in love, little by little?'' . . . Similarly, the shift in perspective from lyrical apostrophes of everyday objects to more distanced, epic accounts of his past, of history, and of God mirrors Malte's own development toward an ''intransitive'' love, and the concluding tableaux of the two sections imply the same: the unicorn, being *subdued* by love, becomes, in the second half, the Prodigal Son, imploring his family *not* to love him. One might add that even the seasons appear to hint at growth in Malte: much as the Prodigal Son is compared to a ''hibernating plant,'' . . . so Malte arrives in Paris in the fall and ends his notebooks sometime in the following spring or summer.

From the forward-looking, utopian close of *Wilhelm Meister* through the subdued and elegiac tones of *Der grüne Heinrich* to the anguished, retrospective visions of *Malte,* the viewpoint of the hero in the nineteenth-century Bildungsroman shifts unerringly from the world without to the world within. The change is signaled in at least three ways: thematically, by the gradual retreat toward the days of one's childhood; structurally, by a turning toward forms dictated by the psychological time of memory—to autobiography, diary, and notebook; and, in terms of the image of the hero, by the transformation of the ''picaro'' into the ''confessor.'' From Wilhelm through Heinrich to Malte the concept of the self shifts imperceptibly from its status as an assumed postulate to what Samuel Beckett has called a ''retrospective hypothesis.'' Moreover, the confessor, due to his increased attention to inner states of the self and his past, often merges with the figure of the artist; his therapeutic, cathartic act of confession actually frees him from the past by putting it into some *form*. . . . Thus the Bildungsroman, mirroring the autobiographical trend of nineteenth-century fiction as a whole, tends to become a *Künstlerroman* [''novel of an artist's development''], as is the case with *Malte.* (pp. 988-89)

> *David H. Miles, ''The Picaro's Journey to the Confessional: The Changing Image of the Hero in the German Bildungsroman,'' in PMLA, 89, Vol. 89, No. 5, October, 1974, pp. 980-92.**

H. R. KLIENEBERGER (essay date 1979)

[*In the following excerpt, Klieneberger distinguishes the modernist aspects of* Malte *from those which place the work in the tradition of Romanticism.*]

For many years after the publication of *Die Aufzeichnungen des Malte Laurids Brigge* in 1910, Rilke's achievement in prose was overshadowed by his lyrical poetry. Rilke's own apologetic remarks about the novel, which were provoked by inquiries from readers, gave currency to the view that *Die Aufzeichnungen* corresponded to the *Duino Elegies* and the *Sonnets to Orpheus* as a photographic negative does to a positive. Moreover, writers on Rilke, down to Else Buddeberg in 1955, were encouraged by Rilke's comments to assume that Malte perished, although this is not apparent from the novel itself, and they concluded that *Die Aufzeichnungen* therefore represented a first and unsuccessful approach to existential problems which were to be resolved in the later poetry. More recent critics, however, . . . played down the association of the novel—for instance, its replacement of plot-structure and chronological sequence by the other formal principles—which it shares with twentieth-century experimental fiction. The question to be considered in this essay is that of the feasibility of separating the articulation of twentieth-century awareness in the novel, which commends it to the modern reader, from those elements of Romantic ideology in it which are to be found also in the lyrical poetry of Rilke and which have gone out of fashion.

The modernity of the novel shows in Rilke's—and Malte's—suspicion of traditional modes of verbalizing perceptions; it clearly links the novel with other manifestations of a crisis of identity in the contemporary Austro-Hungarian empire. . . . [In 1906] a fellow-Austrian, Robert Musil, published *Die Verwirrungen des Zöglings Törless,* an account of the crisis in the life of a schoolboy, occasioned by his incapacity to relate certain emotional and sexual promptings, that alter his experience of existence, to the sphere of consciousness which alone he finds communicable in conventional language, so that he comes to doubt the continuity of his own personality. In *Die Aufzeichnungen,* Malte's dissatisfaction with conventional language is, as in [Hugo von] Hofmannsthal's *Ein Brief* [1901] and in Musil's *Törless,* the result of a process of isolation. But Rilke goes further than his predecessors in developing an original prose-style and a new narrative form for the adequate rendering of his insights, attributed to Malte. The young Dane, who has lost all his relatives and finds himself friendless and impoverished in Paris, develops a nervous sensitivity in which the sights, sounds, and smells of the city, and the trivial manifestations of human proximity that normally pass unnoticed, acquire a strange, menacing significance. But he accepts his new sensitivity, along with the overwhelming fear and anguish that characterize his sense of loneliness, as the condition of true perception. . . . Moreover, Rilke's Malte asserts that the changes he observes taking place in himself are historically significant as reflecting the emergence of a new human sensibility in an era in which traditional social structures and systems of beliefs have collapsed. Pathos alternates with irony, expressed in paradoxical metaphors and images, and the innovatory daring of the prose-style is apparent in the recording of sensations which the reader must recognize as his own though he would not have heard them put into words before. Indeed, the methods of Expressionism are inaugurated in Malte's attempts to make his insights comprehensible by articulating them in ways which involve paradoxical distortions of so-called reality. For instance, he says of a woman who has no time to resume her customary facial expression when, startled by Malte's approaching footsteps, she suddenly lifts her head out of her hands, that she 'hob sich aus sich ab, zu schnell, zu heftig, so daß das Gesicht in den zwei Händen blieb . . .' ['pulled herself too quickly out of herself, too violently, so that her face remained in her two hands . . .'] revealing a 'bloßen wunden

Kopf ohne Gesicht' ['naked flayed head without a face']. . . . And Malte remarks of the noise of a tin-lid rolling on the floor in the room next-door to his—it is inhabited by a Russian student—that 'was diesen Lärm auslöste, jene kleine, langsame, lautlose Bewegung war, mit der sein Augenlid sich eigenmächtig über sein rechtes Auge senkte und schloß' ['what released this noise was that small, slow, soundless movement with which the student's eyelid would of its own accord sink and close over his right eye'] . . . ; the reader must assume that what in fact happens is that a nervous tic, an involuntary closing of his eyelid, prompts the student to throw a tin-lid on the floor where it continues to roll, a recurrent event which drives Malte frantic. A similar paradoxical effect is achieved by Malte's speaking of apparitions and other psychic phenomena as if they were natural, everyday incidents, occasioning no more surprise to him than they would if they occurred in his dreams at night. In these respects, the novel points forward to Kafka's depiction of solitaries for whom an accurately-observed empirical setting and everyday circumstances take on a nightmare quality as if in response to their moods of guilt and dread—the Kafka who emphasized that the verisimilitude he sought to achieve was akin to that experienced in dreams. . . . In his refusal to sentimentalize his hero, his determination to record the abject misery, the nervous irritability, the paranoiac obsessions that are the morbid side-effects of isolation, Rilke anticipates Peter Handke's attempt, in *Die Angst des Tormanns beim Elfmeter* (1970), to trace the collapse of a conventional interpretation of the external world in a process of alienation.

But if Rilke is a pioneer of twentieth-century fiction, he is also the heir and continuator of Romantic traditions in this novel as in much of his poetry. From the beginning, Malte accepts his isolation not only as a means to true perception but as the condition of authentic existence. . . . Malte is an artist in the making, like the protagonists of so many German works of fiction of the eighteenth and nineteenth centuries. If to begin with Malte records, in the main, impressions of his Paris environment, in the later sections of the novel his 'Arbeiten' ['works'] predominate: sketches of various historic figures who, in Malte's view, underwent a process of transformation on coming to terms with their suffering, and thereby achieved the authenticity which eludes him though he aspires to it. (pp. 361-63)

When he is on the verge of a nervous breakdown and falls gravely ill, Malte undertakes to relive certain childhood experiences in order to recover a sense of continuity; but this experiment fails to provide him with the accession of strength and confidence he had expected from it. . . . Readers familiar with Freud's writings will recognize in the childhood predicament of Malte the constituents of the process which leads to inversion: he describes himself as an only child, strongly attached to his mother who partially rejects him in that she makes him feel guilty because he is a boy and not a girl; she makes him impersonate her daughter who had died in infancy; at the same time she prevents him from identifying with his father who is disparaged and kept at a distance. But unlike the novelists of the period who were dedicated to a thorough-going Modernism, Rilke eschews a psychologizing approach and interprets the predicaments of Malte and his historical models in terms of the Romantic conflict between the individual of genius and his environment. The ultimate fate of Malte remains in doubt, but the heroes he writes about triumph over the world which opposes them, a process which is presented as a metaphysical phenomenon, an 'Umschlag' ['sudden change'] into achieved authenticity. What the reader who has assimilated the

discoveries of psychoanalysis must, however, ask himself is whether the inner transformation which is traced in the lives of various historic models is not an extension of the Narcissistic tendency apparent in the infant Malte. Medieval rulers, artists such as Beethoven and the Italian actress Eleonora Duse, are assimilated by Malte to certain figures in the streets of Paris, cripples, beggars, and that blind newspaper-vendor who is marked by 'die durch keine Vorsicht oder Verstellung eingeschränkte Hingegebenheit seines Elends' ['the utter abandonment of his misery, restricted by no precaution or disguise'] . . . ; they come to resemble each other in their abandonment of all concern for human respect, in their achievement of what is presented as total sincerity. This, however, is a provocation in the eyes of society which, we are told, is hostile to the isolated; Malte remembers old paintings, such as those by Hieronymus Bosch, which depict men, daemons, and inanimate objects as conspiring to distract the saint and so prevent him from persevering in his task. In these respects, Malte argues, the modern artist is the heir and successor of the medieval saint. Malte attaches special significance to certain collections of verse, diaries, and other documents, in which a process of inner change in the course of an unhappy love-relationship is recorded by women. . . . Unrequited love is seen, paradoxically, as a preparatory step towards the spiritual love of the contemplatives for whom God is 'nur eine Richtung der Liebe . . . kein Liebesgegenstand' ['only a direction of love . . . not an object of love']. . . . That Rilke offers a therapeutic technique, if of a different kind from that of the psychoanalysts, is borne out by various letters of thanks which he received from lonely people who had learned from his writings to see their painful, humiliating experiences in a positive light. 'Umschlag' is a key concept not only in *Die Aufzeichnungen* but in many of Rilke's poems: a reversal of mood which is said to occur in those who accept and 'überstehen' ['overcome'] their predicament. . . . The authenticity which Malte's models achieve through the acceptance of suffering is its own reward; what in the case of the 'great lovers' he calls an 'eisige Herrlichkeit' ['icy splendor'], he describes elsewhere in the novel as an entry into nature, and into the dimension of a life beyond death. . . . Indeed, all the historic figures whom Malte invokes are credited with having attained an extratemporal stature. There is, therefore, to be found in Rilke a characteristically Romantic 'mythicization' of artists and great men which is unlikely to be acceptable to many present-day readers, however congenial they may find the innovatory modernity of other aspects of the novel. (pp. 363-65)

At times the suggestion is present in the novel as it is in Rilke's poetry that the 'Umschlag' is akin to that sense of enhanced significance experienced in defeat which marks the heroes of tragic drama, and that the serenity which results from it resembles the peace achieved through resignation in the Stoic tradition and some Christian devotional literature; at other times, however, the 'Umschlag' appears rather as a withdrawal into total self-sufficiency, indeed, as a Narcissism rendered in the terms of Romantic metaphysics. (p. 365)

The mirror, which functions so often in Rilke's poetry as an autonomous agent, is a recurrent motif in *Die Aufzeichnungen*. It exposes the defective sense of identity of the boy Malte who is seized with terror at the sight of his own reflection in it. . . . But in the case of the Dame à la Licorne . . . , as in some of the poems, the mirror is a symbol of self-sufficiency, and acts as God does in the case of Marianna Alcoforado; it reflects not only woman's image, but her love which has become 'intransitive', and directs it back into her heart which is thereby enhanced . . . , so that her state of unhappiness becomes one of 'eisige Herrlichkeit'. . . . In Rilke's 'Dinggedichte' ['poems about objects'], the external world has a function analogous to that of the mirror; the self is enhanced by receiving back its own reflection from the objects which it contemplates. The later Rilke calls this process the achievement of 'Weltinnen-raum'; as an experience of the identity of inner and outer world, it is a resuscitation of the Idealistic subjectivism of the first German Romantic movement.

That the Modernism of form and content in *Die Aufzeichnungen* is of one piece with the Romantic ideology, and that to try and separate it out is therefore of no benefit, emerges most clearly from passages in which Malte articulates his aspiration to self-sufficiency. On one occasion, he remarks that it involves the toleration, indeed, the welcoming acceptance of the seemingly negative and repugnant in one's fate and environment. . . . In eschewing selectiveness and evaluation, and so in extending the areas of experience available in art, Rilke belongs with the Modernists. But the same principle of total acceptance is also at the root of the mystique of 'Umschlag', and it led Rilke to reject all socio-political as well as psychoanalytic attempts to alleviate human suffering as spiritually damaging and as, in particular, a threat to the role of art and the artist. (pp. 365-66)

In Rilke's correspondence with Lou Andreas-Salomé, it appears that he considered submitting to psychoanalytical treatment on more than one occasion, but shrank back from it because he feared that if he were 'healed', he might lose the capacity to create poetry. Similarly, it is apparent from his correspondence that there is a connexion between the ideal of intransitive love and his determination to evade lasting historic relationships with women-friends because he feared that a diminution of his isolation and inner autonomy would destroy his creativeness. Romantic ideology is invoked by Rilke to justify the preservation of neurotic defences, of Narcissism, just as in *Die Aufzeichnungen* it is a cult of genius of the kind that had been fashionable in the nineteenth century that is the counterpoise to the threat of disintegration. It is true that in certain respects other pioneers of the modern novel were also heirs of nineteenth-century traditions. James Joyce originated in the Aestheticist movement, as is evident from the ruminations on art and the preciousness of the prose-style in his earlier fiction. Moreover, the aesthetes of the nineties had prepared the way for the stream-of-consciousness technique with their emphasis on passing moods, the sensations of the present moment, and the shared mystical experience of Ulrich and Agathe in Musil's *Der Mann ohne Eigenschaften* is akin to that which figures in the early Hofmannsthal. But the artist in *Ulysses* and in Musil's novel is just as much the object of deflating psychological scrutiny as are the other characters, whereas in *Die Aufzeichnungen* the artist not only occupies a central place among the representatives of authenticity, but he is mythicized in the same kind of way as in the *Duino Elegies,* where he achieves the 'Verwandlung' ['transformation'] of the world which is said to be its 'drängender Auftrag' ['urgent mission'] . . . , and in the *Sonnets to Orpheus,* where he engages in 'Rühmen' ['glorification'] as a quasi-Messianic task. It seems likely, therefore, that the lack of recognition for *Die Aufzeichnungen* as a pioneering venture in twentieth-century fiction is not due merely to the abandonment of the contemporary scene half-way through the novel, but to the inextricable combination of Modernist with Romantic elements that characterizes it. (pp. 366-67)

H. R. Klieneberger, "Romanticism and Modernism in Rilke's 'Die Aufzeichnungen des Malte Laurids Brigge," in The Modern Language Review, *Vol. 74, Part 2, April, 1979, pp. 361-67.*

DIANA FESTA-McCORMICK   (essay date 1979)

[*In the following excerpt, Festa-McCormick discusses the function of the urban setting in* Malte.]

The city of Paris is a drab and sad medley in [*The Notebooks of Malte Laurids Brigge*], a place dominated by loneliness and malady, with faces of anguish along its roads and the recurring image of death. Malte, the protagonist of the story, is here both a spectator and a victim of the city, and his vision is intricately personal and, at the same time, objective and almost detached. Malte's eyes are like those of a camera, selecting details and magnifying them at times, moving along a spectrum of existence dictated by his own inner turmoil and fears. The protagonist's search is both personal and universal, a personal quest that extends beyond the self and reaches for the eternal. Malte's past rests in a twilight of memories of far-away Denmark and of a youth spent in oppressive loneliness. It is only in distorted fashion that he recaptures the morbid fantasies of the child he once was, in isolated and disjointed images that do not add up to the man he has become. When he comes to Paris he is twenty-eight years old, but he still carries within himself an unresolved childhood and the anguish of the incoherent fears that had weighed upon him during the early years of his life. That he must come to terms with that past before the present can hold any meaning for him is clear. But the confrontation with the past means a painful reliving of its torments in the light of an oppressive present, and a reshaping of his Parisian journey through the meandering paths of his Danish ancestry. Day after day will prove a new trial for Malte, seemingly hopeless at first but gradually revealing a glimmer of light in the miasma of city life. His pursuit slowly becomes a resolve, and the truth that he seeks will emerge out of his creative energy. Malte's search leads him to the only possible avenue out of his spectral world of revolving horrors. *The Notebooks* will oppose to the transient aspects of existence a lasting artistic creation.

The tension that is established with the opening words of the work is one that oscillates between recognition of new verities, with an implicit reappraisal of past assumptions, and the lingering doubts that rest upon years of longing and grieving. That tension also arises from contradictory wishes—from a morbid fascination with death and an unavowed but impelling desire to live. "So, then, people do come here in order to live; I would sooner have thought one died here." The Paris that is contemplated through the word "here" is itself a recollection, a memory already, of the present that Malte is in the midst of living. The immediateness of the moment is in fact always pushed back and observed in the light of past experiences. The "here" of this initial sentence is indeed Paris. But Paris, while it stands as a whole, all around, in the streets, the buildings, the people, and even the noises, is cast filtered through an imagination that seeks access to its forbidden world. It is as if Malte were both within and on the outside of Paris, having just arrived and measuring the city with an appraising eye, and seeing it through the fog of years past, real and unreal, vital and decaying at once. . . . Memory is emotionally selective, and Malte's notebook is thus a mirror of his state of mind. His walks along the Parisian avenues and the objects and people he sees are segments of a larger reality only vaguely sensed but still finding no correspondence within. What his eye singles out are recognizable shapes, the same that he carries within and bear heavy upon his soul. (pp. 72-3)

Foreboding and anxiety, the senseless, the grotesque, often hold a fascination that defies the paralyzing effect of their presence. The images that rush to Malte's vision, frightful, frequently macabre, monstrous, and sickening, hold the attraction of a surrealistic world, both dismaying and bewitching, immediate, intimate, and immensely personal.

> I am learning to see, I don't know why it is, but everything penetrates more deeply into me and does not stop at the place where until now it always used to finish. . . .

Malte's ability to discern within reality the hidden layers of the unconscious is new, directly related to the city to which he has come. Paris is the catalyst here that creates, with every event, a mirror of that event; it brings about a kind of emotional dissection that is both inside and outside the event that is contemplated. Malte observes the living portraits of fear, loneliness, and despair that he has always known; but for the first time he sees them, in spite of their familiarity, within a world that is not his own. If it is through his own isolation that he perceives, in the faces around, a reflection of his personal sense of loss and of his dread, he can now observe the random play of dread and loss upon features that are not his own, as phenomena outside of himself, unrelated to any direct experience.

> But the woman, the woman; she has completely collapsed into herself, forward into her hands. . . . The street was too empty; its emptiness was bored; it caught my step from under my feet and clattered about with it hither and yon, as with a wooden clog. The woman startled and pulled away too quickly out of herself, too violently, so that her face remained in her two hands. I could see it lying in them, its hollow form. It cost me indescribable effort to stay with those hands and not to look at what had torn itself out of them. I shuddered to see a face from the inside, but still I was much more afraid of the naked flayed head without a face. . . .

The emptiness of a Parisian street is a "bored" presence with which Malte must reckon. . . . The motion of going through an empty street is a painful discovery with a predictable end; but the steps now become a mission that will eventually lead to the double acceptance of life and death. The street is a guide that tyrannically leads Malte "hither and yon," to a confrontation with suffering and desolation. The woman, caught unaware, reveals a face not composed for Malte's scrutinizing eye; her everyday public mask "remained in her two hands," but inside out, showing the flayed skin and the vulnerability within. This poetic, surrealistic vision of the unknown woman who holds her face in her bare hands—and in so doing offers the portrait of Malte's own helplessness—is an appalling image of pain, but one that suggests an embryonic movement of reconciliation with life. If it is true, in fact, that Malte does not dare to look at "the naked head," and therefore at the total display of what is most hidden and most intimate in a human being, he nevertheless contemplates "those hands" and the segment of gruesome truth they represent.

It is of course difficult to establish to what degree Malte's struggle was that of the author himself. The reader does know that the poet was caught within the double vise of poverty and

unresolved purpose during his stay in Paris, and one can only assume that this accounts for the images of desolation and the aimless wanderings in Malte's world. What is of concern here, however, is the role that the city plays both in projecting the evils with which life is replete and in suggesting the necessity for a measure of acceptance of those evils and a resolution of inner tensions. The city is not a casual background to the quandaries of Malte's existence; it is, rather, the force that brings all strife to the fore and dictates the painful dilemma of choices. Rilke had struggled for clarity there, and had, each day, come closer to heeding the imperious urge for artistic expression. (pp. 74-5)

Caught within Malte's feverish vision, the large French metropolis projects paranoid visions. Malte wanders through them, in and out of objects and sounds, and catches in his frayed nerves all the nuances of their presence. There is an anguished sense of wait, and only an inner turmoil sporadically covers the din of the city. . . . Within the noises, even the mechanical and strident ones, there is hidden the presence of a humanity in disarray, but one that is at least alive with its screams and its calls. In the silence that at night descends suddenly upon a motionless universe, however, Malte watches the terrifying phantoms of his imagination. (p. 76)

Memories, for Rilke as for Proust, are not culled through a cerebral process of a mental storing up of thoughts, but through an eruption of images within the vagaries of the imagination, an associative power of colors, shapes, sounds, and smells that is sudden and often unconscious. But in Proust there is a collective image that gradually emerges, one composed of many layers that rest upon each other with an ever widening and deepening perspective. In Malte's rambling journal, however, there is no focal point, no symbolic cup of tea or kaleidoscopic sun ray upon a pavement to give a point of reference to his "remembrance of things past." The images are disconnected, with no sequential order, each contained in its own frame, frozen in time and immutable in an endless present. Yet little by little a new sense of reality emerges out of Malte's nightmarish contemplations, one that does not consist in an avoidance of but in a willful consenting to the horrors of life.

The image that Malte constantly sees, whenever he looks, the "face in the mirror," is of course his own. His walks along the streets of Paris are hence a kind of pilgrimage, a retracing of each step of the past in the light of the present. The person he addresses at each turn is his other self. That part of his self is still out of reach, on the other side of the psychic cleavage he carries within. But he seeks at each turn a coincidence and a blending with it. "Have I said it before?" . . . he repeats as he tries to bring his intellectual and emotional beings closer to each other. "I sit here and am nothing. Nevertheless this nothing begins to think and thinks, five flights up, on a gray Parisian afternoon . . .". . . . In those thoughts what had been only a dream begins to be a vocation, as Malte sets upon the road that will transmute his anguish into poetry and a work of art. The "gray Parisian" air will not allow him flights of fantasy; he must measure his call with the reality around him, and the reality he had smothered in the early recollections of his youth. "Twelve years old, or at most thirteen, I must have been at the time." . . . Slowly, the tacit suffering of that child of long ago comes to the surface. It is contemplated in dismal solitude by the young man who desperately needs to distance those years in order to face the future. . . . The images that emerge from the distant past, dark, oppressive, bringing along all the repressed pain of the voiceless child that Malte once was, become alive in the equally oppressive Parisian atmosphere. The role of Paris is thus gradually delineated as that of an analyst drawing out of Malte, as with a patient, the reality he must slowly confront. The city's voice is inaudible but imperious, and Malte will heed it. He will look at all the images he carries buried in his consciousness and reappraise them with new maturity and new strength.

Malte says, "I kept on the move incessantly." . . . With self-scrutinizing clarity he knows that the constant act of moving has been his unspoken manner of rejecting a reality too painful to accept. He also knows that all of his perceptive powers are directed by his inner anguish and that he will continue to detect on the outside a replica of the phantoms he carries within. He runs both away and toward those phantoms, realizing that they can no longer be avoided and yet recoiling from their presence. (pp. 76-8)

The line of demarcation between life and death in Malte's world is one tied to the element of fear and, to a lesser degree, to that of longing. Death is that which is fearful, the distortion of images, the corruption of thought—the face of the woman that bewilderingly clings to her two hands, the neighbor's wrestling with the mathematics of time, the shadow weighing in the darkness on the weeping child's bed. . . . Death is the feeling of oppression that emerges from a wall standing sneeringly in the way or the loss of warmth from those one loved. All the figures that had been dear to young Malte have receded into the engulfing shadow of the grave; but as they moved away, Malte has caught their last receding step within his memory and feverish imagination. It is that step, that last motion before eternity, that is within the composition of the wall erected on his path and nourishes the passionate vagaries of his mind: Chamberlain Christof Detlev's ultimate struggle with a force stronger than his, or Maman's last outing to the Schulinses' house. It is of no concern either to the reader or to Malte himself if those images—of grandfather's powerful railings against the impending death or the Schulinses' spectral house in the eerie setting of his youth—are framed within any semblance of empirical reality. They are Malte's tyrannical truth with which he still must come to terms. They are the last erected wall along his way and the last psychic obstacle against creation.

Alone in the foreign capital peopled with shadows, Malte recognizes the nature of death: it resides in loneliness, disarray, and the irrationality of motion constantly at odds with the folly of existence. But the monstrously large Paris itself, when contemplated in the light of the mystery of life, becomes a speck in the realm of eternity. Malte's own losses can thus be assimilated within a larger concept of death, one that is visible upon all the anonymous faces in the streets of Paris. The death of each individual slowly emerges as only a step along the road of unrecorded history, a repetition in time of all the facets of existence. Christof Detlev, Count Brahe, Ingeborg, beautiful Abelone, and even the haunting image of Maman are contemplated, one by one, by Malte, until they blend within a larger frame of reference. Only there are they invested with a measure of their own tenuous continuity and the rightful perspective provided by time and memory. The figures of King Charles VI of France, that of Ivan Grosny and the false Czar that suddenly emerge from the pages of history books upon Malte's consciousness, do not diminish either his personal sense of loss or the importance of the lives of those he had loved. But they can now be viewed in a different light, which embraces a spectrum of existence larger than that of the individual. The

Paris with a thousand deaths and a thousand lives at every corner gradually reveals to Malte a new dimension of death and a measure of life. The milling crowd that seems to have only a semblance of life upon a mask of death imparts a lesson that he has been loath to accept, that of the inseparability of life and death within all visions of eternity. . . . Assertively, the vast city in which Malte has sought refuge has pushed him on. It has led him to weigh the cumulative force of his own past against all that is the past, and to recognize that within a seemingly aimless existence the individual has his own legitimate role. The small universe of his youth in far-away Denmark imparted greatness to familiar figures. That greatness is not diminished with the knowledge of their relative insignificance within the magnitude of life. But the ghosts that once composed Malte's reality are gradually reshaped, "transformed," and given a new perspective through which his fears and hopes assume equitable dimensions. He now notices "certain differences" that separate him from the others, and with this his life assumes a degree of importance it has not known until now. What counts even more is that implicitly the other faces around him assume individual contours too, within the grayness of city life. The city thus becomes a repository of human memory in which Malte has found the very shape of his own past. Paris embodies a condensed reality of life projected through its images of desolation, sickness, and death. "I am a beginner in my own circumstances," recognizes Malte as he considers his private world from the perspective of a larger model of life. He can now identify, within the antlike existence of the city, a coincidence with the strong individualism of the past.

Malte's *Notebooks* is, in the final analysis, his lasting answer to the horrors projected through the magnifying lenses of city existence. Malte does not come to terms with those horrors, and in that respect his efforts are a failure. But in his very act of struggling, his anguish crystallizes into words, and the nightmare of his long Parisian night finds a voice that will be heard long after he himself disappears. (pp. 79-81)

> *Diana Festa-McCormick, "Rilke's 'Notebooks': Paris and the Phantoms of the Past," in her* The City as Catalyst: A Study of Ten Novels, *Fairleigh Dickinson University Press, 1979, pp. 69-88.*

WALTER H. SOKEL (essay date 1980)

[*Sokel is an Austrian-born educator and critic specializing in German language and literature. In the following excerpt, he discusses the emergence of "self" in* Malte.]

A duality seems to run through *The Notebooks* that is most clearly apparent in the contrast between the two families whose union produced Malte—the paternal Brigges and the maternal Brahes. The two grandfathers, Brigge at Ulsgaard and Brahe at Urnekloster, stand at opposite poles in their attitude toward or experience of death, and offer themselves as apt points of departure for examining this duality and its significance.

Malte recalls that old Chamberlain Brigge died his own death. The powerful individuality and authenticity of his whole existence seemed to be manifested in his long-drawn-out dying. But not only he, most members of the Brigges, including even their children, had had their own deaths. Death was for them fruition and fulfillment, and each death confirmed, as it sealed, the unique character of the life it ended.

In contrast to this existentially authentic dying of the Brigges stand not only the anonymous assembly-line deaths in the Parisian hospitals, but also the Brahes' refusal to recognize death at all. At Ulsgaard, the home of the Brigges, everything proclaims the powerful impact of individual personality and the distinctive phases of the individual's life. At Urnekloster, ancestral home of the Brahes, the opposite prevails. Here, one is oblivious of the time of day. Death is not recognized because linear time, dividing existence into the three dimensions of past, present, and future, plays no role. The long-deceased might be expected as dinner guests. (p. 171)

The contradiction between the linear time dimension, implied in Brigge's dying, and the simultaneity of all being, which underlies the Brahe complex of the novel, has escaped attention, despite its importance and the obvious problems it raises. In terms of intellectual history, the Brigges may boast of a truly Nordic genealogy. They derive from the aestheticism of Jens Jacobsen, author of *Niels Lyhne,* through whom the influence of Kierkegaard, a fellow-Dane now more famous than Jacobsen, might have first reached Rilke. This Danish lineage is wedded in Rilke to reminiscences of Nietzsche, mediated to him by their common lady friend, the fascinating Lou Salomé. The Brahe sphere, on the other hand, while pointing ahead to the mysticism of the Duino "experience," is also rooted in the pantheistic penchant present in Rilke's work from its beginnings. The duality expressed by the two families is an instance of "the law of complementaries," which Ulrich Füllebörn has shown to be a basic structural principle of the novel. The Brigges embody the law inherent in the *Gestalt* that grows toward its point of pre-ordained development and constitutes a unique and definite individuality, or in Malte's term "das Eigene," that which is peculiar to the individual. The Brahes, on the other hand, embody the principles of exchangeability of identities, of the commingling of all the forms of the universe, and consequently of the unreality of separateness and distinction. The Brahes experience the melting together of all

contours, which is grotesquely displayed by Mathilde Brahe's overweight body, her somehow overflowing, shapeless flesh. . . . The fact that "das Eigene," one's own distinct individuality, is part of the male line of Malte's descent, while the blurring and mingling of all boundaries mark the female line, would appear as not without significance to anyone familiar with the assumptions on which Rilke's view of the sexes, as expressed—for instance, in his doctrine of love—rests. To develop this aspect of Rilke's thought would lead us too far afield here. Our task is to pursue further the theme of the contrast that the two lines of descent exemplify.

The contrast reappears as an open contradiction in Malte's conflicting views of God. Early in *The Notebooks,* in its nineteenth section, appears a series of questions, each initiated by the words: "Is it possible?"

> Is it possible that there are people who say "God" and mean that this is something they have in common?—Just take a couple of schoolboys: one buys a pocket knife and his companion buys another exactly like it on the same day. And after a week they compare knives and it turns out that there is now only a very distant resemblance between the two—so differently have they developed in different hands. . . .

The passage strikingly resembles a very similar one in Montaigne, in which Renaissance individualism seems to reach its apogee. At the same time, the influence of Jacobsen, and through him of Kierkegaard, cannot be overlooked here. For Malte, God is the opposite of the universal. He is the absolute individual in whom and through whom each individual experiences and reveals his subjectivity as true being; and Malte's rhetorical question: "Is it possible?" expresses his horror at mankind's failure to grasp that ultimate reality is, and must be, utterly individual, unrepeatable, and unique.

However, a remark of Malte's near the end of his notebooks stands in sharp contrast to what has just been established. There Malte says: "Let us be honest about it, then; we have no theatre, any more than we have a God: for this, community is needed." . . . Here the individual is negated as absolute reality, and God, in conformity with the Dionysian principle, to which the theater seems to point, appears as based upon the collective. We find in this contradiction another version of the contrast between the Brigges and the Brahes.

Yet, we shall see that this duality is only apparent. Its two poles not only complement each other; they unite to form a third force in which we shall come to discern, as the unifying theme of *The Notebooks,* the process of the overcoming of the self, the letting go of the ego.

Our concern here will be to examine how the process of the breaking of the self described by Malte reveals the duality of Brigges and Brahes as a unity, consisting of the tension between two poles.

Let us begin with the castaways, those figures of the lowest depths far beneath society, who seem to emerge from the underground into the streets of Paris to haunt Malte and beckon him to follow them into an inconceivable abyss. They function like messengers from future horrors that leave the imagination of the present utterly behind. This future seems to be taking aim at him through them. These homeless beggars and grotesques seem to be grinning at him, winking at him everywhere.

Jens Peter Jacobsen. Etching by Axel Helsted, 1895.

Even the Bibliothèque Nationale fails to protect him from them. They draw him to them with bonds of dread. Disguised as mesmerizing anxiety, an overpowering temptation issues forth from the castaways. With constantly diminishing strength, Malte struggles against their lure. "Who are these people? They are refuse, husks of human beings, whom destiny has spewed up." . . . (pp. 172-74)

The wording of this first characterization of the castaways, given by Malte, already hints at what it is they seem to urge upon him. It is the purging of the ego from his being. He calls them "husks" of human beings, "Schalen," which could also mean "peels" or "shells." This metaphor then conjures a fruit which has lost its inner core and flesh, and has been reduced to the worthless frame of its former being. The metaphor establishes the castaways as the counterpart and opposite of Old Chamberlain Brigge, Malte's powerful paternal grandfather. For the full, ripe, or maturing fruit is the image of his existence, which was full-bodied, unique, and mighty in his death as well as in his life. . . . The castaways are at the opposite pole. They are deprived of that interiority and substance that "everyone" carries within himself. Nothing can make them be compared to an organic being. They are without that which ripens toward fruition and fulfillment of its inner law. The word "refuse" ("Abfälle"), with which they are described, refers in its root meaning to something that has fallen off or been removed and thrown away from something greater to which it originally belonged but now no longer belongs. . . . They exist at the most extreme remove from the world of the Brigges in which life enjoyed the favor of fortune and possessed the time to mature into the fruit of its own death. But the castaways have been robbed of their organic being. They are no longer persons.

In his long letter to Lou Andreas-Salomé of July 18, 1903, Rilke still invests the castaways with a fate. Here he writes of them: "And they were passersby among passersbys, left alone and undisturbed in their fate." In the novel, however, they are already "spewed up by fate (or destiny)"; it is destiny which has thrown them away and made them into "refuse." This is a consistent elaboration of the meaning of "being left alone," which Rilke already expressed in his letter. If we look into the further use of the term "Schicksal" (fate or destiny) in *Malte,* we find that it is called the "inventor" of "patterns and figures," and that it is put in contrast to "life." Whereas the "difficulty" of "destiny" lies in its "complexity," we read that "life is heavy from simplicity." . . . The castaways share their lack of destiny with the saints and the female lovers who are not loved in return. They have become shapelessly simple like "eternal ones." Like the saints and the women, whose love goes unrequited, their lives have ceased to change. "But they maintain themselves almost like eternal ones. They stand at their street corners each day, even in November, and they do not scream because of the winter. Fog comes and makes them indistinct and uncertain: yet they are. I had been away; I had been sick; for me many things had passed; but they have not passed away." . . . The castaways exist in a state in which the unstable self that is subject to linear time, occupied with projects, ambitions, cares, chores, and affairs, no longer is. In this respect, the castaways are like the women lovers who have given up all hope for love requited. These women are likewise "deprived of destiny" and stand as though eternal "next to the beloved man who is subject to metamorphoses." . . . The difference between the castaways and the women lovers lies in the passivity of the former. The castaways endure only passively like "puppets with whom life has played," what the women have "resolutely" chosen for themselves.

Like the saints, the women have deliberately refused destiny, whereas the castaways merely happened to lose it. Circumstances have robbed them of it and made them slowly and gradually "slide down" . . . into the fateless abyss of misery. However, despite the superiority of the unloved lovers *vis-à-vis* the castaways, the result common to both must not be ignored. It is the absence of self that raises both beyond time. Both, after all, are compared to "eternal ones."

Like the unloved lovers, the castaways have, together with the self, thrown off caprice, deception, and shame. When Malte sees the beggar woman daily offering the stump of her arm to the view of the people at sidewalk cafés, he admits to himself his own inability to attain such an utter disregard to self-consciousness and shame. He would lack the strength and indifference for it, ". . . but I would make a vain boast if I claimed to be like them. I am not. I would have neither their strength nor their measure." . . . Having shed the constantly striving and worrying ego, they have allowed being to appear in them. "Yet they *are*," says Malte of them. But through himself, time still passes, many things have happened to him; and with his ego involved, he has been and still is the victim of time which robs and changes all. They, on the other hand, have already traveled so far away from destiny that time no longer occurs in them. From dupes and victims of time, they have become its equals. (pp. 174-76)

We have run ahead from the first appearance of the castaways to the meaning that they will assume for Malte near the end of *The Notebooks.* Between these points lie phenomenological descriptions of the process of losing selfhood. They follow immediately upon the first emergence of the castaways. In a series of infernal scenes, Malte depicts the eruptions and visitations that first threaten and then smash the self. They serve as prefigurations and allusions to his own calling and destiny. The scenes begin with the stranger whose dying Malte witnesses in the dairy café, the creamery, and culminate in the eruption of the St. Vitus's Dance on the Pont du St.-Michel. (pp. 176-77)

The dying man in the creamery, who throws Malte into such shock that he runs away from the scene in panic and races through the streets, is described in this passage:

> The connection between us was established, and I knew that he was stiff with terror. I knew that terror had paralyzed him, terror at something that was happening inside him. Perhaps one of his blood-vessels had burst; perhaps, just at this moment, some poison that he had long dreaded was penetrating the ventricle of his heart; like a rising sun that was changing the world for him. With an indescribable effort I compelled myself to look in his direction, for I still hoped it was all imagination. But then I sprang up and rushed out; for I had made no mistake. . . .

This death in the creamery is a synthesis between the two kinds of death encountered by the reader so far. It combines the anonymous assembly-line dying in the hospitals with the "personal death" of Chamberlain Brigge. Like the death of the chamberlain, the dying in the creamery erupts from within. It explodes, as it were, from the interior space of the individual. It removes its victim from all accustomed things and makes him a stranger to the world. In that sense, his death is like the death of Chamberlain Brigge. On the other hand, this dying is certainly not seen in terms of the ripening of a fruit. It is not at all conceived of in terms of an organic development fulfilling an inner law. Rather, it is experienced as a sudden breakthrough inside. It is not the highest point of growth, but a catastrophe. (p. 177)

In contrast to the imperious death of Old Chamberlain Brigge at Ulsgaard, the silent dying in the creamery is an example of both loss and transcendence of self. In the dying in the creamery the emphasis lies not on the quality and individuality of a personal death, but on dying as a process and on its consequences. The individual and historical aspects of existence, which still found such powerful expression in Old Brigge's dying, lose all significance here. It is the pure happening without a past—the metamorphosis taking place in the present moment—which is described or rather conjured here. The word "perhaps" repeated three times and initiating each of the questions shows that Malte is only able to circumlocute here, and that what is actually occurring must remain conjecture. The three catastrophes evoked—the bursting of a blood vessel, the entrance of poison into the heart, the eruption of a brain tumor—these three catastrophes are speculations surrounding the inconceivable reality. In contrast to the powerful roar of Brigge's dying which dominates the environment and makes this dying unquestionably an event imprinting itself, as did his whole life, upon the world, the dying in the creamery proceeds in a sinister soundlessness. The dying man surrenders defenselessly to what is happening in and to him. (pp. 178-79)

A comparison of the time structure in the death scenes reflected upon and witnessed by Malte is illuminating. In the death of the chamberlain the emphasis is on the linear development which leads from the lived past into the dying present. Living and dying are situated on the same single line. The mass dying in the hospitals is empty present, unconnected with anything preceding or following. But in the anonymous dying of the stranger in the creamery, the present is being swept into a future as yet inconceivable. The tumor bursting in the man is compared to a sunrise "that transformed the world for him." It thus heralds the dawning of a new day, a newborn world. Spine-chilling though it is, this dying is pregnant with a future. We can discern this from the effect this death has upon Malte and the significance it assumes for him. It becomes a call for his rebirth, a milestone on the road to his Damascus. Malte knows that he must obey the call that this death expresses. It is a sign, a signal, which he grasps not conceptually as yet but, as it were, intestinally. The death in the creamery signifies for Malte the need "to change [his] life." (p. 179)

The dying in the creamery, in a sense, becomes a transition from the world of the Brigges to the world of the Brahes. Malte thinks that the dying man might no longer be able to distinguish objects; and it is precisely this inability that makes his dying so horrifying, and yet, from a hidden perspective that only gradually becomes explicit, so exemplary, for Malte. . . . What the Brahes have proudly attained—namely, the transcendence of distinctions between the discreteness of objects—is here still experienced as a loss, as terrifying impotence and negativity. "There was nothing." But even here, Malte realizes that it is the perspective of his own anxiety that posits this experience as a loss, a horror, and an emptiness. He senses and indeed knows that, in place of seeing nothing, a wholly new way of seeing would emerge, a readiness "to see everything differently."

The learning "to see differently" is of course the theme of the book. But it can only come about by a surrender of the ego.

It is a selfless seeing. For Malte it will mean a kind of writing radically different from the one he has practiced so far. His pen will no longer obey the dictation of his conscious will. "But here there will come a day when my hand will be far from me, and when I bid it write, it will write words I do not mean . . . this time I shall be written." . . . For Malte, the poet, that yielding of self, which he has described among the castaways and the women whose love went unrequited, will manifest itself as a profoundly changed form of creativeness. His writing will cease to be "Erlebnisdichtung," which is the expression of the ego and its experience. Malte knows that the time must come when he will have to give up all claim to personal distinction and ambition for his authorship and all self-willed individuality in his style. He will have to renounce the self-pleasing image of creator and lower himself to be mere medium, poor husk, pure vessel of something other and greater than himself.

But Malte's prophecy "but this time I shall be written" poses the question of the identity of that greater author whose medium or whose subject—the distinction is not made—Malte will become. Who is the author who shall write **Malte** or write by means of Malte? The section dealing with the victim of the St. Vitus's Dance on the Boulevard St.-Michel will lead us further in this quest.

The description of the dancer on the Boulevard St.-Michel shows, in anticipation of the fifth elegy, that the self is a will, a concentrated effort at control. The will seeks to maintain an appearance. The victim of the nervous disorder, in whom Malte comprehends himself, is intent on preserving the appearance of a normal existence. The man strains to protect himself against the eruption of an uncontrollable urge to twitch and toss about his limbs. He clings to a cane, which serves him as an instrument of self-control, but also represents the symbol of bourgeois respectability in pre-World War I Europe. He is in Malte's words, "still defending himself," even as Malte himself is desperately resisting the suction issuing from the castaways. "And I am still defending myself," he tells himself, putting a distance between himself and the dying wretch in the creamery. Yet he knows that his defense is as doomed as the spastic's efforts to hide his seizures.

This resistance is identical with the ego, the individual will, the organizing consciousness, seeking to assert its control over the body and over the environment. It is the upkeep of an image of respectability aimed at the others; it is the ambition to avoid becoming an object of derision, contempt, and pity. The self is here identical with appearance and repute. In anticipation of Sartre's concept of "bad faith," the self is a role tailored to the expectations and opinions of others. "This posture [of putting his cane against his back] was not striking; at most it was a little cocky; the unexpected day of spring might excuse that. No one thought of turning round to look; and now all went well. It went wonderfully well." . . . The self corresponds to what Heidegger calls "das Man." It is the crowd turned inward. Anxious regard for people's opinions becomes the yardstick for self-judgment. This self can be equated with the loved ones in Malte's (and Rilke's) doctrine of love, who are dependent on their lovers, try to live up to the role expected of them, and allow their lovers to determine them. Insofar as the lovers tolerate and foster this self-enslavement of the beloved, they themselves are not genuine lovers. Only by transcending the beloved and no longer hoping for love returned can they fulfill the force and freedom that true love is. Short of that, neither partner in a love affair lives authentically, in the freedom and pure activity of emotion that true love is. In the false lovers' case, the self takes its measure from the partner; in the spastic's and in Malte's case, from the others, the impersonal crowd, the faceless "Man" or "people." Insofar as the self depends on the recognition and regard accorded to it by someone else, it is a façade and not a truth, and the defeat of its wish to appear to others in a certain light is, in a sense, a liberation of its truth. This is what the scene with the victim of St. Vitus's Dance shows.

As we have seen, his self consists of his maneuvers to conceal the terrible force that lies waiting inside him. The inward truth in his case is his sickness coiled inside him to be released. The victim's desperate attempt to hide what victimizes him is a form of vanity or shame, a pretense at being what he is not, or what Kierkegaard called the first stage of "the sickness unto death." Malte identifies completely with the victim of the nervous disease. He follows him, anxious and fascinated, down the whole length of the Boulevard St.-Michel, and would like to help him with a portion of his own strength. The thoughts that he projects into the sick man are, of course, all Malte's own thoughts. The sick man is Malte's *alter ego,* literally a projection of his own self and situation. Like the sick man, Malte is anxiously concerned about his external appearance. The same anxiety dominates him as the sick man—the fear of letting it be seen that he is about to lose his footing and slide down into an inconceivably shameful condition. He too makes strenuous efforts not to forfeit the semblance of normality and bourgeois respectability, even though these have long ceased to correspond to his real state of affairs. (pp. 180-82)

[The] afflicted creature on the Boulevard St.-Michel becomes a symbol and prefiguration of Malte's own existence. The wretch's pathetic clinging to his respectability, embodied in his cane, cannot resist the gigantic force welling up in him and waiting to break out from under his pitiful pride. And as he gives in and his will collapses, something incomparably greater, mightier, and truer leaps forth from him. ". . . and then he gave in. His cane was gone, he spread out his arms as if about to take off and fly, and there burst out of him something like a natural force and bent him forward and pulled him back and made him nod and bow, flinging the power of the dance out of him into the crowd. For many people had already gathered around him and I saw him no more." . . . (p. 183)

This is a scene of horror, which leaves Malte utterly empty and exhausted. A human being, with whom the narrator identifies, loses his dignity, in fact his human status. Will and consciousness prove impotent. Man is helplessly handed over to his dreadful disease and to the pitiless derision of the world. A self goes under, literally, when we think of the concluding words of the scene: "For many people had already gathered around him and I saw him no more." The reader is depressed and crushed by this total defeat of human self-control, this total loss of the autonomy of the human will. We share Malte's dreadful melancholy in witnessing the event.

But Rilke gave the advice to read his **Malte** "contre son courant" ["against its current"]. In light of this advice, we must raise the question whether a purely negative evaluation of this scene is justified, no matter how strong the first impression would speak for it. For the depressing content is contradicted by a linguistic structure that clothes and surrounds this destruction of the self with a triumphant exultation. Choice of vocabulary and syntactical structure show the defeat and dissolution of the will as the liberation of an enormous power. The expansive gesture, the spreading out of his arms, with which

the dancer lets go of his cane, indicates relief and liberation. How paltry and false his previous clinging to the cane now appears from the vantage point of this gigantic expansion of arms to wings! The image makes the positive aspect of the ego's destruction appear more significant than the negative meaning suggested by the narrator's perspective and the reader's preconceptions of what man should be. Seen as pure description, the gesture presents a liberation, a broadening and freeing of the figure. In the context, it is a liberation from the constant burden of having to suppress what is strongest within oneself. We have seen how this self had previously been intent on holding back, on keeping down, on covering up, on oppression, pretense, and façade. The main function of the conscious self seemed to be not to allow what was most important inside to become visible—the compulsion to dance that was vibrating in his muscles and nerves.

The simile "as if about to take off and fly" raises the horizontally expansive gesture of the spreading of arms to the vertical dimension of wings going into action. The simile "like a natural force" counteracts all associations of degeneration and negativity implied by the idea of the nervous disorder, and elevates that which the conscious will sought to repress to the rank of a force that not only overwhelms man, but is also in accord with, and part of, nature.

The following phrases, connected by the paratactic conjunctions "and"—"and bent him forward and pulled him back and made him nod and bow"—must of course appear to Malte and to the reader as describing utter horror. For these phrases show man degraded to a puppet and, in the cruellest way, mock our sense of human dignity. However, as Jacob Steiner shows in his discussion of the symbol of the puppet in Rilke's fourth elegy, the puppet embodies for Rilke the highest degree of authenticity. The fact that in the puppet "there is no background (no reaching into interiority and memory) guarantees that appearance and depth are not separated . . . into pretense and actuality, as they are in the human dancer." In **Malte,** too, the puppet or puppetlike condition can be interpreted affirmatively, if the text is read "against the current." The description of the afflicted man's fit, which reduces him to the state of a puppet, is framed, on the one end, by the majestic similes that compare his attack to "a natural force" and, on the other, by the exhilarating metaphor that shows the victim as flinging "the power of the dance" to the crowd. Word order and syntactical structure thus show the following: Negativity—that is, the grotesque reduction and destruction of the human person—is bedded into a highly positive, uplifting, and expansive phrasing. The paratactic arrangement of the sentence most intimately conjoins positive and negative evaluation and, in fact, equates them. The destruction of the individual thus appears as the reverse side of a tremendous expansion and elevation. Destruction becomes, as it were, the necessary precondition for the release of elemental power. The grammatical structure—"something" being the subject, bursting out of the person, and the person being the helpless object in its grip—precisely embodies the existential situation shown. Impersonal force completely dominates the individual. This sentence structure thus represents the total reversal of the accustomed subject-object relationship. Man, who normally conceives himself and is conceived as the subject and ruler of the world of objects, here appears as the defenseless object of the impersonal "something." This "something" attains the rank of "a force of nature." At the same time, it is the donor of the joyous power of the dance. What it takes from the individual, it squanders on the crowd. It transforms man's loss into the enrichment of mankind. (pp. 183-85)

Our reading of the scene on the Pont du St.-Michel shows linguistic formulation in contradiction to the writer's conscious perspective, which, however, filters the scene to the reader. What is actually described stands in contrast to the way it is experienced. It is a striking confirmation of the need to heed Rilke's advice and read his novel *contre le courant*. Throughout the novel, the scenic presentation runs ahead of the conceptually formulated insights. The dance shows in purely scenic terms, without conceptual grasp and comment, something that Malte will later, in the second part of *The Notebooks,* be able to formulate explicitly. In the second part of *The Notebooks* Malte distinguishes between a "bad" fear and a "genuine" (or authentic) fear, a distinction in which [Otto Friedrich] Bollnow sees the heart of the book. This genuine fear increases with "the force which produces it. We have no conception of that force except in our fear." . . . This fear is the token of a power within us that is accessible to our consciousness only negatively, namely as fear. Thus fear is the yardstick for our strength. For this strength "is so utterly inconceivable, so totally opposed to us, that our brain disintegrates at the point where we strain to think it. And yet, for some time now, I have believed that [this fear] is *our own* power, all our power, which is as yet too great for us. . . . we do not know it, but is it not that which is most our own of which we know the least?" . . . (pp. 185-86)

The scene of the dance expresses this insight by its linguistic and visual terms. That which Malte describes there is the eruption of an enormous power that threatens and crushes the self, and makes it disappear. Yet, this power has welled forth from the depths and innermost recesses of the same self that it destroys. It is the self's own power that transcends the empirical ego so far that it can and must be experienced, at least at first, as menacing and destructive strangeness. Even after the encounter in the creamery, Malte had had an inkling of this: "Only one step," he tells himself, "and my profound wretchedness would be bliss." . . . The structure of *The Notebooks* is such that that "bliss" shows itself first as its reverse. In the novel itself, Malte never attains this bliss. It remains mere wish and projection. The last sentence of *The Notebooks* contains the words "not yet." But throughout the metropolitan inferno that Malte has to go through, that possibility of an unknown "bliss" is somehow present, the way, in the "negative theology" of Karl Barth, God speaks to us in and through His absence.

The structure of the dance closely corresponds to the poetics contained in *Malte.* We have already, in connection with the dying in the creamery, referred to the passivity and lack of resisting will, which point to an entirely new way of writing. "There will come a day when my hand will be far from me, and I shall bid it to write, and it will write words I shall not mean." Passivity appears as the poet's openness to his inspiration, which the mind's deliberate intentions would only block. The grievous process of self-abandonment will be the precondition for inspiration. The hand that writes will no longer obey the conscious mind, and it will write down words not intended by the self. And yet, the image of the hand far removed from the self shows that the dissolution of the ego is at the same time a tremendous expansion of the self. For this hand that will refuse to write down the words commanded by the ego will yet be Malte's own hand. It will still belong to him and begin to write at his bidding. Thus the self will not have vanished. It will be removed from the control of that narrow and superficial segment which is conscious intention. It will no longer be subject to what the ego "means." But in exchange, the space between Malte and his hand, which is the self in a larger and greater sense, will be enormous and extend into cosmic reaches.

This future type of writing—what Malte calls "the other interpretation"—can be compared to the wild dance dictated by a deeper force within the victim. As the ego-destroyer *par excellence*, this force is surely "against us." Yet it is "our strength," it is that "which is most our own." The efforts marshaled to repress this power constitute a kind of self-alienation, since they aim at preserving a pretended self, an appearance of "normal" respectability, in place of the real and total self which includes the dance. The pedestrian clinging to his cane and desperately courting the effect he intends to achieve, symbolizes, like Malte himself, that which Heidegger was to call "das Verfallen des Daseins" ("the fallenness of *Dasein*"). This façade, this pretense of health, is not the dancer's "own life," but only an effort to live up to the expectations of others. It is a deception which reality unmasks. His "Eigenstes," his "ownmost" is not the impression he tries to make, but the gigantic power which he seeks to conceal and which is called disease.

When this "ownmost" achieves its eruption, it establishes the possibility of a much more real relationship between the self and the others than the image of "normality" he tried to cultivate. That image amounted to an apparent and negative tie to others. It aimed at a negation, at not arousing attention and derision. Now, however, the barrier of negativity has fallen, and there is an acknowledged link between the dancer and his public. Instead of guarding against being noticed, he flings "the power of the dance" "among the crowd." He infects and moves them, and the crowd literally receives him. We are told that he disappears in it. For Malte's eyes, he has become one with the multitude, and no distinction is left between the self and mankind.

Thus we have arrived at the synthesis of the two apparently antithetical principles embodied in Malte's blood—the Brigge principle of individuation and the Brahe principle of the simultaneity and unity of all states of being. That which is most profoundly our own, the principle of the Brigges, is at the same time that which overwhelms and dissolves us as separate, individual entities. The old chamberlain's "own death" is, on the one hand, the crowning of unique authentic existence. On the other hand, this authenticity is by no means the same as the empirical self or ego, but on the contrary is hostile to it. Growing within him, as the fetus in the womb, his death metamorphoses the personality of old Brigge and makes it strange to all who had known him. His maturing death usurps the self's place. It is no longer Brigge who rules at Ulsgaard, but his death, and that is something very different, as Malte explicitly transcends and annihilates it. Thus the culmination of what is most "our own" is at the same time a falling asunder of ourselves. Fulfillment is transformation and transcendence of that which is fulfilled. That which is most our own is always that which completely transcends our empirical self. It is precisely the Brigges' insistence on the authenticity of "their own" that, if carried out with sufficient thoroughness and consistency, permits the advance toward the realm of the Brahes, where what is our own is no longer felt as distinct from all being. This expansion of the self to a cosmic dimension can only proceed by the devolution of the empirical personality or ego. For, as our analysis of the St. Vitus's Dance scene has shown, the ego is the elaborate concealment of the self's true reality. (pp. 186-88)

> *Walter H. Sokel, "The Devolution of the Self in 'The Notebooks of Malte Laurids Brigge'," in* Rilke: The Alchemy of Alienation, *Frank Baron, Ernst S. Dick, Warren R. Maurer, eds., The Regents Press of Kansas, 1980, pp. 171-90.*

EVA MERRETT FRIEDMAN (essay date 1981)

[*In the following excerpt, Friedman discusses the similarities between the problems of human existence portrayed in* Malte *and those which concerned the philosophers of Existentialism.*]

The alienation of modern man and the enigma of existence have been the cynosure of modern philosophers and thinkers like Kierkegaard, Jaspers, Sartre, and Heidegger. Rainer Maria Rilke grapples with this existential question in the *Notebooks of Malte Laurids Brigge.* In these *Notebooks,* which are concerned with man and his destiny, Rilke the artist confronts reality and lays bare the crisis of existence. Man, stripped to his essence without his facade, is pitted relentlessly against his forlorn existence.

Before one goes more deeply into the problem of human existence as presented in these *Notebooks,* it is essential to observe the form of Rilke's prose work. The style is one of plastic presentation; there is neither the image of the artist's innermost feelings as in the lyric, nor the chronological sequence of a protagonist's destiny as in the epic. Rather, the *Notebooks* appear to be a kaleidoscopic series of pictures and inner visions, which are only loosely bound together. Yet the experiences and perceptions contained in the work do combine to form a unified representation of an inner revelation.... [Rilke] calls this novel a "mosaic" of letters and fragmentary notes. The *Notebooks* then are a kind of personal inventory-taking, while serving at the same time as a pattern for the future. Henceforth, there will merely be different arrangements and dispositions of the stock on hand, but nothing will be lost from the total inventory. Evidence of the importance of this stock-taking may be gathered from the fact that, with the exception of the *Elegies,* no other work drew from the author such abundant, if not altogether consistent self-exegesis. This is not surprising since the *Notebooks* are an amalgam of personal experience. They represent the conscious artistic transformation of experience. It is important, however, that one find in these diaries more than the purely personal thoughts and reminiscences of an anguished poet and more, too, than the mere biography of Rainer Maria Rilke during his sojourn in Paris. The fundamental theme of this seemingly haphazard conglomeration of reflections and experiences is, quite simply, the ontological question of Being or existence.

Now one can understand why these *Notebooks* occupy a focal position in Rilke's total literary output. Having begun them in 1904, he did not complete them until 1910, after a long period of anxiety and anguish.... The *Notebooks* represent for Rilke, as *The Sorrows of Young Werther* represented for Goethe, a literary catharsis. Both Goethe and Rilke place all their spiritual and physical anxieties into the soul of a character created in their own image. The problematical childhood of Rilke is recreated in Malte, who wishes to "realize" his childhood once more. Rilke, however, cautiously denies that this work is totally autobiographical.... There can be no doubt that fiction and autobiography alternate in these reminiscences. The critical

difference between Malte and Rilke lies in the fact that the artist Rilke, like his predecessor Goethe, triumphs in the end, while Malte perishes, although the question of his destruction is uncertain and has been debated by the poet himself. During the course of the *Notebooks* Rilke emerges more and more estranged from his creation, Malte.... Thus, we see in the figure of Malte Laurids Brigge not only a self-portrait of Rilke, but an embodiment of the whole problem of existence.... As Rilke himself states, the *Notebooks* are supposed to be a scheme or projection for existence, a "Daseinsentwurf." He is concerned with the human being's ability to exist, an ability which can realize itself only within finite limits and laws. He explores the tragedy of man's time-bound and basically solitary existence. No matter how writers before Rilke had regarded the world—whether as a cosmos, as evolution, or as an order—they always had a particular understanding of existence.... For Rilke, however, existence as such is no longer seen as self-evident. Rilke felt his spiritually disinherited state to be truly representative of the human condition, particularly in his own age and in its culture, so that it became imperative for him to experience that condition to the full. The relentless pursuit of the existential questions about the individual and his alienation begin in German literature with the *Notebooks.* Rilke's Malte is a unique personification of this "Ausgesetztsein" of a human being separated from all objective existential associations. Thus, he stands as a major literary figure at the beginning of the existential movement particularly as formulated by Heidegger.

Rilke creates in his *Notebooks* poetically what Kierkegaard had pronounced philosophically: "Man is an existent," *ein Existierender.* The central position which the experience of fear occupies in the *Notebooks* can hardly be comprehensible without Kierkegaard's concept of fear.... Rilke's and Malte's fundamental experience, "Urerlebnis", is this fear and anguish. The anxiety of existing, of performing one's existence, "das Dasein zu leisten", becomes the ethical task of both. To the concept of more severe suffering and increased anxiety there is a special signficance attached, for it is that which differentiates the hypersensitive, quasi-seismographic individual from the mere mass.... It is the very nature of life to be fearful and despairing. Images of horror reveal their essential meaning only when one learns to comprehend them as an act of self-discipline. The attempt to harden a hypersensitive, decadent, enervated being is described in Malte Laurids Brigge. In his neurasthenic sensibility Malte recognizes himself as "cowardly," as someone who is far too inclined to turn away and elude the fearful, but who forces himelf to look, whether it is a blind newspaper-vendor or a man struck down by St. Vitus's dance.

In Malte's childhood as well as in Rilke's, mysterious and eerie things, "das Unheimliche," had played a major role. The ghostly encounter in Rilke's youth with the "hand" is a poetic formulation of this experience. Malte finds this experience too full of terror to communicate it to others, because words might bring back the reality of the event. In this situation the child is drawing in a dimly-lit room and then bends down into the darkness under the table in order to search for a lost crayon which had fallen behind it. As the child is groping along the floor, he suddenly comes upon another hand, ghostlike, emerging from the wall that is reaching for his own. Fascinated and then filled with fear, he frantically tries to bring his own hand back to safety and finally succeeds before succumbing, exhausted, to his terror. It is thus the experience of an uncanny object which shocks the human being in his innermost soul.

Essential to note here is the nameless, inexpressible anxiety, which from here on in takes hold of Malte. It will continue to breed fear and terror. This very same eeriness manifests itself again in the masquerade and the reflection in the mirror. Malte designates it as "das Grosse." In Malte's recollections we find the omnipresence of terrifying experience that lurks behind the familiar and apparently harmless surface of things, a mysterious and threatening life. . . . As Heidegger later on will speak of the thrownness, "Geworfenheit," of our life, so Malte describes the sicknesses, the hideousness, the morbidity, and the creeping dehumanization in Paris. . . . Now he encounters reality directly, since he is able to pierce through the deceptive veil of accepted conceptions. The impression touches the point of existence, "den Existenzpunkt," and penetration as well as reflection sets in. This point of existence is filled with anxiety. . . . Now he commences to ask about the existential assumption of the *Dasein* ["existence"]. Malte learns that man is limited to this finite world and separated by an unbridgeable chasm from absolute Being. However, a formulation of Being and man's relation to it does not necessarily indicate an ability to enter into relation with it. (pp. 33-6)

Malte falters, for he cannot assume an active role towards the *Dasein* and is unable to come to grips with the potentials of his existence, of being one's self, (eigentliches Selbstdasein).

Malte's inability to break through and realize his existential potential causes his downfall, although Malte's death or even ultimate disaster is nowhere explicitly made clear. As an artist Malte cannot overcome the negative elements of life, nor, as a human being is he capable of existing in that life. In his all-encompassing anxiety he experiences the enigma and the alienation of the aesthetic existence even more dramatically than Jacobsen's *Niels Lyhne* or Thomas Mann's *Tonio Kröger*. He is an insecure candidate for life, "unsicherer Lebenskandidat," who cannot take a viable position vis-a-vis "the elements of life."

Rilke made it his task to point out and lay bare the inwardness, "Innerlichkeit" of an individual, from the vastness of which existence can constantly replenish itself and eventually make itself invulnerable. In Malte's anguished travels through life Rilke presents the forlornness and alienation of modern man: his anxiety and his defenselessness before the hostile world and his longing for the love of God. But, God is here, as expressed in the parable of the Prodigal Son, one aspect of love, not its object—a concept obviously born under the influence of Kierkegaard. This alienation or fallenness, to use Heidegger's terminology of modern existential man, is aptly expressed in Rilke's own words: "Was im *Malte Laurids Brigge* ausgesprochen eingelitten steht, das its eigentlich nur . . . dies: wie ist es möglich zu leben, wenn doch die Elemente dieses Lebens uns völlig unfasslich sind? Wenn wir immerfort im Lieben unzulänglich, im Entschliessen unsicher und dem Tode gegenüber unfähig sind, wie ist es möglich, *da zu sein?*" ["What is expressed in the suffering that is written into *Malte Laurids Brigge* is really only . . . *This:* how is it possible to live when after all the elements of this life are utterly incomprehensible to us? If we are continually inadequate in love, uncertain in decision and impotent in the face of death, how is it possible to exist?" (Translation by Jane Bannard Greene and M.D. Herter Norton)] (pp. 38-9).

> *Eva Merrett Friedman, "Existence and Alienation in Rilke's 'Notebooks of Malte Laurids Brigge'," in The University of Dayton Review, Vol. 15, No. 1, Spring, 1981, pp. 33-47.*

WILLIAM H. GASS (essay date 1984)

[*Gass is an American fiction writer and critic. Widely praised for the virtuosity of his prose style, he is among the most conspicuous modern proponents of the view that literature's sole meaning lies in the aesthetic forms an author creates with language. This position is developed in two collections of critical essays,* Fiction and the Figures of Life (1971) *and* The World within the Word (1978), *and forms the creative principle of the stories of* In the Heart of the Heart of the Country (1968), *the novel* Omensetter's Luck (1966), *and the long essay* On Being Blue (1976). *As opposed to the representational theory of art, which holds that literature should be a rendering of human experience more or less in the manner of history or journalism, such essays as "The Medium of Fiction" and "Philosophy and the Form of Fiction" disclaim the injunction that fiction should, or indeed is able to, present anything to the reader except an aesthetic pattern composed of rhetorical devices and the poetic qualities of words themselves. This is exemplified by Gass's demonstration in "The Concept of Character in Fiction" that a character may be defined as a series of verbal strategies focusing on a proper noun which in turn serves as one element among many in a larger aesthetic design. Applied to a given work of literature, this critical approach dispenses with psychological, social, moral, or any other consideration which would attempt to offer the meaning of that work in nonliterary terms. While such an abstract account of Gass's work might suggest that his is a purely decorative form of literature, one exclusive of human emotion, he has in fact criticized such writers as Samuel Beckett and Jorge Luis Borges for just such a lack of feeling, and he has made it clear in many of his works that for him the rhetorical substance of literature is perfectly capable of embodying, in aesthetic form, all the passions of life. In the following excerpt, Gass discusses the ways in which Rilke's aesthetic philosophy is revealed in Malte.*]

Rilke had initially thought to title these pages, ***The Journal of my Other Self,*** and in many ways it is a better choice than the one he settled on. The novel we have now is made of two notebooks of nearly equal length, yet none of these entries is very notelike, unless a musical meaning is meant. The prose is too polished, the thought too refined, the sentiments too considered. The prose is constantly pushing at its edges, enlarging its capacities for expression. There can be little doubt, either, that the work is therapeutic and projective; that in its pages Rilke endeavored to confront, and overcome, the nightmares of his present life. True, it is about another self, because even if his surrogate's name has the same phonological shape as his own, it is the northern, Dane-touched Rilke who appears as a character in the novel, not the sensual, southern one; it is not the Malte who sees and speaks of ghosts, but the Rilke who harkens to the Angels, who writes it, and, in writing it, succeeds in escaping its protagonist's ambiguous fate.

Nonetheless, the word 'journal' suggests that these spoon-sized paragraphs are likely to contain doses of daily life's more commonplace medications; and that a familiar temporal progression is going to give a straightforward course to the work; when it is the psychological climate and not the clock that counts. It is a felt world which arises around us. At the same time, the phrase 'of my other self' identifies the author with his fictional agent so narrowly that the wider reaches of neither can be appreciated. Even if every observation in the text has been brought up from its low birth in rude fact, and every thought and feeling is one which Rilke at one time entertained like a guest for lunch; even if some of the transformations come to no more, immediately, than making an address ("11 rue Toullier") into a date ("September 11th, rue Toullier"); the sum of the alterations, omissions, and additions is significant, because Rilke saw and thought and felt strongly about far more things than he permits Malte to see and think and feel. Rilke (as any fine novelist must) will see "all round" his hero the way Henry James once arrogantly claimed to see "all round" Flaubert.

Malte's extraordinary lucidity may mislead us about the bars which frame his vision. There is no Rodin in this book to humble Malte's artistic claims; there is not mention of the glory and the menace of Cézanne, who meant so much to the development of Rilke's art during the time he spent writing this book; there is no intimation of success or greatness; there are no passages, such as those which occur in his letters to Clara, for all their gloomy remonstrances, which evoke the vitality and sensuality of the city.

There is simply a sudden end to the notebooks, as if their author had no interest in beginning a third, or as if the third were lost, or as if Malte Laurids Brigge were no longer alive.

No. Rilke is not Malte. Yet Malte *is* Rilke. Just as matter and mind, for Spinoza, were essential but separate aspects of one natural whole, so Malte is an aspect of Rilke—Rilke seen with one "I". And Malte, when he describes the remaining interior wall of a demolished house (to choose a celebrated example), is penetrating more fully into things that Rilke or Rodin or any one of us would, if we were merely walking by on some Parisian sidewalk, because this vision, like so many others, is an observation taken home, and taken to heart, and held warmly there until it rises like bread. Anyone can stand still and take notes. Quite a different eye or recording hand *constructs one thing out of its response to another*. It is the artful act of composition that creates the emotional knowledge which such passages contain—the metaphors of misery and shame and decay which arise like imagined odors from the wall. Thus Rilke comes into possession of this knowledge in the same moment Malte does; but he does so (and consequently suffers a stroke of synethesia, smelling the ugliness he has just seen) because he is imagining Malte; and Malte, to be Malte, must make these discoveries; must run in horror from this wall which he feels exposes his soul to every passerby like a flung-open coat. One probably cannot say it too often: writing is, among other things, an activity which discovers its object; which surprises itself with the meanings it runs into, and passes sometimes with apologies, or recognizes with a start like an old friend encountered in a strange place.

Rilke has little idea where his project is heading. It has no head: that is the trouble. Bits and pieces of his book are accumulating. They have a thematic and emotional unity. They are uncentered insights. That's all. And the pain of Paris has receded somewhat. To finish his work he will have to return to Paris eventually, but the old wounds won't open as widely as before. How to continue? Worse: why continue? The difficulty is familiar. To re-bleed isn't easy. (pp. xiv-xvi)

At first, Rilke has thought he would attach a small preface to the notebooks indicating to the reader how they had presumably been acquired, but later decided against it, which was wise: first, because to pretend to honesty by calling a mess by its right name will not remove it; second, because the fragmentary and chaotic condition of the text at that time needed no further emphasis (even the suggestion of looseleafery in the novel's name is enough to mislead many critics), and because now Malte's body, as well as the fate of his soul, lies in a deeper darkness than mere dirt or damnation can contrive. (p. xvii)

Back in Paris (it is now 1907), his book begins to mature and to assume a shape, but there is an important change of tone. The second part, or afterhalf, is a progressive transformation of the thematic material of the first. Malte's early obsessions (with alienation, fear, poverty, loneliness, art, disease, death) continue to occupy his thoughts, and figures from the past are still called up; but Malte's meditations on death, for instance, are first mingled with, and then gradually replaced by, his reflections on the notion of a non-possessive passion (the idea of one's own *Tod* ["death"] is supplanted by an ownerless *Liebe* ["love"]); loneliness is more and more that emancipating distance between lovers which we have already seen symbolized in the wave which is both greeting and goodby; alienation begins to look like a defiant freedom; other kinds of dreams, and different ghosts, preoccupy Malte now: the indistinct forms of saintly women, temporally distant kings; while his graphic impressions of Parisian lowlife are overshadowed by his equally intense experiences of ancient texts, often equally grim and macabre, particularly demonstrated by his grisly description of the maggot-infested, rosette-shaped wound in the center of the chest of Charles VI. What is said, early in the first notebook, to be "the main thing" (that is, to survive), is no longer, in the second, "the main thing" at all ("the main thing is just to keep drawing," to remain faithful to one's art). And the initial commandment: to learn to see, is followed by another, later: to take on and learn the task of love.

The final section of the first notebook, and the initial section of the next, are both given over to a description of the *Dame à la Licorne* tapestries which are on display in the Cluny Museum, and to the girls who come to contemplate and sketch them. These pages form a hinge between the novel's two halves. The girls are from good families, Malte imagines, but they have left their homes; no one any longer takes care to see that all the buttons down the backs of their dresses are properly fastened. They are prodigal daughters, entranced momentarily by emblems, by this ethereal, floating, simultaneous, enigmatic world . . . a woven world, static, pictorial, plastic, even as this novel is, although its images are rarely so benign. And the young girls, enamored, begin to draw. The objects they wish to reflect on their tablets, perhaps as the mirror which the woman holds reflects the unicorn and the unicorn's lone white horn back at itself, are, in their way, eternal objects—images which can be safely, purely, loved. Here all passions come to rest like a splash caught by a camera so the wild drops glint like gems, and their frantic rush remains serenely in one place, in the path of a few threads.

In their families, Malte remarks of the girls, religion is no longer possible. "Families can no longer come to God." And in families, if one shares an end or object equally with all its other members, "each gets so shamefully little." And if one tries to gain a little more of liberty or local love or leisure of one's self, disputes will arise. Such thoughts, again, approach those of Spinoza. These girls, before they have known the fat but actually fragile pleasures of the flesh, are able to lose themselves in their drawings for a moment; lose themselves, and thereby realize another kind of love: a love which allows them to take into an almost unfolded soul, like a bee between hesitant petals, "the unalterable life that in these woven pictures has radiantly opened in front of them." Of course, as ordinary girls—as anybody's kids—they want to change, grow up, have their loneliness embraced by another's loneliness; they believe they want to enjoy that promised world where one pleasure is supposed to follow another like sweetmeats tamely to the mouth. Yet not in all young women is the shining, still image of this other—ethereal—love suppressed. And Malte begins to recite the names of his "saved ones," his "blessed"—those whose dedication survives all indifference, cruelty, or rejection, because it contains a love which refuses to enslave or possess its object, but paradoxically insists upon increasing the selfhood, the freedom, the plenty, the being, of what is loved.

Rilke was a rather accomplished caricaturist, even as a child, and his eye is a painterly and plastic one. It is his punishment as a poet not to be able to shape and fondle and bring forth *things*. The lyric poem, too, of which he was one of the last great masters, is only typographically a linear event. Its words interact in all directions to produce an entity whose nature it is to occupy a space—a space which song sings us through like a gracious guide from room to room, but whose structure we grasp as a single simultaneity.

The eyes, the lips, of the reader move, then, and as they move, the music of the work begins; those moving lips sustain it; but, for this great novel, it is as if the eyes were lighting here, then there, upon the surface of a series of tapestries, observing in each place the signs: symbols like the figures of the lion and the lady, the little dog, the silver moons, sung above an oval island. Another significant clue to the character of this fiction is contained in the passage which almost immediately follows Malte's meditation upon *la Dame à la Licorne;* namely, the section in which Malte remembers when his mother unrolled for him the antique pieces of lace she had collected. Malte, even more susceptible to "ecstacy" and loss of self as a child than he will be as an adult, is gratefully absorbed into the realms their lacelight shapes create. He becomes enmeshed in the luxurious leaves and tendrils of one design; he crosses the bleached fields of another, suffering from its chill white winds, its frost. And in the weave where he is happily caught are also the women who sewed and directed and knotted the threads—there, in the linen, in lieu of a lesser heaven. These epitomal pages, which are so occupied with ghostlike, archetypal, and mystical episodes, also include this epiphany of their novel's slow unspooling movement.

Like the tapestries, the laces have a fixed yet enrapturing esthetic design, and their delicate art redeems, from a life of merely "what's expected," those women who might have been otherwise wholly wasted. (pp. xvii-xxi)

Rilke has basely encouraged and nobly earned the affection of many fine women by the time his novel appears in 1910, although their numbers will increase, and although he is fully aware of what these feelings normally mean. His conception of an intransitive love is certainly a defense of his own needs and an apology for his own behavior, but that does not lessen its interest or even increase its novelty, since it is at least as old as the average idea.

Because you are loved, Rilke found (and he interprets the parable of the Prodigal Son in these terms when he chooses to conclude *Malte Laurids Brigge* with it), you are expected to serve your lover, whose feelings have been left like a kitten in your care. Because you are loved, you become the victim of many benevolences which your lover wishes to bestow upon you, but which you are scarcely prepared to receive. Because you are loved, your work, which is a rival much admired but not more jealously betrayed for all that, will have to step aside so that the loving one can be comforted by your attention, assured of your devotion by the degree to which you are pre-

pared to neglect yourself, abandon your principles, release your dreams. Because you are loved you will be offered a physical intimacy which will be perceived as conferring spiritual rights. Because you are loved, you are now fuel for another's fire; and the Prodigal Son does not wish to burn from outward, in. The Prodigal Son flees the embrace of the world, and when he returns he does not desire to be forgiven his departure. *To be loved means to be consumed in flames. To love is to give light with inexhaustible oil. To be loved is to pass away; to love is to endure.* These are Malte Laurids Rilke's hard words. And they have provoked rather stern, angry, and anguished responses.

However, to anyone whose work has to do with the unity of heart and mind in the service of some truth, or the pursuit of some distant ideal of justice or beauty, these words do not seem wide of the mark but rather its eye; for when one compares the concern of the poet for poetry, the philosopher for the good, or that of the physicist for the more abstractly material for mulation of what's finally real, all other adorations (now that the love of the gods has got the go by) come to resemble merely plant or animal appetites; and how well we know those plant and animal appetites! and how they put the objects of their solitude in immediate danger of their teeth, in more distant, slower danger, of their roots.

"Who speaks of victory?" Rilke writes in one of his poems. "To endure is all." The love of God which Malte Laurids Brigge yearns for is actually a license for his own love. Even when the courtly poet loves, in love with love itself and each of its amorous rites, the object of that love, already half imaginary, must nevertheless be worthy. Its pursuit, its contemplation, must furnish the inspiration necessary to sustain the poet's efforts. It need not *do* anything, but it must *be*. Spinoza cannot call "God" some ignominious thing; and although Nature, as that divinity, is certainly indifferent to him, God *is* God, and deserving of the devotion of such a mind as his. When Art or God or the Good return one's love, permission is the substance of it: they have allowed that service simply by meriting it. Rilke's saintly women, who begin by worshipping vain men—earthly objects, leafless twigs—end by transubstantiating them. There is no other way. Malte's choice of deity, it would appear when the novel subsides, has not yet offered him that opportunity. Hence this strenuous attempt, to substitute for his obsession with death the practice of a liberating love, cannot be deemed a success. *The Notebooks'* last words make a dismal sound. *He* [Malte in the guise of the Prodigal Son] *was now terribly difficult to love, and he felt that only One would be capable of it. But He was not yet willing.* Here, the second book breaks off.

It may be that the love which this work asks for is also of the non-possessive kind, although it has certainly received a surfeit of the other sort. In any case, by writing it, Rilke succeeded in furthering the art of fiction so far as to make its continued practice forbidding if not impossible. From its readers, as well, *Malte* requires a wholly different dedication; it requires a *gaze*. Paradoxically, it is just such difficulties which drive us on, so that the novel has become more beguilingly daunting for every age of its existence. As readers too—*look!*—brought to a standstill before the page—how wide, now, we must widen our eyes. (pp. xxi-xxiv)

William H. Gass, in an introduction to The Notebooks of Malte Laurids Brigge *by Rainer Maria Rilke, translated by Stephen Mitchell, Vintage Books, 1985, pp. vii-xxiv.*

ADDITIONAL BIBLIOGRAPHY

Baer, Lydia. "Rilke and Jens Peter Jacobsen." *PMLA* LIV, Nos. 3, 4 (September; December 1939): 900-32, 1133-80.*
　　Examines the impact Rilke's relationship with Danish poet and novelist Jacobsen had on Rilke's life and thought during the years in which he composed *Malte*.

Batterby, K. A. J. *Rilke and France: A Study in Poetic Development.* London: Oxford University Press, 1966, 198 p.
　　A biographical discussion of Rilke's experiences in France, with frequent references to their impact on *Malte*.

Bauer, Arnold. "The Monologue of *Malte Laurids Brigge*." In his *Rainer Maria Rilke,* translated by Ursula Lamm, pp. 69-80. New York: Frederick Ungar Publishing Co., 1972.
　　Draws connections between Malte's perception of Paris and Rilke's admiration of French visual art.

Bethke, Frederick J. "Rilke's *Malte Laurids Brigge* as Prose Poetry." *Kentucky Foreign Language Quarterly* XII, No. 2 (1965): 73-82.
　　Maintains that the relationship of form and content in *Malte* is harmonious and poetic.

Duroche, Leonard L., Sr. "The Perception of Space in Rilke's *Malte Laurids Brigge* and in Kafka." *Perspectives on Contemporary Literature* V (1979): 97-106.*
　　Discusses the "phenomenology of space as an aspect of body-image" in *Malte* and several of Franz Kafka's works.

Garber, Frederick. "Time and the City in Rilke's *Malte Laurids Brigge*." *Contemporary Literature* XI, No. 3 (Summer 1970): 324-39.
　　Examines techniques Rilke employed to structure *Malte*.

Herd, E. W. "An Interpretation of *Die Aufzeichnungen des Malte Laurids Brigge* Based on an Analysis of the Structure." *Seminar* IX, No. 3 (October 1973): 208-28.
　　Contends that a "structural analysis [of *Malte*] shows that the major themes (oppressive reality of the city, childhood, death, and love) are introduced and arranged in such a way as to produce a progressive linear structure, which traces the development of Malte as an artist. At first impotent in the face of the horror of reality, he succeeds, by immersing himself in childhood memories, in overcoming his fear of death and disintegration through a process of learning to see, then to write, and finally to love."

Leppmann, Wolfgang. *Rilke: A Life.* Translated by Russell M. Stockman in collaboration with the author. New York: Fromm International Publishing Corporation, 1984, 421 p.
　　Translation of Leppmann's 1981 biography.

Lyon, Laurence Gill. "Related Images in *Malte Laurids Brigge* and *La Nausée*." *Comparative Literature* XXX, No. 1 (Winter 1978): 53-71.*
　　Compares the imagistic parallels in *Malte* and Sartre's first novel.

Madsen, Borge Gedso. "Influences from J. P. Jacobsen and Sigbjörn Obstfelder on Rainer Maria Rilke's *Die Aufzeichnungen des Malte Laurids Brigge*." *Scandinavian Studies* XXVI, No. 3 (August 1954): 105-14.*
　　Discusses Rilke's familiarity with the works of Danish poet and novelist Jacobsen and Norwegian poet Obstfelder and their impact on the themes of *Malte*.

Mandel, Siegfried. "Love is Fear." In his *Rainer Maria Rilke: The Poetic Instinct*, pp. 78-109. Carbondale and Edwardsville: Southern Illinois University Press, 1965.
　　Discusses the childhood scenes in *Malte*.

Martens, Lorna. "Autobiographical Narrative and the Use of Metaphor: Rilke's Techniques in *Die Aufzeichnungen des Malte Laurids Brigge*." *Studies in Twentieth Century Literature* 9, No. 2 (Spring 1985): 229-50.
　　Argues that "in Malte's notebooks, Rilke creates a new model for autobiographical narrative, where Malte himself figures as the 'absent' subject of book or the 'unnamed' subject of metaphor. Malte gains in authority as a first-person narrator by turning from self-deception to oblique self-presentation, and from referential to figurative language."

Parry, Idris. "Malte's Hand." *German Life and Letters* n.s. II (October 1957): 1-12.
　　Discusses the significance of the hand imagery in *Malte*.

——. "Apollo in the Snail Shell." In her *Hand to Mouth and Other Essays*, pp. 101-15. Manchester, Eng.: Carcanet New Press, 1981.
　　Discusses how Rilke's relationship with sculptor Auguste Rodin influenced his composition of *Malte*.

Peters, H. F. "Hamlet in Paris." In his *Rainer Maria Rilke: Masks and the Man*, pp. 69-95. Seattle: University of Washington Press, 1960.
　　General discussion of the major themes and techniques of *Malte*, the background to its composition, and its significance within the context of Rilke's work.

St. Aubyn, F. C. "Rilke, Sartre, and Sarraute: The Role of the Third." *Revue de Litterature Comparée* XLI, No. 2 (April-June 1967): 275-84.*
　　Compares *Malte* and Nathalie Sarraute's *Portrait d'un inconnu* in light of Jean-Paul Sartre's definition of the "role of the third, the unknown Narrator."

Schoolfield, George C. "Rilke's *Malte* and Schack Staffeldt." *Kentucky Foreign Language Quarterly* III, No. 3 (1956): 136-40.*
　　Considers the minor Danish poet Staffeldt a possible model for Malte.

Shaw, Priscilla Washburn. "The Self." In her *Rilke, Valéry and Yeats: The Domain of the Self*, pp. 3-41. New Brunswick, N.J.: Rutgers University Press, 1964.*
　　Examines factors in Rilke's novel which threaten Malte's developing concept of selfhood.

Wilson, Colin. *The Outsider.* Cambridge, Mass.: Riverside Press, 1956, 288 p.*
　　Important text which centers on the theme of alienation in literature, with references to *Malte*.

Jacques Roumain

1907-1944

Haitian poet, novelist, journalist, essayist, and short story writer.

Roumain was a leader of young Haitian intellectuals who, during the late 1920s and the 1930s, sought Haitian autonomy and an end to the American military occupation of Haiti. His literary themes support his belief in "art for people's sake" and are most strongly presented in the militant, racially conscious poetry of *Bois de'ébène (Ebony Wood)* and the coalescence of Marxist theory and artistic expression found in the novel *Gouverneurs de la rosée (Masters of the Dew)*. A cosmopolite who studied the literatures of Europe, the Americas, and the Caribbean, Roumain sought to create works that were at once indigenous, universal, and in accord with the spirit of Negritude.

Roumain was the oldest of eleven children born to a large landowner and his wife, whose own father was former Haitian president Tancrède Auguste. A member of the upper middle class, he attended one of the most prestigious schools in Port-au-Prince and in 1921 was sent to Grünau in Switzerland to complete secondary school. There Roumain became familiar with and was influenced by the works of Friedrich Nietzsche, Arthur Schopenhauer, Charles Darwin, and Heinrich Heine, and with the art and philosophy of the Near East. An introspective, reflective, and sometimes melancholy student, he wrote poetry during his hours alone, but also participated in a variety of athletic activities, observing that sports satisfied something of the "excess of life which I have." From Grünau he went to Zurich and prepared for advanced studies in engineering, but somewhat abruptly decided to study agronomy in Spain in order to develop his grandfather's land in Haiti. By 1927, mounting Haitian opposition to American occupation and to the conciliatory pro-American government lured Roumain home to join activists fighting for Haitian nationalism.

In 1927 Roumain helped found the Haitian reviews *La trouée: Revue d'interet general* and *La revue indigène: Les arts et la vie* with the goal of politically and culturally educating Haitian youth. *La trouée* proposed to confront major national problems, but Roumain found that its literary standards were weak and that its expression of political ideas ran counter to its stated orientation, so he resigned by the journal's second issue. *La revue indigène* was more successful, in his opinion, publishing poetry and fiction by Roumain and other Haitian contributors as well as French and Latin American literature in translation, with Roumain serving as the principal translator. Roumain also contributed to the leftist newspaper *Le petit impartial*, published by George Petit, who, with Roumain, became vice president and president, respectively, of the *Ligue de la jeunesse patriote haitien*, established to unite divergent social levels of Haitian youth. After an article highly critical of the French clergy appeared in *Le petit impartial*, Roumain and Petit were arrested and held for seven months. Within months of their release they were again arrested, charged with scheduling an unauthorized meeting of more than twenty people.

A series of strikes and civil disorders in Haiti during 1929 and 1930 led the U.S. government to appoint a commission to consider ways to arrange a peaceful transition to a more popular

government in that Caribbean state. Recognized as a nationalist leader, Roumain was among a group of opposition representatives who met with the U.S. commission and chose Eugene Roy as the new provisional president of Haiti in 1930. Roy appointed Roumain head of the Department of the Interior, a position he resigned within a few months to campaign for Sténio Vincent, who won the first presidential election in late 1930 and reappointed Roumain to his former post. During this period Roumain published *La proie et l'ombre, Les fantoches,* and *La montagne ensorcelée,* fiction imbued with his strong sense of the division between the largely mulatto Haitian middle class into which he was born and the black masses with whom he sympathized and identified. His disenchantment with the nationalist government, which had effected no appreciable change in the economic and social conditions of the peasants and laborers after American withdrawal during the mid-1930s, reinforced his growing attraction to communism as prescribed in the writings of Karl Marx and Friedrich Engels. He met with American Communist party officials in the United States, and this, along with his refusal to accept the offer of another government post, brought Roumain under suspicion, leading to surveillance of his movements and inspection of mail and packages intended for him and his associates. Late in 1932 a letter by Roumain detailing a proposed strike by Haitian laborers, scheduled to coincide with the 1933 harvest of the

American Sugar Company's crop, was confiscated. Roumain's subsequent imprisonment was given wide press coverage, inspiring strongly negative sentiment toward him and others who sought to undermine a still popular nationalist government by encouraging the intrusion of communist outsiders. Upon release, Roumain openly declared his allegiance to communism and founded the Haitian Communist party. In 1934 he was arrested, accused of participating in an anti-government communist conspiracy and sentenced by a military tribunal to three years in prison. Communism was outlawed in 1936, and after his release from prison Roumain fled with his wife and son to Belgium.

In Belgium Roumain studied pre-Columbian art and history; after moving to Paris in 1937, he also studied ethnology and other related subjects. While in Paris he associated with such antifascist journalists and intellectuals as André Gide, Romain Rolland, and Louis Aragon, and wrote articles and fiction for European journals. In 1939, just days before France declared war on Germany, Roumain left Paris for the United States. There he met several admiring American writers, including Langston Hughes, whom he would later honor in poetry and who became one of Roumain's translators. Roumain began graduate courses in anthopology at Columbia University, but left for Cuba at the invitation of the communist poet and journalist Nicolas Guillen. After working for a short time as a journalist in Cuba, he returned home to Haiti, which was now under a new government that had offered amnesty to political exiles. Roumain soon established the Bureau de'Ethnologie to oversee the excavation, classification, and study of items found at various archaeological sites related to Haiti's indigenous history. He was later appointed charge d'affairs to Mexico. Roumain died of a heart attack at the age of thirty-seven.

Roumain's poetry and fiction, though limited in quantity by the author's political activities, arrests, and emigrant existence, reflect his changing political ideas and his growing knowledge of world literature. In the early poetry the direct influence of French Romanticism is displayed in the use of established themes, form, and imagery. "Pluie," "Midi," and other animistic poems employ animals and nature to express human emotions, which in these works are predominantly melancholic. In other works, a lone poet or prophet seeks to understand the universe, aspiring to knowledge of an unknown realm outside himself and ultimately despairing of its attainability. This despair is often evoked through mystical or celestial imagery that contrasts light against darkness. Critics note that while many of these works are particularly concerned with traditional forms, others introduce free verse and surrealist elements which were new to Haitian poetry. In later revolutionary and militant poetry, thematic content became the poet's primary preoccupation. Regarded as didactic polemics by most critics, these works self-consciously seek to link nationalist and Negritude movements through the use of the Creole patois spoken by the majority of Haitians and rhythms and images based on African music and dance. Among this later verse, the title poem in the collection *Ebony Wood* makes metaphorical reference to the human "logs" stacked in ships and transported to build the new world; "Nouveau sermon negre," one of Roumain's anticlerical poems, attacks a white-dominated church that brainwashes converts into oppression and servility; and "Sales negres" invokes a catalog of derogatory labels designed to denigrate Africans, Asians, Jews, and others in order to psychologically reinforce misconceptions of racial superiority and inferiority. Although often dividing humanity along racial lines, the poems do distinguish between white oppressors and the white worker,

who is also considered a victim. However, the strong racial sentiment in such poems as "Ebony Wood," which in the end calls for brotherhood among "workers and peasants of all countries," often overshadows hope for interracial reconciliation.

Unlike his poetry, Roumain's fiction was from the beginning concerned with Haitian problems. *La proie et l'ombre* and *Les fantoches* examine the psychology of hopelessly passive young intellectuals, a "lost generation" unable to accept the old ways and unequipped to replace them. Their search for an identity often leads them to petty and sordid diversions in Port-au-Prince after dark. Critics have suggested that the success of these works with Roumain's contemporaries is due more to their recognition, identification and sympathy with the characters than their literary qualities. *La montagne ensorcelée* is set in a peasant village far removed from the urban setting of the early works. While the tension between passivity and action is again central to the story, this novel is considered most notable for Roumain's ambiguous attitude toward the religion of voodoo. Critics note that unlike other literature of the time, which sensationalized specific aspects of voodoo, *La montagne ensorcelée* neither ridicules nor exploits this traditional practice, but instead seriously examines its importance to the Haitian peasant as well as its negative implications in a modern society in which solutions based upon superstition reinforce feelings of powerlessness. Carolyn Fowler considers Roumain's shifts in narrative voice, which she regards as masterfully imperceptible, responsible in large degree for the ambiguity that makes the novel so unsettling: for example, French is used by an objective narrative voice, Creole by the "rational" voice of the peasants who have been exposed to other ways of thinking, and patois by the uneducated peasants, who represent a provincial viewpoint. The peasant novel considered Roumain's masterpiece is *Masters of the Dew*. The traditional plot of the novel renders it easily understandable on a realistic, superficial level, while an intricate system of symbolism lends it literary and psychological depth. Told in poetic language heavily laden with nature imagery, *Masters of the Dew* equates images of drought, barrenness, and hopelessness with the lack of cooperation that lowers the quality of life for feuding families. Many critics contend that the religious symbolism and biblical imagery in the novel support an interpretation of the protagonist Manuel as a Christ figure. Beverley Ormerod and others, however, disagree, and argue that Roumain clearly rejects God as the caretaker of black people in this and other works, and suggest that, in fact, Manuel's religious parents are depicted as symbols of passivity and lack of productivity. J. Michael Dash agrees that the novel expounds obviously socialist ideals, but concludes that such elements as Manuel's gift of water to the village, of productivity through procreation, and peaceful harmony through his refusal to seek revenge serve to move the reader emotionally before they convince intellectually.

Roumain's intellectual dexterity and worldliness lend an experimental quality to works that borrow techniques from the French literary tradition and introduce the distinctive psychological viewpoint of the Afro-Haitian. Answering critics who consider Roumain's works nothing more than ideological tracts, Dash has stated that Roumain's "concern with the individual will and the quest for spiritual fulfillment show the extent to which he was very much a Romantic individualist rather than an ideologue whose main interest was conformity to Marxist ideals. It was really his strong moral conscience that drove him to the secular creed of Marxism. . . . Ultimately Roumain emerges as a modern artist concerned with the fate of the creative imagination in a world of broken continuities."

PRINCIPAL WORKS

La proie et l'ombre (short stories) 1930
Les fantoches (novel) 1931
La montagne ensorcelée (novel) 1931
Gouverneurs de la rosée (novel) 1944
  [*Masters of the Dew,* 1947]
Bois d'ébène (poetry) 1945
  [*Ebony Wood,* 1972]

Translated selections of Roumain's poetry have appeared in the following publications: Fitts, Dudley, ed., *An Anthology of Contemporary Latin-American Poetry;* Collins, Marie, ed., *Black Poets in French;* and Hughes, Langston, and Bontemps, Arna, eds., *The Poetry of the Negro: 1746-1949.*

LANGSTON HUGHES AND MERCER COOK (essay date 1947)

[*Hughes was an American poet, novelist, dramatist, and lyricist whose prolific forty-year career brought him international recognition. Considered one of the leading intellectuals and spokespersons of the Harlem Renaissance literary movement, he has written humorously but insightfully about black people and the relationships between black and white people in America. As a poet, Hughes extolled the beauty and uniqueness of black culture and people, and often imitated the rhythms of jazz and blues in his verse. Among his best known works are the poetry collection* Fine Clothes to the Jew *(1927), the novel* Not Without Laughter *(1930), and his autobiography* The Big Sea *(1940). Hughes has also translated works by such writers as Nicolas Guillen and Roumain, and his own poetry has been compared to Roumain's. Cook, an American critic, editor, and essayist, lived in Haiti and has written and translated works about Haitian literature and culture. He has also written critically about black authors writing in French, English, and African languages. In the following excerpt from their introduction to* Masters of the Dew, *Hughes and Cook praise Roumain's literary achievements.*]

Roumain belonged to one of the first families of Haiti. His grandfather, Trancrède Auguste, had been president of the Republic. Money and position were part of Roumain's heritage. In addition, he had been blessed with the physique of an athlete and the features of a god. It would have seemed only natural for him to adopt the smug, ostrich-like attitude, still prevalent in a few Haitians of his class, who have chosen to ignore the realities of racism and exploitation. Instead, at the outset of his career, he served notice of his militancy by writing polemics inspired by the intense nationalism which the American occupation of his country provoked.

A logical outgrowth of this nationalism was the *Revue Indigène*, which Roumain founded in 1927, thereby inaugurating the new Haitian literature with its increasing awareness of things Haitian, of the African rather than the French background.

> 'Tis a long, long road to Guinée
> And death will guide you there.

So began one of his poems of this period. . . . Likewise, in one of his best known lyrics, **"When the Tom-Tom Beats,"** . . . he asked:

> Do you not feel the sweet magic of the past?
> It is a river which carries you far away from
> the banks and leads you towards the ancestral
> forests.

Other poems, mostly of social protest, appeared in various periodicals, anthologies, and in *Bois d'Ebène,* a booklet of verse posthumously published by the author's widow. In this collection, there is a forceful refrain characteristic of Roumain's revolt:

> que les nègres
> n'acceptent plus
> n'acceptent plus
>
> d'être vos niggers
> vos sales nègres.

Roumain's unusual scientific training, obtained at the Musée de l'Homme and elsewhere, found expression in several monographs, many articles, and in the Haitian Bureau of Ethnology, which he created. As early as 1930 he tried his hand at fiction. His first works—*La Proie et l'Ombre* and *Fantoches*—dealt with the Haitian scene, but in a manner that reflected the influence of the French Decadents. Dominated by a sense of futility and pessimism, these volumes treated primarily of the so-called elite Haitian. The following year, with the publication of *La Montagne Ensorcelée,* he discovered his most effective medium: the peasant novel. Exile, scientific research, imprisonment, the organization of the Haitian Communist Party, and incessant anti-Fascist activity, prevented further experiments in fiction until the Lescot government named him chargé d'affaires in Mexico City, a kind of honorary banishment that would at least keep him out of prison and provide leisure for writing.

Masters of the Dew (Gouverneurs de la Rosée) was written during Roumain's sojourn in the Mexican capital, and published in Haiti shortly after his death. When it became known in Haiti that we were about to translate the novel, offers of assistance came spontaneously from so many admirers of Jacques Roumain that we are unable to name them all. If *Gouverneurs de la Rosée* was to appear in a foreign language, they wanted to help make the translation as faithful as possible. (pp. vii-ix)

> *Langston Hughes and Mercer Cook, in an introduction to* Masters of the Dew *by Jacques Roumain, translated by Langston Hughes and Mercer Cook, Reynal & Hitchcock, 1947, pp. vii-x.*

LINTON WELLS (essay date 1947)

[*In the following excerpt, Wells favorably reviews* Masters of the Dew.]

Langston Hughes and Mercer Cook, with commendable literary acumen, have translated **"Masters of the Dew"** and introduced Jacques Roumain, "poet, novelist, ethnologist, and uncontested leader of Haiti's younger intellectuals," also well-born and well-to-do, whose sympathy for the underdog and whose death almost three years ago at thirty-eight, after years of imprisonment and exile, are said to have inspired the revolution which succeeded in overthrowing the dictatorial Lescot regime.

"Masters of the Dew" is a violently but beautifully written novel about simple but violent-natured people who inhabit a region so barren and politically despoiled only violence can thrive. If the careful and almost literal translation from the Haitian-French makes the English, especially the dialogue, appear stilted and flowery, Roumain's story of the age-old struggle of primitive man against Nature and bad government is, nevertheless, so absorbing as to hold one's interest throughout its 176 pages and arouse sympathy for its characters.

For here, in brief, is the story of Manuel, the elemental Haitian Negro, returned to his eroded, drought-afflicted, poverty-stricken *terre* after fifteen back-breaking years on Cuban sugar plantations, impressed by the fact that there, as well as in Haiti, workers "got nothing but the strength in their arms, not a handful of soil, not a drop of water—except their own sweat." . . .

Manifestly, this book is a Communist tract: "What are we, us peasants?" demands Manuel. "Barefooted Negroes, scorned and mistreated. . . ." Nevertheless, he continues, "We're *this country*, and it wouldn't be anything without us, nothing at all. . . ." "Ignorance and need go together," remarks another character. "If work was a good thing," says still another, "the rich would have grabbed it all up long ago."

But irrespective of the sermon or your views on communism, you will not lay down **"Masters of the Dew"** without a feeling of deepest sympathy for the poor, ignorant, voodoo-ridden, politics-afflicted, mercilessly-exploited Haitian peasant—more than three million of him existing on only 10,000 square miles of fairly well burnt out soil, engaging in debaucheries to forget and making animal sacrifices in an attempt to alleviate his miseries.

If that should prove true, Jacques Roumain, organizer of the Haitian Communist Party, will not have exerted a well-done effort in vain.

> Linton Wells, *"Elemental Men in Haiti,"* in The Saturday Review of Literature, *Vol. XXX, No. 27, July 5, 1947, p. 14.*

EDMUND WILSON   (essay date 1949)

[*Wilson, considered America's foremost man of letters in the twentieth century, wrote widely on cultural, historical, and literary matters, authoring several seminal critical studies. He is often credited with bringing an international perspective to American letters through his widely read discussions of European literature. Wilson was allied to no critical school; however, several dominant concerns serve as guiding motifs throughout his work. He invariably examined the social and historical implications of a work of literature, particularly literature's significance as "an attempt to give meaning to our experience" and its value for the improvement of humanity. Although he was not a moralist, his criticism displays a deep concern with moral values. Another constant was his discussion of a work of literature as a revelation of its author's personality. In* Axel's Castle *(1931), a seminal study of literary symbolism, Wilson wrote: "The real elements, of course, of any work of fiction are the elements of the author's personality: his imagination embodies in the images of characters, situations and scenes the fundamental conflicts of his nature." Related to this is Wilson's theory, formulated in* The Wound and the Bow *(1941), that artistic ability is a compensation for a psychological wound; thus, a literary work can only be fully understood if one undertakes an emotional profile of its author. Wilson utilized this approach in many essays, and it is the most-often attacked element of his thought. However, though Wilson examined the historical and psychological implications of a work of literature, he rarely did so at the expense of a discussion of*

its literary qualities. Perhaps Wilson's greatest contributions to American literature were his tireless promotion of writers of the 1920s, 1930s, and 1940s, and his essays introducing the best of modern literature to the general reader. In the following excerpt from an essay originally published in 1949, Wilson discusses the relative merits of several of Roumain's works.]

I have read only four books of Roumain, two of them, posthumously published, belonging to his late Communist period. *Bois-d'Ebène* . . . is a collection of poems, or rather, of declamations, which somewhat parallels Aimé Césaire's *Cahier*, but fails of the latter's effect of passionate and cruel veracity. Roumain here invokes for the Negro a self-vindication and self-liberation which are simply his own special version of that now too familiar apocalypse, the victory of the proletariat. Except for a few happy images, *Bois-d'Ebène* seems to me unimportant as literature. So does his novel, *Gouverneurs de la Rosée* . . . , which—one assumes, through the efforts of the Communists—has been translated into English, under the title *Masters of the Dew*. This is simply the inevitable Communist novel that is turned out in every country in compliance with the Kremlin's prescription. You have the struggle against the bourgeoisie, the summons of the exploited to class solidarity, the martyr who dies for the cause—in this case, scientific irrigation. The Creole-speaking peasant hero is fired by a social idealism which he is supposed to have learned from a comrade on the sugar plantations of Cuba, but which he expounds with a *Daily Worker* eloquence that would scarcely have been possible in Creole. When one compares *Gouverneurs de la Rosée* with Lespès' *Les Semences de la Colère*, one sees that the experienced agronome (who has evidently been reading Malraux), though he, too, has allied himself with the Communists, has limited himself to observed fact and allowed himself only such sentiments as may be aroused in a sympathetic official by the spectacle of the trials of the peasants, whereas the radical man of letters, Roumain, has indulged himself in a Marxist fantasy. It is quite evident that Jacques Roumain did not know the black peasants well. But he did know the Mulatto bourgeoisie, to which he himself belonged, and his earlier novel, *Les Fantoches* . . . , which deals with the élite of Port-au-Prince, throws so much light on its subject that one regrets it should not have been projected on a more extensive scale. A blasé young man of society aroused to a rabid race-consciousness by the attentions of a visiting Frenchman to his beautiful fiancée—whom, however, he loves only half-heartedly—and her touching but useless attempt to restore his confidence in her by telling him in Creole that she loves him; the strange experience of one of the guests at a big evening party in a splendid house, when he walks by mistake into a sordid chamber, where the grandfather, an aged general, is found setting up lead soldiers and muttering about campaigns—these scenes have been lived and felt. The attempt to make contact with the people—one is often reminded in Haiti of pre-revolutionary Russia—is dramatized more convincingly by one of the episodes of this novel than by the author's own Marxist exploit in writing *Gouverneurs de la Rosée*. Here a black girl who has put up a fight against the amorous son of her Mulatto employers is rescued from the misery to which they have consigned her by an upper-class intellectual, who demonstrates his exceptional nobility by taking her to live with him without making her sleep with him. Another earlier short novel of Roumain's, *La Montagne Ensorcelée* . . . , is somewhat more convincing than *Les Gouverneurs*, because it does take account of the beliefs of the peasants and not merely of their economic situation. (pp. 115-17)

> Edmund Wilson, *"Haiti,"* in his Red, Black, Blond and Olive: Studies in Four Civilizations, Zuñi, Haiti,

Soviet Russia, Israel, *Oxford University Press, 1956, pp. 71-146.**

JACQUES C. ANTOINE (essay date 1951)

[*Antoine, founder and editor of two influential Haitian literary journals of the 1930s and 1940s, is considered a significant figure in the Haitian literary movement of that period. In the following excerpt, Antoine discusses the unique style of* Masters of the Dew *and its influence on the development of Haitian literature.*]

La Trouée, a review of general interest, began publication in June, 1927, under the direction of Richard Salnave. In July of the same year, a literary journal, the *Revue Indigène,* made its bow under the direction of Emile Roumer. Both had more or less the same contributors and were aggressive and merciless in the campaign for the Haitianization of our literature.

Normil Sylvain founded the *Revue Indigène* together with Emile Roumer, Philippe Thoby-Marcelin, Jacques Roumain, Antonio Vieux, Daniel Heurtelou and Carl Brouard. . . . Though the *Revue Indigène* published but six issues and an anthology, its group of writers accomplished as much for Haitian letters as Ronsard and his six friends did for French literature. (pp. 105-06)

On August 18, 1944, fate struck the Young Generation a mortal blow: Jacques Roumain died after an illness of a few days. He scarcely had time to put the finishing touches on some of his writings which he had planned to publish very soon. On December 22 his novel, *Gouverneurs de la Rosée (Masters of the Dew)* appeared, thanks to his widow and one of his brothers, Michel.

The first striking feature of *Gouverneurs de la Rosée* is its style. In *La Famille des Pitite Caille* and *Zoune chez sa Nainnaine,* Justin Lhérisson, in order to make his style sound natural for his characters, most of whom belonged to the lower classes, had interspersed his French text with Creole words and sometimes had introduced expressions in patois. Instead of following this method, Jacques Roumain had endeavored, in *La Montagne Ensorcelée* to merge the two idioms and had produced a Creolized French both in the patois words grammatically integrated in the text, and in the popular turn of his sentences. This is the procedure employed by the Marcelin brothers in *Canapé-Vert.* In *Gouverneurs de la Rosée,* this blending has produced the most beautiful effects.

Even before Cinéas, Jacques Roumain had seized upon a peasant background for the novel referred to and with an artistry which neither Cinéas nor the Marcelin brothers have revealed. In *Le Drame de la Terre,* the lawyer-author has obviously anticipated the role that he intended to play in the novel, and one finds the Marcelin brothers incredulous or impatient as they consider the motives or emotion of their peasants. Jacques Roumain is nowhere in his book; without injecting his views about the actions of his hero, without even appearing on the scene, he has none the less poured all his sympathy for the Haitian peasant into it. He has done this, thanks to an artistry related to magic by its power of evocation and enchantment, and thanks also to the constant balance that he maintains between his own intimate reactions and those of his peasants. Jacques Roumain was a leader of the masses; he was haunted by a vision of a united Haitian people, a vision which dominated his heart and obsessed his mind. The sincerity of the leader who left a life of luxury to become a social menace for his own class, was perhaps responsible for that balance which

allowed his peasants to live in him while he lived in them. His power of suggestion is such that, notwithstanding the reality of his peasants and of the village of Fonds Rouge where the events of *Gouverneurs de la Rosée* take place, a broader world emerges from his pages: the entire Haitian community, of which Fonds Rouge appears as a symbol. And it is in the symbol alone that one sees Jacques Roumain.

The author of *Gouverneurs de la Rosée* has written it for all Haitians and there are words of hope in his book, words which make us vibrate with body, heart, and mind linked by a common bond. (pp. 119-20)

> Jacques C. Antoine, "Literature: From Toussaint Louverture to Jacques Roumain," in An Introduction to Haiti, *edited by Mercer Cook, Department of Cultural Affairs, Pan American Union, 1951, pp. 93-120.**

NAOMI M. GARRET (essay date 1954)

[*In the following excerpt, Garret discusses Roumain's poetic ideals and the themes and techniques employed in his works.*]

Roumain was haunted by a vision of a united Haitian people, a vision which dominated his actions and obsessed his mind; he knew that this could be achieved only by securing a better life for the oppressed masses. As a result, he turned his back upon a life of luxury to become a social menace to his class and a spokesman for the inarticulate masses. His courageous fight for the Haitianization of the total culture of his country won for him the enviable position of uncontested leader of the young intellectuals of Haiti. (p. 107)

In an interview with one of his group, Roumain sets forth his ideas on poetry. For him a poem is a drama which alone is the source of emotion. This dramatic emotion is not to be confused with the artistic emotion that results from satisfaction of a thought well turned; he exacts more than this of a poem. What he wants, he says, is "la force vibrante qui secoue. Le moteur." He cites his **"Cent mètres"** as an example. . . . In his conception, a poet is "un être qui vit. . . C'est le barde antique, adossé aux colonnades et déversant le trop plein de ses sensations. Et c'est pourquoi je me refuserai volontairement à suivre toute règle. Cet oiseau, qu'est la poésie, meurt, en cage."

Relative to the form of a poem, Roumain believes that this should be decided by the prevailing practices of an age. He has no mistaken idea that his group will hit upon the "final form" of Haitian poetry; he knows that they will be considered "vieux jeu" by younger generations.

As one of the leaders of the movement to reconcile Haitians with themselves and with their background, Roumain's ideas on the literature of his country are important. Like others of the young Pléiade, he condemns the past writers of Haiti for their lack of breadth in vision and absence of interest in the people. He credits them with having read French authors only, and only a few of those, whose renown had reached the island republic. He laments their failure to show any interest in the literature of the rest of the world or to keep abreast of the march of literary ideas. (pp. 107-08)

Roumain agrees with Normil Sylvain that it is natural and advisable for Haitian poets to follow the French masters in the forms chosen for their verse. Both of them refute the idea that the French can furnish models of "sensibilité" for Haitians and they advise the study of the works of people whose backgrounds contain elements similar to theirs. Therefore, Roumain advocates the inclusion of Latin-American poets in the reading of intelligent Haitians. . . .

To assist in the education mentioned above, Roumain translated for the readers of *La Revue indigène* selections from several Latin-American poets. . . .

Roumain proves to be the first of his group to become acquainted with the Negro poets of the United States and to realize that their ideas and ambitions are similar to those of Haitians. (p. 109)

Roumain reveals in his poetry the disillusionment, the unrest, and the despair which characterized [his] generation. In **"Insomnie,"** one sees the poet in a state of depression, overwhelmed by a fatigue that is more the result of a heavy heart than of physical exertion. He seems to find rest only in accepting the condition that he is powerless to throw off. . . . (p. 110)

Roumain's desire for the Haitianization of the literature of his country is exemplified in the source of most of the subjects of his poetry. These he found in the traditions and beliefs of the Haitian masses. One of his best known poems, **"Sur le chemin de Guinée,"** is based upon the belief, popular among the peasants, that the soul returns to Guinea after death. The poem abounds with the things the peasant hopes to find upon his return to his ancestral home. . . . The unusual figures of speech—the singular images of sound, sight, and even smell—added to the rhythm of the poem imbue it with a surprising and touching beauty. (pp. 110-11)

The novel, *Gouverneurs de la rosée* . . . , which is considered by some critics as the best work of fiction to come from Haiti, bears out his saying that "Quelle que soit mon oeuvre, c'est à mon sol que je la dédierai." It is a superbly written work growing out of the peasant life of his country. *Bois-d'Ebène,* a small volume of poems, was published by his widow in 1945. Three of these are of special significance; for, they show the later and more militant Roumain who believed firmly in the principle of equality of man, a principle by which he lived and for which he would have willingly died.

The title poem begins by recalling to the Negro, that erstwhile article of commerce, his sufferings and depredation in all parts of the world, "depuis que tu fus vendu en Guinée," of the wanton slaughter of blacks on their long trek from their homeland. . . . They were strengthened by their songs of suffering and of deliverance, songs that were surpassed in power only by the silence of the blacks. . . . It was a silence caused by lynchings and other brutal and savage acts; but this silence, more cutting than the sharpest blade, louder than a cyclone of wild beasts, will not be stilled. It is a formidable power which rises and calls for

> vengeance et châtiment
> un raz de marée de pus et de lave
> sur la félonie du monde
> et le tympan du ciel crevé sous le poing
> de la justice.

Roumain, who could have easily elected to cast his lot among the more privileged, prefers instead to embrace the fate of these exploited pariahs:

> POURTANT
> je ne veux être que de votre race
> ouvriers paysans de tous les pays.

And here, he changes his perspective and alters the aim of his art. A Comintern inspired view of the uniting of the working classes of all nations into a revolutionary international force supersedes his desire for the joining together of the forces of all Haitians into a power for the progress of his country and race. . . . (pp. 112-14)

"Bois-d'Ebène," written in Brussels June 1939, is brutal in its implications and thought provoking as a commentary upon contemporary civilization.

"Sales nègres" speaks in a similar vein of revolt for

> les nègres
> les niggers
> les sales nègres
> . . . en Afrique,
> en Amérique.

and elsewhere, who have been relegated to conditions of degradation and humiliation. All institutions which have aided and abetted the exploitation of the underprivileged are attacked. The Church, which has taught humility and resignation to the "sort maudit" of these outcasts, has not been spared. Since they have never been accepted on terms of equality with the other children in the so-called Christian faith, it is useless for them to continue. . . . (p. 114)

The poet sees the end of the unequitable position of these victims of ignorance and hatred brought about by the revolt of all blacks from the black belts of the United States, the cane fields of the Antilles, and the jungles of Africa. And they will not be alone. . . . (pp. 114-15)

"Nouveau sermon nègre" strengthens the protest against the Church, its practices and its teachings. Church policy has assigned a new role to Christ; He has been taken from the cross where He was crucified between thieves and placed in the den of the thieves whose traits He has assumed. . . . Just as the Church has reversed its character, Negroes will change the character of their songs; revolt will supplant acceptance and resignation. . . . (pp. 115-16)

Jacques Roumain whose command of English acquainted him with the black poets in the United States found in them kindred souls, fighting the same battles as he. He felt a close kinship with Langston Hughes who shared his interest in the common man and whose poems sound a protest against the lot of the latter. . . . It may not be safe to claim that Roumain was directly influenced by the American; it is a fact, nevertheless, that their themes and emotions are the same. Both are preoccupied with the masses instead of with the individual and recognize that the problems of all the underprivileged are similar. They shared a friendship based upon a common cause. One of Roumain's most touching poems is entitled **"Langston Hughes."**

Roumain, in whose veins the blood of his African ancestors had run very thin, cherished this part of his heritage and devoted much energy to ennobling it in the eyes of his compatriots, some of whom were much more skeptical. Turning his back upon material wealth, he dedicated his life to his ideals. He who refused all laws of expediency and of class sang to the country of his forefathers:

> Afrique j'ai gardé la mémoire Afrique
> tu es en moi
> Comme l'écharde dans la blessure
> Comme un fétiche au centre du village.

He begged her to use his gifts in her fight for redemption. . . . (pp. 116-17)

Loved and respected by his group and worshipped by his younger followers, Jacques Roumain has exerted more influence upon the poets among the latter class than any other member of the Pléiade of *La Revue indigène*. (p. 117)

> *Naomi M. Garret, "Representative Poets of the Renaissance: Poets of 'La revue indigène'," in her* The Renaissance of Haitian Poetry, *1954. Reprint by Présence Africaine, 1963, pp. 86-147.**

BEVERLEY ORMEROD (essay date 1977)

> [*In the following excerpt, Ormerod examines the ways in which Roumain's use of symbols, myths, and legends combine literary and socio-political concerns in* Masters of the Dew.]

A recurrent problem of French Caribbean writing is the difficulty of combining purely literary concerns with those of a strong socio-political commitment. Many a *roman à thèse*, here as in metropolitan France, has been more preoccupied with depicting social injustice or historically inspired neurosis than with creating a delicately-wrought work of the imagination. Jacques Roumain's *Gouverneurs de la rosée* may seem, on first acquaintance, to fall into the didactic category, to be a fictional companion piece to the militantly Marxist poems of the same author's *Bois-d'Ébène*. In bold, simple terms, the plot unfolds the story of a Haitian canecutter (familiar figure of Caribbean oppression, emblem of the centuries of slavery), who returns from fifteen years in Cuba to preach a doctrine of protest, self-help and cooperative action to the apathetic, divided and exploited peasants of his native village. The message is transposed from a proletarian to a rural setting, but its political source is readily identifiable. Yet the way in which the revolutionary goal is expressed lifts the reader away from politics to poetry and indicates the strong elements of myth and ritual which underpin the novel: "Nous ferons l'assemblée générale des gouverneurs de la rosée, le grand coumbite des travailleurs de la terre pour défricher la misère et planter la vie nouvelle." . . . Earth and *coumbite*, dew and water, dust and drought are the recurrent symbols through which the hero's adventure is invested with a legendary quality.

The central situation of the novel recalls one of the most ancient mythical motifs: that of the Waste Land. Pre-Christian vegetation cults, as Frazer and later anthropologists have contended, were based upon the concerns of peoples living in hot and often arid regions, dependent upon rain, or, later, irrigation, for the successful pursuit of their agricultural activities. Roumain, who studied at the Institut d'Ethnologie in Paris and undertook research under Paul Rivet of the Musée de l'Homme; who later founded the Haitian Bureau d'Ethnologie and published two anthropological monographs, would certainly have been familiar with the patterns of vegetation myth. Gods who free imprisoned waters, who fall sick and provoke a state of drought, or whose sexual activities are associated with irrigation, are familiar figures in the legends of India and Mesopotamia. (pp. 123-24)

It is immediately apparent that the plight of Fonds-Rouge echoes that of the Waste Land. "Nous mourrons tous . . .—et elle plonge sa main dans la poussière" . . . : from the opening paragraph of the novel, dust and drought are associated with death. The village and the surrounding rural landscape are desolate, the rust-coloured earth laid bare. Parched humans and animals are assailed by the scorching breath of the wind, and by the harsh cries of the crows that circle obsessively above the diseased cactus hedges. The ravaged earth and all her attributes are presented in metaphors of human suffering and torture. . . . In an extension of the metaphor, the drought is associated with loss of sexual fulfilment through the image of the earth as a woman abandoned by her lover. . . . The sexual deprivation suggested here echoes the castration of Adonis and the legendary king's loss of virility; it also establishes by implication a paradigm of the ideal relationship between the peasant and his land, that of lover and mistress which prevailed in the days of the *coumbite*, when, "par un labeur viril" . . . , men forced the earth to yield up its fruits for their pleasure. Even the logical explanation for the drought—the persistent deforestation of the hillsides by the villagers—is expressed in terms of this sexual image. . . . (pp. 124-25)

It is the hero of the novel, Manuel, who perceives this betrayal of the earth and assumes the rôle of her lover: "je suis planté dans cette terre, je suis lié à cette terre." . . . And here the motif of the Waste Land is assimilated into that broader pattern which Joseph Campbell, in *The Hero with a Thousand Faces*, has termed the monomyth. In the standard monomyth the hero undergoes the processes of separation from the everyday world, mystical initiation or supernatural adventure, and triumphant return as a superior being, often bringing back a divine reward. This archetypal pattern is evident at more than one level of the novel. At the narrative level, the hero has already gone through separation from his village and taken part in a collective crisis of self-awareness during his years in Cuba, where the canecutters are for the first time conscious of being exploited and prepared to take militant strike action to improve their working conditions. It is because of this initiation into the world of politics and class struggle that Manuel is no longer able, on his return to Haiti, to accept passively the poverty and natural disasters which beset the villagers, their exploitation by the petty figures of rural authority, and their attitude of patient resignation which is fostered by voodoo and Catholicism alike. He brings with him the seeds of revolutionary change. Light shines on his forehead when he returns home . . . , and this is not only because he is a Christ-figure, an "Emmanuel", as Michel Serres has shown in his study of the novel's Christian imagery, but also because he is an instrument of socio-political illumination. Like Zola's Étienne in *Germinal*, haloed in moonlight as he preaches socialism to the rapt crowds of miners in the forest meeting, Manuel sheds light. . . . (pp. 125-26)

At a further level, however, where narrative merges into myth and symbol, Manuel's initiatory adventure is the discovery of the spring, and the reward which he brings back is the promise of water, of restored fertility, of a renewal of the "vie tarie" . . . of Fonds-Rouge. The image of light recurs in the context of this gift of water . . . , as it will do, with unmistakeable Christian symbolism, in the context of Manuel's sacrificial death. . . . But although Manuel's blood flows to expunge the fratricidal quarrels of the past; although, in renouncing vengeance, he brings peace and good will to the divided village, the novel is not the wholehearted "reprise sans lacune des *Testaments* de la tradition chrétienne" which Serres . . . maintains it to be. Christianity is used in a literary way by Roumain, as a source of traditional symbols; but as a religious system it is derided by his hero, who predicates a paradise where black angels launder the clouds and tidy up after storms, while white angels sing all day or blow into their conventional little trumpets. . . . After the death of Manuel even the devout Annaïse sees God as pitiless and unjust, deaf to black prayers, as destructive as the drought . . .—and old Antoine assents to this rejection of Christian faith with his ironic "Le Bondieu est bon, dit-on. Le Bondieu est blanc, qu'il faudrait dire." . . . Roumain has indeed incorporated important elements of the Christian myth: the idea of a lost Eden (symbolised in the novel by the African-inspired *coumbite*), the parallel between blood and water, the death of a redeemer figure. But Manuel's sacrifice is not made to save his fellow-men from original sin: in forsaking vengeance his obsessive thought is that he must save the water, must not imperil the irrigation scheme which is to restore the land. When, in describing his burial, the novel picks up the Biblical theme of Christ's love for the world, the traditional phrase is given an ironically literal twist: "ces nègres emportent le cercueil, ils emportent leur frère vers cette terre qu'il a tellement aimée, qu'en vérité, il est mort pour elle". . . . If we examine more closely the symbolic value of the earth, the *coumbite*, and the water and dew of the novel, we shall see that Manuel's death, and his relationship with Annaïse, suggest rituals which go back beyond Christianity to the ancient forms of vegetation cult out of which the Christian concept of a redemptive sacrifice was itself to emerge.

We have seen that the drought-ridden, barren earth is personified as a woman deprived of sexual satisfaction. From the moment of his return, Manuel enters into a relationship with the land based on his perception of it. . . . He visualizes the social reform of rural Haiti in terms of a faithful and intimate interaction between the labourer and his plot of earth: images of divorce and desertion . . . express with imperative urgency the plight of those who abandon the land. But the earth is not an easy conquest: like a long-pursued seduction, his patient search for a source of water reflects and moves parallel to his persistent courtship of the hesitant Annaïse. His discovery of the spring is described in terms of sensual excitement: he is like a boy going to his first lovers' rendez-vous, and when he is sure of success, his intense delight finds expression in amorous physical gesture:

> Manuel s'étendit sur le sol. Il l'étreignait à
> plein corps:
> "Elle est lá, la douce, la bonne, la coulante,
> la chantante, la fraîche, la bénédiction, la vie."
> Il baisait la terre des lèvres et riait. . . .
>
> (pp. 126-27)

This symbolic union with earth and water reflects the mythical association of human fertility with that of the land. Ritual springtime couplings in the fields were common in ancient civilizations, which believed that the release of human sexual energy aided the germination of the seed and also provoked rain. Manuel's subsequent sexual union with Annaïse, who lies on the earth above the hidden spring to receive his embrace, repeats in human terms the mystical moment of his finding of the water, and thus assumes a symbolic, ritual nature. Serres . . . asserts that the human coupling represents a cosmic union between sun (Manuel) and water (Annaïse). It is difficult to perceive any association, other than the light symbolism mentioned above, between the hero and the sun; but Manuel is certainly the lover of the water. Annaïse hails him as "Maître de l'eau (qui) connais toutes les sources, même celle qui dormait dans le secret de ma honte" . . . ; the fusion of natural and human worlds here picks up the earlier motif of Manuel's desire for the Haitian peasant to assume mastery over his recalcitrant female environment. . . . (p. 128)

The notion of fertility in the novel is also related to the lost ritual of the *coumbite*, where, in a survival of African tradition, a team of labourers, led by a drummer whose song set the tempo for their digging, used to work together in the fields for the benefit of all the village. Old Bienaimé's memories of the *coumbite* are of a time of plenty, when men went out early in the morning into the lush Guinea grass, barefoot in the cool dew and the gentle light of dawn, amid a landscape whose rich beauty was a reminder of sensual delight. . . . The *coumbite*, at once formal ritual and informal comradeship, and a last link with the lost paradise of African Guinea, symbolised the harmony of man with earth and of man with his human neighbour. The ritual is destroyed by a quarrel over land inheritance which ends in a murder . . . , and this violent loss of fraternity is associated with the coming of the drought and its allied symbols. . . . In Manuel's vision of the future, *coumbite*, water, reconciliation and fertility are inseparably linked. . . . (pp. 128-29)

Water is the pivot of the story at the literal level; as Serres . . . has demonstrated, it assumes a symbolic quality in the denouement through its associations with the Passion of Christ, whose blood is the water of life, and whose self-sacrifice upon the Cross finds many echoes in the circumstances of Manuel's death. A close reading of the novel shows that water and blood are also associated in earlier incidents. Attacked and brutally beaten by the Cuban rural police during his canecutting years, Manuel is sustained by an inner defiant notion of endurance "comme une source de sang, la rumeur inépuisable de la vie." . . . He visualizes the future irrigation canals as a network of veins bringing life to the very depths of the earth. . . . The murder which has divided the village into two hostile factions is like a stream of blood which cannot be crossed . . . ; in persuading them to unite once more for the irrigation project, Manuel presents the water itself as a literal means of redeeming the past bloodshed: "l'eau lavera le sang et la récolte nouvelle poussera sur le passé et mûrira sur l'oubli." . . . In a further symbolic function, stagnant water represents the physical suffering caused by the drought . . .—and also the state of alienation in which the villagers live. . . . In contract to these stagnant pools, the living water will surge through the future canals, as the words of Manuel now flow with hope and promise, "clair comme l'eau courante au soleil." . . . Water also symbolises the control of one's destiny: the exploited Cuban canecutters own no water save their own sweat . . . ; Hilarion fears the irrigation project because it will make the villagers independent of his exploitative money-lending . . . and, petty tyrant to the last, plans to impose a tax upon the new canals. . . . These notions of freedom and renewal through water are summed up in the title of the novel, where water is present in its most poetic form, as dew.

The ambition of being "gouverneur de la rosée" suggests, by its use of the old term for the former colonial ruler, an assumption of independence by the black peasantry at the socio-political level. Implicit in the phrase, however, is the gaining of a god-like authority over the forces of life and death. In the Old Testament, product of a warm and sometimes rainless region, dew has a vital symbolic value: the bestowing of dew is a blessing from God (as in Deut. 33: 13), and the withholding of it is a curse. In a typical instance of divine retribution, the fellow-citizens of the prophet Haggai are punished with drought for failing to rebuild God's temple: "Therefore the heaven over you is stayed from dew, and the earth is stayed from her fruit" (Haggai 1: 10). Likewise old Délira sees God, in syncretic conjunction with the voodoo *loa*, as having control over water and human life. . . . (pp. 129-30)

Manuel's dying vision of the dew projects into the future old Bienaimé's dream of past fruitfulness—"un champ de maïs à l'infini, les feuilles ruisselantes de rosée" . . .—and by willing the renewal of the *coumbite,* he enables the drought of Fonds-Rouge to become part of a positive cycle of suffering and renaissance. The delicate beauty of the dew encapsules the amorous relationship between Manuel and the earth. Dew is associated with the pride of the labourer gazing at his fields . . . , and with the joy of his wife going out at sunrise to gather the fruit of their land . . . ; it is the reward of the peasant who keeps faith with the earth and thus gains control over his own destiny—"un travailleur de la terre sans reproche, un gouverneur de la rosée véritable." . . . Dew stands for fruitfulness, like the water which brings fertility to the land, like Manuel who brings fertility to Annaïse. . . . On the final page of the novel, the child stirs within Annaïse as the first water flows through the canal towards Fonds-Rouge, and the villagers, led once more by their drummer, run alongside shouting and singing with pride. Thus Manuel's death takes its place beside those of the ancient vegetation gods, Tammuz, Attis and Adonis, who, suffering their yearly ritual death and resurrection, symbolise the eternal cycle of sterile winter and fruitful spring, of collective mourning and rejoicing. . . . It is in the light of these traditions that we should view the apotheosis of Roumain's Manuel, whose resurrection is envisaged not in the asexual terms of Christian immortality, but in a sensual fusion with nature. . . . (pp. 131-32)

> *Beverley Ormerod, "Myth, Rite and Symbol in 'Gouverneurs de la rosée'," in L'Esprit Créateur, Vol. XVII, No. 2, Summer, 1977, pp. 123-32.*

MELVIN DIXON (essay date 1979)

[*In the following excerpt Dixon discusses Roumain's use of folk material to "evoke the African presence" characteristic in indigenous and Negritude literature.*]

Edward Brathwaite has distinguished four kinds of New World literature that evoke the African presence: (1) a rhetorical literature, which uses Africa as a mask and only says the word "Africa" or invokes a dream of the Congo, Senegal, Niger, and other place names; (2) the literature of African survival, which "deals quite consciously with African survivals in Caribbean society" but does not reconnect them with the great tradition of Africa; (3) the literature of African expression, "which has its root in the folk, and which attempts to adapt or transform folk material into literary experiment"; and (4) the literature of reconnection by writers who have lived in Africa and the New World and who "are consciously reaching out to rebridge the gap with the spiritual heartland."

Most important of these developments, and the one most applicable to our study, is the "literature of African expression," for here the writer attempts to remake himself as he tranforms folk material into literary experiment. Illustrating this process of self-discovery is Haitian Jacques Roumain, who took as models for his own literary expression the blues references of Langston Hughes, the sermons of James Weldon Johnson (**"Nouveau Sermon nègre"**), and his native Creole culture. Within this pattern of shared influence across linguistic lines one can speak of a cross-fertilization, an intertextuality among works of New World black literature. Not only was Roumain to learn from Hughes about the transformation of musical forms and folk material, but Hughes learned from Roumain, by translating his poetry, how to convey the peculiar Haitian assonance

and sonority in English. In this respect, the poems "The Negro Speaks of Rivers" and **"Guinea"** present opportunities for interesting structural and thematic comparisons.

Both poems invest language with the power of transforming external folk material, atavistic reference, and the speaking voice itself. The speaker in Hughes's poem discovers a personal identity through his participation by means of language in an African past and a New World present. His racial knowledge is not abstract or romantic but grounded in personal and group behavior to create and re-create history. "I've known rivers," the poem begins, *because*

> I bathed in the Euphrates when dawns were young
> I built my hut near the Congo and it lulled me to sleep
> I looked upon the Nile and raised the pyramids above it.

Action within the past gives the poem an authentic voice for the present and rescues the work from an inappropriately romantic perspective. Man actively participates in human history. He earns his identity through the creation of civilization. The history outside him—rivers "older than the flow of human veins"—becomes his through the poem's near incremental repetition of the phrase "my soul has grown deep like the rivers."

Roumain, in a similar lyrical language, charts a journey into the future based on what the speaker in **"Guinea"** has inherited from the past. The word "Guinea" resonates for a Haitian audience not only because it signifies Africa but also because it identifies the popular belief in Haitian folklore that upon death one will journey to Guinea and join the ancestors. The lyrical tone of the poem differs from the more religious language of James Weldon Johnson's "Go Down Death," or Sterling Brown's more colloquial "Sister Lou," but, nevertheless, it initiates Roumain's search for a figurative language to express the form and feeling of his people. The poem is descriptive of one speaker's journey and prescriptive and instructive in the imperative mood for his audience:

> C'est le lent chemin de Guinée
> La mort t'y conduira
> Voici les branchages, les arbres, la forêt
> Ecoute le bruit du vent dans ses longs cheveux
>   d'éternelle nuit.
>
> C'est le lent chemin de Guinée
> Tes pères t'attendent sans impatience
> Sur la route, ils palabrent
> Ils attendent
> Voici l'heure où les ruisseaux grelottent comme
>   des chapelets d'os
>
> C'est le lent chemin de Guinée
> Il ne te sera pas fait de lumineux accueil
> Au noir pays des hommes noirs:
> Sous un ciel fumeux percé de cris d'oiseaux
> Autour de l'oeil du marigot
>   les cils des arbres s'écartent sur la clarté
>   pourrissante.
> Là, t'attend au bord de l'eau un paisible village,
> Et la case de tes pères, et la dure pierre familiale
>   où reposer enfin ton front.
>
> It's the long road to Guinea
> Death takes you down
> Here are the boughs, the trees, the forest
> Listen to the sound of the wind in its long hair
>   of eternal night

It's the long road to Guinea
Where your fathers await you without impatience
Along the way, they talk
They wait
This is the hour when the streams rattle
    like beads of bone

It's the long road to Guinea
No bright welcome will be made for you
In the dark land of dark men:
Under a smoky sky pierced by the cry of birds
Around the eye of the river
    the eyelashes of the trees open on decaying light
There, there awaits you beside the water a quiet village,
And the hut of your fathers, and the hard ancestral
    stone
        where your head will rest at last.

In the repetition of the droning phrase "C'est le lent chemin de Guinée," Roumain establishes a link to Haitian folk culture. And in his use of the "o" sound for near rhyme and rhythm, he approximates the open vowel sounds of the Creole language, as in "La mort t'y conduira."

When Langston Hughes translated the poem, he was particularly sensitive to this use of language and approximated the texture of the open, sonorous speech. Instead of the literal translation of the line to read "death will lead you there," he chose the sonorous, alliterative line "death takes you down" to maintain thematic clarity and to preserve the tonal quality of the language. The speaker in Roumain's original text, as in the translation, discovers a language through which he can experience death on the literal level and passage from the New World to Africa on the symbolic level. His experience is visual and aural: "Here are the boughs, the trees, the forest / Listen to the sound of the wind in its long hair / of eternal night." The speaker comes to know how the wind is animated, personified. And having established a primary contact with nature, he then discerns the voices of his fathers that accompany his passage through a decaying light that signifies no bright welcome. But rather than feeling an existential gloom, the speaker discovers "a quiet village" beside the water and the ancestral stone upon which he will rest. The repeated "long road to Guinea" suggests a passage that will test the speaker and, as in Hughes's "Negro Speaks of Rivers," make his presence one of active and earned behavior until he endures the darkness of his own fears and earns the rewarding, soft darkness of eternal rest.

Roumain's voice in the poem is that of a learned observer, instructing the uninitiated, who may still need to find—in the folk belief of spiritual and cultural redemption—comfort from the psychic dislocation and abandonment of his past in the New World. By its reference to Africa, Hughes's subjective voice affirms, indirectly, the historical, the folkloric, and, directly, the spiritual journey. Roumain is still groping for language that connects more fully to this rite of passage.

Roumain and Hughes were familiar with each other's work, but when Roumain began to write he composed melancholic, meditative verse that described his feelings of alienation upon his return to Haiti from his education abroad. Roumain's early poetry shows his search for a language to illuminate Haitian reality as the poet's own national identity. Other writers of the *Revue Indigène* were helpful to him, but so were writers of the Harlem Renaissance like Hughes and Countee Cullen. When interviewed by the review, Roumain suggested that Haitian writers become more aware of the flourishing North American black poetry. Years later, Roumain described indirectly how he learned from Hughes to depict the black figurative language of the blues. (pp. 33-7)

Roumain's sensitivity to colloquial speech, music, and folklore as a basis for indigenous figurative language is evident in his long, major poem, *Bois d'ébène* and surfaces again as a rhythmic device in his more political piece, **"Sales Nègres"** (**"Dirty Negroes"**). . . . But the creation of the peasant novel was Roumain's greatest achievement in Haitian letters. *Gouverneurs de la rosée* . . . , translated by Langston Hughes and Mercer Cook as *Masters of the Dew* . . . , shows Roumain's masterful transformation of Creole language, music, and folklore into literary experiment.

In *Masters of the Dew* we encounter the peasant greeting of "Honor," which is answered by "Respect" when one peasant visits another. Roumain transforms that dialogue in the text to indicate an exchange of greeting between Manuel, the protagonist, and his homeland of Fonds Rouge. The hero, after fifteen years of working in the cane fields of Cuba, returns to his drought-stricken village and finds water to irrigate the land. The community, however, is divided by a family feud that prevents the peasants from working cooperatively to build an aqueduct now that water is found. Roumain's use of the oral exchange "Honor-Respect" establishes an internal dialogue between Manuel and himself, and an external one with Nature, with whose life forces he renews his primal covenant and from whom he eventually gains redemption in his martyrdom and sustenance for his community:

> (Manuel) was dull of happiness despite the stubborn thoughts that haunted him. He wanted to sing a greeting to the trees: "Growing things, my growing things! To you I say 'Honor!' You must answer 'Respect,' so that I may enter. You're my house, you're my country.
>
> (pp. 38-9)

Roumain's achievement—transforming specific oral, musical, and folk forms into literature—links him to Hughes in the United States, Guillén in Cuba, and Léopold Sédar-Senghor in Senegal. Oral traditions, transformed, are the cultural elements shared by these black writers. They accomplish the very dictum articulated earlier by Jean Price-Mars that "nothing will be able to prevent tales, legends, songs come from afar or created, transformed by us, from being a part of us, revealed to us as an exteriorization of our collective self." (p. 40)

> Melvin Dixon, *"Rivers Remembering Their Sources,"* in Afro-American Literature: The Reconstruction of Instruction, *edited by Dexter Fisher and Robert B. Stepto, The Modern Language Association of America, 1979, pp. 25-43.**

CAROLYN FOWLER (essay date 1980)

[*In the following excerpt from her critical biography of Roumain, Fowler discusses the themes and recurring motifs which appear in both Roumain's poetry and the early fictional works* La proie et l'ombre *and* Les fantoches. *Fowler also examines other aspects of the works, notably characterization.*]

Jacques Roumain's portrayal of the aimlessness of bourgeois existence in *La Proie et l'ombre,* and the implications in his *Les Fantoches* that the "boue gouvernementale" of Haitian politics will remain a real problem after the departure of the marines, were appreciated by his contemporaries, but these works are not typical of the prose literature of the period. *La Proie et l'ombre,* a collection of short stories, appeared in late 1930. (p. 73)

All four stories [in *La Proie et l'ombre*] show essentially the same thematic preoccupations. The protagonists are all young urban intellectuals roaming aimlessly about Port-au-Prince, caught in the empty monotonous pettiness of their existence. Their despair stems from their sense that there is something missing in their lives. They should be capable of more. They are inadequate heroes, incapable of reaching beyond their lives. They realize this in a sudden moment of truth. (p. 77)

The theme of these . . . stories is therefore none other than that already encountered in most of Roumain's poetry of 1927-29. His poetry reflected the hero in various settings: the romantic hero, sensitive, lonely and unhappy; the cosmic hero, just as lonely but reaching beyond himself into the vastness of space, the only bright spot in a universe shrouded in darkness; the valiant hero, fighting for rightful control of his destiny in the society of his compatriots. The hero now, in the early prose, becomes spokesman for a kind of Lost Generation, unable to find fulfillment in the old values and unable to find any new ones, and so existing in a vacuum. It is not the vacuum which ultimately destroys these heroes, but their lucidity about their condition.

But it is not only in the theme that this first prose seems closely related to the early poetry. Certain motifs recur, some of which have appeared in the poetry. Rhythmic buildups into lyric tirades at the moment of lucidity and a use of the self very reminiscent of the lyric or the epic *moi* of Roumain's poetry are also evidence that Roumain's mind is still functioning to a great extent in the poetic mode.

The most impressive of the motifs is the light-darkness antithesis already seen in so much of the poetry. Darkness is announced in the collection's title and enshrouds most of the stories. Occasionally, an image will recall a similar one depicted in the poetry. In "**La Veste**":

> Saivre . . . regarda par la fenêtre. La pluie faisait fondre la lumière du réverbère. De fines aiguilles d'or tombaient. Derrière, la grande nuit vague, le grand silence noir. . . .
>
> (Saivre . . . looked out of the window. The rain was melting the light from the street lamp. Fine needles of gold were falling. Behind, the great vague night, the great black silence.)

We are reminded of the image of the beloved in "**Attente**":

> O les yeux douloureux d'épier le ruisseau d'or
> Que verse sur l'asphalte le réverbère borgne.
>
> (O the eyes sad to watch the golden stream
> which the one-eyed street lamp spills over the asphalt.)

In both passages night, darkness and rain represent vast unending gloom and eternal unfulfilled waiting but are accompanied by the one contrasting spot of light.

Other images found in the poetry seem to repeat themselves with great insistence in the early prose. In reading "**Fragment d'une confession**," one finds oneself immersed in the same poetic universe as in "**Calme**," where the lonely hero, after attempting to reach beyond, finally succumbs. . . . (pp.77-8)

["**Fragment d'une confession**"] also associates silence and space with suspension in time, an association found in much of the early poetry. Expressions such as "courbè sur le passé" suggest the body's futile efforts to escape its contingencies and recall other expressions such as "un homme courbé sur ses désirs morts" ("**Calme**"). The past participate "courbé" recalls other verbs: "je me penche hors de moi" ("**Insomnie**"). The image of the "acrobate tendant les bras vers le but" in this story strongly recalls the images in the early poetry of the outstretched arms, symbolizing the effort sustained, the source of strength called upon to reach the goal. When the arm motif recurs a few paragraphs later, it reveals the failure of the poet's individual effort. And it is at this juncture that the comforting presence of the beloved is invoked:

> . . . Ah, que s'ouvre cette porte et entre une femme aux pas hésitants; qu'elle vienne avec ce mystérieux sourire que je ne connus jamais jusqu'à mon front pesant et mes bras inutiles. . . .
>
> (. . . Ah, that that door might open and a woman enter on hesitant steps; that she might, with that mysterious smile that I never knew, come up to my heavy brow and useless arms. . . .)

Again, we are reminded of certain of Roumain's early poems, which also invoke the comforting presence of the beloved. In the paragraph following, the motif of the hands also appears, symbolizing, as in the poetry, human contact in love:

> Mon Dieu, que s'ouvre cette porte et entre un tout petit enfant et vienne jusqu'à mes genoux et que j'entende sa douce voix malhabile et qu'il mette ses mains puériles sur mon vieux visage. Mon Dieu, peut-être m'aimera-t-il? . . .
>
> (Dear Lord, that that door might open and a very small child come to my knees and that I might hear his sweet, stumbling voice and that he might put his childish hands on my old face. Perhaps, dear Lord, he would love me?)

The story from beginning to end involves the reader in Benoît Carrère's nocturnal quest, up to the moment of final exhaustion at daybreak, when the reader is suddenly catapulted out of the character's private emotional universe by the sudden shift into third-person narrative. The effect is very much like the rhythmic buildup in poems like "**Cent mètres**" and "**Appel**," which implicates the reader in the internal drama of the protagonist and releases him suddenly at the end from involvement in the hero's destiny. "**Fragment d'une confession**" is short, broken up into short stanzaic paragraphs. Given all these considerations, it is perhaps valid to raise the question whether "**Fragment d'une confession**" is not really, after all, a poem.

"**Préface à la vie d'un bureaucrate**," on the other hand, presents an entirely different case. It has a plot, which, however tenuous, functions toward the resolution of a central "problem" announced by the title. It contains as well the usual dialogue and narrative passages and the characterization associated with prose fiction. Yet a lyric interlude interrupts the action toward the end of the story, and at that point the same motif, conveying the same message as in "**Fragment d'une confession**," reappears. (pp. 79-80)

The stories of *La Proie et l'ombre* often evoke gloom and monotony, not solely through surrounding darkness but also through tableaux of an overcast sky and of the sea. Light has an altogether different meaning when it is the diffuse light of day rather than a concentrated spot of light generated by or associated with the solitary, searching hero. In these stories, night typically fades into day, and the day is gloomy, a different form of monotony, as in the opening lines of **"Préface à la vie d'un bureaucrate."** . . . It is not the sunny tropics and the warm, blue-fringed beaches which we see in these stories, but the overcast sky, the murky grey water, the thin, drizzly rain. . . . (pp. 81-2)

If some of the motifs of *La Proie et l'ombre* repeat those of the poetry, others are new. We find over and over in these stories the lonely nocturnal walks through deserted streets contrasted with (sometimes immediately followed by) sudden immersion in a crowd of common folk. The noctambulation represents alienation, whereas the crowds of Creole-speaking blacks represent the Haitian identity which the alienated, intellectual, bourgeois heroes go out nightly in search of. . . . In **"Préface à la vie d'un bureaucrate,"** Michel, on waking, sees his raincoat still dripping from the night's rain, and it reminds him of the moment of his return home. . . . We are not told why the dripping raincoat should remind Michel of his homecoming day, but the fact that the memory directly follows an allusion to nocturnal wanderings is perhaps significant, for it is the same juxtaposition of loneliness followed by sudden immersion in a crowd that we find in other passages in the prose of this period.

Less elaborate but more frequent is the recurrence of the forced smile or laugh. In almost every instance, laughter is hollow, the smile is a sneer or a pose, behind which bitter emptiness is discernible:

Daniel, in **"Propos sans suite"**:

> . . . il éclata de rire. La voix était blanche, tremblait et se brisa avec une sorte de rage. . . .
>
> Le rire fêlé recommençait. . . .
>
> (. . . he burst out laughing. His voice was white; it trembled and broke with a kind of rage.)

Emilio, in **"Propos sans suite"**:

> Emilio fit une curieuse grimace: on eut dit que son rire s'était réfugié dans une ride subite qui tirait ses lèvres, amèrement. . . .
>
> (Emilio made a curious grimace: one would have said that his laughter had taken refuge in a sudden wrinkle which pulled at his lips bitterly . . .)

Michel, in **"Préface à la vie d'un bureaucrate"**:

> Il sourit de ce sourire qui lui était particulier: une sorte de rictus douleureux, qui tirait ses lèvres, d'un côté par deux rides divergents. . . .
>
> Un ricanement intérieur le déchire. . . .
>
> (He laughed that laughter which was peculiar to him: a kind of painful rictus that drew his lips to one side in two divergent wrinkles.
>
> An inner sneer tears at him)

Each succeeding image recalls the ones before it, establishing a kind of metaphoric resonance. The message of empty helplessness in the lives of these young men is transmitted as in

Roumain's early poetry by the indirect means of motif symbolism.

Within the sordidness of the urban setting, here and there images and metaphors allude to the native fruits of Haiti. Such allusions are not usually gratuitous; they give the impression of lush growth and productiveness, of the overabundance resulting from natural, uninhibited growth. These metaphors seem to refocus on that which is indigenous, as contrasted with the gloomy artificiality of intellectualized urban life. Significantly, allusions to fruit occur in passages dealing with women, who themselves are symbols of hope and regenerative power. Sometimes that power is depleted, as in the case of the old peasant woman whom Michel, in **"Préface à la vie d'un bureaucrate,"** had glimpsed the day of his return. But more often, fruit and women still hold the promise of future growth. Crowds of common folk, women, and fruit all seem to represent the essence of Haiti and the source of Haitian life. This symbolism becomes more important as we go from *La Proie et l'ombre* to *Les Fantoches,* where it becomes more closely associated with certain characters and not with others. . . . (pp. 82-4)

Professor Mercer Cook has spoken of the influence of the French Decadents of the turn of the century in *La Proie et l'ombre.* Although Roumain does not speak of such an influence in any of his writings now available to us, certain parallels do exist between his early prose and the Decadents. In their night-time wanderings, Roumain's young heroes often show a propensity for seeking out the dives and hovels of the city. Amid the stale smells of alcohol and cooking grease, the painted prostitutes and flotsam thrown in the sea and washed back up, they comment on man's dismal spiritual state. The heroes of *La Proie et l'ombre* share in common with the Parisians of the turn of the century a feeling that they are witnessing the empty culmination of a civilization. But it is doubtful that the *fin-de-siècle* ethic goes very deeply into the matrix of these stories. The young men of *La Proie et l'ombre* do not seek out depravity because of some genetic degeneracy; they do not seek it as a means of purification or of control over their destinies as do the heroes of the Marquis de Sade and their literary descendants. These young bourgeois of Port-au-Prince are far more humanitarian in their idealism. One is reminded by certain passages more of Baudelarian decadence and fallen angels. (p. 85)

In the heroes of *La Proie et l'ombre,* Jacques Roumain's contemporaries immediately recognized themselves and the author. Almost immediately, the obvious question was posed: Were these stories autobiographical? . . . Quite apart from any examination of its literary merits, young Haitians embraced *La Proie et l'ombre* as a kind of solace. The stories were an esthetization of an inner life which they could recognize as their own.

Carl Brouard avowed that even though only one of the stories was known to him, all of them *seemed* familiar. He agreed with Antonio Vieux that the collection was a "témoignage." But at the same time he implied that that testimonial, the result of Roumain's ability to analyse deep into human motivations, was also the result of Roumain's own analysis of himself. . . . (pp. 86-7)

[Contemporary] judgments seem to be making the same basic assumption. They all see Jacques Roumain the man as a repository for the feelings and aspirations of his generation. The inner life of Jacques Roumain, analyzed and revealed to his peers, reflects the inner life of all of them.

The impulsion of the poet to use himself as model, to effect an esthetic reworking from the specific to the generic, is at the basis of these stories, as it was of the early poetry, and illustrates again their transitional nature. Unlike the poetry, however, these stories have specific characters who move about in more or less well-defined environments (and in the case of **"Préface à la vie d'un bureaucrate,"** must resolve certain problems). This explains why most readers have perceived and drawn meaning from *La Proie et l'ombre* on two levels.

While it seems safe to conclude that the individual soul's journey of the poet-prophet is also a testimony of the anguish of his contemporaries, the relationship between events in the life of the man, Jacques Roumain and those of certain of his characters is by no means as clear. There is strong evidence that certain of the actions and circumstances of some of the characters in *La Proie et l'ombre* parallel those of Jacques Roumain or certain of his associates. (pp. 88-9)

If, in *La Proie et l'ombre,* we find the indirect appeal to the sensitivities of the reader typical of poetry, we also find in it the direct appeal to the reader's powers of analysis typical of prose. While the indirect appeal constitutes an invitation to view the hero from within, to react as one with him, the direct appeal leaves us outside, scrutinizing, not only actions and the motivations for them, but also the milieu in which those actions unfold. In Roumain's first prose publication, the storyteller implicit in the novelist vies still with the impressionmaker implicit in the poet. In *Les Fantoches*, published in 1931, the storyteller comes more clearly into his own, creating more fully developed characters, who move in a better delineated environment and who exteriorize their feelings to a much greater extent through conversation. We find the same motifs of light and dark, of gloomy days and monotonous seas, of nocturnal walks and sudden crowds, of mirthless laughter and fruit and peasant women, as in *La Proie et l'ombre.* But it is more the characters and the opinions they enunciate which carry the theme in *Les Fantoches.*

Les Fantoches traces the lives of three young men: Marcel Basquet, *enfant gâté* of Port-au-Prince society; Santiague, the idealistic and dreamy poet; and Lefèvre, a sincere and dedicated politician. Around them circulate a host of secondary characters, the people who make up their milieu: Irène Estienne, Marcel's sweetheart; Michel Rey, whom we recognize from **"Préface à la vie d'un bureaucrate,"** but now older, resigned, and with a somewhat mellowed cynicism; Jeannette Lange, cool and calculating, who collects lovers almost in her husband's presence; Cosquer, the mathematician, who composes riddles on the theme of life; Albert Lecocq, a Frenchman and Marcel's persistent rival for the attentions of Irène; and Mlle Fattu, Irène's old-maid aunt, ever on the lookout for a suitable match for her ward. The story unfolds through a series of tableaux set in the last years of the American Occupation, just before the national legislative elections of October 1930. (p. 91)

We can recognize in *Les Fantoches* essentially the same theme as in *La Proie et l'ombre.* Lefèvre and Santiague state it in the last pages of the final chapter in a conversation where the word *fantoches* is used twice and which seems intended as the key to the whole book. There is, however, an important difference between this and the fiction published the previous year: the "A quoi bon?" of *La Proie et l'ombre* is no longer an answer but a question which a few courageous men muster enough courage to try to answer. (p. 98)

The book . . . ends on a more optimistic note than any of the stories of *La Proie et l'ombre.* Marcel, Santiague, and Lefèvre,

the principal characters, are the only ones whom we are privileged to glimpse from the inside. Each of the three has a "story" which is in some way resolved at the end: Lefèvre becomes a legislator, Marcel loses Irène, Santiague finds a kind of meaning to existence in befriending Charmantine. Both Marcel and Lefèvre are in conflict, Marcel with himself and Lefèvre with an irrational social system and the irrationality of man, which has spawned it. The poet Santiague has captured through disciplined mental work a kind of visionary equilibrium. He is at a psychological center between the two other men. He is neither happy nor fulfilled; but he is no longer in conflict. But it is Marcel's problem that draws the author's attention. Most of the action involves Marcel, and of the three it is he who must make the most meaningful journey. He is a typical Roumain hero.

Characterization in Roumain's work tends often to be symmetrical or antithetical. The tripartite division of the hero/protagonist in *Les Fantoches* is a case in point. Marcel shares with Santiague a talent for verbal expression. But whereas Santiague becomes absorbed in his writing, Marcel is undisciplined about it and does not believe in what he writes. (pp. 99-100)

Roumain's tendency to pair off opposing characters extends throughout the novel. Lefèvre is at antipodes in every way with his political opponent Marau. Lefèvre is an aristocrat; Marau is a parvenu. Lefèvre appeals to his audience's reason; Marau, to its emotions. Lefèvre's motivations are selfless; Marau's are interested. Lefèvre is quiet and restrained; Marau is loud and boisterous.

Of the two writers, Santiague and Michel Rey, one is productive, the other is a failure. And Marcel wanders between these positive and negative poles. He is attracted very strongly to both. He goes from one to the other, and they both deliver exactly the same message to him: to beware of the empty life he is preparing for himself.

Marcel and Jeannette Lange complement each other in that both are cynical, destructive, and false. They seem to need to destroy in order to convince themselves that they exist. And indeed, they exist only as façades. If Mme Lange is hiding poverty and impotence behind the walls of her stately mansion, Marcel is a *poseur,* as he is called more than once in the novel, and more impressed by Pétion's genteel manners than with Christophe's accomplishments for the new nation of Haiti. Both are going on the pre-Occupation steam generated by their aristocratic backgrounds; the message seems to be that they are running on borrowed time.

Les Fantoches shows also certain affinities with the work of the French Decadents. Mme Lange in particular seems to represent the degenerate end of a noble line. Her seduction of Marcel (who is only one of many) betrays her sadistic character; seduction is her way of controlling and manipulating others. Unlike any of the heroes of *La Proie et l'ombre,* Marcel and Mme Lange purposely inflict pain and destruction. Marcel denies his love for Irène; the only way he can feel competent to cope with it is by turning it on. All of his acts are premeditated; blasé and cynical, he fits rather well a description of the decadent. . . . Of course, the parallel is again valid only on the surface: Marcel's decadent symptoms do not serve as a source of strength to him. Rather, they mask a profound inadequacy to cope with the world and with himself.

In the case of the young women, Roumain has set up an opposition in *Les Fantoches* which he does not pursue in the rest of his fiction. Jeannette Lange and Irène Estiènne, both upper-class, well educated, attractive, and intelligent, may have opposing souls, but this type of opposition does not recur in Roumain's female characterization. What does recur is the antithesis between the bourgeois and the peasant women.

These two classes are invariably cast as representatives of the two extremes of Haitian society: the artificial and the natural, the false and the true. Roumain's young intellectuals are thrown into a dilemma: their need for purity and national-racial identity on the one hand, for intellectual stimulation, fulfillment, and understanding on the other, causes them to fluctuate between one and the other pole. The women of the elite accept unquestioningly the life for which they are destined: a round of parties and evenings on the veranda sipping cool drinks, a world where grace, wit, charm and social standing are ultimate goals. Even Irène, for all her sympathy and intelligence, never gives any indication that she is at variance with these ideals. The women are bewildered and perplexed by the men, who are dissatisfied with that existence but can neither articulate nor actualize anything beyond it. These women are not unsympathetic characters; they are simply products of their upbringing, unquestioning receptacles of the assumptions which rule the society in which they live.

The peasant women are receptacles also, but unlike their European-oriented, upper-class counterparts, they represent the indigenous Haitian. Roumain takes over a device which had existed in Haitian poetry since Oswald Durand, though lately given new life by the generation of 1927, and incorporates it into his fiction: He has his peasant women evoke the native fruits, the free and natural sensuousness and grace of living beings at peace with themselves and their identity. Thus, Charmantine's songs are a long litany of the fruits and streams of the Haitian countryside, and in the nurturing presence of the poet Santiague, they grow as freely and as naturally from her as fruit ripening and falling from a tree. Roumain has a tendency also to describe his peasant women—even the very old ones—in terms of fruits, as . . . with *La Proie et l'ombre*. Such descriptions are much rarer in the case of the young women of the bourgeoisie, who tend to be described more by their mannerisms, their background, their dress. But it is somehow these sophisticated women who emerge as the more credible, the more three-dimensional. The peasant women tend to remain passive, idealized symbols, whereas the bourgeois women act, speak, and *react* to those around them.

The highly developed characterizations in *Les Fantoches* have their beginning far back into the past. Certain characters form a continuity of types. Daniel, Michel Rey, Marcel Basquet are in the main really the same personality but with different names. The hopelessness and despair of each successive character is more elaborately and clearly depicted as those characters acquire more depth under the novelist's pen. We see Michel Rey in youth at his moment of truth, and again, years later, when he has made some sort of compromise with life. His existence clarifies the life ahead for Marcel. That Marcel is a younger edition of Michel is made quite clear in *Les Fantoches* in the beginning chapter where we see the two engaged in conversation at the bar.

Dialogue in Roumain's prose has two functions. Roumain's characters develop certain ideas in such a way that they seem to transmit a covert message to the reader. Roumain makes liberal "borrowings" from his own writing, from theories and experiences that have particularly impressed him or which he is in the process of thinking through. We find, for example,

the Aztec god Huitzilopochtli associated in "**Corrida**" with other images of sacrifice. We find the same god called upon by Michel to illustrate the notion that Christianity shares certain essential traits with pagan rites. Years later, the notion of universal religious practices reappears in more thoroughly thought out form, and as revealed through anthropological investigation, in Roumain's pamphlet: *A Propos de la campagne "antisuperstitieuse"*. And Jacques Roumain the dialectical materialist discussing history as spiral vs history as vertical motion in 1942 newspaper articles ("**Répliques au Révérend Père Foisset**") recalls curiously Marcel Basquet in the copy room of the newspaper *Le Soir,* discussing the implacable determinism of nations and the *"parcours cyclique"* of history. In that same scene, Marcel is made to "borrow" the term *conscience raciale* in one of his essays. *Conscience Raciale* was the title Roumain had given to an essay on which he was working at the time *Les Fantoches* was published. Whether Roumain intended or not, he has invited the reader of *Les Fantoches* to alternate his attention between fictional circumstances and historical author, and thus has given further validity to discussions concerning the extent to which his works are autobiographical.

All of Roumain's literary efforts seem to be an extension of his own desire to do, his desire to push beyond. We see his own attempts to work out ideas and problems through the "borrowings" of his characters. Roumain's need to estheticize his own experiences in order to give ultimate meaning to his aspirations and his ability to sense the continuity between himself and his society rescue his work most of the time from being mere propaganda. (One might perhaps except most of the writings in *Le Petit Impartial*.) Partly because of this felt continuity between himself and others, partly because of the synthesis Roumain seems to have effected between his various activities and his literary expression, he does not distinguish greatly between what his characters do, feel, or say and what he himself does, feels, or says, or wants to convince others of. This synthetic nature of Roumain's own character is responsible for the inevitable (and by no means unjustified) perplexity on the part of the reader as to whether or not he is reading autobiography, whether certain passages at least may not contain autobiographical allusions, whether certain characters "are" Jacques Roumain. . . . Roumain's tendency to display his inner life through his characterizations is also responsible for the sermonizing quality of much of the dialogue; the long harangue on Christophe and the discussion near the end of *Les Fantoches* between Santiague and Lefèvre do not escape it.

Despite the more direct and overt presentation of theme through character and dialogue in *Les Fantoches,* motif symbolism still operates in this novel. Motifs are most noticeable in the final chapter. The hero Santiague appears at the beginning of the chapter, alone in a room bent over a table with a lamp providing the only bright arc of light, with the environing dark, and its negative associations, outside. Later in the scene, Lefèvre will look on Santiague's face and see it illuminated in that light. Santiague's lonely nocturnal walks, his sudden immersion in a crowd of common folk just before he stumbled onto Charmantine, and his alienation and recaptured identity through the peasant woman associated with fruits are all present in this last, important chapter.

The obvious symbolism behind the title is presented in several different ways in this last chapter. When Lefèvre comes in, he flops down into a chair, exhausted:

Son attitude exprimait la plus grande lassitude.
Ses bras pendaient des deux côtés du fauteuil
comme ceux d'un pantin désarticulé. . . .

(His attitude expressed the greatest lassitude.
His arms hung down both sides of the armchair
like those of a disjointed puppet.)

Santiague, speaking of his loneliness, says he peoples it with
the insignificant, wretched folk he meets in his noctambula-
tions:

Ainsi, je meuble ma vie de quelques person-
nages, qu'à certaines heures je fais jouer devant
mon imagination désoeuvrée ou pour me dis-
traire de préoccupations importunes.

Je distribue les rôles à cette petite troupe,
j'invente son destin qui s'accomplit au gré de
ma fantaisie. Ces fantoches m'amusent comme
un Guignol. . . .

(Thus I people my life with a few characters,
which, at certain hours, I parade out in front
of my idle imagination or to distract me from
harassing preoccupations.

I distribute roles to this little troupe. I invent
its destiny, which is accomplished according to
the likings of my fantasy. These puppets amuse
me like a Punch and Judy show.)

The reader will tend to identify Santiague, as a result of this
speech, as a man whose mental discipline leads him to control
rather than be controlled. The author has made us acutely
conscious of puppets, and we are prepared for Lefèvre's statement, several pages later: "Vous êtes . . . le seul parmi nous . . .
qui ne soit pas un fantoche." . . . (pp. 100-05)

Along with the greater preoccupation with characterization,
satire increases. Roumain's gift for incisive commentary manifests itself in *La Proie et l'ombre* and in *Les Fantoches* in his
portrayal of bourgeois existence. . . . But there is also biting
satire for the black Haitian aspiring to break into the middle
class. Santiague remarks of the black politician, Aristide Marau,
who speaks Creole to his mesmerized audience, that his father's
name is Jean-Baptiste Philidor:

Il (Marau) habite maintenant le Chemin des
Dalles et grimpe lentement vers les hauts quar-
tiers dont il prétend exécrer les riches habi-
tants. . . . c'est un grimaud qui enrage de ne
pouvoir faire son petit mulâtre. . . .

(He [Marau] now lives on the Chemin des Dalles
and climbs slowly toward the high sections of
town, whose rich inhabitants he claims to
loathe. . . . he's an ignoramus enraged at not
being able to make his little mulatto baby.)

(pp. 104-05)

But the satire of Haitian modes of existence is most prevalent
and most biting in Roumain's portrayal of middle-aged Haitian
women of the upper classes. They are the repository of all that
Roumain's young men resist—complacent mediocrity, ridiculous ignorance, unwarranted snobbery, fossilized modes of
thought. Michel Rey's reaction before his mother-in-law is seen
again in Marcel's identical response before the spectacle of his
fiancée's aunt. In **"Préface à la vie d'un bureaucrate,"** Mme
Ballin is proud of having, as she says, "vaincu l'atavisme."
(That is, her features show no trace of her African ancestry.) . . . In *Les Fantoches*, Mlle Fattu has come onto the ver-

anda expecting to find Lecocq, Irène's French suitor. Instead,
she finds Marcel, but [is] unable to contain her admiration for
Lecocq. . . . These women are faithful reflectors, incapable of
independent thought or behavior. If the young women do not
exactly show opposition to their set of values, they at least do
not press with such determination; they, at least, attempt to
understand their men. The dowagers make no such concessions, and Roumain renders them ridiculous.

Les Fantoches hangs together primarily because it maintains
the same cast of characters and the same milieu from one
chapter to another. But the book is not yet a fully developed
novel, and this lack is primarily due to the sparseness of plot.
Les Fantoches is really a series of scenes, the drama of which
revolves around the life of Marcel, Santiague, and Lefèvre.
As such, it is a story of love chanced and lost, of personal
tranquility, and of public success and failure. But the weakness
of the structure lies not so much in the lack of plot as in the
fact that we are shifted from the private world of Marcel Basquet to that of the poet Santiague, then to that of Lefèvre. This
occurs at the point where Santiague is deeply moved by his
encounter with the old general hidden in the attic, and again
at the end of the novel, when we enter the private world of
Lefèvre for the first time as, moved by the story of Charmantine, he contemplates Santiague and we are allowed to see his
thoughts.

There are no such structural defects in the case of *La Montagne
ensorcelée,* which, on the contrary, handles admirably such
shifts in point of view. Published the same year, and yet so
different from *Les Fantoches, La Montagne ensorcelée* is a truly
well-written and well-balanced story, with none of the stylistic
excesses which, if they revealed a developing talent and an
intelligent, well-read young author, had marred *La Proie et
l'ombre* and *Les Fantoches*. (pp. 106-08)

> Carolyn Fowler, in her A Knot in the Thread: The
> Life and Work of Jacques Roumain, *Howard Uni-*
> *versity Press, 1980, 383 p.*

J. MICHAEL DASH (essay date 1981)

[*In the following excerpt Dash examines Roumain's poetry, fic-*
tion, and ideological essays, arguing that Roumain's oeuvre was
an expression of the individual imagination typical of the "Ro-
mantic individualist," rather than of mere Marxist socio-political
ideology.]

In the ideological ferment of the post-Occupation period [in
Haiti] it is tempting to see Jacques Roumain as simply an
earnest doctrinaire Marxist whose beliefs provided an antidote
to the excesses of Africanist ideology. (p. 129)

Marxism because of its materialist and relativist explanations
for social and cultural phenomena allowed Roumain to rethink
and challenge many of the received ideas of his generation. It
certainly provided him with the means for refuting the theories
of racial determinism favoured by Griot ideology. He came
closest among his contemporaries to seeing Haiti's racial tensions in their proper perspective—as simply 'l'expression sen-
timentale de la lutte de classes'. The same lucidity is apparent
in his analyses of the voodoo religion, the Catholic Church,
the peasantry and the class from which he came, the Haitian
elite.

However, a closer scrutiny of Roumain's career disturbs this
neat political scenario. Roumain in many ways proves to be a
paradoxical figure, whose relation to orthodox Marxism as well

as the ethno-cultural position of the Griot movement was a complex one. . . . In fact, there is little to distinguish Roumain from his contemporaries in the Occupation period in that they all shared the same anti-establishment sentiments, aggressive populism and fierce nationalism that characterised the late twenties and early thirties. Roumain's blind nationalism in this period led to an anti-rational and xenophobic *prise de position* as is evident in an article such as 'L'éloge du fanatisme' published in *Le Petit Impartial* in 1928. It shows the extent to which Roumain was as much a Maurassian at this time as the later devotees of ethnic and cultural authenticity.

To this must be added the fact Roumain is at his least convincing in his attempts to follow an orthodox Marxist line in his public pronouncements on the writer's role in society. His prescription for literary engagement presents the writer as an activist whose craft is harnessed to an ideological position. In Roumain's own words he simply reflects 'the complexity of the dialectic of social relations, of contradictions and antagonisms of the economic and political structure of a society at a given period'. However this kind of anonymous rhetoric is not reflected in most of Roumain's writing where questions of form and the status of the individual imagination are major preoccupations. His concern with the individual will and the quest for spiritual fulfilment show the extent to which he was very much a Romantic individualist rather than an ideologue whose main interest was conformity to Marxist ideals. It was really his strong moral conscience that drove him to the secular creed of Marxism. He was not the only writer to feel that the moral truth of Marxism represented the will of History itself but to have great difficulty with the regimentation that was demanded. Ultimately Roumain emerges as a modern artist concerned with the fate of the creative imagination in a world of broken continuities.

This pattern of political activism which coexists uneasily with deep poetic longings, so entrenched as to appear at times almost independent of political intention, is evident throughout Roumain's career. . . . For instance, his articles in *Le Petit Impartial* (1927-32) consisted of numerous direct attacks on the treachery of the Catholic Church and the Haitian elite and a glorification of the non-conformity of the young and wild faith in the revolutionary potential of the Haitian masses. This led to a celebration of the ideal of violent revolt in a language not far removed from blank verse: 'Splendid epic struggle. O magnificent adventure to feel oneself surrounded by enemies and to charge their closed ranks and to emerge bloody and victorious.'

This fiery rhetoric was only occasionally echoed, however, in his verse. The only poem that fully incorporates such a violent *prise de position* is **'Appel'** with its Nietzschean invocations. . . . For the most part Roumain's poetry published in *La Trouée* and *La Revue Indigène* in the 1920s was ill-defined ideologically. They could only be seen as 'political' in that they obviously responded to Roumain's aversion for the erudite high culture of the past in which literary creation became simply an 'occupation des pédants'. These early poems can thus be seen as products of his general anti-establishment position at the time, in that, in their understated way, they eschewed the ornate and rigid forms characteristic of the most affected nineteenth century verse. Yet, essentially, these poems present us with a sober, introspective Roumain quite unlike the image of a vengeful *enfant terrible* projected in his strident prose. They are mostly mood poems which give a sharp and usually brief impression of melancholy or quick snatches of landscape. This quiet melancholy pervades much of his early writing. A brief comparison of the poem **'Calme'** and a later short story **'Fragment d'une Confession'** shows the extent to which this mood was cultivated:

> Le soleil de minuit
> de ma lampe. Le temps qui fuit
> n'atteint pas ma quiétude . . .
> Ma table est une île lumineuse
> dans la nuit noire de la silencieuse
> nuit . . .
>
> (The midnight sun
> of my lamp. The passing time
> has no effect on my serenity . . .
> My table is a luminous island
> in the blackness of the silent
> night . . .)

The intimate monologue of the later short story reworks the same theme of loneliness using a similar contrast of the light and the dark:

> la fenêtre ne laisse pénétrer que la nuit, effarouchée à peine par la lampe timide autour de laquelle elle remue comme un sombre papillon.
>
> Me voici dans mon île déserte: ce plat, pale roucher de la table, tout entouré du silence et de l'ombre
>
> (the window only allows the night to enter, hardly frightened by the timid lamp around which it moves like a dark butterfly.
>
> Here I am on my desert island: this flat, pale rock of the table, surrounded by silence and shadow)

Perhaps this early writing provides us with an insight into the underside of a public radical Roumain. This seems most obviously so in the occasional departure from *spleen* poems—the poems that deal with the problem of the individual sensibility in a hostile, uncomprehending world. It is the image of the Romantic individualist that prevails in the poems **'Le Chant de l'homme'** and **'La danse du poète clown'**. The theme of both these poems is the clash between an unheeding world and the poetic consciousness—with the latter predictably the loser. . . . Two possible ways of resolving the conflict are suggested in Roumain's verse. The choice was to be either the retreat into the hallowed world of the creative imagination as is suggested in the poem **'Guinée'** . . . or reach beyond this private world and yield to the demands of one's moral conscience whatever the consequences. The poem **'Miragoane'** cleverly presents the latter solution to the artist's dilemma:

> La chaleur de mille vies intenses
> Monte brutale vers moi. Lourd
> contre mon coeur, un coeur immense
> bat . . .
> —Là-bas, invincible, la mer
> doit.
>
> (The warmth of a thousand intense lives
> rises brutally towards me. Heavy against my heart, an enormous heart
> beats . . .
> —Over there, invincible, the sea sleeps.)

The last line adds a note of fatalism not easily associated with the Utopian impulse evident in Roumain's public pronouncements. It is '**Miragoane**', however, that most persuasively describes the nature of Roumain's engagement and the pulling together of the poet and revolutionary in him. The sentiments of this poem echo throughout the short stories of the early period which invariably deal with the same kind of moral crisis.

It is Marxism that attracts the political activist in Roumain in 1934 and the prelude to this conversion can be seen in the unmistakeable self-scrutiny and dissatisfaction with the provincialism and pretensions of the mulatto élite found in two early collections of short stories, *La proie et l'ombre* . . . and *Les Fantoches*. . . . Roumain's irritation with the narrow and parasitic world of the élite evident in these works would only be later confirmed by Marxist theory. His stories contain numerous caricatures of the Haitian bourgeoisie. With great relish Roumain reduces his protagonists to grotesque puppets. . . . These stories show how the theory of indigenism and anti-elite feeling (because of the elite's 'conscious complicity in the Occupation'), had combined to produce a strong critique of urban society. This is even more significant for Haitian literary history in which the tradition of writing about the city is weak.

Yet, it would be a distortion to see these works as simply sociopolitical satire. The dominant mode is one of irony and the bleak *mise en scène* of the narrative takes us back to concerns initially raised in the early verse. The narrative voice of these works which either take the form of intimate monologues or even edited diaries, is that of a lucid, disabused sensibility but impotent in the face of the *fardeau pesant* of the Haitian milieu. The critique of the mulatto *status quo* is voiced by sensitive young men—Haitian versions of Baudelaire's 'flâneur'. Through these characters Roumain had already begun to assess the true nature of the emotional engagement of those described as 'the young Turks . . . who succumbed to the lure of plush jobs in the corrupt and dictatorial government of Sténio Vincent'. These were the activists of the anti-American movement who Roumain could foresee, would eventually conform to the demands of their society. '**Préface à la vie d'un bureaucrate**' suggests this ironic capitulation in its very title. '**Propos sans suite**' presents us with these scions of wealthy families and their voyeuristic interest in the low life of Port-au-Prince. The coming of daylight only brings a sobering awareness of their sterility, 'useless like these smashed cases, this shattered pottery scattered all over the ground'.

Whereas these early stories reveal Roumain's dissatisfaction with the revolutionary posturing of the radical left of his generation, *La Montagne ensorcelée* . . . was his response to the increasingly popular notion of *l'âme haitienne*, of the Africanists. Simply embracing the peasantry in the name of cultural authenticity was unsatisfactory to Roumain. This novella could easily have been another example of literary regionalism. Roumain's fellow collaborator in *La Revue Indigène*, Phillippe Thoby-Marcelin, made precisely this choice. . . . The peasant world, particularly the supernatural, would be treated differently by Roumain. It is not that this early work always avoids the lurid and melodramatic. In many ways it is heavy-handed when compared with *Gouverneurs de la rosée*. . . . The real innovation is that Roumain refused to view the peasant's relation with the supernatural as a literary curiosity.

He avoids this by making a careful choice in the narrative voice of the story and by a clever orchestration of the stark violence of the denouement. The narration of the text is done to a large extent by the collective voice of the community. Roumain avoids a detached third person narration by imperceptibly surrendering narration to the peasants themselves. His introduction

of the character Desilus clearly illustrates this shift in narrative voice. It moves from a general tableau of peasant life to the specifics of this lonely peasant's world:

> Aujourd'hui, les hommes sont rentrés des champs pour le repas du soir. Dans chaque cabane, les femmes s'affairent autour des chaudrons . . .
>
> Desilus, lui, est assis sous les goyaviers. Il se repaît de leurs derniers fruits . . .
>
> Les jeunes noirs ne sont plus respectueux: ils disent que Desilus a l'esprit dérangé, mais les anciens ne sont pas de cet avis.
>
> Ainsi Tonton Jean qui est mort l'année dernière . . . répétait souvent que Desilus savait beaucoup de choses. Houng!

> (Today, the men have come back from the fields for the evening meal. In each hut, the women are busy around the cauldrons . . .
>
> Desilus is seated under the guava trees. He is filling himself with the last of these fruit . . .
>
> The young men are no longer respectful: they say that Desilus is deranged, but the older ones do not think so.
>
> So Tonton Jean who died last year . . . often repeated that Desilus knew many things. Houng!)

The only precedent for this kind of garrulous realism is Lhérisson's *La Famille des Pitite Caille* which also consciously adopts an oral tradition in the story. The choice of such a narrative view point allows the reader to become an insider in this community rather than the curious voyeur he can so easily be in Marcelin's work.

The denouement sets us straight as to how the author wants us to react to this story of misadventure in a peasant community. The ritual murder of the old woman and her daughter at the end indicates that Roumain saw peasant religion as simply a refuge for the chronic fears of a desolate peasant village. He refused to gloss over the stagnation and impotence that were part of the backward rural society in Haiti. The lingering impression left in the reader's mind is one of human tragedy:

> L'eclair s'abat en sifflant, la tête décollée roule un peu sur l'herbe.
>
> Tous s'enfuient, sauf Balletroy qui regarde, les yeux vides, sa machette, le cadavre, le cadavre, la machette.

> (The flash slashes down with a whistle, the severed head rolls a little on the grass.
>
> They all flee, except Balletroy who stares, eyes empty, his machet, the corpse, the corpse, the machet.)

The message becomes even clearer by the time *Gouverneurs de la rosée* is published as there is a similar refusal to glorify the culture of *Fonds rouge* which is also afflicted by chronic impotence. In spite of all this, Price-Mars's introduction sees the work as simply a 'note émouvante de nouveauté', an example of 'une esthétique haitienne'. Roumain's apprehensions go largely unheeded in the 1930s. Such objective scrutiny could have little impact in a society desperately attempting to regain its self-esteem through pride in the indigenous culture.

The late 1930s in Roumain's life are given over to political activism. This is especially true of the period of exile from Haiti, between 1936 and 1941. The important texts of this period are certainly not literary ones. They all represent dutiful applications of Marxist theory to the specifics of Haiti and the black diaspora. However, even if these works are often unoriginal in thought they do explicitly emphasise the difference between Roumain's ideas and those of the mulatto establishment on one hand and the ethnic 'authentics' on the other. They establish more than anything else the capacity of Marxism to avoid the mystification of race and reach beyond the myopic class and colour conflict towards an objective assessment of Haitian society.

Perhaps the most striking feature of Roumain's three ideological essays *L'Analyse Schématique* . . . , *Le Grief de l'homme noir* . . . , and *A propos de la campagne anti-superstitieuse* . . . is that they all omit the customary reference to the grandeur of the independence struggle or the humiliations of slavery and colonialism. Instead, little time is spent on brooding over the injustice of the colonial past. The following quotation shows clearly that Roumain saw the whole business of slavery as a largely economic phenomenon not a cause for acrimony: 'We will not delay ourselves with the moral side of the matter. That is only really of interest to an individual whose ancestor was a slave.' With this, Roumain closes the subject. Such a document shows a marked contrast with the catalogues of injustice masochistically repeated by the Griot apologists.

The underlying themes in these texts are those of race and religion. Roumain's consistent attitude to these two vexed questions in Haitian society goes back to the orthodox Marxist approach to culture. The Marxist dialectic refutes absolutes and inevitably sees culture in relativist terms—as opposed to the ethnocentric bias of the Africanists, for example. Since culture was conditioned by certain socio-economic circumstances and not an organic process one could appreciate how it manifests itself in terms of religion and racial attitudes. For instance, the voodoo religion was both seen by Roumain as an important manifestation of national culture—specific to Haiti as well as a phenomenon that would disappear if material progress were brought to the Haitian countryside. . . . Roumain observes that there is little to be gained by replacing belief in the voodoo gods by the fear of Hell. Voodoo was simply a product of the peasant's conception of the world. If the latter were changed the attitude to religion as a whole would also be transformed. . . . Roumain in these texts also expressed fears as to how the myth of race could be manipulated for political purposes. In Haiti he saw it as 'the mask under which black and mulatto politicians would like to hide the class struggle'. . . . He instinctively distrusted the nationalism of the traditional élite and also felt, as early as 1934, that a black bourgeoisie was equally capable of using racial identification in order to secure power for themselves. (pp. 129-39)

In this period it is the experience of exile as much as Marxism which exerts an influence on Roumain. His ability to consider the Haitian situation in non-parochial terms but rather in the context of an international system of exploitation results in part from his travels in the late 1930s. . . . He became the prototype of the exiled Marxist writer that would later be reflected in the experience of Jacques-Stéphen Alexis and René Dépestre. This experience also had a marked effect on his creative writing as a change in scale is apparent in all writing that emerges from these later years. The poem '**Madrid**' is our first clue to this shift from the exclusively personal or national concerns of his early work to the broader vision of his last works. The last lines of this tribute to the Spanish people reveal a grand euphoric vision unprecedented in his early writing:

ici que l'aube s'arrache des lambeaux de la nuit
que dans l'atroce parturition et l'humble sang
    anonyme du paysan et de l'ouvrier
nait le monde où sera effacé du front des hommes
    la flétrissure amère de la seule égalité du désespoir.

(here the dawn tears itself from the tatters of the night
in the horrible birth pains and the humble anonymous
    blood
    of the peasant and worker
is born the world in which the withered and bitter
    mark of despair shall be effaced from men's brows.)

The Spanish Civil War was an ideal situation for Roumain in that it could allow him to combine his politics with his romantic conception of individual engagement. As Stephen Spender put it, 'this was a war in which the individual still counted. It was in part an anarchist's war, a poet's war. For this short period the poet and the revolutionary were reconciled.

The last four years of Roumain's life . . . meant an end to his wanderings as an exile and a return to Haiti. This was facilitated by the change of president in Haiti and the anti-Fascist stand taken by the new president, Elie Lescot. By this time Roumain is a writer of international status and certainly the most famous to emerge from the generation of the Occupation. In the comparative quiet of these years Roumain was again able to devote himself to his creative writing. The events of these years show the extent to which Roumain had gone beyond the early iconoclasm of the Occupation years and was now more interested in consolidating early gains than in idealistic revolt and also basically more capable of compromise.

Both his decision to found the Bureau d'Ethnologie (1941) and his later decision to become Lescot's chargé d'affaires in Mexico are characteristic of the later years. (pp. 139-40)

Roumain's literary imagination had also undergone some important changes. The most important of these can be seen in the aesthetic volte-face that his later writing represents. Whereas Roumain's early verse was obviously a product of the modern in poetic styles in that he opted for an immediate and disabused representation of the world and his feelings, his later poetry can be seen as a more conventional, idealised presentation of his subjectivity. The former, private and marginally organised, stand in sharp contrast to the later epic, lyrical offerings of *Bois d'Ebène,* which is aimed to stimulate an international audience rather than shock the local bourgeoisie.

The euphoric humanism and veil of grandeur first seen in '**Madrid**' become the dominant mode in *Bois d'Ebène.* The three poems of this collection are given a symbolic unity through the image of the title. Patience, durability, inscrutability of the 'damnés de la terre' are all suggested in the symbol of ebony wood—'ce masque de silence minéral'. The reification of man is seen in slavery and other forms of exploitation are also suggested by this wood which can be bought and sold on a commercial scale. The versatility of the image also suggests the wider context of universal revolt—the spreading upwards of the flames of a 'forêt de torches funèbres'.

The poems are unified by their utopian impulse and the Marxist imprecations they convey. Roumain, however, chooses a special idiom for each of these political poems. This ranges from the slangy, conversational '**Sales Nègres**' to the shock tactics of '**Nouveau Sermon Nègre**' which is again different from the lyricism and formal cadences of the title poem '**Bois d'Ebène**'. Roumain with his instinctive feel for the poetic—for the lyrical line and the sustained image—is least comfortable with the dramatic monologue of **'Sales Nègres'**. A form that Léon Damas masters so well in *Pigments* Roumain finds alien to his sensibility. He is not the first Marxist who, driven by populist sentiment, opts for the least literary form possible for his verse. The guide to meaning in **'Sales Nègres'** is not metaphor or prosody but the human voice. From the outset its register carefully avoids literary language. . . . The constant repetition of 'nègres', 'niggers', 'sales nègres' in the poem not only ensures that the message is driven home but serves as a kind of incantation which leads to the violent apocalypse at the end. However, whereas oral poetry is so effectively manipulated for protest by Damas, Roumain's poem seems longwinded and loosely constructed.

'Nouveau Sermon Nègre' exploits the symbol of Christ's suffering and the traditional Christian message of acceptance and submission in his declamation of the new revolutionary creed of the oppressed. The poem is constructed around a series of contrasting metaphors. . . . A desecrated Christ serves the materialistic needs of those who oppress. Roumain announces a new world, pure and hallowed, which will replace the tainted world of injustice. One of the more dramatic images of the poem predicts this transition and indicates Roumain's ability to invest an image with emotional force:

> Notre révolte s'élève comme le cri de l'oiseau
> de tempête au-dessus du clapotement pourri des
> marécages . . .
>
> (Our revolt rises like the cry of the storm bird
> over the rotting squelch of the swamps . . .)

Roumain did object to the world of private fantasy of the Surrealists, 'balanced between the traditional poles of eroticism and dream'. He, however, is indebted to them for the way in which they allowed poetic imagery to be set free.

It is the title poem which most obviously reveals Roumain's real resources as a lyrical poet of some standing. Dated 1939, it is more than a revolutionary anthem for the oppressed of the world. It is a poem of exile and dislocation—seen in terms of private experience, the black diaspora and the fate of modern man. It is a successful combination of his didactic urges and the intimate poetic voice of his early years. The most moving poem in the collection, **'Bois d'Ebène'**, has a quality of lived experience which is absent in the anonymous didacticism of the other two pieces. It is unique in this collection in its variations of mood as it moves from contemplation to denial towards the final visionary dawn.

The key to **'Bois d'Ebène'** is, perhaps, the early folk poem **'Guinée'** which represents the artist's retrieval of a state of grace. The same theme informs **'Bois d'Ebène'** which can almost be seen as a sequel to the early poem. **'Bois d'Ebène'** begins with man's fall from this hallowed state. The whole poem can be interpreted as a reenactment of the Fall in secular terms. This is most obviously reflected in the theme of exile which dominates the poem and is presented in a series of images contrasting the sacred pastoral past with the profane industrial present. The poem finds Roumain accepting the Marxist notion of the solidarity of the proletariat . . . but rejecting a rootless materialistic present for a world of spirituality where a state of grace can be restored.

The prelude to the poem (frequently omitted in anthologies which emphasise the more ideological features of the poem) establishes the crucial break with the pastoral serenity of the past. The use of 'pluvieux', 'morne', 'brume', and 'chant funèbre' establishes a bleak *mise en scène* before departure is made explicit—'tu partiras / abandonnant ton village'. The threat of future exile and rootlessness is suggested by the 'foyer éteint'. The exile is never located specifically in his private experience or in ideological terms. The use of the second person singular and the lack of explicit description of landscape make the act of leaving atemporal, remote and charged with universal significance. The emotional impact of this loss and the threat of the strange odyssey ahead can almost be seen as a re-enactment of the Fall. Images of a fleeting world gradually receding suggest both profoundly felt anguish and the larger, metaphysical loss. . . . This evocation of the nostalgia of exile and irretrievable loss is given an explicit historical context as the poem proceeds. The specific reality of the slave trade and on a wider scale man's encounter with a profane, materialistic world are suggested by the images of a grotesque, disorienting culture which replace the fragile echoes of pastoral serenity. . . . The encounter of two different cultures—the pastoral and the industrial, the poetic and the materialistic—is suggested by the dislocation of natural imagery to evoke a hostile, de-humanising universe—decapitated palm trees and withered branches of arms chained by sunlight. It all comes together in the compressed imagery of:

> vingt-cinq mille traverses de Bois-d'Ebène
> Sur les rails du Congo-Océan . . .
>
> (Twenty five thousand sleepers of ebony
> on the rails of the Congo-Ocean)

The 'traverses de Bois-d'Ebène' suggest human railway sleepers which permit an industrial culture to function. **'Congo-Ocean'** introduces the anonymous bodies of slaves stacked below decks for crossing the Middle Passage.

Roumain situates the human drama just outside the context of the revolt of negritude. His anger is not racially directed. He is articulating man's fragility in the face of the dehumanising forces of modern industrial culture. The frequently quoted **'Afrique j'ai gardé ta mémoire'** is more than nostalgia for an ancestral, ethnic past. It is, rather, the desperate identification with the hallowed past lost to the exile. The 'POURTANT' in bold letters that follows simply makes this explicit. By situating his protest in broad universal terms Roumain sharply defines the difference between his position and that of Africanist ideology. The latter also saw modern materialism as incompatible with man's true needs but situates this conflict in terms of an opposition between European materialism and the authentic black soul.

The final movement of the poem centres on a radical shift in mood as strident revolt against this world that makes things of men, asserts itself. Roumain becomes the herald of the future Apocalypse that will put an end to this world. Shades of the *enfant terrible* of the Occupation years emerge as Roumain forsees the end of an epic struggle which involves all men. The 'foyer éteint' of the prelude is rekindled in the vision of fraternity that Roumain now articulates. The first person plural frequently repeated make this new solidarity emphatic. . . . The bleak, misty world of the beginning now yields to a world restored in a blaze of light. This image which underlines the renascence of the end of **'Bois d'Ebène'** in 1939 was also destined to evoke the visionary climax of Roumain's last completed work—*Gouverneurs de la rosée:*

> et la plaine sera l'esplanade de l'aurore
> où rassembler nos forces ecartelées. . . .

(and the plain will be the esplanade of dawn
where our scattered forces can reassemble.)

This is echoed in the final 'coumbite' at dawn in his later novel:
'La plaine était couchée a leurs pieds dans l'embrasement de
midi . . . La savane s'étendait comme une esplanade de lumière
violente.' (The plain lay at their feet in the burning heat of
noon . . . The savanna spread itself like an esplanade of violent
light.)

The humanitarian ideal and open structure of these images show
how far Roumain had moved away from the narrow nationalism
of his early years. Haiti's encounter with American materialism; the African's rootlessness in a disorienting, exploitative
world; the poet culturally unhoused, threatened by sterility of
the modern world, are all phases of the same process. This
conviction becomes the point of departure for *Gouverneurs de
la rosée* which re-states the basic theme raised in **'Bois d'Ebène'**.
(pp. 141-46)

> *J. Michael Dash, "Jacques Roumain: The Marxist
> Counterpoint," in his* Literature and Ideology in Haiti,
> 1915-1961, *Barnes & Noble Books, 1981, pp. 129-55.*

ADDITIONAL BIBLIOGRAPHY

Bostick, Herman F. "Toward Literary Freedom: A Study of Contemporary Haitian Literature." *Phylon* XVII, No. 3 (Third Quarter 1956):
250-56.*
    Discussion of Haitian writers' historical struggle for literary free-
    dom. Bostick parallels the simultaneous movements toward po-
    litical and artistic freedom in Haiti and emphasizes that both move-
    ments draw on African and French influences and reject American
    values. Roumain is regarded as the single greatest influence on
    modern Haitian literature and culture.

Bradley, Francine. "Political Prisoners in Haiti." *The New Republic*
LXXXII, No. 1060 (27 March 1937): 189.
    Letter written by the secretary of the Committee for the Release
    of Jacques Roumain urging readers to send letters of protest on
    behalf of the incarcerated writer and political activist.

Cobb, Martha K. "Concepts of Blackness in the Poetry of Nicolas
Guillen, Jacques Roumain, and Langston Hughes." *CLA Journal* XVIII,
No. 2 (December 1974): 262-72.*
    Links the Cuban, Haitian, and American authors through themes
    of their poetry. Cobb argues that elements of cultural heritage and

historical experience transported from Africa to the Americas re-
    sulted in similarities in the black literary movement in the U.S.,
    Negritude in the French-speaking Caribbean, and negrismo in
    Hispanic America.

Cook, Mercer. "The Haitian Novel." *The French Review* XIX, No.
6 (May 1946): 406-12.*
    Examines the causes and results of the Haitian literary renaissance.
    Cook regards Roumain's *Masters of the Dew* as one of the most
    significant novels to appear in Haiti between 1939 and 1945.

Coulthard, G. R. In his *Race and Colour in Caribbean Literature*,
pp. 39ff. London: Oxford University Press, 1962.
    Scattered discussions of Roumain's poetry and fiction.

Cunard, Nancy. "3 Negro Poets." *Left Review* 3, No. 9 (October
1937): 529-36.*
    Excerpts from antifascist speeches made at the Paris International
    Writers' Congress by Roumain, Langston Hughes, and Nicolas
    Guillen, with notes on their biographical and political backgrounds
    and literary themes.

Dash, J. M. "The Peasant Novel in Haiti." *African Literature Today*,
No. 9 (1978): 77-90.*
    Discusses differences in neo-African cultures and their literatures.
    Dash examines Roumain's fiction as a representative Haitian lit-
    erary expression of the problems of the urban elite and the unique-
    ness of the indigenous peasantry.

Dixon, Melvin. "Toward a World Black Literature & Community."
The Massachusetts Review XVIII, No. 4 (Winter 1977): 750-69.*
    Discussion of black writers, concentrating on political aims and
    artistic expression. Dixon compares the heroes in Roumain's *Mas-
    ters of the Dew* and Claude McKay's *Banjo* to support his ar-
    gument that the survival of the individual in black literature world-
    wide is dependent upon interaction with a community.

Fowler, Carolyn. "Motif Symbolism in Jacques Roumain's *Gouverneurs de la rosée*." *CLA Journal* XVIII, No. 1 (September 1974):
44-51.
    Discusses the universality of *Masters of the Dew* through an ex-
    amination of the novel's symbolism and recurring motifs.

Jahn, Janheinz. "'Indigenism' and 'Negrism'." In his *Neo-African
Literature*, translated by Oliver Coburn and Ursula Lehrburger, pp.
214-38. New York: Grove Press, 1968.*
    Compares the folklorist themes of Roumain's early poetry to his
    later poems extolling the "international solidarity of the working
    class." Jahn traces the roots of the indigenous movement in Hai-
    tian literature and other Caribbean and Hispanic literatures, com-
    paring and contrasting them with simultaneous literary movements
    among black writers worldwide.

Mark Twain

1835-1910

(Pseudonym of Samuel Langhorne Clemens; also wrote under pseudonyms of Thomas Jefferson Snodgrass, Josh, Muggins, Soleather, Grumbler, and Sieur Louis de Conte) American novelist, short story and novella writer, journalist, essayist, memoirist, autobiographer, and dramatist.

The following entry presents criticism of Twain's *Adventures of Huckleberry Finn.* For a complete discussion of Twain's career, see *TCLC,* Volumes 6 and 12.

Considered Twain's masterpiece and one of America's greatest novels, *Adventures of Huckleberry Finn* is also regarded as the first significant American work to break with European literary traditions. The novel's semiliterate narrator, vernacular dialogue, forthright depiction of the hypocrisy and brutality of American life, and unrefined frontier humor were sufficiently radical at the time of its publication to warrant the novel's banishment from numerous libraries as "the veriest trash." These very improprieties, however, eventually became the basis for critical acclaim and initiated the divergence of the American novel from European conventions. According to Ernest Hemingway, "All modern American literature comes from one book by Mark Twain called *Huckleberry Finn....* There was nothing before. There has been nothing as good since."

Twain began writing *Huckleberry Finn* immediately after the publication of *The Adventures of Tom Sawyer* in 1876. *Huckleberry Finn* was intended as a sequel to the popular children's book, which chronicled the adventures of a mischievous but good-hearted boy and his companions in a Mississippi Valley town modeled after Twain's boyhood home of Hannibal, Missouri. According to Twain, Huck, a minor figure in the earlier story, was inspired by the real-life Tom Blankenship, and Twain's description of Tom in his *Autobiography* could serve equally well for Huck: "He was ignorant, unwashed, insufficiently fed; but he had as good a heart as ever any boy had. His liberties were totally unrestricted. He was the only really independent person—boy or man—in the community." *Huckleberry Finn* records Huck's adventures as he accompanies Jim, an escaped slave, down the Mississippi in a quest for freedom. Amid abundant social satire, the narrative focuses on Huck's developing moral independence from the teachings of his society, and critics concur that *Huckleberry Finn* far surpasses *Tom Sawyer* in the depth of both its main character and its themes. Twain rapidly completed about four hundred pages of the narrative in the summer of 1876. He then lost interest in the story and set the book aside, writing to his friend and editor William Dean Howells: "I like it only tolerably well, as far as I have got, and may possibly pigeonhole or burn the ms. when it is done." The novel remained unfinished for the next seven years while Twain devoted the bulk of his creative energy to *A Tramp Abroad, The Prince and the Pauper,* and numerous minor literary projects. In 1883 his enthusiasm for *Huckleberry Finn* suddenly returned, perhaps prompted by an 1882 visit to Hannibal, and he completed the novel in a few months. Scholars note that Twain appeared unaware of the magnitude of his accomplishment in *Huckleberry Finn.* Although he admitted of the book that "modesty compels me to say it's a rattling good one," during the summer of its completion he demon-

strated equal or greater enthusiasm for a variety of now-forgotten literary projects and business enterprises, such as the marketing of a history game he had invented for his daughters.

Dissatisfied with his previous publishers, Twain resolved to publish *Huckleberry Finn* himself in time for the Christmas season of 1884. British publication proceeded on schedule in early December, but American publication was delayed until the following February by the discovery of an obscene alteration in one of the illustrations. The incident was widely publicized and according to Michael Patrick Hearn "tainted the novel's reputation long before its official publication." Critical reception of *Huckleberry Finn* was mixed, but most commentators agreed with the *Springfield Republican* that "the trouble with Mr. Clemens is that he has no reliable sense of propriety." The public library of Concord, Massachusetts, banned the novel "as rough, coarse, and inelegant, dealing with a series of experiences not elevating, the whole book being more suited to the slums than to intelligent, respectable people." Commentators note that although Twain was hurt by the typically vicious tone of critical response, he professed to be undisturbed by the reviews and by the Concord Library's well-publicized banishment, which he called "a rattling tip-top puff" that "will sell 25,000 copies for us sure." His lack of concern proved well-founded: critical opinion had no effect on the novel's popular success, which was overwhelming. *Huckleberry Finn* became the best-selling book of Twain's career, and has remained one of the most popular American novels ever written.

In addition, critical reaction to the work has gradually evolved from initial hostility to nearly universal acclaim. Modern critics generally agree that the artistry of *Huckleberry Finn* far surpasses that of Twain's other works, which were more highly admired during his lifetime. Although the book lacks a formal structure, being composed of a series of loosely-connected episodes, the narrative achieves a high degree of unity through the repetition and interplay of various themes and motifs. Many critics find Huck's narrative voice to be the novel's most unique and distinctive aspect. Huck's naive, unadorned observations provide much of the book's characteristic humor and irony, and through Huck's innocent eyes Twain was able to present a fresh vision of American life. Particularly innovative was Twain's use of vernacular throughout the narrative: although dialect had often been used in the works of nineteenth-century Southern authors for quaint and humorous effects, in *Huckleberry Finn* Twain became the first to sustain the use of vernacular speech throughout an entire novel. His lifelong fascination with the spoken word is evident in his careful rendering of seven distinct forms of Southern dialect, and critics attribute much of the novel's freshness and vividness to Twain's sensitivity to the poetry of everyday language.

Twain described *Huckleberry Finn* as "a book of mine where a sound heart & a deformed conscience come into collision & conscience suffers a defeat," and most critics agree that Huck's moral development provides the novel's central theme. At the outset of their journey, Huck's attitudes toward Jim are those of the prevailing white majority toward slaves. He considers Jim his intellectual and social inferior and has little conception of him as a human being. Through a series of episodes strengthening Huck's awareness of Jim as an individual, however, Huck progresses from uncritical acceptance of traditional attitudes and morals to an independent moral stance in direct defiance of social conventions. In the novel's climactic scene Huck reflects on the wickedness of what he has done in "stealing a poor old woman's nigger," but after tortuous deliberation resolves to help his friend escape even though he knows that "people that acts as I'd been acting about that nigger goes to everlasting fire." Critics consider the paradox of Huck's decision, in which he makes a supremely moral choice while convinced of the immorality of his actions, to be the novel's most brilliant example of Twain's ironic skill. The episode also emphasizes the book's dominant thematic conflict, the contrast between the cruelty of life on shore and the fundamental decency of life on the raft, where Huck and Jim exercise a code of behavior free from the strictures of society. Huck and Jim's journey is generally considered a symbolic repudiation of the corrupt society of the Mississippi Valley, and the novel as a whole is often regarded as a condemnation of civilization.

A frequent topic of critical discussion is the role played by Jim in Twain's novel. Although it is generally agreed that Jim's emancipation from slavery is of secondary importance in the narrative to Huck's emancipation from society, critics disagree over Jim's exact function in the novel. Several critics have argued that Jim's purpose is solely to provide opportunities for the development of Huck's character: it is Jim's place in society as an escaped slave that precipitates Huck's moral crisis, as he attempts to reconcile his knowledge of Jim as a human being with the teachings of his society. The most controversial reading of Jim's place in the novel is provided by Leslie Fiedler,

who asserts that Jim's relationship with Huck is homosexual. Most critics discount Fiedler's theory and uphold that of Kenneth Lynn, who contends that one of the book's dominant themes is Huck's search for a father figure, and that through their travels Jim gradually becomes Huck's father-surrogate. The figure of Jim has prompted further controversy in recent years by critics who contend that *Huckleberry Finn* is replete with racial stereotypes and that Jim in particular is portrayed as a "comic stage Negro" similar to the ignorant and gullible characters in nineteenth-century minstrel shows. Twain apologists counter that Jim is one of the few adults in the novel portrayed in a favorable light, and that his exhibition of such qualities as compassion, logic, and self-sacrifice forms a distinct and obvious contrast with the callousness, gullibility, and greed demonstrated by the novel's white characters. Defenders of *Huckleberry Finn* further argue that Twain's introduction of racial stereotypes into the novel was an intentional attempt to expose the bigotry of Southern society through satire.

In addition to racism, Twain's satire was loosed in *Huckleberry Finn* on several interrelated themes that recur throughout his works: the evils of aristocracy, Southern gentility, and romantic literature. Twain blamed romantic literature, particularly the novels of Walter Scott, for the backwardness of the South, maintaining that such literature "sets the world in love with dreams and phantoms; with decayed and swinish forms of religion; with decayed and degraded systems of government; with the sillinesses and emptinesses, sham grandeurs, sham gauds, and sham chivalries of a brainless and worthless long-vanished society." In his depiction of the Grangerfords, Southern aristocrats who simultaneously adhere to a strict code of etiquette and conduct a murderous feud with a neighboring family, Twain exposed the chivalric mentality he found so repellent in Southern society. Through the introduction of the King and the Duke, confidence men posing as dethroned royalty who use the raft as a base from which to perpetrate their frauds, Twain continued his attack on aristocracy and simultaneously expressed contempt for the equally foolish and brutal lower classes of the South. The townspeople victimized by the King and the Duke are both gullible and vicious, and the cruelty of life on shore appears in sharp contrast to the idyllic nature of life on the raft, further emphasizing the novel's conflict between civilization and freedom.

The novel's concluding section, in which Jim is captured and Tom Sawyer returns to the story to mastermind his escape, has fueled a seemingly endless controversy over Twain's intention. Critical dissatisfaction generally centers on the novel's abrupt change of tone: Huck and Jim's quest for freedom is suddenly superceded by a farcical parody of romantic literature, as Tom designs an elaborate escape based on such adventure stories as *The Count of Monte Cristo*. The action is dominated by Tom, whose values are distinctly those of the society against which Huck and Jim have rebelled, and their journey is rendered pointless by the deathbed repentance of Miss Watson, Jim's owner, who grants his freedom. Although such critics as Lionel Trilling and T. S. Eliot have defended the conclusion as formally appropriate, Bernard DeVoto has asserted that "in the whole reach of the English novel there is no more abrupt or more chilling descent." Among the conclusion's most vehement detractors is Leo Marx, who maintains that the ending "jeopardizes the significance of the entire novel." In submitting to Tom's childish sense of adventure, Marx argues, Huck and Jim lose the dignity and individuality that they had developed on the river. Furthermore, as Miss Watson is an outstanding example of the hypocrisy of valley society, her freeing of Jim "accomplishes a vindication of persons and attitudes symbolically repudiated when they set forth downstream." Marx considers the conclusion a failure on the part of Twain, who, "having revealed the tawdry nature of the great valley, yielded to its essential complacency." Other critics attribute less significance to the concluding sequence, maintaining that the entire episode is merely a technical device allowing Twain both to further his attack on romanticism and to conclude the novel, and that Huck's final decision to "light out for the Territory" signals his successful emancipation from conventional society. More critics, however, agree with James M. Cox, who considers Huck's initiation into society, rather than his escape from it, to be the book's dominant theme, and therefore finds "an inexorable and crushing logic inherent in the ending." Yet another position on the issue is taken by A. E. Dyson, who considers the traditional view of *Huckleberry Finn* as a clearly-drawn contrast between corrupt society and independent morality to be an oversimplification. Dyson maintains that the novel portrays various gradations of morality, not a stark contrast between good and evil, and that through Miss Watson's change of heart Twain sought to emphasize that "actual humane progress does come about, whether we like it or not, through muddled insights, muddled kindlinesses, muddled actions, as much as from the straightforward vindication of ideals."

While scholars debate the philosophical issues raised in what they consider one of the masterpieces of American literature, the novel's enduring popularity continues to defy Twain's definition of a classic as "a book that people praise and don't read." Claude M. Simpson has described *Huckleberry Finn* as a book that "has miraculously managed to transcend most of its limitations," and summarizes the qualities contributing to the novel's enduring appeal: "Its language is vernacular, raised to an uncommon power of effectiveness; its milieu is heavy with local color, but wrenched free of condescension; its hero is a poor-white isolato whose simplicity of vision never blinds him to innate truths; its dedication to adventure assures us surface excitement which cannot obscure an underlying critique of human nature. Twain builded better than he knew. He could never again quite duplicate the triumph."

(See also *Contemporary Authors*, Vol. 104; *Dictionary of Literary Biography*, Vol. 11: *American Humorists, 1800-1950*; Vol. 12: *American Realists and Naturalists*; Vol. 23: *American Newspaper Journalists, 1873-1900*; and *Yesterday's Authors of Books for Children*, Vol. 2.)

[BRANDER MATTHEWS] (essay date 1885)

[*An American critic, playwright, and novelist, Matthews wrote extensively on world drama and served for a quarter century at Columbia as professor of dramatic literature, becoming the first holder of the first such position at any American university. Matthews was also a founding member and president of the National Institute of Arts and Letters. Matthews, whose criticism is both witty and informative, has been called "perhaps the last of the gentlemanly school of critics and essayists" in America. In the following excerpt, Matthews favorably reviews* Huckleberry Finn.]

The boy of to-day is fortunate indeed, and, of a truth, he is to be congratulated. While the boy of yesterday had to stay his stomach with the unconscious humour of *Sandford and Merton*, the boy of to-day may get his fill of fun and of romance and of adventure in *Treasure Island* and in *Tom Brown* and in *Tom*

Sawyer, and now in a sequel to *Tom Sawyer,* wherein Tom himself appears in the very nick of time, like a young god from the machine. Sequels of stories which have been widely popular are not a little risky. *Huckleberry Finn* is a sharp exception to this general rule. Although it is a sequel, it is quite as worthy of wide popularity as *Tom Sawyer*. An American critic once neatly declared that the late G. P. R. James hit the bull's-eye of success with his first shot, and that for ever thereafter he went on firing through the same hole. Now this is just what Mark Twain has not done. *Huckleberry Finn* is not an attempt to do *Tom Sawyer* over again. It is a story quite as unlike its predecessor as it is like. Although Huck Finn appeared first in the earlier book, and although Tom Sawyer reappears in the later, the scenes and the characters are otherwise wholly different. Above all, the atmosphere of the story is different. *Tom Sawyer* was a tale of boyish adventure in a village in Missouri, on the Mississippi river, and it was told by the author. *Huckleberry Finn* is autobiographic; it is a tale of boyish adventure along the Mississippi river told as it appeared to Huck Finn. There is not in *Huckleberry Finn* any one scene quite as funny as those in which Tom Sawyer gets his friends to whitewash the fence for him, and then uses the spoils thereby acquired to attain the highest situation of the Sunday school the next morning. Nor is there any distinction quite as thrilling as that awful moment in the cave when the boy and the girl are lost in the darkness, and when Tom Sawyer suddenly sees a human hand bearing a light, and then finds that the hand is the hand of Indian Joe, his one mortal enemy; we have always thought that the vision of the hand in the cave in *Tom Sawyer* is one of the very finest things in the literature of adventure since Robinson Crusoe first saw a single footprint in the sand of the seashore. But though *Huckleberry Finn* may not quite reach these two highest points of *Tom Sawyer,* we incline to the opinion that the general level of the later story is perhaps higher than that of the earlier. For one thing, the skill with which the character of Huck Finn is maintained is marvellous. We see everything through his eyes—and they are his eyes and not a pair of Mark Twain's spectacles. And the comments on what he sees are his comments—the comments of an ignorant, superstitious, sharp, healthy boy, brought up as Huck Finn had been brought up; they are not speeches put into his mouth by the author. One of the most artistic things in the book—and that Mark Twain is a literary artist of a very high order all who have considered his later writings critically cannot but confess—one of the most artistic things in *Huckleberry Finn* is the sober self-restraint with which Mr. Clemens lets Huck Finn set down, without any comment at all, scenes which would have afforded the ordinary writer matter for endless moral and political and sociological disquisition. We refer particularly to the account of the Grangerford-Shepherdson feud, and of the shooting of Boggs by Colonel Sherburn. Here are two incidents of the rough old life of the South-Western States, and of the Mississippi Valley forty or fifty years ago, of the old life which is now rapidly passing away under the influence of advancing civilization and increasing commercial prosperity, but which has not wholly disappeared even yet, although a slow revolution in public sentiment is taking place. The Grangerford-Shepherdson feud is a vendetta as deadly as any Corsican could wish, yet the parties to it were honest, brave, sincere, good Christian people, probably people of deep religious sentiment. Not the less we see them taking their guns to church, and, when occasion serves, joining in what is little better than a general massacre. The killing of Boggs by Colonel Sherburn is told with equal sobriety and truth; and the later scene in which Colonel Sherburn cows and lashes the mob which has set out to lynch him is one of the most vigorous bits of writing Mark Twain has done.

In *Tom Sawyer* we saw Huckleberry Finn from the outside; in the present volume we see him from the inside. He is almost as much a delight to any one who has been a boy as was Tom Sawyer. But only he or she who has been a boy can truly enjoy this record of his adventures, and of his sentiments and of his sayings. Old maids of either sex will wholly fail to understand him or to like him, or to see his significance and his value. Like Tom Sawyer, Huck Finn is a genuine boy; he is neither a girl in boy's clothes like many of the modern heroes of juvenile fiction, nor is he a "little man," a full-grown man cut down; he is a boy, just a boy, only a boy. And his ways and modes of thought are boyish. As Mr. F. Anstey understands the English boy, and especially the English boy of the middle classes, so Mark Twain understands the American boy, and especially the American boy of the Mississippi Valley of forty or fifty years ago. The contrast between Tom Sawyer, who is the child of respectable parents, decently brought up, and Huckleberry Finn, who is the child of the town drunkard, not brought up at all, is made distinct by a hundred artistic touches, not the least natural of which is Huck's constant reference to Tom as his ideal of what a boy should be. When Huck escapes from the cabin where his drunken and worthless father had confined him, carefully manufacturing a mass of very circumstantial evidence to prove his own murder by robbers, he cannot help saying, "I did wish Tom Sawyer was there, I knowed he would take an interest in this kind of business, and throw in the fancy touches. Nobody could spread himself like Tom Sawyer in such a thing as that." Both boys have their full share of boyish imagination; and Tom Sawyer, being given to books, lets his imagination run on robbers and pirates and genies, with a perfect understanding with himself that, if you want to get fun out of this life, you must never hesitate to make believe very hard; and, with Tom's youth and health, he never finds it hard to make believe and to be a pirate at will, or to summon an attendant spirit, or to rescue a prisoner from the deepest dungeon 'neath the castle moat. But in Huck this imagination has turned to superstition; he is a walking repository of the juvenile folklore of the Mississippi Valley—a folklore partly traditional among the white settlers, but largely influenced by intimate association with the negroes. (pp. 153-54)

The romantic side of Tom Sawyer is shown in most delightfully humorous fashion in the account of his difficult devices to aid in the easy escape of Jim, a runaway negro. Jim is an admirably drawn character. There have been not a few fine and firm portraits of negroes in recent American fiction, of which Mr. Cable's Bras-Coupé in the *Grandissimes* is perhaps the most vigorous, and Mr. Harris's Mingo and Uncle Remus and Blue Dave are the most gentle. Jim is worthy to rank with these; and the essential simplicity and kindliness and generosity of the Southern negro have never been better shown than here by Mark Twain. Nor are Tom Sawyer and Huck Finn and Jim the only fresh and original figures in Mr. Clemens's new book; on the contrary, there is scarcely a character of the many introduced who does not impress the reader at once as true to life—and therefore as new, for life is so varied that a portrait from life is sure to be as good as new. That Mr. Clemens draws from life, and yet lifts his work from the domain of the photograph to the region of art, is evident to any one who will give his work the honest attention which it deserves. Mr. John T. Raymond, the American comedian, who performs the character of Colonel Sellers to perfection, is wont to say that there is scarcely a town in the West and South-West where some

man did not claim to be the original of the character. And as Mark Twain made Colonel Sellers, so has he made the chief players in the present drama of boyish adventure; they are taken from life, no doubt, but they are so aptly chosen and so broadly drawn that they are quite as typical as they are actual. They have one great charm, all of them—they are not written about and about; they are not described and dissected and analysed; they appear and play their parts and disappear; and yet they leave a sharp impression of indubitable vitality and individuality. No one, we venture to say, who reads this book will readily forget the Duke and the King, a pair of as pleasant "confidence operators" as one may meet in a day's journey, who leave the story in the most appropriate fashion, being clothed in tar and feathers and ridden on a rail. Of the more broadly humorous passages—and they abound—we have not left ourselves space so speak; they are to the full as funny as in any of Mark Twain's other books; and, perhaps, in no other book has the humourist shown so much artistic restraint, for there is in *Huckleberry Finn* no mere "comic copy," no straining after effect; one might almost say that there is no waste word in it. (p. 154)

> [Brander Matthews], "Huckleberry Finn," in The Saturday Review, *London, Vol. LIX, No. 1527, January 31, 1885, pp. 153-54.*

[ROBERT BRIDGES]   (essay date 1885)

> [In the following excerpt, Bridges finds Huckleberry Finn *a work filled with grim episodes that belie Twain's reputation as a humorist.*]

Mark Twain is a humorist or nothing. He is well aware of this fact himself, for he prefaces the *Adventures of Huckleberry Finn* with a brief notice, warning persons in search of a moral, motive or plot that they are liable to be prosecuted, banished or shot. This is a nice little artifice to scare off the critics—a kind of "trespassers on these grounds will be dealt with according to law."

However, as there is no penalty attached, we organized a search expedition for the humorous qualities of this book with the following hilarious results:

A very refined and delicate piece of narration by Huck Finn, describing his venerable and dilapidated "pap" as afflicted with delirium tremens, rolling over and over, "kicking things every which way," and "saying there was devils ahold of him." This chapter is especially suited to amuse the children on long, rainy afternoons.

An elevating and laughable description of how Huck killed a pig, smeared its blood on an axe and mixed in a little of his own hair, and then ran off, setting up a job on the old man and the community, and leading them to believe him murdered. This little joke can be repeated by any smart boy for the amusement of his fond parents.

A graphic and romantic tale of a Southern family feud, which resulted in an elopement and from six to eight choice corpses.

A polite version of the "Giascutus" story, in which a nude man, striped with the colors of the rainbow, is exhibited as "The King's Camelopard; or, The Royal Nonesuch." This is a good chapter for lenten parlor entertainments and church festivals.

A side-splitting account of a funeral, enlivened by a "sick melodeum," a "long-legged undertaker," and a rat episode in the cellar.

> *[Robert Bridges], "Mark Twain's Blood-Curdling Humor," in* Life Magazine. *Vol. V, No. 113, February 26, 1885, p. 119.*

WILLIAM LYON PHELPS   (essay date 1910)

[*Phelps was for over forty years a lecturer on English at Yale. His early study* The Beginnings of the English Romantic Movement *(1893) is still considered an important work and his* Essays on Russian Novelists *(1911) was one of the first influential studies of the Russian realists. From 1922 until his death in 1943 he wrote a regular column for* Scribner's Magazine *and a nationally syndicated newspaper column. During this period, his criticism became less scholarly and more journalistic, and is notable for its generally enthusiastic tone. In the following excerpt, Phelps praises the literary skill evidenced in* Huckleberry Finn.]

Although Mark Twain has the great qualities of the true humorist—common sense, human sympathy, and an accurate eye for proportion—he is much more than a humorist. His work shows high literary quality, the quality that appears in first-rate novels. He has shown himself to be a genuine artist. He has done something which many popular novelists have signally failed to accomplish—he has created real characters. His two wonderful boys, Tom Sawyer and Huckleberry Finn, are wonderful in quite different ways. The creator of Tom exhibited remarkable observation; the creator of Huck showed the divine touch of imagination. Tom is the American boy—he is "smart." In having his fence whitewashed, in controlling a pool of Sabbath-school tickets at the precise psychological moment, he displays abundant promise of future success in business. Huck, on the other hand, is the child of nature, harmless, sincere, and crudely imaginative. His reasonings with Jim about nature and God belong to the same department of natural theology as that illustrated in Browning's *Caliban*. (pp. 107-08)

Mark Twain has so much dramatic power that, were his literary career beginning instead of closing, he might write for us the great American play that we are still awaiting. The story of the feud between the Grangerfords and the Shepherdsons is thrillingly dramatic, and the tragic climax seizes the heart. The shooting of the drunken Boggs, the gathering of the mob, and its control by one masterful personality, belong essentially to true drama, and are written with power and insight. The pathos of these scenes is never false, never mawkish or overdone; it is the pathos of life itself. Mark Twain's extraordinary skill in descriptive passages shows, not merely keen observation, but the instinct for the specific word—the one word that is always better than any of its synonyms, for it makes the picture real—it creates the illusion, which is the essence of all literary art. (p. 109)

Tom Sawyer and *Huckleberry Finn* are prose epics of American life. The former is one of those books—of which *The Pilgrim's Progress, Gulliver's Travels,* and *Robinson Crusoe* are supreme examples—that are read at different periods of one's life from very different points of view; so that it is not easy to say when one enjoys them the most—before one understands their real significance or after. Nearly all healthy boys enjoy reading *Tom Sawyer,* because the intrinsic interest of the story is so great, and the various adventures of the hero are portrayed with such gusto. Yet it is impossible to outgrow the book. The eternal Boy is there, and one cannot appreciate the nature of

boyhood properly until one has ceased to be a boy. The other masterpiece, *Huckleberry Finn,* is really not a child's book at all. Children devour it, but they do not digest it. It is a permanent picture of a certain period of American history, and this picture is made complete, not so much by the striking portraits of individuals placed on the huge canvas, as by the vital unity of the whole composition. If one wishes to know what life on the Mississippi really was, to know and understand the peculiar social conditions of that highly exciting time, one has merely to read through this powerful narrative, and a definite, coherent, vivid impression remains. (pp. 110-11)

> *William Lyon Phelps, "Mark Twain," in his* Essays on Modern Novelists, *The Macmillan Company, 1910, pp. 99-114.*

ALBERT BIGELOW PAINE   (essay date 1912)

[*Paine was Twain's secretary and the author or editor of six books on Twain's life and works. Although his authorized biography* Mark Twain *(1912) is no longer considered the definitive work on Twain due to its adulatory tone and numerous factual errors, Paine is credited with recording a great deal of first-hand information on Twain that might otherwise have been lost. In the following excerpt, Paine discusses some of the qualities that make* Huckleberry Finn *a superior work of literature.*]

The story of *Huck Finn* will probably stand as the best of Mark Twain's purely fictional writings. A sequel to *Tom Sawyer,* it is greater than its predecessor; greater artistically, though perhaps with less immediate interest for the juvenile reader. In fact, the books are so different that they are not to be compared—wherein lies the success of the later one. Sequels are dangerous things when the story is continuous, but in *Huckleberry Finn* the story is a new one, wholly different in environment, atmosphere, purpose, character, everything. The tale of Huck and Nigger Jim drifting down the mighty river on a raft, cross-secting the various primitive aspects of human existence, constitutes one of the most impressive examples of picaresque fiction in any language. It has been ranked greater than *Gil Blas,* greater even than *Don Quixote;* certainly it is more convincing, more human, than either of these tales. Robert Louis Stevenson once wrote, "It is a book I have read four times, and am quite ready to begin again to-morrow."

It is by no means a flawless book, though its defects are trivial enough. The illusion of Huck as narrator fails the least bit here and there; the "four dialects" are not always maintained; the occasional touch of broad burlesque detracts from the tale's reality. We are inclined to resent this. We never wish to feel that Huck is anything *but* a real character. We want him always the Huck who was willing to go to hell if necessary, rather than sacrifice Nigger Jim; the Huck who watched the river through long nights, and, without caring to explain why, felt his soul go out to the sunrise. (pp. 793-94)

Take the story as a whole, it is a succession of startling and unique pictures. The cabin in the swamp which Huck and his father used together in their weird, ghastly relationship; the night adventure with Jim on the wrecked steamboat; Huck's night among the towheads; the Grangerford-Shepherdson battle; the killing of Boggs—to name a few of the many vivid presentations—these are of no time or literary fashion and will never lose their flavor nor their freshness so long as humanity itelf does not change. The terse, unadorned Grangerford-Shepherdson episode—built out of the Darnell-Watson feuds [in *Life on the Mississippi*]—is simply classic in its vivid casualness, and the same may be said of almost every incident on that long river-drift; but this is the strength, the very essence of picaresque narrative. It is the way things happen in reality; and the quiet, unexcited frame of mind in which Huck is prompted to set them down would seem to be the last word in literary art. To Huck, apparently, the killing of Boggs and Colonel Sherburn's defiance of the mob are of about the same historical importance as any other incidents of the day's travel. When Colonel Sherburn threw his shotgun across his arm and bade the crowd disperse Huck says:

> The crowd washed back sudden, and then broke all apart and went tearing off every which way, and Buck Harkness he heeled it after them, looking tolerable cheap. I could a staid if I'd a wanted to, but I didn't want to.
>
> I went to the circus, and loafed around the back side till the watchman went by, and then dived in under the tent.

That is all. No reflections, no hysterics; a murder and a mob dispersed, all without a single moral comment. And when the Shepherdsons had got done killing the Grangerfords, and Huck had tugged the two bodies ashore and covered Buck Grangerford's face with a handkerchief, crying a little because Buck had been good to him, he spent no time in sentimental reflection or sermonizing, but promptly hunted up Jim and the raft and sat down to a meal of corn-dodgers, buttermilk, pork and cabbage, and greens. . . . (pp. 795-96)

Able critics have declared that the psychology of Huck Finn is the book's large feature: Huck's moral point of view—the struggle between his heart and his conscience concerning the sin of Jim's concealment, and his final decision of self-sacrifice. Time may show that as an epic of the river, the picture of a vanished day, it will rank even greater. The problems of conscience we have always with us, but periods once passed are gone forever. Certainly Huck's loyalty to that lovely soul Nigger Jim was beautiful, though after all it may not have been so hard for Huck, who could be loyal to anything. Huck was loyal to his father, loyal to Tom Sawyer of course, loyal even to those two river tramps and frauds, the King and the Duke, for whom he lied prodigiously, only weakening when a new and lovelier loyalty came into view—loyalty to Mary Wilks.

The King and the Duke, by the way, are not elsewhere matched in fiction. The Duke was patterned after a journeyman-printer Clemens had known in Virginia City, but the King was created out of refuse from the whole human family—"all tears and flapdoodle," the very ultimate of disrepute and hypocrisy—so perfect a specimen that one must admire, almost love, him. "Hain't we all the fools in town on our side? and ain't that a big enough majority in any town?" he asks in a critical moment—a remark which stamps him as a philosopher of classic rank. We are full of pity at last when this pair of rapscallions ride out of the history on a rail and feel some of Huck's inclusive loyalty and all the sorrowful truth of his comment: "Human beings *can* be awful cruel to one another."

The "poor old king" Huck calls him, and confesses how he felt "ornery and humble and to blame, somehow," for the old scamp's misfortunes. "A person's conscience ain't got no sense," he says, and Huck is never more real to us, or more lovable, than in that moment. Huck is what he is because, being made so, he cannot well be otherwise. He is a boy throughout—such a boy as Mark Twain had known and in some degree had been. One may pettily pick a flaw here and

there in the tale's construction if so minded, but the moral character of Huck himself is not open to criticism. And indeed any criticism of this the greatest of Mark Twain's tales of modern life would be as the mere scratching of the granite of an imperishable structure. *Huck Finn* is a monument that no puny pecking will destroy. It is built of indestructible blocks of human nature; and if the blocks do not always fit, and the ornaments do not always agree, we need not fear. Time will blur the incongruities and moss over the mistakes. The edifice will grow more beautiful with the years. (pp. 797-98)

Albert Bigelow Paine, "Huck Finn Comes Into His Own," in his Mark Twain, a Biography: The Personal and Literary Life of Samuel Langhorne Clemens, Vol. II, *Harper & Brothers Publishers, 1912, pp. 793-98.*

WALDO FRANK (essay date 1919)

[*Frank was an American novelist and critic who was best known as an interpreter of contemporary civilization, particularly that of Latin America. A socialist and supporter of various radical groups in the United States, he was a founding editor of the* Seven Arts *(1916-17), a leftist, avant-garde magazine of literature and opinion. One of Frank's most significant works of criticism,* Our America *(1919), derides the "genteel tradition" in American letters and is considered an influential work for its support of realism in the nation's literature. In the following excerpt from that work, Frank proclaims* Huckleberry Finn *a great American epic.*]

[*Huckleberry Finn*] must go down in history, not as the expression of a rich national culture like the books of Chaucer, Rabelais, Cervantes, but as the voice of American chaos, the voice of a precultural epoch. Mark Twain kept this book long at his side. Ostensibly, it was the sequel to *The Adventures of Tom Sawyer* which appeared in 1875. "Huck" came nine years later. In it for once, the soul of Mark Twain burst its bonds of false instruction and false ideal, and found voice. Mark Twain lived twenty-six years longer. That voice never spoke again.

Huckleberry Finn is the simple story of a young white lad, born on the banks of the Mississippi who, with an escaped slave named Jim, builds a raft and floats down the mighty current. Mark Twain originally had meant it to be nothing else: had meant it for the mere sequel of another tale. But his theme was too apt a symbol. Into it he poured his soul.

Huck is a candid ignorant courageous child. He is full of the cunning and virtue of the resilient savage. He wears the habiliments of the civilization from which he comes, loosely, like trinkets about his neck. He and his companion build a raft and float. At night they veer their craft into the shallows or sleep on land. They have many adventures. The adventures that Huck has are the material of pioneering life. He always *happens* upon them. At times, he is a mere spectator: at times enforced accessory. Always, he is passive before a vaster fact. Huck is America. And Huck *floats* down the current of a mighty Stream.

Huckleberry Finn is the American epic hero. Greece had Ulysses. America must be content with an illiterate lad. He expresses our germinal past. He expresses the movement of the American soul through all the sultry climaxes of the Nineteenth Century.

The Mississippi with its countless squalid towns and its palatial steamboats was a ferment of commingled and insoluble life.

All the elements of the American East and all the elements of Europe seethed here, in the hunt of wealth. A delirium of dreams and schemes and passions, out of which shaped our genius for invention and exploitation. The whole gamut of American beginnings ran with the river. And Huck along. One rises from the book, lost in the beat of a great rhythmic flow: the unceasing elemental march of a vast life, cutting a continent, feeding its soil. And upon the heaving surface of this Flood, a human child: ignorant, joyous and courageous. The American soul like a midge upon the tide of a world. (pp. 38-40)

> *Waldo Frank, "The Land of the Pioneer," in his* Our America, *Boni and Liveright, Publishers, 1919, pp. 13-58.**

CARL VAN DOREN   (essay date 1921)

[*Van Doren is considered one of the most perceptive critics of the first half of the twentieth century. He worked for many years as a professor of English at Columbia University and served as literary editor and critic of the* Nation *and the* Century *during the 1920s. A founder of the Literary Guild and author or editor of several American literary histories, Van Doren was also a critically acclaimed historian and biographer. Howard Moss wrote of him: "His virtues, honesty, clarity and tolerance, are rare. His vices, occasional dullness and a somewhat monotonous rhetoric, are merely, in most places, the reverse coin of his excellence." In the following excerpt, Van Doren ranks* Huckleberry Finn *among America's greatest novels.*]

In richness of life *Tom Sawyer* cannot compare with [*Huckleberry Finn*]. The earlier of the two books keeps close home in one sleepy, dusty village, illuminated only, at inconvenient moments, by Tom Sawyer's whimsies. But in *Huckleberry Finn* the plot, like Mark Twain's imagination, goes voyaging. Five short chapters and Huck leaves his native village for the ampler world of the picaresque. An interval of captivity with his father—that unpleasant admonitory picture of what Huck may someday become if he outgrows his engaging youthful fineness—and then the boy slips out upon the river which is the home of his soul. There he realizes every dream he has ever had. He has a raft of his own. He has a friend, the negro Jim, with the strength of a man, the companionableness of a boy, and the fidelity of a dog. He can have food for the fun of taking it out of the water or stealing it from along the shore. He sleeps and wakes when he pleases. The weather of the lower Mississippi in summer bites no one. At the same time, this life is not too safe. Jim may be caught and taken from his benefactor. With all his craft, Huck is actually, as a boy, very much at the mercy of the rough men who infest the river. Adventure complicates and enhances his freedom. And what adventure! It never ceases, but flows on as naturally as the river which furthers the plot of the story by conveying the characters from point to point. Both banks are as crowded with excitement, if not with danger, as the surrounding forest of the older romances. Huck can slip ashore at any moment and try his luck with the universe in which he moves without belonging to it. Now he is the terrified and involuntary witness of a cruel murder plot, and again of an actual murder. Now he strays, with his boy's astonished simplicity, into the Grangerford-Shepherdson vendetta and sees another *Romeo and Juliet* enacted in Kentucky. In the undesired company of the "king" and the "duke," certainly two as sorry and as immortal rogues as fiction ever exhibited, Huck is initiated into degrees of scalawaggery which he could not have experienced, at his age, alone; into amateur theatricals as extraordinary as the Royal

Nonesuch and frauds as barefaced as the impostures practised upon the camp-meeting and upon the heirs of Peter Wilks. After sights and undertakings so Odyssean, the last quarter of the book, given over to Tom Sawyer's romantic expedients for getting Jim, who is actually free already, out of a prison from which he could have been released in ten minutes, is preserved from the descent into anticlimax only by its hilarious comic force. As if to make up for the absence of more sizable adventures, this mimic conspiracy is presented with enough art and enough reality in its genre studies to furnish an entire novel. That, in a way, is the effect of *Huckleberry Finn* as a whole: though the hero, by reason of his youth, cannot entirely take part in the action, and the action is therefore not entirely at first hand, the picture lacks little that could make it more vivid or veracious.

In the futile critical exercise of contending which is the greatest American novel, choice ordinarily narrows down at last to *The Scarlet Letter* and *Huckleberry Finn*—a sufficiently antipodean pair and as hard to bring into comparison as tragedy and comedy themselves. Each in its department, however, these two books do seem to be supreme. *The Scarlet Letter* offers, by contrast, practically no picture; *Huckleberry Finn,* no problem. Huck undergoes, it is true, certain naggings from the set of unripe prejudices he calls his conscience; and once he rises to an appealing unselfishness when, in defiance of all the principles he has been taught to value, he makes up his mind that he will assist the runaway slave to freedom. But in the sense that *The Scarlet Letter* poses problems, *Huckleberry Finn* poses none at all. Its criticism of life is of another sort. It does not work at the instigation of any doctrine, moral or artistic, whatever. As Hawthorne, after long gazing into the somber dusk over ancient Salem, had seen the universal drama of Hester and Dimmesdale and Chillingworth being transacted there, and had felt it rising within him to expression, so Mark Twain, in the midst of many vicissitudes remembering the river of his youthful happiness, had seen the panorama of it unrolling before him and also had been moved to record it out of sheer joy in its old wildness and beauty, assured that merely to have such a story to tell was reason enough for telling it. Having written *Life on the Mississippi* he had already reduced the river to his own language; having written *Tom Sawyer,* he had got his characters in hand. There wanted only the moment when his imagination should take fire at recollection and rush away on its undogmatic task of reproducing the great days of the valley. Had Mark Twain undertaken to make another and a greater *Gilded Age* out of his matter, to portray the life of the river satirically on the largest scale, instead of in such dimensions as fit Huck's boyish limitations of knowledge, he might possibly have made a better book, but he would have had to be another man. Being the man he was, he touched his peak of imaginative creation not by taking thought how he could be a Balzac to the Mississippi but by yarning with all his gusto about an adventure he might have had in the dawn of his days. Although he did not deliberately gather riches, riches came. (pp. 172-75)

> *Carl Van Doren, "Mark Twain," in his* The American Novel, *The Macmillan Company, 1921, pp. 157-87.*

JOHN ERSKINE   (essay date 1927)

[*Erskine was a distinguished American educator, musician, and author. In the following excerpt, originally published in 1927, he compares* Tom Sawyer *with* Huckleberry Finn *and explores the latter novel's principal themes and techniques.*]

"You don't know about me without you have read a book by the name of *The Adventures of Tom Sawyer;* but that ain't no matter," says Huckleberry Finn. He is quite right. We can understand his masterly story even if we have not read the book to which it is the sequel, but most Americans have read both, and a comparison of them helps us to see the greatness of the later one. In the preface to *Tom Sawyer* Mark Twain tells us he is drawing on his own memories of boyhood, and hopes to entertain young readers, but he adds that older folk may be interested in the picture of the Middle West, around 1850, and in the incidental record of the odd superstitions which were then prevalent among children and slaves.

In *Huckleberry Finn* the superstitions still appear, and the story certainly fascinates boys and girls, but mature readers value it for the rich picture of human nature, a satirical picture, if you will, but mellow and kind. In the preface to this book Mark Twain calls our attention to the various dialects the characters use, but it is hard not to believe his own interest was chiefly in providing us with our first and still our best account of Main Street—of the small community, narrow as to their virtues and their vices, and starved in their imaginations, all but the children and the most childlike among them.

Since the *Adventures of Tom Sawyer* and the later book have the same background and much the same characters, it looks as though Mark Twain must have discovered his true subject during the eight years which separated the stories. Huckleberry Finn tells us far more than he knows; through his naive confessions we see the panorama of his world and become sophisticated. We are really studying ourselves. In the earlier books, however, we have episodes of boyhood, rather loosely strung together, with one terrific stroke of melodrama to help out the plot. No doubt *Tom Sawyer* would be enjoyed by young people even if *Huckleberry Finn* did not lend it fame and keep it alive, but taken by itself it now seems a rather poorly constructed book. The story is built up with anecdotes, each one complete in itself, and none developed beyond the point of the joke.

In this early book Tom Sawyer interests us by his love of mischief and by his exuberant fancy. He contrives more than the usual share of histrionics; other boys make believe, but Tom dramatizes his boyish sentimentality on the grand scale, and we have the suspicion that by emphasizing and isolating the boy, Mark Twain gets the total picture of life out of focus, and makes it difficult for us to interpret the exceptional events in terms of the normal parts of his story.

These comments on the earlier book may help us to see why we instinctively admire *Huckleberry Finn.* The same elements reappear, the same characters, though new persons enter the tale, the same scene is described, though Huckleberry and the negro Jim have their chief adventures down the river on a raft, and the spirit of adventure in boyhood again is the central theme of the book. But this time the elements are arranged in a proportion which convinces us, and we are sure the picture is true.

When you sit down to write a novel, you find you must have something besides characters and a plot; you must have a philosophy of life. . . . There are novelists who believe that humdrum experience, the typical daily round of all of us, is the proper material for fiction, and that the novelists, by bearing down hard on it, may bring out the grain of significance under the smooth-worn surface. Another kind of artist portrays the average life remorselessly, to show that it is even less significant than it seems. He is the satirist, and he shows himself frequently in American literature to-day, a strong critic of narrowness and meanness, especially as observed in village life. A third kind of story-teller, with perhaps the same dislike of what is familiar and trite, turns resolutely to fresh material, to the unusual event; he looks, as we say, for an escape from the world which shuts him in.

In *Huckleberry Finn* Mark Twain is all three kinds of story-teller at once. He gives us a kindly picture of men and women in very small towns along the river, people with no heroic experience, who yet find their lives of considerable importance to themselves.

There is a satiric picture, too, an intermittent glimpse into the smallness of human nature. Huckleberry has learned how to make use of men by appealing to their mean side. When the two oarsmen come near the raft and almost discover the runaway slave, Huckleberry saves Jim by inviting them to come on board and minister to the crew. There's a mild case of smallpox, he explains, and the two men row away, after giving him forty dollars, to salve their conscience for thus denying the appeal of the sick.

The way in which the realistic elements and the satiric are combined with extraordinary adventure might well be the envy and the admiration of any novelist. The quiet river towns which Mark Twain remembered from his youth had something of the frontier still; violent death varied the monotony, from time to time, and the outcasts of older parts of the world chanced along, for shelter, or for a last opportunity to play their tricks in a place where they weren't known. The law-abiding portions of the community would condemn such interruptions of the peace, but they would also be fairly hardened to them. If a novelist tried to tell us now that the performance of the two quacks in *Romeo and Juliet*, or in the *Royal Nonesuch*, was ever accepted by any American community we should probably decline to believe him. But when we watch these rascals and their doings through the eyes of Huckleberry Finn, we are free to believe them as exceptional as we please, yet we understand perfectly why the boy took them for granted. Huckleberry has had a bringing-up which has prepared him to be surprised at nothing. We know that his approach to life is peculiar; if his judgments are not those of the average person, we know why they aren't, and we know just how far they depart from the normal, and he has our sympathy. Mark Twain manipulated his material, therefore, so that the most outrageous melodrama could present itself as matter of fact, through the mediium of Huckleberry's temperament, and even while we are rearranging the values, and discerning what the boy was blind to, we like him, and concede that he is true to life.

He is not supposed to be an average boy, like Tom Sawyer; he is the son of the village drunkard, a waif who grows up uneducated and uncared for, so far as the community can see. (pp. 263-67)

Huckleberry's mother does not exist, so far as the story is concerned. We may imagine her the victim of her husband's brutality, if we are so inlined, and we may endow her with enough virtues to account for her son's kind heart and gentle instincts. But Mark Twain is at his best when he leaves her history a blank. Huckleberry's isolation is complete, and we are under no compulsion to measure him by the accustomed traditions of society.

The handling of the romantic or melodramatic elements in the story can be admired from another angle also. Though the life of the small village may seem unduly quiet, it is the person from the city who chiefly finds it dull; the people involved in it often are aware of excitements. Of course the excitements come at long intervals, and they are cherished most often as scandal. Every small community has its stories about this woman or that man, stories which are often wild enough and improbable, but they really happened. But if a whole and steady view of life seems to us desirable, we can admire the way in which Mark Twain allows us to enjoy the wild adventures of Huckleberry, and at the same time shows us, in the not too remote background, a just picture of the folks who will talk about such experiences, but to whom they will never come. It is extraordinary that this balance is preserved through so long a succession of wild episodes; but even at the end, we still are aware of some surprise when a new accident occurs, we still consider ourselves the inhabitants of a quite normal world.

Several technical devices for securing this sense of the normal, for convincing us that the eccentric character is eccentric, no matter how often he appears, can easily be recognized by any one who knows the formulas of literary criticism. We can see, for example, that the characters speak for themselves. Though Huckleberry is telling the story, he reports conversations fully, and rarely makes a comment. This is the ancient rule for rendering character vividly, but it is easier to state the principle than to follow it. (pp. 268-69)

It would be in the sound tradition of criticism to say also that Mark Twain established a human scale throughout by descriptions of nature. The broad and changing river, the starry nights, the fogs, the glorious storms, refer us constantly to a scheme of things against which man even at his best would seem small. (p. 270)

But when we have said this about the descriptions of nature in the story, we ought to add that perhaps Mark Twain put them in for no other reason than his love of them. The joy in grand aspects of weather is so evident that their effect on the story may well have been a happy result, not altogether intended. It is a pagan love of nature—and we might say, a typically American love of the thing for itself, without asking what it means.

The book owes more of its fame than we sometimes recognize to the portrait of the negro, Jim, who runs away from a good home and from the neighborhood of his wife and children because he has reason to fear he may be sold down the river. He is the one elaborate picture we have of the negro slave before the war, and in a community in which owner and slave alike take slavery very much for granted. Mrs. Stowe's famous book is full of correct observation; she gives us no doubt a fair account of slavery at its happiest—along with other reports which some Southerners will always think exaggerated. But *Uncle Tom's Cabin* remains a discussion of slavery as an issue in justice; the problem colors every sentence in the book. There must have been thousands of families in which the issue never suggested itself. That is the version of slavery which Mark Twain has given us—the picture of good Christian homes in which the slaves were as natural an incident as any other human relation. Even as propaganda, if *Hucklebrry Finn* had been written early enough to serve that purpose, it would have been more subtly convincing than Mrs. Stowe's book, for the dramatic method, without preaching of any kind, here stirs the emotions deeply. (pp. 270-71)

Though our sympathy for the slave is profound, we are allowed to see the negro on more sides of his character than Mrs. Stowe may have been aware of. She knew that the colored race was deeply religious, but she took religion to mean the reading of the Bible and the attendance in a Christian church. Uncle Tom is religious in this sense. What we have more recently learned to appreciate, the wealth of folk-lore, superstition and mysticism which still seems to be the inheritance of negroes, even when they live among the whites, Mrs. Stowe did not portray. Mark Twain makes the most of it; he shows us the African in Jim, the ignorance which to the casual white seems absurd, but which really is connected with powers the white does not share. Altogether he is a wonderful creation, the more remarkable for the matter-of-fact way in which he is presented, without emphasis or exaggeration. He does not take the important place in the scene—Huckleberry remains the hero of the story, but when we have laid the book down, the patient inscrutable black, with his warm heart and his childlike wisdom, remains not the least vivid of our memories.

Whether the portrait of the Grangerfords and the Shepherdsons, in their famous feud, is true to historical fact, those must decide who know the regions of the South before the war where this feud is supposed to occur. But there is no question that the persons seem real, and that the satire on the follies of human nature bites rather deep in this part of the story. Here again the fact that Huckleberry is telling the story serves to secure a splendid literary effect. Nothing in the book is told with greater restraint, and nothing is quite so tragic. The restraint is art, but it seems the work of nature, because Huck wishes, as he says, to hurry over the details—he tries not to remember them for fear they may spoil his sleep. Yet out of the tragedy the reader seizes a noble emotion. When you reflect on the wickedness of feuds and duels, as on the wickedness of war, you may be troubled that a noble emotion should be roused by such material, but when you let yourself go uncritically you can enjoy the courage, the chivalry, the romance which Mark Twain has put into this episode.

At the end of the story Tom Sawyer reappears. He comes to the place where Jim has been captured as a runaway slave, and Huck is hoping to contrive an escape. Tom happens to know that Jim is no longer a slave, but a freeman. The idea of getting him out of his prison, however, is too fruitful to be resisted; Tom begins to make believe—the log cabin becomes a dungeon—the methods of release must be as elaborate as though there were a moat and high walls to cross, and valiant guards to beat down. From this point on, the story lags. The adventures which Tom imagines are cheap after the real dangers Huck and Jim have gone through. We wonder whether this effect of anticlimax was accidental or intended. Did Mark Twain wish to draw this comparison between the genuine experience and the fanciful? Whether he did or not, the contrast is there.

For that reason I have thought it not unjust to compare the two stories to the advantage of *Huckleberry Finn.* We always think of them together, and here at the close of his masterpiece the author sets the two boys side by side for us to look at. *Tom Sawyer* is a fine story, but the other is one of those books which occur all too rarely in a national literature, a book so close to the life of the people that it can hold any reader, and yet so subtle in its art that the craftsman tries to find out how it was done. I don't see why we shouldn't recognize it as a masterpiece now, without waiting for posterity to cast any more votes. Indeed, we thought a while ago that the ballot was closed. But recently it has been suggested that Mark Twain, poor man, missed his full development as an artist, that American life in his time was not sophisticated enough in matters of art to demand of him perfect workmanship, or to applaud when he gave it. Well, that sort of argument breaks down when we ask to see what men have written who were more fortunately placed than he, and when we set their work beside his. Some things he wrote will suffer by the comparison, but not the *Adventures of Huckleberry Finn*. (pp. 272-74)

> John Erskine, "Huckleberry Finn," in his The Delight of Great Books, *The World Publishing Co.*, 1941, pp. 263-74.

BERNARD DeVOTO (essay date 1932)

[*An editor of the* Saturday Review of Literature *and longtime contributor to* Harper's Magazine, *DeVoto was a highly controversial literary critic and historian. A man whose thought enraged much of America's literary establishment during the 1930s and 1940s, he was frequently motivated by anger at authors he considered ignorant of American life and history. As a critic, he admired mastery of form and psychological subtlety in literature. His own work is characterized by its scholarly thoroughness and by its vigorous, infectious style. DeVoto is the author of two influential studies of Twain,* Mark Twain's America *(1932) and* Mark Twain at Work *(1942). The first, written in response to Van Wyck Brooks's* Ordeal of Mark Twain *(1920), presents a portrait of American frontier life and humor of the mid-nineteenth century, demonstrating this background to have been beneficial to Twain's literary development. The second book, written after scrutiny of Twain's manuscripts, examines the composition of* Tom Sawyer *and* Huckleberry Finn. *In the following excerpt from* Mark Twain's America, *DeVoto compares characters and incidents in* Huckleberry Finn *to those in Twain's previous works and discusses the artistic failures and achievements of the novel.*]

The kernel of *Huckleberry Finn* is in a speech of Huck's toward the end of *Tom Sawyer*. At the foot of the dead-limb tree t'other side of Still-House branch, he doubts the value of finding buried treasure. "Pap would come back to thish yer town some day and get his claws on it if I didn't hurry up, and I tell you he'd clean it out pretty quick." *Old Times on the Mississippi*, contains a passage as integral with Huck's journey as anything in his book, and *Life on the Mississippi*, written over the period when Huck was gestated, has many incidents on their way to fruition. The Darnell-Watson feud is the Grangerford-Shepherdson trouble in chrysalis, a desultory tale told by a passenger as the *Gold Dust* passes through the chute of Island Number 8. On the upstream voyage as yet anonymous strollers forecast David Garrick the younger and Edmund Keen the elder. John A. Murrell's inheritors hint at revenge in the staterooms of a wrecked steamboat and other creatures of midnight presage the turmoil of search and escape through underbrush. Nor are these volumes the only ones in which pupal stages of incidents in *Huckleberry Finn* may be observed: most of the books that precede have passages of premonition. Why not? It was a book he was foreordained to write: it brought harmoniously to a focus everything that had a basic reality in his mind.

The opening is just *Tom Sawyer* and pretty poor *Tom Sawyer* at that. Huck's report of his emotions while ghosts are talking to him in the wind is a promise of what is to come, but Tom Sawyer's gang commenting on *Don Quixote* lacks the fineness of its predecessor. Discussions of ransom and Tom's exposition of Aladdin's lamp are feeble; such finish as they have comes from Huck's tolerant but obstinate common sense, here making its first experiments. But no flavor of the real Odyssey appears until Miss Watson forbids him to avert by magic the bad luck

made inevitable by spilled salt, thus precipitating his trouble, and he immediately finds in the snow the impression of a boot heel in which nails make a cross to keep off the devil. . . . It is expedient to list here the book's obvious faults. After a first half in which, following the appearance of old man Finn, no touch is unsure, Mark's intuition begins to falter occasionally. When the Duke has Louis XVII learn a Shakespearian speech compounded out of Sol Smith and George Ealer, high and poetic reality lapses into farce. (Predictably. The humorist's necessity to write burlesque had frequently ruined fine things in the earlier books.) The King's conversion is weakened by his use of pirates instead of the neighborhood church which his predecessor Simon Suggs had more persuasively employed. (Predictably. The necessity to carry a joke into cosmic reaches had betrayed him often enough before.) Huck's discourse on the domestic manners of royalty is a blemish. (Extravaganza had diluted satire in many earlier contexts.) Huck's confusion when he tries to lie to the harelipped girl is perfunctory. (Improvisation had substituted for structure sufficiently often in Mark's previous fiction.) The concluding episodes of the attempted fraud on the Wilks family are weak in their technical devices—the manipulation required to postpone the detection of imposture for instance, is annoying. Thereafter the narrative runs downhill through a steadily growing incredibility. The use of ghosts, the deceptions practiced on Aunt Sally and Uncle Silas, the whole episode built around the delivery of Jim from prison—all these are far below the accomplishment of what has gone before. Mark was once more betrayed. He intended a further chapter in his tireless attack on romanticism, especially Southern romanticism, and nothing in his mind or training enabled him to understand that this extemporized burlesque was a defacement of his purer work. His boundless gusto expended itself equally on the true and the false. . . . Predictably. It has been observed that he was incapable of sustained and disciplined imagination. One could expect it no more reasonably here than in *The Innocents Abroad*. (pp. 310-12)

The title announces the structure: a picaresque novel concerned with the adventures of Huckleberry Finn. The form is the one most native to Mark Twain and so best adapted to his use. No more than Huck and the river's motion gives continuity to a series of episodes which are in essence only developed anecdotes. They originate in the tradition of newspaper humor, but the once uncomplicated form becomes here the instrument of great fiction. The lineage goes back to a native art; the novel derives from the folk and embodies their mode of thought more purely and more completely than any other ever written. . . . [The] life of the southwestern frontier was umbilical to the mind of Mark Twain. The blood and tissue of *Huckleberry Finn* have been formed in no other way. That life here finds issue more memorably than it has anywhere else, and since the frontier is a phase through which most of the nation has passed, the book comes nearer than any other to identity with the national life. The gigantic amorphousness of our past makes impossible, or merely idle, any attempt to fix in the form of idea the meaning of nationality. But more truly with *Huckleberry Finn* than with any other book, inquiry may satisfy itself: here is America.

The book has the fecundity, the multiplicity, of genius. It is the story of a wandering—so provocative a symbol that it moved Rudyard Kipling to discover another sagacious boy beneath a cannon and conduct him down an endless road, an enterprise that enormously fell short of its model. It is a passage through the structure of the nation. It is an exploration of the human race, whose adjective needs no explicit recording. It is an adventure of pageantry, horror, loveliness, and the tropisms of the mind. It is a faring-forth with inexhaustible delight through the variety of America. It is the restlessness of the young democracy borne southward on the river—the energy, the lawlessness, the groping ardor of the flux perfectly comprehended in a fragment of lumber raft drifting on the June flood. In a worn phrase—it is God's plenty.

The arrival of Huck's father lifts the narrative from the occupations of boyhood to as mature intelligence as fiction has anywhere. The new interest begins on a major chord, for old man Finn is the perfect portrait of the squatter. Behind him are the observations of hundreds of anonymous or forgotten realists who essayed to present the clay-eaters or piney-woods people, as well as a lifelong interest of Mark Twain's. It is amazing how few pages of type he occupies; the effect is as of a prolonged, minute analysis. There is no analysis; a clear light is focused on him and the dispassionate, final knowledge of his creator permits him to reveal himself. We learn of him only that he had heard about Huck's money "away down the river", but a complete biography shines through his speech. This rises to the drunken monologue about a government that can't take a-hold of a prowling, thieving, white-shirted free nigger. The old man subsides to an attack of snakes, is heard rowing his skiff in darkness, and then is just a frowsy corpse, shot in the back, which drifts downstream with the flood.

Something exquisite and delicate went into that creation—as into the casuals of the riverside. Mrs. Judith Loftus is employed to start Huck and Jim upon their voyage. She is just a device, but she outtops a hundred-odd patient attempts of fiction to sketch the pioneer wife. In her shrewdness, curiosity, initiative and brusque humanity one reads an entire history. Mere allusions—the ferryboat owner, the oarsmen who flee from smallpox, even raftsmen heard joking in the dark—have an incomparable authenticity. There is also the crowd. The loafers of Brickville whittle under the store fronts. They set a dog upon a sow that has "wholloped" herself right down in the way and "laugh and look grateful for the noise." Presently a bubble rises through this human mire: the drunken Boggs, the best-naturedest old fool in Arkansaw, comes riding into Brickville, on the wawpath. Colonel Sherburn finds it necessary to shoot him; and then, in one of the most blinding flashlights in all fiction, a "long, lanky man, with long hair and a big white fur stovepipe hat on the back of his head" rehearses the murder. "The people that had seen the thing said he done it perfect." So Buck Harkness leads a mob to Sherburn's house for a lynching but the Colonel breaks up the mob with a speech in which contempt effervesces like red nitric.

But in such passages as this, the clearly seen individuals merge into something greater, a social whole, a civilization, seen just as clearly. Pokeville, where the King is converted at the camp-meeting, Brickville, and the town below the P'int where a tanner has died are one with Dawson's Landing and Napoleon—but more concentrated and thereby more final. It seems unnecessary to linger in consideration of this society. At the time of its appearance in 1885 a number of other novelists, perhaps fecundated by *The Gilded Age,* were considering similar themes. The name of any one of them—Charles Egbert Craddock or Mary E. Wilkins or Edward Eggleston will do—is enough to distinguish honest talent from genius. The impulse weakened under the aestheticism of the Nineties, and it was not till after the World War that the countryside again received consideration in these terms. To set Brickville against Gopher Prairie or Winesburg is to perceive at once the finality of Mark Twain. The long lanky man in a white stovepipe hat who rehearses the death of Boggs has recorded this society with an unemotional certainty beside which either Mr. Lewis's anger or Mr. Anderson's misery seems a transitory hysterics.

The completeness of the society must be insisted upon. One should scrutinize the family of the dead tanner and their friends and neighbors, and orient them by reference to the family of Colonel Grangerford. The Wilkses belong to the industrious respectability of the towns. Their speech and thinking, the objects of their desire, the circumstances of their relationships are the totality of their kind. The funeral of Peter Wilks is, as fiction, many themes blended together; it is, among them, a supreme exhibition of the midcontinental culture of its time—almost an archaeological display. When the undertaker tiptoes among the mourners to silence a howling dog and returns to whisper "He had a rat", something final has been said about this life. But Colonel Grangerford is a gentleman. Incidentally to the feud, which is the principal occupation of this episode, Southern gentility is examined. James's Basil Ransom was an embraced tradition; Colonel Grangerford is a reality. His daughter's elopement, a device for the precipitation of the plot, is out of fiction; the feud itself, with all the lovingly studied details of the scene, are from life. Gentility decorates the parlor with Emmaline Grangerford's verse and sketches. Its neurons show in the management of more than a hundred niggers quite as positively as in the parlor, or in the ceremonies of family intercourse and the simple code of honor, so indistinguishable from that of the Iroquois, which results in mass murder.

The portraiture which begins among the dregs with old man Finn ends with the Grangerfords. Between these strata has come every level of the South. What is the integrity of an artist? It would seem to consist in an intelligence which holds itself to the statement of a perceived truth, refusing to color it with an emotion of the artist's consequent to the truth. . . . These scenes are warm with an originality and a gusto that exist nowhere else in American fiction, and yet they are most notable for Mark Twain's detachment. There is no coloration, no resentment, no comment of any kind. The thing itself is rendered. If repudiation is complete, it exists implicitly in the thing.

The differentiation of the speech these people use is so subtly done that Mark had to defend himself against an accusation of carelessness. He did not want readers to "suppose that all these characters were trying to talk alike and not succeeding." Superlatives are accurate once more: no equal sensitiveness to American speech has ever been brought to fiction. But a triumph in dialect is after all one of the smaller triumphs of novel-writing, and the important thing to be observed about Huckleberry's speech is its achievement in making the vernacular a perfect instrument for all the necessities of fiction. Like Melville, Mark Twain could write empty rhetoric enough when the mood was on him, and the set pieces of description in the travel books are as trying as the McGuffey selections which may have influenced them, while a willingness to let tears flow menaces a good many effects elsewhere. Yet his writing is never mediocre and is mostly, even in the least pretentious efforts, a formidable strength. Beginning with *Life on the Mississippi* it becomes, as Mr. Ford has remarked, one of the great styles of English literature. No analysis need be made here: its basis is simplicity, adaptability, an intimate liaison with the senses, and fidelity to the idioms of speech. Against the assertions of criticism, it should be remembered that such a style is not developed inattentively, nor are infants born with one by God's providence. Mark's lifelong pleasure in the peculiarities of language, which has distressed commentators, was the interest of any artist in his tools. . . . The successful use of an American vernacular as the sole prose medium of a masterpiece is a triumph in technique. Such attempts have been common in two and a half centuries of English fiction, but no other attempt on the highest level has succeeded. In this respect, too, *Huckleberry Finn* is unique. Patently, American literature has nothing to compare with it. Huck's language is a sensitive, subtle, and versatile instrument—capable of every effect it is called upon to manage. Whether it be the purely descriptive necessity of recording the river's mystery, or the notation of psychological states so minute and transitory as the effect on a boy of ghosts crying in the wind, or the fixation of individuality in dialogue, or the charged finality that may be typified by the King's "Hain't we got all the fools in town on our side? And ain't that a big enough majority in any town?"—the prose fulfills its obligation with the casual competence of genius. The fiction of Mark Twain had brought many innovations to the national literature—themes, lives, and interests of the greatest originality. This superb adaptation of vernacular to the purposes of art is another innovation, one which has only in the last few years begun to have a dim and crude but still perceptible fruition.

A tradition almost as old as prose narrative joins to the novel another tributary of world literature when a purely American wandering brings two further creatures of twilight to the raft. The Duke of Bilgewater and the Lost Dauphin were born of Mark's inexhaustible delight in worthlessness, but are many-sided. Pretension of nobility is one of his commonest themes, here wrought into pure comedy. The Duke is akin to characters in the other books; the King embodies a legend widespread and unimaginably glorious on the frontier. The ambiguity surrounding the death of Louis XVII gave to history riots, dynasties and social comedies that still absorb much reverence in Florence and Paris. It gave mythology a superb legend, which at once accommodated itself to American belief. Up the river from New Orleans, one of the most pious repositories of allegiance, stories of the dethroned Bourbon gratified believers during three generations. The legend must have entertained Mark's boyhood but the circumstances of his Dauphin suggest that he more enjoyed the appearance of Eleazar Williams, who became an international celebrity in 1853. The whole course of his life probably gave him no more satisfying exhibition of the race's folly than the discovery of a Bourbon king in the person of this Mohawk half-breed turned Christian and missionary, who had systematically defrauded his church and his people. The story is one of the occasional ecstasies with which history rewards the patient mind.

The two rogues are formed from the nation's scum. They are products of chance and opportunity, drifters down rivers and across the countryside in the service of themselves. The Duke has sold medicines, among them a preparation to remove tartar from the teeth; he has acted tragedy and can sling a lecture sometimes; he can teach singing-geography school or take a turn to mesmerism or phrenology.when there's a chance. The King can tell fortunes and can cure cancer or paralysis by the laying on of hands; but preaching, missionarying, and the temperance revival are his best lines. American universals meet here; once more, this is a whole history, and into these drifters is poured an enormous store of the nation's experience. They have begotten hordes of successors since 1885 but none that joins their immortality. They belong with Colonel Sellers: they are the pure stuff of comedy. Their destiny is guile: to collect

the tax which freedom and wit levy on respectability. Their voyage is down a river deep in the American continent; they are born of a purely American scene. Yet the river becomes one of the world's roads and these disreputables join, of right, a select fellowship. They are Diana's foresters: the brotherhood that receives them, approving their passage, is immortal in the assenting dreams of literature. Such freed spirits as Panurge, Falstaff, Gil Blas and the Abbé Coignard are of that fellowship; no Americans except the Duke and the Dauphin have joined it. None seems likely to.

Yet the fabric on which all this richness is embroidered is the journey of Huck and Jim down the Mississippi on the June rise. There, finally, the book's glamour resides. To discuss that glamour would be futile. In a sense, Huck speaks to the national shrewdness, facing adequately what he meets, succeeding by means of native intelligence whose roots are ours—and ours only. In a sense, he exists for a delight or wonder inseparable from the American race. This passage down the flooded river, through pageantry and spectacle, amidst an infinite variety of life, something of surprise or gratification surely to be met with each new incident—it is the heritage of a nation not unjustly symbolized by the river's flow. Huck sleeping under the stars or wakefully drifting through an immensity dotted only by far lights or scurrying to a cave while the forest bends under a cloudburst satisfies blind gropings of the mind. The margin widens to obscurity. Beyond awareness,

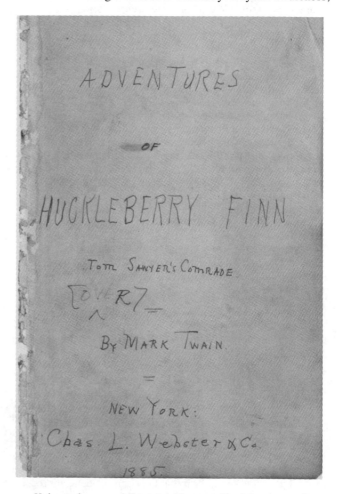

Holograph copy of Twain's title page for Adventures of Huckleberry Finn.

a need for freedom, an insatiable hunger for its use, finds in him a kind of satisfaction. At the margin, too, the endless flow speaks for something quite as immediate. It is movement, not quiet. By day or darkness the current is unceasing; its rhythm, at the obscure margin, speaks affirmatively. For life is movement—a down-river voyage amidst strangeness.

Go warily in that obscurity. One does not care to leave Huck in the twilight at such a threshold, among the dim shapes about which no one can speak with authority. Unquestionably something of him is resident there—with something of Tom, the disreputables, Colonel Sellers and some others. But first he is a shrewd boy who takes a raft down the Mississippi, through a world incomparably alive. With him goes a fullness made and shaped wholly of America. It is only because the world he passes through is real and only because it is American that his journey escapes into universals and is immortal. His book is American life formed into great fiction. (pp. 313-20)

> *Bernard DeVoto, "The Artist as American," in his* Mark Twain's America and Mark Twain at Work, *Houghton Mifflin Company, 1967, pp. 298-322.**

EDGAR LEE MASTERS   (essay date 1938)

[*Masters was one of the first major twentieth-century American authors to use the theories of modern psychology to examine human thought and motivation. A prolific writer, he is best known for the monumental poetic cycle* Spoon River Anthology (1915), *a collection of free-verse epitaphs on the men and women buried in a small-town churchyard. Through its sardonic attack on provincial dullness and spiritual sterility,* Spoon River Anthology *strongly influenced the literature of the 1920s. In the following excerpt, Masters criticizes* Huckleberry Finn *as an artistically flawed work of fiction.*]

I concur in the judgment of Arnold Bennett on *Tom Sawyer* and *Huckleberry Finn,* namely that they are "episodically magnificent," but as complete works of art quite inferior, though I should not say quite inferior, but rather that they fall off from what they might have been made. I regret to say that they are not as consistently and sustainedly created and executed as Stevenson's *Treasure Island.* (p. 122)

Some judges of books place *The Adventures of Huckleberry Finn* above *Tom Sawyer.* I think the latter book comes nearer being a rounded and consistent work. Twain put a note of explanation to *Huckleberry Finn* in regard to the dialects which he employed in writing it. He was not the relator as in *Tom Sawyer,* but the story comes from the mouth of Huck. "In this book," wrote Twain, "a number of dialects are used, to wit: the Missouri negro dialect; the extremest form of the backwoods, Southwestern dialect; the ordinary 'Pike county' dialect; and four modified varieties of the last. The shadings have not been done in a haphazard fashion, or by guesswork, but painstakingly, and with the trustworthy guidance and support of personal familiarity with these several forms of speech."

Twain had a keen mimetic sense, an acting ability. Indeed, his humor depends upon these histrionic equipments. His memory was excellent, and his opportunity to know how the people of Missouri and Arkansas talked could not have been better. Yet I venture that he went wrong many times in this book in choosing words for Huck and the other characters in it. A few instances may be cited.

Would Huck, in speaking of his feelings, say "very well satisfied"? Would he not rather say, "and feelin' all right"?

Would he use the word "reticule" instead of saying "one of them things they keep needles in, ratacoul or something"? Would he not say "et" instead of "eat"? Would he not say "the lightning showed her very plain," instead of "the lightning showed her very distinct"? . . . There are passages, too, in the book where Twain is unmistakably talking and not Huck. They are too well expressed and compact for the unlettered brain of Huck to give utterance to. So Huck would say "the other feller," not "the other fellow." He would likely speak of sheet lightning as "winking and spreading," not as "squirting." At the outset in this book Twain accomplished one of those strokes of genius which cannot be too much praised. It is the talk between old Man Finn and Huck in the river shack concerning the money which Huck has from treasure hunting, which Judge Thatcher controls as trustee for Huck. Listen to the ragged old drunkard:

> "Ain't you a sweet-scented dandy, though? A bed, and bedclothes, and a look'n glass; and a piece of carpet on the floor—and your father got to sleep with the hogs in the tanyard. I never see such a son. I bet I'll take some o' these frills out o' you before I'm done with you. Why, there ain't no end to your airs—they say you're rich. Hey? how's that?"
>
> "They lie—that's how."
>
> "Looky here—mind how you talk to me; I'm standing about all I can stand now—so don't gimme no sass. I've been in town two days, and I ain't heard nothing but about you bein' rich. I heard about it away down the river, too. That's why I come. You git me that money tomorrow—I want it."

Here Twain employs [the humorous trick in which] . . . the aggressor is posed as the aggrieved person. Poor Huck stands shivering with fear as his father heaps guilt upon his innocent life. (pp. 129-31)

This book is rich in episodes. There is a wonderful account of a Southern feud, and excellent descriptions of rooms and furnishings in houses down the Mississippi. Huck's boyish word picture of the river is very wonderful. And there is a graphic relation of a camp meeting of the time drawn true to life, just as they were held and appeared in Illinois, in Missouri, and Arkansas.

At about this point in the book invention runs mad, it becomes so preposterous that all belief is paralyzed. The antics of the Duke and the Dauphin, their Shakespearean acting, and the money they are credited with earning at little towns down the Mississippi strain belief. How is the human race satirized by the depiction of such types as the Duke and the Dauphin? If that is not accomplished, what remains but pure nonsense?

The Duke and the Dauphin pose as the heirs of an old man down on the Mississippi. Thus there is treasure again. They get the money, $6000, and hide it in a bed tick in the house of the deceased. Huck takes the money from the bed tick and puts it in the coffin of the deceased, and it is buried with the body. The corpse is then dug up and the money restored to the rightful heirs as the Duke and the Dauphin are exposed in their villainy and posing. There are more plotting and transparent lying than were ever before in the same number of pages. Tom Sawyer arrives on the scene pretending that he is Sid, Huck meanwhile having been taken for Tom. The Duke and the

Dauphin are tarred and feathered. Nigger Jim, whom Huck has been trying all along to rescue from being sold down the river, is placed in a log house on the lawn of the Phelps house, where all this incredible stuff has taken place. It is here that the tale breaks down, and with a superfluity of invention. It is so absurd that illusion lifts off and away and the scene appears in a kind of naked silliness. Jim is fed everything, even sawdust, while incarcerated, and is made the bedfellow of toads, snakes, and rats which Tom and Huck introduce into the cabin as a part of the necromancy by which Jim may be released from the prison of the cabin. Tom is shot in the leg in one of the scrambles about Jim, and Huck goes for the doctor and tells a story about the matter that could not fool an idiot. The reader is supposed to believe it enough to laugh. Sister Damrell, one of the *dramatis personae* at the Phelps house, talks just like Aunt Polly in **Tom Sawyer.** She says on an occasion, "them's the very words—they all heard me." That's the way old Finn talked too. Aunt Sally Phelps is a replica of Aunt Polly; and finally Aunt Polly appears on the scene, and thus St. Petersburg in a measure is moved down the Mississippi. (pp. 134-36)

> *Edgar Lee Masters, in his* Mark Twain: A Portrait, *Charles Scribner's Sons, 1938, 259 p.*

CLIFTON FADIMAN   (essay date 1940)

[*Fadiman became one of the most prominent American literary critics during the 1930s with his insightful and often caustic book reviews for the* Nation *and the* New Yorker *magazines. He also reached a sizable audience through his work as a radio talk-show host from 1938 to 1948. In the following excerpt, originally published as an introduction to the 1940 Heritage Press edition of* Huckleberry Finn, *Fadiman examines the aspects of the novel that make it a uniquely American work.*]

This is the book with which we as a literary people begin. Two thousand years from now American professors of literature—if such still exist—will speak of **Huckleberry Finn** as English professors of literature now speak of Chaucer. For **Huckleberry Finn** is our Chaucer, our Homer, our Dante, our Virgil. It is the source of the stream, the seed-bed, the book which, read or unread, has influenced a thousand American writers, the first great mold within which the form and pattern of our speech were caught. It has spawned both Hemingway and Mickey Spillane.

First-rate writers existed on this continent before **Huckleberry Finn.** But **Huckleberry Finn** is the first important work written out of a simple, vast unconsciousness of the existence of any country except ours. It is not traditionless, buts its traditions all have their roots in the Mississippi Valley. It is the nearest thing we have to a national epic.

And what an extraordinary national epic it is! It has its Achilles, but he is a fourteen-year-old boy. The hero has his Patroclus, but Patroclus is an illiterate Negro. It has its Kings and Dukes, but they are frauds and through them the whole principle of aristocracy (a principle upon which national epics rest) is ridiculed. It has its voyages and explorations, but they are undertaken on a raft. Its central episode is not some feat of high emprise, upon which rests the fate of a people, but an elaborate hoax involving the unnecessary freeing of a Negro slave. And the tone of this epic! Not a heroic phrase, no elevation, no invocation to the Muses. On the contrary, a style casual, conversational, the first completely unliterary style to appear on the American continent. "I sing of arms and the man" begins the noble Virgilian strain. And how does our *Aeneid* begin?

"You don't know about me without you have read a book by the name of **The Adventures of Tom Sawyer;** but that ain't no matter. That book was made by Mr. Mark Twain, and he told the truth, mainly. There was things which he stretched, but mainly he told the truth." These sentences announce the birth of a literature.

Yes, from one point of view, its language is the most important thing about **Huckleberry Finn,** more important than its humor, its characters, its story. For its language *is* in a way the humor, the characters, the story. Just as the Declaration of Independence (let us hope) contains in embryo our whole future history as a nation, so the language of **Huckleberry Finn** (another declaration of independence) expresses our popular character, our humor, our slant. This is the way we talk and think in those moods when we are most remote from our European or African beginnings. The smoking-car conversation, the Rotary Club address, the talk at a church social, the spiel of the traveling salesman, the lingo of Broadway—whatever is uniquely of this country has a smack, a tang, a flow, an accent, a rhythm, that go back to the language of **Huckleberry Finn.** For its language is not merely a comic device intended to convey the character of a rather unevenly educated boy of fourteen. It has in it the casual drawl of the frontier, the irreverent intonation of the democratic idea, and an innocent disregard of all the traditions of European writing. When Huck, complaining over the widow's preference for cooking each kind of food by itself, says, "In a barrel of odds and ends it is different; things get mixed up, and the juice kind of swaps around, and the things go better," when he says this, we know we are listening to the idiom of a separate civilization.

Perhaps the word civilization is a bad one, for this book—and here lies its troubling appeal to us—is an epic of rebellion against civilization. We have become a people of cities and motorcars and vacuum cleaners and two-week vacations and commutation tickets. But that is not the way we began, and despite our childish delight in gadgetry, we have a deep hankering for the forest, the river, the rifle out of which this country came. **Huckleberry Finn** is our most typical novel precisely because it expresses this hankering. The typical novels of France or England or Russia are novels of civilization. They assume the permanence of certain sophisticated societal relations. **Huckleberry Finn,** on the contrary, is a book about primitive things: small boys and food and weather and murders and darkness. Though produced in the century of Balzac, Tolstoy, and Thackeray it is more akin to the *Odyssey* or the Norse myths than to any of the representative great novels of the European tradition.

Here, in this rambling tale about the unimportant adventures of a boy who will probably not amount to much when he grows older (except that he will never grow older) are the matters, the myths, the deep conflicts of the American people: the influence of the frontier, the unresolved problem of the Negro, the revolt against city-convention, the fascinated absorption in deeds of violence, the immense sense of a continent cut in two by a vast river, the type-figure of the self-sufficient frontiersman, the passion for exploration, the love of the hoax, the exaggeration, and the practical joke, the notion of basic social equality, the enskying of youth. (pp. 129-31)

> *Clifton Fadiman, "Lead-Ins: A Note on 'Huckleberry Finn',"* in his Party of One, The World Publishing Company, 1955, pp. 129-31.

VAN WYCK BROOKS   (essay date 1947)

[*An American critic and biographer, Brooks is noted chiefly for studies of such writers as Twain, Henry James, and Ralph Waldo*

Emerson, and for his influential commentary on the history of American literature. His career can be divided into two distinct periods: in the first, from 1908 to 1925, Brooks was primarily concerned with the negative impact of European Puritanism on the development of artistic genius in America. Brooks argued that the puritan conscience in the United States, carried over from Europe, produced an unhealthy dichotomy in American writers that resulted in a literature split between stark realism and what he called "vaporous idealism." He maintained that in reality America had no culture of its own, and that American literature relied almost exclusively on its European heritage. During this period Brooks published his controversial *Ordeal of Mark Twain* (1920), in which he argued that Twain's life was not the unmitigated success portrayed in Albert Bigelow Paine's biography, but rather the ordeal of a literary genius repressed by his mother and wife and stifled in his literary development by America's false puritanical standards. Critical disagreement and Brooks's revised perception of American literary history led him to temper his argument somewhat in the second edition of the book, published in 1933 (see excerpt in TCLC, Vol. 6). Brooks eventually came to see much in America's past as unique and artistically valuable, and he called for a return in literary endeavors to the positive values of Emerson, as opposed to the modern pessimism of such writers as T. S. Eliot and James Joyce. In the following excerpt from his* Makers and Finders: A History of the Writer in America (1936-1952), Brooks considers* Huckleberry Finn *the source of much of modern American literature. For a disagreement with Brooks's characterization of the novel as the product of Twain's "fathomless naivety," see the excerpt by F. R. Leavis (1952).]

Mark Twain with his fathomless naivety prepared the ground, as Whitman did, for a new and unique American art of letters, in a negative way with *The Innocents Abroad,* in a positive way with the Western writings in which he contributed to establish and foster this art. For *Huckleberry Finn,* with *Tom Sawyer* and the first part of *Life on the Mississippi,*—books that were all composed before 1885,—were germs of a new American literature with a broader base in the national mind than the writers of New England had possessed, fine as they were. As the literary centre of gravity of the country shifted slowly westward and the Western writers in time came into their own, one found traces of Mark Twain in their rhythms, in their vision, in their choice of themes, in their mode of seeing and recording what they heard and saw. *Huckleberry Finn* with its panorama of river-towns and river-folk was the school of many a later Western writer: the imaginative world of Sherwood Anderson was largely based upon it and the style of Ernest Hemingway owed much to it as well. By his recreation of the frontier life in the great central continental Mississippi valley, by his skill in recapturing its speech and its turns of mind,— the accent and the manner of the world he had known as a child,—Mark Twain preempted for later writers a realm that was theirs by right of birth but might never have been theirs for literature if he had not cleared the way. (pp. 296-97)

[Did] Mark Twain really admire the "booming" nineteenth century, sturdy and great as he sometimes said it was,—the civilization the "Connecticut Yankee" stood for? Privately he said it was shabby and mean, cruel and hypocritical, and he wished he could see it in hell, for it belonged there. Was it not the moral of *Huckleberry Finn* that all civilization is a hateful mistake, something that frustrates life and stands in its way, something that did not "work" for Huck, the hero of the tale, who had to return to his barrel to save his life? Was not this one of the reasons for the vast vogue of *Huckleberry Finn* in the disillusioned years that followed the first world war, when the very conception of civilization lost all its charm for countless minds for whom honesty implied a reversion to a primitive existence? (p. 460)

Van Wyck Brooks, "Mark Twain in the West" and "Mark Twain in the East," in his The Times of Melville and Whitman, E. P. Dutton & Co., Inc., 1947, pp. 283-300, 448-64.

F. R. LEAVIS   (essay date 1952)

[*Leavis is an influential contemporary English critic. His critical methodology combines close textual criticism with predominantly moral, or social-moral, principles of evaluation. Leavis views the writer as that social individual who represents the "most conscious point of the race" in his or her lifetime. More importantly, the writer is one who can effectively communicate this consciousness. Contrary to what these statements may suggest, Leavis is not specifically interested in the individual writer per se, but rather with the usefulness of his or her art in the scheme of civilization. The writer's role in this vision is to promote what Leavis calls "sincerity"—or, the realization of the individual's proper place in the human world. Literature which accomplishes this he calls "mature," and the writer's judgment within such a work he calls a "mature" moral judgment. From the foregoing comments it should be clear that Leavis is a critic concerned with the moral aspects of art, but a number of his contemporaries, most notably René Wellek and C. S. Lewis, have questioned the existence of a moral system beneath such terms as "maturity" and "sincerity." Leavis's refusal to theorize or develop a systematic philosophy has alienated many critics and scholars from his work. In the following excerpt, Leavis disagrees with Van Wyck Brooks's contention that* Huckleberry Finn *is a naive work repudiating civilization (see excerpt dated 1947).*]

I have to say that *Huckleberry Finn* as I read it is a very different kind of work from that offered us by Mr. Brooks [in his five-volume study *The Makers and Finders: A History of the Writer in America* (see excerpt dated 1947)]. I cannot help thinking that my *Huckleberry Finn* is the greater work, and my Mark Twain a greater artist. In *The Times of Melville and Whitman* we are told:

> He was the frontier story-teller, the great folk-writer of the American West, and he raised to a pitch unrivalled before him the art of oral story-telling and then succeeded in transferring its effects to paper.

Yes, but it won't do to suggest that the art of *Huckleberry Finn* is a naive art, or that there is anything naive or simple about the outlook of the author. And to the question, "Was it not the moral of *Huckleberry Finn* that all civilization is a hateful mistake?" . . . one can only answer that to come away from the book with *that* would be to have simplified it into something very different from the great work of art it is.

It wasn't Huck who wrote *Huckleberry Finn;* the mind that conceived *him* was mature, subtle, and sophisticated. Mark Twain had had very wide and varied experience of men and the world, and he was not only a shrewd observer; he observed out of a ripe wisdom. If he was tender-hearted, he had, when his genius was engaged, too firm a hold on reality to indulge any sentimental bent. And when Mr. Brooks, in *The Confident Years,* calls *Huckleberry Finn* "that paean to the inborn goodness of man, or the goodness of boys peculiarly as nature made them," and makes it a document that justifies the grouping of Mark Twain with Emerson and Whitman, one can only protest against a disastrous misrepresentation. There is nothing simple or simplifying about the moral outlook of *Huckleberry Finn.* The irony is sophisticated: faced with a (for him) inescapably complex situation, Mark Twain is intent on doing justice to the complexity. It might be said that the essential theme of the book, that which makes it a world classic, is the complexity of ethical valuation in any society that has a complex tradition. Mark Twain, that is, though so unmistakably and profoundly American, writes out of a full continuity with the European past.

One way of enforcing the truth of this account is to compare *Huckleberry Finn* with another book of Mark Twain's, one that I very much admire though Mr. Brooks dismisses it with contempt: *Pudd'nhead Wilson*. It is "about" murder and detection, just as *Huckleberry Finn* is "about" boys' adventures on the Mississippi; but it is an ironical masterpiece, and the irony is essentially that of *Huckleberry Finn;* the ethical preoccupation is the same. But in *Pudd'nhead Wilson,* Mark Twain, instead of making his conventions out of the frontiersman's art of story-telling as he knew it, adopts a style and a convention of sophisticated literary tradition, and handles them with the supreme skill of a writer perfectly at home in them. And when one goes back to *Huckleberry Finn* it should be plain that to have made out of a Western vernacular the instrument that Mark Twain made, and used for such purposes, required an author of the cultural background and intellectual sophistication necessary to the writing of a *Pudd'nhead Wilson*. There is no paradox in the putting of such an instrument to such a use. The society that formed Mark Twain, and is depicted by him in *Huckleberry Finn,* might have been "frontier," but it had kept a vigorous hold on its heritage of civilization. (pp. 471-72)

> *F. R. Leavis, "The Americanness of American Literature: A British Demurrer to Van Wyck Brooks,"*
> *in* Commentary, *Vol. XIV, No. 5, November, 1952, pp. 466-74.**

LEO MARX (essay date 1953)

[*In the following excerpt, Marx discusses the controversial conclusion of* Huckleberry Finn, *contesting favorable assessments of the ending made by Lionel Trilling (see Additional Bibliography) and T. S. Eliot (see TCLC, Vol. 6).*]

The Adventures of Huckleberry Finn has not always occupied its present high place in the canon of American literature. When it was first published in 1885, the book disturbed and offended many reviewers, particularly spokesmen for the genteel tradition. In fact, a fairly accurate inventory of the narrow standards of such critics might be made simply by listing epithets they applied to Clemens' novel. They called it vulgar, rough, inelegant, irreverent, coarse, semi-obscene, trashy and vicious. So much for them. Today (we like to think) we know the true worth of the book. Everyone now agrees that *Huckleberry Finn* is a masterpiece: it is probably the one book in our literature about which highbrows and lowbrows can agree. Our most serious critics praise it. Nevertheless, a close look at what two of the best among them have recently written will likewise reveal, I believe, serious weaknesses in current criticism. Today the problem of evaluating the book is as much obscured by unqualified praise as it once was by parochial hostility.

I have in mind essays by Lionel Trilling and T. S. Eliot. Both praise the book, but in praising it both feel obligated to say something in justification of what so many readers have felt to be its great flaw: the disappointing "ending," the episode which begins when Huck arrives at the Phelps place and Tom Sawyer reappears. There are good reasons why Mr. Trilling and Mr. Eliot should feel the need to face this issue. From the point of view of scope alone, more is involved than the mere "ending"; the episode comprises almost one-fifth of the text.

The problem, in any case, is unavoidable. I have discussed *Huckleberry Finn* in courses with hundreds of college students, and I have found only a handful who did not confess their dissatisfaction with the extravagant mock rescue of Nigger Jim and the denouement itself.The same question always comes up: "What went wrong with Twain's novel?" Even Bernard DeVoto, whose wholehearted commitment to Clemens' genius is well known, has said of the ending that "in the whole reach of the English novel there is no more abrupt or more chilling descent." Mr. Trilling and Mr. Eliot do not agree. They both attempt, and on similar grounds, to explain and defend the conclusion.

Of the two, Mr. Trilling makes the more moderate claim for Clemens' novel. He does admit that there is a "falling off" at the end; nevertheless he supports the episode as having "a certain formal aptness." Mr. Eliot's approval is without serious qualification. He allows no objections, asserts that "it is right that the mood of the end of the book should bring us back to the beginning." I mean later to discuss their views in some detail, but here it is only necessary to note that both critics see the problem as one of form. And so it is. Like many questions of form in literature, however, this one is not finally separable from a question of "content," of value, or, if you will, of moral insight. To bring *Huckleberry Finn* to a satisfactory close, Clemens had to do more than find a neat device for ending a story. His problem, though it may never have occurred to him, was to invent an action capable of placing in focus the meaning of the journey down the Mississippi.

I believe that the ending of *Huckleberry Finn* makes so many readers uneasy because they rightly sense that it jeopardizes the significance of the entire novel. To take seriously what happens at the Phelps farm is to take lightly the entire downstream journey. What is the meaning of the journey? With this question all discussion of *Huckleberry Finn* must begin. It is true that the voyage down the river has many aspects of a boy's idyl. We owe much of its hold upon our imagination to the enchanting image of the raft's unhurried drift with the current. The leisure, the absence of constraint, the beauty of the river— all these things delight us. "It's lovely to live on a raft." And the multitudinous life of the great valley we see through Huck's eyes has a fascination of its own. Then, of course, there is humor—laughter so spontaneous, so free of the bitterness present almost everywhere in American humor that readers often forget how grim a spectacle of human existence Huck contemplates. Humor in this novel flows from a bright joy of life as remote from our world as living on a raft.

Yet along with the idyllic and the epical and the funny in *Huckleberry Finn,* there is a coil of meaning which does for the disparate elements of the novel what a spring does for a watch. The meaning is not in the least obscure. It is made explicit again and again. The very words with which Clemens launches Huck and Jim upon their voyage indicate that theirs is not a boy's lark but a quest for freedom. From the electrifying moment when Huck comes back to Jackson's Island and rouses Jim with the news that a search party is on the way, we are meant to believe that Huck is enlisted in the cause of freedom. "Git up and hump yourself, Jim!" he cries. "There ain't a minute to lose. They're after us!" What particularly counts here is the *us*. No one is after Huck; no one but Jim knows he is alive. In that small word Clemens compresses the exhilarating power of Huck's instinctive humanity. His unpremeditated identification with Jim's flight from slavery is an unforgettable moment in American experience, and it may be said at once that any culmination of the journey which detracts from the urgency and dignity with which it begins will necessarily be unsatisfactory. Huck realizes this himself, and says so when, much later, he comes back to the raft after discovering that the Duke and the King have sold Jim:

> After all this long journey . . . here it was all come to nothing, everything all busted up and ruined, because they could have the heart to serve Jim such a trick as that, and make him a slave again all his life, and amongst strangers, too, for forty dirty dollars.

Huck knows that the journey will have been a failure unless it takes Jim to freedom. It is true that we do discover, in the end, that Jim is free, but we also find out that the journey was not the means by which he finally reached freedom.

The most obvious thing wrong with the ending, then, is the flimsy contrivance by which Clemens frees Jim. In the end we not only discover that Jim has been a free man for two months, but that his freedom has been granted by old Miss Watson. If this were only a mechanical device for terminating the action, it might not call for much comment. But it is more than that: it is a significant clue to the import of the last ten chapters. Remember who Miss Watson is. She is the Widow's sister whom Huck introduces in the first pages of the novel. It is she who keeps "pecking" at Huck, who tries to teach him to spell and to pray and to keep his feet off the furniture. She is an ardent proselytizer for piety and good manners, and her greed provides the occasion for the journey in the first place. She is Jim's owner, and he decides to flee only when he realizes that she is about to break her word (she cannot resist a slave trader's offer of eight hundred dollars) and sell him down the river away from his family.

Miss Watson, in short, is the Enemy. If we except a predilection for physical violence, she exhibits all the outstanding traits of the valley society. She pronounces the polite lies of civilization that suffocate Huck's spirit. The freedom which Jim seeks, and which Huck and Jim temporarily enjoy aboard the raft, is accordingly freedom *from* everything for which Miss Watson stands. Indeed, the very intensity of the novel derives from the discordance between the aspirations of the fugitives and the respectable code for which she is a spokesman. Therefore, her regeneration, of which the deathbed freeing of Jim is the unconvincing sign, hints a resolution of the novel's essential conflict. Perhaps because this device most transparently reveals that shift in point of view which he could not avoid, and which is less easily discerned elsewhere in the concluding chapters, Clemens plays it down. He makes little attempt to account for Miss Watson's change of heart, a change particularly surprising in view of Jim's brazen escape. Had Clemens given this episode dramatic emphasis appropriate to its function, Miss Watson's bestowal of freedom upon Jim would have proclaimed what the rest of the ending actually accomplishes—a vindication of persons and attitudes Huck and Jim had symbolically repudiated when they set forth downstream.

It may be said, and with some justice, that a reading of the ending as a virtual reversal of meanings implicit in the rest of the novel misses the point—that I have taken the final episode too seriously. I agree that Clemens certainly did not intend us to read it so solemnly. The ending, one might contend, is simply a burlesque upon Tom's taste for literary romance. Surely the tone of the episode is familiar to readers of Mark Twain. The preposterous monkey business attendant upon Jim's

"rescue," the careless improvisation, the nonchalant disregard for common-sense plausibility—all these things should not surprise readers of Twain or any low comedy in the tradition of "Western humor." However, the trouble is, first, that the ending hardly comes off as burlesque: it is *too* fanciful, *too* extravagant; and it is tedious. For example, to provide a "gaudy" atmosphere for the escape, Huck and Tom catch a couple of dozen snakes. Then the snakes escape.

> No, there warn't no real scarcity of snakes about the house for a considerable spell. You'd see them dripping from the rafters and places every now and then; and they generly landed in your plate, or down the back of your neck. . . .

Even if this were *good* burlesque, which it is not, what is it doing here? It is out of keeping; the slapstick tone jars with the underlying seriousness of the voyage.

Huckleberry Finn is a masterpiece because it brings Western humor to perfection and yet transcends the narrow limits of its conventions. But the ending does not. During the final extravaganza we are forced to put aside many of the mature emotions evoked earlier by the vivid rendering of Jim's fear of capture, the tenderness of Huck's and Jim's regard for each other, and Huck's excruciating moments of wavering between honesty and respectability. None of these emotions are called forth by the anticlimactic final sequence. I do not mean to suggest that the inclusion of low comedy per se is a flaw in *Huckleberry Finn*. One does not object to the shenanigans of the rogues; there is ample precedent for the place of extravagant humor even in works of high seriousness. But here the case differs from most which come to mind: the major characters themselves are forced to play low comedy roles. Moreover, the most serious motive in the novel, Jim's yearning for freedom, is made the object of nonsense. The conclusion, in short, is farce, but the rest of the novel is not.

That Clemens reverts in the end to the conventional manner of Western low comedy is most evident in what happens to the principals. Huck and Jim become comic characters; that is a much more serious ground for dissatisfaction than the unexplained regeneration of Miss Watson. Remember that Huck has grown in stature throughout the journey. By the time he arrives at the Phelps place, he is not the boy who had been playing robbers with Tom's gang in St. Petersburg the summer before. All he has seen and felt since he parted from Tom has deepened his knowledge of human nature and of himself. Clemens makes a point of Huck's development in two scenes which occur just before he meets Tom again. The first describes Huck's final capitulation to his own sense of right and wrong: "All right, then, I'll *go* to Hell." This is the climactic moment in the ripening of his self-knowledge. Shortly afterward, when he comes upon a mob riding the Duke and the King out of town on a rail, we are given his most memorable insight into the nature of man. Although these rogues had subjected Huck to every indignity, what he sees provokes this celebrated comment:

> Well, it made me sick to see it; and I was sorry for them poor pitiful rascals, it seemed like I couldn't ever feel any hardness against them any more in the world. It was a dreadful thing to see. Human beings can be awful cruel to one another.

The sign of Huck's maturity here is neither the compassion nor the skepticism, for both had been marks of his personality from the first. Rather, the special quality of these reflections is the extraordinary combination of the two, a mature blending of his instinctive suspicion of human motives with his capacity for pity.

But at this point Tom reappears. Soon Huck has fallen almost completely under his sway once more, and we are asked to believe that the boy who felt pity for the rogues is now capable of making Jim's capture the occasion for a game. He becomes Tom's helpless accomplice, submissive and gullible. No wonder that Clemens has Huck remark, when Huck first realizes Aunt Sally has mistaken him for Tom, that ''it was like being born again.'' Exactly. In the end, Huck regresses to the subordinate role in which he had first appeared in *The Adventures of Tom Sawyer*. Most of those traits which made him so appealing a hero now disappear. He had never, for example, found pain or misfortune amusing. At the circus, when a clown disguised as a drunk took a precarious ride on a prancing horse, the crowd loved the excitement and danger; ''it warn't funny to me, though,'' said Huck. But now, in the end, he submits in awe to Tom's notion of what is amusing. To satisfy Tom's hunger for adventure he makes himself a party to sport which aggravates Jim's misery.

It should be added at once that Jim doesn't mind too much. The fact is that he has undergone a similar transformation. On the raft he was an individual, man enough to denounce Huck when Huck made him the victim of a practical joke. In the closing episode, however, we lose sight of Jim in the maze of farcical invention. He ceases to be a man. He allows Huck and ''Mars Tom'' to fill his hut with rats and snakes, ''and every time a rat bit Jim he would get up and write a line in his journal whilst the ink was fresh.'' This creature who bleeds ink and feels no pain is something less than human. He has been made over in the image of a flat stereotype: the submissive stage-Negro. These antics divest Jim, as well as Huck, of much of his dignity and individuality.

What I have been saying is that the flimsy devices of plot, the discordant farcical tone, and the disintegration of the major characters all betray the failure of the ending. These are not aspects merely of form in a technical sense, but of meaning. For that matter, I would maintain that this book has little or no formal unity independent of the joint purpose of Huck and Jim. What components of the novel, we may ask, provide the continuity which links one adventure with another? The most important is the unifying consciousness of Huck, the narrator, and the fact that we follow the same principals through the entire string of adventures. Events, moreover, occur in a temporal sequence. Then there is the river; after each adventure Huck and Jim return to the raft and the river. Both Mr. Trilling and Mr. Eliot speak eloquently of the river as a source of unity, and they refer to the river as a god. Mr. Trilling says that Huck is ''the servant of the river-god.'' Mr. Eliot puts it this way: ''The River gives the book its form. But for the River, the book might be only a sequence of adventures with a happy ending.'' This seems to me an extravagant view of the function of the neutral agency of the river. Clemens had a knowledgeable respect for the Mississippi, and, without sanctifying it, was able to provide excellent reasons for Huck's and Jim's intense relation with it. It is a source of food and beauty and terror and serenity of mind. But above all, it provides motion; it is the means by which Huck and Jim move away from a menacing civilization. They return to the river to continue their journey. The river cannot, does not, supply purpose. That purpose is a facet of their consciousness, and without the mo-

tive of escape from society, *Huckleberry Finn* would indeed ''be only a sequence of adventures.'' Mr. Eliot's remark indicates how lightly he takes the quest for freedom. His somewhat fanciful exaggeration of the river's role is of a piece with his neglect of the theme at the novel's center.

That theme is heightened by the juxtaposition of sharp images of contrasting social orders: the microcosmic community Huck and Jim establish aboard the raft and the actual society which exists along the Mississippi's banks. The two are separated by the river, the road to freedom upon which Huck and Jim must travel. Huck tells us what the river means to them when, after the Wilks episode, he and Jim once again shove their raft into the current: ''It *did* seem so good to be free again and all by ourselves on the big river, and nobody to bother us.'' The river is indifferent. But its sphere is relatively uncontaminated by the civilization they flee, and so the river allows Huck and Jim some measure of freedom at once, the moment they set foot on Jackson's Island or the raft. Only on the island and the raft do they have a chance to practice that idea of brotherhood to which they are devoted. ''Other places do seem so cramped and smothery,'' Huck explains, ''but a raft don't. You feel mighty free and easy and comfortable on a raft.'' The main thing is freedom.

On the raft the escaped slave and the white boy try to practice their code: ''What you want, above all things, on a raft, is for everybody to be satisfied, and feel right and kind towards the others.'' This human credo constitutes the paramount affirmation of *The Adventures of Huckleberry Finn,* and it obliquely aims a devastating criticism at the existing social order. It is a creed which Huck and Jim bring to the river. It neither emanates from nature nor is it addressed to nature. Therefore I do not see that it means much to talk about the river as a god in this novel. The river's connection with this high aspiration for man is that it provides a means of escape, a place where the code can be tested. The truly profound meanings of the novel are generated by the impingement of the actual world of slavery, feuds, lynching, murder, and a spurious Christian morality upon the ideal of the raft. The result is a tension which somehow demands release in the novel's ending.

But Clemens was unable to effect this release and at the same time control the central theme. The unhappy truth about the ending of *Huckleberry Finn* is that the author, having revealed the tawdry nature of the culture of the great valley, yielded to its essential complacency. The general tenor of the closing scenes, to which the token regeneration of Miss Watson is merely one superficial clue, amounts to just that. In fact, this entire reading of *Huckleberry Finn* merely confirms the brilliant insight of George Santayana, who many years ago spoke of American humorists, of whom he considered Mark Twain an outstanding representative, as having only ''half escaped'' the genteel tradition. Santayana meant that men like Clemens were able to ''point to what contradicts it in the facts; but not in order to abandon the genteel tradition, for they have nothing solid to put in its place.'' This seems to me the real key to the failure of *Huckleberry Finn.* Clemens had presented the contrast between the two social orders but could not, or would not, accept the tragic fact that the one he had rejected was an image of solid reality and the other an ecstatic dream. Instead he gives us the cozy reunion with Aunt Polly in a scene fairly bursting with approbation of the entire family, the Phelpses included.

Like Miss Watson, the Phelpses are almost perfect specimens of the dominant culture. They are kind to their friends and relatives; they have no taste for violence; they are people capable of devoting themselves to their spectacular dinners while they keep Jim locked in the little hut down by the ash hopper, with its lone window boarded up. (Of course Aunt Sally visits Jim to see if he is "comfortable," and Uncle Silas comes in "to pray with him.") These people, with their comfortable Sunday-dinner conviviality and the runaway slave padlocked nearby, are reminiscent of those solid German citizens we have heard about in our time who tried to maintain a similarly *gemütlich* ["comfortable, placid"] way of life within virtual earshot of Buchenwald. I do not mean to imply that Clemens was unaware of the shabby morality of such people. After the abortive escape of Jim, when Tom asks about him, Aunt Sally replies: "Him? . . . the runaway nigger? . . . They've got him back, safe and sound, and he's in the cabin again, on bread and water, and loaded down with chains, till he's claimed or sold!" Clemens understood people like the Phelpses, but nevertheless he was forced to rely upon them to provide his happy ending. The satisfactory outcome of Jim's quest for freedom must be attributed to the benevolence of the very people whose inhumanity first made it necessary.

But to return to the contention of Mr. Trilling and Mr. Eliot that the ending is more or less satisfactory after all. As I have said, Mr. Trilling approves of the "formal aptness" of the conclusion. He says that "some device is needed to permit Huck to return to his anonymity, to give up the role of hero," and that therefore "nothing could serve better than the mind of Tom Sawyer with its literary furnishings, its conscious romantic desire for experience and the hero's part, and its ingenious schematization of life. . . ." Though more detailed, this is essentially akin to Mr. Eliot's blunt assertion that "it is right that the mood at the end of the book should bring us back to that of the beginning." I submit that it is wrong for the end of the book to bring us back to that mood. The mood of the beginning of *Huckleberry Finn* is the mood of Huck's attempt to accommodate himself to the ways of St. Petersburg. It is the mood of the end of *The Adventures of Tom Sawyer,* when the boys had been acclaimed heroes, and when Huck was accepted as a candidate for respectability. That is the state in which we find him at the beginning of *Huckleberry Finn.* But Huck cannot stand the new way of life, and his mood gradually shifts to the mood of rebellion which dominates the novel until he meets Tom again. At first, in the second chapter, we see him still eager to be accepted by the nice boys of the town. Tom leads the gang in re-enacting adventures he has culled from books, but gradually Huck's pragmatic turn of mind gets him in trouble. He has little tolerance for Tom's brand of make-believe. He irritates Tom. Tom calls him a "numbskull," and finally Huck throws up the whole business:

> So then I judged that all that stuff was only just one of Tom Sawyer's lies. I reckoned he believed in the A-rabs and the elephants, but as for me I think different. It had all the marks of a Sunday-school.

With this statement, which ends the third chapter, Huck parts company with Tom. The fact is that Huck has rejected Tom's romanticizing of experience; moreover, he has rejected it as part of the larger pattern of society's make-believe, typified by Sunday school. But if he cannot accept Tom's harmless fantasies about the A-rabs, how are we to believe that a year later Huck is capable of awe-struck submission to the far more extravagant fantasies with which Tom invests the mock rescue of Jim?

After Huck's escape from his "pap," the drift of the action, like that of the Mississippi's current, is *away* from St. Petersburg. Huck leaves Tom and the A-rabs behind, along with the Widow, Miss Watson, and all the pseudo-religious ritual in which nice boys must partake. The return, in the end, to the mood of the beginning therefore means defeat—Huck's defeat; to return to that mood *joyously* is to portray defeat in the guise of victory.

Mr. Eliot and Mr. Trilling deny this. The overriding consideration for them is form—form which seems largely to mean symmetry of structure. It is fitting, Mr. Eliot maintains, that the book should come full circle and bring Huck once more under Tom's sway. Why? Because it begins that way. But it seems to me that such structural unity is *imposed* upon the novel, and therefore is meretricious. It is a jerry-built structure, achieved only by sacrifice of characters and theme. Here the controlling principle of form apparently is unity, but unfortunately a unity much too superficially conceived. Structure, after all, is only one element—indeed, one of the more mechanical elements—of unity. A unified work must surely manifest coherence of meaning and clear development of theme, yet the ending of *Huckleberry Finn* blurs both. The eagerness of Mr. Eliot and Mr. Trilling to justify the ending is symptomatic of that absolutist impulse of our critics to find reasons, once a work has been admitted to the highest canon of literary reputability, for admiring every bit of it. (pp. 423-34)

How does it happen that two of our most respected critics should seem to treat so lightly the glaring lapse of moral imagination in *Huckleberry Finn*? Perhaps—and I stress the conjectural nature of what I am saying—perhaps the kind of moral issue raised by *Huckleberry Finn* is not the kind of moral issue to which today's criticism readily addresses itself. Today our critics, no less than our novelists and poets, are most sensitively attuned to moral problems which arise in the sphere of individual behavior. They are deeply aware of sin, of individual infractions of our culture's Christian ethic. But my impression is that they are, possibly because of the strength of the reaction against the mechanical sociological criticism of the thirties, less sensitive to questions of what might be called social or political morality.

By social or political morality I refer to the values implicit in a social system, values which may be quite distinct from the personal morality of any given individual within the society. Now *The Adventures of Huckleberry Finn,* like all novels, deals with the behavior of individuals. But one mark of Clemens' greatness is his deft presentation of the disparity between what people do when they behave as individuals and what they do when forced into roles imposed upon them by society. Take, for example, Aunt Sally and Uncle Silas Phelps, who consider themselves Christians, who are by impulse generous and humane, but who happen also to be staunch upholders of certain degrading and inhuman social institutions. When they are confronted with an escaped slave, the imperatives of social morality outweigh all pious professions.

The conflict between what people think they stand for and what social pressure forces them to do is central to the novel. It is present to the mind of Huck and, indeed, accounts for his most serious inner conflicts. He knows how he feels about Jim, but he also knows what he is expected to do about Jim. This division within his mind corresponds to the division of the novel's moral terrain into the areas represented by the raft on the one hand and society on the other. His victory over his "yaller dog" conscience therefore assumes heroic size: it is a victory over the prevailing morality. But the last fifth of the novel has the effect of diminishing the importance and uniqueness of Huck's victory. We are asked to assume that somehow freedom can be achieved in spite of the crippling power of what I have called the social morality. Consequently the less importance we attach to that force as it operates in the novel, the more acceptable the ending becomes.

Moreover, the idea of freedom, which Mr. Eliot and Mr. Trilling seem to slight, takes on its full significance only when we acknowledge the power which society exerts over the minds of men in the world of *Huckleberry Finn.* For freedom in this book specifically means freedom from society and its imperatives. This is not the traditional Christian conception of freedom. Huck and Jim seek freedom not from a burden of individual guilt and sin, but from social constraint. That is to say, evil in *Huckleberry Finn* is the product of civilization, and if this is indicative of Clemens' rather too simple view of human nature, nevertheless the fact is that Huck, when he can divest himself of the taint of social conditioning (as in the incantatory account of sunrise on the river), is entirely free of anxiety and guilt. The only guilt he actually knows arises from infractions of a social code. (The guilt he feels after playing the prank on Jim stems from his betrayal of the law of the raft.) Huck's and Jim's creed is secular. Its object is harmony among men, and so Huck is not much concerned with his own salvation. He repeatedly renounces prayer in favor of pragmatic solutions to his problems. In other words, the central insights of the novel belong to the tradition of the Enlightenment. The meaning of the quest itself is hardly reconcilable with that conception of human nature embodied in the myth of original sin. In view of the current fashion of reaffirming man's innate depravity, it is perhaps not surprising to find the virtues of *Huckleberry Finn* attributed not to its meaning but to its form.

But "if this was not the right ending for the book," Mr. Eliot asks, "what ending would have been right?" Although this question places the critic in an awkward position (he is not always equipped to rewrite what he criticizes), there are some things which may justifiably be said about the "right" ending of *Huckleberry Finn.* It may be legitimate, even if presumptuous, to indicate certain conditions which a hypothetical ending would have to satisfy if it were to be congruent with the rest of the novel. If the conclusion is not to be something merely tacked on to close the action, then its broad outline must be immanent in the body of the work.

It is surely reasonable to ask that the conclusion provide a plausible outcome to the quest. Yet freedom, in the ecstatic sense that Huck and Jim knew it aboard the raft, was hardly to be had in the Mississippi Valley in the 1840's, or, for that matter, in any other known human society. A satisfactory ending would inevitably cause the reader some frustration. That Clemens felt such disappointment to be inevitable is borne out by an examination of the novel's clear, if unconscious, symbolic pattern. Consider, for instance, the inferences to be drawn from the book's geography. The river, to whose current Huck and Jim entrust themselves, actually carries them to the heart of slave territory. Once the raft passes Cairo, the quest is virtually doomed. Until the steamboat smashes the raft, we are kept in a state of anxiety about Jim's escape. (It may be significant that at this point Clemens found himself unable to continue work on the manuscript, and put it aside for several years.) Beyond Cairo, Clemens allows the intensity of that anxiety to diminish, and it is probably no accident that the fainter it becomes, the more he falls back upon the devices of low comedy. Huck and Jim make no serious effort to turn north, and there are times (during the Wilks episode) when Clemens allows Huck to forget all about Jim. It is as if the author, anticipating the dilemma he had finally to face, instinctively dissipated the power of his major theme.

Consider, too, the circumscribed nature of the raft as a means of moving toward freedom. The raft lacks power and maneuverability. It can only move easily with the current—southward into slave country. Nor can it evade the mechanized power of the steamboat. These impotencies of the raft correspond to the innocent helplessness of its occupants. Unresisted, the rogues invade and take over the raft. Though it is the symbolic locus of the novel's central affirmations, the raft provides an uncertain and indeed precarious mode of traveling toward freedom. This seems another confirmation of Santayana's perception. To say that Clemens only half escaped the genteel tradition is not to say that he failed to note any of the creed's inadequacies, but rather that he had "nothing solid" to put in its place. The raft patently was not capable of carrying the burden of hope Clemens placed upon it. (Whether this is to be attributed to the nature of his vision or to the actual state of American society in the nineteenth century is another interesting question.) In any case, the geography of the novel, the raft's powerlessness, the goodness and vulnerability of Huck and Jim, all prefigure a conclusion quite different in tone from that which Clemens gave us. These facts constitute what Hart Crane might have called the novel's "logic of metaphor," and this logic—probably inadvertent—actually takes us to the underlying meaning of *The Adventures of Huckleberry Finn.* Through the symbols we reach a truth which the ending obscures: the quest cannot succeed.

Fortunately, Clemens broke through to this truth in the novel's last sentences:

> But I reckon I got to light out for the territory ahead of the rest, because Aunt Sally she's going to adopt me and civilize me, and I can't stand it. I been there before.

Mr. Eliot properly praises this as "the only possible concluding sentence." But one sentence can hardly be advanced, as Mr. Eliot advances this one, to support the rightness of ten chapters. Moreover, if this sentence is right, then the rest of the conclusion is wrong, for its meaning clashes with that of the final burlesque. Huck's decision to go west ahead of the inescapable advance of civilization is a confession of defeat. It means that the raft is to be abandoned. On the other hand, the jubilation of the family reunion and the proclaiming of Jim's freedom create a quite different mood. The tone, except for these last words, is one of unclouded success. I believe this is the source of the almost universal dissatisfaction with the conclusion. One can hardly forget that a bloody civil war did not resolve the issue.

Should Clemens have made Huck a tragic hero? Both Mr. Eliot and Mr. Trilling argue that that would have been a mistake, and they are very probably correct. But between the ending as we have it and tragedy in the fullest sense, there was vast room for invention. Clemens might have contrived an action which left Jim's fate as much in doubt as Huck's. Such an ending would have allowed us to assume that the principals were defeated but alive, and the quest unsuccessful but not abandoned. This, after all, would have been consonant with the symbols, the characters, and the theme as Clemens had created them—and with history.

Clemens did not acknowledge the truth his novel contained. He had taken hold of a situation in which a partial defeat was inevitable, but he was unable to—or unaware of the need to—give imaginative substance to that fact. If an illusion of success was indispensable, where was it to come from? Obviously Huck and Jim could not succeed by their own efforts. At this point Clemens, having only half escaped the genteel tradition, one of whose pre-eminent characteristics was an optimism undaunted by disheartening truth, returned to it. *Why* he did so is another story, having to do with his parents and his boyhood, with his own personality and his wife's, and especially with the character of his audience. But whatever the explanation, the faint-hearted ending of *The Adventures of Huckleberry Finn* remains an important datum in the record of American thought and imagination. It has been noted before, both by critics and non-professional readers. It should not be forgotten now. (pp. 438-40)

> Leo Marx, "Mr. Eliot, Mr. Trilling, and 'Huckleberry Finn'," in The American Scholar, Vol. 22, No. 4, Autumn, 1953, pp. 423-40.

JAMES M. COX   (essay date 1954)

[*Cox is an American educator and critic specializing in American literature. In the following excerpt, he discusses the theme of Huck's initiation into society.*]

The Adventures of Huckleberry Finn is one of those rare books which are at once acceptable to the intelligentsia and to that celebrated American phenomenon, the average citizen; it is a book which even anti-literary children read and enjoy. Even if the language of the book should eventually be lost or, worse still, replaced by convenient abridgements, the memory of Huck Finn would still survive among us like some old and indestructible god. In the popular imagination, however, Huck Finn does not exist by himself, but is accompanied by Tom Sawyer, his other half. These two figures are not imagined as individuals; they are conceived as identical twins who roam about the earth stealing jam, beating up sissies, playing hooky, and raising hell in general. Furthermore, the Tom-Huck image exists in terms of Tom Sawyer; the real Huck Finn who floated down the Mississippi with Nigger Jim has been shuffled under the rather trivial aegis of the Bad Boy.

Yet there is a grim logic behind this discomforting shift, for if Huck stands uncomfortably next to Tom Sawyer at least he has been there before. Indeed he even adopted Tom Sawyer's name during those rather flat final chapters of *Huckleberry Finn*. After Huck reached his unknown destination, the Phelps farm, the only terms on which he could exist were Tom's terms, and, driven to distraction by the hemming forces which threatened to annihilate him, he gave up his freedom to be free. In order to save himself, the fugitive played the part of Tom Sawyer and in playing it he completed his long, arduous, and disillusioning initiation. (p. 389)

The Adventures of Huckleberry Finn is a conscious continuation and extension of *Tom Sawyer*. As he begins his own story, Huck carefully recounts the events of his immediate past. After mentioning the discovery of gold he goes on to say:

> The Widow Douglas she took me for her son, and allowed she would sivilize me; but it was rough living in the house all the time, considering how dismal regular and decent the widow was in all her ways; and so when I couldn't

stand it no longer I lit out. I got into my old rags and my sugar hogshead again, and was free and satisfied. But Tom Sawyer he hunted me up and said he was going to start a band of robbers, and I might join if I would go back to the widow and be respectable. So I went back.

Here is the argument of the entire novel—all that follows revolves around this major theme, Huck's initiation into respectable society. The tragic irony of the novel is Huck's inner awareness that membership in the cult will involve the dissolution of his character and the denial of his values.

Huck is hardly situated comfortably at the Widow Douglas where Miss Watson plies him with frontier puritanism on the one hand and Tom Sawyer confronts him with bourgeois romanticism on the other, when his ruthless father suddenly appears demanding Huck's money which is happily drawing interest, having been shrewdly invested by Judge Thatcher. Pap's onslaught is momentarily halted by the young judge who, fresh from the East, attempts to reform the outcast drunkard. In a chapter significantly entitled "Pap Starts in on a New Life" the whole initiation and rebirth theme is launched on a tragicomic note. The beautiful spare room in the judge's home is opened to Pap and great is the celebration by the judge's family as Pap jubilantly begins the new life, but during the night he slips out of the beautiful room, trades his new coat which they have given him for a jug of "forty-rod," and climbs back into the room, gets terribly drunk, finally falls off the porch roof into the yard—"and when they come to look at that spare room they had to take soundings before they could navigate it." After this fearful fall from respectability, Pap seizes Huck, whom he considers as property suddenly become valuable, transports him to a log hut up the river, and imprisons him. He treats Huck so violently that Huck finally stages a mock murder of himself in order to escape. This fake murder is probably the most vital and crucial incident of the entire novel. Having killed himself, Huck is "dead" throughout the entire journey down the river. He is indeed the man without identity who is reborn at almost every river bend, not because he desires a new role, but because he must re-create himself to elude the forces which close in on him from every side. The rebirth theme which began with Pap's reform becomes the driving idea behind the entire action.

Coupled with and inseparable from the theme of rebirth is the central image of death. Huck has hardly assumed the role of outcast when he meets Jim, who is also in frantic flight (interestingly enough, Jim is considered in terms of property too; his motive for escaping was fear of being sold down the river for $800.00), and the two fugitives watch the house of death float by on the swollen Mississippi. When Jim carefully covers up the face of the dead man in the house, the second major image of the novel is forged. These two images, rebirth and death, provide a frame for all succeeding episodes of the arduous initiation. As Huck and Jim move down the river, an oncoming steamboat crashes into their raft, forcing the two outcasts to swim for their lives. From this baptism Huck emerges to enter the new life at the Grangerfords under the name of George Jackson. His final act in that life is to cover the dead face of Buck Grangerford much as Jim had covered Pap's face in the house of death. When the Duke and King come aboard, their unscrupulous schemes force Huck and Jim to appear in new disguises; but the image of death is never absent. It confronts Huck in the little "one-horse town" in Arkansas where Colonel Sherburn shoots the drunken Boggs in cold blood.

Holograph copy of Twain's manuscript for Adventures of Huckleberry Finn.

When the townspeople lift Boggs from the street and take him to the little drug store, Huck peers in through the window to watch him die. The Peter Wilks episode involves the same central images. The Duke and the King disguise themselves as foreign kinsmen of the deceased Wilks and they force Huck to play the role of an English valet. The final scene of the episode takes place in the graveyard where the mob of townsmen has gathered to exhume the buried Wilks in an effort to discover whether the Duke and King are impostors. A flash of lightning reveals the dead man with the gold on his breast where Huck had hidden it. The man who has Huck in charge forgets his prisoner in his zeal to see corpse and gold; Huck takes full advantage of the moment and runs out of that world forever.

Finally, at the Phelps farm the initiation is completed. Huck is reborn as Tom Sawyer and this time no image of death appears. The Duke and the King are far back in his past and the wheel has indeed come full circle. Jim is imprisoned in a cabin much like the one in which Pap locked Huck; Tom Sawyer himself comes to the rescue in the role of Sid Sawyer; the entire household, though not the same as the one in which the novel began, is related to it through strong blood ties. The full import of this initiation becomes more clearly evident when the differences between Huck and Tom Sawyer are examined.

All of Tom Sawyer's world has been imported into this novel, but with the addition of Huck as narrator and protagonist and Jim as his companion, Tom's world is seen in sharp perspective. Huck and Jim may have to live in that world but they are not of it, and their very detachment creates a larger and deeper universe of which Tom Sawyer's values are but a part. True, Huck is finally overtaken by the society represented by Tom, but his heroic flight and his inner resistance give dignity to his submission. Huck is, after all, incorruptible and though his body is finally captured by the society which "wants" him so, it has not got his name affixed to it; as the novel ends, the real Huck who cannot die is ready to "light out for the territory," to continue his restless flight from "sivilization." Tom Sawyer's initiation had been routine, had merely confirmed his membership in a society to which he already latently belonged; Tom's whole attitude toward his initiators was . . . one of self-consciousness, even affectation. Huck's initiation, on the other hand, is forced upon him; his drama is different in that it is drama, not play; everything is at stake in an elemental conflict where the values of one world are pitted against the values of another. And Huck's humor is deeper and greater because it is underlain by the pathos and tragedy of his situation.

Huck is, in the deepest sense, an outcast. Although Tom is an orphan, he at least has relatives who recognize his credentials and have adopted him. Huck has only Pap, the drunkard, the outcast himself, whose eyes shine through his tangled, greasy hair "like he was behind vines." Pap attains intense symbolic stature in his brief but violent pilgrimage:

> . . . There warn't no color in his face where his face showed; it was white; not like another man's white, but a white to make a body's flesh crawl— a tree toad white, a fish-belly white. As for his clothes—just rags, that was all.

There is in this description a supernatural quality which links up to Melville's whale. His ways are not so much evil as they are inscrutable; he has somehow gotten consumed by the very creature he set out to conquer and out of the dark union between himself and the River the divine Huck has sprung; Huck certainly belongs more to the river than to the society along its banks, but this in no way makes of him a Rousseauistic child of nature. His lineal descendancy from Pap removes him from the garden of innocence, but if it implies his connection with violence and terror, it also puts him in touch with the deeper human forces which cannot be neatly filed under sociological headings. He has "connections" which, though they do not enable him to get ahead in an acquisitive society, give him a depth and a reality which far surpass anything Tom Sawyer has dreamed of.

Both boys fall back on a world of superstition, but Huck's rituals are naturally inherited while Tom's are appropriated from books. Tom's whole life is an imitation of the romances he has read or heard in the middle class society of which he is a part. The drab and empty life of St. Petersburg forces Tom's mind into an irretrievable past and he pathetically attempts to revive dead chivalry in blighted prairie air. Huck's whole code is, on the contrary, part of him, and he reacts sensitively to life about him. Instead of importing life and law from outside worlds, he invests the objects and people of his world with a life of their own. The difference between Tom Sawyer and Huckleberry Finn is the difference between the primitive and the effete imagination. Tom's drive to dominate his companions, the quality which marks him a devotee at the shrine of William James's bitch goddess, arises from the imitative aspect of his mind. The artificial application of a foreign code demands its strict inflexibility. When Tom organizes his gang at the beginning of the novel he is helpless before the independent machinery of his code; even when the machinery obviously will not work, he insists on its use. In his desire to free Jim according to "the rules," Tom displays utter disregard for him as a human being. The ultimate irony emerges when Huck discovers Tom has known Jim was legally free all the time. This discovery explains the deep mystery to Huck who has been wondering all along why Tom Sawyer would "lower hisself" by helping a runaway slave. Through Huck's apparently innocent eyes we get an intimate glimpse into the soul of Tom Sawyer and we see an appalling relationship between Tom and Colonel Sellers, George Babbitt, and, I suppose, Willy Loman.

It is inevitable that Tom should assume Sid Sawyer's role when he reappears at the end of the novel. Sid, Tom's half-brother, was the Good Boy of *Tom Sawyer;* he was the eternal prude, the darling of a puritan Sunday School. Yet for all Tom's apparent romantic revolt, his values are Sid's values and though he retains illusions of himself he shows unmistakably that he really is Sid's half-brother. In the closing chapters of the novel Tom's very words become "respectable" and "principle," "regular" and "duty."

> . . . The thing for us to do is just to do our
> *duty,* and not worry about whether anybody
> *sees* us do it or not. Hain't you got no principle
> at all?

Huck's relationship to Tom is much more distant. True, there are times when he attempts to emulate Tom Sawyer. Even when he stages his own murder he is conscious that Tom Sawyer would think it was right proud. He sometimes treats Jim the way Tom might treat him. He puts the rattlesnake in Jim's bed and sees the terrifying results. When the two of them board the *Walter Scott,* Huck consciously plays the role of the adventurous Tom much to the dismay of Jim. After Huck and Jim become separated in the fog, Huck attempts to deceive Jim into believing that the separation is a product of Jim's fertile imagination, but Jim humiliates him in the famous passage which ends:

> Dat truck dah is trash; en trash is what people
> is dat puts dirt on de head er dey frens en makes
> 'em ashamed.

Most of the time, however, Huck is living on too thin a margin to afford Tom's luxurious romances. His motives, arising from his struggle for survival, allow him to indulge in no impracticalities, but he knows the fugitive must rely on magic and superstition to propitiate the inscrutable powers which confront him. The wedding of the practical and the magical gives Huck's character a mobility in the constricting circumstances which envelop him. But all his mobility is not enough, for the forces which pursue him are as relentless as the Mississippi's current. They appear in the forms of the Duke and King, the Grangerfords and Shepherdsons and their feud, Judith Loftus, even Jim. Every living thing becomes a source of danger to the lost boy without a name. Huck's remarkable observation upon first seeing the Duke and King coming toward him at a run reveals the terror of his plight:

> . . . Just as I was passing a place where a kind
> of a cowpath crossed the crick, here comes a
> couple of men tearing up the path as tight as
> they could foot it. I thought I was a goner, for

> whenever anybody was after anybody I judged
> it was *me*—or maybe Jim.

Because Huck completely lives his rituals, because he participates to the tips of his fingers in a struggle for survival, and because his whole world and all its values are at stake, he transcends the empty rituals of Tom Sawyer's universe and achieves mythic significance.

When he wearily walks into the Phelps yard and is once more faced with the inevitable proposition of creating himself, he feels his string playing out. At Judith Loftus', at the Grangerfords', before the King and Duke, Huck, the man without identity, had been able to choose his disguise from a vast store of verbal masks which he kept ready at hand; but at the Phelps home even his name has been chosen and he bewilderingly attempts to discover who he is. As he stands before Aunt Sally trying to solve the riddle of his identity, he feels so tight and uncomfortable that he almost wishes he were dead:

> . . . Well, I see I was up a stump—and up it
> good. Providence had stood by me this fur all
> right, but I was hard and tight aground now. I
> see it warn't a bit of use to try to go ahead—
> I'd got to throw up my hand. So I says to
> myself, here's another place where I got to resk
> the truth.

The swirl of events never allows him to "resk the truth" (the phrase itself suggests the ironic plight of Huck's position throughout the novel): Uncle Silas Phelps arrives at this precise moment and Huck finds to his delight and amazement that he is supposed to be Tom Sawyer. The very language Huck uses at this point suggests the myth behind the humor:

> By jings, I almost slumped through the floor!
> But there warn't no time to swap knives; the
> old man grabbed me by the hand and shook,
> and kept on shaking. . . . But if they was joyful,
> it warn't nothing to what I was; for it was like
> being born again, I was so glad to find out who
> I was.

There is bitter irony in Huck's assumption of Tom's name because the values of Tom Sawyer are so antithetical to the values of Huck Finn; in the final analysis, the two boys cannot exist in the same world. When Huck regains his own identity at the very end of the novel he immediately feels the compulsion to "light out for the territory" because he knows that to be Huck Finn is to be the outcast beyond the paling fences. From Mark Twain's point of view in this novel, Tom Sawyer civilization involves obedience, imitation, and is directly opposed to a dynamic and creative frontier imagination. In Tom Sawyer's triumph, the hard core of Mark Twain's later disillusion and pessimism is already evident. Although Huck Finn may escape to the territory, the whole outline of the frontier is receding westward before the surge of small town culture, and it is indeed doomed country into which Huck must retreat.

Huck Finn cannot be reduced to historical proportions, however, even though there is much in the novel for the historian. The territory to which Huck refers is more than a diminishing area in nineteenth century America. It is a metaphoric equivalent of the broader and deeper vision which Huck and Jim represent. To be in the "territory" is not to be in heaven, for the wilderness and waste places have their perils for the sojourner, as Pap's presence fearfully testifies, but it is to escape the dehumanizing forces of the little towns; it is to be stripped of the pride encouraged by a sterile respectability and to feel absolute humility in the face of the awful unseen powers. Huck and Jim are the only real human beings in the novel—they are human because they can still feel and because they possess a heightened sensitivity to the promises and terrors of life. The characters whom they encounter, with the exception of the young and innocent, have an angularity and rigidity which mark them as grotesques. The blind spots of the eminently respectable become proving grounds for the avaricious; the pretentious righteousness of one group merely encourages the brutal sensationalism of another. Only Huck and Jim possess wholeness of spirit among the horde of fragmentary personalities which parade through the novel. The society which hotly pursues Huck and Jim knows that they possess the real secrets—that is why it so desperately wants to "own" them.

And if Tom has taken Sid's role and Huck has been forced to take Tom's in this rather discouraging progression, who is left to take Huck's place? Fifteen years later Mark Twain could not answer the question, for his imagination had been consumed by what Bernard DeVoto calls the symbols of despair. There is someone, however, to take Huck's place in this novel; he is, of course, that primitive of primitives, Jim. He stands in relation to Huck in this novel much as Huck stood in relation to Tom in *Tom Sawyer,* and is in many ways the central figure of the book. It is to Jim that Huck retreats as if to a savior; he it is who mothers Huck as they travel down the big river; and he it is who, knowing secretly that Huck's Pap is dead forever, takes Huck to his own bosom to nourish him through the ordeal of being lost. Acting as Huck's foster father, Jim brings to that role a warmth and gentleness which Huck had never known under the brutal masculinity of his real father. Near the end of the novel, after Jim has accompanied and protected Huck on their perilous journey, how appropriate it is that he should be led back to the Phelps plantation, following his temporary escape with Tom, arrayed in the dress which the boys had stolen from Aunt Sally. The incident points up the ambivalent nature of Jim, emphasizing his role of motherly father to Huck. Leslie Fiedler, looking at the novel as an American myth of love, has searchingly explored this ambivalent relationship.

Jim is also one of the two great human forces in the book. By means of his truth and sincerity, the fraud and hoax of the world along the river banks are thrown into sharp relief. Probably the finest example of Jim's function as a moral norm occurs on the raft just before the King and Duke meet the country boy who unwittingly directs them into the Peter Wilks exploit. Huck awakens at daybreak one morning to see Jim grieving to himself. Jim finally tells him that a whacking sound he heard on shore reminded him of the time he disciplined his little daughter for not obeying a command. Upon repeating his command to no avail, Jim finally struck the child down, only to find that her recent attack of scarlet fever had left her deaf and dumb:

> Oh, Huck, I burst out a-crying en grab her up in my arms, en say, 'Oh, de po' little thing! De Lord God Almighty forgive po' ole Jim, kaze he never gwyne to fogive hisself as long's he live!' Oh, she was plumb deef en dumb, Huck, plum deef en dumb—en I'd ben a-treat'n her so!

Immediately after this burst of genuine remorse, the Duke and the King launch their expedition to rob the Wilks daughters of their inheritance by pretending to be Peter Wilks' foreign kinsmen. The Duke poses as a deaf mute. By employing the same device he used so successfully in *Tom Sawyer,* Twain establishes a subtle and exquisite relationship between the two episodes. Through Jim's sensitivity the entire Wilks episode is thrown into much more precise focus. Indeed, Jim is the conscience of the novel, the spiritual yardstick by which all men are measured. As the two fugitives move down the river, Huck's whole moral sense grows out of and revolves around the presence of Jim, and his ability to measure up signifies his worth. Huck's whole sense of wrong, his feeling of guilt are products of his intimate association with Jim—his companionship with the runaway slave makes possible his moral growth.

Many critics, intent on seeing Jim as a symbol of the tragic consequences of slavery, have failed to see that he is much more than this. He is that great residue of primitive, fertile force turned free at the end of the novel at the very moment Huck is captured. That Mark Twain recognized in the Negro a new American protagonist is evident not only in his creation of Jim, but in his interesting return to the whole problem of slavery in *Pudd'nhead Wilson.* Certainly Jim and Thomas à Becket Driscoll stand solidly behind Faulkner, Robert Penn Warren, and Richard Wright. Having been thrown from his secure place within the social structure, Jim will be the new fugitive which the bourgeoisie will, with a great deal of hesitation, wish to make respectable.

There is an inexorable and crushing logic inherent in the ending of *Huckleberry Finn.* T. S. Eliot, in his remarkable introductory essay to the Cressett Library edition of the novel [see *TCLC,* Vol. 6], remarked the inevitability of the final chapters, but failed to enlarge upon the generalization. Most critics agree that the ending is much weaker than the rest of the book, as indeed it is, but often they mistakenly gauge that weakness. Certainly Tom's reappearance itself does not weaken the ending. Any comprehensive vision of the book will, it seems to me, consider Tom's presence at the end not only vital but inevitable. The flatness of the ending results from Tom's domination of the action and the style. As soon as he appears, his whole aggressive spirit bids for position, and although Mark Twain attempts to use Huck to exploit the ironies of the situation, Tom's seizure of the style damages the tenor of the novel. It is a stylistic rather than a structural flaw, a failure in taste rather than in conception.

Mark Twain's failure in taste at this particular juncture bears further consideration. *Huckleberry Finn* is without question his greatest work, and diametric opposition of Tom and Huck is eminently clear. The substitution of Tom's humor for Huck's vision indicates that Mark Twain, though aware of the two sets of values, could not keep a proper balance between them because of his fascination with Tom Sawyer. In turning over the narration to Huck Finn he had turned to the incorruptible part of himself which was not for sale and could not be bought. The opening paragraph of the novel indicates that he was not entirely unaware of what he was about:

> You don't know about me without you have read a book by the name of *The Adventures of Tom Sawyer;* but that ain't no matter. That book was made by Mr. Mark Twain, and he told the truth, mainly. There was things which he stretched, but mainly he told the truth.

"Mainly he told the truth." In this novel Mark Twain tried to tell the whole truth through Huckleberry Finn. Although Tom Sawyer makes his presence too much felt at the end of the novel, Mark Twain saw his whole truth with supreme vision. Because of the deeply human values which are at stake, neither the satire nor the humor is tainted by the scoffing disillusion and the adolescent cynicism in which he finally foundered. The unobtrusive formal perfection allows the novel to retain the primitive power and immediacy of the myth which it recreates; its impact strikes us in the profoundest areas of our consciousness, and we are reminded of the darkness and the terror and the violence which walk the virgin forest where the American dream lies waiting, aware and unaware. (pp. 394-405)

> *James M. Cox, "Remarks on the Sad Initiation of 'Huckleberry Finn'," in* The Sewanee Review, *Vol. LXII, No. 3, Summer, 1954, pp. 389-405.*

FRANK BALDANZA   (essay date 1955)

[*Baldanza is an American critic and educator. In the following excerpt, he examines the narrative structure of* Huckleberry Finn.]

The much-vexed question of the structure of *Huckleberry Finn* has received both distinguished and penetrating attention; T. S. Eliot [see *TCLC*, Vol. 6] and Lionel Trilling [see Additional Bibliography] have defended the plot as a whole in their introductions to editons of the novel, and Leo Marx has ably replied to both [see excerpt dated 1953]. James Cox [see excerpt dated 1954] and Philip Young [see Additional Bibliography] have attempted symbolic and psychological interpretations which make passing comments on structure. I should like to suggest, however, that both groups of critics, although they have made valuable exploratory searches, have neglected the one aspect of the structure which is perhaps the most rewarding to investigate.

In the first place, as Edgar Goold points out in regard to Twain's theory of the novel:

> Concerning plot construction and related matters Clemens's contribution is of somewhat lesser significance for the writer of fiction than the uninitiated might expect. . . . His own temperament and training did not tend to develop in him the ability to plan carefully and practice the sustained concentration necessary for tight and well-developed plots.

That this failure in planning out his plots had a temperamental basis is corroborated, perhaps, by Twain's virulent antipathy to the total work of such a careful planner as Jane Austen. But many other critics, of whom I choose James Cox as representative, argue that the structure of *Huckleberry Finn* is determined by the interplay of sets of symbols—civilization and the frontier, gentility and barbarism, freedom and bondage, and the like. These ideas certainly play a major part in the development of the book because they are, in a certain sense, what the book is about; but the question ought to be in what way Twain uses these ideas. Bernard DeVoto, who assures us that "Mark Twain was not a systematic thinker," finds him "as feeble a novice as ever ventured into [metaphysics]." He goes on to say that

> . . . there is a type of mind, and the lovers of *Huckleberry Finn* belong to it, which prefers experience to metaphysical abstractions and the thing to its symbol. Such minds think of *Huckleberry Finn* as the greatest work of nineteenth century fiction in America precisely because it is not a voyage in pursuit of a white whale but

a voyage among feudists, mobbers, thieves, rogues, nigger-hunters, and murderers, precisely because Huck never encounters a symbol but always some actual human being working out an actual destiny.

But even if we overlook Twain's antisymbolic cast of mind (in which we should hardly be justified), we find that his own ambivalence blurs the neatness of whatever categories we set up. Even though we interpret the book as a "sad initiation" into society, we are baffled by the final sentence in which Huck lights out for the territory; if he has adamantly resisted the culture of the towns, then he is not in any sense "initiated." and if we try to see the book as a progression toward Jim's liberation, we must ask why the Boggs episode, the Shepherdson-Grangerford feud, and the Wilks interlude, which compose the bulk of the central portion, are so remarkably irrelevant to the thesis. Even toward the close of the book, Huck is scandalized by Tom's easy acquiescence in the escape plot, and invokes the wrath of society on such behavior. The resolution of these dilemmas is perhaps to be found in Twain's own ambivalences, but an analysis of these leads us into biography or psychology and inevitably away from *Huckleberry Finn*. Nevertheless, if we hold to any aesthetic standards at all, we hardly have the right to make extravagant claims for a book which we must admit in the same breath is negligible as a work of art.

Let us for a moment abandon the search for any plotted or symbolic or psychological unity in the novel and return to what we know about Mark Twain's temperament and about his habits of composition; in this way we can more easily make an inductive study of the kind of structure he put into the novel, rather than impose from the outside some preconceived pattern. Bernard DeVoto, who gave an entire book to Twain's work habits, tells us that. . .

> He had little ability to impose structure on his material; he could not think and feel it through to its own implicit form. He got 'ideas' for books, stories, or sketches and jotted them down in his notebooks where they survive by the hundred, promising or feeble but almost always undeveloped. He caught fire easily and when an 'idea' inflamed him, he attacked it with verve and enthusiasm, trusting to luck, providence, or his demon to make it good.

We might say, as many have said, that the picaresque form would certainly be the ideal genre for such a talent, and that in the kind of episodic, spurting movement of such tales Twain would find his best vehicle; however, at the best, such an "explanation" of the structure of the book consists simply in the substitution of one word for another.

Let us rather try to see whether the very *élan* of his improvisation did not often carry him forward through a form which is implicit in his method. In Chapter VIII of his suggestive *Aspects of the Novel*, E. M. Forster remarks the same method as the fundamental source for the structure of Marcel Proust's *A la Recherche du Temps Perdu*. Like Twain's great river novel, "the book is chaotic, ill constructed, it has and will have no external shape. . . ." But Forster finds that "it hangs together because it is stitched internally, because it contains rhythms." The parallel is enforced by what Forster tells us of Proust's work habits, because he attributes the quality of rhythm in the novel to a type of temperament that accords precisely with what we have already found in Goold's and DeVoto's descriptions of Mark Twain: "I doubt that it can be achieved by the writers who plan their books beforehand, it has to depend on a local impulse when the right interval is reached." Local impulse and lack of planning, the two prime characteristics of Twain's genius, then, ought to produce in his novel effects parallel to those rhythmic stitchings that Forster finds so exquisite in the work of the great French novelist. (pp. 347-50)

I propose to show that without advanced planning, and spurred by momentary impulses, Mark Twain—in all probability unconsciously—constructed whole passages of **Huckleberry Finn** on an aesthetic principle of repetition and variation. Because the process was unconscious, it does not attain the regularity of Proust's employment of the Vinteuil theme, and we must also remember that Twain was working on a much smaller scale than the seemingly inexhaustible French analyst. But to take one simple example, we remember how Huck early in the book saws his way out of his father's cabin undetected because he works behind a blanket that is stretched over the wall; toward the end of the book, Jim's escape is managed through a hole dug beneath the cabin, again disguised by a hanging blanket. Regardless of how we justify the correspondence on other grounds, it remains as a repetition of an earlier incident with a variation: it is, as Forster remarks, the variation which gives a sense of freshness and surprise, but it is the repetition that ravishes the memory, and, in its implicit assumption of order, it perhaps gives hope too.

If we survey the total bulk of such correspondences in the novel, we find that they bear out our earlier assumption that they occur as unplanned, impulsive repetitions, sometimes seemingly enforcing a moral lesson, and other times existing simply as abstract aesthetic flourishes. An example of the latter is Tom's gratuitous insistence on having a rattlesnake to keep Jim company in the Phelpses' cabin, which recalls, solely for the aesthetic pleasure involved, the great to-do earlier in the book over the rattlesnake skin and over Jim's being bitten in the heel.

The largest group of repetitions centers about the situations in which Huck encounters rogues on his side trips. Here we might distinguish several themes, all of which are involved with the self-defeating nature of evil, as exemplified in Chaucer's "Pardoner's Tale." We need not assume that Twain chose such material for its profound moral significance, however; probably it was simply what came to hand and what he knew would please his readers. For the first of these themes, we might use one of Twain's chapter headings, "Better let blame' well alone": if Huck and Jim had not boarded the *Walter Scott* they would have been better off. In the same way, Bill and Packard would have made a clean getaway if they had not returned for Turner's share of the money, thus giving Huck and Jim the chance to take their boat, and consequently abandoning them ironically to the fate they had reserved for Turner. This greedy lingering at the scene of the crime in order to squeeze out every last cent is repeated subtly, and with a variation, when the Duke and the Dauphin, not content with the huge sum of gold, remain at the Wilks home in order to auction the goods and clean up the small change; it is repeated even more subtly, and with even wider variation, when Tom refuses to free Jim the easy way, but lingers in order to fulfil all the conditions of his rigorous code, and suffers a bullet wound because of his greed for glory. This last example, too, shows how the aesthetic requirements of the novel dovetail with the meaning: most critics have been content with explaining the final passages of the novel solely in terms of Tom's romanticism, but with the need for rhythm in mind, we can see that Twain chose—again, probably unconsciously—to manage the incident so that it echoed the previous patterns of "better let blame' well alone."

A second major repetitive theme is that of desertion. Just as Bill and Packard lack even the honor of thieves in their plan to abandon Turner, so, on the third night of the "Royal Nonesuch" performance, Huck and the Duke flee the theater before the performance; Huck thinks that they are abandoning the Dauphin to an angry crowd, but to his immense surprise, he finds the Dauphin asleep in the wigwam on the raft. Later in the book, when another angry mob has the three of them in tow in the graveyard at the end of the Wilks episode, Huck flees when he has the chance, and when the Duke and the Dauphin catch up with him at the opening of Chapter XXX, they make the same accusation that Turner might have made to his companions, and that the Dauphin might have made to Huck and the Duke after the Nonesuch flight. "'Tryin' to give us the slip, was ye, you pup! Tired of our company, hey?'" The elaborate argument on who has a right to desert whom is a kind of climactic repetition of the whole theme in the book, although Twain reserves one more repetition, as a kind of coda, for the splitting up of Tom and Jim and Huck after their flight from the Phelpses.

To these two themes of lingering for spoils and abandoning companions we might add a third, which perhaps approaches patterning more nearly than any of the others—that of the crowd. But again, I think we can see that each individual treatment of a crowd incident was impulsive on Twain's part, and that any pattern we find in the repetitions is either unconsciously or accidentally ordained. The first large crowd is that on the boat searching for Huck's body, a "good" crowd of friends (with the exception of Pap) bent on a mission of mercy: "Pap, and Judge Thatcher, and Bessie Thatcher, and Joe Harper, and Tom Sawyer, and his old Aunt Polly, and Sid and Mary, and plenty more." Then the first nuance of possibly evil motivations on the part of a crowd is indicated in Mr. Loftus's proposed search of the island to get the reward for Jim's capture. Later we descend to the cowardly violence of the Sherburn lynching manqué, of the odoriferous Nonesuch mob, and of the stupid avengers of the Wilks family; after the tarring and feathering of the royal impostors, we return to the "good" crowd in the final chapters where the farmers and their garrulous wives congregate to help Mr. Phelps. The variation in this employment of crowds is rich and inexhaustible; they are all foiled, regardless of the quality of their motives, except the mob that metes out justice to the Duke and the Dauphin; they are all impressionable and stupid, and their little ruses, like the plan of the first Nonesuch crowd, are all pitifully inadequate. The two "good" crowds which appear at the opening and the closing of the book, do attain their ends, but in so indirect a fashion that they are rendered ridiculous: in the first case, Huck muses that the bread filled with quicksilver *did* reach him, and that the widow's and the parson's prayers *were* answered after a fashion; and in the latter case the crowd *did* finally solve the mystery, but only by pure accident. At the center of the problem, though, is the example of the Shepherdson-Grangerford "crowd"; whether Twain intended it or not, this central incident in the book embodies all the paradoxes of motivation that impelled the other crowds, because it is by a code of honor that these two groups defeat themselves, even as the rogues defeated themselves by lack of a code.

And, in speaking of the gullibility of the crowd and the roguery of the tricksters, we are reminded that before any of these examples of man's baseness occur in the book, Huck, in Chapter XV, gulls Jim himself, and in Huck's conscience-stricken reaction to Jim's eloquent rebuke, Twain sets the pattern for our reaction to the complicated roguery of the vagabonds.

These examples are perhaps sufficient to suggest the kind of rhythm that pulses through the novel by repetition and variation; it remains to indicate that just as such repetitions were conceived unconsciously or accidentally on the author's part, so their influence on the reader may be largely without his conscious attention to the means by which he is beguiled into finding the book somehow ordered within his recollection, but by an order he cannot explain very clearly in terms of conventional plotting or symbols.

Thus it is unnecessary to survey in detail the abundantly burgeoning variations on change of identity, on superstition and prophecy, and on lying which stitch one chapter to another in the reader's memory. One could nearly make a parlor game of searching out minor correspondences like Huck's dressing as a girl when he visits Mrs. Loftus, and Tom's later insistence on Huck's assumption of the "yaller wench's frock" when he delivers the note to the Phelpses. The very proliferation of such repetitions, in fact, proves that Twain had no control over them and that they simply flowed from his pen as exuberant impulse. What is more, it seems to me that this principle of repetition, as in the preceding example, gives some dignity and power to what had heretofore been excused as the blemishes of a feverishly melodramatic imagination.

It remains to note that in at least one case the principle of repetition rays out to include unconscious recollection of culture tales as well as incidents treated earlier in the novel; this should not suprise us, because Blair and DeVoto have shown how the Royal Nonesuch incident was derived from an obscene frontier tale. In the present case, we remember that the critics who emphasize the symbolic structure of the book are quick to point out that Huck is "dead" throughout the book as far as the rest of his friends know. When Jim sees him for the first time, he falls to his knees and entreats the ghost to leave him. The same reaction, with a significant variation, occurs to Tom when he sees Huck toward the end of the book in Chapter XXXIII. . . . Tom's doubts on the corporeality of Huck, besides recalling those of Jim, obviously parallel those of his biblical namesake, and this Doubting Thomas satisfies himself in the same way as his predecessor, by feeling of his body. This is, too, an oblique recall of the previous references to Moses and Solomon and the biblical kings. There is no real need to see Huck as a Christ figure, especially since he is Tom's disciple, rather than the reverse; we need only note the fact of Twain's repeating a situation already familiar to his readers simply out of the exuberance of his aesthetic faculty.

If this explanation of the structure of *Huckleberry Finn* has any further recommendation, it is that in accepting it we completely exonerate ourselves—as few other critics can claim to do— from the ominous threats that open the novel: "Persons attempting to find a motive in this narrative will be prosecuted; persons attempting to find a moral in it will be banished; persons attempting to find a plot in it will be shot." (pp. 350-55)

> Frank Baldanza, "The Structure of 'Huckleberry Finn'," in American Literature, Vol. XXVII, No. 3, November, 1955, pp. 347-55.

RICHARD P. ADAMS (essay date 1956)

[*Adams was an American critic and educator. In the following excerpt, he discusses the thematic, structural, and symbolic unity of* Huckleberry Finn.]

[*Huck Finn*] has a symbolic pattern or organization of imagery, not a plot in the traditional sense. (p. 88)

The most obvious element of structure in *Huck Finn,* and the one most often noticed, is the picaresque journey down the river, full of inconsequently interspersed and apparently aimless adventures. But it is dangerous to say that much and stop, for the inconsequence does not preclude a plan, and the aimlessness is only apparent. Trilling, in discussing the special qualities of the river as a road, points out some profitable directions for further inquiry [see Additional Bibliography]. The important thing, he says, is that the river is a moving road,

> . . . and the movement of the road in its own mysterious life transmutes the primitive simplicity of the form: the road itself is the greatest character in this novel of the road, and the hero's departures from the river and his returns to it compose a subtle and significant pattern. The linear simplicity of the picaresque novel is further modified by the story's having a clear dramatic organization: it has a beginning, a middle, and an end, and a mounting suspense of interest.

Trilling perhaps oversimplifies the linear quality of the picaresque novel as Clemens knew it, but he does not overestimate the complexity of *Huck Finn,* and his observations on the "living" quality of the river and on the alternation of Huck's river and shore experiences are valuable clues.

Another clue, of perhaps even greater value, is furnished by James M. Cox's discussion of Huck's "initiation" [see excerpt dated 1954]. According to Cox, the "fake murder" that Huck stages in order to get away from his father "is probably the most vital and crucial incident of the entire novel," and Cox's observations on this event come close to defining the basic structure of the boy's growth and which carries the weight of the incidents and the imagery throughout, is a pattern of symbolic death and rebirth. As Cox points out, the central action on the river begins with Huck's pretended death. It ends with his mistaken recognition as Tom by Aunt Sally Phelps, when he feels that "it was like being born again, I was so glad to find out who I was." This pattern is kept in the focus of the reader's attention, as Cox also observes, by repeated deaths and escapes occurring between, before, and after the main events.

The pattern of death and rebirth is reinforced by the pattern Trilling observes in Huck's departures from and returns to the river; only we need to reverse Trilling's terms, for it is Huck's departures from and returns to shore which are cognate and parallel to the pattern of death and rebirth. The same pattern provides the framework for the "clear dramatic organization" which Trilling notices, and it roughly determines the kind of beginning, middle, and end that the story has. Putting Cox and Trilling together, and oversimplifying for the sake of initial clarity, we can state a more nearly complete definition of the structure of *Huckleberry Finn.* The beginning is Huck's life on shore in and around the village of St. Petersburg with the Widow Douglas and Pap. The middle, initiated by Huck's fake death, is his withdrawal from the life of society and civilization to the river; this withdrawal is repeated after each of his adventures on land. The end is his equivocal rebirth, his qualified return, under a false identity and with many reservations, to civilized life at the Phelps plantation.

The pattern of death and rebirth is also intimately concerned in the "mounting suspense of interest" which Trilling notes. The theme of the book . . . is the same as that of *Tom Sawyer:* the growth of a boy to manhood, and his final acceptance of adult moral responsibilities. In this connection the pattern of death and rebirth is more than a technical device. In the tradition of romantic literature, to which *Huck Finn* belongs, it is a form with a meaning. The growth of a boy to manhood is perhaps the most popular of all themes for romantic fiction, and the structure which best expresses it is that of the death-and-rebirth pattern. The reason for this association is based in romantic philosophy, according to which the individual human personality is conceived as an organism, which cannot undergo a fundamental change of any kind without being totally reconstituted. Its old self "dies" and its new self, an unpredictably different organism, is "born." Huck's initiation, his transformation from boy to man, is such a change. It is a radical reconstitution of his moral attitude toward the society in which he lives. He grows, therefore, during the time of crucial change, by "dying" out of society, withdrawing into nature on the river, and then returning or being "reborn" into society with a new and different attitude toward it.

It should not have to be said that this return is by no means an uncritical accceptance of conventional social values. The process of Huck's moral growth is, in fact, most emphatically indicated by his decision, made on three separate but closely related occasions, to free Jim from slavery, which is an act of rebellion against society. In a superficial sense the three decisions are the same, but each means more than the one before, because Huck knows more about the society he is deciding to oppose and because he sees more fully and clearly the implications of the decision and its probable consequences.

The context, which becomes increasingly solid and massive as Huck's knowledge increases, is a complex interrelationship of social, cultural, political, and economic forces. We might skeletonize it by making three simple statements, which we can then elaborate. First, slavery is evil. Second, the pseudo-aristocratic society of the ante-bellum South which fosters and depends on slavery is also evil. Third, the sentimental cultural veneer with which that society conceals its evil from itself, if not from others, is evil as well. These propositions apply with increasing cogency to Huck's three decisions, as he learns more about the character and workings, the concrete personal meanings and moral values, of Southern slave-holding aristocracy. The relations among these three intertwined thematic strands in *Huck Finn* are so complex and pervasive that a thorough explication of them would be longer than the book. I shall not try to exhaust them here, but rather to indicate their general character and, by exploring a few of them in some detail, to show how they work.

Huck's first decision to help Jim escape is made casually enough in the process of his own flight from civilization and from the domination of his father. When he comes across his fellow runaway on Jackson's Island, he is so glad to have his lonesomeness relieved by any sort of company that he hardly thinks of difficulties. "'People would call me a low-down Abolitionist and despise me for keeping mum,'" he admits to Jim, "'—but that don't make no difference. I ain't a-going to tell, and I ain't a-going back there, anyways.'" But even this first and easiest decision is preceded by a fairly substantial development of motives and of symbolic motifs. Huck has been introduced to respectable society at the Widow's, where gentility is manifested painfully to him in regular hours, formal meals, and stiff clothing. When Miss Watson tells him about the bad place, he says he wishes he were there. "She got mad then, but I didn't mean no harm. All I wanted was to go somewheres. . . ." Later the same night, in harmony with the fake murder which is to come, he says, "I felt so lonesome I most wished I was dead." Then, in the planning and organization of Tom Sawyer's gang, we see Huck's indirect exposure to the culture of popular books and the sentimental proprieties of "high-toned" robbery and exploitation. Tom and the gang, of course, are completely unrealistic about the crimes they propose to commit, and blissfully unaware that crime, as gilded by the popular romances, is morally wrong. Farther on, Huck is regaled with Pap's reverse snobbishness on the subject of education and with his poor-white's groundless assertion of superiority over the much better educated "free nigger."

These lights and others like them are placed so as to reveal what Clemens considered to be the characteristic weaknesses, follies, and injustices of prewar Southern society. The essentially false and hypocritical gentility of the would-be aristocracy, the febrile and morally confusing sentimentalism of its favorite literature, and the crime of slavery which was the real basis of its economic and social system are continually brought home to Huck and the reader, in all kinds of dramatic, representative, and symbolic ways. The incidents are not haphazardly chosen or arranged. Each has its revealing gleam to contribute to Huck's unconsciously dawning awareness of the true values of the civilization to which he is being asked to belong. The result is that he runs away and, without any great misgivings at first, agrees to help Jim do the same.

The second decision is made necessary by a qualm of conscience. The fugitives are approaching Cairo, or think they are, and they both believe that Jim is almost free. Says Huck, "It hadn't ever come home to me before, what this thing was that I was doing. But now it did; and it stayed with me, and scorched me more and more." The point of difficulty is that freeing Jim involves robbing his owner, Miss Watson, of the eight hundred dollars he is worth on the market; and Jim makes the difficulty greater by threatening to have his children stolen, if necessary, by an Abolitionist. Huck is immediately and properly horrified. "It most froze me to hear such talk. . . . Here was this nigger, which I had as good as helped to run away, coming right out flat-footed and saying he would steal his children—children that belonged to a man I didn't even know; a man that hadn't ever done me no harm." The juxtaposition of "his" and "belonged' in this sentence, so carefully calculated to drive home the shocking injustice of property rights in human flesh, should not obscure the fact that there is a real moral issue. The great wrong of slavery does not make the lesser wrong of robbery right; a point which most pre-Civil War anti-slavery propagandists preferred to overlook. The issue is resolved by the fact that Huck finds himself unable to turn Jim in, for reasons which he does not fully understand but which the reader can surmise. To put it most simply, his human feelings are stronger than the commercial morality with which they are in conflict— as of course they should be. Unable to do entirely right, he chooses the lesser evil and goes on helping Jim.

When he repudiates his own conscience in this way, Huck takes a long step farther in his repudiation of Southern society, which has formed his conscience. He says to himself, in his usual innocent way, "what's the use you learning to do right when it's troublesome to do right and ain't no trouble to do wrong, and the wages is just the same? . . . So I reckoned I wouldn't bother no more about it but after this always do whichever come handiest at the time.'' The innocence is of Huck, not Clemens, and it represents a remarkably keen penetration into the difficult question of personal or individual morality in relation to social conventions. Huck realizes in practice, though never in conscious theory, that the question is not one of simple conflict between the individual and the mass, or the social institution, but that the two interpenetrate, and that the individual conscience is usually an ally of the social pressure for conformity.

Thoreau, in "Civil Disobedience," feels himself on solid ground when his conscience tells him to oppose the extension of slavery and the government that sanctions and promotes it. "If," he says, "the injustice . . . is of such a nature that it requires you to be the agent of injustice to another, then, I say, break the law." That seems comparatively easy; all that is needed is the courage to stand up against the government, which Southerners have always had in abundance. But, when the ante-bellum conscience is formed in Missouri instead of Massachusetts, the battle becomes intensely complicated. Its lines are drawn mostly inside the personality, which is then divided against itself. As Trilling remarks, it is the paradox in Huck's own thinking, by the terms of which he does right by doing what he thoroughly believes, in his conscious mind, to be wrong, that makes his character heroic and Clemens's satire brilliant. His battle is desperate, his victory sublime. If it is fine to follow as Thoreau does the dictates of conscience over law, it is finer and much more difficult to follow those of the right over conscience and law combined.

It is fair to say, as it is for the first decision, that everything leading up to this second one contributes to Huck's preparation for making it as he does. We can examine the process most efficiently, perhaps, by focussing on one incident, and tracing its relations to see how they bear on the larger meanings of the action. Let us take, for example, the adventure of Huck and Jim with the murderers on the wrecked steamboat *Walter Scott*.

This event has a number of bearings, mostly ironic, on the related themes of aristocracy and sentimental literature. One of the antipathies which Clemens cherished most warmly and flourished most often was his detestation of Sir Walter Scott and all or almost all his works. In *Life on the Mississippi* Scott is blamed for having checked the "wave of progress" in the South with his propaganda for medieval feudalism, which, according to Clemens, "sets the world in love with dreams and phantoms; with decayed and swinish forms of religion; with decayed and degraded systems of government; with the sillinesses and emptinesses, sham grandeurs, sham gauds, and sham chivalries of a brainless and worthless long-vanished society." The reality behind these shams was, Clemens felt, a sordid and quite common crime. He remarked in a notebook entry, probably made in 1888, that the establishment of a monarchy "is the same sort of crime that surprise and seizure of a weak community's property by a robber gang, and the conversion of the community itself into slaves, is. . . . A monarchy is perpetuated piracy. In its escutcheon should always be the skull and crossbones."

In these terms, the presence of three murderous robbers on a wrecked steamboat named *Walter Scott* is neatly satirical. It echoes, on a note of considerably greater seriousness, the earlier activities of Tom's gang, one of which is a seizure of doughnuts and jam from "a Sunday-school picnic, and only a primer class at that," which Tom insists is a rich caravan— as if that would make the act less shamefully cruel. The Amer-

ican function of Scott and others like him, Clemens implies, is to excuse and gloss over the exploitation of slaves and poor whites, and to glamorize the exploiters as Southern chivalry. The actual behavior of the slave-owning class, according to Clemens's double-edged suggestion, is on the one hand as evil as that of a gang of thieves and murderers, and on the other as silly as that of Tom's infatuated band.

Part of the loot of the *Walter Scott*, which the robbers unknowingly bequeath to Huck and Jim, is a number of appropriate books "about kings and dukes and earls and such, and how gaudy they dressed, and how much style they put on, and called each other your majesty, and your grace, and your lordship, and so on, 'stead of mister. . . ." Huck's reading to Jim from these books leads to a good deal of talk about Solomon and his wisdom, which Jim rather shrewdly questions, and about Louis XVI and "the dolphin," which prepares for the later advent of the bogus king and duke. The whole incident, in all its ramifications, contributes to the satirical exploration in Huck's experience of the various meanings, pretended and real, false and true, of the aristocratic idea in the South.

This incident is balanced as well as followed by the much more important one of Huck's separation from Jim in the fog and practical joke in making Jim think that it was a dream. In this event Huck is made to realize that Jim is a proud and sensitive human being, not livestock or chattel goods, and that the joke has been a cruel and humiliating betrayal of a friend's feelings. Corrupted by his life in a slave society and by the propaganda with which that society tries to justify the crime of slavery, Huck has never before considered that a slave might have feelings as worthy of respect as anyone else's. The speech in which Jim shows him his error, full of simple dignity and a pathos that beautifully consists with its righteous indignation, opens Huck's eyes in a way that is likely to stay in his memory. His reaction is worthy. "It was fifteen minutes," he says, "before I could work myself up to go and humble myself to a nigger; but I done it, and I warn't ever sorry for it afterward, neither. I didn't do him no more mean tricks, and I wouldn't done that one if I'd 'a' knowed it would make him feel that way." This realization, occurring shortly before the second decision to help Jim escape, makes any other decision practically impossible. With his indirect, unconscious realization of the falseness of aristocracy to balance his new awareness of the humanity of the slave, Huck would find it the meanest trick of all to betray Jim and send him back into the status of a piece of property to be exploited by the robber gang which is the reality behind the sham front of Southern aristocracy.

The third and final decision is led up to by a more personal and extensive experience of upperclass Southerners than before. Shortly after the second crisis, Huck and Jim realize that they have passed Cairo in the fog, but before they can do anything to get back, the raft is wrecked by a steamboat and they are separated again. Huck finds himelf ashore, beginning a new phase of the story and of his education. His shore adventures alternate, from this point on, with repeated escapes to the river, until he comes to the Phelps plantation. These adventures bring him more dramatically than before into contact, and more often into conflict, with aristocrats of various kinds. The increase of experience, knowledge, and understanding which he gains in this phase leads convincingly to his ultimate decision to repudiate aristocratic society by freeing its victim Jim.

The first aristocrats he meets in person, leaving aside the Widow, Miss Watson, and Judge Thatcher, are the Grangerfords, by

Twain's copy of Adventures of Huckleberry Finn, *marked for oral delivery. Courtesy of The Mark Twain Papers, The Bancroft Library.*

whom he is strongly impressed and who are genuinely impressive in many ways. They have the typical aristocratic virtues: they are dignified, hospitable, proud, handsome, cultured (after a fashion), courteous, devout, and kind to strangers and dependents. But the more Huck learns of them, the more uneasy he becomes about their character and behavior. Clemens, through Huck's observations and comments, gradually undercuts the value of their culture. The description of the house, which is parallel to the account of "The House Beautiful" in *Life on the Mississippi,* is a skillful piece of irony. Huck admires the place immensely, while Clemens mercilessly exposes the queer mixture of arrogant show and pathetic provincialism that it presents to even a moderately sophisticated eye. The description leads up to and is ludicrously topped off by Huck's account of Emmeline Grangerford's esthetic misdeeds in crayon and verse, of the graveyard school run wild and gone to seed. The cultural pretensions of the aristocracy are, by this report, sufficiently harmless in themselves but crude, anachronistic, and highly absurd from any civilized modern point of view.

The feud which is going on between the Grangerfords and the Shepherdsons is a much more serious matter, and it does not depend on the same kind of irony for its effect. It is as deeply horrifying to Huck as it could possibly be to Clemens. The brutal killing of the two boys makes Huck so sick that he cannot even tell about it in detail without getting sick again; and his admiration for the better qualities of the aristocrats is more than canceled by this result of their violence.

The incident is a direct expression of feeling on the part of its author. In *Life on the Mississippi* Clemens goes somewhat out of his way to comment on a published opinion that the South had "the highest type of civilization this continent has seen. . . ." He demonstrates the hollowness of the brag in a footnote with "Illustrations of it thoughtlessly omitted by the advertiser," consisting of newspaper accounts of four fights in which five Southern gentlemen were killed and one injured, with the usual incidental damage to bystanders, reference also being made to four other murders and one nonfatal stabbing in previous engagements involving some of the same gentlemen. The people concerned were of the highest class that Southern civilization had produced, including a general and his son, a bank president, a college professor, and "two 'highly connected' young Virginians" who fought a duel with butcher knives. It is from this kind of violence that Huck escapes to the river again, wishing that he "hadn't ever come ashore that night to see such things. I ain't ever going to get shut of them—lots of times I dream about them." Clemens had often dreamed about some violent episodes he witnessed as a boy.

Huck's reaction leads to one of his most lyric descriptions of the freedom, comfort, and beauty of the river, and the loveliness of life on a raft. But evil comes into this world also, in the shape of the two confidence men who palm themselves off as "the rightful Duke of Bridgewater" and "the late Dauphin . . . Looy the Seventeen, son of Looy the Sixteen and Marry Antonette," and who take over in the true aristocratic, robber-gang fashion. The cream of the jest is that the duke's claim is accepted by the other rogue so that he may in turn make his higher claim. The cream of the cream is that the duke then has to admit the king's superior status and rights in order that both may exploit the plebeian members of the little commonwealth. But the richest layer of all is Huck's good naturedly cynical accommodation to the whole arrangement. He sees immediately what frauds these are, but he is pleased when the duke knuckles under; "for what you want, above all things, on a raft, is for everybody to be satisfied, and feel right and kind towards the others."

Clemens's feeling about the kind of imposition practiced—or at least attempted—here is given in another notebook entry: "There are shams and shams; there are frauds and frauds, but the transparentest of all is the sceptered one. We see monarchs meet and go through solemn ceremonies, farces, with straight countenances; but it is not possible to imagine them meeting in private and not laughing in each other's faces." The fraud practiced by the bogus king and duke is no different from the frauds put over by real kings and dukes, except that the latter are bigger. As Huck explains to Jim, after the confidence men have worked over their first town together, they are lucky not to have Henry VIII on their hands, for he was a really accomplished crook; "'If we'd 'a' had him along 'stead of our kings he'd 'a' fooled that town a heap worse than ourn done. I don't say that 'ourn is lambs, because they ain't, when you come right down to the cold facts; but they ain't nothing to *that* old ram, anyway.'" This observation reinforces the point already made, implicitly, that the Grangerfords and Shepherdsons, by their more serious imitation of aristocratic ways, are only presenting a more pernicious version of something which at best is a sham and a fraud.

Perhaps the most emphatic impression of the ugly side of Southern chivalry is given by the incident in which Huck witnesses the cold-blooded murder of old Boggs by Colonel Sherburn. Boggs is a noisy but harmless fool, Sherburn a fine example of aristocratic pride—brave and intelligent in his own way, but narrow, selfish, inconsiderate, harsh, and brutal. It is, again, a sickening scene, and it is based on a murder that Clemens witnessed as a boy. But it may be that the importance of the incident for the satirical aspect of the book lies mainly in the character of the townspeople, who are by and large a degraded lot. "There couldn't anything wake them up all over," says Huck, "and make them happy all over, like a dog-fight—unless it might be putting turpentine on a stray dog and setting fire to him, or tying a tin pan to his tail and see him run himself to death." They try half-heartedly to get Boggs to stop his offensive yelling and go home, but they also perversely enjoy the shooting and the old man's death, the view of the body in the drug store window, and the reenactment of the murder by one of the onlookers. When they go to Sherburn's house with the announced intention of lynching him, he lectures them contemptuously and drives them off with a shotgun, which he does not have to fire.

His contempt seems justified, on the face of things. These are the same people who, after hooting the Shakespearean efforts of the king and duke, prove ripe for the Royal Nonesuch hoax. The duke, in his estimate of them, agrees with Sherburn. He prints at the foot of his handbill "LADIES AND CHILDREN NOT ADMITTED," remarking, "'There . . . if that line don't fetch them, I don't know Arkansaw!'" It does. But the deeper point is not explicitly stated here, or anywhere else in *Huck Finn,* nor is it fully understood, we may suppose, by either Sherburn or the duke. They see well enough that the people are ignorant, cowardly, and gullible; they do not see that the reason for that fact is the apparently opposite fact that an ar-

istocracy is in power. Clemens, however, was aware of it and well convinced that poverty, both of the flesh and of the spirit, is the mirror image of aristocratic splendor and that universal cruelty is inevitably characteristic of any society divided into rigid classes with hereditary inequalities of function, privilege, and status.

This principle is explaind more clearly in *A Connecticut Yankee.* The Yankee is shocked at the way poor peasants in Arthurian England rush out, heedless of right or justice, and help each other hang their neighbors in their lord's behalf, apparently unable "to see anything horrible about it.". . . The Yankee also remarks that "It is enough to make a body ashamed of his race to think of the sort of froth that has always occupied its thrones without shadow of right or reason," and what Clemens obviously means is that any respectable race would blow such froth to the moon before letting it settle into power.

Huck, whose background is about as purely poor-white as it could be, is given almost exactly the same words—"It was enough to make a body ashamed of the human race"—to describe his feelings about the next incident. The king and duke are having a fine run of initial success in playing their confidence game on the Wilks girls and most of their neighbors. It is a game that Huck perfectly understands, and he becomes so much ashamed of himself for being involved in it, though unwillingly, that he takes the risky measure of telling the truth in order to break it up. The most painful aspect of the affair applies directly to the theme of slavery, being the inhumanity of the fake aristocrats in the sale of the Wilks family slaves, "the two sons up the river to Memphis, and their mother down the river to Orleans." Huck says again that "it most made me down sick to see it. . . . I can't ever get it out of my memory, the sight of them poor miserable girls and niggers hanging around each other's necks and crying. . . ." The reader is likely to recall, as Clemens must have done, that this is not something only fakers do; it is precisely what Miss Watson does in planning to sell Jim "down to Orleans"; the general truth is that, as the Connecticut Yankee remarks in another place, "a privileged class, an aristocracy, is but a band of slaveholders under another name." The function of the king and duke is to show this basic identity, and underscore its meaning. Are these two scoundrels the most absurd, unmitigated, bare-faced buffoons of wickedness imaginable? So, Clemens wishes us to feel and understand, are all aristocrats. Kings, dukes, pirates, robbers, confidence men, and slaveholders are the same, and all sorry. Anyone who respects them is a fool, anyone who fears them is a coward, and anyone who supports them or submits to them is a slave himself.

Huck is none of these things, though he is almost infinitely good-natured and accommodating. He goes along with the king and duke as well and as long as he can, and he feels sorry for them when the mob escorts them out of town, in tar and feathers, on a rail. But he spoils their game with the Wilkses, and he leaves them when the king sells Jim into bondage again. For him, their function has been to complete his education in the social realities of slavocracy and to put the finishing touches on his preparation for the final decision he has to make. They have done the job effectively; he is ready now to see Jim through to freedom in spite of anything. Unconsciously, but with deep conviction, he understands the society to which by accident of birth he belongs, and refuses to submit to it.

On this last occasion, Huck sees his problem as being more difficult than it has ever seemed to him before, because it presents itself to him in terms of the religious sanction which the institution of slavery enjoyed in the prewar South. His conscience, unable to win the battle alone, now tells him, in accordance with the Sunday-school teaching he feels he should have had, "'that people that acts as I'd been acting about that nigger goes to everlasting fire.'"'. . . Huck has easily won out over public opinion, less easily over public opinion reinforced by his own conscience. The addition of the Deity to the list of powers with which he has to contend raises his battle to its ultimate pitch of intensity.

His first maneuver is to pray for the improvement of his character, but he realizes at once that the plea is hypocritical. To make it good, he writes a letter to Miss Watson to tell her where Jim is, but he gets to thinking about Jim's goodness and loyalty and kindness, and all the times they have helped each other, and again he makes up his mind.

> I was a-trembling, because I'd got to decide, forever, betwixt two things, and I knowed it. I studied a minute, sort of holding my breath, and then says to myself:
>
> "All right, then, I'll *go* to hell"—and tore it up.
>
> It was awful thoughts and awful words, but they was said. And I let them stay said; and never thought no more about reforming.

With this decision, the middle or river section comes to its conclusion, and the ending of the book begins.

Clemens obviously had difficulty handling the ending. The reason seems to be that once Huck's final decision is made there is no longer any important part for Jim to play. His function in relation to the theme has been to test, or to furnish occasions when events would test, Huck's growing moral strength and mature independence. When that has been done, to the last possible extreme, Jim needs simply to be got out of the book as quickly and as unobtrusively as possible. Instead, Clemens plays up Tom Sawyer's long, elaborate, and almost meaningless escape plot. The final solution to the problem, the disclosure that Miss Watson has died and freed Jim in her will, is all that is needed, and the less said about it the better. And yet the escape plot is not altogether irrelevant. It furthers and completes the satire on sentimental literature, from which Tom draws his inspirations. It caps the ridicule of aristocratic pretensions by identifying Jim, the imprisoned slave, with the noble persons on whose renowned adventures his liberation is modeled. It is an immense expression of contempt for adult society, so easily and so thoroughly hoodwinked by a pair of audacious children; and the more absurd Tom's antics become, the more the satire is built up. It is as much an attack on conventional respectability as Huck's discomforts at the Widow Douglas's, or his observations on the culture of the Grangerfords, or his rebellion against slavery itself.

Huck's attitude at the end is a mixture, full of ironies and reservations of many kinds. Having made the great decision to repudiate society, physically, morally, and spiritually, he can hardly return to it without equivocation. In a sense, his acceptance of the name and status of Tom Sawyer on the Phelps plantation is a return, but it is made on completely false premises. Also Huck is glad in a way to submit to Tom's leadership and direction. The burden of lonely responsibility has weighed long and heavily. But he is not fooled for a minute into thinking that there is any validity in Tom's adherence to bookish or aristocratic authority. "'When I start in to steal a nigger,'"

he says, "'I ain't no ways particular how it's done so it's done. What I want is my nigger . . . and I don't give a dead rat what the authorities thinks about it nuther.'" He has arrived at maturity and self-sufficiency, and he is poised at the end in a delicate balance, ready at any moment "to light out for the territory" in order to escape Aunt Sally's threatened continuation of the civilizing process begun by the Widow Douglas.

This aspect of the conclusion is exactly right. It would have been wrong—impossible in fact—for Clemens to bring the story to a stop, as he might have tried to do by having Huck accept the moral values of society and return to it uncritically in a "happy ending." The whole process of his development runs counter to any such result. The impression that Clemens has to leave, and does leave, in the reader's mind and feelings is that Huck will continue to develop. He will escape again, as many times as he needs to, from society and any of its restrictions which would hamper or prevent his growth. He will die and be reborn whenever his character needs to break the mold that society would place upon it. Accordingly, the structure of the story is left open; the conclusion is deliberately inconclusive.

Frank Baldanza, who has made the most direct attack so far on the problem of structure in *Huck Finn* [see excerpt dated 1955], believes that the basic principle can be defined as rhythmic repetition, with variation and development, of many thematic motifs, which have the effect of stitching the book together internally. He further suggests that each recurrence "was impulsive on Twain's part, and that any pattern we find in the repetitions is either unconsciously or accidentally ordained." My analysis would seem to bear out the observation that rhythmic, varied, and developmental repetition is important. It is not basic to the structure, but it certainly does support it and supply it with a texture of rich and complex harmony. However, this effect is not and cannot possibly be accidental; it fits too well with the larger thematic repetition of Huck's decision. And I suspect very strongly too that Clemens must have been aware of it, in some way, as being appropriate to the pattern of the work he meant to make. A close examination will show that the motifs most often repeated are those most intimately concerned with the aristocracy-slavery-sentimentalism relationship. Moreover the variations add up to a steady intensification of Huck's and the reader's awareness of the injustice, the hypocrisy, and the general moral ugliness and weakness of Southern society before the war. This intensification provides the milieu and the measure of Huck's development through the death-and-rebirth pattern from irresponsible boyhood to moral maturity.

The total result of these thematic, structural, and symbolic workings is a novel which has a remarkably high degree of consistency, coherence, and unity. Its theme is the growth of an individual personality. Its crisis is the moral decision, repeated three times, to repudiate the conventions of society and do the individually, humanly right thing. Its rising interest is given by the sharply increasing complexity of the individual awareness of the implications of such an action. Its structure is defined by the extinction of the old childish organization of mind and feelings, the symbolic death of the individual as he was, his withdrawal from society into nature, and his reconstitution, or symbolic rebirth, on a higher and more mature level of organization, as a better, more capable person. The theme and structure are concretely embodied and related in the texture, which reinforces both with a rhythmically repeated and varied pattern of appropriate motifs and images. The functional, organic interrelations of all these factors must have something to do with the effect of unity which readers generally feel in *Huckleberry Finn,* but which we are now only beginning to understand and be able to explain. (pp. 89-103)

> *Richard P. Adams, "The Unity and Coherence of 'Huckleberry Finn'," in* TSE: Tulane Studies in English, *Vol. VI, 1956, pp. 87-103.*

RALPH ELLISON (essay date 1958)

[*Ellison is the author of the highly acclaimed novel* Invisible Man *(1952). Considered among the most significant works of postwar American fiction,* Invisible Man *concerns a black American's search for identity as an individual as well as his struggle against racial prejudice. The following excerpt is from Ellison's essay* "Change the Joke and Slip the Yoke," *which was written in response to an essay by American critic Stanley Edgar Hyman concerning, as Ellison has paraphrased it, "the relationship between Negro American literature and Negro American folklore." In his essay, Ellison discusses Twain's portrayal of Jim as a fictional rendition of the stage blacks in minstrel shows.*]

In the Anglo-Saxon branch of American folklore and in the entertainment industry (which thrives on the exploitation and debasement of all folk materials), the Negro is reduced to a negative sign that usually appears in a comedy of the grotesque and the unacceptable. As Constance Rourke has made us aware, the action of the early minstrel show—with its Negro-deprived choreography, its ringing of banjos and rattling of bones, its voices cackling jokes in pseudo-Negro dialect, with its nonsense songs, its bright costumes and sweating performers—constituted a ritual of exorcism. Other white cultures had their gollywogs and blackamoors but the fact of Negro slavery went to the moral heart of the American social drama and here the Negro was too real for easy fantasy, too serious to be dealt with in anything less than a national art. The mask was an inseparable part of the national iconography. Thus even when a Negro acted in an abstract role the national implications were unchanged. His costume made use of the "sacred" symbolism of the American flag—with red and white striped pants and coat and with stars set in a field of blue for a collar—but he could appear only with his hands gloved in white and his face blackened with burnt cork or greasepaint.

This mask, this willful stylization and modification of the natural face and hands, was imperative for the evocation of that atmosphere in which the fascination of blackness could be enjoyed, the comic catharsis achieved. The racial identity of the performer was unimportant, the mask was the thing (the "thing" in more ways than one) and its function was to veil the humanity of Negroes thus reduced to a sign, and to repress the white audience's awareness of its moral identification with its own acts and with the human ambiguities pushed behind the mask. (pp. 48-9)

It is not at all odd that this black-faced figure of white fun is for Negroes a symbol of everything they rejected in the white man's thinking about race, in themsleves and in their own group. When he appears, for example, in the guise of Nigger Jim, the Negro is made uncomfortable. Writing at a time when the blackfaced minstrel was still popular, and shortly after a war which left even the abolitionist weary of those problems associated with the Negro, Twain fitted Jim into the outlines of the minstrel tradition, and it is from behind this stereotype mask that we see Jim's dignity and human capacity—and Twain's complexity—emerge. Yet it is his source in this same tradition which creates that ambivalence between his identification as

an adult and parent and his "boyish" naïveté, and which by contrast makes Huck, with his street-sparrow sophistication, seem more adult. Certainly it upsets a Negro reader, and it offers a less psycho-analytical explanation of the discomfort which lay behind Leslie Fiedler's thesis concerning the relation of Jim and Huck in his essay "Come Back to the Raft Ag'in, Huck Honey!" [see *TCLC*, Vol. 6].

A glance at a more recent fictional encounter between a Negro adult and a white boy, that of Lucas Beauchamp and Chick Mallison in Faulkner's *Intruder in The Dust,* will reinforce my point. For all the racial and caste differences between them, Lucas holds the ascendency in his mature dignity over the youthful Mallison and refuses to lower himself in the comic duel of status forced on him by the white boy whose life he has saved. Faulkner was free to reject the confusion between manhood and the Negro's caste status which is sanctioned by white Southern tradition, but Twain, standing closer to the Reconstruction and to the oral tradition, was not so free of the white dictum that Negro males must be treated either as boys or "uncles"—never as men. Jim's friendship for Huck comes across as that of a boy for another boy rather than as the friendship of an adult for a junior; thus there is implicit in it not only a violation of the manners sanctioned by society for relations between Negroes and whites, there is a violation of our conception of adult maleness.

In Jim the extremes of the private and the public come to focus, and before our eyes an "archetypal" figure gives way before the realism implicit in the form of the novel. Here we have, I believe, an explanation in the novel's own terms of that ambiguity which bothered Fiedler. Fiedler was accused of mere sensationalism when he named the friendship homosexual, yet I believe him so profoundly disturbed by the manner in which the deep dichotomies symbolized by blackness and whiteness are resolved that, forgetting to look at the specific form of the novel, he leaped squarely into the middle of that tangle of symbolism which he is dedicated to unsnarling, and yelled out his most terrifying name for chaos. Other things being equal, he might have called it "rape," "incest," "parricide" or—"miscegenation." It is ironic that what to a Negro appears to be a lost fall in Twain's otherwise successful wrestle with the ambiguous figure in black face is viewed by a critic as a symbolic loss of sexual identity. Surely for literature there is some rare richness here. (pp. 50-1)

Discussions of folk tradition and literature which slight the specific literary forms involved seem to me questionable. . . . [Novelists] in our time are more likely to be inspired by reading novels than by their acquaintance with any folk tradition.

I use folklore in my work not because I am Negro, but because writers like Eliot and Joyce made me conscious of the literary value of my folk inheritance. My cultural background, like that of most Americans, is dual (my middle name, sadly enough, is Waldo).

I knew the trickster Ulysses just as early as I knew the wily rabbit of Negro American lore, and I could easily imagine myself a pint-sized Ulysses but hardly a rabbit, no matter how human and resourceful or Negro. And a little later I could imagine myself as Huck Finn (I so nicknamed my brother) but not, though I racially identified with him, as Nigger Jim, who struck me as a white man's inadequate portrait of a slave. (p. 58)

> *Ralph Ellison, "Change the Joke and Slip the Yoke," in his* Shadow and Act, Random House, 1964, pp. 45-59.*

KENNETH S. LYNN   (essay date 1958)

[An American literary scholar whose works evidence his conservative principles, Lynn is the general editor of Houghton-Mifflin's "Riverside Literature" series and the author of numerous essays and books on American life and letters. In the following excerpt, he discusses the incompatibility of Jim's quest for freedom and Huck's search for a father.]

The first episode from **"Huckleberry Finn"** to appear in print was the chapter about Huck and the raftsmen that Twain casually excised from the still-uncompleted novel and threw—as he phrased it—into **"Life on the Mississippi."** The purpose of the transposition was to illustrate "keelboat talk and manners" as they had existed in the 1840's, but Twain could hardly have chosen a more significant chapter for introducing what he liked to call "Huck Finn's Autobiography" to the world, because in his prodigally wasteful American way, Twain improved a good book at the cost of looting his masterpiece of an episode of extraordinary richness, of great beauty and humor, which sets forth in a parable the two major themes of the novel.

The chapter begins immediately after Huck and Jim's terrifying experience of getting lost in the fog. Drifting down an unfamiliar and "monstrous big river," the boy and the Negro decide that Huck should find out where they are by swimming over to a huge raft they have seen in the distance and gathering the information by eavesdropping. Under cover of darkness, Huck reaches the raft, climbs on board without being noticed, and settles down to listen to the talk of the raftsmen, to their colossal boasting, their roaring songs, and above all, to the fantastic tall-tale about a man named Dick Allbright and the mysterious barrel that followed him on the river wherever he went rafting, bringing terror and death to his companions. Nothing, the teller of the tale assures his audience, could keep the barrel off Dick Allbright's trail or mitigate its inexorable fatality, until finally a raft captain swam out to the barrel and hauled it aboard. Inside its wooden walls, the captain and his men found a stark-naked baby—"Dick Allbright's baby; he owned up and said so. 'Yes,' he says, a-leaning over it, 'yes, it is my own lamented darling, my poor lost Charles William Allbright deceased,' says he—for he could curl his tongue around the bulliest words in the language when he was a mind to.... Yes, he said, he used to live up at the head of this bend, and one night he choked his child, which was crying, not intending to kill it—which was prob'ly a lie—and then he was scared, and buried it in a bar'l, before his wife got home, and off he went, and struck the northern trail and went to rafting; and this was the third year that the bar'l had chased him."

Crouched in the darkness, naked and afraid, Huck seems utterly apart from these coarse, rough men, but the fantasy of violence and terror which the raftsman has spun for the scoffing delight of his fellows nevertheless vitally involves the runaway boy, for the story tells, after all, of a man who locked up his son, and of a naked child floating down the river in search of its father. That Huck has escaped to his fabulous voyage by making his Pap think he has been murdered only completes his identification with the dead baby who was somehow "reborn" in the river, an identification which he makes explicit when, suddenly seized from his hiding-place and surrounded by strange men demanding to know his name, Huck jokingly replies, "Charles William Allbright, sir." Always in Twain the best jokes reveal the profoundest connections, and with the release of laughter triggered by Huck's superbly-timed joke the chapter not only reaches its humorous climax, but we are suddenly made aware that through Huck we have been eavesdropping on a parable of the search for the father and of death by violence and rebirth by water which takes us to the very heart of the novel.

Yet even this awareness does not exhaust the richness of the riverman's story. The symbolic connection between Huck Finn and the tall-tale beautifully exemplifies how Mark Twain could exploit for the purposes of high art the tradition of Southwestern humor; but it also reveals that behind the novel there stands the Bible. A baby in a barrel afloat on a great, continental river: beyond a raftsman's fantasy we discern the infant Moses in the ark of bulrushes hidden in the Nile. Through that association we can understand that Twain was doing a great deal more than simply setting up a magnificent joke when he began **"Huckleberry Finn"** with a chapter entitled "I Discover Moses and the Bulrushers"; for although Huck soon loses all interest in Moses, "because I don't take no stock in dead people," the humorous introduction of the Biblical story effectively announces the sombre theme of death and rebirth, with its attendant implications of slavery and freedom, and inextricably associates Huck with the Mosaic saga of an infant who "died" and was reborn in the river, and who grew up to lead an enslaved people to freedom.

The Moses theme unfolds in a series of initiations. A new life, a fresh start, is constantly being attempted by Huck; in the course of his journey down the river he assumes a dazzling variety of roles, becoming by turns George Peters, George Jackson, a young girl, an English valet, and finally, Tom Sawyer. But just as Pap's spiritual rebirth culminates in a quite literal fall from grace (dead drunk, off a porch-roof), so Huck's initiations run a cycle from birth to death. His "new life" at the Widow's terminates with his simulated murder in the cabin where Pap has locked him up; his identity as George Jackson is concluded by the blood bath at the Grangerford's; his masquerade as an English valet is abandoned in a graveyard. The same cyclical movement marks the drama of liberation. From the time that Tom and Huck tie up Jim "for fun" at the beginning of the novel until they make a game out of liberating him from the cabin on the Phelpses' farm at the very end of the book, Jim moves in and out of one bondage after another. But these sine wave movements from birth to death and from freedom to slavery that give the novel its characteristic rhythm take place within the framework of a larger movement that carries Huck and Jim simultaneously toward triumph and tragedy. When Moses led the Israelites to freedom he also moved toward his prophesied appointment with death; the great paradox of **"Huckleberry Finn"** is that Huck and Jim's voyage toward freedom takes them due south, into the very heart of the slave country, and that the triumphant liberation of Jim inexorably enforces the tragic separation of the boy and the Negro. As W. H. Auden has observed [see Additional Bibliography], the final meaning of **"Huckleberry Finn"** is that freedom and love are incompatible, which is another way of saying that the liberation theme and the search for the father theme are tragically at odds.

The search theme is officially introduced when Judge Thatcher and the Widow Douglas go to court to get permission to take Huck away from his Pap. Who should be his parents, the respectable aristocrats who are no blood relation to Huck, or his violent, drunken father? Nothing less than a human life is at stake; the decision would seem to call for the wisdom of Solomon. Echoing Huck's judgment of Moses, Nigger Jim "doan' take no stock" in the wisdom of Solomon, yet in the chapter entitled "Was Solomon Wise?" our laughter at Jim's stupidity carries with it the realization that the search theme also has a connection with the Bible. Jim regards it as utter foolishness that Solomon should have attempted to settle the parenthood dispute by offering to cut the child in two—"De 'spute warn't 'bout half a chile, de 'spute was 'bout a whole chile; en de man dat think he kin settle a 'spute 'bout a whole chile wid a half a chile doan' know enough to come in out'n de rain." As well as being marvelously funny, the speech throws into Biblical perspective the entire problem of parenthood with which the novel is concerned.

Like Solomon, Huck listens for the voice of truth and the accents of love as a means of identifying the true parent he seeks, but neither side in the legal contest so identifies itself, and therefore when Huck escapes to the river he is fleeing, as Twain once pointed out, both a "persecuting good widow" and his "persecuting father." Encountering Jim, Huck is at first amused and exasperated by the black man's ignorance, but part of the great drama of their relationship is Huck's gathering awareness that Jim is always right about all the things that really matter, about how certain movements of the birds mean a storm is coming, about the dangers of messing with snakes, and the meaning of dreams. But if Jim's relationship to Huck is fatherly in the sense that he constantly is correcting and admonishing the boy, forever telling him some new truth about the world, he is identified even more unmistakably as Huck's father by the love that he gives him. Just as Huck is searching for a father, so Jim is attempting to rejoin his family, and he lavishes on the love-starved river waif all of his parental affection, calling Huck honey, and petting him, and doing "everything he could think of for me." Jim's ludicrous horror at Solomon's apparent willingness to split a child in two is, as it turns out, a humorous statement of his loving care for the integrity of his white child.

The moral center of the novel focuses in the intense relationship between Huck and Jim, but as in Gogol's "Dead Souls," the panoramic sweep of Huck's journey in search of his father also opens to view a whole civilization, and the wrath of Twain's judgment of that civilization is the novel's most Biblical quality. Entering many houses in his quest for truth and love, Huck calls only the raft his home, a fact which symbolizes at the broadest reach of social implication Twain's massive condemnation of the society of the Great Valley as he knew it in the tragic quarter of a century before the Civil War.

When, at the beginning of the novel, Huck is sworn into Tom Sawyer's gang and introduced to Miss Watson's piousness, he is thereby initiated into the two mysteries of the society which offer—respectively—an institutionalized version of truth and love: romanticism and religion. For Tom, life is a circus, a romantic adventure story. Turnips are "julery" and Sunday School picnickers are "Spanish merchants and rich A-rabs," and Tom denounces Huck as a "numskull" for his literal-mindedness about these marvels. Huck, however, who understands that the fine spectacle of lights twinkling in a village late at night means that "there was sick folks, maybe," knows that romanticism is a way of faking the nature of reality, and when he temporarily forgets this, when he disregards Jim's warning and boards an abandoned steamboat to have an adventure of which Tom Sawyer would have approved, he comes close to losing his life. (The fact that the steamboat is named the "Walter Scott" is scarcely accidental, for in **"Life on the Mississippi"** Twain had already blasted the Scott-intoxication of the South as "in great measure responsible" for the Civil

War.) But the novel's bitterest attack on the romantic imagination occurs in two interrelated and successive chapters, 21 and 22. In the latter chapter, Huck goes to a circus, sees a drunken man weaving around the ring on a horse, and is terribly distressed, although the crowd roars with delight. But it is not Huck's charming naïveté in not recognizing that the drunkard is a clown that Twain condemns, it is the callousness of the crowd. For this circus scene depends upon the preceding chapter, which really does involve a drunk, the drunken Boggs, who weaves down the street on horseback, shouting insults at Colonel Sherburn. When Sherburn mortally wounds Boggs, a crowd gathers excitedly around the drunkard to watch him die. Everyone is tremendously pleased—except Huck, and the dying man's daughter. Thus by this juxtaposition of episodes, each of which contrasts the boy's sympathetic concern with the gleeful howling of the crowd, does Twain lay bare the depravity of a society that views life as a circus, as some kind of romantic show.

For Miss Watson, life is a moral certainty. Bible readings and daily prayers fill her smug world with assurances. She tells Huck that if he will pray every day he will get whatever he asks for, and when he prays for fish hooks without being able to "make it work," she calls him a fool, just as Tom had called him a numskull. Yet it is Miss Watson, prattling of Providential mercy, who treats Nigger Jim severely, who despite her promise to him that she would never sell him away from his wife and children, can't resist the sight of a stack of money and agrees to sell him down the river. If romanticism is a lie, religion is a monumental lovelessness, a terrible hypocrisy. When Huck goes to church with the Grangerfords, the minister preaches a sermon on brotherly love to a congregation made up of men armed to the teeth and panting to kill one another; when the King pretends he is infused with Divine grace in order to con the camp meeting, he is only acting out Miss Watson's hypocrisies on the level of farce. But once again, as in his attack on life as a circus, Twain's most withering blast at lovelessness and hypocrisy is delivered by juxtaposing two chapters with a vengeance.

The last paragraph of chapter 23 is perhaps the most poignant moment in the entire novel, for it is here that Jim relates to Huck how his daughter, after recovering from scarlet fever, became a mysteriously disobedient child. Even when Jim had slapped her and sent her sprawling she refused to obey his orders, but just as he was going for her again, he realized what was wrong: "De Lord God Amighty forgive po' ole Jim, kaze he never gwyne to fogive hisself as long's he live! Oh, she was plumb deef en dumb, Huck, plumb deef en dumb—en I'd ben a-treat'n her so!" On the last page of chapter 24, the King and the Duke launch their scheme for robbing the Wilks girls of their inheritance, with the King pretending to be a parson and the Duke acting the part of a deaf mute. When viewed beside Jim's sorrow and compassion for his deaf-and-dumb daughter, the spectacle of the two frauds talking on their hands is sickening—"It was enough," says Huck, "to make a body ashamed of the human race."

In the end, Huck turns his back on the corruption of society, but his tragedy is that in the very moment of doing so he loses Jim. In one of the numerous sequels to the novel that Twain obsessively sketched out in his later years, Jim has somehow been caught again and Huck fantastically plans to free him by changing places with him and blacking his face. But the sad reality of the novel is that such a masquerade is an impossible dream; once Jim has reached the promised land of freedom,

Huck is forever separated from his black father by the tragedy of race. It is scarcely necessary to know that in still another contemplated sequel Twain envisioned Huck as a broken, helplessly insane old man in order to sense that at the conclusion of the novel Huck's voyage has become as doomed in its way as Captain Ahab's, and that in lighting out for the Territory without Jim beside him he flees with "all havens astern." (pp. 425-31)

Kenneth S. Lynn, "Huck and Jim," in The Yale Review, Vol. XLVII, No. 3, Spring, 1958, pp. 421-31.

HENRY NASH SMITH   (essay date 1962)

[Smith is an American educator and the literary executor of the Mark Twain Estate. He is currently serving on an editorial committee at work on The Mark Twain Papers, which are being published in fifteen volumes by the University of California Press. In the following excerpt, he discusses the characters of Pap and Colonel Sherburn and comments on the novel's conclusion.]

A number of characters besides Huck are presented in greater depth than is necessary either for purposes of satire or for telling the story of his and Jim's quest for freedom. Perhaps the most striking of these is Pap Finn. Like most of the book, Pap comes straight out of Mark Twain's boyhood memories. We have had a glimpse of him as the drunkard sleeping in the shade of a pile of skids on the levee in the opening scene of **"Old Times on the Mississippi."** His function in the plot, although definite, is limited. He helps to characterize Huck by making vivid the conditions of Huck's childhood. He has transmitted to his son a casual attitude toward chickens and watermelons, a fund of superstitions, a picaresque ability to look out for himself, and even the gift of language. Pap takes Huck away from the comfort and elegance of the Widow's house to the squalor of the deserted cabin across the river, and then by his sadistic beatings forces the boy to escape to Jackson's Island, where the main action of the flight with Jim begins. After the three chapters which Pap dominates (5-7) we do not see him again except as a corpse in the house floating down the river, but Huck refers to him several times later, invoking Pap's testimony to authenticate the aristocratic status of the Widow Douglas, and to support the family philosophy of "borrowing."

In the sociological scheme of the novel Pap provides a matchless specimen of the lowest stratum of whites who are fiercely jealous of their superiority to all Negroes. His monologue on the "govment" in Chapter 6, provoked by the spectacle of the well-dressed free negro professor from Ohio, seizes in a few lines the essence of Southern race prejudice. Huck shrewdly calls attention to his father's economic code. When the flooded river brings down part of a log raft, he says: "Anybody but Pap would 'a' waited and seen the day through, so as to catch more stuff; but that warn't Pap's style. Nine logs was enough for one time; he must shove right over to town and sell," mainly in order to buy whiskey.

But these documentary data supply only a minor part of the image of Pap in **Huckleberry Finn.** He provides some of the most mordant comedy in the book. The fashion in which he gives himself away in the monologue on "govment" is worthy of Jonson or Molière. . . . Even when the comedy verges on slapstick it retains its function as characterization. Pap is so completely absorbed in his diatribe that he barks his shins on the pork barrel:

He hopped around the cabin considerable, first on one leg and then on the other, holding first one shin and then the other one, and at last he let out with his left foot all of a sudden and fetched the tub a rattlin kick. But it warn't good judgment, because that was the boot that had a couple of his toes leaking out of the front end of it; so now he raised a howl that fairly made a body's hair raise, and down he went in the dirt, and rolled there, and held his toes; and the cussing he done then laid over anything he had ever done previous. He said so his own self afterwards. He had heard old Sowberry Hagan in his best days, and he said it laid over him, too; but I reckon that was sort of piling it on, maybe.

Pap's detached evaluation of his own accomplishment in swearing gives to his character an almost medieval flavor. In all his degradation he conceives of himself as enacting a role which is less a personal destiny than part of an integral natural-social reality—a reality so stable that he can contemplate it as if it were external to him. On election day he was drunk as a matter of course; it was an objective question, like an effort to predict the weather, whether he might be too drunk to get to the polls. When he settles down for a domestic evening in the cabin, he "took the jug, and said he had enough whiskey there for two drunks and one delirium tremens."

But when the delirium comes, it belies the coolness of his offhand calculation. Huck's description of the drunkard's agony is a nightmare of neurotic suffering that blots out the last vestige of comedy in Pap's image and relates itself in Huck's mind to the ominous sounds he had heard from his window in the Widow's house. . . . (pp. 125-27)

Pap's hallucinations externalize inner suffering in images of ghosts and portents. Presently he sees in Huck the Angel of Death and chases him around the cabin with a knife "saying he would kill me, and then I couldn't come for him no more." In fact, the mystery of Pap's anguished psyche has had a supernatural aura all along. He is in a sense a ghost the first time we see him, for his faceless corpse has been found floating in the river; and immediately before his dramatic appearance in Huck's room Jim's hair-ball oracle has announced, "Dey's two angels hoverin' roun' 'bout him. One uv 'em is white en shiny, en t'other one is black. De white one gits him to go right a little while, den de black one sail in en bust it all up. A body can't tell yit which one gwyne to fetch him at de las'." Coming early in the story, at a time when Mark Twain had apparently not yet worked out the details of the plot, this sounds as if he had in mind the possibility of involving Pap more elaborately in the course of events. But aside from the relatively minor incidents that have been mentioned, what the angels might have led Pap to do is never revealed.

He does, however, have an important thematic function. He serves as a forceful reminder that to be a vernacular outcast does not necessarily bring one into contact with the benign forces of nature. Physical withdrawal from society may be plain loafing, without moral significance. Huck's life with Pap in the cabin foreshadows his life with Jim on the raft, but lacks the suggestion of harmony with the natural setting. . . . More explicitly, Pap's denunciation of Huck for the civilized habits the Widow and Miss Watson have imposed on him is a grotesque version of vernacular hostility toward the conventions of refined society:

Starchy clothes—very. You think you're a good deal of a big-bug, *don't* you? . . . You're educated, too, they say—can read and write. You think you're better'n your father, now, don't you, because he can't? . . . you drop that school, you hear? I'll learn people to bring up a boy to put on airs over his own father and let on to be better'n what *he* is . . . First you know you'll get religion, too. I never see such a son.

This adds another nuance to the book by suggesting that civilized values have something to be said for them after all.

The extent to which Mark Twain's imagination was released in *Huckleberry Finn* to explore multiple perspectives upon the Matter of Hannibal and the Matter of the River can be realized if one compares Pap with the sociologically similar backwoodsmen observed from the steamboat in **"Old Times."** These "jeans-clad, chills-racked, yellow-faced miserables" are merely comic animals. Pap is even more degraded than they are, lazier, more miserable, but he is not an object of scorn. The fullness with which his degradation and his misery are presented confers on him not so much a human dignity—although it is also that— as the impersonal dignity of art.

In relation to the whole of *Huckleberry Finn*, Pap serves to solidify the image of Huck's and Jim's vernacular paradise by demonstrating that Mark Twain is aware of the darker possibilities confronting them when they escape from the shore to the river. The mass of superstitions with which Pap is so vividly connected (we recall the cross of nails in his boot heel to ward off the devil), standing in contrast to the intimations of blissful harmony with nature in the passages devoted to Huck and Jim alone on the raft, keeps that lyrical vision from seeming mere pathetic fallacy. And the appalling glimpse of Pap's inner life beneath the stereotype of the town drunkard makes him into what might be called a note of tragic relief in a predominantly comic story.

It has become a commonplace of criticism that the drastic shift in tone in the last section of *Huckleberry Finn,* from Chapter 31 to the end, poses a problem of interpretation. The drifting raft has reached Arkansas, and the King and the Duke have delivered Jim back into captivity. They make their exit early in the sequence, tarred and feathered as punishment for one more effort to work the "Royal Nonesuch" trick. Tom Sawyer reappears by an implausible coincidence and takes charge of the action, which thereafter centers about his schemes to liberate Jim from confinement in a cabin on the plantation of Tom's Uncle Silas Phelps.

These events have for their prelude a vivid description of Huck's first approach to the Phelps place:

> When I got there it was all still and Sunday-like, and hot and sunshiny; the hands was gone to the fields; and there was them kind of faint dronings of bugs and flies in the air that makes it seem so lonesome and like everybody's dead and gone; and if a breeze fans along and quivers the leaves it makes you feel mournful, because you feel like it's spirits whispering—spirits that's been dead ever so many years—and you always think they're talking about *you*. As a general thing it makes a body wish *he* was dead, too, and done with it all. . . .

This passage has much in common with Huck's meditation before his open window in Chapter I. They are the two most vivid expressions of his belief in ghosts, and in both cases the ghosts are associated in his mind with a deep depression not fully accounted for by the context of the story.

It would be reasonable to suppose that the cause of Huck's depression is the failure of his long effort to help Jim toward freedom. The reader knows that even if Huck could manage to rescue Jim from the Phelpses, they face insuperable difficulties in trying to make their way back up the Mississippi to free territory. Yet oddly enough, Huck does not share this estimate of the situation. He is confident he can find a way out of the impasse: "I went right along, not fixing up any particular plan, but just trusting to Providence to put the right words in my mouth when the time come; for I'd noticed that Providence always did put the right words in my mouth if I left it alone." Somewhat later, Huck points out to Tom that they can easily get Jim out of the log cabin by stealing the key, and "shove off down the river on the raft with Jim, hiding daytimes and running nights, the way me and Jim used to do before. Wouldn't that plan work?" Tom agrees: "Why, cert'nly it would work, like rats a-fighting. But it's too blame' simple; there ain't nothing *to* it. What's the good of a plan that ain't no more trouble than that?"

The tone as much as the substance of the references to the problem of rescuing Jim makes it plain that Huck's view of his predicament cannot account for his depression as he approaches the Phelps plantation. The emotion is the author's rather than Huck's, and it is derived from sources outside the story. In order to determine what these were we must consult Mark Twain's autobiographical reminiscences. The Phelps place as he describes it in the novel has powerful associations for him because it is patterned on the farm of his Uncle John A. Quarles where he spent summers as a boy. "I can see the farm yet, with perfect clearness," he wrote in his *Autobiography*.

> I can see all its belongings, all its details; the family room of the house, with a "trundle" bed in one corner and a spinning-wheel in another—a wheel whose rising and falling wail, heard from a distance, was the mournfulest of all sounds to me, and made me homesick and low spirited, and filled my atmosphere with the wandering spirits of the dead.

Additional associations with the Quarles farm are recorded in Mark Twain's **"The Private History of a Campaign That Failed,"** written a few months after the publication of *Huckleberry Finn*. This bit of fictionalized autobiography describes his experiences as second lieutenant of the Marion Rangers, a rather informal volunteer militia unit organized in Hannibal in the early months of the Civil War. The Quarles farm is here assigned to a man named Mason:

> We stayed several days at Mason's; and after all these years the memory of the dullness, and stillness, and lifelessness of that slumberous farm-house still oppresses my spirit as with a sense of the presence of death and mourning. There was nothing to do, nothing to think about; there was no interest in life. The male part of the household were away in the fields all day, the women were busy and out of our sight; there was no sound but the plaintive wailing of a spinning-wheel, forever moaning out from some

distant room—the most lonesome sound in nature, a sound steeped and sodden with homesickness and the emptiness of life.

The emotional overtones of the memories recorded in **"The Private History"** are made more explicit in a letter Mark Twain wrote in 1890:

> I was a *soldier* two weeks once in the beginning of the war, and was hunted like a rat the whole time . . . My splendid Kipling himself hasn't a more burnt-in, hard-baked and unforgettable familiarity with that death-on-the-pale-horse-with-hell-following-after which is a raw soldier's first fortnight in the field—and which, without any doubt, is the most tremendous fortnight and the vividest he is ever going to see.

But while there are references to fear of the enemy in **"The Private History,"** they are mainly comic, and the dullness and lifelessness that afflict the neophyte soldiers at the Mason farm do not suggest the feeling of being hunted like a rat. More significant, perhaps, is an incident Mark Twain places a few pages later in **"The Private History."** Albert B. Paine says it was invented; and it does have the air of fiction. But it reveals the emotional coloring of the author's recollections. He relates that he fired in the dark at a man approaching on horseback, who was killed. Although five other shots were fired at the same moment, and he did not at bottom believe his shot had struck its mark, still his "diseased imagination" convinced him he was guilty. "The thought shot through me that I was a murderer; that I had killed a man—a man who had never done me any harm. That was the coldest sensation that ever went through my marrow."

Huck also experiences a strong and not easily explicable feeling of guilt a few pages after his arrival at the Phelpses'. When he sees the Duke and the King ridden out of the nearby town on a rail, surrounded by a howling mob, he says:

> It was a dreadful thing to see. Human beings *can* be awful cruel to one another . . . So we poked along back home, and I warn't feeling so brash as I was before, but kind of ornery, and humble, and to blame, somehow—though *I* hadn't done nothing. But that's always the way; it don't make no difference whether you do right or wrong, a person's conscience ain't got no sense, and just goes for him *anyway*. If I had a yaller dog that didn't know no more than a person's conscience does I would pison him.

The close linkage of the Phelps and Mason farms with Mark Twain's memory of the Quarles place strongly suggests that Huck's depression is caused by a sense of guilt whose sources were buried in the writer's childhood. It is well known that Mark Twain was tormented all his life by such feelings. A fable written in 1876, **"The Facts Concerning the Recent Carnival of Crime in Connecticut,"** makes comedy of his sufferings; but they were serious and chronic. In his twenties, because of an imaginary error in administering an opiate, he had insisted he was to blame for the death of his brother from injuries received in the explosion of a steamboat. Later he accused himself of murdering his son Langdon when he neglected to keep him covered during a carriage ride in cold weather, and the child died of diphtheria.

But why was Mark Twain's latent feeling of guilt drawn up into consciousness at a specific moment in the writing of **Huckleberry Finn**? The most probable explanation is that at this point he was obliged to admit finally to himself that Huck's and Jim's journey down the river could not be imagined as leading to freedom for either of them. Because of the symbolic meaning the journey had taken on for him, the recognition was more than a perception of difficulty in contriving a plausible ending for the book. He had found a solution to the technical problem that satisfied him, if one is to judge from his evident zest in the complicated pranks of Tom Sawyer that occupy the last ten chapters. But in order to write these chapters he had to abandon the compelling image of the happiness of Huck and Jim on the raft and thus to acknowledge that the vernacular values embodied in his story were mere figments of the imagination, not capable of being reconciled with social reality. To be sure, he had been half-aware from the beginning that the quest of his protagonists was doomed. Huck had repeatedly appeared in the role of a Tiresias powerless to prevent the deceptions and brutalities he was compelled to witness. Yet Providence had always put the right words in his mouth when the time came, and by innocent guile he had extricated himself and Jim from danger after danger. Now the drifting had come to an end.

At an earlier impasse in the plot Mark Twain had shattered the raft under the paddle wheel of a steamboat. He now destroys it again, symbolically, by revealing that Huck's and Jim's journey, with all its anxieties, has been pointless. Tom Sawyer is bearer of the news that Jim has been freed in Miss Watson's will. Tom withholds the information, however, in order to trick Huck and Jim into the meaningless game of an Evasion that makes the word (borrowed from Dumas) into a devastating pun. Tom takes control and Huck becomes once again a subordinate carrying out orders. As if to signal the change of perspective and the shift in his own identification, Mark Twain gives Huck Tom's name through an improbable mistake on the part of Aunt Sally Phelps. We can hardly fail to perceive the weight of the author's feeling in Huck's statement on this occasion: "it was like being born again, I was so glad to find out who I was." Mark Twain has found out who he must be in order to end his book: he must be Tom.

In more abstract terms, he must withdraw from his imaginative participation in Huck's and Jim's quest for freedom. If the story was to be stripped of its tragic implications, Tom's perspective was the logical one to adopt because his intensely conventional sense of values made him impervious to the moral significance of the journey on the raft. Huck can hardly believe that Tom would collaborate in the crime of helping a run-away slave, and Huck is right. Tom merely devises charades involving a man who is already in a technical sense free. The consequences of the shift in point of view are strikingly evident in the treatment of Jim, who is subjected to farcical indignities. This is disturbing to the reader who has seen Jim take on moral and emotional stature, but it is necessary if everything is to be forced back into the framework of comedy. Mark Twain's portrayal of Huck and Jim as complex characters has carried him beyond the limits of his original plan: we must not forget that the literary ancestry of the book is to be found in backwoods humor. As Huck approaches the Phelps plantation the writer has on his hands a hybrid—a comic story in which the protagonists have acquired something like tragic depth.

In deciding to end the book with the description of Tom's unnecessary contrivances for rescuing Jim, Mark Twain was certain to produce an anticlimax. But he was a great comic writer, able to score local triumphs in the most unlikely circumstances. The last chapters have a number of brilliant touches—the slave who carries the witch pie to Jim, Aunt Sally's trouble in counting her spoons, Uncle Silas and the ratholes, the unforgettable Sister Hotchkiss. Even Tom's horseplay would be amusing if it were not spun out to such length and if we were not asked to accept it as the conclusion of *Huckleberry Finn.* Although Jim is reduced to the level of farce, Tom is a comic figure in the classical sense of being a victim of delusion. He is not aware of being cruel to Jim because he does not perceive him as a human being. For Tom, Jim is the hero of a historical romance, a peer of the Man in the Iron Mask or the Count of Monte Cristo. Mark Twain is consciously imitating *Don Quixote,* and there are moments not unworthy of the model, as when Tom admits that "we got to dig him out with the picks, and *let on* it's case-knives."

But Tom has no tragic dimension whatever. There is not even any force of common sense in him to struggle against his perverted imagination as Huck's innate loyalty and generosity struggle against his deformed conscience. Although Mark Twain is indulgent toward Tom, he adds him to the list of characters who employ the soul-butter style of false pathos. The inscriptions Tom composes for Jim to "scrabble onto the wall" of the cabin might have been composed by the Duke:

> 1. Here a captive heart busted.
> 2. Here a poor prisoner, forsook by the world and friends, fretted his sorrowful life.
> 3. Here a lonely heart broke, and a worn spirit went to its rest, after thirty-seven years of solitary captivity.
> 4. Here, homeless and friendless, after thirty-seven years of bitter captivity, perished a noble stranger, natural son of Louis XIV.

> While he was reading these noble sentiments aloud, "Tom's voice trembled . . . and he most broke down."

Mark Twain's partial shift of identification from Huck to Tom in the final sequence was one response to his recognition that Huck's and Jim's quest for freedom was only a dream: he attempted to cover with a veil of parody and farce the harsh facts that condemned it to failure. The brief episode involving Colonel Sherburn embodies yet another response to his disillusionment. The extraordinary vividness of the scenes in which Sherburn figures—only a half-dozen pages all told—is emphasized by their air of being an intrusion into the story. Of course, in the episodic structure of *Huckleberry Finn* many characters appear for a moment and disappear. Even so, the Sherburn episode seems unusually isolated. None of the principal characters is involved in or affected by it: Jim, the Duke, and the King are offstage, and Huck is a spectator whom even the author hardly notices. We are told nothing about his reaction except that he did not want to stay around. He goes abruptly off to the circus and does not refer to Sherburn again.

Like Huck's depression as he nears the Phelps plantation, the Sherburn episode is linked with Mark Twain's own experience. The shooting of Boggs follows closely the murder of "Uncle Sam" Smarr by a merchant named Owsley in Hannibal in 1845, when Sam Clemens was nine years old. Although it is not clear the he actually witnessed it, he mentioned the incident at least four times at intervals during his later life, including one retelling as late as 1898, when he said he had often dreamed

about it. Mark Twain prepares for the shooting in *Huckleberry Finn* by careful attention to the brutality of the loafers in front of the stores in Bricksville. "There couldn't anything wake them up all over, and make them happy all over, like a dogfight—unless it might be putting turpentine on a stray dog and setting fire to him, or tying a tin pan to his tail and see him run himself to death." The prurient curiosity of the townspeople who shove and pull to catch a glimpse of Boggs as he lies dying in the drugstore with a heavy Bible on his chest, and their pleasure in the re-enactment of the shooting by the man in the big white fur stovepipe hat, also help to make Bricksville an appropriate setting for Sherburn's crime.

The shooting is in Chapter 21, and the scene in which Sherburn scatters the mob by his contemptuous speech is in the following chapter. There is evidence that Mark Twain put aside the manuscript for a time near the end of Chapter 21. If there was such an interruption in his work on the novel, it might account for a marked change in tone. In Chapter 21 Sherburn is an unsympathetic character. His killing of Boggs is motivated solely by arrogance, and the introduction of Boggs's daughter is an invitation to the reader to consider Sherburn an inhuman monster. In Chapter 22, on the other hand, the colonel appears in an oddly favorable light. The townspeople have now become a mob; there are several touches that suggest Mark Twain was recalling the descriptions of mobs in Carlyle's *French Revolution* and other works of history and fiction. He considered mobs to be subhuman aggregates generating psychological pressures that destroyed individual freedom of choice. In a passage written for *Life on the Mississippi* but omitted from the book Mark Twain makes scathing generalizations about the cowardice of mobs, especially in the South but also in other regions, that closely parallel Sherburn's speech.

In other words, however hostile may be the depiction of Sherburn in Chapter 21, in chapter 22 we have yet another instance of Mark Twain's identifying himself, at least partially, with a character in the novel other than Huck. The image of Sherburn standing on the roof of the porch in front of his house with the shotgun that is the only weapon in sight has an emblematic quality. He is a solitary figure, not identified with the townspeople, and because they are violently hostile to him, an outcast. But he is not weaker than they, he is stronger. He stands above the mob, looking down on it. He is "a heap the best dressed man in that town," and he is more intelligent than his neighbors. The scornful courage with which he defies the mob redeems him from the taint of cowardice implied in his shooting of an unarmed man who was trying to escape. Many members of the mob he faces are presumably armed; the shotgun he holds is not the source of his power but merely a symbol of the personal force with which he dominates the community.

The Colonel's repeated references to one Buck Harkness, the leader of the mob, whom he acknowledges to be "half-a-man," suggest that the scene represents a contest between two potential leaders in Bricksville. Harkness is the strongest man with whom the townspeople can identify themselves. In his pride Sherburn chooses isolation, but he demonstrates that he is stronger than Harkness, for the mob, including Harkness, obeys his command to "*leave*—and take your half-a-man with you."

Sherburn belongs to the series of characters in Mark Twain's later work that have been called "transcendent figures." Other examples are Hank Morgan in *A Connecticut Yankee;* Pudd'nhead Wilson; and Satan in *The Mysterious Stranger.* They exhibit certain common traits, more fully developed with the passage of time. They are isolated by their intellectual superiority to the community; they are contemptuous of mankind in general; and they have more than ordinary power. Satan, the culmination of the series, is omnipotent. Significantly, he is without a moral sense—that is, a conscience, a sense of guilt. He is not torn by the kind of inner struggle that Huck experiences. But he is also without Huck's sound heart. The price of power is the surrender of all human warmth.

Colonel Sherburn's cold-blooded murder of Boggs, his failure to experience remorse after the act, and his withering scorn of the townspeople are disquieting portents for the future. Mark Twain, like Huck, was sickened by the brutality he had witnessed in the society along the river. But he had an adult aggressiveness foreign to Huck's character. At a certain point he could no longer endure the anguish of being a passive observer. His imagination sought refuge in the image of an alternative persona who was protected against suffering by being devoid of pity or guilt, yet could denounce the human race for its cowardice and cruelty, and perhaps even take action against it. The appearance of Sherburn in *Huckleberry Finn* is ominous because a writer who shares his attitude toward human beings is in danger of abandoning imaginative insight for moralistic invective. The slogan of "the damned human race" that later became Mark Twain's proverb spelled the sacrifice of art to ideology. Colonel Sherburn would prove to be Mark Twain's dark angel. His part in the novel, and that of Tom Sawyer, are flaws in a work that otherwise approaches perfection as an embodiment of American experience in a radically new and appropriate literary mode. (pp. 127-37)

> *Henry Nash Smith, in his* Mark Twain: The Development of a Writer, *Cambridge, Mass.: The Belknap Press, 1962, 212 p.*

CHADWICK HANSEN (essay date 1963)

[*Hansen is an American educator and author of works on American history, literature, and folk culture. In the following excerpt, he examines the characterization and narrative function of Jim.*]

An understanding of Jim's character is by no means a simple matter; he is a highly complex and original creation, although he appears at first sight very simple. We meet him first as the butt of a practical joke played by Tom Sawyer, in Chapter II. While Jim is sleeping Tom takes three candles from the Widow's kitchen, leaving a five-cent piece on the table to pay for them. Then he slips Jim's hat off and hangs it on the limb of a tree over his head. Afterwards, Jim decides that his sleep was a trance induced by witches, who rode him all over the world and hung his hat on a limb "to show who done it," and he believes that the devil himself has left the five-cent piece. His version of the episode makes him a very important man in the Negro community. "Jim was most ruined, for a servant," says Huck, "because he got so stuck up on account of having seen the devil and been rode by witches."

The Jim of this first episode is a recognizable type-character, the comic stage Negro, a type who has trod the less reputable boards of the American theatre almost from its beginnings and who is still with us in the grade B movie and in certain television and radio programs. His essential quality in this particular case is that he feels no humiliation as a result of Tom's trick. His ignorance protects him from the mental pain of humiliation and enables him to turn the trick into a kind of triumph. If Jim had suffered as a result of the trick into a kind of triumph—a false triumph, to be sure, but still a triumph. If Jim had suffered as a result of the trick, we—the audience—would be inclined

to feel pity for him. But since he does not suffer we are free to laugh at the incongruity between his account of the event and the reality. We are free to laugh at him, that is, because his ignorance is so sub-human that he cannot feel mental pain. (pp. 45-6)

Jim is still the stage Negro the next time we see him, when Huck asks Jim to have the hair-ball tell his fortune, but our attitude toward him is very much qualified, since in this episode Huck believes as firmly in Jim's magical powers as does Jim himself. In the first episode the audience was asked to think of itself as white men laughing at old Jim, the comical nigger. Here we are asked to think of ourselves as men, laughing at human ignorance and superstition. We could attribute Jim's ignorance to his color in the first episode; here we must attribute it to his humanity. Perhaps this is overstating the case, since the reader who does not wish to recognize the direction Twain is taking might feel that Huck himself is not fully human; he is only a child, and a White Trash child at that. It seems to me, however, that it requires considerable insensitivity to think of Huck as less than human, even at this early stage in the narrative, and in any case the direction of Twain's development of our attitude toward Jim is clear.

We see Jim next on Jackson's Island, where two episodes deserve particular notice. In the first of them Jim and Huck have been discussing "signs," and Jim predicts that he will be rich because he has hairy arms and a hairy breast. Then he gives us an account of his "specalat'n" in stock—livestock—and in a bank. The dialogue might have come from any minstrel show, and Jim has lost his money like any other stage Negro. But the conversation ends with Jim's reflection that "I's rich now, come to look at it. I owns mysef, en I's wuth eight hund'd dollars. I wisht I had de money, I wouldn' want no mo'." With this statement we move outside the world of low comedy, and Jim becomes something more than the ordinary stage Negro.

Twain has done enough by now to prepare us for the first of the tricks Huck plays on Jim. Huck kills a rattlesnake and curls it up on the foot of Jim's blankets. He expects, of course, that Jim will react like any other stage Negro. His eyes will bug out; his teeth will chatter; his knees will knock together; and Huck will have a good healthy laugh. But we are dealing now with someone who is more than a stereotype. "When Jim flung himself down on the blanket . . . the snake's mate was there, and bit him."

Huck is sorry and ashamed for what he has done. He throws the snakes away in the bushes, "for I warn't going to let Jim find out it was all my fault, not if I could help it." But he does *not* blame himself for failing to understand that Jim is a human being, who can be hurt if you play a stupid trick on him. There is something much simpler for which Huck can blame himself, and whenever he can, Huck will use Ockham's razor. "I made up my mind," he says, "I wouldn't ever take aholt of a snakeskin again with my hands, now that I see what had come of it." From this he proceeds to speculating on whether it isn't just as foolhardy to look at the new moon over your left shoulder.

> Old Hank Bunker done it once, and bragged
> about it; and in less than two years he got drunk
> and fell off the shot tower and spread himself
> out so that he was just a kind of a layer, as you
> may say; and they slid him edgeways between
> two barn doors for a coffin, and buried him so,

so they say, but I didn't see it. Pap told me.
But anyway, it all come of looking at the moon
that way, like a fool.

With the entrance of Hank Bunker we are back in the world
of slapstick comedy, and we can recognize how very little
Huck understands of what has happened. But the episode has,
I think, made some impression. That snake-skin continues to
haunt Huck's consciousness far down the river.

At the beginning of Chaper XIV we discover that Jim has a
good deal of common sense, when he complains to Huck of
how dangerous it is to go looking for the sort of adventures to
be found on the *Walter Scott.* Huck has to admit that Jim is
right. ''He was most always right; he had an uncommon level
head for a nigger.'' Having begun the chapter with Jim's ''uncommon level head,'' Twain fills the rest of it with the dialogues on whether Solomon was wise and why a Frenchman
doesn't talk like a man, which William Van O'Connor condemns as a cheap and inappropriate ''minstrel show, end-men
sort of humor'' [see *TCLC*, Vol. 12].

Now there is a considerable distance between the world of the
minstrel show and the world of William Van O'Connor, and
most of that distance is, of course, to Mr. O'Connor's credit.
But the distance is so great that it prevents him from seeing
the ways in which these dialogues *are* appropriate. Jim is ''down
on Solomon'' for threatening to cut a child in two, and this is
plainly preparation for our later discovery that Jim cares very
much for his own children, and blames himself for having been
unintentionally cruel to his daughter.

The dialogue on why a Frenchman doesn't talk like a man is
much more complicated. In order to understand it we must
remember the conventions of the minstrel show, where Mr.
Bones, although he seems at first sight to be abysmally ignorant
in comparison to Mr. Interlocutor, is actually very clever and
usually wins the arguments, just as Jim does. But what is
important is not that Mr. Bones wins again; what is important
is the terms in which the argument is won. Huck argues that
since a cat and a cow ''talk'' differently, and since it is ''natural
and right'' that they should do so, it is equally ''natural and
right'' for a Frenchman to talk differently from an American.
Huck's unstated assumption is that ethnic difference is founded
in nature, and has, therefore, the same magnitude and necessity
as difference in species. Jim immediately spots the fallacy. He
agrees that there is a basic difference between a cat and a cow,
which requires that they ''talk'' differently. But he asks:

''Is a Frenchman a man?''

''Yes,'' says Huck.

''*Well*, den! Dad blame it, why doan' he *talk*
like a man? You answer me *dat!*''

Jim recognizes, and Huck does not, that all men share a common humanity. When we remember that this argument has
been over differences in human language, when we remember
that Twain boasted at the beginning of the book of accurately
reproducing seven discrete dialects, and when we remember
how thoroughly man is divided from man in the society of the
Mississippi Valley, this little dialogue takes on an extraordinary
richness of meaning.

But Huck's only conclusion is that ''you can't learn a nigger
to argue.'' He does not understand how he has been beaten,
since, as Henry Nash Smith has clearly demonstrated, he is
incapable of handling abstract ideas. But the careful reader will

notice that while Huck is not capable of handling abstract ideas,
Jim is. Chapter XIV is clearly minstrel show humor, and the
Jim of this chapter is equally clearly Jim as Mr. Bones. But
within the framework of minstrel show dialogue Twain has
created a cluster of meaning both significant and appropriate.

How much do we know about Jim at the end of Chapter XIV?
We know that his character is partially a type-character, the
comic stage Negro, but that it extends far beyond the limits of
that type. We know that his superstitions are shared by some
whites. We know that he is human enough to suffer physical
pain. We know that he has a considerable amount of common
sense, and that within the rather severe limits of his knowledge
he is capable of handling abstract ideas. We know also that
the ideas he expresses—that there is a kind of wealth in owning
oneself, and that all men share a basic humanity—are most
appropriate to his own situation.

Huck, of course, has learned much less than the reader. At the
level of conscious thought, which is his weakest point, Huck
has learned only that it is bad luck to handle a snake-skin, that
Jim has ''an uncommon level head for a nigger,'' and that in
spite of his common sense ''you can't learn a nigger to argue.''
But in Chapters XV and XVI Huck is placed in situations where
he, as well as the reader, is forced to learn something new
about Jim.

Chapter XV is devoted to the justly famous episode in which
Huck is separated from Jim in a fog. He gets back to the raft
while Jim is asleep, and convinces him that the whole experience was a dream, which Jim proceeds to ''interpret.'' Then

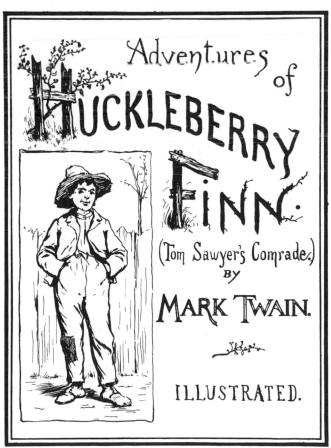

Original cover design for Adventures of Huckleberry Finn.

Huck points to the rubbish on the raft, evidence that the experience was real. He asks Jim what *it* means, and gets ready to laugh. But the laughter does not come. Instead, Jim tells him that "dat truck dah is *trash*; en trash is what people is dat puts dirt on de head er dey fren's en makes 'em ashamed." Not the least of Twain's achievements is his ability to give such dignity and force to Negro dialect (not that Negro dialect in itself is weak or undignified; but literary use of it has generally been both). The Jim of this episode, although he still speaks in the dialect of the stage Negro, is not the stage Negro, but man in the abstract, with all the dignity that belongs to that high concept, and he teaches Huck that it is painful, not funny, to play childish tricks on human dignity. Huck says,

> It was fifteen minutes before I could work myself up to go and humble myself to a nigger—but I done it, and I warn't ever sorry for it afterwards, neither. I didn't do him no more mean tricks, and I wouldn't done that one if I'd a knowed it would make him feel that way.

"If I'd a knowed." It is easy to penetrate Huck's feelings, but it is almost impossible to penetrate his mind. The idea that he hadn't really known Jim has penetrated, however, and it comes briefly to the surface of Huck's mind in Chapter XVI, when he wrestles for the first time with his "deformed conscience." Huck thinks,

> Here was this nigger which I had as good as helped to run away, coming right out flat-footed and saying he would steal his children—*children that belonged to a man I didn't even know;* a man that hadn't ever done me no harm. [my italics]

The ambiguity is evidence that Huck's mind has been touched at last. And when Jim calls him "de bes' fren' Jim's ever had" and "de on'y white genlman dat ever kep' his promise to ole Jim," Huck's reaction is "I just felt sick." Huck is not one to overstate his emotions; "sick" is as strong a term as he ever uses for them. He uses it here, and when he watches the Grangerford boys being butchered, and when the King and the Duke are ridden on a rail, and when he sees the farmers sitting with their guns in the Phelps' parlor. Jim's appeal to his friendship and his honor, coming immediately after he has betrayed Jim with a stupid trick and is about to betray him again, hits Huck very hard indeed. It makes it impossible for Huck to continue to be totally ignorant of who Jim is, and it makes it possible for him to win this first battle with his conscience.

There are four more passages which seem to me essential to an understanding of Twain's development of Jim's character. First, we have Jim laughing when Huck is washed overboard by a wave (Chapter XX). Huck was in no danger, so there is nothing vicious in Jim's laughter. All Huck can do is grumble that Jim "was the easiest nigger to laugh that ever was." The episode is one more illustration of Twain's fondness for playing brilliant variations on themes from folk humor. In this case he has simply and skilfully reversed the roles, making the white man rather than the Negro the butt of the humor.

Second, and more complex, is Jim's grief over his unintentional mistreatment of his four-year-old daughter (Chapter XXIV). He had told her to close the door, and when she didn't move, he struck her. Then he discovered that scarlet fever had left her deaf, and he tells Huck his reaction to this discovery:

> "Oh, Huck, I bust out a-cryin' en grab her up in my arms, en say, 'Oh, de po' little thing! de Lord God Amighty fogive po' ole Jim, kaze he never gwyne to fogive hisself as long's he live!' Oh, she was plumb deef en dumb, Huck, plumb deef en dumb—en I'd been a-treat'n her so!"

To understand what Twain is doing in this passage, we must remember that the popular culture of Twain's time was far more apt to sentimentalize family relationships than the popular culture of our own time. The sick or dying child; the old drunkard who deserves kindness because he is "somebody's grandpa"; mother; the young girl with her child in her arms thrown out in the snow by the stern arm of father—these figures are, by and large, no longer with us. . . . [Since] that time the popular song has largely abandoned family sentimentality and devoted itself almost exclusively to the emotional spasms of the pubescent. It is easy for us to see how Twain is using popular culture when Huck describes Emmeline Grangerford's drawings and poetry, partly because the intention is so plainly satirical, and partly because Emmeline's emotions differ only in detail rather than in kind from those of the girls in present-day popular songs. But we must make a somewhat greater effort here.

Huck's reaction to Jim's feelings for his family is worth noticing. "I do believe he cared just as much for his people as white folks does for their'n," says Huck. "It don't seem natural, but I reckon it's so." "It don't seem natural." As on so many other occasions, Huck is more right than he knows, since, at the level we have been discussing, Jim's feelings are anything but "natural"; they are as conventional as they could possibly be. And yet they are convincing, primarily, I think, because they are given to us in Jim's language rather than in the "soul-butter" style which is used in "grieving" over two other children: William Dowling Botts, deceased, and Charles William Allbright, deceased (the latter is the baby in the barrel in the excised raftsman passage). Twain has produced here a variation on one of the tritest popular themes of his time, and has made it effective and genuine by giving it to Jim. He has achieved the unique distinction of producing the most magnificently written piece of *schmalz* in all American literature, and with it he has added one more dimension to Jim's character.

Third is a facet of Jim's character which is presented to us at many points, but is most completely described during Huck's second struggle with his conscience. This is the Jim who is kind and gentle, who stands Huck's watch on top of his own and always calls Huck "honey." This is Jim as Negro Mammy, and like several of the other faces of Jim it is a skilful variation on a type-character from folk and popular culture.

Fourth, and finally, we have the Jim who is capable of noble action, who sacrifices his freedom in order to save Tom's life. Like the Jim whom Huck tries to make a fool of on the raft, this Jim is man in the abstract, and in both cases he manages to assume this high role while remaining "nigger" Jim, the runaway slave. (pp. 47-55)

Jim is, in part, the comic stage Negro who can be made the butt of Tom's childish humor. But he is also a second Negro type, Mr. Bones, whose cleverness enables him to turn the joke back on the Interlocutor. He is also a third Negro type, the kindly old colored Mammy, the protector of the white child. He is a fourth type, the sentimental family man who weeps for the suffering of his own child. And he is a fifth type, man in the abstract—natural man, if you wish—with the reasoning power, the dignity, and the nobility that belong to that high abstraction. "Begin with an individual," said F. Scott Fitzgerald, "and before you know it you find that you have created a type; begin with a type, and you find that you have created—nothing." But what happens when you begin with *five* types?

Given Mark Twain's genius for piling theme-with-variations on top of theme-with-variations you arrive at a character who is relatively consistent, who manages to retain his identity through all of his varying roles. You arrive at a character who is human, unlike the type-characters of low comedy, since he can feel both mental and physical pain. You arrive at a character who is capable of a curious and highly original kind of development as he passes from the lower role to the next higher. But you do not, by any stretch of the imagination, arrive at a fully-rounded character.

It should be recognized that it is by no means easy to create a fully-rounded character for the fictional Negro. He is easily handled if you confine him to the limits of the low comedy type. And he is also easily handled if, like Harriet Beecher Stowe, you make him "the lowly," a person who is not a character in his own right but an object of the white man's character—more specifically, an object of the white man's Christian charity, a person whose chief non-minstrel characteristic is his desire for that freedom the author wishes to grant him. But if you try to make him more, he still tends to lapse into a type. Faulkner generally uses the name "Sambo" in speaking of the Negro in *Intruder in the Dust*, and even Dilsey, in *The Sound and the Fury*, is made generic by the characterization "they endured." The Negro's own attempt to discover his identity has been the central problem for the Negro author; it dominates the fiction of Richard Wright, and it is the central theme of Ralph Ellison's *Invisible Man*. But all of this is somewhat beside the point, because I do not believe that Jim's function in the novel requires that he be a fully-rounded character.

Before considering the question of Jim's function in the novel it is necessary to ask another question that has been asked many times before: why didn't Twain let Jim escape to the free states? He could have had him paddle across the river to the Illinois shore. He could have had him go up the Ohio river at Cairo. He could have sent him north when Huck found a canoe below the Grangerford plantation, just before the Duke and Dauphin came aboard. Since it was, after all, Mark Twain who made the book up, he could have sent Jim north at any point and in any manner he chose. And it would have been easy to start Jim north, since Jim's purpose is much more specific than Huck's. Huck is escaping from civilization, but the direction of that escape is, through most of the novel, a matter of supreme indifference to him. Jim is escaping from slavery in order to avoid being sold south, away from his family, and he intends to deliver his family from slavery as well. The fact of the matter is that it cost Twain a good deal of trouble, particularly at Cairo, to prevent Jim's more specific intention from dominating the novel. One can sense his relief once he gets Jim past Cairo and settled at the river's pace. And I don't think there can be any question here of Twain's not knowing what he was doing.

Huckleberry Finn is not primarily an anti-slavery novel, but certainly it is that in part, and it is my contention that letting Jim go north would spoil the anti-slavery theme and much more as well. Remember that Twain has given us, very early in the novel, a picture of the northern free Negro. In Pap's drunken tirade against the government we learn that the free Negro in Ohio is a college professor who talks all kinds of languages and knows everything, and the reader is being asked, of course, to contrast this to the situation of the Negro—and the white man—in a slave society. Now, with all due respect to Jim's virtues, including his mental ones, it must be recognized that Jim would tarnish this bright image the moment he set foot on Ohio soil. Jim is simply not college professor material.

Furthermore, how is Jim to accomplish his purpose? He intends to work and buy his family out of slavery, but he is an unskilled laborer, and he would have to save every penny for the rest of his life before he would have enough to buy one child. This could, I suppose, be made the theme of a very moving piece of fiction, but surely it is better suited to almost any other talent than Mark Twain's. Or suppose that Jim had taken the other alternative that has occurred to him, of getting an abolitionist to "steal" his family. Such a course would take us unavoidably into the realm of abolitionist ideas, and we have already seen that our narrator, Huck, is incapable of handling ideas. Twain could not report them to us without doing great violence to Huck's established character.

More important, this is a novel in which two innocents encounter every kind of viciousness and hypocrisy whenever they come in contact with society. If Twain had sent them north he would have had to face the issue of northern viciousness and hypocrisy, and surely this would have confused the anti-slavery theme. Whereas, by keeping them on the river he can admit through Colonel Sherburn that northerners have their own vices without in any way obscuring the reader's impressions of what was wrong with slave society.

Finally, and most important, this is not primarily an anti-slavery novel, nor even a novel in which two innocents encounter a corrupt society, although it is partly that. But first of all it is a novel about a boy escaping from civilization—from a civilization in which slavery is only the most conspicuous cruelty. Remember, however, that the escape is not complete. Twain referred to the book as a conflict between "a sound heart & a deformed conscience," and Huck's conscience still belongs to society. What is Jim's function in this novel? I think it is, quite simply, to be the white man's burden. I do not intend that phrase ironically. I mean that Jim's function is quite literally to be Huck's moral burden. Jim may, and does, disappear from Huck's view temporarily, but he always returns. And finally, by his constant presence, and his constant decency, and his constant humanity he forces Huck to do something more than drift with the river. He forces Huck to come to grips with that part of himself that belongs to society, forces him "to decide, forever, betwixt two things," forces him to decide to go to hell rather than betray his fellow human being. (pp. 55-8)

Chadwick Hansen, "The Character of Jim and the Ending of 'Huckleberry Finn'," in The Massachusetts Review, *Vol. V, No. 1, Autumn, 1963, pp. 45-66.*

LEO B. LEVY (essay date 1964)

[In the following excerpt, Levy discusses Huck's conscience and the relationship between his personal moral code and the principles of his society.]

Nearly all discussion of *Adventures of Huckleberry Finn* consists of an extension and elaboration of Mark Twain's description of it as "a book of mine where a sound heart & a deformed conscience come into collision & conscience suffers a defeat." Huck Finn, according to Coleman O. Parsons, "is the protesting battleground on which conscience, custom, and law (the Moral Sense in different aspects) clash with primal sympathy, the impulsive will to freedom. . . ." This view is amplified in Henry Nash Smith's introduction to the Riverside edition of the novel, in which Huck Finn is presented as a version of "natural man" coming into conflict with all the powers of conventional society and transcending them (at least in part) by virtue of a spontaneous and untutored goodness. Synonymous with society is conscience as Twain conceives it, the "unerring monitor" that at once educates the individual and enslaves him. In Professor Smith's words, "Huck's spontaneously good heart has dictated his actions, but his conscience has remained depraved, for it represents the community."

There is no doubt about the correctness of this formulation as an expression of Mark Twain's thought or as a necessary guide to a sound interpretation of the novel. Even so, criticism of the novel has suffered from too much insistence upon its schematic and doctrinal elements. Bernard DeVoto has argued that Twain's relationship to the ideas he entertained was not so simple as is sometimes imagined, and Parson's image of Twain as Prometheus "chained to a rock no less by the irreconcilability of his simple ideals and his complex wants than by manmade codes" suggests that the connection between the man of ideas and the creative artist was oblique and tentative. Certainly there is much in *Adventures of Huckleberry Finn* that the avowed ideological intention of the book will not support; its substructure of imagery and symbol supplies a complicating set of emotional attitudes that at times overshadows the rather simple conceptual framework.

It has been observed by others that the equation between "Civilization" and "the Shore" as contrasted with "Freedom" and "the River" is by no means unequivocal. Equally important as a symptom of moral uncertainty or ambiguity in the novel is the role played by Pap. When Huck rejects the "two Providences" of Miss Watson and the Widow Douglas, he places himself at the disposal of his father, who by an act of violence—kidnapping—becomes the effective means of his escape. His reaction to his father is decidedly less sharp than his antagonism toward the two women who offer him an alternative between fear of "the bad place" and a policy of unselfish aid to others. Without the intervention of Pap, Huck apparently would have made the adjustment to school and village: "The widow said I was coming along slow but sure and doing very satisfactory. She said she warn't ashamed of me." At this early point, despite Huck's premonitions of disaster in the offing, the civilizing process is nearly complete; Twain may intend that we feel a twinge of regret as Pap tears up the picture that Huck has earned "for learning my lessons good." But Huck is happy to leave the Widow and enjoys his captivity: "It was kind of lazy and jolly, laying off comfortable all day, smoking and fishing, and no books to study."

Though the idyll of freedom-in-captivity is soon marred by Pap's intolerable brutality and Huck's resentment of his three-day imprisonment in the cabin, Huck makes no moral judgment of this father who lies drunk with the hogs in the tanyard, screams horribly in delirium tremens, and beats him unmercifully. Huck has learned, he later says, to let such people have their own way—a strangely guarded pronouncement compared,

for example, to the openness of his judgments of the King and the Duke. Perhaps it is fear, but more probably a profound acquiescence that leads to the impersonality of Huck's description, "A body would a thought he was Adam, he was just all mud." This reverses the image of natural, Adamic man in the philosophy upon which Twain draws: Pap is man in his natural depravity—but he *is* natural; the term is not reserved for the honorific connotations it has when applied to Huck. The dirt, brutality, and degeneracy of the father become not only the means of Huck's departure from civilization; they remain abiding characteristics of the experiences that follow his plunge into the "freedom" that is antithetical to the social restraints he has cast off.

Were it not for the image that fixes Pap as symbolic of natural depravity, it would be possible to see him as a pariah hopelessly debased by the community itself—but that is the view of the sentimental reformers upon whom Twain heaps his scorn. His relationship to his son is deeply rooted in his natural condition; man, as seen in the two halves, father and son, is irremediably evil or irremediably good. With Jim, the three form a trio of outcasts; but Jim, as a slave, is a social outcast in a sense that Pap and Huck are not; the supreme test of Huck's humanity that Jim's situation provides accordingly has a primarily social meaning. Nothing in the novel seems more inevitable than the gradual envelopment of Huck and Jim in fellowship and trust—a bond at once so strong and yet so delicate that many critics have found it embarrassing, and have thus taken refuge in the grossly simplifying labeling of it as founded on "sublimated homosexuality" or the need for a "father surrogate." It accounts for more to say that Huck's need for freedom is as real as Jim's, and that their relationship is the recognition and fulfillment of mutual needs so strong that they can transcend racial barriers. The all-important question is whether Huck's decision to help Jim escape is the ultimately rebellious and isolating experience it is ordinarily understood to be, or a socializing decision through which he begins to discover a deeper bond with society than any he has known.

That these bonds are never quite dissevered is indicated in the passage (in chapter viii) in which Huck outwits the search party by eating the bread which has been sent forth upon the waters to find his corpse. Like all tricksters, Huck is dependent upon those he deceives. But he does not know this; in sublime unconsciousness he devours the loaf of Baker's bread—a highly artificial product—("what the quality eat—none of your lowdown corn-pone"), finding nourishment and strength preliminary to the great trials that lie ahead, having with equal symbolic point shaken out "the little dab of quicksilver" which has weighted the bread—the poison of society. It is significant too that Huck carefully saves a portion of the bread for future consumption. Those critics who understand Huck's deception of the search party as inaugurating a symbolic death and consequent rebirth are often led into an over-insistence upon the themes of alienation and separation. James M. Cox, for example, presents an unduly simplified reading with his view that "the argument of the entire novel" centers in "Huck's initiation into respectable society" [see excerpt dated 1954]. This perspective exaggerates the way in which the initiation theme operates by sentimentalizing the differences between Huck (and Jim) and the other characters, or "society." The claim that "Huck is 'dead' throughout the entire journey down the river" enlarges an element of plot (Huck's deception) into a dominant symbolic motif; but why may not other details, circumstantial to the same deception, be drawn upon as symbolic cues as well, and to other ends? The eating of the bread as symbolic of dependence and affiliation opens another area of meaning, one which also recognizes that the belief of the Widow and the others that Huck is dead is the ironical condition necessary to the maturing and emergence of Huck's true self, a process which can fairly be called a kind of rebirth.

Huck's joy at his release from the restrictions of society is, at first, immense, but the passages which usually are understood to express this liberating experience—the idyll of drifting on the raft with Jim and the eloquent hymns to nature in chapters ix and xix—have been pressed too hard in the service of the contrast between "civilization" and "freedom." Leo Marx, for instance, writes that "Huck, when he can divest himself of the taint of social conditioning (as in the incantatory account of sunrise on the river), is entirely free of anxiety and guilt" [see excerpt dated 1953]. But similar passages, though less extended, occur earlier than the raft episode (in chapter ii, for example, Huck describes the river by the village, "a whole mile broad, and awful still and grand.") He cannot be said to be "free of anxiety and guilt" until late in the novel when he irrevocably joins himself to the cause of Jim's freedom. An idyll, after all, is an escape, not necessarily from society, but certainly from reality—any reality. The magnificent sections to which Marx refers owe their greatness to the fact that they are vernacular modifications of the ancient pastoral tradition expressing man's oneness and unity with nature. As such they suspend, rather than resolve, the moral tensions of the book; they are symbolic of the quite limited freedom that occupies the interval between Huck's escape and the various ordeals that define the trials that ensue.

Such a view does not detract from the genuineness of Huck's responses to the river and to his natural environment; in fact, it is partly through these responses that we are able to visualize him in his continuing involvement in a remarkably hazardous world, a relationship at once practical, moral, and aesthetic. The most striking of the pastoral episodes, with all their evocative and static power, are followed by events that are grim and sordid. The memorable description of a summer storm ("It would get so dark that it looked all blue-black outside, and lovely; and the rain would thrash along by so thick that the trees off a little ways looked dim and spider-webby") has for its sequence the horror of the drifting frame-house with its dead man—Huck's father—and its woeful litter. The hymn to the sunrise terminates in the terrifying appearance of the King and the Duke. These contrasts are woven into a pattern of designed interrelatedness that diminishes rather than sustains the alleged "polar opposition between the River and the Shore, between freedom and bondage."

The problem of freedom and bondage is psychological rather than geographical, centering upon the impulses within Huck that from the beginning stubbornly resist all attempts to shape him into conformity. Freedom for Huck is first of all a need to elude those stern guardians of authority, Miss Watson and the Widow Douglas, to evade the proscriptions that define the developing super-ego. Freedom is largely the absence of constraint, and therefore empty of positive meaning apart from the opportunities it gives to grow autonomously. Huck, after heroic struggles with the internalized form of society, his conscience, flowers as the perfectly natural being whose decency and humanity guide him through the circles of hell that make up the evils and terrors of organized society. This apparently is what Twain means, but it is not much help in constructing a picture of Huck—if it is possible to do so—formed and conditioned by his society, rather than magically exempted from its influence.

One evidence of that conditioning is that Huck often seems compulsively rebellious, a fact connected with his often-noted failures of self-esteem, exaggerated loneliness, and acute depression. Feelings of worthlessness and guilt invite from Huck a willingness to take the punishment meted out for his delinquencies, as if he alone knew how well he deserved to be punished. One wonders about the measure of irony intended, for example, in Huck's comment on the consequences of playing hookey: " . . . the hiding I got next day done me good and cheered me up." Much of the discouragement that colors his outlook is expressed in his something more than humorous addiction to superstitious signs, particularly those omens of ill-luck that confirm his bleakness, his tendency to worry and to retreat into self-reproach. Some part of him feels that he ought to be able to live up to the counsel on the efficacy of prayer and the desirability of helping others. His choice of the Widow's Providence is accompanied by the acknowledgment that "I couldn't make out how he was agoing to be any better off than what he was before, seeing I was so ignorant and so kind of low-down and ornery."

Huck's spells of downheartedness all but disappear once he is free of the paralyzing grip of the Widow. They persist, however, in that ever-active conscience over which he achieves victory—or so it is usually understood—with his decision to destroy the note he has written betraying Jim to his owner, Miss Watson. The stirrings that lead Huck to his courageous avowal, "All right, then, I'll *go* to hell," correspond to a casting off, in Twain's terms, of everything that he has accepted of the laws, prescriptions, and codes that govern society. The triumph of decency is the shedding of conventional morality; immorality, paradoxically, is the source of virtue. Much of the ironical force of the novel focuses upon this discrepancy; but it is precisely at this point that a difficulty presents itself.

Many of Twain's short stories illustrate his conception of conscience as a destructive force. In **"Was It Heaven? Or Hell?,"** a doctor persuades two ladies to ignore the promptings of conscience and thereby comfort their dying niece; in **"The Facts Concerning the Recent Carnival of Crime in Connecticut,"** persecuting conscience is uproariously throttled; and in **"The Man That Corrupted Hadleyburg,"** the men of conscience are in reality the slaves of their own avariciousness. In *Huckleberry Finn*, however, the notion that Huck behaves morally because he has set aside the dictates of conscience is more difficult to accept. R. P. Adams, noting that Huck's conscience has been formed by the mores of Southern society, praises his momentous decision by declaring that "If it is fine to follow as Thoreau does the dictates of conscience over law, it is finer and much more difficult to follow those of the right over conscience and law combined" [see excerpt dated 1956]. This is essentially the argument of most critics on this point; but it raises the question of whether or not a distinction between "dictates of the right" as opposed to "dictates of conscience" is valid. It is sometimes said that Huck acts out of simple affection for Jim; but affection does not determine a moral attitude. It is more reasonable to say that Huck defies "conscience" on the basis of an unformulated but very real sense of responsibility—to the notion that it is wrong, for example, to contribute to the enslavement of another human being. And this is a matter of conscience too, to which we may assume Huck's experiences with Jim have contributed in a fundamental way.

Twain and his critics alike are guilty of verbal quibbling when they propose that Huck's loyalty to Jim is not the work of conscience. What Huck violates is not conscience, but those demands of society that oppose it. Huck is in effect forced to alienate himself from the community in order to satisfy the needs of conscience; his depression and nagging sense of worthlessness express that alienation. But society and morality are not always at odds. On two occasions, Twain reverses his point of view and invites an approving judgment of conscience, once when it prompts Huck to intervene in behalf of Mary Jane and her family in the fraud perpetrated by the King and the Duke ("My mind's made up: I'll hive that money for them or bust"), and again in a more complex way when Huck sees the King and the Duke "astraddle of a rail," tarred and feathered. Huck's bewilderment at his feelings—he knows he isn't responsible for the fate of the two impostors but nevertheless feels guilty—gives him an opportunity to exclaim on the deviousness of conscience and to conclude that "It takes up more room than all the rest of a person's insides, and yet ain't no good, nohow." But, clearly, the point of Twain's irony here is to let us admire Huck's humaneness and revulsion at the cruelty of men to one another, both of which his conscience expresses. Evidently, then, conscience is something more than the voice of the depraved community.

The process psychologists call introjection—the internalization of social law—is never complete. Huck's rebelliousness obviously exceeds what we might want to call the norm, but his conscience is in the service of his needs for association as well as his needs for separation. There is no way to determine how much the operation of conscience in particular cases is due to internal or external forces. J. C. Flugel, an exponent of the psychoanalytic school, defines conscience (and its dual sources) as "something within the self that demands obedience to its claims and at the same time something the nature of which is determined by social and moral influences from outside." Twain and the psychoanalysts agree that conscience is an often unreliable guide, but for different reasons; the psychoanalysts because they regard it as archaic and irrational, and Twain, in accordance with his assumptions concerning man in a natural state, because he usually regards it as the expression of social restrictions that are inherently evil.

Twain is particularly concerned with the enormous and crippling guilt that conscience can engender. His perception of the ways in which conscience becomes the tool of organized hypocrisy led him to the hope, expressed through Huck Finn, that moral decision independent of the workings of conscience is possible. In carrying out this idea, Twain relies upon vaguely Rousseauistic conceptions of freedom and moral spontaneity which, however inadequate in themselves, serve him as a viable dramatic medium. *Adventures of Huckleberry Finn* is not a literary masterpiece because it testifies to conceptions of natural man; these ideas are the successful means to the end of projecting and dramatizing a moral struggle that culminates in a totally convincing picture of a hero who grasps a truth that allows him to have the experiences of brotherhood and love. How Huck achieves that condition is as much a mystery as the question of his "true self." There are no psychological explanations of the qualities that make Huck Finn a universal hero. The pessimism which leads Twain to believe that the brotherhood exemplified in Huck and Jim can survive only outside organized society may indeed be justified. But it is meaningless to suppose as Twain does that the strength and independence that lead his protagonist to his momentous choices do not have their sources in society itself. Conscience indeed makes cowards of us all—except that, rarely, it also creates heroes of the stature of Huckleberry Finn. (pp. 383-91)

Leo B. Levy, "Society and Conscience in 'Huckleberry Finn'," in Nineteenth-Century Fiction, *Vol. 18, No. 4, March, 1964, pp. 383-91.*

WILLIAM R. MANIERRE (essay date 1964-65)

[*In the following excerpt, Manierre challenges the dominant critical view of Huck's moral development.*]

Any critical evaluation of *Adventures of Huckleberry Finn* that assumes either that Jim is the protagonist or that his quest for freedom is the core of the novel is, simply, in error. Huck Finn, the titular hero, is the major character; his quest for freedom, not Jim's, is the thematic center. Jim's quest adumbrates Huck's but exists on a different level. Jim's escape from physical slavery is achieved by a kind of Miss Watson *ex machina;* but Huck's escape from mental and emotional slavery is categorically denied. In spite of its forced happy tone, the ending is not happy; it is profoundly pessimistic. As Albert E. Stone remarks, Huck "has achieved the ultimate ironic escape—out of his own social and moral identity into the protective coloration of 'sivilization's' fair-haired boy."

Huck's acceptance, in the final chapters, of Tom's romantic and sentimental methods does not restore precisely the mood or the situation of the beginning. There is a difference, and that difference is all-important. In the opening chapter we learn that Huck, fed up with "sivilization," has already "lit out," not "for the Territory" but to his "old rags" and "sugar-hogshead" and has been mighty "free and satisfied." "But Tom Sawyer, he hunted me up and said he was going to start a band of robbers, and I might join if I would go back to the widow and be respectable. So I went back." But at this stage, Huck is still capable of renouncing—of resigning from—Tom's gang and of recognizing Tom's "lies" for what they are. At the end of the book he is not. He has undergone his initiation, has been reborn, but less into manhood than into society. When he "goes back" in the concluding chapters, he goes back to stay.

Very much a part of his character, along with his pragmatic turn of mind, is Huck's basic adaptibility. For all his yen for freedom and the life of slothful ease and dirt, he is a natural born joiner. He "joins" Tom's gang; he "joins" Jim; later, he "joins" the Grangerfords; later still he "joins" Mary Jane Wilks and her cause; finally, he "joins" society, presumably for good. In fact, even at the start he was well on his way to joining society. Though he "hated" school at first, it is not long before he finds that he can "stand it." Though he continued to like "the old ways best," he soon finds himself liking "the new ones, too, a little bit." He even stops "cussing." But of course he is adaptable to Pap's ways too; he "joins" Pap; and only breaks with him because of external circumstances: Pap's drunkenness and brutality. But he had also left "sivilization" because of circumstances beyond his control. Not Huck's action but Pap's had separated him from the dull regularity of washing, eating on plates, and combing up. Similarly, his separations from the Grangerfords and, later, from Mary Jane, were not the results of free choice on Huck's part but of external forces beyond his control. Indeed, the most painful burden of the book is that escape from society can be but partial and temporary at best because of the nature both of society and of the average man. Unlike Natty Bumpo, Huckleberry Finn does not like to be alone.

Huck's "moral growth" has, I believe, been vastly over-estimated. When he first realizes that Jim has "run off," Huck announces, apparently without serious inner qualms, "I ain't agoing to tell, and I ain't agoing back there anyways." Later, of course, his conscience gives him trouble, but, ironically enough, only after he has come to think of Jim as a human being. ". . . what's the use you learning to do right, when it's troublesome to do right and ain't no trouble to do wrong, and the wages is just the same? I was stuck. I couldn't answer that. So I reckoned I wouldn't bother no more about it, but after this always do whichever came handiest at the time." . . . And it came "handiest" to him to forget all about Jim while having exciting times with Buck Grangerford.

Certainly Huck attains a kind of moral grandeur when, after fighting his conscience, he tears up the letter to Miss Watson. "It was a close place. . . . I was a trembling, because I'd got to decide, forever, betwixt two things, and I knowed it. I studied a minute, sort of holding my breath, and then says to myself: 'all right, then, I'll *go* to Hell'." . . . What makes this episode significant is that, this time, the decision has not been easy. For the moment, Huck is really involved. But in view of his easy acceptance of Tom's methods throughout the last ten chapters, we are forced to ask ourselves how seriously this "moral climax" is to be taken. We remember that elsewhere in the book Huck has dedicated his life to "evil," has, in fact, earlier expressed a clear preference for Hell to Heaven. "Then she told me all about the bad place, and I said I wished I was there. . . . Well, I couldn't see no advantage in going where she was going, so I made up my mind I wouldn't try for it." . . . I believe that such flippancy seriously qualifies the significance of his later decision to tear up the letter and go to Hell for Jim's sake. Furthermore, since Huck has been actively helping Jim to escape ever since the eighth chapter, his moral struggle at this point seems somehow out of place. What seems to have increased in him—(else why the intensity of the struggle?)—is precisely his respect for the dictates of conscience which represent not his recognition of Jim as man but as slave. Heart, of course, wins out, but the very fight put up by conscience suggests that Huck is, at this point, almost ready to return to "sivilization" for good. The return, symbolized by Huck's "rebirth" as Tom Sawyer, is an ironic assumption of the concluding chapters.

Henry Nash Smith's reminder . . . that "it is Tom . . . [not Huck] . . . who conceives the plan to 'go for howling adventures amongst the Injuns, over in the Territory, for a couple of weeks or two,'" has been all too often ignored. So too with his further caution that "when Huck says he means to set out ahead of the others, there is nothing in the text to indicate that his intention is more serious than Tom's." In fact, the erroneous thesis that Huck's final remark about "the Territory" demonstrates some kind of achieved freedom has attained almost the stature of an American myth. R.W.B. Lewis states that "in those novels [of Cooper] where the setting is the untracked American forest, the world always lies all before the hero, and normally, like Huck Finn, he is able to light out again for the 'territories'." And "Surely," remarks Allen Guttman, "Thoreau would have treasured . . . [this] . . . book . . . [in which] . . . freedom from possessions is achieved. . . . The story ends—as everyone remembers—with Huck's final rejection of civilization. He lights out 'for the Territory' before Aunt Polly [sic] can shut him within the four walls of a meretricious culture. Huck Finn, who had not a great deal to leave behind, took to the open road and sought a more primitive world." Unfortunately, however, the facts are otherwise. The text provides considerable evidence that Huck's concluding assertion is little more than delusion and that the values which

finally dominate his mind and the book as well are precisely those of Tom Sawyer, those of a hypocritical, misguided, immoral, slave-holding and materialistic social order; just those, in short, that Thoreau most despised.

Tom's original plan in the event of a successful "evasion" was "for us to run [Jim] down the river, on the raft, and have adventures plum to the mouth . . . and then, [and only then, to] tell him about his being free." . . . Tom's intention to "pay [Jim] for his lost time" sufficiently reveals the materialistic basis of Tom's reasoning. When he pays Jim for being such a patient prisoner, Jim's and Huck's complete satisfaction with the terms suggests the degree of their acceptance of Tom's version of a quid pro quo—the degree, that is, of their mental and emotional slavery to all that Tom represents. One remembers Tom's leaving "five cents on the table to pay . . . [for] . . . three candles" and his later insistence that Huck "give the niggers a dime" for a watermelon already appropriated. But the value of a "free nigger's" freedom, though greater than that of candles or watermelons, can still be estimated in financial terms and Tom is so generous as to "give Jim forty dollars" for his late, patient captivity.

Particularity here reminds the reader of other contexts in which the number forty has appeared. "Who nailed him?" asks Huck after learning of Jim's capture. . . . "It was an old fellow . . . [who] . . . sold out his chance on him for forty dollars." Huck's response, which immediately precedes the gripping conflict between heart and conscience that culminates in his decision to "*go* to Hell," is eloquent. "Here it was all come to nothing, everything all busted up and ruined, because they could have the heart to serve Jim such a trick as that, and make him a slave again . . . for forty dirty dollars." . . . Identity of figure forces attention to the similarity between Tom's "approved" action in the last chapter and the King's earlier, "disapproved" betrayal. But the "approval" exists only within the ironic moral dialectic—the total reversal of values—that is the key to the book's essential meaning.

After Tom is wounded, Jim insists on risking his newly acquired "freedom." "Well, den, dis is de way it look to me, Huck. Ef it wuz *him* dat 'us bein' sot free, en one er de boys wuz to git shot, would he say, 'Go on en save me, nemmine 'bout a doctor f'r to save dis one?' Is dat like Mars Tom Sawyer? Would he say dat? You *bet* he wouldn't! *Well,* den, is *Jim* gwyne to say it? No, sah—I doan' budge a step out'n dis place, 'dout a *doctor;* not if it's forty year!'" . . . . The figure forty suggests comparison of Jim's action and motivation with those of Tom and of the King; while Huck's immediate response—"I knowed he was white inside"—forces, indeed, a moral general application.

In the context of this book, in the context of pleasure derived from lynchings and feuds and cruelty to animals, the highest compliment Huck can bestow is actually, though unconsciously, insulting. As a commentary on Jim's mind, moreover, Huck's compliment implies his own and Jim's total enslavement by the values of their slave-holding environment. . . . Of his plan to keep this "free nigger" unaware of his "freedom" for as long as he can, Tom "said it was the best fun he ever had in his life . . . ; and said if he only could see his way to it we would keep it up all the rest of our lives and leave Jim to our children to get out; *for he believed Jim would come to like it better and better the more he got used to it*" (my italics). Jim offers no objections; he "couldn't see no sense in the most of it, but he allowed we was white folks and knowed better than him." . . . (pp. 341-45)

The doctor's subsequent betrayal of Jim is relevant here both as thematic parallel and as mark of Huck's ultimate capitulation to moral blindness. The doctor's touching account of Jim's sacrifice of freedom for the sake of his "friend" effectively also poses the conflicting values with which the book has been concerned. "I got to have *help*, somehow; and the minute I says it, out crawls this nigger . . . and says he'll help, and he done it, too, and done it very well. . . . But I dasn't [leave], because the nigger might get away, and then I'd be to blame. . . . I never see a nigger that was a better nuss or faithfuller, and yet he was resking his freedom to do it. . . . I liked the nigger for that . . . ; a nigger like that is worth a thousand dollars." . . . At the first opportunity, the doctor, with the help of two men who arrived, "as good luck would have it" while "the nigger [was] sound asleep," overpowers Jim and returns him to slavery.

Huck's response to this crushing account reflects complete domination by the forces of conscience and consequent blindness to the higher responsibilities and values of humanity, personal relationship, heart. "I was mighty thankful to that old doctor for doing Jim that *good* turn; and I was glad it was according to my judgment of him, too; because I thought he had a *good heart* in him and was a *good* man." . . . The irony and reversal of values in this passage do not require comment. Twain's statement that in this book "a deformed conscience . . . suffers defeat . . . [when it] . . . comes into collision . . . [with] a sound heart" reflects his own unawareness of what his book actually says. Like others who accept the myth of Huck's "freedom," Twain was doubtless thinking in terms of the decision to "*go* to Hell," not in those of the last twelve chapters.

Huck's new commitment to the values of the establishment is demonstrated less by his acceptance of Tom's methods of "freeing" Jim than by the moral unawareness that now makes him incapable either of recognizing evil when confronted by it or of distinguishing between degrees of responsibility.

When, in Chapter 41, the doctor heads for the island in order to tend the wounded Tom, Huck is convinced that he must rejoin his friends as soon as possible if Jim's freedom is to be preserved. When he learns that the doctor has not returned during the night, Huck sees at once that it "looks powerful bad for Tom" and that he must "dig out for the island, right off." He is immediately trapped, however, and forced by circumstances and Uncle Silas to return to the plantation. That night Aunt Sally "works" him with sentimentality and an appeal to the chivalric code of honor. "The door ain't going to be locked, Tom; and there's the window and the rod; but you'll be good, *won't* you? And you won't go? For *my* sake?" (Twain's italics). Here again is the appeal to goodness as defined by a system that embraces human slavery. Tom, we remember, refuses to "stand by and see the rules broke—because right is right, and wrong is wrong, and a body ain't got no business doing wrong when he ain't ignorant and knows" . . . Huck, on the other hand, ignorant and ornery and kind of low down and mean, has often found the "rules" exactly contradictory to the dictates of his heart and a dedication to "wickedness" the necessary consequence. But the horrible thing is that he is losing his ignorance (innocence) and coming, in Tom's and Aunt Sally's and society's terms precisely, to "know better." Only three pages after Aunt Sally's appeal to the "good" we find Huck "thankful" for the "good heart" of the "good man" who did Jim the "good turn" of delivering him back into slavery and to the gentle mercies of those who,

like Old Mrs. Hotchkiss, allows that "as for the niggers that wrote it . . . I'd take 'n' lash'm t'll—'" and of others who would have "got their satisfaction" by lynching Jim if it had not been for the possibility that they might subsequently also have to pay for him." . . . (pp. 345-46)

Aunt Sally appeals to Huck's responsibility to herself. Clearly, however, as a case of conscience this problem is easily resolved. For one thing, Aunt Sally's concern stems almost entirely from her erroneous belief that she is addressing Tom Sawyer. In any event, there can be no question but that Huck has a much higher responsibility to Jim at this moment than to Aunt Sally. This higher responsibility is compounded by that to Tom who, with a bullet in his leg, has now been missing for close to twenty-four hours. Furthermore Huck is fully aware of the need for haste. From every point of view—except that of the establishment—there is only one right place for Huck to be and that is—not "within the four walls of a meretricious culture"—but with his two friends and in the full knowledge of being outside the law. I do not believe that Thoreau would have rejoiced at Huck's decision.

Lapsing into that "other" language of the novel's verbal dialectic, Huck capitulates. "Laws I *wanted* to go, bad enough, to see about Tom [he has forgotten Jim again], and was all intending to go; but after that, I wouldn't a went, not for kingdoms.

"But she was on my mind, and Tom was on my mind. . . . I . . . see her setting there by her candle in the window with her eyes towards the road and the tears in them. . . . I could . . . only . . . swear that I wouldn't never do nothing to grieve her any more. . . . I waked up at dawn, and slid down, and she was there yet, and her candle was most out, and her old gray head was resting on her hand and she was asleep." . . . On the next page Jim is brought back in chains.

Mr. Smith describes this other language as "a burlesque of the exalted rhetoric of the official culture . . . the 'higher' language . . . or . . . 'soul-butter' mode of speech . . . [which all] . . . the characters . . . [in this novel use] . . . when . . . they try to claim for themselves a false pathos . . . , when they fall into pretense." . . . Huck's lapse into such language at this juncture demonstrates—as does his failure to act—the pitiful fact that he is now "thinking" in the "approved" fashion. He ignores his higher responsibilities both to Tom and to the forgotten Jim in order to avoid hurting the feelings of a woman who believes him to be—not Huckleberry Finn—but the conformist Tom Sawyer. His indulgence in that sort of sentimental orgy which the book constantly denounces as one mark of social corruption and which is the exact antithesis of everything that has defined Huck's naturally pragmatic turn of mind and of everything in his personality that formerly enabled him to achieve, even momentarily, a degree of moral grandeur suggests that Aunt Sally is not so far wrong as might at first appear.

As Thoreau well knew, nothing so firmly welds one's commitment to the establishment as does the possession of worldly goods. But Huck, having "not a great deal to leave behind," takes "to the open road . . . [to seek] . . . a more primitive world." And "Thoreau would have treasured . . . [this] . . . book . . . [in which] . . . freedom from possession is achieved." But, unfortunately for this thesis, the suggestion "to light out for the Territory" stems not from Huck but from Tom, who limits the journey's duration to "a couple of weeks or two." Of far greater significance, however, is Huck's initial response to the suggestion. "I says, all right, that suits me, but I ain't got no money for to buy the outfit.'' Huckleberry Finn unable to take a business man's weekend in the country because he lacks the MONEY to buy an ''outfit!'' Self-reliance has somehow departed. Poor Thoreau! Poor Huck! He has indeed come a long way towards social maturity during the course of this novel. ''I ain't got no money for to buy the outfit, and I reckon I couldn't get none from home [a most significant word in context], because it's likely Pap's been back before now, and got it all away from Judge Thatcher and drunk it up.'' Tom's answer is reassuring. Not only is Huck's capital secure but during his voyage to freedom it has been quietly accruing interest. In fact, Huck is one of the wealthiest persons in what he now inadvertently refers to as ''home.'' ''It's all there, yet—six thousand dollars and more.'' And not even Pap, who, we remember, was the only force that stopped the Widow Douglas from civilizing Huck in the first place, can take it from him now; for Pap is dead and as Jim, the faithful darky, says, ''you k'n git yo' money when you wants it.''

On this same concluding page, moreover, Jim has been appropriately served: his physical chains struck off and his psychological chains reaffirmed in suitable financial terms. ''Tom give Jim forty dollars for being prisoner for us so patient . . . and Jim was pleased most to death . . . and says:

'''*Dah,* now, Huck, what I tell you?—what I tell you up dah on Jackson islan'? I *tole* you I . . . ben rich wunst, en gwineter to be rich agin.''' Forty dollars for Jim and ''six thousand . . . and more'' for Huck—a quite proper proportion.

The incipient revolution never quite came off; the establishment was never seriously disturbed. At the book's end, Huck is not, as Mr. Trilling wouuld have us believe, ''the servant of the river-god.'' Quite the contrary. He now serves Mammon. His announced liberation is as meaningless as the huckster's Sunday mouthings of a Christian ethic. (pp. 346-48)

> *William R. Manierre, '''No Money for to Buy the Outfit': 'Huckleberry Finn' Again,''* in Modern Fiction Studies, *Vol. X, No. 4, Winter, 1964-65, pp. 341-48.*

A. E. DYSON (essay date 1965)

[*Dyson is an English literary critic who has explained that while he formerly adhered to an ideology of ''liberal humanism,'' he has for some time considered himself a ''traditionalist'' and a Christian. ''Literature is a celebration,'' Dyson has stated. ''Almost everything that makes life rich was said or written or created by people who are no longer living; almost all the color and joy came from religious men.'' In the following excerpt, Dyson discusses irony in* Huckleberry Finn.]

If Shakespeare's 'fatal Cleopatra' was the quibble, Mark Twain's was the practical joke, or so his readers at times are tempted to think. 'How could he?' we wonder, as we move towards the end of **Huckleberry Finn.** It is not only that our sense of Jim's dignity is outraged as he is sacrificed to Tom Sawyer's nigger-minstrel antics, nor is it merely reluctance to concede that Huck's exquisite sense of values, tested and proved throughout the novel, can fail once more before Tom's adolescent and unreflecting romanticism. What worries us most of all, I think, is the suspicion that a great work of art is being sold out to a schoolboy sense of fun. Tom himself might conceivably turn Jim's predicament into a farce. He hasn't lived through the experience of the raft, morally he is less sensitive than Huck. He knows, moreover, that Jim is already freed, so that his attitude is at least understandable in human terms. But

how can Huck and Jim accept the situation as they do? How, above all, can Mark Twain? We look back at that most famous and disregarded of warnings from writer to reader at the beginning ('Persons attempting to find a motive in this narrative will be prosecuted; persons attempting to find a moral in it will be banished; persons attempting to find a plot in it will be shot'), and wonder.

The ending has not, however, lacked its distinguished defenders. T. S. Eliot and Lionel Trilling have both found the return from Huck's world to Tom Sawyer's structurally appropriate. 'It is right,' says Eliot, 'that the mood of the book should bring us back to the beginning' [see *TCLC*, Vol. 6]; 'a certain formal aptness,' comments Trilling [see Additional Bibliography]. Leo Marx, in an interesting recent essay, has taken them both to task for this [see excerpt dated 1953]. What really counts in a novel, he thinks, is not structural but moral appropriateness, and in this the end of **Huckleberry Finn** is lacking. It is here that I tend for my own part to differ from him, as to some extent from all the critics I have read on the work. Lionel Trilling's general moral claim for **Huckleberry Finn** is that it tells the truth, and to my mind this claim extends to the ending not in the somewhat desultory way he suggests, but as part of the logic and texture of the whole book. The raft, paradoxically idyllic though life on it seems, has to tie up somewhere; and if one honestly favours the whole truth, the return to land at the end, with its lessening tension and its gradual descent from clear-cut decencies and responsibilities to the more muddled ones of everyday life is the only ending that will really, over a long period, ring true.

But this is to jump ahead: best to start, perhaps, from the irony, which is the clearest clue to Mark Twain's intentions that we have, providing a far firmer unity for the work than it gets from the pleasantly picaresque and rambling plot. Twain's sense of the incongruous rubs shoulders with the practical joke at many points, but it also ranges through much of the spectrum of irony, sometimes seeming most at home as it approaches the tragic. 'Everything human is pathetic,' as Twain himself once wrote. 'The secret source of humour itself is not joy but sorrow. There is no humour in heaven.' Ernest Hemingway, taking his cue perhaps from this, has gone to the extreme of seeing **Huckleberry Finn** as a novel moved by its own powerful insights in one direction, and wrested away again only by the deliberate sabotage of the author. 'If you read it,' he says, 'you must stop where the nigger Jim is stolen by the boys. This is the real end. The rest is cheating' [see *TCLC*, Vol. 6]. Yet the true state of affairs, I believe, is that Mark Twain followed the fluctuations of human fortune more subtly than this or any similar view allows. His irony approaches both the comic and the tragic, as most truly great irony does, but it finally rests in neither. Its essential insight can be more usefully linked with the 'whole fortune' of Huck and his father, as Jim tells it at dead of night, using a hair ball out of the fourth stomach of an ox.

> Yo' ole father doan' know, yit, what he's a-gwyne to do. Sometimes he spec he'll go 'way, en den agin he spec he'll stay. De bes' way is to res' easy en let de ole man take his own way. Dey's two angels hoverin' roun' 'bout him. One uv' em is white en shiny, en t'other one is black. De white one gits him to go right, a little while, den de black one sail in en bust it all up. A body can't tell, yit, which one gwyne to fetch him at de las'. But you is all right.

You gwyne to have considable trouble in yo'
life, en considable joy. Sometimes you gwyne
to git hurt, en sometimes you gwyne to git sick;
but every time you's gwyne to git well agin. . . .

Mark Twain, like Jim's hair ball, responds to life as a gamble,
with good and bad endlessly struggling together, neither actually winning, but neither cancelling the other out. The two
angels hover, and there is no telling which will come to fetch
us at the last. The fate of Huck's father is dubious, but Huck
himself? If he takes the rough along with the smooth all will
be well with him, though death in one form or another will be
waiting at the last. As a philosophy of life we are normally
inclined, I believe, to think of such ideas as naïve, and one of
Twain's triumphs is to show how much better they stand up
to actual experience than the more sophisticated beliefs of Miss
Watson and the widow. Throughout *Huckleberry Finn* good
and evil are shown co-existing in Nature as well as in man.
The squirrel Huck sees as a natural friend, the snake as a natural
enemy: why?—because the one he can live with, embracing
its faults with his tolerance, and the other he can't. There is
an acceptance of fact here which is not only part of Huck's
unsentimental common sense, but part too of the common sense
of Mark Twain himself manipulating the irony. Most human
minds gravitate towards either optimism or pessimism; there
is a constant temptation to think that either good or bad will
'win' in the end. Mark Twain, like Huck, does not share this
view—which is why his irony never settles in either a comic
or a tragic mould, and why his ending is deliberately less
conclusive than either would require.

Doubts about the ending of *Huckleberry Finn* cluster around
another misconception, not dissimilar to the one of Hemingway
I have been considering. This is the very common error of
regarding the novel as a simple contrast between *two* worlds—
the one civilised, insensitive and corrupt, the other uncivilised,
sensitive and humane. The widow, 'dismal, regular and decent'
as Huck calls her, is seen as typical of the former, Huck himself
and Jim as typical of the latter. Tom Sawyer, while having
many fine qualities, belongs basically to the widow's world;
and Twain's irony is taken to be the playing off of the genuine
against the conventional, the good, if one likes, against the
bad.

Now though this is true in that the values achieved on the raft
are used for an ironic survey of society at large, I am convinced
that to put the matter so simply is misleading. For one thing
it overlooks, as most criticism does, the importance of the
Duke, the King and Huck's father. These are all much further
away from the 'respectable' folk than Huck himself is, yet they
are the most decisively evil characters in the book. One has
only to recall them to be aware that Jim stands less hope of
mercy from this group than he does from Miss Watson and
Tom, and that a straight choice of 'outsider' against 'insider'
is not at all what is being presented. Nor is this all. The eventual
freeing of Jim comes about not through the journey on the raft,
but through a change of heart in his former owner. The method
by which it happens is muddled, the insights behind it are less
pure, to put the matter mildly, than those of the raft, yet the
fact of freedom comes from Miss Watson's dying request, and
from the camp of the respectable. In allowing this, Mark Twain
is not 'selling out' the rest of the novel, as some commentators
assume, but simply being faithful to the realism which makes
us trust him all along. Respectable morality, though muddled
and sometimes cruel, does have certain ideals behind it: the
ideals, indeed, which Huck himself embodies in a purer form,

outside society, and paradoxically in defiance of it. The world
of the widow and of Miss Watson might be blinkered, and
provided with blind eyes for all occasions; it might recoil with
horror from its own more Christian ideals when despite every
precaution it catches sight of them. But it is myopic rather than
totally blind, thoughtlessly rather than wilfully cruel. Miss
Watson's request in her will is the beginning, maybe, of a
challenge to the system of slavery from inside; a moment without which no purer moral protest, however noble, would stand
much hope of eventually winning the majority to its side. If
we think historically, we shall see that her dying decision to
free Jim, despite the fact that he has sinned both against herself
and against the economic system by escaping, may be as important a landmark on the road to emancipation as the dangerous quest for freedom on the raft itself. Actual humane
progress does come about, whether we like it or not, through
muddled insights, muddled kindliness, muddled actions as much
as from the straightforward vindication of ideals. Twain's ending draws attention to this, too, and it is part of the whole truth
he has to tell.

At the end, the values of the raft are assimilated to the pattern
of life seen steadily and as a whole. Could Mark Twain really
have shown Huck and Jim simply winning through to freedom,
without violating history and contriving an ending we should
have doubted? Could any conceivable ending, on the other
hand, have really betrayed the realities of the raft, in such a
way that we should retrospectively doubt them? The final balance is one in which we see what has been acheived on the
raft as real rather than illusory, yet exceptional rather than
normative. And this, I am sure, is what the author intended.

For consider the journey itself. During the course of it, Huck
and Jim are living in a very special world, from which almost
all the distinctive data of human living have been removed.
There is no sex on the raft, no politics, no formal worship, no
money, no status. There are no traditional sanctions, either.
Huck is unimpressed by dead people, including Moses; even
his Conscience turns out to be a Trojan Horse smuggled in by
the enemy, not a genuine moral inheritance from the past. There
is, however, in this apparent vacuum, and in the strenuous
business of survival which occupies it, a fundamental human
decency at work which is the ground for all good manifestations
of sex, politics, worship, money, status, wherever they occur.
In being driven outside society, Huck and Jim are given an
occasion to transcend it. Their tenderness and affection for one
another is the condition of all good relationships, private or
public; their sensitivity to the grandeur and mystery of nature
and to the suffering of men is the condition for all true reverence; their deep sense of responsibility, and their natural
dignity, are a condition for all uses of money and status that
can ever deserve respect. In the world of the raft, they represent
a type of pre-morality; a decency outside civilisation, which
is both a seed for all that grows good inside it, and a touchstone
for all that turns bad. To achieve the raft, Huck has to renounce
everything—his father, his money, even his official life; Jim,
to achieve it, has to be betrayed even by his owner, and to be
driven to complete isolation. In the ensuing events, totally
exiled from humanity, the two of them achieve the highest type
of relationship of which humanity is capable. The paradox
involved in this is not overlooked; it is, indeed, the impetus
of much of the irony. Yet Huck and Jim are not mistaken for,
or presented as, a norm. Their morality cannot exist permanently without social contexts, and when it returns to these it
will be unable, perhaps, to exist as purely and unambiguously
as it does on the raft. At the end, they return to the world

where their values, never articulate at the best of times, will become clouded again by the mesh of actuality. When this happens, the raft will remain as a memory, and as a leaven. And this, in fact, is what happens. We are left with the assurance that there is, in man, a power for good as well as bad and that good is worth fighting for; we are not left with the assurance that the power for good is normally or easily followed, or that it will necessarily win.

But at this point we must approach Mark Twain's irony more directly. At one end of the scale, as we know, there are the practical jokes—the simple incongruities of fooling people which are usually associated with Tom Sawyer, though Huck can be his uneasy partner at times. Tom Sawyer has often been called a 'romantic', and so he is, if one uses the word to mean, not necessarily with disrespect, the adolescent and the immature. In a fairly obvious way, he is a distinguished example of a type familiar in British boys' books of the period—healthy, good natured, full of animal spirits, a born leader of men. He flirts with the terrible as he does with Becky Thatcher, courting death and glory without being entirely aware of what he is doing, and without therefore being entirely serious. His immaturity is ironically underlined, yet Mark Twain sympathises with Tom in important ways. He likes his boisterousness, his courage, his lively fancy, his sentimentality, his *joie de vivre*. Tom is the sort of lad that Dr Arnold would also have been happy with at Rugby; a Christian boy?—hardly, a Christian gentleman?—yes, given time, that is just what he will be. His unreflecting, limited but not uncostly decency is a pre-eminently respectable virtue; unlikely, as Huck knows, to engage in such eccentric enormities as nigger emancipation, especially at this stage of history, but to be relied on nonetheless for goodwill to all men in so far as expediency and the general good permit. His immaturity is of the type which, properly nurtured, passes unscathed through adolescence into manhood, protecting the ruling class by and large, with all its gifts, its virtues and its opportunities, from producing too many radicals, intellectuals, artists and others disruptive of the *status quo*. He is a good empire-building type; an adventurous extrovert, as Mark Twain himself was; far more fit than Huck to be running the world, and far more likely to be doing so. Even his naughtiness exists, as one critic has pointed out, only inside the limits that he knows are expected of him. And his make-believe, like his jesting, goes to show that though his fancy is lively, his imagination—and especially his moral imagination—is dulled and conventional. Moral imagination—the response to people and to events with direct insight and sympathy—is exactly, of course, the quality in which Huck excels. This is why Huck is never wholly at ease with Tom, though he naturally looks up to him. It is also why Huck is peculiarly fitted to see the deepest moral truths, though he is at the same time peculiarly unfitted to articulate them, or to set about making them prevail.

Practical joking, and its implications, is only the start of our enquiry. Mark Twain's sense of the discrepancies between one world and another goes beyond the gulf between schoolboy fantasy and reality; the more basic gulf between Tom and Huck is the clue that leads towards the heart of the matter. Consider, for example, the following passage, in which two essentially adult worlds are held in sharp contrast.

> Then Miss Watson she took me in the closet
> and prayed, but nothing come of it. She told
> me to pray every day, and whatever I asked for
> I would get it. But it warn't so. I tried it. Once
> I got a fish-line, but no hooks. It warn't any

Original frontispiece illustration for Adventures of Huckleberry Finn.

good to me without hooks. I tried for the hooks three or four times, but somehow I couldn't make it work. By and by, one day, I asked Miss Watson to try for me, but she said I was a fool. She never told me why, and I couldn't make it out no way.

I set down, one time, back in the woods, and had a long think about it. I says to myself, if a body can get anything they pray for, why don't Deacon Winn get back the money he lost on pork? Why can't the widow get back her silver snuff-box that was stole? Why can't Miss Watson fat up? No, says I to myself, there ain't nothing in it. I went and told the widow about it, and she said the thing a body could get by praying for it was 'spiritual gifts'. This was too many for me, but she told me what she meant— I must help other people, and do everything I could for other people, and look out for them all the time, and never think about myself. This was including Miss Watson, as I took it. I went out in the woods and turned it over in my mind a long time, but I couldn't see no advantage about it—except for the other people—so at last I reckoned I wouldn't worry about it any more, but just let it go. Sometimes the widow would take me on one side and talk about Providence in a way to make a body's mouth water; but maybe next day Miss Watson would take hold and knock it all down again. I judged I could see that there was two Providences, and a poor chap would stand considerable show with the widow's Providence, but if Miss Watson's got him there warn't no help for him any more. I thought it all out, and reckoned I would belong to the widow's, if he wanted me, though I couldn't make out how he was a-going to be any better off then than what he was before, seeing I was so ignorant and so kind of low-down and ornery.

The irony here is not generated by Huck's conscious attitude. When he sees through people himself, as he often does, it is only after 'thinking it all out', and then with a shrewd and charitable insight far removed from any tone that would lead to irony, or that an ironist himself would adopt. Though Huck tells the story, in other words, the irony comes directly from the author behind Huck; it is a communication to the reader in which the narrator has no share. Where, then, is the irony aimed? Are the widow and Miss Watson its targets? To some extent, yes; their piety is unreflecting, and their dealings with Huck are less than intelligent. Yet they mean well, as Huck correctly allows, and their belief in prayer and in Providence is not entirely discredited, though it is damaged, by Huck's reflections. Might the irony, then, be at the expense of Huck? On a superficial reading we are tempted to think so, and it is here that Mark Twain's most basic moral trap exists for the reader: if we think that Huck is the victim, we are in fact the victims ourselves. For Mark Twain is neither here nor elsewhere a civilised man glancing with superior amusement at ignorance—his is not the irony of a Gibbon, or a Lytton Strachey; nor is he an indulgent father smiling at the errors of a favorite child—still less is it the irony of a Lamb. Though at first sight Huck's reasoning is deceptively schoolboyish, a moment's reflection reveals not its folly, but its wisdom. For one thing, he pays the widow and Miss Watson the compliment of taking them seriously, even though what they say sounds to him like nonsense. He has the humility and readiness to learn without which any educaton, however sophisticated, cannot be more than a sham. But then again, he has shrewdness and independence of judgement, the qualities which are at the root of his remarkable moral honesty and intelligence. Testing what he has been told against his own experience of life and his own observation of people, he finds grave reasons for doubting it. These doubts are anything but ill-informed cynicism; they have a seriousness which places the traditional piety of Miss Watson and the widow very exactly, and it must be admitted very damagingly, for what they are. Huck's own 'religious' awareness is governed by things he knows—the mysterious grandeur of the river, the stars in the night sky, the age-old folk-lore of good and bad omens, which fit in with his sense of the splendours and uncertainties of life better than doctrines of prayer that he can't make to work, and tales of Providence, Heaven and Hell that relate to no experiences he has had.

Huck is serious and honest, then; he is also kind and gentle. It is these latter qualities which make the word 'wisdom' rather than 'common sense' seem appropriate. He is sure that Miss Watson and the widow are doing their best to educate him, and he has no wish to hurt them by arguing. Whenever he can, he gives them the benefit of the doubt. Prayer does work, perhaps, for some folk, but not for the likes of him. This possibility he accepts unselfconsciously and without bitterness. The fact that he does so is part of the irony, but his obtuseness

at this level, unlike that of (say) Gulliver, reflects nothing but credit on himself.

What one sees in this passage, more than anything else, is Huck's selflessness and humanity, all the richer for the paradoxical form they take. For though he applies tests of self-interest to prayer and Providence, and is quick to see that Miss Watson herself is less disinterested than she might think, it is his good sense, not his greed, that is proved. His real selflessness can be easily seen in the readiness with which he accepts himself as 'low-down and ornery' without, however, making this an excuse for bitterness or irresponsibility, and in the fine natural courtesy towards others which he invariably has. A similar important paradox inheres in his lies. 'I never seen anybody but lied, one time or another', he comments, but his own lies are always related to a deeper honesty: fidelity to fact and to good sense as he sees them. His lies, are, in fact, worked out in the face of much he is asked to believe, evasive action taken not because he is wilful or stupid, but because he is generous and alive. They are a technique for surviving in a largely immoral world with as little unpleasantness for himself and for everyone else as possible. Jim, who shares Huck's predicament, shares his attitude to lying. His greeting to Huck when he first meets him during the escape, and thinks he must be a ghost, is a splendid example of the type of lie which includes in almost equal measure an instinct for survival, a deference to fact however unexpected, genuine courtesy even to one as beyond the pale as a ghost, and a sense that one outcast ought to be able to appeal to the sympathy and goodwill of another, even if naked truth isn't wholly expedient. 'Doan' hurt me—don't! I hain't ever done no harm to a ghos'. I alwuz liked dead people, en done all I could for 'em. You go en git in de river agin, whah you b'longs, en doan' do nuffin to Ole Jim, 'at 'uz alwuz yo' fren'.'

What, then, characterises this irony most? It does not score points against people as its main aim, and is wholly untainted with the assumption of superiority. At root, it is a juxtaposing of two or more real worlds at points where they do not, and cannot, meet. Both worlds exist, and though Huck's is the more virtuous, that of Miss Watson and the widow is the more usual. The irony offers a rich realism, the 'whole truth', as I am calling it; but the whole truth shot through with a moral awareness without which such a description of it would not be deserved, and with a charity rare among writers who use irony at all.

The inevitable question concerning Mark Twain's values now presents itself. How far is **Huckleberry Finn** the expression of a clear preference, either for radicalism or for the noble savage? The answer is not clear-cut. If one tries Mark Twain out with some radical causes of the present day, he can sometimes seem reactionary. He would have been anti-apartheid, of course; if his irony is committed to any obvious 'cause' it is that. But he might well have been for hanging rather than against it, on the familiar grounds, abundantly clear in his work, that reformers interested only in kindness overlooked the grim realities of human evil, against which society must protect itself strongly, even ruthlessly, to survive. Huck's charity, it is true, transcends this, by way of an equally ruthless honesty on the other side. Confronted with the murderers trapped on the boat, he reflects: 'I began to think how dreadful it was, even for murderers, to be in such a fix. I says to myself, there ain't no telling but I might come to be a murderer myself, yet, and then how would I like it?' And when the Duke and the King have perpetrated every possible treachery against both himself and Jim, he can still spare them compassion in their own misery and suffering. But Mark Twain himself, on the whole, feels that murderers and others like them deserve what they get; as to the do-gooders like the new judge who thinks he can reform Huck's father by kindness, they come in for frequent satiric treatment at his hands.

Mark Twain takes evil seriously, in other words, and he believes that strong social law is necessary to combat it, even though law will be tainted with the defects of the class who make it. This becomes more obvious when one thinks of the really anti-social figures in *Huckleberry Finn.* Huck's father, the Duke and the King are all failures, who stand outside society not because they are too honest for it, like Huck, or unjustly discriminated against by it, like Jim, but simply because they are lazy, vicious, and by nature parasitic. The passage in which Huck's father fulminates against the Government for tolerating an educated 'nigger' is irony of the straightforwardly boomerang kind, and of him, as of the other scoundrels in the book, there is no good word to be said. Though Huck understands and pities them, and sees himself partly in the same boat, he certainly does not approve of them, and he is nothing like them himself. In an important sense, they represent what happens when the respectable virtues are rejected outright—the good like duty, justice, responsibility along with the bad—and for Twain the last state is clearly worse than the first.

Huck himself, and to a great extent Jim, are wholly different from this. They represent not the rejection of society's highest values, but their fulfilment. The irony here is that society rejects Huck for being too good; by living up to its own ideals he becomes unfamiliar, and offers a challenge which can easily be mistaken for something stupid, or sceptical, or subversive. On the raft, Huck and Jim become what Lionel Trilling has called a 'community of saints'; yet their values come not from the civilised society which is supposed to encourage saints, but from the older incentive of a common danger, a common humanity, a common predicament.

It is here that the most penetrating ironic effects take place. The fact that Huck thinks himself worse, rather than better, than his fellows leads to the major irony that from first to last he sees the help he gives Jim as a sin; and the notion of selling Jim back into bondage can repeatedly present itself as a prompting to repentance and virtue. There are the harrowing moments when he wavers; and the final victory when he says 'All right, I'll go to Hell then' is all the more powerful for being unrecognised by Huck himself as savouring of either paradox or irony.

Nor should one underestimate the nature of Huck's stand at this moment. A large part of the country's economy depended on slavery, and one knows for a fact that even tender consciences have difficulty in seeing very clearly when this is so. Again and again the point is underlined. The question is asked, 'Anyone hurt?', and Huck answers, quite naturally, 'No mum; one nigger killed.' The doctor towards the end of the tale assumes that recapturing a runaway slave is a more pressing moral duty than attending to a patient. Huck himself is horrified to think that Tom Sawyer might have degenerated into a 'nigger stealer', and is relieved to discover that this is not so. All of this may be slightly exaggerated for purposes of the irony, but truth can sometimes defy a satirist to improve upon it for his purpose. The depth to which an economic condition causes moral blindness is deeper, at any rate, than Huck's conscious moralising can reach. Huck really thinks he *is* being wicked,

and the irony here cuts straight from writer to reader, by-passing Huck himself, though enhancing his stature.

One can see, from this central point, what Mark Twain is really doing. Though he rejects ideals that strike him as facile or dangerous, he holds passionately to the conviction that underlies all true radical feeling: namely, that all men should be treated as equally human, irrespective of the natural or man-made barriers of colour, class, belief or what you will. That men are not equally good he acknowledges, and that some are too bad to be tolerated he also admits. But that a man should be despised simply for being brought up in poverty, like Huck, or for being the wrong colour, like Jim, fills him with outrage. In presenting the pair of them as the salt of the earth he is making a most profoundly radical point. He is also doing more. The decency of Huck and Jim offers some hope for the human species itself: an original virtue, perhaps, constantly departed from, and paradoxically exiled, yet ultimately not to be eradicated from the human heart.

The episode I now want to consider is the very famous one, felt by many readers to be the high point of the novel's greatness. Huck, having been separated from Jim in a fog, and been mourned by him as dead, returns, and plays a joke of Tom Sawyer's kind. (It is very similar, in fact, to the one played by Tom Sawyer on Aunt Polly in the earlier book.) Jim's honest joy at seeing him again he puts down to drink: he hasn't been away, he says, Jim must have imagined it all. So great is Jim's trust in Huck, that he sits thinking for five minutes, and then decides to believe Huck before the evidence of his own senses. 'Well, den, I reck'n I did dream it, Huck; but dog my cats ef it ain't de powerfullest dream I ever see.' Huck allows Jim to give an account of the 'dream', together with an ingenious interpretation, and at the end, by pointing out certain things which do not fit in, makes Jim realise that he has been fooled. The episode continues as follows.

> Jim looked at the trash, and then looked at me, and back at the trash again. He had got the dream fixed so strong in his head that he couldn't seem to shake it loose and get the facts back into its place again, right away. But when he did get the thing straightened around, he looked at me steady, without ever smiling, and says:

> 'What do dey stan' for? I's gwyne to tell you. When I got all wore out wid work, en wid de callin' for you, en went to sleep, my heart wuz mos' broke bekase you wuz los', en I didn' k'yer no mo' what become er me en de raf'. En when I wake up en fine you back agin', all safe en soun', de tears come en I could a got down on my knees en kiss' yo' foot I's so thankful. En all you wuz thinkin' 'bout wuz how you could make a fool uv ole Jim wid a lie. Dat truck dah is *trash;* en trash is what people is dat puts dirt on de head er dey fren's en makes 'em ashamed'.

> Then he got up slow, and walked to the wigwam, and went in there, without saying anything but that. But that was enough. It made me feel so mean I could almost kissed *his* foot to get him to take it back.

> It was fifteen minutes before I could work myself up to go and humble myself to a nigger—but I done it, and I warn't sorry for it after-

wards, neither. I didn't do him no more mean tricks, and I wouldn't done that one if I'd a knowed it would make him feel that way.

Almost any comment on this is bound to be clumsy; it is one of the most memorable moments in literature. In Tom Sawyer's world, a joke of this type would be more or less in order; personal relationships matter less, affections, emotions, sensibility are all blunted or suppressed to the necessary degree. Here, on the raft, it is supremely wrong, as Huck comes to *feel*, as usual without entirely understanding why. In fact, the lies he has told Jim are not his type of lies, and his moral imagination has for once let him down. The law of the raft has been broken, and personal affection sacrificed to a cheap, though not malicious, victory on points. The behavior of Huck and Jim at this moment, free as it is of the sentimentality or the embarrassment which normally surrounds and inhibits such feelings, is both moving and authentic. The values of the raft here reach a moment of undeniable and unforgettable reality.

Mark Twain's irony, I have insisted, is a direct communication between the writer and reader. No one at all in the novel, including Huck, knows that the raft is a place of virtue; it is the secret communication of the irony. Mark Twain's greatness as a writer can be demonstrated from the skill with which he uses Huck's obtuseness about his own worth as part of his own technique, yet enhances rather than damages him as a person in so doing. It can also be shown from the lack of any arbitrary traps in his work of the Swiftian kind. The reader is challenged wholly at the level of moral response; failure to perceive the direction of the irony is indistinguishable from failure to perceive Huck's virtue. The irony is, indeed, a forcing into the consciousness of readers more educated than Huck himself the reality, as he embodies them, of their own ideals.

The end of the novel, I have contended, is the final insight that Twain has to offer, the final twist of his technique towards truth. It is right, psychologically and historically as well as structurally, that Tom Sawyer should come into the ascendant again; he is, after all, a leader, and Huck and Jim will naturally start trusting him again more than they trust themselves. We can be sure, however, that whatever happens to Huck, as the long process of 'civilising' him starts afresh, he will be a good man. The values which Twain's irony have been establishing will stand more chance of survival because he is in the world, even though they will never have an unambiguous victory. There will be a redemptive possibility at the heart of what Mark Twain elsewhere calls the 'damned human race', underlying the cruelty, the muddle and the squalor. Naïve cynicism, like naïve idealism, will not after all have the last word.

For the rest? Goodness might not have a sure triumph, Mark Twain seems to imply, but it has some claim on the universe nonetheless. Huck's enjoyment of life, his honesty, his reverence and charity deserve to be respected; whatever happens he will somehow be all right, as Jim says when telling his fortune. The claim might be solely by way of our own human moral sense; the Mississippi itself will flow on, caring little who worships and enjoys it and who does not. Yet Huck and Jim, with whatever indifference the river might return their worship, remain undefeated, and one feels it is right that they should. This, too, is part of Mark Twain's feeling for life; a reason why Hemingway is wrong to say he cheats at the end, why Dr Leavis, Lionel Trilling and others are right to find him one of the great writers of moral health. (pp. 96-111)

A. E. Dyson, "Mark Twain: 'Huckleberry Finn' and the Whole Truth," in his The Crazy Fabric: Essays in Irony, *St. Martin's Press, 1965, pp. 96-111.*

STUART B. JAMES (essay date 1969)

[*In the following excerpt, James examines Huck as an example of the uniquely American individualist described by Alexis de Tocqueville.*]

In his early 19th century work *Democracy in America*, Alexis de Tocqueville was often critical of what Americans saw, and still tend to see as a distinguishing characteristic of our nation: American individualism. Tocqueville saw latent in that individualism dispersive forces that might conceivably sever not only a person's connecting ties with history and tradition but could set each man apart from his social comrades and render him at last alone in what Tocqueville called the feverish chaos of a democratic world. "Among democratic nations," Tocqueville wrote in a well-known passage,

> new families are constantly springing up, others are constantly falling away, and all that remain change their condition; the woof of time is every instant broken and the track of generations effaced. Those who went before are soon forgotten; and of those who will come after, no one has any idea: the interest of man is confined to those in close propinquity to himself.... Not only does democracy make every man forget his ancestors, but it hides his descendents and separates his contemporaries from him; it throws him back forever upon himself alone and threatens in the end, to confine him entirely within the solitude of his own heart.

(p. 19)

Mark Twain's Huckleberry Finn is [a] Tocquevillean democrat, in flight in the vastness of American space, drifting down that grand and savage River, deeper and deeper into the society into which he has been born and which he has come to hate. Huckleberry Finn feels nothing for the generations that went before him; Miss Watson and the Widow Douglas are only to be escaped from; he cares not a wit for the past because like Moses in the Bulrushers, it is dead. We hear nothing of his mother; he is an orphan at fourteen and, considering his father, should have been one long before that. His only close companions are Tom Sawyer, a cruel little American smart-aleck and know-it-all whom Huck ironically worships, and Nigger Jim, a sad, generous, and ignorant Negro, something of the shaping hand of Harriet Beecher Stowe upon him, who, like Faulkner's Dilsey Gibson, can only endure. At the end of the novel, as everyone knows, Huck announces like the good separatist that he is, that he is going to light out for the territory to escape Aunt Sally's threat that she is going to civilize him. But the vast emptiness and loneliness of that territory may well fulfill for him the Tocquevillean prophecy that he will be thrown back upon himself alone and confined at last within the solitude of his own heart.

In the figure of Huckleberry Finn we see ... [an] American fictional character at odds with and fleeing from the culture in which he grew up. But when we ask the question, What are his responsibilities to this culture, we hit a snag. Because as everyone knows, the civilizing that Aunt Sally threatens Huck with means simply that the boy is to be shaped to fit the ugly posture of a slave society, that ante-bellum South where slavery was sanctioned by law. If, as Cooper remarked, no civilization can be without law, Twain's book asks us to consider the moral tenor of that law and its ramifications for the culture as a whole. And it is hardly too much to say that the White laws governing slavery in the ante-bellum South imprisoned a high proportion of its society, the Blacks, in a state of nature where their lives remained solitary, poor, nasty, brutish, and short.

Twain's book dramatizes Thoreau's suggestion that men standing completely within an institution, never distinctly and nakedly behold it. The book suggests, too, that laws are often only the legal articulation of men's economic and psychic needs; and that law can become the machine that works for the benefit of the power group of a society. And the peculiar historical moment with which Twain deals throws into relief the fact that the people who most desperately need the protection of the law have little or no voice in its formulation.

Twain makes crystal clear that the full configuration of this society, including its laws, is but the enlarged reflection of the individual hearts and minds which make up that society. Twain, like so many southern writers, works with caricature, but his caricatures are but the blown-up sketches of traits lodged in us all: The moral blindness of Aunt Sally; the self-deception of Tom Sawyer; the ugly hunger for violence of the Bricksville crew; the economic exploitations of the King and the Duke; the saccharine piety that hangs over this world like a miasma; and everywhere evidences of the enslavement of Black bodies and the enslavement of White minds. There men are asked to believe in and celebrate that most grotesque of all marriages: Christianity and Slavery. The laws of this society gain an immense force from their religious underledging. The southern God not only insists that human slavery is a practice of which he approves but that any questioning of that practice will be met with unbelievable punishment. The Sunday School that Huck would have attended had he been a "better" boy, would have taught him that anyone who frees Blacks "goes to everlasting fire."

We know that the boy refused to turn his friend Jim back into slavery. But that refusal was an act against the law, and not only southern law. When in 1850 Congress passed the Fugitive Slave Law, Ralph Waldo Emerson recorded in his journal, "All I have and all I can do shall be given and done in opposition to the execution of (this) law. . . . This filthy enactment was made in the 19th century, by people who could read and write. I will not obey it, by God." The Sage of Concord and the fourteen year old ragamuffin from St. Petersburg, Missouri, saw eye-to-eye on this matter of the Fugitive Slave Law. But Emerson apparently confined his rebellion to the pages of his journal; Huck tested his loyalty in the bitter event and became in his own and in his society's eyes a subversive, dangerous to the social order and liable to punishment legally administered. Yet nearly all readers agree that Huckleberry Finn might rightfully join those figures of history who have struck a blow for human freedom. He refused to sacrifice his friend to an abstract principle, that law of the state which, sadly enough, he believed in his heart to be right. If Huck, under the pressure of cultural habit, knows he is going to everlasting fire for his act of helping Jim, we, of course, know differently. It was Dante who placed Cassius and Brutus in the lowest circle of Hell, but not for subversive action against the state, but because they betrayed their friend.

Twain's novel carries a tremendous moral suggestion and a tremendous moral force. The polarization between the boy and the society is justly complete. (pp. 34-7)

[History] has taught us that the danger of high idealism lies in its adoption of means at dramatic odds with its stated ends.

But with Huckleberry Finn the solution is the old fictional solution. He lights out for the territory and, in running, deserts his friend whom he has so greatly championed.

His language is marked by that very stereotypic blindness that stigmatizes the society he will desert. The highest praise he can give his Black friend is that he is white inside. Asked by Aunt Sally if anyone was hurt in a steamer accident, he answers, "No'm. Killed a nigger." He goes along with Tom Sawyer's adolescent and shocking treatment of Jim in the closing chapters of the book, the whole episode a grotesque foreshadowing of the place of the free Black as a plaything of a cruel and morally adolescent White society. In the end, in good separatist fashion, Huck will abstract himself from the dung heap of this slave society. He thus declares himself free from any responsibility to a culture which holds, still in virtual slavery, the only morally sensitive person he ever knew and the only real friend he ever had.

The clowning at the end of the novel is American clowning of the Sut Lovingood variety. It does not obscure Jim's suffering, but has hidden from too many readers the fact that that very attractive All-American boy Huckleberry Finn, like so many of our fictional heroes, has fallen from grace and in his essentially selfish bid for personal salvation has turned his back on the tedious and discouraging attempts by men to create a just and humane social order. The boy—and we say this in sadness because he is a boy, yet remember the immensity of the shadow he casts—the boy is yet another example of that ruinous individualism to which Tocqueville addressed himself, an individualism which "at first only saps the virtues of public life," Tocqueville wrote, "but in the long run it attacks and destroys all others and is at length absorbed in downright selfishness." (pp. 38-9)

> Stuart B. James, "The Politics of Personal Salvation: The American Literary Record," in The Denver Quarterly, Vol. 4, No. 2, Summer, 1969, pp. 19-45.*

KEITH M. OPDAHL   (essay date 1979-80)

[Opdahl is an American critic and educator. In the following excerpt, he discusses the pattern of child-adult relations in Huckleberry Finn.]

A fascinating new approach to *The Adventures of Huckleberry Finn* found its voice in the turbulent Sixties. At least a dozen critics probed the psychology of America's favorite young tourist Huck Finn. What they found when they examined his language and fantasy was disturbing: the freckle-faced lad is a nervous wreck. His famous decision for Jim ("'All right, then, I'll *go* to hell'") is not really noble, for Huck is motivated less by love or justice than a need for companionship (Campbell Tatham) or a family (Eric Solomon) or creature comforts (Martha Banta). Huck is, to use the terms such critics use, "passive" or "unheroic"; he is "wounded and damaged"; his relationship with Jim is unconsciously "homoerotic," or he's "in love with death."

All of these innovative critics share a psychological view of Huck and tend to measure his actions by the light of his motives. What others dismiss as the foibles of youth, these critics take as weakness or pathology. Many focus on Huck's family life, pointing out that Twain's fiction is informed by a sublimation of hostility toward the father, expressed by competition with the brothers (Robert Regan's *Unpromising Heroes*) or that Huck seeks a father (Eric Solomon) or that Huck needs more than anything to become independent of the father (Ray B. Browne). If the Mississippi is "the River God," as T. S. Eliot told us in 1950 [see *TCLC,* Vol. 6], it is also (to Barchilon and Kovel) the great mother.

Are we justified in probing the internal Huck? May we treat this novel as though it were written by Henry James or Herman Melville? Surprisingly perhaps, the answer must be yes. (pp. 613-14)

[Perhaps] the most conclusive evidence of psychological content is the many ways in which the novel is dream-like. Such, at least, I would like to argue. The novel *is* a dream, from first to last. It opens with Jim's comic dream and proceeds to pap's murderous one. Huck persuades first Jim and then Silas Phelps that they are dreaming. Tom and Huck wander at night, living out their dreams, and Huck and Jim, on those long, "dreamy" afternoons, live a daydream of peace and freedom. (p. 614)

The actual events, in fact, may be dream-like. Here we need remember only Huck's fake death and the deliberate calm with which he works. Kenneth Lynn notes exactly the kind of meaning we associate with dreams when he tells us the pig is a stand-in for pap, who after Huck's escape (we later learn) is killed. Huck and Jim "float" down the river. Adults appear unexpectedly as in a dream and even (locked in their own nightmare) try to kill Huck. Such scenes as Huck watching the adults search for his body are dream-like (as Huck eats the loaves of bread superstitiously floated to find his body and the boat fires its cannon in his face), and such images as the stranger sleeping on Jackson's Island, the robbers in lamplight, and Jim painted blue, have the mute, vivid quality of nightmares. (pp. 615-16)

The novel is also a dream in the way in which the same material is thrashed over and over, as events and characters appear a second and even a third time, first in play and then in deadly reality. Huck plays robber with Tom and then meets real robbers; Huck and Jim discuss kings shortly before they meet the "real" one. Jim flees to freedom in the novel proper, and then must submit to Tom's cruel play-acting at the novel's end. Such duplication, though enclosed in what is clearly a realistic novel, repeats the patterns of dream, as does the equally peculiar way in which major characters like Huck and Jim shift roles, appearing first in one light and then another. In a way, the notorious reversals in character in the last third of the novel merely continue the dream-like shifts we've already seen.

We'd probably be surprised, given this dream-like tone, if the novel did *not* contain a psychological bias. And indeed, Twain's dreamy (or nightmarish) tone is essential to his themes, one of the most important of which derives from the fact that **Huck Finn** is a children's book, with a special focus on child-adult relations. As in a nightmare, the adults are dangerous. When Huck is kidnapped from the widow, he loses the protection of the St. Petersburg middle class; when he flees pap, he loses *all* adult protection, fulfilling the child's dream of freedom (as he relishes his camp on Jackson's Island) and the child's nightmare of vulnerability. Of all the magnificent ideas that make this novel go, Huck's vulnerability might be the key. When he fakes his death, Huck dies as a social being; outside the community, unable to seek its protection, Huck has broken the magic circle. He can defend himself only by his wits.

Thus the novel dramatizes Huck's defenselessness among treacherous adults. Again and again as he weaves and dodges in a world in which loafers set fire to stray dogs, Huck is trapped by dangerous men—pap, the robbers, the king and duke, the Phelpses' neighbors. Part of this hostility is a joke, of course: told he may join Tom's gang only if he has family to kill, Huck offers up Miss Watson—"they could kill her." But the joke expresses something real and even points to the pattern of this novel. Each set of adventures clusters about a single adult, so that as Huck passes from one to the other, the novel breaks into six sections—each following the same general pattern of events. In each section, Huck passes through three clearly defined stages.

In every case, first of all, the grown-up initially frightens Huck, even the widow surprisingly enough, since Huck originally feared boredom in her house and so had to be lured into it by Tom Sawyer's promise of a robber band. Pap's first appearance is terrifying, as Huck sees first the heelprint and then in his room that fishbelly face—his disreputable blood returning to haunt him. Even the loving Jim gives Huck a start, for the boy sees at first a smoking fire which terrifies him, and then a man wrapped in a blanket. The Grangerfords threaten to shoot the boy ("Three big men with guns pointed at me"), and the duke and the king, fleeing a posse, carry danger behind them. Once aboard the raft, they take over. And in the concluding episode, the Phelpses are a special danger because they might discover Huck's lie, and they confuse him by calling him "Tom Sawyer."

Secondly, in each case the adult proves not to be the threat he'd seemed. Huck always learns to enjoy his new life. He gets used to the widow, enjoys pap's easy ways, has long talks with Jim—who as a fugitive is the only adult who is no threat, since he's dependent on Huck—and admires the Grangerford's living room, going so far as to try his hand (like Emmeline) at writing poetry. Does he dream of replacing the dead daughter? He has a good time with the king, too, at first, and plays endless pranks on the Phelpses with the newfound Tom Sawyer.

But then (with one exception) the adults turn ugly indeed, becoming a real threat. Miss Watson pecks at him so much, Huck says, "I most wished I was dead." The delirious pap tries to kill him. Jim, though loving, creates a threat by his visibility—as a Black he attracts the notice of strangers and brings the posse sneaking over to Jackson Island. The king forces Huck into the Wilks swindle, which almost gets them all lynched, and the Phelpses, warned by Tom Sawyer that armed robbers will steal Jim, ask armed neighbors to fight the bandits, and so cause the hail of bullets that almost kills the Black and the boys. Once again, in what is really the novel's emotional climax (involving fifteen hostile grownups), adults prove murderous.

Is such a pattern more than a coincidence? It's a formula certainly, for it provides Twain with all sorts of thrills, and plays on the child's fear of adults. First the threat, and then a comfortable comic interlude, and then real danger—Twain had discovered a formula which he uses to good effect in such escapades as the boarding of the wrecked "Walter Scott," which appears at first to be dangerous, and then a lark, and then—as the raft slips its mooring—a threat all too real.

If this pattern is a formula, however, it's also a revelation of the emotional nightmare at the center of the novel. All of the adults, or at least the males, are a single character: the father. The men break into two groups, each of which is a threat: the lower-class men (pap and the king) because of booze and dishonesty, and the middle- or upper-class men (Thatcher, Robinson, and Bell) because Huck is on the wrong side of the law. The dream-like murder of Boggs, who is similar to pap in drunkenness and posturing, by a Sherburn who has the rigidity and anger of, say, Doctor Robinson, might even be viewed as a confrontation of the two types. Twain's shift to the circus in that episode reflects the novel's flickering, nightmarish quality as another drunk also risks his life—this time magically transforming himself into a handsome acrobat by the kind of sudden shift we'd almost come to expect.

Thus the form and tone of the novel parallel the insight of Peter Beidler that Huck identifies with a suffering child. Each adventure keeps Huck knocked off balance, making him suffer the emotion of fear. More importantly, each father figure fails Huck, so that Huck becomes the opposite of the picaro, not a traveling rogue but a traveling sufferer, careening from one panic to another. Twain's art reinforces this impression, as Twain gives his sharpest, most detailed description to the adults who terrorize the boy.

Can any children's book exist without ambivalence toward adults? Like the raft inside, the novel tips one way and then another. Huck is caught between the widow and pap, the middle and lower classes, the river and shore, a woman and masculine freedom. He accepts the widow, and then flees; he accepts pap, and then escapes. Jim, the Grangerfords, the king, and even the Phelpses all appear in one light to Huck and then another, so that the structure of the novel is a kind of throbbing, as Huck himself goes back and forth. Huck fears Jim and then loves him; mocks Jim and then feels sorry; saves Jim and then begins to turn him in. Sherburn is admirable standing up to the crowd; he's despicable shooting Boggs. Huck admires a daring Southern aristocrat in Grangerford, but isn't so sure in the wake of the bloodbath.

Such ambivalence is natural to Twain's art, since Twain proceeded on a principle of contrast, alternating peace and fear, humor and melodrama, "Was Solomon Wise?" with "Honest Loot from the 'Walter Scott,'" And yet the ambivalence embodies Huck's psychology, too, for Huck is deeply in need of a family and yet quick to take flight. Huck needs a father, but the intensity of his need drives him away. He is so dependent, he would be smothered by a family (as he is actually dominated by these adults). We could argue that the physical threat of the father dramatizes a psychological one, as Huck creeps close, feels himself endangered (physically and emotionally), and flees. That he must flee, that pap will kill him or the king abuse him, objectifies the psychological truth, given Huck's dependency. The melodrama and the psychology add up to a single nightmare, which I suppose must belong to Twain, or at least to the Twain who identified with Huck's voice.

Is it possible that Huck feels resentment at the way these adults treat him? Surely not, if Huck is the fantasy of peace and generosity we believe him to be. Huck embodies the longing Twain felt when he looked back on his youth: Huck alone among Twain's protagonists does not share the aggression and ambition of "The Unpromising Hero" (though without brothers to stand in for the father, Huck must confront the father himself). Huck is our national dream of rest, floating down that river and giving up the social struggle in order to *be*, to accept the biological existence which need not prove anything.

Or is Huck too good? Although Huck is bored, threatened, terrified, shot at, and run over, he never complains and is never embittered. He's never angry or malicious. He's *sorry*: the spectacle of human cruelty makes him sad. He remains one of the great portraits in world literature of the good man—made possible, perhaps by his youth.

And yet this very goodness might explain our uneasiness with the novel. Given the treatment he receives, we'd *expect* Huck to feel resentment; is it possible that like many self-sacrificing people he carries a burden of unarticulated anger? One of the remarkable aspects of this novel is how often Huck blunders, hurting himself. He takes a false name and forgets it. As the king's English valet he attempts a detailed description of English life. He insists on boarding the wrecked steamboat and is the one who ties the raft the night it breaks loose and floats past the Ohio, botching Jim's chance for freedom.

Huck clearly turns a certain amount of anger against himself—he feels guilty a good part of the time. Is it possible that he carries a burden of unconscious hostility? Or is it Twain who feels this anger? We really ought to distinguish in this curious novel between Huck's voice—which is never angry—and the events which occur. Huck is gentle; the novel ranges from social satire to outright cruelty. In a way, the basic problem in this book is the peculiar exchange between Huck's voice, which is the style, and the novel's plot, which goes off in its own direction, contradicting Huck's tone. Suppose we forget for a moment Huck's kindly voice and generous nature and examine only the events. Would we discover a hidden resentment or hostility?

The spectacle of Huck passing from person to person—some six adults in all—implies some kind of rejection. At the same time that Huck saves his life by fleeing, he punishes them. Surely Huck (or Twain behind him) realizes that his fake murder makes the St. Petersburg adults grieve. In the scene in which Huck examines the adults sadly searching for his body, pap stands beside Judge Thatcher and Aunt Polly (with the widow strangely missing); the three grieve together, for they are (in Huck's emotions) the same—the older people who have power over him. It's significant that the boat fires a cannon in Huck's face, committing another "wrong." Twain gives the youth the child's ultimate weapon: "You'll be sorry when I'm dead"—and thus imagines Huck punishing everyone who abused him.

Twain also imagines Huck doing direct harm to adults. We remember the way Huck teases Jim—again and again, in the course of the novel—but we forget that Huck hurts Jim physically. It's Huck who puts the dead rattlesnake in Jim's blankets, forgetting that the live mate will curl up with the corpse. Twain thus has his youth contrive a poisonous snake in Jim's blanket—a snake that almost costs Jim his life.

High spirits? Certainly—Huck gives no clue to bad feeling. It's a prank. And yet the fantasy contained in the events clearly exists. Huck never tells Jim that he put the dead snake in his blanket, but he does talk a lot about "handlin' snake-skin," referring to a molted skin he found. That skin causes all their misfortune, Huck says, confessing his guilt to a related act. It's as though Huck unconsciously knew what he was up to.

Twain involves Huck in other adult disasters too. Huck carries the note that rekindles the Grangerford-Shepherdson feud and, in a curious scene, fails to watch out for the Shepherdsons after Buck had asked him to stand lookout. The Shepherdsons catch Buck and his cousin off guard, chase them to the river, and use their bodies for target practice.

Tom Blankenship, the young boy after whom Huck Finn was modeled, lived in this house, close to the Clemens family. Courtesy of Mark Twain Home Board, Hannibal, MO.

Huck turns against the duke and king, too, stealing back the gold for the orphans. The widow, pap, Jim, the Grangerfords, and the king are all in some way worse off for associating with Huck. They deserve it, of course; and Huck is *not* aware of his acts. And yet the adult pain is real. We're reminded that when Huck calls himself Charles William Allbright, he identifies with not only a murder victim but a child seeking ghostly vengeance. Again and again in this complex book, Huck is taken for a ghost or the Angel of Death. Pap, Jim, and Tom all at some point feel fear upon seeing Huck.

Let us distinguish between Huck and Mark Twain, who controls these events, and continue to believe in Huck's goodness. In a curious way, Twain's remarkable style is too good, for we are so dazzled by it, so taken with the tone and detail, that we forget the contrivance and anger. Or let us say that Huck has a darker, unconscious side which he cannot control and of which not even Twain was aware. Why can't Huck be as complicated as anyone else? In a way, given the hostile world in which he wanders, it is not Huck's resentment that is striking in this novel, but the fact that he does not fight back at all. He's too humble, we say, too young to fight—forgetting that children are more prone to anger and resentment than adults, which is why we use the word "childish." Huck's voice is in reality middle-aged, with the mellow wisdom that comes with years.

Or let us say that the novel is a dream, with the peculiar dualities, the leaps and jumps and gaps that permit the dreamer to express illicit emotions. Freud argued that all dreams are wish fulfillment and become nightmares when the dreamer suffers an inner conflict. Huck's dream here is of love, as adult after adult takes him in (and even pap gives Huck a good life of a sort), and of self-pity as the adults fail him. It is also a dream of revenge against the dangerous fathers—note how often Huck is given power over adults, even though he doesn't exercise it. He has Jim at his mercy, and holds a gun on pap, and fools everyone with his fake murder. His disguises give him a kind of power, as do his pranks, with or without Tom Sawyer. On the "Walter Scott" Huck has the power of life and death over the robbers, and in the Wilks trial he has a similar power over the duke and king. Having exercised the ultimate power of the child by running away from St. Petersburg, Huck does the same to Aunt Sally Phelps when she desires to adopt him—this after witnessing her grief when he and Tom had disappeared the night of Jim's escape.

Modern researchers tell us that dreams are essential to mental health, almost as though we had to express the emotions there, or so review or order our experience. *Huck Finn* provides such a function for children. It objectifies and expresses some otherwise illicit or unadmirable impulses, a function that is one source of its power. Such expression was also an important function to Mark Twain, who wished to have it both ways, really, to create a daydream of goodness with a Huck who is generous, unassuming, unafraid—clearly without malice—and a fantasy of vengeance, as the plot expresses resentment, hostility, or the anger we know was close to eruption in Twain at this time. Huck's ignorance made this possible, as did Twain's running exchange between river and shore. But so, too, did the implicit dream-like nature of Huck's narrative, with its poker face, its sudden unexplained shifts, and its return again and again to the theme of the destructive and symbolically destroyed father.

To be aware of this hidden anger, I think, is to understand several puzzling events, such as the fact that Huck in his first lie claims to have been abused by adults or the fact that when Huck lies about Jim—even sweet Jim—he claims the Black threatened to cut out his liver. A latent anger explains why Huck feels guilty when he sees the king and duke tarred and feathered, for in the dream logic of the book Huck *is* guilty, even though he had no actual part in it.

But most of all the novel's unconscious anger explains the problematical last section of the book, following Huck's separation from the king. Although Ernest Hemingway advised the reader to stop reading at the point at which Jim is sold, because "the rest is just cheating," critics have had a wonderful time discovering the theme that ties the last episode to the main text and so justifies it. Huck begins in society, some critics claim, and so should end there. The novel is a study of thievery, culminating in this last theft. It's a study of illusions, such as Tom now attempts to weave. Greed, racism, a shifting identity, are all neatly tied together by this last adventure.

And yet it's clear that the quality of writing falls off. The decline begins with the Wilks swindle, which is full of coincidence and melodrama (and over which Twain labored desperately). Although it contains some pleasant bits, such as the country women apologizing for their cooking or the dog howling during the funeral (and the undertaker's stage whisper, *"He had a rat!"*), it is below Twain's earlier standard. Twain in this episode gives more dialogue and less description. He's plotty, with a lot of movement that betrays the author's labor. With few exceptions, he no longer takes the time to describe—to develop his scenes.

We might deduce that the last third of the novel was written in haste and fatigue. But the problem is a matter of tone as well, as we might see in a comparison of Huck's description of the Phelpses' corn field ("... flies in the air that makes it seem so lonesome and like everybody's dead") with his earlier description of the river, with the world emerging lyrically from darkness. In the last part of the novel Huck's voice no longer conceals the novel's unhappy emotions. Because the joke goes on too long, the cruelty—of an unhappy man—shines through. Twain's vision has darkened, and though he tries to get back to his joke, he can't make it. The love that would redeem the laughter is missing; the smile stiffens, and the light-hearted joke goes sour.

The novel also fails because Twain struggled to return to his original, hidden theme. Because Silas Phelps is bumbling, the last part of the novel lacks a single strong father figure and so lacks focus, as though this were the theme that galvanized Twain's imagination. Or is it the lack of an *evil* father? Without an Injun Joe or pap or king to give form to his fantasies of adult aggression, Twain has no justification for the children's hostility, as Tom and Huck play pranks that humiliate. Neither

Jim nor the Phelpses, all of whom are tormented by the [...] deserve the treatment they get. What had been appropr[...] Huck sought to stay alive is now gratuitous. This migh[...] be the significance of Huck assuming Tom's name, for Tom, resenting any authority outside of books, acts out the child's hostility toward all adults, male or female, kindly or not. Tom suggests (in this Victorian era) that Aunt Sally is sexually easy: "They all said, kiss her," Tom says of Aunt Sally to her face, "and said she'd like it. They all said it—every one of them." For Huck to become Tom means that corrosive emotions previously hidden now spill into view.

Nor does Twain have an excuse for the adults threatening the young. Believing in a strong ending and sensing what his real tale had been, Twain groped for a final crystallizing act of adult aggression. He had to rely on the contrivance of Tom Sawyer's note warning the Phelpses of armed robbers, and then the appearance of fifteen armed farmers to shoot at the ostensibly well-meaning boys. The adults attack in a blaze of bullets; the children respond by disappearing, resorting once more to their ultimate weapon: "You'll be sorry when I'm dead." Just as Huck earlier had seen the adults mourn him, and as Huck and Tom in *Tom Sawyer* had seen the whole town mourning them at their funeral, Huck has a glimpse of the exhausted, worried Aunt Sally, dozing as she sits up all night awaiting news of her missing charges. Clearly, in the face of all this contrivance, Twain missed a really evil character, the true villain of his novel up to the Phelps episode, a father figure with his terrifying face lit by candle-light and his presence trapping the endangered Huck.

Does such a view of *Huckleberry Finn* diminish the novel as a whole? I don't think it has to, unless one is a moralist of the most genteel sort. Huck is fourteen; such feelings of confusion and resentment are natural. We could say rather that *Huck Finn* is grounded in a struggle that is psychological and mythic. Huck slides from one adult male to another, as we've seen, from Judge Thatcher to pap to Jim and to Grangerford, settling finally on the king—the ultimate, generic father—and then Tom Sawyer playing a father-like role. As in a dream, in something of the same way "The Wasteland" has a single protagonist. *Huck Finn* has a single antagonist—all of these characters are the same. They are all fathers, all figures of authority, playing much the same role in Huck's life. If Huck chooses for Jim, risking eternal Hell, he surmounts obstacles much larger than his conditioning in racism. He surmounts his own deeply felt resentment toward fathers. To accept Jim's humanity, Huck must rise above the lesson taught by much of his own experience—the suspicion and hostility that so many of these adults deserve. He must break out of his nightmare. That he does, that for these few, brief moments he chooses *for* the father, may be viewed as an even greater testimony to Jim's humanity and Huck's kind heart than we'd realized. (pp. 616-24)

Keith M. Opdahl, "'You'll Be Sorry When I'm Dead': Child-Adult Relations in 'Huck Finn'," in Modern Fiction Studies, *Vol. 25, No. 4, Winter, 1979-80, pp. 613-24.*

FREDERICK WOODARD AND DONNARAE MacCANN (essay date 1984)

[*Woodard is an American critic and educator. MacCann is an American author of books on children's literature. In the following excerpt, they discuss racism in* Huckleberry Finn.]

Scholars and other commentators have generally maintained that Mark Twain's *The Adventures of Huckleberry Finn* is a broadly humanistic document. Twain's ability as a humorist and stylist, his effective satires and his advocacy—at times—of improved conditions for Black Americans have contributed to this judgment.

However, in spite of the countless analyses of *Huck Finn,* the influence of ''blackface minstrelsy'' on this story is either barely mentioned or overlooked entirely, even though the tradition of white men blackening up to entertain other whites at the expense of Black people's humanity is at the center of *Huck Finn*'s portrayal of Jim and other Blacks. . . .

Minstrel performers were an important cultural influence in the last century. They were featured in circuses and other traveling shows, as well as in the afterpieces and entr'actes of the formal, ''high art'' theaters. . . .

Minstrel actors blackened their faces with burnt cork and wore outlandish costumes. They swaggered about the stage boasting nonsensically about minor accomplishments or fabricating tales of grandiose deeds; they had riotous celebrations; they mutilated the English language; and they quarreled vehemently over trivial issues.

Nineteenth century American minstrelsy drew upon European traditions of using the mask of blackness to mock individuals or social forces. The conventions of clowning also played a part, since clowns in many cultures have blackened or whitened their faces, exaggerated the appearance of the mouth, eyes and feet, used rustic dialects, and devised incongruous costumes. Clowns have filled a variety of social and aesthetic functions, but U.S. blackface performers have been unique in their single-minded derogation of an oppressed group. In the U.S., aspects of African American culture were incorporated into the minstrel routines in a highly distorted form. The resulting ridiculous or paternalistic portrayals of Black Americans were particularly appealing to the white theater-going audience. . . .

Twain called these blackface minstrel routines a ''joy.'' ''To my mind,'' he said, ''minstrelsy was a thoroughly delightful thing, and a most competent laughter-compeller. . . .'' He described the broad dialect as ''delightfully and satisfyingly funny.'' As to the typical violent quarrels between two minstrel protagonists, Twain wrote:

> . . . a delightful jangle of assertion and contradiction would break out between the two; the quarrel would gather emphasis, the voices would grow louder and louder and more and more energetic and vindictive, and the two would rise and approach each other, shaking fists and instruments and threatening bloodshed. . . . Sometimes the quarrel would last five minutes, the two contestants shouting deadly threats in each other's faces with their noses not six inches apart, the house shrieking with laughter all the while at this *happy and accurate imitation of the usual and familiar negro quarrel. . . .* [emphasis added]. . .

Twain wrote his laudatory remarks about minstrelsy in 1906, just four years before his death. Like many other authors, he was apparently influenced by this tradition throughout his life, even as he argued for more humane conditions for Black Americans and Africans.

Twain's own career as a stage performer gave him a close tie with minstrelsy. Stage performances were a major source of income and status for Twain, and these performances were often based on ''readings'' of his works, a ''lecture'' style that was extremely popular at that time. (p. 4)

It is not surprising to find that episodes in *Huck Finn* which read like skits in a minstrel show were probably written after most of the novel was completed, and at a time when Twain was planning a return to the stage with a new tour. These episodes—''King Sollermun,'' ''Balum's Ass,'' ''how a Frenchman doan' talk like a man,'' Jim's ''rescue'' by Huck and Tom Sawyer—would fit neatly into a Twain-style lecture tour, and it seems quite likely that they were created with the taste of theater audiences in mind.

The novel's concluding farcical scenes—in which Huck and Tom concoct a nonsensical plan to help Jim, the runaway slave—insured the book's success on and off the stage. As Twain wrote his wife about reading these rescue scenes: ''It is the biggest card I've got in my whole repertoire. I always thought so. It went abooming. . . .''

The depiction of Blacks in *Huck Finn* matches those of numerous minstrel plays in which Black characters are portrayed as addlebrained, boastful, superstitious, childish and lazy. These depictions are not used to poke fun at white attitudes about Black people; Jim is portrayed as a kindly comic who *does* act foolishly.

Early in the story, for example, Tom Sawyer moves Jim's hat to a nearby tree branch while he is sleeping. When Jim wakes he claims that witches put him in a trance and rode him over the state; he then elaborates this story several times until he finally claims that witches rode him all over the world and his back was ''all over saddleboils.''

Throughout the book, Jim is presented as foolish and gullible, given to exaggeration. After Jim and Huck get lost in the fog, an event Jim ''painted . . . up considerable,'' Huck tells Jim their frightening experience was only a dream. Jim believes him, even when he sees evidence that the experience was real:

> He had got the dream fixed so strong in his head that he couldn't seem to shake it loose and get the facts back into its place again right away.

Twain has already established that Huck fulfills the role of a youthful, ''unreliable'' narrator; however, these comments about Jim *seem* accurate because they are backed up by Jim's own befuddled statements and actions. For example, Jim exclaims: ''Is I *me,* or who *is* I? Is I heah, or what *is* I? Now dat's what I wants to know.''

Similarly, when the Duke and Dauphin come aboard the raft, Huck sees that they are ''lowdown humbugs and frauds,'' but says it ''warn't no use to tell Jim,'' who is childishly proud to serve royalty.

Chapter eight is like a whole series of minstrel routines. First Jim explains how he speculated in stock, but the stock—a cow—died. Then he invested in a banking operation run by a black swindler and lost more money. He gives his last dime to ''Balum's Ass; one er dem chuckleheads, you know. But he's luck, dey say. . . .'' Balum's Ass gives the dime to the church when he hears a preacher say ''whoever give to de po' len' to de Lord, en boun' to git his money back a hund'd times.''

The closing chapters serve a thematic purpose as Twain strengthens his attacks on the violence and hypocrisy of adult "civilization." Jim is a convenient instrument in the concluding burlesque, but his docile behavior reinforces his role as a dimwit—and hence as an audience pleaser. Jim could have walked away from his confinement many times, but he acts only under the direction of the white children—the implications being that he so dotes on the children that he will sacrifice his survival to their games, that he is helpless without white assistance and that he can think only on a child's level.

The farcical rescue scenes point up the unequal nature of the Huck/Jim relationship, but it is not the only time that Twain treats Huck and Jim as less than equal partners. For example, Huck makes no effort to find the raft after it is run down by a steamboat and the two are separated. He doesn't grieve over Jim's apparent death and doesn't express any relief when the two are reunited, although Jim nearly cries because he is so glad to see Huck alive.

Literary critics calling Jim the novel's one and only noble adult are usually focusing on Jim's kindness toward Huck and Tom. With that image in mind, critics credit Twain with a broadly liberal perspective, but in fact, the "sympathy" that *Huck Finn* evokes for Jim is part of what minstrelsy is all about. "Stage Negroes" were shaped by their creators, according to Alan Green, so that they *would* be viewed sympathetically. Who would not feel affection for a "permanently visible and permanently inferior clown who posed no threat and desired nothing more than laughter and applause at his imbecile antics"? Blacks had to be a source of hilarity for whites, says Green, in order for whites to cease feeling guilt and anxiety.

It's true that Jim is admirable because he is not an inveterate schemer, like most of the other people in the book. Jim also often makes more sense than other characters. For instance, when he argues with Huck about how Frenchmen talk, Jim is the more logical. But this debate "plays" like the dialogue in a minstrel show because Jim has the information base of a child (*i.e.*, Jim believes English to be the world's only language).

When Twain was working on *The Adventures of Tom Sawyer* in 1874, he wrote noted author and editor William Dean Howells, his literary advisor, about his technique: "I amend dialect stuff by talking and talking and *talking* it till it sounds right." The "right" sound, however, was the sound of a white person playing a "stage Negro"—a sound that fit white expectations. The mock Black "dialect" in *Huck Finn* turns the humor into caricature and makes Jim's every appearance stereotypical. Jim's language is largely made up of either so-called nonstandard words or so-called "eye dialect"—words that look peculiar in print, as when "wuz" replaces "was." This eye dialect reinforces the notion that a character is stupid rather than merely poorly educated.

When Huck and Jim are both satirized in the chapter on having "a general good time," the language tends to isolate Jim as a fool. Huck reads from books salvaged from a sinking steamboat and we see the highly nonsensical result of his learning experiences in a country school. Jim's garbled impression of the Scriptures is similarly revealed, and there is a nice give-and-take between the two vagabonds throughout the whole scene. But while we can easily laugh at Huck's very human confusion in this episode, it is more difficult to see the human side of Jim because of the exaggerated dialect. For example, Jim says:

> A harem's a bo'd'n-house, I reck'n. Mos' likely
> dey has rackety times in de nussery. En I reck'n

de wives quarrels considerable; en dat 'crease de racket. Yet dey say Sollermun de wises' man dat ever liv'. I doan' take no stock in dat. Bekase why: would a wise man want to live in de mids' er sich a blimblammin' all de time?

Jim's attempt to escape slavery contributes a strong element of suspense in the early part of the novel, and Twain has an opportunity to comment on that institution. To a certain degree Twain offers a comic/serious protest against slavery, although we must remember that this issue had been decided by the Civil War some 20 years earlier. There are some brilliantly ironic stabs at slavery, but the plot line that focuses on Jim's escape is scuttled when the Duke/Dauphin burlesque takes over. This plot change occurs at the very moment Jim and Huck might have escaped in a newly acquired canoe. Instead, Huck goes in search of strawberries and then performs one of the most illogical acts in the story: he brings the false Duke and Dauphin to the raft he and Jim are living on. If the original plot line had remained important, good-hearted Huck *might* have sympathized with the desperate con men and he *might* have rowed them to some safer location, but it is hard to believe that he would suddenly contradict all his efforts to keep Jim out of sight.

Twain scholar Henry Nash Smith argues that the escape plan is aborted because Huck and Jim are virtually the captives of the Duke and Dauphin. The text does not support this thesis, however, since Huck and Jim ignore several opportunities to follow though with their original plan while the Duke and Dauphin are working their confidence tricks on the river towns.

When Tom Sawyer reenters the story, Huck helps him carry out the farcical, futile escape plan. Because Jim's escape is not actually a high priority, Tom and Huck play at heroics based upon Tom's favorite adventure stories, affording Twain an opportunity to satirize such tales. When the boys actually release Jim, armed slavehunters are on the premises and the "rescue" has no chance of success. "The unhappy truth about the ending," writes Leo Marx in *The American Scholar*, ". . . is that the author, having revealed the tawdry nature of the culture of the great valley, yielded to its essential complacency" [see excerpt dated 1953].

Jim is in fact, finally free because his owner dies and frees him in her will. Thus his liberator turns out to be a slaveholder, the very sort, writes Leo Marx, "whose inhumanity first made the attempted escape necessary."

The fact that Huck decides to "go to hell" rather than turn Jim in—to make, in other words, an eternal sacrifice for Jim—is often treated by critics as a superb evocation of anti-slavery sentiment. But to reach this interpretation, readers must not only ignore the characterization of Jim; they must also arbitrarily withdraw their attention from Twain's thematic and narrative compromises throughout the last fifth of the novel. Since Huck's concern for Jim all but disappears in the farcical "rescue" sequence, and since it is finally a slaveholder who is presented as the true rescuer, the "going to hell" pronouncement seems more closely related to Twain's many satirical commentaries on religion than to an overriding interest in the slave question. (In the incomplete novel "Tom Sawyer's Conspiracy," Twain uses Tom and Huck brilliantly as a means of debunking religion, while Jim is again a minstrel side-kick.)

Because *Huck Finn* is very contradictory as an anti-slavery work, it is important for readers, and for teachers especially, to examine the larger context of the "freedom" theme. This means pin-pointing the text's cultural biases—the white supremacist beliefs which infuse the novel and which are not difficult to discover in a close reading. Notions of racial and cultural superiority appear in **Huck Finn** in the various ways that Twain undercuts Jim's humanity: in the minstrel routines with Huck as the "straight man," in the generalities about Blacks as unreliable, primitive and slow-witted, in the absence of appropriate adult/child roles, in Jim's vulnerability to juvenile trickery, and in the burlesqued speech patterns.

One of the most controversial aspects of **Huck Finn** is Twain's use of the term "nigger." As with every detail of the novel, the term needs to be examined in relation to its context. Huck uses "nigger" as it was used by white people to ridicule Blacks. When Huck says, "it was fifteen minutes before I could work myself up to go and humble myself to a nigger," he is rising slightly above his cultural conditioning by making an apology, but at the same time the reader sees him caught up in that bigoted culture by his use of a label that whites understood as pejorative.

A serious problem arises, however, in the fact that Jim refers to himself and other Blacks as "niggers," but the self-effacement inherent in his use of this term is not presented as a Black survival tactic. If Twain did not recognize the Black American use of such language as part of the "mask" worn to disarm whites, he was, like Huck, caught unwittingly in the bigoted system that he could not always transcend. If he understood this strategy, but left out any hint of this awareness in order to please a white audience, then he compromised his literary integrity. (pp. 5-7)

It is important here to note Twain's use of irony. Some statements which seem blatantly racist are the most highly ironic. For instance, when Huck responds to Aunt Sally's query about an accident, "Anybody hurt?" with the statement, "No'm. Killed a nigger," a double layer of irony strengthens Twain's commentary. Aunt Sally replies, "Well, it's lucky; because sometimes people do get hurt," and the reader can easily discern the social conditioning behind Huck's denial of Black humanity, as well as the extraordinary indifference that makes Aunt Sally's idea of "luck" a bitterly ironic indictment of slavery. Similarly, one of the most potent comments on slavery occurs when Jim threatens to steal his own children and Huck responds:

> Here was this nigger which I had as good as helped to run away, coming right out flat-footed and saying he would steal his children—children that belonged to a man I didn't even know; a man that hadn't ever done me no harm.
>
> (pp. 7-8)

When looking at **Huck Finn,** it is important to consider Twain's upbringing and milieu. Twain himself emphasized the importance of early "training." Significantly, he lamented the fact that his mother would never abandon her support of slavery, but he defended her by saying, "Manifestly, training and association can accomplish strange miracles." Huck himself emphasizes the importance of how people are "brung up." Tom was not "brung up" to free a "nigger" unless that slave was already legally free; the Dauphin was not "brung up" to deliver lines from Shakespeare properly; and kings, says Huck, "are a mighty ornery lot. It's the way they're raised." While Twain was in some respects a renegade, he was also "brung up" in a period in which opposition to slavery was a controversial

position, and in which sensitivity to other issues of racial injustice was severely limited. (p. 8)

Like many of his white contemporaries, Twain clearly had ambivalent attitudes about Blacks. On the one hand, we see his efforts to help Black college students financially, to aid a Black college, to publicly support the reputation of Black leader Frederick Douglass and to speak out boldly and progressively (*e.g.*, there is a "reparation due," said Twain, "from every white to every black man"). Yet he could not shake off some persistent white supremacist notions. In **Huck Finn,** Twain's ambivalence is recorded in the degrading minstrel elements on the one hand and in the anti-slavery theme on the other. (p. 10)

> *Frederick Woodard and Donnarae MacCann, "'Huckleberry Finn' and the Traditions of Black-face Minstrelsy," in* Interracial Books for Children Bulletin, *Vol. 15, Nos. 1 & 2, 1984, pp. 4-13.*

J. C. FURNAS (essay date 1985)

[*Furnas is an American novelist, biographer, critic, and historian. In the following excerpt, he provides a retrospective of criticism on* Huckleberry Finn *and the critical issues and controversies surrounding the novel. Excerpts from many of the critical commentaries mentioned or alluded to by Furnas may be found in the Mark Twain entries included in* TCLC, *Volumes 6 and 12, as well as in the present volume.*]

Credentials first: I am a Finnophile first-class. At the age of nine in a Pullman car on the way to Florida in 1915, I read **The Adventures of Huckleberry Finn** (Tom Sawyer's Comrade) and have never been the same since. The ensuing seventy years have widened my acquaintance with American literature. Yet if forced to choose only one piece of American writing to be spared from an otherwise clean-sweep annihilation, I'd never hesitate. For many that is at least an understandable choice. It is anything but original. Long since, H. L. Mencken, T. S. Eliot, Ernest Hemingway, F. R. Leavis ("one of the great books of the world") have celebrated it far beyond my poor power to add or to detract. Yet if most of what is usually promulgated about that remarkable work is sound, we primitive Finnophiles are dismayingly misguided.

Late last year while having a nightcap with a college classmate of whom I see less than I'd like, I learned for the first time, though not to my surprise, that he agreed that, alone among Mark Twain's works, **Huckleberry Finn** does justice to his extraordinary talent. We got to quoting chunks of it to each other: The loafers' drowsy maunderings at the ferry landing; Pap's blast at the "govment"; Jim's contempt for the wisdom of Sollermun; the lovely passage beginning, "It was a monstrous big river down there. . . ." We further agreed that today's—and yesterday's as far back as the 1920s—accepted wisdom about the book not only misrepresents but obscures its virtues.

Maybe we were experiencing ESP. A few days later my *New York Times Book Review* proclaimed a landmark of which we had been unaware—1985 as the hundredth anniversary of the American publication of **Huckleberry Finn.** The same annus mirabilis also included the hundredth birthday of Ring Lardner and the three hundredth of Johann Sebastian Bach and George Frideric Handel. All received appropriate attention. But when the final precincts have reported, **Huckleberry Finn** will probably be a squeakily close second, at worst. The University of California Press published three new editions with various refinements. The University of Missouri Press published a twenty-five-warhead book of essays on Huck. Chicago's Goodman Theatre revived a stage version produced by the local Organic Theatre ten years ago; Huck got double publicity from that, for inevitably it revived the controversy over whether its consistent use of *nigger* makes him unacceptable. A vast musical version alleged to cost three million dollars came to Broadway. The National Geographic Society set up a **Huckleberry Finn** exhibit in Washington. It felt as though Tom Sawyer had called in a Madison Avenue PR wizard to make sure Huck got his centenary just due. Heaven knows he deserves it, heaped up and running over—but a *just* due. Too often the terms in which he is celebrated make one wonder what book the climbers on the bandwagon are talking about.

For, all too many of them, however sure they are that it is a masterpiece, cannot accept it as is—an unruly, lopsided, half-inadvertent joy too sui generis to hold still even for the label "picaresque novel." Only its brilliant central portion carries the full range of its virtues. The first twenty-five pages are just warmed-over **Tom Sawyer**. When Pap arrives in Huck's bedroom, the magic begins and weaves gorgeous spells for more than two hundred pages. But the concluding ninety pages, though sometimes irresponsibly funny, are an exasperating reprise of Tom Sawyerishness that, as Stephen Leacock said and Ernest Hemingway agreed, spoils things.

That is the work under discussion. The reader is assumed to be well versed in it. The underprivileged (those who are certain about who Mrs. Judith Loftus was) are urged to do themselves the favor of rereading.

After some preliminary rumblings, the tonesetting opening gun of the doings came when the *New York Times Book Review* asked Norman Mailer to celebrate **Huckleberry Finn**. Most of his piece whimsically sketched its influence on American writing. But his last two paragraphs took off into what I had been flinchingly expecting—a rehash of orthodox criticism that set the keynote:

> Few works of literature can be so luminous without the presence of some majestic symbol. . . . We are presented with the best river ever to flow through a novel . . . larger than a character, the river is a manifest presence, a demiurge to support the man and the boy, a deity to betray them, feed them, all but drown them, fling them apart, float them back together. The river winds like a fugue through the marrow of the true narrative which is nothing less than the ongoing relation between Huck and the runaway slave, this Nigger Jim whose name embodies the very stuff of the slave system itself—his name is not Jim but Nigger Jim. The growth of love and knowledge between the runaway white and the runaway black is . . . full of betrayal and nourishment, separation and return. So it manages to touch that last fine nerve of the heart where compassion and irony speak to one another and thereby give a good turn to our most protected emotions.

> . . . One comes to realize all over again that the near-burned-out, throttled, hate-filled affair between whites and blacks is still our great national love-affair. . . . **Huckleberry Finn** frees us to think of democracy and its sublime, terrifying promise.

Mailer flawed his credentials as a Finnophile by admitting that at the age of ten or so he much enjoyed **Tom Sawyer,** but **Huckleberry Finn** as a sequel sadly disappointed him; and then in college he was puzzled by the high regard nearly everyone who taught American Lit. "professed for it. Obviously I was waiting for an assignment from the New York Times." (That is the reverse of my experience; I read **Tom Sawyer** second and thought it much inferior, and still do.) Evidence is strong that Mailer not only reread the book at the paper's behest but also explored the commentaries with which critical enterprise has cumbered it. Maybe he also recalled bits of those American Lit. lectures in Sever Hall. Anyway, the above carries the authentic flavor of not a justified Finnophilia but an overwrought Finnomania.

For a symptomatic error: Mailer's overplayed "Nigger Jim" motif has no standing in court. No such label appears in **Huckleberry Finn**. It is exactly wrong to say "his name is not Jim but Nigger Jim." Lowercase "nigger" is freely used, of course, as an intrinsic (however distasteful nowadays) part of Huck's supple, shapely, back-homey idiom. Others, black and white, refer to Jim as "nigger"; but Mark Twain's text designates him only as "Jim" or "Miss Watson's Jim"; no racial tag, no capitalized "Nigger Jim" to make him the archetype symbol of black slavery. The only capitalization involved is his notion that to achieve freedom will make him rich, for he will then own himself, and a slave trader had offered Miss Watson $800 for him. Yet that "Nigger Jim" distortion is curiously common in the accumulated literature—used by, among others, Hemingway, Ralph Ellison, Lionel Trilling, Leslie Fiedler. It typifies in miniature the liberties so often taken with the book in hopes of squaring it with such critical clichés as Mailer purveys in dwelling on the river-as-symbol and the erotic overtones of black/white. The prurient tingle in that last may stem from Fiedler's essay, conspicuous a generation ago, "Come Back to the Raft Ag'in, Huck Honey"—a model of impertinence (in both senses) that lumped Huck/Jim, Ishmael/Queequeg, Leather-Stocking/Chingachgook, and Dana/Hope as intertwisted symbols of latent homosexuality in cronyism between whites and nonwhites.

But the general tenor of Mailer's overture actually goes back much further, almost three generations, to Waldo Frank's *Our America* (1919). Its hot-news statement was that **Huckleberry Finn** is:

> the voice of American chaos. . . . Mark Twain had meant it for the mere sequel of another tale . . . but his theme was too apt a symbol. . . . Huck is America. And Huck floats down the current of a mighty Stream . . . is the American epic hero . . . an illiterate lad . . . expresses our germinal past . . . the movement of the American soul through all the sultry climates of the Nineteenth Century. . . . The whole gamut of American beginnings ran with the river. And Huck along. One rises from the book lost in a great rhythmic flow . . . and upon the heaving surface of this Flood . . . the American soul like a midge upon the tide of the world.

That really belongs in the *New Yorker*'s "How's That Again?" department. How can chaos have anything so integrated as a voice? "The whole gamut of American beginnings"? For its first century and a half our America had little to do with the Mississippi. "One rises from the book lost in a great rhythmic flow"? One does so deploring Mark Twain's imposing on the reader that coda of thirty-thousand words of contrived farce. "Illiterate lad"? Frank must have meant *uncultivated,* for Huck has learned to read and write; his gleanings from the books found in the wrecked steamboat set off entertaining discussion between him and Jim. About the only element that stands scrutiny is the description of the Father of Waters as a "mighty Stream." It was those wild swings that not only began but have permeated in spirit the tradition of irresponsible rhapsody ever since, enhancing the epiphany of *Huckleberry Finn:* no gold and no myrrh, but lots of Frankincense.

Until *Our America* set those symbols tinkling, Finnophiles had been content to call the book something gloriously close to the Great American Novel that literary patriots longed for. By 1913, for instance, John Macy, eminent critic and liberal friend of good writing, rated it "the greatest piece of American fiction . . . one of the unaccountable triumphs of creative power that happen now and again." But once Frank had shown the way to lily gilding, throngs of disciples came heaping their extravagances—some imitative, some innovative—on their leader's. Thirty years ago Leo Marx had reason to complain that "the problem of evaluating the book is as much obscured by unqualified praise as it once was by parochial hostility"—meaning that hostility of the librarians of the 1890s who rejected it as "unqualified trash." Further apropos, Kenneth S. Lynn later protested that "the only trash connected with *Huckleberry Finn* is what emanates from the teachers thereof" and ascribed at least part of the trouble to "professional interpreters of literature [lacking] a sense of humor."

Among them such interpreters have given Ole Man River quite a beating, working up the world's first 2,348-mile cliché. Though Macy had early deplored a tendency to call *Huckleberry Finn* "an Odyssey of the Mississippi," in 1931 Constance Rourke's widely acclaimed *American Humor* said it "gave to the great flood of the Mississippi an elementary place in the American experience, with the river a dominating fantasy, with the small human figures as prototypes of those untethered wanderers who had appeared so often on the popular horizon." If that really means anything, it casts Huck, Jim, Huck's drunken rattlesnake of a father, and Colonel Sherburn as abstract walk-ons in a World's Fair pageant cobbled together round a river theme. Ever since, the symbol seekers have clogged the Mississippi with pretentious metaphor and simile; a fair sample is Pascal Covici's: "Just as the river flows between slave and free territory [as it doesn't during most of the book], so Huck's soul balances between an infinite series of opposites."

F. R. Leavis took high ground when seeing in Huck's story "a central theme . . . the complexity of ethical values in a society with a complex tradition." Trilling raised the ante: the novel "has the truth of moral passion [and] . . . deals directly with the virtue and depravity of man's heart." His credentials were better than Mailer's: "One may read [*Huckleberry Finn*] at ten and then annually ever after, and each year find that it is as fresh as before." But he goes on, ominously, "Each year adds a new growth of meaning," and likens the first-time reader to an Athenian boy growing up with the *Odyssey.* To cue in his river motif, Trilling quotes Eliot about the Mississippi as "a strong brown god" and proceeds: "Huck himself is the servant of the river-god and he comes very close to being aware of the divine nature of the being he serves. . . . The river itself is only divine; it is not ethical and good. But its nature seems to foster the goodness of those who love it and try to fit themselves into its ways." This could be a Wagnerian libretto starring Heidi.

Trilling also joined the movement to inflate Jim into a figure from an anti-racist WPA mural: "In Jim [Huck] finds his true father . . . the boy and the negro slave form a family, a primitive community—and it is a community of saints." Somewhat later Kenneth Rexroth formally ushered Huck's adventures into the lecture-room Valhalla: "It would have been impossible for Mark Twain not to have had Homer constantly in mind. . . . Huck and Jim are obviously Crusoe and Friday reborn. . . . Twain's novel occupies the same symbolic universe as Whitman's *Passage to India.*" No doubt Sam Clemens read one or another translation of Homer, but I know of nothing in his writings to show it. And if there are two important American writers less alike than Mark Twain and Walt Whitman, it would have to be Finley Peter Dunne and Theodore Dreiser.

The effect—and doubtless the purpose—of all that sort of thing is so to blur the actual nature of the text in question that it will sound like a blend of *Moby-Dick* and *Uncle Tom's Cabin* ghosted by Thomas Wolfe, its chief merits consisting of the river-symbolism and the way Nigger Jim as essence of black slavery causes Huck's soul to bud and blossom. That might make a notable book, but it would not be *Huckleberry Finn.* If it were, those elements would dominate the text; whereas, in fact, of its roughly one hundred and ten thousand words, a rough workup shows only three thousand dealing with the river in any manner suggesting a pervasive symbol; and only twenty-two hundred dealing with slavery, including the deservedly famous long passage about Huck's decision to go to hell in order to stay on Jim's side. Clearly the river and Jim-as-slave are only minor, though priceless, matters recurring off and on—indeed hit-or-miss—in an overflowing, rambling yarn.

Waldo Frank, Lionel Trilling, and Norman Mailer may serve as benchmarks between which some sixty years of academic busywork has evolved several other gratuitous mythologies. More may be hovering, for so far, nobody has imaginatively exploited the book's thunderstorms, a specialty of Mark Twain's. (And how well he did them!) His patent delight in meteorological turmoil could afford some candidate for a Ph.D. God-knows-what pregnant surmises. For present purposes, however, most of the orthodox range is succinctly packaged in a purchase I recently made at the bookstore of a famous university town: *Cliffs Notes on Huckleberry Finn* by James L. Roberts of the University of Nebraska's department of English—one of that teeming series of handbooks supplying apprehensive students with synopses of and deep thoughts about *Beowulf, The Catcher in the Rye, Anna Karenina, Don Quixote.* . . . Its text is unsettlingly shaky on the exact meanings of words, using *persecute* for *prosecute, instigate* for *initiate, imitate* for *impersonate* and calls the King's and the Duke's treacherous sale of Jim back into slavery their "final calumny." But it is a thorough $2.75 worth.

Dutifully it leads off with ". . . the Odyssey down the river . . . immediately takes upon [*sic*] a mythical quality" and touches all bases from then on. "Birth and rebirth" are soon symbolizing away, starting when Huck fakes being murdered to get away from Pap and then, on Jackson's Island, enjoys the attempt to find his presumably waterlogged body. Every time he assumes a false identity to get out of trouble, birth and rebirth raise their chubby little hands. Pap carries two layers of significance: first he symbolizes the brutality of the civilization that Huck mistrusts—Pap being the least civilized figure Mark Twain could draw—then later is alleged to provide an antithetic parallel to Jim's dismay over having struck his deaf daughter. The name of the wrecked steamboat, *Walter Scott,* betokens Mark Twain's scorn for the Author of *Waverley*. The ease with which the King and the Duke impose on others shows how "only through the sentimentalizing and the gullibility of the general public can such rogues flourish." Huck's shying away from "sivilization" correlates with Jim's "quest of freedom from slavery." The fits of loneliness that Huck, reasonably enough, associates with the unrelievedly empty expanse of river must be further linked to "the vastness of the frontier . . . and the formidable forests which surrounded the settlements"—neither of which elements has a part in the story. The masterly pages about the Grangerford house and Emmeline as poet and artist—one of the most delightful pieces of writing in English—are adduced merely as part "of Twain's technique of using Huck as a realistic reporter . . . [and] satire against those who have . . . bad taste in almost everything." The undertaker, rat, and dog at the Wilks funeral—one of the funniest things ever written—is solemnly identified as "the first significant American satire on the sentimentality of funeral customs." All this is derivative, of course, distilled off from a mash of the handbook's elders and betters; but that makes it an invaluable museum of Finnomania.

Those *Cliffs Notes* thus supply what it is advisable to regurgitate at exam time. But this *Huckleberry Finn* item will soon need revision. That fresh-off-the-press *Hundred Years of Huckleberry Finn* has added to the compost 180,000 more words from twenty-five qualified scholars.

The editor's preface asks: "Do we really need . . . another couple of dozen essays on that novel" and then assures itself that the following contributions triumphantly show "how inexhaustible a source of the need for fresh commentary *The Adventures of Huckleberry Finn* has been, is, no doubt will be." No doubt. Once established, perpetual motion takes a lot of braking.

Allison R. Ensor's able account of the illustrations that have visually interpreted Huck, Jim, Aunt Sally, et al. over the last century has value for even the mere Finnophile. So has David Sewell's expert discussion of the subtle variations of Mark Twain's manipulations of language. Beyond that, however, the book suggests numerous well-meaning blind men so engrossed in elaborating farfetched insights that if the elephant were to walk out on them they'd hardly notice.

Among them a certain professor of English, who dabbles in psychoanalysis and naturally leans heavily on Freud's *Totem and Taboo*, describes Huck as testing "the affection of Jim, his totemic second father, in the masculine Sacred Forest of Jackson's Island, then in the feminine coils of the river monster." But it is an unalloyed professor of English who, noting that the late Peter Wilks left three daughters, suggests that the whole Wilks episode is "an inverse duplication of King Lear." For another professor, the name Finn, admittedly drawn from the town drunk of Mark Twain's boyhood, nevertheless implies "Huck's association with the river and the fish on which he and Jim depend . . . with its reference to a legendary Gaelic warrior . . . it also implies that a former grandeur lies behind the family debased by . . . Pap Finn." Still another professor treats Pap at more respectful length in his highly original analysis of an alcoholic psychopath: he represents "anarchic individualism . . . because he feels none of the positive ties of family and affection. . . ."

Though he has had no academic training, Huck comes up with some pretty breathless subtleties; for instance, he detects "an underlying kinship between Emmeline's speedy tributes for

[*sic*] the dead and Buck's monomaniacal haste to kill a Shepherdson." From observing the King and the Duke he deduces "that the confidence man is no longer a marginal predator but a national symbol of the American character." Or, less actively, in the trendy light of the 1980s, he "represents the typically helpless victim of a world in which nightmare, absurd quests for identity, alienation, and apocalypse are the facts of daily life." But he comes down with a thud as still another essayist denigrates him and associates: He is only "a dimly comprehending fumbler and stooge"; Tom Sawyer "a dominating knave"; Jim "a victim." Indeed Tom is "the true protagonist" of this novel—in which he appears in less than a third of its length.

These givers of good measure customarily speak as though the patterns they ascribe to the text are Mark Twain's doing. If so, in writing *Huckleberry Finn* he consciously meant: to teach "that whereas utopianism is possible, utopians are not"; to "lead us to comprehend how the Civil War was possible"; to inculcate "the hard lessons about accumulated wealth that he thought Americans . . . were in need of learning." Even a temporary reference to the biblical Moses in the early section is seized on as Mark Twain's "clear prefiguration of Huck's . . . mission . . . helping Jim to gain freedom." And—take a long breath here—the book as a whole embodies his "understanding of human life . . . as . . . a precarious continuity in which identity is maintained only by our willingness to accept definition of ourselves from the norms of society and the expectations of others." Now exhale.

The other possibility is, of course, that such speculations detect and describe the symptoms of subliminal struggles within the writer's mind or emotional depths, however labeled, which implies that, among them, this scratch committee of earnest specialists in literature can deduce from the outside and, long after the fact, what Mark Twain had in mind, or what his maimed psyche hoped to saddle him with. It all makes *Huckleberry Finn* a cryptopsychodrama riding seven mutually contradictory ways at once. Fortunately we don't need to guess what Mark Twain would have said about this amateur psychiatrists' grab bag. He led off the first edition of *Huckleberry Finn* with this "Notice": "Persons attempting to find a motive in this narrative will be prosecuted; persons attempting to find a moral in it will be banished; persons attempting to find a plot in it will be shot." And you should see what ingenious squirmings occur when a loyal significance seeker goes to the mat with that.

Another gnarly problem for the *Huckleberry Finn* industry is that brought up by *Cliffs Notes* in review question number nine, as well as by several of the experts in *One Hundred Years of Huckleberry Finn*: "If the purpose of the trip down the river is to gain freedom for Jim, why do they continue deeper and deeper into slave territory?"

The simple, maybe adequate, answer is that Mark Twain usually wrote in bursts of improvisation. He was not the man to bother reflecting that, if keeping Jim from being sold down the river—his stated reason for running away—was primary, all he had to do the first dark night was catch a drift log and swim to the free-soil Illinois shore from Jackson's Island before Huck ever found him there. Indeed, Jim makes it clear that he has some such intention: "I'd . . . swim asho', en take to de woods on de Illinois side." Had he thus tried his luck, however, all Mark Twain's suddenly new plans for Huck and Jim together would have miscarried. Further, this question illuminates the book's inadequacy as the sermon-after-the-fact against slavery that it is often thought to be; as a devoted student of it recently wrote: "The principal purpose was to describe an ignorant 14-year-old boy's awakening to the injustices of slavery." That is a worthy purpose, and Mark Twain had come to hate what slavery had been, as certain of his other works show. But if that was what he had in mind for *Huckleberry Finn*, he had a strange way of going at it.

Back to review question number nine. It is likely that, on picking up the unfinished draft of *Huckleberry Finn* after it had lain fallow for years, he sent Huck and Jim's raft past Cairo, the last vestige of free soil, because he was obeying an imperative impulse to show readers the raffish settlements along the lower Mississippi that he had known as a river pilot. Since this resulted in the central narrative that is perhaps America's best book, *bravo!* But it blurred the values of Jim's predicament. Worse, Tom Sawyer reenters the story fifty thousand words later and embarks on frivolous claptrap to free Jim in spite of Tom's being aware, as Huck and Jim are not, that on her deathbed Miss Watson has already freed him. Those capers cut the emotional ground from under the freedom-for-good-old-Jim issue and identify Mark Twain as the most irresponsible great writer since Shakespeare, who was so heedless about the way his plays got printed. Yet, the over-subtilizers being what they are, many a critic unable to accept this has sought to maintain that, looked at creatively, the misbegotten ending really symbolizes the values of the trip-down-the-river—or some such casuistry. Whereas what Leo Marx wrote thirty years ago remains starkly true: "To take seriously what happens on the Phelps farm is to take lightly the entire downstream journey."

Huck's growing affection for Jim and Jim's loyalty to Huck creep up on the reader just as they should. That has set certain observers—most cogently Philip Foner—nominating him the hero of the story. Even if one limits "hero" to the classic meaning of "principal male character," the notion is unsound; if there is a hero, Huck is it. That Mark Twain had nothing like a Jim-hero in mind is obvious, as the Tomfoolery on the Phelps place leaches away the dignity that Huck has sensed in Jim during the trip down the river. The basis for Jim-as-hero was scant anyway. The first few pages show him as pretentiously self-impressed by his own exaggerations of superstitious delusions. Some of the E. W. Kemble illustrations that Mark Twain personally insisted on (more numerous in the first edition than in subsequent trade editions) make Jim a pop-eyed, grinning semi-caricature. Saying that he was "white inside" and "had an uncommon level head for a nigger" is as far as Huck goes toward what today's standards would prefer. Toward the end Jim regains some dignity by risking return to slavery in order to get Tom's wound looked after. By the last time we see him, he has reverted to the chuckleheaded superstitions of the first chapter. In *Tom Sawyer Abroad*, a feeble sequel, Mark Twain returns him to the kind of dispute that led Huck to say: "You can't learn a nigger to argue." Ralph Ellison had cause to write: "I could imagine myself as Huck Finn . . . but not Nigger Jim . . . a white man's inadequate portrait of a slave."

The customary Huck image also shows disconcerting flaws. Can "the sensitive and suffering Huck" really serve as "a conscience for an entire era and culture," as Frank Baldanza asserted? DeLancey Ferguson was much closer to the actuality: Mark Twain, he writes, "simply took a clever and uninhibited boy and let the whole world of the Mississippi happen to him." His willingness to go to hell for Jim is notably overplayed. It is not mounting revulsion against slavery, as such, but generous defiance for personal reasons of the "sivilization" that he already dislikes and of which slavery, as he knows it, is an integral part. Trilling saw this: "He no more condemns slavery than Tristram and Lancelot condemn marriage." What happens to Huck is often character revealing, never character developing—never a flash of light on the road to Damascus. It is often laid down that major characters in great fictions should mature or degenerate or somehow shift levels of emotional leverage. By that criterion this very great fiction falls short. Huck begins and ends as the atomic, incorrigible maverick, an archetype that, one hopes—anxiously—can resist any amount of academic wear and tear.

Discussion of what Huck would do or feel under given circumstances is, of course, a tribute to his creator. Thus to be speculated about like a real person happens to only the aristocracy of fictional characters: Hamlet, Falstaff, Iago, Rebecca Sharp, Beatrix Esmond, Anna Karenina, Julien Sorel. . . . In that fourth dimension not only is personality distilled to a proof higher than real people usually show, it can also jar the rest of the cast into acting over their heads. One comes to know Queen Gertrude only after Hamlet drags her into his magnetic field. That is why none of Mark Twain's major characters outside *Huckleberry Finn*—not Roxy or Hank Morgan or Colonel Sellers—persists in the memory like the minor ones passing through Huck's orbit: not only Jim and Pap, but Mrs. Loftus and Aunt Sally and even Buck Harkness, that paragon of trenchant pantomime.

Those special vividnesses come of refraction through the pellucid but also prismatic Huck-medium in the first person. This kind of narrative makes two stern demands: The narrator, like Huck, may say he is writing for print, but his text must come out like speech sublimated without losing texture and informality. And all the while he chats away, his soul and ways of thinking and feeling must covertly emerge until the reader knows him rather better than he probably knows himself. In all those respects Huck sits among the royalty of first-persons, along with Barry Lyndon, Lorelei Lee, Gully Jimson, and Jack Keefe. This is fast company, but his way with his unadorned native speech is beyond comment. Its virtues persist in many pages of that misbegotten final section as a half reason for being reconciled to its presence. Under his surefooted sentences well up the many affinities of congenial words and the unaccountable, ever-various throb of our astonishing native tongue. In the last few pages before Tom's jiggery-pokery begins, Huck is reconnoitering the Phelps plantation:

> It was all still and Sunday-like, and hot and sunshiny; the hands was gone to the fields; and there was that kind of faint dronings of bugs and flies in the air that makes it seem so lonesome and like everybody's dead and gone; and if a breeze fans along and quivers the leaves it makes you feel mournful because you feel like it's spirits whispering—spirits that's been dead ever so many years—and you always think they're talking about *you*. As a general thing it makes a body wish *he* was dead too, and done with it all. . . . I went around and clumb over the back-stile by the ash-hopper and started for the kitchen. When I got a little ways I heard the dim hum of a spinning wheel wailing up and sinking along down again; and then I knowed for certain I wished I was dead—for that *is* the lonesomest sound in the world.

Never mind the ash-hopper and the spinning wheel and the superstitious set of the poor-white mind as cultural data. The same voice in other keys can strike brisk and savory: a certain kind of meat tastes like "old cold cannibal"; the King and the Duke "took on about that dead tanner like they'd lost the twelve disciples"; "most folks don't go to church only when they've got to, but a hog is different." Hats off. Shoes off the feet. That bush is really burning.

Strange that all those hundreds of thousands of words conscientiously spun out about *Huckleberry Finn* for the edification of others should practically ignore the things that make it great. The spinners necessarily suggest the proverbial musicologist so intent on the score that he doesn't hear the music. Indeed in this case, the score has small relation to the music: not enough river, too little anti-slavery parable. . . . What's printed in the novel seems far from what Professor Procrustes was lecturing about yesterday. In that sense Mailer may have been right about his American Lit. first time around.

Such muttering is probably futile. Literary fashions, like others, have their own momentum. That new *Huckleberry Finn* musical is entitled—what else?—*Big River*. George F. Will, the *Newsweek* columnist, weighs in asking: "Is the steamboat that wrecks Huck's raft—his pristine island of self-government— a symbol of the machine destroying Huck's garden?" Whereas years ago Justin Kaplan cast that steamboat as "the image of avenging society." Whereas, further, in *Hundred Years* Jeffrey Steinbrink suggests that the smashup betokens "a frenzy of anger, frustration, and resignation" overcoming Mark Twain because his plot wouldn't behave to suit him. Actually what it probably symbolizes is the storyteller's wish to get Huck ashore without Jim so he can spend a while with the Grangerfords.

The Finnophile can only stubbornly stand on the credo drawn up by Bernard DeVoto, a sound, if often overextended, stalwart: "There is a type of mind, the lovers of *Huckleberry Finn* belong to it, which prefers experience to metaphysical abstractions and the thing to its symbol. Such minds think of *Huckleberry Finn* as the greatest work of nineteenth century fiction in America precisely because it is not a voyage in pursuit of a white whale but a voyage among feudists, mobbers, thieves, rogues, nigger-hunters and murderers, precisely because Huck never encounters a symbol but always some actual human being working out an actual destiny."

Huck called the King's running off at the mouth at the Wilk's house "soul-butter and hogwash." That phrase kept occurring to me as I prowled back through the thickets of Frankincense. (pp. 517-24)

> *J. C. Furnas, "The Crowded Raft: 'Huckleberry Finn' & Its Critics," in* The American Scholar, *Vol. 54, No. 4, Autumn, 1985, pp. 517-24.*

ADDITIONAL BIBLIOGRAPHY

Altenbernd, Lynn. "Huck Finn, Emancipator." *Criticism* I, No. 4 (Fall 1959): 298-307.
  Maintains that the ending of *Huckleberry Finn* is an allegory of the Civil War.

Alter, Robert. "Heirs of the Tradition." In his *Rogue's Progress: Studies in the Picaresque Novel*, pp. 106-34. Cambridge, Mass.: Harvard University Press, 1964.*
  Contends that "the picaresque tradition [realized] a kind of apotheosis in Mark Twain's *Huckleberry Finn*" and that Huck "is an embodiment of all the virtues potential in the distinctively picaresque situation."

Auden, W. H. "Huck and Oliver." *The Listener* L, No. 1283 (1 October 1953): 540-41.
  Contrasts the typically American attitudes evidenced in *Huckleberry Finn* toward nature, morality, time, and money with their European counterparts. Auden finds in the novel's conclusion "a kind of sadness, as if freedom and love were incompatible."

Barchilon, Jose and Kovel, Joel S. "*Huckleberry Finn*: A Psychoanalytic Study." *Journal of the American Psychoanalytic Association* 14, No. 4 (October 1966): 775-814.
  Psychoanalytic study of the novel's main characters.

Barnett, Louise K. "Huck Finn: Picaro as Linguistic Outsider." *College Literature* VI, No. 3 (Fall 1979): 221-31.
  Examines the conflict between Huck and society in terms of language, asserting that the language of society serves primarily to reinforce group values and attitudes rather than to convey truth, and that Huck's ultimate withdrawal from civilization "is a fitting response to a society of fools and knaves and to that language which serves their purposes."

Bell, Millicent. "*Huckleberry Finn*: Journey without End." *The Virginia Quarterly Review* 58, No. 2 (Spring 1982): 253-67.
  Maintains that Huck's rejection of the society represented by Tom results in a loss of identity, which is regained at the end of the novel by Huck's "last relapse, nearly without protest, into the character of Tom Sawyer's comrade, accepting Tom's name and serving Tom's imagination."

Bellamy, Gladys Carmen. "Acceptance *versus* Rejection." In her *Mark Twain as a Literary Artist*, pp. 326-51. Norman: University of Oklahoma Press, 1950.
  Discusses *Huckleberry Finn* in terms of its "three thematic units": the episodes in St. Petersburg, the journey downriver, and Jim's escape from the Phelps farm.

Bier, Jesse. "'Bless You Chile': Fiedler and 'Huck Honey' a Generation Later." *Mississippi Quarterly* XXXIV, No. 4 (Fall 1981): 456-62.
  Response to Leslie Fiedler's 1948 essay "Come Back to the Raft Ag'in, Huck Honey!" [see *TCLC*, Vol. 6] in which Fiedler alleged a homoerotic relationship between Huck and Jim. Bier argues that Jim's relationship to Huck is that of a surrogate father rather than a lover.

Blackburn, Alexander. "The Symbolic Confidence Man." In his *The Myth of the Picaro: Continuity and Transformation of the Picaresque Novel, 1554-1954*, pp. 145-200. Chapel Hill: University of North Carolina Press, 1979.*
  Considers *Huckleberry Finn* "almost a nihilistic book," arguing that Huck's decision to help Jim escape is a surrender to conscience through which Huck "loses forever the power to be Huck, a free human being capable of choice."

Blair, Walter. *Mark Twain and Huck Finn*. Berkeley and Los Angeles: University of California Press, 1960, 436 p.
  Examines "the forces which gave *Adventures of Huckleberry Finn* its substance and form"—specifically, Twain's life, reading, and other writings between 1874 and 1884.

Browne, Ray B. "Huck's Final Triumph." *Ball State Teachers College Forum* VI, No. 1 (Winter 1965): 3-12.
  Contends that the novel's main theme is Huck's search for intellectual and spiritual freedom from the civilization of the antebellum South, and demonstrates the novel's ending to be necessary to the development of this theme.

Brownell, Frances V. "The Role of Jim in *Huckleberry Finn*." *Boston University Studies in English* I (Spring-Summer 1955): 74-83.
  Maintains that Jim's primary function in the novel is to "further the characterization of Huckleberry Finn: by his presence, his personality, his actions, his words, to call forth from Huckleberry

Finn a depth of tenderness and moral strength that could not otherwise have been fully and convincingly revealed to the reader."

Cecil, L. Moffitt. "The Historical Ending of *Adventures of Huckleberry Finn:* How Nigger Jim Was Set Free." *American Literary Realism 1870-1910* XIII, No. 2 (Autumn 1980): 280-83.
    Finds Jim's emancipation to be a symbolic representation of the abolition of slavery.

Christopher, J. R. "On the *Adventures of Huckleberry Finn* as a Comic Myth." *Cimarron Review,* No. 18 (January 1972): 18-27.
    Analyzes the novel in terms of Northrup Frye's theory of the comic myth.

Cox, James M. "Southwestern Vernacular." In his *Mark Twain: The Fate of Humor,* pp. 156-84. Princeton, N.J.: Princeton University Press, 1966.
    Discusses Twain's integration of serious themes into the humorous narrative of *Huckleberry Finn.*

Fetterley, Judith. "Disenchantment: Tom Sawyer in *Huckleberry Finn."* *Publications of the Modern Language Association* 87, No. 1 (January 1972): 69-74.
    Examines Tom's transformation from an imaginative leader in *Tom Sawyer* to a petty tyrant obsessed with a strict code of right and wrong in *Huckleberry Finn.* Fetterley concludes that Twain reveals through Tom, as well as through the Grangerfords and Miss Watson, "his sense of the inevitable connection between moralism, the language of right and wrong with its inevitable concomitant of self-righteousness, and the fact, the act, of aggression."

Frantz, Ray W. "The Role of Folklore in *Huckleberry Finn."* *American Literature* XXVIII, No. 3 (November 1956): 314-27.
    Demonstrates how Twain's use of folklore is important to the development of the novel's structure, plot, themes, and characters.

Fraser, John. "In Defence of Culture: *Huckleberry Finn."* *The Oxford Review,* No. 6 (Michaelmas 1967): 5-22.
    Counters prevailing critical opinion in asserting that the book is neither an attack on romanticism nor an attack on culture.

Gargano, James W. "Disguises in *Huckleberry Finn."* *The University of Kansas City Review* XXVI, No. 3 (March 1960): 175-78.
    Observes that the many situations in the novel in which characters assume disguises in order to manipulate others "are not merely humorous interludes; they are the vehicle of Twain's indictment of human dissimulation and gullability."

Geismar, Maxwell. "The River and the Raft." In his *Mark Twain: An American Prophet,* pp. 66-109. Boston: Houghton Mifflin Co., 1970.
    Discusses the writing of *Huckleberry Finn* and the novel's principal themes and techniques.

Gerber, John C., ed. *The Merrill Studies in "Huckleberry Finn."* Columbus, Ohio: Charles E. Merrill Publishing Co., 1971, 121 p.
    Selected criticism from 1885 to 1968, including essays by Van Wyck Brooks ("Mark Twain: A Frustrated Spirit"), H. L. Mencken ("One of the Great Masterpieces of the World"), and Leslie Fiedler ("Accommodation and Transcendence"), several of which are included in *TCLC.*

Gullason, Thomas Arthur. "The 'Fatal' Ending of *Huckleberry Finn."* *American Literature* 29 (March 1957): 86-91.
    Contends that Twain's primary objective in the concluding chapters of the novel was to contrast the romantic tradition represented by Tom with the realistic tradition represented by Huck.

Hearn, Michael Patrick. Introduction to *The Annotated Huckleberry Finn,* by Mark Twain, pp. 1-50. New York: Clarkson N. Potter, Inc./Publishers, 1981.
    Informative discussion of the writing, publication, and critical reception of the novel, profusely illustrated with photographs of Twain and his associates and with illustrations from various editions of *Huckleberry Finn* and Twain's other works.

Howell, Elmo. "Uncle Silas Phelps: A Note on Mark Twain's Characterization." *The Mark Twain Journal* XIV, No. 2 (Summer 1968): 8-12.
    Presents Twain's ambivalent view of slavery, which he considered wrong in principle but portrayed in *Huckleberry Finn,* through slaveowners such as the Phelps family, in a sympathetic light.

Kolb, Harold H., Jr. "Mark Twain, Huck Finn, and Jacob Blivens: Gilt-Edged, Tree-Calf Morality in *The Adventures of Huckleberry Finn."* *The Virginia Quarterly* 55, No. 4 (Autumn 1979): 653-69.
    Discusses the development of Twain's view of morality as reflected in his works and speculates that his increasing cynicism may have been responsible for the problematic ending of *Huckleberry Finn,* in which Twain "was reluctant to let his hero triumph" and intentionally lowered "the vision of humanity, of moral possibility, attempted in the earlier sections."

Krause, Sydney J. "Huck's First Moral Crisis." *The Mississippi Quarterly* XVIII, No. 2 (Spring 1965): 69-73.
    Analyzes two episodes in the novel: Huck fooling Jim in the fog, and Huck saving Jim from the slave hunters. Krause maintains that Huck's remorse after the first episode is the result of purely psychological factors, while his decision in the second results from his awakening moral consciousness.

Krauth, Leland. "Mark Twain: The Victorian of Southwestern Humor." *American Literature* LIV, No. 3 (October 1982): 368-84.
    Demonstrates how in *Huckleberry Finn* Twain purged traditional Southwestern humor of its profanity and vulgarity and maintains that Huck is "Mark Twain's version of the eighteenth-century Man of Feeling."

Lynn, Kenneth S. "You Can't Go Home Again." In his *Mark Twain and Southwestern Humor,* pp. 198-245. Westport, Conn.: Greenwood Press, Publishers, 1959.
    Examines the novel's principal themes and techniques.

Mailer, Norman. "Huckleberry Finn, Alive at 100." *The New York Times Book Review* (9 December 1984): 1, 36-7.
    Emphasizes the modernity of *Huckleberry Finn.* Mailer compares the novel with the works of such authors as Ernest Hemingway, John Steinbeck, and J. D. Salinger and ironically asserts that *Huckleberry Finn* "would be superb stuff if only the writer did not keep giving away the fact that he was a modern young American working in 1984."

Mark Twain Journal, Special Issue: Black Writers on "Adventures of Huckleberry Finn" One Hundred Years Later 22, No. 2 (Fall 1984): 1-52.
    Contains essays by eight critics, including David L. Smith on "Huck, Jim, and American Racial Discourse," Kenny J. Williams on *"Adventures of Huckleberry Finn;* or, Mark Twain's Racial Ambiguity," and Arnold Rampersand on *"Adventures of Huckleberry Finn* and Afro-American Literature."

Marks, Barry A., ed. *Mark Twain's "Huckleberry Finn".* Boston: D. C. Heath and Co., 1959, 108 p.
    Contains essays by ten critics, including James M. Cox, Frank Baldanza, and Richard P. Adams, many of which are included in *TCLC.*

Marx, Leo. "The Pilot and the Passenger: Landscape Conventions and the Style of *Huckleberry Finn."* *American Literature* XXVIII, No. 2 (May 1956): 129-46.
    Contends that much of the novel's greatness lies in Twain's synthesis of an aesthetic and emotional view of nature with an analytic and practical view recognizing nature as a potentially destructive force. Marx concludes that Twain's successful combination of these elements results in "a book, rare in our literature, which manages to suggest the lovely possibilities of life in America without neglecting its terrors."

Matthews, Brander. Introduction to *The Adventures of Huckleberry Finn,* by Mark Twain, pp. ix-xx. New York: Harper & Brothers Publishers, 1918.
    Biographical and critical essay.

McMahan, Elizabeth E. "The Money Motif: Economic Implications in *Huckleberry Finn*." *The Mark Twain Journal* XV, No. 4 (Summer 1971): 5-10.
 Examines Twain's use of money to facilitate action and characterization as well as to emphasize his indictment of greed in the novel.

Miller, Bruce E. "*Huckleberry Finn*: The Kierkegaardian Dimension." *Illinois Quarterly* 34, No. 1 (September 1971): 55-64.
 Argues that Huck's spiritual development parallels that of the Kierkegaardian "knight of faith."

Millichap, Joseph R. "Calvinistic Attitudes and Pauline Imagery in *The Adventures of Huckleberry Finn*." *The Mark Twain Journal* XVI, No. 1 (Winter 1971-72): 8-10.
 Examines elements of *Huckleberry Finn* that reflect a Calvinistic view of man's fallen nature.

Modern Fiction Studies: Mark Twain, Special Number XIV, No. 1 (Spring 1968): 1-140.
 Issue devoted to studies of *Huckleberry Finn*, including essays by Martha Banta ("Escape and Entry in *Huckleberry Finn*"), William R. Manierre ("Huck Finn, Empiricist Member of Society"), and Peter G. Biedler ("The Raft Episode in *Huckleberry Finn*").

More, Olin Harris. "Mark Twain and Don Quixote." *Publications of the Modern Language Association of America* XXXVII, No. 2 (June 1922): 324-46.*
 Traces the influence of Miguel Cervantes's novel on *Huckleberry Finn* and Twain's other works.

Ornstein, Robert. "The Ending of *Huckleberry Finn*." *Modern Language Notes* LXXIV, No. 8 (December 1959): 698-702.
 Argues that in the novel's final chapters Twain abandoned his role as social critic and "through his characterization of Tom confessed his commitment to a social order from which (unlike Huck) he saw no possible escape."

Patterson, Robert G. "Death on the Mississippi." *Psychological Perspectives* 7, No. 1 (Spring 1976): 9-22.
 Compares the ritualistic aspects of Huck's falsified death in the cabin and Buck Grangerford's murder with early Greek and Roman initiation rituals and attributes the novel's universal appeal to the archetypal nature of its themes.

Power, William. "Huck Finn's Father." *The University of Kansas City Review* XXVIII, No. 2 (December 1961): 83-94.
 Demonstrates Pap Finn's importance to the structure of the story, maintaining that *Huckleberry Finn* "draws much of its strength from tension between the hero and his father."

Pritchett, V. S. "The American Puritan." In his *In My Good Books*, pp. 175-82. London: Readers' Union/Chatto & Windus, 1943.
 Discusses *Huckleberry Finn* as Twain's reaction against American Puritanism. Although Pritchett considers the novel a comic masterpiece, he also observes that the book "is lacking in that civilized quality which you are bound to lose when you throw over civilization—the quality of pity," with the result that "one is left with the cruelty of American humor."

Remes, Carol. "The Heart of *Huckleberry Finn*." *Masses & Mainstream* 8, No. 11 (November 1955): 8-16.
 Considers a repudiation of slavery to be the novel's central theme.

Santayana, George. "Tom Sawyer and Don Quixote." *The Mark Twain Quarterly* IX, No. 2 (Winter 1952): 1-3.*
 Compares Tom and Huck with Don Quixote.

Sapper, Neil. "'I Been There Before': Huck Finn as Tocquevillian Individual." *The Mississippi Quarterly* XXIV, No. 1 (Winter 1970-71): 35-45.
 Discusses Huck as an example of the American individualist described by Alexis de Tocqueville.

Schmitz, Neil. "The Paradox of Liberation in *Huckleberry Finn*." *Texas Studies in Literature and Language* XIII, No. 1 (Spring 1971): 125-36.

Examines the antithetical natures of Huck's and Jim's individual quests for freedom.

Schornhorn, Manual. "Mark Twain's Jim: Solomon on the Mississippi." *The Mark Twain Journal* XIV, No. 3 (Winter 1968-69): 9-11.
 Disagrees with prevailing readings of the "Was Solomon Wise?" episode as purely minstrel comedy. Schornhorn maintains that the incident is integral both to the positive development of Jim's character and to the plot.

Sidnell, M. J. "Huck Finn and Jim: Their Abortive Freedom Ride." *The Cambridge Quarterly* 2, No. 3 (Summer 1967): 203-11.
 Maintains that Huck and Jim's journey on the raft represents life as it should be but is not, and that the novel's end is an appropriate return to the real world—"the trivially vicious world of Tom Sawyer's America."

Simpson, Claude M., ed. *Twentieth Century Interpretations of "Adventures of Huckleberry Finn": A Collection of Critical Essays*. Englewood Cliffs, N.J.: Prentice-Hall, 1968, 119 p.
 Contains essays by seventeen critics, including Bernard DeVoto, Leo Marx, and Henry Nash Smith, several of which are included in *TCLC*.

Spengemann, William C. "The Backwoods Angel: *Adventures of Huckleberry Finn*." In his *Mark Twain and the Backwoods Angel: The Matter of Innocence in the Works of Samuel Clemens*, pp. 61-83. Kent State University Press, 1966.
 Examines the theme of the innocent individual in conflict with corrupt society.

Stein, Allen F. "Return to Phelps Farm: *Huckleberry Finn* and the Old Southwestern Framing Device." *The Mississippi Quarterly* XXIV, No. 2 (Spring 1971): 111-16.
 Defends the novel's ending as an intentional reworking of the traditional Southwestern framing device, which Twain uses to criticize conventional society by portraying the superficial peacefulness of St. Petersburg and the Phelps farm as a subtle counterpart to the overt violence of the core story.

Tanner, Tony. "Huck Finn and the Reflections of a Saphead." In his *The Reign of Wonder: Naivety and Reality in American Literature*, pp. 155-86. Cambridge, England: Cambridge at the University Press, 1965.
 Contrasts Tom's stylish social conformity with Huck's naive and independent humanity.

Tenney, Thomas Asa. *Mark Twain: A Reference Guide*. Boston: G. K. Hall & Co., 1977, 443 p.
 Comprehensive annotated bibliography of Mark Twain criticism through 1974.

Trilling, Lionel. "Huckleberry Finn." In his *The Liberal Imagination: Essays on Literature and Society*, pp. 104-17. New York: Viking Press, 1950.
 Examines Huck as "a servant of the river-god." Trilling maintains that Huck's "very intense moral life may be said to derive almost wholly from his love of the river."

Wasiolek, Edward. "The Structure of Make-Believe: *Huckleberry Finn*." *The University of Kansas City Review* XXIV, No. 2 (December 1957): 97-101.
 Discusses the contrast between the "fluid, uncaught, unpredictable stuff of life on the river" and the "still, rigid, formalized imitation of life on shore."

Wiggins, Robert A. "The Craft of *Huckleberry Finn*." In his *Mark Twain: Jackleg Novelist*, pp. 57-71. Seattle: University of Washington Press, 1964.
 Analyzes technical aspects of the novel.

Young, Philip. "Adventures of Huckleberry Finn." In his *Ernest Hemingway*, pp. 181-212. New York: Rinehart & Co., 1952.
 Compares Hemingway and Hemingway character Nick Adams to Huck Finn.

H(erbert) G(eorge) Wells

1866-1946

(Also wrote under pseudonyms of Sosthenes Smith, Walter Glockenhammer, and Reginald Bliss) English novelist, short story writer, historian, essayist, autobiographer, and critic.

Wells is best known today as one of the progenitors of modern science fiction who foretold an era of chemical warfare, atomic weaponry, and world wars. *The Time Machine, The Invisible Man, The War of the Worlds, The Island of Doctor Moreau,* and several other works in Wells's canon are classics in the field of science fiction that have profoundly influenced the course of the genre. Although his science fiction works are predominantly informed by a pessimistic, apocalyptic vision which proved the major shaping force on the classic dystopian fiction of the twentieth century, in later speculative works such as *The World Set Free, The Shape of Things to Come,* and *Guide to the New World* Wells developed an ideal of a potential utopian millennium which he believed to be attainable by humankind. Among his other nonfiction works illustrative of this vision, *The Outline of History,* a history of the world written to demonstrate the needlessness of national boundaries and to offer hope for world peace, is Wells's most famous and controversial. As a polemicist, Wells's strident advocacy of free love and of socialism, as well as his attacks on what he considered the stifling moral constraints of society, are credited with contributing to the liberalization of modern Western culture.

Wells was born into a lower-middle-class Cockney family in Bromley, Kent, a suburb of London. Struggling to escape the unrewarding, below-stairs existence that defeated his parents, Wells attended London University and the Royal College of Science, where he studied zoology. One of his professors, the noted biologist T. H. Huxley, instilled in Wells a belief in social as well as biological evolution which Wells later cited as the single most important and influential aspect of his education. After graduation from London University, Wells wrote a biology textbook and tried his hand at writing fiction, contributing short stories to several magazines. The serialization of his short novel *The Time Machine* brought Wells his first substantial critical notice—he was hailed as a literary genius by a critic for the *Review of Reviews*—and launched his career. The writing of science fiction and science fantasies occupied the earliest part of his career and brought him great popular and critical attention. As his popularity grew, Wells was enabled by his burgeoning fame to meet Arnold Bennett, Joseph Conrad, and other prominent authors of the day, with whom he exchanged criticism and opinions on the art of writing. His own theory and style of writing was basically journalistic and was acquired while serving under editor Frank Harris as literary critic at the *Saturday Review*. Believing that it is important to continuously place copy before the reading public, even if one's concerns are soon outdated and forgotten, Wells gradually turned from fiction of entertainment to address the social and political problems of England and the world. Several socially concerned, comedic novels followed the science fiction works; in such novels as *The Wheels of Chance, Kipps: The Story of a Simple Soul,* and *The History of Mr. Polly,* Dickensian, lower-middle-class characters are depicted living at odds with the

downtrodden society in which the author had himself been raised. A socialist, Wells joined the Fabian Society in 1903, but left the group after fighting a long, unsuccessful war of wit and rhetoric over some of the society's policies with his friend, the prominent Fabian and man of letters Bernard Shaw. Wells's socialist thought, combined with a belief in the gradual perfection of humanity through evolution and scientific innovation, is expressed in the serious fiction and prognostications that gradually succeeded the humorous character novels during the first decade of the twentieth century. By 1914, through such works as *Anticipations of the Reaction of Mechanical and Scientific Progress upon Human Life and Thought, A Modern Utopia,* and *The New Machiavelli,* Wells was established in the public mind as a leading proponent of socialism, world government, free thought, and free love, and as an enemy of many elements of Edwardian thought and morality.

Before World War I, Wells's name was commonly linked with that of Shaw as an advocate of the new, the iconoclastic, and the daring. But the war and its aftermath of widespread disillusionment upset his optimistic vision of humankind. During the war, as evidenced by the essay *God the Invisible King* and the novel *Mr. Britling Sees It Through,* Wells turned temporarily to belief in God—a belief that he later vigorously repudiated. His postwar ideas on humanity's perfectibility were modified to stress the preeminent importance of education in bringing about progress. In his ambitious two-volume work *The Outline of History*, a work written to further the cause of world peace, Wells attempted to illustrate the commonality of the origins and histories of the world's peoples. The subject of much critical discussion, *The Outline of History* sparked one of the most celebrated literary debates of the 1920s, between Wells and his longtime antagonist, the Catholic polemicist Hilaire Belloc. Objecting to Wells's naturalistic, Darwinian view of world history, Belloc attacked the *Outline* as a simpleminded, nonscientific, anti-Catholic document. A war of mutual refutation was fought by both writers in the pages of several books and essays. Ironically, although much of the scientific community now affirms Wells's biological theses as presented in the *Outline*, during the mid-1920s the preponderance of scientific evidence supported the biological theories of Belloc, who, in the minds of many critics, bested Wells in their exchange of polemical broadsides. Throughout the 1920s and 1930s, Wells's works became progressively less optimistic about the future of humanity and increasingly bitter, as is evident in such satiric novels as *The Croquet Player* and *The Holy Terror*. The advent of World War II increased Wells's despondency about the future, and his last book, *Mind at the End of Its Tether*, predicts the destruction of civilization and degeneration of humanity. Wells died in London in 1946.

Critics believe that Wells's reputation as a writer of fiction rests upon his early works of science fiction and science fantasy, and on his humorous character novels. The "scientific romances," as Wells called them, were enormously popular upon first appearance and continue to be widely read. They have been the subject of numerous adaptations in other artistic media. Perhaps the most successful such adaptation was the Mercury Theater's famous radio broadcast of *The War of the Worlds*, directed by Orson Welles on Halloween night, 1938; tuning in late to the program, many listeners across the United States panicked in the face of what they believed was an actual Martian invasion of the earth. With their use of such fantastic devices as encounters with aliens, invisibility, and time travel, Wells's scientific romances have fascinated readers and have influenced the work of several generations of science fiction writers. While Wells did not invent speculative fiction positing technological advances, his early science fiction pioneered the fictional exploration of such complex issues as the impact of technology on human affairs and the moral responsibility of scientists for the potentially harmful applications of their research. Wells's science fiction is also noted for its sophisticated, Swiftian satire of the author's own culture and times. *The War of the Worlds*, for example, has been noted for Wells's drawing of parallels between the relentless, destructive advance of the technologically advanced Martian invaders and the one-sided military successes of the British Army over poorly armed Tasmanian Islanders during the years of Britain's colonialist expansion. The greatest formative influence on Wells's science fiction was Huxley's philosophical interpretation of Darwinian evolutionary theory. Huxley contended that the evolutionary process will not inevitably lead to the social or moral improvement of humankind, but that the course of life on earth, like the life of any organism, follows a pattern of quickening, maturing, and ebbing, all of which may be charted as a parabolic curve, with the degenerative downward slope of the curve a natural part of the process. At a time when the notion was seriously advanced that "everything had been discovered"—that only refinements of existing scientific and technological advances remained to be made—Huxley's "cosmic pessimism" was a disturbing thought, implying as it did that humanity was poised on the brink of a plunge into decadence and oblivion. Wells adopted this chilling concept in the stories and scientific romances that he wrote in the 1890s, such as *The Time Machine, When the Sleeper Wakes,* "A Story of the Days to Come," and *The First Men in the Moon*. Although in his later utopian fiction Wells adopted a millenial vision, these earliest works reflecting Huxley's cosmic pessimism are probably Wells's best-known and have proved the primary influence on the classic twentieth-century dystopian novels of Yevgeny Zamyatin, Aldous Huxley, and George Orwell.

Although Wells's character novels, according to most critics, lack psychological subtlety and are not as well constructed as his science fiction works, Wells is praised for the humor and sympathy for common individuals which is displayed throughout them. The publication of *The History of Mr. Polly* in 1910, according to many critics, marked the end of Wells's literary ascension. His novels had by that time taken on a pedantic nature, and many of his subsequent works, such as *Joan and Peter* and *The World of William Clissold*, examined contemporary social problems in a didactic way that drew the scorn of many critics of the era. However, *Tono-Bungay*, an ambitious portrayal of social and political decay, stands out among Wells's social novels and serves as a bridge between his character and expository fiction. The subject of numerous interpretations, *Tono-Bungay* has been called by many critics Wells's greatest novel. From the turn of the century until his death, Wells wrote social and political criticism and prognostications. Of these, *The War That Will End War* gave the world, through its title, a cynical catch-phrase for obstinate, benevolent naiveté in the face of widespread human corruption—a characteristic criticized often in Wells's social fiction and nonfiction. For all his concern over the future of the human race, critics remain uncertain as to whether Wells actually believed that humanity could be improved. There is evidence that, like the Time Traveller of his first major work, Wells believed that even if life is indeed a meaningless, dualistic struggle, "it remains for us to live as though it were not so."

In spite of the pessimism that pervades many of his works, Wells is regarded as one of the most prominent champions of the early twentieth-century spirit of British liberal optimism. With the possible exception of Shaw, perhaps no other author of his day so effectively captured the exuberant sense of release from Victorian conventions and morals. The continued popularity of his books, the tremendous body of criticism devoted to them, and the liberalizing effect that much of his work had on Western thought combine to make Wells one of the major figures in modern literature.

(See also *TCLC*, Vols. 6 and 12; *Contemporary Authors*, Vol. 110; *Dictionary of Literary Biography*, Vol. 34: *British Novelists, 1890-1929—Traditionalists;* and *Something about the Author*, Vol. 20.)

PRINCIPAL WORKS

Text-book of Biology   (nonfiction)   1893
Select Coversations with an Uncle, Now Extinct, and Two Other Reminiscences   (short stories)   1895
The Time Machine   (novel)   1895
The Wonderful Visit   (novel)   1895
The Island of Dr. Moreau   (novel)   1896
The Wheels of Chance   (novel)   1896
The Invisible Man   (novel)   1897
The War of the Worlds   (novel)   1898

When the Sleeper Wakes: A Story of the Years to Come
(novel) 1899; also published as *The Sleeper Awakes*
[revised edition], 1910
Love and Mr. Lewisham (novel) 1900
*Anticipations of the Reaction of Mechanical and Scientific
Progress upon Human Life and Thought* (essay)
1901
The First Men in the Moon (novel) 1901
Mankind in the Making (essays) 1903
The Food of the Gods, and How It Came to Earth (novel)
1904
Kipps: The Story of a Simple Soul (novel) 1905
A Modern Utopia (essay) 1905
The Future in America: A Search after Realities (essays)
1906
In the Days of the Comet (novel) 1906
*First and Last Things: A Confession of Faith and Rule of
Life* (essay) 1908
New Worlds for Old (essay) 1908
*The War in the Air and Particularly How Mr. Bert
Smallways Fared While It Lasted* (novel) 1908
Ann Veronica (novel) 1909
Tono-Bungay (novel) 1909
The History of Mr. Polly (novel) 1910
The Country of the Blind, and Other Stories (short stories)
1911
The New Machiavelli (novel) 1911
Marriage (novel) 1912
The War That Will End War (essays) 1914
The Wife of Sir Isaac Harmon (novel) 1914
The World Set Free (novel) 1914
Boon [as Reginald Bliss] (sketches) 1915
The Research Magnificent (novel) 1915
Mr. Britling Sees It Through (novel) 1916
God the Invisible King (essay) 1917
*The Soul of a Bishop: A Novel (with Just a Little Love in It)
about Conscience and Religion and the Real Troubles of
Life* (novel) 1917
Joan and Peter: The Story of an Education (novel) 1918
The Outline of History. 2 vols. (history) 1919-20
The Undying Fire (novel) 1919
Men Like Gods (novel) 1923
The World of William Clissold (novel) 1926
Mr. Blettsworthy on Rampole Island (novel) 1928
The Open Conspiracy (essay) 1928
*The Autocracy of Mr. Parham: His Remarkable Adventures
in This Changing World* (novel) 1930
The Bulpington of Blup (novel) 1932
The Shape of Things to Come (essays) 1933
Experiment in Autobiography (autobiography) 1934
The Croquet Player (novel) 1936
The Holy Terror (novel) 1939
All Aboard for Ararat (novel) 1940
Guide to the New World (essay) 1941
Mind at the End of Its Tether (essay) 1945
*Arnold Bennett and H. G. Wells: A Record of a Personal
and a Literary Friendship* (letters and criticism)
1960
*George Gissing and H. G. Wells: Their Friendship and
Correspondence* (letters and criticism) 1961

THE SPECTATOR (essay date 1896)

[*The following review of* The Island of Doctor Moreau *illustrates
the assumption made by critics that the novel served some didactic
purpose such as promoting antivivisectionism.*]

The ingenious author of **The Time Machine** has found in [**The
Island of Dr. Moreau**] a subject exactly suited to his rather
peculiar type of imagination. When he tried to conceive the
idea of making a man of the nineteenth century *travel* in time,
so that he was at the same moment both contemporary with
and far removed from the people of a prehistoric age, he conceived an idea which was really quite too self-contradictory to
be worked out with any sort of coherence. But in this little
book he has worked out a notion much less intrinsically incoherent, and though impossible, yet not so impossible as to
be quite inconceivable. In other words, the impossibility is of
a less unworkable order, though it is also much more gruesome.
He has taken a few of the leading methods of the modern
surgery and exaggerated them in the hands of an accomplished
vivisector into a new physiological calculus that enables its
professor to transmute various animals into the semblance of
man. . . . It should be explained that the accomplished vivisector described has found a small island in the Pacific far out
of the track of ordinary mariners where he can practise his
gruesome manipulations of living organisms without fear of
being disturbed. . . . Of course, the real value for literary purposes of this ghastly conception depends on the power of the
author to make his readers realise the half-way stages between
the brute and the rational creature, with which he has to deal.
And we must admit that Mr. Wells succeeds in this little story
in giving a most fearful vividness to his picture of half-created
monsters endowed with a little speech, a little human curiosity,
a little sense of shame, and an overgrown dread of the pain
and terror which the scientific dabbler in creative processes
had inflicted. There is nothing in Swift's grim conceptions of
animalised man and rationalised animals more powerfully conceived than Mr. Wells's description of these deformed and
malformed creations of Dr. Moreau, repeating the litany in
which they abase themselves before the physiological demigod
by whom they have been endowed with their new powers of
speech, their new servility to a human master, and their profound dread of that "house of pain" in which they have been
made and fashioned into half-baked men. The hero of the story,
who has been thrown into Dr. Moreau's grisly society, comes
suddenly on the huts of these spoiled animals who have been
fashioned into a bad imitation of men, and hears them proclaim
their new law in the following creed: . . .

'Not to go on all-Fours; *that* is the Law. Are we not
Men?'
'Not to suck up Drink; *that* is the Law. Are we not
Men?'
'Not to eat Flesh nor Fish; *that* is the Law. Are we not
Men?'
'Not to claw Bark of Trees; *that* is the Law. Are we not
Men?'
'Not to chase other Men; *that* is the Law. Are we not
Men?' . . .

'*His* is the House of Pain.
His is the Hand that makes.
His is the Hand that wounds.
His is the Hand that heals.' . . .

Our readers may gain from this passage some faint idea of the
power with which this grim conception of the mauling and

maiming of brutes into bad imitations of human beings has been worked out by Mr. Wells. It is, of course, a very ingenious caricature of what has been done in certain exceptional efforts of human surgery,—a caricature inspired by the fanaticism of a foul ambition to remake God's creatures by confusing and transfusing and remoulding human and animal organs so as to extinguish so far as possible the chasm which divides man from brute. Mr. Wells has had the prudence, too, not to dwell on the impossibilities of his subject too long. He gives us a very slight, though a very powerful and ghastly, picture, and may, we hope, have done more to render vivisection unpopular, and that contempt for animal pain, which enthusiastic physiologists seem to feel, hideous, than all the efforts of the societies which have been organised for that wholesome and beneficent end. Dr. Moreau is a figure to make an impression on the imagination, and his tragic death under the attack of the puma which he has been torturing so long, has a kind of poetic justice in it which satisfies the mind of the reader. Again, the picture of the rapid reversion to the brute, of the victims which Dr. Moreau had so painfully fashioned, so soon as the terrors of his "house of pain" are withdrawn, is very impressively painted. Altogether, though we do not recommend *The Island of Dr. Moreau* to readers of sensitive nerves, as it might well haunt them only too powerfully, we believe that Mr. Wells has almost rivalled Swift in the power of his very gruesome, but very salutary as well as impressive, conception. (pp. 519-20)

> *A review of "The Island of Dr. Moreau," in* The Spectator, *Vol. 76, No. 3537, April 11, 1896, pp. 519-20.*

ARNOLD BENNETT   (essay date 1897)

[*Bennett was an Edwardian novelist who is credited with bringing techniques of European Naturalism to the English novel. His reputation rests almost exclusively on* The Old Wives' Tale *(1908) and the Clayhanger trilogy (1910-16), novels set in the manufacturing district of Bennett's native Staffordshire that tell of the thwarted ambitions of those who endure a dull, provincial existence. In the following excerpt, originally published September 29, 1897, in the journal* Woman, *Bennett provides a largely favorable review of* The Invisible Man.]

Like most of Mr. H. J. [*sic*] Wells's novels and stories, [*The Invisible Man*] is based upon an Idea—the Idea that a man by a scientific process can make himself invisible. The Idea is not a new one—I think I have met with it several times before—but it is worked with an ingenuity, a realism, an inevitableness, which no previous worker in the field of "grotesque romance," has ever approached, and which surpasses in some respects all Mr. Wells's former efforts. The strength of Mr. Wells lies in the fact that he is not only a scientist, but a most talented student of character, especially quaint character. He will not only ingeniously describe for you a scientific miracle, but he will set down that miracle in the midst of a country village, sketching with excellent humour the inn-landlady, the blacksmith, the chemist's apprentice . . . , the doctor, and all the other persons whom the miracle affects. He attacks you before and behind, and the result is that you are compelled to yield absolutely to his weird spells.

The Invisible Man thought he was going to do great things when he devisualised himself (he did, in fact, terrorise a whole district), but he soon found his sad error, and his story is one of failure, growing more pathetic and grimmer as it proceeds; the last few pages are deep tragedy, grotesque but genuine. The theme is developed in a masterly manner. The history of

the man's first hunt in London for clothes and a mask wherewith to hide his invisibility, is a farce dreadful in its significance, but this is nothing to the naked, desperate tragedy of his last struggle against visible mankind. Indeed, the latter half of this book is pure sorrow. The invisible man is no longer grotesque, but human. One completely loses sight of the merely wonderful aspect of the phenomena in watching the dire pathos of his loneliness in a peopled world. Mr. Wells has achieved poetry.

Although the book contains the best work the author has done, it is not free from slight blemish. Mr. Wells seems to be losing his affectionate care for the minutiae of style, a surprising lapse in a man trained under W. E. Henley. Thus one finds: "he was contempla*ting*, try*ing* on a pair of boots." "The *ones* he had were a very comfortable fit." There is also a split infinitive. Moreover, Mr. Wells seems actually to have overlooked a scientific point. If the man was invisible his eyelids must have been transparent, and his eyes, without their natural shield, must speedily have become useless from simple irritation. This difficulty ought to have been got over. These things are of course trifles, but they deserve attention. (pp. 258-59)

> *Arnold Bennett, "Bennett's Review of 'The Invisible Man'," in* Arnold Bennett and H. G. Wells: A Record of a Personal and a Literary Friendship *by Arnold Bennett and H. G. Wells, edited by Harris Wilson, University of Illinois Press, 1960, pp. 258-59.*

W. T. STEAD   (essay date 1898)

[*Stead was the founder and editor of the* Review of Reviews. *In the following excerpt from the April, 1898, issue of that journal, Stead offers a discussion of Wells's gruesome tendencies in his fiction.*]

Mr. Wells, as a novelist, cannot be said to deal in pleasant themes. He is a professor of the gruesome, a past master in the art of producing creepy sensations. I leave out of account his book *The Island of Doctor Moreau,* which ought never to have been written, and which Mr. Wells would consult his own reputation by withdrawing from circulation. But that is only an extreme instance of the note of the horrible, the weird and the uncanny which characterise all his writings. There is his story of *The Invisible Man,* for instance, the subject of which is a discovery by which it was possible for man to render himself absolutely invisible while retaining his body and all his faculties. The hero of this novel having possessed himself of this extraordinary gift, finds it a very dubious advantage. His invisibility did not extend to his raiment, and it was therefore necessary for him either to go stark naked, if he would be completely invisible, or else sacrifice the advantages of his invisibility without securing the ordinary commonplace advantages of visibility by dressing himself, and concealing the invisible void where the face should have been seen. The story is worked out with much ingenuity; but as if by irresistible gravitation towards the unpleasant, the invisible man passes through a series of disastrous experiences, until finally he goes mad, and is beaten to death as the only way of putting an end to a homicidal maniac with the abnormal gift of invisibility.

But Mr. Wells is a seer of gruesome visions. He spends his life imagining what would happen if one of the laws of Nature were altered just a little—with terrifying results. One of the latest of his tales, [**"The Star"**], which appeared in the Christmas number of the *Graphic,* described the devastation that was wrought by the swoop of a blazing star so near the earth that its heat melted the snow on the Himalayas and swept hundreds of millions to sudden death. He has caught the trick of describing events which only exist in his imagination with the technical precision of a newspaper reporter. Leaving to the ordinary journalist the chronicling of the happenings of every day, he soars into space of Four Dimensions, and exults in nothing so much as in readjusting the familiar environment of daily life to the circumstances of a world altered, it may be only in one important particular, from that in which we live. Stories work out in his brain as a kind of mathematical problem. If human nature under such conditions evolved such results, what results would be evolved if this, that, or the other condition were revolutionised? And it must be admitted that Mr. Wells works out his problems with a skill which leaves all his rivals far behind. (pp. 61-2)

W. T. Stead, in an extract from H. G. Wells: The Critical Heritage, *edited by Patrick Parrinder, Routledge & Kegan Paul, 1972, pp. 61-2.*

THE CRITIC, NEW YORK (essay date 1898)

[*An anonymous American reviewer of* The War of the Worlds *notes the innovative nature of the "quasi-scientific novel" as a literary form.*]

Following in the wake of the sciences for half a century is a new species of literary work, which may be called the quasi-scientific novel. From M. Verne's prophetic submarine boat to Mr. Waterloo's prehistoric caveman, one could classify a score of romances which try to put into imaginative form the latest results in science and mechanics. Like all literature, too, the new novel is not content with presenting living embodi-

ments of truth, but is fain to make guesses at the future. It is as yet experimental, and is quite too young to have produced an enduring masterpiece. The whole group can claim nothing that will live very far into the next century. It is hopelessly doomed, not more by its lack of artistic breadth of treatment than by its slipshod style, which betrays all the haste of the daily "leader" to get into type.

Had Mr. Wells not been forestalled by Mr. Du Maurier, he would probably have called the novel before us ["**The War of the Worlds**"] "The Martians." It is the story of the invasion of our earth by a company of intelligent beings from Mars. . . . Having created an atmosphere of reality for his story, the author proceeds in journalistic style to tell of the coming of the first cylinder. "Flying swiftly and steadily towards me across that incredible distance, came the thing they were sending us." Though the mysterious projectile fell near London, its arrival did not cause the sensation that an ultimatum to Spain would have done. Ten cylinders, each thirty yards in diameter and containing five Martians, arrived at intervals of twenty-four hours.

The war which ensues is melodramatic and shamefully one-sided. The strangers fight in vast spider-like engines, a hundred feet high, which stride along with the speed of a limited express. In each of these "boilers on stilts" sat the guiding intelligence of the machine, smothering cities with seas of poisonous black smoke, and wiping out of existence artillery and battleships with his heat-ray, a sort of search-light which burned. As the gunner said, it was soon all up with humanity; we were beaten by superior mechanical genius. After completely subjugating humanity, the Martians are attacked from an unexpected quarter, and fall victims to our invisible allies, the bacteria. This is highly satisfactory and the happiest stroke in the plot.

Mr. Wells's conception of the Martians is not only daring as a piece of imaginative work, but interesting for its deduction from biological laws. . . . The highest intelligence in Mars, through the processes of evolution, is embodied in what is scarcely more than a huge round head with large protruding eyes, and a mouth surrounded by sixteen whip-like tentacles—a kind of octopus that is all brain. The complex apparatus of digestion is dispensed with, for he injects directly into his veins the blood of living creatures, including man. The interest of Mr. Wells's work is divided between the excitement of the story and speculations on the differentiated forms of life on this and other planets.

The author has written an ingenious and original work. Now and again in the intervals of a colloquial or hysterical style, one comes upon passages of sweetness and virility. The book has the tone of intense modernity, with notes of convincing realism and morbid horror. One misses the simplicity of Gulliver and the epic impressiveness of the stories of Sodom and Mt. Carmel. It is an Associated Press dispatch, describing a universal nightmare.

A review of "The War of the Worlds," in The Critic, *New York, Vol. XXIX, No. 844, April 23, 1898, p. 282.*

Wells in 1895.

G. K. CHESTERTON (essay date 1902)

[*Regarded as one of England's premier men of letters during the first half of the twentieth century, Chesterton is best known today as a colorful bon vivant, a witty essayist, and the creator of the Father Brown mysteries and the fantasy* The Man Who Was

Thursday *(1908). Much of Chesterton's work reveals his childlike joie de vivre and reflects his pronounced Anglican and, later, Roman Catholic beliefs. His essays are characterized by their humor, frequent use of paradox, and chatty, rambling style. Chesterton and Wells were longtime friends and adversaries; while they maintained a friendship which lasted from the early 1900s until Chesterton's death in 1936, the two were at sword's-point over most social and political issues of their era, with Wells's materialistic socialist views ever at odds with Chesterton's orthodox Christian and Distributist beliefs. In the following excerpt from a review written before the beginning of his friendship with Wells, Chesterton criticizes* The First Men in the Moon *for the lack of human interest engendered by the characters. Angered by this review, Wells wrote a letter to his friend Arnold Bennett, saying, in part: "I've just read this new light Chesterton on ME in the* Pall Mall Magazine *& Really, you know, he's an ass. . . . His judgement does not penetrate, it's sham."*]

Mr. H. G. Wells has . . . almost every intellectual faculty for the estimate of the tendency of society; but he has a deep and not easily definable deficiency which is well exhibited in the fact that he can contemplate apparently with contentment the idea that society will be dominated eventually by a race of sombre and technical experts—a race, as it were, of glorified gasfitters, without gaiety, without art, without faith. The best chance of analysing this deficiency lies in studying Mr. Wells's novels, and it so happens that a typical novel comes within our scope. He continues in *The First Men in the Moon* . . . his great series of the thousand romances that lie secreted in *The Origin of Species.* Mr. H. G. Wells is, of course, a profoundly interesting and representative man of this age. The conception at the back of his mind appears to be essentially the same as that of Swift. Swift, in *Gulliver's Travels,* sought to show how, by merely altering the standards and proportions of life, by conceiving a hypothetical man forty feet high, and another hypothetical man five inches high, you could make the whole position of humanity ridiculous, and confound all the principles of heaven and earth. *Gulliver's Travels* is, indeed, the great Bible of scepticism, and worthy to be the greatest literary work of the most polished and most futile of centuries. Mr. Wells achieves this same conception—the conception of the confusion of standards—but not by means of Swift's big men and little men, which were merely abstract figures, like the figures of a geometrical diagram. He attains this confusion of standards by means of the whole roaring and bewildering vision of the universe as seen by science. His world is indeed a kind of opium-dream.

The First Men in the Moon is an account written with astonishing animation and lucidity of a visit to our satellite conducted by purely scientific methods. In dealing with the inhabitants of the moon, Mr. Wells exhibits in a very clear way the difference . . . between the old sceptical and satiric romance and the new. Such writers as Lucian or Rabelais or Swift would have used the moon as a mere convenience, an empty house among the planets in which to put the angels or elfins of some human allegory, a mere silver mirror in which would have been glassed, under monstrous shapes and disguises, all that was passing upon the earth. Mr. Wells's satiric method is the new one; it inaugurates almost a new method, which might be called biological satire. He represents the moon creatures as being more or less what he conjectures that such creatures would, by the laws of nature, have become. They are beings like walking toadstools or horribly magnified animalcula; beings with heads like huge bubbles, which grow bigger as they think; beings who divide among themselves the senses and the powers of man, who have one specialist to see and another specialist

to hear, and another specialist to count. The weakness of the book is that of nearly all Mr. H. G. Wells's books, and it arises out of his sceptical attitude. As a human story it is lifeless. The men who conduct the expedition are as distant, as monstrous, and as cold as the wan populace of the moon. A curious cold light of indifference, a curious cold air of contentment and unconcern, lies upon the whole wild narrative. We read of the blood-curdling idea of a man left behind on the moon, but we do not read it with any of the basic and primeval human emotions with which we should read of our brother, born of our own kindly race, whirling in space at the mercy of the blind tournament of the spheres. We do not care what becomes of the man; we feel that he and the moon monsters are both about as basically heartless and dreary as each other. This is a real misfortune, or punishment of the sceptical attitude, for you cannot write a romance or a story of adventure without human interest. The common modern notion that a romance is simply a string of brute incidents, fights, voyages, and discoveries, is an error which is responsible for cartloads of bad imitations of Dumas and Scott. A set of adventures is nothing unless we have first gained a working and approximate human interest in the adventurer. . . . *The First Men in the Moon* fails, in spite of a wealth of world-wide fancy and gigantesque logic, for lack of that one feeling which one of the older and more humane romances would have made us feel—the feeling of man returning after his nightmare of space and finding this common earth glowing all round him like a fire-lit room. (pp. 134-35)

> G. K. Chesterton, *in a review of "The First Men in the Moon," in* The Pall Mall Magazine, *Vol. XXVI, No. 105, January, 1902, pp. 133-36.*

ROBERT H. SHERARD (INTERVIEW WITH JULES VERNE) (interview date 1903)

[*Verne is acknowledged as one of the world's first and most imaginative science fiction writers. Although his fantastic adventures were originally considered children's fiction, new translations have led to critical assessment of Verne's works as serious expressions of his concern with the potential for destruction inherent in the technological advances of the machine age. Verne described in his fiction such devices as the submarine, television, and helicopter that later came into being much as he imagined them, which helped to establish the critical tendency to evaluate science fiction according to the accuracy of its forecasts. Verne is commonly linked with Wells as one of the progenitors of modern science fiction, though Verne often repudiated any comparison between their works, as in the following excerpt from an interview in which he stresses that his own works have a sound scientific basis lacking in the works of Wells.*]

It was inevitable, as Jules Verne remarked, that I should speak to him about Wells.

'*Je pensiez bien que vous alliez me demander cela,*' he said. 'His books were sent to me, and I have read them. It is very curious, and, I will add, very English. But I do not see the possibility of comparison between his work and mine. We do not proceed in the same manner. It occurs to me that his stories do not repose on very scientific bases. No, there is no *rapport* between his work and mine. I make use of physics. He invents. I go to the moon in a cannon-ball, discharged from a cannon. Here there is no invention. He goes to Mars in an airship, which he constructs of a metal which does away with the law of gravitation. *Ça c'est très joli,*' cried Monsieur Verne in an animated way, 'but show me this metal. Let him produce it.' (pp. 101-02)

Robert H. Sherard, in an interview with Jules Verne on October 9, 1903, in H. G. Wells: The Critical Heritage, *edited by Patrick Parrinder, Routledge & Kegan Paul, 1972, pp. 101-02.*

J. D. BERESFORD   (essay date 1915)

[*Beresford was an English architect and author of short stories, plays, poems, and nearly forty novels. He was best known and is most remembered for his science fiction. An admirer of Wells, Beresford often dealt with the same themes as his more famous contemporary. His most popular work,* The Hampdenshire Wonder *(1911), treats the Wellsian theme of a superintelligent child sprung from an ordinary background, while his novel* Goslings *(1913), conerning the effects of an extraterrestrial encounter, has been compared with* The War of the Worlds. *In the following excerpt from his critical biography of Wells, Beresford offers an early overview of Wells's scientific and utopian fiction.*]

Mr Wells' romances have little or nothing in common with those of Jules Verne, not even that peculiar quality of romance which revels in the impossible. (p. 17)

Mr Wells' experiments with the relatively improbable have become increasingly involved with the social problem, and it would be possible to trace the growth of his opinions from this evidence alone, even if we had not the valuable commentary afforded by his novels and his essays in sociology. . . . The later works have been so defensive and, in one sense, didactic that one is apt to forget that many of the earlier books, and all the short stories, must have originated in the effervescence of creative imagination. (pp. 17-18)

[Wells] prefaced his romances by a sketch in the old *Pall Mall Gazette,* entitled **The Man of the Year Million,** an a priori study that made one thankful for one's prematurity. After that physiological piece of logic, however, he tried another essay in evolution, published in 1895 in book form under the title of **The Time Machine**—the first of his romances.

The machine itself is the vaguest of mechanical assumptions; a thing of ivory, quartz, nickel and brass that quite illogically carries its rider into an existing past or future. We accept the machine as a literary device to give an air of probability to the essential thing, the experience; and forget the means in the effect. The criterion of the prophecy in this case is influenced by the theory of "natural selection." Mr Wells' vision of the "Sunset of Mankind" was of men so nearly adapted to their environment that the need for struggle, with its corollary of the extermination of the unfit, had practically ceased. Humanity had become differentiated into two races, both recessive; one, the Eloi, a race of childlike, simple, delicate creatures living on the surface of a kindly earth; the other, the Morlocks, a more active but debased race, of bestial habits, who lived underground and preyed cannibalistically on the surface-dwellers whom they helped to preserve, as a man may preserve game. The Eloi, according to the hypothesis of the Time Traveller, are the descendants of the leisured classes; the Morlocks of the workers. . . . All this is in the year 802,701 A.D.

The prophecy is less convincing than the wonderful sight of the declining earth some million years later, sinking slowly into the dying fires of the worn-out sun. . . . And the picture is made more horrible to the imaginative by the wonder whether the summit of the evolutionary curve has not already been reached—or it may be passed in the days of the Greek philosophers.

The Time Machine, despite certain obvious faults of imagination and style, is a brilliant fantasy; and it affords a valuable picture of the young Wells looking at the world, with his normal eyes, and finding it, more particularly, incomplete. At the age of twenty-seven or so, he has freed himself very completely from the bonds of conventional thought, and is prepared to examine, and to present life from the detached standpoint of one who views it all from a respectable distance; but who is able, nevertheless—an essential qualification—to enter life with all the passion and generosity of his own humanity.

And in **The Wonderful Visit**—published in the same year as **The Time Machine**—he comes closer to earth. That ardent ornithologist, the Rev. K. Hilyer, Vicar of Siddermouth, who brought down an angel with a shot-gun, is tenderly imagined; a man of gentle mind, for all the limitations of his training. The mortalised angel, on the other hand, is rather a tentative and simple creature. He may represent, perhaps, the rather blank mind of one who sees country society without having had the inestimable privilege of learning how it came about. His temperament was something too childlike—without the child's brutality—to investigate the enormous complexities of adjustment that had brought about the conditions into which he was all too suddenly plunged by a charge of duck-shot. He came and was filled with an inalterable perplexity, but some of his questions were too ingenuous; and while we may sympathise with the awful inertia of Hilyer before the impossible task of explaining the inexplicable differences between mortal precept and mortal practice, we feel that we might, in some cases at least, have made a more determined effort. . . . But the wounded angel, like the metal machine, is only a device whereby the searching examination of our author may be displayed in an engrossing and intimate form. And in **The Wonderful Visit,** that exuberance we postulated, that absorption in the development of idea, is more marked; in the unfolding of the story we can trace the method of the novelist.

Indeed, the three romances that follow discover hardly a trace of the social investigator. **The Island of Dr Moreau, The Invisible Man** and **The War of the Worlds** are essays in pure fantasy, and although the first of the three is influenced by biology I class it unhesitatingly among the works of sheer exuberance. Each of these books is, in effect, an answer to some rather whimsical question, and the problem that Dr Moreau attempted to solve was: "Can we, by surgery, so accelerate the evolutionary process as to make man out of a beast in a few days or weeks?" And within limits he found that the answer was: "Yes."

In the seclusion of his island, and with the poor assistance of the outlawed medical student, Montgomery, Dr Moreau succeeded in producing some creditable parodies of humanity by his operations on pigs, bulls, dogs and other animals. These cut and remoulded creatures had something of the appearance and intelligence of Homo Sapiens, and could be maintained at that level by the exercise of discipline and the constant recital of "the Law"; left to themselves they gradually reverted to the habits and manners of the individual beasts out of which they had been carved. We may infer that some subtle organic chemistry worked its determination upon their uncontrolled wills, but Mr Wells offers no explanation, psychic, chemical or biological, and I do not think that he intended any particular fable beyond the evident one that, physically, one species is as like to the next as makes no matter. What Moreau did well another man might have done better. It is a good story, and the adventures of the marooned Prendick, alone, are sufficient justification for the original conception. (I feel bound to note, however, the absurd comments of some early reviewers who seemed to imagine that the story was a defence of vivisection.)

The next romance [*The Invisible Man*] . . . seeks to answer the question: "What could a man do if he were invisible?" Various attempts to answer that question had been made by other writers, but none of them had come to it with Mr Wells' practical grasp of the real problem; the earlier romantics had not grappled with the necessity for clothes and the various ways in which a material man, however indistinguishable his body by our sense of sight, must leave traces of his passage. The study from beginning to end is finely realistic; and even the theory of the albino, Griffin, and in a lesser degree his method of winning the useless gift of invisibility, are convincing enough to make us wonder whether the thing is not scientifically possible. As a pure romance set in perfectly natural surroundings, *The Invisible Man* is possibly the high-water mark of Mr Wells' achievement in this kind. He has perfected his technique, and the interest in the development of the story works up steadily to the splendid climax, when the form of the berserker Griffin returns to visibility, his hands clenched, his eyes wide open, and on his face an expression of "anger and dismay," the elements—as I choose to think—of man's revolt against imprisonment in the flesh. It is worth while to note that by another statement, the same problem is posed and solved in the short story called *The Country of the Blind*.

The War of the Worlds . . . , although written in the first person, is in some ways the most detached of all these fantasies; and it is in this book that Mr Wells frankly confesses his own occasional sense of separation. "At times," says the narrator of the history, "I suffer from the strangest sense of detachment from myself and the world about me, I seem to watch it all from the outside, from somewhere inconceivably remote, out of time, out of space, out of the stress and tragedy of it all." That sense must have remained with him as he wrote the account of the invading Martians, so little passion does the book contain. The vision, however, is clear enough and there is more invention than in many of the other romances. The picture of the Martians themselves develops in one direction the theory of human evolution expressed in *The Man of the Year Million*. The expansion of the brain case, and the apotheosis of pure intellect, devoid, so far as we can judge, of any emotional expression, are the steadily biological deductions that we should expect from the Wells of this period. The fighting machines of these incomprehensible entities, the heat ray and the black smoke, are all excellent conceptions; and the narrative is splendidly graphic. But only in the scenes with the curate, when the narrator is stirred to passionate anger, and in his later passages with the sapper, do we catch any glimpses of the novelist intrigued with the intimate affairs of humanity. Even the narrator's brother, in his account of the escape with two women in a pony-carriage, has become infected with that sense of detachment. The two women are strongly differentiated but leave little impression of personality.

The fact that I have made this comment on lack of passion in describing one of these earlier romances is indicative of a particular difference between Mr Wells' method in this sort and the method of the lesser writer of fantasias. The latter, whatever his idea, and it may be a brilliant idea, is always intent on elaborating the wonder of his theme by direct description. Mr Wells is far more subtle and more effective. He takes an average individual, identifies him with the world as we know it, and then proceeds gradually to bring his marvel within the range of this individual's apprehension. We see the improbable, not too definitely, through the eyes of one who is prepared with the same incredulity as the reader of the story, and as a result the strange phenomenon, whether fallen angel, invisible man, converted beast or invading Martian, takes all the shape of reality. That this shape is convincing is due to the brilliance of Mr Wells' imagination and his power of graphic expression; the lesser writer might adopt the method and fail utterly to attain the effect; but it is this conception of the means to reach the intelligence and senses of the average reader that chiefly distinguishes these romances from those of such writers as Jules Verne. Our approach to the wonderful is so gradual and so natural that when we are finally confronted with it the incredible thing has become inevitable and expected. Finally, it has become so identified with human surprise, anger or dismay that any failure of humanity in the chief person of the story reacts upon our conception of the wonderful intrusion among familiar phenomena.

Now, this power of creating the semblance of fact out of an ideal was too valuable a thing to be wasted on the making of stories that had no purpose beyond that of interesting or exciting the reader with such imaginations as the Martians, whose only use was to threaten humanity with extinction. . . . So he began tentatively at first to introduce a vivid criticism of the futility of present-day society into his fantasies, and the first and the least of these books was that published in 1899 as *When the Sleeper Wakes*, a title afterwards changed to *The Sleeper Awakes*. (pp. 20-33)

The first appearance of Graham the Sleeper, tormented then by the spectres and doubts that accompany insomnia, is made so credible that we accept his symptoms without the least demur; his condition is merely unusual enough to excite a trembling interest. Even the passing of his early years of trance does not arouse scepticism. But then we fall with one terrific plunge into the world of A.D. 2100, and, like Graham, we cannot realise it. Moreover this changed, developed world has a slightly mechanical air. The immense enclosed London, imagined by Mr Wells, is no Utopia, yet, like the dream of earlier prophets, it is too logical to entice us into any hallucination; and we come, fatally, to a criticism of the syllogism. (pp. 33-4)

The main theme is the growing division between Capital and Labour. The Giant Trust—managing the funds accumulated in Graham's name, a trust that has obtained possession of so immense a capital that it controls the chief activities of the world—is figured in the command of a certain Ostrog, who, with all the dependents that profit by the use of his wealth and such mercenaries as he can hold to himself, represents one party in opposition to the actual workers and producers, generically the People. The picture is the struggle of our own day in more acute form; the result, in the amended edition, is left open. "Who will win—Ostrog or the People?" Mr Wells writes in the Preface referred to above, and answers: "A thousand years hence that will still be just the open question we leave to-day." (pp. 34-5)

In *The Sleeper Awakes*, even in the revised version, the sociological theory is still mechanical, the prophecy at once too logical, and at the same time deduced from premises altogether too restricted. The world of A.D. 2100 is the world of to-day, with its more glaring contrasts still more glaringly emphasised; with its social incongruities and blindness raised to a higher power. And all that it lacked has been put into a romance called *In the Days of the Comet*. . . . (p. 36)

The great change wrought by the coming of the Comet might be sentimentally described as a change of heart; I prefer to call it a change of reason. All the earlier part of the work, which is again told in the first person, presents the life of a Midland industrial area as seen by one who has suffered it. The Capital-Labour problem bulks in the foreground, and is adequately supported by a passionate exposition of the narrowness and misery of lower-middle-class life in the jumble of limitations, barriers and injustices that arise from the absolute ownership of property. Also, into this romance—the only one, by the way—comes some examination of the relations of the sexes. And all this jumble is due, if we are to believe the remedy, to human misunderstanding. The influence of the Comet passed over the earth, and men, after a few hours of trance, awoke to a new realisation. (pp. 36-7)

[Every] person on the earth had been miraculously cured of their myopia and astigmatism. They saw beauty and the means to still more perfect beauty, and, seeing, they had but to believe and the old miseries vanished. . . . The lesson—I cannot deny that the book is didactic—of the change wrought by the comet is that man should find the full expression of his personality in sympathy and understanding. The egotism remains, but it works to a collective end. . . .

War is necessarily touched upon in this book as an inevitable corollary to the problems of personal and a fortiori of national property; but the real counterblast against wholesale fratricide was reserved for the following romance, published in 1908.

The War in the Air definitely disclosed a change of method that was adumbrated in its predecessor. The agent of experience is still retained in the person of Bert Smallways, but the restrictions imposed by the report of an eye-witness have become too limiting, and, like Hardy in *The Dynasts,* Mr Wells alternates between a near and a distant vision. . . . So the intimate, personal narrative of Smallways' adventures is occasionally dropped for a few pages; Mr Wells shuts off his magic-lantern and fills the interval with an analysis of larger issues.

And the issues are so vital, the *dénouement* so increasingly probable, that, despite all the exaggerations necessary in a fiction of this kind, the warning contained in this account of a world-war is one that must remain in the minds of any thoughtful reader. (pp. 39-41)

Indeed, I think that *The War in the Air* is the greatest of Mr Wells' achievements in fantasy that has a deeper purpose than mere amusement. The story is absorbing and Smallways a perfectly conceived character, recommendations that serve to popularise the book as a romance; but all the art of the construction is relevant to the theme, and to the logical issue which is faced unflinchingly. . . . In the book now under consideration the conception is too wide for any such lapses into the maudlin. British interests play an insignificant part in the drama. We have to consider war not as an incident in the history of a nation, but as a horrible disgrace in the history of humanity.

And war is the theme also of *The World Set Free* . . . , but it leads here to a theory of reconstruction of which we have no sight in the earlier work. The opening chapters describe the inception of the means, the discovery of the new source of energy—a perfectly reasonable conception—that led to the invention of the ''atomic bomb,'' a thing so terribly powerful and continuous in its action that after the first free use of it in a European outbreak, war became impossible. As a romance, the book fails. The interest is not centred in a single character, and we are given somewhat disconnected glimpses of various

phases in the discovery of the new energy, in its application, and of the catastrophes that follow its use as an instrument of destruction. The essay form has almost dominated the method of the novelist, and consequently the essential parable has not the same force as in *The War in the Air.* Nevertheless, the vision is there, obscured by reason of its more personal expression. . . . (pp. 42-4)

The First Men in the Moon . . . is little more than a piece of sheer exuberance. The theory of the means to the adventure and the experience itself are both plausible. There are a few minor discrepancies, but when the chief assumption is granted the deductions will all stand examination. . . . The exposition of lunar social conditions cannot be taken very seriously. Specialisation is the keynote; the production by education and training, of minds, and, as far as possible, bodies, adapted to a particular end, and incapable of performing other technical functions. The picture of this highly developed state, however, is not such as would tempt us to emulation. As a machine it works; as an ideal it lacks any presentation of the thing we call beauty. The apotheosis of intelligence in the concrete example leaves us unambitious in that direction. (pp. 46-8)

The Sea Lady . . . stands alone among Mr Wells' romances. The realistic method remains, but the conception is touched with a poetic fancy of a kind that I have not found elsewhere in these books. The Venus Annodomini who came out of the sea at Folkestone in the form of an authentic mermaid was something more than a mere critic of our civilised conventions. She was that, too. . . . But she was also the personification of ''other dreams.'' She had ''the quality of the open sky, of deep tangled places, of the flight of birds . . . of the high sea.'' She represented to one man, at least, ''the Great Outside.'' And, if we still find a repetition of the old statement in that last description, it is, nevertheless, surrounded with a glamour that is not revealed in such books as *In the Days of the Comet.* The ideal that is faintly shadowed in *The Sea Lady* is more ethereal, less practical; the story, despite the naturalistic, half-cynical manner of its recountal, has the elements of romance. (pp. 49-50)

We come, finally, without any suggestion of climax, to *The Food of the Gods.* . . . The food was produced, casually in the first instance, by two experimenters who served no cause but that of their own inquisitive science. One of them, Redwood, had become intrigued by the fact that the growth of all living things proceeded with bursts and intermissions. . . . And Bensington, the other experimenter, succeeded in separating a food that produced regular instead of intermittent growth. It was universal in its effects, influencing vegetable as well as animal life; and in the course of twenty years it produced human giants, forty feet high. This is a theme for Mr Wells to revel in, and he does, treating the detail of the first two-thirds of the book with a fine realism. Like Bensington, he saw, ''behind the grotesque shapes and accidents of the present, the coming world of giants and all the mighty things the future has in store— vague and splendid, like some glittering palace seen suddenly in the passing of a sunbeam far away.'' The parable is plain enough, but the application of it weakens when we realise that so far as the merely physical development goes, the food of the gods is only bringing about a change of scale. If we grant that this ''insurgent bigness'' must conquer the world, the final result is only humanity in the same relation to life that it now occupies. . . . (pp. 51-2)

The change of scale, however, so long as it was changing, presents in another metaphor the old contrasts. The young giants, the Cossars and Redwood, looking down on common humanity from a vantage-point some thirty to forty feet higher than the "little people," are critical by force of circumstances; and they are at the same time handicapped by an inability to comprehend the thing criticised. They are too differentiated. . . . (p. 53)

I think the partial failure of *The Food of the Gods* to furnish any ethical satisfaction is due to the fact that in this romance Mr Wells has identified himself too closely with the giants; a fault that indicates a slight departure from normality. The inevitable contrast between great and little lacks a sympathy and appreciation we find elsewhere. "Endless conflict. Endless misunderstanding. All life is that. Great and little cannot understand one another" is the true text of the book; and it implies a weakness in the great not less than in the little; a weakness that is hardly exonerated by the closing sentence: "But in every child born of man lurks some seed of greatness—waiting for the food." I find a quality of reasonableness in the little people's antagonism to the blundering superiority of those giants.

To the tail of these romances I may pin the majority of Mr Wells' short stories. The best of them are all included in the collection published under the title of *The Country of the Blind*. In this form Mr Wells displays nothing but the exuberance of his invention. In the Preface to the collection he defines his conception of short-story writing as "the jolly art of making something very bright and moving; it may be horrible or pathetic or funny, or beautiful, or profoundly illuminating, having only this essential, that it should take from fifteen to twenty minutes to read aloud." I can add nothing to that description, and would only take away from it so much as is implied by the statement that I cannot call to mind any one of these stories which is "profoundly illuminating" in the same sense that I would certainly apply the phrase to some of the romances. Jolly and bright they undoubtedly are, but when they are moving, they provide food for wonder rather than for enlightenment. (pp. 54-6)

I feel no shade of hesitation when I say that H. G. Wells is a great writer. His fecundity, his mastery of language, his comprehension of character are gifts and abilities that certain of his contemporaries have in equal, or in some particulars in larger measure. But he alone has used his perfected art for a definite end. He has not been content to record his observations of the world as he has seen it, to elaborate this or that analysis of human motive, or to relate the history of a few selected lives. He has done all this, but he has done infinitely more by pointing the possible road of our endeavour. Through all his work moves the urgency of one who would create something more than a mere work of art to amuse the multitude or afford satisfaction to the critic. His chief achievement is that he has set up the ideal of a finer civilisation, of a more generous life than that in which we live; an ideal that, if it is still too high for us of this generation, will be appreciated and followed by the people of the future. (pp. 115-16)

> *J. D. Beresford, in his* H. G. Wells, *Henry Holt and Company, 1915, 127 p.*

MARK R. HILLEGAS   (essay date 1967)

[*Hillegas is an American educator and critic. As author and editor of such studies as* The Future as Nightmare: H. G. Wells and the Modern Anti-Utopians (1967) *and* Shadows of the Imagination: The Fantasies of C. S. Lewis, J. R. R. Tolkien, and Charles Williams (1969), *Hillegas displays his concern with examining*

Wells, photographed during the First World War. Courtesy of Martin Wells.

the relationship of scientific and technological advances to human life. In the following excerpt, he defines the concept of "the Wellsian imagination" and discusses the essentially non-Wellsian ways in which Wells attacked human complacency in his early science fiction works.]

Wells turned naturally and easily to the writing of science fiction because he possessed what demands to be called "the Wellsian imagination." This Wellsian imagination is the key to his science fiction as well as to the nature of its impact, and I shall attempt to describe it briefly.

Wells is, of course, closely identified with a particular vision of a utopian World State, a vision which is important in explaining his relationship to the anti-utopians. . . . What I am dealing with now, however, is a quality, a way of looking at things, which was first described at length by Van Wyck Brooks in 1915 [see Additional Bibliography]. This quality, which must surely be a chief characteristic of the mind scientifically educated, is detachment. As Brooks remarked about Wells's fiction in general, and as we would say particularly about his scientific romances, future histories, and utopias, Wells saw men chemically and anatomically, the world astronomically. Brooks also put it another way: it is the distinction between the intellectual, who views life in terms of ideas, and the artist, who views life in terms of experience. Generally speaking, the intellectual dominated Wells's writings, though sometimes— most continuously in *Tono-Bungay, Kipps,* and *Mr. Polly*—the artist took over. But it must be emphasized that this distinction between "intellectual" and "artistic" refers to the angle at which reality is viewed, not to the quality of writing. Even at his most "intellectual," as in, say, *The Time Machine,* Wells was capable of vividness in both conception and expression. *The Time Machine,* though it differs greatly from ordinary fiction, has some right to the title of "art."

Surely the single most spectacular manifestation of this detached quality of the Wellsian imagination is its preoccupation with the future. This preoccupation, which is central to many of Wells's writings, is most enthusiastically explained in "**The Discovery of the Future,**" a lecture Wells delivered at the Royal Institution in January 1902, which was published in *Nature* the next month. In this lecture, Wells distinguished between two kinds of minds. The first, oriented to the past, regards the future "as sort of black nonexistence upon which the advancing present will presently write events." It is the legal mind, always referring to precedents. The second kind of mind, oriented to the future, is constructive, creative, organizing. "It sees the world as one great workshop, and the present is no more than material for the future, for the king that is yet destined to be." Finally, Wells predicted what might be accomplished if the future-oriented mind were given freedom to express itself:

> All this world is heavy with the promise of greater things, and a day will come, one day in the unending succession of days, when beings who are now latent in our thoughts and hidden in our loins, shall stand upon this earth as one stands upon a footstool and shall laugh and reach out their hands amidst the stars."

(In the context of that entire lecture, this passage is not, incidentally, the expression of simple optimism it can easily be taken to be.)

Along with the detached imagination and its preoccupation with the future go certain clearly defined and inevitable values and interests. Wells—not surprisingly for a former student and admirer of T. H. Huxley—was a supreme rationalist and believer in science and the scientific method, a Francis Bacon reborn. And so for Wells, as for one of his Utopians in *Men Like Gods,* there was no way out of the cages of life but by knowledge— knowledge of man himself and of man in relation to the things about him. Naturally the Wellsian imagination is drawn to certain characteristic subjects. It is fascinated by the revelations of man's place in time and space given to us by science, fascinated by the vistas of astronomy, particularly the death of the world and the vastness of interstellar space, fascinated by the vision of geological epochs, the evolution of life, and the early history of man vouchsafed by geology, paleontology, and archaeology.

The first, brilliant fruit of this Wellsian imagination were the scientific romances and stories written in the 1890's which led, in their turn, by a complicated process which also involved reaction against the Wellsian utopias, to the major anti-utopias of the twentieth century.

Ironically, Wells's early scientific romances and stories present a vision of man's nature, his place in the universe, and the power of science which is the complete antithesis of the vision that by the 1930's was commonly considered Wellsian. "Wellsian," it need hardly be said, came to connote a utopia filled with super-gadgets, mechanical wonders, run by an elite of

scientists and engineers for the good of the people (the kind of thing the public saw in the tasteless movie made by Alexander Korda, *Things to Come*). The application of science had almost automatically brought this heaven on earth, which was inhabited by a finer race of human beings, who had inevitably evolved to their state of near perfection. Neither in spirit nor in detail are Wells's stories and romances at all similar to this commonly accepted notion of the Wellsian vision.

Odd as it may seem in view of the later widespread identification of Wells with scientific optimism, knowledgeable commentators have long been aware of the darkness which actually permeates much of the early science fiction—the stories and the great scientific romances like *The Time Machine, The Invisible Man, The Island of Dr. Moreau, The War of the Worlds,* and *The First Men in the Moon.* In the 1890's several reviewers, one of whom was W. T. Stead, were quick to note Wells's pessimism and "the gloomy horror of his vision" [see excerpt dated 1898]. Certain later critics have been well aware that the Wells of the scientific romances is not "Wellsian." (pp. 13-17)

To understand the darkness and pessimism of the early stories and scientific romances, we must remember that they were written against the background of grave social injustice and economic distress, socialist agitation and labor unrest. Fifty years after Disraeli had written of the "two nations," England still consisted chiefly of the rich and the poor. At the bottom of the social heap were the exploited multitudes of the industrial proletariat, who, in spite of the fact that conditions had improved incredibly since the "Hungry Forties," still led horribly deformed and meaningless lives. Above them were the energetic and upward aspiring middle class, cramped by the conditions of their existence only at the bottom levels of the class. At the summit, the "unpremeditated, successful, aimless Plutocracy" led sterile lives of unproductive leisure. The middle and upper classes, who were seldom their brothers' keepers and usually ignored the inhabitants of the Abyss, managed, in the face of worsening conditions during these last years of the nineteenth century, to hold to their faith in "progress," managed to believe that things were somehow improving. In his scientific romances and stories written at this time, Wells set about vigorously to attack this late Victorian complacency, for in his opinion there was no greater enemy of progress than a belief in inevitable progress. He launched this attack, as I have pointed out elsewhere [see Additional Bibliography], from what is best described as the "cosmic pessimism" of T. H. Huxley. (p. 18)

In Huxley's philosophy of evolution there is an element of grave doubt about the outcome of the cosmic or evolutionary process—his "cosmic pessimism"—which was exactly suited to Wells's aesthetic and didactic purposes in the stories and scientific romances written in the 1890's. And it is this "cosmic pessimism" which inspired the details in the scientific romances (chiefly *The Time Machine, The Island of Dr. Moreau, When the Sleeper Wakes* and "**A Story of the Days To Come,**" and *The First Men in the Moon*) that are repeated in the works by Forster, Zamyatin, Huxley, Orwell, and others and that make these romances by Wells something like the first modern anti-utopias.

By the 1880's Huxley had clearly formulated his idea that the evolutionary process will never lead to moral or social improvement, for cosmic nature is the "headquarters of the enemy of ethical nature" and the only chance for social and ethical progress is the "checking of the cosmic process at every step" and the substitution for it of the ethical. But, as Houston Peterson remarked [in his *Huxley, Prophet of Science* (1932)], Huxley had ''no fantastic hopes'' for the success of any such effort. The savagery in civilized men will not easily be eradicated because their cosmic nature is the outcome of millions of years of evolutionary training, while control of the cosmic process by manipulating the human organism is out of the question. Occasionally Huxley became so pessimistic that he would almost have welcomed ''some kindly comet'' to sweep the whole affair away. (pp. 19-20)

The detached Wellsian imagination, obsessed by the Huxleyan cosmic pessimism, led Wells in the 1890's to produce two categories of attack on human complacency. The first and larger group contains stories chiefly of pure menace, and excellent fiction they are indeed, being among the very best things of this sort ever written. The second category, closely related to the first, consists of works anti-utopian in their assault on optimism.

The germ of the stories of menace, and probably of the one romance of the same type, is contained in an article Wells published in the *Pall Mall Gazette*, Septemter 25, 1894, and entitled **''The Extinction of Man,''** an article which relates these stories and the romance to Wells's interest in the future. Wells began **''The Extinction of Man''** by questioning man's complacent assumption of his continued existence on this planet in the light of the evidence from geology: ''in no case does the record of the fossils show a really dominant species succeeded by its own descendants.'' It is the familiar lesson of geology; again and again forms of life have risen to dominance, only to vanish away and be replaced by other forms:

> What has usually happened in the past appears to be the emergence of some type of animal hitherto rare and unimportant, and the extinction, not simply of the previously ruling species, but of most of the forms that are at all closely related to it. Sometimes, indeed, as in the case of the extinct giants of South America, they vanished without any considerable rivals, victims of pestilence, famine, or, it may be, of that cumulative inefficiency that comes of a too undisputed life.

And so Wells came to caution his readers against the ''too acceptable view of man's certain tenure of the earth for the next few million years or so.'' As possible threats, he cited, among others, the evolution of the ant and the cephalopod, thus foreshadowing two of his stories, **''The Empire of the Ants''** and **''The Sea Raiders.''** (pp. 21-2)

And so Wells wrote numerous stories of menace. **''The Empire of the Ants''** (1905) describes a race of intelligent ants in the upper region of the Amazon who are beginning a march on civilization—''new competitors for the sovereignty of the globe.'' **''The Sea Raiders''** (1896) purports to be a ''true account'' of the attack on the coast of Devon and Cornwall of giant man-eating octupuses. **''The Flowering of the Strange Orchid''** (1894) deals with a man-eating plant; **''In the Avu Observatory''** (1894) with a giant and hostile bat; **''The Valley of the Spiders''** (1903) with a deadly floating spider. But the best of the stories is **''The Star''** (1897), which deals, in remarkably solid, concrete detail, with the catastrophic approach to the earth of a large body of matter from the depths of space beyond the solar system.

Disaster also comes from outer space in the one scientific romance of pure menace type that Wells wrote and which is closely related to **''The Star''** and **''The Sea Raiders''**—the enormously effective **The War of the Worlds**. . . . In plot and fictional technique it bears some resemblance to Defoe's *A Journal of the Plague Year:* both novels are offered as eye-witness accounts of a great disaster which befalls mankind and particularly the inhabitants of London. In each case the disaster had a special topical interest at the time of publication: an outbreak of the plague in 1720 in Marseilles set Londoners to recalling the horror of 1665, while in the 1890's popular interest in Mars as the abode of life was, because of Schiaparelli's earlier discovery of the ''canals,'' so intense that it at times amounted to a mania. At the same time this interest combines with a fascination for stories of an invasion of England which began, as I. F. Clarke has shown in *Voices Prophesying War*, with Sir George Chesney's ''Battle of Dorking'' (1872). (pp. 22-3)

Much more important for our purposes than the story of menace is the second category of Wellsian attack on human complacency, in which Huxleyan cosmic pessimism generates images and ideas central to the twentieth-century anti-utopian tradition. The major works in this ''cosmic pessimism'' category are **The Time Machine, The Island of Dr. Moreau, When the Sleeper Wakes, ''A Story of the Days To Come,''** and **The First Men in the Moon.** (pp. 24-5)

The Time Machine ... [is] the first of Wells's scientific romances and perhaps the most nearly faultless example of the kind of fiction with which we are concerned. Its vitality and literary power are enormous, its credibility almost perfect, and, inspired by Huxleyan cosmic pessimism, it is rich in significant meanings. It is worth discussing its technique, not only to show how this kind of fiction works, but also to explain why **The Time Machine** had such an enormous impact on the twentieth century anti-utopia.

''For the writer of fantastic stories to help the reader to play the game properly,'' Wells wrote, ''he must help him in every possible unobtrusive way to *domesticate* the impossible hypothesis. He must trick him into an unwary concession to some plausible assumption and get on with his story while the illusion holds.'' This is exactly Wells's technique in **The Time Machine**.

And so the story begins in the solid, upper-middle-class atmosphere of the Time Traveler's home, as he is expounding to his guests after dinner the mysteries of the geometry of Four Dimensions:

> ''I do not mean to ask you to accept anything without reasonable ground for it. You will soon admit as much as I need from you. You know of course that a mathematical line, a line of thickness *nil*, has no real existence. They taught you that? Neither has a mathematical plane. These things are mere abstractions.''
>
> ''That is all right,'' said the Psychologist.
>
> ''Nor, having only length, breadth, and thickness, can a cube have a real existence.''
>
> ''There I object,'' said Filby. ''Of course a solid body may exist. All real things—''
>
> ''So most people think. But wait a moment. Can an *instantaneous* cube exist?'' . . .

Before we know what has happened, we are tricked into the concession that Time could be another, a Fourth Dimension, along which one might travel as one does the other three dimensions. All we need is a vehicle.

And so Wells invented the Time Machine, thereby becoming the father of a new genre, the modern story of time travel. The invention was a major leap of the imagination, and it grew not only out of contemporary interest in the geometry of four dimensions but also the great vogue at the time for tales of the future. Such stories existed, of course, at least as early as Mercier's *L'An 2440* (1772), but their wide popularity began only with Edward Bellamy's *Looking Backward* (1888). In the late 1880's and early 1890's, dozens of these stories were written, and at least two besides *Looking Backward* are significant as literature: W. H. Hudson's *A Crystal Age* (1888) and William Morris's *News from Nowhere* (1891). **The Time Machine** is a natural evolution from all these stories and an improvement on them, for in each the visitor arrives in the future by means of such clumsy devices as dream, hypnosis, accident, or trance. Wells's machine is considerably more suitable, given the sophisticated requirements for plausibility of a new scientific and mechanical age. It may possibly have been suggested to him by the space vehicle of the cosmic voyage, obviously a related genre. (pp. 25-7)

It is impossible, really, to do justice to the perfection of Wells's effort to ease the reader into a willing suspension of disbelief in [the] first two framing chapters. All one can do is list some of the elements: the common-sense character of the narrator; the solid atmosphere of his home; the characterization of the guests to give them sufficient—but not too much—individuality for the purposes of the story; the skillful use of incidental details to create the air of reality. This same perfection continues in the next section, the journey through time to the year 802,701, and, indeed, throughout the rest of the romance.

In the description of the journey through time, Wells's powers of concretization, apparent throughout the story, are at their highest. The journey begins, as do most journeys into space in fiction and reality, with a shock at departure: "I drew a breath, set my teeth, gripped the starting lever with both hands, and went off with a thud." . . . The sensations of time travel are those of motion through space, and at first the Time Traveler finds them distinctly unpleasant. He has a feeling of helpless headlong motion and the horrible anticipation of an imminent collison. Later, the unpleasant nature of time travel begins to wear off and the Traveler experiences the kind of exhilaration felt by many voyagers through space in fiction from Domingo Gonsales and Cyrano de Bergerac to Elwin Ransom. Finally he watches awestruck the accelerated sequence of celestial phenomena. He sees the moon spinning swiftly through her quarters from new to full, the alternation of day and night merging into one continuous grayness, the sky taking on a wonderful deepness of blue, and the sun, like a streak of fire, burning a brilliant arch in space. As his velocity increases at a tremendous rate, he becomes apprehensive and decides to stop, and in his panic slows the machine down too suddenly. Traveler and machine go toppling over into the world of 802,701. Thunder rumbles and hail hisses around him as he sits on the grass of what seems to be a little garden.

This world, as we will see later, is central to the meaning of **The Time Machine**. Suffice it now to say that it is a disillusionment to the Traveler. Instead of a world far advanced beyond ours, he finds that in 802,701 mankind has evolved into two degenerate species: above ground, the Eloi, delicate little creatures with the intellect of a five-year-old; and below

ground, the pale, ape-like Morlocks, who leave their subterranean world only at night. It is the sunset of mankind.

But at first glance, the earth in 802,701 seems to be a garden of Eden. Everywhere are beautiful flowers and fruit, and no hostile insects or animals—nature is seemingly in perfect subjugation to man. The weather is mild and warm, apparently because the earth is now closer to a sun into which have fallen one or more of the inner planets. Gone are the smaller houses and cottages of our time; instead our descendants live in magnificent, ornate palace-like buildings "dotted about among the variegated greenery." These are the buildings of utopia and the first manifestation of Wells's familiar preoccupation with housing and the physical features of the future.

But a second look reveals that it is only a ruined splendor. All human artifacts are slowly crumbling. Some of the buildings are already gone: "a great heap of granite, bound together by masses of aluminium, a vast labyrinth of precipitous walls and crumbled heaps, amidst which were thick heaps of very beautiful pagoda-like plants." And even the many still-standing buildings, in which the surface people live, are decaying. . . . (pp. 27-9)

Even more of a ruined splendor are the people the Time Traveler finds living in this great garden—the Eloi. Fragile little creatures perhaps four feet tall, they pass their time "in playing gently, in bathing in the river, in making love in a half-playful fashion, in eating fruit and sleeping." Human vigor and energy have passed into languor and decay.

In time the Traveler learns the purpose of the mysterious wells and towers scattered across the country: these structures are part of the ventilation system for a subterranean world, in which live the other degenerate descendants of men, the Morlocks. They are strange little beings whose pallid bodies are "just the half-bleached colour of the worms and things one sees preserved in spirit in a zoological museum." They are chinless, and in their faces are set "great lidless, pinkish grey eyes." At night they leave their subterranean world to hunt down Eloi for food.

Slowly the Time Traveler pieces together the history of mankind's horrible degeneration, a degeneration which has occured because mankind, as T. H. Huxley feared, was ultimately unable to control the cosmic or evolutionary process. It is Huxley's cosmic pessimism which gives meaning and permanence to this first anti-utopia of the modern mechanical and scientific age. For all its exuberance and vitality of imagination, **The Time Machine** is a bleak and sober vision of man's place in the universe. By the year 800,000, the world, at least above ground, had become intelligent and co-operative, truly a modern utopia. Nature had been subjugated and man had readjusted the balance of animal and vegetable life to suit his needs. Disease, hardship, and poverty were eliminated. With the attainment of security and freedom from danger, man's restless energy turned to art, and for a time a great culture flourished. But it was a utopian age which could never last because the upperworlders ignored another of Huxley's warnings [from his "Evolution and Ethics"]: "If we may permit ourselves a larger hope of abatement of the essential evil of the world . . . I deem it an essential condition of the realization of that hope that we cast aside the notion that escape from pain and sorrow is the proper object of life." And so came languor and decay. The struggle to conquer nature had developed human intelligence, strength, and courage. But when the battle had been won, there was no force to select the most fit. In the new state of balance and security, intellectual and physical power were out of place. The weak were as well equipped as the strong, in fact even better equipped, for the strong were fretted by an energy for which there was no outlet. And so the inhabitants of the utopia above ground evolved to feeble prettiness, a process which constitutes one of the major criticisms in the twentieth century of the idea of utopia. The perfection and ease of utopia, say many of its critics—like Forster in "The Machine Stops"—can only lead to degeneration and decay.

But this was only half the explanation of the world of 802,701. The development of the Morlocks had followed a somewhat different course, and here the story becomes social criticism and very much a product of the 1890's, the years of increasing Socialist protest. The Eloi and Morlocks grew apart, just as earlier in the nineteenth century the widening of the social difference between capitalist and laborer had become more pronounced. As technology and industrialization progressed, factories went underground and with them their workers, who in time became adapted to the subterranean life and no longer came out into the light of day. . . . ([The] beginning of this process in the twenty-second century is later portrayed by Wells in the complementary stories, **When the Sleeper Wakes** and "**A Story of the Days To Come.**") Above ground the Haves pursued pleasure, comfort, and beauty; below ground the Have-Nots became continually adapted to the conditions of their labor. While the upper-worlders drifted to physical and mental ineffectiveness, the lower-worlders drifted to mere mechanical industry. However, since machines, no matter how perfect, require some intelligence to maintain, the Morlocks managed to retain some of their original intellectual strength, and, when the process of feeding the underworld became disrupted, the cosmic process reasserted itself and the Morlocks emerged to eat the Eloi. The world of 802,701 presents Huxley's trajectory of evolution some distance past the highest point, but still far from the end.

Escaping from the Morlocks, the Time Traveler pushes the levers in the wrong direction and rushes off into the even more distant future. The hand marking a thousand years sweeps by like the second hand on a watch, and he sees the earth nearing the end of the falling portion of Huxley's trajectory of evolution, thus bringing us to the idea which haunted Wells, Huxley, and others at the end of the nineteenth century—the death of our world. (pp. 29-32)

It is hard to exaggerate the significance of **The Time Machine**. Although Bellamy's *Looking Backward*, as Chad Walsh has said, inspired a great number of dystopias like Konrad Wilbrandt's *Mr. East's Experiences in Mr. Bellamy's World* and Richard C. Michaelis's *Looking Forward*, which show the evils of a socialist future, their impact was slight since all were trivial as works of art. In the 1880's or 1890's the only vivid pictures of the future—besides Wells's—were utopias or utopian romances: *Looking Backward, News from Nowhere,* and *A Crystal Age*. **The Time Machine** was thus the first well-executed, imaginatively coherent picture of a future worse than the present, a picture at the same time generally anti-utopian in its tendencies. Indeed, in imaginative qualities it excels later anti-utopias, such as even *We* and *Brave New World*, being both more successful in domesticating the incredible and more poetic in its conception. Its coherence and power explain why it not only contributed numerous details and images to twentieth-century anti-utopias but made available to the literary consciousness a new form (science fiction) and suggested one use for this form (the attack on utopias). (pp. 33-4)

Mark R. Hillegas, in his The Future as Nightmare: H. G. Wells and the Anti-Utopians, *Oxford University Press, 1967, 200 p.*

ROBERT L. PLATZNER   (essay date 1969)

[*In the following excerpt, Platzner examines the extent to which Kipling's* Jungle Books *were a significant influence on Wells's* The Island of Doctor Moreau.]

The probable source of at least one striking episode in H. G. Wells's **The Island of Dr. Moreau**—the narrator's initial meeting with the Beast Folk and the "Saying of the Law"—has been traced by one of the more scholarly and perceptive of Wells's critics, Bernard Bergonzi, to Kipling's *Jungle Books* [see *TCLC*, Vol. 6]. Bergonzi finds Wells drawing upon and perhaps parodying Kipling's image of an articulate beast society, and both the facts of contemporaneity (**The Island of Dr. Moreau** was published scarcely a year after *The Second Jungle Book*) and of Wells's known interest, at least at this stage in his career, in popular literary fashion, render this inference based on "internal" evidence even more probable. What I would propose in this essay is something further, however. For one thing, the number of narrative details borrowed or transformed by Wells is greater than most readers are aware of. But more significantly, the relationship between Kipling's *Jungle Books* and Wells's bleak island fable is built around philosophical as well as literary satire.

If one were to regard the impact of Kipling's tales on Wells's imagination at the level of mere literary invention, it would seem remarkable how much sinister suggestiveness Wells found in Kipling's unoffending nursery tales. For the animal world Kipling describes—I am thinking now specifically of the "Mowgli" tales—is essentially harmonious. In fact, the law of the jungle, its codes of honor and the pervasive hatred of *moral* treachery (something distinct from animal cunning), is the implicit theme of each of these stories, and the entire course of Mowgli's "natural" education is the discovery of the logic behind jungle instinct. . . .

Kipling never attempts to exclude the tooth and claw struggle for food or life that dominates animal life. What he does deny (or simply fails to perceive) is any form of *gratuitous* cruelty that is part of the "natural" pattern of animal life. . . . When sin and guilt do enter the jungle, it is man who is usually seen as the carrier of these diseased fears and longings. (p. 19)

No thematic summary, of course, can even suggest the compelling charm or the final pathos of the Mowgli stories, but even so brief a discussion can accurately convey the sustaining teleology of the whole. For it is just this aspect of *The Jungle Books*—Kipling's faith in the purposiveness of the natural universe and in man's place in that universe—that must have appeared so appallingly sentimental and unreflective to Wells. Whatever we have been able to reconstruct of Wells's world view during the first decade of his career suggests that he must have found *The Jungle Books* grotesquely false, biologically and morally. Whether one attributes the bleakness and recurrent apocalyptic fixations of Wells's early science fiction to *fin-de-siècle* pessimism or to a more systematically reasoned theory of cosmic degeneration derived from T. H. Huxley, or to both, the explicit metaphysical assumptions of **The Island of Dr. Moreau** are, roughly, antithetical to those of *The Jungle Books*. Man, as Wells saw him, is set adrift in a universe of chance, and in spite of human intelligence and will he can achieve no final victory over a cosmos devoid of Mind; nor can he finally

Claude Rains as Dr. Griffin, the title character in the 1933 film version of The Invisible Man. *Copyright © by Universal Pictures, a Division of Universal City Studios, Inc. Courtesy of MCA Publishing Rights, a Division of MCA Inc.*

overcome his own evolutionary heritage, those regressive animal instincts that civilization can modify but never eliminate. The moral and even biological insanity of Wells's mad scientist, Dr. Moreau, consists essentially in his refusal to concede that the "mark of the beast" can never be removed.

Given this grounding of Wells's imagination in nearly total skepticism, it is not difficult to see why the Mowgli stories were transmogrified in Wells's desolate parable; what remains is to trace how these changes were made. Let us consider first, then, the jungle society Moreau has established on his nameless island. In what appears to be at once a reduction and inversion of Kipling's rather subtle metaphoric animal characterizations (Bagheera, Baloo, and Kaa resemble recognizable human types but are never confined allegorically to that resemblance and are therefore acceptable as animal types as well) Wells reduces his Beast Folk to the status of human caricatures; they do not simply remind us of men, they *are* men, and in an even deeper sense they represent the condition of man. Of course, the process by which the Beast Folk came to be endowed with speech and human emotions (or perhaps one ought to say "humanoid" response) is "scientifically" elaborated through Moreau's discourse on the "limits of individual plasticity." But to Prendick, and I believe ultimately to the reader as well, the Beast Folk

appear, at first through ignorance and later in a kind of Swiftian hallucination, to be men who have been somehow animalized.

More precisely, one should describe Wells's satiric purpose here as an attempt to create an image of *homo sapiens* that is as near the evolutionary threshold of animality as possible, stripped (as are Swift's Yahoos) almost literally of the protective covering of civilized behavior. Civilization presents itself to Prendick's "maddened" brain as little more than a disguised jungle, but we are obviously meant to regard his reaction (as we are meant to regard Gulliver's) as mythically truthful *because* of its insane revulsions and distortions:

> When I lived in London the horror was well-nigh insupportable. I could not get away from men. . . . I would go into the streets to fight with my delusion, and prowling women would mew after me, furtive craving men glance jealously at me, weary pale workers go coughing by me, with tired eyes and eager paces like wounded deer dripping with blood, old people, bent and dull, pass murmuring to themselves, and all unheeding a ragged tribe of gibing children. Then I would turn aside into some chapel, and even there, such was my disturbance, it

seemed that the preacher gibbered Big Thinks even as the Ape Man had done. . . . And even it seemed that I, too, was not a reasonable creature, but only an animal tormented with some strange disorder in its brain, that sent it to wander alone, like a sheep stricken with the gid.

What happens in this passage and at similar moments in *The Island of Dr. Moreau* is what Kipling termed "letting in the jungle," but in quite another context. For Kipling's jungle represented a microcosm of order, a refuge from human inhumanity. Moreau's island, however, has no refuge, for civilization and the jungle are one; the huts and the "society" that has been established there are practically all that can be called remotely human. Moreau, in his godlike, "remorseless" cruelty and madness, is above (or at least beyond) humanity, while Montgomery, in his self-pity and suicidal drunkenness is perhaps more degraded than the beasts that serve him and finally kill him. There is nothing in Prendick's terrestrial environment, either on the island or back in England (just another "island"), that reflects his internalized image of human reason or compassion or gives evidence of a transcendent purposiveness. In desperation, Prendick finally turns to both chemistry and astronomy for some assurance of cosmic laws that exist before or beyond animal life. Once again, Wells has inverted Kipling's myth by placing even the possibility of a teleological ordering outside of "Nature."

The "Law" that does in fact exist in the Wellsian jungle—and here we encounter obvious and direct parody—is a grotesque litany of forbidden abominations. In place of the positive urging of Kipling's jungle law, that sense of honor and obligation that forms the basis of the heroic in jungle life, we find a series of commandments that deform and thwart rather than simply control natural impulse:

> "Not to go on all-Fours; *that* is the Law. Are we not Men?"
>
> "Not to suck up Drink; *that* is the Law. Are we not Men?"
>
> "Not to eat Flesh nor Fish; *that* is the Law. Are we not Men?"
>
> "Not to claw Bark of Trees; *that* is the Law. Are we not Men?"
>
> And so from the prohibition of these acts of folly, on to the prohibition of what I thought were the maddest, most impossible and most indecent things one could well imagine. . . .

Law is repression, Prendick discovers, but no repressive mechanism or ritual can hold out against the force of instinct. And the eruption of animal instinct is horrifying and traumatic to Wellsian sensibilities; so much so, that many of the later Utopian romances exhaust credibility in attempts to escape the ape and tiger within.

Parody of *The Jungle Books* becomes far more savage once Prendick has been accepted as a member of the island "family." In a satiric perversion of Mowgli's education, Prendick is forced to study the bared-teeth reality of the struggle for existence as it appeared to a post-Darwinian intellect. As I have noted, there are moments in *The Jungle Books* when animal ferocity is either dramatized or alluded to, but this realization of the necessary violence of nature is almost always accompanied by a recognition that only through this life-or-death grappling can courage or intelligence be displayed. Think of the trampling of Shere Khan, of Baloo and Bagheera fighting with the *Bandar-log* at the Cold Lairs, or of the pack warring to the death with the red dogs, therefore, as both the model and satiric target for the hunting of the Leopard Man in *The Island of Dr. Moreau:*

> So, panting, tumbling against rocks, torn by brambles, impeded by ferns and reeds, I helped to pursue the Leopard Man, who had broken the Law, and the Hyena-Swine ran, laughing savagely, by my side. I staggered on, my head reeling, and my heart beating against my ribs, tired almost to death, and yet not daring to lose sight of the chase, lest I should be left alone with this horrible companion. I staggered on in spite of infinite fatigue and the dense heat of the tropical afternoon. . . .

The excitement and blood lust of the Beast Folk, their obvious enjoyment when Moreau chooses a victim onto whom they can transfer their own guilt and hatred, are all physically and morally revolting. The Wolf-Bear's cry of "none escape" is, of course, part of the Law they chant (and it clearly recalls Kipling's precept "Sorrow never stays punishment") but the deeper meaning of this warning—and of the Law itself—becomes clear only at this moment, when "punishment" and gratifying torture are interchangeable. The hunt is thus judged and described in terms of civilized ethics with no sense of incongruity: it is ugly and sadistic and wholly "natural."

This feeling of bitter estrangement from the animal world (or from animality) is experienced even more acutely in the episodes following Moreau's death. Once again, Wells turns to the Mowgli tales for significant details and incidents that can be at once exploited and mocked. Thus Prendick, in a chapter entitled "Alone with the Beast Folk," confronts the animals in a manner reminiscent of the mature Mowgli—now that Moreau is gone he is "master of the jungle"; but in what does his control of these beasts consist? Apart from his revolver and whip, Prendick finds (as did Mowgli) that he can intimidate some of the animals by staring at them—a piece of fanciful zoology Kipling reiterates continually throughout *The Jungle Books*. But Prendick's most potent weapon, again like Mowgli's, is his intelligence or, more exactly and ironically, his talent for lying. Realizing that to survive he must somehow establish an ascendancy over the beasts that is based on fear, Prendick pretends that Moreau has not merely died, but that he has also been resurrected:

> "He is not dead," said I, in a loud voice. "Even now he watches us."
>
> This startled them. Twenty pairs of eyes regarded me.
>
> "The House of Pain is gone," said I. "It will come again. The Master you cannot see. Yet even now he listens above you."
>
> "True, true!" said the Dog Man.
>
> They were staggered at my assurance. An animal may be ferocious and cunning enough, but it takes a real man to tell a lie. . . .

The almost Gulliver-like naïveté of this confession demonstrates how skillfully Wells grafted Swiftian insight onto Kiplingesque matter.

The isolation that Prendick experiences is far more terrible than Gulliver's or Mowgli's. Gulliver can at least revive the memory of the Houyhnhnm ideal by speaking with his stable horses, and Mowgli, although he must return to civilization, carries within a code of honor and fidelity that protects him from the moral decay of the village. Prendick, however, cannot appeal to any norm, without or within. His delusion of universal bestiality—an anthropological variant of original sin—prevents him from turning to the moral consciousness of society. Nor can he turn inward. In his own way he has been animalized, and he confesses: "I was almost as queer to men as I had been to the Beast People. I may have caught something of the natural wildness of my companions." . . . Although man does "return to man" at the conclusion of *The Island of Dr. Moreau,* he returns in fact to a disfigured yet truthful image of his own "reversion." In Wells's despairing vision there is no way out of the jungle, and the jungle itself is a place of horror.

Neither Wells nor Kipling offers us a more truthful or more verifiable myth in his jungle vision, although I suspect *The Island of Dr. Moreau* is more relevant (if not more congenial) to contemporary philosophical tastes. I feel sure, though, that Wells regarded his romance in just this way: as an act of debunking, a scraping away of the surface illusions of the romantic imagination, an experiment in shock therapy that would communicate vile truths to the uncritical Victorian mind. It should be clear, therefore, why *The Jungle Books* must have seemed so rich a repository of delusions. Kipling's sequestered world of beast and man affirms natural intimacies yet never questions identities: Mowgli may belong and not belong to the jungle, but in either case he is never an outcast. Kipling will not permit him to reject his humanity, for it is only by remaining a half-brother to the animal world that he can effect a reconciliation between the jungle and civilization. For Wells, such a reconciliation evidently portended the nightmare of racial devolution. (pp. 20-2)

Robert L. Platzner, "H. G. Wells's 'Jungle Book':
The Influence of Kipling on 'The Island of Dr. Mo-
reau'," in The Victorian Newsletter, *No. 36, Fall,*
1969, pp. 19-22.

DARKO SUVIN (essay date 1975)

[*Suvin has edited and contributed to numerous studies of science fiction. In the following excerpt, he surveys Wells's science fiction works, focusing on* The Time Machine.]

H. G. Wells's first and most significant SF cycle (roughly to 1904) is based on the vision of a horrible novum as the evolutionary sociobiological prospect for mankind. His basic situation is that of a destructive newness encroaching upon the tranquillity of the Victorian environment. Often this is managed as a contrast between an outer framework and a story within the story. The framework is set in surroundings as staid and familiarly Dickensian as possible, such as the cozy study of *The Time Machine,* the old antiquity shop of "**The Crystal Egg,**" or the small towns and villages of southern England in *The War of the Worlds* and *The First Men in the Moon.* With the exception of the protagonist, who also participates in the inner story, the characters in the outer frame, representing the almost invincible inertia and banality of prosperous bourgeois England, are reluctant to credit the strange newness. By contrast, the inner story details the observation of the gradual, hesitant coming to grips with an alien superindividual force that menaces such life and its certainties by behaving exactly

as the bourgeois progress did in world history—as a quite ruthless but technologically superior mode of life. (p. 208)

As Wells observed, the "fantastic element" or novum is "the strange property or the strange world." The strange property can be the invention that renders Griffin invisible, or, obversely, a new way of seeing—literally, as in "**The Crystal Egg,**" "**The Remarkable Case of Davidson's Eyes,**" and "**The New Accelerator,**" or indirectly, as the Time Machine or the Cavorite sphere. It is always cloaked in a pseudo-scientific explanation, the possibility of which turns out, upon closer inspection, to be no more than a conjuring trick by the deft writer, with "precision in the unessential and vagueness in the essential"—the best example being the Time Machine itself. The strange world is elsewhen or elsewhere. It is reached by means of a strange invention or it irrupts directly into the Victorian world in the guise of the invading Martians or the Invisible Man. But even when Wells's own bourgeois world is not so explicitly assaulted, the strange novelty always reflects back on its illusions; an SF story by Wells is intended to be "the valid realization of some disregarded possibility in such a way as to comment on the false securities and fatuous self-satisfaction of everyday life."

The strange is menacing because it looms in the future of man. Wells masterfully translates some of man's oldest terrors—the fear of darkness, monstrous beasts, giants and ogres, creepy crawly insects, and Things outside the light of his campfire, outside tamed nature—into an evolutionary perspective that is supposed to be validated by Darwinian biology, evolutionary cosmology, and the fin-de-siècle sense of a historical epoch ending. Wells, a student of T. H. Huxley, eagerly used alien and powerful biological species as a rod to chastize Victorian man, thus setting up the model for all the Bug-Eyed Monsters of later chauvinistic SF. But the most memorable of those aliens, the octopuslike Martians and the antlike Selenites, are identical to "**The Man of the Year Million**" in one of Wells's early articles (alluded to in *The War of the Worlds*): they are emotionless higher products of evolution judging us as we would judge insects. In the final analysis, since the aliens are a scary, alternative human future, Wellsian space travel is an optical illusion, a variation on his seminal model of *The Time Machine.* The function of his interplanetary contacts is quite different from Verne's liberal interest in the mechanics of locomotion within a safely homogeneous space. Wells is interested exclusively in the opposition between the bourgeois reader's expectations and the strange relationships found at the other end: that is why his men do land on the Moon and his Martians on Earth.

Science is the true, demonic master of all the sorcerer's apprentices in Wells, who have—like Frankenstein or certain folktale characters—revealed and brought about destructive powers and monsters. From the Time Traveller through Moreau and Griffin to Cavor, the prime character of his SF is the scientist-adventurer as searcher for the New, disregarding common sense and received opinion. Though powerful, since it brings about the future, science is a hard master. Like Moreau, it is indifferent to human suffering; like the Martians, it explodes the nineteenth-century optimistic pretentions, liberal or socialist, of lording it over the universe. . . . For Wells human evolution is an open question with two possible answers, bright and dark; and in his first cycle darkness is the basic tonality. The cognitive "match" by whose small light he determines his stance is Darwinian evolution, a flame which fitfully illumines man, his hands (by interaction of which with the brain and the eye he evolved from ape), and the "patch he stands on." Therefore Wells could much later even the score by talking about "the anticipatory inventions of the great Frenchman" who "told that this and that thing could be done, which was not at that time done"—in fact, by defining Verne as a short-term technological popularizer. From the point of view of a votary of physics, Wells "invents" in the sense of inventing objective untruths. From the point of view of the evolutionist, who does not believe in objects but in processes—which we have only begun to elucidate—Verne is the one who "invents" in the sense of inventing banal gadgets. For the evolutionist, Nemo's submarine is in itself of no importance; what matters is whether intelligent life exists on the ocean floor (as in **"In the Abyss"** and **"The Sea Raiders"**). Accordingly, Wells's physical and technical motivations can and do remain quite superficial where not faked. Reacting against a mechanical view of the world, he is ready to approach again the imaginative, analogic veracity of Lucian's and Swift's story-telling centered on strange creatures, and to call his works "romances." Cavorite or the Invisible Man partake more of the flying carpet and the magic invisibility hood than of metallurgy or optics. The various aliens represent a vigorous refashioning of the talking and symbolic animals of folktale, bestiary, and fable lore into Swiftian grotesque mirrors to man, but with the crowning collocation within an evolutionary prospect. Since this prospect is temporal rather than spatial, it is also much more urgent and immediate than Swift's controlled disgust, and a note of fairly malicious hysteria is not absent from the ever-present violence—fires, explosions, fights, killings, and large-scale devastations—in Wells's SF.

The Time Machine . . . , Wells's programmatic and (but for the mawkish character of Weena) most consistent work, shows his way of proceeding and his ultimate horizon. The horizon of sociobiological regression leading to cosmic extinction, simplified from Darwinism into a series of vivid pictures in the Eloi, the giant crabs, and the eclipse episodes, is established by the Time Traveller's narration as a stark contrast to the Victorian after-dinner discussions in his comfortable residence. The Time Machine itself is validated by an efficient forestalling of possible objections, put into the mouth of schematic, none too bright, and reluctantly persuaded listeners, rather than by the bogus theory of the fourth dimension or any explanation of the gleaming bars glimpsed in the machine. Similarly, the sequence of narrated episodes gains much of its impact from the careful foreshortening of ever larger perspectives in an ever more breathless rhythm. . . . Also, the narrator-observer's gradually deepening involvement in the Eloi episode is marked by cognitive hypotheses that run the whole logical gamut of sociological SF. From a parodied Morrisite model ("Communism," says the Time Traveller at first sight) through the discovery of degeneration and of persistence of class divisions, he arrives at the anti-utopian form most horrifying to the Victorians—a run-down class society ruled by a grotesque equivalent of the nineteenth-century industrial proletariat. Characteristically, the sociological perspective then blends into biology. The laboring and upper classes are envisioned as having developed into different races or indeed species, with the Morlocks raising the Eloi as cattle to be eaten. In spite of a certain contempt for their effeteness, the Time Traveller quickly identifies with the butterfly-like upper-class Eloi and so far forsakes his position as neutral observer as to engage in bloody and fiery carnage of the repugnant spider-monkey-like Morlocks, on the model of the most sensationalist exotic adventure stories. His commitment is never logically argued, and there is a strong suggestion that it flows from the social consciousness of Wells himself. . . . Instead, the Time Traveller's attitude is powerfully supported by the prevailing imagery—both by animal parallels, and by the pervasive open-air green and bright colors of the almost Edenic garden (associated with the Eloi) opposed to the subterranean blackness and the dim reddish glow (associated with the Morlocks and the struggle against them). Later in the story these menacing, untamed colors lead to the reddish-black eclipse, symbolizing the end of the Earth and of the solar system. The bright pastoral of the Eloi is gradually submerged by the encroaching night of the Morlocks, and the Time Traveller's matches sputter out in their oppressive abyss. At the end, the unforgettable picture of the dead world is validated by the disappearance of the Time Traveller in the opaque depths of time.

Many of these devices reappear in Wells's other major works. The technique of domesticating the improbable by previews on a smaller scale, employed in the vivid vanishing of the model machine, is repeated in the introduction to the Grand Lunar through a series of other Selenites up to Phi-oo, or to Moreau's bestial people through the brutal struggles in the boat and through the ship captain, or to the Cavorite sphere's flight through the experimental explosion raising the roof. The loss of the narrator's vehicle and the ensuing panic of being a castaway under alien rule (in *The War of the Worlds* this is inverted as hiding in a trap with dwindling supplies) recurs time and again as an effective cliff-hanger. Above all . . . , Wells's whole first cycle is a reversal of the popular concept by which the lower social and biological classes were considered as "natural" prey in the struggle for survival. In their turn they become the predators: as laborers turn into Morlocks, so insects, arthropods, or colonial peoples turn into Martians, Selenites, and the like. This exalting of the humble into horrible masters supplies a subversive shock to the bourgeois believer in Social Darwinism; at the same time, Wells vividly testifies that a predatory state of affairs is the only even fantastically imaginable alternative. (pp. 208-13)

The human/animal inversion comes openly to the fore in *The Island of Dr. Moreau* . . . with admirable Swiftian stringency. Dr. Moreau's fashioning of humans out of beasts is clearly analogous to the pitiless procedures of Nature and its evolutionary creation. He is not only a latter-day Dr. Frankenstein but also a demonically inverted God of Genesis, and his surgically humanized Beast Folk are a counterpart of ourselves, semibestial humans. Wells's calling their attempts to mimic the Decalogue in the litanies of "The Saying of the Law" and their collapse back into bestiality a "theological grotesque" indicates that this view of mankind's future reversed Christian as well as socialist millennialism into the bleak vistas of an evolution liable to regression. *The Island of Dr. Moreau* turns the imperial order of Kipling's *Jungle Book* into a degenerative slaughterhouse, where the law loses out to bestiality.

Wells's next two famous SF novels, though full of vivid local color, seem today less felicitous. Both have problems of focusing. In *The Invisible Man* . . . the delineation of Griffin hesitates between a man in advance of his time within an indifferent society and the symbol of a humanity that does not know how to use science. This makes of him almost an old-fashioned "mad scientist," and yet he is too important and too sinned against to be comic relief. The vigor of the narration, which unfolds in the form of a hunt, and the strengths of an inverted fairy tale cannot compensate for the failure of the supposedly omniscient author to explain why Griffin had got into the position of being his own Frankenstein and Monster at the same time. In this context, the dubious scientific premises (an invisible eye cannot see, and so forth) become distressing and tend to deprive the story of the needed suspension of disbelief. *The War of the Worlds* . . . , which extrapolates into xenobiology the catastrophic stories of the "future wars" subgenre discussed in chapter 7, descends in places to a gleeful sensationalism difficult to stomach, especially in its horror-fantasy portraiture of the Martians. The immediate serialization in the US yellow press, which simply suppressed the parts without action, made this portraiture the most influential model for countless later Things from Outer Space, extendable to any foreign group that the public was at that moment supposed to hate, and a prototype of mass-media use of SF for mindless scare-mongering (inaugurated by Orson Welles's famous 1938 broadcast). The novel's composition is marred by the clumsy system of two eyewitness narrators, improvised in order to reconcile the sensational immediacy and the necessary over-view. Of course, *The War of the Worlds* also contains striking and indeed prophetic insights such as the picture of modern total warfare, with its panics, refugees, quislings, underground hidings, and an envisaged Resistance movement, as well as race-theory justifications, poison gas, and a "spontaneous" bacteriological weapon. (In other tales, Wells—a lifelong lover of war games—added air warfare, tanks, atom bombing of a major city, and other bellicose devices.)

Except for the superb late parable **"The Country of the Blind,"** . . . Wells's sociobiological and cosmological SF cycle culminated in *The First Men in the Moon*. . . . It has the merit of summarizing and explicating openly his main motifs and devices. The usual two narrators have grown into the contrast-ing characters of Bedford, the Social-Darwinist speculator-adventurer, and Cavor, the selfless scientist in whom Wells manages for once to fuse the cliché of absent-mindedness with open-mindedness and a final suffering rendered irremediable by the cosmic vistas involved. The sharply focused lens of spatial pinpointing and temporal acceleration through which the travelers perceive the miraculous growth of Lunar vege-tation is the most striking rendering of the precise yet won-dering scientific regard often associated with the observatories and observation posts of Wells's stories. The Selenites not only possess the Aesopian fable background and an endearing gro-tesqueness worthy of Edward Lear's creatures, they are also a profound image of sociopolitical functional overspecialization and of an absolute caste or race State, readily translatable from insect biology back into some of the most menacing tendencies of modern power concentration. Most Swiftian among Wells's aliens, they serve a double-edged satire, in the authentic tone of savage and cognitive indignation. . . . The usual final es-trangement fuses biological and social disgust into Bedford's schizophrenic cosmic vision of himself "not only as an ass, but as the son of many generations of asses" (chap. 19). Par-allel to that, Cavor formulates most clearly the uselessness of cosmic as well as earthly imperialism, and articulates a refusal to let science go on serving them (had this been heeded, we would have been spared the Galactic Empire politics and swashbuckling of later SF). Finally, Bedford's narration in guise of a literary manuscript with pretenses to scientific ve-racity, combined with Cavor's narration in guise of interpla-netary telegraphic reports, exhibit openly Wells's ubiquitous mimicry of the journalistic style from that heyday of early "mass communications"—the style of "an Associated Press dispatch, describing a universal nightmare" [see excerpt from *The Critic* dated 1898].

Yet such virtuosity cannot mask the fundamental ambiguity that constitutes both the richness and the weakness of Wells.

Is he horrified or grimly elated by the high price of evolution (*The Island of Dr. Moreau*)? Does he condemn class divisions or simply the existence of a menacing lower class (*The Time Machine*)? Does he condemn imperialism (*The First Men in the Moon*) or only dislike being at the receiving end of it (*The War of the Worlds*)? In brief, are his preoccupations with vi-olence and alienation those of a diagnostician or of a fan? Both of these stances coexist in his works in a shifting and often unclear balance. For example,—to translate such alternatives into an immediate determinant of narration—Wells's central morphological dilemma in the years of his first and best SF cycle was: which is the privileged way of understanding the world, the scientifically systematic one or the artistically vivid one? Faced with the tension between "scientific" classification and "artistic" individuation, a tension that remained constant (albeit with different outcomes) throughout his life, Wells had already in 1891 satirized the deterministic rigidity in his essay **"The Universe Rigid"** and gone on to find a first compromise in his **"The Rediscovery of the Unique"** and its successive avatars in **"The Cyclic Delusion," "Scepticism of the Instru-ment,"** and *First and Last Things*. . . . These articles attempt to formulate the deep though unclear pulls which Wells at his best reconciled by opting for representativeness, for fusing individuum and species into socially *and* biologically typical figures like the Time Traveller, but which he often left unre-conciled.

Wells's SF makes thus an aesthetic form of hesitations, inti-mations, and glimpses of an ambiguously disquieting strange-ness. The strange novum is gleefully wielded as a sensational scare thrown into the bourgeois reader, but its values are finally held at arm's length. In admitting and using their possibility he went decisively beyond Verne, in identifying them as hor-rible he decisively opposed Morris. Wells's SF works are clearly "ideological fables" [the phrase is Patrick Parrinder's], yet he is a virtuoso in having it ideologically both ways. His satis-faction at the destruction of the false bourgeois idyll is matched by his horror at the alien forces destroying it. He resolutely clung to his insight that such forces must be portrayed, but he portrayed them within a sensationalism that neutralizes most of the genuine newness. Except in his maturest moments, the conflicts in his SF are therefore transferred—following the Social-Darwinist model—from society to biology. This is a risky proceeding which can lead to some striking analogies but . . . as a rule indicates a return to quasi-religious eschatol-ogy and fatal absolutes. Wells expressed this, no doubt, in sincerely Darwinist terms, but his approach is in fact marked by a contamination of echoes from a culturally sunken medieval bestiary and a Miltonic or Bunyanesque color scheme (dark and red, for example, as satanic) with the new possibilities of scientific dooms (compare the Ruskinian Angel of *The Won-derful Visit* . . . , presented as an alien from a parallel world). The annihilation of this world is the only future alternative to its present state; the present bourgeois way of life is with scientific certainty leading the Individualist *homme moyen sen-suel* ["the average nonintellectual man"] toward the hell of physical indignity and psychic terror, yet this *is* still the only way of life he can return to and rely on, the best of all the bad possible worlds. Thus Wells's central anxious question about the future in store for his Everyman—who is, characteristically, a bright, aggressive, White, middle-class male—cannot be re-solved as posed. His early SF can present the future only as a highly menacing yet finally inoperative novum, the connection with its bearers (Time Traveller, Moreau, Griffin, Martians, Selenites, or Cavor) being always broken off. Formally, this impasse explains his troubles with works of novel length: his most successful form is either the short story or the novelette, which lend themselves to ingenious balancings on the razor's edge between shock and cognitive development. In them he set the pace for the commercial norms of most later SF (which adds insult to injury by calling such works novels).

Wells's later SF abandoned such fragile but rich ambiguity in favor of short-range extrapolations. His first attempt in that direction, *When the Sleeper Wakes* . . . , was the most interesting. Its picture of a futuristic megalopolis with mass social struggles led by demagogic leaders was "a nightmare of Capitalism triumphant" and an explicit polemic against Bellamy's complacent optimism about taming the organizing urge and the jungle of the cities. In Wells's complex corporate capitalism "everything was bigger, quicker and more crowded; there was more and more flying and the wildest financial speculation." Since Wells's sketch of the future was full of brilliant and detailed insights (as, for example, those about competing police forces and stultifying mass media) that turned out to be close to actual developments in the twentieth century, this novel became the model for anti-utopian anticipation from Zamyatin and von Harbou to Heinlein and Pohl. But Wells's imaginative energy flagged here at the crucial narrative level: the observer-hero waking after two centuries behaves alternatively like a savior (suffering his final passion on an airplane instead of a cross) and vacillating liberal intellectual. The jerky plot concerns itself primarily with the adventure of a beautiful soul in the future, and is thus coresponsible for a spate of similar inferior SF with more rugged heroes who are given wonderful powers and who experience sentimental entanglements. "A Story of Days To Come" . . . and "A Dream of Armageddon" . . . , told wholly from inside the same future, are not much more than an exploitation of that interesting locale for sentimental tales seen from the bottom, respectively the top, of society. Wells's later SF novels—though even at their worst never lacking flashes of genuine insight or redeeming provocation—do not attain the imaginative consistency of his first cycle. In *The Food of the Gods* . . . the fundamental equation of material and moral greatness is never worked out. His series of programmatic utopias, from *A Modern Utopia* . . . to *The Holy Terror* . . . , has interesting moments, especially when he is describing a new psychology of power and responsibility such as that of the "Samurai" or the "holy terror" dictator. However, its central search for a caste of technocratic managers as "competent receivers" for a bankrupt capitalist society oscillates wildly from enlightened monarchs or dictators, through Fabian-like artists and engineers, to airmen and Keynesians (in *The Shape of Things to Come* . . .): millennium has always been the most colorless part of Christian apocalypse. What is worst, Wells's fascinated sensitivity to the uncertain horizons of humanity gives only too often way to impatient discursive scolding, often correct but rarely memorable. A visit to young Soviet Russia (where his meeting with Lenin provided an almost textbook example of contrasts between abstract and concrete utopianism) resulted in the perhaps most interesting work in that series, *Men Like Gods* . . . , where Wells gave a transient and somewhat etiolated glimpse of a Morris-like brightness. But his work after the first World War vacillated, not illogically for an apocalyptic writer, between equally superficial optimism and despair. His position in the middle, wishing a plague on both the upper and the working classes, proved singularly fruitless in creative terms—though extremely influential and bearing strange fruit in subsequent SF, the writers and readers of which mostly come from precisely those "new middle classes" that Wells advanced as the hope of the future.

With all his strengths and weaknesses Wells remains the central writer in the tradition of SF. His ideological impasses are fought out as memorable and rich contradictions tied to an inexorably developing future. He collected, as it were, all the main influences of earlier writers—from Lucian and Swift to Kepler, Verne, and Flammarion, from Plato and Morris to Mary Shelley, Poe, Bulwer, and the subliterature of planetary and subterranean voyages, future wars, and the like—and transformed them in his own image, whence they entered the treasury of subsequent SF. He invented a new thing under the sun in the time-travel story made plausible or verisimilar by physics. He codified, for better or worse, the notions of invasion from space and cosmic catastrophe (as in his story "The Star" . . .), of social and biological degeneration, of fourth dimension, of future megalopolis, of biological plasticity. Together with Verne's *roman scientifique*, Wells's "scientific romances" and short stories became the privileged form in which SF was admitted into an official culture that rejected socialist utopianism. True, of his twenty-odd books that can be considered SF, only perhaps eight or nine are still of living interest, but those contain unforgettable visions (all in the five "romances" and the short stories of the early sociobiological-cum-cosmic cycle): the solar eclipse at the end of time, the faded flowers from the future, the invincible obtuseness of southern England and the Country of the Blind confronted with the New, the Saying of the Law on Moreau's island, the wildfire spread of the red Martian weed and invasion panic toward London, the last Martian's lugubrious ululations in Regent's Park, the frozen world of "The New Accelerator," the springing to life of the Moon vegetation, the lunar society. These summits of Wells's are a demonstration of what is possible in SF, of the cognitive shudder peculiar to it. Their poetry is based on a shocking transmutation of scientific into aesthetic cognition, and poets from Eliot to Borges have paid tribute to it. More harrowing than in the socialist utopians, more sustained than in Twain, embracing a whole dimension of radical doubt and questioning that makes Verne look bland, it is a grim caricature of bestial bondage and an explosive liberation achieved by means of knowledge. Wells was the first significant writer who started to write SF from within the world of science, and not merely facing it. Though his catastrophes are a retraction of Bellamy's and Morris's utopian optimism, even in the spatial disguises of a parallel present on Moreau's island or in southern England it is always a possible future evolving from the neglected horrors of today that is analyzed in its (as a rule) maleficent consequences. . . . For all his vacillations, Wells's basic historical lesson is that the stifling bourgeois society is but a short moment in an impredictable, menacing, but at least theoretically open-ended human evolution under the stars. He endowed later SF with a basically materialist look back at human life and a rebelliousness against its entropic closure. For such reasons, all subsequent significant SF can be said to have sprung from Wells's *Time Machine*. . . . (pp. 213-21)

Darko Suvin, "Wells as the Turning Point of the SF Tradition," in his Metamorphoses of Science Fiction: On the Poetics and History of a Literary Genre, *Yale University Press, 1979, pp. 208-21.*

FRANK McCONNELL   (essay date 1981)

[*McConnell is an American literary and film critic. In the following excerpt, he examines some major influences on and tendencies within Wells's science fiction.*]

H. G. Wells has been called the father, the one authentic genius, even the Shakespeare of science fiction. All these judgments can be called into question. But even today, when science fiction is attracting more first-rate writers than ever and is taken more seriously by "official" literary critics than ever, the burden of proof is still on the person who wants to question such judgments, not the one who affirms them. Wells's first novel, *The Time Machine* . . . , was an immediate success. Between 1895 and 1914 he produced, among many other works, a series of "scientific romances" that, by the outbreak of the First World War, had helped to make him one of the best-selling and most controversial writers of his time. And the influence of those novels and stories on what came to be called "science fiction" continues to be nothing less than gigantic.

If science fiction is, as some defenders argue, mainly important as technological prophecy, Wells's record is impressive. *The Time Machine* can be read, as we shall see, as a prophecy of the effects of rampant industrialization on that class conflict which was already, in the nineteenth century, a social powder keg. Disraeli had warned—and Marx had demonstrated—that the industrialized state was in danger of becoming two nations, the rich and the poor; but the real horror, Wells warns, is that they might become two races, mutually uncomprehending and murderously divided. In *The War of the Worlds* . . . he hinted at, and in later stories fully anticipated, the disastrous innovations the discovery of flight could bring to the business of warfare. In *When the Sleeper Wakes* . . . he predicted a future society in which devices very like video cassettes have replaced printed books, and an ignorant populace is force-fed censored news through things he calls "Babble Machines." In **"The Land Ironclads"** . . . he predicted the use of armored tanks in war (he later got involved in a long and futile lawsuit, claiming royalties for the "invention" of the tank). Long before "ecology" became a fashionable phrase and concern, Wells was using it as one of the common concepts of his utopias. And in *The World Set Free* . . . perhaps his most celebrated anticipation—he invented the phrase "atomic bomb," and detailed with some accuracy the apocalyptic power of chain reaction weapons or, in his phrase, "continuing explosives."

But there are other ideas of science fiction beyond the weatherman's standard of accurate forecasting. Some very good science-fiction writers never do manage a prophecy that later history ratifies. And the rest, Wells included, guess wrong at least as often as they guess right. We can say that science fiction matters not just because of the occasional random prediction of technological innovation, but because it seriously examines the implications of scientific and technological development *as a whole* for our lives, and our sense of the nature and goals of our lives. "The history of science," write Robert Scholes and Eric S. Rabkin in their book, *Science Fiction*, "is also the history of humanity's changing attitudes toward space and time. It is the history of our growing understanding of the universe and the position of our species in that universe." Science fiction, then, like science itself, is a facet of the history of the human spirit. It is an authentic fiction for our time, whose visionary tales are not so much visions of "things to come" as versions of things as they are *right now,* though seen against the immense backdrops of geological time and sidereal space (which are, after all, the true stage on which the human drama is played).

This is a more or less sociological definition of the genre, and under its terms too, Wells is not only primary but preeminent. *The Island of Doctor Moreau* . . . and *The Invisible Man* . . .

are versions, respectively horrible and tragicomic, of the conflict between knowledge and goodness, what less perceptive minds than Wells's have cheapened into the "mad scientist" theme. With penetrating insight into the problems besetting technology not only in his own time but in ours, Wells asks: though we demonstrably can do almost anything we want to do, may we do anything we want or is there still, in some deep sense, such a thing as Forbidden Knowledge? This is, of course, the theme of Mary Shelley's *Frankenstein* (1818), which also has claims to being the "first" novel of science fiction. But Wells's treatment, though no subtler or "greater" than Mary Shelley's, takes on an added force by being embedded in the giant fabric of his lifelong discussion of human science, human morality, and their conflict. Once again in *The War of the Worlds* and *The First Men in the Moon* . . . he imagined extraterrestrial aliens who are not just the picturesque bug-eyed bogeymen of later science fiction at its simplest, but projections of the possible deformity of the human species if present trends toward bloodless intellectualism, the fissure of heart and head, were to continue. And beginning with *The Food of the Gods* . . . and *A Modern Utopia* . . . , and continuing nearly to the end of his life, he gave us a series of novels of more and more homiletic, more and more strenuous and urgent social analysis and prophecy whose explicit aim was to change the course of history, bringing human science into congruity with human moral development and thereby saving the world from a second, total, perhaps final world war.

These later utopias are not, by any means, his best books. Most of them are long out of print, and they are not often discussed in histories of science fiction. But that may be a mistake. Flawed though they are, they are flawed honorably. Wells's passion for social reform could overweigh his instincts as a storyteller; his desire to convince the reader could get in the way of his ability to keep the reader reading. But if all these later books in part (and some of them throughout) are muscle-bound, it is because they are strong. And if we wish to regard science fiction seriously as a sociological form, we have to remember that Wells, more than any other writer in the genre, tried to harness the powers of narrative to the great tasks of social change and man's salvation. (pp. 3-6)

Through a combination of historical moment and personal strategy, [Wells] transformed the scientific and social controversy of his time into an extended fable of apocalypse and terror that is sometimes grim and sometimes ennobling in its vision of the human condition, but always compelling and crafted with immense skill. And it is in terms of this artistry that he looms largest over the later development of science fiction. (pp. 6-7)

Nevertheless, there are some preliminary qualifications to be made about Wells and science fiction. The first, to which I have already alluded, is that Wells didn't really *write* "science fiction." The term was invented by Hugo Gernsback, who founded *Amazing Stories* in 1926. By that time Wells's output of "scientific romances" had dwindled to an occasional heavily sociological utopian novel every few years. (Of course, this was "dwindling" only for a man like Wells, who between 1895 and 1946 wrote an average of three books a year.)

This qualification is a version, perhaps, of the old cliché that Plato was no Platonist, Marx no Marxist. But it makes a difference. Because the form had not been named yet, it was freer to associate itself with the great mainstream tradition of storytelling. After Gernsback named science fiction, making it both a suburb and a ghetto of fiction itself, it would be many years before a writer in the field would unblushingly admit a sense of his own continuity with the works of Lucan, Rabelais, Swift, and Voltaire. Wells could, and often did, avow this debt.

The second qualification is implicit in the first. Those works of Wells that exercise the greatest influence on later science fiction were all written during the first twenty years of his fifty-year career as a writer and make up only a small percentage of his total output. (p. 7)

Wells, then, was the heir to not only the Victorian apotheosis of the Will, but its Darwinian negation. In his brief encounter with formal education, he studied at the newly formed Normal School of Science (now the Royal College of Science) under Thomas Henry Huxley, Darwin's defender and popularizer. It was an experience he never forgot. Those doubts, despairs, and depressions that the official, liberal myth of Victorianism had managed to suppress were openly admitted, in the wake of science after Darwin, to be the central and inescapable condition of human life. Defeat was man's lot, man's fate, and, if he was strong enough to face it, man's supreme test. So that if Wells was a true Victorian in his faith in the power of Will, he was also a true Edwardian in his open doubt about the final usefulness of that faith when weighed against the inexorable processes of uncaring nature. The narrator of *The Time Machine* says of the Time Traveller that he "thought but cheerlessly of the Advancement of Mankind, and saw in the growing pile of civilisation only a foolish heaping that must inevitably fall back upon and destroy its makers in the end." There speaks the evolutionary theorist, the connoisseur of futility. But, the narrator himself continues, "If that is so, it remains for us to live as though it were not so." And there speaks the romantic, the exponent of Will, the man who never stopped hoping that there might after all be some final appeal against entropy, against fate, against the Second Law of Thermodynamics.

Those two voices continue their debate in Wells's work to the very end of his life, and their uncertain contest is one of the great dramas of his writing. (pp. 10-11)

Think . . . of his projected epitaph: "God damn you all: I told you so." It is not just an epitaph, it is an open letter to the world. And what, after all, *did* he tell us? Well, just this: that the major disease of modern man is that his scientific and technological expertise has outstripped his moral and emotional development; that the human race, thanks to its inherited prejudices and superstitions and its innate pigheadedness, is an endangered species; and that mankind must learn—*soon*—to establish a state of worldwide cooperation by burying its old hatreds and its ancient selfishness, or face extinction.

Today, these assertions are not shocking. They might appear in a presidential campaign speech or an address to the United Nations. (They would probably not be taken seriously, of course, but they have entered the realm of consoling pieties, buzzwords that do not raise eyebrows.) And even when Wells first uttered them, they were not being uttered for the first time. Wells was a brilliant man, but he was not an original thinker. His gift was for *imagining,* for realizing firmly, almost visually, the implications of his age's philosophy and science and for communicating those implications to his readers with the urgency of myth. The same may be said of Shakespeare.

If there was something permanently Victorian in Wells's optimism and permanently Edwardian in his qualifications of that optimism, there is nevertheless something distinctively modern about the whole man. (pp. 11-12)

Wells with Alexander Korda in 1935. The Illustrated News Picture Library.

Wells's major science fiction appeared between 1895 and the outbreak of World War I in 1914. It is . . . the Wells of these two decades . . . who seems, as years go by, to have the surest claim to permanence. But if the Wells of these years matters to us as much as he does, if he seems more and more one of us, it is because at the beginning of his career, he was so brilliantly and completely one of *them*—"they" being our ideological and spiritual ancestors around the turn of the century.

In the utopian novels he wrote after this period, he liked to refer to the origins of the modern era as the "Age of Confusion" (in *Men Like Gods*) or the "Age of Frustration" (in *The Shape of Things To Come*). And confusing, frustrating, upsetting the intellectual life of the years 1895-1914 certainly was. In an important study of *The Early H. G. Wells,* Bernard Bergonzi indicates the relationship between the scientific romances and that set of attitudes, emotions, and opinions tagged, by the people who held them, *fin de siècle* [see TCLC, Vol. 6]. (p. 32)

Wells caught this tone in his first scientific romances. *The Time Machine, When the Sleeper Wakes,* and *The First Men in the Moon* show us, through the eyes of eccentric, nervous, *fin de siècle* men, future human civilizations where technology has obliterated all struggle (for the rich at least), and yet where the beneficiaries of that gift have declined below the horizon of the really human. As Graham, the "sleeper" of *When the Sleeper Wakes,* dies he pronounces a single grim judgment on the men of the future struggling for their freedom: "Weak men." *The Island of Doctor Moreau, The Invisible Man,* and *The War of the Worlds* show us not a future de-evolving toward weakness and mass suicide, but rather the explosion of the technological future *into* the present. The eruption of science's cold equations and bitter wisdom into the world of the everyday corrodes the comfortingly "normal" through the sheer power of its murderous efficiency. "Cities, nations, civilisations, progress—it's all over," shrieks the artilleryman to the narrator of *The War of the Worlds* as the Martians rampage toward London. "That game's up. We're beat."

In *The Food of the Gods, In the Days of the Comet,* and *The World Set Free,* Wells was to give these elementary situations a more positive, hopeful turn. And later still he was to make situations like these the vehicles for a full-scale attempt to save mankind from itself. But it is nevertheless true that his science fiction, always, remained an elaboration of one of these two central themes: a man of the present is cast or voyages into a possible future organization of mankind, or the future of mankind somehow invades or possesses—and tests—the resilience and vitality of men of the present. It is a sign of Wells's genius that these two archetypal situations are also, with very few exceptions, the two elementary forms of all science fiction written after him. It is also a sign of his genius that these archetypes are ones he inherited, and creatively transformed, from the anxious, self-doubting, apocalyptic *fin de siècle* world of his youth.

But Bergonzi's discussion of this end-of-the-century, end-of-the-world sensibility explains only part of the early Wells's science fiction. Queen Victoria died in 1901—she could hardly have chosen a more symbolic date—and was succeeded by her portly, self-indulgent, and (at least at first) liberal son, Edward VII. Wells himself described the transition from the late Victorian to the Edwardian spirit: "Queen Victoria was like a great paper-weight that for half a century sat upon men's minds, and when she was removed their ideas began to blow about all over the place haphazardly." Of course, there had been forward-looking, enthusiastic architects of social change before 1900, and there remained many celebrants of degeneration and decay after that date. But the total effect of the transition was largely of the sort Wells describes. William Bellamy, an important critic of Edwardian fiction, sees the transition as one from a culture-bound to a culture-free or "post-cultural" mental environment. While late Victorians had lived with the claustrophobic sense of a cultural inheritance too rich and too consolidated to allow for personal freedom, Edwardians—having survived the reign of the old Queen and lived past the magic year 1900—enjoyed a sense of new beginnings and of individual self-realization that often implied a possibility of personal fulfillment outside the conventional sanctions of society.

There is much justice in this description of the Edwardian mood, particularly since it allows us to see the close connection between the passions, enthusiasms, and warring ideologies of the Edwardian period and later twentieth-century movements of the same "post-cultural" sort. As Samuel Hynes observes in *The Edwardian Turn of Mind,* "virtually everything that is thought of as characteristically modern already existed in England by 1914: aircraft, radiotelegraphy, psychoanalysis, Post-Impressionism, motion picture palaces. . . ." The late Victorians, we can say, lived through and acted out all the modes of anxiety and despair that were to characterize the coming century; and the Edwardians—who were by and large the same people—felt and articulated that century's greatest expectations.

Here, too, Wells managed to be quintessentially a man of his time. . . . [His] personal revolution, his lifelong sexual adven-

turism, became full-fledged in the years just after the turn of the century. And parallel to this private transformation is a transformation in the tone of his speculative fiction. He begins to think not just in terms of the disasters awaiting technological man in his quest for survival, but of the chances available to him for transcendence, for final victory over the stern dictates of history and the struggle for existence. It is no accident then, following this argument, that to this period also belong the best of Wells's "realistic" novels: *Kipps* in 1905, *Tono-Bungay* and *Ann Veronica* in 1909, and *The History of Mr. Polly* in 1910. In these books he takes the common stuff of existence in an industrial society as his theme, without the apocalyptic trappings of voyages through time or invasions from beyond the atmosphere, and manages to demonstrate convincingly that the apocalyptic spirit, regardless of the trappings, is still there— that the life of the middle class in England is *already,* as he writes, moving toward a future which must be either radically liberating or radically destructive for the individual psyche.

His "realistic" novels of this period, in other words, should be read along with his more explicitly scientific romances, since they explore many of the same themes with only a slight change of tone. Stylistically, Wells was a shapeshifter. He seldom wrote the same sort of book twice, and if he did, the second one was usually a parody or inversion of the first. But ideologically, he was a remarkably consistent man. From his first books to his last, in despair or in optimism, his theme was obsessively that of middle-class man's chances for survival in a world which through the accumulated weight of technology and the inexorable pressures of evolutionary history threatens his life. If there is a single question to which all Wells's books are addressed, it might be phrased as this one: How shall Man live through his own coming of age? (pp. 33-5)

Wells's fiction, from its beginning, was also intimately related to the currents of social theory and reform which characterized the waning years of the century. (p. 43)

It has been a cliché for some time now to say that the nineteenth century "discovered" history as a science. And like many clichés, this one is fundamentally true. Historians of the late eighteenth and early nineteenth century, partly because of the upheavals in European society and culture taking place around them, began to regard the study of history as more than simply the preservation of the past or even the understanding of the present through the past. History, it came to be believed, might be approached with the same analytical rigor and, perhaps, predictive efficiency that had been so brilliantly employed in the physical sciences since Sir Isaac Newton. (p. 44)

[Wells] was by both class and temperament a revolutionary soul. He was also a true nineteenth-century ideologue, at least to the extent of insisting on "finished ideas" as the only possible basis for social action or social planning. But he was also—as Lenin is reported to have called him—a petty bourgeois. He mistrusted the brute force and inarticulate aspirations of the laboring class—that "mass man" whose existence Marx had discovered and whose destiny he had hymned as world dominion. He mistrusted the figure of the bomb-toting, metaphysically inclined terrorist (or "anarchist" or "nihilist," to use the age's catchphrases), the man willing to commit the unspeakable for the sake of a theory. And, perhaps most of all, he mistrusted theory itself. A voracious assimilator of systems and abstractions, he was nevertheless skeptical of any system whose complexity appeared to overweigh its application to the observable and observed facts of the life around us. This pragmatism, or empiricism, has been often described as a particularly "English" as opposed to Continental trait of mind; or it may also be explained as the special genius for observation of the novelist, as opposed to the social scientist or philosopher. At any rate, it is one of the hallmarks of Wells's distinctive vision of social possibilities, and of the chance for utopia. From the beginning, he believed in the necessity and the reality of social change, or revolution. But to the end, he wanted his revolution to be both rational and sensible, both total and civilized.

It can be argued that Wells expressed his fears of revolutionaries most fully in his fiction of the 1890s, and his hopes for revolution most fully in his fiction of the Edwardian years and afterward. Just as the Eloi of *The Time Machine* are partly a vision of the aesthetes and decadents of the literary and artistic world, the cannibalistic Morlocks who prey upon the Eloi are a much more explicit projection of the proletariat, the "mass man" whose emergence Wells feared. His dislike and suspicion of the dedicated "scientific" anarchist are the basis of one of his early short stories, **"The Stolen Bacillus."** . . . And his suspicion of abstraction, of theory without humanity, may fairly be said to run through all his early fiction. Griffin, the anti-hero of *The Invisible Man,* and Dr. Moreau of *The Island of Doctor Moreau* are both ferociously intelligent men—the former a physicist, the latter a biologist—who erect upon their scientific discoveries plans for a new world empire, a new order of things, only to find their structures collapse on them in a suicidal rubble. In *The War of the Worlds* and *The First Men in the Moon* Wells shows us alternate societies—the octopuslike Martians and the insectlike Selenites—that have been built upon an absolutely efficient, rational collectivism, and which are equally anti-human (there is an important anticipation of both these books in his 1896 story, **"In the Abyss"**).

It is **"The Stolen Bacillus,"** though, that best catches his attitude toward social revolution. This very short story tells how a pale-faced anarchist steals a phial containing what he thinks is a deadly concentration of cholera bacteria. He intends to empty it into the London water system. But the phial breaks in the cab in which he is making his escape; undaunted, the anarchist greedily swallows the few drops of liquid in the bottom of the phial and charges off amidst the busy London crowds, himself now a living instrument of death and contagion, shouting "Vive l'Anarchie!" Only then do we learn that the phial did not really contain cholera bacteria, but rather a dose of a new compound whose only effect is to turn its recipient bright blue.

What began as a tale of terror ends as a joke: but a joke with a serious point. Men and women really did dread anarchy, and particularly the threat presented by the figure of the anarchist, that outwardly normal, rational man who might, unsuspected, be harboring thoughts and plans of the most unspeakable violence and hatred. If revolution, even in its maddest aspects, could now be "rational"—i.e., philosophically planned and supported—then it was, to all intents and purposes, invisible. Wells's invention of the Invisible Man had been an early, very resonant expression of this fear: the invisible minister of apocalypse, the hyperintelligent terrorist, part of whose terror is that you can't see him. Joseph Conrad, in his novel of 1907, *The Secret Agent,* and G. K. Chesterton in his novel of 1908, *The Man Who Was Thursday,* would both treat the theme of anarchy in ways perhaps suggested by *The Invisible Man:* in terms, that is, of its fundamentally frightening aspects of normality, its terrible quality of being unrecognizable until it is too late.

"The Stolen Bacillus" is a reassuring version of the same situation. The anarchist, for all his dedication and care, has made a stupid blunder; a blunder, moreover, that henceforth will render him immediately, unequivocally recognizable. He will be bright blue, an all too visible man.

We can see the difference between *The Invisible Man* and **"The Stolen Bacillus"** as part of the difference between the despairing and the optimistic halves of Wells's sensibility. But **"The Stolen Bacillus"** is also reassuring because it insists that anarchists and their like are not to be feared: their own excessive hatreds will lead them into comically excessive postures of impotent violence. But, the story insists, they will be led into these absurdities because of the workings of a slower, surer, and ultimately more total revolution, the revolution of scientific thought, which is changing the world daily by making the animosities and class hatreds of the past irrelevant. The scientist who prepares the "blue" solution does not know he is thwarting anarchy. But he is, and the single-minded blindness of his research is revealed to be also the wisdom of history (Hegelian theme), its comic judgment upon the impulse to mass murder.

Wells, then, heir to a century of metaphysical and social revolutionaries, was impelled to a version of revolution much quieter, much more explicitly middle class, than many which were abroad in his time. This can be thought of as a very *English* taste in revolution, though Wells was tumultuous enough in his personal life and far-ranging enough in his social vision to alienate or scandalize the more conservative of his revolutionary English friends. (pp. 47-9)

A number of his early critics were disturbed by the frequency and level of violence in Wells's scientific romances, and the incidence of violence has continued to be an easy cliché for critics discussing his work. And it is true that, especially from *The War of the Worlds* through the utopian visions of *The War in the Air, The World Set Free, Men Like Gods,* and *The Shape of Things To Come,* he imagined a period of chaos and apocalyptic warfare as the inevitable prelude to the establishment of a just state. Indeed, there was something in Wells that took a real delight in scenes of Old Testament-scale destruction and pillage. He wrote to a friend during the composition of *The War of the Worlds,* "I'm doing the dearest little serial for Pearson's new magazine, in which I completely wreck and sack Woking—killing my neighbours in painful and eccentric ways—then proceed via Kingston and Richmond to London, which I sack, selecting South Kensington for feats of peculiar atrocity." It is a lighthearted summary of the book's plot but also an accurate one, and the "feats of peculiar atrocity" Wells enjoyed imagining—or symbolically doing, as the letter makes plain—would characterize his fiction for the rest of his life. (p. 51)

It is important to understand the special quality of violence in Wells's prophecies. In book after book he describes a future that lurches toward a Golden Age across a no man's land of war, pestilence, and reversion to bestiality. But he insists that the ordeal by violence, though highly likely, is not necessary. Again and again in his utopias, there occur observations to the effect that if men had only understood themselves better, had only formed clear and useful concepts of their place in the universe, the Golden Age might have been reached without such an appalling waste of life. "If we had only *seen*": that is the sentiment whose melancholy harmony runs through all his future histories, and it is the central connection between his science fiction and his other writing, where he tried to *make* people see how the kingdom of man could be established without the spilling of blood. For all the violence of his imagination Wells differed from most social visionaries, from the author of the Book of Revelations down to and including Marx, in that he did not believe, or would not let himself believe, that the Golden Age had to be preceded by a Last War. But he feared it would be.

To comprehend the full complexity of his attitude, we must examine a third aspect of Wells's intellectual background, perhaps the most important one. As an heir to the problems and perils of the aesthetic tradition, and to the expectations and fears of nineteenth-century socialism, he would doubtless have written brilliant and successful books. But it is impossible to imagine the Wells we know without Science (the capital "S" put there by Wells's attitude toward it), and particularly without the awesome edifice of Darwinian evolutionary theory. (pp. 52-3)

From *The Time Machine* on, it was generally recognized that no writer had so completely or so perceptively taken Darwin to heart. Wells may not have been the first man to acknowledge the importance of Darwinian theory for the future of civilization and the business of fiction, but he was certainly the first to acknowledge and assimilate that theory, in all its corrosive effect upon ideas of what fiction was for and about. (p.54)

Darwin's great defender T. H. Huxley—Wells's tutor in his first year at the Normal School of Science—examined the problem of the soul of man under evolutionary principles more explicitly. In 1893 Huxley delivered one of his most famous and most influential lectures, "Evolution and Ethics." It is probably the fullest statement of Darwinian principles as they affect moral and political concerns, and it is a very important anticipation of Wells's own thought on these matters—indeed, it is probably one of the chief influences. (p. 60)

Man's proper role, said Huxley, is not to imitate but to resist the cosmic process, to oppose, however unavailingly, the moral force of his tiny microcosm to the cruel exigencies of the cosmos at large. To say this is to argue that, in a universe governed by the Second Law of Thermodynamics, consciousness is the only power that resists the tendency of all things to spin their way down to the level of least energy. It is also to argue that the human enterprise—culture, art, intelligence—is both totally "artificial" and, in being totally artificial, totally "natural." This is the crucial paradox on which Wells's science fiction—and, indeed, his lifework—is based. . . . (p. 63)

Frank McConnell, in his The Science Fiction of H. G. Wells, *Oxford University Press, 1981, 235 p.*

JOHN HUNTINGTON (essay date 1982)

[*Huntington is an American critic and educator who has written studies of modern science fiction. In the following excerpt, he discusses the encounter between human and nonhuman life forms as a central event in Wells's science fiction.*]

To even a casual reader of Wells it must be obvious that the meeting with alien life is a frequent, even a dominant theme for him. There are, of course, important stories that do not explicitly imagine some strange, new, nonhuman being, but such stories mark the exception rather than the rule. Eloi, Morlocks, Beast People, Martians, Selenites in the novels and the multitude of strange creatures—curiously seldom humanoid—in the stories constitute a tribe that owns an important territory of Wells's imagination. Once we start to think of the subject we can find that bit by bit the domination of aliens

expands until even the supposed exceptions fit into the scheme. We can move from Martians to Morlocks to Eloi, so why not on to primitive natives and to anarchists? And, taking the same sized steps, why not the blind people in "**The Country of the Blind**" or even the invisible man in the novel of that name? Or to move in another direction, one can step from the Octopuslike Martians to the organized octopi in "**The Sea Raiders**" to the military ants in "**The Empire of the Ants**" to the blood-sucking orchid in "**The Flowering of the Strange Orchid**" to the cholera bacillus in "**The Stolen Bacillus.**" We can see that in a sense Wells's stories and novels aspire to a rendering of all the possibilities of human confrontation with other forms of (conscious) life.

The very completeness of the web suggests that Wells is interested in trying out the various bonds and antipathies that can exist between beings. In general in the short stories he deals with creatures with whom no communication is possible (ants, octopi, orchids, Aepyornis). In the novels, however, he sets up a system of relationships between humans and creatures who one way or another express an aspect of what we value in humanity while at the same time remaining alien. . . . In the Martians of *The War of the Worlds,* the Selenites of *The First Men in the Moon,* and the beast men of *The Island of Doctor Moreau,* Wells focuses on precise attractions and antipathies: the Martians, while physically repulsive, are superior to humans in intellect; the Selenites, also repulsive, are skilled in social organization; the beast men occupy a middle ground, uneasily human in appearance, dully human in intellect.

In general Wells's heroes feel a bond with creatures like the Eloi, who share the human appearance, but antipathy with creatures who, whatever their intellect, look nonhuman. As we shall see, one of the processes of the novels is to transcend that instinct. Also, the higher the intellect of the alien, the more threatening it is. This is important because a paradox develops: the more intellectually superior creatures are, that is, the more capable they are of establishing an ethical relationship with other forms of being, the more likely they are to engage in evolutionary competition, while creatures of inferior intellectual accomplishment are occasionally able to achieve a more ethical relationship.

Every confrontation between the human and the nonhuman involves the evolutionary-ethical puzzle. The nonhuman, as a different species, exists in an unstable relationship with the human, and insofar as the human's and nonhuman's needs overlap the two are going to compete and a struggle for survival is going to occur. As Huxley argues, ethical questions are out of place in pure nature. . . . If humanity were living simply in a state of nature no one could blame it for brutality or domination. But humanity's intelligence, Huxley argues, leads to a civilization in which the ethical imperative replaces the evolutionary.

Wells's early fiction probes two questions that arise out of such issues. The first is, when, if ever, do the demands of survival obviate the ethical criteria? When is nonethical behavior justified? In a curious way this question is not limited to conflicts between different species. The confrontation between human and nonhuman is simply a type for a whole series of confrontations which includes those between humans of different races, nationalities, and classes. It may not be extravagant to say that all difference leads to imbalance and the threat of domination and generates the puzzle of evolution and ethics.

If human intellect leads to ethics, it is reasonable to expect alien intelligence also to be ethical. The second question is, at what point, if any, does the nonethical behavior of the alien obviate the human's ethical imperative? The solutions to such questions must come from moralists; the role of Wells's fiction is not to answer such questions but to create structures that make us rethink them.

Wells's main probings of the ways evolutionary and ethical imperatives conflict and of the kinds of obligations that can extend across species difference occur in the novels, but the tale, **"Aepyornis Island"** gives neat, concise expression of the problem and its ramifications and demonstrates how the work will establish opposite expressions as a way of setting up and balancing the situation. The main narrator in **"Aepyornis Island,"** a man appropriately named Butcher, recounts how he was stranded on an atoll for four years, the first two of which he spent in the company of a growing giant bird, the Aepyornis, now, alas, extinct. The core story tells how much Butcher enjoyed the bird's company ("You'd be surprised what an interesting bird that Aepyornis chick was"), the difficulties that occurred as the bird reached full growth (he was "about fourteen feet high to the bill of him, with a big broad head like the end of a pickaxe"), and the final battle between the two when the bird got ornery. Butcher takes the bird's unpleasant disposition to heart:

> I don't suppose I ever felt so hurt by anything before or since. It was the brutal ingratitude of the creature. I'd been more than a brother to him. I'd hatched him, educated him. A great gawky, out-of-date bird! and me a human being—heir of the ages and all that.

This little passage is interesting for the way it combines a genuine affection with a more questionable pride. Butcher tries to link himself and the bird ("I'd hatched him") and set himself apart from him ("And me a human being"). By naming the chick Friday, Butcher has worked a similar double transformation: he has raised a pet to human status and lowered a companion to servant status. When Friday becomes truly murderous and prevents him from coming on shore, Butcher devises a bolo, snags the bird's gawky legs, upends him, and saws through his throat with his pen knife. But no sooner has he won the battle for survival than he regrets his victory:

> I don't like to think of that even now. I felt like a murderer while I did it, though my anger was hot against him.
>
> (pp. 58-60)

> With that tragedy loneliness came upon me like a curse. Good Lord! you can't imagine how I missed that bird. I sat by his corpse and sorrowed over him, and shivered as I looked round the desolate, silent reef. I thought of what a jolly little bird he had been when he was hatched, and of a thousand pleasant tricks he had played before he went wrong. I thought if I'd only wounded him I might have nursed him round into a better understanding. If I'd had any means of digging into the coral rock I'd have buried him. I felt exactly as if he was human. As it was, I couldn't think of eating him, so I put him in the lagoon, and the little fishes picked him clean.

Here the identification across the species difference is clear and powerful. In place of competition he envisions companionship, and in place of justified self-defense he sees murder.

The puzzle this simple event expresses is brought into clear prominence by the contrast afforded by the subplot of the story. Butcher and two "native chaps" originally set off looking for fossil eggs. When one of the natives, bitten by a centipede, drops and breaks an egg, Butcher "hit[s] him about rather." In revenge the two natives try to abandon Butcher on the island. Butcher shoots one and later finds the other dead from the centipede bite. Butcher never thinks of calling the killing of the native murder, nor does he ever regret beating the native. By disregarding the ethical view of his atrocities, Butcher is, in effect, enforcing a separation between himself and the natives and treating them as nonhuman. Thus, the subplot mirrors, in the sense of echoing and reversing, the main plot in which Butcher feels impelled to stress the link between himself and the large bird. The story probes the issue of ethical obligation by presenting us with two opposite extremes: a savage and callous murder treated without ethical considerations, and a justifiable act of evolutionary self-defense treated ethically.

That Butcher cannot eat Friday is one of the signs of a closeness that overrides species difference. Throughout Wells's early work cannibalism is a test of difference: if cannibalism or the fear of cannibalism is involved (as with the Morlocks and the Eloi), then the two species are really one, but if it is not involved, then they are separate. Cannibalism is a transformation of the sense of murder Butcher felt: if the other species is different from ours, murder is not involved, but if it is the same, then murder is involved. The problem is raised acutely near the beginning of *The War of the Worlds*. The narrator has met a group of soldiers and told them about the Martians. They get into a discussion: (pp. 61-2)

> "Ain't they got any necks, then?"
>
> (p. 62)
>
> I repeated my description.
> "Octopuses," said he, "that's what I calls 'em. Talk about fishers of men—fighters of fish it is this time!"
> "It ain't no murder killing beasts like that," said the first speaker....

The separation between Martians and men is made from two directions here. Since the Martians use their weapons to "cook" men, they are themselves drawing a line, otherwise they would be cannibals. But also the fishiness of the Martians allows the first speaker to avoid the accusation of murder.... The point to be made is that it doesn't matter which way the hierarchy goes so long as there is a clear division. Even if the Martians are superior to humans, the evolutionary "doctrine" of survival of the fittest justifies killing them. According to these soldiers, ethics enters only if the two are of the same species.

In other parts of *The War of the Worlds* this ethically sterile situation is challenged. As the narrator points out, it is disgusting to watch the Martians kill and use human beings for food: "I think," he modestly cautions, "that we should remember how repulsive our carnivorous habits would seem to an intelligent rabbit." The role of victim leads us to give an ethically weighted significance to even the most purely evolutionary situation. The special perspective enjoined by *The War of the Worlds* places humanity, not at the top of the natural hierarchy, but in a middle position, the predator of lower nature (ants, wasps, rabbits, dodoes, even Tasmanians) and the victim of the superior Martians. This structure makes us acutely aware of the ethical horror of natural evolutionary behavior and makes us reconsider the relations that can exist across species lines.

Near the end of *The War of the Worlds* the narrator has a moment in which he experiences the possibility of a different way of dividing life, a way which cuts across species and acknowledges the bonds of intelligence that transcend biology. As the last Martian dies, the narrator, wandering through a London deserted of all intelligent life except for the marginal figures of wild dogs and black, carnivorous birds, becomes aware of how much the Martians themselves can be seen as partners to humanity rather than as enemies: "Night, the mother of fear and mystery, was coming upon me. But while that voice sounded the solitude, the desolation had been endurable; by virtue of it London had still seemed alive, and the sense of life about me had upheld me." . . . If there is division in species, there is a union in intellect, and, for a moment anyway, the narrator perceives the quality of this latter union as more important than the competitive division. As the novel ends all the machinery of decline and fall that has been set up and which we have been led to anticipate to be designed for humanity, comes down on the Martians; the tragedy of the novel is theirs.

In *The Island of Doctor Moreau* the sympathy with nonhumans is rendered more difficult by the absence of anything like real human intellect in the Beast Men. But that lack does not mean that no bonds exist. If in *The War of the Worlds* the reader moves from the easy antipathy of the soldiers, based on appearance, to the moment of union on the basis of intellect, in *The Island of Doctor Moreau* the reader studies the middle ground in which the relation of human and alien is always problematic. The novel develops a symmetrical system in which for every symbolic link between human and beast there is a symbolic separation, and often the very terms of union contain within them the seeds of division.

The basic symmetry of the situation is clear; for one half of the novel Prendick feels uneasy about the beast men because he thinks that they are humans who have been surgically modified by Doctor Moreau, and then for the second half of the novel he has anxieties because he is aware that they are not human at all, but humanized animals. While the nature of the biological link occupies much of Prendick's and our attention, and while from a Wilberforcean point of view it should make a major difference whether the beast men are degenerate humans or superior animals, the issue is ultimately irrelevant in determining the obligations that exist between humans and beast men.

Though the humans on the island hold themselves aloof from the beast men, the distinction they maintain is always in danger of being blurred. When Prendick first sees M'ling he perceives him as a "misshapen," "deformed man with a black face" and a "singular voice." Even when one knows exactly which is which the distinction keeps slipping away. . . . Similarly, the beast men are confused about Prendick's status: they check his hands to see if they are malformed . . . , and in the huts they debate, not whether Prendick is human, but to what level of beast man he belongs. . . . For all the biological differences between humans and beast men, the final enforcer of their separation is the revolver, the "fire that kills."

The law that the beast men recite seems to set up a neat, systematic distinction between human and beast, but in fact it creates an illusion of separation:

> Not to go on all-Fours; *that* is the Law. Are we not Men?
> Not to suck up Drink; *that* is the Law. Are we not Men?

> Not to eat Flesh or Fish; *that* is the Law. Are we not Men?
> Not to claw Bark of Trees; *that* is the Law. Are we not Men?
> Not to chase other Men; *that* is the Law. Are we not Men?. . . .

The ironies of this attempt to cross a biological boundary by means of ethical self-definition are multiple. First, there is an inherent paradox in the law itself: only a nonhuman would need such a rule to be human. And the law describes a line that is disproven in the very act of invocation, for we are aware that those here asserting "are we not men?" are definitely not men. Clearly, what defines the human is something other than what these monstrosities assert; they draw a line, but it is a trivial one. And finally, despite its precision, the line marks nothing, for in the course of the novel we see real humans repeatedly trespass across the boundary the law establishes. We see Prendick himself on all fours; Montgomery teaches M'ling how to cook a rabbit; at the beginning of the novel we see men in a lifeboat planning cannibalism, and it is only because they are clumsy that cannibalism does not occur. When he is rescued at the beginning of the novel Prendick drinks something that "tasted like blood," and at the end of the novel Montgomery drinks brandy the way beasts drink blood. Throughout the novel the activity of distinguishing between human and beast is mirrored by the activity of bridging that carefully defined boundary.

Such trespass does not, however, disqualify the distinction; human and beast constitute a difference even if the line between them cannot be clearly established biologically or the criteria of distinction settled. Humans can act bestial, and perhaps, though it is a rarer event, beasts can act humanely. M'ling is a possible instance of the latter: as the situation on the island gets more chaotic, he becomes more faithful to Montgomery, protecting him with his presence and perhaps even dying in his defense. . . . The possibility of bestial humanity is exquisitely rendered by the Captain of the *Ipecacuanha* who as captain should be a figure of civilized authority but turns out to be a drunken brute. Like the beast men, he invokes a "law": "I'm captain of the ship—Captain and Owner. I'm the law here, I tell you—the law and the prophets." . . . Later, just as the beast men fall away from their law and attack humans, the Captain abandons the law he has invoked: "Law be damned! I'm king here." . . . In place of civilized order the Captain asserts aggressive, impulsive force. His language gets childish and repetitive: he calls Prendick "Mr. Shut Up," a phrase that the beast men will proudly use . . . , and finally out of pure malice he casts Prendick adrift. Though his biology and his social role qualify him for humanity, the Captain is morally and intellectually bestial.

Montgomery and Prendick more consciously bridge the line between human and beast. Montgomery is able to regard the beast men "as almost normal human beings" . . . and, never a very pleasant man himself, he becomes so generally misanthropic that towards the end he casts his lot with the beast men even going so far as to burn the boats to prevent a return to humankind. . . . His most radical jumbling of the distinction occurs . . . when, leaving the teetotalling Prendick, he turns to the beast men and invites them: "drink, ye brutes! Drink, and be men." . . . We prove our humanity by degenerating beneath it.

At the end of the novel Prendick the prig performs a similar but opposite re-vision; like Montgomery he becomes a misanthrope, but whereas Montgomery joins the beasts to escape the human, Prendick, like Gulliver, sees beasts when he looks at humans: "I go in fear. I see faces keen and bright, others dull or dangerous, others unsteady, insincere; none that have the calm authority of a reasonable soul. I feel as though the animal was surging up through them; that presently the degradation of the Islanders will be played over again on a larger scale." He has left London for the country because,

> in London the horror was well-nigh insupportable. I could not get away from men; their voices came through windows; locked doors were flimsy safeguards. I would go out into the streets to fight with my delusion and prowling women would mew after me, furtive craving men glance jealously at me, weary pale workers go coughing by me, with tired eyes and eager paces like wounded deer dripping blood. . . . Then I would turn aside into some chapel, and even there, such was my disturbance, it seemed that the preacher gibbered Big Thinks even as the Ape Man had done; or into some library, and there the intent faces over the books seemed but patient creatures waiting for prey. Particularly nauseous were the blank expressionless faces of people in trains and omnibuses; they seemed no more my fellow-creatures than dead bodies would be, so that I did not dare to travel unless I was assured of being alone. And even it seemed that I, too, was not a reasonable creature, but only an animal tormented with some strange disorder in its brain, that sent it to wander alone, like a sheep stricken with the gid. . . .

Wells here adapts a favorite device of satire, but how has civilized humanity earned the accusation of bestiality in the novel? Or what justifies Prendick's skewed vision? The deep point of the passage is not simply satiric, but ontological: it is the confusion of animal and human, the collapse of all claim that a biological difference earns a moral position.

The dichotomy of human and animal is a kind of conceptual pun that crops up, almost inevitably, perhaps even unconsciously in the novel's language. Like some of Milton's puns, the second, discovered meaning is narrower and more precise than the first, more obvious meaning. For instance, when Prendick, after he has learned of the animal origin of the beast men, calls them "inhuman monsters," . . . he is at once making an emotional statement of moral and aesthetic revulsion and stating the cool facts: they are biologically "inhuman" and they are literally monsters. At another time, when he thinks the beast men are degenerate humans, he can in his revulsion accidently express the paradoxical truth when he remarks on "the inhuman face of the man." . . . Toward the end of the novel Montgomery gives an important and telling ironic twist to the word "human" when he observes that he and Prendick have ethical responsibilities toward the beast men even though they are physically threatened by them: "We can't massacre the lot,—can we?" Montgomery asks bitterly. "I suppose that's what *your* humanity would suggest?" . . . The pun here works on the evolution-ethics contradiction. In an evolutionary context Prendick's "humanity" pits him against the beast men and survival at all costs is his final imperative. Later when Montgomery is dead and he is alone, Prendick "had half a mind to make a massacre of them." . . . The other meaning of humanity sarcastically alludes to the usual hypocrisy of supposedly ethical humanity in slaughtering other creatures.

Just as the narrator of *The War of the Worlds* has a moment when by an act of sympathy he bridges the separation that has dominated the novel, so Prendick achieves a moment of true connection in spite of separation. Both moments occur when the other dies, but Prendick's is rendered especially difficult by the fact that he is not simply the witness of the other's death, but its killer. After he understands the genetic nature of the beast men, Prendick, assisting in the hunt for the leopard man who has reverted to carnivore, by chance comes upon him hiding:

> I saw the creature we were hunting. I halted. He was crouched together into the smallest possible compass, his luminous green eyes turned over his shoulder regarding me.
>
> It may seem a strange contradiction in me I cannot explain the fact—but now, seeing the creature there in a perfectly animal attitude, with the light gleaming in its eyes, and its imperfectly human face distorted with terror, I realized again the fact of its humanity. In another moment other of its pursuers would see it, and it would be overpowered and captured, to experience once more the horrible tortures of the enclosure. Abruptly I slipped out my revolver, aimed between his terror-struck eyes and fired. . . .

The moral dynamics are complex here, but it is clear that Prendick is performing an act of mercy. In the face of evolutionary chaos in which the animal and the human overlap and in which the conflicting obligations of evolution and ethics have become hopelessly tangled, Prendick responds with simple sympathy for a fellow creature, "perfectly animal" but endowed with the "fact of its humanity." Here the word "humanity" has broken free from any question of biological descent: instead of a pun that poses a puzzle, the word here challenges the whole evolutionary criterion. And yet Prendick's ethically motivated act is cold-hearted slaughter. The ethical impulse is contaminated by an almost spontaneous violence; when Moreau complains that Prendick should not have killed the beast, Prendick evades both Moreau's point and the ethical one: "I'm sorry,' said I, though I was not. 'It was the impulse of the moment.'"

The Island of Doctor Moreau, while it may be Wells's most systematic study of the evolutionary dilemma, arrives at no conclusions. The prevailing mood is of a confused flux: the beast men are frightening and pitiful; Moreau is heroic and tyrannical; all Prendick can do is get sullen. The darkness of the book comes not from a real pessimism, but from a kind of muddiness that the inconclusive yet systematic separations and crossings create. . . . All imperatives are pointless here where the most humane gesture is to kill. And if evolutionary and moral aimlessness occupies the center of the novel, the imagery of the beginning and the end expresses the problem exactly. Prendick begins and ends adrift: the oarless, open boat in the midst of a vast expanse of empty sea is a fitting image for the universe Moreau's genius has created.

If biology poses a clear distinction between human and nonhuman which is then overcome, intellect may offer a no less problematic criterion for discrimination. In *The Island of Doctor Moreau* the separation of human and beast is paralleled by the deep problem posed by Moreau himself, and to a slighter degree Montgomery. Moreau's genius is thwarted by society, and so he preys on society. As an intellect with no ethical sensibilities, Moreau is like the Martians, but without the physiological difference that enforces separation in *The War of the Worlds.* It is his action, not his appearance, that has driven Moreau apart. Whereas in the case of the Martians and the beast men the imaginative achievement of the novel is to bridge the antipathy physiology establishes, in the case of Moreau that gulf has been neutralized. To a certain extent the problem has been reversed: now the imaginative achievement is to get past an urge to admire Moreau as an exceptional human and to see how inhumane he is. In this respect, *The Island of Doctor Moreau* is structurally like *The Time Machine* in that the antithetical urges to see separation and to see union balance. But the important question of how a man like Moreau "fits" civilization is largely ignored in the novel. Wells isolates him on his island where he can play God without the inconvenience of considering his relation to civilization. Though he attains a certain grandeur, he looms as an outcast in the tradition of Victor Frankenstein, tormented and alienated by his genius and his egoism, but Wells does not follow Shelley into the psychology of such a figure.

Yet, if Moreau alludes to issues left largely undeveloped in the novel, he still represents an important figure in Wells's logic: he is the most complex alien, the isolated scientist, the exceptional human. We see him in the Time Traveller; we see him in Cavor in *The First Men in the Moon;* and he is studied most concentratedly in Griffin in *The Invisible Man.* The figure will always attract and bother Wells. While the value placed on the isolated genius shifts radically in different works, logically he remains constant: he is always solitary against a crowd. The ambiguities inherent in the figure are those generated by

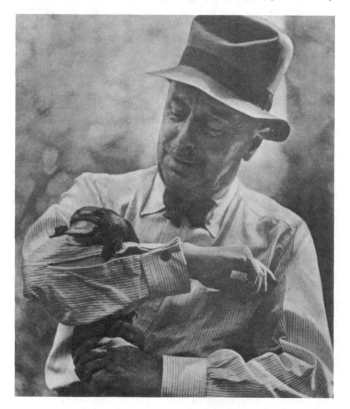

Wells, in 1939, holding a duck-billed platypus. From H. G. Wells: Aspects of a Life, *by Anthony West.*

the individual in society: he saves society and he plagues it; society nurtures him and it frustrates and persecutes him.

But if the scientist figure has a variety of permutations in different works, in each work he is inflexible and undergoes remarkably little revaluation. Griffin becomes more homicidal as the novel progresses until Kemp realizes that the conflict is evolutionary: "Griffin contra mundum" ["Griffin against the world"]. But such change is simply the following out of the beginning potential, and it is apt that this is the one novel in which we never experience the kind of reversal of sympathies that is so important to the others. In his early work the question that interests Wells is not how to think about the exceptional person, but how to think about civilization, and the genius is mainly interesting for the pressure he puts on the mechanisms of civilization. (pp. 62-70)

> *John Huntington, in his* The Logic of Fantasy: H. G. Wells and Science Fiction, *Columbia University Press, 1982, 191 p.*

CATHERINE RAINWATER (essay date 1983)

[In the following excerpt, Rainwater closely examines Wells's indebtedness to Poe for many elements in his early science fiction.]

In his early **"Popularising Science"** . . . , H. G. Wells acknowledges Edgar Allan Poe as one of his literary precursors. Wells believes that "the fundamental principles of construction that underlie such stories as Poe's 'Murders in the Rue Morgue,' or Conan Doyle's 'Sherlock Holmes' series, are precisely those that should guide a scientific writer." Despite this and later such acknowledgements, the subject of Poe's influence on Wells has received almost no critical attention. This lack of scholarship is especially curious since, according to David Y. Hughes and Robert M. Philmus, Wells considers Poe's "fundamental principles of construction" to underlie several of his own science-fiction works. Throughout Wells's lengthy career, his indebtedness to this American author becomes increasingly apparent; numerous direct and indirect allusions to Poe and to his works occur within Wells's novels, early and late. . . .

Some of Wells's early works containing significant echoes of Poe's fiction—especially "Ms. Found in a Bottle" (1833), "Ligeia" (1838), "The Fall of the House of Usher" (1839), "A Descent into the Maelstrom" (1841), and *The Narrative of Arthur Gordon Pym* (1838)—include a short story, **"The Red Room"** . . . , three scientific romances, *The Time Machine* (1895), *The Island of Dr. Moreau* . . . , and *The First Men in the Moon* . . . , and a social novel, *Tono-Bungay.* . . . (p. 35)

These early works of Wells suggest Poe's influence in three general areas: Wells develops symbolic settings and spatial metaphors suggesting psychological terrain; he questions conventional notions about objective reality and individual identity through the use of spatially disoriented or otherwise unreliable narrators; and finally, he ponders the role of language in creating, sustaining, and sometimes even destroying human reality and identity. Perhaps the image of the "white sphinx" in *The Time Machine* most paradigmatically suggests Poe's influence on Wells's early works. This strange icon recalls the "white god" at the end of Poe's *Pym* and, like the "white god," implies much about the complex relationship between the human mind and phenomena.

During the years between 1895 and 1901, Wells appears most affected by Poe's technique of creating settings and situations that obscure the boundaries between phenomenal reality and human imaginative states. As he blurs usual distinctions between phenomena and his characters' imaginings, Wells emulates Poe in exposing as simplistic the conventional philosophical attitude which considers the human mind as affected by, but not profoundly affecting, the world outside. Both authors insist upon the highly important function of the mind in making and sustaining the external world humans assume they merely inhabit. Poe and Wells show that when the mind ceases to operate in its usual modes, the face of the external world can change, often irrevocably. Owing to the effects of dreams, drugs, art, intense emotions, encounters with extraterrestrials, or exotic adventures in strange environments, Poe's and Wells's characters often find themselves unable to sustain any notions about the external world that conform to their expectations and assumptions. Indeed, characters sometimes discover the complex interdependence between mental activity and so-called objective reality; like Prendick in *Moreau,* they might also discover that sobriety or the return to familiar surroundings does not guarantee full psychological reorientation. On the contrary, Poe and Wells (in his early period) suggest that when consciousness is even temporarily disordered, notions about reality can be permanently altered, often undesirably. Furthermore, characters who experience the disruption of their notions about reality also suffer the destructive disorganization of personal identity and linguistic ability.

One early story, **"The Red Room,"** particularly suggests Wells's affinities with Poe. Except for a few subtle stylistic differences (amid a number of striking stylistic similarities), **"The Red Room"** might have been written by Poe himself. The narrator of the story spends the night in a haunted room, developed as a Poe-esque spatial metaphor for a human mind debilitated by terror. Initially skeptical about haunted rooms and somewhat boastful of his own rationality, the narrator follows the confusing directions of Lorraine Castle's "grotesque custodians," first down a shadowy hallway, then up a spiral staircase, and finally through a "long, draughty subterranean passage" lit only by a few flickering candles. Like the narrator of "The Fall of the House of Usher," he admits being "affected" by the environment as he proceeds through this Gothic labyrinth of a house. He redoubles his efforts to maintain a "matter-of-fact" attitude against the growing impression of a sinisterly animate quality in the furniture and statuary of the castle. During the night he combats his fear of the darkness by burning seventeen candles, but a shadowy presence seems bent on extinguishing them and rendering him hysterical. The narrator becomes more and more the victim of his own state of mind in a remote and claustrophobic chamber where terror "seal[s his] vision" and "crush[es] the last vestiges of reason from [his] brain." In an attempt to escape the room he stumbles against a piece of furniture, experiences a "horrible sensation of falling," and remains unconscious until dawn when, rescued by his hosts, he is compelled to admit that the room is indeed haunted, not by a ghost but by "the worst of all things that haunt poor mortal man . . . *Fear!*". . . . (pp. 35-6)

Wells could not have devised a more Poe-like haunting; "FEAR" debilitates Roderick Usher and several other Poe characters who are, after all, the victims of their own imaginations. Their emotions preside over rational judgment, and their subsequent actions often cause permanent changes in their external worlds. Along with Usher, consider as well Poe's narrator in "The Tell-Tale Heart" (1843). His paranoid delusions about an old man's supposed "evil eye" eventually dominate his thoughts and actions until he finally commits murder and effects his own capture by the police. The psychological state of the narrator in **"The Red Room"** similarly accounts for his panic, subsequent head wound and near self-destruction.

Wells's psychological horror story exhibits further resemblances to Poe's fiction. Echoing Poe's narrators in works such as "The Tell-Tale Heart," the speaker in **"The Red Room"** emphasizes his own lucidity under the most bizarre circumstances, even as language fails him and the nature of his experiences obviates such clarity. Unable to gauge the extent of his mental deterioration within an environment "too stimulating for the imagination" and only partially illuminated by firelight and candlelight, the narrator insists upon his own objectivity even while admitting that he "fancies" he hears noises. He declares, "I was in a state of considerable nervous tension, although to my reason there was no adequate cause for the condition. My mind, however, was perfectly clear." . . . (pp. 36-7)

This passage reveals a Poe-esque conception of how the human psyche evinces rational and emotional components working independently, even somewhat against one another. Now well documented by Darrel Abel, G. R. Thompson and others is Poe's penchant for developing characters symbolizing rational and nonrational aspects of mind. . . . The works of Freud significantly reinforce this same theory of human psychology in Wells's writings subsequent to 1914; however, **"The Red Room"** strongly implies Wells's primary indebtedness in the early works to Poe for his ideas about human psychology. In **"The Red Room"** Wells ironically exposes the narrator's subjectivity while proclaiming his objectivity. (p. 37)

Like his short story **"The Red Room,"** some of Wells's best known scientific romances—*The Time Machine, The Island of Dr. Moreau, The First Men in the Moon*— exploit Poe-esque narrative techniques. Each of these works relies heavily upon a narrator's altered state of consciousness for successful effects, whether such a state results from heightened emotion, as in **"The Red Room,"** or from some other source, such as drugs or dreams. Most of the central characters in Wells's early works undergo profound and somewhat permanent disorientation experiences which provoke fundamental questions about reality and personal identity. Further evidence of Poe's influence upon Wells during these early years arises in the numerous spatial metaphors occurring throughout Wells's works; some of these metaphors seem borrowed directly from Poe's writings while others are perhaps carefully fashioned after Poe models.

Like the speaker in **"The Red Room,"** the narrator of *The Time Machine* shows much confidence in his own objectivity despite the fantastic nature of his experiences. The wary reader, however, finds reasons to suspect him of naivete. In fact, neither the narrator nor the Time Traveller, whose story the narrator relates, inspires reader confidence in his objectivity. The Traveller, of course, does not really try to convince his listeners of the accuracy of his own account, for he warns them that they hear only his interpretations of essentially incomprehensible experiences in the eighty-third century. The narrator, however, insists upon the veracity of his report of the Traveller's behavior. Although he distrusts the Time Traveller, owing to some deceptive quality lurking beneath the latter's "lucid frankness," the narrator vehemently denies the possibility of being tricked or deceived.

The narrator's opening remarks inform us that he hears the Traveller's story and sees the miniature model of the time machine in a firelit parlor after dinner when "thought runs gracefully free of the trammels of precision." Agreeing with the Medical Man that people are more credulous by night than by day, the narrator, in language strikingly reminiscent of Poe's in its tendency to undercut subtly the very assertions it proffers, nevertheless insists "It appears incredible to me that any kind of trick . . . could have been played upon us under these conditions." . . . Mitigating the certainty implied in the narrator's emphatic tone is the subjectivity he reveals through the words "appeared . . . to me" (a phrase, incidentally, which occurs in Poe's "Usher" under quite similar circumstances. After he is already "infected" with Roderick's hysteria, Poe's narrator announces that "it appeared" to him that strange noises, such as those described in the "Ethelred" tale, emanated from some remote region of the house). Here the narrator unwittingly reveals exactly what the Time Traveller feels compelled to admit, that any reporter is limited to descriptions of mere appearances. Furthermore, the "conditions" the narrator finds conducive to objectivity are, in fact, quite the opposite; for when the Traveller shows his guests the miniature time machine and later the full-scale apparatus, the demonstration takes place by candlelight and lamplight, to which the narrator refers contradictorily as "brilliant" and "shadowy."

Within the framework of the narrator's less-than-reliable report lies the Time Traveller's presumably verbatim account of his adventures among the Eloi, an account by the Traveller's admission quite open to question. Besides admitting that by necessity he imposes his own nineteenth-century interpretations upon the phenomena he observes in the distant future, the Traveller reports a dramatic experience of psychological disorientation prior to arriving among the Eloi. His account, ostensibly an effort at objective reporting, actually serves further to envelope his narrative in an impenetrable shroud of mystery. As he pulls the levers sending his vehicle forward through time, he feels a "nightmare sensation of falling. . . . An eddying murmur filled my ears, and a strange, dumb confusedness descended on my mind." . . . All of these "peculiar sensations . . . merged at last into a kind of hysterical exhilaration," characterized by "a certain curiosity" and "a certain dread," which "at last . . . took complete possession of me." . . . Wells's Time Traveller resembles many of Poe's narrators who are often adversely affected psychologically even before they begin to experience the series of events comprising the substance of their narratives. In fact, the Time Traveller's "peculiar sensations" are quite similar to those reported by the old man in Poe's "A Descent into the Maelstrom" and by the narrator of "Ms. Found in a Bottle," both of whom fall through a vortex of ocean, experience terror, hysteria, paralysis, dread, and finally a calm curiosity enabling them to make a self-proclaimed "objective" account of their surroundings and feelings. Such objectivity, however, becomes increasingly dubious as the details of their narratives unfold.

Narrative unfoldings in Wells's works uncover even more evidence of Poe's influence. In *The Time Machine* Wells devises a geographical landscape functioning as a Poe-esque symbol of psychological terrain, and he develops a mysterious white icon perhaps deliberately reminiscent of the one Poe's Pym encounters at the end of his voyage. As we have seen in the story **"The Red Room,"** wherein a labyrinthine haunted castle corresponds to the uncharted regions of the human mind, quite early Wells begins to understand Poe's use of spatial metaphor in exposing the artificiality of all clear-cut distinctions between mind and world, or interior and exterior realms.

The world of the Eloi consists exclusively of the surface of their planet. At first the Traveller assumes that this surface is the whole world, but as he begins to detect the Eloi's fear of darkness and to discover the curious shafts leading down into the interior of the planet, he gradually realizes that a powerful subterranean force rules all. Malevolent, shapeless beings who emerge at night to feed on the docile Eloi, the Morlocks control absolutely the lives of the surface creatures by instilling in them a fear of the unknown. Just as Poe in such works as "Usher," "The Cask of Amontillado," "The Tell-Tale Heart," "The Black Cat" (1843) and *Pym* suggests that recessed, subterranean regions of the mind exert much control over conscious behavior, Wells in this work develops the same notion in showing how the gentle, insipid Eloi are so easily manipulated by the subterranean Morlocks' demonic force, a force Wells quite significantly describes in another work as "the Unseen." For Poe and for Wells, an "unseen" interior force can often prevail over exterior forms and appearances.

In *The Time Machine* Wells employs the image of the white sphinx to illustrate the ways in which appearances intimate but never disclose the "unseen" forces informing them. The white sphinx, like the white figure at the conclusion of Poe's *Pym*, confronts the observer with the task of discovering its meaning. The Traveller sees the sphinx as a key to the mysteries he observes in the future, and he senses that a look inside will reveal not only the hiding place of his time machine, but also the terms for understanding the strange world into which he has ventured. Like the image Pym confronts, however, the white sphinx forces the Traveller to explore his own interior, to discover the extent to which the human mind projects meanings onto the exterior world. Pym's narrative discloses no ultimate knowledge derived from contemplation of a white god but intimates the processes of the mind as it seeks some ultimate knowledge it believes may exist independently of itself. Likewise, the hermetically sealed white sphinx finally discloses nothing but forces the Traveller to understand that exterior phenomena may be without meaning other than that imposed by the questing mind. Thus the Traveller wishes to communicate to his dinner guests that his narrative consists largely of his own interpretations of experience. But the naive narrator fails to hear this message even as he reports it, for he maintains faith in his own ability to report "objective" truth. Like the "editors" of *Pym*, this narrator argues for the "veracity" of a report designed specifically to challenge all traditional notions of narrative veracity.

Having much in common with the Time Traveller, Prendick in Wells's *Moreau* emerges as another narrator whose story is filtered to the reader through the subjective haze of a Poe-esque disorientation designed to obscure accepted boundaries between mind and phenomena. Whereas the Time Traveller visits an exotic environment many centuries in the future, Prendick visits an island extant within his own era but every bit as remote from his reality as the future is remote from the Time Traveller's. Like the Traveller, he suffers a series of increasingly disorienting experiences, ranging from eight days' exposure to the elements in a dinghy lost at sea, to an alternating feverish/alcoholic delirium; his confusion grows as he discovers the subjects of Dr. Moreau's vivisectionist experiments which change animals into near-humans (and later Prendick into something not quite an animal). Prendick witnesses a complete breakdown of the accepted boundaries between animal and human mentality—the result of Dr. Moreau's misguided visionary experiments. Between the time when he disappears and reappears eleven months later, the fabric of Prendick's reality steadily unravels, leaving him in the end like Montgomery, "an outcast from civilization," his perceptions of himself, humanity and the world irrevocably altered.

Significantly, many of the disorienting experiences resulting in Prendick's loss of reality closely parallel those of Pym of Poe's *The Narrative of Arthur Gordon Pym.* Like Pym, Prendick drifts for days in a lifeboat where he and his companions are finally driven to cannibalism. Before they are able to kill and eat their victim, however, the men fall out of the boat and drown, leaving Prendick alone to be rescued by the strange crew of the *Ipecacuanha.* Already delirious, Prendick is nourished on alcohol by Montgomery, a passenger aboard the ship and protege of Dr. Moreau. Like Pym, who as a castaway drinks port wine and notices its effects on the other men but denies that it has any effect on himself, Prendick sees Captain Davis' intoxication but remains completely unaware that he himself has been fed alcohol. Indeed, insisting that he never drinks alcohol, Prendick still cannot explain why all his memories of events aboard the *Ipecacuanha* lack important "connexions." Like Pym, he must piece together fragments.

Also identically with Pym, Prendick finds himself on an island where his already tenuous hold on reality weakens and dissolves altogether. The events on Moreau's island, recalling those on Pym's Tsalal, fail to conform to any of Prendick's standards of reality, and Prendick quite often has to interpret the fantastic in terms of the familiar, the reality he knew before coming to Moreau's island. Just as Pym attempts to identify forms of life on Tsalal, including the peculiar white, scarlet-clawed animal at which the natives call out, "Tekeli-li," Prendick tries to assign names and meanings to the strange but, he assumes, natural sights and sounds he witnesses. However, on Moreau's island, which is soporifically warm and suspends Prendick in a trance-like state, the expected "laws of nature" do not apply, for they have been humanly altered by Moreau. Furthermore, Moreau's attempts to keep his vivisectionist activities secret from Prendick magnify the distortion of Prendick's perceptions of the events going on about him, his memories of inexplicable sights and sounds intermingle with the contents of his dreams, and in turn the island environment becomes "altered to [his] imagination." . . . His subsequent account of the ordeal acknowledges language as the primary tool for wresting meaning out of a chaos of memories. Before he can logically organize and interpret his experiences for the reader, he faces the difficult task of finding language which will serve adequately to describe them. Like the narrator of *The Time Machine,* Prendick struggles with language because he believes in objective "truth." An episode apparently drawn directly out of Poe's *Pym,* however, exposes as completely illusory Prendick's notion that he or anyone can narrate objectively. During his final hours on Moreau's island, Prendick despairs of finding any suitable materials from which to construct a raft or boat, but one day he spies a small sail to the southwest of the island and begins frantically to signal for aid. Although he sees men in the boat, they seem oddly unresponsive to his cries and gestures. Prendick finds out why only when the boat drifts near enough for him to capture it—the occupants are dead. Just as Pym and his comrades desperately hail a ship full of carrion, Prendick similarly seeks help from what appears to be a rescue boat. Even though the vessel itself turns out to be the means of his escape from the island, deceptive phenomenal appearances cause Prendick to misinterpret what he sees (or thinks he sees) before his eyes. Repeatedly, Prendick's experiences teach him what the Time Traveller learns from the white sphinx— the meanings we attribute to exterior phenomena actually arise within us; narrative is never the objective report of "truth"

but is instead the subjective record of the human mind's interactions with the "white sphinx" of outward form.

The First Men in the Moon is another early work in which a narrator's profound disorientation immediately precedes an almost complete loss of identity and an attempt to recount the entire ordeal in narrative form. As in *Moreau,* Wells in *First Men* contrives a narrator who suffers increasing difficulties in the use of language and, owing to the strange character of his actual experiences, in distinguishing between "real" and dreamed events. (pp. 37-41)

When [Bedford] finally leaves the earth with Cavor, he remarks several times that the experience is "like the beginning of a dream;" . . . later he reports that enroute to the moon both he and Cavor were "in a sort of quiescence that was neither waking nor slumber" as they "fell through a space of time that had neither night nor day in it, silently, softly and swiftly down towards the moon." . . .

Already disoriented when they step onto the moon's surface, Bedford and Cavor complicate their conditions by drinking the latter's "sickly tasting" concoction to prevent moonsickness and by eating "fleshy red" moon flora which renders them totally incoherent. Later, very aware of his previous intoxication, Bedford wonders is some of his experiences were dreamt owing to the fungus they had eaten. (p. 41)

It is significant that Cavor's messages emanate not from the surface of the moon, but from its interior, a subterranean labyrinth where the controlling lunar beings reside. (Like the Morlocks, the Selenites dwell beneath the surface of their world and feed on surface life.) Cavor's telegraphed messages describe the interior of the moon as a type of supernal region reached by travelling in a diminishing spiral direction through huge lunar caverns, the environment growing "less and less material" all the time. Recalling Poe's Tsalal in *Pym,* this lunar/supernal region is a labyrinth of chasms illuminated by phosphorescent rocks and water. At the lowest point in the Grand Lunar chamber lies "a lake of heatless fire, the waters of the Central Sea, glowing and eddying in strange perturbation. . . . In this innermost cavern resides the Grand Lunar, a god-like being which Wells develops emblematically to coalesce cosmos (exterior) and mind (interior) in the same fashion as Poe coalesces the mind of Roderick with the House of Usher. The chamber is a cavernous rocky enclosure suggestive of a skull and housing the Grand Lunar whose form is that of a luminous disembodied brain. However, owing to the vastness of the cavern and to its indistinct, dimly lit boundaries (a chamber calling to mind a similar one in Poe's "Usher," where the narrator struggles to see the "remoter" parts of the "large and lofty" room), the Grand Lunar also reminds Cavor of a star floating in a "blaze of incandescent blue."

Such presumably are the "facts" about the moon. Before stumbling into a well-prepared Poe-esque trap of textual veracity, however, a reader should pause to observe the vague origins of ostensibly factual data. Wells's narrative is a Poe-esque baroque, a highly detailed body of information arising out of and encircling an indistinct, unfathomable center composed of a series of complex interiors. The narrator of the opening chapters of *First Men* is a man whose mind has been affected first by an "implosion," then by intoxicating drink, and overall by the exotic lunar atmosphere. Following his return to earth, Bedford's narrative, now completely unreliable owing to the grudge he bears Cavor, becomes an amalgam of his own and his former companion's distorted points of view. Because Bedford believes Cavor maligns him in the telegraphed communications from the moon, Bedford edits Cavor's messages to his own advantage. All narrative information emanates first from the mind of Bedford, then from the mind of Cavor, and finally from the interior of the moon, a region emblematically suggesting a vast, cosmic mind. Thus, as in a Poe text, any careful reader attempting to distinguish between reliable and unreliable narrative data must suddenly realize that narrative reflects no "truth" at all but the processes of the mind confronting phenomena and pursuing certainty which is not forthcoming.

Like the disoriented characters themselves, the reader must traffic in a jumble of possibilities within a narrative comprised of dreams, hallucinations, and two men's very different interpretations of their experiences. In the same manner as so many of Poe's works, *First Men* draws the reader into a text which proffers "objective" reportage and "truth" but immediately frustrates attempts to locate any such "truth." Such a narrative states no meaning but involves the reader in a search for meaning which, like Cavor's final communication, remains a "secret." Ultimately the reader shares the dilemma of Bedford when, in a passage evoking an episode in Poe's *Pym*, he receives from Cavor a partially intelligible message scribbled in blood. Just as Bedford must decipher this fragmentary note, the reader must deal with the many disjunctions occurring within Bedford's text which, conflated with Cavor's telegraphed communications, finally degenerates into silence as the Selenites deliberately scramble the already feeble signals; containing their forever inaccessible "secret," these signals drift out into the "impenetrably dark" expanse of the universe.

Although *The Time Machine, Moreau,* and other works deal tangentially with such questions of language and text, *First Men* represents Wells's first scientific romance to evince sustained, complex concern with these matters. (A social novel, *Love and Mr. Lewisham,* published only a year earlier in 1900, also exhibits a pervasive interest in language.) Cavor's language floating through the dark silence of space possesses a "secret" which it will never render up. This "secret" at the heart of language gradually becomes the focus of Wells's preoccupation with "the unseen." Perhaps because of this interest in language, from about 1900 on Wells's works rely less and less upon conventionally Gothic or fantastic accoutrements to embody "the unseen." Instead they begin to explore language itself as the most profound revealer and concealer of the mysteries of existence. In *Tono-Bungay,* when Wells's narrator resigns himself at last to ultimate inarticulateness after a sustained effort to state "something" (a word he and other characters repeat in frustration) which remains ineffable, he expresses Wells's own most consistently maintained attitude toward language as a powerful force forever seeking a forever-elusive mystery "at the heart of life." Such a notion of language comprises a fundamental affinity between Wells and his predecessor Poe. (pp. 42-3)

> Catherine Rainwater, "Encounters with the 'White Sphinx': Poe's Influence on Some Early Works of H. G. Wells," in English Literature in Transition, Vol. 26, No. 1, 1983, pp. 35-51.

BRIAN ALDISS (essay date 1985)

[*Aldiss is an English novelist, short story writer, critic, and editor who is best known for his science fiction novels and criticism. In the following excerpt, Aldiss discusses* In the Days of the Comet *as a constructive fantasy expressing Wells's hopes for a utopian future.*]

Once his book of essays, *Anticipations,* had been published in 1901, Wells was listened to increasingly as a prophetic voice, competent to speak about the real world, rather than to indulge merely in his ingenious fantasies. *In the Days of the Comet* is a balance between the dissatisfactions and hope of the real world, and constructive fantasy. It's a visionary novel. Visionary novels are always disappointing in some way, since words never correspond exactly to either facts or wishes; but this is a prize exhibit of the species.

Wells's first readers were most struck by his vision of the new world emerging, a world of free love and social equality. We in our generation are more likely to be impressed by his portrait of things as they were—and by their resemblance to today. The comet has yet to come.

A profile of the novel appears disarmingly simple, a case of 'Look here upon this picture, and on this'. We are shown the old world; the comet passes; we are shown the new world. There is a Biblical directness in the parable: 'We shall all be changed, in a moment, in the twinkling of an eye.' The comet is the mechanism which carries us from the one picture to the other, and Wells is properly off-hand in his pseudo-scientific talk of the nitrogen in the comet's tail having its benevolent effects upon mankind.

This sensible method of argument by contrast is one that others have followed, before and since. We hope for a better world, we see it clear. But how to get there? Wells in 1906 could see no bridge to utopia; he forged a miracle instead, with legitimate didactic intent.

This forging is performed with great literary skill—something with which Wells is too little credited (though Nabokov and Eliot have acknowledged Wells's powers). The strengths of the book have also been widely underestimated, even by those writers and readers who traffic in comets and similar wonders.

The story is told in Wells's easy manner. After a crisis, we get the throwaway remark, 'Then, you know, I suppose I folded up this newspaper and put it in my pocket', which catches without pretension the absent-minded listlessness following a lover's quarrel. The prose grows more spirited when Wells's traditional dislikes are paraded. Despite many attempts at it since, no one has bettered Wells's description of places where commerce has invaded nature—perhaps because he finds a kind of desolate beauty there. (pp. iv-v)

The plain tale of Leadford's thwarted affair with Nettie, and of his love which turns to hatred, is enough to allow Wells to string out before us a series of ghastly cameos, the finest of which is probably the picture of the industrial Midlands, when twilight settles over a tawdry scene of sheds, factories, terrace houses, and blast furnaces. . . . (p. v)

Such passages brim with imaginative energy. In his book *Language of Fiction,* David Lodge makes an eloquent defence of *Tono-Bungay,* which Wells was to publish only three years after *In the Days of the Comet.* Lodge points out that there is a way of reading Wells, just as there is of reading Henry James, and speaks of *Tono-Bungay* as a 'Condition of England' novel: a novel neglected because its style, its whole thrust, does not accord with preconceived ideas of the English novel as formulated by James and F. R. Leavis. To a large extent, the same principle applies to *In the Days of the Comet.*

All its vivid imagery of physical chaos serves a purpose directly geared to the meaning of the novel. It links the tangible world with the chaos of mankind's thinking, and in particular with Leadford's lost and murderous state of mind. As we are told, 'the world of thought in those days was in the strangest condition, it was choked with obsolete inadequate formulae, it was tortuous to a maze-like degree with secondary contrivances and adaptations, suppressions, conventions, and subterfuges. Base immediacies fouled the truth on every man's lips.' Clarity was blocked as thoroughly as the way to the sea.

Over the chaos shines the comet, growing larger night by night. It forms a contrast to the 'dark compressed life' on which it shines. Wells wrote with the predicted 1910 appearance of Halley's Comet in mind. Equally topical for us is the miners' strike, with its pickets and attacks on cars. Wells's power as a fantasist derives from his firm grip on the world-as-it-is.

Since *In the Days of the Comet* was not well received when it first appeared, as frequently happens when visionary books are set before a largely unprepared public, it seems appropriate to offer a new reading of the novel to a new set of readers.

This is not exactly a 'Condition of England' novel, although in some respects it may be seen as a precursor of *Tono-Bungay.* Rather, it is a skilfully conducted 'Condition of Mind' novel. The Change effected by the comet is a change of mind. Descriptions of physical states are always linked to mental states—as when the hideous towns are designated 'cities men weep to enter'. The sick mind of the people before the Change is dramatized cunningly in a variety of ways as it drifts towards war, the ultimate waste, the ultimate confusion. 'Humanity choked amidst its products.'

This sickness of mind is nowhere better embodied than in the character of its central figure, Willie Leadford, who tells the story. On the first page of his narrative, Leadford speaks of his 'crude, unhappy youth'. Throughout the story until the Change, he reveals himself as brutal, troubled, murderous, and ineffective. This is precisely the state of the world in which he lives. Despite the tide of bottled emotions, everything is reduced to pettiness. (pp. vi-vii)

Leadford is deliberately not elaborately characterized. The same applies to the few other actors—a point to which we return later. But on the details encumbering Leadford's physical existence Wells is sharply precise. We particularly understand the nature of this 'dark and sullen lout', as he calls himself, by his treatment of his mother, the woman who endures much to ensure her son's comfort, minimal though that comfort is.

The portrait of Mrs Leadford is undoubtedly based on Wells's memory of his mother at Atlas House in Bromley, Kent, where he was born. The exasperated love he felt for her is always present, nowhere more so than in the description of the old woman's dreadful kitchen. Even George Orwell never bettered that kitchen of Mrs Leadford's, where the business of deforming the human soul is carried on quite as efficiently as in any factory. Mrs Leadford is growing old in her foul kitchen. Her hands are distorted by ill-use. She coughs. She shuffles about in badly fitting boots. Even her son wants nothing to do with her.

Wells turns to the historic present for the climax of these scenes of domestic misery. Leadford, betrayer and betrayed, says, 'And while she washes up I go out, to sell my overcoat and watch in order that I may desert her.'

In the Days of the Comet is full of such compelling moments, which crystallize the whole point of the book while being sufficiently powerful in themselves as moments of tragi-comedy in Wells's best manner.

So the entire first part of the novel represents an acute and brilliantly drawn picture of the mind of England and the industrialised countries at the turn of the century. Leadford, taken up with his wretched emotional relationships and his socialism, pays little attention to the comet drawing nearer to Earth. His counter-weight, Parload, is the astronomer; it is through Parload that we see the contrast between earthly squalor and heavenly beauty, while Leadford is still having trouble with his boots.

The comet arrives and brings the Change. Wells now draws the utopia that could be. He was always a master of symbols, in his swift, careless-seeming way. Among the first objects the changed Leadford sees are a discarded box of pills and a wrecked battleship, a 'torn and battered mass of machinery' now lying amid ploughed-up mountains of chalk ooze. From the destruction of the old mind grows a better one.

Despite all these excellent preparations, the utopian world of might-be is a shadowy place when we come to it. Wells has to resort ultimately to traditional stereotype, to a place with trees of golden fruit and crystal fountains, tenanted by people who look exalted. He confronts a difficulty which Dante and Milton faced before him; the *Inferno* and *Paradise Lost* have more readers than a thousand *Paradisos* and *Paradise Regaineds.* Not only is a better world hard to realise, even on paper, but Wells had addressed himself particularly to that subject in the previous year, with the publication of *A Modern Utopia.*

A Modern Utopia is a full-fleshed blueprint for a better, healthier, and happier world, in which a regulated capitalist economy is presided over by an elite (the 'samurai'). Since it appeared in 1905, *A Modern Utopia* has been much sneered at. Many of the book's ideas are sensible and rational—in a word, Wellsian; but an irrational streak in us prevents us putting our knowledge into practice on any effective scale. Wells was essentially rather a simple person (an adjective he applies affectionately to Kipps), and it was this simplicity which gave him the confidence to put forward his less-than-simple plans for mankind, generally in the expectation that they would be immediately taken up.

The rather shadowy utopia to which we are introduced at the end of [*In the Days of the Comet*] contains two well-dramatized elements not markedly present in *A Modern Utopia,* the death of warfare and an outspoken argument for free love. The argument for free love is carried on into the 'frame' of the story for extra emphasis.

Critics have accused Wells of wanting war. Certainly he was obsessed with war, almost as greatly as we are in our time. Certainly in 1914 he applauded the call to arms, as many people did—and wrote a rather silly book whose title coined a cliché, *The War that Will End War.* But nobody reading *In the Days of the Comet* would call him a war-monger. I am thinking particularly of the lovely moment after the Change when the common soldiery, on its way to war—as it might be, in Flanders—returns to consciousness by the roadside.

The men do not fall into ranks. They discuss the causes of war with incredulity. 'The Emperor!' they exclaim. 'Oh, nonsense! We're civilized men . . . Where's the coffee?'

It did not work out that way in 1914. Halley's Comet passed without effect.

But the new thing in Leadford's utopia which caught the attention in 1906 was love, not war.

Wells advocates free love: cleverly, he has a woman put forward the argument. Nettie is changed from a rural faceless creature to a 'young woman of advanced appearance' (to borrow a description jokingly applied to Christina Alberta in Wells's later novel, *Christina Alberta's Father*). She puts forward the argument tentatively at first, but in the end conclusively: marriage is not what she wants; she wants to love where she chooses; she wants both Leadford and his rival. 'Am I not a mind that you must think of me as nothing but a woman?' (pp. vii-ix)

A word should be said finally about the form of *In the Days of the Comet*. Although it has been referred to here, as elsewhere, as a novel, it is in fact a separate if allied form, a novella. A novella, as properly understood, restricts itself to a single situation or event. It has few characters, and they mainly function in a symbolic role: the protagonist, the woman as love object, the rival, the mother, the statesman, and so on. Goethe's *Elective Affinities* is a good example of a novella. And *In the Days of the Comet* is a rare English example of the mode—a much more perfect example than has hitherto been recognised.

In it, H. G. Wells shows his characteristic dissatisfaction with the existing order, his spirited hatred of the mess we have got ourselves into, his striving for better things. No doubt if he were alive today he would still find ample reason for dissatisfaction, hatred, striving. (p. x)

> *Brian Aldiss, in an introduction to* In the Days of the Comet *by H. G. Wells, The Hogarth Press, 1985, pp. iii-x.*

PATRICK PARRINDER   (essay date 1985)

[*In the following excerpt, Parrinder discusses some elements central to Wells's fictional portrayals of utopian or paradisaical societies.*]

Visions in which the whole human race—not just, as in *A Modern Utopia*, part of it—has been made, or appears to have been made, "wise, tolerant, noble, perfect" appear at least twice in Wells's fiction. There is, first of all, the fleeting vision (set in the same pastoral Thames Valley landscape as *News from Nowhere*) of the world of the Eloi as an arcadian Communism at the beginning of *The Time Machine*—a vision no sooner entertained than it is brutally destroyed. Wells portrayed a more genuinely arcadian paradise in his later utopian romance *Men Like Gods*. . . . While *The Time Machine* shows a degenerate future for humanity, *Men Like Gods* shows the species at a higher level of evolution than it has yet attained. The political system is a form of anarchism. The intellectual capacity of the utopians is reflected in unimaginable (and, on Wells's part, unimagined) achievements in science and in the arts. They communicate by means of telepathic mindspeech. These utopians are the natural descendants of the intellectual aristocracy, the "fine Olympians" (*Tono-Bungay* . . .) whom Wells saw as the highest products of the civilization of the English country-house. Their utopia is almost destroyed by the belligerence of a party of English visitors, led by a splendid caricature of Winston Churchill—the unacceptable face of the country-house ethic.

Mr Barnstaple, Wells's protagonist, says of the utopia of *Men Like Gods* that "By all outward appearance this might be a Communism such as was figured in a book we used to value on earth, a book called *News from Nowhere* by an Earthling named William Morris. It was a graceful impossible book." . . . Something that Wells can hardly have failed to notice in *News from Nowhere* is its idyllic portrayal of sexual relationships. A defining feature of the Earthly Paradise in Wells is that, going farther than Morris, he shows his utopians enjoying complete freedom from the emotional disturbances caused by sexual passion. In *The Time Machine*, there is the brother-and-sister relationship between the Time Traveller and the childlike Weena. The hero of *The History of Mr Polly* . . .—the unlikely survivor of a suicide bid, a major fire, and three desperate fights—finds peace and contentment at the Potwell Inn, a mildly Rabelaisian paradise which he inhabits on terms of asexual companionship with the Fat Woman.

Wells's two formal utopias, *A Modern Utopia* and *Men Like Gods*, were each followed a year later by a sort of unofficial pendant, *In the Days of the Comet* . . . and *The Dream* . . . respectively, stressing not the perfection of social organization in a utopia but the contrast between the individual contentment it would offer and the emotional storm and stress of 20th-century life. (In addition, the two "pendant" novels are plotted on a time-axis between present and future, whilst the formal utopias show their characters travelling in space between the Earth and a parallel world.) *The Dream* describes a vision of present-day life experienced by Sarnac, an Olympian living in A.D. 4000 who is staying with his mistress Sunray and their friends at a holiday resort. In his dream, Sarnac becomes Harry Mortimer Smith, an embattled 20th-century man whose emotional turmoil ends in his becoming the victim of a crime of passion. The dream is scarcely comprehensible to the Olympians, whose life consists of rational, non-possessive sexual companionship in a state of continual nudity. Just as this follows out the implications of *Men Like Gods* for individual life, so *In the Days of the Comet* builds on the botanist's experience in *A Modern Utopia*, showing how the coming of the Earthly Paradise supersedes sexual possessiveness and the problem of jealousy.

In the Days of the Comet is narrated by Willie Leadford, a young man from the Potteries who becomes murderously jealous after his girl-friend, Nettie, goes off with another man. After the "Change" brought about by the green vapors of the comet, Willie is at first as unreceptive to utopian ideas of sexuality as the botanist of *A Modern Utopia* had been. When Nettie proposes to divide her attentions between her old lover and her new one, Willie is unable to accept, and goes back home to his mother. Finally, however, his infatuation is cured and he becomes a contented participant in a sexual foursome consisting of Nettie, his male rival, and a new partner, Anna Reeves, who becomes the mother of his children.

For Willie the rites of passage to utopian sexuality include the renewal of his relationship with his mother, her death, and the transference of his affections to Anna, who had been his mother's nurse. It is a regression to childlike love. . . . There is, perhaps, a similarly regressive and childlike element in all Wells's representations of utopian sexuality. The Fat Woman in *Mr Polly* is a mother-substitute, and Weena (like all the Eloi) is there to be treated as a baby sister. Sexually at least, Wells is at one with William Morris in representing the Earthly Paradise as a place of "second childhood," an "epoch of rest" where humanity is stuck, becalmed if not actually degenerating. (pp. 120-22)

No sooner has Wells created an Earthly Paradise, than he or his characters feel moved to destroy it. The destructive element in his writing has been widely noted. V. S. Pritchett has observed, "There are always fist-fights and fires in the early Wells. Above all, there are fires" [see *TCLC*, Vol. 6]. The fires symbolize the potentially unharnessable energy released by the technological exploitation of nature. Man is the "fire-making animal," as Wells puts it in the chapter of *The World Set Free* . . . which introduces the discovery of nuclear energy and is, significantly, entitled "The Sun Snarers." . . . Fires in Wells are almost always deliberately started. The Time Traveller sets off a conflagration by his injudicious use of matches stolen from a ruined science museum. The Martians in *The War of the Worlds* start fires by means of the Heat-Ray. Mr Polly sets his own house on fire. In *Men Like Gods* . . . Arden and Greenlake are killed by an explosion. Lurking in these examples is the suggestion that humankind is strengthened by going through the fire (it is a measure of the degeneracy of the Morlocks and of Weena that they perish so miserably by it). *In the Days of the Comet* shows an interesting attempt by Wells to turn the purging fire into a wholly positive symbol. There the new age opens with the semi-annual Beltane festivals in which all the accumulated materials of life before the Change are systematically burnt. The only articles to be spared these "Phoenix fires" . . . are carefully disinfected and preserved in museums.

Very different, however, are the Wellsian fist-fights, which symbolize human recalcitrance and resistance to utopia. Man's unregenerate belligerence and competitiveness appears on two principal levels, those of nationalism or imperialism and of sexuality. In *Men Like Gods,* Catskill and his party almost destroy utopia as a result of their attempts to colonize it and plant the League of Nations' flag. In *A Modern Utopia* and *In the Days of the Comet,* sexual rapacity is the destroying force. While Wells's scientific romances contain many scenes of actual fist-fights, the "soap-bubble" of *A Modern Utopia* is pricked by a virtual fist-fight, due to the botanist's jealous rage when he sees his beloved's double with another man. The narrator has to apply both verbal and physical restraints. . . . At the moment when the fight is about to erupt, Utopia vanishes. Wells, it seems, cannot portray a paradisal society without an ironic sub-plot asserting the "perpetuity of aggressions" as it is realized in the violence and self-assertion of the contemporary world. Often, too, violence and self-assertion in his novels have a specific survival-value. It is only in advanced technological societies that these qualities threaten species destruction. (pp. 122-23)

Wells's utopian worlds are joined to our empirical world either in time (the glimpse of the future) or in space (the parallel world somewhere else in the cosmos). This means that, far from simply negating our world or forming an ironic antithesis, they fit together with our world into a greater whole. Utopia is a "hopeful stage, leading to a long ascent of stages" (*A Modern Utopia* . . .); it is "but one of countless universes that move together in time, that lie against one another, endlessly like the leaves of a book" (*Men Like Gods* . . .). To know all these stages, worlds, or universes would necessitate the development of a synthetic human consciousness, infinitely extensible in space and time. The Wellsian motifs of space- and time-travel are, therefore, not so much metaphoric or ironic as synecdochic. That is, each world that Wells invents or that his narrators visit is a "part" whose ultimate significance lies in its belonging to a greater whole. No Wellsian utopia is an end in itself, and no paradise is ever conclusively lost or regained.

Behind each individual manifestation of the utopian spirit is an ultimate utopia based on "developments of power and activity upon which at present we can set no limits nor give any certain form" [as Wells wrote in *The Open Conspiracy*]. Many of Wells's texts end with the expression of an open-ended cosmic mysticism which promises knowledge of the super-universe consisting of all the topias and utopias possible to man. (p. 125)

Patrick Parrinder, "Utopia and Meta-Utopia in H. G. Wells," in Science-Fiction Studies, *Vol. 12, No. 36, July, 1985, pp. 115-28.*

ADDITIONAL BIBLIOGRAPHY

Aldiss, Brian W. "The Man Who Could Work Miracles: H. G. Wells." In his *Billion Year Spree: The True History of Science Fiction*, pp. 113-33. New York: Schocken Books, 1974.
> Survey of the milieu in which Wells's science fiction was written, initial critical reaction, and Wells's place within modern science ficion.

Aldridge, Alexandra. "Origins of Dystopia: *When the Sleeper Wakes* and *We*." In *Clockwork Worlds: Mechanized Environments in SF,* edited by Richard D. Erlich and Thomas P. Dunn, pp. 63-84. Westport, Conn.: Greenwood Press, 1983.*
> Examines Wells's *When the Sleeper Wakes* and Zamyatin's *We* as archetypal and extremely influential dystopian novels.

Batchelor, John. "H. G. Wells." In his *The Edwardian Novelists,* pp. 119-49. New York: St. Martin's Press, 1982.
> Discussion of the theme of escape in several of Wells's major novels.

Bellamy, William. "*The Time Machine*" and "H. G. Wells." In his *The Novels of Wells, Bennett and Galsworthy: 1890-1910*, pp. 51-70, 114-43. New York: Barnes & Noble, 1971.
> Critical studies of *The Time Machine, In the Days of the Comet, Kipps, Tono-Bungay,* and *The History of Mr. Polly.*

Bergonzi, Bernard. "*The Time Machine:* An Ironic Myth." *Critical Quarterly* 2, No. 4 (Winter 1960): 293-305.
> Study of *The Time Machine* emphasizing the fantastic and romantic elements of the novel over the scientific.

———, ed. *H. G. Wells: A Collection of Critical Essays.* Englewood Cliffs, N.J.: Prentice-Hall, 1976, 182 p.
> Ten important essays on Wells and his work, including discussions by Bernard Bergonzi and Robert M. Philmus.

Bleiler, E. F. Introduction to *Three Prophetic Novels of H. G. Wells,* by H. G. Wells, edited by E. F. Bleiler, pp. vii-x. New York: Dover Publications, 1960.
> Discusses the prophetic nature of some of Wells's major science fiction.

Borrello, Alfred. *H. G. Wells: Author in Agony.* Carbondale: Southern Illinois University Press, 1972, 137 p.
> Close examinations of all phases of Wells's writing career.

Brome, Vincent. *H. G. Wells: A Biography.* London: Longmans, Green and Co., 1952, 255 p.
> A biography containing interesting personal glimpses into Wells's life and including many examples of the critical reception of his works.

Brooks, Van Wyck. *The World of H. G. Wells.* New York: Mitchell Kennerley, 1915, 189 p.
> Critical and biographical study focusing on the development of Wells's social and political thought as discernible in his fiction.

Clear, Claudius. "The Fantastic Fiction; or, 'The Invisible Man'." *The Bookman* (London) VI, No. 3 (November 1897): 250-51.

Enthusiastic early review of *The Invisible Man* that notes the inevitability of this kind of speculative fiction in an "age of inventions" and scientific advances.

Collins, Christopher. "Zamyatin, Wells and the Utopian Literary Tradition." *The Slavonic and East European Review* XLIV, No. 103 (July 1966): 351-60*
Notes Zamyatin's acknowledgment of Wells as the master of "classical Utopianism, social satire, scientific fantasy, and the adventure novel."

Costa, Richard Hauer. "The Rescue of H. G. Wells." *English Literature in Transition, 1880-1920, Special Series*, No. 3 (1985): 42-58.
Thorough survey of recent major critical and biographical studies of Wells.

Crossley, Robert. "Famous Mythical Beasts: Olaf Stapledon and H. G. Wells." *The Georgia Review* XXXVI, No. 8 (Fall 1982): 619-35.*
Examination of the correspondence between Stapledon and Wells and a comparison of their fiction.

Eisenstein, Alex. "*The Time Machine* and the End of Man." *Science-Fiction Studies* 3, No. 9, Part 2 (July 1976): 161-65.
Argues that the apocalyptic final scene of *The Time Machine*, which is usually interpreted as a depiction of the extinction of humankind, is in fact intended to show humanity's final evolutionary stage.

Farrell, John K. A. "H. G. Wells as an Historian." *The University of Windsor Review* II, No. 2 (Spring 1967): 47-57.
Appraisal of *The Outline of History* and *The Shape of Things to Come*, finding the former suspect as a work of history because of oversimplification and lack of documentation, and the latter a surprisingly prophetic book.

Ford, Ford Madox. *Letters of Ford Madox Ford*. Edited by Richard M. Ludwig. Princeton: Princeton University Press, 1965, 335 p.
Contains several letters from Ford to Wells that offer criticism of the latter's works.

Freeman, John. "H. G. Wells." In his *The Moderns: Essays in Literary Criticism*, pp. 53-101. 1917. Reprint. Freeport, N.Y.: Books for Libraries Press, 1967.
A critical examination of Wells's canon, emphasizing his social and humorous novels and his nonfiction.

Gerber, Richard. *Utopian Fantasy: A Study of English Utopian Fiction since the End of the Nineteenth Century*. London: Routledge & Kegan Paul, 1955, 162 p.*
Study attempting to demonstrate that English utopian fiction derives from "a comprehensive utopian imagination and view of life." Included is a discussion of Wells's major futuristic fiction.

Gilbert, James B. "Wars of the Worlds." *Journal of Popular Culture* X, No. 2 (Fall 1976): 326-36.
Examines the successive treatments of Wells's novel *The War of the Worlds* as a radio drama and a motion picture, noting the ways in which the work was distorted to suit changing times.

Hillegas, Mark R. "The First Invasions from Mars." *Michigan Alumnus Quarterly Review* LXVI, No. 14 (27 February 1960): 107-12.*
Historical placement of Wells's novel *The War of the Worlds* as only the second novel to depict "the invasion of Earth by immensely superior" extraterrestrial beings.

Hughes, David Y. "H. G. Wells and the Charge of Plagiarism." *Nineteenth-Century Fiction* 21, No. 1 (June 1966): 85-90.
Discussion of some charges of plagiarism against Wells, arguing that coincidence, coupled with Wells's tendency to employ topical materials, explains the instances.

———. "Bergonzi and After in the Criticism of Wells's SF." *Science-Fiction Studies* 31, No. 9, Part 2 (July 1976): 165-74.
Survey of the major critical and biographical books written about Wells between 1960 and 1976.

Hume, Kathryn. "The Hidden Dynamics of 'The War of the Worlds'." *Philological Quarterly* 62, No. 3 (Summer 1983): 279-92.

Explores the symbolic content of some images and events in *The War of the Worlds*.

Kagarlitski, J. *The Life and Thought of H. G. Wells*, translated by Moura Budberg. London: Sidgwick & Jackson, 1966, 210 p.
Revised and expanded version of the first book-length critical and biographical study of Wells published in Russia.

Kemp, Peter. *H. G. Wells and the Culminating Ape*. New York: St. Martin's Press, 1982, 225 p.
Documents Wells's interpretation of human needs, including food, sex, congenial habitat, and survival.

Mackenzie, Norman, and Mackenzie, Jean. *The Time Traveller: The Life of H. G. Wells*. London: Weidenfeld and Nicolson, 1973, 487 p.
A detailed and complete biography of Wells.

Macy, John. "H. G. Wells and Utopia." In his *The Critical Game*, pp. 269-76. New York: Boni and Liveright, 1922.
An essay on Wells's vision of Utopia as set forth in *The World Set Free*.

Mirsky, D. S. "H. G. Wells and History." *The Criterion* XII, No. 46 (October 1932): 1-9.
Views Wells as an exponent of bourgeois attitudes.

Parrinder, Patrick. "Imagining the Future: Zamyatin and Wells." *Science-Fiction Studies* 1, No. 1 (Spring 1973): 17-26.*
Examines some shared characteristics of Zamyatin's and Wells's science fiction.

———, ed. *H. G. Wells: The Critical Heritage*. London: Routledge & Kegan Paul, 1972, 351 p.
A collection of important reviews and studies of Wells's work.

Platzner, Robert L. "H. G. Wells's 'Jungle Book': The Influence of Kipling on *The Island of Dr. Moreau*." *The Victorian Newsletter*, No. 36 (Fall 1969): 19-22.*
Suggests that Wells drew extensively from Kipling's *The Jungle Book* in constructing episodes of *The Island of Doctor Moreau*.

Priestley, J. B. "H. G. Wells." *The English Journal* XIV, No. 2 (February 1925): 89-97.
Characterizes Wells as "a trinity of persons": the scientific romancer, the creative comic genius, and the sociologist; and discusses which of these personae was foremost in the creation of the major works.

Scholes, Robert, and Rabkin, Eric S. "A Brief History of Science Fiction." In their *Science Fiction: History, Science, Vision*, pp. 3-99. New York: Oxford University Press, 1977.*
Surveys the origins of science fiction and briefly discusses the thematic concerns treated in Wells's major science fiction novels.

Shelton, Robert. "The Mars-Begotten Men of Olaf Stapledon and H. G. Wells." *Science-Fiction Studies* 11, No. 1 (March 1984): 1-14.*
Compares human-Martian confrontations in Wells's *The War of the Worlds* and *Star-Begotten* with those in Stapledon's *Last and First Men*, noting the authors' mutual indebtedness to one another.

Sherman, Stuart P. "The Utopian Naturalism of H. G. Wells." In his *On Contemporary Literature*, pp. 50-84. New York: Henry Holt and Co., 1917.
Unfavorable assessment of the ideas presented in Wells's fiction.

Smith, Page. "The Millennial Vision of H. G. Wells." *Journal of Historical Studies* II, No, 1 (Winter 1968-69): 23-4.
Characterizes Wells's reflections on the future as overly optimistic.

Snow, C. P. "H. G. Wells." In his *Variety of Men*, pp. 63-85. New York: Charles Scribner's Sons, 1967.
Snow's reminiscences of conversations with Wells, and a brief biography.

Suvin, Darko. "*The Time Machine* versus *Utopia* as a Structural Model for Science Fiction." *Comparative Literature Studies* X, No. 4 (December 1973): 334-52.*

Close structural examination of *The Time Machine*, concluding that all science fiction has sprung from this novel.

Suvin, Darko, and Philmus, Robert M., eds. *H. G. Wells and Modern Science Fiction*. Lewisburg, Pa.: Bucknell University Press, 1977, 277 p.

A collection of essays concerning Wells's influence on, and comparative stature within, modern science ficion. Included are essays on "The Garden in Wells's Early Science Fiction," by David Y. Hughes and "Evolution as a Literary Theme in H. G. Wells's Science Fiction," by J. P. Vernier, as well as annotated listings of Wells's scientific writings.

Wagar, W. Warren. *H. G. Wells and the World State*. 1961. Reprint. Freeport, N.Y.: Books for Libraries Press, 1971, 301 p.

Examination of Wells's role as a prophet of a new utopian world order. Wagar provides extensive discussion of Wells's social philosophy.

Weeks, Robert P. "Disentanglement as a Theme in H. G. Wells's Fiction." *Papers of the Michigan Academy of Science, Arts, and Letters* XXXIX (1954): 439-44.

Defines the Time Traveller—a character striving to break out of a specific physical, chronological, or social sphere—as an archetypal Wells character that recurs through much of Wells's fiction.

West, Anthony. *H. G. Wells: Aspects of a Life*. London: Hutchinson, 1984, 405 p.

Painstaking and unsparing but self-interested biography of Wells by Wells's son.

West, Geoffrey. *H. G. Wells*. New York: W. W. Norton & Co., 1930, 287 p.

Portrait written in consultation with Wells.

[Williams, Basil.] "New Novels: *The Island of Doctor Moreau*." *The Athenaeum*, No. 3576, (9 May 1896): 615-16.

Representative early review of *The Island of Doctor Moreau*, questioning the validity of repulsive and horrible details that are seemingly included for their own sake.

Wilson, Harris, ed. *Arnold Bennett and H. G. Wells: A Record of a Personal and a Literary Friendship*. Urbana: University of Illinois Press, 1960, 290 p.*

An insightful collection of articles and letters by Bennett and Wells.

Woolf, Virginia. "Modern Fiction." In her *The Common Reader*, pp. 207-18. New York: Harcourt, Brace and Co., 1925.*

An appraisal of Wells as a "materialist" who makes "the trivial and transitory appear the true and the enduring."

Zamyatin, Yevgeny. "H. G. Wells." Translated by Mirra Ginsburg. *Midway* 10, No. 1 (Summer 1969): 97-126.

Translation of a 1955 revision of a 1922 essay praising Wells's fantastic and speculative novels as modern versions of traditional fairy tales.

Appendix

The following is a listing of all sources used in Volume 19 of *Twentieth-Century Literary Criticism*. Included in this list are all copyright and reprint rights and acknowledgments for those essays for which permission was obtained. Every effort has been made to trace copyright, but if omissions have been made, please let us know.

THE EXCERPTS IN TCLC, VOLUME 19, WERE REPRINTED FROM THE FOLLOWING PERIODICALS:

The Academy, v. XLVI, October 20, 1894; v. LXIII, October 25, 1902.

American Literature, v. XXVII, November, 1955. Copyright © 1955, renewed 1983, Duke University Press, Durham, NC. Reprinted by permission.

American Magazine, v. 74, June, 1912.

American Mercury, v. XXXI, April, 1934.

The American Review, v. II, December, 1933.

The American Scholar, v. 22, Autumn, 1953 for "Mr. Eliot, Mr. Trilling, and 'Huckleberry Finn'" by Leo Marx. Copyright © 1953, renewed 1981, by the United Chapters of Phi Beta Kappa. Reprinted by permission of the author./ v. 54, Autumn, 1985 for "The Crowded Raft: 'Huckleberry Finn' & Its Critics" by J. C. Furnas. Copyright © 1985 by the author.

The Antigonish Review, n. 13, Spring, 1973 for "The Religious Thought of Lionel Johnson" by Gary H. Paterson; n. 39, Autumn, 1979 for "Spiritual Decadence? Some Religious Poetry of John Gray" by Gary H. Paterson. Copyright 1973, 1979 by Gary H. Paterson. Both reprinted by permission of the publisher and the author.

The Athenaeum, n. 4690, March 19, 1920.

The Aylesford Review, v. VII, Winter, 1965-Spring, 1966 for "On Re-reading 'Park'" by Brocard Sewell, O. Carm. Reprinted by permission of the author.

The Baker Street Journal, n.s. v. 27, March, 1977. © copyright 1977 by The Baker Street Irregulars. All rights reserved. Reprinted by permission.

The Bookman, London, v. X, April, 1896; v. XIII, February, 1898.

The Bookman, New York, v. I, June, 1895; v. XX, February, 1905; v. XXV, June, 1907; v. XXVII, July, 1908; v. XXXVI, October, 1912; v. XLIV, September, 1916.

THE EXCERPTS IN TCLC, VOLUME 19, WERE REPRINTED FROM THE FOLLOWING BOOKS:

Aldiss, Brian. From an introduction to *In the Days of the Comet*. By H. G. Wells. Hogarth Press, 1985. New introduction copyright © Brian Aldiss 1985. All rights reserved. Reprinted by permission of The Hogarth Press.

Alford, Norman. From *The Rhymers' Club*. Cormorant Press, 1980. Copyright © by Norman Alford 1980. All rights reserved. Reprinted by permission of the author.

Antoine, Jacques C. From ''Literature: From Toussaint Louverture to Jacques Roumain,'' in *An Introduction to Haiti*. Edited by Mercer Cook. Department of Cultural Affairs, Pan American Union, 1951.

Barson, Alfred T. From *A Way of Seeing: A Critical Study of James Agee*. University of Massachusetts Press, 1972. Copyright © 1972 by Alfred Turner Barson. All rights reserved. Reprinted by permission.

Beach, Joseph Warren. From *The Outlook for American Prose*. The University of Chicago Press, 1926.

Bennett, Arnold. From ''Bennett's Review of 'The Invisible Man','' in *Arnold Bennett and H. G. Wells: A Record of a Personal and a Literary Friendship*. By Arnold Bennett and H. G. Wells, edited by Harris Wilson. University of Illinois Press, 1960.

Beresford, J. D. From *H. G. Wells*. Henry Holt and Company, 1915.

Bergonzi, Bernard. From *The Turn of a Century: Essays on Victorian and Modern English Literature*. Barnes & Noble, 1973. © Bernard Bergonzi, 1973. All rights reserved. Reprinted by permission of Barnes & Noble Books, a Division of Littlefield, Adams & Co., Inc. In Canada by permission of A. D. Peters & Co. Ltd.

Bleiler, E. F. From an introduction to *Best ''Thinking Machine'' Detective Stories*. By Jacques Futrelle, edited by E. F. Bleiler. Dover, 1973. Copyright © 1973 by Dover Publications, Inc. All rights reserved. Reprinted by permission.

Bleiler, E. F. From an introduction to *Great Cases of the Thinking Machine*. By Jacques Futrelle, edited by E. F. Bleiler. Dover, 1976. Copyright © 1976 Dover, Inc. Reprinted by permission.

Bloomfield, Paul. From an introduction to *The Essential R. B. Cunninghame Graham*. By R. B. Cunninghame Graham, edited by Paul Bloomfield. Jonathan Cape, 1952.

Bosschère, Jean de. From an introduction to *The World of Jean de Bosschère: A Monograph*. By Samuel Putnam. The Fortune Press, 1932.

Boyd, Ernest. From *Ireland's Literary Renaissance*. Revised edition. Alfred A. Knopf, 1922.

Brooks, Cleanth, Jr., and Robert Penn Warren. From *Understanding Fiction*. Appleton-Century-Crofts, Inc., 1943. Copyright 1943 by F. S. Crofts & Co., Inc. Renewed 1970 by Cleanth Brooks and Robert Penn Warren. Reprinted by permission of Prentice-Hall, Inc., Englewood Cliffs, N.J.

Brooks, Van Wyck. From *The Times of Melville and Whitman*. E. P. Dutton & Co., Inc., 1947.

Burdett, Osbert. From *The Beardsley Period: An Essay in Perspective*. Boni and Liveright, 1925.

Butler, E. M. From *Rainer Maria Rilke*. The Macmillan Company, 1941.

Cargill, Oscar. From *Intellectual America: Ideas on the March*. Macmillan, 1941. Copyright 1941 by Macmillan Publishing Co., Inc. Renewed 1969 by Oscar Cargill. All rights reserved. Reprinted with permission of Macmillan Publishing Company.

Cevasco, G. A. From *John Gray*. Twayne, 1982. Copyright 1982 by Twayne Publishers. All rights reserved. Reprinted with the permission of Twayne Publishers, a division of G. K. Hall & Co., Boston.

Charlesworth, Barbara. From *Dark Passages: The Decadent Consciousness in Victorian Literature*. The University of Wisconsin Press, 1965. Copyright © 1965 by the Regents of the University of Wisconsin. Reprinted by permission.

Chesterton, G. K. From *Autobiography*. Hutchinson & Co., Ltd., 1936, Hutchinson of London, 1969. 1936 edition © Gilbert Keith Chesterton. Renewed 1964 by Dorothy Edith Collins. 1969 edition © Dorothy Edith Collins. Reprinted by permission of Miss D. E. Collins.

Appendix

Macdonald, Dwight. From *On Movies*. Da Capo Press, 1981. Copyright © 1969 by Dwight Macdonald. All rights reserved. Reprinted by permission of the publisher and The Literary Estate of Dwight Macdonald.

MacLeish, Archibald. From a foreword to *Permit Me Voyage*. By James Agee. Yale University Press, 1934. Copyright, 1934, by Yale University Press. Copyright © renewed 1962 by Mia Fritsch Agee. All rights reserved. Reprinted by permission of Houghton Mifflin Company.

Mann, Thomas. From a preface to *The Case of Mr. Crump*. By Ludwig Lewisohn. E. W. Titus, 1926.

Masters, Edgar Lee. From *Mark Twain: A Portrait*. Charles Scribner's Sons, 1938. Copyright 1938 Edgar Lee Masters. Copyright renewed © 1965 by Ellen C. Masters. All rights reserved. Reprinted with the permission of Charles Scribner's Sons.

McConnell, Frank. From *The Science Fiction of H. G. Wells*. Oxford University Press, 1981. Copyright © 1981 by Oxford University Press, Inc. Reprinted by permission.

Mersand, Joseph. From *The Play's the Thing*. The Modern Chapbooks, 1941.

More, Paul Elmer. From *Shelburne Essays, first series*. G. P. Putnam's Sons, 1904.

Moreau, Geneviève. From *The Restless Journey of James Agee*. Translated by Miriam Kleiger with Morty Schiff. Morrow, 1977. Copyright © 1977 by William Morrow and Company, Inc. All rights reserved. Abridged by permission of William Morrow & Company, Inc.

Nassaar, Christopher S. From *Into the Demon Universe: A Literary Exploration of Oscar Wilde*. Yale University Press, 1974. Copyright © 1974 by Yale University. All rights reserved. Reprinted by permission.

Nelson, James G. From *The Early Nineties: A View from the Bodley Head*. Cambridge, Mass.: Harvard University Press, 1971. Copyright © 1971 by the President and Fellows of Harvard College. All rights reserved. Excerpted by permission.

Olivero, Federico. From *Rainer Maria Rilke: A Study in Poetry and Mysticism*. W. Heffer & Sons, Ltd., 1931.

Paine, Albert Bigelow. From *Mark Twain, a Biography: The Personal and Literary Life of Samuel Langhorne Clemens, Vol. II*. Harper & Brothers, 1912. Copyright, 1912 by Harper & Row, Publishers, Inc. Renewed 1940 by Dora T. Paine. All rights reserved. Reprinted by permission of Harper & Row, Publishers, Inc.

Parker, W. M. From *Modern Scottish Writers*. Edited by W. M. Parker. W. Hodge & Co., 1917.

Phelps, William Lyon. From *Essays on Modern Novelists*. Macmillan, 1910. Copyright 1910 by Macmillan Publishing Company. Renewed 1939 by William Lyon Phelps. All rights reserved. Reprinted with permission of Macmillan Publishing Company.

Pound, Ezra. From a preface to *Poetical Works of Lionel Johnson*. By Lionel Johnson, edited by Ezra Pound. Elkin Mathews, 1915.

Putnam, Samuel. From *The World of Jean de Bosschère: A Monograph*. The Fortune Press, 1932.

Quinn, Arthur Hobson. From *A History of the American Drama, from the Civil War to the Present Day: Vol. II*. F. S. Crofts & Co., Publishers, 1936. Copyright, 1927, 1936, by F. S. Crofts & Co., Inc. Copyright renewed 1964 by Arthur Hobson Quinn, Jr. Reprinted by permission of Irvington Publishers, Inc. and the Literary Estate of Arthur Hobson Quinn.

Rilke, Rainer Maria. From a letter to L. H. on November 8, 1915, in *Letters of Rainer Maria Rilke: 1910-1926, Vol. 2*. By Rainer Maria Rilke, translated by Jane Bannard Greene and M. D. Herter Norton. Norton, 1948. Copyright © 1947, 1948 by W. W. Norton & Company, Inc., New York, N.Y. Renewed 1975 by M. D. Herter Norton. Reprinted by permission of W. W. Norton & Company, Inc.

Rilke, Rainer Maria. From a letter to Lou Andreas-Salomé on December 28, 1911, in *Letters of Rainer Maria Rilke: 1910-1926, Vol. 2*. By Rainer Maria Rilke, translated by Jane Bannard Greene and M. D. Herter Norton. Norton, 1948. Copyright © 1947, 1948 by W. W. Norton & Company, Inc., New York, N.Y. Renewed 1975 by M. D. Herter Norton. Reprinted by permission of W. W. Norton & Company, Inc.

Rose, William. From "Rilke and the Conception of Death," in *Rainer Maria Rilke: Aspects of His Mind and Poetry*. Edited by William Rose and G. Craig Houston. Sidgewick & Jackson, Ltd., 1938.

Rosenblatt, Roger. From *Black Fiction*. Cambridge, Mass.: Harvard University Press, 1974. Copyright © 1974 by the President and Fellows of Harvard College. All rights reserved. Excerpted by permission.

Ruoff, Gene W. From "'A Death in the Family': Agee's 'Unfinished' Novel," in *The Fifties: Fiction, Poetry, Drama*. Edited by Warren French. Everett/Edwards, Inc., 1970. Copyright © 1970 by Warren French. All rights reserved. Reprinted by permission.

Santayana, George. From *The Middle Span: Persons and Places, Vol. II*. Charles Scribner's Sons, 1945. Copyright, 1945, by Charles Scribner's Sons. Renewed 1972 by the Literary Estate of George Santayana. All rights reserved. Reprinted with permission of The MIT Press and The Literary Estate of George Santayana.

Shafer, Robert. From an introduction to *Reviews & Critical Papers*. By Lionel Johnson, edited by Robert Shafer. E. P. Dutton, Inc., 1921.

Shafer, Robert. From *Paul Elmer More and American Criticism*. Yale University Press, 1935. Copyright 1935 by Yale University Press. Renewed 1963 by Robert Shafer. All rights reserved. Reprinted by permission.

Shaw, Bernard. From *Three Plays for Puritans*. Brentano's, 1906.

Sheed, Wilfrid. From "Collected Short Prose of James Agee," in *The Morning After: Selected Essays and Reviews*. Farrar, Straus and Giroux, 1971. Copyright © 1971 by Wilfrid Sheed. All rights reserved. Reprinted by permission of Farrar, Straus and Giroux, Inc.

Sinclair, May. From an introduction to *The Closed Door*. By Jean de Bosschère, translated by F. S. Flint. John Lane Company, 1917.

Smith, C. Alphonso. From *O. Henry Biography*. Doubleday, Page, 1916. Copyright 1916 by C. Alphonso Smith. All rights reserved. Reprinted by permission of Doubleday & Company, Inc.

Smith, Henry Nash. From *Mark Twain: The Development of a Writer*. Cambridge, Mass.: Belknap Press, 1962. Copyright © 1962 by the President and Fellows of Harvard College. All rights reserved. Excerpted by permission.

Sokel, Walter H. From "The Devolution of the Self in 'The Notebooks of Malte Laurids Brigge'," in *Rilke: The Alchemy of Alienation*. Frank Baron, Ernst S. Dick, Warren R. Maurer, eds. Regents Press of Kansas, 1980. © copyright 1980 by The Regents Press of Kansas. Reprinted by permission.

Stanford, Derek. From an introduction to "Friends that Fail Not," in *Critics of the 'Nineties*. Edited by Derek Sanford. John Baker, 1970. © 1970 Derek Stanford. Reprinted by permission of A. & C. Black (Publishers) Ltd.

Stott, William. From *Documentary Expression and Thirties America*. Oxford University Press, 1973. Copyright © 1973 by Oxford University Press, Inc. Reprinted by permission.

Suvin, Darko. From *Metamorphoses of Science Fiction: On the Poetics and History of a Literary Genre*. Yale University Press, 1979. Copyright © 1979 by Yale University. All rights reserved. Reprinted by permission.

Symons, Julian. From *Mortal Consequences: A History—From the Detective Story to the Crime Novel*. Harper & Row, 1972. Copyright © 1972 Julian Symons. All rights reserved. Reprinted by permission of Harper & Row, Publishers, Inc. In Canada by Curtis Brown Ltd., London on behalf of Julian Symons.

Thornton, R.K.R. From *The Decadent Dilemma*. Edward Arnold, 1983. Copyright © R.K.R. Thornton 1983. All rights reserved. Reprinted by permission.

Van Doren, Carl. From *The American Novel*. Macmillan, 1921. © 1921 by Macmillan Publishing Co., Inc. Copyright renewed 1949 by Carl Van Doren. All rights reserved. Reprinted with permission of Macmillan Publishing Company.

Watts, Cedric. From *R. B. Cunninghame Graham*. Twayne, 1983. Copyright 1983 by Twayne Publishers. All rights reserved. Reprinted with the permission of Twayne Publishers, a division of G. K. Hall & Co., Boston.

West, Herbert Faulkner. From *A Modern Conquistador: Robert Bontine Cunninghame Graham, His Life and Works*. Cranley & Day, 1932.

Wilson, Edmund. From *Red, Black, Blond and Olive: Studies in Four Civilizations, Zuñi, Haiti, Soviet Russia, Israel*. Oxford University Press, Inc., 1956.

Wood, Frank. From *Rainer Maria Rilke: The Ring of Forms*. University of Minnesota Press, 1958. © copyright 1958 by the University of Minnesota Press. All rights reserved. Reprinted by permission.

Wyatt, David. From *Prodigal Sons: A Study in Authorship and Authority*. The Johns Hopkins University Press, 1980. Copyright © 1980 by The Johns Hopkins University Press. All rights reserved. Reprinted by permission.

Zamyatin, Yevgeny. From *A Soviet Heretic: Essays*. Edited and translated by Mirra Ginsburg. University of Chicago Press, 1970. © 1970 by The University of Chicago. All rights reserved. Reprinted by permission of The University of Chicago Press.

ISBN 0-8103-2401-6